VOLUME

24

U–Vult
pages 1-408

Compton's Encyclopedia

and Fact-Index

Compton's Learning Company, a division of
Encyclopædia Britannica, Inc.
Chicago · Auckland · Geneva · London · Manila
Paris · Rome · Seoul · Sydney · Tokyo · Toronto

1989 EDITION COMPTON'S ENCYCLOPEDIA

COPYRIGHT © 1989 by COMPTON'S LEARNING COMPANY
DIVISION OF ENCYCLOPÆDIA BRITANNICA, INC.

Library of Congress Catalog Card Number: 87-73073
International Standard Book Number: 0-85229-494-8
Printed in U.S.A.

THE UNIVERSITY OF CHICAGO
COMPTON'S ENCYCLOPEDIA IS PUBLISHED WITH THE EDITORIAL ADVICE
OF THE FACULTIES OF THE UNIVERSITY OF CHICAGO

"Let knowledge grow from more to more and thus be human life enriched"

PHOTOS: Row 1: Flip Schulke—Black Star. Row 2: (center right) James Mason—Black Star; (far right) Giraudon—Art Resource/EB Inc. Row 4: (right) AP/Wide World. Row 5: (center) W.H. Hodge.

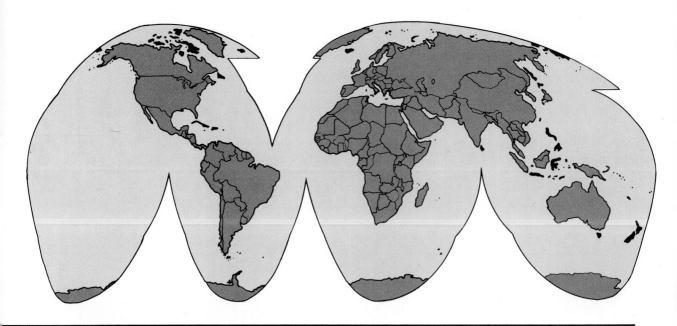

HERE AND THERE IN VOLUME 24

From the A-1 satellite to the zygote cell, thousands of subjects are gathered together in Compton's Encyclopedia and Fact-Index. Organized alphabetically, they are drawn from every field of knowledge. Readers who want to explore their favorite fields in this volume can use this subject-area outline. While it may serve as a study guide, a specialized learning experience, or simply a key for browsing, it is not a complete table of contents.

Arts

Paolo Uccello	2
Sigrid Undset	8
Utopian Literature	260
Maurice Utrillo	261
Paul Valéry	268
Anthony Van Dyck	277
Jan van Eyck	277
Vincent van Gogh	278
Ralph Vaughan Williams	284
Lope de Vega	284
Diego Velasquez	289
Ventriloquism	300
Giuseppe Verdi	302
Paul Verlaine	303
Jan Vermeer	303
Jules Verne	320
Paolo Veronese	320
Heitor Villa-Lobos	356
François Villon	356
Virgil	358

Antonio Vivaldi	385
Vocal Music	386
Voltaire	407
Kurt Vonnegut, Jr.	408

Physical Science

Uranium	230
Harold Clayton Urey	238
Vacuum	267
Valley	269
Vanadium	270
James A. Van Allen	271
Volcano	402

Living Things

Vanilla	278
Vegetables	285
Venus's-Flytrap	301
Vertebrates	323
Vine	357

Violet 357
Vireo 358

Medicine

Ulcer 7
Urinary System 239
Vaccines 264
Andreas Vesalius 326
Veterinary Medicine 330
Rudolf Virchow 358
Virus 379
Vitamins 380

Technology and Business

Valve 269
Vanderbilt Family 276
Vending Machine 290
Video Recording 335

Geography

Ubangi River 2
Uganda 3
Ukrainian Soviet Socialist Republic 4
Ulaanbaatar 6
Union of Soviet Socialist Republics 18
United Arab Emirates 67
United Kingdom 68
United States 88
Ural Mountains 229
Uruguay 240
Utah 243
Utrecht 261
Uzbek Soviet Socialist Republic 262
Valencia 268
Valley Forge 269
Valparaiso 269
Lake Van 270
Vancouver 274
Vancouver Island 275
Vanuatu 279
Varanasi 279
Vatican City 280
Venda 290
Venezuela 291
Venice 297
Veracruz 301
Verdun 302
Vermont 304
Americus Vespucius 326
Mount Vesuvius 326
Vicksburg 331
Victoria 334
Lake Victoria 334

Victoria Falls 335
Vienna 338
Vientiane 340
Vietnam 341
Virginia 359
British Virgin Islands 378
United States Virgin Islands 378
Vistula River 380
Vladivostok 385
Volga River 406
Volgograd 406

History

Walter Ulbricht 7
Underground Railroad 7
Mariano G. Vallejo 268
Martin Van Buren 272
Vandals 276
Getulio Vargas 279
Denmark Vesey 326
Giambattista Vico 332
Victor Emmanuel 332
Victoria 333
Congress of Vienna 340
Vietnam War 347
Vikings 351
Pancho Villa 356
Julius Vogel 400
John Vorster 408

Social and Political Science

United Nations 80
United States Constitution 194
United States Government 208
Veterans' Affairs 327
Veto 331

Potpourri

Unidentified Flying Object 8
Unification Church 9
Uniforms and Insignia 10
Unitarian Universalist Association 67
Universities and Colleges 222
Urban Planning 233
Vatican Councils 283
Vegetarianism 289
Palace of Versailles 320
Veterans' Organizations 328
Vocation 390
Vocational Training 398
Voice 400
Volleyball 407
Voodoo 408

EXPLORING VOLUME 24

This self-portrait of Vincent van Gogh was completed shortly before his eyesight failed and his bouts of depression increased. How did the painter die? 278.

Venice is centered on islets in the middle of a lagoon. How many canals make up the streets of the city? 297.

The United States Constitution is preserved under sealed glass. What so-called errors were later found in the Constitution signed in 1787? 198.

Name the surgeon whose dissection of cadavers revolutionized medicine. 326.

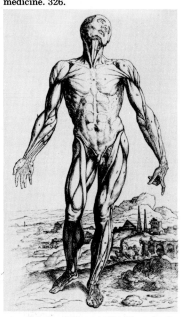

What is the largest Christian church in the world? 280.

This replica of an 8th-century Viking ship was built with the customary dragon-shaped prow and striped sail on a single mast. Why were the Norsemen's ships pointed at each end? 351.

What is the largest palace in France, and why did it serve as a royal residence for only a century? 320.

Which Flemish painter of religious subjects on wooden panels perfected the technique of working in oils? 277.

From the article UNIFORMS AND INSIGNIA

The letter U

is a descendant of the letter V, which is discussed later in this volume. Relatives of U are F, W, and Y. The original forms of the sign in the Egyptian hieroglyphic, Phoenician, and Greek writings are shown in the illustrations numbered (1), (2), and (3) respectively.

For a time the Romans used one sign (4) for three sounds, namely "u," "v," and "w." For example, they wrote the name "Julius" as IVLIVS.

In late Roman times Latin scribes made the capital letter as V but rounded the small letter (5). People of the Middle Ages chose the pointed form for the consonantal "v" and the rounded form for the vocalic "u." To make the change complete, they added small "v" and capital U to their writing (6). This distinction of the four signs passed into English writing unchanged. The English small "u" is a copy of the capital, except that in handwriting it is connected to adjoining letters.

Y 1	Y 2
V 3	V 4
Vu 5	vU 6

'The Flood' is a fresco painted by Paolo Uccello in the Green Cloister of the church of Santa Maria Novella in Florence in about 1448. The work represents a transition from the decorative Gothic style to the newer and bolder forms of the Renaissance.

UBANGI RIVER. One of the major rivers of Central Africa, the Ubangi is the largest right-bank tributary of the Congo (Zaire) River. With the Uele River, its headstream, the Ubangi flows for more than 1,400 miles (2,250 kilometers) before it empties into the Congo. (For maps, *see* Africa; Zaire.)

The Ubangi is formed at the confluence of the Bomu and Uele rivers on the northern border of Zaire. The river forms part of Zaire's northern border with the Central African Republic as it flows westward. After passing through the Zongo rapids, the river turns southward and flows through Bangui, the capital of the Central African Republic. The lower course of the Ubangi flows southwestward and forms part of the border between Zaire and Congo before it empties into the Congo River west of Lake Tumba.

The Ubangi begins as a wide river that is navigable for about 100 miles (160 kilometers) from Yakoma, Zaire, to Banzyville, Zaire. Beyond the rapids navigation begins again at Bangui. From Bangui the river is dotted with small islands and is navigable for the remainder of its length. The German botanist Georg Schweinfurth traveled the river in 1870, and Wilhelm Junker, a Russian explorer, determined in 1882–83 that it is part of the Congo River system.

UCCELLO, Paolo (1397–1475). The works of the Florentine painter Paolo Uccello represent a combination of two distinct styles—the basically decorative late Gothic and the heroic early Renaissance. Long considered significant primarily for his new means of rendering perspective, Uccello also possessed a genius for decoration that later historians found to be an even greater contribution.

Paolo di Dono was born in Pratovecchio, near Florence, in 1397. He was later nicknamed Uccello, meaning "bird," because of his paintings of birds and animals. By the time he was 10, he was an apprentice in the workshop of the sculptor Lorenzo Ghiberti, who was at work on his famous bronze doors for the baptistery of the Florence cathedral. There is no record of Uccello's training as a painter, but he had joined a confraternity of painters in 1414 and the next year became a member of the Arte dei Medici e degli Speziali, the official painters' guild.

Uccello's earliest frescoes, now in poor condition, are in the Green Cloister of Santa Maria Novella in Florence. They represent episodes from the creation and are in the late Gothic style. From 1425 to 1431 Uccello worked as a mosaicist in Venice, but all of his work there has been lost. In 1436 he completed a monochrome fresco in the Florence cathedral of an equestrian monument to Sir John Hawkwood. Hawkwood had commanded Florentine troops in the late 14th century. A few years later Uccello painted four heads of prophets around a huge clock on the cathedral's west wall and contributed designs for two stained-glass windows in the cupola.

After a brief trip to Padua in 1447, Uccello returned to the Green Cloister of Sta. Maria Novella. 'The Flood', a fresco with two separate scenes united by a rapidly receding perspective, shows the influence of Donatello's reliefs in Padua. More than any other painting, 'The Flood' illustrates the problems of grafting the rapidly developing heroic style of the Renaissance onto the older decorative style.

Uccello's best-known paintings are three panels (about 1457) of the battle of San Romano, which represent the victory in 1432 of Florentine forces over those of Siena. Renaissance elements—such as sculptured forms and bits of broken perspective—and the elaborate decorative patterns typical of the Gothic style are both present in this work (*see* Painting). The panels have since been separated, and each now resides in a different European museum.

In his last years Uccello received few commissions, and he executed only minor works. He died in Florence on Dec. 10, 1475.

UFO *see* UNIDENTIFIED FLYING OBJECT.

UGANDA. A republic and a member of the Commonwealth since independence in 1962, Uganda must cope with internal rivalries among its traditional kingdoms and tribes. It has suffered under frequent changes of leadership, a brutal dictatorship, invasion by Tanzania, and

finally civil war. The landlocked country is bordered on the west by Kenya, on the north by Sudan, on the east by Zaire, and on the south by Rwanda, Tanzania, and Lake Victoria.

Landscape

The country consists of a broad open plateau between 3,500 and 5,000 feet (1,000 and 1,500 meters) above sea level underlain by ancient crystalline rocks. It is a land of many lakes and swamps, which cover about 15 percent of the total area. The waters of Lake Victoria and Lake Kyoga overflow into the upper reaches of the Nile River. On the west boundary a large rift valley and the mountain range Ruwenzori are associated with dormant volcanoes. In this valley are found Lake Edward (Idi Amin), Lake George, and Lake Albert (Mobuto Sese Seko). To the east a similar rift valley marks the end of the Uganda plateau. Mount Elgon is a high volcano (14,178 feet, or 4,321 meters) on the edge of this rift. To the north the plateau slopes gently toward southern Sudan and the great swamp As Sudd.

Located on both sides of the equator, all regions of Uganda except the extreme east and north receive abundant rainfall, which lasts from nine to eleven months of the year. Around Lake Victoria and in the western mountains, some 50 inches (127 centimeters) of annual rainfall enables farmers to grow food crops throughout the year. On Ruwenzori and the high volcanoes there is permanent snow cover. Temperatures over most of the country are modified by the great height, making it comfortable despite its closeness to the equator.

At one time much of southern Uganda and the lower slopes of the mountains were covered with tropical rain forests. These were steadily cleared for farming so that only a few scattered areas survive today. To the north, as rainfall decreases, the vegetation changes to tall, grassy woodlands. Unusual forms of giant plant life occur on Ruwenzori and Mount Elgon.

Wild animals of all kinds were once abundant, but forests have been cleared, eliminating many habitats, and animals have been driven off the grassy woodlands. People have also hunted game for meat and trophies. A few national parks have been established as wildlife preserves. The largest is Kabarega (Murchison Falls), an area on either side of the Victoria Nile River where large herds of elephant overgraze the woody grasslands.

People

Ugandan society is largely rural, though there are several cities, including Kampala, Entebbe, and Jinja. The greater part of the population is concentrated in a wide band around the shores of Lake Victoria. It is difficult to count the total population because of the internal strife, but in the mid-1980s it was estimated to be about 15.5 million. Large numbers of refugees have been lost to neighboring countries. With an annual growth rate of more than 3 percent, half of the population are under the age of 16 years. Life expectancy is 49 years, and infant mortality is 110 per thousand live births. Some 15 percent of the population are estimated to be urban. Kampala is the main commercial center and capital city, while most industry is concentrated in Jinja (*see* Kampala).

The Bantu-speaking peoples are concentrated in the south and southwest and are the largest group. They include the Ganda, Soga, Nyoro, and Nkole. To the north and east are Nilotic and Nilo-Hamitic peoples, composed of many different tribes. The dominant languages are Luganda (spoken by the Ganda) and Swahili, the East African lingua franca. English is used throughout the country as the official language.

The country has become increasingly Christian (78 percent) under the influence of Protestant and Roman Catholic missionaries. About 7 percent of the population are Muslims. More than half of Uganda's people are literate, the result of the Christian missions and British colonial rule. Makerere University in Kampala has played a leading role in training Ugandans in medicine and engineering as well as in law and the arts. There is one daily newspaper, printed in English and Luganda, while the government-run radio and television stations offer programs in English, Swahili, and Luganda.

The Ruwenzori Mountains extend for about 80 miles (129 kilometers) along the border of Uganda and Zaire.

Regina Power—Shostal Associates

3

Economy

Most of Uganda's people are farmers, producing either food or export crops. Except on the lower slopes of volcanic mountains, soils are not rich. The good reliable rains make farming possible. Food crops consist of corn, millets and sorghum, maniocs and other root crops, and bananas. People usually grow enough for their families and have a surplus for sale in local markets.

Cash crops were introduced in about 1900 and quickly became a major part of the economy. While a number of plantations (estates) were established, it was the small farmer who took to producing robusta coffee for export. Cotton, tea, and sugarcane followed, providing regular income for most Ugandans.

Cattle represent another major part of Ugandan life. The western part of the country (Ankole) is known for its large-horned Sanga cattle. Elsewhere nagana, or sleeping sickness, which is carried by the tsetse fly, restricts the number of animals.

On such lakes as Victoria and Kyoga commercial fishing is a major activity. There are only a few areas that still yield quality hardwoods for local use.

There are no extensive mineral deposits except copper. It was mined at Kilembe, 125 miles (200 kilometers) west of Kampala, and transported to Jinja, where a smelter converted it to exportable metal. Unfortunately the mine has ceased production. Uganda exports substantial deposits of apatite and mines tungsten, beryl, and tin on a small scale. There are also unexploited deposits of high-grade iron ore at Kigesi.

Because Uganda has no fossil fuels, a hydroelectric power plant was built on the Victoria Nile at Owens Falls, near Jinja and Kampala, opening in 1954. Grain milling, food processing, textiles, and copper concentrates became the main industries of Jinja, while Kampala concentrated on such light industries as brewing and manufacturing import substitutes. Unrest makes it difficult to maintain production.

The need for Uganda to have an outside link for its exports and imports was recognized in the 1890s. The British government provided funds to complete a railroad from Mombasa on the east coast across what is now Kenya to Kisumu on Lake Victoria by 1902, using indentured East Indian laborers. Lake steamers from Uganda made connections at Kisumu. The Busoga Railway, the first railroad within Uganda, was completed in 1912, linking Jinja and Lake Kyoga. When the main line was realigned through Tororo in 1928, it joined the Busoga at Mbulamuti, offering a better outlet for cotton exports. In 1948 a line was extended to Kasese to bring out the Kilembe copper ores. The country is covered by a 17,000-mile (27,000-kilometer) network of roads, some 4,000 miles (6,400 kilometers) of which are paved. An international airport is located at Entebbe.

History

From the 15th century, rival kingdoms in what is now Uganda were gradually overcome by the well-organized state of Buganda, ruled by a *kabaka,* or king, with an animist religion. Arab traders arrived in the 1840s, and the *kabaka,* Mutesa I, adopted some of the teachings of Islam in 1867. He allowed Anglican missionaries to teach Christianity in 1877, followed by Roman Catholics in 1879. After Mutesa died in 1884, there was serious rivalry between the Muslims, Anglicans, and Catholics.

The British, worried by German penetration of the region, set up the British East Africa Company in Buganda in 1890. The area that is now Uganda was declared a protectorate in 1894 to control the Upper Nile and Egypt, which was also under the British.

After World War II Ugandans prepared for independence, which came in 1962. A general election was held, and a Westminster-Cabinet style government under Milton Obote was formed. A republic was declared in 1963, with the *kabaka,* Mutesa II, as president and Milton Obote as prime minister. In 1966, with the support of the army under Colonel Idi Amin, Obote suspended the constitution, made himself executive president, forced the *kabaka* to flee the country, and nationalized many of the banks and industries. In 1971 Amin deposed Obote and during the next seven years expelled 40,000 East Indians and slaughtered at least 300,000 Ugandans. Amin's army was attacked by troops from Tanzania in 1979, forcing him to flee the country. Obote returned to the presidency, but he was unable to restore unity and was deposed in July 1985 by Tito Okello.

The National Liberation Army, led by Yoweri Museveni, a prominent member of the Ankole tribe, took control of Kampala in January 1986 after an extensive field campaign in the south and southwest.

Museveni banned all political parties until a general election promised for 1990 and began a program of economic reforms. Attempted coups by dissident groups disrupted many areas, however, reducing the exports of cash crops. Intermittent border disputes with Kenya continued as well.

UKRAINIAN SOVIET SOCIALIST REPUBLIC. The second most populous of the soviet republics after the Russian S.F.S.R., the Ukrainian Soviet Socialist Republic lies in the southwestern  corner of the European part of the Soviet Union. Extending over 233,100 square miles (603,700 square kilometers), it is the third largest of the soviet republics in area. Often called the Ukraine, it is bounded by the Belorussian S.S.R. on the north; the Russian S.F.S.R. on the east; the Sea of Azov, the Black Sea, the Moldavian S.S.R., and Romania on the south; and Hungary, Czechoslovakia, and Poland on the west. Occupying less than 3 percent of Soviet territory, the republic produces more than one fifth of the Soviet industrial and agricultural output and a quarter of its grain. The capital and largest city is Kiev (population, 1986 estimate, 2,495,000). (*See also* Kiev.)

Landscape. Geographically part of the East European Plain, the Ukraine's only highlands are the Carpathian Mountains in the west and the Crimean Mountains in the south. Consisting of several parallel ranges, the Ukrainian Carpathians include Mount Hoverla—at 6,762 feet (2,061 meters), the republic's highest point. The majority of forest lands are in the Carpathian region. Mountain passes provide routes for both highways and railroads. Lowlands extend along the shores of the Black and Azov seas.

Major rivers include the Dnepr, Dnestr, Donets, and Bug. They all drain southward toward the Azov and Black seas. The rivers are vital as a source of water supply, transportation, and hydroelectricity.

Lying in a temperate continental climate zone, the Ukraine's mean January temperatures are about 26° F (−3° C) in the southwest and 18° F (−8° C) in the northeast. The mean July temperatures are about 73° F (23° C) in the southwest and 66° F (19° C) in the northeast. The southern shores of the Crimea have a warm Mediterranean-type climate.

The steppe (grasslands) zone in the south, constituting about 40 percent of the republic, is covered with black soils (chernozems), some of the most fertile soils in the world. More than three fourths of the steppe zone is under cultivation. Because of occasional dry spells, large areas are irrigated.

The conservation of natural resources is given high priority, and the Ukraine has several steppe and forest preserves and game reserves. The Nikitsky Botanical Garden near the city of Yalta is known for its plants from almost every country in the world.

People. Ukrainians, the second most numerous ethnic group in the Soviet Union after the Russians, make up more than three fourths of the population of the republic. Belonging to the East Slavic language group, Ukrainian is related to Russian and Polish. Russians make up less than a quarter of the population. Most Ukrainians are members of the Eastern Orthodox church. The population density is among the highest in the Soviet Union, especially in the highly industrialized Donets River basin and Dnepr River lowland. Principal cities in addition to Kiev are Khar'kov, Odessa, Donetsk, and Dnepropetrovsk. (*See also* Khar'kov; Odessa.)

Education and health services are provided by the government. Education is compulsory between the ages of 7 and 17, and the literacy rate is almost 100 percent. Ukrainian is the major language of instruction. There are about 140 institutions of higher learning, including the A.M. Gorky State University in Khar'kov (1805) and the Kiev T.G. Shevchenko State University (1834). The Kiev-Mogila Academy (1632) has long been a major center of learning. The Ukrainian S.S.R. Academy of Sciences coordinates the work of numerous scientific institutions.

Economy. Highly mechanized and specialized agriculture produces grains, commercial crops, and

A statue of an athlete adorns the Park of Physical Culture in Khar'kov, in the Ukrainian S.S.R.

Jerry Cooke

livestock products. Modern farming methods—with tractors, trucks, and grain-harvesting combines—are widely used. The republic has long been the principal granary of the Soviet Union, producing such grains as wheat, rye, barley, oats, corn, millet, and buckwheat. The Ukraine ranks first in the Soviet Union in cultivation of sugar beets. Other crops are flax, cotton, tobacco, hemp, soybeans, and hops. Potatoes, a food staple, are also grown for making starch and alcohol; sunflowers are cultivated for their seed oil and latex. Grapes, medicinal and essential-oil plants (mint, coriander, lavender, roses), and vegetables are also grown on a large scale. Mechanized poultry farming, beekeeping, sericulture (silkworm raising), and pond fishing contribute increasingly to the republic's economy. Large numbers of cattle are raised for meat and milk. Mink and silver-black fox are raised on specialized state farms.

The Ukraine ranks among the world's richest areas of manganese-bearing ores. Extensive iron ore, coal, and petroleum deposits also exist. Other minerals include titanium ores, bauxite, potash, rock salt, and sulfur. Much of the Ukraine's industry is concentrated in the Donets Basin, where rich deposits of coal, limestone, and iron ore exist. The Krivoy Rog area is noted for its iron-ore mines, the Nikopol area for manganese ore, and the Ruthenia district for oil, salt, and natural gas deposits.

The Ukrainian ferrous-metal industry produces nearly half of the Soviet Union's cast iron, about two fifths of its steel, and about a quarter of its steel pipe. Other major industries are machine building, metalworking, metallurgy, and the processing of energy fuels. Manufactured items include diesel railway engines, tractors, television sets, chemicals, fertilizers, machine tools, radio and electronic equipment, turbines, aircraft, aluminum, motor vehicles, textiles, garments, shoes, paper, and pulp. Sugar-beet processing, winemaking, and distilling are the chief food-processing industries. Nearly 30 percent of all wine made in the Soviet Union comes from the Ukraine. Kiev is known for its flour and textile mills, sugar refineries, glass works, and tobacco factories; L'vov for its breweries and distilleries; and Odessa for its shipyards. Almost all of the energy for Ukrainian industry is provided by fossil fuels.

Railroads are the chief means of transportation for both passengers and freight. The heaviest concentration of railroads is in the Donets Basin. A network of good highways connects all industrial centers. An international airport is at Borispol near Kiev; air transport connects the Ukraine with other soviet republics. Major tourist attractions are the coasts of the Black and Azov seas, the Crimea and Carpathian regions, and the cities of Kiev and L'vov.

History. The Ukraine, meaning "borderland," was centered around the Kievan state in the 9th century. The region was successively held by Tatars from 1240 to 1340 and by Lithuanians and Poles (1340–1654). With the partition of Poland in the late 18th century, Russia acquired most of the Ukraine. In 1917, during the Russian Revolution, an independent Ukrainian republic was proclaimed. It was made part of the Union of Soviet Socialist Republics on Dec. 30, 1922. Later its territory was expanded by acquiring areas of Czechoslovakia, Poland, and Romania. The Crimea was taken over in 1954.

On April 26, 1986, a catastrophic nuclear-reactor meltdown occurred at the Chernobyl nuclear power plant, 80 miles (129 kilometers) north of Kiev. A fire burned out of control and released radioactive materials that spread over vast sections of Central and Eastern Europe and Scandinavia. Government secrecy surrounding the accident led to conflicting stories concerning the number of related deaths, extent of evacuation, and fears in neighboring countries. Population (1986 estimate), 50,994,000.

ULAANBAATAR, Mongolia.

H.K. Bruske—Artstreet

A monument to the revolutionary leader Damdiny Suhbaatar stands in the square named for him in Ulaanbaatar.

Formerly known as Urga, Ulaanbaatar is the capital and largest city, as well as an autonomous municipality, of Mongolia. Surrounded by mountains, Ulaanbaatar stands on a windswept

plateau and covers an area of 770 square miles (2,000 square kilometers). Situated in the north-central part of the country, it is located on the northern bank of a shallow and swift-flowing river, the Tuul Gol, at an altitude of 4,430 feet (1,350 meters). Several dikes were built along the river to control drainage and to protect the city from water seepage. More than half of Mongolia's total urban population lives in Ulaanbaatar.

The modern city was planned with Soviet help. There are large squares and avenues. The majority of the buildings are white, and the architecture shows the influence of the Soviet Union. Located in the heart of the city is Suhbaatar Square, the site of a neoclassic Palladian government building, the National Theater,

and a marble mausoleum containing the remains of heroes of the Mongolian Communist revolution. In the center of the square is an equestrian statue of Suhbaatar, who helped establish the provisional communist regime in 1921. Educational and cultural institutions include the Mongolian State University, the Academy of Sciences, and several professional and technical schools.

Ulaanbaatar is the major industrial and transportation center of the country and accounts for nearly half of Mongolia's industrial output. The Ulaanbaatar Industrial Combine is a complex of industries that produces leather, carpets, felt, soap, textiles, footwear, glass, furniture, pharmaceuticals, garments, cement, iron and steel, and bricks. There are also motor-vehicle repair yards, a distillery, a brewery, and printing facilities. Food-processing factories include meat-packing, bread-baking, and flour-milling plants. The leading trade center of Mongolia, Ulaanbaatar receives almost 70 percent of the country's total imports.

Ulaanbaatar is served by an international airport. A railroad connects it with Peking and Moscow. It is linked by highways with other cities in Mongolia.

The city originated as a seasonal home of the Mongolian princes. In 1639 with the construction of Da Khure, or Great Monastery, it became a permanent settlement. For almost 200 years the monastery was the residence of the *bodgo-gegen,* the high priest or "living Buddha" of the Buddhist-Lamaist religion to which Mongols adhere. The Russians called the city Urga, meaning "headquarters" in Mongolian, and it developed as a major trade center for camel caravans. In 1860 a Russian consulate was established. In 1911 Ulaanbaatar was the chief center of Outer

Mongolian revolt against the Ch'ing, or Manchu, Dynasty of China, and it declared itself independent. From 1911 to 1924 it was called Niislel Khureheh, or "Capital of Mongolia." In 1921 it became the capital of an independent state under Russian protection. When Mongolia was declared a republic in 1924, Ulaanbaatar, which means "Red Hero," was made its capital. Flooding caused extensive damage in 1966. Population (1985 estimate), 488,200.

ULBRICHT, Walter (1893–1973). The ruler of the German Democratic Republic, or East Germany, from 1949 until his retirement in 1971 was Walter Ulbricht. He was born in Leipzig on June 30, 1893. After grade school he became an apprentice carpenter. At age 15 he joined the Workers' Youth Organization of the Social Democratic party, and joined the party itself in 1912. Ulbricht served on the Eastern Front in World War I. In 1919 he became a founder of the German Communist party and worked as a party organizer. In the mid-1920s he went to Moscow for training in party operations. Back in Germany in 1928, Ulbricht was elected to the Reichstag (national legislature).

When Adolf Hitler came to power in 1933 Ulbricht fled to Paris. By 1935 he was again in Moscow. He served in the International Brigades opposing Francisco Franco's forces in the Spanish Civil War (1936–39). He spent World War II in the Soviet Union but returned to Germany in 1945 to help reestablish the Communist party. When the German Democratic Republic was formed in October 1949, Ulbricht became deputy prime minister and general secretary of the Socialist Unity party. In 1960 a Council of State, with Ulbricht as chairman, was formed to replace the presidency. The Berlin Wall was built during his rule (see Berlin). Ulbricht helped make East Germany one of the most prosperous of the Soviet bloc nations. He died in East Berlin on Aug. 1, 1973.

ULCER. A potentially serious condition, an ulcer is a break in the skin or mucous membrane with a loss of surface tissue and the disintegration and sloughing off of the epithelial tissue, leaving an open sore. Ulcers can occur in any tissue or organ as the result of injury, disease, or chronic irritation or inflammation. The most common type in humans is peptic ulcers found in the gastrointestinal tract.

Peptic ulcers occur most frequently at the beginning of the duodenum, in the lower stomach, and in the lower end of the esophagus (see Digestive System). Normally, these organs are protected by mucous membranes that provide a barrier against gastric acids and digestive enzymes and by alkaline secretions from the small intestine and pancreas that neutralize gastric juices.

A peptic ulcer results when either too much acid and pepsin (a digestive enzyme of gastric juice) are secreted or when the mucosal barrier is weakened and becomes unable to protect against the acid-pepsin complex. Most duodenal ulcers are thought to be caused by excessive secretion of acid and pepsin.

Gastric ulcers, on the other hand, occur in patients who have a normal or even slightly lower secretion of gastric acid but whose stomach mucosa have a reduced resistance to digestion.

Heredity plays a strong role in the development of ulcers. Offspring of people who secrete excessive amounts of gastric acid or who have diminished mucosal protection are also likely to show the same symptoms. Chronic stress and anxiety can stimulate the body to produce excessive amounts of stomach acid, which, in susceptible individuals, can lead to duodenal and esophageal ulcers.

Medical treatment for ulcers is generally a combination of stress reduction and the use of antacid drugs, along with forbidding cigarette smoking and avoiding the use of alcohol, aspirin, and other substances that can break down the mucosal barrier. Surgery is used in only the most extreme cases.

ULTRAVIOLET RAYS *see* LIGHT; RADIATION.

UNDERGROUND RAILROAD. For more than four decades before the American Civil War, there was an organized system in the Northern states established to help escaped slaves reach places of safety in the North and in Canada. It was called the Underground Railroad because its activities were carried on in secret and because railway terms were used to describe the system in order to disguise the real nature of the operation.

Once slaves reached Canada they were free from the prosecution mandated by the Fugitive Slave Acts. These statutes, passed by Congress in 1793 and 1850, provided for the capture and return of slaves who escaped into free states or into federal territories. To counteract these laws, personal-liberty laws were passed by some Northern states. Although these personal-liberty laws could not make slaves free, they did hamper federal officials and judges in implementing the Fugitive Slave Acts.

The Underground Railroad extended throughout 14 Northern states from Maine to Nebraska, but its heaviest activities were concentrated in Pennsylvania, Ohio, Indiana, New York, and the New England states. The freed slaves were called "freight," routes were called "lines," stopping places were "stations," and those who helped the slaves along the way were "conductors." Slaves were helped from one transfer place to another until they reached Canada. Hundreds of slaves avoided the overland journey by traveling to New England as stowaways on ships from Southern ports. From New England they made their way to New Brunswick, Canada.

Those who were most active in helping slaves to escape by way of the "railroad" were Northern abolitionists and other antislavery groups, including members of several Protestant denominations, especially Quakers, Methodists, and Mennonites. The Quaker leader Thomas Garrett is reputed to have helped about 2,700 slaves escape to freedom. Some former slaves were also active in the system. One of these was Harriet Tubman (*see* Tubman). Estimates of the total number of slaves who reached freedom by way of the Underground Railroad vary between 40,000 and 100,000.

UNDSET, Sigrid (1882–1949). The author Sigrid Undset was noted for her writings against Nazism as well as for her novels. When the Germans invaded Norway in 1940, she had to flee. She went first to Sweden and then to the United States, where she remained for five years.

Sigrid Undset was born on May 20, 1882, in Kalundborg, Denmark, of Norwegian ancestry. Her father was Dr. Ingvald Martin Undset, a renowned archaeologist. Sigrid grew up in Christiania (now Oslo), Norway. She worked for an electrical engineering firm for ten years before she married. It was only after she married artist Anders Svarstad and started a family that she began to write. Her early novels dealt with the place of women in the middle class. They included 'Jenny' (1911) and 'Images in a Mirror' (1917).

After these early books, Undset turned her attention to the past and wrote the historical novels on which her reputation rests. The author's greatest work was the trilogy 'Kristin Lavransdatter'. The first volume, 'The Bridal Wreath', appeared in 1920; the second, 'The Mistress of Husaby', in 1921; and the third, 'The Cross', in 1922. A grim and foreboding novel about the Middle Ages, it won world acclaim. Undset became a Roman Catholic convert shortly after the third novel was published. Her next large novel was 'The Master of Hestviken' (1925–27). She was given the Nobel prize in literature in 1928. She died on June 10, 1949, in Lillehammer, near Oslo.

UNEMPLOYMENT *see* EMPLOYMENT AND UNEMPLOYMENT.

UNIDENTIFIED FLYING OBJECT (UFO). Almost every civilization that has kept a written history has recorded the sighting of strange objects and lights in the skies. Today, unexplained aerial phenomena are generally referred to as unidentified flying objects, or "flying saucers." Descriptions of UFOs have ranged from glowing wheels to colored balls of light to cigar-, disk-, or crescent-shaped "craft." One of the first well-documented UFO sightings occurred in 1561 in Nuremberg, Germany. A broadsheet published that year describes red, blue, and black balls or "plates," crosses, and tubes that appeared to battle each other in the sky over the city.

The term flying saucer was coined in 1947. A businessman named Kenneth Arnold told reporters that while flying a private plane near Mount Rainier in Washington he saw nine objects flying over the mountain in formation and at a speed of more than 1,600 miles (2,600 kilometers) per hour. Arnold described the objects as moving like "a saucer skipping across the water." After that first report, Arnold's description was shortened and it soon became popular to call all UFOs flying saucers.

The United States government has records of thousands of UFO sightings, including photos of alleged UFOs and interviews with people who claim to have seen them. Since UFOs were considered a potential security risk, the report on these sightings was originally classified as secret. When the report was later declassified it showed that 90 percent of all UFO sightings could be easily explained. Most of the sightings turned out to be celestial objects, such as stars or bright planets like Venus, or atmospheric events such as auroras or meteors falling through the atmosphere. Many other sightings turned out to be such objects as weather balloons, satellites, aircraft lights, or formations of birds. Often these sightings were accompanied by unusual weather conditions.

In 1948 the United States Air Force began the government's first official UFO panel, Project Sign, which studied 243 sightings. It was replaced by Project Grudge, which investigated another 244 UFOs. In March 1952 the most ambitious of the UFO panels, Project Blue Book, was organized by the Air Force. The panel employed a number of scientists, including physicists, engineers, meteorologists, and an astronomer. Project Blue Book had three main goals: (1) to explain all reported sightings of UFOs; (2) to decide if UFOs posed a threat to the national security of the United States; and (3) to determine whether UFOs were using any advanced technology that the United States could use.

By the mid-1960s UFO reports were more numerous than ever. For the first time they were coming in regularly from places outside the United States, including Canada, Sweden, the Soviet Union, and Australia. In February 1966 another UFO panel was convened. Like the others, this panel determined that the vast majority of UFO reports were either mistakes or outright hoaxes.

A few scientists publicly disagreed with the panel's conclusions. This group, which included James E. McDonald, a meteorologist at the University of Arizona, and J. Allen Hynek, an astronomer at Northwestern University, maintained that since a few of the most reliable UFO reports had never been clearly explained, this was definite proof that Earth was being visited by extraterrestrials.

The dissenting scientists' opinion was received coldly by the mainstream scientific community. In 1968 the United States Air Force asked Edward U. Condon, a physicist at the University of Colorado, to head a panel studying the extraterrestrial hypothesis (*see* Extraterrestrial Life). The committee's final report, 'A Scientific Study of UFOs', which covered detailed investigations of 59 UFO sightings, was reviewed by a special committee of the National Academy of Sciences and released in early 1969. The 37 scientists who contributed to the report interviewed UFO witnesses and studied physical and photographic evidence. The report, also known as the Condon Report, concluded that not only was there no evidence of extraterrestrial control of UFOs but also that no further UFO studies were needed.

Courtesy of the Aerial Phenomena
Research Organization, Inc., Tucson, Ariz.

UNIFICATION CHURCH

Based on the recommendations of the Condon Report, Project Blue Book was closed in December 1969. By the time the project was disbanded, it had amassed 80,000 pages of information on 12,618 reported UFO sightings or events, each of which was ultimately classified as "identified" with a known astronomical, atmospheric, or artificial phenomenon, or as "unidentified," including cases in which information was insufficient. Currently, the United States government does not have any programs studying UFOs. The largest group still studying the phenomenon is the Center for UFO Studies, organized in 1973 and now located in Northfield, Ill. The only other official and fairly complete records of UFO sightings were maintained in Canada, where they were transferred in 1968 from the Canadian Department of National Defense to the Canadian National Research Council. The Canadian records totalled about 750 in the late 1960s. Less complete records have been maintained by scientists in Great Britain, Sweden, Denmark, Australia, and Greece.

According to a United States Air Force guide published on the subject, the reliability of witnesses is one of the main considerations in all UFO sightings. Also of note are the number of witnesses, how long they saw the UFO, how far away they were from the sighting, and the weather conditions at the time of the sighting. One of the most common features of UFO reports is that witnesses often insist that the objects they saw were under intelligent control. People frequently come to this conclusion because, like Kenneth Arnold who saw flying saucers above Mt. Rainier, they believe they see objects flying in formation or toward some other object or changing direction or speed dramatically and intentionally.

People have a natural desire to explain and understand everything they see. This is why visual sightings of UFOs are the least reliable. It is well known that the unaided human eye plays tricks bordering on hallucinations. A bright light, such as the planet Venus, often appears to move, though a clamped telescope or a sighting bar shows it to be fixed. Visual impressions of distance are also highly unreliable, being based on assumed size. Reflections from windows and eyeglasses can provide superimposed views. Optical defects can turn point sources of light into apparently saucer-shaped objects. Such optical illusions, and the psychological desire to interpret visual images, are known to account for many visual UFO reports.

Radar sightings, while more reliable in certain respects, fail to discriminate between physical objects and meteor trails, tracks of ionized gas, rain, or thermal discontinuities. Furthermore, several effects can give false radar echoes: electronic interference, reflections from ionized layers or clouds, and reflections from regions of humidity, as in a cumulus cloud. Even "contact events"—in which activities besides sighting were reported—have been found most frequently to involve dreams or hallucinations; the reliability of such reports depends heavily on whether there were two or more independent witnesses.

Lenticular clouds hanging over São Paulo, Brazil, can easily be mistaken for unidentified flying objects.

UNIFICATION CHURCH. Members of the Unification church are often called "Moonies" because the organization was founded by the Korean evangelist Sun Myung Moon. The name, which is considered derisive and insulting by the group, has been used because many people consider the church to be a cult. The official name of the organization is the Holy Spirit Association for the Unification of World Christianity.

The movement was founded in South Korea in 1954 but shifted its headquarters to Tarrytown, N.Y., in 1971. Moon had been a member of the Presbyterian church in North Korea. After World War II he began teaching doctrines contrary to Presbyterian beliefs and was excommunicated (deprived of his church membership) in 1948. In his preaching he claimed that in about 1936 he had a vision of Jesus Christ in which he was given the mission of saving the world from Satanism—which he identified with communism. Moon was imprisoned in North Korea, but in 1950 he escaped and fled to South Korea. There his book 'The Divine Principle' was published in 1952. This book became the sacred scripture of the Unification church.

The unification movement has the goal of establishing the rule of God on Earth. Moon declared that work toward this goal was initiated by Jesus, but that his crucifixion prevented its completion (see Jesus Christ). Completion of the mission, according to Moon, has been entrusted to him and his wife, Hak Ja Han, who are together called the lord and lady of the Second Advent.

The Unification church is a highly disciplined organization, and it operates a network of missions, cultural undertakings, and commercial enterprises. The members, mostly young people, are expected to work and to raise funds. In 1981 the church's request for tax-exempt status in the United States was denied when an appellate court ruled that the organization is mainly political in nature rather than religious.

The Queen's guards troop the colors on the Horse Guards Parade grounds in London.

UNIFORMS AND INSIGNIA. When Sloan Wilson used the title 'The Man in the Gray Flannel Suit' for his 1955 novel, he was suggesting that the ordinary business suit—as worn by eager young executives looking for promotions—had attained the status of a uniform. It had become a distinctive type of clothing worn by a whole class of individuals engaged in similar tasks. A uniform is a specially designed type of clothing that has the purpose of designating what the wearer does.

In some cases uniforms carry insignia. An insignia is some kind of badge, usually made of cloth or metal, that indicates rank, specialty, or unit for military personnel. Indications of rank are also worn on some nonmilitary uniforms, such as those worn by police officers.

Uniforms are normally associated with people in military service. But there are many other vocations that require them. Among the uniforms most commonly seen by the public are those worn by police officers and fire fighters. Bus drivers and postal employees also wear company uniforms. People who work in restaurants—waiters and waitresses, bartenders, cooks, and busboys—often wear uniforms. Children who are in the Boy Scouts, Girl Scouts, Camp Fire, and other youth organizations wear the uniforms of their organizations, and sometimes the uniforms have insignia indicating some achievement (*see* Youth Organizations). Some children wear uniforms to school. The clothing worn by priests and nuns in the Roman Catholic church can be considered uniforms. Employees of fast-food restaurants, such as McDonald's, Burger King, and Kentucky Fried Chicken, wear uniforms designed by their companies. Airline personnel, from the pilots to the ground crews that clean the cabins, wear company uniforms. Train conductors the world over wear uniforms. Uniforms are also worn by high school and college bands, sports teams, forest rangers, security guards, and auto mechanics.

Military Uniforms

The modern standing army, in contrast to hired mercenaries, made its appearance at about the time of the Thirty Years' War in the early 17th century (*see* Army, "Development of Standing Armies"). At the same time, the elements of today's military uniforms came into use. Previous to the emergence of the full-fledged uniform, armies had used different kinds of insignia as identifying marks. These served to distinguish friend from foe. Colored sashes worn at the shoulder or around the waist were the insignia used in Denmark, Sweden, Spain, and a few other countries.

The uniforms of a high school marching band in Chicago's Saint Patrick's Day parade suggest a military origin.

Military units, in the absence of strong central governments, adopted their own forms of dress. Most of them were very colorful: bright reds, greens, yellows, and blues were common. Regimental loyalties became strong. Units wore their uniforms as a badge of honor. Only with the growth of strong central governments did it become possible to create national uniforms for the armed services. When this happened, regimental identification was relegated to insignia.

The colorful uniforms proved a hazard when gunfire improved. The British soldiers fighting in the American Revolution quickly learned how visible a target a bright red uniform could be, as rebels dressed in dark colors fired at them seemingly out of nowhere. During the 19th century battle dress became more drab as firepower became more accurate. Today's battle and work uniforms tend to vary from gray to shades of green for army personnel around the world. The other branches of the military, however, have their own distinctive uniforms: Air Force blue and Navy blue and white. Drab gray-greens will probably remain standard for land-based fighting units.

United States

Army. Nineteenth-century Army uniforms were dark blue. The olive-drab color was adopted in 1902. In 1957 it was replaced by what is called Army green. One reason for the change was that many civilians were wearing parts of old uniforms for work clothes. The olive-drab shade thus had lost much of its distinction as a military symbol. Modern armed services have similar uniforms for male and female officers and enlisted personnel since the branches of the military were integrated. The basic types of uniform are: service; utility, or battle dress; and dress.

The basic green service uniform, for both officers and enlisted personnel, is made of wool and worn year-round. It includes a coat cut somewhat like a civilian's single-breasted suit coat. The standard necktie is black in summer or winter, as are shoes. The utility, or battle dress, uniform of four-color camouflage material is worn while on duty on military installations and in battle. The trousers worn with the utility uniform are tucked into blousing straps above the combat boots.

Army dress blue and white uniforms are authorized for both enlisted personnel and officers and are worn both on duty and at less formal social gatherings. Formal dress includes white or blue mess uniforms and white or blue evening mess uniforms.

Ranks of officers are indicated by insignia on shoulder loops or collars. Rank insignia of specialists and noncommissioned officers (NCOs) is worn on both sleeves.

On or off the post either a cloth garrison cap or a visored service cap may be worn. A peaked camouflage cap is worn with the utility uniform. The service-cap insignia, slightly different for officers and for enlisted personnel, features the United States coat of arms. The garrison cap often carries a unit crest. In combat a kevlar helmet is worn, while the helmet liner may be worn by itself in nontactical training.

Official colors of branch or corps are worn on various uniform components, such as the dress aiguillette. Light blue stands for infantry; yellow for armor; scarlet for field artillery; orange piped with white for signal corps; cobalt blue piped with golden yellow for chemical corps; and scarlet piped with white for corps of engineers.

Air Force. Except for insignia, Air Force officers and airmen dress alike. The service uniform is dark blue. It includes a coat, matching trousers, light blue shirt, dark blue necktie, and service cap. Green fatigues are worn in the field and on duty when the service uniform is inappropriate.

For semiformal functions, a blue uniform is worn with white shirt and black bow tie. There are black

Chefs in the finest restaurants wear distinctive headgear as part of their otherwise plain uniforms.

RANK INSIGNIA OF THE

	E-1	E-2	E-3	E-4	E-5	E-6	E-7	E-8	E-9	E-9‡	W-1	W-2
	ENLISTED MEN										**WARRANT**	
AIR FORCE	(NO INSIGNIA) AIRMAN BASIC	AIRMAN	AIRMAN FIRST CLASS	SERGEANT / SENIOR AIRMAN	STAFF SERGEANT	TECHNICAL SERGEANT	MASTER SERGEANT	SENIOR MASTER SERGEANT	CHIEF MASTER SERGEANT	CHIEF MASTER SERGEANT OF THE AIR FORCE	WARRANT OFFICER W-1	CHIEF WARRANT OFFICER W-2
ARMY	(NO INSIGNIA) PRIVATE E-1	PRIVATE E-2	PRIVATE FIRST CLASS	CORPORAL / SPECIALIST 4	SERGEANT	STAFF SERGEANT	PLATOON SERGEANT OR SERGEANT FIRST CLASS	FIRST SERGEANT / MASTER SERGEANT	COMMAND SERGEANT MAJOR / SERGEANT MAJOR	SERGEANT MAJOR OF THE ARMY	WARRANT OFFICER W-1	CHIEF WARRANT OFFICER W-2
MARINE CORPS	(NO INSIGNIA) PRIVATE	PRIVATE FIRST CLASS	LANCE CORPORAL	CORPORAL	SERGEANT	STAFF SERGEANT	GUNNERY SERGEANT	FIRST SERGEANT / MASTER SERGEANT	SERGEANT MAJOR / MASTER GUNNERY SERGEANT	SERGEANT MAJOR OF THE MARINE CORPS	WARRANT OFFICER W-1	CHIEF WARRANT OFFICER W-2
NAVY AND COAST GUARD *	SEAMAN RECRUIT	SEAMAN APPRENTICE	SEAMAN	PETTY OFFICER THIRD CLASS	PETTY OFFICER SECOND CLASS	PETTY OFFICER FIRST CLASS	CHIEF PETTY OFFICER†	SENIOR CHIEF PETTY OFFICER	MASTER CHIEF PETTY OFFICER	MASTER CHIEF PETTY OFFICER OF THE NAVY	WARRANT OFFICER W-1	CHIEF WARRANT OFFICER W-2

* Rank marks of Coast Guard officers bear a shield in place of the Navy star.
† Gold strips indicate 12 or more years of good conduct.
‡ Only one person in each branch of the service holds this rank.
§ Navy only.

U. S. ARMED FORCES

OFFICERS | COMMISSIONED OFFICERS

W-3	W-4	O-1	O-2	O-3	O-4	O-5	O-6	O-7	O-7 O-8	O-9	O-10	SPECIAL
CHIEF WARRANT OFFICER W-3	CHIEF WARRANT OFFICER W-4	SECOND LIEUTENANT	FIRST LIEUTENANT	CAPTAIN	MAJOR	LIEUTENANT COLONEL	COLONEL	BRIGADIER GENERAL	MAJOR GENERAL	LIEUTENANT GENERAL	GENERAL	GENERAL OF THE AIR FORCE
CHIEF WARRANT OFFICER W-3	CHIEF WARRANT OFFICER W-4	SECOND LIEUTENANT	FIRST LIEUTENANT	CAPTAIN	MAJOR	LIEUTENANT COLONEL	COLONEL	BRIGADIER GENERAL	MAJOR GENERAL	LIEUTENANT GENERAL	GENERAL	GENERAL OF THE ARMY
CHIEF WARRANT OFFICER W-3	CHIEF WARRANT OFFICER W-4	SECOND LIEUTENANT	FIRST LIEUTENANT	CAPTAIN	MAJOR	LIEUTENANT COLONEL	COLONEL	BRIGADIER GENERAL	MAJOR GENERAL	LIEUTENANT GENERAL	GENERAL	
CHIEF WARRANT OFFICER W-3	CHIEF WARRANT OFFICER W-4	ENSIGN	LIEUTENANT JUNIOR GRADE	LIEUTENANT	LIEUTENANT COMMANDER	COMMANDER	CAPTAIN	COMMODORE	REAR ADMIRAL	VICE ADMIRAL	ADMIRAL	FLEET ADMIRAL§

13

INSIGNIA OF BRANCH OR SPECIALTY— U.S. ARMED FORCES

U.S. ARMY

INSIGNIA OF BRANCH

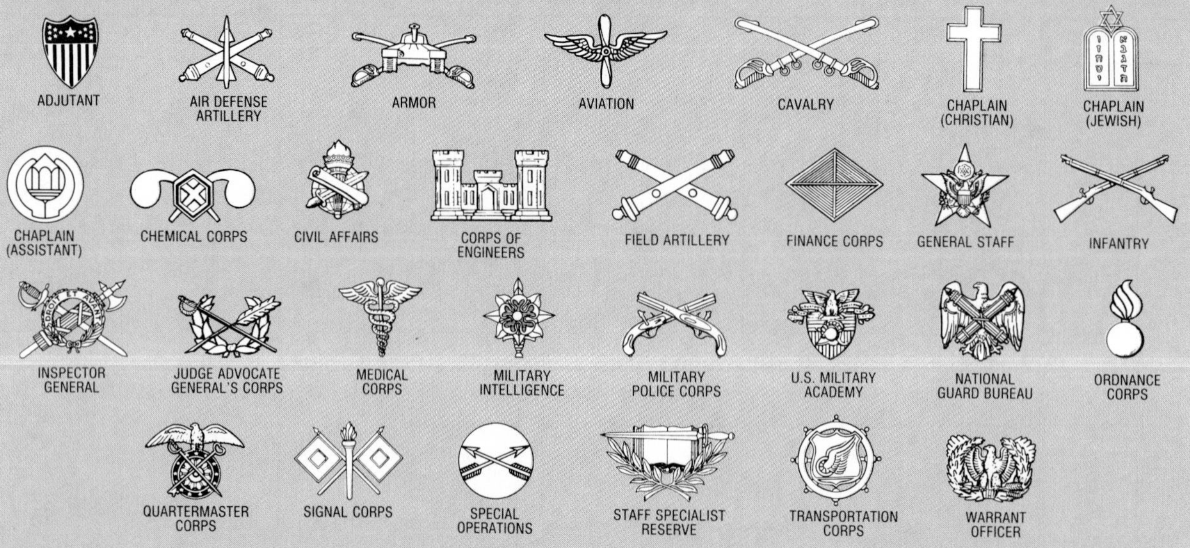

ADJUTANT
AIR DEFENSE ARTILLERY
ARMOR
AVIATION
CAVALRY
CHAPLAIN (CHRISTIAN)
CHAPLAIN (JEWISH)
CHAPLAIN (ASSISTANT)
CHEMICAL CORPS
CIVIL AFFAIRS
CORPS OF ENGINEERS
FIELD ARTILLERY
FINANCE CORPS
GENERAL STAFF
INFANTRY
INSPECTOR GENERAL
JUDGE ADVOCATE GENERAL'S CORPS
MEDICAL CORPS
MILITARY INTELLIGENCE
MILITARY POLICE CORPS
U.S. MILITARY ACADEMY
NATIONAL GUARD BUREAU
ORDNANCE CORPS
QUARTERMASTER CORPS
SIGNAL CORPS
SPECIAL OPERATIONS
STAFF SPECIALIST RESERVE
TRANSPORTATION CORPS
WARRANT OFFICER

BADGES

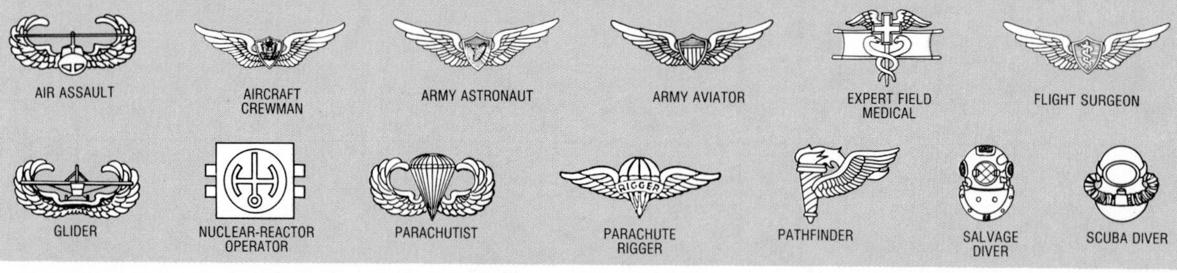

AIR ASSAULT
AIRCRAFT CREWMAN
ARMY ASTRONAUT
ARMY AVIATOR
EXPERT FIELD MEDICAL
FLIGHT SURGEON
GLIDER
NUCLEAR-REACTOR OPERATOR
PARACHUTIST
PARACHUTE RIGGER
PATHFINDER
SALVAGE DIVER
SCUBA DIVER

U.S. AIR FORCE

ENLISTED AIRCREW MEMBER
SENIOR ENLISTED AIRCREW MEMBER
CHIEF ENLISTED AIRCREW MEMBER
OFFICER AIRCREW MEMBER
SENIOR OFFICER AIRCREW MEMBER
MASTER AIRCREW MEMBER
SPECIALIST, EXPLOSIVE ORDNANCE DISPOSAL
SUPERVISOR, EXPLOSIVE ORDNANCE DISPOSAL
MASTER, EXPLOSIVE ORDNANCE DISPOSAL
FLIGHT SURGEON
SENIOR FLIGHT SURGEON
CHIEF FLIGHT SURGEON
NAVIGATOR OR AIRCRAFT OBSERVER
SENIOR NAVIGATOR OR SENIOR AIRCRAFT OBSERVER
MASTER NAVIGATOR OR MASTER AIRCRAFT OBSERVER
FLIGHT NURSE
SENIOR FLIGHT NURSE
CHIEF FLIGHT NURSE
PILOT
SENIOR PILOT
COMMAND PILOT
BASIC AIR-TRAFFIC CONTROLLER
PARACHUTIST
WEAPONS CONTROLLER
SECURITY POLICE
CHAPLAIN (CHRISTIAN)
CHAPLAIN (JEWISH)
MISSILE
DENTIST
NURSE
PHYSICIAN

INSIGNIA OF BRANCH OR SPECIALTY— U.S. ARMED FORCES

U.S. NAVY

LINE DEVICES

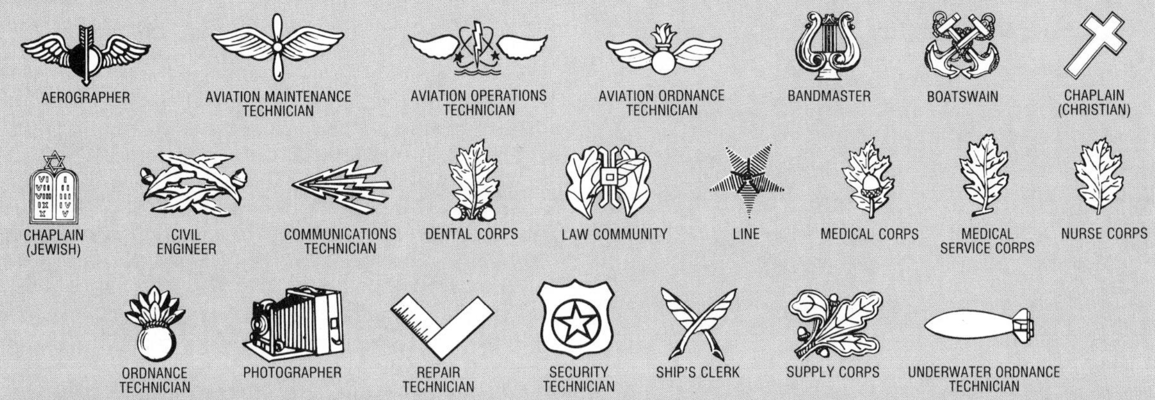
AEROGRAPHER
AVIATION MAINTENANCE TECHNICIAN
AVIATION OPERATIONS TECHNICIAN
AVIATION ORDNANCE TECHNICIAN
BANDMASTER
BOATSWAIN
CHAPLAIN (CHRISTIAN)
CHAPLAIN (JEWISH)
CIVIL ENGINEER
COMMUNICATIONS TECHNICIAN
DENTAL CORPS
LAW COMMUNITY
LINE
MEDICAL CORPS
MEDICAL SERVICE CORPS
NURSE CORPS
ORDNANCE TECHNICIAN
PHOTOGRAPHER
REPAIR TECHNICIAN
SECURITY TECHNICIAN
SHIP'S CLERK
SUPPLY CORPS
UNDERWATER ORDNANCE TECHNICIAN

SPECIALTY MARKS

AIRCREW SURVIVAL EQUIPMENT MAN
AIR-TRAFFIC CONTROLLER
AVIATION BOATSWAIN'S MATE
AVIATION ELECTRONICS TECHNICIAN
AVIATION FIRE-CONTROL TECHNICIAN
AVIATION MAINTENANCE ADMINISTRATION MAN
AVIATION ORDNANCEMAN
AVIATION SUPPORT EQUIPMENT TECHNICIAN
BOATSWAIN'S MATE
BOILER TECHNICIAN
BUILDER
CONSTRUCTION ELECTRICIAN
CONSTRUCTION MECHANIC
CRYPTOLOGIC TECHNICIAN
DAMAGE CONTROLMAN
DATA-PROCESSING TECHNICIAN
DENTAL TECHNICIAN
DISBURSING CLERK
ELECTRICIAN'S MATE
ELECTRONICS TECHNICIAN
ELECTRONICS WARFARE TECHNICIAN
ENGINEERING AID
ENGINEMAN
EQUIPMENT OPERATOR
FIRE-CONTROL TECHNICIAN
GAS TURBINE SYSTEM TECHNICIAN
GUNNER'S MATE
HOSPITAL CORPSMAN
HULL MAINTENANCE TECHNICIAN
ILLUSTRATOR DRAFTSMAN
INSTRUMENTMAN
INTELLIGENCE SPECIALIST
INTERIOR COMMUNICATIONS ELECTRICIAN
JOURNALIST
LEGALMAN
LITHOGRAPHER
MACHINERY REPAIRMAN
MACHINIST'S MATE
MESS MANAGEMENT SPECIALIST
MINEMAN
MISSILE TECHNICIAN
MUSICIAN
NAVY COUNSELOR
OPERATIONS SPECIALIST
OPTICALMAN
PATTERNMAKER
PERSONNELMAN
POSTAL CLERK
QUARTERMASTER
RADIOMAN
SHIP'S SERVICEMAN
SIGNALMAN
SONAR TECHNICIAN
STEELWORKER
STOREKEEPER
TORPEDOMAN'S MATE
TRADESMAN
UTILITIES MAN
YEOMAN

Giansanti—Sygma

The uniforms of the Swiss Guard in Vatican City have remained virtually unchanged for centuries.

or white mess dress uniforms and ceremonial dress uniforms for formal functions. A black formal dress uniform also may be worn.

Navy. The regular service uniforms of the Navy are blue. Grades above first-class petty officers wear a double-breasted tunic with white shirt and dark necktie. Naval aviation officers wear a green uniform while on flight duty. Enlisted personnel below the rank of chief petty officer wear dungarees for work. Summer work and service uniforms for all other Navy personnel are khaki. Khaki or dungarees are worn during submarine duty.

Petty officers and nonrated men wear a loose-fitting jumper with a square sailor collar. The collar and the sleeves of the dress jumper are trimmed with three stripes. The undress jumper has a plain collar. For several years the trousers had zippers, but in 1956, at the request of many sailors, the official trousers were changed back to the traditional 13-button "broad fall front." For shore patrol or field duty, trousers are

tucked into khaki leggings. Officers and chief petty officers wear a visored cap. First-class petty officers and lower grades wear a round white hat with a brim that turns up all around.

There are white service uniforms for both enlisted personnel and officers, and full-dress uniforms for officers and chief petty officers. A white dinner jacket and blue trousers may be worn.

Navy ranks of commissioned and warrant officers are indicated by the number and size of gold stripes worn on the lower sleeve or on shoulder boards. The stripes are black on the naval aviation green uniform. Collar insignia, like those of the Army for equivalent rank, are worn on Navy officers' summer uniforms. Enlisted personnel wear rating badges on their left sleeves.

Marine and Coast Guard. The Marine Corps uniform is similar to that of the Army. The winter uniform consists of forest green wool coat and trousers, khaki shirt, and necktie. The blue dress uniform includes a dark blue coat, piped in red, with a standing collar. Trousers are light blue, with a red stripe for noncommissioned and commissioned officers. A khaki cap is worn with the summer service uniform and a forest green cap in winter. With the blue uniform a blue cap is worn in winter and a white cap in summer. The Marine Corps emblem is a globe resting on an anchor, surmounted by an eagle. Rank and insignia are similar to those of the Army.

The Coast Guard wears the same uniforms and insignia of grade as the Navy, with some minor changes. A Coast Guard shield is used on officer and warrant officer insignia where a Navy star would appear on Navy uniforms. Other variations are in buttons, some sleeve insignia, cap devices, and shoulder marks.

Service ornaments. Members of the Army may wear specific ornaments on their sleeves to denote special service. A gold overseas service bar may be worn horizontally on the right sleeve for each six months active overseas duty with the Army in World War II and during the Korean and Vietnam wars.

The dress uniform for a United States Marine honor guard contrasts greatly with the battle dress of khaki with camouflage markings of the Army's 82nd Airborne Division at Fort Bragg, N.C.

Photos, Camerique

Midshipmen on parade (below) at the United States Naval Academy in Annapolis, Md., wear their navy blue field uniforms with white hats. Students at the Air Force Academy near Colorado Springs, Colo., (right) wear field uniforms of Air Force blue with matching hats.

Enlisted personnel of the Army wear a diagonal service stripe (hash mark) on the lower left sleeve for each three years of service. The Marine Corps and Navy wear a service stripe for each four years of service. (*See also* Medals and Decorations.)

Great Britain and the Commonwealth

The dress uniforms of the British armed forces are among the most colorful in the world. They have been changed very little over the years, and they bear markings and symbols that may be traced far back into the history of Great Britain.

The uniforms of the guards regiments are among the best known. Londoners and tourists throng to Buckingham Palace to watch the changing of the guards. These soldiers of the Queen wear brilliant red jackets and blue-striped trousers. Regular headdress for all five of the regiments is a tall bearskin hat.

Plumes on the bearskin identify the various regiments. The Grenadiers' bearskin has a 6-inch (15-centimeter) white plume of goat's hair on the left side. The Coldstream Guards have a red plume on the right side. The Irish Guards' bearskin has a 6-inch Saint Patrick's blue plume of cut feathers on the right side. The Welsh Guards have a 9-inch (23-centimeter) white plume with a 2-inch (5-centimeter) green band on the left side of the headdress. Scots Guards have no plumes on their bearskins.

The buttons on the English dress uniforms also have special significance. Evenly spaced tunic buttons are the mark of the Grenadier. The other guards wear buttons in groups of twos, threes, fours, or fives to indicate their regiment. Full dress for the Scots Guards is a brilliant Highland uniform with kilts.

Regular summer and winter uniforms for the British Army are khaki. A darker shade is used for battle dress. Uniforms of the British Navy are the familiar navy blue. Those of the Air Force are air force blue. The same general pattern of color and style is used in other Commonwealth nations, with certain exceptions. One celebrated variation is the slouch hat of the Australian Army. Insignia of rank on Commonwealth uniforms are somewhat similar to those used in the United States. British NCOs wear stripes on their sleeves. British officers, depending upon their service or class of uniform, wear insignia of rank on the shoulder, lower arm, or collar in the same general positions used on United States military dress.

Before Canada's military forces were unified in 1968, its uniforms were similar in cut and colors to those worn by the armed forces of Great Britain. However, for the development of a national identity within the newly instituted Canadian Armed Forces, a dark green dress uniform was introduced. All members of the Canadian forces wear the common dress uniform. Fatigue uniforms are worn for land, sea, and air units. Members of the Mobile Command, the land forces of the Canadian Armed Forces, wear combat dress resembling that worn by United States infantrymen.

The Blues and Royals are one of the two regiments of Household Cavalry stationed at the Horse Guards in London.

The Kremlin in Moscow is the seat of government for the Soviet Union. Originally a large fortress complex dating from the 12th century, it is situated on the Moscow River.

UNION OF SOVIET SOCIALIST REPUBLICS

UNION OF SO-VIET SOCIAL-IST REPUBLICS (U.S.S.R.). The Union of Soviet Socialist Republics, or Soviet Union, is a country glutted with superlatives. With 8.6 million square miles (22.4 million square kilometers), it is the world's largest country. With a sixth of the Earth's landmass, it is exceeded in size by only three geographic phenomena: Eurasia (Europe and Asia considered as a single continent), Africa, and North America—each a continent. Making up half of Europe and nearly two fifths of Asia, the Soviet Union represents the lion's share of the Eurasian continent (41 percent). It is 2.4 times the size of the United States and contains the third largest population on Earth after China and India. On Jan. 1, 1987, the Soviet Union claimed a population of 282 million people, nearly 40 million more than that of the United States, the fourth most populous country.

Preview

The article Union of Soviet Socialist Republics is divided into the following sections:

Introduction 18
The Land 21
Climate, Vegetation, and Animal Life . . 25
People and Culture 29
Economy 39
Government 47
History 49
Bibliography 56
Fact Summary 57
Political Maps 59–66
For a brief review of essential information about the Union of Soviet Socialist Republics, *see* UNION OF SOVIET SOCIALIST REPUBLICS FACT SUMMARY.

This article was contributed by Victor L. Mote, Professor of Geography and Political Science, University of Houston, and Fellow, Slavic Research Center, University of Hokkaido, Japan.

18

The Soviet Union's size ensures a generous endowment of natural features and raw materials. The country also has some of the world's highest mountains and lowest basins, largest plains and broadest tablelands, driest deserts and wettest swamps, purest waters and saltiest seas, longest rivers and deepest lakes, greatest grasslands and most extensive forests. The Soviet resource base is by far the world's most extensive, ensuring self-sufficiency for its people in most resources for dozens, if not hundreds, of years. The Soviet Union is usually first or second in the annual production of the majority of the world's strategic raw materials.

Yet, superior size can be a disadvantage: quality often yields to quantity. Raw materials, no matter how abundant, must be accessible and economical to exploit. Supplies that are far away from consumers require efficient transportation networks. Large countries need effective communications to maintain smooth political control.

Immensity and Diversity

The Soviet Union stretches from Wisla (Vistula) Bar in Kaliningrad oblast (19° E.) in the west to Ratmanova (Big Diomede) Island (169° W.) in the east. The 171 degrees of longitude span 5,700 miles (9,180 kilometers) and eleven time zones. If the Soviet Union could be placed atop North America so that Leningrad was over Anchorage, Alaska, the Chukchi Peninsula would lie close to Oslo, Norway—fully halfway around the globe at the 60th parallel. Put another way, when Leningraders are eating their evening meal on any given day, Soviet Eskimo are breakfasting on the next. From its southernmost point at 35° N. to the tip of its northernmost islands at 82° N., the Soviet Union extends nearly 3,700 miles (6,000 kilometers).

Befitting the world's largest country, Soviet borders are the longest of any nation—37,000 miles (60,000 kilometers)—more than two thirds of them seacoast. The vast majority of the coastal boundary, however, is frozen for up to ten months yearly. Access to the world's oceans is both difficult and expensive.

Perhaps more significant than sheer size are its relative location and orientation to other industrial nations. Three fourths of the country is north of the 50th parallel. Except for Alaska no part of the United States is so far north. Moscow, the capital of the Soviet Union, is in the latitude of Edmonton, Alta., while Leningrad's latitude approximates that of Anchorage, Alaska. Given its high-latitude position, the Soviet Union resembles Canada more than it does the United States. Yet Moscow is as close to Washington, D.C., as it is to Seattle, Wash. Seattle in turn is as close to Leningrad as it is to Vladivostok. Leningrad and Vladivostok are almost as far away from each other as they are from Seattle.

This north-south "military" axis contrasts sharply with the Soviet Union's historical east-west axis of domestic commerce and migration. These movements have been funnelled between the Arctic's frozen seas and the deserts and mountain barriers of the south.

Size again explains why three fourths of the country is more than 250 miles (400 kilometers) from the sea, which strongly affects its continental climate.

Its size also emphasizes great distances between and among geographic phenomena. Although in its totality the Soviet Union displays great beauty and diversity of landforms, climate, vegetation, and soils, close up it can be very dull because of the space and time required between changes. Variety spread thinly over a massive land can be monotonous. Three fourths of the country, for example, is a vast plain at less than 1,500 feet (450 meters) in elevation. The typical Soviet landscape is a flat-to-rolling countryside, the mountains relegated to the borders and the area east of the Yenisey River. The Ural Mountains, which divide Europe from Asia, are no higher than 6,200 feet (1,890 meters) and form only a modest barrier to passing air masses and human interaction. The average elevation for the country as a whole is 1,406 feet (430 meters), ranging from −433 feet (−132 meters) on the bottom of the Caspian Sea's Karagiye Depression to 24,590 feet (7,495 meters) atop Mount Communism in the Pamir Range of Central Asia.

Eurasian Collectivists

In a mostly landlocked, huge northerly landmass bound on the north and east by icy, uninviting seas, on the south by rugged mountains, and on the west by a generally flat, open land border, the people who have coped with the territory now occupied by the Soviet Union have overcome great difficulties. As if the environment did not pose problems enough, historically the inhabitants have had to deal persistently with the threat of foreign invasion. At first the invaders were Asiatic nomadic horsemen. Since the 1800s they have come as modern armies from Europe. Whether troubled by the hostile environment or attacked by hostile armies, the peoples of the East European Plain typically met danger collectively rather than as individuals. Village life-style and group cooperation have been the rule rather than the exception throughout the history of most Eastern Slavic nations, including those who live in this part of Russia.

Leaders of collectivist societies believe that the welfare of the collective—meaning all of society—is more important than individual liberties. Everyone's basic needs are taken care of by the governing body. In the modern Soviet state "basic needs" include such services as education, medical care, and transportation. Housing is inexpensive, and food supplies, though relatively expensive, are subsidized and generally available. In collective societies equal rights and shares among individuals and communities matter more than do individual freedoms. Everyone in such communities is supposed to have enough, but no one has very much because the resources are distributed equally. People's lives improve when the quality and quantity of resources increase and society overall progresses. Without the market principle to guide the economy, central authorities shape the direction of this progress. These authorities are supposed to be fair

In the vast extent of the Soviet Union are several areas almost totally unfit for agriculture. Some of the Pripyat' Marshes (top left)in the Belorussian S.S.R. have been reclaimed, but the area has low population density. The autumn tundra in the far north of Siberia (top right) is already frozen. Horses (left) quench their thirst at a well in the desert area of the Mangyshlak Peninsula in the Kazakh S.S.R.

Photos, Tass/Sovfoto; (top left) E. Kobyak; (top right) S. Belyavoi; (left) V. Granovsky

and rational in their decision making, but many times they are arbitrary and sometimes despotic. Without the traditions of English common law, free enterprise, and an emphasis on human rights, only a handful of Russian intellectuals ever toyed with the concepts of individual freedom, initiative, and innovation. The brief experiment with capitalism in the late 1800s and early 1900s was limited to a few major cities and was too ineffective to have lasting influence.

In this sense, as with their geography, Russians are uniquely neither European nor Asian—they reflect a truly Eurasian character. They have an Oriental sense of patience. Their religion sprang from Byzantium, not Rome. They never had a Renaissance. They only experimented fleetingly with free enterprise and never with democracy. On the eve of the Bolshevik Revolution in 1917, two of three Russians were peasant collectivists, and four of five lived in rural villages of fewer than 15,000 residents. Perhaps socialism was tailor-made for what was then czarist Russia.

In his last unpublished writings, in 1881, Karl Marx apparently thought so, and later on Lenin knew so.

The Soviet Union not only looms large on world maps but also composes the Earth's second (or third) largest economy and competes well for military superiority. Since 1960 it has taken an increasingly major role in international commerce, as its trade turnover quintupled to 131 billion rubles (170 billion mid-1980s United States dollars). A member of the United Nations together with the Ukrainian and Belorussian Soviet Socialist Republics (S.S.R.s) since 1945, it is a powerful political force.

For good or bad it was the first country in the world to espouse the causes of Marxist-Leninist socialism. Beginning as an impoverished country, the Soviet Union has made spectacular strides since the Bolshevik Revolution in 1917. Marxism-Leninism thus appeals to leaders of some developing countries as a viable alternative to capitalism—nations where there are many dispossessed and impoverished people, where a few have most of the wealth, or where the leadership is unresponsive to the needs of the masses. The Soviet constitution openly supports "wars of liberation" wherever and whenever they occur, and impoverished, militant intellectuals are often only too happy to accept that support. Viewed as either a powerful rival or a threat, the presence of the Soviet Union cannot be ignored.

In the 1980s the Soviet Union began to change. Following decades of repression, political favoritism, and bureaucratic stagnation, the Soviet government after 1984 was given an injection of fresh new leadership. General Secretary Mikhail Gorbachev promised a vast array of *perestroika,* or "restructuring," that in his words is "absolutely essential" if the Soviet Union is to remain competitive in the world economy. A more open policy of *glasnost,* or "openness," was encouraged. A host of peace proposals were proffered, resulting in a major nuclear arms reduction agreement with the United States.

THE LAND

The Soviet Union is the classic example of the geographic "too theory." It is a massive, land-based, high-latitude subcontinent. Essentially a large rectangle, the country consists of a slightly interrupted plain for more than half of its extent, flanked in the south and east by plateaus and mountains. The country's underbelly (Central Asia) is a desert and "too dry." Western Siberia is so flat and poorly drained that it contains the world's largest bog, the Vasyugan, which is "too wet." This is also true of the Pripyat' (or Pinsk)

Marshes in Belorussia, which frustrated Napoleon's and Adolf Hitler's invading armies. The winters of the north country, eastern Siberia, and much of the Soviet Far East are so long—six to ten months—that well over half of the country is "too cold" for farming. The southern mountains are "too high" and rugged except for seasonal pastoralists. Because three quarters of the people live in the western third of the country, most of Siberia is "too far" away to justify economic development. Overlapping all the "toos" on a map displays an *ecumene,* or habitable area, that represents only about 10 percent of the country. This *ecumene* is most often called the Fertile Triangle.

Surface Features

The Soviet Union contains two stable blocks—the Eastern European and Siberian platforms. The suture that ties the two platforms together is the 250-million-year-old Ural Mountain chain. Around these platforms are folded mountain systems of younger ages. The platforms' ancient rocks (more than 550 million years old) are exposed on the Fenno-Scandian Shield, in the southern Urals, and on Siberia's Aldan and Anabar shields. The youngest materials are the sediments of the Azov-Caspian, Turanian, and West Siberian plains.

The European part of the Soviet Union is covered by sediments except in the northwest (Kola-Karelia) and in the foothills of the Carpathian Mountains (Volyno-Podol'sk Upland), where resistant outcrops appear. The highest elevations outside the Urals in the west are in the Khibin Mountains of the Kola Peninsula—

Topography

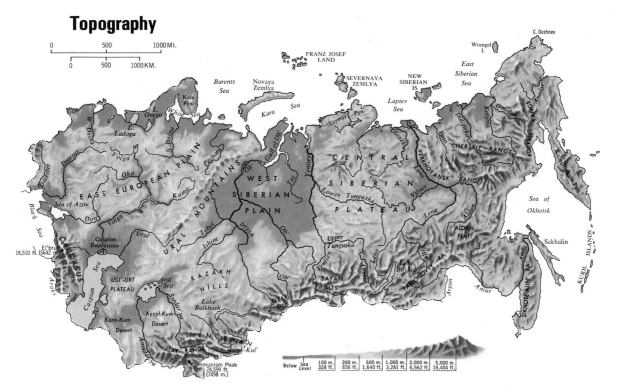

Mount El'brus, at 18,481 feet (5,633 meters), is Europe's highest peak. It is located in the Greater Caucasus mountain range between the Black and Caspian seas.

Tass/Sovfoto

3,000 feet (900 meters). Elsewhere the region consists of low-lying plains and peat bogs except in the Valday Hills, with a maximum elevation of 1,138 feet (347 meters); the Smolensk-Moscow Ridge and the Central Russian Upland—both less than 1,000 feet (300 meters); and the pre-Volga Heights. The Valday Hills and Smolensk-Moscow Ridge are morainal deposits that trapped meltwater from Pleistocene glaciers and created pro-glacial lakes and marshes. The Smolensk-Moscow Ridge, representative of the only dryland route between Moscow and Warsaw, Poland, divides the Pripyat' Marshes into two sections.

In cross section the Ukraine resembles a shallow bowl that swells with the Carpathians in the west, bottoms out in the Dnepr River valley, and rises again in the Donets and pre-Azov heights. The Donets Heights, which reach elevations of 1,200 feet (366 meters), are known for coal deposits. The Ukrainian Shield and Azov-Caspian Lowland flank the uplands in the south and east.

On the southern lip of the Crimean Peninsula begins the first of a long string of bordering mountain ranges that penetrate into eastern Siberia and the Soviet Far East. The Crimean, or Yaila, Mountains are separated from the Greater Caucasus by the Kerch' Peninsula and Kerch' Strait. The Greater Caucasus are flanked on the north by the broad Stavropol' Upland, the home of Mikhail Gorbachev. Many of the mountains of the range are igneous, including Mount El'brus—at 18,481 feet (5,633 meters), the highest peak in Europe. In the south the Great Caucasus sink into the Transcaucasian depression that contains the Colchis Lowland of the Georgian S.S.R., the Suram Massif that links the Greater and Lesser Caucasus in the Armenian S.S.R., and the Kura Lowland that runs from Tbilisi, Georgia, into Azerbaijan. The Colchis is known for the legend of the Golden Fleece. The Armenian Plateau spreads southward from the Lesser Caucasus into Turkey and Iran.

The chain of high mountains continues beyond the Caspian Sea with Turkmenia's Greater Balkhan and Kopet Dag ranges. These ranges slope northeastward into the deserts of the Kara-Kum and Kyzyl-Kum. Flowing through these wastelands and the Turanian Lowland of the Aral Sea are the Amu-Dar'ya and Syr-Dar'ya rivers. The Aral and Caspian seas are separated by the barren Ustyurt Plateau.

There is no natural barrier along the Afghan border with the Turkmen S.S.R. The once-high mountain chain blends into lower foothills that rise abruptly as the Hindu Kush inside Afghanistan. In the Tadzhik S.S.R. the Hindu Kush are tied together with the Himalayas in the Pamir Knot, the country's highest mountain range and the focus of South Asia's great system of alpine mountains. Here along with Mount Communism is Lenin Peak, which rises to 23,406 feet (7,134 meters). The Pamir glaciers provide the meltwaters that feed the Amu-Dar'ya.

The Uzbek S.S.R.'s Fergana Basin is shaded in the south by the Alay Range that separates Tadzhikistan from the Kirgiz S.S.R. On the north the fertile valley, irrigated by the Syr-Dar'ya, is sheltered by the lofty Tian Shan, China's "Heavenly Mountains." The Tian Shan rank among the world's most earthquake-prone systems. Nestled in the mountainous interior is one of the world's highest lakes, Issyk-Kul'.

As the Tian Shan veer eastward into China, the landscape descends quickly into the Ili River valley and the Balkhash Basin. It was along the Ili River and through the Dzungarian Gates that many Asiatic nomads rode into the modern Kazakh S.S.R. From Lake Balkhash north and west, these nomads would have ascended the Kazakh Upland.

The Kazakh Upland supplies the western headwaters of the Ob'-Irtysh river system. One of the tributaries, the Tobol, occupies a natural trough, the Turgay Gate, that divides the Kazakh Upland from the southern Urals.

The Ural Mountains are low-lying remnants of much higher ranges. The northern Urals are highest. The central Urals are lowest and are the location of the main transportation routes including the Trans-Siberian Railroad. The southern Urals are of medium elevation but broad. For more than 200 million years the once-mighty Urals have been attacked by the Volga-Kama system and the rivers of the Ob' network. Sediments have filled basins on both sides of the divide, but none so remarkably as the West Siberian Plain.

For 1,000 miles (1,600 kilometers) from the Urals to the Yenisey, and for 1,200 miles (1,900 kilometers) north to south, the West Siberian Plain never rises more than 600 feet (180 meters) above sea level. The Ob' River and its tributaries flow slowly across this massive "pool table" into the Arctic Ocean. When the southern tributaries swell with meltwater in the spring, the main trunk, the Ob', is still ice-dammed in the north. The flooding is extensive, creating the world's largest sphagnum bog, the Vasyugan Swamps, on the world's largest plain.

East of the Yenisey River lies the Central Siberian Plateau, from which flow the major tributaries of the Yenisey and Lena. In the south the mountain arc continues as the Altai Range, where the Ob' River is born. Two arms of the Altai system confine a valley of the Tom' River, a right-bank tributary of the Ob'. Within the valley (the Kuznetsk Basin), deposits of high-quality coal have been unearthed. The Altai merges with the Sayan Range in the east.

The centerpiece of the region beyond the Sayans is Lake Baikal, or Baykal, which lies in an active rift valley that is separating at a rate of 1 to 2 inches (2.5 to 5 centimeters) per year. Baikal's surface area is not very impressive—the size of Belgium—but it is the world's deepest lake. More than 1 mile (1,600 meters) deep in the late 1980s, Baikal gets deeper by the earthquake, and in several million years it will become a new ocean. It contains a fifth of the world's fresh water—more water than all five of the Great Lakes combined. If Baikal could be drained, it would take all the rivers of the Earth nearly a year to fill it again. Truly unique on Earth, Baikal is home to more than 1,700 species of plants and animals, two thirds of which can be found nowhere else.

Lake Baikal forms a tectonic divide. In the west is the pre-Baikal Upland. In the east is Transbaikalia, which merges in the southeast with the Yablonovyy Range. Swinging arclike first eastward and then northward along the coast of the Sea of Okhotsk are the Stanovoy, Dzhugdzhur, and Kolyma ranges. The Anadyr', Koryak, and Kamchatka ranges compose the Chukchi and Kamchatka peninsulas. The latter is one of the Earth's most volcanically active regions. This is also true of the Kuril (derived from the Russian verb "to smoke") Islands. In the southeast the Amur River is flanked in the north by the Bureya Range and in the south by the Sikhote-Alin'. Deep in the interior along the eastern bank of the Lena is the Verkhoyansk Range that links with the Cherskiy Range.

In eastern Siberia lowlands are dispersed. The Central Siberian Lowland divides the same-named upland from the hilly Taymyr Peninsula. The Lena River creates the Central Yakut Lowland in its middle course near Yakutsk. Likewise the Kolyma Lowland is the product of the Kolyma River's winding course. Along the Amur is the fertile Zeya-Bureya Plain, and along the Ussuri River, a right-bank tributary of the Amur, is the Ussuri Lowland.

Major Rivers and Lakes

Of its 150,000 rivers, the Soviet Union contains five of the world's 17 longest. Of these five the shortest, the Volga, is the most famous—not only because it is the longest river in Europe but also because of its major role in Russian history. The other four are in Asia: Ob'-Irtysh, Amur, Lena, and Yenisey. These respectively rank fourth, seventh, eighth, and twelfth among the world's longest rivers. All but the Amur flow northward into the Arctic Ocean. The "Mother Volga" flows southward but into the world's largest "lake," the landlocked, saltwater Caspian Sea. Finally, 336 rivers flow into Lake Baikal, and only one, the mighty Angara, a tributary of the Yenisey, flows out. If all 336 influents ceased to flow, it would take the Angara 307 years to drain the lake.

The "land of lakes" is in Karelia south to the Valday Hills. Here Pleistocene glaciers left thousands of bodies of water as they receded. The largest of these are Lake Ladoga and Lake Onega. Other sizable lakes are found in Central Asia and southern Kazakhstan (Aral Sea, Lake Balkhash, and Issyk-Kul').

Natural Resources

The resource base of the Soviet Union is truly impressive. Because of its size and diversity, the country is self-sufficient in almost every raw material. Ironically it is least well supplied with agricultural resources, a function of both its high-latitude position and its climatic types. Soviet farmers have had increasing difficulty harvesting sufficient food

Siberia's Lake Baikal is the world's deepest lake and holds one fifth of the world's fresh water.

© Boyd Norton

Khabarovsk, on the Amur River in the Soviet Far East, was founded in 1858 and today is a large industrial center.

for both people and livestock, and the government consistently imports livestock feed from the West to meet the deficit.

Soviet forests include 82 billion cubic meters of wood, or 34 percent of the world's reserves, including 58 percent of the world's coniferous forests. Only a few of these forests are accessible, and a large proportion of the trees are noncommercial.

Perhaps the Soviet Union's greatest single resource is natural gas. The country contains two fifths of the world's gas reserves and leads in its production, having surpassed the United States in 1983. The natural gas deposits are unfortunately not convenient to the markets. Four fifths of the reserves are in the lower Ob' River basin north of the Arctic Circle in permafrost. One field in this remote region, Urengoy, has 10 percent of the Earth's natural gas reserves.

The proved reserves of petroleum represent 10 to 12 percent of the world's total, and the country leads in production. Western Siberia, this time in the middle Ob', again contains most of the reserves and produces 60 percent of current output. One field, Samotlor, traditionally yields 25 percent of Soviet production. Soviet oil production is hampered by not only high transportation costs but also unsatisfactory results from late explorations.

The country ranks second in coal reserves (behind the United States) and third in production (behind the United States and China). Most of the coal mined is either bituminous or anthracite (78 percent). Lignite composes the rest. Two fifths of the mines are strip mines. Although declining, the Donets Basin leads the country in coal production. The best-quality coal comes from the Kuznetsk Basin, the second leading producer. The country's largest coal deposits are on the remote Central Siberian Plateau.

The country has long ranked first in iron-ore production and became the world's leading steel producer in the early 1970s. The greatest iron-ore reserves are in the Kursk Magnetic Anomaly between Kiev and Moscow. The Krivoy Rog Basin southeast of Kiev is the leading producer. Other major iron-ore reserves are in the southern and northern Urals.

The country also leads the world in the production of ferroalloys that go into steelmaking. It typically yields about a third of the world's manganese from the Ukraine and Transcaucasus, a quarter of the chromite from the Urals, a fifth of the nickel from the Kola Peninsula and lower Yenisey River region (Noril'sk), and 5 to 10 percent of the cobalt—mainly from Siberia.

The Soviet Union usually is second in world copper, lead, and zinc production. Major copper-producing centers are in eastern Kazakhstan, Central Asia, Noril'sk, and the Urals. The main lead and zinc producers are in eastern Kazakhstan, the Caucasus, and the Soviet Far East.

Although second in production of aluminum, it is only about 60 percent self-sufficient in the principal aluminum raw material, bauxite. Soviet bauxite mines are in the northwest, the Urals, and in Kazakhstan, but they must be supplemented by the mining of lower-quality ores (nephelite, alunite). The country thus is a net importer of bauxite and alumina for the aluminum industry.

The country also ranks second in the production of tin and tungsten, though it is not well endowed with either. These are found principally in the Soviet Far East. Also found there and in eastern Siberia are such precious minerals as gold, platinum-group metals, and diamonds. The Soviet Union is a close competitor with South Africa for world supremacy in these minerals.

In all, the country in the 1980s was in first or second place in the world production of 28 of the 36 most strategic raw materials. No other country is so well endowed.

Difficult Environments

No country on Earth has a more difficult total environment. Virtually no place in the country is immune to natural hazard: long winters, excessive cold, permafrost, long distances (high transport costs), earthquakes, mudslides, landslides, avalanches, frost, drought, floods, snow problems, icings, and so forth. The geographic "too theory" notes the severity of the environments of Central Asia, the swamps, and almost all of Siberia. In Central Asia agriculture cannot be practiced without irrigation. In the west swamps must be drained at great cost. In eastern Siberia structural foundations cannot be laid unless they are anchored in the permafrost.

Environmental constraints add greatly to economic development costs. In the most severe environments salaries must be raised three to seven times above the average wage to induce workers to leave the comforts of the European heartland. Labor is typically deficient in those areas. To compensate for the lack of workers, more machinery must be used. Usually this machinery is a special variety, suited to the harsh conditions, and thus expensive (15 to 60 percent above average). Servicing the machinery is also expensive (25 percent of the value of the equipment). All this means that benefits from investment accrue very slowly. Labor deficits also imply longer construction periods of double or triple the normal time. Jobs that guarantee more immediate return on investment have priority over local cultural needs and amenities, but without the latter development sites are harried by the rapid turnover of labor. Construction costs spiral well beyond the country's means.

CLIMATE, VEGETATION, AND ANIMAL LIFE

The Soviet Union's continental proportions dramatically influence its climates. Except for the tundra, Crimea, Transcaucasia, and extreme southeast, more than 90 percent of the country has a continental type of climate. Continental climates exhibit extreme differences between winter and summer temperatures and have low precipitation that peaks in summer. The harshness of the climates increases from west to east as the moderating influence of the Atlantic Ocean decreases. Leningrad on the Gulf of Finland has a 45° F (25° C) difference between the July and January means and 19 inches (48 centimeters) of annual precipitation. Yakutsk in eastern Siberia contrasts with a 112° F (65° C) range of temperature and only 4 inches (10 centimeters) of precipitation.

The country's climates range from the cold, windy tundra north of the Arctic Circle to the balmy subtropics of western Georgia; from the arid continental deserts of Central Asia to the mid-latitude monsoon of the Maritime province opposite Japan. The southern Crimea has a Mediterranean climate. The vast bulk of the country, however, experiences a climate characterized by long, cold winters (with snow), brief springs and falls, and mild to cool, moist summers.

Precipitation

The country's open western border, uninterrupted except for the low Urals, permits Atlantic winds and air masses to penetrate as far east as the Yenisey River. In winter these air masses bring moderation and relatively heavy snow to many parts of the European section and western Siberia. Meanwhile most of eastern Siberia and the Soviet Far East are blanketed by a dense, cold high-pressure cell called the Siberian, or Asiatic, High. This huge high-pressure ridge forces the Atlantic air to flow northward into the Arctic and southward against the southern mountains. As a result neither much snow nor much wind affects the deep interior of Siberia in the winter. The exceptions are found along the east coast (Kamchatka, the Kurils, and Maritime province).

As the Eurasian continent heats faster in summer than the surrounding oceans, the pressure cells shift position: the continent becomes dominated by low pressure and the oceans by high pressure. Moist air masses flow onto the land, bringing summer thunderstorms to most Soviet regions. Exceptions are the

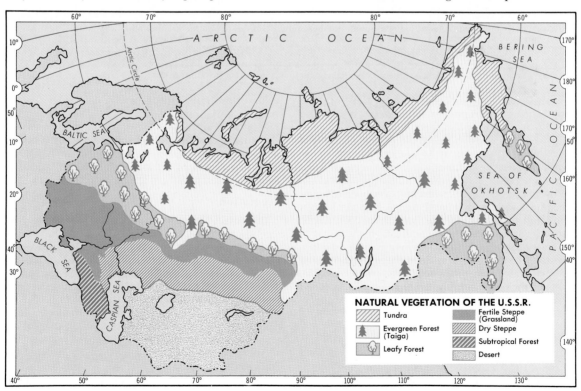

NATURAL VEGETATION OF THE U.S.S.R.

Tundra, Evergreen Forest (Taiga), Leafy Forest, Fertile Steppe (Grassland), Dry Steppe, Subtropical Forest, Desert

25

All photos except bottom right, Bruce Coleman Inc.; (top left) Erwin and Peggy Bauer; (top right) Francisco Erize; (bottom left) Robert L. Dunne; (bottom center) L.L. Rue III; (bottom right) Tom McHugh—Photo Researchers

The Eurasian lynx (top left) is found today in sizable numbers only in Siberia. It, like the musk ox of the northern tundra (top right), is an endangered species, which the Soviet government is trying to preserve. The river otter (bottom left), one of the ablest swimmers in the animal kingdom, may grow to 5 feet (1.5 meters) in length. The Old World brown bear (bottom center) lives now mostly in the mountainous areas of Europe and northern Asia. It is the type of bear often trained for circuses. The mountain goat, or tur (bottom right), thrives in the high mountainous regions of the Himalayas.

eastern Black Sea coast and much of Central Asia. Like Southern Europe the latter areas receive an autumn or winter peak of precipitation. The heaviest rains come later in summer from west to east, often occurring in July or August in western Siberia. In the Soviet Far East the summer wet monsoon yields more than 75 percent of its average annual precipitation.

The most generous, reliable, and evenly distributed precipitation falls in a land wedge that runs from Leningrad to Moscow to the Carpathian Mountains. Here 20 inches (51 centimeters) of precipitation is virtually guaranteed yearly. Elsewhere such amounts are rare. The heaviest quantities are in southwestern Georgia—more than 90 inches (230 centimeters). The least—3 inches (7 centimeters) or less—is recorded in the Central Asian deserts and parts of northeastern Siberia.

Temperature

In winter, temperatures become colder from west to east, the warmest being along the Black Sea, the southern Caspian seaboard, and along the Iran-Afghanistan border. Temperatures along the Pacific coast are little moderated because of sea ice and the tendency for air masses to move from west to east.

In summer, temperatures tend to cool with higher latitudes, with the warmest averaging more than 80° F (27° C) in southern Turkmenistan. Simultaneously the coldest temperatures are recorded in the tundra.

Vegetation

The Soviet Union includes almost every variety of vegetation except for tropical types. In the tundra the warmest average monthly temperature dips below 50° F (10° C), the cold threshold for trees. Tundra consists of mosses, sedges, lichens, grasses, and stunted trees. The Soviet tundra fringes the Arctic coast and exists above the timberline in the mountains.

With 40 percent of its territory clad in forests of all types, the country contains three fifths of the world's coniferous forests. From the Russian language the northern coniferous forest is called taiga. West of the Urals the taiga contains pine, spruce, and fir. East of the Urals the species mix becomes more cold tolerant, including spruce, fir, Siberian stone pine, and larch. Larch, a deciduous conifer, loses its needles in winter and survives well on permafrost. Where the taiga is cleared by loggers, it is often invaded by quick-growing birch or aspen.

Almost all of the tundra and taiga zone is underlain by permafrost. Where sunlight is deficient and snow cover—which insulates the subsurface—is not deep, moisture within the soil down to bedrock may exist in a perpetually frozen state. Only the upper few feet of the ground surface thaws with warmer temperatures. Just under half of the country and more than two thirds of Siberia must deal with permafrosts of varying thicknesses that decrease and become more sporadic from north to south and east to west. Permafrost naturally hinders farming, structural engineering, road construction, and many other activities.

South of the taiga summers are longer and in the west, wetter, allowing for a greater variety of trees. In the European section the forest is invaded by broadleaf species, including hornbeam (Carpathians only), oak, ash, maple, linden, poplar, birch, and aspen. Siberia is noted for its lack of mixed forest.

Still farther south the conifers eventually reach their existence threshold, and all that remain are broadleaf trees of the varieties mentioned above. In western Siberia a broadleaf forest of birch and aspen divides the taiga from the steppe. In the European section most of the broadleaf forest and much of the mixed-forest belt have been cleared for farming.

Conditions become steadily drier approaching the southern borders. Trees first become clumped into copses separated by tall- to medium-height grasses (forest steppe) and then disappear altogether. The Soviet steppe, a short- to medium-height grassland, is one of the world's great biomes, consisting of the Earth's richest endowment of chernozem soils (mollisols). Virtually no virgin steppe remains, having been plowed for agriculture long ago. The steppe forms the heart of the Fertile Triangle.

The steppe finally merges with the mountains and deserts of the south-central Soviet Union. The deserts include those of the pre-Caspian Lowland and Central Asia, where dry-land vegetation survives, including the saxaul tree.

Special vegetation complexes are found in the unusual climates of the southern Crimea, Transcaucasia, and the Maritime province of the Soviet Far East. The Crimea and Transcaucasus are noted for their Mediterranean and subtropical plant species: eucalyptus (imported from Australia), Russian olive, oleander, rhododendron, Italian cypress, beechnut, tung, citrus, and a host of others. The Maritime province has such unusual species as the Amur cork tree.

Soils

Soils are the product of underlying bedrock, slope, climate, and vegetation. True soil (solum) is a suitable mixture of organic and inorganic ingredients: neither sand nor peat is true soil. Most climates, if the vegetation is typical, yield a zonal soil, or a soil that is predictably in place as a response to climatic factors.

True soil is hard to find in the Soviet tundra. The soils are either mechanically weathered bedrock (lithosols) or bog-type soils on permafrost (cryaquepts). Neither is suitable for farming—even if the tundra's growing season were longer than its normal 60 days.

The taiga likewise possesses soils with little agricultural potential. These are either highly acidic nodzols (spodosols) or mountain or permafrost soils determined by factors other than climate. The growing season is longer in the taiga than in the tundra but still only suitable for root crops and hardy, quick-ripening produce. Berries and mushrooms grow wild in the taiga.

The mixed and broadleaf forest soils are also acidic and podzolized (gray and brown alfisols) but historically have been easily tilled. They also are combined with a growing season (120-day minimum) that per-

People wait in line to buy chickens and other farm produce in Tashkent, Uzbek S.S.R. The open markets in some of the southern republics help prevent the food shortages often found in other parts of the Soviet Union.

Bruce Gordon—Photo Researchers

The Cathedral of the Assumption, founded in the 12th century and completed in the 18th, was one of the few historic buildings in and around Smolensk to survive the ravages of World War II.

mits one harvest per field per year. They must be fertilized with lime if cultivated often. These soils merge with increasingly fertile soils on the margins of the forests and grasslands (forest steppe).

The steppe has rich black loams known as "black earths," or chernozems (mollisols). These soils have been naturally fortified by wind-driven loess and the steady decomposition and accumulation of humus from prairie grasses. Below is also limestone from ancient seabeds. These factors—combined with a semiarid climate that leaves the soluble nutrients near the surface instead of draining them away—make the richest soil on Earth. With proper irrigation they yield bumper harvests. Otherwise dry-farming techniques must be used, whereby fields are plowed one year in every two or three years and allowed to lie idle when not in crops. The Soviet chernozems are the key to the Fertile Triangle.

Approaching the arid margins of the steppe, the soils are chestnut and later brown, with much reduced humus layers. These degraded chernozems also may be cultivated but at a much higher risk because of reduced water content. The climate also entails greater risk: one year out of three brings drought.

Soviet desert regions are noted for gray and red aridisols that must be irrigated. In Central Asia—with growing seasons of 200 days or more—double-cropping with irrigation of quick-ripening crops is theoretically possible.

Red and yellow alfisols (krasnozems) are typical of the humid subtropics of Georgia (Colchis Lowland). Like the soils of the forests, these also require basic fertilizers such as lime and potash. This is one of the very few regions of the country where exotic crops (citrus, tea, tobacco, and so on) may be raised naturally. Variants of these soils are also typical of the Mediterranean climate of the southern Crimea.

The soils of the Fertile Triangle, making up most of the country's arable land, are susceptible to erosion. This is particularly true of the soils containing loess. Wind and water erosion are endemic to the steppes and forest steppes. Summer thunderstorms are often "gully washers" that, true to the name, have created some of the world's most extensive gully networks in the rolling hills of the Central Black Earth and the Ukraine. The same areas are prone to sukhoveys—hot, dry winds that carry loess-laden duststorms deep into the Fertile Triangle. In places, up to a quarter of the arable land has been badly eroded.

Animal Life

The variety of animal life in the Soviet Union is impressive—ranging from ice-bound polar bears to migrant flamingos, from snow geese to snow leopards, from musk ox to gazelles. Since the 1970s the Soviets have cooperated with several countries in trying to preserve the polar bear, snow goose, and musk ox—all natives of the Soviet tundra.

The taiga is especially plentiful in wildlife, including the northern deer, lynx, brown bear, sable, river otter, wolverine, moose, wolf, and many birds. Although the country has its share of endangered species, it has had surprisingly few recent extinctions. Two of these occurred in the taiga, when 18th-century Russian hunters and seamen decimated the populations of a kind of sea cow, known as Steller's sea cow, and the spectacled cormorant on the Commander Islands.

The mixed and broadleaf forests host the European deer (European elk), Siberian deer (*macal*), Sika deer, roe deer, polecat, Eurasian badger, European forest cat, marten, beaver, bison, and the rare molelike desman. Here beaver harvests are strictly controlled (at 10 to 12 percent of the total population per year). Soviet conservationists have been successful in regenerating herds of European bison (wisent).

The steppe is home to the saiga (a Central Asian antelope), Corsac fox, Pallas cat, Caspian cane cat, a variety of polecats, European hare, marmot, giant mole-rat, pika, gazelle, and many migrant birds. Within the last 400 years the steppe has been the setting for at least two more extinctions: the wild auroch and the wild tarpan—sometimes wrongly identified as the rare Przewalski horse, which is an eastern tarpan. The last wild tarpan herd was eliminated in 1870, and only the zoo-bred Przewalski horse survives. Cross-breeding programs have developed near-replicas of the original wild auroch, the ancestor of domestic cattle, the last of which was killed in 1627.

On Soviet deserts are found the desert fox, jackal, gopher (suslik), Karakul sheep, camel, sand rat and other rodents, hedgehog, and many reptiles and birds. Especially rare desert species include the hyena, the caracal, the cheetah, and the *kulan* (wild ass).

The mountain zones have abundant wildlife. In addition to many of the species already mentioned, the Caucasus region claims the chamois, a mountain goat called *tur,* the Dagestan ibex, and the Priasiatic leopard. Central Asian mountains yield the Markhor sheep, the shy (and rare) snow leopard (*iribis*), Asian red wolf, the argali, and snow sheep. In 1984 an exchange of captive snow leopards between the United States and the Soviet Union increased zoo-bred stocks of the animal.

Nestled in the mountains of eastern Siberia, Lake Baikal is home to more than 1,700 species, two thirds of which are unique in the world. One is the Baikal seal, the world's only freshwater seal. The Soviets have strict rules regulating its bagging—less than 1 percent of the population per year.

The mountains of the Far East are noted for the world's largest cat, the Amur, or Siberian, tiger and the rare Asiatic black bear. The Amur tiger may number 150 on Soviet refuges. It is joined by other endangered cats: the Far East leopard and Amur forest cat.

PEOPLE AND CULTURE

On Jan. 1, 1987, the population of the Soviet Union was 282 million, the third largest in the world after China and India. There were 17 million more women than men, but most of the imbalance was from the age group 55 and older.

Undergoing rapid industrial expansion from 1922, the Soviet Union changed from a very rural economy—82 percent—to a society in which two out of three people live in cities. This is the result of migration from farms to the cities. Whereas in 1922 virtually all rural dwellers were farmers, nonfarmers now outnumber farmers by a ratio of 77 to 23. This means that one Soviet farmer supports three nonfarmers who live in the countryside as well as in cities. (In the United States one farmer supports 113 nonfarmers.)

Urbanization has been accompanied by modernization. Until the 20th century czarist Russia demographically resembled an underdeveloped country, exhibiting high birth rates (45 per one thousand),

A large portrait of Lenin stands outside an apartment complex at Bratsk in Siberia, site of one of the largest hydroelectric projects in the world.

© Boyd Norton

L. Werner—Shostal Associates

The city of Sochi, founded in 1896, is now the heart of a resort area on the coast of the Black Sea.

high death rates (about 30 per one thousand), and high infant mortality rates (more than 100 per one thousand), with natural increase rates of more than 15 per one thousand. In the Soviet period (post-1917) all variables decreased until about 1965, when for some reason reported rates of death and infant mortality began to rise again. In 1986 the number of births were 20 per one thousand and the number of deaths, 9.8. The natural increase rate thus stood at 10.2 per one thousand, slightly higher than that of the United States.

Such averages hide regional variations. Slavs and Balts reflect very slow natural increase rates that ranged between 4 and 8 per one thousand, whereas the traditionally Muslim republics of Central Asia and Azerbaijan recorded Third World growth rates of between 20 and 35 per one thousand. Child mortality—including infant mortality and deaths of children up to age 5—apparently peaked in 1979 and by 1987 was once again in decline.

Society and the Family

As in most developed industrial countries, the integrity of the Soviet family has been under stress. Prior to the 1917 Revolution, families were large and extended, including several generations. Land was divided into strips that were allocated to households by the village elders. The amount of peasant land was fixed, and as the farm population increased the size of the individual strips decreased. Frustration over the size and quality of land created a sense of pessimism among the tightly knit peasant families. Nevertheless some peasants became successful landowners (kulaks). Some other families migrated to Siberia to seek a new life.

In the late 1920s private property was abolished, agriculture was collectivized, and industrialization reached frenzied proportions. Civil war (1918–20) fragmented many families, and more of the same

came late in the decade. Under Joseph Stalin some attempts were made to erase the institution of the family altogether.

Since the 1950s the average size of most families has decreased to fewer than four members. Families are smallest among the Slavs and Balts and largest among Muslim groups. Many households continue to include one or more elderly persons, perpetuating the tradition of the extended family. This is especially true in rural and farm areas. In cities—because of crowding, economics, or both—parents wait longer to have children. The Soviet abortion rate ranks very high. Divorce has soared from one in ten marriages in 1960 to one in two or three. Because of the imbalance between the sexes, older women may have trouble finding a new spouse. Most of these problems are associated with the city-dwelling Slavic and Baltic peoples. Rural residents and Muslim peoples in particular are less likely to suffer these strains.

In the 1950s Soviet citizens ate far less meat, milk, eggs, fish, fruit, and vegetables than did most Europeans. By the late 1980s they still consumed less meat and fruit and more grain and potatoes. Even among its Eastern European allies, the Soviet Union ranks below Czechoslovakia, Hungary, Yugoslavia, Poland, and Bulgaria in per-capita meat consumption. Soviet citizens eat less fruit than the Irish, who are the lowest fruit consumers in Western Europe.

Cities

Despite a total population 3.6 times smaller, the Soviet Union has an urban population almost the size of China's—186 million. In 1987 the country included 55 cities with populations of more than 500,000 and 23 with more than 1 million residents. The largest is Moscow, the Soviet and Russian capital, with an estimated 1987 population of 8.8 million. Greater Leningrad has about 5 million, and Kiev, the capital city of the Ukraine, contains more than 2.5 million. The fourth largest Soviet city is Tashkent, the capital of Uzbekistan in Central Asia. The largest cities (500,000 or more) are growing the most rapidly. (See also Kiev; Leningrad; Moscow; Tashkent.)

Controlled, predictable growth is the key to the planned development of the Soviet city. Attempts have been made to limit the growth of large cities. They include the requirement that citizens over 15 carry internal passports or similar documents, without which they theoretically cannot migrate between cities. Also required of city dwellers is the *propiska,* or "permit to reside," in a given city, without which housing cannot be obtained legally even for a short period. The government may also refuse to invest in new industry in a large city. Without new jobs, the city theoretically cannot grow.

Despite these measures the big cities continue to grow by the addition of both legal and illegal residents. Part of the reason is that Soviet cities have no shortage of jobs—just of laborers. According to a 1935 decree Moscow, for instance, was to have a population of no more than 5 million. By 1987 the city's population was 75 percent larger. Most Soviet people want to live in Moscow because it is the "center of their universe." If there is a way to live there, they will somehow find it.

Urbanization has varied according to region and republic. Remote, environmentally severe areas like Siberia are generally very urban (75 percent or more). The economically developed Baltic and Slavic republics also exhibit urban ratios of 75 percent or more. Moldavia, Transcaucasia (except for Armenia), and the Central Asian republics reflect urban shares of 55 percent or less. The most rural republic is Tadzhikistan, where only one in three persons lives in a city. The republic also records the highest natural increase rate.

Ethnic and Language Groups

Although the Soviet Union contains more than 100 different ethnic groups, most are very small.

According to the 1979 census, only 52 ethnic groups numbered 100,000 or more. Of these, 23 exceeded 1 million. Among the six largest groups ethnic (and Russified) Russians led all others with 137 million, followed by Ukrainians (42 million), Uzbeks (12 million), Belorussians (9 million), and Kazakhs and Tatars with more than 6 million each.

Ethnicity is a complex concept. People may be classified according to physical traits (race), material culture (food, possessions, and ways of life), spiritual culture (religion), language, or political development. In physical appearance the Soviet people range from the fair, blue-eyed Balts in the northwest to those with swarthy, brown-eyed Mediterranean traits in the south, who merge with the fallow-skinned, almond-eyed Mongoloids in the east. There are sedentary hunters on the Arctic coast, nomadic reindeer herders in the tundra and taiga, nomadic hunters in the taiga, sedentary fishermen along large rivers and coasts,

Some of the most striking examples of religious architecture in the world can be found in the Soviet Union. The Church of the Virgin of Tikhvin (top left), the Church of the Trinity in Kiev (bottom left), and the Cathedral at the Trinity-St. Sergius monastery in Zagorsk (bottom right) are associated with the Russian Orthodox Church. The mausoleum of Timur Lenk in Samarkand (top right), however, shows the strong Muslim infuence that dominates some of the southern republics.

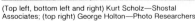
(Top left, bottom left and right) Kurt Scholz—Shostal Associates; (top right) George Holton—Photo Researchers

31

Residents of Moscow often keep
up on current events by reading
newspapers that have been posted
on public bulletin boards.

Norman Myers—Bruce Coleman Inc.

nomadic herdsmen in the steppes, sedentary farmers
in the temperate zone, seminomadic mountaineers,
and irrigationists in the dry steppes and deserts.

Although the Soviet Union is an officially atheistic
country, from 50 million to 90 million people may
belong to one religion or another, according to Soviet
government estimates in the early 1980s. Compared
to 1917 only one out of seven Russian Orthodox
churches is active. There are only 400 operating synagogues and mosques. The largest religious groupings
are Muslims (up to 35 million), Russian Orthodox
(30 million), Baltic Roman Catholics and Lutherans
(5 million), and Baptists and Jews (1 million). A few
million belong to other religions.

Of the ten linguistic stocks recognized in the
world, at least four exist in the Soviet Union. About
three fourths of the population belong to the Indo-
European linguistic stock, including Slavic, Baltic,
Germanic, Romance, Greek, Armenian, Iranian, and
Indic branches.

The second largest (and fastest-growing) stock is
Altaic, containing the Turkic, Mongol, and Tungus-
Manchu branches. The Uralic stock comprises Finns,
Ugrians, and Samoyeds. Almost the entire Caucasian
(or Japhetic) stock is confined to the Soviet Union.
Even the tiny Chukchi-Kamchatka family is native
to the country. Three of the minority languages—
Korean, Chinese, and Semitic—have their main pop-
ulations outside the Soviet Union.

Although an estimated 200 languages and dialects
are spoken, Russian is the official language, or lingua
franca, of the country. It is taught in all schools.
According to the 1979 census, Russian was the primary language for 153 million people, of whom 137
million were ethnic Russians and 16 million were
Russified from other ethnic groups. In addition 61
million claimed to speak Russian fluently as a second
language. Thus 82 percent of the Soviet population
had command of the Russian language.

In an age of nationalism every nationality aspires
to independent statehood. The non-Russian peoples
have been appeased with a hierarchy of administrative units. Fifteen have been granted a soviet socialist
republic (S.S.R.) that, according to the constitution,
is most like a sovereign nation-state. Twenty others
possess the status of an autonomous soviet socialist
republic (A.S.S.R.), which provides some cultural autonomy. Still others are recognized as autonomous
oblasts (A.O.) or autonomous okrugs (A.OK.), by which
ethnic homelands are officially acknowledged but
little else. Many groups—like the Germans, Poles,
Koreans, Bulgarians, Greeks, Hungarians, and Romanians—do not have homelands within the Soviet
Union. Other officially designated homelands are only
nominal in purpose. The Tatar A.S.S.R., for example,
includes only a quarter of the Soviet Tatars, and the
Jewish A.O. in the Soviet Far East is only 5 percent Jewish.

Much has been made of the political significance of
the slow demographic growth of the ethnic Russians
and the rapid growth of the other ethnic groups, notably the Muslim groups—especially in Central Asia.
Ethnic Russians, who are about half of the total population, make up at least three fifths of the leadership
of the Communist party. Of the 21 leading party and
government officials (Politburo and Secretariat) in
early 1988, not one was a Muslim or from a Muslim republic. There were 20 Eastern Slavs (Russian,
Ukrainian, and Belorussian) and one Georgian. Of the
Eastern Slavs, 17 were Russian, 2 were Belorussian,
and 1 was Ukrainian. The rapid rate of population
increase in Central Asia implies that at least one out
of every four Soviet citizens in the year 2000 will
be from a Muslim background. Already a third of
the 18-year-old Soviet Army recruits come from such
a heritage. These facts may prove meaningless: the
Russians under the czars were a minority in their own
country for many years.

Russian Language

Russian, the language of the Great Russian people, is one of the three families of the Eastern Slavic branch of the Indo-European linguistic stock, which includes Russian, Ukrainian (Little Russian), and Belorussian (White Russian). The roots of the Russian language are some 3,000 to 4,000 years old. In the late 1980s perhaps 235 million Soviet citizens, together with an estimated 5 million Russian-speaking emigrants in Europe, Asia, and North America spoke the language fluently.

As a result of the work on Old Church Slavonic begun by Saints Cyril and Methodius in the 800s, the Russians in AD 988 received Christianity in their own language. Russian thus was influenced strongly by Greek (by way of Byzantium) and the language of the Eastern Orthodox church. Russian was shaped by the 300-year occupation of the country by Mongol-Tatars. Through the years it was also influenced by Polish, German, French, Italian, and Latin. Since World War II it has borrowed many American terms. In turn Russian exerted its own influence on Old Church Slavonic, on other Soviet languages, and on tongues spoken in nearby countries.

The earliest written texts (Chronicles) originated in the 1100s as a mixture of original Russian and Old Church Slavonic. Peter the Great made his mark on the language by altering the Old Church Slavonic alphabet in the early 1700s. Peter's alphabet was further simplified in 1918 to form the current system of 33 letters.

Literature

The Russian language reflects a rich oral literary tradition, consisting of proverbs, folk tales, legends, and heroic ballads that may be traced to the earliest Eastern Slavic tribes. The oldest surviving Russian manuscripts date from the time when Kiev was the cultural center of Russia (988–1240). From that time until the reign of Peter the Great (1682–1725), written literature was mainly the handmaiden of the Russian Orthodox church. The only major secular work was 'The Lay of the Host of Igor', produced in the late 1100s. Many manuscripts and historical records are believed to have been destroyed or lost during the Mongol occupation (1248–1480), a period representing the dark ages of Russian political and cultural development.

The Mongol yoke isolated the Russian church from the rest of Christendom. Unique forms of worship emerged. An attempt to re-Westernize the church stimulated the autobiography of a courageous theologian, 'The Life of the Archpriest Avaakum, by Himself', which was published (1672–73) just before Peter's reforms.

The social upheaval that accompanied the reign of Peter the Great helped to divorce the Russian literary language from Old Church Slavonic, spurring secular writing traditions. In the 1700s there were works by Mikhail Lomonosov, Nikolai Karamzin, Gavriil Derzhavin, Ivan Krylov, and Denis Fonvizin. Aleksandr Radishchev's 'A Journey from St. Petersburg to Moscow' (1790), social commentary that reflected the growing concerns of Russian intellectuals over autocracy and serfdom, is considered one of the first examples of revolutionary literature.

Golden Age. The 1800s are recognized as the Golden Age of Russian literature, a time when it developed a conscience, especially regarding serfdom and the downtrodden. The "Russian Shakespeare," Aleksander Pushkin, blended European and native Russian influences to perfection, inspiring his successors to perpetuate what he could not in the span of his short life. He died in a duel at age 38. A truly great poet, Pushkin's best works include a novel in verse,

The final scene of Nikolai Rimski-Korsakov's opera 'Legend of the Invisible City of Kitezh' is staged at the Bolshoi Theater in Moscow. The Bolshoi is the leading theater for opera and ballet in the Soviet Union. Founded in the 1770s, the company has survived the Revolution of 1917 and two world wars.

V. Mastyukov—Tass/Sovfoto

The Kirov Ballet in
Leningrad performs a scene
from 'Notre Dame de Paris'
by Maurice Jarre.

'Eugene Onegin' (1825–33), a prose tale, 'The Captain's Daughter' (1836), and a play, 'Boris Godunov' (1831), the basis for Modest Musorgski's opera. (*See also* Pushkin.)

"Russia's Byron," Mikhail Lermontov, also died in a duel—in 1841 at the even earlier age of 26. Lermontov began writing at a very early age and produced a legacy that belied his years. As a soldier in the early Caucasian Wars, he wrote the short novel 'A Hero of Our Time', one of the first examples of Russian realism. Yet he is considered Russia's greatest Romanticist, and he was the first Russian poet to describe not only the beauty of the Caucasus Mountains but also Caucasian culture and folk art. Some critics believe that had he lived longer Lermontov would have been even greater than Pushkin. (*See also* Lermontov.)

Other great writers of the Golden Age include the humorist and prose writer Nikolai Gogol ('Dead Souls', 1842) and the satirist Ivan Goncharov ('Oblomov', 1859). Gogol is known as the father of the Russian novel. Both Gogol and Goncharov cleverly unmasked the corruption and misery of the underprivileged that existed in Russia by the mid-1800s, paving the way for the great works of Ivan Turgenev, Fedor Dostoevski, Leo Tolstoi, Anton Chekhov, Maksim Gorki, and Aleksandr Blok. (*See also* Gogol.)

Whereas Gogol and Goncharov were poignant social critics in an age of massive censorship, subsequent writers became embroiled in arguments over how to eliminate the problems. Solutions came in two forms: copy the West or use time-honored examples of Russian goodness and wisdom, an approach called Slavophilism. The former was international in orientation, the latter isolationist and nationalistic. Ivan Turgenev was the most articulate spokesman for the Westernizers. His many stories and novels represent his quest for a leader capable of solving Russia's political and social problems. (*See also* Turgenev.)

Fedor Dostoevski was a spokesman for the Slavophiles, and his work strongly shows the influence of Russian Orthodox Christianity. He fiercely opposed reliance on foreign influences and imports. He recognized the value of native culture, but he was not completely against everything foreign. His novels reflect his ideas: 'Crime and Punishment' (1866), 'The Idiot' (1868), 'The Possessed' (1871–72), and 'The Brothers Karamazov' (1879–80). Reading both Turgenev and Dostoevski is an excellent way to understand the way things were before the Russian Revolution in 1917. (*See also* Dostoevski.)

After an early life marked by ribaldry and adventure, Leo Tolstoi was inspired by the Russian rural landscape, the nobility, and the peasantry. Whereas Dostoevski's slum-dwelling urbanites are complex, unhealthy, and abnormal, Tolstoi's characters are mostly simple, easily understood provincial folk. Dostoevski wrote with humility; Tolstoi wrote with authority, combining the ideologies of Westernism and Slavophilism, synthesizing them into his own philosophy—Tolstoism. His best novels are 'War and Peace' (1865–69) and 'Anna Karenina' (1875–77). The former consistently is regarded by many literary critics as "the world's greatest novel." (*See also* Tolstoi.)

Silver Age. Anton Chekhov, Maksim Gorki, and the poet Aleksandr Blok wrote works that overlapped the 19th and 20th centuries. With them came another literary and artistic revival, designated sometimes as Russia's Silver Age.

Chekhov wrote about the fundamental social dichotomies of his time: ruralism versus urbanization; the decaying life-styles of the Russian nobleman versus the upstart, crude, and practical world of the merchants of the new industrial age. Among his works 'Three Sisters' (1901) and 'The Cherry Orchard' (1904) most cogently reveal the stress of these conflicts. (*See also* Chekhov.)

Both Chekhov and Gorki believed that Russia's future lay in further industrialization, but Gorki showed more sympathy for the working class (proletariat) than for the merchant capitalists. Considered the champion of the Russian working man and honored by the early Bolsheviks, Gorki unmasked the corruption of capitalism in such novels as 'Mother' (1907). (*See also* Gorki.)

Blok's abstract, sometimes bizarre, poetry sprang from the Russian symbolist movement of the 1890s. It arrived at a time when no outstanding Russian novels had been written for many years. The symbolists were devoted to abstract expressionism and a rejection of realism. They formed a bridge between Russia's Golden Age and Soviet literature.

Soviet period. Traditionally Soviet literature has served the political regime. In 1932 all Soviet writers were organized into the Union of Soviet Writers, which was guided by the Stalinist doctrine of "socialist realism." Under this concept writers were required to participate fully and prominently in building socialism. Those who did not conform were to be expelled from the Writer's Union, as happened to the poet Anna Akhmatova in 1946 and Boris Pasternak in 1958. Pasternak, who was offered the Nobel prize for 'Doctor Zhivago' (1957), was expelled after his novel was published in the West. (*See also* Pasternak.)

Gorki, who was a friend of Lenin, dedicated the remainder of his life to salvaging the remnants of Russian culture and to encouraging new Soviet authors. He became the dean of Soviet writers in 1928, and when he died in 1936 Soviet literature was well established. He was succeeded as dean of literature by Aleksei Tolstoi.

Tolstoi, Vladimir Mayakovski, Panteleimon Romanov, Fedor Gladkov, Valentin Katayev, and Boris Pilnyak each dealt with propagandistic and pragmatic themes, as illustrated by Gladkov's novel 'Cement' (1926). Also emerging along with Pasternak in the prewar period was Mikhail Sholokhov, a Don Cossack, who won the Nobel prize for literature in 1965 for such works as 'And Quiet Flows the Don' (4 vols., 1928–40) and 'Virgin Soil Upturned' (2 vols., 1932–60). Sholokhov's novels describe Cossack life in the civil war and the period of collectivization.

The postwar period brought modest liberalization under Nikita Khrushchev. The unconventional poets Yevgeny Yevtushenko and Andrei Voznesensky arose (*see* Yevtushenko). Although Pasternak was never allowed to claim his Nobel prize and died an "unperson" in 1960, Alexander Solzhenitsyn was allowed to publish 'One Day in the Life of Ivan Denisovich', a short novel about the inmates of a Stalinist prison camp. Later Solzhenitsyn also was expelled from the Writer's Union for his "anti-Soviet" novels 'The Cancer Ward' and 'The First Circle'. Having been offered the Nobel prize for literature in 1971, he was forced to emigrate from the Soviet Union in the early 1970s in order to accept it formally. (*See also* Solzhenitsyn.)

The most significant postwar literary movements leaned toward naturalism. "The village prose writers" include Fyodor Abramov and Valentin Rusputin. Such writers as Vasily Shukshin wrote about the lives of ordinary citizens in a highly original way. The *byt'* (life quality) writers wrote about the lives of Soviet intellectuals. The works of Yuri Trofonov, for example, focus on the post-Stalin era and question the validity of Marxism-Leninism in modern life.

There were further expulsions of outstanding Soviet writers in the 1970s and 1980s. Along with Solzhenitsyn, Vladimir Maksimov, Vasily Voynovich, and Aleksandr Zinoviev were forced to immigrate to the West. Another émigré, Joseph Brodsky, won the Nobel prize for his poetry in 1987.

The Mikhail Gorbachev administration's policy of *glasnost* (openness) stimulated literary liberalization from 1985. Measures included the posthumous reinstatement of Pasternak and the publication of 'Doctor Zhivago', as well as much more freedom of expression for all writers. (*See also* Russian Literature.)

Visual Arts

Like literature, Russian art was the servant of the Orthodox church until the reign of Peter the Great. Until then borrowings from the Scythians, Sarmatians, Huns, and Turko-Mongols were the basis for the rich background of folk art that entered the liturgical tradition by way of embroidery, metalwork, leatherwork, wood carving, and some bas-relief sculpture.

Youngsters from grade-school age upward are enrolled at the school for circus performers in Moscow.

Burt Glinn—Magnum

Tass/Sovfoto

French is among the foreign languages that are taught in a seventh-grade class.

Painting and sculpture. Sculpture did not play a role in Russian art until relatively recent times because the church forbade the display of the human body in three-dimensional form. This also explains why the figures in icons are so two-dimensional in appearance. A serious art, icon painting was brought to its zenith as a Russian art form in the 14th and 15th centuries by Theophanes the Greek and Andrei Rublev. Until the late 1600s the icon and the mosaic were the Russian artist's sole outlet.

Modern westernized painting and sculpture date from Peter's reforms after 1700. Perhaps the most famous Russian artist in the last 200 years was Ilya Repin (1844–1930). The stress on "socialist realism" in art as well as literature hampered artistic creativity from 1917. Modern art typically was banned and forced underground. Gorbachev, however, permitted public exhibits of Soviet modern art.

Architecture. Byzantium also influenced Russian architecture, but Russian buildings from the outset had a higher, narrower silhouette than their Byzantine models. Russians experimented with the dome, which was derived from the nomadic yurt (felt tent). This led to the onion-shaped outer shell that is seen on most Russian domed churches.

Early Russian architecture cannot be divided into periods like Gothic or baroque. Rather it sprang from different city centers: Kiev, Novgorod, Moscow, and later Saint Petersburg (Leningrad). Soviet buildings are pragmatic products of standardized architecture, largely the result of the need to build fast after the decimation of World War II. Some Stalinist "wedding cake" architecture dots the streets of Moscow. Since the 1960s more innovative architectural styles have appeared around the country.

Performing Arts

Ballet began as court entertainment in 1732, spreading to the wealthy estates in the middle of the century. Simultaneously imperial ballet theaters and companies were created. In the 1800s the distinctive style of Russian ballet was strongly influenced by French, Italian, and Swedish choreographers and dancers, including Marius Petipa, the so-called "father of modern ballet." Only late in the century did the first Russian choreographers arise—Lev Ivanov and Michel Fokine (*see* Fokine).

The great Russian dancers asserted themselves at the same time—Anna Pavlova and Vaslav Nijinsky—and truly Russian ballet reached a high technical and stylistic level. In 1909 the impresario Sergei Diaghilev founded the Ballets Russes and took Russian ballet to the capitals of Europe (*see* Diaghilev; Nijinsky; Pavlova).

Soviet ballet continues the 19th-century traditions. The Bolshoi Ballet in Moscow and the Kirov in Leningrad are famous throughout the world. (*See also* Ballet; Dance.)

Theater originally was inspired by folk entertainment. Peasant companies performed for serfs and nobility alike, sometimes traveling from estate to estate. Later Russian theater was influenced by foreign models much like the ballet. The first Russian dramatists appeared about 1750. Under Catherine the Great (1762–96), herself an author of comedies, theater reached new highs, but most of the works were of foreign origin. Great Russian comedy came in the 1800s with the work of Aleksandr Griboedov ('Woe from Wit', 1833) and Nikolai Gogol ('The Inspector General', 1836). (*See also* Drama, "The Drama in Czarist Russia.")

At the end of the century Konstantin Stanislavsky founded the Moscow Art Theatre, where Russian theater art came of age. Realistic plays produced here, among them the works of Chekhov and Gorki, stimulated the modern "method" school of acting (*see* Acting). Experimental theater, including the works of producer-director Vsevolod Meyerhold and fellow constructivists, flourished through the early Soviet period. As in literature under Stalin, all experimental theater was replaced by socialist realism. The Gorbachev administration allowed the performance of controversial works. The Soviet Union claims more theaters than any other country. Plays are performed both in Russian and in minority languages.

Music. Russian and Soviet opera have combined music with theater and sometimes ballet to create a visual display that ranks among the best in the world. The Soviet people are great lovers of music. Almost all ethnic minorities in the Soviet Union have their own national instruments and musical traditions.

Because musical instruments were forbidden in Russian Orthodox church services, Russian music and consequently opera were delayed in development as an art form until more recent times. Typically Russian choruses chanted and sang without accompaniment except for an occasional drum beat. Secular vocal music did not develop until the 1800s. Since then Russian operas, symphonies, instrumental compositions, and art songs have flourished. Most are based on the melodic and rhythmic patterns of Russian folk music and nationalistic themes. The latter have been particularly stressed during the Soviet period.

The most ancient Russian folk instrument was a kind of zither, the *gusli*. Other traditional stringed instruments are the *domra, gudok,* and balalaika. The last, a triangular three-stringed, short-necked instrument, was made popular in the 1800s in both city salons and in the countryside. Wind instruments include the flutelike *dudka* and *suirel*.

Russian music came of age in 1836 with the performance of Mikhail Glinka's 'A Life for the Czar', today called 'Ivan Susanin'. Glinka also produced a musical fairy tale based on Pushkin's poem 'Ruslan and Lyudmila' (1842), but Glinka's operas contain many examples of Italian style.

The Russian nationalist school was founded by Modest Musorgski with the production of the opera 'Boris Godunov' (1869). Musorgski was one of a group of Russian composers who critics at the time called the Five. The group included Mili Balakirev, Nikolai Rimski-Korsakov, Aleksandr Borodin, and César Cui. Balakirev is noted for his classical renderings of Russian folk music. Rimski-Korsakov developed Orientalism to near perfection in his fairy-tale operas and in the brilliant symphonic suite 'Sheherazade'. Borodin also followed this pattern in his opera 'Prince Igor'. Cui composed miniature forms. (*See also* Musorgski; Rimski-Korsakov.)

Not one of the Five, but the most famous of all Russian composers is Peter Ilich Tchaikovsky, composer of the well-known '1812' overture, among many other works, including symphonies, symphonic poems, operas, ballets, concertos, and piano pieces. Distinctively Russian, Tchaikovsky's melancholic lyricism was perpetuated by the music of Sergei Rachmaninoff, the last of the Russian romantic composers. (*See also* Rachmaninoff; Tchaikovsky.)

Famous Russian and Soviet composers of the 20th century have been Igor Stravinsky, Sergei Prokofiev, Nikolai Miaskovsky, Nikolai Medtner, Dimitri Shostakovich, and Aram Khachaturian. A resident of France and the United States for most of his creative life, Stravinsky is best known for 'The Rite of Spring' (1913). Prokofiev's most famous works of the Soviet period are 'Peter and the Wolf' and the ballet 'Romeo and Juliet'. Miaskovsky wrote 27 symphonies, most of them known only in the Soviet Union. Shostakovich, who wrote his first symphony at the age of 19, composed 15 symphonies, some of which received criticism for not following the line of socialist realism. Orientalism reached a new high in the hands of Khachaturian, an ethnic Armenian. Modern Soviet composers number in the hundreds. As in the West, most specialize in writing popular songs and dances. (*See also* Prokofiev; Shostakovich; Stravinsky; Music, Classical, "Russian Nationalists" and "Music in the 20th Century.")

The Soviet Union has more permanent opera and ballet companies than any other country. The Soviet government has encouraged all its ethnic minorities to develop their musical talents, including the revival of native instrumental music and dance. All ethnic capitals and many other cities have music halls. More than 30 cities have large opera and ballet theaters, where there are performances of both traditional and international works.

Cinema. The Soviet Union also leads the world in the number of movie theaters. Soviet film made its mark in the early 1900s. Sergei Eisenstein directed such innovative films as 'Potemkin', 'Ivan the Terrible', and 'Alexander Nevsky', whose realism and technique continue to influence filmmakers worldwide (*see* Eisenstein).

Since World War II, because of the great tragedy of the war, vast numbers of Soviet films have dealt with wartime themes. Among these 'The Ballad of a Soldier' and 'The Cranes Are Flying' gained international critical acclaim. Under Gorbachev nearly three fourths of the leadership of the Filmmakers' Union changed. A reexamination of a number of films dealing with previously forbidden topics, such as portrayals of the Stalin era, led to their release or rerelease.

Television, which is entirely state-controlled, reflects the official viewpoint of the top leadership. Traditionally it has been very much like public television in the West, though many more movies and sporting events are shown. Most Soviet citizens receive only two channels: the main, Moscow channel and a local channel. Moscow and Leningrad have third stations.

Soviet television during the Gorbachev administration became much more interesting, objective, and candid. Gorbachev was the first Soviet leader to use television for popularizing his policies. Under his leadership television news analysts reported natural disasters and accidents. They were also much more informative, objective, and entertaining in their coverage of events in the rest of the world.

Education

Before the Revolution education was generally available to only a privileged few. In 1913 only 6

Two physicians and two nurses consult on a case at the Cardiovascular Sanitorium for Children in Moldavian S.S.R.

M. Potyrnike—Tass/Sovfoto

A farmer takes his sheep to pasture on a traditional Russian farm (top left). Wheat is being harvested (top right) on a state farm in the Russian S.S.R. Workers on a collective farm, or kolkhoz (left), pour fresh milk into containers for shipment in the Ukrainian S.S.R.

(Top left) Tass/Sovfoto; (top right) Jack Novak—Shostal Associates; (left) John L. Strohm—Shostal Associates

percent of the total population of czarist Russia were in schools of all types. In 1987 two out of five Soviet citizens were enrolled in classes. As late as 1920 only 44 percent of the population in the age group 9 to 49 were literate. By 1987 the literacy rate had grown to more than 99 percent.

Primary and secondary education. Education is free or provided at minimal cost. Under the education reforms of the 1980s, Soviet children enter primary school (now grades one to four) at age 6 and are required to continue through the eleventh grade. By age 11 the pupil will have undertaken work projects and will have visited a factory. This aspect of the educational reform is an attempt to rectify a glaring deficiency in the old system: one new laborer in four entered the work force with insufficient vocational training. Prior to 1986 all school-age children finished an "incomplete" secondary educational program (through grade eight), with most (89 percent) finishing a "complete" secondary program to grade

ten in general high schools, specialized high schools, or trade schools. Since 1970 about one high school graduate in six has attended a college or university, with most students receiving government stipends as well as free room and board.

Typically Soviet education is designed to meet the needs of the state. Pupils are taught the principles of Marxism-Leninism along with their formal courses. The Gorbachev reforms reemphasized this.

All boys and girls take the same subjects during their first four years in school: Russian grammar, reading, writing, arithmetic, drawing, singing, history, geography, natural science, and physical education. They go to school six days a week and wear uniforms. It is in the fifth grade that the differences between Soviet educational standards and those of the United States become pronounced. Biology, physics, chemistry, and foreign languages are added to the course load. By the tender age of 10 pupils decide what languages they will pursue for the rest of their school years—usually English, French, or German. At age 14 four of five Soviet pupils have strong backgrounds in biology, algebra, geometry, physics, and chemistry. They also have studied the fundamentals of politics and the framework of the Soviet constitution.

Elementary and secondary schools are run by the ministries of education in each republic. Their activities are coordinated by the Ministry of Education of the Russian Republic.

Preschool. Nearly 60 percent of Soviet preschoolers are enrolled in some kind of child-care center or nursery. In the mid-1980s the facilities were nearly twice as available to city children as to rural children. The centers and nurseries are subsidized by Soviet trade unions, but unlike other forms of schooling they are not free to users. Parents pay 2 to 12 rubles (3 to 15 United States dollars) per month tuition to ensure that their children are well supervised while they both work. Child-care centers are for children between the ages of six months and 3 years. Nurseries or kindergartens are for children from 3 to 6 (formerly 7) years old. In addition to being taught to appreciate their parents and how to play with each other, preschoolers and kindergartners learn the rudiments of the Russian language, some English, and a little Soviet history. Preschools of all types are supervised by the Ministry of Public Health.

Higher education. In the late 1980s there were 69 Soviet universities with 587,000 students enrolled. Students who have finished the full 11-year program, and who rank in the top 20 percent of their graduating class, take difficult college entrance examinations. Students ranking lower may be eligible later if they take additional secondary school courses. Other students can go to *technicums,* which train technicians for industrial work, nursing, dentistry, agronomy, and primary school teaching. Entrance examinations are also required for these schools. Workers acquiring *technicum* training have the best chance of obtaining supervisory jobs in industrial plants.

University students spend from five to six years studying their professions. Training is highly specialized from the outset. Seven percent of the students study medicine (80 percent of these are women), about 10 percent study agriculture, and 30 percent prepare to be teachers and so on. Students take only the courses that pertain to their interests.

Health Care

The Soviet Union has the most extensive system of medical care in the world. The country leads in the ratio of physicians and hospital beds to population. The system is characterized, however, by growing quantities of simple facilities, cheap labor (physicians, more than 80 percent of whom are women, are near the bottom of the pay scale and make less than the average factory worker), low technology, and emphasis on large volumes of basic services.

A source of national pride, medical care is supposed to be inflation-free and free of charge to all Soviet citizens. In practice, however, patients desirous of receiving better treatment often pay physicians "on the left" (*nalevo*).

Between 1970 and 1985 the number of physicians increased from 27 per 10,000 persons to 42, and the number of hospital beds from 109 to 130. Despite the impressive numbers, complaints about overcrowded hospitals where patients lie in corridors, about long lines at polyclinics, and about shortages of medicines and medical personnel are sent by the thousands to the Soviet Ministry of Health. Such statistics reflect a health-care system that not only lacks the high technology usually found in the developed industrial world but one that may not be adequate to treat many common ailments. There is a relatively high incidence, for example, of rickets, respiratory ailments, influenza, and pneumonia. Kidney dialysis machines are in extremely short supply, X-ray equipment lacks lead shielding, and disposable hypodermic needles are rare. Manually carried stretchers—not rollaways—are still used. Even bed linens are at times in scarce supply. Many drugs that can be bought over the counter in any pharmacy in the West are extremely rare in the Soviet Union.

Sophisticated medical care traditionally has been available to high-ranking members of the Communist party, and the general public is aware of this imbalance. Gorbachev set out to correct this system of privileges, deeming it unsuitable for a socialist society.

There was radical improvement in health between 1945 and 1964, but this was followed by rises in age-specific mortality rates and declining life expectancy through 1984. The rate of deaths from heart disease more than doubled between 1960 and 1983, and cancer deaths were also much higher. Gorbachev placed health care high on his agenda of reforms. He made sweeping personnel changes in the Ministry of Health, and hundreds of administrators and hospital workers were dismissed. Wages for medical personnel were slated to increase "substantially." His anti-alcohol campaign resulted in generally better health. The mortality rate has fallen since 1984, and there are indications that age-specific death rates are down and life expectancy is up.

ECONOMY

The Soviet Union is in many ways an economic paradox. It ranks first or second in the output of most of the world's strategic minerals. It has long led the world in cement and iron-ore production. During the 1970s it outstripped the United States in the output of steel, petroleum, and mineral fertilizers. In the 1980s it overtook the United States in the extraction of natural gas. Its ferroalloys, used in making steel, compete with the southern third of Africa for world supremacy in production. It also has taken the lead in the output of some manufactures—for example, tractors, woolen cloth, and butter. Its machine construction is numerically second only to the United States, and its chemical industry made spectacular advances from the early 1960s. All of these industrial resources and manufactured products have laid the foundation for a mighty military complex that, according to some experts, is the strongest in the world.

There is no question that the Soviet Union has taken great strides industrially in the 20th century. On the eve of the Revolution czarist Russia was a country of poor peasant farmers. They represented 69 percent of a population that was 87 percent rural. Despite the fact that in 1913 it ranked as the fifth largest industrial country, Russia registered a per capita income that was less than a sixth that of the United States—among the poorest countries of Europe.

The country has always performed poorly in agriculture. The reasons are varied, but a major factor is weather. Canada has similar, but not identical, weather patterns in its farm belts, but Canada's population is less than 10 percent that of the Soviet Union. Canada can afford to leave much of its farm land in regenerative fallow.

The problem is not one of investment. The Soviet government spends more money on agriculture (30 percent of gross national product, or GNP) than any other industrial country but has not reaped equivalent benefits. Agriculture and defense allocations are estimated to be nearly half of all Soviet investment. (The equivalent figure in the United States is less than 10 percent.) When a crop failure occurs in the Soviet Union, it ripples through the economy like an earthquake—and there have been as many as six crop failures since 1970.

Food is the most essential consumer good. Except for agriculture Soviet planners traditionally have neglected the consumer sector, emphasizing heavy industry instead. The result is an economy dominated

Timber is floated from forest to mill on the Vychegda River in the northern part of the Russian S.S.R.

S. Gubsky—Tass/Sovfoto

by a massive and successful military-heavy industrial base coupled with a pervasive agricultural base that has at best muddled through. Little else has been left for other consumer goods, and many goods that are produced are of such poor quality that few want to buy them. The economy therefore consists of a developed world industries and armed forces sector and a Third World consumer sector—an economic paradox.

Agriculture

The performance of Soviet agriculture has been called rhapsodic. Farming is conducted in an environment that differs from that of the Western world: short growing seasons, low annual temperatures, and lack of balance in the distribution of precipitation. Such constraints restrict the availability of good farm land and create variations in food supply. The farm sector is vexed both by unreliable natural conditions and by a lack of work incentives for the farmer. Farm output in Soviet times consequently has resembled a boom-or-bust cycle that steadily rose between 1945 and 1978 but has since flattened.

Soviet agriculture is huge. It obtains a third of total annual investment and employs nearly 30 percent of the labor force. Farm production alone claims 20 percent of annual investment and a similar share of the labor force, compared to less than 5 percent for both in the United States. Soviet farmers cultivate about a third more land than American farmers, but their average yield per acre is only 56 percent of that in the United States.

The lack of farm productivity, a problem that dates from czarist times, has affected trade in agricultural produce. Once a major exporter of grain and other farm products, the Soviet Union has become one of the world's largest importers of farm commodities. Experts claim that these failures are tied not only to the physical limitations of the agricultural base and poor wages for farmers, but also to a bureaucracy that meddles in the affairs of farm managers; a poor infrastructure, including roads, storage facilities, and housing; a low quality of life; and poor performance of farm-support industries.

Traditional farming. A major stumbling block in the development of Soviet socialism was the backwardness of agriculture. Small peasant farms, fragmented into widely dispersed, tiny strips of plowland, dominated the rural landscape. Since the farms were mainly sown to grain, fodder crops were scarce, pastures were often overgrazed, and the livestock sector was impoverished. Tools and methods were feudal: in most areas sickles, scythes, and wooden plows were still in use, and chemical fertilizers were almost unknown. The obsolete three-field system of crop rotation (spring grain—winter grain—fallow), which dated from the 1500s, was evident virtually everywhere. In some areas (the colder north and Siberia), a two-field system (spring grain—fallow) was used. In Transcaucasia and Central Asia traditional subtropical and irrigation farming and semi-subsistence grazing of sheep prevailed.

All of this backwardness stemmed from the oppressive system of serfdom that existed in Russia between the 1500s and 1861. Under serfdom Russian noblemen were granted title to their landholdings by the czar in exchange for military or bureaucratic service. The landholding included all the peasants, or serfs, who lived on the land, who in turn were obliged to work for the lord in exchange for their right to work small farm strips. Serfs were bought or sold, moved by the landlord at will, had no legal rights, and yet had to pay taxes to the state. Ironically, as serfdom intensified in Russia, feudalism withered away in Western Europe. Like slavery in the United States, the economic basis for serfdom finally was discredited, and the peasants were emancipated in 1861.

Although peasants were legally free after 1861, most stayed in farming. The nobleman's estate was carved into peasant land—for which the nobleman was paid handsomely by the state—and noble property, which often became a large commercial farm worked by hired peasants. On the peasant land the authority of the noble landlord was replaced by the village commune (*mir* or *obshchina*). The commune, composed of the village elders, collected the redemption payments (a form of mortgage payment) from its peasant members. These payments were made at high interest for a period of no less than 40 years.

The commune held woodland, pastures, and plowland in common. Only the cottages, sheds, tools, animals, and garden plots adjacent to houses belonged to the peasant households. Members had access to the commons and at the commune meetings were allocated randomly distributed strips of plowland until the next reallocation. The choice of strips for a household was left to chance by drawing straws. As the number of households grew, the size of the strips was smaller. By the early 1900s the average size of a peasant holding was ridiculously small.

There were, however, scattered bits of technical and commercial progress. Large, successful gentry estates existed in the Baltic; there were rich sugarbeet plantations in the Ukraine; and, in the steppes of the southern Ukraine, northern Caucasus, and Volga, mechanized grain farms flourished. In the vicinity of Moscow and St. Petersburg (Leningrad), multiple crop rotations added fodder grasses and potatoes to the three-field system, and better livestock herds were the result. In Central Asia new irrigation projects allowed creation of commercial cotton plantations. A significant number of hardworking peasants became private landowners, and many of the fragmented farms were consolidated, especially after 1905. This modernization and "stratification of the peasantry"—the enrichment of the few at the expense of the many—were described and disdained by Lenin. Lenin argued that because of these trends and others Russia was ripe for a proletarian revolution.

Socialist agriculture. Serfdom and the installation of the peasant commune after 1861 encouraged collectivism in agriculture. Whether because of their village life-style, the harshness of physical conditions,

Fishermen along the Volga River catch sturgeon for the lucrative caviar market.

or some other reason, Russian farmers had always worked as a unit rather than as individuals.

Socialized farming, consisting of collective and state farm systems, was established during the 1930s. During the 1920s, under Lenin's New Economic Policy (NEP), a mixed farming economy arose in which land was nationalized but peasant farming prevailed. By 1928 more than 98 percent of the farm population and the sown area were nonsocialized. Joseph Stalin feared an entrenchment of private farming, and in his First Five-Year Plan (1928–33) he demanded radical collectivization of agriculture. By 1938, 93.5 percent of all peasant households were on collective or state farms.

The foundations of socialized agriculture rest in the teachings of Karl Marx (1818–83), who believed that scale economics operate in agriculture in the same way that they do in industry. Marx believed that large farms, like large factories, produce goods more cheaply than small ones. Marx's dream of the future included the organization of all workers into "industrial armies" working on large agricultural enterprises to produce food for their comrade workers in the cities—all "in accordance with a common [state] plan."

By the mid-1980s the socialized sector of Soviet agriculture included 98 percent of the system of farms—68 percent state farm land and 30 percent collective farm land. The remaining 2 percent was in nonsocialized private plots that belonged to state and collective farm workers and urban residents.

The *kolkhoz,* or collective farm, consists of a number of member families who are granted perpetual rights to rent-free state land. Membership is a birthright, and children normally are given membership on

A marine preserve for breeding scallops and other seafood has been established in the Primorsky Territory between China and the Sea of Japan.

Yu Muravin—Tass/Sovfoto

their 16th birthday. Typically families live in small, individual cottages clustered in villages. Adjacent to each cottage is a rectangular private plot. *Kolkhoz* members are usually assigned to brigades, which are responsible for a production center such as a dairy or crop production program. Often a brigade includes all the members of a village. Workers receive wages based on the number of hours contributed along with bonuses and production incentives.

A collective farm averages 12,350 acres (5,000 hectares), of which 7,400 acres (3,000 hectares) are in crops. They may include some 500 households, usually in more than one rural settlement within the limits of the farm. The total number of collective farms in the Soviet Union is about 26,000. Formerly there were many more, but some have been converted to state farms and others consolidated. These trends continue.

The *sovkhoz,* or state farm, is the Marxian ideal: a state-operated "factory in the fields." *Sovkhoz* workers are state employees and are paid wages from state funds. They too receive year-end bonuses if annual production exceeds targets.

The *sovkhoz* is normally much larger than the *kolkhoz*—typically about 42,000 acres (17,000 hectares). In the mid-1980s there were 23,000 state farms. In contrast to the *kolkhoz* headquarters, which ordinarily is a village, the center of the *sovkhoz* is a collection of apartments, dormitories, administrative buildings, and a cultural center.

Working units on the *sovkhoz* are also organized according to the brigade system, with permanently assigned personnel performing specific tasks. They are often assigned to the *sovkhoz* system upon graduation from a technical school in a distant town or city.

As the favored, truly "proletarian," agricultural organization, the number of state farms has grown since the 1950s. They lend themselves to central control.

Private agriculture. Known officially as the personal subsidiary holding, the private plot consists of a small parcel of land around a village dwelling. The maximum size of a private holding cannot exceed 1.2 acres (0.5 hectare), or slightly larger than an American football field. The average size is only about 0.75 acre (0.3 hectare). This includes the land occupied by the cottage. Most of the land is taken up by kitchen gardens, but the private holding may also include a cow, a pig, and up to ten sheep and goats.

In the mid-1980s there were 32 million Soviet families (*kolkhozniki, sovkhozniki,* and urbanites) operating some form of private plot. Composing only about 2 percent of the agricultural area, private plots yielded 64 percent of the Soviet potato crop (much of which was fed to pigs); 58 percent of the fruit; 33 percent of the vegetables; 1 percent of the grain; 19 percent of the consumed beef; 40 percent of the pork, mutton, and goat meat; 38 percent of the poultry meat; 30 percent of the milk; and 32 percent of the eggs.

Gorbachev assigned high priority to improving efficiency and reducing the enormous costs of food production. A major element of his program was to shift the share of investment away from farms and into development of the rural infrastructure, food processing, and agricultural supportive industries (machinery and chemicals). He also restructured the agricultural hierarchy under a single superministry—Gosagroprom. Gorbachev strongly supported economic incentives instead of administrative directives as a means of regulating enterprise activity.

Crops. The principal food crops are grains (mainly wheat, rye, rice, buckwheat, and millet), potatoes, sugar beets, and vegetables. The Soviet Union is the world's largest producer of wheat—both winter and spring varieties.

Grains comprised 55 percent of the sown area in the mid-1980s, including 23 percent in wheat, 14 percent in barley, 6 percent in oats, and 12 percent in other grains and pulses. Grain acreage has declined since 1980, and the area sown to feed crops (grasses, silage, green corn, and other fodder) has increased. The area sown to industrial crops—like cotton, sugar beets, flax, hemp, and sunflowers—has declined slightly as has the acreage in potatoes and vegetables.

Livestock. Since 1955 Soviet leaders have placed heavy emphasis on increased production of meat and dairy products. Livestock herds have increased steadily, but production has been erratic. Two thirds of the livestock are equally divided between dairy cows and beef cattle; pigs make up 17 percent and poultry 16 percent. Between 1980 and 1985, 55 percent of all the domestic and imported grain was used to feed livestock. The remainder of the feed came in the form of hay and silage.

Agricultural regions. Most agriculture is in the Fertile Triangle, but the country may be divided into regions according to specialization. Well over half the country—from just north of Leningrad to Lake Baikal and mainly north of the Amur River to Sakhalin and the Kuril Islands—consists of forests and tundra where there is little agriculture beyond reindeer herding, extensive dairying, and raising root crops. An exception is Yakutia, where cattle and horses are raised on natural pasture and hay in forest clearings. Spring grains are also raised in sheltered river valleys.

Within the mixed and broadleaf forests—stretching from Leningrad and L'vov to Irkutsk—flax, potatoes, oats, rye, barley, hay, and livestock are raised. In the heart of the Fertile Triangle, the steppes and forest steppes yield wheat, sugar beets, sunflowers, corn, and livestock. Winter wheat is raised primarily west of the Volga. Spring wheat grows in northern Kazakhstan and Siberia. The central Ukraine is known for sugar beets. Prized sunflowers grow in a belt running from Rostov-on-the-Don to Kuybyshev. Corn yields are best in the North Caucasus and on the fringe of the Black Sea.

The humid subtropics of the Colchis and Lenkoran' lowlands in Transcaucasia are known for citrus, tea, tobacco, grapes, other fruits and vegetables, corn, rice, and livestock. The deserts (dry subtropics) of Central Asia are noted for irrigated cotton, rice, alfalfa, sugar beets, and a host of other exotic crops. These crops plus dry-farmed wheat are also raised in the semiarid mountain forelands of Central Asia, including the Fergana Basin. Here seasonal livestock raising is also conducted. The Amur River valley and the Maritime province of the Soviet Far East are noted for wheat, sugar beets, soybeans, rice, grain sorghums, and livestock.

Forestry

The Soviet Union contains the largest domestic forest in the world: roughly 80 billion cubic meters of wood, or 34 percent of world reserves, including 58 percent of the world's coniferous forest. Forestry industries suffer from bad distribution. Only a fifth of the forest is in the Urals and European Russia, closest to the markets, whereas 80 percent is in Siberia. Of the annual cut of up to 425 million cubic meters, two thirds is in the Urals and European Russia and one third in Siberia.

Soviet loggers consistently "mine" their forests, and 346 million acres (140 million hectares) await reforestation. The huge reserve of forest has been taken for granted by the cumbersome state bureaucracy. Much of the forest is cut over and diseased, and the vast majority of the healthy forest remains inaccessible.

Fishing

Fish is a major element in the Soviet diet. Until 1955 most of the fish came from domestic fishing grounds, but Soviet fishing fleets have expanded enormously. They are now on every ocean in the world and vie with Japan for world leadership in the annual harvest. Nearly 90 percent of the Soviet catch comes from marine fisheries—chiefly the Pacific Ocean, north Atlantic, and east central Atlantic. Most of the remaining catch is from the Caspian, Black, and Azov seas.

The stocking of inland lakes and streams and the establishment of fish farms and hatcheries have been emphasized since the 1960s. By 1980 more than 320 freshwater fish farms, with a surface area of about 371,000 acres (150,000 hectares), had been created in ponds, reservoirs, and ditches. Soviet aquaculturists have been successful in increasing the productivity of these farms by adding nutrients to the water.

Coal is dug with large power shovels from an open-pit mine in the Yakut Autonomous Soviet Socialist Republic.

Tass/Sovfoto

E. Kotlyakov—Tass/Sovfoto

The iron and steel works is one of the metal production facilities in Almalyk, Uzbek S.S.R.

Fish hatcheries along the Volga River have helped to restore populations of the valuable caviar-producing sturgeon, whose numbers were reduced after construction of large dams on the river.

Mining

Mining is a far more significant sector of the Soviet economy than it is in other developed countries. This is partly because consumption and services are weakly developed and partly because the Soviet raw-material base is extensive and relatively inexpensive to exploit. Apart from shortages of barite, bauxite, fluorspar, tin, and tungsten, the Soviet mining industry is well endowed with virtually every other mineral.

The major obstacle to Soviet mining is the geographic disparity between regions of supply and demand. This problem is sometimes compounded by the need to haul minerals over long distances. A quarter of the country—including the Urals, Transcaucasia, and the rest of the European Soviet Union—contains three fourths of the population, four fifths of industrial and agricultural production, but only one fourth of the resources. Kazakhstan and Central Asia contain 14 percent of the population, 18 percent of the area of the country, 7 percent of the industry, 11 percent of the agriculture, and less than one tenth of the raw-material base. Siberia, with a mere 11 percent of the population, has 57 percent of Soviet territory and upward of 67 percent of all the resources. Its industrial and agricultural products account for 13 and 8 percent, respectively.

Coal. In the mid-1980s the Soviet Union was third in the world in coal production (after the United States and China), its industry having fallen on hard times from the late 1970s. The country has the largest quantity of coal resources of any nation, but most of the fuel is in inaccessible deposits in eastern Siberia and is inferior brown coal (lignite). Eastern regions yield more than half of all Soviet coal. Long-distance rail transport is required to reach consumers in the Urals and beyond.

Iron and steel. The Soviet iron-and-steel industry is heavily concentrated in the European section and the Urals, where most of the iron-ore reserves are found (Kursk Magnetic Anomaly, Krivoy Rog, and the southern Urals). The Soviet Union has long led the world in iron-ore production and has led in steel production since 1970.

Petroleum and natural gas. From the 1960s there has been a spectacular increase in the production of petroleum and natural gas. The Soviet Union leads in world output of both. This rapid development is the result of drilling operations in western Siberia—the Middle Ob' Basin. As of 1964 no oil was produced in western Siberia. In 1986 nearly 400 million metric tons were produced in the region, or 65 percent of Soviet output. Other oil-producing areas include the Volga-Urals region, the Caspian Basin (both on- and offshore), and the Timan-Pechora region.

Natural gas, not oil, has paced the growth in Soviet energy. The country contains as much as a third of the world's natural gas reserves and in the early 1980s outstripped the United States in output. Again the driving force has been western Siberia—the Lower Ob' Basin. In the 1960s western Siberia yielded a mere trace of natural gas but by 1985 it produced 58 percent of the country's output. By the year 2000 the region is projected to provide 75 percent of production. Other regions of natural gas include the Lower Volga, Central Asia, the southern Urals, and the Timan-Pechora complex.

Hydroelectricity

Although hydroelectric development began in the European section, Siberia has the greatest potential. Most of this is concentrated in the Yenisey-Angara Basin of central Siberia. The Siberian development program involved the construction of some of the world's largest dams—Bratsk, Krasnoyarsk, Ust'-Ilimsk, Sayanogorsk, and Boguchany—and the establishment of such associated power-consuming industries as aluminum reduction and wood-pulp manufacture. Half of Siberia's electricity is from hydroelectric installations. There are other major dams along the Volga and Dnepr rivers and on fast-moving streams in the high mountains of Transcaucasia and Central Asia.

Manufacturing

Before the 1917 Revolution only 2 percent of the population worked in factories. Nearly four fifths of industrial activity was situated in only five regions:

The petrochemical industry is one of the largest productive enterprises in Tatar Autonomous Soviet Socialist Republic.

Jack Novak—Shostal Associates

Moscow, St. Petersburg (Leningrad) and the Baltic region, the southern and eastern Ukraine (including the Donbas), the Urals, and the northwestern Ukraine (including Kiev).

Until 1928 this pattern changed only slightly. Lenin's State Plan for Electrification established electric power in peripheral areas, but most new industry was light manufacturing.

Stalin's early five-year plans before World War II promoted heavy industry and indelibly changed the industrial landscape. Two thirds of all new projects were heavy industrial enterprises or power plants. Of 370 major industrial construction projects begun between 1928 and 1940, more than a third were located in former peripheral areas, and nearly two fifths were in new towns.

Foreseeing the threat of war, Stalin hurriedly tried to disperse the industrial base from the vulnerable European section to the east. His abbreviated Third Five-Year Plan (1938–42) stressed this need, and the war accelerated the process. Between July and November 1941, 1,500 factories were moved from Soviet Europe to eastern areas: the Urals (667), Turkestan (308), western Siberia (244), and eastern Siberia (78). After the war these factories stayed in place, but the need for reconstruction and new construction in the west took priority over eastern development until the 1960s.

By the 1960s the current pattern was set. About 40 percent of manufacturing is concentrated in the central industrial district—including Moscow and Gorky—where diversified machine building, textiles, and chemicals are produced. Perhaps 15 percent of Soviet manufacturing is in the southern and eastern Ukraine, where there is metallurgy, machine building, chemicals, and food processing. The Volga-Urals region—concentrating on chemicals, machinery, metallurgy, and wood processing—may produce another 15 percent. The Leningrad area, with its skilled labor force, manufactures more than 5 percent, including electronics, instruments, diversified machinery, textiles, and wood products. Eighty percent of Soviet manufacturing is still centered in the European section of the country. By the mid-1980s Siberia had only 11.7 percent of the industry, and Kazakhstan and Central Asia accounted for the rest of the Soviet Union's output.

Ust-Ilimsk became a city in 1973 when construction began on the dam and hydroelectric plant on the Angara River.

E. Bryukhanenko—Tass/Sovfoto

45

Jonathan T. Wright—Bruce Coleman Inc.

A woman works on an automobile assembly line in a factory built with the help of Western European industrialists.

Distribution and Trade

In the past the State Planning Agency (GOSPLAN) decided what products various enterprises in the different industrial branches would manufacture. The agency set weekly, monthly, and annual production targets, which plant managers had to meet or surpass.

Changes under Gorbachev include a liberalized target system. An annual target is now set by GOSPLAN, but how plant managers fulfill the target is their responsibility. In the past state procurement agencies took most of the output, but the state's share is now 25 percent and below. Factories deal directly not only with suppliers but also with retailers without interference from above. Success is based on profit. On Jan. 1, 1988, subject to legislation passed in 1987, all Soviet enterprises switched to local cost accounting (khozcaschet) and self-financing, both of which had been done at the central level.

A cooperative and private industrial sector was encouraged by Gorbachev as well. Cooperative markets in agriculture have existed for many years. Most of the produce from private plots is sold in the collective farm market at much higher prices than in state stores.

The Soviet Union usually reflects a favorable foreign trade balance except in years of crop failure. Such trade is only a small share of Soviet GNP—less than 10 percent. Most trade is with socialist countries (58 percent), but 30 percent is with developed capitalist countries and 12 percent with Third World countries. Healthy trade balances are maintained with socialist and Third World countries, but there are trade deficits with developed capitalist countries, exchanging raw materials for finished products and technology. Because of this and the lack of convertibility of the ruble, the Soviet Union in 1986 maintained the eleventh largest foreign debt. It continually seeks internationally exchangeable currencies to pay for imports of technology from Western nations and Japan.

Transportation

The Soviet domestic transportation system is the most heavily used in the world. It carries three times as much freight per ton-kilometer (a measure of freight hauled over distance), for instance, as does the network in the United States. The expansion of the country's rail, pipeline, river, and maritime programs has been ambitious and largely successful. Yet historically the Soviet government has placed a low priority on transportation in relation to other branches of the economy. This has had an adverse effect, especially on the railroads, which carry 47 percent of all freight and 37 percent of all passengers. Since 1938 added rail traffic has outstripped the construction of new track by a factor of 24.

Railways. Railway construction began in Russia in 1837 with a short line between St. Petersburg and Tsarskoye Selo (now Pushkin). By 1913 more than 40,000 miles (70,000 kilometers) of track were in operation. With few exceptions (the Trans-Siberian, Trans-Caspian, and others), the overwhelming majority of lines were concentrated in European Russia. With the fall of the czar, railroad building continued under Soviet rule. By 1985 the length of the Soviet system surpassed 90,000 miles (145,000 kilometers), but it was still little more than half the trackage of the United States.

Without sufficient track to absorb the rapidly expanding demand, Soviet planners called for increasing train weights and lengths, but this caused safety problems. This in turn affected the relative performance of the railroads. In 1940, 85 percent of ton-kilometers were by rail; by the 1980s the share fell to less than half. The principal cargoes of Soviet railroads are coal, building materials, and refined petroleum products.

Pipelines. The chief contributor to the shift in the transport balance is the pipeline. Until 1955 nearly 65 percent of the country's energy needs were satisfied by coal combustion, and a large portion of the oil was hauled by rail. A decision to convert from the burning of coal to oil and gas stimulated an unprecedented demand for trunk pipelines. Pipeline length increased from 10,000 miles (16,000 kilometers) to more than 160,000 miles (260,000 kilometers) in 1986. Later expansion was between the Ob' Basin and the West, including Eastern and Western Europe.

Roads and highways. The neglect of motor vehicle transportation has been characterized as "the greatest weakness" in the Soviet transportation network. Soviet roadways always have been few in number, and they rank among the poorest in the world. (Most farm-to-market roads in the United States are superior to the Moscow-Leningrad Highway.) The roads are especially bad in farming regions, causing delays in bringing harvests to markets.

Although inadequate, surfaced roads continue to expand. Their share of all roads increased from 40 percent in 1971 to 72 percent in 1985, but the term hard surfaced includes anything from gravel on rural roads to concrete city streets.

For years the majority of Soviet motor vehicles were trucks, but there was a fivefold growth of passenger cars between 1970 and 1983. In the early 1980s there were about 14 million passenger cars, a per capita figure ten times smaller than in the United States and a fifth smaller than in Mexico. A third of the cars belonged to government officials. Several million trucks haul only about 6 percent of the freight over an average distance of 10 miles (16 kilometers). Railroads must carry the bulk of the small and short-distance traffic, for which they are ill-suited.

Rivers. In 1913 Russian waterways carried nearly half as many shipments as were carried by rail. By 1982 the number had dropped to 7.6 percent. While expressing enthusiasm for waterway transport, Soviet leaders have given it low priority, particularly as regards investment in boats and port facilities. Most Soviet rivers freeze solidly for at least 80 days a year. The major inland waterway, the Volga, for example, freezes for from three to five months. Inland waterways are no longer a significant factor in the overall transport balance, carrying only 3 percent of the freight and 0.5 percent of the passengers.

Maritime. Soviet marine shipments grew rapidly between 1950 and 1970—from 23rd in world shipping to 6th place. The Soviet Union is bounded by the sea for 70 percent of its border, but much of the coastline is either frozen for part of the year or lacks good harbors. Much of the effort in expanding its maritime activity from 1970 was in lengthening the navigation season of the Northern Sea Route in the Arctic Ocean. Frozen solidly for as long as nine months of the year, the route is kept navigable with atomic icebreakers, which lead convoys of conventional icebreakers and freighters between Murmansk, Dudinka, and Noril'sk. Soviet maritime shipping accounts for as much as 14 percent of all freight haulage. The principal basins are the Black and Azov seas (43 percent of maritime tonnage), the Caspian Sea (20 percent), the Baltic Sea (15 percent), the Far East (14 percent), and the northern seas (8 percent).

Air. Soviet aviation carries an increasingly large share of passenger traffic but only a trace of the overall freight. Limited to the mail and high-value, low-weight materials and finished products, airlines haul little more than 80 million tons of freight each year, compared to nearly 4 billion tons shipped by rail. After the pipelines, however, aviation is the fastest-growing branch of transportation. Most of the increase is in intercity passenger flights.

The Soviet airline Aeroflot is the largest airline in the world. It employs 400,000 people and operates more than 6,500 aircraft of all types that fly to 3,500 domestic locations and 84 foreign countries.

Communications

In the early 1980s there were 89 telephones per 1,000 Soviet citizens. Only Brazil and Mexico among the major nations of the world reported lower ratios. All countries of Western Europe recorded more than 300 telephones per 1,000 citizens.

Radio and television are much better distributed—more than 300 units per 1,000 persons. This is better than all other advanced industrial countries except the United States, Japan, Canada, and Great Britain. The Soviet Union has its own telecommunications satellites. Usually within two years of the establishment of an urban settlement in a remote area such as northeastern Siberia, television transmitters beam video. Virtually all settlements receive the Moscow channel and a local or regional channel.

As many as 5 million personal computers are slated to be allocated to secondary and vocational-technical schools by the year 2000. They will not be available for home use. Their purpose is to foster computer literacy to enhance the country's economic performance.

GOVERNMENT

The capital city of the Soviet Union is Moscow, and the government is headquartered in Moscow's Kremlin. This medieval fortress served as the center of Russian government until 1712 and again became the capitol of the Soviet state after 1918 (*see* Kremlin).

The Soviet state has a dual structure: one part is represented by the Communist party, and the other is the official government organization. Each side has a parallel hierarchy in the shape of a pyramid. In theory power flows upward from the broad base, but in reality all major officials of government are members of the party, and high-level party officials make the major decisions.

Communist Party

The Communist party is an elite organization. Its membership rarely exceeds from 6 to 12 percent of the population. Membership is regarded as a privilege and a reflection of high moral character and leadership qualities. Persons 18 years of age and older may join the party. They must be recommended by three party members in good standing and approved by the regional party organization. Young persons between

The Trans-Siberian Railroad, begun in 1891, stretches for 5,786 miles (9,311 kilometers) from Moscow to Vladivostok.

Ken Proctor—Shostal Associates

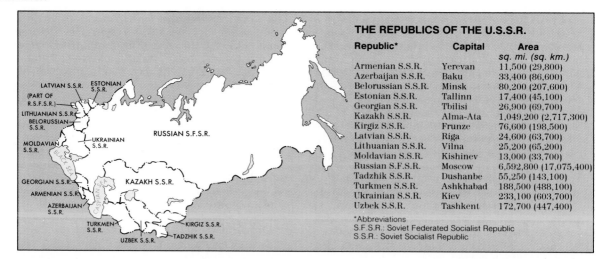

THE REPUBLICS OF THE U.S.S.R.

Republic*	Capital	Area sq. mi. (sq. km.)
Armenian S.S.R.	Yerevan	11,500 (29,800)
Azerbaijan S.S.R.	Baku	33,400 (86,600)
Belorussian S.S.R.	Minsk	80,200 (207,600)
Estonian S.S.R.	Tallinn	17,400 (45,100)
Georgian S.S.R.	Tbilisi	26,900 (69,700)
Kazakh S.S.R.	Alma-Ata	1,049,200 (2,717,300)
Kirgiz S.S.R.	Frunze	76,600 (198,500)
Latvian S.S.R.	Riga	24,600 (63,700)
Lithuanian S.S.R.	Vilna	25,200 (65,200)
Moldavian S.S.R.	Kishinev	13,000 (33,700)
Russian S.F.S.R.	Moscow	6,592,800 (17,075,400)
Tadzhik S.S.R.	Dushanbe	55,250 (143,100)
Turkmen S.S.R.	Ashkhabad	188,500 (488,100)
Ukrainian S.S.R.	Kiev	233,100 (603,700)
Uzbek S.S.R.	Tashkent	172,700 (447,400)

*Abbreviations
S.F.S.R.: Soviet Federated Socialist Republic
S.S.R.: Soviet Socialist Republic

the ages of 15 and 27 may become members of the Young Communist League (Komsomol).

Although at 20 million members the Communist party is relatively small, it affects all aspects of Soviet life through the primary party organization (PPO). Composed of three or more members, PPOs are found in factories, offices, military platoons, and on farms.

In accordance with the Leninist principle of "democratic centralism," PPO members elect a secretary who represents them at the next higher level (*raykom* or *gorkom*). At each ensuing level a secretary is chosen until the top of the party pyramid is reached. Each level of the hierarchy (*rayon* or city, oblast or *kray,* republic or region) has a congress. Republic or regional congresses elect deputies to the all-union congress of the Communist party of the Soviet Union. The all-union party congress, which meets once every five years, elects members of the Central Committee, which in turn selects the Secretariat.

Standing committees at each level of hierarchy are staffed by full-time party functionaries. The party apparatus consists of about 300,000 employees. The *apparatchiki,* as these people are called, compose the bulk of party officers. They are guided in their work by the Secretariat, which handles the day-to-day implementation of decisions made by the Politburo.

The Politburo is the highest administrative unit in the Communist party and the most powerful Soviet political body. Like those of the Secretariat, its members are selected by the Central Committee. Members of the Central Committee or of its Politburo make all major state decisions. Some Politburo members are also members of the Secretariat. The first secretary of the Secretariat is also general secretary of the Politburo. Decisions made by the Politburo are binding on all persons and units below. Simultaneously its decrees are automatically ratified by the parallel government structures.

Government Organization

The government bureaucracy consists of both elective and appointive bodies. Among the elective bodies is the two-chamber Supreme Soviet (Council), which has 1,500 members who meet twice a year in Moscow. One chamber, the Soviet of the Union, is a body whose 750 deputies are elected on the basis of one representative for every 375,000 people. The other chamber is the Soviet of Nationalities, whose 750 deputies represent a given national administrative unit—Russians, Tatars, Uzbeks, and so on. The relative allocation of the 750 seats on the Soviet of Nationalities depends on the rank of a given ethnic group on the "nationalities ladder." Each of the 15 soviet socialist republics (S.S.R.s) has 32 deputies; autonomous S.S.R.s, 11 deputies each for 20 units; autonomous oblasts, five deputies each for eight units; and autonomous okrugs, one deputy each for ten units.

The two houses are elected popularly once every five years by more than 180 million voters, 90 percent of whom are non-party members. To be eligible to vote, citizens must be at least 18 years of age. Voting is done in secret, and at least 97 percent of the electorate turn out to vote.

Candidates—both party and non-party members—are carefully screened by the local heads of the Communist party. Each office on the ballot lists the name of a single party-approved nominee, but there is room for write-ins. Candidates must be at least 23 years old. Of those elected to the Supreme Soviet, 80 percent are party members. Gorbachev called for and experimented with multi-candidate elections.

The two annual sessions of the Supreme Soviet last only a few days. The Presidium of the Supreme Soviet is elected at a joint meeting of the two chambers. It acts as a legislative body when the Supreme Soviet is not in session. The Presidium approves or ratifies legislation proposed by the ministries and central administrations of government. Its senior ranking member is the president of the Supreme Soviet, who more often than not is also the party's general secretary.

The Supreme Soviet is nominally the highest legislative body. Although debate occurs in the Supreme Soviet, it has never vetoed legislation proposed by the Council of Ministers. Such legislation has already been approved by the Presidium. No legislation has ever originated with the Supreme Soviet, though technically it can.

Among appointive bodies the highest is the Council of Ministers, most of whose members are also high-ranking officials in the Communist party and are usually members of the Central Committee. Ministers, who have been previously screened by the party, are proposed to the Supreme Soviet by the chairman of the Council of Ministers through the Presidium. They are automatically approved.

The Council of Ministers is the chief executive body of Soviet government. Alone, or jointly with the Central Committee of the Communist party, it formally issues all major legislative and administrative orders. These are automatically ratified by the Supreme Soviet.

Members of the Council of Ministers head the various ministries, commissions, and committees of government that run day-to-day activities. Each minister deals with the affairs of a specific branch of the economy or of a given region.

Key appointive administrative posts like those of the Council of Ministers are filled only with the approval of the Communist party. Appointive positions, which cannot be filled without party consent, are called "nomenclature jobs." Executives who are part of the *nomenklatura* rank among the most powerful members of Soviet society.

Gorbachev restructured the ministries. His purpose was to streamline them and make them more efficient. Former bureaucrats were recycled into other more productive sectors of the economy.

The Council of Ministers has its own Presidium of a dozen or more members, which is comparable in size and function to the Politburo on the party side. The chief executive of the Presidium of the Council of Ministers is called the chairman or premier. The premier inevitably is a ranking member of the Politburo.

Under a nominally federal system, better called federative, each of the 15 republics also has a Supreme Soviet. There is also a system of regional and local soviets.

Justice is administered by the Supreme Court of the Soviet Union, the Supreme Court of each of the union republics, regional courts, and by local peoples' courts. Special officials called procurators supervise the courts to make sure that state law is strictly observed. Judges are elected by the Supreme Soviet of the Soviet Union for a period of five years. The procurator general serves for seven years.

International Relations

Soviet leaders have believed that capitalist countries are inherently expansionist and that they threaten Soviet security. Relations with the West typically have been undermined by an air of suspicion and hostility—the Cold War. The Cold War has not turned hot because the Soviets believe that capitalism inevitably will collapse from its own inherent weaknesses and flaws. This explains the special rela-

tionship of the Soviet state with the socialist countries of Eastern Europe and with Communist parties elsewhere. It also provides some understanding of the intense Soviet interest in the developing world, in which countries are seeking ways to modernize but are already predisposed against capitalism because of its association with their colonial pasts.

Nonideological considerations also play a role in explaining Soviet policy toward the West, toward ruling and non-ruling Communist parties, and toward developing countries in Asia, Africa, and Latin America. Nonideological considerations include the protection of Soviet security—defense by buffer, the need for extensive foreign trade to obtain exchangeable currency, and the desire for prestige and recognition as a global superpower.

The Gorbachev administration has shown a willingness to rethink its interpretation of relations with capitalist countries. Historically relations with the West have improved when the Russian or Soviet economy needed help: the early 1700s under Peter the Great, the late 1700s under Catherine the Great, between 1890 and 1917 under Nicholas II, the 1930s under Stalin, and the 1970s under Brezhnev. The difference between the improvements made in the past and Gorbachev's is that the latter seems to have less ideological orthodoxy, greater sincerity, honesty, and far less hostility—including statements and acts of accommodation.

HISTORY

In antiquity the territory that now constitutes the Soviet Union was occupied by the cultural hearths of four major linguistic stocks: Indo-Europeans (Germans, Slavs, and others) north of the Black Sea; Uralians (Finns, Ugrians) in the environs of the Ural Mountains; Altaic peoples (Turks, Mongols) in southwestern Siberia; and Caucasians (Georgians, Abkhaz) in Transcaucasia. During the two millennia before the Christian era, the Indo-Europeans spread into the Middle East (Iran and Afghanistan) and South Asia. Simultaneously the Uralic group diffused to the north and northwest and the Altaic group to the east, south, and southwest. Some of the Caucasian peoples crossed the mountains onto the forelands north of the Greater Caucasus Mountains.

In what is now Soviet Europe, an Indo-European group called the Cimmerians developed a semisedentary society on the forest and steppe boundary. They may have been the people who first domesticated the horse about 1000 BC. Eventually in the grasslands they coupled herding with grain cultivation. Another Indo-European group, the Tripolyans, raised wheat and millet in the forest clearings located northwest of the Cimmerians.

In 600 BC this pleasant setting was upset by an invasion by a Persian Indo-European nomadic group, the Scythians. Thus began a series of invasions by Indo-Europeans, Altaic groups, and one Uralic (Ugrian) group that persisted for 18 centuries. German scholars call this period "the peoples' migrations." It was a period that molded and established the distinctive patchwork of more than 100 different nationalities that now inhabit the Soviet Union.

Slavs

Slavic origins are obscure. They evidently diffused from their homeland north of the Carpathian Mountains at the beginning of the Christian era. Some tribes moved eastward into the Ukraine, Belorussia, and Russia. There they met Finnic tribes, whom they pushed farther north. By the 3rd and 4th centuries the steppes and forests of the region south and west of contemporary Moscow were home to various eastern Slavs. By AD 600 Slavic trading villages were on all the rivers west of the Ural Mountains.

Slavic ethnic distinction probably crystallized during a period of prolonged peace brought about by the domination of the Volga trade route by the Khazars— Pax Khazarica, 720–860. Lively commerce was carried on between Scandinavia and Baghdad by way of the Volga, and the Khazars kept the route safe from marauding nomads. In time the Khazar dominion stretched as far west as the Dnepr River, the focus of Slavic culture in the Antes Confederation.

Beginnings of the Russian Empire

Long before the rise of the first Slavic state— Kievan Rus'—during the latter 800s, southern Russia was occupied by Cimmerians, Scythians, Sarmatians, Goths, Huns, Turkic Bulgars, Avars, and Khazars. The Slavs endured them all. Loosely knit and socially bound mainly by extended families, the Slavs seemed to be interested only in farming and welcomed the protection they received from powerful warriors like the Khazars. But as soon as their protector fell from grace they became vulnerable.

During Pax Khazarica Scandinavians traded not only with Baghdad but with Byzantium by way of the Dnepr. These Norsemen, or Varangians, as the Slavs called them, traveled inland through lakes and rivers, hauling their boats overland from one body of water to the next. At Novgorod they portaged to the Dnepr watershed, which led them to the Black Sea. Near Kiev the Dnepr bends eastward and is plagued by rapids, forcing the Varangians to make another portage at Kiev.

In the 800s the Slavs were in complete turmoil. They had great respect for the Varangians, and the people of Novgorod asked the Norsemen for a ruler to organize them. The Scandinavians sent Rurik, chieftain of the Rus' trading company, in 862—the year from which the Russians date their first dynasty. Shortly after Rurik's death his relative Oleg became grand duke of Novgorod and soon added Kiev to his domains, making it his capital. During the next century the influence of Kiev was felt from the Danube to the Volga.

Kievan Rus' (878–1240)

In 988 Vladimir, grand prince of Kiev, became a Christian in the Byzantine (Eastern Orthodox) tradi-

Courtesy of the Lenin State Library, Moscow

In the battle of Kulikovo on Sept. 8, 1380 (shown in a 16th-century manuscript illumination), Russian forces defeated the Tatars of the Golden Horde.

tion. Greek missionaries moved into Russia, bringing their religion, art and architecture, and the Cyrillic alphabet. For the next four centuries Kievan Rus' developed into a well-organized, democratic, urban, commercial society. At the height of its glory in the 11th century, Kievan Rus' was populated by 7 to 8 million people, including the cities of Kiev, Novgorod, and Smolensk. It was the largest and most populous state in Europe.

In the 12th century Kievan Rus' began to decay because of a fragmented power structure and the inability to ward off attacks from steppe nomads. Moreover the Volga River trade route began to experience rebirth. A new trading center grew at Moscow. Between 1237 and 1240 Kievan Rus' was finally crushed by the onslaught of the Mongolians, who were also known as Tatars. The Mongolians were under the leadership of Batu, grandson of Ghengis Khan. The once-flourishing populace either perished or fled into the neighboring forests.

Mongol Yoke (1237–1480)

The Mongols formed a kingdom with a capital at Sarai on a tributary of the Volga River. The influence of the Golden Horde was felt almost everywhere in Russia. They did not attempt to settle the land but exacted tribute through Russian intermediaries. Asian customs and ways of thought became a part of Russian culture, but as long as they paid tribute the Russians were free to practice their religion and native customs.

The Golden Horde soon split into three separate Tatar hordes focused on Kazan', Astrakhan', and the Crimea. Although they controlled the Moscow area, they never gained control of Novgorod. During the Mongol yoke Nougorod joined the European trading consortium, the Hanseatic League, and flourished.

In time the Tatars began to weaken because of war and internal discord. The principality of Muscovy (Moscow), nestled deep in the forest at the hub of all the major trade routes, developed at the expense of the Tatars' decline. Muscovite princes, who efficiently collected the tribute demanded by the Tatar Khans, enhanced their coffers through reward and fraud. As descendants of the Rurik line, Muscovite princes came to be looked upon by the people as justified leaders of all Russians.

From the beginning of his reign, Ivan the Great (1462–1505) refused to pay tribute to the Tatars. In 1480 the Tatars sent an army against him, but the army withdrew without a battle. Ivan added Novgorod to his domains and spread Muscovy's rule to the Arctic. (*See also* Ivan.)

First Czars

Ivan IV, called the "the Terrible" because of his savage cruelty, crowned himself czar—the Russian word for Caesar—and ruled Muscovy from 1533 to 1584. Russian sovereigns now ruled "by the grace of God" as absolute monarchs, responsible to the Almighty alone. Ivan defeated the Khanates of Kazan' in 1552 and Astrakhan' in 1556, making the Volga a wholly Russian river. In the 1580s he spread Muscovy's rule into Siberia, but the West proved too strong. He futilely engaged the Swedes, and Kiev still lay deep within the powerful Polish-Lithuanian kingdom.

Ivan IV killed one of his sons, and another died at age 9. The remaining son, Fedor, was feeble, and, after reigning as czar for 14 years, he died childless. Thus ended the House of Rurik.

Boris Godunov was elected to succeed Fedor. He consolidated Russia's territorial gains, but, soon after he came to power, drought, famine, and plague killed half a million people in Muscovy. Peasants fled their villages, leaving their holdings in weeds. In response Godunov decreed that the peasants were forbidden to leave the estates on which they were born. The peasants were thus bound to the soil, and serfdom began.

Godunov died in 1605. His successor was murdered within a few months. Leaderless Russia was rife with dissension. For the next eight years it coped with civil wars, Cossack raids in the south, Polish invaders, and impostors pretending to be sons of Ivan IV and trying to claim the throne. The frustrated Russians in 1610 temporarily accepted the son of the Polish king as czar, but Russian guerrilla forces later ousted the foreigners.

Romanov Dynasty (1613–1917)

The Russian nobility sought a new bloodline for the aristocracy. They found it in Mikhail Romanov, who was a young nobleman (*boyar*). Thus began the Romanov Dynasty, which ruled until 1917. (*See also* Romanov Dynasty.)

Peter and Catherine the Great. The Russian Empire is usually dated from the reign of Peter the Great (1689–1725) and with it the beginning of modern Russian history. Peter defeated the Swedes and gained an outlet to the Baltic Sea. He founded a navy, introduced factories, reformed the administrative machinery, and organized a modern army. He forced education upon his officers and members of his court, many of whom could not read. He created a new Russian capital—St. Petersburg (Leningrad)—on the Gulf of Finland. (*See also* Peter the Great.)

Peter died in 1725. His work survived almost half a century of incompetent rulers. Then Catherine the Great (1762–96) came to the throne. She again took up the task of reform. Her armies defeated the Crimean Tatars in 1792. (*See also* Catherine the Great.)

Alexander I and Nicholas I. The reign of Alexander I (1801–25) began in the spirit of Peter and Catherine, both of whom were Westernizers. Plans were drawn for a Duma, or representative assembly, to propose new laws. He had begun to carry out his program when Russia became involved in the Napoleonic wars. Reform was then abandoned. (*See also* Alexander.)

Alexander's successor, Nicholas I (1825–55), devoted his attention to protecting Russia against what he considered corrupting Western ideas. All democratic reform was suppressed.

In 1854 Russia became involved in the disastrous Crimean War, which lasted more than two years. The

The first czar of Russia, Ivan IV, was a ruthless authoritarian known in history as Ivan the Terrible.

Sovfoto

A statue of Peter the Great in Leningrad is one of the many memorials to the enlightened ruler and reformer.

Russian people were tired of war, and the serfs rose against the landowners and burned and pillaged their estates. (*See also* Crimean War; Nicholas.)

Emancipation of the Serfs (1861). Alexander II (1855–81) succeeded Nicholas I. He was the greatest czarist reformer in Russian history. His reforms began with the emancipation of the serfs in March 1861, giving liberty to some 40 million people.

The long years of tyranny and lack of progress, however, had produced discontent, especially among the young with university educations. Revolutionary activity, which had been brewing since an unsuccessful revolt against the czar in December 1825, developed rapidly, and in 1881 Alexander II was assassinated by a bomb hurled at his carriage. He was succeeded by his son Alexander III (1881–94), a Slavophile and no friend of reformers. Under Alexander III revolutionary organizations were completely suppressed—but not revolutionary feeling. (*See also* Alexander.)

First Duma. Nicholas II (1894–1917) was the last of the Romanovs. In 1904 Russia and Japan went to war over rights in the Far East. The war was unpopular in Russia, and the country suffered a terrible defeat, encouraging greater revolutionary activity. (*See also* Russo-Japanese War.)

Although small, a new factory laboring class was organized by the revolutionaries. Peasants sympathized and helped. Mutinies broke out in the army and navy. Manufacturers and landlords demanded reforms that would satisfy workers, peasants, and soldiers. After a general strike, climaxing the Revolution of 1905,

Nicholas called for the election of a Duma as proposed by his ancestor Alexander I a century before.

In August 1914 Russia went to war against Germany and Austria over conflicting claims in the Balkans. The peasants and workers at first accepted it without protest, but great military failures resulted because of the Russian government's inability to supply and equip its armies. Millions of Russian lives were sacrificed. The attitude of the public toward the war and the government changed.

Food shortages in March 1917 stimulated mass rioting in the capital (then called Petrograd). Soldiers deserted the government and joined the people. The Duma demanded that the czar step down. Nicholas II abdicated his throne on March 15, and he and his family were exiled. (*See also* Nicholas; World War I.)

Revolution and the Soviet Union

The March 1917 revolution was over within a week with little bloodshed. For a time the government was in the hands of the nonsocialist Constitutional Democrats. In July, however, power passed to Alexander Kerensky. Kerensky wanted to continue the war, but the Russian people did not.

Bolsheviks take power. At this point a group of socialists schooled in the doctrines of Karl Marx filtered into Petrograd. Many had been in exile both in Russia and abroad. They were few in number, though their name Bolsheviks means "majority men." They were extremely well organized and dedicated, and they had a program.

Vladimir Ilich Ulyanov (Lenin) was the Bolsheviks' undisputed leader. Lenin aimed to overthrow Russia's infant capitalist system, which he would then replace with a dictatorship of the proletariat (workers) based on the principles that had been espoused by Marx. (*See also* Lenin.)

October Revolution. Thousands of revolutionary soviets (councils) had sprung up all over Russia. The Bolsheviks carried on propaganda campaigns among them. By October 1917 the party controlled the majority of the soviets of Petrograd and Moscow.

On October 25 the second All-Russian Congress of Soviets was scheduled to meet in Petrograd. Early that morning Red Guards poured into the city, surrounded the Winter Palace, and occupied the railroad stations, the ministries, and the state bank. When the Congress of Soviets met that night, Lenin was proclaimed premier. The event is called the October Revolution because Russia still used the old calendar. According to the calendar now in use, the event took place on November 7. (*See also* Russian Revolution.)

The October Revolution itself was over in a week, and fighting was limited to the major cities. Eight months later the former czar and his entire family were executed in the Urals city of Yekaterinburg (Sverdlovsk).

The new government assumed ownership of all land and took control of industry. In March 1918 a treaty of peace was signed with the Germans at Brest-Litovsk. By the terms of the treaty Russia recognized

Germany's claims to the Caucasus and Ukraine. In addition, Russia agreed to give up Poland and the Baltic states and to pay huge indemnities.

Civil war and famine. Between 1918 and 1922 the Bolsheviks were confronted with civil war, intervention by troops of 15 foreign countries, and terrible famine. "White" armies composed of soldiers loyal to the czar challenged the Bolshevik "Red" armies. The White armies were supplied by foreign interventionists—including British, American, and Japanese representatives—and were quite successful at first. After the surrender of Germany in 1918, Poland invaded Belorussia. The Reds finally defeated the Whites, the interventionists withdrew, and Lenin made peace with Poland. On Dec. 30, 1922, the Union of Soviet Socialist Republics was officially established.

In economic chaos, Russia had suffered a drought in 1921, causing widespread famine and disease. The American Relief Administration, under the direction of Herbert Hoover, fed millions, but many people died. In 1921 Lenin inaugurated the New Economic Policy (NEP), encouraging individual initiative in the farm sector. The NEP temporarily reinvigorated the Soviet economy by providing sufficient food for both city and countryside.

Stalin Years

Lenin died in 1924, and a struggle for leadership began between Joseph Stalin and Leon Trotsky. As secretary of the Central Committee of the Communist party, Stalin stripped Trotsky of power and exiled him in 1928. (*See also* Stalin; Trotsky.)

Stalin continued Lenin's NEP until 1928. Fearing the entrenchment of a capitalist class in agriculture, however, he initiated the First Five-Year Plan. The plan called for rapid growth in heavy industry and collectivization of agriculture.

The last known photograph of Czar Nicholas II was taken after his abdication of the throne early in 1917.

Rather than yield their livestock to the new collectives, many farmers slaughtered them. A man-made famine resulted. In 1932 about 3 million people died of starvation in the Ukraine alone. Nevertheless, when the First Five-Year Plan ended in 1932, the government announced that great progress had been made. Peasant resistance had been smashed, and the country was on the road to industrialization.

Stalin meanwhile tightened his grip on the government and the Red Army by means of a series of purges. In 1935 and 1936 alone nearly 500,000 people were executed, imprisoned, or forced into labor camps. He further consolidated his position through the Great Purge trials (1936–39). Through this system of trials and terror, Stalin eliminated all of his rivals. He systematically employed the services of the secret police (today the KGB) to root out "political criminals."

Stalin's foreign policy was equally ruthless. Like Lenin, he believed that the Soviet state would never be totally secure until the entire world was communist. Many nations were disturbed by the activity of the Third, or Communist, International, known as the Comintern. The Comintern directed the activities of Communist parties outside the Soviet Union. It gathered information by espionage, caused labor troubles and other civil discord, and undermined governments.

In Germany the Communist party played a major part in helping to destroy the Weimar Republic. Its destruction, however, brought Adolf Hitler, an outspoken anti-Communist, to power. Stalin then began to advocate "collective security" and ordered the

Lenin, left, founded the Soviet Union in 1917. Joseph Stalin, his successor, right, ruled until 1953.

Comintern to tone down its propaganda. Until then the United States refused to recognize the Soviet Union. With the apparent change in the Communist program, President Franklin D. Roosevelt granted recognition in 1933, and in 1934 the Soviet Union joined the League of Nations.

Stalin-Hitler pact. On Aug. 23, 1939, Stalin and Hitler signed a Soviet-German nonaggression pact. This assured Hitler that he would not have to fight a war on two fronts. On September 1 the Nazis attacked Poland, and World War II began. Shortly thereafter Soviet troops occupied eastern Poland.

In November the Soviets attacked Finland and defeated the Finns in three months of bitter fighting. In 1940 Soviet authorities annexed the Baltic states—Latvia, Lithuania, and Estonia—and a part of Romania—Moldavia.

Germany invades Russia. Unable to defeat Great Britain, the Nazis invaded the Soviet Union on June 22, 1941, in pursuit of the rich granaries of the Ukraine and the petroleum fields of the Caucasus. By November the Germans had reached the suburbs of Moscow. In the north, aided by the Finns, they had surrounded Leningrad. In the south, aided by the Romanians, they reached Stalingrad (now Volgograd) in 1942.

That spring supplies from the United States and Great Britain poured into the Soviet Union. Soviet fighting men were soon fed and outfitted by the very

Statues at the Mamayev Memorial in Volgograd commemorate Soviet soldiers who died in the Battle of Stalingrad.

capitalists who were so much despised by Stalin. By the end of the war, the United States alone had given more than 11 billion dollars of Lend Lease aid to the Soviet Union.

Ultimately the Germans were defeated by Lend Lease aid, severe winter weather, and a scorched earth policy. Early in 1943 the Red Army forced the surrender of 22 enfeebled German divisions at Stalingrad. Counterattacking on all fronts, Soviet forces reached Berlin victoriously in 1945. No one knows exactly what the Soviet war losses were, but it has been estimated that 20 million soldiers and civilians died directly because of the war and as many as 15 million births were not realized because of it.

Yalta and Potsdam. In February 1945 Stalin met with Roosevelt and British Prime Minister Winston Churchill at Yalta on the Crimean Peninsula. Stalin promised to enter the war against Japan three months after the end of hostilities in Europe. The Soviets turned against Japan on Aug. 8, 1945. The Red Army fought no battles, but when Japan surrendered on September 2 it had moved into northern Korea and into much of Manchuria.

After Germany's unconditional surrender, representatives of the Soviet Union, the United States, and Great Britain met again—at Potsdam, a suburb of Berlin. At this conference Germany and Austria were both divided into four zones—each zone to be occupied by one of the "big three" nations and France. Although entirely within the Soviet German sector (East Germany), Berlin was also carved into four parts. (*See also* World War II.)

Eastern Europe. At Yalta and Potsdam Stalin promised that in Soviet-occupied Europe there would be civil liberties, free elections, and representative governments. In all of these countries, however, Moscow-trained political leaders supported by the Red armies succeeded in gaining power. Anti-Communists were soon dead, in jail, or in exile.

As a concession to foreign opinion, the Comintern was dissolved in 1943. In 1947 it was revived under a new name, the Cominform (Communist Information Bureau). It controlled the Soviet satellite nations of Eastern Europe.

Cold War. The Soviet Union was a charter member of the United Nations and one of the "big five" on the Security Council. In the council Soviet representatives used their veto power to halt disarmament plans and to prevent action against Soviet aggression. It also blocked efforts to write peace treaties for Germany and Austria.

In 1948 Stalin tried to drive the Western powers out of Berlin by blockading the city and starving the people. Britain and the United States broke the blockade, bringing in food by air. (*See also* Cold War.)

On April 4, 1949, the United States, Canada, and most of the countries of Western Europe signed a pact creating the North Atlantic Treaty Organization (NATO), which provided that an armed attack against any one of them should be considered an attack against them all. This alliance checked Soviet expansion in Western Europe—but the Soviet Union was compensated by large gains in Asia.

Marxism-Leninism in Asia. In 1924 Outer Mongolia had become a "people's republic." North Korea was quickly communized after 1945. From Manchuria Soviet forces were partially withdrawn to allow the Chinese Communists to take over much of the industrial area to use as a base for operations against the Nationalists in the Chinese civil war. Chinese Communists finally drove the Nationalist government off the mainland and set up a government modeled on that of the Soviets. In February 1950 Communist China and the Soviet Union signed a treaty of friendship, alliance, and mutual assistance.

The United Nations created the republic of South Korea when the Soviets refused to allow free elections in a unified Korea. On June 25, 1950, Soviet-trained North Koreans, using Soviet tanks and equipment, invaded South Korea. The United Nations was able to take action against the aggression because the Soviets boycotted the Security Council.

Khrushchev: the Curious Reformer

Stalin died on March 5, 1953. Party leaders announced that the nation would be ruled by a committee, headed by Georgi M. Malenkov. Nikita S. Khrushchev seemed to be the least of the ruling group. In a few days, however, Malenkov "voluntarily" resigned the key post of first secretary of the party, and Khrushchev took over. Malenkov kept his title of premier, but two years later Khrushchev forced Malenkov to resign even that position. Nikolai Bulganin took Malenkov's place.

In 1956 Khrushchev, in what was considered a very bold move at the time, denounced Stalin in a speech before the Communist party congress. He also dissolved the Cominform. Several satellite countries were at once encouraged to strike out for more independence. The Poles rioted, and the Hungarians launched a full-scale revolt that the Soviet army quickly suppressed.

AFP Photo

Ronald Reagan and Mikhail Gorbachev shake hands after signing the INF treaty in Moscow on June 1, 1988.

Khrushchev next moved against his enemies in the government. In July 1957 Malenkov was further demoted along with the foreign minister, Vyacheslav M. Molotov, and other prominent leaders. In March 1958 Khrushchev ousted Bulganin and took the title of premier himself.

Soviet strides in science and technology scored propaganda victories and aroused concern in the West. The successful test of an intercontinental ballistic missile was announced in August 1957. In October Sputnik I, an artificial Earth satellite, rocketed into orbit. In 1959 Soviet scientists launched the first manmade planet, and in 1961 they sent the first human into orbit around the Earth.

In 1958 and 1959 Soviet leaders demanded that Western troops be removed from Berlin. Later Khrushchev made friendship visits to the United States and Asia. Hoping to promote a summit meeting of heads of state, he did not press the Berlin demands. But the four-power conference collapsed in May 1960.

Soviet soldiers are given a welcome home ceremony on their return from fighting in Afghanistan. The Soviet withdrawal of troops began in May 1988 after a war of 8½ years.

P. Robert—Sygma

In 1961 Soviet officials ordered a wall built between East and West Berlin. Ignoring a "no testing" agreement with the West, they also resumed nuclear weapons tests. In 1962 United States President John F. Kennedy demanded that Soviet offensive missiles be withdrawn from Cuba. Facing a United States naval blockade of Cuba and the threat of nuclear war, Khrushchev yielded.

In 1960 the Communist party congress narrowly endorsed Khrushchev's doctrine of peaceful coexistence with the West. Soviet representatives signed a limited nuclear test-ban treaty with the Western nations in 1963. The following year Khrushchev was ousted. (*See also* Khrushchev.)

Brezhnev to Gorbachev

Leonid I. Brezhnev succeeded Khrushchev as first secretary (now called general secretary) with Aleksei N. Kosygin as premier. In 1966 the Soviets landed an unmanned vehicle on the moon and sent a satellite into moon orbit. In 1968 they led a Warsaw Pact invasion of Czechoslovakia to halt that country's liberal movement. Relations with China deteriorated during the 1960s but improved again in the 1980s.

During the Brezhnev years there was emphasis on détente with the West along with a massive arms buildup. In the 1970s and early 1980s the Soviet government came under international pressure for suppressing dissent within the country and restricting the emigration of Jews. In 1979 the Soviets invaded Afghanistan to preserve a newly established Marxist regime. (*See also* Brezhnev.)

Although Brezhnev had singled out Konstantin Chernenko as his successor, Yuri Andropov became general secretary after Brezhnev's death in 1982. Chernenko, who had replaced Andropov as second secretary, succeeded Andropov, who died in 1984. When Chernenko died in 1985, the second secretary was Mikhail S. Gorbachev. (*See also* Andropov; Chernenko; Gorbachev.)

As general secretary Gorbachev established himself as the most polished Soviet leader since Lenin. In December 1987 he obtained with the United States the first voluntary bilateral arms reduction agreement in 700 years of human history—the INF treaty. He called for the elimination of all nuclear arms by the year 2000. He withdrew Soviet forces from Afghanistan. He was determined to reform the domestic economy. A master of diplomacy, he knew the value of good public relations. (*See also* the various articles on individual republics and other geographic areas, cities, and geographic features.)

BIBLIOGRAPHY FOR U.S.S.R.

Books for Children

Bernstein, J.E. Dmitry: a Young Soviet Immigrant (Houghton, 1981).
Gillies, John. The Soviet Union: the World's Largest Country (Dillon, 1985).
Jackson, W.A.D. Soviet Union, rev. ed. (Fideler, 1983).
Kronenwetter, Michael. Capitalism vs. Socialism (Watts, 1986).
Lye, Keith. Take a Trip to Russia (Watts, 1982).

McGuire, Leslie. Catherine the Great (Chelsea House, 1986).
Resnick, Abraham. Lenin: Founder of the Soviet Union (Children's, 1987).
Resnick, Abraham. Russia: a History to 1917 (Children's, 1983).
Resnick, Abraham. The Union of Soviet Socialist Republics (Children's, 1984).
Riordan, James. Soviet Union (Silver Burdett, 1987).
Ryabko, E. We Live in the European U.S.S.R. (Bookwright, 1984).
Smith, Samantha. Journey to the Soviet Union (Little, 1985).
Stanley, Diane. Peter the Great (Macmillan, 1986).
Stein, R.C. Invasion of Russia (Children's, 1985).
Zhitkov, Boris. How I Hunted the Little Fellows (Dodd, 1979).

Books for Young Adults and Teachers

Alexeyeva, Ludmilla. Soviet Dissent: Contemporary Movements for National, Religious, and Human Rights (Wesleyan Univ. Press, 1985).
Berlin, Isaiah. Russian Thinkers (Penguin, 1979).
Billington, J.H. The Icon and the Axe (Random, 1970).
Brown, Archie and others, eds. The Cambridge Encyclopedia of Russia and the Soviet Union (Cambridge Univ. Press, 1982).
Carrère d'Encausse, Hélène. Decline of an Empire (Harper, 1981).
Cohen, S.F. Rethinking the Soviet Experience: Politics and History Since 1917 (Oxford Univ. Press, 1986).
Cole, J.P. Geography of the Soviet Union (Butterworth, 1984).
Dallin, Alexander. The Gorbachev Era (Stanford Alumni Assoc., 1986).
Demko, G.J. and Fuchs, R.J., eds. Geographical Studies on the Soviet Union (Univ. of Chicago Department of Geography, 1984).
Dienes, Leslie and Shabad, Theodore. The Soviet Energy System (Halsted Press, 1979).
Gorbachev, Mikhail. Perestroika (Harper, 1987).
Gregory, P.R. and Stuart, R.C. Soviet Economic Structure and Performance (Harper, 1981).
Harris, C.D. Cities of the Soviet Union (Rand, 1970).
Hewett, E.A. Reforming the Soviet Economy: Equality Versus Efficiency (Brookings, 1987).
Hoffmann, E.P. and Laird, Robbin. The Politics of Economic Modernization in the Soviet Union (Cornell Univ. Press, 1982).
Hough, J.F. and Fainsod, Merle. How the Soviet Union Is Governed (Harvard Univ. Press, 1979).
Hough, J.F. Opening up the Soviet Economy (Brookings, 1988).
Jensen, R.G. and others, eds. Soviet Natural Resources in the World Economy (Univ. of Chicago Press, 1983).
Kaiser, R.G. Russia (Pocket Books, 1984).
Katz, Zev and others. Handbook of Major Soviet Nationalities (Free Press, 1975).
Komarov, Boris. The Destruction of Nature in the Soviet Union (M.E. Sharpe, 1980).
Lapidus, G.W., ed. Women, Work, and Family in the Soviet Union (M.E. Sharpe, 1982).
Massie, Suzanne. Land of the Firebird (Simon & Schuster, 1982).
Nogee, Joseph, ed. Soviet Politics (Praeger, 1985).
Plotkin, Gregory. Cooking the Russian Way (Lerner, 1986).
Pond, Elizabeth. From the Yaroslavsky Station (Universe, 1984).
Resnick, Abraham. Siberia and Soviet Far East: Unmasking the Myths (G.E. McCuen, 1985).
Riasanovsky, N.V. A History of Russia, 4th ed. (Oxford Univ. Press, 1984).
Sagers, M.J. and Green, M.B. The Transportation of Soviet Energy Resources (Rowman, 1986).
Shabad, Theodore. Basic Industrial Resources of the U.S.S.R. (Columbia Univ. Press, 1969).
Smith, Hedrick. The Russians (Ballantine, 1984).
Swearingen, Roger, ed. Siberia and the Soviet Far East (Hoover Institution, 1987).
Treadgold, D.W. Twentieth Century Russia (Westview, 1987).
Whiting, A.S. Siberian Development and East Asia (Stanford Univ. Press, 1981).
Wolfe, B.D. Three Who Made a Revolution (Stein & Day, 1986).
Wood, Alan, ed. Siberia: Problems and Prospects for Regional Development (London, Methuen, 1987).
Zaslavsky, Victor and Brym, R.J. Soviet-Jewish Emigration and Soviet Nationality Policy (St. Martin, 1983).
ZumBrunnen, Craig and Osleeb, Jeffrey. The Soviet Iron and Steel Industry (Rowman, 1986).

U.S.S.R. Fact Summary

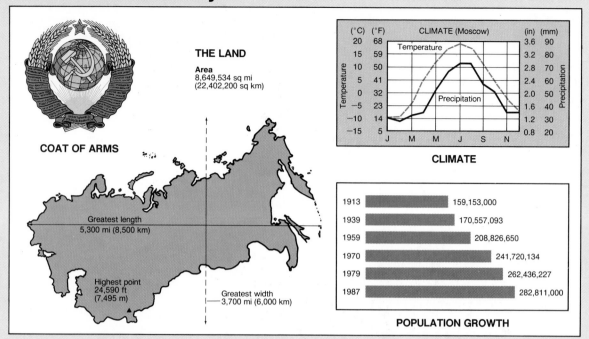

THE LAND

Area
8,649,534 sq mi
(22,402,200 sq km)

COAT OF ARMS

Greatest length
5,300 mi (8,500 km)

Highest point
24,590 ft
(7,495 m)

Greatest width
3,700 mi (6,000 km)

CLIMATE (Moscow)

CLIMATE

1913	159,153,000
1939	170,557,093
1959	208,826,650
1970	241,720,134
1979	262,436,227
1987	282,811,000

POPULATION GROWTH

Official Name: Union of Soviet Socialist Republics.

Capital: Moscow.

Coat of Arms: Hammer and sickle on globe represent industrial and agricultural workers; star above it represents authority of Communist party. On scroll binding sheaves of wheat, in languages of each of the 15 republics: "Workers of the world, unite!" Adopted 1923.

Flag: On red field, yellow hammer and sickle with star above (*see* Flags of the World).

Anthem: 'Gimn sovyetskovo soyuza' (Anthem of the Soviet Union).

NATURAL FEATURES

Borders: *Coast*—27,000 miles (43,450 kilometers); *land frontier*—11,000 miles (17,700 kilometers).

Natural Regions: East European Plain, West Siberian Lowlands, Turgay Plateau, Kazakh Uplands, Turan Plain, Central Siberian Plateau.

Major Ranges: Altai, Carpathians, Caucasus, Chersky, Crimean Hills, Kopet-Dag, Pamir, Sayan, Stanovoy, Sredinny, Tian Shan, Ural, Yablonovy.

Notable Peaks: Communism Peak, 24,590 feet (7,495 meters); Victory (Pobedy), 24,406 feet (7,439 meters); Lenin Peak, 23,406 feet (7,134 meters); El'brus, 18,481 feet (5,633 meters); Dykh-Tau, 17,070 feet (5,203 meters).

Major Rivers: Amur, Angara, Dnepr, Lena, Ob', Volga, Yenisey.

Major Lakes: Aral Sea, Baikal, Balkhash, Caspian Sea, Issyk-Kul', Ladoga, Onega.

Climate: Diversified, influenced by complex topography. Seven climatic zones—*tundra* (along Arctic coast), long, bitter winters and short summers; *taiga* (north-central half of country), long, severe winters and short spring and summer; *steppe* (parts of Ukraine, Kazakhstan, and Soviet Europe), cold winters and hot, dry summers; *Mediterranean* (Crimean coast), cool, rainy winters and hot, dry summers; *subtropical* (Black Sea coast), heavy annual rainfall; *semidesert* (north of Caspian Sea), low annual rainfall and high evaporation rate; *desert* (Central Asia), cold winters and very hot summers.

THE PEOPLE

Population (1987 estimate): 282,811,000; 32.9 persons per square mile (12.7 persons per square kilometer); 65.6 percent urban, 34.4 percent rural.

Vital Statistics (rate per 1,000 population): *Births*—19.6; *deaths*—9.7; *marriages*—9.8.

Life Expectancy (at birth): *Males*—64.0 years; *females*—73.0 years.

Major Languages: Russian, Ukrainian, Uzbek, Belorussian, Kazakh.

Ethnic Groups: Russian, Ukrainian, Uzbek, Belorussian, Kazakh, Tatar.

Major Religions: Atheism and no religion, Russian Orthodoxy, Islam, Protestantism, Roman Catholicism, Judaism.

MAJOR CITIES (1986 estimate)

Moscow (8,714,000): capital of nation and of Russian S.F.S.R.; industrial, cultural, political, scientific, and educational center; Gorky Park; Tretyakov Gallery; Pushkin Fine Arts Museum; Bolshoi Theater of Opera and Ballet (*see* Moscow).

Leningrad (4,904,000): major seaport, on Neva River; cultural, educational, and industrial center; famous for 18th-century palaces and churches (*see* Leningrad).

Kiev (2,495,000): capital of Ukrainian S.S.R.; major port, on Dnepr River; transportation, industrial, administrative, and scientific center (*see* Kiev).

Tashkent (2,077,000): capital of Uzbek S.S.R.; one of country's oldest cities; industrial, educational, and cultural center; Lenin Square; Revolution Garden; Islamic center (*see* Tashkent).

Baku (1,722,000): capital of Azerbaijan S.S.R.; on Caspian Sea; built up from ancient fortress; industrial and oil-processing center (*see* Baku).

Khar'kov (1,567,000): agricultural collection point; educational, cultural, and manufacturing center; A.M. Gorky University (*see* Khar'kov).

Minsk (1,510,000): capital of Belorussian S.S.R.; administrative center of Minsk Oblast; industrial, educational, and cultural center; Belorussian State Theater of Opera and Ballet (*see* Minsk).

Gorky (1,409,000): manufacturing and educational center; fortress and cathedral (*see* Gorky).

Novosibirsk (1,405,000): administrative center of Novosibirsk province; industrial, educational, and scientific center; Akademgorodok science center (*see* Novosibirsk).

Sverdlovsk (1,315,000): administrative center of Sverdlovsk Oblast; transportation, educational, and industrial center (*see* Sverdlovsk).

U.S.S.R. Fact Summary

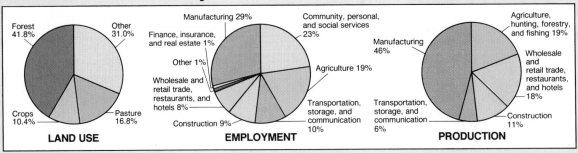

LAND USE
- Forest 41.8%
- Other 31.0%
- Crops 10.4%
- Pasture 16.8%

EMPLOYMENT
- Manufacturing 29%
- Finance, insurance, and real estate 1%
- Other 1%
- Wholesale and retail trade, restaurants, and hotels 8%
- Construction 9%
- Community, personal, and social services 23%
- Agriculture 19%
- Transportation, storage, and communication 10%

PRODUCTION
- Manufacturing 46%
- Agriculture, hunting, forestry, and fishing 19%
- Wholesale and retail trade, restaurants, and hotels 18%
- Construction 11%
- Transportation, storage, and communication 6%

ECONOMY

Chief Agricultural Products: *Crops*—wheat, rye, rice, buckwheat, millet, potatoes, sugar beets, vegetables, flax, oats, barley, hay, sunflowers, corn, tobacco, cotton. *Livestock and fish*—cattle, poultry, pigs, freshwater fish and seafood, caviar.

Chief Mined Products: Natural gas, petroleum, coal, iron ore, manganese, chromite, nickel, cobalt, copper, lead, zinc, bauxite, tin, tungsten, gold, platinum, diamonds.

Chief Manufactured Products: Cement, iron and steel, refined petroleum, mineral fertilizers, tractors, textiles, chemicals, machinery, metal products, wood products, electronic equipment.

Chief Imports: Bauxite, alumina, agricultural products, machinery, transportation equipment, consumer products, foodstuffs, ores, concentrates, metal products, iron and steel, textile yarns.

Chief Exports: Gold; vehicles; transportation, agricultural, and communications equipment; lifting machinery; electrical machinery; metallic ores and concentrates; fuel; timber products.

Chief Trading Partners: East Germany, Czechoslovakia, Bulgaria, Poland, Hungary.

Monetary Unit: 1 ruble = 100 kopecks.

EDUCATION

Schools: Compulsory for children ages 6 through 17. Free at all levels: primary, secondary (general, technical, and vocational), and university (admittance by examination).

Literacy: About 99 percent of population.

Leading Universities: Moscow State University; Leningrad State University; Kiev State University; Tashkent State University; Gorky State University.

Notable Libraries: Lenin State Library, Moscow; Saltykov-Shchedrin Public Library, U.S.S.R. Academy of Sciences, both in Leningrad; Gorky Scientific Library, Moscow State University.

Notable Museums and Art Galleries: Central Lenin Museum, Central Museum of the Revolution, Armory Museum in the Kremlin, State Historical Museum, State Pushkin Museum of Fine Arts, State Tretyakov Gallery, Exhibition of National Economic Achievements, Moscow; Hermitage, State Russian Museum, Leningrad; Kiev State Museum of Ukrainian Art, Kiev State Museum of Russian Art.

GOVERNMENT

Form of Government: Federal socialist republic.

Constitution: Adopted 1917.

Chief of State: President (chairman of the Supreme Soviet).

Head of Government: Premier (chairman of the Council of Ministers).

Cabinet: Council of Ministers, appointed by Supreme Soviet.

Legislature: Supreme Soviet, composed of Soviet of the Union and Soviet of Nationalities; semiannual sessions. *Soviet of the Union*—750 elected members, term, 5 years. *Soviet of Nationalities*—750 elected members, term, 5 years. Presidium, elected from among deputies, acts as supreme state authority.

Judiciary: *Supreme Court*—chairman, vice-chairmen, members, and people's assessors, elected for 5-year terms by Supreme Soviet. Other courts include Supreme Courts of Union Republics and of Autonomous Republics; territorial, regional, and city courts; courts of autonomous regions and of autonomous areas; district people's courts; and military tribunals.

Political Divisions: 15 union republics, 20 autonomous republics, 8 autonomous *oblasts* (regions), 10 autonomous *okrugs* (administrative areas), and 129 *krays* (territories) and *oblasts*.

Voting Qualification: Age 18.

PLACES OF INTEREST

Akhunbabayev Square: in Tashkent; area of Turkish and Islamic culture; 16th-century institution of higher education; nearby monument and theater in honor of 15th-century Turkish poet.

Belovezhskaya Pushcha National Park: in Belorussian S.S.R.; best-preserved remnant of primeval European lowland forest; trees hundreds of years old; breeding center of rare European bison.

Bolshoi Theater of Opera and Ballet: in Moscow; internationally renowned company, founded 1776; ballet company usually performs in Palace of Congresses in the Kremlin.

Cathedral of Saint Sophia: in Kiev; completed in 1037 and reconstructed in 17th century; now a museum; frescoes and mosaics.

Gorky Park of Culture and Leisure: in Moscow; largest of city parks, located on Moskva River; lawns, flowers, fun fair.

Great Palace of Peter the Great: near Leningrad, in Petrodvorets; built 1714–28 in Baroque style, reconstructed in mid-1700s; gardens, statues, Grand Cascade of the Samson Fountain; Summer and Winter palaces in city proper.

GUM Department Store: in Moscow; name stands for Gosudarstvenny Universalny Magazin (state universal store), U.S.S.R.'s largest department store; huge mall complex houses over 150 shops; built 1888–94, with ornate bridges and gangways, chandeliers.

Kirov Opera and Ballet Theatre: in Leningrad; on west side of Theater Square; resident company enjoys international reputation.

Kremlin: in Moscow; center of city, on bank of Moskva River; built in 12th century as fort; largest concentration of historic buildings in U.S.S.R. (*see* Kremlin).

Lake Baikal: near Irkutsk; world's largest lake, by volume; 395 miles (636 kilometers) long; supports indigenous plant and animal life, including freshwater seals.

Lenin Square: in Tashkent; government buildings; Alleya Paradov (Boulevard of Parades); nearby is Revolution Garden.

Pechorskaya Lavra (Monastery of the Caves): in Kiev; founded in early 11th century; one of most famous monasteries in Russian history; still in use; catacombs, museum, 18th-century bell tower.

Peter and Paul Fortress: in Leningrad; on Neva River; city's first structure, founded in 1703; Cathedral of St. Peter and St. Paul; nearby is Lenin Park, home of Leningrad Zoo, planetarium, theaters.

Red Square: in Moscow; major center for political and social events; originally a marketplace; nearby are Kremlin, Lenin Mausoleum, state historical museum.

St. Basil's Cathedral: in Moscow; southern end of Red Square; built 1555–61, during Ivan the Terrible's reign; now a museum.

Stolby Reservation: in Russian S.F.S.R.; area of pillarlike rock formations in spurs of Vostochny Sayan range of Sayan Mountains.

Teberda Reservation: in Russian S.F.S.R.; area of peaks, glaciers, meadows; northern slopes of Great Caucasus; brown bear, deer.

Television Tower: in Moscow; tallest structure in U.S.S.R.; near All Union Television Center, site of television and cinema studios.

Theater Square: in Tashkent; one of major focal points of city; site of Navoi Academic Bolshoi Theater of Opera and Ballet.

UNION OF SOVIET SOCIALIST REPUBLICS*

Name	Grid	
Abakan, 151,000	J	4
Abkhaz A.S.S.R., 535,000	E	5
Adimi	O	5
Adygey Aut. Obl., 426,000	D	5
Adzhar A.S.S.R., 385,000	E	5
Aginsk Aut. Okrug, 78,000	M	4
Aginskoye	M	4
Akmolinsk (Tselinograd), 276,000	H	4
Aksha	M	4
Aktyubinsk, 248,000	F	4
Alakol (lake)	J	5
Aldan	N	4
Aldan (plateau)	N	4
Aldan (river)	O	3
Aleksandrovsk-Sakhalinskiy	P	5
Alexandra Land (isl.)	E	1
Aleysk	J	4
Alga	F	5
Allakh-Yun'	O	3
Allaykha	P	2
Alma-Ata, 1,108,000	H	5
Altay (mts.)	J	5
Ambarchik	R	3
Amderma	F	3
Amga	O	3
Amu-Dar'ya (river)	G	5
Amur (river)	O	4
Anadyr'	S	3
Anadyr' (gulf)	T	3
Anadyr' (mt. range)	S	3
Anadyr' (river)	S	3
Andizhan, 288,000	H	5
Angara (river)	K	4
Angarsk, 262,000	L	4
Anzhero-Sudzhensk, 262,000	J	4
Aral (sea)	F	5
Aral'sk	G	5
Archangel, 416,000	E	3
Arctic (ocean)	K	1
Argun' (river)	M	4
Arkticheskiy Institut (isls.)	H	2
Armavir, 172,000	E	5
Armenian S.S.R., 3,412,000	E	6
Artem, 73,000	O	5
Artemovskiy	M	4
Arzamas, 108,000	E	4
Ashkhabad, 382,000	F	6
Asino	J	4
Astrakhan', 509,000	E	5
Atbasar, 34,316	G	4
Atka	Q	3
Atrek (river)	F	6
Ayaguz	J	5
Ayan	O	4
Ayon (isl.)	R	2
Azerbaijan S.S.R., 6,811,000	E	5
Azov (sea)	D	5
Bagdarin	M	4
Baku, 1,115,000	F	5
Balashov, 99,000	E	4
Balkhash, 84,000	H	5
Balkhash (lake)	H	5
Baltic (sea)	B	4
Balturino	K	4
Barabinsk	H	4
Baranovichi, 154,000	C	4
Barents (sea)	D	2
Barnaul, 596,000	J	4
Bashkir A.S.S.R., 3,895,000	F	4
Batumi, 135,000	E	5
Baunt	M	4
Baykal (lake)	L	4
Baykal (mt. range)	L	4
Baykit	K	3
Baykonur	G	5
Bayram-Ali	G	6
Belgorod, 293,000	D	4
Belogorsk, 71,000	N	4
Belomorsk	D	3
Beloretsk, 75,000	F	4
Belorussian S.S.R., 10,078,000	C	4
Beloye (lake)	D	3
Belyy (isl.)	G	2
Berdichev, 89,000	C	5
Berezniki, 200,000	F	4
Berezovo	G	3
Bering (sea)	S	4
Bering (strait)	U	3
Beringovskiy	T	3
Bet-Pak-Dala (desert)	H	5
Birobidzhan, 82,000	O	5
Biysk, 231,000	J	4
Black (sea)	D	5
Blagoveshchensk, 202,000	N	4
Bobruysk, 232,000	C	4
Bodaybo	M	4
Bol'shevik (isl.)	K	2
Bol'shoy Lyakhov (isl.)	P	2
Bolvanskiy Nos (cape)	G	2
Boris Vil'kitskiy (strait)	L	2
Borisoglebsk, 69,000	E	4
Borzya, 249,000	M	4
Bratsk, 249,000	L	4
Bratsk (reservoir)	L	4
Brest, 238,000	C	4
Bryansk, 445,000	D	4
Bugul'ma, 88,000	F	4
Bukhara, 220,000	G	5
Bulun	N	2
Buryat A.S.S.R., 1,030,000	L	4
Buzuluk, 82,000	F	4
Caspian (sea)	F	6
Caucasus (mts.)	E	5
Chagda	O	4
Chapayevo	F	4
Chapayevsk, 87,000	F	4
Chara	M	4
Chardzhou, 166,000	G	6
Cheboksary, 414,000	E	4
Chechen-Ingush A.S.S.R., 1,119,000	E	5
Chelkar, 17,236	F	5
Chelyabinsk, 874,000	G	4
Chelyuskin (cape)	M	2
Cheremkhovo, 73,000	L	4
Cherepovets, 315,000	D	4
Cherkessk, 107,000	E	5
Chernigov, 291,000	D	4
Chernobyl	D	4
Chernovtsy, 254,000	C	5
Chernyshevsk	M	4
Cherskiy (mt. range)	P	3
Chimbay	F	5
Chimkent, 389,000	H	5
Chita, 349,000	M	4
Chu (river)	H	5
Chukchi (pen.)	T	3
Chukchi (sea)	T	2
Chukchi Aut. Okr., 157,000	R	3
Chul'man	N	4
Chulym (river)	J	4
Chumikan	O	4
Chuna (river)	K	4
Chunya (river)	K	3
Chuvash A.S.S.R., 1,330,000	E	4
Communism (peak)	H	6
Crimea (pen.), 2,397,000	D	5
Dagestan A.S.S.R., 1,768,000	E	5
Daugavpils, 128,000	C	4
De Long (strait)	S	2
Dezhnev (cape)	T	3
Dikson	J	2
Dmitriy Laptev (strait)	O	2
Dnepropetrovsk, 1,182,000	D	5
Dnieper (river)	D	5
Dniester (river)	C	5
Dolinsk	P	5
Don (river)	E	5
Donets (river)	D	5
Donetsk, 1,090,000	D	5
Drogobych, 76,000	C	5
Druzhina	P	3
Dudinka	J	3
Dushanbe, 582,000	G	6
Dvina, Northern (river)	E	3
Dvina, Western (river)	C	4
Dzerzhinsk, 281,000	E	4
Dzhalal-Abad	N	4
Dzhalinda	N	4
Dzhambul, 315,000	H	5
Dzhelinda	M	2
Dzhetygara	G	4
Dzhezkazgan, 105,000	G	5
Dzhugdzhur (mt. range)	O	4
East Siberian (sea)	S	2
Ege-Khaya	O	3
Ekibastuz, 141,000	H	4
Ekimchan	O	4
Elista, 85,000	E	5
Emba (river)	F	5
Engel's, 182,000	E	4
Erivan, 1,168,000	E	6
Estonian S.S.R., 1,556,000	C	4
Etorofu (isl.)	P	5
Evenki Aut. Okrug, 22,000	K	3
Faddeyevskiy (isl.)	P	2
Fergana, 203,000	H	5
Finland (gulf)	C	4
Fort-Shevchenko	F	5
Franz Josef Land (isls.)	E	1
Frolovo	E	5
Frunze, 632,000	H	5
Gasan-Kuli	F	6
George Land (isl.)	E	1
Georgian S.S.R., 5,266,000	E	5
Gizhiga	R	3
Gol'chikha	J	2
Gomel', 488,000	D	4
Gor'kiy, 1,425,000	E	4
Gorno-Altay Aut. Oblast	J	4
Gorno-Altaysk	J	5
Gorno-Badakhshan Aut. Oblast, 151,000	H	6
Gorodok	L	4
Graham Bell (isl.)	G	1
Grodno, 263,000	C	4
Groznyy, 404,000	E	5
Gubakha	F	4
Gulistan, 51,000	G	5
Gur'yev, 150,000	F	5
Gusinoozersk	L	4
Gyda (pen.)	H	2
Gydan (Kolyma) (mt. range)	Q	3
Gydy	H	2
Hiiumaa (isl.)	C	4
Igarka	J	3
Ilanskiy	K	4
Ili	H	5
Ili (river)	H	5
Ilimsk	L	4
Iman	O	5
Imandra (lake)	D	3
Indiga	E	3
Indigirka (river)	P	3
Industrial'nyy	R	4
Inta, 58,000	G	3
Iolotan	G	6
Irkutsk, 609,000	L	4
Irtysh (river)	H	4
Ishim, 65,000	H	4
Ishim (river)	G	4
Ishimbay, 67,000	F	4
Isil'-Kul'	H	4
Issyk-Kul' (lake)	H	5
Ivano-Frankovsk, 225,000	C	5
Ivanovo, 479,000	E	4
Izhevsk, 631,000	F	4
Izmail, 90,000	C	5
Japan (sea)	O	6
Jewish Aut. Oblast, 216,000	O	5
Kabardin-Balkar A.S.S.R., 732,000	E	5
Kachug	L	4
Kagan	G	6
Kakhovka (res.)	D	5
Kalachinsk	H	4
Kalakan	M	4
Kalinin, 447,000	D	4
Kaliningrad, 394,000	B	4
Kalmuck A.S.S.R., 329,000	E	5
Kalmykovo	F	5
Kaluga, 307,000	D	4
Kamchatka (pen.), 443,000	Q	4
Kamensk-Ural'skiy, 204,000	G	4
Kamenskoye	R	3
Kamyshin, 119,000	E	4
Kamyshlov	G	4
Kandalaksha	C	3
Kanin (pen.)	E	3
Kanin Nos (cape)	E	3
Kansk, 108,000	K	4
Kara (sea)	G	2
Kara-Bogaz-Gol (gulf)	F	5
Kara-Kalpak A.S.S.R., 1,139,000	G	5
Kara-Kum (canal)	G	6
Kara-Kum (desert)	F	5
Karabekaul	G	6
Karachay-Cherkess Aut. Oblast, 402,000	E	5
Karaganda, 633,000	H	5
Karaginskiy (isl.)	R	4
Karasuk	H	4
Karelian A.S.S.R., 795,000	D	3
Karkaralinsk	H	5
Karshi, 141,000	G	6
Karskiye Vorota (str.)	F	2
Kaunas, 417,000	C	4
Kazach'ye	O	2
Kazakh S.S.R., 16,244,000	G	5
Kazalinsk	G	5
Kazan', 1,068,000	F	4
Kazandzhik	F	6
Kem'	D	3
Kemerovo, 520,000	J	4
Kerki	G	6
Kezhma	K	4
Khabarovsk, 591,000	O	5
Khakass Aut. Oblast, 555,000	J	4
Khandyga	O	3
Khanka (lake)	O	5
Khanty-Mansi Aut. Okrug, 1,125,000	H	3
Khanty-Mansiysk	H	3
Khar'kov, 1,587,000	D	4
Kharovsk	D	3
Khatanga	L	2
Kherson, 358,000	D	5
Kheta (river)	K	2
Khilok	M	4
Khiva	F	5
Khodzheyli, 55,000	F	5
Kholmsk, 50,000	P	5
Khorog	H	6
Kiev, 2,544,000	D	4
Kirensk	L	4
Kirgiz S.S.R., 4,143,000	H	5
Kirov, 421,000	E	4
Kirovabad, 270,000	E	5
Kirovograd, 269,000	D	5
Kiselevsk, 128,000	J	4
Kishinev, 663,000	C	5
Kizel'	F	4
Kizyl-Arvat	F	6
Klaipėda, 201,000	B	4
Klyuchevskaya Sopka (vol.)	Q	4
Kokchetav, 127,000	H	4
Kola (pen.)	D	3
Kolguyev (isl.)	E	3
Kolomna, 159,000	D	4
Kolpashevo	J	4
Kolyma (mt. range)	Q	3
Kolyma (river)	Q	3
Komandorskiye (isls.)	R	4
Komi A.S.S.R., 1,247,000	F	3
Komi-Permyak Aut. Okrug, 161,000	F	4
Komsomolets (isl.)	L	1
Komsomol'sk, 136,000	O	4
Kondopoga	D	3
Kopeysk, 99,000	G	4
Korf	R	3
Korkino	G	4
Korsakov	P	5
Kortkeros	F	3
Koryak (mt. range)	S	3
Koryak Aut. Okrug, 40,000	R	3
Koslan	E	3
Kostroma, 276,000	E	4
Kotel'nyy (isl.)	O	2
Kotlas, 69,000	E	3
Kotuy (river)	L	3
Kovel', 66,000	C	4
Kovrov, 158,000	E	4
Kozhevnikovo	L	2
Krasino	F	2
Krasnodar, 623,000	E	5
Krasnokamsk, 58,000	F	4
Krasnotur'insk, 66,000	G	3
Krasnoural'sk	G	4
Krasnovishersk	F	3
Krasnovodsk, 59,000	F	5
Krasnoyarsk, 899,000	K	4
Kremenchug, 230,000	D	5
Krivoy Rog, 698,000	D	5
Kudymkar	F	4
Kul'sary	F	5
Kuma (river)	E	5
Kungur, 83,000	F	4
Kupino	H	4
Kura (river)	E	6
Kurgan, 354,000	G	4
Kurgan-Tyube, 55,000	G	6
Kuril (isls.)	P	5
Kursk, 434,000	D	4
Kushka	G	6
Kustanay, 212,000	G	4
Kutaisi, 220,000	E	5
Kuybyshev, 1,280,000	F	4
Kuybyshev (res.)	F	4
Kyakhta	L	4
Kyusyur	N	2
Kyzyl, 80,000	K	4
Kyzyl-Kum (desert)	G	5
Kzyl-Orda, 189,000	G	5
La Pérouse (strait)	P	5
Labytnangi	G	3
Ladoga (lake)	D	3
Laptev (sea)	N	2
Latvian S.S.R., 2,647,000	C	4
Lena (river)	N	3
Leninabad, 157,000	G	5
Leninakan, 228,000	E	5
Leningrad, 4,393,000	D	4
Leninogorsk, 69,000	J	5
Leninsk-Kuznetskiy, 169,000	J	4
Leninskoye	O	5
Lenkoran'	E	6
Lesozavodsk	O	5
Liepāja, 114,000	B	4
Lipetsk, 465,000	E	4
Lithuanian S.S.R., 3,641,000	C	4
Lopatka (cape)	Q	4
Lower Tunguska (river)	K	3
Luga	D	4
Lutsk, 185,000	C	4
Luza	E	3
L'vov, 767,000	C	4
Lys'va, 77,000	F	4
Magadan, 148,000	P	4
Magdagachi	N	4
Magnitogorsk, 430,000	G	4
Makhachkala, 320,000	E	5

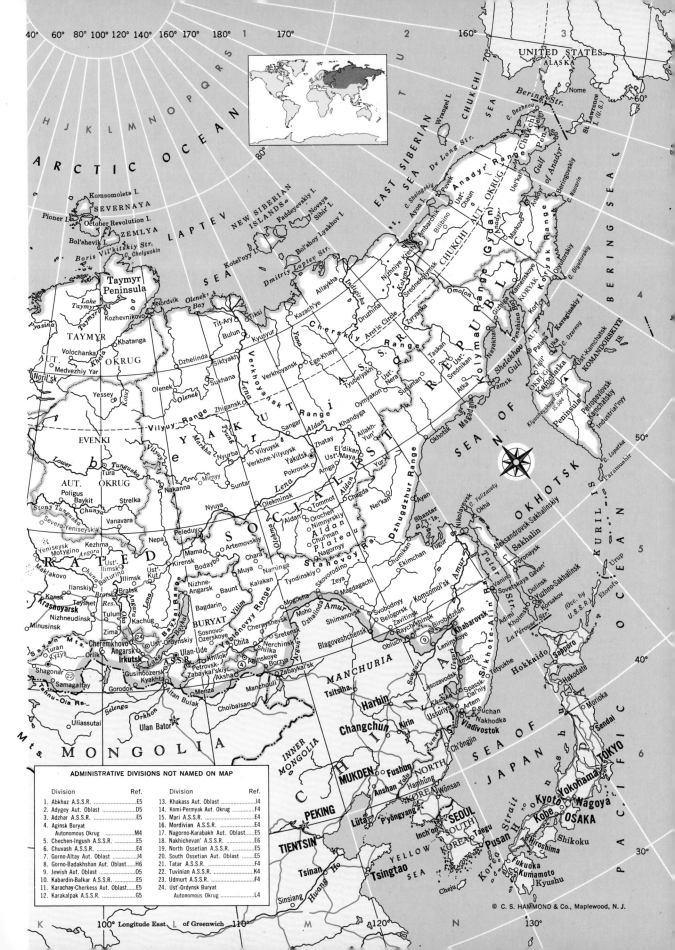

Makinsk	G 4	Omutninsk	F 4	Sikhote-Alin' (mt. range)	O 5	Tyubelyakh	O 3
Maklakovo	K 4	Onega	D 3	Siktyakh	N 3	Tyumen', 456,000	G 4
Mama	M 4	Onega (lake)	D 3	Simferopol', 338,000	D 5	Tyung (river)	M 3
Mangyshlak (pen.)	F 5	Onega (river)	D 3	Skovorodino	N 4	Udmurt A.S.S.R., 1,587,000	F 4
Mari A.S.S.R., 739,000	E 4	Onguday	J 4	Slavgorod	H 4	Uelen	T 3
Markha (river)	M 3	Ordzhonikidze, 313,000	E 5	Slobodskoy	E 4	Uel'kal'	S 3
Markovo	S 3	Orel, 335,000	D 4	Smolensk, 338,000	D 4	Ufa, 1,092,000	F 4
Mary, 89,000	G 6	Orenburg, 537,000	F 4	Sochi, 317,000	D 5	Ukhta, 105,000	F 3
Matochkin Shar (strait)	F 2	Orlik	K 4	Sokol	E 4	Ukrainian S.S.R., 51,201,000	C 5
Maykop, 145,000	D 5	Orochen	N 4	Solikamsk, 108,000	F 4	Ulan-Ude, 300,000	L 4
Mednogorsk	F 4	Orsk, 273,000	F 4	Sortavala	C 3	Ul'yanovsk, 589,000	E 4
Medvezhiy Yar	K 2	Osh, 209,000	H 5	Sosnogorsk	F 3	Ural (mts.)	F 4
Medvezh'yegorsk	D 3	Ostrogozhsk	E 4	Sosnovo-Ozerskoye	M 4	Ural (river)	F 5
Megion	H 3	Oymyakon	O 3	South Ossetian Aut. Oblast, 99,000	E 5	Ural'sk, 201,000	F 4
Melekess	F 4	Ozernoy (cape)	R 4	Sovetskaya Gavan'	P 5	Urgench, 123,000	F 5
Menza	L 5	Palana	R 4	Spassk-Dal'niy, 60,000	O 5	Urup (isl.)	Q 5
Mezen'	E 3	Panfilov	H 5	Srednekolymsk	Q 3	Ussuri (river)	O 5
Mezen' (river)	E 3	Paramushir (isl.)	Q 4	Sretensk	M 4	Ussuriysk, 158,000	O 5
Michurinsk, 103,000	E 4	Pärnu	C 4	Stalingrad (Volgograd), 988,000	E 5	Ust'-Chaun	R 3
Millerovo	E 5	Pavlodar, 331,000	H 4	Stalino (Donetsk), 1,090,000	D 5	Ust'-Ilimsk, 105,000	L 4
Minsk, 1,543,000	C 4	Pechenga	D 2	Stanislav (Ivano-		Ust'-Kamchatsk	R 4
Minusinsk, 72,000	K 4	Pechora, 64,000	F 3	Frankovsk), 225,000	C 5	Ust'-Kamenogorsk, 321,000	J 5
Mirnyy	M 3	Pechora (river)	F 3	Stanovoy (mt. range)	N 4	Ust'-Kara	G 3
Mogilev, 359,000	D 4	Peipus (lake)	C 4	Stavropol', 306,000	E 5	Ust'-Kut, 58,000	L 4
Mogocha	N 4	Peleduy	M 4	Stepanakert	E 6	Ust'-Maya	O 3
Moldavian S.S.R., 4,185,000	C 5	Penza, 540,000	E 4	Stepnyak	H 4	Ust'-Nera	P 3
Molodechno, 87,000	C 4	Penzhina (bay)	R 3	Sterlitamak, 251,000	F 4	Ust'-Ordynskiy	L 4
Monchegorsk, 65,000	C 3	Perm', 1,075,000	F 4	Stony Tunguska (river)	K 3	Ust'-Ordynskiy Aut.	
Mordvinian A.S.S.R., 964,000	E 4	Petropavlovsk, 233,000	G 4	Strelka	L 3	Okrug, 129,000	L 4
Moscow (cap.), 8,614,000	D 4	Petropavlovsk-		Suchan	O 5	Ust'-Port	J 2
Motygino	K 4	Kamchatskiy, 252,000	R 4	Sukhana	M 3	Ust'-Srednikan	Q 3
Mozyr'	C 4	Petrovsk-Zabaykal'skiy	L 4	Sukhumi, 130,000	D 5	Ust'-Urt (plateau)	F 5
Murgab	H 6	Petrozavodsk, 264,000	D 3	Sumy, 268,000	D 4	Uvat	G 4
Murgab (river)	G 6	Pevek	S 3	Suntar	M 3	Uzbek S.S.R., 19,026,000	G 5
Murmansk, 432,000	D 3	Pinsk, 116,000	C 4	Surgut, 227,000	H 3	Vanino	P 5
Muya	M 4	Pioner (isl.)	J 2	Susuman	P 3	Velikiy Ustyug	E 3
Muynak	F 5	Pobeda (mt.)	J 5	Sverdlovsk, 1,331,000	F 4	Velikiye Luki, 113,000	D 4
Nadym (river)	H 3	Podol'sk, 209,000	D 4	Svobodnyy, 78,000	N 4	Vel'sk	E 3
Nagorno-Karabakh Aut.		Pokrovsk	N 3	Syktyvkar, 224,000	F 3	Ventspils	B 4
Oblast, 180,000	E 5	Poligus	K 3	Sym	J 3	Vereshchagino	K 3
Nakhichevan', 51,000	E 6	Poltava, 309,000	D 5	Syr-Dar'ya (river)	G 5	Verkhne-Vilyuysk	N 3
Nakhichevan' A.S.S.R., 278,000	E 6	Polyarnyy	D 3	Syzran', 174,000	E 4	Verkhniy Ufaley	F 4
Nakhodka, 152,000	O 5	Ponoy	E 3	Tadzhik S.S.R., 4,807,000	H 6	Verkhoyansk	N 3
Nal'chik, 236,000	E 5	Poronaysk	P 5	Taganrog, 295,000	D 5	Verkhoyansk (mt. range)	N 3
Namangan, 291,000	H 5	Potapovo	J 3	Takhta-Bazar	G 6	Vilna, 566,000	C 4
Naminga	M 4	Prikumsk	E 5	Taldy-Kurgan, 113,000	H 5	Vilyuy (mt. range)	M 3
Napas	J 4	Prokop'yevsk, 278,000	J 4	Tallinn, 478,000	C 4	Vilyuy (river)	L 3
Narodnaya (mt.)	G 3	Przheval'sk, 64,000	H 5	Tambey	G 2	Vilyuysk	N 3
Nar'yan-Mar	F 3	Pskov, 202,000	C 4	Tambov, 305,000	E 4	Vinnitsa, 383,000	C 5
Naryn	H 5	Pur (river)	H 3	Tannu-Ola (mt. range)	K 5	Vitebsk, 347,000	D 4
Navarin (cape)	T 3	Pushkin, 97,000	C 4	Tara	H 4	Vitim (river)	M 4
Nebit-Dag, 85,000	F 6	Pyasina (river)	J 2	Tarko-Sale	H 3	Vladimir, 343,000	D 4
Nel'kan	O 4	Pyatigorsk	E 5	Tartu, 113,000	C 4	Vladivostok, 615,000	O 5
Nenets Aut. Okrug, 54,000	F 3	Raychikhinsk	O 5	Tashauz, 110,000	F 5	Volga (river)	E 5
Nepa	L 4	Riga, 900,000	C 4	Tashkent, 2,124,000	G 5	Volgograd, 988,000	E 5
Nerchinsk	M 4	Riga (gulf)	C 4	Taskan	Q 3	Volochanka	K 2
New Siberian (isls.)	P 2	Rostov, 1,004,000	D 5	Tatar (strait)	P 4	Vologda, 278,000	E 4
Nikolayev, 501,000	D 5	Rovno, 233,000	C 4	Tatar A.S.S.R., 3,568,000	F 4	Vol'sk, 66,000	E 4
Nikolayevsk	P 4	Rubtsovsk, 168,000	J 4	Tatarsk	H 4	Vorkuta, 112,000	G 3
Nimnyrskiy	N 4	Ruch'i	E 3	Tayga	J 4	Voronezh, 872,000	E 4
Nizhne-Angarsk	M 4	Rudnyy, 118,000	G 4	Taymyr (lake)	K 2	Voroshilovgrad, 509,000	E 5
Nizhneudinsk	K 4	Russian S.F.S.R., 145,311,000	D 4	Taymyr (pen.)	L 2	Votkinsk, 101,000	F 4
Nizhniy Tagil, 427,000	G 4	Ryazan', 508,000	E 4	Taymyr (river)	K 2	Voy-Vozh	F 3
Nizhniye Kresty	Q 3	Rybachiy (pen.)	D 2	Taymyr Nat'l Okrug, 55,000	K 2	Vyborg, 81,000	C 3
Nordvik	M 2	Rybinsk, 254,000	D 4	Tayshet	K 4	Vyshniy Volochek, 70,000	D 4
Noril'sk, 181,000	J 3	Rybinsk (res.)	D 4	Taz (river)	J 3	Western Dvina (river)	C 4
North Ossetian A.S.S.R., 619,000	E 5	Rzhev, 70,000	D 4	Tazovskoye	J 3	White (sea)	D 3
Northern Dvina (river)	E 3	Saaremaa (isl.)	B 4	Tbilisi, 1,194,000	E 5	Wiese (isl.)	H 1
Novaya Kazanka	F 5	Sakhalin (isl.), 709,000	P 4	Tedzhen	F 6	Wilczek Land (isl.)	G 1
Novaya Sibir' (isl.)	Q 2	Salekhard	G 3	Temir	F 5	Wrangel (isl.)	T 2
Novaya Zemlya (isls.)	F 2	Sal'sk, 62,000	E 5	Temir-Tau, 228,000	H 4	Yablonovyy (mt. range)	M 4
Novgorod, 228,000	D 4	Samagaltay	K 4	Tengiz (lake)	G 4	Yakut A.S.S.R., 1,034,000	N 3
Novokuznetsk, 589,000	J 4	Samarkand, 588,000	G 5	Termez, 72,000	G 6	Yakutsk, 188,000	N 3
Novomoskovsk, 147,000	E 4	Sangar	N 3	Ternopol', 197,000	C 5	Yamal (pen.)	G 2
Novorossiysk, 179,000	D 5	Saransk, 323,000	E 4	Tetyukhe	O 5	Yamal-Nenets Aut.	
Novosibirsk, 1,423,000	J 4	Sarapul, 111,000	F 4	Tigil'	Q 4	Okrug, 430,000	H 3
Novouzensk	E 4	Saratov, 918,000	E 4	Tiksi	N 2	Yamsk	Q 4
Novozybkov	D 4	Sary-Su (river)	G 4	Tit-Ary	N 2	Yana (river)	O 3
Novyy Port	G 3	Sayan (mts.)	K 4	Tobol (river)	G 4	Yaroslavl', 634,000	D 4
Nukus, 152,000	G 5	Segezha	D 3	Tobol'sk, 82,000	G 4	Yartsevo	J 4
Nyandoma	E 3	Semipalatinsk, 330,000	J 4	Tokmak, 71,000	H 5	Yelets, 119,000	D 4
Nyda	H 3	Serakhs	G 6	Tommot	N 4	Yelizavety (cape)	P 4
Nyurba	M 3	Serov, 103,000	G 4	Tomsk, 489,000	J 4	Yenisey (river)	J 3
Nyuya	M 3	Serpukhov, 142,000	D 4	Tot'ma	E 4	Yeniseysk	K 4
Ob' (gulf)	H 3	Sevastopol', 350,000	D 5	Troitsk, 91,000	G 4	Yermak	H 4
Ob' (river)	G 3	Severnaya Zemlya (isls.)	L 1	Tselinograd, 276,000	H 4	Yessey	L 3
Obluch'ye	N 5	Severo-Yeniseyskiy	K 3	Tsimlyansk (res.)	E 5	Yoshkar-Ola, 243,000	E 4
October Revolution (isl.)	L 2	Severodvinsk, 239,000	E 3	Tskhinvali	E 5	Yuzhno-Sakhalinsk, 166,000	P 5
Odessa, 1,141,000	D 5	Severoural'sk	G 3	Tugur	O 4	Zabaykal'sk	M 5
Oka (river)	L 4	Shadrinsk, 87,000	G 4	Tula, 538,000	D 4	Zaporozh'ye, 875,000	D 5
Okha	P 4	Shagonar	K 4	Tulun, 56,000	L 4	Zavitinsk	O 4
Okhotsk	P 4	Shakhty, 225,000	E 5	Tura	L 3	Zaysan	J 5
Okhotsk (sea)	P 4	Shantar (isls.)	O 4	Turan	K 4	Zeya	N 4
Olekma (river)	N 4	Shar'ya	E 4	Turgay	G 5	Zhatay	O 3
Olekminsk	N 3	Shelagskiy (cape)	R 2	Turkestan, 77,000	G 5	Zhdanov, 529,000	D 5
Olenek	M 3	Shelekhov (gulf)	Q 4	Turkmen S.S.R., 3,361,000	F 6	Zhelaniye (cape)	H 2
Olenek (bay)	N 2	Shenkursk	E 3	Turtkul'	G 5	Zhigansk	N 3
Olenek (river)	M 3	Shevchenko, 161,000	F 5	Turukhansk	J 3	Zhitomir, 287,000	C 4
Olyutorskiy (cape)	S 4	Shilka	N 4	Tuvinian A.S.S.R., 289,000	K 4	Zima	L 4
Omolon (river)	Q 3	Shimanovsk	N 4	Tym (river)	J 3	Zlatoust, 206,000	F 4
Omsk, 1,134,000	H 4	Shiauliai, 140,000	C 4	Tyndinskiy	N 4	Zyryanka	Q 3
		Siberia (region), 25,737,000	M 3				

*All population figures are taken from the latest census or estimate available.

UNION OF SOVIET SOCIALIST REPUBLICS*
(EUROPEAN PART)

Abdulino	H 4
Abez'	K 1
Achikulak	G 6
Agdam	G 6
Agryz	H 3
Akhaltsikhe	F 6
Akhtubinsk, 53,000	G 5
Akhtyrka	E 4
Alagir	F 6
Alatyr'	G 4
Alchevsk (Kommunarsk), 126,000	E 5
Aleksandriya, 95,000	D 5
Aleksandrov, 66,000	E 3
Aleksandrov Gay	G 4
Alekseyevka	E 4
Aleksin, 72,000	E 4
Ali-Bayramly, 51,000	G 7
Al'met'yevsk, 128,000	H 3
Alushta	D 6
Amderma	K 1
Anapa	E 6
Andreyevka	H 4
Apatity, 80,000	D 1
Apsheron (pen.)	H 6
Apsheronsk	F 6
Araks (Araxes) (river)	G 7
Archangel (Arkhangel'sk), 416,000	F 2
Armavir, 172,000	F 5
Armenian S.S.R., 3,412,000	F 6
Armyansk	D 5
Artemovsk, 91,000	E 5
Arzamas, 108,000	F 3
Astara	G 7
Astrakhan', 509,000	G 5
Atkarsk	G 4
Aykino	H 2
Azerbaijan, S.S.R., 6,811,000	G 6
Azov, 81,000	E 5
Azov (sea)	E 5
Babayevo	E 3
Bakhchisaray	D 6
Bakhmach	D 4
Baku, 1,115,000	H 6
Balakhna	F 3
Balaklava	D 6
Balakovo, 188,000	G 4
Balashov, 99,000	F 4
Baltic (sea)	B 3
Baltiysk	A 4
Baranovichi, 154,000	C 4
Barents (sea)	D 1
Barysh	G 4
Bataysk, 98,000	E 5
Batumi, 135,000	F 6
Belaya (river)	H 3
Belaya Tserkov', 194,000	C 5
Belebey, 51,000	H 4
Belev	E 4
Belgorod, 293,000	E 4
Belgorod-Dnestrovskiy, 54,000	D 5
Belomorsk	D 2
Beloretsk, 75,000	J 4
Belorussian S.S.R., 10,078,000	C 4
Beloye (lake)	E 2
Belozersk	E 3
Bel'tsy, 157,000	C 5
Belush'ya Guba	H 1
Bendery, 130,000	C 5
Berdichev, 89,000	C 5
Berdyansk, 133,000	E 5
Berezina (river)	C 4
Berezniki, 200,000	J 3
Berislav	D 5
Beslan	F 6
Bezhetsk	E 3
Birsk	J 3
Black (sea)	D 6
Blagodarnoye	F 5
Bobrinets	D 5
Bobruysk, 232,000	C 4
Boguchar	F 5
Bolkhov	E 4
Bologoye	D 3
Borislav	B 5
Borisoglebsk, 69,000	F 4
Borisov, 140,000	C 4
Borisovka	E 4
Borovichi, 64,000	D 3
Borzhomi	F 6
Brest, 238,000	B 4
Bryansk, 445,000	D 4
Bug (river)	B 4
Bug (river)	D 5
Bugrino	G 1
Bugul'ma, 88,000	H 4
Buguruslan, 53,000	H 4
Buturlinovka	F 4
Buy	F 3
Buynaksk, 53,000	G 6
Buzuluk, 82,000	H 4
Bykhov	C 4
Caspian (sea)	G 6
Caucasus (mts.)	F 6
Central Ural (mts.)	J 2
Cēsis	C 3
Chadyr-Lunga	C 5
Chagoda	E 3
Chapayevsk, 87,000	G 4
Cheboksary, 414,000	G 3
Cherepovets, 315,000	E 3
Cherkassy, 287,000	D 5
Cherkessk, 107,000	F 6
Chernigov, 291,000	D 4
Chernobyl	D 4
Chernovtsy, 254,000	C 5
Chervonograd, 71,000	B 4
Cheshskaya (bay)	G 1
Chiatura	F 6
Chir (river)	F 5
Chistopol', 65,000	H 3
Chizha	F 1
Chkalov (Orenburg), 537,000	J 4
Chortkov	B 5
Chudovo	D 3
Chukhloma	F 3
Chusovoy, 59,000	J 3
Crimea (pen.), 2,397,000	D 5
Danilov	E 3
Daugavpils, 128,000	C 3
Davlekanova	H 4
Demidov	D 3
Derbent, 83,000	G 6
Desna (river)	D 4
Divnoye	F 5
Dmitrov, 64,000	E 3
Dmitrovsk-Orlovskiy	D 4
Dneprodzerzhinsk, 279,000	D 5
Dnepropetrovsk, 1,182,000	D 5
Dnieper (river)	D 5
Dniester (river)	C 5
Dno	D 3
Dobrush	D 4
Dolgiy (island)	J 1
Don (river)	F 5
Donets (river)	E 5
Donetsk, 1,090,000	E 5
Drogobych, 76,000	B 5
Dubna, 64,000	E 3
Dubna	E 4
Dubovka	G 5
Dvina (bay)	E 1
Dykh-Tau (mt.)	F 6
Dzaudzhikau (Ordzhonikidze), 313,000	F 6
Dzerzhinsk, 281,000	F 3
Dzhankoy, 51,000	D 5
Dzhul'fa	G 7
El'brus (mt.)	F 6
Elista, 85,000	F 5
El'ton	G 5
Engel's, 182,000	G 4
Erivan, 1,168,000	F 6
Estononian S.S.R., 1,556,000	C 3
Fastov, 55,000	C 4
Feodosiya, 83,000	D 5
Finland (gulf)	C 3
Frolovo	F 5
Furmanov	F 3
Gadyach	D 4
Gagarin	D 3
Gagra	E 6
Galich	F 3
Gaysin	C 5
Gdov	C 3
Gelendzhik	E 6
Genichesk	E 5
Georgian, S.S.R., 5,266,000	F 6
Georgiu-Dezh, 54,000	E 4
Glazov, 98,000	H 3
Glubokoye	C 3
Glukhov	D 4
Gomel', 488,000	D 4
Gori, 62,000	F 6
Gorki	D 4
Gor'ki (Gorki), 1,425,000	F 3
Gorlovka, 345,000	E 5
Gornyatskiy	K 1
Gorodets	F 3
Gorodok	D 3
Goryn' (river)	C 4
Gremyachinsk	J 3
Grodno, 263,000	B 4
Groznyy (Grozny), 404,000	G 6
Gryazi	F 4
Gryazovets	F 3
Gubakha	J 3
Gudauta	F 6
Gukovo, 72,000	F 5
Gus-Khrustal'nyy, 76,000	F 3
Hiiumaa (Dagö) (island)	B 3
Ichnya	D 4
Ilek (river)	J 4
Il'men (lake)	D 3
Imandra (lake)	D 1
Indiga	G 1
Inta	K 1
Inza	G 4
Ishimbay, 67,000	J 4
Ivano-Frankovsk, 225,000	B 5
Ivanovo, 479,000	F 3
Izhevsk, 631,000	H 3
Izhma	H 1
Izmail, 90,000	C 5
Izyaslav	C 4
Izyum, 63,000	E 5
Jekabpils	C 3
Jelgava, 72,000	B 3
Kadiyevka (Stakhanov), 112,000	E 5
Kagul	C 5
Kakhovka	D 5
Kalach	E 5
Kalevala	D 1
Kalinin, 447,000	E 3
Kaliningrad, 394,000	B 4
Kalinkovichi	C 4
Kaluga, 307,000	E 4
Kama (river)	H 2
Kamenets-Podol'skiy, 101,000	C 5
Kamenka	F 1
Kamenka	F 4
Kemensk-Shakhtinskiy, 75,000	E 5
Kamyshin, 119,000	F 4
Kanash, 53,000	G 3
Kandalaksha	D 1
Kandalaksha (gulf)	D 1
Kanin (pen.)	G 1
Kanin Nos (cape)	F 1
Kapsukas	B 4
Kapydzhik (mt.)	G 7
Kara (sea)	K 1
Karachayevsk	F 6
Karachev	E 4
Kargopol'	E 2
Karpogory	F 2
Karskiye Vorota (strait)	J 1
Kashin	E 3
Kasimov	F 4
Kaspiysk, 61,000	G 6
Kaspiyskiy	G 5
Kaunas, 417,000	B 4
Kazan', 1,068,000	G 3
Kazatin	C 5
Kazbek (mt.)	F 6
Kem'	D 2
Kerch', 173,000	E 5
Keret'	D 1
Kesten'ga	D 1
Khachmas	G 6
Khal'mer-Yu	K 1
Khalturin	G 3
Khar'kov, 1,587,000	E 5
Kharovsk	F 3
Khasavyurt, 74,000	G 6
Kherson, 358,000	D 5
Khmel'nitskiy, 230,000	C 5
Kholm	D 3
Khoper (river)	F 4
Khorol	D 5
Khotin	C 5
Khvalynsk	G 4
Kiev, 2,544,000	D 4
Kil'din (island)	D 1
Kiliya	C 4
Kimovsk	E 4
Kimry, 61,000	E 3
Kinel'	H 4
Kinel' (river)	H 4
Kineshma, 105,000	F 3
Kingisepp	C 3
Kirillov	E 2
Kirov	D 4
Kirov, 421,000	G 3
Kirovabad, 270,000	G 6
Kirovakan, 169,000	G 6
Kirovo-Chepetsk, 89,000	H 3
Kirovograd, 269,000	D 5
Kirovsk	D 1
Kirsanov	F 4
Kishinev, 663,000	C 5
Kislovodsk, 110,000	F 6
Kizel'	J 3
Kizlyar	G 6
Klaipėda, 201,000	B 3
Klimovichi	D 4
Klintsy, 72,000	D 4
Kobrin	B 4
Kobuleti	F 6
Kohtla-Järve, 78,000	C 3
Kola (pen.)	E 1
Kolguyev (island)	G 1
Kologriv	F 3
Kolomna, 159,000	E 4
Kolyma (river)	J 1
Kommunarsk, 126,000	E 5
Komrat	C 5
Kondopoga	D 2
Königsberg (Kaliningrad), 394,000	B 4
Konosha	F 2
Konotop, 93,000	D 4
Korosten', 72,000	C 4
Koslan	G 2
Kostroma, 276,000	F 3
Kotel'nich	G 3
Kotel'nikovo	F 5
Kotlas, 69,000	G 2
Kotovsk	C 5
Kotovsk	F 4
Kovel', 66,000	C 4
Kovrov, 158,000	F 3
Kozhva	J 1
Kramatorsk, 198,000	E 5
Krasino	H 1
Krasnoarmeysk	G 4
Krasnodar, 623,000	E 6
Krasnograd	E 5
Krasnokamsk, 58,000	H 3
Krasnoslobodsk	F 4
Krasnovishersk	J 2
Krasnyy Liman	E 5
Krasny Yar	G 5
Kremenchug, 230,000	D 5
Krichev	D 4
Krivoy Rog, 698,000	D 5
Krolevets	D 4
Kronshtadt	C 3
Kropotkin, 73,000	F 5
Krymsk	E 6
Kuba	G 6
Kuban' (river)	E 5
Kubeno (lake)	E 3
Kudymkar	H 3
Kulebaki	F 3
Kuma (river)	G 5
Kumertau, 62,000	J 4
Kunda	C 3
Kungur, 83,000	J 3
Kuolayarvi	D 1
Kupyansk	E 5
Kura (river)	G 6
Kuressaare	B 3
Kursk, 434,000	E 4
Kushchevskaya	E 5
Kutaisi, 220,000	F 6
Kuvandyk	J 4
Kuybyshev, 1,280,000	H 4
Kuybyshev (res.)	G 4
Kuyto (lake)	D 2
Kuznetsk, 98,000	G 4
Kuzomen'	E 1
Labinsk, 58,000	F 6
Ladoga (lake)	D 2
Lakhdenpokh'ya	C 2
Lapland (region)	D 1
Latvian S.S.R., 2,647,000	B 3
Lebedin	D 4
Lebedyan'	E 4
Lendery	D 2
Leninakan, 228,000	F 6
Leningrad, 4,393,000	C 3
Leninogorsk, 61,000	H 4
Leninsk	G 5
Lenkoran'	G 7
Lepel'	C 4
Leshukonskoye	G 2
Lesnoy	D 1
L'gov	E 4
Lida, 81,000	C 4
Liepāja, 114,000	B 3
Likhoslavl'	E 3
Lipetsk, 465,000	E 4
Lisichansk, 124,000	E 5
Lithuanian S.S.R., 3,641,000	B 3
Livny, 51,000	E 4
Lodeynoye Pole	D 2
Lovat' (river)	D 3
Lozovaya, 68,000	E 5
Lubny, 58,000	D 4
Luga	C 3
Lukoyanov	F 3
Luninets	C 4
Lutsk, 185,000	B 4
Luza	G 2
L'vov, 767,000	B 5
Lyskovo	F 3
Lys'va, 77,000	J 3
Lyubotin	E 4
Lyudinovo	D 4
Madona	C 3
Makar'yev	F 3
Makeyevka, 455,000	E 5
Makhachkala, 320,000	G 6
Makharadez	F 6
Malaya Vishera	D 3
Malmyzh	G 3
Maloarkhangel'sk	E 4
Malyye Karmakuly	H 1
Mansel'ka (mts.)	C 1
Manturovo	F 3
Manych-Gudilo (lake)	F 5
Marganets, 55,000	E 5
Mariupol' (Zhdanov), 529,000	E 5
Marks	G 4
Maykop, 145,000	F 6
Mednogorsk	J 4
Medveditsa (river)	F 4
Medvezh'yegorsk	D 2
Melekess	G 4
Melenki	F 3
Meleuz	J 4
Melitopol', 174,000	D 5
Memel (Klaipėda), 201,000	B 3
Mena	D 4
Merefa	E 5
Mezen'	F 1
Mezen' (river)	G 1
Mezhdusharskiy (island)	H 1
Michurinsk, 103,000	E 4
Mikhaylovka, 58,000	F 4
Millerovo	F 5
Mineral'nye Vody, 75,000	F 6
Mingechaur, 78,000	G 6
Minsk, 1,543,000	C 4
Mirgorod	D 5
Mogilev, 359,000	C 4
Mogilev-Podol'skiy	C 5
Moksha (river)	F 4
Moldavian S.S.R., 4,185,000	C 5
Molodechno, 87,000	C 4
Molotov (Perm'), 1,075,000	J 3

*All population figures are taken from the latest census or estimate available.

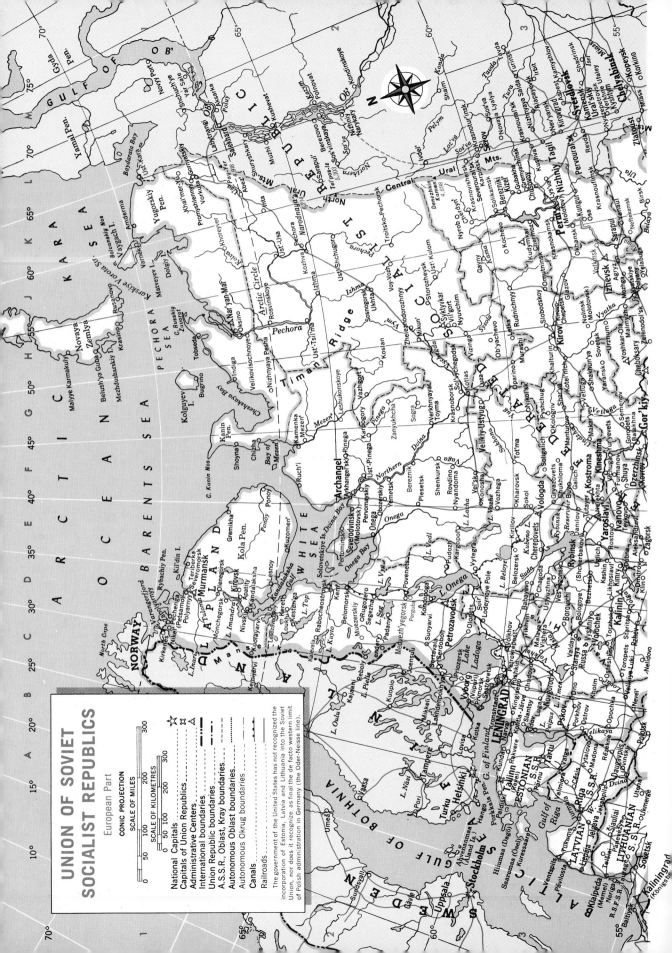

UNION OF SOVIET SOCIALIST REPUBLICS

European Part

CONIC PROJECTION

SCALE OF MILES
0   50   100   200   300

SCALE OF KILOMETRES
0 50 100   200   300

National Capitals
Capitals of Union Republics
Administrative Centers
International boundaries
Union Republic boundaries
A.S.S.R., Oblast, Kray boundaries
Autonomous Oblast boundaries
Autonomous Okrug boundaries
Canals
Railroads

The government of the United States has not recognized the incorporation of Estonia, Latvia and Lithuania into the Soviet Union, nor does it recognize as final the de facto western limit of Polish administration in Germany (the Oder-Neisse line).

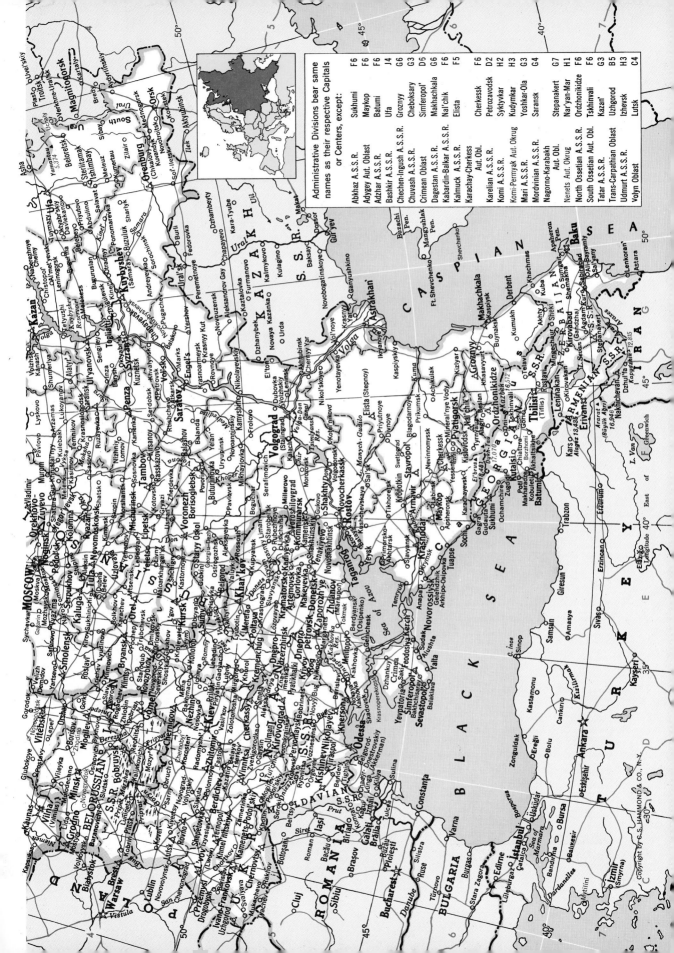

Place	Ref
Monchegorsk, 65,000	D 1
Morozovsk, 51,000	F 5
Morshansk, 51,000	F 4
Moscow (Moskva) (cap.), 8,614,000	E 3
Moskva (river)	E 3
Mozhaysk	E 3
Mozhga	H 3
Mozyr'	C 4
Msta (river)	D 3
Mtsensk	E 4
Mukachevo, 88,000	B 5
Murashi	G 3
Murmansk, 432,000	D 1
Murom, 124,000	F 3
Naberezhnye Chelny, 480,000	H 3
Nakhichevan', 51,000	F 7
Nal'chik, 236,000	F 6
Naro-Fominsk, 60,000	E 3
Narva, 81,000	C 3
Nar'yan Mar	H 1
Nelidovo	D 3
Nerekhta	F 3
Nevel'	D 3
Nevinnomyssk, 116,000	F 6
Nezhin, 81,000	D 4
Niemen (river)	B 4
Nikel'	C 1
Nikolayev, 501,000	D 5
Nikolayevskiy	G 4
Nikol'sk	G 3
Nikol'skoye	G 5
Nikopol', 157,000	D 5
Nivskiy	D 1
Nizhniy Lomov	F 4
Nizhni Novgorod (Gor'kiy), 1,425,000	F 3
Nizhnyaya Pesha	G 1
Noginsk, 122,000	E 3
North Ural (mts.)	K 1
Northern Dvina (river)	F 2
Nosovka	D 4
Novaya Kakhovka, 53,000	D 5
Novaya Zemlya (islands)	H 1
Novgorod, 228,000	D 3
Novgorod-Severskiy	D 4
Novoanninskiy	F 4
Novocherkassk, 188,000	F 5
Novograd-Volynskiy	C 4
Novogrudok	C 4
Novokuybyshevsk, 112,000	G 4
Novomoskovsk, 147,000	E 4
Novopolotsk, 90,000	C 3
Novorossiysk, 179,000	E 6
Novoshakhtinsk, 106,000	E 5
Novotroitsk, 105,000	J 4
Novoukrainka	D 5
Novouzensk	G 4
Novovolynsk, 54,000	B 4
Novozybkov	D 4
Novyy Bug	D 5
Nyandoma	F 2
Nyuvchim	H 2
Oboyan'	E 4
Obruch	C 4
Ob'yachevo	G 2
Ochamchire	F 6
Odessa, 1,141,000	D 5
Oka (river)	F 4
Oktyabr'sk	G 4
Oktyabr'skiy, 106,000	H 4
Olenogorsk	D 1
Olonets	D 2
Omutninsk	H 3
Onega	E 2
Onega (bay)	E 2
Onega (lake)	E 2
Onega (river)	E 2
Oni	F 6
Opochka	C 3
Ordzhonikidze, 313,000	F 6
Orekhovo-Zuyevo, 137,000	E 3
Orel, 335,000	E 4
Orenburg, 537,000	J 4
Orgeyev	C 5
Orsha, 123,000	D 4
Qrsk, 273,000	J 4
Osel (Saaremaa) (isl.)	B 3
Osipenko (Berdyansk), 133,000	E 5
Osipovichi	C 4
Ostashkov	D 3
Ostrogozhask	E 4
Ostrov	C 3
Otradnyy	H 4
Paldiski	B 3
Panevėžys, 122,000	B 3
Pärnu	C 3
Pãvilosta	B 3
Pavlovo, 72,000	F 3
Pavlovsk	F 4
Pay-Yer (mt.)	K 1
Pechenga	D 1
Pechora, 64,000	J 1
Pechora (river)	H 1
Pechora (sea)	H 1
Peipus (lake)	C 3
Penza, 540,000	F 4
Perm', 1,075,000	J 3
Pervomaysk, 79,000	D 5
Pervomayskiy	F 2
Petrokrepost'	D 3
Petrovsk	G 4
Petrovskoye	F 5
Petrozavodsk, 264,000	D 2
Petsamo (Pechenga)	D 1
Pinega	D 1
Pinega (river)	G 2
Pinsk, 116,000	C 4
Piryatin	D 4
Plesetsk	F 2
Pochep	D 4
Podol'sk, 209,000	E 3
Polonnoye	C 4
Polotsk, 80,000	C 3
Poltava, 309,000	D 5
Polyarnyy	F 1
Ponoy	F 1
Ponomarevka	H 4
Porkhov	C 3
Postavy	C 3
Poti	F 6
Povenets	E 2
Povorino	F 4
Prikumsk	F 6
Priluki, 73,000	D 4
Primorsk	C 2
Primorsko-Akhtarsk	E 5
Priozersk	D 2
Pripet (marshes)	C 4
Pripyat' (Pripet) (river)	C 4
Privolzhskiy	G 5
Priyutnoye	F 5
Priyutovo	H 4
Promyshlennyy	K 1
Prut (river)	C 5
Psel (river)	D 4
Pskov, 202,000	C 3
Pudozh	E 2
Pugachev	G 4
Pushkin 97,000	D 3
Pyatigorsk, 121,000	F 6
Pyatikhatki	D 5
Pytalovo	C 3
Rabocheostrovsk	D 1
Radomyshl'	C 4
Rakhov	B 5
Rakvere	C 3
Rasskazovo	F 4
Rechitsa, 71,000	D 4
Rêzekne	C 3
Riga, 1,004,000	B 3
Riga (gulf)	B 3
Rogachev	D 4
Romny, 53,000	D 4
Roslavl', 61,000	D 4
Rossosh', 55,000	E 4
Rostov	E 3
Rostov, 1,004,000	F 5
Rosvinskoye	H 1
Rovdino	F 2
Rovno, 233,000	C 4
Rovnoye	F 4
Rtishchevo	F 4
Rubezhnoye, 72,000	E 4
Ruch'yi	F 1
Rudnichnyy	H 3
Rugozero	D 2
Rusanovo	J 1
Russian Sov. Fed. Soc. Rep., 145,311,000	F 3
Russkiy Zavorot (cape)	H 1
Rustavi, 147,000	G 6
Ruzayevka, 53,000	F 4
Ryazan', 508,000	E 4
Rybachiy (pen.)	D 1
Rybinsk, 254,000	E 3
Rybinsk (reservoir)	E 3
Rybnitsa, 58,000	C 5
Rzhev, 70,000	D 3
Saaremaa (island)	B 3
Sabirabad	G 6
Safonovo, 56,000	D 3
Saki	D 5
Salavat, 153,000	H 4
Sal'sk, 62,000	F 5
Sal'yany	G 7
Samara (river)	H 4
Saransk, 323,000	G 4
Sarapul, 111,000	H 3
Saratov, 918,000	G 4
Sarny	C 4
Sasovo	F 4
Seg (lake)	D 2
Segezha	D 2
Semenov	F 3
Sengiley	G 4
Serafimovich	F 5
Serdobol' (Sortavala)	D 2
Serdobsk	F 4
Serpukhov, 142,000	E 4
Sestroretsk	C 2
Sevan (lake)	G 6
Sevastopol', 350,000	D 6
Severodvinsk, 239,000	E 2
Severomorsk, 55,000	D 1
Seym (river)	D 4
Shakhty, 225,000	F 5
Shakhun'ya	G 3
Shar'ya	G 3
Shatsk	F 4
Shatura	E 3
Shcherbakov (Rybinsk), 254,000	E 3
Shchigry	E 4
Sheki, 54,000	G 6
Shemakha	G 6
Shenkursk	F 2
Shepetovka	C 4
Shostka, 87,000	D 4
Shoyna	F 1
Shumerlya	G 3
Shuya, 72,000	F 3
Siauliai, 140,000	B 3
Sibay	J 4
Simferopol', 338,000	D 6
Sisola (river)	H 2
Skadovsk	D 5
Skopin	F 4
Slantsy	C 3
Slavgorod	D 4
Slavuta	C 4
Slavyansk, 144,000	E 5
Slavyansk (-na-Kuban'), 57,000	E 5
Slobodskoy	H 3
Slutsk, 55,000	C 4
Smela, 76,000	D 5
Smolensk, 338,000	D 4
Sochi, 317,000	E 6
Sokol	F 3
Sol'-Iletsk	J 4
Soligalich	F 3
Solovetskiye (islands)	E 1
Sol'vychegodsk	G 2
Sorochinsk	H 4
Soroki	C 5
Sortavala (Serdobol')	D 2
Sosnogorsk	H 2
Sosnovka	F 4
South Ural (mts.)	J 4
Sovetsk	G 3
Sovetsk	C 4
Stalingrad (Volgograd), 988,000	F 5
Staliniri (Tskhinvali)	F 6
Stalino (Donetsk) 1,090,000	E 5
Stalinogorsk (Novomoskovsk), 147,000	E 4
Staraya Russa	D 3
Staritsa	D 3
Starobel'sk	E 5
Starodub	D 4
Staryy Oskol, 167,000	E 4
Stavropol', 306,000	F 5
Stepanakert	G 7
Stepnoy (Elista), 85,000	G 5
Sterlitamak, 251,000	J 4
Storozhevsk	H 2
Stupino	E 4
Suda (river)	E 3
Sudak	E 6
Sukhinichi	E 4
Sukhona (river)	F 2
Sukhumi, 130,000	F 6
Sumgait, 234,000	G 6
Sumy, 268,000	E 4
Suoyarvi	D 2
Sura (river)	G 4
Svir' (river)	D 2
Sychevka	D 3
Syktyvkar, 224,000	H 2
Syzran', 174,000	G 4
Taganrog, 295,000	E 5
Tallinn, 478,000	C 3
Tambov, 305,000	F 4
Tartu, 113,000	C 3
Taurage	B 3
Tbilisi, 1,194,000	G 6
Telavi	G 6
Telšiai	B 3
Temnikov	F 4
Temryuk	E 5
Ternopol', 197,000	C 5
Tetyushi	G 4
Teykovo	F 3
Tiflis (Tbilisi), 1,194,000	F 6
Tikhoretsk, 67,000	F 5
Tikhvin, 70,000	D 3
Tilsit (Sovetsk)	B 4
Timan (ridge)	H 1
Tiraspol', 173,000	D 5
Tirlyanskiy	J 4
Togliatti, 627,000	G 4
Tokmak	D 5
Top (lake)	D 1
Toropets	D 3
Torzhok, 51,000	D 3
Tot'ma	F 3
Troitsko-Pechorsk	D 4
Trubchevsk	D 4
Tskhinvali	F 6
Tuapse, 64,000	E 6
Tukums	B 3
Tula, 538,000	E 4
Tul'chin	C 5
Tuloma (river)	D 1
Tutayev	E 3
Tuymazy	H 4
Tyrnyauz	F 6
Ufa, 1,092,000	J 4
Ufa (river)	J 4
Ugleural'skiy	J 3
Uglich	E 3
Ukhta, 105,000	H 2
Ukmergé	C 3
Ukrainian S.S.R., 51,201,000	D 5
Ul'yanovsk, 589,000	G 4
Uman', 89,000	D 5
Undzha (river)	G 3
Ural (mts.)	J 2
Ural (river)	J 4
Uryupinsk	F 4
Usa (river)	K 1
Usman'	E 4
Ust'-Kulom	H 2
Ust'-Pinega	F 2
Ust'-Tsil'ma	H 1
Ust'-Usa	J 1
Ustyuzhna	E 3
Utena	C 3
Uzhgorod, 111,000	B 5
Uzlovaya, 63,000	E 4
Vaga (river)	F 2
Valday	D 3
Valday (hills)	D 3
Valga	C 3
Valmiera	C 3
Valuyki	E 4
Vasil'kov	D 4
Vaygach (island)	K 1
Vazhgort	G 2
Velikaya (river)	F 2
Velikiy Ustyug	F 2
Velikiye Luki, 113,000	D 3
Velikovisochnoye	H 1
Velizh	D 3
Vel'sk	F 2
Ventspils, 52,000	B 3
Verkhnyaya Toyma	G 2
Ves'yegonsk	E 3
Vetluga (river)	G 3
Vichuga, 51,000	F 3
Viipuri (Vyborg), 81,000	C 2
Vileyka	C 4
Vilna (Vilnius), 566,000	C 4
Vinnitsa, 383,000	C 5
Vitebsk, 347,000	C 3
Vladimir, 343,000	F 3
Vodl (lake)	E 2
Volga (river)	G 5
Volga-Don (canal)	F 5
Volgodonsk, 179,000	F 5
Volgograd, 988,000	F 5
Volkhov	D 3
Volkhov (river)	D 3
Volkovysk	B 4
Vologda, 278,000	F 3
Vol'sk, 66,000	G 4
Volzhsk, 60,000	G 3
Volzhskiy, 257,000	F 5
Vorkuta, 112,000	K 1
Vorona (river)	F 4
Voronezh, 872,000	E 4
Voroshilovgrad, 509,000	E 5
Vorskla (river)	E 4
Votkinsk, 101,000	H 3
Vozhe (lake)	F 2
Vozhega	F 2
Voznesensk	D 5
Vyatka (river)	H 3
Vyatskiye Polyany	H 3
Vyaz'ma, 57,000	D 3
Vyborg, 81,000	C 2
Vychegda (river)	G 2
Vyg (lake)	E 2
Vyksa, 60,000	F 3
Vym' (river)	H 2
Vyshniy Volochek, 70,000	D 3
Vytegra	E 2
Western Dvina (river)	C 3
White (sea)	E 1
Yalta, 89,000	D 6
Yamantau (mt.)	J 4
Yanaul	J 3
Yaransk	G 3
Yaroslavl', 634,000	E 3
Yartsevo	D 3
Yefremov, 58,000	E 4
Yegor'yevsk, 73,000	E 3
Yelabuga	H 3
Yelan'	F 4
Yelets, 119,000	E 4
Yelgava (Jelgava)	B 3
Yenakiyevo, 117,000	E 5
Yenotayevka	G 5
Yershov	G 4
Yessentuki, 84,000	F 6
Yevpatoriya, 106,000	D 5
Yeysk, 77,000	E 5
Yoshkar-Ola, 243,000	G 3
Yug (river)	G 2
Yugorskiy (pen.)	K 1
Yur'yevets	F 3
Zagorsk, 113,000	E 3
Zaporozh'ye, 875,000	E 5
Zelenodol'sk, 93,000	G 3
Zhdanov (Mariupol'), 529,000	E 5
Zheleznodorozhnyy 90,000	H 2
Zherdevka	F 4
Zhigulevsk	G 4
Zhitomir, 287,000	C 4
Zhlobin, 52,000	D 4
Zhmerinka	C 5
Zhodino, 51,000	C 4
Zilair	J 4
Znamenka	D 5
Zolotonosha	D 5
Zugdidi	F 6
Zvenigorodka	D 5

*All population figures are taken from the latest census or estimate available.

UNITARIAN UNIVERSALIST ASSOCIATION.

In 1961 two religious groups in the United States merged to form the American Unitarian Universalist Association. Of the two, the Unitarians appeared earlier, having their roots in Europe's 16th-century Reformation. The Universalists were first established in the United States in 1779 by a former English Methodist, John Murray.

Both Unitarianism and Universalism are based on ideas that originated early in the history of Christianity. The chief Unitarian doctrine is, as the name indicates, the unity or oneness of God. In the 4th century Arias, a priest from Alexandria, Egypt, taught that Jesus Christ was a man chosen by God but in no sense a deity himself. This teaching was condemned as heresy by most Christian theologians of the time, but it persisted and emerged again during the 16th century. Some liberal followers of the Reformers Martin Luther and John Calvin taught the unity of God. Persecuted by the major Reformation churches and by the Roman Catholic church as well, some of these followers took refuge in Poland. There a Unitarian group called the Minor Reformed Church was formed in 1565. After 1579 the group was led by the Italian exile Faustus Socinus, who formulated the basic teachings of the denomination. The Polish Unitarians were persecuted and driven into exile by the Counter-Reformation in the 16th century.

Unitarianism became established in Hungary in the late 1500s and in the British Isles in the early 1600s. In the United States it arose as a reaction against the emotionalism of the Great Awakening of the mid-18th century (see Revivalism). One of its influential founders was Charles Chauncy, minister of First Church in Boston, Mass., for 60 years. Other powerful influences were William Ellery Channing and Ralph Waldo Emerson.

Universalism's roots are in the teachings of the 3rd-century Christian theologian Origen, who taught at Alexandria. He denied everlasting punishment for unbelievers. He taught instead that the whole universe will be restored to God at the end of time. This doctrine also persisted as a minor strain in Christianity, though it was condemned by the major denominations. It had no influence in North America, however, until it was first preached by George de Benneville, Elhanan Winchester, and John Murray. Their preaching, like Charles Chauncy's, was a reaction against 18th-century revivalism and its preaching of everlasting punishment for unbelievers. Universalist teaching was shaped by Hosea Ballou, a former Baptist, in his 'A Treatise on Atonement' (1805), 'An Examination of the Doctrine of Future Retribution' (1834), and other writings.

There is no official statement of belief for Unitarians and Universalists. Each congregation is independent, though it is a member of the association. Some congregations maintain beliefs and rituals based on the Bible, while others emphasize human social improvement and scientific progress. All members are devoted to individual freedom, reason, and tolerance.

UNITED ARAB EMIRATES.

A union of seven Arab kingdoms on the eastern coast of the Arabian Peninsula, the United Arab Emirates consists of Abu Dhabi, Dubai, Sharjah, Ajman, Umm al-Qaiwain, Ras al-Khaimah, and Fujairah emirates. The capital and the largest town of the federation is Abu Dhabi. Bordered by Qatar and the Persian Gulf on the north, Saudi Arabia on the west and south, and Oman on the east and northeast, the United Arab Emirates covers an area of about 32,300 square miles (83,600 square kilometers).

The country's relief consists of a low-lying, flat desert coastal plain. The climate is hot and dry. Summer temperatures may reach 114° F (46° C). Annual rainfall averages only 3 to 4 inches (7.6 to 10 centimeters). Natural vegetation is very sparse.

The native population, largely of Arab descent, follows Islam, the official religion. A large number of people still practice a nomadic lifestyle. Arabic is the official language, but Hindi, Urdu, and Persian are also widely spoken. A large portion of the work force consists of foreign skilled laborers. The United Arab Emirates University is the country's only institution of higher learning.

Petroleum is the chief economic resource of the region. Proven reserves of petroleum and natural gas are among the world's largest. Production is largely concentrated in Abu Dhabi, Dubai, and Sharjah. Since the discovery of petroleum in the late 1950s, the country has undergone extensive modernization. Because of huge profits from petroleum exports, the United Arab Emirates has one of the world's highest per capita gross national products.

Less than 0.2 percent of the land can be cultivated. Wheat, barley, millet, fruits, and vegetables are grown with the aid of irrigation. Date palm and alfalfa are produced in oases. Fishing is of some economic significance. Dubai, with an extensive transit trade, is the chief seaport.

The area became known as the Trucial Coast in 1853 when the Treaty of Maritime Peace in Perpetuity was signed. From 1873 to 1947 the region was administered by British India and after 1947 by the London Foreign Office. Each of the states maintained full internal control, however. In 1960 the Trucial States Council was formed, with representation from each state. The British vacated in 1971, and the Trucial States became a federal union known as the United Arab Emirates. Ras al-Khaimah joined in 1972, and Bahrain and Qatar became independent states. Each of the seven emirates is governed by its own hereditary ruler. The highest federal authority lies with the Supreme Council of Rulers, which consists of the rulers of the seven emirates. Population (1987 estimate), 1,856,000.

© Jim Pickerel—CLICK/Chicago

The United Kingdom legislature meets in the New Palace of Westminster, better known as the Houses of Parliament.

UNITED KINGDOM

UNITED KINGDOM.
The United Kingdom of Great Britain and Northern Ireland is the political union of England, Scotland, Wales, and Northern Ireland. It is not a federation but a unitary state, and its inhabitants elect members to represent them in a parliament that meets in London. Scotland, Wales, and Northern Ireland, however, retain a degree of autonomy in running some of their own affairs.

History

The first union of separate states in the British Isles took place in 1301, when Wales was joined to England by the creation of the title of prince of Wales for the son of Edward I of England. Wales was not officially incorporated with England, however, until 1536. In 1603 James VI of Scotland became king of England (as James I), uniting Scotland and England under one ruler and creating the so-called Union of the Crowns. Scotland retained its own parliament until 1707, when the parliaments of the two states were formally united. Although this union was opposed by many Scots, it gave them entry to the larger world of English politics and business. The name Great Britain was officially adopted for this union; when Ireland was added to Great Britain by the Act of Union of 1801, the title United Kingdom of Great Britain and Ireland was introduced.

As a result of Irish demands for independence, the Irish Free State was declared in 1922. The six north-

This article was contributed by Ian M. Matley, Professor of Geography, Michigan State University, East Lansing.

ern counties of Ireland, which had a predominantly Protestant population, remained as part of the United Kingdom but were officially named Northern Ireland. The present title for the union of England, Scotland, Wales, and Northern Ireland—the United Kingdom of Great Britain and Northern Ireland—dates from 1927. Northern Ireland sent representatives to the London Parliament but had its own legislature and executive to deal with domestic matters. In 1972, because of continuing political and religious problems in Northern Ireland, the London Parliament suspended the Northern Ireland Parliament and established its own direct control over the province.

In 1885 a secretary of state was appointed to look after Scottish affairs. There are separate departments in Scotland for home affairs, health, agriculture, fisheries, education, and economic development. The Scottish legal system is also separate from the English system.

In 1964 a Welsh Office was established to oversee matters of interest to Wales. The office is headed by a secretary of state for Wales.

The Channel Islands and the Isle of Man do not belong to the United Kingdom. They are direct dependencies of the Crown, or sovereign, and have their own legislative and taxation systems. (For a general history, *see* England, "History.")

Constitution

The United Kingdom does not have a written constitution like that of the United States. The British constitution is formed partly by statutes, or legislative enactments of Parliament; partly by common law, based on decisions of courts of law; and partly by practices and precepts, which are known as conventions. These conventions are not part of the law of the country but are nevertheless necessary for running the machinery of government. Because the constitution is not written, it can be adapted as necessary either by an act of Parliament or by the general acceptance of a new convention.

There are three organs of government in the constitution: the legislature, the executive, and the judiciary. The legislature consists of Parliament, which is the supreme authority in the country. The executive consists of the Cabinet members and other ministers who make and direct the policy of the country, along with government departments and local authorities. The judiciary determines common law and also interprets statutes.

The Crown

The Crown is the supreme power in the legislature, the executive, and the judiciary. The sovereign is also the head of the established Church of England and is commander in chief of the armed forces. In practice, however, the present queen, Elizabeth II, acts only on the advice of her ministers and cannot reject or ignore their advice. These restrictions on the powers of the sovereign are the result of several centuries of confrontation and interaction between the sovereign and Parliament. In effect the United Kingdom is governed by her majesty's government in the queen's name.

The queen still has several significant functions. She calls and dissolves Parliament, and she opens a new session with a speech from the throne. This speech is not written by her, however, but by the government in power, and it outlines the government's policy for the forthcoming session of Parliament. Similarly, the queen confers honors—in the form of peerages, knighthoods, and decorations—that are given on the advice of the government and that often reward people for services to the political party in power. She can award some honors herself, however—such as the Order of the Garter. She appoints judges, army officers, diplomats, and officials of the Church of England also on advice.

Although the queen has in fact little authority of her own, she is kept informed of events and is sometimes consulted by the government in power. The queen has the advice of a Privy Council, which consists of ministers of the government and other persons recommended by the government in power. In the event of an inconclusive national election, the queen may be required to choose a new prime minister.

In addition to her other functions the queen is head of the Commonwealth, which consists of a number of states that formerly belonged to the British Empire. The Commonwealth includes such countries as Australia, Canada, and New Zealand and a number of smaller states such as Jamaica, the Bahamas, and Fiji. The queen is represented in these countries by governors-general, who are not members of the United Kingdom government and who act independent of it. The United Kingdom government cannot interfere in the affairs of a Commonwealth country, except in the case of such dependencies as the Falkland Islands and Gibraltar, which have not achieved complete independence from the United Kingdom.

The history of the monarchy plays a large part in the history of the British Isles. The present sovereign is a descendant of Sophia—the electress of Hanover—whose son came to the British throne in 1714 as George I. Sophia was the nearest Protestant descendant of James I, her grandfather. The Act of Settlement in 1701 provided for the accession to the throne of Sophia and her heirs in order to ensure a Protestant monarchy. By this act all sovereigns must be members of the Church of England. The act also strictly limited the role of the sovereign in the government of the country. In 1917 the royal family dropped their German titles and took the name of the House of Windsor because of the unpopularity of everything German during World War I.

The queen and her family members are largely supported by the state. Parliament annually approves allowances for members of the royal family. The queen's private expenditures come partly from her own funds and partly from an inheritance known as the Duchy of Lancaster. The prince of Wales receives revenues from another estate—the Duchy of Cornwall.

Parliament

In theory the queen functions as the supreme legislative authority through Parliament. In practice, however, the queen and Parliament rarely come together, except at the openings of Parliament sessions. Parliament consists of two houses—the House of Commons and the House of Lords.

The House of Commons consists of 650 members—523 from England, 72 from Scotland, 38 from Wales, and 17 from Northern Ireland. The United Kingdom is divided into a number of constituencies, each of which returns one member to Parliament. All persons

Queen Elizabeth II invested Prince Charles, kneeling, with the title prince of Wales on July 1, 1969, at Caernarvon Castle.

Photo Trends

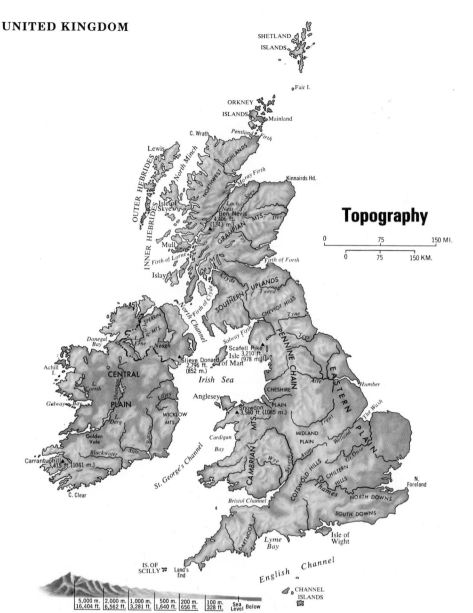

Topography

0   75   150 MI.

0   75   150 KM.

| 5,000 m. 16,404 ft. | 2,000 m. 6,562 ft. | 1,000 m. 3,281 ft. | 500 m. 1,640 ft. | 200 m. 656 ft. | 100 m. 328 ft. | Sea Level | Below |

over the age of 18 are eligible to vote for a member from their local constituency. The number and size of constituencies occasionally change with variations in population. Members receive a salary and hold their seats for the duration of a Parliament. A general election for all members must be held at least every five years but may be called at any time within that period. For example, a government may face a general election if it is defeated in some major issue by a vote in Parliament.

The speaker of the House of Commons is elected by the members and acts as the president of the House. Other elected and appointed officials look after the running of the House. Members of Parliament are controlled by their party whips, who round up members before a vote and organize debates in the Commons.

Members of the House of Commons belong to one of the British political parties. The party that wins the majority of parliamentary seats forms a government with the party leader as prime minister. Of the remaining parties, the one with the largest number of seats becomes the official opposition.

The party in power in the late 1980s was the Conservative party, led by Margaret Thatcher, who was elected in 1987 as prime minister for a third term. She was the longest continuously serving prime minister in the 20th century. The Conservatives under Thatcher held power since 1979.

The Labor party was the largest minority party in the government of the late 1980s. Its leader was Neil Kinnock. The Labor party advocates socialism and supports the nationalization of basic industries and services. In general it opposes the power of big business. Many of its members would like to abolish the House of Lords and the annual awards of titles and honors. The party supports higher rates of unemployment compensation, old-age pensions, and other forms of welfare. It was responsible for the establishment in 1948 of the United Kingdom's free medical service, known as the National Health Service. The party gains much of its support from the trade unions, but it has been troubled with internal divisions and decreasing numbers of trade-union members. It lost many votes in the 1987 election because of its controversial defense policy, which called for partial British unilateral disarmament. The main strongholds of Labor support are in the industrial north of England, in Scotland, and in southern Wales.

The Social Democratic party (SDP) is an offshoot of the Labor party. Its members regard Labor and its policies as too left-wing. The SDP allied with the Liberal party in order to attract voters in the 1987 elections but gained fewer votes than it had hoped.

There are small nationalist parties in Scotland and Wales—the Scottish National party and the Welsh Nationalist party, Plaid Cymru. In Northern Ireland there are several parties, including the Ulster Unionist party, the Ulster Democratic Unionist party, and the Social Democratic and Labor party. There are also some small far-left parties in Britain—such as the Communist party, the Socialist Workers' party, and the Workers' Revolutionary party—which play no real role in present-day politics.

The House of Lords has more than 1,100 members. These include hereditary peers, or nobles by inheritance or birth; life peers, or individuals with nonhereditary titles conferred by the Crown; law lords; and archbishops and senior bishops of the Church of England. All hereditary peers may attend sessions, but only those Irish peers who also hold an English or Scottish peerage may attend. Peers receive no salary. In practice no more than about 380 peers regularly attend sessions. In the House of Lords the lord chancellor fulfills the same role as does the speaker in the Commons.

The functions of Parliament are to make laws, to appropriate money for various state purposes, and to provide a forum for debate. Debates in the House of Commons are controlled by the speaker.

Legislation is initiated by the introduction of bills in either house. In general most bills are introduced by the government, though members may introduce their own bills. Finance bills can only be introduced in the Commons. A bill is given three readings in the house in which it is introduced; if passed, it is sent to the other house, where it is submitted to the same procedure. If a bill is passed by both houses, it becomes law. In theory the sovereign has a right to veto a bill, but this has not occurred since the 18th century. Likewise the House of Lords has little power to stop or delay bills that have been passed by the Commons. It is hoped that the members of the Lords—often senior political figures who have been knighted for their services—will use their experience to suggest amendments to a bill. The Lords cannot interfere with a money bill or with a bill that has been passed by the Commons in two consecutive sessions.

There has been talk of abolishing the House of Lords because of its limited role and because its members are not elected and represent, at least in part, an aristocracy that no longer plays a major role in British life. No action has been taken, however, except to limit further the power of the Lords.

There are a number of committees appointed by the House of Commons to conduct various kinds of business. Some of these committees are permanent; others—the select committees—are appointed temporarily to examine special matters.

The Government

The head of the government is the prime minister. (The title of prime minister dates back to the 18th century.) The prime minister is the leader of the majority party in Parliament and has the power to appoint and dismiss ministers. The prime minister is the main representative of the government and recommends the appointment of some senior judges and of senior clergy of the Church of England. The prime minister also draws up the annual list of honors, which are usually awarded on New Year's Day.

The prime minister selects a Cabinet of ministers. The Cabinet develops the government's policies, which are presented as proposed legislation to Parliament, and exercises control over government departments. Meetings of the Cabinet are held in private, and strict secrecy is maintained. Some matters are discussed by Cabinet committees, which consist of the ministers involved. The Cabinet Office handles the records of Cabinet meetings and provides information to ministers. To maintain stability the Cabinet must act as a collective group and issue unanimous statements and policies. If a minister does not agree with Cabinet policies, that minister must resign.

Ministers head government departments and are responsible for the work of those departments. The ministers must be prepared to answer questions about their departments in the House of Commons. Ministers who sit in the House of Lords have a parliamentary secretary whose responsibility is to answer questions raised in the Commons. This system of parliamentary

Prime Minister Margaret Thatcher, right, consults with Foreign Secretary Sir Geoffrey Howe.

Rex Features/© RDR Productions

71

control over government departments discourages inefficiency and irresponsibility.

There are many government departments of various sizes and complexity. Major departments include the Treasury, which handles the country's finances; the Ministry of Defence; the Ministry of Health, which operates the National Health Service; the Home Office, which controls the police and other law-and-order institutions; the Foreign Office; and the Post Office. There are several Scottish and Northern Irish departments. A Welsh Department of the Ministry of Education deals with special aspects of Welsh education.

Most of the work of government departments is carried out by members of the civil service. Because none of the positions held by civil servants is an elective or political appointment, a change in government does not affect a department's staff.

Local Government

Local government is carried out primarily by locally elected councils. There are numerous administrative divisions, each with its own council. The largest division is the county; it has a county council. There are also borough councils, rural district and urban district councils, district town councils (in Scotland), and parish councils. These councils are responsible for providing such services as garbage disposal, water supplies, sewerage, and street cleaning. They also administer the police and fire services as well as education, certain health services, and housing.

In 1974 seven metropolitan district councils were established for certain large cities and their regions, including London, Manchester, and Liverpool. The Greater London Council was the largest such council. These councils were abolished in 1980, and their work was passed to borough and district councils and to joint authorities.

Members of councils are elected and generally belong to one of the major political parties. Councils in some of the large cities consist predominantly of Labor members. The actions of some left-wing councils

in London and Liverpool have created considerable controversy. The Conservative government's breakup of the metropolitan councils is seen as a way of removing left-wing influence.

Income for the operation of local government comes partly from the national government and partly from property taxes, which are known as rates. The system of property taxation is to be abolished and replaced by charges that will be levied by local authorities on adults residing in their areas.

The Judiciary

The judiciary is independent of the legislature and the executive. No one—not even the sovereign—can control or influence the courts' operations or decisions. The judicial system is administered by the lord chancellor (who is a government minister) and by the home secretary. The lord chancellor recommends candidates for various judicial appointments.

The legal system of Scotland differs in many ways from that of England and Wales; however, both systems have civil and criminal divisions, and both use the jury system for trying persons accused of serious crimes. The legal system of Northern Ireland is similar to that of England and Wales.

In England and Wales the courts most often used for civil cases are the county courts. Cases that involve large sums of money, however, are heard in one of the divisions of the High Court of Justice. There is a Court of Appeal, from which a further appeal is possible to the House of Lords, the United Kingdom's Supreme Court of Appeal for civil cases.

Criminal cases involving minor offenses may be tried without a jury in magistrate's courts. Other cases may be heard in Courts of Assize. These courts are served by judges who travel around county towns or by so-called courts of Quarter Sessions, which convene four times a year in a number of counties and boroughs. In London the Central Criminal Court handles cases for the capital city and its surrounding districts. A Court of Criminal Appeal also exists.

In Scotland most civil cases are heard in sheriff courts, which are somewhat similar to English county courts. Minor civil matters are often tried by a justice of the peace. The supreme civil court is the Court of Session, from which appeals may be made to the House of Lords.

Minor criminal cases in Scotland are handled by the sheriff courts, with or without a jury. More serious criminal cases go to the High Court of Judiciary, located in Edinburgh. Its judges may also try cases in other towns. Appeals are heard by a group of judges, and there is no appeal possible to the House of Lords.

In August the Edinburgh Castle esplanade is the scene of the annual military tattoo, or musical drill and parade.

Karen Phillips—CLICK/Chicago

BIBLIOGRAPHY FOR THE UNITED KINGDOM

Britain, an Official Handbook (Central Office of Information, annual).
Evans, R.H. Government (Vista Books, 1964).
Harvey, Jack and Bather, L. The British Constitution (St. Martin, 1964).
Ingle, Stephen. The British Party System (Basil Blackwell, 1987).
Whitaker's Almanack (Whitaker, annual).
(*See also* bibliographies for **England; Wales.**)

United Kingdom Fact Summary

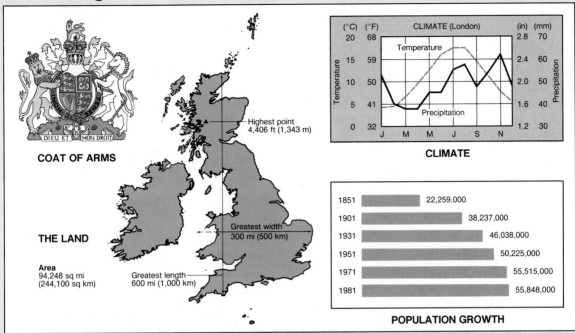

COAT OF ARMS

DIEU ET MON DROIT

THE LAND

Area
94,248 sq mi
(244,100 sq km)

Highest point
4,406 ft (1,343 m)

Greatest width
300 mi (500 km)

Greatest length
600 mi (1,000 km)

CLIMATE

(°C)	(°F)	CLIMATE (London)	(in)	(mm)
20	68		2.8	70
15	59	Temperature	2.4	60
10	50		2.0	50
5	41	Precipitation	1.6	40
0	32	J M M J S N	1.2	30

POPULATION GROWTH

1851	22,259,000
1901	38,237,000
1931	46,038,000
1951	50,225,000
1971	55,515,000
1981	55,848,000

Official Name: United Kingdom of Great Britain and Northern Ireland.

Capital: London, England.

Coat of Arms: Quartered shield with England represented by two of the quarters and Scotland and Ireland each represented by one quarter; supported by a crowned golden lion for England and a unicorn for Scotland; a garter encircles the shield. The Royal motto, *Dieu et mon droit* is beneath the arms. Took present form in 1837.

Flag: Union Jack, a combination of the red and white crosses of the patron saints of England, Scotland, and Ireland (*see* Flags of the World).

Anthem: 'God Save the King (Queen)'.

NATURAL FEATURES

Coastline: *Total*—5,130 miles (8,257 kilometers); *England and Wales*—2,410 miles (3,880 kilometers); *Scotland*—2,500 miles (4,023 kilometers); *Northern Ireland*—220 miles (354 kilometers).

Natural Regions: Scottish Highlands, Lowlands, and Uplands; Lake District; Antrim Plateau; Lleyn Peninsula; Gower Peninsula.

Major Ranges: Brecon Beacons, Cambrian Mountains, Grampian Mountains, Mourne Mountains, Pennines, Sperrin Mountains.

Notable Peaks: Ben Nevis, 4,406 feet (1,343 meters); Snowdon, 3,560 feet (1,085 meters); Scafell Pike, 3,210 feet (978 meters); Ben Lomond, 3,192 feet (973 meters); Cader Idris, 2,927 feet (892 meters); Slieve Donard, 2,796 feet (852 meters); Plynlimon, 2,468 feet (752 meters).

Major Rivers: Bann, Dee, Erne, Severn, Teifi, Thames, Towy, Trent, Tweed, Wye.

Major Lakes: Bala, Lomond, Lower Lough Erne, Neagh, Upper Lough Erne, Vyrnwy, Windermere.

Climate: *Northern Ireland*—temperate, maritime; cool and humid conditions. *England*—rainy and temperate; mild winters; cool summers. *Scotland*—cool, rainy, windy; winds from the southwest make the climate warmer than it would otherwise be so far north; autumn and winter are the wettest seasons; west coast receives the most rainfall. *Wales*—influenced by mountains and nearness to the sea; mild winters; cool summers; west coast has high rainfall; higher mountain regions can have cold winters with heavy snow.

THE PEOPLE

Population (1987 estimate): 56,878,000; 603.5 persons per square mile (233.0 persons per square kilometer); 91.5 percent urban, 8.5 percent rural.

Vital Statistics (rate per 1,000 population): *Births*—13.3; *deaths*—12.2; *marriages*—6.9.

Life Expectancy (at birth): *Males*—71.4 years; *females*—77.2 years.

Major Language: English (official).

Ethnic Groups: white, Indian, West Indian, Pakistani, African, Chinese, Bangladeshi, Arab.

Major Religion: Protestantism.

MAJOR CITIES (1985 estimate)

London, England (5,100; Greater London, 6,767,500): capital of the United Kingdom; international financial center; huge port; Buckingham Palace; Tower of London; Westminster Abbey; Saint Paul's Cathedral; Houses of Parliament; National Gallery; British Museum (*see* London).

Birmingham, England (1,008,000): industrial center; metal manufacturing; machinery; engines; iron roofs; girders; railway cars; automobiles; Birmingham Repertory Theater; City Art Gallery; University of Birmingham (*see* Birmingham, England).

Glasgow, Scotland (773,800): largest city in Scotland; center for commerce and industry; chief port city of western Scotland; textiles; food and beverages; tobacco; chemicals; engineering; printing; Kelvingrove Art Galleries and Museum; Hunterian Museum; Glasgow School of Art; University of Glasgow (*see* Glasgow).

Leeds, England (710,000): wool cloth; iron; boots; shoes; felt; ready-made clothing; stock and corn exchanges; music festivals; Civic Theater; City Museum; City Art Gallery; University of Leeds (*see* Leeds).

Sheffield, England (539,000): fine steel cutlery; steel; plated ware; iron and brass goods; clothing; canned foods; paint and varnish; chemicals; shopping and cultural center; Sheffield University (*see* Sheffield).

Liverpool, England (492,000): large port in industrial region; textiles; machinery; chemicals; flour milling; agriculture; shipbuilding and repair; engineering works; Walker Art Gallery; University of Liverpool (*see* Liverpool).

Bradford, England (464,400): textile and clothing industries; Cartwright Memorial Hall; University of Bradford; Bolling Hall (*see* Bradford).

Manchester, England (451,100): a leading seaport and industrial area of England; engineering; printing; electrical products; machine tools; chemicals; financial and banking center; railway hub; Manchester University (*see* Manchester, England).

United Kingdom Fact Summary

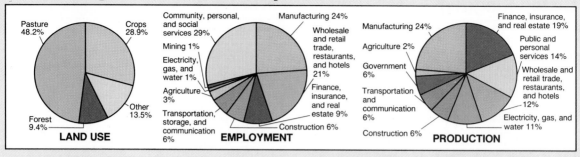

LAND USE
- Pasture 48.2%
- Crops 28.9%
- Other 13.5%
- Forest 9.4%

EMPLOYMENT
- Community, personal, and social services 29%
- Manufacturing 24%
- Wholesale and retail trade, restaurants, and hotels 21%
- Mining 1%
- Electricity, gas, and water 1%
- Agriculture 3%
- Finance, insurance, and real estate 9%
- Transportation, storage, and communication 6%
- Construction 6%

PRODUCTION
- Manufacturing 24%
- Agriculture 2%
- Government 6%
- Transportation and communication 6%
- Construction 6%
- Finance, insurance, and real estate 19%
- Public and personal services 14%
- Wholesale and retail trade, restaurants, and hotels 12%
- Electricity, gas, and water 11%

Edinburgh, Scotland (439,700): capital of Scotland; center of medicine, law, banking, insurance, tourism; Edinburgh Castle; National Gallery; Royal Scottish Academy; University of Edinburgh (*see* Edinburgh).

Bristol, England (394,000): port city; industrial and educational center; sugar refining; tobacco processing; cocoa and chocolate making; wine bottling; glass, porcelain, and pottery making; aircraft design and construction; University of Bristol (*see* Bristol).

ECONOMY

Chief Agricultural Products: *Crops*—apples, barley, flax, hops, oats, pears, plums, potatoes, rapeseed, raspberries, strawberries, sugar beets, vegetables, wheat. *Livestock and fish*—beef cattle, dairy cows, pigs, poultry, sheep, freshwater fish and seafood.

Chief Mined Products: Basalt, chalk, china clay, clay, coal, copper, dolomite, granite, grit and conglomerate, gypsum, iron ore, lead salt, limestone, natural gas, petroleum, rock salt, sand and gravel, silver, tin ore, tungsten, zinc.

Chief Manufactured Products: Aircraft, automobiles, beer, chemicals, china, engines, helicopters, hovercraft, iron and steel, machinery, missiles, nonferrous metals, paper, refined petroleum, rope and twine, ships, space-exploration equipment, textiles.

Chief Imports: Metallic ores, except iron ore; food.

Chief Exports: China, automobiles and other vehicles, woolen goods, steel, electrical and mechanical machinery, tractors, scientific instruments, chemicals, petroleum.

Chief Trading Partners: United States, West Germany, France, The Netherlands.

Monetary Unit: 1 pound sterling = 100 new pence.

EDUCATION

Schools: Free, compulsory education for children ages 11 to 16.

Literacy: Virtually 100 percent of population.

Leading Universities: Cambridge University, Cambridge; Open University, Milton Keynes; Oxford University, Oxford; University of Birmingham; University of Edinburgh; University of Glasgow; University of Leeds; University of Liverpool; University of London; Victoria University of Manchester.

Notable Libraries: Birmingham Public Libraries, Birmingham; British Library, Guildhall Library, Westminster City Library, London; Cambridge University Library, Cambridge; Glasgow District Libraries, Glasgow; Leeds City Libraries, Leeds; National Library of Scotland, Edinburgh; National Library of Wales, Aberystwyth; Oxford University Library, Oxford.

Notable Museums and Art Galleries: British Museum, National Gallery, Natural History Museum, Science Museum, Tate Gallery, Victoria and Albert Museum, London; City Art Gallery, Birmingham; City Art Gallery, City Museum, Leeds; Hunterian Museum, Kelvingrove Art Galleries and Museum, Glasgow; National Gallery, Royal Scottish Academy, Edinburgh; Walker Art Gallery, Liverpool.

GOVERNMENT

Form of Government: Constitutional Monarchy.

Constitution: Partly unwritten and wholly flexible.

Chief of State: Sovereign; inheritance of the Crown is governed by an order of succession under which the sovereign's sons and their descendants have precedence over the daughters.

Head of Government: Prime Minister; appointed by the sovereign.

Cabinet: consists of about 20 ministers, selected by the prime minister.

Legislature: Parliament, composed of House of Lords and House of Commons; annual sessions. *Lords*—1,172 members, seats are inherited and appointed. *Commons*—650 elected members, term, 5 years.

Judiciary: Each country has its own legal system; courts include House of Lords, High Court of Justice, Court of Appeal, Courts of Assize, Courts of Quarter Sessions, Central Criminal Court, Court of Criminal Appeal, sheriff courts, Court of Session, High Court of Judiciary.

Political Divisions: England—39 nonmetropolitan counties; Northern Ireland—26 districts; Scotland—9 regions; Wales—8 counties.

Voting Qualification: Age 18.

PLACES OF INTEREST

Bath, England: resort city on the River Avon; one of the most elegant and architecturally distinguished of British cities; Georgian buildings; 16th-century abbey church; hot mineral springs.

Belfast, Northern Ireland: capital of Northern Ireland; port city; shopping, retail, educational, commercial, entertainment, and service center for Northern Ireland (*see* Belfast).

Caernarfon, Wales: in Gwynedd County; castle has been the site, since 1911, of the investiture of the prince of Wales.

Channel Islands: in English Channel off the northwest coast of France; famous for breeds of cattle that originated on them (*see* Channel Islands).

Cornwall: county in southwestern England jutting into the Atlantic Ocean; popular resort area; contains Land's End, the traditional southwestern extreme of Great Britain.

Fens: reclaimed marshland area of about 1,400 square miles (3,600 square kilometers) in eastern England; rivers and drainage channels throughout the region; rich agricultural area; nature reserves.

Giant's Causeway: striking natural formation on the northern coast of Northern Ireland; consists of thousands of columns of basalt rock.

Lake District: in Cumbria County, England; scenic region and national park; mountains, lakes, valleys.

Loch Lomond: on the southern edge of the Scottish Highlands; Scotland's largest lake; scenery ranges from rugged, glaciated mountains in the north to softer, well-wooded hills and islands in the south.

Lough Neagh: in east-central Northern Ireland; largest lake in the British Isles; oldest recorded artifacts of humans in Ireland have been recovered from one of the lake's bays.

Oxford, England: on the Thames River; home of Oxford University, one of the world's greatest educational institutions (*see* Oxford).

Parliament Square: in London; site of the Houses of Parliament and Westminster Abbey; the Parliament building has 1,100 rooms; the abbey, a Gothic church, is the site of the coronation of kings and queens.

Saint Andrews, Scotland: home of the Royal and Ancient Club, the world's ultimate authority on golf, founded in 1754; Old Course is the most famous of the four main golf courses.

Stonehenge: prehistoric monument near Salisbury, England; circular setting of large standing stones surrounded by an earthwork; built about 1800–1400 BC; assumed to have been constructed as a place of worship; thought to have been a type of astronomical clock or calendar for predicting the seasons (*see* Stonehenge).

Wight, Isle of : tourist resort in the English Channel; known for its beauty and pleasant climate; golf, yachting (*see* Wight, Isle of).

York Minster: in York, England; largest medieval church in England; built between the 13th and 15th centuries.

UNITED KINGDOM AND IRELAND

ENGLAND*

Abergavenny, 14,398	E	5
Abertillery, 28,351	E	5
Abingdon, 29,558	F	5
Accrington, 59,141	G	1
Aire (river)	F	4
Aldeburgh, 2,918	G	4
Alderney (isl.)	E	6
Aldershot, 222,157	F	5
Aldridge-Brownhills, 17,589	G	3
Alnwick, 7,188	F	3
Alton, 14,366	F	5
Altrincham, 39,693	G	2
Ambleside, 3,188	E	3
Andover, 30,932	F	5
Appleby, 2,401	E	3
Arundel, 2,788	F	5
Ashford, 45,962	G	5
Ashington, 28,116	F	3
Ashton-under-Lyne, 44,196	G	2
Avon (river)	F	4
Axminster, †4,594	E	5
Aylesbury, 52,914	F	5
Ayre (Isle of Man) (point)	D	3
Bacup, 14,099	G	1
Bakewell, 3,961	G	2
Banbury, 38,191	F	4
Banstead, 35,679	B	6
Barking, 149,930	C	5
Barnet, 292,441	B	5
Barnsley, 128,157	F	4
Barnstaple, 24,878	E	5
Barrow-in-Furness, 50,625	E	3
Barton-on-Humber, 8,524	F	4
Basildon, 95,338	G	5
Basingstoke, 73,492	F	5
Bath, 87,161	F	5
Battle, †5,141	G	5
Bebington, 62,236	F	2
Beccles, 10,815	G	4
Bedford, 77,014	F	4
Bedlington Sta.	E	3
Bedworth, 29,277	F	4
Belper, 17,426	F	4
Berwick-on-Tweed, 12,989	F	3
Beverley, 19,687	F	4
Bewdley, 8,752	F	3
Bexhill-on-Sea, 35,402	G	5
Bexley, 214,078	C	5
Bideford, 13,993	D	5
Biggleswade, 10,954	F	4
Birkenhead, 280,521	F	2
Birmingham, 920,398	G	3
Bishop Auckland, 23,898	E	3
Bishop's Castle, †1,405	E	4
Bishop's Stortford, 22,791	G	5
Blackburn, 110,254	G	1
Blackpool, 262,675	F	1
Blandford Forum, 7,310	E	5
Blaydon, 16,734	F	3
Bletchley, 38,273	F	4
Blyth, 35,056	F	3
Bodmin, 12,269	D	5
Bognor Regis, 53,175	F	5
Bollington, 6,628	G	2
Bolton, 143,921	G	2
Bootle, 70,610	F	2
Boston, 34,453	F	4
Bournemouth, 327,807	F	5
Brackley, 6,663	F	4
Bradford, 295,048	H	1
Braintree and Bocking, 31,139	G	5
Brandon and Byshottles, †17,996	F	3
Brent, 253,275	B	5
Brentwood, 51,643	C	5
Bridgwater, 31,011	E	5
Bridlington, 28,970	F	3
Bridport, 10,791	E	5
Brightlingsea, 7,297	G	5
Brighton, 137,985	F	5
Bristol, 387,977	E	5
Bristol (channel)	E	5
Bromley, 282,334	B	6
Bromsgrove, 25,177	G	3
Buckingham, 6,554	F	5
Bungay, 4,116	G	4
Burnley, 77,127	G	1
Burntwood, †26,075	G	2
Burton upon Trent, 59,595	G	2
Burtonwood, 4,593	G	2
Bury, 62,181	G	2
Bury Saint Edmunds, 31,178	G	4
Bushey, 15,760	B	5
Buxton, 20,282	G	2
Camborne-Redruth, 34,774	D	5
Cambridge, 106,673	G	4

Camden, 172,014	B	5
Cannock, 54,583	G	2
Canterbury, 36,507	G	5
Canvey Island, 35,338	G	5
Carlisle, 73,233	E	3
Caterham and Warlingham, 30,344	B	6
Channel (isls.), 133,000	E	6
Chard, 9,402	E	5
Chatham, 66,063	G	5
Cheadle and Gatley, 59,828	G	2
Chelmsford, 92,479	G	5
Cheltenham, 88,687	F	5
Chertsey, 10,247	B	6
Cheshunt	B	5
Chester, 92,102	F	2
Chester-le-Street, 34,975	E	3
Chesterfield, 74,180	F	4
Chichester, 27,241	F	5
Chigwell, 9,866	C	5
Chippenham, 21,532	F	5
Chorley, 33,708	G	2
Christchurch, 33,529	F	5
Cirencester, 13,783	F	5
Clacton-on-Sea, 40,313	G	5
Cleethorpes, 33,347	F	4
Clitheroe, 13,729	G	1
Cockermouth, 7,174	E	3
Colchester, 88,847	G	5
Colne, 19,173	G	1
Colne (river)	B	5
Colne Valley	G	2
Congleton, 23,590	G	2
Coventry, 322,573	F	4
Cowes, 16,278	F	5
Crediton, 6,198	E	5
Crewe, 59,352	G	2
Crewkerne, 6,070	E	5
Cromer, 7,173	G	4
Crosby, 53,853	F	2
Croydon, 300,508	B	6
Cuckfield, 2,909	F	5
Darlington, 86,358	F	3
Dartford, 63,064	C	5
Dartmouth, 5,581	E	5
Darwen, 31,094	G	1
Deal, 26,548	G	5
Dee (river)	E	4
Derby, 220,681	F	4
Derwent (river)	F	3
Devizes, 12,707	F	5
Devonport	D	5
Dewsbury, 50,046	H	2
Diss, 5,541	G	4
Don (river)	F	4
Doncaster, 133,178	F	4
Dorchester, 14,225	E	5
Dorking, 14,830	F	5
Douglas (Isle of Man), 19,944	D	3
Dover, 34,304	G	5
Dover (strait)	G	5
Downham Market, 4,678	G	4
Driffield, 9,100	F	4
Dudley, 187,367	G	3
Dungeness (prom.)	G	5
Dunstable, 48,629	F	5
Durham, 41,178	F	3
Ealing, 279,846	B	5
East Dereham, 11,910	G	4
East Grinstead, 24,183	G	5
East Retford, 19,380	F	4
Eastbourne, 90,653	G	5
Eastleigh, 58,914	F	5
Ebbw Vale, 21,145	E	5
Eccles, 37,792	G	2
Eden (river)	E	3
Egham, 21,810	B	5
Ellesmere Port, 65,803	F	2
Ely, 9,122	G	4
Enfield, 258,770	B	5
English (channel)	E	6
Epping, 10,409	C	5
Epsom and Ewell, 66,872	B	6
Esher, 46,847	B	6
Eston, 37,633	F	3
Eton, †3,559	F	5
Evesham, 15,280	F	4
Exeter, 91,938	E	5
Exmouth, 28,661	E	5
Eye, 1,731	G	4
Falmouth, 18,548	D	5
Fareham, 88,609	F	5
Farnham, 34,852	F	5
Faversham, 15,985	G	5
Felixstowe, 24,461	G	5
Filey, 5,213	F	3
Flamborough (head)	G	3
Fleetwood, 28,136	E	4

Folkestone, 43,998	G	5
Frinton and Walton, 12,689	G	5
Frome, 19,817	E	5
Fulwood	G	1
Gainsborough, 20,593	F	4
Gateshead, 91,893	F	3
Glastonbury, 6,807	E	5
Glossop, 30,040	G	2
Gloucester, 108,150	E	5
Godalming, 18,882	F	5
Goole, 19,508	F	4
Gosport, 70,705	F	4
Grantham, 31,095	F	4
Grasmere	E	3
Gravesend, 53,638	C	5
Great Torrington, 4,130	D	5
Great Yarmouth, 62,429	G	4
Greenwich, 212,987	B	5
Grimsby, 92,429	F	4
Guernsey (isl.), 53,268	E	6
Guildford, 56,652	F	5
Hackney, 180,434	B	5
Halesowen, 57,532	G	3
Halifax, 77,354	G	1
Halstead	G	5
Haltemprice, 9,308	F	4
Hammersmith, 148,447	B	5
Haringey, 203,553	B	5
Harrogate, 64,915	F	4
Harrow, 195,478	B	5
Hartlepool, 92,133	F	3
Harwich, 17,329	G	5
Haslemere, 10,617	F	5
Hastings, 76,678	G	5
Havering, 239,344	C	5
Hebden Royd, †8,960	G	1
Helston, 8,656	D	5
Hemel Hempstead, 80,340	F	5
Hereford, 48,976	E	4
Hertford, 21,606	F	5
Hexham, 9,177	E	3
High Wycombe, 107,824	F	5
Hillingdon, 230,159	B	5
Hinckley, 35,611	F	4
Hitchin, 33,744	F	5
Holbeach, †4,689	F	4
Holsworthy, 1,647	D	5
Honiton, 6,627	E	5
Horncastle, 4,247	F	4
Hornsea, 7,301	F	4
Horsham, 38,565	F	5
Hounslow, 200,829	B	5
Hove, 67,137	F	5
Hoylake, 24,620	F	2
Huddersfield, 148,544	G	2
Hull, 325,485	F	4
Humber (river)	G	4
Hunstanton, 4,069	F	4
Huntingdon, 14,648	F	4
Hyde, 30,551	G	2
Hythe, 16,655	G	5
Ilfracombe, 10,424	D	5
Ilkeston, 34,840	F	4
Ipswich, 131,131	G	4
Irish (sea)		
Islington, 160,890	B	5
Jarrow, 31,213	F	3
Jersey (isl.), 72,970	E	6
Keighley, 49,267	H	1
Kendal, 24,203	E	3
Kenilworth, 18,917	G	3
Kensington and Chelsea, 138,837	B	5
Keswick, 5,645	E	3
Kettering, 45,389	F	4
Kidderminster, 50,746	G	3
King's Lynn, 37,966	G	4
Kingston-upon-Hull (Hull), 325,485	F	4
Kingston-upon-Thames, 132,547	B	6
Kington, 2,067	E	4
Kirkby, 52,609	F	2
Kirkham, 8,537	F	1
Knaresborough, 12,994	F	4
Knutsford, 13,751	G	2
Lambeth, 246,426	B	5
Lancaster, 44,447	E	3
Land's End (prom.)	D	5
Launceston, 6,092	D	5
Leamington, 57,347	F	4
Leatherhead, 42,629	B	6
Ledbury, 5,032	E	5
Leeds, 448,528	H	1
Leek, 18,535	E	4
Leicester, 328,835	F	4
Leigh, 42,929	G	2
Leominster, 8,681	E	4
Lewes, 14,971	F	5
Lewisham, 231,324	B	5

Leyland, 37,151	F	1
Lichfield, 25,738	G	2
Lincoln, 81,305	F	4
Liskeard, 6,335	D	5
Litherland, 21,918	F	2
Littlehampton, 46,632	F	5
Liverpool, 510,306	F	2
Lizard (head)	D	6
Loftus, 5,640	F	3
London (Greater)		
(capital), 6,713,165	B	5
Longridge, 7,170	G	1
Loughborough, 46,122	F	4
Louth, 13,304	F	4
Lowestoft, 59,875	G	4
Ludlow, 7,580	E	4
Lundy (isl.), †52	D	5
Luton, 164,743	F	5
Lyme (bay)	E	5
Lyme Regis, 4,801	E	5
Lymington, 11,955	F	5
Lymm, 10,024	G	2
Lynton, †2,075	E	5
Lytham St. Anne's, 40,136	F	1
Macclesfield, 48,071	G	2
Maidenhead, 60,461	F	5
Maidstone, 87,068	G	5
Maldon, 14,754	G	5
Malton, 4,136	F	3
Malvern, 30,470	E	4
Man (isl.), 64,679	D	3
Manchester, 448,604	G	2
Mangotsfield, 28,758	F	5
Mansfield, 155,466	F	4
March, 14,236	G	4
Margate, 54,980	G	5
Market Drayton, 9,047	E	4
Marlborough, 5,411	F	5
Marple, 18,684	G	2
Maryport, 9,890	E	3
Matlock, 13,867	F	4
Melksham, 13,300	E	5
Melton Mowbray, 23,592	F	4
Mersey (river)	F	2
Merton, 166,100	B	6
Middleton, 51,437	G	2
Middlewich, 8,203	G	2
Minehead, 11,211	E	5
Monmouth	E	5
Morecambe and Heysham, 42,057	E	3
Morpeth, 14,496	F	3
Mounts (bay)	D	6
Nantwich, 12,023	G	2
Nelson, 30,494	G	1
Nene (river)	F	4
Neston, 14,979	F	2
New Mills, 8,454	G	2
New Windsor	F	5
Newark, †24,246	F	4
Newbury, 31,894	F	5
Newcastle	E	4
Newcastle-on-Tyne, 203,591	E	3
Newham, 209,494	B	5
Newhaven, 10,773	F	5
Newmarket, 16,129	G	4
Newport, 116,658	E	5
Newport (Isle of Wight), 118,594	F	5
Newquay, 15,209	D	5
Newton Abbot, 20,744	E	5
North Somercotes, †1,327	G	4
North Walsham, 7,941	G	4
Northallerton, 13,858	F	3
Northampton, 155,694	F	4
Northfleet, 21,413	C	5
Northwich, 32,832	G	2
Norwich, 173,286	G	4
Nottingham, 598,867	F	4
Nuneaton, 60,948	F	4
Oakengates, 26,907	E	4
Oakham, 8,035	F	4
Okehampton, 4,213	D	5
Oldham, 107,830	G	2
Ormskirk, 22,715	F	2
Oswestry, 13,264	E	4
Ottery Saint Mary, 4,034	E	5
Ouse (river)	G	4
Oxford, 119,909	F	5
Padstow, 2,447	D	5
Peel (Isle of Man)	D	3
Penrith, 12,290	E	3
Penzance, 19,210	D	5
Peterborough, 114,733	F	4
Plymouth, 242,560	E	5
Poole, 124,974	F	5
Portsmouth, 413,143	F	5
Potters Bar, 22,681	B	5
Poulton le Fylde, 18,604	F	1

*All population figures are taken from the latest census or estimate available. †Population of parish

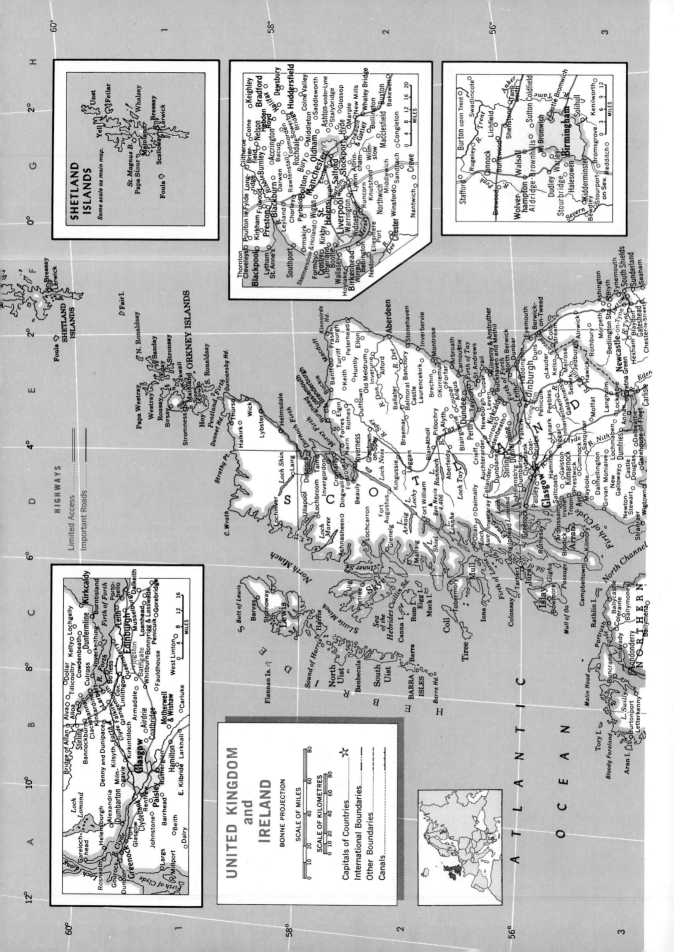

UNITED KINGDOM and IRELAND

BONNE PROJECTION

SCALE OF MILES

SCALE OF KILOMETRES

Capitals of Countries............
International Boundaries............
Other Boundaries............
Canals............

HIGHWAYS
Limited Access ============
Important Roads ------------

SHETLAND ISLANDS

Same scale as main map.

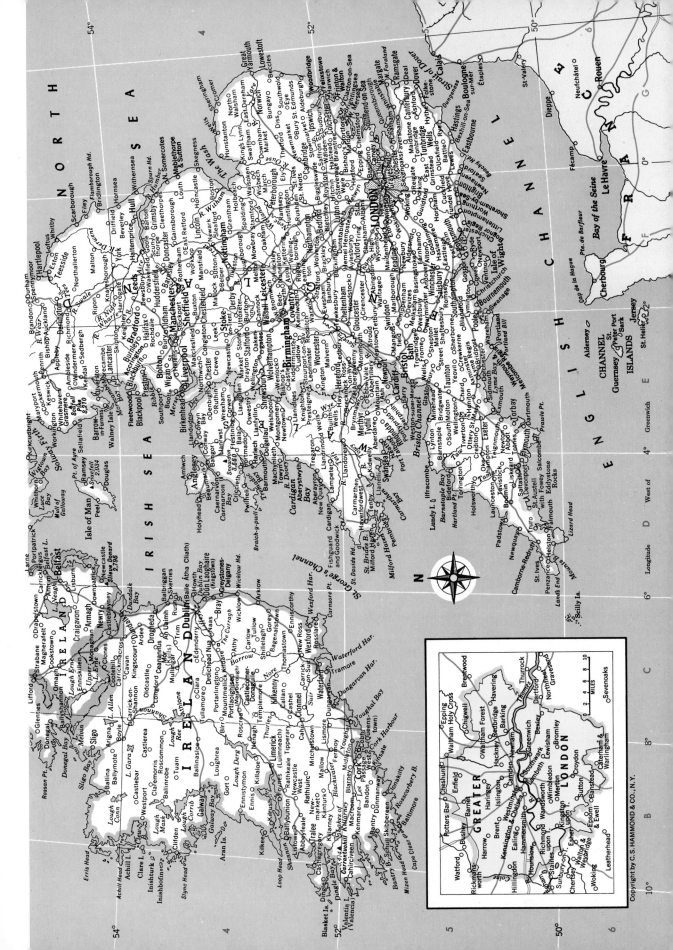

Preston, 168,405	F	1
Queensborough	G	5
Ramsey, 5,934	F	4
Ramsey (Isle of Man), 5,934	D	3
Ramsgate, 37,398	G	5
Rawtenstall, 21,437	F	2
Reading, 198,341	F	5
Redbridge, 228,542	C	5
Redditch, 61,875	G	3
Reigate, 48,913	F	5
Richmond, 7,700	E	3
Richmond-upon-Thames, 159,693	B	5
Rickmansworth, 15,948	A	5
Ripon, 13,232	F	3
Rochdale, 97,942	G	2
Rochester, 24,402	G	5
Romsey, 15,039	F	5
Ross-on-Wye, 8,430	E	5
Rothbury, †1,733	E	3
Rotherham, 123,312	F	4
Royston, 12,993	F	4
Rugby, 59,723	F	4
Rugeley, 23,810	G	2
Runcorn, 64,216	G	2
Rushden, 22,434	F	4
Ryde, 19,843	F	5
Rye, 4,299	G	5
Saddleworth, †21,839	G	2
Saffron Walden, 12,058	G	4
Saint Albans, 77,187	F	5
Saint Austell with Fowey, 20,585	D	5
Saint Helens, 172,890	F	2
Saint Helier (Jersey I.)	E	6
Saint Ives, 12,278	G	4
Saint Ives, 10,985	D	5
Saint Neots, 12,566	F	4
Saint Peter Port (Guernsey I.)	E	6
Salcombe, 2,193	D	5
Salford, 98,343	G	2
Salisbury, 37,831	F	5
Saltash, 12,460	D	5
Sandbach, 13,753	G	2
Sark (isl.)	E	6
Scafell Pike (mt.)	E	3
Scarborough, 38,048	F	3
Scilly (isls.)	C	6
Scunthorpe, 79,684	F	4
Seaford, 16,652	G	5
Seaham, 21,884	F	3
Sedbergh, †1,665	E	3
Sevenoaks, 24,588	C	6
Severn (river)	E	5
Shaftesbury, 4,951	E	5
Sheffield, 477,257	F	4
Shenstone, †2,042	G	3
Shepton Mallet, 6,306	E	5
Sherborne, 7,614	E	5
Sheringham, 7,138	G	4
Shoreham-by-Sea	F	5
Shrewsbury, 59,169	E	4
Sidmouth, 11,434	E	5
Skegness, 13,127	G	4
Skelmersdale and Holland, 42,609	F	2
Skipton, 13,185	F	4
Sleaford, 8,348	F	4
Snaefell (Isle of Man) (mt.)	D	3
Solihull, 94,613	G	3
South Molton, 3,611	E	5
South Shields, 87,125	F	3
Southampton, 214,802	F	5
Southend-on-Sea, 156,969	G	5
Southport, 90,962	F	2
Southwark, 211,840	B	5
Southwold, 3,877	G	4
Sowerby Bridge, 11,290	F	2
Spalding, 18,340	F	4
Spennymoor, 18,643	F	3
Spurn (head)	G	4
Stafford, 62,242	G	2
Staines, 52,815	B	5
Stalybridge, 23,668	G	2
Stamford, 16,393	F	4
Stevenage, 75,367	F	5
Stockport, 136,792	G	2
Stoke-on-Trent, 275,168	E	4
Stone, 12,203	E	4
Stour (river)	G	4
Stourbridge, 55,499	G	3
Stourport-on-Severn, 17,933	G	3
Stowmarket, 11,050	G	4
Stratford-on-Avon, 21,732	F	4
Street, 9,543	E	5
Stroud, 38,228	E	5
Sudbury, 17,911	G	4
Sunbury-on-Thames, 28,436	B	6
Sunderland, 195,896	F	3
Sutton, 167,100	B	6

Sutton Coldfield, 103,097	G	3
Sutton-in-Ashfield, 39,622	F	4
Swadlincote, 33,739	G	2
Swaffham, 4,798	G	4
Swale (river)	F	3
Swanage, 9,640	F	5
Swindon, 128,493	E	5
Tamar (river)	D	5
Tame (river)	G	3
Tamworth, 63,553	G	3
Taunton, 48,863	E	5
Tavistock, 8,798	D	5
Taw (river)	D	5
Tees (river)	F	3
Teesside, 382,690	F	3
Tetbury, †4,498	E	5
Tewkesbury, 9,568	F	4
Thames (river)	F	5
Thetford, 19,593	G	4
Thornton Cleveleys, 26,787	F	1
Thurrock, 127,105	C	5
Tiverton, 14,982	E	5
Todmorden, 11,972	G	2
Tonbridge, 34,491	G	5
Torbay, 98,311	E	5
Totnes, 6,247	E	5
Trent (river)	F	4
Tring, 10,738	F	5
Trowbridge, 27,476	E	5
Truro, 18,557	D	5
Tunbridge Wells, 58,141	G	5
Tyne (river)	F	3
Tynemouth, 17,783	F	3
Uckfield, †7,853	G	5
Ulverston, 11,970	E	3
Uttoxeter, 10,013	F	4
Ventnor, 6,458	F	5
Wakefield, 75,838	F	4
Wallasey, 62,531	F	2
Walsall, 178,852	G	3
Walsoken, †1,084	G	4
Waltham Forest, 215,947	B	5
Waltham Holy Cross	B	5
Walton and Weybridge, 50,402	B	6
Wandsworth, 254,898	B	5
Wantage, 9,872	F	5
Ware, 15,471	F	5
Wareham, 2,798	E	5
Warley	G	3
Warminster 15,222	E	5
Warrington, 130,333	F	2
Warwick, 21,990	F	4
Wash, The (bay)	G	4
Watford, 110,244	B	5
Wear (river)	F	3
Welland (river)	F	4
Wellingborough, 38,772	F	4
Wellington, 10,567	E	5
Wellington	E	4
Wells, 8,374	E	5
Wells	G	4
Welwyn	F	5
Wenlock	E	4
West Bromwich, 154,531	G	3
West Mersea, 5,292	G	5
Westbury, 9,545	E	5
Westminster, 191,098	B	5
Weston-super-Mare, 62,261	E	5
Weymouth and Melcombe Regis, 39,712	E	5
Whaley Bridge, 3,744	G	2
Wharfe (river)	F	3
Whitby, 13,377	F	3
Whitehaven, 27,925	E	3
Whitstable, 26,451	G	5
Widnes, 55,926	F	2
Wigan, 88,901	G	2
Wight (isl.), 118,594	F	5
Wilmslow, 28,933	G	2
Wimbledon	B	5
Winchester, 35,664	F	5
Windermere, 7,956	E	3
Windsor (New Windsor)	F	5
Winsford, 26,532	G	2
Wirral, 339,494	F	2
Wisbech, 23,191	G	4
Withernsea, 6,013	G	4
Woking, 81,773	B	6
Wokingham, 30,773	F	5
Wolverhampton, 265,631	G	3
Wolverton, 18,696	F	4
Woodbridge, 9,772	G	4
Woodstock, 3,143	F	5
Worcester, 76,350	E	4
Workington, 26,123	E	3
Worksop, 34,993	F	4
Worthing, 92,056	F	5

Wye (river)	E	4
Yare (river)	G	4
Yeovil, 36,597	E	5
York, 126,377	F	4

IRELAND

Achill (isl.), 3,101	A	4
Allen (lake)	B	3
An Uaimh, 4,124	C	4
Aran (isl.), 803	B	3
Aran (isls.)	B	4
Arigna	B	3
Arklow, 9,444	C	4
Athlone, 9,444	C	4
Athy, 4,920	C	4
Bagenalstown, 2,510	C	4
Baile Atha Cliath (Dublin) (cap.), 525,882	C	4
Balbriggan, 5,582	C	4
Ballina, 6,856	B	3
Ballinasloe, 6,374	B	4
Ballybunion, 1,364	B	4
Ballymote, 1,098	B	3
Ballyshannon, 2,675	B	3
Baltimore, 234	B	4
Bandon, 2,055	B	5
Bantry, 2,862	B	5
Barrow (river)	C	4
Birr, 3,679	B	4
Blackwater (river)	B	4
Blarney, 1,980	B	5
Blasket (isls.)	A	4
Boyle, 1,737	B	3
Bray, 22,853	C	4
Buncrana, 3,141	C	3
Cahir, 2,120	B	4
Cahirciveen, 1,428	A	5
Callan, 1,431	C	4
Carlow, 11,722	C	4
Carrantuohill (mt.)	B	5
Carrick-on-Shannon, 2,037	B	3
Carrick-on-Suir, 5,566	C	4
Carrickmacross, 1,768	C	3
Cashel, 2,436	C	4
Castlebar, 6,409	B	4
Castleblayney, 2,425	C	3
Castlecomer-Donaguile, 1,548	C	4
Castlegregory, 181	B	4
Castlerea, 1,874	B	4
Cavan, 3,240	C	4
Ceanannus Mór, 2,623	C	4
Clara, 2,596	C	4
Clare (isl.), 127	A	4
Claremorris, 2,036	B	4
Clear (cape)	B	5
Clew (bay)	B	4
Clifden, 796	B	4
Clonakilty, 2,698	B	5
Clones, 2,329	C	3
Clonmel, 12,407	C	4
Cobh, 6,587	B	5
Conn (lake)	B	3
Cootehill, 1,554	C	3
Cork, 136,344	B	5
Corrib (lake)	B	4
Curragh (racecourse)	C	4
Derg (lake)	B	4
Dingle, 1,358	A	4
Donegal, 1,956	B	3
Donegal (bay)	B	3
Drogheda, 23,247	C	4
Droichead Nua, 5,780	C	4
Dublin (capital), 525,882	C	4
Dún Laoghaire, 54,496	D	4
Dundalk, 25,663	C	4
Dungarvan, 6,631	C	4
Dunmanway, 1,493	B	5
Edenderry, 3,452	C	4
Ennis, 6,223	B	4
Enniscorthy, 5,014	C	4
Ennistymon, 1,104	B	4
Erris (head)	A	3
Fermoy, 3,106	B	4
Foyle (lake)	C	3
Foynes, 775	B	4
Galway, 37,835	B	4
Gara (lake)	B	4
Glenties, 843	B	3
Gorey, 2,588	C	4
Gort, 1,095	B	4
Greystones-Delgany, 7,442	D	4
Howth	D	4
Inishbofin (isl.), 195	A	4
Inishturk (isl.), 7	A	4
Irish (sea)	D	4
Kanturk, 1,976	B	4

Kells (Ceanannus Mór), 2,623	C	4
Kenmare, 1,123	B	5
Kildare, 4,016	C	4
Kilkee, 1,389	B	4
Kilkenny, 9,466	C	4
Killaloe, 1,022	B	4
Killarney, 7,693	B	4
Killarney (lakes)	B	4
Kilrush, 2,753	B	4
Kingscourt, 1,267	C	4
Kingstown (Dún Laoghaire), 54,496	D	4
Kinsale, 1,765	B	5
Lee (river)	B	5
Letterkenny, 6,444	C	3
Liffey (river)	C	4
Lifford, 1,461	C	3
Limerick, 60,736	B	4
Lismore, 919	B	4
Listowel, 3,542	B	4
Longford, 3,998	B	4
Loughrea, 3,377	B	4
Luimneach (Limerick), 60,736	B	4
Macroom, 2,495	B	5
Malin (head)	C	3
Mallow, 6,572	B	4
Maryborough, 4,049	C	4
Mask (lake)	B	4
Midleton, 3,214	B	5
Mitchelstown, 3,106	B	4
Mizen (head)	B	5
Monaghan, 6,177	C	3
Mountmellick, 2,954	C	4
Mullingar, 7,854	C	4
Naas, 8,345	C	4
Nenagh, 5,717	B	4
New Ross, 5,386	C	4
Newcastle West, 3,380	B	4
Newmarket, 1,025	B	4
Oldcastle, 894	C	4
Passage West, 3,584	B	5
Portarlington, 3,386	C	4
Portlaoighise (Maryborough), 4,049	C	4
Queenstown (Cobh), 6,587	B	5
Rathkeale, 1,879	B	4
Rathluirc, 2,874	B	4
Ree (lake)	B	4
Roscommon, 1,673	B	4
Roscrea, 4,201	B	4
Rosscarbery (bay)	B	5
Rosslare, 779	C	4
Rush, 3,864	C	4
Schull, 502	B	5
Shannon (river)	C	4
Shillelagh, 299	C	4
Skerries, 5,793	D	4
Skibbereen, 2,130	B	5
Sligo, 17,232	B	3
Templemore, 2,425	C	4
Thomastown, 1,308	C	4
Thurles, 7,352	B	4
Tipperary, 4,984	B	4
Tralee, 16,495	B	4
Tramore, 5,635	C	4
Trim, 2,144	C	4
Tuam, 4,366	B	4
Tullamore, 7,901	C	4
Tullow, 2,281	C	4
Valentia (Valencia) (isl.), 718	A	5
Waterford, 38,473	C	4
Westport, 3,378	B	4
Wexford, 11,417	C	4
Wicklow, 5,178	C	4
Youghal, 5,870	B	5

NORTHERN IRELAND

Antrim, 22,342	C	3
Armagh, 12,700	C	3
Ballycastle, 3,284	C	3
Ballymena, 28,166	C	3
Ballymoney, 5,679	C	3
Belfast, 295,223	D	3
Carrickfergus, 17,633	D	3
Coleraine, 15,967	C	3
Cookstown, 7,649	C	3
Craigavon, 10,195	C	3
Downpatrick, 8,245	D	3
Draperstown, 1,300	C	3
Enniskillen, 10,429	C	3
Erne (lake)	C	3
Foyle (inlet)	C	3
Larne, 18,224	D	3
Limavady, 8,015	C	3
Lisburn, 40,391	D	3
Londonderry, 62,697	C	3
Magherafelt, 5,044	C	3
Melvin (lake)	B	3

*All population figures are taken from the latest census or estimate available. †Population of parish.

Neagh (lake) C 3
Newcastle, 6,246 D 3
Newry, 19,426 C 3
Omagh, 14,627 C 3
Portrush, 5,114 C 3
Rathlin (isl.) C 3
Slieve Donard (mt.) D 3
Strabane, 10,340 C 3
Upper Erne (lake) C 3

SCOTLAND*

Aberdeen, 203,612 F 2
Aberfeldy, 1,613 D 2
Achnasheen D 2
Airdrie, 45,747 B 1
Alexandria, †26,329 A 1
Alford E 2
Alloa, 26,428 B 1
Alva, 4,874 B 1
Alyth, 2,289 E 2
Annan, 8,314 E 3
Arbroath, 24,119 E 2
Ardee C 4
Ardrossan, 11,421 D 3
Armadale, 9,527 B 1
Arran (isl.) 3,700 D 3
Auchterarder, 2,904 D 2
Awe (lake) D 2
Ayr, 49,522 D 3
Ballater, 1,218 E 2
Balmoral Castle E 2
Banchory, 4,890 E 2
Banff, 3,938 E 2
Bannockburn B 1
Barra (isl.), 1,339 C 2
Barrhead, 18,418 A 1
Barvas C 1
Bathgate, 14,477 C 1
Beith, †5,742 A 1
Benbecula (isl.) C 2
Biggar, 1,938 E 3
Birsay E 1
Blair-Atholl E 2
Blairgowrie and Battray, 7,184 E 2
Bo'ness, 14,641 C 1
Bowmore C 3
Braemar E 2
Brechin, 7,692 E 2
Bressay (isl.) G 1
Bridge of Allan, 4,694 B 1
Brodick D 3
Buckhaven and Methil, 18,265 E 2
Buckie, 7,839 E 2
Burghead, 1,380 E 2
Burntisland, 5,865 C 1
Callander, 2,520 D 2
Campbeltown, 6,098 C 3
Canna (isl.) C 2
Carluke, †11,674 B 1
Carnoustie, 9,225 E 2
Castle Douglas, 3,521 D 3
Clackmannan, 3,258 B 1
Clyde (firth) D 3
Clyde (river) E 3
Clydebank, 51,854 A 1
Coatbridge, 50,957 B 1
Coldstream, 1,645 E 3
Coll (isl.) C 2
Colonsay (isl.) C 2
Coupar Angus, 2,186 E 2
Cowdenbeath, 12,272 C 1
Crail, 1,181 E 2
Crieff, 5,477 E 2
Cromarty D 2
Cuillin (sound) C 2
Culross B 1
Cumnock and Holmhead, 9,650 D 3
Cupar, 6,637 E 2
Dalbeattie, 3,917 E 3
Dalkeith, 11,255 C 1
Dalmally D 2
Dalmellington, †1,425 D 3
Dalry, †5,856 A 1
Dee (river) E 2
Denny and Dunipace, 23,158 B 1
Dingwall, 4,842 D 2
Dollar, 2,486 B 1
Don (river) E 2
Dornoch D 2
Dufftown, 1,643 E 2
Dumbarton, 23,430 A 1
Dumfries, 32,100 E 3
Dunbar, 6,035 E 2
Dunblane, 6,855 D 2
Duncansby (head) E 1
Dundee, 174,375 E 2
Dunfermline, 52,227 C 1
Dunnet (head) E 1
Dunoon, 9,369 A 1
Duns, 2,253 E 3
Eday (isl.) E 1
Edinburgh, 419,187 C 1
Eigg (isl.) C 2
Elgin, 18,908 E 2
Ellon, 6,319 E 2
Eyemouth, 3,398 F 3
Fair (isl.) F 1
Falkirk, 36,880 B 1
Fauldhouse, †5,036 C 1
Fetlar (isl.) H 1
Flannan (isls.) C 1
Forfar, 12,770 E 2
Forres, 8,354 E 2
Fort Augustus D 2
Fort William, 11,061 D 2
Forth (firth), 2,890 E 2
Forth (river) C 1
Forth and Clyde (canal) B 1
Fortrose, 1,332 D 2
Foula (isl.) G 1
Fraserburgh, 12,512 E 2
Fyne (firth) D 2
Galashiels, 12,244 E 3
Galloway, Mull of (prom.) D 3
Galston, 5,311 D 3
Garelochhead, †2,072 A 1
Gatehouse-of-Fleet E 3
Gigha (passage) D 3
Girvan, 7,795 D 3
Glasgow, 765,030 B 1
Gleneig D 2
Gourock, 11,203 A 1
Grangemouth, 21,599 B 1
Grantown-on-Spey, 2,034 E 2
Greenock, 59,016 A 1
Gretna Green, 2,811 E 3
Haddington, 8,139 E 3
Halkirk E 1
Hamilton, 51,718 B 1
Hawick, 16,364 E 3
Hebrides (isls.), 44,344 C 2
Helensburgh, 16,621 A 1
Helmsdale E 1
Hoy (isl.), 519 E 1
Huntly, 3,952 E 2
Inner (sound) D 2
Innerleithen, 2,468 E 3
Inveraray D 2
Inverbervie, 1,799 E 2
Invergordon, 4,067 D 2
Inverkeithing, 5,770 C 1
Inverness, 40,010 D 2
Inverurie, 7,680 E 2
Iona (isl.), 268 C 2
Irvine, 32,968 D 3
Islay (isl.) C 3
Jedburgh, 4,069 E 3
Johnstone, 42,669 A 1
Jura (isl.) D 3
Keith, 4,407 E 2
Kelso, 5,648 E 3
Kilmarnock, 52,083 D 3
Kilmory D 3
Kilrenny and Anstruther, 2,962 E 2
Kilsyth, 10,538 B 1
Kincardine, †3,166 B 1
Kingussie, 1,229 D 2
Kinnairds (head) F 2
Kinross, 3,496 E 2
Kirkcaldy, 46,522 C 1
Kirkcudbright, 3,427 E 3
Kirkintilloch, 33,148 B 1
Kirkwall, 5,995 E 1
Kirriemuir, 5,326 E 2
Laggan D 2
Lairg D 1
Lanark, 9,806 E 3
Langholm, 2,615 E 3
Larbert B 1
Largs, 9,905 A 1
Larkhall, †16,216 B 1
Lauder E 3
Laurencekirk, 1,329 E 2
Leith C 1
Lerwick, 7,561 G 1
Leven, 8,624 E 2
Lewis and Harris, 23,390 C 1
Linlithgow, 9,543 B 1
Linnhe (firth) D 2
Little Minch (sound) C 2
Livingston, 38,954 C 1
Loanhead, 6,159 C 1
Lochbroom D 2
Lochcarron D 2
Lochgelly, 7,334 C 1
Lochgilphead, 2,461 D 2
Lochinver D 1
Lochmaben, 1,713 E 3
Lochy (lake) D 2
Lockerbie. 3,561 E 3
Lomond (lake) A 1
Long (firth) A 1
Lorne (firth) D 2
Lossiemouth and Branderburgh, 6,847 E 2
Luce (bay) D 3
Lybster E 1
Macduff, 3,887 E 2
Mainland (isl.), 14,279 E 1
Mallaig D 2
Maree (lake) D 2
Maybole, 4,798 D 3
Melrose, 2,345 D 3
Millport, 1,472 A 1
Milngavie, 12,067 B 1
Minch, The (sound) C 2
Moffat, 2,051 E 3
Moniaive D 3
Montrose, 12,325 E 2
Moray (firth) D 2
Motherwell and Wishaw, 30,676 B 1
Muck (isl.) C 2
Mull (isl.), 2,605 D 2
Musselburgh, 19,081 C 1
Nairn, 7,705 E 2
Ness (lake) D 2
Nevis (mt.) D 2
New Galloway D 3
Newburgh, 2,002 E 2
Newton-Stewart, 3,246 D 3
North Berwick, 5,162 E 2
North Minch (sound) D 1
North Ronaldsay (isl.) E 1
North Uist (isl.), †1,454 C 2
Oa, Mull of (prom.) C 3
Oban, 8,111 D 2
Old Meldrum, 1,356 E 2
Orkney (isls.), 19,056 E 1
Paisley, 84,954 A 1
Papa Stour (isl.) G 1
Papa Westray (isl.) E 1
Peebles, 6,692 E 3
Penicuik, 17,607 C 1
Pentland (firth) E 1
Perth, 43,010 E 2
Peterhead, 17,085 E 2
Pitlochry, 2,621 E 2
Port Glasgow, 22,580 A 1
Portobello C 1
Portpatrick D 3
Portree, †1,505 C 2
Prestwick, 13,599 D 3
Queensferry, 7,540 C 1
Rannoch (lake) D 2
Renfrew, 21,458 A 1
Rosneath, †1,439 A 1
Rothes, 1,425 E 2
Rothesay, 5,455 D 3
Rousay (isl.) E 1
Rum (isl.) C 2
Rutherglen B 1
Saint Andrews, 11,369 E 2
Saint Magnus (bay) G 1
Saltcoats, 12,834 D 3
Sanday (isl.) E 1
Sanquhar, 2,082 E 3
Scapa Flow (chan.) E 1
Selkirk, 5,437 E 3
Shetland (isls.), 27,277 G 1
Shiel (lake) D 2
Shin (lake) D 1
Skye (isl.), 8,139 C 2
Solway (firth) E 3
South Ronaldsay (isl.) E 1
South Uist (isl.), †2,223 C 2
Spey (river) E 2
Stirling, 38,842 B 1
Stonehaven, 7,922 E 2
Stornoway, 8,638 C 1
Stranraer, 10,873 D 3
Strathy (point) D 1
Stromness, 1,832 E 1
Stronsay (isl.) E 1
Tain, 3,486 D 2
Tay (firth) E 2
Tay (river) E 2
Tayport, 3,029 E 2
Thurso, 8,896 E 1
Tillicoultry, 6,161 B 1
Tiree (isl.) C 2
Tobermory C 2
Troon, 14,233 D 3
Turriff, 3,683 E 2
Tweed (river) E 3
Uig C 2
Ullapool, †1,146 D 2
Unst (isl.) H 1
West Linton C 1
Westray (isl.) E 1
Whalsay (isl.) H 1
Whitburn, 12,610 C 1
Whithorn, 983 D 3
Wick, 7,900 E 1
Wigtown, 1,015 D 3
Wrath (cape) D 1
Yell (isl.) G 1

WALES*

Aberayron, 1,445 D 4
Aberdare, 31,684 E 5
Aberystwyth, 11,170 D 4
Amlwch, 3,418 D 4
Anglesey (isl.) D 4
Bala, 1,852 E 4
Bangor, 13,002 D 4
Barmouth, 2,142 D 4
Barry, 46,520 E 5
Beaumaris, 1,450 D 4
Brecknock E 5
Bristol (chan.) E 5
Brynmawr, 5,537 E 5
Builth Wells, 2,253 E 4
Caernarvon, 9,431 D 4
Caernarvon (bay) D 4
Caerphilly, 39,065 E 5
Cardiff, 266,267 E 5
Cardigan, 3,842 D 4
Cardigan (bay) D 4
Carmarthen, 14,491 D 5
Chepstow, 12,457 E 5
Colwyn Bay, 27,683 E 4
Conway, 13,462 E 4
Corwen, †2,187 E 4
Criccieth, 1,577 D 4
Dee (river) E 4
Denbigh, 7,783 E 4
Dolgellau, 2,318 E 4
Dovey (river) D 4
Ffestiniog, 5,414 E 4
Fishguard and Goodwick, 4,935 D 5
Harlech, †1,356 E 4
Haverfordwest, 13,871 D 5
Hay, 1,302 E 4
Holyhead, 12,652 D 4
Irish (sea) D 4
Kidwelly, 2,680 D 5
Knighton, 2,761 E 4
Lampeter, 1,976 D 4
Llandovery, 1,695 D 5
Llandrindod Wells, 4,438 E 4
Llandudno, 14,372 E 4
Llanelli, 24,009 D 5
Llanfyllin, 1,210 E 4
Llangollen, 3,072 E 4
Llanidloes, 2,418 E 4
Llanrwst, 2,946 E 4
Machynlleth, 1,998 D 4
Merthyr Tydfil, 39,483 E 5
Milford Haven, 13,927 D 5
Montgomery, 1,035 E 4
Mountain Ash, 23,547 E 5
Neath, 19,521 E 5
New Quay, 775 D 4
Newtown, 8,961 E 4
Pembroke, 15,576 D 5
Pontypridd, 33,128 E 5
Port Talbot, 40,261 E 5
Portmadoc D 4
Presteigne, 1,501 E 4
Pwllheli, 4,003 D 4
Rhondda, 71,611 E 5
Ruthin, 4,450 E 4
Saint Brides (bay) D 5
Saint Davids (head) D 5
Saint George's (chan.) D 4
Snowdon (mt.) D 4
Swansea, 282,605 D 5
Teifi (river) D 4
Tenby, 4,823 D 5
Towy (river) E 5
Towyn D 4
Tregaron E 4
Tremadoc (bay) D 4
Usk (river) E 5
Welshpool, 7,326 E 4
Wrexham, 40,928 E 4
Wye (river) E 4

*All population figures are taken from the latest census or estimate available. †Population of parish or district.

UNITED NATIONS

UNITED NATIONS. The United Nations (UN) is an association of independent national states. It was formed by the victorious nations of World War II to keep the peace their efforts had won. Its supreme goal is to end war.

It was expected that the great powers would work together to keep the peace. Instead, disagreements between the Soviet Union and the West created a state of international tension called the Cold War (*see* Cold War). The Soviet Union's goal was to spread its Communist system throughout the world. The Western nations, led by the United States, joined together to resist Communist expansion. Both sides built up their armaments, including atomic weapons. Nevertheless, the United Nations has made progress toward world cooperation and has adapted to changing circumstances that were not dreamed of by its founders.

Origin of the United Nations

In 1941 United States President Franklin Delano Roosevelt and British Prime Minister Winston Churchill, meeting secretly, issued the Atlantic Charter (*see* Atlantic Charter). The charter looked forward to the "abandonment of the use of force" and a "permanent system of general security."

In 1942, representatives of 26 countries, calling themselves the United Nations, signed a pledge in Washington, D.C., to defeat the Axis and to uphold the principles of the Atlantic Charter.

In 1944, representatives of the Big Four (China, Britain, the Soviet Union, and the United States) drew up plans for a world organization when they met at Dumbarton Oaks, a private mansion in Washington, D.C.

In February 1945, at Yalta, the Big Three (Britain, the Soviet Union, and the United States) agreed on voting procedure (the veto in the Security Council) and called for a conference to draw up a charter.

On April 25, 1945, the United Nations Conference on International Organization opened in San Francisco. Delegates of 50 nations discussed and modified the original Dumbarton Oaks proposals. On June 26 the United Nations Charter was completed and signed. On July 28, 1945, the United States Senate voted 89 to 2 to ratify the charter.

By Oct. 24, 1945, the required number of nations had ratified the charter and the United Nations came officially into existence. October 24 has been celebrated as United Nations Day since 1948. Some countries set aside seven days—United Nations Week—for educational and social programs.

The United Nations Charter

The preamble of the United Nations Charter sets forth the aims of the organization. The charter itself states the basic principles and purposes, defines the membership, and establishes the six principal departments, or "organs."

The original members numbered 51. The charter provides that "all other peace-loving states" can become members on the recommendation of the Security Council if approved by a two-thirds vote of the General Assembly. The Assembly, on recommendation of the Security Council, can expel a member that has persistently violated the principles of the charter.

Amendments to the charter require a vote of two thirds of all the members of the General Assembly. Then the amendment must be ratified by two thirds of the member states, including all five permanent members of the Security Council.

Each member nation contributes to the main budget and to the budget of each agency to which it belongs. The scale of contributions, based partly on ability to pay, is set by the General Assembly. Some states pay less than half of one percent. The United States pays one fourth; the Soviet Union pays 10.2 percent; the United Kingdom pays 4.86 percent.

The Six Basic Organs

The General Assembly, largest of the six basic organs, is the great deliberative body of the United

---

PREAMBLE—UNITED NATIONS CHARTER

WE THE PEOPLES OF THE UNITED NATIONS DETERMINED

 to save succeeding generations from the scourge of war, which twice in our lifetime has brought untold sorrow to mankind, and

 to reaffirm faith in fundamental human rights, in the dignity and worth of the human person, in the rights of men and women and of nations large and small, and

 to establish conditions under which justice and respect for the obligations arising from treaties and other sources of international law can be maintained, and

 to promote social progress and better standards of life in larger freedom,

AND FOR THESE ENDS

 to practice tolerance and live together in peace with one another as good neighbors, and

 to unite our strength to maintain international peace and security, and

 to ensure, by the acceptance of principles and the institution of methods, that armed force shall not be used, save in the common interest, and

 to employ international machinery for the promotion of the economic and social advancement of all peoples,

HAVE RESOLVED TO COMBINE OUR EFFORTS TO ACCOMPLISH THESE AIMS.

 Accordingly, our respective Governments, through representatives assembled in the city of San Francisco, who have exhibited their full powers found to be in good and due form, have agreed to the present Charter of the United Nations and do hereby establish an international organization to be known as the United Nations.

Nations. It is linked up with all the other organs and it elects part or all of their membership. It may discuss any subject within the scope of the charter, except those disputes that are being dealt with by the Security Council. After voting, it may pass on its recommendations to other organs or to member governments.

All member states are represented in the Assembly. Each state may have up to five representatives but only one vote. Decisions on important questions (listed in the charter) require a two-thirds majority of members present and voting. Other questions are decided by a simple majority of those voting.

The Assembly meets in regular annual ses-

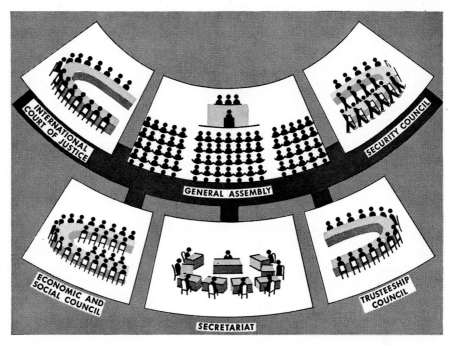

The International Court of Justice is a world court. The General Assembly is the "parliament of the world." The Security Council is charged with maintaining peace. The Economic and Social Council seeks to promote the welfare of all peoples. The Secretariat has administrative responsibilities. The Trusteeship Council supervises certain non-self-governing territories.

sions and in such special sessions as occasion may require. It elects its president for each session.

The Security Council has the primary responsibility for maintaining world peace and security. Every member of the United Nations is pledged to accept and carry out the Council's decisions.

The Security Council has 15 members. Five nations—the United Kingdom, China, France, the Soviet Union, and the United States—have permanent seats. Of the other ten, five are elected each year by the General Assembly for two-year terms; five retire each year. Each member has one vote. On all routine (procedural) matters, approval requires nine "yes" votes. On all other matters, the nine "yes" votes must include the votes of all five permanent members. Thus, each of the Big Five has a veto power. Any one of them can block even the discussion of an action that it disapproves. A party to a dispute, however, must abstain from voting.

Any state, even if it is not a member of the United Nations, may bring a dispute to which it is a party to the notice of the Security Council. If the Council finds there is a real threat to peace, or an actual act of aggression, it may call upon the members of the United Nations to cut communications with the countries concerned or break off trade relations (economic sanctions). If these methods prove inadequate, the charter states that the Council may take military action against the offending nation by air, sea, and land forces of the United Nations.

Every member of the United Nations was pledged by Article 43 to supply the Council with armed forces on

its call. These forces were to be directed by a Military Staff Committee, consisting of the chiefs of staff (or their representatives) of the five permanent members.

The International Court of Justice (also known as the World Court) is the "supreme court" of the United Nations. Its permanent seat is in The Netherlands at The Hague (*see* Hague Peace Conferences). The court consists of 15 judges (no two from one nation) elected by the General Assembly and the Security Council. The judges serve for nine years (five retiring every third year) and they may be reelected. Nine judges make a quorum and questions are decided by a majority vote.

Any states—even nonmembers—may bring disputes to the court for judgment. Both parties must first agree to allow the court to try the case. Should one of them fail to accept the judgment of the court, the other may appeal to the Security Council for enforcement. The court serves also as the legal adviser to the General Assembly, Security Council, and other United Nations organs.

The Economic and Social Council is devoted to the constructive tasks of peace—achieving higher standards of living, improving health and education, and promoting respect for human rights and freedoms throughout the world. It works under the authority of the General Assembly and reports to it. The Assembly elects 9 of the council's 27 members each year. They serve three-year terms.

The Economic and Social Council is assisted by its own commissions and by independent specialized agencies. (*See* list at the end of this article.)

The Secretariat carries on the day-to-day business of the United Nations and assists all the other organs. At its head is the Secretary General, the chief administrative officer of the United Nations. He is appointed by the General Assembly upon recommendation of the Security Council. His staff numbers thousands of workers, from many countries.

The Trusteeship Council seeks to protect the interests of people who live in trust territories and to lead them toward self-government. It receives reports from the administering authorities, examines petitions, and sends out visiting missions. Its members are elected by the General Assembly.

A non-self-governing territory becomes a trust territory through an individual trusteeship agreement with the United Nations. The Trust Territory of the Pacific Islands (administered by the United States) is defined as a "strategic area" and is under the authority of the Security Council. All other trust territories are under the General Assembly. (For list, *see* Trusteeships in Fact-Index.)

The United Nations Headquarters

The General Assembly decided in February 1946 to locate the permanent headquarters of the United Nations in the United States. The Secretariat set up temporary quarters first at Hunter College in New York City, then at Lake Success, Long Island. The General Assembly met at Flushing Meadow, N. Y.

Various sites were proposed for a permanent home. The question was dramatically settled in December 1946 when John D. Rockefeller, Jr., offered a six-block tract in midtown New York City as an $8,500,000 gift. New York City contributed additional land along the East River and rights to the water front. The 18-acre site extends from the river to First Avenue and from East 48th Street to East 42d Street.

Construction was financed by an interest-free loan of 65 million dollars from the United States. The cornerstone was laid Oct. 24, 1949. The Secretariat was completed in 1951. In 1952 the General Assembly and the Conference Building were completed.

The buildings were designed by a group of international architects headed by Wallace K. Harrison of the United States. Built of glass, marble, steel, and aluminum, they are functional and modern, with dramatic contrasts of form and mass.

The General Assembly is long and low, with concave sides and a sloping roof surmounted by a dome. The public entrance, at the north, leads to a large lobby. The south front is a great window looking out on the Delegates' Garden and the Circular Fountain. The vast hall, under the domed ceiling, is decorated with murals by Fernand Léger, a French artist.

The long, low Conference Building, on the riverside, built of metal and glass, has chambers for the Security Council, the Economic and Social Council, and the Trusteeship Council. This building connects the General Assembly with the 39-story Secretariat.

A new library was dedicated in 1961. It was named after Secretary-General Dag Hammarskjöld, who was killed in a plane crash earlier that year.

An International Enclave

The United Nations site was made international territory by agreement with the United States government. It is patroled by United Nations guards in gray uniforms, who come from all parts of the world.

The United Nations has its own post office and issues its own stamps. The stamps are designed to acquaint people with the work of the United Nations.

All but a few meetings are open to the public. Visitors may obtain tickets by telephoning in advance or by writing to United Nations, New York 10017.

THE UNITED NATIONS IN ACTION

The General Assembly opened its first session in London, Jan. 10, 1946. Trygve Lie, foreign minister of Norway, was elected the first secretary-general.

The Council Fails to Provide Armed Forces

The charter called for armed forces, contributed by the member states, to carry out the decisions of the Security Council. The forces were to be directed by a Military Staff Committee, consisting of the chiefs of staff of the five permanent Council members.

The Security Council in 1946 set up the committee and asked it to draw up plans. Russia blocked agreement in the Committee. The Council was so divided that it did not even discuss the Committee's problems.

On the podium are the president of the Assembly and the secretary general. The delegates occupy ten rows, with desks.

By dialing on his earphone, a delegate can listen to translations of speeches in English, French, Spanish, Russian, or Chinese.

E. Carle—Shostal Associates

The United Nations Headquarters near the East River in New York City opened in 1952. The tall building is the Secretariat; the low one the General Assembly.

Efforts at Disarmament and Atomic Control

The General Assembly set up the Atomic Energy Commission to plan control of atomic weapons. The United States in 1946 submitted to the Commission a plan for an international authority to supervise each stage of atomic production. Russia proposed instead to ban completely both the production and the use of atomic weapons. It also refused to submit to any effective inspection or control.

Deadlock in the Security Council

It had been expected that the Big Five in the Security Council would work together to keep the peace. Time after time, however, Russia used the overriding veto to block action favored by the other four powers.

The Council faced its first test when Iran demanded that Russia withdraw the troops it had stationed there during World War II. The Russian delegate walked out of the Council. Nevertheless Russian troops did leave Iran before the year ended.

In December 1946 Greece complained that Communist states on its borders were supporting the guerrillas that had plunged Greece into civil war (see Greece). The United States called on the Council to end the strife, if necessary by "enforcement action." Russia's veto again made the Council powerless.

The Rise of the General Assembly

To end Russian obstruction, the nations began to take their problems to the vetoless General Assembly. The Assembly, under the charter, can only discuss and recommend; it cannot take action. Unlike the Council, however, it represents all the member na-tions; and its resolutions can influence world opinion.

One of the earliest political disputes considered by the Assembly was the problem of Korea. In 1947 it called for elections in the divided nation and sent a commission to observe them. North Korea, which was under Russian domination, refused to admit the commission. Elections were held in South Korea, and a national government was set up.

The Assembly also sent an investigating committee to Greece after Russia vetoed the continuance of the Security Council's committee.

Social Welfare and Human Rights

The social welfare program of the United Nations embraces a wide variety of activities. Its agencies and commissions have given aid to many thousands of refugees and cared for needy children in many countries. They are concerned also with education, health, forced labor and slavery, equal rights for women, and the protection of minorities.

To promote and encourage respect for "human rights and fundamental freedoms," the General Assembly issued as a proclamation the 'Universal Declaration of Human Rights' (Dec. 10, 1948). In 1950 it proclaimed December 10 Human Rights Day.

A convention to prevent and punish *genocide* was submitted to member governments for ratification in 1948. Genocide was defined as an attempt to destroy "a national, ethnical, racial, or religious group."

Development Aid and "Atoms for Peace"

Technical, economic, and social aid to developing countries is provided by the United Nations Development Programme. Twelve international organizations share in its operations. Typical of the aid they provide are studies of a nation's resources and advice on agricultural methods, industrial programs, engineering projects, and procurement of capital.

In 1953 President Eisenhower proposed to the General Assembly that it should set up an agency to further the peaceful uses of nuclear energy. In 1956, delegates from 81 countries, including Russia, approved the statute of the International Atomic Energy Agency. The purpose of the agency is to exchange scientific information and pool materials.

The Partition War in Palestine

Palestine, an Arab land, came under British rule after World War I. Britain allowed the Jews to establish a "national home" there. After World War II thousands of refugees from Europe poured in. Unable to keep the peace between Arabs and Jews, Britain in 1947 turned the problem over to the General

MEMBERSHIP

	Chile*	Honduras*	Nepal (1955)	Spain (1955)
Afghanistan (1946)	China*†	Hungary (1955)	Netherlands*	Sri Lanka (1955)
Albania (1955)	Colombia*	Iceland (1946)	New Zealand*	Sudan (1956)
Algeria (1962)	Comoros (1975)	India*	Nicaragua*	Suriname (1975)
Angola (1976)	Congo (1960)	Indonesia (1950)	Niger (1960)	Swaziland (1968)
Antigua and Barbuda	Costa Rica*	Iran*	Nigeria (1960)	Sweden (1946)
(1981)	Cuba*	Iraq*	Norway*	Syria*‡
Argentina*	Cyprus (1960)	Ireland (1955)	Oman (1971)	Tanzania (1961)◆
Australia*	Czechoslovakia*	Israel (1949)	Pakistan (1947)	Thailand (1946)
Austria (1955)	Denmark*	Italy (1955)	Panama*	Togo (1960)
Bahamas (1973)	Djibouti (1977)	Ivory Coast (1960)	Papua New Guinea	Trinidad and
Bahrain (1971)	Dominica (1979)	Jamaica (1962)	(1975)	Tobago (1962)
Bangladesh (1974)	Dominican Republic*	Japan (1956)	Paraguay*	Tunisia (1956)
Barbados (1966)	Ecuador*	Jordan (1955)	Peru*	Turkey*
Belgium*	Egypt*‡	Kampuchea (1955)	Philippines*	Uganda (1962)
Belize (1981)	El Salvador*	Kenya (1963)	Poland*	Ukrainian S.S.R.*
Belorussian S.S.R.*	Equatorial Guinea	Kuwait (1963)	Portugal (1955)	U.S.S.R.*
Benin (1960)	(1968)	Laos (1955)	Qatar (1971)	United Arab
Bhutan (1971)	Ethiopia*	Lebanon*	Romania (1955)	Emirates (1971)
Bolivia*	Fiji (1970)	Lesotho (1966)	Rwanda (1962)	United Kingdom*
Botswana (1966)	Finland (1955)	Liberia*	St. Christopher	United States*
Brazil*	France*	Libya (1955)	and Nevis (1983)	Uruguay*
Brunei (1984)	Gabon (1960)	Luxembourg*	St. Lucia (1979)	Vanuatu (1981)
Bulgaria (1955)	Gambia (1965)	Madagascar (1960)	St. Vincent and the	Venezuela*
Burkina Faso (1960)	Germany, East (1973)	Malawi (1964)	Grenadines (1980)	Vietnam (1977)
Burma (1948)	Germany, West (1973)	Malaysia (1957)	São Tomé e Príncipe	Western Samoa (1976)
Burundi (1962)	Ghana (1957)	Maldives (1965)	(1975)	Yemen, People's
Cameroon (1960)	Greece*	Mali (1960)	Saudi Arabia*	Democratic
Canada*	Grenada (1974)	Malta (1964)	Senegal (1960)	Republic of (1967)
Cape Verde (1975)	Guatemala*	Mauritania (1961)	Seychelles (1976)	Yemen Arab
Central African	Guinea (1958)	Mauritius (1968)	Sierra Leone (1961)	Republic (1947)
Republic (1960)	Guinea-Bissau (1974)	Mexico*	Singapore (1965)§	Yugoslavia*
Chad (1960)	Guyana (1966)	Mongolia (1961)	Solomon Islands (1978)	Zaire (1960)
	Haiti*	Morocco (1956)	Somalia (1960)	Zambia (1964)
		Mozambique (1975)	South Africa*	Zimbabwe (1980)

*Charter member, 1945. †Seat originally held by Republic of China; replaced by People's Republic of China in 1971. ‡One seat held jointly by Egypt and Syria as United Arab Republic, 1958–61. §Part of Malaysia, 1963–65. ◆Tanganyika (admitted 1961) and Zanzibar (admitted 1963) merged as Tanzania in 1964.

Assembly. The Assembly recommended dividing Palestine into separate Arab and Jewish states.

On May 14, 1948, the Jews proclaimed their state of Israel. The Arab states at once launched a war against Israel to block partition. The United Nations mediator, Count Folke Bernadotte, was assassinated in Jerusalem. Ralph Bunche, as acting mediator, persuaded both sides to sign armistice agreements in 1949; but there was no real peace. The Arab states refused to recognize Israel, and fighting continued. (*See also* Palestine; Israel; Bunche.)

Shortly after World War II fighting broke out in the Netherlands Indies. The Security Council called on the Dutch and Indonesians to cease hostilities, but the war continued until 1949. The United Nations helped to achieve the settlement that made Indonesia an independent republic (*see* Indonesia).

United Nations mediation brought about a ceasefire in Kashmir between India and Pakistan in 1949; but India would not allow a plebiscite to be held to determine whether the people of Kashmir wanted to join India or Pakistan (*see* Jammu and Kashmir).

The charter named the Republic of China one of the five permanent members of the Security Council. At the end of 1949 Chinese Communists completed their conquest of the Chinese mainland. The Nationalist Chinese government retreated to Formosa.

Russia demanded the immediate expulsion of the Nationalist delegate and the seating of the delegate from the new People's Republic. The United States was opposed. In protest Russia boycotted for several months all United Nations bodies on which Nationalist China was represented.

The Security Council was called into emergency session on Sunday, June 25, 1950, after North Korea had invaded the Republic of Korea, which the United Nations had sponsored. The Council called on the North Koreans to withdraw, and it also authorized member states of the United Nations to furnish military aid to South Korea. (*See also* Korean War.)

Secretary–General Trygve Lie resigned in 1952. Dag Hammarskjöld, Sweden's minister of state, was elected to succeed him. He was reelected in 1957.

The Assembly Broadens Its Powers

In 1950, during the war in Korea, the General Assembly adopted the Uniting for Peace Resolution. Whenever the Security Council was unable to act against aggression because of the veto, a majority of its members could call an emergency session of the Assembly. The Assembly could recommend "collective measures," including the use of armed force.

These powers were used in the Middle East after Egypt's nationalization of the Suez Canal in 1956. The Assembly set up the United Nations Emergency Force (UNEF). UNEF's first task was to supervise the withdrawal from Egypt of the Israeli, French, and British forces. (*See also* Egypt; Suez Canal.)

Russia and several other nations refused to help pay the cost of the UNEF operation. They claimed that the Assembly could not legally authorize or impose assessments for peace-keeping forces.

A revolt against the government of Hungary in October 1956 had been followed by Russian armed intervention. Russia vetoed a Security Council resolution calling upon it to withdraw. The General Assem-

Norway's Trygve Lie (top left) was the UN's first
secretary-general (1946–52), followed by Dag Hammarskjöld
of Sweden (top right), who died in 1961; U Thant of Burma
(bottom left) served as secretary-general from 1961–72, and
Javier Pérez de Cuéllar of Peru (bottom right) since 1981.

bly then requested that United Nations observers be permitted to visit Hungary. The request was ignored. (*See also* Hungary.)

In 1959 Red China crushed a Tibetan revolt. The Assembly called for "respect for the fundamental human rights of the Tibetan people." China ignored the resolution. (*See also* Tibet.)

The Congo Intensifies Financial Problems

A peace-keeping force for the Republic of the Congo (now Zaire) was authorized by the Security Council after that strife-torn nation asked for help in 1960 (*see* Zaire, Republic of). The Assembly later levied assessments on United Nations members to pay the cost of the United Nations Operation in the Congo (Opération des Nations Unies au Congo, or ONUC). As in the case of UNEF, the Soviet Union called such assessments illegal and refused to pay them. This time France was among the nations that supported the Soviet position.

The United Nations attempts to raise funds included approval of a 200-million-dollar bond issue late in 1961. The next year the International Court of Justice, in an advisory opinion, held that the General Assembly had the legal right to divide peace-keeping costs among the members. The nonpaying nations, however, maintained their stand.

Early in the ONUC operation, the Soviet Union charged that Hammarskjöld supported pro-Western Congolese. The Soviets demanded Hammarskjöld's dismissal as secretary-general. Then they wanted to abolish the post itself and substitute a so-called *troika* (a three-man governing body) representing Western, Soviet, and neutralist members.

Soviet pressure for a "troika" was continued even after Hammarskjöld's death, in a plane crash in Africa, in September 1961. However, U Thant of Burma was made acting secretary-general in November. Thant's prestige was increased by his intervention between the United States and the Soviet Union in the 1962 Cuban crisis (*see* Cuba). In November 1962 he was elected secretary-general.

Membership in the United Nations swelled in the early 1960's. An influx of new African and Asian nations led to new voting-bloc alignments. It also led to heavy competition for the six nonpermanent seats in the Security Council and for the 18 seats in the Economic and Social Council.

Late in 1963 the General Assembly approved a proposed amendment to the United Nations charter. The amendment provided for a 15-member Security Council and a 27-member Economic and Social Council. The slow process of ratification began. Approval of the amendment by all permanent members of the Security Council and by two thirds of all United Nations members was completed in 1965.

Meanwhile, as a stopgap measure, the General Assembly began permitting two nations to share a regular two-year term on the Council. For example, Czechoslovakia began a term in 1964 and yielded its seat to Malaysia after a year.

Other United Nations activities in this period included a peace-keeping mission to Yemen in 1963 and a survey, preceding the formation of Malaysia, of public opinion in North Borneo (Sabah) and Sarawak. (*See also* Yemen Arab Republic; Malaysia.)

In West (Netherlands) New Guinea a period of United Nations control ended, and the territory, renamed West Irian, was turned over to Indonesia. In October 1963, the United States, the Soviet Union, and Britain registered the partial nuclear test ban treaty with the United Nations.

The Security Council in March 1964 authorized a peace-keeping force and a mediator for Cyprus, where Greek and Turkish Cypriots were battling. It avoided the problem of financing that had arisen over UNEF and ONUC by agreeing that part of the costs would be paid by Cyprus and by the nations supplying troops. The rest would be met through voluntary contributions. (*See also* Cyprus.)

Search for a Financial Compromise

On June 30, 1964, the last United Nations troops left the Congo. Expenditures for ONUC had reached more than $381\frac{1}{2}$ million dollars, and UNEF costs were running at about 18 million dollars a year. The unpaid assessments for these operations had left the United Nations on the brink of bankruptcy.

The Economic and Social Council of the United Nations

THE ECONOMIC AND SOCIAL COUNCIL (ECOSOC) performs its functions with the aid of the specialized agencies, commissions, and other bodies listed below.

SPECIALIZED AGENCIES

The specialized agencies are international, independent, self-governing organizations that work with the United Nations. The Economic and Social Council coordinates their activities.

International Labor Organization (ILO). Founded 1919. Brought into relationship with the United Nations in 1946. ILO brings together government, labor, and management to solve problems, and makes recommendations concerning pay, working conditions, trade union rights, safety, woman and child labor, and social security. It also assists governments in economic development by missions and fellowships. Headquarters, Geneva, Switzerland.

Food and Agriculture Organization of the United Nations (FAO). Founded 1945. Brought into relationship with the United Nations in 1946. FAO seeks to increase production from farms, forests, and fisheries and to improve distribution. It also provides expert assistance to governments and works to improve nutrition. Headquarters, Rome, Italy.

United Nations Educational, Scientific, and Cultural Organization (UNESCO). Founded 1946. Brought into relationship with the United Nations in 1946. UNESCO seeks to broaden the base of education throughout the world, to bring the benefits of science to all countries, and to encourage cultural interchange. National Commissions act as liaison groups between UNESCO and the educational, scientific, and cultural life of their own countries. Headquarters, Paris, France.

International Civil Aviation Organization (ICAO). A provisional organization began work in August 1945 and was replaced by the permanent body (ICAO) in April 1947. Brought into relationship with the United Nations in 1947. ICAO encourages use of safety measures, uniform regulations for operation, and simpler procedures at borders. It promotes the use of new technical methods and equipment and participates in the United Nations technical assistance program. Headquarters, Montreal, Canada.

International Bank for Reconstruction and Development (IBRD) or World Bank. Founded in 1945, began work in 1946. Brought into relationship with the United Nations in 1947. The World Bank furthers economic development of members by granting loans for productive projects and by furnishing technical advice. It also promotes private foreign investment and world trade. Headquarters, Washington, D. C.

International Finance Corporation (IFC). Founded in 1956. Closely affiliated with the World Bank. It underwrites and invests in private industry in underdeveloped countries and plays a leading role in helping industrial development banks. Headquarters, Washington, D. C.

International Development Association (IDA). Established in 1960, it is an affiliate of the World Bank. It lends money on more flexible terms than those of the Bank but uses the same high standards of planning and execution in considering loans. Headquarters, Washington, D. C.

International Monetary Fund (IMF). Founded in 1945, began work in 1946. Brought into relationship with the United Nations in 1947. The Fund promotes international monetary cooperation and stabilized currencies. It sells currency to members for international trade and offers help on financial problems. Headquarters, Washington, D. C.

World Health Organization (WHO). An Interim Commission, formed in 1946, carried out preparatory work for WHO. The permanent WHO was brought into relationship with the United Nations in 1948. WHO acts as a world clearinghouse for medical and scientific information; sets international standards for drugs and vaccines; administers international sanitary regulations governing land, sea, and air traffic; and, on government request, helps fight disease in any country. Headquarters. Geneva, Switzerland.

Universal Postal Union (UPU). Founded 1874. Brought into relationship with the United Nations in 1948. Unites member countries into a single postal territory and fixes international postal rates. Every member agrees to transmit the mail of other members by the best means available. UPU's International Bureau is a clearinghouse for international postal accounts. Headquarters, Bern, Switzerland.

International Telecommunication Union (ITU). Created 1932 by merging International Telegraph Union (founded 1865) and International Radiotelegraph Union (1906). Brought into relationship with the United Nations in 1947. ITU promotes international cooperation in telecommunications, allocates radio frequencies, and seeks to establish the lowest possible rates. Headquarters, Geneva, Switzerland.

World Meteorological Organization (WMO). International Meteorological Organization (IMO), the predecessor of WMO, was founded 1878. WMO founded 1951. Brought into relationship with the United Nations in 1951. WMO promotes international cooperation in establishing worldwide networks of meteorological stations and rapid weather-data exchange. Headquarters, Geneva, Switzerland.

Inter-Governmental Maritime Consultative Organization (IMCO). Came into formal existence in 1959 when 21 nations ratified its convention, drawn up in 1948. IMCO encourages safety measures and seeks the removal of shipping restrictions. Headquarters, London, England.

COMMISSIONS

The commissions study matters referred to them by the Council and submit detailed reports and recommendations. The *economic* bodies are concerned with raising living standards. The *social* groups aim to raise cultural and educational levels, to improve health, and to further respect for justice and human rights and freedoms.

Regional Commissions. Economic commissions were established in 1947, one for Europe (ECE, Economic Commission for Europe) and one for Asia and the Far East (ECAFE). In 1948 one for Latin America was created (ECLA). One for Africa (ECA) was created in 1958. In 1974 ECAFE was reorganized as the Economic and Social Commission for Asia and the Pacific (ESCAP) and the Economic Commission for Western Asia (ECWA). Among their concerns are food production, industrial development, and trade.

Functional Commissions. Commission on the Status of Women; Commission on Narcotic Drugs; Statistical Commission; Commission for Social Development; Population Commission; Commission on Human Rights and its Subcommission on Prevention of Discrimination and Protection of Minorities.

OTHER BODIES

International Atomic Energy Agency (IAEA). Founded in 1957 as an autonomous agency. IAEA furthers peaceful uses of atomic energy. Headquarters, Vienna, Austria.

United Nations Children's Fund (UNICEF). Established in 1946 to carry out war relief in Europe. Now concerned with the welfare of children in the developing countries. Headquarters, New York City.

International Trade Organization (ITO). Establishment of ITO postponed, but many nations are parties to the General Agreement on Tariffs and Trade (GATT).

Among the other special bodies are: United Nations World Food Council, established in 1974; United Nations High Commissioner for Refugees (UNHCR), established in 1950; United Nations Conference on Trade and Development (UNCTAD), established in 1964; United Nations Emergency Operation, established in 1974; United Nations Research Institute for Social Development (UNRISD), established in 1964; United Nations Institute for Training and Research (UNITAR), established in 1965; United Nations Fund for Population Activities (UNFPA), established in 1967, since 1972 under the United Nations Development Programme (UNDP); United Nations Environment Programme (UNEP), established in 1973.

The United States was bringing pressure against the Soviet Union, France, and 11 other holdouts. It wanted to invoke against them Article 19 of the United Nations charter. This article provides that a nation two years in arrears in the payment of contributions "shall have no vote" in the General Assembly.

The 19th session of the Assembly opened in December 1964 after two postponements. To avoid a showdown between the United States and the Soviet Union on the issue of finances, the United Nations carried on its business without formal voting. To keep the question of Article 19 from arising, decisions were made by consensus. New Security Council members were chosen by balloting outside the Assembly hall. The Assembly set up a Special Committee on Peace-Keeping Operations to seek a solution to the financing problem.

The United Nations After 1965

The 20th anniversary year of the United Nations was marred by the first withdrawal from the organization—Indonesia quit in March 1965 as a protest against the seating of Malaysia on the Security Council. (Indonesia resumed its membership in 1966.)

The General Assembly concluded its 19th session on Sept. 1, 1965. The Assembly approved a formula set up by the peace-keeping committee to end the dispute on Article 19. This formula provided that Article 19 would not be invoked against delinquent members and that UNEF would be maintained by voluntary contributions. The United States accepted this solution.

The 20th session of the General Assembly was faced with a crisis in November, when Rhodesia (now Zimbabwe) declared itself independent from Great Britain rather than grant the colony's black majority additional voting rights. The Security Council voted for economic sanctions against Rhodesia in 1965, and in 1966 imposed mandatory sanctions—the first in United Nations history (see Zimbabwe). Another crisis confronting the 20th session was the outbreak of hostilities between India and Pakistan. In 1966, United Nations observers supervised troop withdrawals to the 1949 cease-fire line.

During the 21st session Secretary-General U Thant was persuaded to accept a second term. A treaty was negotiated to ban nuclear weapons from outer space.

From 1966 onward the United Nations made repeated attempts to end the protracted military struggle in Vietnam. The organization also sought to reestablish stability in the Middle East, where war erupted briefly between Israel and a number of Arab states in 1967. (See also Vietnam War; Israel.)

In 1968 the Assembly voted to change the name of South West Africa to Namibia and condemned South Africa for continuing to defy a 1966 United Nations resolution terminating South Africa's mandate over the area. It also called upon members to break off relations with South Africa. (See also Namibia.)

In June 1968 the Assembly approved a treaty to prevent the proliferation of nuclear weapons. Later

Courtesy of the United Nations

UN multinational peacekeeping forces use a tank to patrol southern Lebanon, one of the world's worst trouble spots.

in the year the Soviet Union and Hungary vetoed a Security Council resolution condemning the August 1968 entry of Soviet-led troops into Czechoslovakia.

In 1971, after years of debate, the Assembly voted to admit the People's Republic of China into the United Nations. The country on the mainland replaced the Republic of China (on the island of Taiwan), which had been expelled by the same vote. U Thant announced his retirement. Kurt Waldheim of Austria succeeded him as secretary-general (see Waldheim).

War again broke out in the Middle East in October 1973, and the United Nations appealed for a cease-fire in place. A 7,000-man UNEF was sent to the Suez Canal area. After a cease-fire in mid-1974, the UNEF moved into the Golan Heights buffer zone to patrol the troop disengagement. In November 1975 the Assembly adopted a controversial resolution branding Zionism as "a form of racism and racial discrimination." Another controversy arose in March 1980 when the United States supported a resolution condemning Israeli settlements in Arab territory.

The Office of the United Nations High Commissioner for Refugees was awarded its second Nobel peace prize in 1981. Waldheim, who had been reelected in 1976, failed in his attempt to gain an unprecedented third term as secretary-general. He was succeeded by Javier Pérez de Cuéllar of Peru in December 1981; Pérez de Cuéllar was reappointed in 1986.

By 1985 there were 159 members in the United Nations; only the Comoros, Solomon Islands, and Vanuatu do not maintain permanent missions at the United Nations headquarters in New York City. In 1986, Swiss voters rejected a proposal that Switzerland join the United Nations; the key issue was whether membership would threaten the country's policy of neutrality.

BIBLIOGRAPHY FOR THE UNITED NATIONS

Angell, R.C. The Quest for World Order (Univ. of Mich. Press, 1979).
Carroll, Raymond. The Future of the United Nations (Watts, 1985).
Finger, S.M. Your Man at the UN: People, Politics and Bureaucracy in the Making of Foreign Policy (N. Y. Univ. Press, 1980).
Finger, S.M. American Ambassadors at the UN, 2nd ed. (Holmes and Meier, 1987).
Finkelstein, L.S., ed. Politics in the United Nations System After Forty Years (Duke, 1988).
Hovet, Thomas and Erica. A Chronology and Fact Book of the United Nations: 1941–1985, 7th ed. (Oceana, 1986).
Luard, Evan. The United Nations: How It Works and What It Does (St. Martin, 1985).

UNITED STATES

UNITED STATES.
The United States represents a series of ideals. For most of those who have come to its shores, it means the ideal of freedom—the right to worship as one chooses,
the right to seek a job appropriate to one's skills and interests, the right to be judged equally before the law. It means the ideal of the frontier, of overcoming obstacles—taming the West, making the deserts bloom, curing diseases, voyaging to the planets. It means the ideal of progress—that life in America will ever be better; that political, social, and economic institutions will improve through hard work, fair play, and honest endeavor. It means the ideal of democracy—the right to be heard as an individual, the right to cast a ballot in a free election, the right to dream of better things and better days. In order to understand the United States, it is necessary to review its significance as a place and the role that its ideals have played in its development.

Landscape

The mainland United States is located between Mexico on the south and Canada on the north and between the Atlantic and Pacific oceans. Two of its 50 states, however, are far removed from the continental core: the Hawaiian Islands, 2,400 miles (3,900 kilometers) from San Francisco, are surrounded by the Pacific Ocean; Alaska, in the northwestern corner of North America, is nearly 700 miles (1,100 kilometers) from Seattle. If the outlying states are included, the area is 3,679,192 square miles (9,529,063 square kilometers), making the United States the fourth largest country in the world. The United States also ranks fourth in population. At the 1980 census its population was 226,504,825. The American landscape has

The United States exhibits a great diversity of landmarks and monuments. The contrast between Devil's Tower, Wyo. (top left), a flat Iowa cornfield (top right), Yellowstone National Park (center left), and Niagara Falls (bottom right) is striking. Mount Rushmore, in South Dakota (center) and the Statue of Liberty in New York City (bottom left) are well known by sight to nearly every American. Young twins celebrate an old-fashioned Fourth of July (center right).

evolved over millions of years. Mountains have risen to great heights only to be worn down by the forces of erosion. Rivers have changed course. Plains and plateaus have been alternately raised and lowered. Glaciers have moved over the land, cutting giant creases into America's crust. They have created new landforms and moved precious soil from one location

Preview

The article United States is divided into the following sections:

Introduction 89
Landscape 89
  Physiographic Provinces 90
  Climate 95
  Vegetation 100
  Soils 102
Regions 102
  New England 103
  Middle Atlantic 106
  The South 109
  North Central Plains 119
  Great Plains 123
  Rocky Mountains 126
  Western Basins and Plateaus 128
  North Pacific 134
  South Pacific 137
  Alaska 142
  Hawaii 145
Peoples and Cultures 148
International Relations 152
History 153
Bibliography 186
Fact Summary 188
Political Map 190–93

For a brief review of essential information about the United States, *see* UNITED STATES FACT SUMMARY.

This article was contributed by Daniel Jacobson, Professor of Geography, Michigan State University, East Lansing, and author of 'Great Indian Tribes' (1970), 'The Hunters' (1974), 'The Fishermen' (1975), 'The Gatherers' (1977), 'Indians of North America' (1983), and 'The North Central States' (1984).

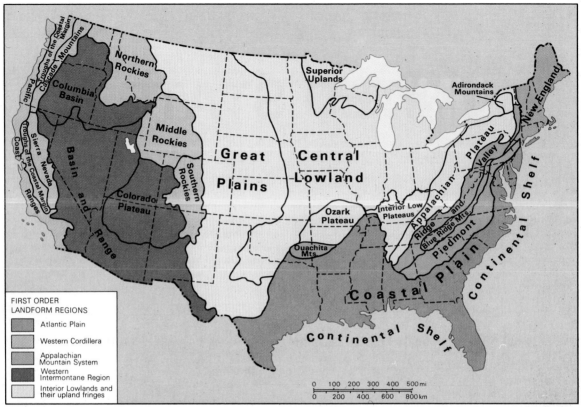

Physiographic regions of the United States

to another. Wetlands have become deserts; arid wastes have become filled with lakes. Landscape changes have often meant extinction for native plants and animals, and their replacements have been forced to adapt to new environments. Change is an axiom of the American landscape.

PHYSIOGRAPHIC PROVINCES

The United States is dominated by a range of old mountains and plateaus—the Appalachians—that runs north and south on the east side of the North American continent and young ranges of lofty mountains—the Rockies, Cascades, and Sierra Nevada—that run north and south in the western quarter of the continent. The great interior lowland extends from the Canadian Shield to the Gulf of Mexico. These dominant mountain and lowland areas have helped to define what are called the physiographic provinces of the United States.

Atlantic and Gulf Coastal Plain

The Atlantic and Gulf Coastal Plain extends 2,200 miles (3,540 kilometers) from Cape Cod to the Rio Grande. Its western layers border the Piedmont of the Appalachian Highlands, but a portion extends in a wide swath in the lower Mississippi River valley from Cairo, Ill., to the Gulf of Mexico and westward to the Balcones escarpment in Texas. An extensive continental shelf exists offshore. The elevation is low

and the relief minimal. The eastern shore features the glacier deposits of Long Island; the estuaries of New York, Delaware, and Chesapeake bays and Albemarle and Pamlico sounds; and the sea islands off Georgia. From Cairo, Ill., to the gulf the Mississippi slopes only 8 inches per mile (12.6 centimeters per kilometer), near the gulf fewer than 6 inches (9.5 centimeters). The river meanders and has formed numerous oxbow lakes, and south of New Orleans the river has created a vast and growing delta.

Appalachian Highlands

Immediately to the west of the Atlantic Coastal Plain is the Piedmont, followed on the west in turn by the Blue Ridge, the Ridge and Valley, and the Appalachian Plateau—all sub-provinces of the Appalachian Highlands. New England and the Adirondacks, located farther north, are also included.

North of the Potomac River the Piedmont looks down—often 100 to 200 feet (30 to 60 meters)—on the Coastal Plain. Rivers coming off the Piedmont drop to the lower elevations in waterfalls. The fall line is an imaginary line connecting the waterfalls. Washington, D.C., Philadelphia, and Baltimore are fall-line cities, as are Richmond, Raleigh, Columbia, and Macon farther south.

From the fall line elevations rise steadily westward over a hilly terrain to 1,100 and 1,200 feet (335 and 365 meters) near the Blue Ridge boundary. In the

Vacationers relax on the rocky Atlantic coastline (top) near Ogunquit, Me. Hill climbers (bottom) reach the top of a bluff on the glacial Lake of the Clouds in the Porcupine Mountains of Michigan's Upper Peninsula. The landform is part of the Canadian Shield, or Laurentian Highlands.

Tim Moran

The Rocky Mountains near Aspen, Colo., rise to heights of more than 14,000 feet (4,270 meters) above sea level.

north the Palisades of the Hudson, opposite New York City, and the Watchung Mountains of northern New Jersey are considered part of the Piedmont. So too is Georgia's Stone Mountain.

The eastern scarp, or line of cliffs, of the Blue Ridge, from Pennsylvania to Georgia, stands 1,000 to 1,500 feet (300 to 460 meters) above the Piedmont. In western North Carolina a number of peaks tower more than 6,000 feet (1,800 meters). Mount Mitchell, the highest peak, stands 6,684 feet (2,037 meters) above sea level. In the west the old rocks of the Blue Ridge meet the younger folded rocks of the Ridge and Valley Province.

The Ridge and Valley extends from the Saint Lawrence River southward to Alabama. It is characterized by a series of linear ridges that are arranged in a northeast to southwest progression and includes their accompanying valleys. The Great Valley portion includes Lake Champlain, a part of the Hudson River, and the Lebanon, Cumberland, Shenandoah, Tennessee, and Coosa valleys.

At the Allegheny Front the Appalachian Plateau stands 3,000 feet (900 meters) above the Ridge and Valley. The plateau itself has been much dissected by streams and appears mountainous in places. The Kanawha River, for example, lies 1,000 to 1,500 feet (300 to 460 meters) below the Appalachian Plateau surface. The highest parts of the plateau are in the Catskill Mountains, and the most scenic perhaps are the Finger Lakes—both in New York State.

New England and the Adirondacks have been modified by glaciation. Kettle holes, kame and esker hills, and drumlin ridges are common. New England is famous for its rockbound coast. In places small isolated mountains called monadnocks rise above the general level of the land, as in Mount Monadnock, N.H. (*See also* Appalachian Highlands.)

Central Lowlands

The Central Lowlands extend from the Appalachian Highlands westward to the Great Plains and from the Interior Highlands northward to the Canadian Shield. Elevations tend to be low. They range from 1,000 feet (300 meters) in the extreme east, to 500 feet (150 meters) at the Mississippi River, and to only 2,000 feet (600 meters) near the Great Plains boundary. Much of the province was glaciated, which helped to create the Great Lakes and the kame-and-kettle topography. In the far north the Red River Valley, famous for its spring wheat, is a remnant of glacial Lake Agassiz. Where the glaciation did not strike, as in the driftless area of Wisconsin, such unusual landforms as natural bridges, arches, and occasional monadnocks occur. The plains east and west of the Mississippi are mantled with loess, a wind-deposited silt long subject to erosion.

Interior Highlands

Unlike the landforms of the Appalachian Highlands, the topography of the Interior Highlands is oriented east and west. The linear ridges of the Ouachita Mountains, 2,600 feet (790 meters) high, stand 1,500 feet (460 meters) above the Arkansas River; the Boston Mountains stand 2,000 feet (600 meters) above the Arkansas and White rivers. On the Ozark Plateau both Iron Mountain and Pilot Knob are more than 1,000 feet (300 meters) high. Local relief varies from 800 to 900 feet (240 to 270 meters), and the topography in general is similar to that of the Appalachian Highlands.

Lake Superior Uplands

The Lake Superior Uplands are part of the Laurentian Highlands, or Canadian Shield. They are found in northeastern Minnesota, northern Wisconsin, and the Upper Peninsula of Michigan. Glacial lakes are common. Ranges of iron ore include Cuyuna, Mesabi and Vermilion, Gogebic, Marquette, and Menominee.

Great Plains

The Great Plains extend from Montana and North Dakota southward to Texas. In the north the eastern boundary is the Missouri Coteau, which stands 500 feet (150 meters) above the Central Lowlands. In Texas the eastern boundary is marked by the Balcones escarpment. In Kansas and Nebraska the boundary is barely noticeable. The horizontal layers of the plains rise constantly to the west—from 2,000 feet (600 meters) on the eastern margin to nearly 5,000 feet (1,500 meters) where they strike the Rocky Mountains. The High Plains between Nebraska and Texas, however,

A large hayfield (top) near Grandview, Mo., is close to the center of the Great Plains, perhaps the most vital and productive farming region on Earth. The plains are a stark contrast to the lush tropical vegetation (bottom) in the rich, volcanic soil of the Hawaiian Islands.

Topography

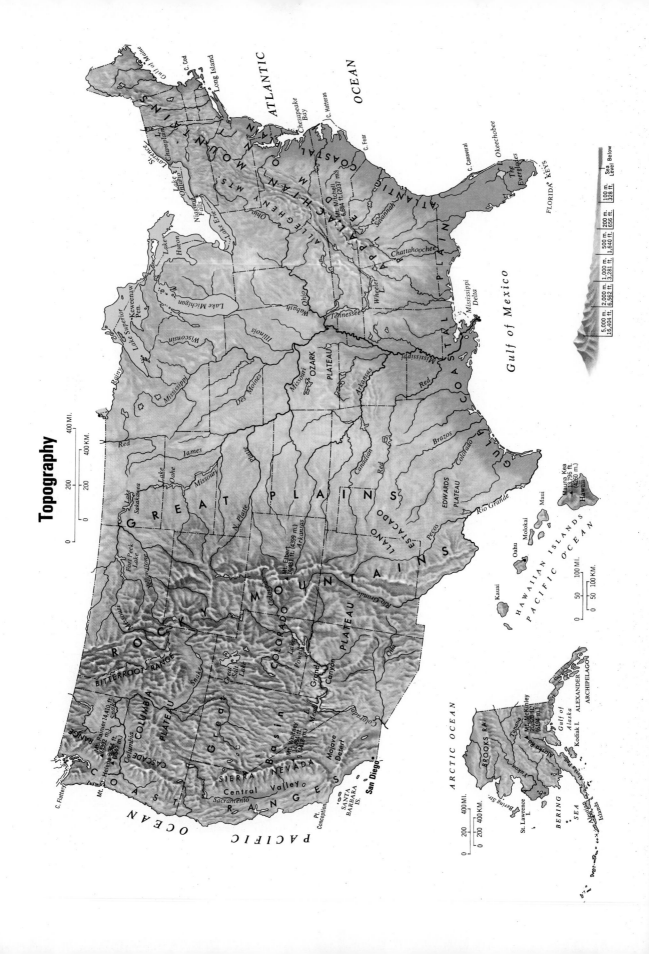

ATLANTIC OCEAN

Gulf of Maine
C. Cod
Long Island
C. Cod

WHITE MOUNTAINS
Lake Champlain
St. Lawrence
Lake Ontario
Niagara Falls
Lake Erie
Chesapeake Bay
C. Hatteras

ALLEGHENY MTS
APPALACHIAN MOUNTAINS
Mt. Mitchell
6,684 ft.(2037 m.)
C. Fear

PIEDMONT
ATLANTIC COASTAL PLAIN

C. Canaveral
Okeechobee
The Everglades
FLORIDA KEYS

Ohio
Chattahoochee
Savannah
Wheeler L.
Tennessee

Lake Huron
Lake Michigan
Keweenaw Pen.
Lake Superior
Rainy
Mississippi
Des Moines
Wisconsin
Illinois
Wabash

OZARK PLATEAU
Mississippi
Arkansas
Red
Mississippi Delta

Gulf of Mexico

Red
James
Missouri
Lake Oahe
Lake Sakakawea

GREAT PLAINS

Red
N. Platte
Missouri
Canadian
Red
Arkansas
Brazos
Colorado
EDWARDS PLATEAU
LLANO ESTACADO
Pecos
Rio Grande

Fort Peck Lake
Yellowstone

ROCKY MOUNTAINS
Mt. Elbert
14,431 ft. (4399 m.)
Columbia
COLORADO PLATEAU
Grand Canyon
Colorado
Rio Grande
Lake Powell
Lake Mead
Gila

BITTERROOT RANGE
Missouri
Snake
Great Salt Lake
Great Basin

COLUMBIA PLATEAU
Columbia
Snake

CASCADE RANGE
Mt. Rainier 14,410 ft.
(4392 m.)
Mt. St. Helens 8,364 ft.
(2549 m.)

Mt. Whitney
14,494 ft.
(4418 m.)
SIERRA NEVADA
Mojave Desert
Central Valley
Sacramento
San Diego

COAST RANGES
C. Flattery
Mt. Olympus
Pt. Conception
SANTA BARBARA IS.

PACIFIC OCEAN

Scale bars (upper)
400 MI.
400 KM.
200
200
0

Elevation legend
| 5,000 m. 16,404 ft. | 2,000 m. 6,562 ft. | 1,000 m. 3,281 ft. | 500 m. 1,640 ft. | 200 m. 656 ft. | 100 m. 328 ft. | Sea Level Below |

HAWAIIAN ISLANDS
PACIFIC OCEAN
Kauai
Oahu
Molokai
Maui
Mauna Kea
13,796 ft.
(4205 m.)
Hawaii

100 MI.
100 KM.
50
50
0

ARCTIC OCEAN
BROOKS RANGE
Gulf of Alaska
Mt. McKinley
20,320 ft.
(6194 m.)
ALASKA RANGE
Tanana
Yukon
Kodiak I.
Alexander ARCHIPELAGO
St. Lawrence I.
Bering Str.
BERING SEA
Aleutian Islands

400 MI.
400 KM.
200
200
0

are conspicuously flat and indicate little erosion. Western Nebraska has sand hills, and western South Dakota has its Black Hills—an outlier of the Rocky Mountains that stands 4,000 feet (1,200 meters) above the level of the plains. (*See also* Great Plains.)

Rocky Mountains

The Rocky Mountains tower from 2,000 to 8,000 feet (600 to 2,400 meters) above the Great Plains. In bold, rugged ranges they stand more than 14,000 feet (4,270 meters) above sea level. They look down upon the Cordilleran Plateaus to the west. The Colorado Front, Sangre de Cristo, Laramie, Wind River, and Wasatch ranges and the Uinta, Bighorn, and Bitterroot mountains are all parts of the Rocky Mountain system. One of the few major breaks in the system can be found at South Pass in the Wyoming Basin— a favorite route of the settlers moving west. (*See also* Rocky Mountains.)

Cordilleran Plateaus

West of the Rockies are the Cordilleran Plateaus: the Colorado Plateau, the Great Basin, and the Columbia River and Snake River Plateau. The horizontal layers of the Colorado Plateau have been cut by the Colorado River to form the Grand Canyon, in places 6,000 feet (1,800 meters) deep and from 5 to 15 miles (8 to 24 kilometers) wide. The plateau is a land of dissected mesas, domed mountains, arches and natural bridges, stone monuments, and spires. Monument Valley in northwestern Arizona is a case in point. Shiprock in New Mexico rises 500 feet (150 meters) above the surrounding surface.

The Great Basin lies between the Rocky Mountains and the Sierra Nevada. It is made up of numerous north-south-trending ranges that rise 3,000 to 5,000 feet (900 to 1,500 meters) above the basin floor, or to 10,000 feet (3,000 meters) above sea level. In former times much of the area was covered by Lake Bonneville, of which the Great Salt Lake is a remnant. Western Nevada was covered by Lake Lahontan. Pyramid, Winnemucca, Honey, North Carson, and Walker lakes are remnants of it.

Farther north is the Columbia River and Snake River Plateau, essentially a great lava flow. The Snake River has cut a deep canyon in the lava, and the Columbia River also crosses the plateau. Conspicuous features are the Craters of the Moon and the Grand Coulee.

Pacific Mountain System

Included in the Pacific Mountain System are the Sierra Nevada and Cascade Range on the east and the Coast Ranges on the west. Between them are Puget Sound and the Willamette Valley in the north and the Valley of California in the south. Also included are the Salton Sea and the Sonoran Desert. (*See also* Cascade Range; Coast Ranges; Sierra Nevada.)

The Sierra Nevada stands high above the present-day landscape. Eleven peaks rise more than 14,000 feet (4,270 meters) above sea level. North of the Si-

erras are the Cascades, separated into northern and southern sections by the gorge of the Columbia River. Crater Lake and Wizard Island are prominent features of the southern Cascades. Mt. Rainier, Mt. Adams, Mt. St. Helens, and Mt. Baker are prominent volcanic peaks of the northern Cascades.

The Puget Sound-Willamette Valley lowland lies between the northern Cascades and the Coast Ranges. The 400-mile- (640-kilometer-) long Valley of California lies between the Sierra Nevada and the Coast Ranges. The San Andreas Fault is located in the Coast Ranges. Movement in the fault in 1906 caused the San Francisco earthquake.

The Salton Sea was caused by a break in the right bank of the lower Colorado River in 1905. Colorado River water flowed into the Salton trough. In 1907 the flow from the river was checked, and the Salton Sea has been shrinking ever since. Most of the Sonoran Desert is located in northwestern Mexico.

Alaska

The Pacific Mountain system also appears in southern Alaska. The Alaska Range-Aleutian Islands province is a northern extension of the Coast Ranges; Cook Inlet and the Copper River lowland are northern extensions of the Puget Sound-Willamette Valley area; and to the north is an extension of the Cascades. The Alaska interior is an extension of the Cordilleran Plateaus. The Brooks Range is the northern outlier of the Rocky Mountains, and the Arctic Central Plain has its equivalent perhaps in the Great Plains. The trend of the provinces in Alaska, however, is different: the mountains and lowlands run east and west. Mt. McKinley, at 20,320 feet (6,194 meters) the highest peak in North America, is located in the Alaska Range. (*See also* Alaska Range.)

Hawaiian Islands

The Hawaiian Islands are really mountain peaks formed from lava that stand above the junction of two submarine ridges. The oldest islands are in the west, the youngest in the east. Thus the volcanic peaks on the island of Hawaii stand highest above sea level: Mauna Kea, 13,796 feet (4,205 meters), and Mauna Loa, 13,680 feet (4,170 meters). Both are still active. The peaks on Oahu and Kauai are much lower, as they have been reduced by erosion. The older islands are also flanked by coral reefs. There is a small coastal plain on Oahu and a significant harbor at Pearl Harbor.

CLIMATE

The United States is affected primarily by air masses that blow southward from Canada, north- and eastward from the Atlantic Ocean and the Gulf of Mexico, and westward from the Pacific Ocean. In winter cold blasts of Arctic air make their presence felt in the northern parts of the country. In late summer winds of hurricane force from the Caribbean strike the Atlantic and Gulf coasts. Occasionally they strike even farther north. In all seasons the westerlies affect the climate and weather of much of the country.

Phil Degginger—CLICK/Chicago

A vital role is also played by the topography. For example, the westerly winds, charged with the waters of the Pacific, run into the Cascades and leave much precipitation on the western, or windward, side of the mountains. The eastern, or leeward, side therefore receives little precipitation. Portland, Ore., averages 40 inches (100 centimeters) of precipitation per year, The Dalles only 13 inches (33 centimeters). The Sierra Nevada range leaves the Great Basin relatively dry. Nevada City, Calif., averages 48 inches (122 centimeters); Carson City, Nev., only 9 inches (23 centimeters). The Great Plains lie in the so-called rain shadow of the Rocky Mountains. Accordingly Coeur d'Alene, Idaho, receives 22 inches (56 centimeters); Great Falls, Mont., but 15 inches (38 centimeters).

In general the 100th meridian tends to separate a wet East from a much drier West. New Orleans receives more than 60 inches (152 centimeters) of precipitation per year; Miami more than 55 inches (140 centimeters); Birmingham, Ala., more than 50 inches (127 centimeters); Boston, New York City, and Washington, D.C., all more than 40 inches (102 centimeters); Chicago and Saint Louis more than 30 inches (76 centimeters); but Bismarck, N.D., only 16 inches (41 centimeters), Wichita, Kan., 28 inches (71 centimeters), and Albuquerque, N. M., but 8 inches (20 centimeters). There is much precipitation, however, in the extreme Northwest. Seattle averages more than 35 inches (90 centimeters) per year.

Frequent rainfall gives the ferns and other vegetation at Cape Disappointment (left), at the southern tip of Washington State along the Pacific Ocean coast, the appearance of a rain forest. The colorful Badlands National Park in South Dakota (below), however, is in a very arid region.

Tim Moran

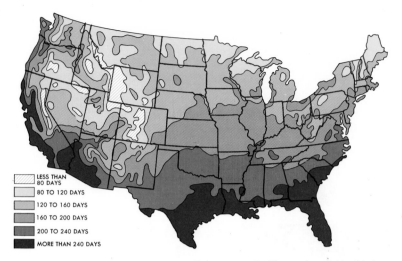

LESS THAN 80 DAYS
80 TO 120 DAYS
120 TO 160 DAYS
160 TO 200 DAYS
200 TO 240 DAYS
MORE THAN 240 DAYS

The yearly number of days without killing frost is affected by mountains and bodies of water, as well as by latitude. Frost-free days in Alaska (not shown) range from 60 to 180. Hawaii (not shown) has a year-round growing season except on high peaks.

In both Alaska and the Hawaiian Islands, precipitation varies considerably. Sitka, for example, records 87 inches (221 centimeters), Nome 17 inches (43 centimeters), and Barrow less than 5 inches (13 centimeters). Downtown Honolulu records but 20 inches (51 centimeters) of rain, but more than 200 inches (508 centimeters) are often recorded in the surrounding hills. Waialeale on Kauai averages more than 480 inches (1,219 centimeters), making it one of the wettest places on Earth.

Temperatures also vary considerably. The average January temperature in Miami, for example, is 68° F (20° C); New Orleans 55° F (13° C); New York City 33° F (0.6° C); Chicago 27° F (−3° C); Phoenix 52° F (11° C); Denver 31° F (−0.6° C); Seattle 40° F (5° C). The average July temperature in Miami is 82° F (28° C); New Orleans 83° F (28° C); New York City 77° F (25° C); Chicago 75° F (24° C); Phoenix 91° F (32° C); Denver 73° F (23° C); Seattle 65° F (18° C). Fairbanks, Alaska, averages −11° F (−24° C) in January, 60° F (16° C) in July. Honolulu averages 72° F (22° C) in January, 79° F (26° C) in July, moderated by the Pacific Ocean.

Temperature and precipitation regimes help to define the climatic regions of the mainland United States of which there are nine—four east of the 100th meridian, five west of it. Tropical Savanna, Humid Subtropical, Humid Continental Warm Summer, and Humid Continental Cool Summer are found east of the 100th meridian; Steppe, Desert, Western High Areas, Mediterranean, and Marine West Coast regions are found west of it. Alaska is made up of Subarctic and Tundra regions. The Hawaiian Islands are part of an Oceanic region.

Tropical Savanna

The southern portion of Florida is Tropical Savanna, which is a tropical wet and dry climate with one distinct dry season—winter. Miami receives 55 inches (140 centimeters) of rain, but most of it falls in the summer half year and the early fall because of the hurricane influence. Nine of the 55 inches, however,

fall in October. The winter half year is relatively dry. Temperatures are uniformly high.

Humid Subtropical

Humid Subtropical is a warm, temperate, rainy climate with no distinct dry season. This climate affects the region that covers the Atlantic and Gulf Coastal Plain, most of Appalachia, and the Interior Highlands. Its western boundary lies approximately at the 100th meridian. The 40 inches (102 centimeters) of precipitation in Washington, D.C., is fairly evenly distributed throughout the year. The same is true for Charleston's 49 inches (124 centimeters) and New Orleans' 60 inches (152 centimeters). There is no dry season. Temperatures vary considerably between northern and southern locations.

Humid Continental Warm Summer

The Humid Continental Warm Summer region lies north of the Humid Subtropical. Its northern border runs just south of lakes Erie and Michigan and includes the area between western Pennsylvania and Kansas, Nebraska, and South Dakota west to the 100th meridian. The region has a cold climate, though summers are warm and winters humid. Pittsburgh averages 35 inches (89 centimeters) of precipitation evenly distributed throughout the year. The average temperature for January is 31° F (−0.6° C), but July's average is 74° F (23° C). Omaha, Neb., averages 28 inches (71 centimeters) of precipitation. The average temperature for January is 22° F (−6° C), but it is 77° F (25° C) in July.

Humid Continental Cool Summer

The Humid Continental Cool Summer region lies north of the Humid Continental Warm Summer region. It includes northern New England, the Great Lakes area, and portions of Minnesota and North Dakota west to the 100th meridian. A cold climate with cool summers and humid winters characterizes the region. Marquette, Mich., averages 32 inches (81 centimeters) of precipitation per year, much of it

Goose Lake Prairie near Morris, Ill., is part of the tall-grass prairie of Illinois. The grasslands of the Great Plains stretch from Illinois to Wyoming and from Montana and the Dakotas south to Texas.

in the form of snow during the winter. The average temperature in January is 16° F (−9° C), in July only 65° F (18° C). In Duluth, Minn., there is 26 inches (66 centimeters) of precipitation per year, with much snow. January temperatures average 1° F (−17° C); July temperatures, like Marquette's, average 65°.

Steppe

Steppe is a mid-latitude cold-and-dry region in which there is usually a winter drought. The region covers the Great Plains, much of the Great Basin, and portions of the Columbia and Snake River Plateau. Helena, Mont., receives less than 14 inches (36 centimeters) of precipitation per year. Nine inches (23 centimeters) of the total falls between April and September. The winter months are very dry. Helena's average temperature in January is 20° F (−7° C); in July it is 68° F (20° C). Boise, Idaho, receives only 12 inches (30 centimeters) of precipitation per year but receives most of it in the winter half, showing a strong influence from the Pacific Ocean. Boise's average January temperature is 29° F (−17° C); in July it is 74° F (23° C).

Desert

Desert includes portions of the Great Basin, the Salton Sea area, southern Arizona and New Mexico, and the Sonoran Desert. Precipitation is meager, and temperatures are high. Yuma, Ariz., receives less than 4 inches (10 centimeters) of rain per year, most of it coming in the winter half. The months between April and July are very dry. In January Yuma's average temperature is 53° F (12° C); in July, 91° F (33° C).

Western High Areas

The Western High Areas include the northern Rockies, the Sierra Nevada, and the Cascades. The region, like the Humid Continental Cool Summer, is cold with cool summers and humid winters.

Mediterranean

Classic Mediterranean has three times as much rain in the wettest month of winter as in the driest month of summer. The climate in most of western California comes close to this definition. San Francisco records 21 inches (54 centimeters) of precipitation per year, 18 inches (46 centimeters) in the winter half. January receives 4.4 inches (11 centimeters); there is no precipitation in July. January temperatures average 50° F (10° C); the temperature in July averages only 57° F (14° C). San Diego, much farther south, records only 10 inches (25 centimeters) of precipitation per year, most of it in the winter months. The summers are very dry. January temperatures average 55° F (13° C); the July temperature climbs to only 67° F (19° C) and in August to only 69° F (21° C).

Marine West Coast

Marine West Coast is a warm, temperate, rainy climate. Most of the precipitation occurs in the winter half year, and there is little during the summer months. The region lies west of the Cascades between northern California and the Canadian border. Olympia, Wash., receives 52 inches (132 centimeters) of precipitation per year. Nearly half falls from November through January, and less than 2 inches

(5 centimeters) is recorded in July and August. The average temperature in January is 38° F (3° C); in July, 63° F (17° C). Portland, Ore., records nearly 44 inches (112 centimeters) of precipitation per year, including nearly 20 inches (51 centimeters) from November through January. The average temperature in January is 39° F (4° C); in July, 67° F (19° C). Precipitation is extremely heavy on the western slopes of the Olympic Mountains.

Subarctic

An extension of the Marine West Coast extends northward into Canada and southeastern Alaska. Sitka records 87 inches (221 centimeters) of precipitation per year, 42 inches (107 centimeters) from September through December. The average January temperature is 33° F (0.6° C), the July average only 55° F (13° C). But most of central Alaska can be classified as Subarctic, a cold climate with relatively little precipitation and short, cool summers. Fairbanks receives only 11 inches (28 centimeters) of precipitation fairly evenly distributed throughout the year. August, however, is usually the rainiest of the months. The average January temperature is −11° F (−24° C); the July, 60° F (16° C). Nome, on Norton Sound, records 17 inches (43 centimeters) of precipitation fairly evenly distributed throughout the year, but August is the rainiest of the months. The average temperature in January is 3° F (−16° C); in July, 50° F (10° C). In

the Aleutian Islands there is a very different climatic regime: at Dutch Harbor 56 inches (142 centimeters) of precipitation, much of it in the winter half year, and average temperatures in January of 32° F (0° C) and in July of 51° F (11° C).

Tundra

Essentially a polar climate with little precipitation and low temperatures, the Tundra's average temperature in the warmest month is below 50° F (10° C). Barrow, on the Arctic Ocean, records a total precipitation of 4 inches (11 centimeters), an average January temperature of −16° F (−26° C), and a July average of 40° F (4° C).

Oceanic

The Pacific Ocean keeps the trade winds that blow across the Hawaiian Islands filled with water. There is much precipitation in the islands. The Pacific also plays a major role in modifying the islands' temperatures. Location in the low latitudes helps to make the islands tropical, and topography—the leeward and windward effects—plays a significant role in precipitation at particular places. At Hilo, on the island of Hawaii, precipitation averages 140 inches (356 centimeters) per year. March alone produces 14 inches (36 centimeters), November nearly 14 inches, and June, the month with the least precipitation, nearly 8 inches (20 centimeters). There are climatic stations

Kettle Moraine State Forest (left), noted as a wildlife refuge in southeast Wisconsin, is resplendent with pine trees and other evergreens. The strawberry cactus (right) is an example of the sparse vegetation that covers the ground in Big Bend National Park, Texas.

(Right) Courtesy of the Texas Tourist Agency; photo, Richard Reynolds; (left) Cathy Melloan—EB Inc.

on the same island that produce more than 200 inches (500 centimeters) and some with less than 20 inches (51 centimeters). Mauna Kea and Mauna Loa are often covered with snow. Honolulu, on Oahu, records 23 inches (58 centimeters), most in the winter half year. The January temperature averages 72° F (22° C), July only 79° F (26° C). Other climatic stations on Oahu and those on the other islands show great differences in precipitation amounts. The temperatures, however, remain equable. Unlike many areas in the tropics, the climate of the Hawaiian Islands can be described as very pleasant.

VEGETATION

Plants tend to adapt to particular precipitation and temperature regimes, hence to particular climatic regions. Topographic and soil conditions are also of consequence. Through adaptation plant formations or plant communities are formed. They may contain a number of different species from which a dominant, or climax, vegetation emerges. In the humid climates the climax vegetation is likely to be the forest; in the subhumid areas the grasses; in the deserts the desert grasses and shrubs. In much of the United States the climax, or natural, vegetation has been removed. Forests have been cut, grasslands destroyed by fire, and new plants and crops introduced to many of the country's regions. Nevertheless, five vegetation regions are distinguished in the coterminous United States: Subtropical Evergreen Forest, Mid-latitude Deciduous Forest, Coniferous Forest, Grasslands, and Desert. Alaska adds a sixth, Tundra; and the Hawaiian Islands a seventh, Oceanic.

Subtropical Evergreen Forest

The Subtropical Evergreen Forest includes much of the Atlantic and Gulf Coastal Plain and the Tropical Savanna and Humid Subtropical climatic regions. The tip of southern Florida is marked by a mangrove forest; cypress is found along the streams. Broom, saw, and marsh grasses line the coasts. The dominant tree in the interior is the southern, or yellow, pine, known for its strength compared to other conifers. Some oaks and gums are interspersed among the evergreens— probably because of particular soil conditions.

Mid-latitude Deciduous Forest

The Mid-latitude Deciduous Forest extends from southern New England to eastern Texas and eastern Iowa. It includes the Ohio and much of the Mississippi River valleys. Its northern border is south of lakes Michigan and Erie. Before European and American settlement the area was covered with a wide variety of deciduous trees: oak, maple, walnut, beech, hickory, ash, tulip, poplar, and others. Much of the original forest was stripped by indiscriminate cutting and was ravaged by fire. Only remnants are left.

Coniferous Forest

The Coniferous Forest lies north of the Mid-latitude Deciduous Forest. It extends from northern New England to the Great Lakes and Minnesota. Portions of the Western High Areas and the Marine West Coast are also included, as is the central interior of Alaska. Conifers dominate—spruce and fir in northern Maine; white pine in Michigan and Wisconsin; ponderosa pine and Douglas fir in the Western High Areas; redwoods in northern California; and Douglas fir, hemlock, and red cedar in the Marine West Coast. White-pine cutting was at its peak in the 1890s in Michigan, and by 1910 most of the trees were gone. The conifers in the Western High Areas remain, as do the tallest trees in the world—the redwoods—most of which are on private land. In the 1960s Redwood National Park was created in an effort to preserve the trees. Hemlock, spruce, and cedar continue to dominate the coasts of Oregon and Washington, while the Douglas fir is predominant inland.

Grasslands

Grass—tall-grass prairie and short-grass prairie-steppe—marked the land from Iowa west to Wyoming and from Montana and North Dakota south to Texas. A portion of the tall-grass prairie is included in the so-called Prairie Wedge in Illinois; short-grass prairie-steppe is found in eastern Oregon, Washington, and western Idaho in the Palouse Hills. The Central Valley of California is also part of the Grasslands. In the moister eastern parts big bluestem was the most characteristic grass. In the drier Great Plains grama, buffalo, and bunch grasses were dominant. The deep and tangled root systems of these grasses made the prairies especially difficult to plow; yet most of the tall-grass prairie was brought under cultivation. Ranching and winter wheat (Texas to Nebraska) and spring wheat (the Dakotas) are dominant enterprises in the drier prairie-steppe. Wheat is grown under dry-farming methods in the Palouse Hills. Fruit, nut, and vegetable crops replaced the native grasses in the Central Valley of California.

Desert

Deserts cover most of the Interior Plateau. They are found in the lee of the Cascades, in the Great Basin, and south into southwestern Texas and California. These areas tend to be scrublands dominated by sage and short grass. Varieties of cactus are found in the arid southwest, and mesquite is familiar in western Texas. Upslope in the plateau country are piñon and juniper and at higher elevations ponderosa pine and Douglas fir.

Tundra

The tundra in Alaska extends along the shores of the Arctic Ocean, the Bering Strait, and southward to the Aleutian Islands. It is treeless. Grasses, lichens, and mosses dominate the vegetation. Tundra is also found at high elevations in the Lower 48.

Oceanic

Isolation, a temperate climate, and great environmental variations created a unique vegetation pattern

Sheep grazing in the Big Horn Mountains in Wyoming (top) are eating grasses that grow in aridisols, pale-colored soils that produce sparse vegetation. The tundra in Denali State Park in Alaska (bottom) is an example of inceptisol soil, a type also found in the Rocky Mountains.

101

in the Hawaiian Islands. There are several thousand native plants, most found nowhere else in the world. Plumeria, ornamental hibiscus, coconut, and taro—which are closely associated with the islands—are exotics introduced from elsewhere. Much of the native vegetation has been destroyed by both human and animal predators.

SOILS

Soil is the natural medium in which plants grow. No two soils are exactly alike, but similar soils form under similar environmental conditions. The parent rock, topography, living matter, age of materials, and climate all contribute to soil formation. Soils are so complex that classification is a problem. The following classification is based on the Seventh Approximation of the United States Department of Agriculture.

Spudosols

Spudosols, acidic and low in nutrients, tend to develop in cool, moist places. Accordingly they are found under the Coniferous Forest region in northern New England and in the Great Lakes area of northern Michigan, Wisconsin, and Minnesota. Spudosols also appear in central Florida.

Ultisols

The ultisols have been much weathered and leveled. They are highly acidic but can be productive. They are found in the heavy moisture areas of southern Florida and on the Atlantic and Gulf Coastal Plain, excluding the lower Mississippi Valley where udalfs tend to dominate. They are also found under coniferous forests in the Cascade Range and Sierra Nevada on the West coast.

Alfisols

Udalf soils are the soils of the mid-latitude forests and forest-grassland borderlands. The udalfs occur in humid climates with at least one moisture-deficient period. Like the ultisols they are somewhat acidic, but applications of lime can make them quite fertile. They underlie the Mid-latitude Deciduous Forest from New York State to eastern Iowa and Missouri. They are also the dominant soil type in the lower Ohio and lower Mississippi valleys.

Boralf soils were formed under the forest cover at considerably lower temperatures. They are acidic but have little agricultural potential. They can be found in west-central Wisconsin and east-central Minnesota.

Ustalfs exist in warmer areas where there are strong seasonal variations in precipitation. They are found primarily in Texas, Oklahoma, and New Mexico.

Xeralfs are brownish, reddish soils that form in Mediterranean climates (hot dry summers and cool moist winters). They are quite productive and are found in the Great Valley and southern California.

Inceptisols

The alfisol boralfs merge into inceptisols (also soils of the humid regions) under the spruce-fir forests of the Rocky Mountains. They in turn merge into still another inceptisol at the higher elevations—cryaquepts in the tundra. Inceptisols dominate in the Appalachians.

Vertisols

Vertisols are clayey soils that occasionally crack (open and close) over time, depending on the weather. They can be found along the Gulf coast in southwestern Louisiana and southeastern Texas; in Mississippi, Alabama, and Arizona; in the Coast Ranges of California; and in the Hawaiian Islands.

Mollisols

The mollisols are the thick, dark brown to black, high-nutrient soils of the Grasslands. They are naturally fertile and are conducive to growing cereal crops. Mollisols are found on the Great Plains, in the Illinois Wedge, and in the area east of the Cascade Range. The fine wheat crops of the Palouse Hills, for example, are grown on mollisols.

Aridisols

The pale-colored aridisols form in areas of little moisture and sparse vegetation. They are low in organic matter. Aridisols are found in much of the Great Basin and in Wyoming, eastern Colorado, New Mexico, Arizona, and southern California. Grazing is the ideal form of land utilization, but crops can be grown under irrigation.

Inceptisols of Alaska and Hawaii

Aquepts are wet inceptisols associated in Alaska with low temperatures and little precipitation. Permafrost, or permanently frozen ground, increases soil wetness. Outside southeastern Alaska, the Aleutian Islands, and the Brooks Range, aquepts are the dominant soil in Alaska.

Because of the great variety of climates, topography, and land cover in the Hawaiian Islands, there is also a multiplicity of soils. Oxisols, with high organic and clay content, are prominent in the older western islands. They are found on the windward eastern side of Kauai and on Oahu's Schofield Plateau planted in pineapples. Histisols, light soils that hold water well, can be found on Kauai, Oahu, and Hawaii. The inceptisols include soils of great diversity and are common on the newer Hawaii. The variety andepts occurs on or near active volcanoes and develops from volcanic ash.

Regions

Physiographic provinces and climatic, vegetation, and soil regions provide a way of organizing a complex set of data that deals with the physical characteristics of the United States. Many other regions have also been delineated. There are economic, cultural, and sociocultural regions; there are political, manufacturing, and dialect regions. There are regions where one religion or another has had a strong influence. There are obviously many others.

New
England

Eric Carle—Shostal/EB Inc.

The picturesque White Mountains extend across north-central New Hampshire and into Maine. The highest elevations in the Northeast are in this range.

New England's coast was settled by the Pilgrims and the Puritans in the 17th century. The Pilgrims established Plymouth in 1620; the Puritans founded Salem in 1628. Charlestown and Boston (1630) were settlements in the Massachusetts Bay Colony. By 1700 New Englanders had moved into eastern New Hampshire and southeastern Maine, Roger Williams had founded Providence (1636) in Rhode Island, and settlers had moved into Connecticut and Vermont.

Portions of the forest were cut, and attempts were made to farm the land. The work was backbreaking and the yields poor. New Englanders in the interior, inured to the land, continued to farm. Near the coast they farmed too, but they turned increasingly to the sea. The sea offshore was full of cod, herring, menhaden, mackerel, mussels, and lobsters. New Englanders built ships of native lumber, challenged the seas, and fished the area between the coast and the Grand Banks.

It can be said that New England grew through the 18th and 19th centuries—and into the 20th—in two parts: the New England of the rural interior, of the rivers and lakes, the glacial soils, the little towns and villages, the small self-sufficient farms; and the New England that faced the sea, that became increasingly world conscious, urban, and sophisticated. (*See also* articles on individual states.)

Rural Scene

The farmers worked from before dawn to after dusk. They milked cows, cut wood, prepared maple trees for sugaring; they plowed and harrowed the fields, planted vegetables, cared for apples and peaches in the orchard; they raised chickens and turkeys, pigs, sheep, and cattle. Summer was haying time and autumn the time of harvest. Equally busy were the farmers' wives. They were responsible for all the household chores, churning butter, tending fires, and caring for children. Good times were few: attendance at town hall or Grange meetings, visits to the country store or post office, winter skating, sleigh riding and bobsledding, summer swimming in ponds or streams.

When the western lands opened after the building of the Erie Canal in 1825, many of these farmers abandoned New England. They moved into New York State, into Michigan and the West. Some remained and continued to practice farming as it had been practiced for generations.

Truck and tobacco farming became significant on the Connecticut River terraces. Onions were a popular truck crop. Leaf tobacco, grown from a variety of Cuban imports, was planted under the shade of cheesecloth screens. The product was found to be admirable for cigar manufacture and became a bestseller. Blueberries, grown in acidic soils on lands formerly covered with spruce, became a specialty crop in eastern Maine. In the bogs and swamps of southeastern Massachusetts, cranberries began to flourish. Rhode Island reds, used for breeding, helped to inaugurate a significant interest in poultry production.

Potatoes—for the potato starch industry and for seed—became a major crop in cool, moist Aroostook County in northern Maine. The potatoes were farmed in a three-year rotation—potatoes, followed by oats, then hay, and back to potatoes. Oats and hay were fed to the animals; potatoes were strictly a money crop, a fine example of an agricultural specialty. Potato farmers fell on hard times during the 1950s and 1960s. Competition from potato farmers in Idaho and Oregon was keen. The number of farms in Aroostook

Fishing for scallops (top) and other seafood off the coast of Nantucket Island, Mass., is one of the mainstays of New England's economy. Potatoes are still harvested near cool, moist Aroostook County, Me. (bottom).

County dropped from more than 4,500 to 1,300. There were a few good potato years in the mid-1970s.

Another specialty area lies in western Vermont—in the Champlain Lowland. It is devoted to dairying. Until World War I Vermont dairymen were most concerned with the production of butter and cheese. Milk production predominated after the war. Mild, moist summers favor the growth of fodder crops like hay, and milk cows thrive.

Urge to the Sea

Hearty New Englanders took readily to the sea. They built the masts and spars for their early ships of pine and the ribs and hull from tough oak. In the 18th century the schooner was already plying Atlantic waters. New England sailors, having made their catches on or near the Grand Banks, sailed to the Mediterranean with dried cod and salt herring; on the Guinea coast of Africa they purchased slaves and brought them to the West Indies and the American South; they purchased sugar, molasses, and rum in the Indies to bring to New England ports. Boston and Newport, R.I., became centers of the slave trade.

New Englanders later sailed the famous clipper ships. They sent their sealers and whalers from New London and Mystic, Conn., and New Bedford and Nantucket, Mass., to the seas of the world. In local waters fishermen netted the menhaden—also for its oil—the famous porgy, as New Englanders termed it.

In 1900 New England fishing was centered in Boston and Gloucester. Gloucester supported a fleet of 400 ships. Lobstering in Maine and oystering in Connecticut continue to be significant enterprises. Haddock, cod, mackerel, redfish, hake, flounder, and pollack are still brought into New England's ports.

Manufacturing

Capital earned on the seven seas helped to establish New England manufacturing. Samuel Slater, recently arrived from England, in 1790 established near the falls of the Blackstone River at Pawtucket, R.I., the first cotton manufacturing center in America (*see* Slater). The first spinning machines were driven by hand or animal power but were later replaced by the water wheel. Manufacturing centers grew up at the widely scattered water-power sites. By 1800, 29 other mills were operating in and around Pawtucket; by 1810 62 were in operation and 25 others were being built. The War of 1812 and later the Civil War spurred the manufacturing industries. New England factories turned out most of the war's necessities: rifles, cartridges, and bayonets; uniforms, overcoats, shoes, socks, and caps; tents and flags.

By the time of the Civil War, factories were beginning to locate near tidewater. The use of the steam engine and the need for imported coal made the move possible and necessary. New England factories were to be dominated by the tall smokestack well into the 20th century.

Like the farmers in the rural interior, mill hands in urban New England worked hard. Yankees, Irish,

French Canadians, and later immigrants from Eastern and Southern Europe—Poles, Greeks, and Portuguese—all contributed to the textile mills. They worked 12-hour days in the weaving or carding rooms—often standing. Amid the dust and lint they suffered from respiratory diseases. They often lived in company houses. Many of the workers were women.

The largest textile plant in the world—the Amoskeag Manufacturing Company—was located in Manchester, N.H. There were large mills in Lowell, Lawrence, and Fall River, Mass., and many others in smaller communities. The largest loom room in the world—covering 9 acres (3.6 hectares), with 4,000 looms—stood in Salem, Mass. Textiles became a mainstay in the economy of New England.

There were other manufactures—specialties—at which New Englanders also excelled: shoes, machines, woolens, brass, and hardware. Lynn, Brockton, and Haverhill, Mass., were famous for leatherware—shoes and boots; Athol, Mass., for fine machine tools; Lawrence, Lowell, and Holyoke, Mass., and Woonsocket and Providence, R.I., for woolens and worsteds; and Danbury, Conn., for felt hats. The Naugatuck Valley in Connecticut was known for brass and hardware—the greatest center at New Britain. St. Johnsbury, Vt., made scales; Waltham, Mass., watches; Holyoke, paper; and Cambridge, books.

Much of the old New England manufacturing collapsed over time. The textile industry succumbed to competition from the South. Southern workers, who were nonunion, worked longer hours for lower wages. Land in the South cost less, and rents and taxes were lower. Southern realists knew that the future lay in synthetics. New England spindles began to move to Southern climes. In 1935 the Amoskeag Company declared bankruptcy. By 1950 New England had lost nearly 150,000 jobs in the textile industry. Eight-hundred little firms, however, still work in the area.

The shoe industry also succumbed. Part of it moved west, but shoes could be made less expensively—and just as well—in Spain, Italy, and the Far East. It is noteworthy that some 60,000 people are still employed making New England's shoes. Other industrial enterprises simply hang on—many fighting for their lives. New England's thrust today—after the bad recession years of the 1970s, when unemployment in Rhode Island was more than 16 percent and in Massachusetts more than 12 percent—is in high-tech industries, electronic components, machinery, and plastics.

Boston and Megalopolis

Boston became the hub of New England very early. All roads, including railroads, led to the city. Boston was a leading market and manufacturing community. Wool was bought and sold; woolens, worsteds, and leather footwear were made; books and magazines were published; the port was alive with foreign commerce and with ships engaged in the coastwise trade. By 1900 Boston had more than 500,000 people; by 1935 more than 800,000. After a marked decline, the city came back physically superior and better able to cope with its problems. By 1980 Boston's population had fallen to 641,071, but its metropolitan area numbered nearly 3 million. (*See also* Boston.)

Boston is part of the great megalopolis that extends from near Richmond, Va., to Portland, Me.—a great urban region in itself. Also included are Providence, Warwick, and Pawtucket, R.I.; Springfield, Chicopee, and Holyoke, Mass.; and Hartford, New Haven, and West Haven, Conn. In 1980 New England's overall population was just under 12½ million.

The Future

New England's economy can be called mature. It has long passed from the agricultural to the industrial state. New England has numerous problems: few natural resources, no coal or petroleum, high electric power costs, and much apathy and scepticism. At the same time New England has many assets: an educational system from elementary to graduate school that is first rate, great pools of capital, the ability to make precision products, a magnificent historical heritage, and a beautiful countryside that lends itself to tourism. New England can look to its past with pride; it can also look to its future with promise.

Rock of Ages granite quarry is near Barre, Vt., which has been a center of the nation's granite quarrying since 1812.

Courtesy of the State of Vermont

Middle Atlantic Region

Cary Wolinsky—CLICK/Chicago

Johnstown, Pa., became a major steel-producing city in the 1860s, but this industry declined after World War II.

The Middle Atlantic Region—made up of the states of New York, New Jersey, Pennsylvania, Delaware, Maryland, and the District of Columbia—was largely settled in the 17th century by a number of European peoples: the Dutch in the Hudson River valley and New Amsterdam (New York); the English on Long Island, neighboring New Jersey, and Maryland; the Swedes in the lower Delaware Valley; and the Germans and Scots-Irish in Pennsylvania. Each of these groups practiced its own religion. (*See also* articles on individual states.)

The region thrived on commerce. New Amsterdam collected furs from the interior and shipped them to Holland as early as 1626. Baltimore shipped Chesapeake Bay tobacco to England and grain, hams, and barrel staves to the West Indies. Philadelphia grew as a grain-shipping port, as did Wilmington, Del. The interior region thrived on general farming, on mining the rich anthracite and bituminous coal deposits, and on the growth of heavy industry—particularly iron and steel. There are perhaps two parts to the Middle Atlantic Region—one commercially oriented that faces the sea and is part of the great megalopolis that extends from Portland to near Richmond; the other dominated by the Appalachian Highlands and the Allegheny Plateau and Lakes Erie and Ontario that is part of the great American manufacturing belt.

Iron Manufacture Moves Westward

Iron was made in the Pine Barrens of southern New Jersey beginning late in the 17th century. Bog iron was used. Power was derived from the streams, and fuel in the form of charcoal was obtained from the forests. The reducing agents, or flux, were oyster and clam shells found along the Jersey shore. The furnaces, when in blast, operated day and night. The forges produced bar iron and pig iron. Many operated well into the 19th century.

But the movement westward had already begun into the anthracite iron district: Scranton, Shomokin, Allentown, and Pottsville, Pa., where anthracite was the fuel and limestone the flux. Although pig iron was made in Pittsburgh as early as 1812, it was not until 1859 that the first coking coal furnace was employed using the famous Connellsville coke. With the new coking coal Pittsburgh began to flourish as an iron-making center.

Erie Canal

New York City, Philadelphia, and Baltimore were all rivals for the trade of the growing interior—the Ohio River valley and the West. Location favored New York in the struggle. It could tap the lowest route through the highlands by way of the Mohawk Depression. The 363-mile (584-kilometer) Erie Canal was constructed from 1817 to 1825 along the Mohawk between the Hudson River and Lake Erie. Prices for carrying grain from the Middle West to New York began to fall. New York City began to grow rapidly, as did the communities built on and near the canal: Albany, Schenectady, Utica, Syracuse, Rochester, Buffalo, and others. In 1836 a million bushels of Western grain were unloaded in Buffalo; 4 million in 1840. Transshipped to canal boats, the grain was sent to New York City, where it was processed into flour. The canal cities also attracted the railroads. Competition between canal and rail was keen. Fares were kept low. Rail traffic in New York State did not surpass canal traffic until 1870.

Agriculture

Meanwhile, because of the region's growth, there was a call for more and more agricultural produce. The sandy soils of the Coastal Plain, the long growing season, and the proximity of a huge urban market proved favorable for the development of truck farming. Western Long Island, the Pine Barrens of New Jersey, and Delaware's three counties began to produce a wide variety of truck crops, including potatoes and cauliflower, sweet corn and onions, cabbages and tomatoes. Cranberries were a mainstay in New Jersey's bog area; watermelons were equally significant in Kent County, Del. So widespread was truck farming in New Jersey that the nickname the Garden State was adopted by the state. Truck farming continues as a major resource. The sandy soils are fertilized with lime, and products are marketed by cooperatives. Much of the produce goes into canning in the Baltimore and Camden, N.J., centers.

A significant agriculture also grew in eastern Pennsylvania. It was dominated by wheat, rye, oats, barley, buckwheat, hemp, and flax. Fruit orchards and vegetable gardens were maintained, as were forage crops. Cattle, pigs, sheep, and horses were raised. In Lancaster County the Pennsylvania Dutch raised tobacco in a four-year rotation—wheat, clover, and corn, followed by potatoes and tobacco. Amish and Mennonite farmers still cling tenaciously to old European farming techniques and to many of their social customs.

In the highlands to the west, agriculture is devoted to corn, pigs, and chickens and to stock raising and dairying. Notable are the vineyards in the vicinity of the Great Lakes and orchards devoted to apples, peaches, and plums—the Niagara Fruit Belt.

Coal and Steel

Anthracite, or hard coal, early used in the iron industry, became a favorite fuel because it is smokeless. It was widely used in the Middle Atlantic Region and in New England. In the peak production years of 1916 and 1917, nearly 100 million tons were taken from eastern Pennsylvania. The industry employed more than 150,000 people. The anthracite towns were prosperous and progressive, but competition from fuel oil and natural gas cut into the need for anthracite. Production fell, and so did employment in the coalfields. By the 1950s production was down to 30 million tons per year, and fewer than 70,000 were employed. Today anthracite mining is minimal. The old anthracite towns have lost a significant resource.

In the bituminous coal area of western Pennsylvania, there have been many ups and downs. Production and employment remained high in the early years of the 20th century, fell sharply during the Great Depression (1930–39), rose again during World War II, only to decline again. Bituminous coal, or soft coal, unlike anthracite, burns with a smoky flame, contains sulfur, and gives off a sulfurous smell. It was not suitable for home use or for direct use in the iron-making furnaces of the 19th century. When heated with no air present, however, the sulfurous gases and other impurities can be eliminated. This discovery led to the beehive oven that draws its heat from the burning of the gases from the coals. Some coals, of course, are better than others. Connellsville coke, found near Chestnut Ridge southeast of Pittsburgh, proved to be the best of the coking coals. Before long beehive coking ovens began to dot the western Pennsylvania countryside.

New technology in iron and steel continued to develop—the Bessemer converter and the open-hearth furnace. To meet the growing demand for steel—especially for steel rails—western Pennsylvanians turned to northern Michigan and later to the Lake Superior district in Minnesota—the great Mesabi Range—for their iron ores. They brought in metallurgical limestone from Michigan and used the local Connellsville coke for fuel. Because it takes twice as much coke as iron ore to produce a heat of steel, Connellsville coke helped to root the iron and steel industry in western Pennsylvania, especially in and near Pittsburgh.

Consolidation of all phases of the industry took place with the formation of the United States Steel Corporation in 1901. To protect the industry a pricing system known as Pittsburgh Plus was introduced. All steel companies—no matter where they were located—based their prices on those quoted by United States Steel at Pittsburgh. Companies located elsewhere also had to add the cost of transportation to Pittsburgh. The system, which further rooted the iron and steel industry to the Pittsburgh area, was not abandoned until 1924.

In later years mammoth steel plants, using foreign iron ores, were built near Baltimore and Philadelphia. Buffalo, on Lake Erie, had long been a great steel-making center. Bad times have since come to the steel-making communities, and many plants have shut down, with others struggling. Most are trying to diversify their industries. Pittsburgh has moved from a heavy industry base to one focused on basic research.

Cities

New York City, Philadelphia, Baltimore, and Washington, D.C., are the dominant cities in the eastern portion of the Middle Atlantic Region. Pittsburgh and Buffalo dominate the western portion.

New York City. A traveler to New York City pointed out in the 1840s that "Every Western man on his first visit to New York will be struck with the immensity of the place." This is still true. In 1840 New York's population numbered only 312,710; by 1980 the city numbered more than 7 million, the metropolitan area more than 9 million. The city and metropolitan area are served by the Port of New York Authority, which spills over into New Jersey. Newark and Elizabeth, the northeastern counties of New Jersey, Long Island, and portions of southern New York State and Connecticut are all part of the New York metropolitan area. (*See also* New York, N.Y.)

Philadelphia, at the junction of the Delaware and Schuylkill rivers, was the largest and wealthiest of American cities during colonial times. It also served briefly as the capital of the United States (1790–1800). Its growth was steady and impressive. Much of today's growth, however, is in Philadelphia's suburbs. In 1980 the city itself had a population of nearly 1.7 million, the metropolitan area more than 4.7 million. (*See also* Philadelphia.)

Baltimore, on the Patapsco River near Chesapeake Bay, developed early as a commercial center. Tobacco was the earliest of the trade commodities. In the 19th century—taking advantage of favorable freight rates and rail connections with the Western interior—the city became a handler and exporter of grain and coal. Baltimore grew rapidly. But time, as in the other large Middle Atlantic Region centers, took its toll. By the 1950s Baltimore was a dying city. It fought back, it cleared 33 acres (13 hectares) downtown to build the Charles Center. It renovated the Inner Harbor. Baltimore is coming back. In 1980 it had just short of 800,000 people and its metropolitan area more than 2 million. (*See also* Baltimore, Md.)

Washington, D.C., is a unique city. It was created to serve as the capital of the nation on land donated by the states of Maryland and Virginia. The city grew as the nation's political power and governmental functions grew. A city of tree-studded thoroughfares, parks, open spaces, and beautiful public buildings, Washington is a symbol of the United States and has become a significant tourist center. In 1980 its population totaled more than 600,000, its metropolitan area more than 3 million. (*See also* Washington, D.C.)

Pittsburgh. The geographer J. Russell Smith described Pittsburgh and the neighboring mill towns as "a land of fire." With burning coke ovens, smoke, flaming furnaces, and white hot pouring metal, Pittsburgh was the steel city, the smoke city. Coal smog hung everywhere. Residents knew in the 1940s that Pittsburgh was dying and that something had to be done to save it. A strong smoke abatement program was passed. Railroads were barred from firing their coal-burning engines in or near the city.

When diesel engines replaced coal burners, the air above Pittsburgh became remarkably clear. Old slum dwellings were torn down, new low-cost housing was erected, and many old houses were rehabilitated. A new and sparkling Gateway Center rose in the Golden Triangle, the central business district bounded by the Allegheny and Monongahela rivers. Pittsburgh was a city reborn. In 1980 the population numbered more than 400,000, and there were more than 2 million in the metropolitan area. (*See also* Pittsburgh.)

Buffalo, at the mouth of the Niagara River on Lake Erie, began to grow rapidly after the completion of the Erie Canal in 1825. Grain, brought to its docks from the Middle West, was milled in Buffalo and shipped to the Eastern seaboard. Lumber mills, tanneries, furniture factories, iron foundries, and breweries marked the beginnings of a diverse manufacturer. Heavy industry came to the city in 1904 with the Lackawanna Iron and Steel Company. By the 1920s Buffalo was producing steel, railroad cars and engines, automobiles, and airplanes. Taking advantage of the hydroelectric power at nearby Niagara Falls, the city became a leading manufacturer of aluminum and chemicals.

It was the St. Lawrence Seaway (1959) that dealt a major blow to Buffalo's economy. Ships moving through the Great Lakes by way of the Welland Canal into Lake Ontario could bypass Buffalo's docks—and did. The glory days were over. In 1950 Buffalo had a population of 532,000; in 1980 the city had been reduced to less than 360,000 but with a metropolitan area of some 1.2 million. (*See also* Buffalo, N.Y.)

The Future

The Middle Atlantic Region, like New England, has a mature economy in a post-industrial era. Government defense contracts, ventures in space, and funds for technological development have passed to centers in the sunbelt. Its population growth has slowed. Many people have left its major cities and have moved to the suburbs or left the region. But renovation and rehabilitation are occurring in individual centers. Baltimore and Pittsburgh are models in that respect.

Cranberries are harvested each fall in southern New Jersey. Berry picking begins in September and continues until late October.

Phil Degginger—CLICK/Chicago

The South

Courtesy of the Georgia Department of Industry and Trade; photo, Bob Busby

At 729 feet (222 meters), the waterfall in Amicalola Falls State Park near Dawsonville, Ga., is the highest in the state. The park is one of about 40 in the state.

The South can be divided into three separate entities. The traditional South extends from Virginia to eastern Texas and swings northward to include much of Arkansas and western Tennessee and Kentucky. The southern portions of the Appalachian Highlands make up another division, and the Gulf Coast and Florida form a third. (*See also* articles on individual states.)

Traditional South

Hot, humid, and blessed with a long growing season and a variety of soils, the South from its beginnings was marked for agriculture. In Virginia and North Carolina tobacco became the chief crop. In the sea islands off the coast of South Carolina and Georgia, rice and indigo were planted. The English and Scots-Irish settlers who had been granted large estates, developed the so-called plantation system of land tenure. Because the labor requirements on plantations were great, blacks were imported from Africa and the West Indies to work the fields. Thus the cornerstones of Southern culture and land use—an agricultural base, a white population that stemmed largely from the British Isles and was overwhelmingly Protestant, the plantation system, and a black population that served as slaves—were laid early. In 1793 Eli Whitney, working as a tutor on a Georgia plantation, invented the cotton gin. This machine, which separates the seeds from the cotton, makes the production of cotton easier and its sale price much lower (*see* Whitney, Eli). Cotton growing on a large scale (it was grown earlier in small amounts) spread widely in the South and became yet another cornerstone in Southern culture and land use.

Movement westward. After the Revolutionary War the lands beyond the Appalachians were opened to settlement. Southerners from Virginia and the Carolinas moved into Kentucky and Tennessee. Early in

the 19th century Georgians were following the Old Federal Road into the Black Belt of Alabama. In the western locales Southerners attempted to reproduce the culture of the South. In the Blue Grass of Kentucky and the Nashville Basin of Tennessee, black slaves cleared the fields and planted and harvested the crops. Grains, tobacco, and hemp were the major plantings. They were often shipped down the Mississippi River to New Orleans for export. In the dark chalky soil of the black belt, cotton and plantation agriculture were dominant. Black slaves formed a majority of the population. Dallas County, Ala.,—the leading cotton producer—was 76 percent black in 1860.

Farther west in and around Natchez, Miss., cotton also helped to produce a wealthy plantation society. A bit farther north in the Yazoo-Mississippi Delta (known simply as the Delta to Mississippians), settlement was long delayed by Indian occupation and frequent flooding. But the rich soil and flat land eventually enticed the cotton planters to the area. A wealthy slave-holding society arose. In a number of delta areas black slaves outnumbered the white population ten to one.

In the less-favored hill country of the South, there were no plantation houses, little cotton, and few slaves. Poorer farmers planted sorghum, peas, beans and potatoes, oats, barley, and rye. They raised razorbacks (pigs). Obviously not all of the South's farmers worked plantations, owned slaves, and raised cotton.

Rise and demise of King Cotton. For plantation owners and hill-country farmers momentous changes were in the offing. During the Civil War (1861–65) the South's military forces were beaten on the battlefield, and black slaves were given their freedom. Following the war the South was subjected to Northern rule. On the farms, however, most blacks continued to work for white landowners, often as tenant farmers. Some whites, on the other hand, retreated into themselves.

109

Cotton is harvested by machine in Arkansas, one of the leading cotton states of today's South.

They became advocates of white supremacy, formed the Ku Klux Klan, and sought refuge in the Democratic party. Cotton continued to be the South's major crop. It was King Cotton, and the entire region was often called the cotton belt.

In 1892 little insects—boll weevils—crossed the Rio Grande from Mexico and invaded the cotton belt. The infant larvae ate their way into the unripe cotton pods, thereby spoiling the crop. By 1921 the South was entirely infested. Cotton production began to decline markedly; yields per acre fell sharply. Five years after the boll weevils arrived in Louisiana 75 percent of the state's cotton crop had been destroyed; ten years after the arrival two thirds of Georgia's cotton crop was no more. King Cotton's long reign had been brought to an end. The Old South was dead. In its place a New South would rise.

Old South to New South. Growing industrialization and urbanization, government policies and wars, and mechanization and diversification in agriculture helped to change the Old South to the New South. The process was slow and often painful.

Cotton mills had been erected in the 1840s at Charleston and Columbia, S.C., in Petersburg and Richmond, Va., in Augusta and Columbus, Ga., and Huntsville and Florence, Ala. Richmond had its flour mill, and little iron works dotted the nearby Appalachians. By the 1880s Southern towns were vying

with one another (they offered a free site, exemption from taxes, and only minor regulations) for the construction of new factories. Wherever these factories were built tenant farmers and mountain families moved to the new sites. In 1880 there were only 184 cotton textile mills in the South; by 1900 the number of mills had increased to 416.

There were murmurings in lumber and iron and steel. In the 1890s furniture was already being made in North Carolina. High Point emerged as the leading center a decade later. In the southern Appalachians of Alabama (economically part of the traditional South), good coking coal, iron ore, and limestone were found in conjunction—a most unusual occurrence. In 1871 pig iron furnaces and a rolling mill were constructed in Birmingham. Former black slaves, poor whites, and European immigrants (from the British Isles and Southern Europe) were all attracted to the iron-making center. In spite of a strike by area miners against mine owners in 1894, Birmingham's industrial base continued to grow. The first open-hearth furnace was built in 1899. In 1907 Birmingham's iron-and-steel complex became part of United States Steel.

There were major changes in tobacco making. Factories that made chewing and smoking tobacco and snuff in Virginia, North Carolina, and Kentucky had predated the Civil War. Closed during the war, they soon reopened. By the 1880s new machines were stemming the leaf, packaging and labeling the products. A cigarette-rolling machine replaced the hand rolling of the past. The industry was becoming highly mechanized and standardized. It was centered in Durham, N.C. A virtual monopoly was formed (cigars not included) with the organization of the American Tobacco Company in 1910.

Meanwhile the railroads, shattered during the Civil War, were revamped. Mileage in the South was doubled, and the gauge was changed to conform with the general pattern of the country. Despite being controlled by Northern capital, the rejuvenation of the railroads helped change the Old South to the New.

A number of the changes came slowly. Relationships between the races, for example, had hardened. Jim Crow, or segregation, laws were designed to create two separate societies in the South—one white, the other black. Separate areas in which to live, separate railroad cars, drinking fountains, hospitals, restaurants, schools, even separate cemeteries—separate but equal in theory but certainly not in practice.

During the 1930s the United States government made great efforts to spur development in the South. The Tennessee Valley Authority (TVA), set up in 1933, was an attempt at regional rejuvenation. A program of improved river navigation and flood control was planned. Low-cost electricity was provided as well as reforestation and improved use of marginal lands. TVA helped provide for the industrial growth of the entire Tennessee Valley. It later housed the final stages of the Manhattan Project, which during World War II was in charge of developing the atomic bombs manufactured at Oak Ridge.

A wide variety of New Deal measures helped considerably. Projects of the Public Works Administration (PWA) and the Works Progress Administration (WPA) were particularly helpful. New roads, bridges, airports, post offices, and schools were built. Employment was stimulated. The Civilian Conservation Corps (CCC) planted trees and drained swamps. The Agricultural Adjustment Acts of 1935 and 1938, designed to limit agricultural output and maintain high prices, were perhaps less successful.

World War II and its aftermath brought further changes. Tractors and power tools became conspicuous on the farms. Cotton was sown by mechanical seeders and weeded by flame throwers. Airplanes dusted the fields with insecticides. The cotton crop—smaller than in previous decades—was harvested by mechanical pickers. Tobacco continued to be a significant crop. Rice growing was also significant in Louisiana, Arkansas, and Mississippi; sugarcane in Louisiana. Diversification also played a role in the changes. Nuts, fruits, and vegetables became money-making crops: pecans and peanuts; apples, pears, peaches, and grapes; potatoes and sweet potatoes. There were truck crops needed to supply the growing urban markets: tomatoes, beans, cabbages, asparagus, squash, cauliflower, and cucumbers. There was spectacular growth in broiler chicken and turkey production in Georgia, the Carolinas, and Tennessee. Farmers—using better grasses, fodder, and fertilizers—raised beef cattle, milk cows, sheep, and pigs. Soybeans were rotated with rice, wheat, or corn. In 1981 farmers earned 3.5 billion dollars on soybeans; cotton earned 1.1 billion dollars the same year.

The industrial scene was also changing. As early as 1950 E.I. du Pont de Nemours had opened its new air-conditioned orlon processing plant in Camden, S.C. It employed 950 people—half from Camden itself and half from the surrounding cotton and tobacco lands. Before long Camden was building a new junior high school and a new high school for blacks. It built new sewer lines and removed its outdoor privies. New drive-in theaters, furniture stores, and supermarkets were built. Ministers noted that church membership increased. Most significant, the 12-foot (3.7-meter) marble Confederate monument was moved from the middle of Broad Street to a new site in the park. The New South had come to Camden.

Industrial parks mushroomed—more than 100 in Georgia alone. Research Triangle Park was organized in Durham, Chapel Hill, and Raleigh, N.C. Local development districts were formed in many places. They recommended improvements in schools, hospitals, public utilities, and recreational facilities. Small plants were encouraged to move to small towns. The South was getting richer, more urbanized, less dependent on agriculture, and more dependent on commerce and industry.

In spite of many economic improvements, the old race problem did not disappear. In 1954 the Supreme Court declared in Brown *vs.* Board of Education of Topeka that school segregation and the "separate but equal" doctrine were both unconstitutional. White southerners were outraged. In Montgomery, Ala., in 1955, Rosa Parks refused to give up her seat on a bus to a white man. She was arrested. Martin Luther King, Jr., led a boycott against the Montgomery bus system. Mass protests were held all over the South. The Civil Rights Movement was born. The struggle goes on, but fewer blacks are now leaving the South. Many are even returning. Much has been done to strengthen relations between the races, though there is much yet to be done.

Cities. The South has a number of large seaport cities (Norfolk, Va., and Charleston, S.C.); several located on major rivers (Memphis, Tenn., and Louisville, Ky.); and any number that might be called cities of the interior (Atlanta, Ga.; Nashville, Tenn.; Birmingham, Ala.); and the urban complexes at Greensboro, Winston-Salem, and High Point, at Charlotte and Gastonia, and at Raleigh and Durham—all in North Carolina—and at Greenville and Spartanburg, S.C. With the single exception of Charleston, the populations of all of these metropolitan areas exceed 500,000. The Memphis and Louisville metropolitan areas number more than 900,000; Atlanta's metropolitan area population is more than 2 million. (*See also* Birmingham, Ala.; Charleston, S.C.; Charlotte, Greensboro; Louisville; Memphis; Nashville; Norfolk; Raleigh, N.C.; Winston-Salem.)

Atlanta, founded in 1845 on the rail line to Chattanooga and the West, was burned to the ground during General William T. Sherman's march to the sea in 1864. Restored, it became the South's major rail and distribution center. But growth was slow. In the 1920s and again in the 1950s Forward Atlanta programs were launched. The boosterism worked, and growth during the 1960s was phenomenal. New office buildings, warehouses, manufacturing plants, and housing of all kinds changed the physical look of the city. Atlanta became a leading financial and air transportation center and the showplace of the New South. (*See also* Atlanta.)

The future. The traditional South is a region transformed. It has passed from Old South to New South in little more than a half century. In a sense it has become less Southern and more integrated into the national scene and economy. The old cotton kingdom has long since passed into oblivion, and a new agriculture has appeared in its place. The South has become a significant manufacturing area. As part of the new sunbelt it continues to attract new industries and new residents.

In the future the traditional South's newfound wealth must be better distributed. Strong efforts are needed to improve education and health. Much attention must be paid to the continued improvement of relations between the races.

Appalachia

The Appalachian mountain system extends in a northwest-southeast direction from New York to northern Alabama. The northern portions are part of

The Blue Ridge Mountains stretch from Pennsylvania to northern Georgia. The range is one segment of the Appalachian Mountains.

the Middle Atlantic Region. The southern portions—West Virginia, western Virginia and North Carolina, eastern Kentucky and Tennessee, the northwestern corner of Georgia, and northern Alabama—are part of Appalachia.

Appalachia is dominated by topography—by the Blue Ridge in the east; the Great Valley, of which the Shenandoah, the James, the New, and the Tennessee valleys are parts; the Ridge and Valley (shale and sandstone ridges, limestone valleys); and to the west the rumpled lands of the Appalachian Plateau. Early travelers thought of the rugged mountains as barriers to movement, but they found in the Great Valley a long but relatively easy passage south. They also found the gaps through the mountains that led westward, one of which—the Cumberland Gap—led settlers to the blue grass of Kentucky and beyond.

Many of the settlers—predominantly Scots-Irish, English, and Germans—chose to remain in the Great Valley itself. Some moved to the neighboring Blue Ridge, and others pushed westward by way of the river valleys into the Ridge and Valley section. They occupied the small isolated valleys and put their land into farms. Their holdings were small, the yields only enough for subsistence. Americans moving westward late in the 18th and early 19th centuries joined the earlier settlers. When the valley lands were taken up, the lower ridges were occupied. These too proved conducive only to subsistence farming. The mountaineers—in valley and ridge alike—became isolated from the world of the Coastal Plain, from the developing Old South, and from the Great Valley itself. Life was turned inward. Independence, family, love of land and community, pride, loyalty, a deep Protestant faith, and a conservative life-style became the hallmarks of the mountain folk. When West Virginia joined the Union as a state in 1863, it adopted as its motto, *Montani semper liberi,* "Mountaineers are always free."

Bituminous coal. The mountaineers occupied the plateau country of West Virginia and the hill country of eastern Kentucky and Tennessee. Mountain folk moved into the neighboring hill country of Georgia and Alabama. One of the early discoveries was bituminous coal. By the 1840s coal from eastern Kentucky was already being moved down the Kentucky River by barge. In 1883 the Baby Mine was opened in Pocahontas, Va., only a mile (1.6 kilometers) from the West Virginia state line. Before long southern West Virginia was bristling with coal mines, loading tipples, and slag heaps. There were Princeton and Bramwell, Gary, Caretta, and War, Tralee and Matewan—coal to feed the Pittsburgh mills. In 1900, 5 million tons of coal were taken from West Virginia. Forty collieries and 3,000 beehive coking ovens were at work. These were boom days for the mountaineers.

Boom days were also present in the coal country of eastern Tennessee (Coal Creek in Anderson County), eastern Kentucky, and northern Alabama. The white mountaineers were joined (as in West Virginia) by black and immigrant miners. Coal, limestone, and iron ore at Red Mountain helped to form the foundations of Birmingham.

First boom and then bust. Mechanization, increased production of petroleum and natural gas as energy fuels, and a drop in coal prices led to increased unemployment in the mining areas. West Virginia and eastern Kentucky were particularly hard hit from 1950 to 1960. Poverty stalked the region. Out-migration was substantial as the mountaineers moved to the manufacturing towns of the Middle Atlantic Region and the Middle West. Not until the late 1970s and early 1980s was there a revival in coal production, due mostly to the great rises in oil prices beginning in 1973. Shaft mining where necessary and strip mining where possible were the methods. Much effort went into reclamation. The precious Appalachian land was to be cared for—preserved.

TVA once more. A major effort to rejuvenate Appalachian land and the South in general had been made earlier by the TVA in the 1930s. Plentiful power, a moderate climate, inland location (little vulnerability by land or sea), low land costs, and a good labor supply (mostly mountaineer women) led the famed Manhattan Project to Oak Ridge. By 1945, when Oak Ridge's atomic bomb burst over Hiroshima, the eastern Tennessee community had a population of 75,000. Dams and reservoirs in a "giant stairway" reshaped the Tennessee River watershed. Power began to flow into the nearby hill country; navigation on the river was improved; new industries were attracted to Knoxville and Chattanooga. Alcoa, using the awesome power supplied by TVA, built an aluminum plant in the area. TVA began to produce artificial fertilizers—a boon to the region. The Tri-Cities—Bristol, Johnson City, and Kingsport—became the home of significant manufacturing plants. Oak Ridge today, though substantially reduced in size, still produces fuel for nuclear power plants, millions of gallons of cooling water, and billions of kilowatt-hours of electricity. It remains the headquarters of the United States Atomic Energy Commission.

Farming. In the narrow steep valleys of the Ridge and Valley, where cropland is limited, general farming predominates. Emphasis often is on fodder for livestock. Corn is a major crop. Tobacco, tomatoes, cabbages, and apples are raised for sale, but the market is limited and incomes tend to be low. On the ridges where good air drainage exists, tree farming—peaches and apples—is significant. Farmers often are part-time operators. They have additional employment in nearby towns.

In the fertile limestone soils of the Great Valley, farming is quite different. The small farms of the Shenandoah Valley, for example, are marked by tilled fields, neat fences, freshly painted houses, and big barns. For years wheat was the major crop, but competition from the Great Plains eventually forced it to play second fiddle. Wheat is still grown, but corn, clover, and bluegrass are also major crops. Shenandoah Valley grains, cattle, and dairy produce are shipped to Great Britain, France, and local markets.

The lower Shenandoah Valley is famous for its apples. Several million apple trees bear excellent fruit in the Winchester and Martinsburg areas. In sharp contrast to the farmers of the Ridge and Valley, farmers here use the machines of the new technology. They have mechanical pickers and bulk loaders, and they spray the fruit to eliminate rust, scab, mildew, mites, and codling moths. Nearby Old Order Mennonites continue to farm using more traditional methods.

Farther south near the Virginia-Tennessee border, the tougher land is given over to pasture and the raising of cattle and sheep. In Alabama and Georgia a little cotton is grown.

Great Kanawha Valley. The availability of natural resources—salt brine and water, vitreous clay, bituminous coal, natural gas, and petroleum—helped to locate the chemical industry in West Virginia's Great Kanawha Valley. Hydroelectric power was also a major consideration. The hub of the chemical industry is at Charleston, where rail, highway, pipeline, and barge connections are easily made. Chemical plants—producing sulfuric acid, caustic soda, ammonia, chlorine, ether, and hydrochloric acid—line the banks of the narrow Kanawha at unequal intervals.

Watts Bar Dam, built to harness the waters of the Tennessee River, is one of the hydroelectric projects built and operated by the Tennessee Valley Authority (TVA).

Joe Viesti—Viesti Associates, Inc.

A powerful tugboat, viewed from the Sunshine Bridge, pushes 35 barges up the Mississippi River toward Baton Rouge, La.

Nearby are nylon, plastics, and rubber plants. Not far removed are glass factories and ferro-alloy processing establishments.

The Ohio River valley also has its chemical plants, asphalt and cement-making factories, oil depots, and good farmland between the manufactures. At Weirton two basic oxygen furnaces produce some of the finest of American steels. Wheeling is also a steel-making center.

Appalachian Regional Commission. In the early 1960s there were marked differences in the economy, culture, and quality of life in Appalachia. There were also common problems: isolation, poverty, low educational attainment, poor health-care delivery systems, and increasing deterioration of the physical environment. To combat these ills the Appalachian Regional Commission (ARC) was established in 1965. The ARC set as its first tasks the improvement of the highway system and the general betterment of the quality of life in the region.

In a single decade more than 1,000 miles (1,600 kilometers) of new roads were completed. New manufactures attracted to the region were built near the new roads, half of them no more than 10 minutes away. The new roads provided easier access to manufacturing sites, hospitals, schools, environmental projects, and recreational facilities. A report in 1975 pointed out that poverty had decreased, out-migra-

tion trends had been reversed, numerous jobs had been added, and per capita income had increased. There were more high school graduates and a greater number of practicing physicians.

While the new roads and improvements in the quality of life benefited the region considerably, numerous problems remained. A good portion of the region's population was still dispersed, pockets of poverty remained, there were wide discrepancies in per capita income, schools still lagged behind those in many parts of the nation, there was still much substandard housing, and more and better medical services were needed.

In-migration. People are now moving into Appalachia. Newcomers more than replace those who leave. Most are young people eager to try their hand at farming. Some are white-collar workers and professionals—physicians, nurses, lawyers, teachers. Others are retirees drawn by the beautiful rural setting. There are also returnees, those born and bred in Appalachia, who left for employment elsewhere and are now returning home. Appalachia is changing rapidly. The loss of its once cherished isolation and the new in-migration may even change the distinctive character of the Appalachian people.

Urbanization. Appalachia does not abound in cities but remains largely rural. There are, of course, significant urban clusters. Knoxville's metropolitan area numbers nearly 500,000. Chattanooga and the Tri-Cities—Bristol, Johnson City, and Kingsport—each has more than 425,000 inhabitants. The Huntington, W. Va., metropolitan area numbers more than 300,000, and Charleston has nearly 275,000. Urbanization throughout the region is on the rise. (*See also* Charleston, W. Va.; Chattanooga; Knoxville.)

The future. The impact of the ARC is significant. Isolation has broken down, and regional identity has become stronger. The growing need for coal strengthened the region's economy. In-migration is now greater than out-migration, and the future looks brighter in many ways. Further improvements are needed, however, in schools, health services, and housing, and tourism needs greater development.

Gulf Coast and Florida

The Gulf Coast and Florida, sometimes called the Humid Subtropical Coast, extends from southeastern Georgia to the southeast coast of Texas. It includes all of the Florida peninsula; the southern portions of Alabama, Mississippi, and Louisiana; and the entire southeast Texas coast. The northern boundary with the traditional South, difficult to demarcate, can be set approximately at a line where the growing season is 250 frost-free days. Areas within the Gulf Coast and Florida normally have more than 270 frost-free days. In southern Florida and southeastern Texas the frost-free days often number more than 320.

Largely because of location the region's climate is marked by high average temperatures, abundant sunshine, and much precipitation that falls as rain during the summer half year—more than 55 inches (140 centimeters). The soils are either fine sandy loams or rich silt loams. The topography is low and flat. These factors, coupled with the long growing season, help to make the region an ideal place for growing certain crops. The eastern portions of the region—Florida in particular—have developed tourism and the idea of the vacation land. The western portions have contributed mineral development, particularly petroleum, natural gas, salt, and sulfur.

Agriculture. American Indians planted maize, squash, and beans here for centuries. Europeans introduced the exotics. In the 16th century Spaniards brought the fig, olive, and orange to Sapelo Island off the Georgia coast. They planted figs, pomegranates, guavas, plantains, lemons, limes, and oranges in their gardens at St. Augustine. In Louisiana in the 18th century the French planted indigo, cotton, tobacco, and rice. They became successful sugarcane planters.

Commercial ventures in citrus fruits under American auspices date from the 19th century. Orange groves were planted on both sides of the St. Johns River in northeastern Florida. In late December 1894, however, the area was struck by the Big Freeze. After a period of warm, moist weather, temperatures suddenly dropped from 60° F (16° C) to 14° F (−10° C) over a three-day period. Most of the orange trees were destroyed by the frost, and grove owners made no effort to restore them. In 1893–94 Florida had shipped more than five million boxes of oranges north; in 1894–95 fewer than three million boxes were shipped; and by 1895–96 the number had been reduced to only 147,000. The Big Freeze had killed orange growing in Florida's north. Grove owners were forced to move south into the lake region of central Florida.

Today central Florida produces the vast majority of oranges, grapefruit, tangerines, and mandarins grown in the United States. There is also a significant citrus fruit harvest in southeastern Texas. Fewer and fewer oranges are shipped north to be sold as fresh fruit. Instead they are processed (often into frozen concentrate) and then shipped.

The Big Freeze also gave birth to an enlarged truck and vegetable farming capability. Florida—and other Gulf Coast sites—are planted with potatoes, lettuce, tomatoes, green beans, spinach, and celery. Specialty crops are shipped north by rail and highway in winter when the Middle Atlantic Region remains unproductive. Celery, for example—grown on well-drained muck land, irrigated, and fed with heavy applications of fertilizers—is shipped north from Sanford in Seminole County, Florida's celery delta.

Sugarcane is a tall perennial grass. It is at home in the wet tropics under much rain—50 to 65 inches (127 to 165 centimeters)—and with a dry season that brings maturity and high sugar content. Because frost is an ever-present danger in Louisiana, the cane is planted for each crop. It is harvested in the immature stage before the sugar content is highest. Sugarcane is grown in the Mississippi Delta and in the Everglades of Florida. Because of high costs of production and harvesting, sugarcane farming in the region was long protected by tariffs. Federal controls were removed in 1974, and expansion ceased because competition from other world sources is too keen.

Rice is an annual grass. There are thousands of varieties—all summer crops. In Louisiana rice does best on the level prairie west of the Mississippi Delta. Rice growing is aided here by heavy fertile soils, an impervious subsoil, and high temperatures. Because rainfall is less than adequate, rice is grown under irrigation. Plowing, planting, threshing, and combining are all done by machine. Elton, La., has three large rice dryers. Rice is also grown farther north outside the region in Arkansas, Mississippi, and eastern Texas.

For years beef cattle grazed on the poor natural grasses of central and northern Florida. Florida beef,

A shrimp boat unloads its catch onto a conveyor belt for processing at a packing plant near Ocean Springs, Miss.

Cameramann International

115

The spherical Spaceship Earth dominates part of Epcot Center in Walt Disney World, near Orlando, Fla. The theme park is one of the most popular tourist sites in the United States.

often of poor grade, was shipped to Cuba. The market began to decline in the 1920s, and Florida ranchers had to learn to produce beef that was acceptable to the domestic market. They started by attempting to eradicate tick fever, a disease caused by a protozoan parasite. Florida cattle were driven through dipping vats. It took 21 years to free Florida cattle from the tick. In the interim ranchers improved the pastures and bred the Florida cows with Brahman bulls (and other breeds) to create a fine beef cattle type. The number of cattle sold in Florida increased markedly.

Tourism. Americans love to run to the sun during the winter months. The Florida peninsula, Mississippi Riviera, and New Orleans are primary tourist attractions with hotels, motels, restaurants, natural and artificial beaches, and Disneyworld. This brings billions of dollars.

Henry M. Flagler saw the opportunities early. In 1885 he built the Hotel Ponce de Leon in St. Augustine, Fla. In 1891 his rival, Henry B. Plant, built the Tampa Bay Hotel on the Gulf coast. Before long wealthy Northern sun worshippers were going to the South by train—to St. Augustine, Palm Beach (where Flagler built the Breakers), and ultimately Key West (1912).

By the 1920s there was a land boom in Florida. Many speculators bought and sold lots, and there were new tourists to make purchases. Not until 1926 did the bubble burst. Following the lean tourist years of the Great Depression and World War II, a new land boom ensued with a new tourist boom. Miami became a major tourist attraction. Sun worshippers now traveled to Florida—and to other points in the region—by plane, auto, truck, and train. In 1982 tourist dollars spent in Florida numbered more than 21 billion.

The sun and other amenities also attracted a permanent and growing population to the peninsula. In 1950 Florida's population was 2.8 million; by 1960 it was 4.9 million, the highest increase over the decade for any state in the nation. And there was no abatement—by 1987 the population had swelled to more than 12 million, and Florida had become the 4th largest state.

Petroleum and natural gas. In 1901 the oil-gushing Spindletop salt dome was brought in 80 miles (129 kilometers) east of Houston, Tex. Other gushers in the vicinity followed. Hundreds of companies were formed to begin the oil search along the Texas-Louisiana coast. In 1930 the East Texas field, one of the richest in the country, began production.

Shortly after World War II the first offshore drilling rig was put into operation off the Louisiana coast (1947). Louisianans (primarily Cajuns and a few Indians) and Mississippians manned the rigs. They put in 12-hour days at one- or two-week stretches. They worked, ate, and slept on the offshore platforms. The work was rewarding but dangerous. A blowout could bring disaster, and accidents were common.

Offshore drilling moved farther and farther out to sea. Some rigs were put up in 150 feet (46 meters) of water and were located as far as 18 miles (29 kilometers) from shore, producing the major political problem of who controls the tidelands oil—the nation or the states. Strictly speaking Florida and Texas can claim a 9-mile (14.5-kilometer) seaward limit; Louisiana, Alabama, and Mississippi are restricted to a 3-mile (5-kilometer) limit. Legal limits have obviously been disregarded, and the problem has not yet been solved. Meanwhile offshore tracts have been opened to commercial bidding all along the Gulf and Atlantic coasts of the region.

Natural gas is often found in conjunction with oil; it is also found in independent gas fields. In former years it was considered a dangerous by-product of petroleum and was burned off. Because it burns cleanly and is convenient to use, natural gas grew considerably as an energy fuel. Whereas crude oil can be shipped to refineries in barrels, barges, tank cars, oceangoing tankers, trucks, and by pipeline, it is feasible to ship natural gas only by pipeline. Accordingly, a vast network of natural gas pipelines (and a lesser number of oil pipelines) extends from Texas and Louisiana to Northern markets. Both are also refined and used for industrial and domestic purposes within the region.

Salt and sulfur. Salt is found in the salt domes between the lower Mississippi Valley and the lower Rio Grande Valley. On Avery Island, Iberia Parish, La., the salt deposits were discovered in 1791. They were widely used during the Civil War. Today salt is used in the manufacture of sodium sulphate, soda ash, caustic soda, and hydrochloric acid. It is also used in the manufacture of glass, paper, steel, and brick; it is used in refrigeration and in water softeners. At Avery Island a shaft has been sunk to the 500-foot (152-meter) level (the salt dome base may extend to 2,200 feet, or 670 meters). Visitors are welcome to view the salt deposits.

Sulfur is another mineral of the salt domes. It occurs in deposits hundreds of feet thick between 700 and 2,000 feet (200 and 600 meters) below the surface in eastern Texas and southwestern Louisiana. Efforts at ordinary shaft mining proved impossible. Quicksand was a problem. The mining is done today using a method called the Frasch process (*see* Sulfur). Sulfur is widely used in the chemical (sulfuric acid) and other industries.

Manufacturing. Proximity to raw materials helped to locate the vast petrochemical industry on the west Gulf coast. Oil refineries are located in an arc between Pascagoula, Miss., and Corpus Christi, Tex. Refineries are located near the edges of the oil fields. They are usually port cities with access to deepwater and ocean shipping. Baton Rouge and New Orleans, La., and Houston, Port Arthur, and Corpus Christi, Tex., are examples. The refineries—and the nearby natural gas processing plants—are responsible in turn for the location of plants that make plastics, anti-freeze, insecticides, and pharmaceuticals.

Proximity to salt and sulfur resources led to the location of plants making sulfuric acid, superphosphate fertilizers, and synthetic rubber. A chemical corridor grew between Baton Rouge and New Orleans. The Houston Ship Channel is lined with refineries, oil terminals, and warehouses. They manufacture petrochemicals that range from fertilizers to jet airplane fuel. Prosperity in the petrochemical industry fluctuates widely with the price of oil.

The eastern part of the region has lagged behind in manufacturing industries, but they are growing. In Florida, for example, products range from processed food to electrical equipment, pulp and paper, chemicals for fertilizers, and cigars.

The area around Houston, Tex., has abundant oil and natural gas to support a huge petrochemical industry. The plants turn out compounds to make plastics, synthetic rubber, and other products.

Bob Thomason—CLICK/Chicago

Trade. The region provides access to Anglo-America from the south—Cuba is only 90 miles (145 kilometers) from Florida, and Mexico sits on the border of Texas. Latin Americans and Latin American products can move to the United States coast with ease. Sea communications are also open with other parts of the world. Added access to the interior is provided by the Mississippi River.

New Orleans' wharfs reflect the great seaborne trade. Coming up river are raw sugar and molasses, coffee and bananas, jute and sisal, and bauxite for aluminum plants. Going down river are cotton and flour, farm machinery, and trucks and buses. Mobile, Ala., with the best natural harbor on the Gulf coast, ships cotton and lumber and receives bauxite and many other items. Galveston, Tex., ships cotton, wheat, and sulfur. Houston sends oil, petrochemicals, oil-drilling supplies, cotton, grain, hides, and synthetic rubber to the world. It receives coffee, natural rubber, textiles, paper, and a myriad of other goods in return. There is also much barge traffic on the Intracoastal Waterway between Houston and the Mississippi River.

Cities. The population of the metropolitan area of one city in the region approaches 3 million (Houston). There are four metropolitan areas that have more than 1 million (Miami, Tampa-St. Petersburg, New Orleans, and Fort Lauderdale-Hollywood, Fla.). There are two metropolitan areas with populations in the 700,000s (Jacksonville and Orlando, Fla.), West Palm Beach-Boca Raton, Fla., numbers more than 500,-000. Baton Rouge and Mobile exceed 400,000. The urban dominance of Texas, Florida, and Louisiana within the region is clear. (See also Baton Rouge; Fort Lauderdale; Jacksonville; Mobile; Orlando; Saint Petersburg; Tampa.)

Houston was founded in 1836 and named for General Sam Houston, the victor over the Mexicans at San Jacinto (see Houston, Sam). It served as the first capital of the Texas Republic (1837–39). Cotton was its first leading export, but oil became number one during the 20th century, following the dredging of Buffalo Bayou and the creation of the Houston Ship Channel (1914). A great boost was given the city in the 1960s when the National Aeronautics and Space Administration (NASA) located the manned space center there. Houston, from Mission Control, monitors space flights (see National Aeronautics and Space Administration).

The city's growth has been phenomenal. Population was only 79,000 in 1910 and 292,000 in 1930. By 1960 it was more than 900,000 and more than 1 million in 1980. (See also Houston, Tex.)

Miami was founded on the site of Fort Dallas, built to wage war on the Seminoles in 1870. In 1896 Henry M. Flagler built the Royal Palm Hotel there. The harbor was dredged and the city incorporated the same year. By the second decade of the 20th century, Miami was booming. The city survived the land speculations of the 1920s and the devastating hurricanes of 1926 and 1935. Tourists, most of them arriving from the North by rail, continued to come.

In 1959, as a result of the Castro revolution in Cuba, there was an influx of Cubans—by sea and air—into the city. Over the years they continued to come—perhaps as many as 600,000. Many settled in what came to be called Miami's "Little Havana." They and the "boat people," who arrived from Cuba and Haiti in 1980, are major factors in Miami's growing economy—in business, construction, finance, and manufacturing. Miami, Miami Beach, and Miami International Airport are linked by a 20½ mile (33-kilometer) overhead rail line. In the mid-1980s the city had nearly 400,000 people, and its metropolitan area numbered more than 1.7 million.

New Orleans, the oldest of the large cities in the region, was founded by the French in 1718. The Spaniards occupied the city in 1763; it became French again in 1800 and part of the United States in 1803. Between 1810 and 1840 the growth of New Orleans exceeded that of any other American city. By 1840 it was the third largest city in the United States. It controlled the Mississippi River and shipped cotton from the South and foodstuffs from the Middle West to markets on the East coast and Europe.

During the Civil War Northern forces captured the city, but it was the railroads in the North that brought an end to New Orleans' ascendancy. They broke the monopoly that New Orleans had on the Mississippi River traffic. Northern manufacturing centers grew rapidly, and by the 1890s New Orleans was only the 13th largest American city.

New Orleans did not succumb but maintained the heavy bulk grain traffic on the river and continued to export cotton. It cultivated Latin American trade. Coffee and bananas became import items on the docks, and Latinos themselves became residents of the Creole city. The port was rebuilt, and the city began to spread.

New Orleans remains an enchanting city. The Vieux Carre, or French Quarter, is a tourists' delight. The central business district underwent numerous changes in the 1970s and 1980s—a new skyline was born. Port facilities were modernized, and manufacturing grew. In the mid-1980s New Orleans had a population of nearly 560,000; its metropolitan area numbered well over 1 million. (See also New Orleans.)

The future. The eastern portion of the Gulf Coast and Florida region prospered largely because of sun, citrus fruit and vegetable agriculture, and the development of tourism. The western portion prospered largely because of its proximity to large petroleum and natural gas resources and the development of petrochemical industries. But there are problems even in paradise. The sun induced a large population to descend on the region. Florida is growing very rapidly, and the population tends to be of retirement age. In addition to the problem of population growth, there are problems with the exploitation of oil and natural gas. Prices from foreign competition run low. Unemployment in the Texas and Louisiana fields runs high, perhaps spelling difficulty for the petrochemical industries.

North Central Plains

Tom Dietrich—CLICK/Chicago

Soybeans, in the foreground, and corn are the two main crops that are produced on the plains of Illinois.

The North Central Plains—often called the Middle West—are the heartland of America. The region lies between the Ohio River and the Great Lakes and stretches to beyond the 95th meridian. Included are eight states: Ohio, Indiana, Illinois, Michigan, Wisconsin, Minnesota, Iowa, and Missouri. The eastern portions of North Dakota, South Dakota, Nebraska, and Kansas are excluded here and are discussed in the Great Plains section of this article. (*See also* articles on individual states.)

Environment

The North Central Plains are a flat to gently rolling land. Glaciers planed the hills, filled the valleys, and scooped out the Great Lakes. In the driftless area (southwestern Wisconsin and nearby Minnesota, Iowa, and Illinois) the land remains hilly and rugged. There is also high ground in the iron ranges of Michigan, Wisconsin, and Minnesota. But for the most part the North Central Plains are a level land suitable for machine agriculture.

The climate and soils help. Summer days are hot, evenings warm, and rainfall moderate—fine attributes for growing corn. Winters are cold, snowy, and often severe, but the growing season lasts for approximately 170 days. In a region so large climatic conditions vary. Alfisols—good fertile soils—were established under the original hardwood forest (oak, hickory, beech, and maple) in the east. The dark and extremely fertile mollisols formed under the tall grass of the prairie west of the Wabash River in Indiana. The region is also well endowed with rich minerals (iron ore, limestone, coal, lead, and zinc), wood (white pine), and water resources.

Indian tribes long lived in the area north of the Ohio River. They planted maize, squash, and beans; hunted in the forests; and fished the lakes and streams. The French, the earliest of the European arrivals, built a series of missions and forts (Sault Sainte Marie, Saint Ignace, Fort Michilimackinac, and Fort Pontchartrain) in the Great Lakes country (17th century). The English moved into the Ohio River valley. In an epic struggle between the two—the French and Indian War from 1756 to 1763—the English were victorious. After the Revolutionary War the area became American (Treaty of Paris, 1783).

Northwest Territory

To deal with the new land, Congress, under the Articles of Confederation, passed the Ordinance of 1785. Under the ordinance the new area was surveyed into townships 6 miles (9.7 kilometers) square, each of which was subdivided into 36 lots, or sections. A section was made up of 640 acres (259 hectares). Potential buyers could buy a section for 1 dollar per acre, but few Americans of that day could put up 640 dollars or more to meet the purchase price. The lots were therefore purchased by absentee land speculators (Ohio Company of Associates, Scioto Company, and Symmes Patent, among them), which sold the lots to make a profit. After the land was surveyed it was quickly occupied. Marietta, Ohio, laid out at the conjunction of the Muskingum and Ohio rivers in 1788, was soon a thriving community—by 1810 it could boast of nearly 200 houses.

The Ordinance of 1787 provided a temporary government for the Northwest Territory. It provided that from three to five states could be carved from its limits. The ordinance also provided for the civil rights of the territory's inhabitants—religious freedom was guaranteed, slavery was prohibited, and education was encouraged.

119

An Amish family walks by Bonneyville Mill Park in Bristol, Ind. The Amish are noted for their well-run and very productive farms in several Midwestern states.

Cathy Melloan—EB Inc.

Americans moved from southern Ohio into southern Indiana and Illinois by way of the Ohio River. After the building of the Erie Canal, they moved into Michigan. They moved into southwestern Wisconsin and neighboring Illinois to exploit the lead ores—they founded Galena, Ill. They pushed into Iowa and Minnesota. The Louisiana Purchase of 1803 sent Americans into Missouri and into areas farther west.

Rise of the Corn Belt

The earliest settlers north of the Ohio River were subsistence farmers. Before long, however, they began to send their produce to market. A system of agriculture evolved that was well adapted to the environment of the Middle West. It was based on a three-year rotation of crops (corn, small grains, and hay). Kingpin in the rotation was corn. The small grains were winter wheat in the southern parts of the region and oats in the northern parts. Winter wheat was in constant demand, could be shipped over long distances without spoilage, and brought a good price. Oats were used as horse feed and, with corn, as feed for cattle and sheep. The hay crops—clover and alfalfa—completed the rotation. As a system the three-year, three-crop rotation was diffused to the prairie lands. And as a system it gave rise to the so-called corn belt, where growing corn—and raising pigs—became part of the ritual of farm life.

Dairy Belt

Agricultural evolution followed a different pattern in Wisconsin. Yields on the farmers' prime crop—winter wheat—began to decline. Crops were hit by the chinch bug and plant diseases. Costs began to

climb. To stem the tide farmers began to raise sheep, pigs, or beef cattle. They planted corn, hay, and oats. Then they turned to the dairy cow. Jerseys, Holsteins, and Guernseys were brought in to stock the herds. By 1890 milk cows could be found on 90 percent of Wisconsin's farms. In the process Wisconsin's farmers began to produce butter and cheese. They shipped the products by way of Chicago to New York City and even to London. Wisconsin became a prime dairying state and continues to call itself "America's dairyland."

Values

From the farm population of the Middle West came a set of distinct values. Hard work is one. As farmers Midwesterners toiled from dawn to dusk, and on dairy farms they worked seven days a week. "Work hard and prosper," was the motto. The family is important, perhaps the crux of the value system. Efficiency and progress are also essentials. Corn belt farmers adopted the latest machines when they came into being, and they adapted quickly to the use of fertilizers and pesticides. They helped build a number of America's great universities dedicated to agriculture, including Michigan State University, the first of the land-grant institutions (1855). They were conservative politically; they supported the Republican party. They went to church on Sunday.

Corn Belt to Corn-Soybean Belt

Great changes were coming to the American heartland. Soybeans, for example, replaced the small grains and hay in crop rotation. By the 1970s soybeans had become part of a new two-year corn-soybean rotation. The old three-year, three-crop rotation was all but a memory. Southern Illinois and northern Missouri were planting more acres in soybeans than in corn. A new corn-soybean belt was developing in the Middle West.

Meanwhile much progress had been made in corn hybridization. By 1939, 75 percent of Iowa's corn crop was in hybrid corn, and during World War II the figure went to nearly 100 percent. At the same time the mechanical corn picker and ultimately the picker-sheller (it picks, husks, and shells corn in one operation) came into general use. Midwestern farms became larger and the number of farmers fewer. Many farms are now owned by agribusiness corporations, though family farmers still produce up to 60 percent of the farm goods in the region.

Early Manufactures

Early farmers concentrated first on obtaining salt. They also made flour in the gristmill and cut lumber in the sawmill; they made whiskey, beer, and ale; they tanned leather and manufactured paper for newsprint; they produced woolen goods and linens at home; and they made rope from locally grown hemp.

With the growth of towns there was a tendency to locate the factories within them. Cincinnati became an early manufacturing center. By 1826 it was sending many factory-made goods to the East: flour, pork, whiskey, hats, clothing, and furniture. At Ironton, Ohio, ironmakers (using Hanging Rock Iron District ores) were producing hammers, cooking utensils, and shoe lasts. In the years prior to the Civil War Cyrus

Hall McCormick built and sold his reaper and Jerome I. Case his thresher (*see* McCormick, Cyrus Hall). In Milwaukee they brewed beer, milled flour, and made a wide variety of lumber products.

Iron and Steel

Michigan's master surveyor William A. Burt, noting the fluctuations in his magnetic compass, discovered the iron ore of the Lake Superior district at Negaunee in 1844. Bloom iron was made on the spot, and by 1858 a local blast furnace was at work. But most of the rich ore was sent south through the canal at Sault Sainte Marie (1855). The canal permitted the ore-carrying ships to negotiate the 21-foot (6.4-meter) drop between Lake Superior and Lakes Michigan and Huron. Negaunee ores fed the distant furnaces in Pittsburgh and vicinity. Further exploration led iron seekers to the Menominee Range in 1877, the Gogebic and Vermillion ranges in 1884, and to the great Mesabi Range in 1892.

In 1907 the United States Steel Corporation, looking for an optimum location for its new steel plant, selected a Great Lakes site on the Indiana dunes at Gary. Iron ore could be brought by water from the Lake Superior district; limestone could be dug from quarries on Lake Huron; coal could be brought from Illinois by rail. Gary prospered, and so did the iron-and-steel industry in the Great Lakes area. More and more iron ore passed through the Soo locks; more and more iron and steel was made at Great Lakes centers. In 1904 the Great Lakes region produced more than

Barge traffic moves down the Ohio River and under the bridges connecting Cincinnati, Ohio, with Kentucky, on the way to the Mississippi River and the Gulf Coast near New Orleans.

J.F. Photo—CLICK/Chicago

16 percent of the raw steel made in the United States. By 1929 it was more than 23 percent and rising. The biggest reason was the success of a new transportation device—the automobile.

Automobile

Attempts to build a mechanically driven vehicle that could move with ease over a hard surfaced road—swiftly and safely—were made in both Europe and the United States. One such builder was Ransom E. Olds, who wanted to make a vehicle that was inexpensive, durable, and easy to operate. In 1900 in his plant in Detroit, Mich., he built and tested the "curved dash runabout," the first of the cars to carry the name Oldsmobile. In 1901 the Olds firm made 425 runabouts; in 1904 it made 5,508.

Meanwhile Henry Ford was experimenting. In 1903 he organized the Ford Motor Company. In 1908 the company produced the famous Model T—the "tin lizzie." It was made of alloy steels, was powered by a four-cylinder engine, could go forward and backward, and was operated with foot pedals. It was black in color. Ford standardized the parts—wheels, axles, engines, nuts and bolts. All were made alike and were put together on a moving assembly line. The Model T was mass produced. In 1908 Ford built 5,986 cars. Each one sold for 850 dollars. By 1916 Ford was building more than 500,000 cars annually. Each sold for 360 dollars. Ford had helped to make a revolution; he had brought the possibility of owning an automobile to nearly every American. (*See also* Ford, Henry.)

Olds and Ford helped to centralize the automobile industry in the Detroit area. So large did it become that, like Pittsburgh's iron-and-steel industry, it spilled over. Flint, Pontiac, Lansing, and Jackson—all in Michigan—became automobile manufacturing centers. The industry spread to Cleveland and Toledo, Ohio, to South Bend and Indianapolis, Ind., to Kenosha, Wis., and to Chicago.

Taconite

The high-grade iron ores of the Lake Superior district were fast disappearing. Millions upon millions of tons of ore were taken from the iron ranges. Shortly after World War II Minnesota turned to low-grade ores—the taconites. The work of the mines experiment station at the University of Minnesota made their use possible, and the taconites became significant in the manufacture of iron and steel (*see* Iron and Steel Industry, "Types of Ores.")

Cities

Immigration from Europe in the late 19th and early 20th centuries helped to swell the population of the Middle West's cities. Chicago was a big city in 1880 with more than 500,000 people, but more than a million people were living there in 1890. Detroit, Milwaukee, Cleveland, and Columbus all grew between 60 and 80 percent during the same period. Minneapolis-St. Paul tripled in size. Twelve of America's largest cities were located in the Middle West in

1890. By 1980 ten Midwestern cities had metropolitan areas with populations of more than a million—with Detroit exceeding 4 million and Chicago more than 7. (*See also* Cincinnati; Cleveland; Columbus; Indianapolis; Kansas City; Milwaukee; Minneapolis; Saint Louis; Saint Paul.)

Chicago dates from 1830. In 1837, when it was incorporated as a city, it already had 4,000 people. It was a lumbering and meat-packing center. The addition of rail lines boosted the city's growth, and it became a center of the grain trade. In 1865 the Union Stock Yards were completed. Shortly thereafter Cyrus McCormick built his new agricultural implement plant along the Chicago River. By 1870 the city had a population of nearly 300,000.

Tragedy struck the following year when at least a third of the city was destroyed by fire. Chicago was rebuilt in brick and iron. In 1883 the first skyscraper in the nation was built, and in the Columbian Exposition of 1893 Chicago showed its new face to the world. The city grew. In 1910 Chicago's population was already more than 2 million, and by 1930 it was more than 3 million. (*See also* Chicago.)

Detroit was founded by the French in 1701. The British took over in 1760 and were not dislodged until 1796. Like Chicago, Detroit had its fire—in 1805—and it too was quickly rebuilt. The little community began to grow as a manufacturing center after the opening of the Erie Canal. Wagons, carriages, ships, and furniture were made. Then work began in iron and steel, railroad cars, copper, and brass. Detroiters made paints, pills, and stoves.

The beginning of the 20th century was marked by the ascendancy of the automobile and the work of Olds and Ford. On Jan. 14, 1914, Ford announced that each of his workers would be paid 5 dollars per day—an astounding figure for the time—for an eight-hour day. Job seekers streamed to the city. During World War II the city was dubbed "the arsenal of democracy." It made tanks, guns, and Liberator bombers in a mighty war effort. The war brought many blacks and Southern whites to the city. Detroit's population was more than 1.6 million in 1940 and peaked in 1950 at more than 1.8 million. (*See also* Detroit.)

The Future

The Middle West has its difficulties. There is trouble on the farms, in the factories, and in the cities. People are deserting the American heartland for the sunbelt, especially Florida, Texas, and California. Agribusiness continues to grow, and family farms continue to diminish. The iron-and-steel and automobile industries are retooling and modernizing. They are turning to robotics and are placing new emphasis on quality and productivity. There is a trend toward diversification: computers, electronics, communications, and microbiology—the hi-techs—are booming and growing, as are service industries. Retraining and new training for the job market are needed. Although great strides have been made, there is further need for revamping the region's cities.

Great Plains

Joe Viesti—Viesti Associates, Inc.

Longhorn cattle graze on the Yo Ranch in Texas. Texas still leads the nation in cattle raising, though livestock graze most of the year over all the Great Plains.

The Great Plains region lies between the North Central Plains and the South on the east and the Rocky Mountains on the west. It stretches from the Edwards Plateau and the hill country of central Texas to the Canadian border. The Great Plains include much of the area covered by Texas, Oklahoma, Kansas, Nebraska, North and South Dakota, New Mexico, Colorado, Wyoming, and Montana. (*See also* articles on individual states.)

Physiographically the region rises very gradually from east to west. On the eastern margins elevations of 1,500 feet (460 meters) are recorded and in the foothills of the Rocky Mountains 4,000 to 5,000 feet (1,200 to 1,500 meters). But there are many variations. The Black Hills of South Dakota rise 4,000 feet above the surrounding countryside; the Sand Hills of western Nebraska, a large area of dunes and grass, also stand above the neighboring terrain. The high plains are generally flat—the Llano Estacado extremely so. Irregular features mark the Badlands of North Dakota. The high plains are dissected by a number of west-to-east flowing rivers. Two of these—the Platte and the Arkansas—served as roadways westward.

The climate, like the physiography, varies considerably. The eastern portions of the Great Plains are wetter than the western portions. Forty inches (100 centimeters) of rain may fall on eastern Kansas in a given year while southwestern Kansas may receive less than 20 inches (50 centimeters). The variability is also great. One year's rainfall does not necessarily match another's. The region frequently suffers from drought, and tornadoes are common. Blizzards, in winter—much snow, high winds, low temperatures—are another hazard. The length of the growing season also varies considerably—from more than 240 days in central Texas to fewer than 100 days in Montana and North Dakota.

The decreasing precipitation east to west is reflected in differences in the natural vegetation. The bluestem grasses are the response to the heavier precipitation in the prairie; the grama grasses are adaptations to the drier areas in the steppe. Underlying both are the excellent soils of the Great Plains, the extremely fertile mollisols that cover most of the region and the ultisols in the farthest west.

Great American Desert

For years the facts related above were unknown to most Americans. Their perceptions of the region were drawn from descriptions left by early travelers. Zebulon Pike wrote that the prairies beyond the Missouri "may become in time as celebrated as the sandy wastes of Africa." Edwin James, the geographer of the Stephen H. Long expedition, wrote that "it is almost wholly unfit for cultivation." Maps published prior to the Civil War often called the Great Plains area the "Great American Desert." It was a region deemed unfit for settlement and habitation—barren and unproductive.

Sod-House Frontier

In the 1840s there was a town-building mania in the central plains (Kansas and Nebraska). Towns and imaginary towns were laid out. People in the East were encouraged to move to Kearney, Bellevue, and Plattsmouth, Neb., and to Emporia and Eureka, Kan. In 1856 the first settlement was attempted at Sioux Falls, S.D. By 1858 settlers were moving into eastern North Dakota.

In the wooded areas log cabins were built. But as settlers moved into the grasslands proper—especially after the passage of the Homestead Law in 1862—the homesteaders came to depend more and more on sod for house building. The sod house became the symbol of the new frontier. Corrals, henhouses, pigpens, corncribs, and windbreaks were also made of sod, as were schools and churches. By 1900, however, the "soddies" were no more. They were rapidly replaced by frame, brick, and stone structures. The size of individual land holdings also greatly increased.

123

Cattle

From the earliest days southern Texas cattlemen sent their steers and cows to feed on the open range. When the land was taken up by farms, the cattlemen moved north to central Texas. Long before the Civil War, Texas cattle (a mix between hardy Hispanic breeds and meatier Anglo breeds) were being driven north. After the war drovers delivered cattle to the nearest railhead (Abilene and other sites in Kansas), from which they were sent to slaughterhouses in the North and East.

By the 1880s most of the open range had been fenced. Large companies, controlled by outside capital, ran the new ranches, as they were called. Drovers were no more; they were replaced by north-south rail lines. Before long (1900) many ranches were giving way to farms—to wheat and cotton production.

Wheat

Farmers experimented with different kinds of crops. They experimented with corn, and they planted winter wheat in early autumn. It survived the cold winters and was harvested in late June and early July. They pushed it to its environmental limits. When Mennonites from southern Russia arrived in the 1870s, they introduced a special variety—Turkey red—that did extremely well in the Kansas earth. Because of the water scarcity in western Kansas, farmers permitted the fields to lie fallow every other year.

Turkey red succeeded. It helped to spawn a winter wheat belt in the Great Plains. By the early years of the 20th century, the belt extended from central Oklahoma, through Kansas, into southern Nebraska. About 75 percent of the cropland is devoted to winter wheat. Farmers also raise corn, alfalfa, milo, barley, and sorghum for forage to fatten cattle. Grain eleva-

tors in Hutchinson, Kan., remain full in late June. Winter wheat, the cash crop, is sent to American mills and then shipped abroad.

Farther north spring wheat is the chief crop. It helped to form a spring wheat belt that includes western Minnesota, northeastern South Dakota, most of North Dakota, northeastern and north-central Montana, and portions of the Prairie Provinces of Canada. Spring wheat is planted in the spring, does well during the summer rains, and ripens in the autumn. The environment—like that of the winter wheat belt—is filled with many perils: frost, hail, drought, dust, rust, and grasshoppers. There are good years and bad.

In what is called Montana's Triangle—between Great Falls, Havre, and Cut Bank—for example, homesteaders had exceptionally good farm years in 1915 and 1916. In 1917 and 1918 there was less rain. The next year was extremely dry, and crop yields were poor. Many people left the area. The 1930s brought dust-bowl conditions. Today—during good rain years—the Triangle is covered with endless fields of spring wheat.

In the area between the winter wheat and spring wheat belts, oats is the leading crop. South of the winter wheat belt cotton and sorghum are raised. North Dakota farmers raise sugar beets and potatoes. Turkey raising is also a specialty.

Irrigation

In a region where precipitation is critical, irrigation is a significant factor in crop production. Farmers tap the Oglala aquifer that underlies the Great Plains for water. More than 50,000 wells in and around Lubbock, Tex., for example, supply water for the most productive cotton region in the country. Farther north sugar beets are grown under irrigation from water derived from wells and the Platte River. In Colorado the Big

Combines harvest wheat in Montana. Spring wheat is the chief crop in northern Montana, parts of the Dakotas, and western Minnesota, as well as in the Prairie Provinces of Canada.

Courtesy of Montana Travel Promotion

Courtesy of the Kansas Department of Commerce

Grain elevators alongside railroad tracks in Kansas City, Kan., suggest the dominance of wheat in the state's economy.

Thompson Project, which carries water from the west side of the Front Range of the Rocky Mountains to the east side, provides water for irrigation on the Great Plains, as does the Missouri Valley Project.

Ranching

In the dry, western nonirrigated, nonfarming areas of the Great Plains, ranching continues to dominate the economy. Ranches vary considerably in size from a few thousand acres to several hundred thousand. The smaller ranches are in the wettest areas, with the larger ones on the drier fringes. Ranchers must have an adequate water supply, enough winter feed for their animals, and a headquarters (including a ranch house, corrals, and sheds) from which to operate. A huge feedlot, where 200,000 cattle may be fed simultaneously, can require 2 million gallons of water daily and hundreds of thousands of tons of silage, alfalfa, and corn to maintain the operation. A large ranch may have many cowhands. The roundup, branding, dipping the animals in chemically treated water to provide protection from ticks, riding the pens to check for crippled or sick cattle—these are the jobs of the cowhand. The horse is still a significant vehicle, the helicopter becoming more so. The cowboy's job may not be over until he deposits the livestock at the nearest packinghouse.

The Edwards Plateau is unique ranch country. Sheepmen were the first to enter in the 1880s. Then came the settlers in the 1890s. They drilled water wells, set up windmills and water tanks, and brought in cattle and Angora goats. Today cattle enjoy the tall grasses, sheep the shorter grasses, goats the shoots and leaves of shrubs—all three often on a single ranch.

Energy Sources

The Great Plains are underlain with significant energy resources—petroleum, natural gas, and low-grade coal. The mid-continent oil fields are located in southwestern Kansas, the Oklahoma Panhandle, and northern Texas. There are other reserves in the Williston Basin of North and South Dakota and in Wyoming. Natural gas is found in abundance in the mid-continent field along the southeastern New Mexico-Texas border. There are major subbituminous and lignite deposits in North Dakota, Wyoming, and Montana. There are coal seams in Montana that range from 10 to 50 feet (3 to 15 meters) in thickness. The major landowner is the federal government, though the Burlington Northern Railroad owns some of the land, and there are large deposits of coal on a number of Indian reservations.

Cities

The Great Plains area is not one that is dynamically urban. Farms, ranches, and small towns dominate the region. Cities tend to be peripheral, lying on the region's margins, for example, Dallas-Fort Worth, the largest metropolitan area in the Great Plains, as well as San Antonio, Tex.; Oklahoma City and Tulsa, Okla.; and Austin, Tex. Wichita, Kan., is perhaps more a city of the region than others. (*See also* Austin, Tex.; Oklahoma City; San Antonio; Tulsa; Wichita.)

Both Dallas and Fort Worth date from the 1840s. During the Civil War the Confederate Army maintained a headquarters in Dallas. The city's orientation—largely because of Texas cotton—has been with the South. Fort Worth boomed as a cattle town. Drovers on the way to Abilene bedded their herds just outside town and purchased supplies here. Its orientation was with the Great Plains.

Dallas grew with the discovery of petroleum in eastern Texas and during and after World War II with the establishment of aircraft and electronics industries. Meat packing, milling, and shipping of grain were responsible for Fort Worth's initial growth. In the 20th century came industrialization and diversification. By 1980 the population in the Dallas-Fort Worth metropolitan area numbered nearly 3 million. (*See also* Dallas; Fort Worth.)

The Future

The future in the Great Plains rests with the farm, the ranch, and energy sources. For the farmer land values continue to drop, and farm foreclosures mount. On the ranches the grand scale of operations may be a problem. Oil and gas operations are troubled by low prices. Coal operations may meet the demands for energy in the future.

Rocky Mountains

Longs Peak stands in Rocky Mountain National Park in Colorado. At 14,256 feet (4,345 meters), it is the highest point in the park.

The Rocky Mountains extend in a northwest-southeast direction from the Brooks Range in Alaska, across Canada, and in a widening mass into Idaho and Montana and southward to north-central New Mexico. The Rocky Mountains region includes parts of Colorado, Idaho, Montana, New Mexico, Utah, and Wyoming. (*See also* articles on individual states.)

The Rockies—like the Great Plains—were originally merely a barrier to be crossed. The lures—California and Oregon—were strong. The Oregon Trail took potential settlers through the mountains over South Pass; traders on the Santa Fe Trail avoided the mountains if possible or viewed them from the mountain division. But the mountains, it was discovered, had lures of their own—valuable mineral ores.

Gold

Gold was discovered on Cherry Creek near present-day Denver, Colo., in 1858. In the following spring the rush was on for the "Pikes Peak diggings." Placer, or gulch, mining—the use of pick and pan in the streams—was not particularly rewarding and all but ceased by 1865. In 1859, however, a rich lode of gold-bearing quartz was discovered near Central City. The proven veins were tapped as miners built their homes in the surrounding hills and gulches. The mining went deeper, and the ores became more complex.

Concentrates contained silver, copper, and lead as well as gold. With the coming of the railroads, which brought heavy mining machinery, fuel, and other supplies to the diggings, more mining properties were developed. To treat the complex ores, crushing mills, concentration plants, and smelters were added.

Denver grew as a mining and supply center. Central City, in the heart of the gold-mining area, was booming. Churches, schools, a hotel, and even an opera house were built for a community of about 10,000. The same was true for other mining communities. The problems inherent with deep mining—the high cost of building shafts and tunnels, draining groundwater, and providing ventilation—discouraged the mine operators, and by 1900 most of Central City's business houses and homes were empty. The best of the mining days were over.

Copper

At Butte Hill in the northern Rockies of Montana, miners were panning for gold early in the 1860s. Silver was also discovered. When the miners moved into the deeper deposits in the 1870s, they found the rich copper ores. By the 1890s hundreds of miles of tunnels had been dug into the ore veins. Copper was needed to provide wire for the newly emerging electrical industries.

Butte, like other mining communities, lived through years of boom and bust. Price changes, depletion of high-grade ores, and changes in technology produced either one or the other. During World War I, for example, with many immigrant miners at work and prices of copper high, Butte had a population of 90,000. It was Montana's largest city. In the 1940s, with low prices for copper, thousands were forced to leave the mines. By the 1950s the huge Berkeley Pit—a mile (1.6 kilometers) wide and 1,500 feet (460 meters) deep—was beginning to encroach upon and swallow the old city.

Butte copper is still coming out of the mines with low-grade ores. The mines have been mechanized, and there are fewer miners. In 1980 Butte's population was reduced to 37,000. Both Billings and Great Falls, Mont., were larger.

Other Minerals

The Rocky Mountains region is a storehouse for other minerals: silver, lead, zinc, tungsten, carnotite (it yields uranium and vanadium), and molybdenum. There are huge reserves of phosphate, used in making fertilizer, and large reserves of oil shale.

At Climax, Colo., at elevations between 11,000 and 13,600 feet (3,350 and 4,150 meters), molybdenum is exposed. The metal, a major alloy used in the steel industry, came into prominence during World War I for armor plating. Daily ore production is more than 35,000 tons—only 6 pounds (3 kilograms) of molybdenum are extracted for each ton of ore mined.

The chief silver-producing area in the nation is the Coeur d'Alene district in northern Idaho. The chief phosphate deposits are found in southwestern Wyoming and southeastern Idaho. Oil shales are in southwestern Wyoming, northwestern Colorado, and neighboring Utah.

Agriculture

Agriculture began in the Rocky Mountains region as a response to the arrival of miners. The miners had to be fed, and agriculture expanded accordingly. Ranching and farming grew in the piedmont areas. The farms were irrigated gardens. A number of agricultural colonies were formed, but few were successful.

Agriculture today is quite successful in particular places. In San Luis Park (Valley), for example, at 8,000 feet (2,400 meters) in southern Colorado, the temperatures favor a high-quality iceberg lettuce crop, grown under irrigation. Alfalfa, field peas, and potatoes are also raised, as are cattle and sheep—for both local and distant markets.

In the valleys of western Colorado, alfalfa, potatoes, wheat, barley, and alfalfa again are grown in rotation. The wheat and potatoes are sold, the barley and alfalfa fed to the sheep. A number of valleys do well in growing fruits—especially peaches.

Most farm income in the region, however, is derived from livestock. While sugar beets, for example, are raised primarily for sugar, the tops and beet pulp provide feed for the animals.

Forestry

The highest quality trees are located in the more humid Northern Rockies. Because distances to potential markets are so great and water transportation is lacking, the timber is used locally—chiefly for mine props and railroad ties. Much of the forest land throughout the region is owned by the federal government, and conservation plays a significant role in preservation and development.

Tourism

The Rocky Mountains region is an all-year wonderland for tourists. The scenery is often breathtaking. Sightseeing, hunting, fishing, and mountain climbing are popular activities in summer. Skiing at Sun Valley, Idaho, in the Sawtooth Range, created the first American winter resort. New resorts quickly followed at Jackson Hole, Wyo., and throughout Colorado's Rockies in such towns as Vail, Aspen, and Steamboat Springs.

The Southern Rockies offer a number of notable attractions: Rocky Mountain National Park, Garden of the Gods, Mountain of the Holy Cross, and the Royal Gorge of the Arkansas River—all in Colorado. The Central Rockies has the oldest of the national Parks—Yellowstone, with its volcanic peaks, hot springs, geysers, petrified forests, and Yellowstone Lake and Yellowstone Falls. In the Northern Rockies is the equally delightful Waterton-Glacier International Peace Park.

Denver

One would not expect to find large cities high in the mountains, and there is none. Denver—more properly a peripheral city of the Great Plains—is the gateway to the Rocky Mountains region and styles itself as the Mile-high City.

Denver was founded just after the placer gold discoveries in Cherry Creek in 1858. Many seekers of gold, silver, and other minerals passed through the city on their way to the mining areas. By the end of the 19th century, Denver had become a processing, shipping, and distribution center for agricultural products. Its stockyards were widely known; it was a leading meat-packing center. By 1980 Denver's population was just under 500,000 but with a metropolitan area of more than 1.6 million. (*See also* Denver.)

The Future

The future must deal with possibilities in mining, agriculture, and tourism. Mining the world over is a boom-and-bust industry. The resources can only go so far and can only last so long. The prospects in agriculture, however, appear bright. There is room for growing valley crops—fruits and vegetables, potatoes, and dairy products—and there is room to produce wool and meat and wheat. The region can support a greater population than it now has. Tourism provides economic possibilities, as the region is an area of spectacular beauty.

Western Basins and Plateaus

Joe Viesti—Viesti Associates, Inc.

Canyon de Chelly National Monument in northeastern Arizona was established in 1931. The site contains cliff dwellings of prehistoric cultures.

The Great Basin, the Semiarid Southwest, the Colorado Plateau, and the Columbia Plateau are all included in the Western Basins and Plateaus region. Within are Arizona, Nevada, most of New Mexico, and portions of Colorado and Utah, southern and northwestern Idaho, northeastern Oregon, and eastern Washington. The entire region lies between the Rocky Mountains on the east and the Sierra-Cascade mountain system on the west. Semiaridity is a mark of the entire region. Rainfall ranges from an arid 5 inches (13 centimeters) or less in southwestern Arizona to more than 15 inches (38 centimeters) in the Palouse Hills (eastern Washington and neighboring Idaho). The growing season also varies considerably— from 365 days on the lower Colorado River to fewer than 100 days in the extreme north. (*See also* articles on individual states.)

Great Basin

The Great Basin, situated between the Rocky Mountains and the Sierra Nevada, actually consists of many basins—more than 100—separated by high ridges that trend in a north-south direction. The crests of the ridges average between 8,000 and 10,000 feet (2,400 and 3,000 meters) in elevation. The basin

floors are higher than the Appalachian Mountains. A peculiar characteristic of the physiography is interior drainage—none of the streams has an outlet to the sea. The Humboldt, Truckee, Carson, Walker, Owens, Bear, Weber, and Sevier rivers, however, all carry water throughout the year. Vegetation varies with altitude and latitude. Sagebrush is common in the north; piñon and juniper are found on the slopes. In the south creosote bush, greasewood, and the Joshua tree flourish. The Great Basin, like the Rocky Mountains, is rich with minerals. Gold and silver, copper and iron, coal, barite, perlite, pumice, and gypsum can all be found here. The region was and remains the home of the Shoshone and Paiute Indians.

Gold and silver. Spaniards entered the Great Basin in the 18th century. Peter Skene Ogden of the Hudson's Bay Company was on the Humboldt River in 1828. Americans moved into the area over the California Trail in the 1840s—especially after the California gold discoveries. With the discovery of the great Comstock Lode and the building of Virginia City, Nev., in 1859, more Americans came. Silver City, Gold Hill, and Dayton sprang up. Nevada became a state in 1864, and Chinese laborers pushed the new railroad across the Humboldt Sink. The Central Pacific Railroad united with the Union Pacific at Promontory Point, Utah, on May 10, 1869. When peak production was reached at the Comstock mine in the 1870s, 1,500 miners were employed. By 1877 the high-grade silver and gold ores were all but exhausted, and by 1881 only the poorer ores remained.

Mormons. Meanwhile the Mormons, searching for Zion, had moved into the eastern Great Basin between the Rocky Mountains and Great Salt Lake. In 1847 Brigham Young declared to his followers that "This is the place." In a few short years the area was studded with flourishing farms—all under irrigation. Salt Lake City, laid out by Young on a magnificent scale, was booming—by 1865 it had about 20,000 people. Mormon settlers were pushing west- and southward into Nevada, California, and Arizona and northward into Idaho. While non-Mormons also crossed the region on the California Trail and settled within it, there is little question that the Mormons created a Mormon culture region in the Great Basin, which is firmly in place today.

Bingham. While Young cautioned against "godless" enclaves—the mines—a copper mine was opened for production in Bingham Canyon, 20 miles (32 kilometers) southwest of Salt Lake City. It has been in production continuously since 1865 and is the largest single copper mine in North America. The open-pit mine—it resembles a huge amphitheater—is more than ½ mile (0.8 kilometer) deep and stretches for 2½ miles (4 kilometers). It is served by 166 miles (267 kilometers) of standard-gauge railroad track. The ores are low-grade and are sent to a concentrator near Salt Lake City.

Semiarid Southwest

The Semiarid Southwest includes the upper Rio Grande Valley and the plateau country that surrounds it, the valleys of the Gila and Salt rivers and nearby mesas and buttes, and the lower Colorado River valley. American Indians, Hispanics, and Anglos have impressed their cultures on the region. As delimited here, the Semiarid Southwest is made up of the states of Arizona and New Mexico. The Colorado River portion is covered in the South Pacific Region.

American Indian cultures in the area emerged from four subcultures: Mogollon (north-central Arizona into New Mexico), Anasazi (northern Arizona and New Mexico), Hohokam (the desert of southern Arizona and neighboring Mexico), and Patayan (Colorado River Valley). The hallmark of the culture in each was the introduction of cultivated plants—especially maize, squash, gourds, and, later, red kidney beans. The plants were probably dispersed from a center in the Mogollon Mountains. As it developed the Southwestern tradition also included the pit house and the making of pottery. The pit house ultimately gave way to the pueblo.

Present-day Indians of the region are direct descendants of the original inhabitants. The Pueblo peoples stem from the Anasazi; the Pima and Papago from the Hohokam; the Yuma, Havasupai, and others from the Patayan. The original Mogollon most likely merged with the other peoples.

Hispanics. Spaniards arrived in the area in the 16th century. They established Santa Fe in 1610. They sent missionaries to the Pueblos. Indians began to learn

Grand Canyon National Park in Arizona was established in 1893. The huge gorge was carved by the Colorado River and is noted for the shapes and colors of its rocks.

Tim Moran

Monument Valley (top), on the Arizona-Utah border, has mesas and spires standing several hundred feet high. Bryce Canyon National Park (bottom) in southwestern Utah was established in 1923. Instead of having one canyon, the park contains a number of natural amphitheaters with stone columns and walls sculpted by erosion.

the Spanish language and the catechism. Wheat and fruit-tree planting were introduced, as were horses, cattle, and sheep. Apaches raided the pueblos, and there were frequent rebellions. In 1680 there was the Pueblo Revolt, during which the Spaniards left the area, only to return in added strength in 1692. In the succeeding century Indian and Spanish cultures grew side by side, but the Spanish population began to outgrow the Indians. In 1846 United States troops entered the region.

Anglos. As part of the United States, Indian lands were controlled by Congress. The Pueblos could not alienate or sell them. Experts were sent to the region to teach improved farming methods, including irrigation, ditch building, dam construction, and well digging. Protestant missionaries appeared. The federal government offered the Indians free schools and hospitals. Hispanics found the treatment of the Indians difficult to understand—they felt discriminated against. In 1881 two railroads were built into the region. In the 20th century the credit system and the cash economy enveloped the area.

Today the Pueblos remain. Zuni is served with electric power and has a modern water supply. Farms are cultivated by machine. The Hopi continue to live on the mesas. With newfound wealth in petroleum, natural gas, coal, and uranium, the Navajo are prosperous. Meanwhile the Hispanics—legal and illegal—continue to arrive from Mexico. Illegals may number as many as 5 million—perhaps more. United States citizenship is now available to some of them. By 1980 more than 36 percent of New Mexico's population had Spanish surnames, Arizona's more than 16 percent. Anglos continue to move to the Semiarid Southwest—nearly a million to Arizona alone between 1970 and 1980. Phoenix doubled in size between 1950 and 1960 and doubled again during the next decade. Between 1970 and 1980 the gain was 60 percent.

Cultural diversity is the hallmark of the area. Other characteristics include the charm of the desert, the irrigation projects of the Gila and Salt rivers, minerals, the lure of the sun (tourism), and growing urbanization that shows no signs of abatement.

Colorado Plateau

The Colorado Plateau is a transition area between the Semiarid Southwest, the Rocky Mountains, the Great Basin, and the plateaus to the north. Northern Arizona, southeastern Utah, southwestern Colorado, and northwestern New Mexico—the Four Corners area—are included. Plateaus, canyons, and escarpments mark the region. The Grand Canyon of the Colorado River is a distinctive feature.

Summers are quite warm, winters cold. Precipitation is normally less than 15 inches (38 centimeters). The growing season averages between 90 and 180 days, but freezing temperatures occur in any season. Drought and floods are common.

Indians were here early. Spaniards and Americans followed. Officers of the Corps of Topographical Engineers learned much about the area in the 1840s

and 1850s. The great surveys were conducted after the Civil War. Rails and roads were pushed across the plateau.

Widely distributed are deposits of petroleum and gas, oil shale, uranium, and coal. Coal-burning electric plants serve the Four Corners area. Residents are concerned about pollution and about the future of their water resources. On Black Mesa the coal-mine operators tap an aquifer at 3,000 feet (900 meters). Water is also taken from the Colorado River. More and more tourists visit the Colorado Plateau, attracted by the Grand Canyon (*see* Grand Canyon).

Columbia Plateau

The Columbia Plateau is made up of a variety of landforms—small plateaus, broad valleys and basins, upfolded ridges, and flat plains—whose common denominator is the basaltic lava flow. Included are the Columbia Plain, the Central Highlands, the High Lava Plains, the Palouse Hills, and the Channeled Scablands. Major rivers are the Columbia, Clearwater, and Okanogan. The region lies between the Cascade Mountains and the Rocky Mountains and north of the Great Basin. As such it includes portions of eastern Washington and Oregon and neighboring Idaho.

Early days. At Five Mile Rapids, near The Dalles on the Columbia River, Indians had netted and speared salmon for centuries. Lewis and Clark, moving overland from Missouri, observed them in 1805–06; and David Thompson of the North West Company, coming south from Athabasca Pass, met them in 1811. In the years that followed pioneers settled in Oregon's Willamette Valley. When gold was discovered near the Clearwater in 1860, potential miners and others ascended the Columbia into the plateau. The Dalles and Walla Walla (farther into the interior) came into prominence as portals to the mining region. Little mining communities blossomed; Lewiston, Idaho, grew as a supply center. The earliest settlers raised livestock—pigs, sheep, horses, mules, and burros—and other farmers soon were planting crops.

Dry farming. Disturbed by winter kill in the low-lying areas, farmers turned to the higher lands—the Palouse Hills among them—for their wheat crops. They experimented. They planted in the fall and harvested in the spring; they planted in the spring and harvested in the fall. They planted little club and bluestem. They planted year in and year out on the same acres. There was enough precipitation—about 20 inches (50 centimeters), most of it falling during the winter half year—for dry farming. The summers were quite dry. Yields were high—40 to 45 bushels per acre—and the farmers prospered. In later years they learned to leave some acres fallow each year. With improvements in transportation—especially rail—Palouse and Columbia Plain wheat was shipped to the Pacific coast and other points for distribution and export.

In the 1950s Palouse farmers began to plant seed peas. They also raised oats and barley. They might maintain a garden, a few cows, and some poultry.

131

A dairy cow nurses its calf on a farm near Moscow, Idaho.

Don L. Crawford—CLICK/ Chicago

Irrigation. In the drier areas of the Columbia Plateau—8 to 10 inches (20 to 25 centimeters) of precipitation—farming can only be carried on under irrigation. During the 1930s work was begun on the Grand Coulee Dam on the Columbia River (see Grand Coulee Dam). In 1952 water from its reservoir was delivered for the first time to more than a million acres (405,000 hectares) of land south of the Grand Coulee. Well planned, the irrigated acres avoided areas of poor soils and alkali traps. Sugar beets, potatoes, and alfalfa are all grown on the irrigated acres.

In the dry western corners of the plateau are the Yakima and Wenatchee valleys, which specialize in growing apples under irrigation. Well advertised and well packaged, Washington's apples are marketed in the East and abroad.

Tourism

Like the Rocky Mountains, the Western Basins and Plateaus offer much for the tourist. Indian communities have developed their own hotel facilities and guides. The annual Inter-Tribal Ceremonial at Gallup, N.M., involves some 30 Indian groups. Santa Fe and Taos, N.M., are popular resorts.

Arizona offers old mining communities at Globe-Miami, Ajo, and Bisbee. Phoenix and Tucson lead trav-

Lake Mead on the Colorado River is actually the reservoir formed by Hoover Dam. Located on the Arizona-Nevada border, it is the heart of Lake Mead National Recreation Area.

Cameramann International

The Temple in Salt Lake City, Utah, is headquarters for the Mormons. The building was completed in 1893 and is used for various religious ceremonies. Nearby stand a museum, assembly hall, visitors' center, and the famous Tabernacle.

Courtesy of the Utah Travel Council

elers to the Painted Desert and the Petrified Forest. The Grand Canyon, Bryce Canyon, and Zion national parks are unforgettable experiences.

Las Vegas and Reno are famous for legal gambling. Hoover Dam on the Colorado River is near Las Vegas. Salt Lake City and Great Salt Lake are also prime tourist attractions. Farther north the lava outcrops on the Colorado Plateau, Grand Coulee Dam, and Hanford, Wash., the atomic-energy city, attract visitors.

Cities

City growth was substantial in the region after World War II. The largest city, Phoenix, has a metropolitan area population of more than 1.5 million. Salt Lake City, Tucson, Las Vegas, Albuquerque, and Spokane are other population centers. (*See also* Albuquerque; Las Vegas; Spokane; Tucson.)

Phoenix, on the Salt River, was founded on the site of an ancient Hohokam settlement in 1867 and incorporated as a city in 1881. It replaced Prescott as the territorial capital of Arizona in 1889. The city's growth may have been insured by the development of irrigation agriculture in the surrounding area. In 1911 the rock masonry, multipurpose Roosevelt Dam (storage for irrigation, power generation, flood control, and recreation) was completed. Auxiliary dams were constructed downstream. Farmers flocked to the irrigated acres. When Arizona became a state in 1912, Phoenix became the capital. It also became the supply town for the area's farmers.

Growth was slow until World War II, when, as part of the emerging sunbelt, the city began to grow considerably. Manufacturers of small, high-value products relished the climate of the Valley of the Sun. Electronics, computer, aircraft, furniture, aluminum, and chemical manufacturers moved to Phoenix. It became known nationwide as a retirement center, health resort, and vacation wonderland. (*See also* Phoenix.)

Salt Lake City was laid out on a site nearly 12 miles (19 kilometers) square at the foot of the Wasatch Mountains in 1847. Ten-acre (21-hectare) blocks, divided into eight lots of 1¼ acres (0.5 hectare) each, and Temple Square were parts of the original plan. Space was at a premium. In the 1850s the city became a supply point for travelers moving west on the California Trail. By 1865 there were 20,000 inhabitants. Many buildings were already in place, and the famous temple was rising from its foundations. In 1896 Salt Lake City became the capital of Utah. The Mormon influence is visible everywhere: the Mormon Temple and Tabernacle, the church office building, the monument at the foot of the Wasatch that records the words of Brigham Young, "THIS IS THE PLACE." In 1980 the metropolitan area's population numbered nearly 1 million. (*See also* Salt Lake City.)

The Future

The future of the Western Basins and Plateaus may well depend on the appropriate handling of natural resources—particularly water. In 1980 Arizona passed a comprehensive water-planning law. Wells are metered and withdrawal fees charged. Water rights can be sold to urban and industrial users. If this does not occur, the state can buy the farm land (with the water rights) and retire the land from agriculture. Arizona's hope is to reduce sharply the amount of irrigated land and therefore the use of water by the 21st century. The state also supports the Central Arizona Project—an aqueduct that carries Colorado River water to the Valley of the Sun.

In the Great Basin and on the Columbia Plateau, there is also great concern about water and future development. On the Colorado Plateau citizens worry about the strip-mining of coal, possible pollution of the atmosphere, and the large quantities of water needed for the production of power.

133

North Pacific Region

Pat Allen—CLICK/Chicago

North Cascades National Park is part of the Cascade Range. The range extends from northern California through Oregon, Washington, and British Columbia.

The North Pacific Region extends from northern California to southeastern Alaska. The region includes the coastal mountains, the Puget Sound-Willamette Valley, and the Cascade Range. Northern California is covered in the section on the South Pacific Region and southeastern Alaska in the Alaska section. Considered here is the area between the Cascades and the Pacific Ocean, or the western parts of the states of Oregon and Washington. (*See also* articles on individual states.)

Physical Earth

The region is marked by the rugged north-south Coast Ranges that flank the Pacific Ocean, the higher north-south-trending Cascade Range to the east, and the intervening Puget Sound-Willamette Valley trough. The Columbia River—which flows across the region for more than 750 miles (1,200 kilometers) before emptying into the Pacific—cuts across the Cascades and the Coast Ranges and forms part of the boundary between Oregon and Washington.

Because the rain-bearing winds blow at right angles against the mountains creating what is called orographic rainfall—particularly in the winter months—the North Pacific Region can be very wet. More than 130 inches (330 centimeters) of rain annually is not uncommon on the Pacific coast. In the high Olympic Mountains—above 6,000 feet (1,800 meters)—up to 200 inches (500 centimeters) have been recorded. On the lee side of the mountains, rainfall is much less. Portland, Ore., averages only 39 inches (99 centimeters); Seattle, Wash., only 32 inches (81 centimeters). The western flanks of the Cascades are very wet, the eastern flanks quite dry. Much of the air over the wet land is damp and cloudy. Summers tend to be cool; winters are warm for the latitude.

Heavy precipitation has helped to produce magnificent strands of timber: Douglas fir, west coast hemlock, western red cedar, and Sitka spruce. The drier Puget Sound area was forested early, while much of the Willamette Valley lay in grass. The soils are highland with good structure, a fair supply of humus, and good quantities of mineral plant food.

Especially significant are the waters of the region—both ocean and river—for fishing and collecting. Salmon and halibut have been caught here from time immemorial. The Makah and others were hunters of the whale, seal, and sea otter; Indian peoples collected clams, crabs, and oysters in the shallow bays and on the beaches. Fishing continues to be a major industry in the region.

Early Settlement

The Pacific Northwest coast was known to Europeans in the 16th century. The first European to set foot in what is now Washington State was probably the Spaniard Bruno Hecate, who landed on the Olympic Peninsula in 1775. The English navigator George Vancouver named and explored Puget Sound in 1792. Lewis and Clark reached the Columbia River in 1805, and Americans under John Jacob Astor established a fur post at Astoria on the Columbia River in 1811. The first American settlement parties arrived by sea. Later journeys were made over the Oregon Trail. By 1845 there were already 8,000 Americans in the Willamette Valley and vicinity. In June 1846 the boundary dispute with Great Britain was settled, and the 49th parallel was established as the boundary between the United States and the British possessions. Americans were attracted to the Pacific Northwest when Congress passed the Oregon Donation Land Law in 1850, giving 640 acres (260 hectares) of land to a married man or 320 acres (130 hectares) to a single man if he settled on the land by December. Settlement boomed accordingly. Oregon was admitted to the Union in 1859, Washington in 1889.

Agriculture

Good fortune smiled on the early settlers in the Willamette Valley. They planted and harvested wheat, clover, and potatoes. Wheat was the prime crop. They sold it to the Russians in Alaska, to the fur traders on the Columbia River, and to Hawaiians and Californians. The valley proved excellent for general farming—grain, grass, and hay—and for raising livestock. In time specialty crops were introduced—loganberries, raspberries, strawberries, blackberries, and cherries. They were shipped fresh to Portland and other markets, and they were canned or brined. Strawberries were perhaps the biggest money crop. Most were sold to local processing plants. Plums were grown, and prunes were dried, canned, and later frozen. Nursery products, hops, and peppermint were other specialty crops.

Grain and hay are the major crops today. Oats and barley replaced wheat in significance. They are fed to milk cows, as dairying is the chief source of income on many farms. Beef cattle, sheep, and poultry are also raised. Berry crops continue to be raised, as are walnuts and filberts. Oregon grapes, grown in the lee of the Coast Range, are used in the manufacture of Oregon wine. In October they are blown from the vines by helicopter downdrafts.

In the Puget Lowland the mild rainy winters and the long cool summers favor grazing and high milk production. Eggs are of significance. In western Washington farmers are also dairymen. Where land costs are high, fruits and vegetables are raised, including lettuce. Bulbs—tulips and daffodils—are grown in the rich black soil of the Puyallup Valley by farmers of Dutch origin.

Lumbering

Lumber has helped to power the economy of the region. The Douglas fir trees—towering between 200 and 350 feet (60 and 100 meters)—clothe the area between the coast and the Cascades. Interspersed are west coast hemlock and Western red cedar. On the eastern side of the Cascades are ponderosa pine, aspen, and cottonwood.

In the early days lumbermen hacked away at the lower trunks with axes, then used the platform and two-man saw, and turned ultimately to the base with power saws. Today the entire industry is mechanized. The automatic chipper strips a log of its bark and branches and cuts it into convenient sizes for further processing. Massive log movers load the logs onto trucks and railroad cars.

Loggers once cut everything in their path. Today logging is controlled. Clear, or patch, logging is a common method. A small swath is cut in the forest, providing natural reseeding. Conservationists maintain that the areas cut remain unsightly, are subject to erosion, and are not available for recreational use. Many private companies use tree farming. When trees are cut, others are planted in their place.

Douglas fir, ideal for most construction needs, is the major soft-wood species. West coast hemlock,

Haystack Rock is a prominent rock formation off the coast at Cannon Beach in Oregon. The beach was named for a cannon that washed ashore from a shipwreck in 1846.

Breck Kent—Earth Scenes

135

also used in construction, is significant in the pulp industry. It is used in the manufacture of rayon, cellophane, photographic film, and tissue paper as well as high-grade book and magazine paper. Western red cedar, which resists decay, is used in shingles, siding, and exterior paneling.

Oregon probably has more standing saw timber and produces more logs, lumber, and plywood than any other state. Formerly the leading pulp producer, Washington now ranks second to Georgia. In both states lumber remains a gigantic economic enterprise.

Fishing

Salmon spawn in fresh water, fatten over a three- or four-year period in the ocean, and return to their places of birth. On the Columbia River—and other Pacific Northwest streams—Indian fishermen went after the sockeye with dip net, seine, and spear. They then preserved their catches. The idea was not lost on American businessmen. The first salmon cannery was established on the Columbia River in 1867. Canneries sprouted all along the river and in coastal communities, and salmon canning became a major industry. Hundreds of thousands of cases of Columbia River and Puget Sound salmon were sent to market in the late 19th and early 20th centuries.

Later in the 20th century catches were much reduced. Overfishing, stream pollution, and the building of high dams interfered with the life cycle of the salmon. Yields were cut in half. Today there are many more salmon canneries farther north—along the British Columbia and Alaska coasts—than in either Oregon or Washington.

The supplies of halibut, mackerel, flounder, and herring have also made significant contributions to the economy of the region. In 1976 the federal government extended the line of exclusive American offshore fishing rights to the 200-mile limit. Foreign competition provoked the action.

Manufacturing

Early manufacturing was based on forest (lumbering) and agriculture (food processing). Manufacturing has since diversified, with concentrations in the Portland and Seattle areas. Work in metals, freeze-dried foods, chemicals, machinery, and electronics has increased. Low-cost electric power enabled aluminum reduction to secure a foothold, and the building of ships and aircraft is of major significance.

The Boeing Company in Seattle is a major builder of both commercial and military aircraft. As a manufacturing enterprise Boeing dominates the city, the entire "Pugetopolis" between Oregon and Canada, and perhaps the whole state of Washington. Founded in 1916, Boeing has had many periods of boom and near bust. During World War II there were 45,000 at work in Boeing plants. In 1945 the federal contracts expired. In the 1950s Boeing revived with commercial jet transports and began to build Saturn V rockets and Minuteman ICBMs. Employment swelled to 72,000, but by 1960 it had dropped to 58,000 and then

to 50,000. In 1968—with the model 747 airplane—Boeing employment reached 95,000, with ups and downs in the 1970s and 1980s. Boeing is an economic barometer for the entire Pacific Northwest.

Tourism

Tourism may be the fastest growing industry in the region. Mountains, valleys, and seacoast attract hunters, campers, boaters, fishermen, and skiers. There are the beauties of the national parks: Crater Lake in Oregon; Olympic, North Cascades, and Mount Rainier in Washington. There is the quiet green of the Willamette Valley, the robust activity of Puget Sound, the San Juan Islands, and Mount Saint Helens.

Cities

Two metropolitan areas dominate the Pacific Northwest—Seattle-Everett and Portland. Pugetopolis is an urban world: Seattle-Everett is joined by Olympia (Washington's capital city), Tacoma, Bremerton, and Bellingham. Portland is joined on the Willamette River by Eugene and Salem (Oregon's capital city). (*See also* Olympia; Salem; Tacoma.)

Seattle is situated on seven hills and looks out on both the Cascades and the Olympic Mountains. Mount Rainier can be seen from the city on clear days. Between its founding in 1851 and the arrival of the transcontinental railroad in 1884, Seattle served as a lumber town. Its growth was slow until the boom days of the Alaska gold rush (1897–98). Ties with Alaska have been strong ever since. In 1890 Seattle had a population of 42,000; by 1910, 250,000. Seattle grew as a trade, transportation, and manufacturing center. Its deepwater port facility was one of the first to be computerized and to support containerized freight. It supplies markets in the Orient and Alaska's Prudhoe Bay. By 1980 the metropolitan area numbered more than 1.6 million. (*See also* Seattle.)

Portland was founded at the juncture of the Willamette and Columbia rivers in 1845. It grew to tap the trade of both rivers. Its links with the wheat belt in eastern Washington, the development of the salmon industry, and the arrival of the transcontinental railroad in 1883 assured its growth. Like Seattle, Portland is a trade, transportation, and manufacturing center. When the sandbars at the mouth of the Columbia River were removed, it became an ocean port with miles of deepwater frontage. During World War II it became a leading shipbuilding center. By 1988 the metropolitan area numbered more than 1.2 million people. (*See also* Portland.)

The Future

Former Governor Tom McCall's oft-quoted remark provides a statement for the future. "Welcome to Oregon. . . . Travel, visit, drink in the great beauty of our state. But for God's sake, don't move here." Limiting the growth of the region in order to maintain the quality of life is a priority. The North Pacific Region continues to rely on its traditional industries but will continue to diversify.

South Pacific Region

Ken McKowen

Gulls and other birds crowd secluded Agate Beach in northern California. The beach is in Patrick's Point State Park, not far from Humboldt Bay.

The South Pacific Region consists exclusively of California. Included within this extraordinary region are the Sierra Nevada, Great Central Valley, and Coast Ranges; a Mediterranean climate; one area much like the Semiarid Southwest, another akin to the Pacific Northwest; Indians, Hispanics, Mexicans, and Anglos; gold; citrus fruits; irrigation; Los Angeles and San Francisco; and Hollywood and Silicon Valley. (*See also* California.)

The Sierra Nevada range forms the towering eastern wall of California. The western side rises gently from the Great Central Valley; the eastern side shows a series of high steep cliffs to the Great Basin. To the north and south of Mount Whitney—14,495 feet (4,418 meters) high—elevations decline somewhat. A great number of canyons have been formed by the westward-flowing rivers—Yosemite, Merced, and Kings canyons among them.

The rugged Coast Ranges, which are much lower than the Sierra Nevada, run along the coast. Between the ridges and the Pacific there are small valleys and plains—Los Angeles and San Francisco are both located in such areas.

The Great Central Valley, sometimes called the Sacramento-San Joaquin Valley, is 450 miles (725 kilometers) long and about 50 miles (80 kilometers) wide. It should not be thought of as one continuous expanse of level land, for there is much topographic variety. Most of the Great Central Valley is devoted to agriculture.

The climate in California is essentially Mediterranean, but there are great differences within the physiographic divisions, and the climate varies considerably from north to south. In the Sierra Nevada there is heavy precipitation and much snow. During the rainless summer the Sierras form a great reservoir for much of central and southern California. In the Coast Ranges temperatures decrease and rainfall increases from south to north. San Luis Obispo, for example, receives 21 inches (53 centimeters) of precipitation, and at Eureka 37 inches (94 centimeters) is recorded. With the cold California Current flowing offshore and the westerly winds blowing onshore, San Francisco maintains a mean July temperature of 59° F (15° C), and the range is less than 10° F (5° C) for the entire year—a boon for tourists. The climate in the Great Central Valley, on the other hand, is markedly continental. At Bakersfield in the south the mean temperature for July is 83° F (28° C), and the mean January temperature is 47° F (8° C)—a range of 36° F (20° C). Precipitation averages 6 inches (15 centimeters). At Redding in the north the mean temperature for July is 82° F (28° C), and the mean January temperature 45° F (7° C)—but the precipitation is 37 inches (94 centimeters).

Spaniards and the Missions

California was the home of a great number of small Indian tribes in prehistoric times. The Spaniards, moving northward from Lower California in Mexico, established the mission system among them. The Indians were induced to congregate in a town, where under clerical discipline they were taught the Roman Catholic religion, the Spanish language, and the rudiments of the white man's culture. At the center of the mission stood the church. Around it were the missionary's house; the Indian quarters; granaries and storerooms; workshops for carpentry, weaving, and blacksmithing; and rooms for making pottery, candles, and soap. Beyond lay the corrals, irrigated fields, and grazing lands. The first mission in California was established in 1769 at San Diego by the Franciscan Junípero Serra (*see* Serra). Ultimately 21 missions were established in California. In 1776 the mission and presidio, or fort, were founded at Yerba Buena (San Francisco).

137

The Edwards Mansion stands amid the orange groves near Redlands, Calif., part of the Southern citrus belt.

Gold

The Spaniards found little gold in California. It was James W. Marshall who discovered the little flecks of yellow while excavating for a sawmill along the tailrace in the American River that would ignite the Gold Rush of 1849. Rancheros and farmers flocked to the diggings. Entire communities in California were depopulated. Some struck it rich on Feather River. President James K. Polk announced the findings in his annual message to Congress on Dec. 5, 1848, and the stampede was on. Gold seekers arrived in California by way of Cape Horn and across the Isthmus of Panama. They arrived by way of the California, Old Spanish, and Gila Route trails. In 1849 some 40,000 potential miners flocked into San Francisco. California would never be the same again.

The gold discoveries brought an end to California's isolation. They brought new elements (many foreign) and a substantial increase in California's population. They helped to create new towns and villages. They provided incentives for vigorous transportation development and permanently altered California's (and the world's) price structure. The gold discoveries also helped to inaugurate agriculture, lumbering, and commerce in the northern part of the state.

Development of Agriculture

North. During the Spanish regime rancheros raised cattle in the Sacramento River valley. They exported hides and tallow. The lower river, which joins the San Joaquin to form the delta at San Francisco Bay, was little used. Tidal and poorly drained, the area was covered with a reedy grass called tule, willows, live oaks, and vines. American farmers reclaimed the area—diking and ditching helped—and planted rice in the 1870s. On the upper Sacramento they planted wheat in the late fall and harvested it in the dry summer. They raised barley to feed the draft animals.

Farmers were also at work in the coastal valleys. Imitating the farmers of the Spanish missions, they raised wine grapes and planted prune plum trees. The Napa Valley was already covered in a sea of vineyards by 1865. In the Santa Clara Valley wheat was growing and orchards of plums and other fruits were being laid out.

South. In the missions near Los Angeles (San Juan Capistrano, San Gabriel, and San Fernando), the Spaniards planted olives, citrus fruits, and wine grapes. They raised cattle, horses, and sheep. In 1851 the Mormons founded San Bernardino in the nearby mountains, where wheat was planted and grapes raised. When the settlers were recalled to Utah in 1857, San Bernardino all but disintegrated. Later settlers had some success in the 1870s, when artesian water sources were discovered and citrus fruit trees planted. Freezes, hot and cold air blasts from the mountains, and even occasional snowfalls put an end to the ventures. Farmers turned to grapes, dairying, and general farming.

The San Fernando Valley was planted in olives, grapes, and fruit trees. Anaheim became successful with wine grapes and winemaking, but in 1884 the vine disease crippled the vineyards. Success returned with the introduction of the Valencia orange in 1889.

Agriculture moved slowly into the San Joaquin Valley. Wheat was planted in the Kings River and Fresno areas but proved unsuccessful. Conditions, however, were ideal—intense sunlight, dry air, and moisture derived from irrigation—for raisin grapes. The Fresno area became a world leader in the production of raisins.

Citrus fruits. In 1860 there were only 4,000 orange trees in all of California. Growth was rapid, however, after the introduction of the navel orange—seedless, good color, and fine taste—near Riverside in 1873. By 1880 there were 17,000 orange trees in California, more than 3,000 lime trees, and nearly 2,500 lemon trees. Most were located in the Riverside-Los Angeles area, but they had already spread to the Great Central Valley.

Further growth was assured with the completion of the transcontinental railroads—Union Pacific, Southern Pacific, and Santa Fe—and the introduction in 1889 of the refrigerated boxcar. During the 1908–09 season 15 million boxes of citrus fruits were shipped east by rail. The fruits were marketed cooperatively through the California Fruit Growers' Exchange (established 1893), now the Sunkist Fruit Growers' Exchange (1952), whose Sunkist trade name is famous the world over.

Water. Water is a California nemesis, a California savior. It is needed in huge amounts for farms, urban areas, and industrial enterprises—particularly in the dry southern parts of the state. Los Angeles, for example, went early to the Sierra Nevada to bring water from Owens Valley—nearly 200 miles (320 kilometers) away—to the city by way of the Los Angeles Aqueduct (1913). Fifteen years later eleven communities in the coastal south formed the Metropolitan Water District to insure an adequate water supply for the area. Under its auspices the Colorado River Aqueduct carries water from Parker Dam to the coastal cities (1939).

But the irrigated farms were the biggest water users. In the 1940s work was begun on the Central Valley Project, designed to transfer Sacramento River water south to the dry San Joaquin Valley. Shasta Dam was built to impound the waters of the Sacramento River; Friant Dam, the waters of the San Joaquin. Water from the Sacramento was then sent south in the Delta-Mendota Canal. From Mendota, water was sent north to irrigate the lower San Joaquin Valley. When the Friant-Kern Canal—160 miles (260 kilometers) long—was completed, water could be carried south to the upper San Joaquin Valley. Near the Mexican border irrigation waters from the Colorado River feed into the Coachella Canal to supply the Coachella Valley, the All-American Canal supplies water to the Imperial Valley, and the California Aqueduct carries water from the delta to the western parts of the San Joaquin Valley and the coastal south.

So great is the water nemesis that plans to secure water from other sources—the Columbia and Snake rivers, the sea, Antarctica—frequently surface. There are also proposals for carrying more water from north to south within the state, but northern Californians are opposed. They are concerned about their own water needs in the 21st century.

Agriculture Today

Despite water problems California leads the nation in agricultural production: citrus fruits and grapes; peaches, pears, cherries, and plums; figs, dates, and avocados; walnuts and almonds; cantaloupes, tomatoes, lettuce, asparagus, artichokes, carrots, cauliflower, celery, and peas; rice in the Sacramento Valley; cotton in the Imperial Valley, Riverside County, and the southern part of the San Joaquin Valley; and livestock, poultry, and dairying. Enough milk, cream, butter, cheese, ice cream, and condensed milk is produced to care adequately for the state's population. California's agriculture is a remarkable achievement.

Meanwhile urban and industrial expansion have claimed much of the former farmland. Encroachments have been made on the citrus orchards in the Los Angeles Basin. Farmland fell to new housing developments, airport runways, industrial sites, and even to the building of a new college campus.

There are fewer farmers. Mechanization has made deep inroads. Lettuce and cotton are picked by machine. Fruit sorters are electronic; box movers are automatic. While the number of farms and farmers has declined sharply, the need for migrant labor remains. In the vineyards César Chavez emerged as a force in upholding the interests of the farm worker.

Manufacturing

Lumber mills and flour mills, wagon and carriage "factories," tanneries and leatherworking establishments were among the early manufacturing enterprises. Californians also made textiles (woolen goods) and explosives for the mines and engaged in sugar refining and cigar making. They made large and small iron products. At the Vulcan Iron Works in San Francisco they made locomotives.

In the 20th century energy sources—petroleum from Los Angeles and vicinity and electricity trans-

Towers of calcium carbonate in Moon Lake, Calif., were exposed after the lake was used as a source for water.

John Gerlach—CLICK/Chicago

Workers inspect computer chips at LSI Logic Corporation, a company in the part of California known as Silicon Valley.

mitted from the Colorado River—helped to boost the Los Angeles area as a prime manufacturing center. Petroleum refining, motion picture production, automobile assembly, meat packing, the making of rubber tires and tubes, printing and publishing, and the making of machinery and machine shop products all became significant industrial pursuits. In San Francisco petroleum refining was also the leading manufacturing enterprise. It was followed by the canning of fruits and vegetables, meat packing, printing and publishing, baking bread, and making tin cans, tin ware, paints, and varnishes.

World War II had a great impact on manufacturing. Aircraft were produced at many locations in the Los Angeles Basin. Shipbuilding was prominent in San Francisco and the bay area. An integrated steel mill was built at Fontana. The war effort was also responsible for the growth of other manufactures: airplane parts, electrical machinery, rubber goods, sheet metal, and light metal products.

Today California is deeply involved in food processing, canning, quick-freezing fruits, and winemaking. It packages raisins, prunes, figs, dates, and apricots. It manufactures tires, plastics, drugs, furniture, airplanes, radios and television sets, and record players and tape decks. It is still very much involved in motion-picture production.

Hollywood

Hollywood is the place of fantasy and dreams. It is California. D.W. Griffith brought his troupe—Mary Pickford among them—to the community in 1910. The first all-California film was shot at the Mission San Gabriel. Between January and April 1910, 21 films were produced at California locations—the missions, oilfields, seacoast, Pasadena, and the Sierra Nevada. Weather and light, physiography, and architecture—southern California seemed to have it all. Cecil B. De Mille's troupe included such stars as Gloria Swanson, Ramon Navarro, Wallace Beery, and Walt Disney. The movie industry was set for a long run. By the 1920s it was making more money than was the orange crop.

The community continues to produce and distribute major films. It is a leading producer of television films. CBS (Columbia Broadcasting System) and NBC (National Broadcasting Company) both have facilities in Hollywood and Burbank.

Silicon Valley

The nation's scientists found that silicon (refined from quartz) can be used in making the electronic switches (transistors) that can control and amplify electrical signals. Digital watches, calculators, and computers are the result. The hub of these industries today is the so-called Silicon Valley, which rings San Francisco Bay from Palo Alto to San Jose. More than 80 chip (a sliver of silicon packed with hundreds of thousands of transistors) manufacturers are located in the area. Chip, computer, and software companies include such names as Apple, Intel, IBM, and Hewlett-Packard. These industries thrive, but competition is keen. The talented and creative are lured here. Like Hollywood, Silicon Valley is a piece of California.

Tourism

California offers amazing year-round opportunities for tourists: swimming, skiing, hunting, fishing, and mountain climbing; magnificent scenery—mountains, deserts, valleys, and seacoast—a photographer's delight. There are Balboa Park and its famous zoo in San Diego; Knott's Berry Farm, Marineland, and Disneyland; Death Valley and Yosemite and Lassen Volcanic national parks. There are also Imperial Valley, Coachella Valley, and the Salton Sea; the redwoods; and the cities of Los Angeles, San Diego, and San Francisco.

Cities

More than 90 percent of its population live in cities. The Los Angeles-Long Beach metropolitan area numbers nearly 7.5 million people. San Francisco-Oakland is home to more than 3 million. Other large metropolitan areas include Anaheim-Santa Ana-Garden Grove, San Diego; Riverside-San Bernardino-Ontario; San Jose, reported to be the fastest-growing community in the United States; Sacramento; Oxnard-Simi Valley-Ventura; and Fresno. A megalopolis already exists between San Diego and Santa Barbara—nearly 200 miles (320 kilometers) of continuous city. California is people; it is urban (*See also* Anaheim; Fresno; Long Beach; Oakland; Riverside; Sacramento; San Diego; San Jose.)

Los Angeles. The pueblo of Los Angeles was founded in 1781. In 1846, during the Mexican War, Commodore Robert F. Stockton entered the pueblo and claimed it for the United States. In 1850, the same year that California became a state, Los Angeles was incorporated as a city. In the 1870s and 1880s the city was linked to the east by the transcontinental railroads. The 1890s brought the petroleum discoveries that prompted the city's growth. By the 1920s the movie industry was solidly in place.

Los Angeles' development and appearance was sharply influenced by the automobile. Many individual communities have come together to form the general metropolis. Most of the housing is single-family even among the poor. Los Angeles County has the heaviest concentration of automobiles in the world; it also has a far-flung freeway network to support them.

The city has become a leading financial, trade, and manufacturing center. It ranks first in the country in the manufacture of aircraft and aircraft parts and is a leading garment center (sportswear). Anglos are a minority in the population. There are well over 2 million Mexican Americans, as well as many other Hispanics, and numerous Asians. There are many ethnic neighborhoods. (*See also* Los Angeles.)

San Francisco. Mission Dolores and the nearby presidio were erected at Yerba Buena in 1776. An American force captured the community during the Mexican War (1846), and Yerba Buena became San Francisco the following year. Gold discoveries in 1848 led to growth. San Francisco's waterfront was known to be rough and tumble—vigilantes patrolled the area.

The growing city was engulfed by earthquake and fire on April 18, 1906, virtually demolishing the central business district—28,000 buildings were destroyed and 400 people killed. Recovery, however, came quickly. By the 1920s automobile ferries operated between Sausalito, Oakland, Berkeley, and San Francisco; from Richmond to San Rafael; and across the Carquinez Straits. The Bay and Golden Gate bridges were not completed until 1937. In World War II the city served as the chief embarkation point for troops leaving for the Pacific. For residents and tourists alike San Francisco is a delight, with cable cars, Chinatown, Telegraph Hill, Fisherman's Wharf, excellent restaurants, Ghirardelli Square, the Cow Palace, Golden Gate Park, and the National Maritime Museum. (*See also* San Francisco.)

The Future

While the growth rate may have peaked, there are still those who see California as Paradise. Both Americans and immigrants will continue to move here, and newcomers will find most of the amenities they seek. They will also discover the chief problems—the continuing need for water and the encroachment of the urban areas on the farmland. They will learn about smog and hear about preservation. They will also hear about California as a cultural center and a leader in the arts, sciences, hi-tech, and education.

Lake Tahoe, on the Nevada-California border in the northern Sierra Nevada, has been developed as a tourist resort. The lake is 22 miles (35 kilometers) long and 12 miles (19 kilometers) wide.

Mike McCabe—CLICK/Chicago

Alaska

Glacier Bay extends about 50 miles (80 kilometers) along the coast of southeastern Alaska. It contains 16 active tidal glaciers descending from the St. Elias Mountains.

Alaska differs markedly from the "Lower 48," or the coterminous United States. It is distinguished by its physical characteristics, history, people, relative isolation, and size. The population of the state is comparatively small, and distances are formidable. (*See also* Alaska.)

Physiography

Much of Alaska is dominated by plateau and mountain country. The core is made up of the Central Plateau, which is drained by the valleys of the Yukon and Kuskowim rivers and their tributaries. North of the plateau is the broad and formidable east-west-trending Brooks Range—which runs the breadth of the state—and north of it the relatively low-lying Arctic Slope. South of the plateau is the Alaska Range and south of it the Pacific Mountains, which include the Aleutian Range, the Kenai-Chugach Mountains, the St. Elias Mountains, and the Coast Mountains.

Summit elevations in the Brooks Range vary from 5,000 to 6,000 feet (1,500 to 1,800 meters) above sea level. The mountains rise conspicuously above the Central Plateau and even above the Arctic Plateau in the immediate north. The Alaska Range towers even more conspicuously above the Central Plateau. Mount McKinley—20,320 feet (6,194 meters)—is the highest peak in North America and a birthplace of glaciers (*see* McKinley, Mount). In the Aleutian Range—elevations of 3,000 to 6,000 feet (900 to 1,800 meters)—there are a number of active volcanoes. There is also found the Valley of Ten Thousand Smokes.

Farther east are awesome heights once more—Mount St. Elias towers 18,008 feet (5,489 meters) above the sea. Many glaciers descend from the range to form the Malaspina Glacier, which breaks off in the ocean to form icebergs. The Coast Mountains in Alaska's Panhandle are akin to the mountains of the Pacific Northwest. There is little coastal plain in Alaska. Most of what there is can be found on the flat, featureless Arctic Slope.

Climate

Climatic conditions vary considerably among the physiographic provinces. At Fairbanks in the interior of the Central Plateau, the January average temperature is a very cold −17° F (−27° C), and the July average is only 60° F (16° C). Rainfall is meager—17 inches (28 centimeters) and the growing season short (90 days). On the Arctic Slope temperatures are even lower—in winter −17° F (−27° C) and in summer 40° F (4.4° C). A growing season is virtually nonexistent (17 days), and precipitation is less than 5 inches (13 centimeters). Throughout northern Alaska permafrost—or permanently frozen ground—is a significant environmental condition. Subsoils may be frozen to 1,000 feet (300 meters) or more in depth. In the warm summer the upper few feet melt, causing a gooey sludge to form. Pipes break, floors heave, and walls crack.

At Anchorage, between the Alaska Range and the Kenai-Chugach Mountains, the average January temperature is 11° F (−12° C) and 57° F (14° C) in July. But the growing season is longer than at Fairbanks—110 days and precipitation averages 15 inches (38 centimeters). In the neighboring Matanuska Valley agriculture is practiced.

At Dutch Harbor in the Aleutian Islands, temperatures are modified by the warm Kuroshio, or Japan Current. January temperatures average 32° F (0° C) and July temperatures 51° F (11° C). In the Panhandle temperatures vary little, but precipitation varies considerably. Juneau, like its sister communities in the Alaskan Panhandle, averages about 29° F (−2° C) in January, 57° F (14° C) in July. Rainfall here is recorded at 91 inches (230 centimeters), and the growing season is 172 days. Sitka, however, records 87 inches (221 centimeters) of rainfall, Ketchikan 150 inches (381 centimeters), and Little Port Walker, near the southeastern tip of Baranof Island, 221 inches (561 centimeters).

Peoples

The original inhabitants of Alaska were Indians, Eskimo, and Aleuts—all of whom adapted well to the northern environment. The interior peoples became hunters primarily; those facing the sea—like the Tlingit in the Panhandle—became fishermen. They trapped or harpooned salmon, caught candlefish in nets, and scoured beaches for clams and crabs.

First to meet the native peoples in force were the Russians. In the 18th century Russian fur traders found their way to the Aleutian Islands. They quickly subdued the Aleuts and exploited the available sea otters. In 1799 Alexander Baranof, governor of the Russian American Company, built Redoubt Archangel Michael on Sitka Sound. The Tlingit resisted bravely but succumbed. At Sitka, where the Russian presence was direct, a number of the Tlingit joined the Russian Orthodox church. They went to school and planted gardens in potatoes, turnips, and cabbages. Then their world changed once again—the United States purchased Alaska from the Russians for 7.2 million dollars.

The Americans came—home seekers, miners, fur traders, ship owners, lawyers, cooks, and gamblers—eager to exploit the newly bought land. They set up restaurants, saloons, and trading stores. But neither the army (1867–77) nor the navy (1879–84) was able to keep order. Civilian authority arrived in 1884 with passage of the Organic Act.

Gold, Copper, and the Railroads

Discoveries of gold helped to spur Alaska's settlement. The first major gold strike was made near Juneau in 1880. Others followed at Forty Miles River (1886), Circle City (1893) in the Yukon drainage, and the Klondike in 1897 in nearby Canada. Gold was also discovered near Nome (1899–1900) on the Seward Peninsula and near Fairbanks (1902) on the Tanana River. Juneau, Nome, and Fairbanks owe their origin and continued existence to the gold discoveries. Alaska's population started to mount. Only slightly more than 32,000 in 1890, it leaped to more than 63,000 by 1900—largely gold inspired.

Even more wealth was available in the copper ores on Copper River. A rail line was built from Cordova on the coast nearly 200 miles (320 kilometers) north to the mines. The builders were J.P. Morgan and the Guggenheim interests, or the Alaska Syndicate. A second railroad was later built between Seward, Anchorage, and Fairbanks (1923). Alaskans were much concerned about transportation. They wanted rail links through Canada with the Lower 48. There was talk of building a railroad across Bering Strait to connect with the Trans-Siberian Railroad, but the Soviets rejected the proposal.

Fisheries

Fishing is a leading money-maker for the Alaskan economy. The cod provided the call for fishermen in 1865, the salmon shortly thereafter. Salmon canner-ies were built as early as 1878. Fishing was intense and competitive. There were cries of overfishing and possible depletion. In 1924 the United States Fish and Wildlife Service was given supervisory and enforcement powers over all Alaskan fishing. Fifty percent of the salmon were to be permitted to move upstream to spawn, but the depletion continued. In 1953 the canneries packed fewer than three million cases—the second lowest total in 42 years—and soon Japanese fishermen were engaged in Alaskan waters.

Today efforts are being made to raise salmon in hatcheries, but many fishermen are turning to the king crab for their livelihood. The demand is great, and the catch is an all-year-long activity. Halibut, shrimps, and herring are other significant Alaskan catches. On the Pribilof Islands, Aleut fishermen continue to make their fur-seal kills.

Lumber

The potential for exploiting the western hemlock, Sitka spruce, and western red cedar was apparent from Alaska's earliest days. Great distances to Lower 48 markets and high transportation costs, however, limited development. World War I pointed out the critical need for pulp and paper, and in 1922 a small mill was put into operation near Juneau. It could not be sustained, however, because of high labor and transportation costs and was forced to shut down.

Kamishak Bay in Alaska has an extensive fishing commerce involving the processing of shrimp, king crab, and salmon.

Phil Degginger—CLICK/Chicago

Not until the 1950s was a viable pulp and paper mill completed near Ketchikan. A Japanese-owned mill that ships pulp to Japan is located at Sitka. The Japanese have invested heavily in Alaskan timber.

Agriculture

Distances, freight costs, limited population, and a harsh climate have typically discouraged agriculture in Alaska. Frost is a common deterrent, the soil lacks nutrients, and fertilizer costs are high. In order to succeed agriculture must be limited to suitable areas and must be subsidized. Agricultural experiment stations were established in various parts of Alaska and continued at Fairbanks and in the Matanuska Valley.

In 1935, 202 colonists—fresh from the relief rolls of Michigan, Wisconsin, and Minnesota—journeyed to the Matanuska Valley. It is protected by mountains on three sides and open only to Cook Inlet. Each family was provided with 40 acres (16 hectares), a house, a barn, farming equipment, and stock. Adjustments were not easy to make, but by 1937 the settlers were raising wheat, barley, and oats, carrots, turnips, and potatoes—thus serving the local market at Anchorage. A larger market was later established with the building of a large military base at Fort Richardson (1940).

There is little farming in the Matanuska Valley—and therefore in Alaska—today. Much of the farmland has been subdivided into lots—sacrificed to the growth of Anchorage. The prospects for future agricultural development are not promising.

Petroleum

Oil seepages were known in Alaska from the 1830s. At Katalla on the Gulf of Alaska east of Cordova, oil was refined between 1911 and 1931. President Warren G. Harding set aside 37,000 square miles (95,-830 square kilometers) on the Arctic Slope as Naval Petroleum Reserve No. 4. In 1957 oil was discovered on the Kenai Peninsula. In the late 1960s five fields were working in the Kenai-Cook Inlet area (nine fields were also yielding natural gas). In 1968 Atlantic Richfield brought in the monumental discovery 10,-000 feet (3,000 meters) deep at Prudhoe Bay on the Arctic Slope. Not until passage of the Alaska Native Claims Settlement Act of 1971 and Congressional approval in 1973, however, were the companies free to build the pipeline to carry the oil from the Arctic Slope to Valdez.

The pipeline, one of the most sophisticated ever built, crosses three mountain ranges, goes under several hundred rivers and streams, and passes through areas of intense earthquake activity. Because of permafrost the pipeline must be elevated over much of the distance and insulated with polyurethane coverings. These measures serve to protect both the permafrost and the pipeline. Under the rivers it is jacketed in concrete. Maintenance (welding the pipe, repairing leaks, and so on) is costly. About 1.2 million barrels of oil, however, pass through the pipeline to Valdez each day. It is shipped to West coast ports.

Land Claims

Alaska became a state in 1959 and was invited by the federal government to select 103 million acres (41.7 million hectares) of land for itself out of the Alaska domain. The selection process began in the 1960s. The native peoples were dismayed. They would certainly be the biggest losers, but the Eskimo, Indians, and Aleuts—organized in the Alaska Federation of Natives (1966)—began to fight back. They made their own demands: 40 million acres (16 million hectares) of land for themselves, 500 million dollars from the federal treasury, and a 2 percent royalty on all minerals taken from lands that they did not directly own. The native peoples wanted clear title to their own land and compensation for those lands taken from them in the past.

Opposition to the native peoples was formidable, but they were supported by the oil companies that wanted to proceed with the building of the Prudhoe Bay-Valdez pipeline, Alaska's Congressional delegation, and by civil rights groups. The struggle was bitter, but the native groups won. A bill passed both houses of Congress in 1971. The 40 million acres were divided among 200 native villages. Each village became a corporation, and 12 regional corporations carried out developmental plans. Nearly 500 million dollars was awarded the villages over an 11-year period, and the 2 percent royalty was assured.

Doyon (it built a 2.3-million-dollar structure in Fairbanks), Bristol Bay, and Bering Straits are among the 12 regional corporations. The natives of Alaska became stockholders in a land-rich and a possibly cash-rich enterprise.

Cities

The only city of any size in Alaska is Anchorage. In the mid-1980s it had a population of about 230,000. Because of its strategic location, it has become a crossroads in world aviation. It is also headquarters of the Alaska Railroad, a major seaport, and a trucking center. The interior city of Fairbanks is Alaska's second largest city, and Juneau in the Panhandle is the capital. (*See also* Anchorage; Fairbanks; Juneau.)

The Future

Alaska's economy will continue to benefit from its natural wealth: petroleum, natural gas, fish, and lumber. Oil will continue to flow from the Arctic Slope. New discoveries are likely in the Beaufort and Bering seas and the Gulf of Alaska. Natural gas finds will become increasingly significant. Alaska is rich in many other minerals as well: coal, gold, mercury, platinum, copper, silver, uranium, and tungsten—and capital will be needed for development. Alaska will continue to benefit from the United States military and administrative presence, which pours millions of dollars into the economy. It will benefit from tourism. With the 12 regional corporations, Alaska's native peoples will be brought into the American mainstream. Alaskan society will become increasingly urban.

Hawaii

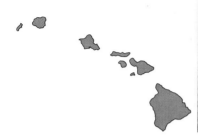

Tom Nebbia—CLICK/Chicago

The sea cliffs of the 20-mile- (32-kilometer-) long Na Pali Coast on Kauai are best seen by hikers or from a helicopter, since there are no roads with automobile access.

The Hawaiian Islands stretch for more than 1,600 miles (2,575 kilometers) across the mid-Pacific Ocean about 2,400 miles (3,860 kilometers) from the mainland United States. They are the visible peaks of a gigantic range of submarine volcanic mountains. Lowest and oldest (geologically) in the west, they become higher and younger toward the east. Mauna Loa in easternmost Hawaii, an active volcano, peaks at 13,680 feet (4,170 meters) above sea level. From west to east the major islands include: Niihau, Kauai, Oahu, Molokai, Lanai, Kahoolawe, Maui, and Hawaii. In the distant west between Kure Island and Niihau is a small group of lesser-known islands, pinnacles, and shoals. (*See also* Hawaii.)

Climate

Latitude, elevation, the trade winds, and the surrounding seas play key roles in the climate of the islands. Honolulu, for example, is south of the Tropic of Cancer. The angle of the sun's rays changes little from season to season, the days are about the same length, and the sea moderates the temperatures. The average temperature in Honolulu in January is 72° F (22° C) and in July a moderate 79° F (26° C).

The big differences occur in the amount of rainfall, in which the trade winds and mountains (orographic precipitation) are significant. Honolulu receives 23 inches (58 centimeters) of rain annually, most of it in the winter half year. Within the metropolitan area there are places that receive less than 20 inches (50 centimeters) and others that receive more than 120 inches (300 centimeters). On the big Island (Hawaii) Hilo records 140 inches (356 centimeters), another station only 14 inches (36 centimeters), and still another 230 inches (584 centimeters).

In general the climate is unusually pleasant for the tropics. There is little uncomfortable heat. Frost rarely occurs below 4,000 feet (1,200 meters). Only in winter are the high peaks covered with snow. Tornadoes, hurricanes, and typhoons never occur.

Peoples

Before the Christian Era the West Polynesians (Lapita culture), after a long stay in Tonga-Samoa, began to send their canoes eastward. They discovered and colonized the Marquesas Islands in about 200 BC. From the Marquesas—as East Polynesians—they occupied the Society Islands and the Hawaiian group in about AD 300.

Archaeological evidence from Hawaii and Oahu confirms that early Hawaiians were fine farmers who raised taro, sweet potato, varieties of banana, breadfruit, sugarcane, yam, and coconut and were expert fishermen who caught fish and shellfish. As they moved from the wetlands to the drylands, large irrigation works and dryland field systems were developed. By AD 1100 the population had reached 20,000, and by the 17th century it was more than 200,000. A class society had come into being, and chiefdoms operated throughout the islands.

A kingdom emerged under Kamehameha, and *hoales*—European foreigners—appeared in the islands for the first time. The English navigator Captain James Cook landed on Kauai in 1778, and French, Americans, and others followed. Americans, using Hawaiian sandalwood, participated in trade with China and later engaged in the whaling trade. Meanwhile the first of the Protestant missionaries arrived in Hawaii in 1820. They taught Hawaiians the rigid New England moral code and how to read and write. Hiram Bingham, one of their number, was an advisor to the monarchy.

Under *hoale* influence the native Hawaiian population began to decline. Measles, smallpox, syphilis, and tuberculosis swept the islands. During Captain Cook's

145

Kilauea, on the big island of Hawaii, is the world's largest active volcanic mass. The summit has collapsed to form a shallow depression about 3 miles (5 kilometers) long and 2 miles (3 kilometers) wide. The volcano has frequent, nonexplosive eruptions.

E.R. Degginger—Earth Scenes

first visit as many as 300,000 Hawaiians inhabited the islands. One hundred years later the number had dwindled to 71,000. Planters of sugarcane, pressed for a labor source, turned to Asia. The first contract workers from China arrived in 1852, and the Japanese followed in 1868. In 1898 the United States annexed the islands, but Asian numbers continued to mount. By 1971—despite the World War II years—Japanese constituted nearly 35 percent of the population, native Hawaiians and part native Hawaiians 21 percent, Caucasians 19 percent, Filipinos nearly 9 percent, and Chinese 6 percent. The figures changed considerably during the late 1970s and 1980s through a population surge from the American mainland. Nearly 40 percent of the population are now Caucasians, and the Japanese number about 25 percent. Native Hawaiians have been the biggest losers and Filipinos the biggest gainers. Chinese percentages remain about the same. Marriages between the ethnic groups are characteristic of the islands. There is little ethnic prejudice.

Sugarcane

Sugarcane was brought to the islands by the original West Polynesians. It was planted near house sites, where it acted as a windbreak. Early attempts to make sugar—crystalline sugar—were unsuccessful. The first successful milling operation was begun on Kauai in 1935. With growth and dispersal Oriental immigrants were brought to work the fields. When the Reciprocity Treaty was signed in 1876, which allowed unrefined sugar to enter the United States duty free, the market for the sugar crop was assured.

Sugarcane is grown commercially on Hawaii, Maui, Oahu, and Kauai in climates that range from wet to relatively dry. In the relatively dry leeward areas, furrow, drip, and other forms of irrigation are used. The best yields are obtained from the irrigated fields. Planting and harvesting are done mechanically. The cane is milled locally but refined at the California and Hawaiian Sugar Refining Corporation's plant in Crockett, Calif. There is a small refinery at Aiea, Oahu, to supply local needs.

Pineapples

Efforts were made to diversify the one-crop (sugar) economy. Rubber, coffee, and sisal were planted but were not grown successfully. Pineapples were raised for the gold miners in California in 1849 and 1850, but planters did not make a profit. It was left for James Dole, who planted 60 acres (24 hectares) of pineapples on Oahu in 1899, to inaugurate a successful commercial venture. The Hawaiian Pineapple Company was organized in 1901, a cannery built in 1903, and other packers joined to market pineapples in the United States. Pineapple growing later spread from Oahu to Lanai, Molokai, Kauai, and Maui.

Pineapples are planted by hand at elevations up to 3,000 feet (900 meters) in areas where precipitation may average only 25 inches (64 centimeters). Irrigation is not necessary. Harvesting is also done by hand. Crowns are removed in fruit destined for canneries and left on for the fresh fruit market. Fresh pineapples are shipped to the American mainland in refrigerated containers in five days or by air in a few hours. There are local canneries in Honolulu and on Maui. The largest pineapple plantation in the world—16,000 acres (6,475 hectares)—is on Lanai. It ships its product to the Dole cannery in Honolulu.

The islands also grow papayas, macadamia nuts, coffee, and fruits and vegetables for the local market. Cattle and pigs are raised, as are poultry for meat and eggs. Flowers and other nursery products are also raised.

Tourism has had a visible effect on sugarcane and pineapple acreages. Land purchases for hotel and condominium development have encroached on the farmland. The trend is likely to continue.

Tourism

The tropical climate, fine beaches, volcanoes, beautiful scenery, friendly people with a multiethnic culture, and an aloha spirit have all enticed tourists to the islands. But the development was slow. Not until 1866 was the first hotel—Volcano House—built on Hawaii. The following year steamship service was begun with the United States. The Hawaiian Hotel was built in Honolulu in 1872, and the Seaside Annex was completed on Waikiki Beach in 1894. Others followed swiftly. A big burst in tourism came with the inauguration of transpacific flight in 1936. But it was the aftermath of World War II, jet travel, and statehood in 1959 that brought the tourists. By 1952 there were only 52,000 annual visitors, but by 1965 the number had increased to more than 600,000 and by 1970 to more than 1.7 million. In 1980 the islands had nearly 4 million visitors, well over half from the American mainland, more than 500,000 from Japan, and nearly 300,000 from Canada. Other Asians and Western Europeans were also among the visitors, and all injected an imposing 3 billion dollars into the economy.

Military

The military plays a major role in the islands. Nearly 6 percent of the land area is either owned or leased by the armed forces. On Oahu 26 percent of the land is either owned or leased by the federal government. The Commander in Chief Pacific (CINCPAC) is located in the Honolulu area. Pearl Harbor, Hickham Air Force Base, and Schofield Barracks are well-known military properties. The largest military base in the islands is the Pohakuloa Training Area in Hawaii.

The number of Army, Navy, Air Force, Marine Corps, and Coast Guard personnel varies, but the impact on the economy is always great. Much money is spent by these personnel, in the local communities, and thousands of civilian jobs are made available by the military presence.

The military also serves as a major tourist attraction. There are military museums at Pearl Harbor, Schofield Barracks, and Fort Derussy, and on Armed Forces Day visitors may tour the bases and inspect the ships and docks.

Honolulu

The Hawaiian Islands are dominated by a single urban center—80 percent of the islands' people live in Honolulu. The second city is Hilo with a population of only 37,000.

Honolulu began as a small fishing village and grew with the sandalwood trade and as a supply center for foreign shipping. It became a city and Kamehameha's capital in 1850, but in 1860 its population was only 14,000. Shortly after the islands' annexation by the United States, Honolulu's population leaped to 39,000: 23 percent Chinese, 21 percent Hawaiian, 16 percent Japanese, 12 percent Portuguese, 11 percent partly Hawaiian, and 18 percent Caucasian other than Portuguese—a rare ethnic mix.

The city did not begin its boom years until after World War II and statehood for the islands in 1959. Land is scarce and expensive, housing for low-income families is inadequate, and the cost of living is high; yet this queen city of the islands continues to thrive. By 1980 its metropolitan area exceeded 762,000. (*See also* Honolulu.)

The Future

Tourism, the military, sugarcane, and pineapples will continue to dominate the economy of the islands—but all have their problems. Tourism is subject to fluctuations in the mainland (and world) economy, and the military is subject to budget and policy decisions. Urban land use is eating into the sugarcane and pineapple fields. With the population increasing, energy needs are greater. Near Puna on the Big Island, geothermal sources are being tapped, and enough energy is available to supply the island of Hawaii and perhaps the other islands as well. Questions have arisen whether Hawaii should encourage manufacturers with high energy needs to locate here, and whether energy should be sold to the other islands.

Hanauma Bay on the island of Oahu is a former volcanic crater, one side of which has been washed away by the sea. Today it is a popular tourist spot.

Robert J. Western—CLICK/ Chicago

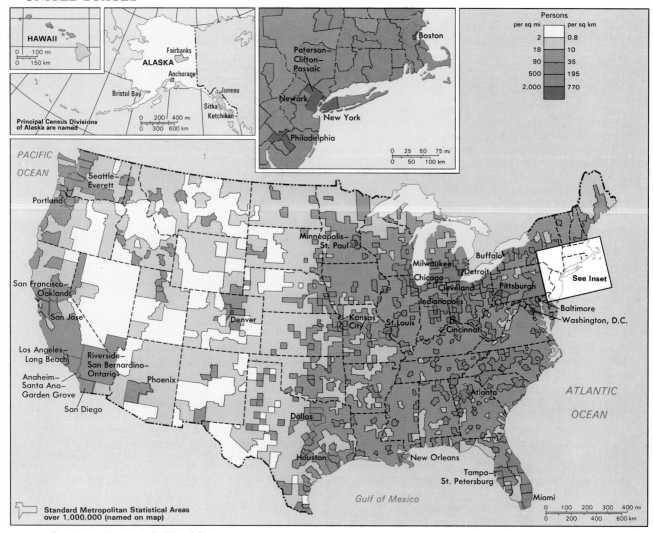

Population density of the United States

PEOPLES AND CULTURES

North America was first settled by immigrants from Asia—the American Indians between 50,000 and 15,000 years ago. A fleshing tool discovered at Old Crow Flat in the Yukon drainage, Alaska—the oldest known artifact in North America—has been radio-carbon dated at 27,000 years before the present. The Indians became hunters on the Great Plains and hunters and gatherers in the Great Basin and nearby California. As fishermen they occupied the Columbia River Valley and the North Pacific Region. Farming was established in the Semiarid Southwest and diffused to the South, the Middle Atlantic Region, and New England. Maize, squash, and beans were the favored crops. At the time of the European discoveries, there were perhaps 2 million or more American Indians in what is now the coterminous United States.

Spanish settlements were established in Florida and in the Semiarid Southwest. The English settled in the South, the Middle Atlantic Region, and New England; the Dutch, Swedes, and Finns in the Middle Atlantic Region; the French on the Gulf coast and in the Mississippi Valley. The onslaught of Europeans brought chaos and devastation to the Indians. They succumbed to disease and warfare, their life patterns were changed, and most were driven west to the forests and prairies beyond the Appalachians.

Blacks from Africa were transported to Virginia as early as 1619. By 1790 they were a majority in the South and made up 20 percent of the American population. Their numbers continued to climb with the adoption of the cotton culture in the South.

Between 1830 and 1850 the population of the United States increased from 13 million to 23 million. Some 2.5 million immigrants—most from Great Britain and, after the potato famine, from Ireland—set sail for America during these years. The Irish provided much brawn for their adopted land. They helped dig the canals, prepare track for the new railroads, and man the steamboats. They settled in the manufacturing towns and worked in the factories. As many of them were Roman Catholics, they were much disliked by the majority Protestants of the time. They went into politics in New York City, Philadelphia, Baltimore, and Boston.

Meanwhile Germans moved into the Ohio Valley and Great Lakes areas. They published and read their own newspapers, met at the local beer gardens, fought the public school movement, and organized their own school system. French Canadians went south into the New England mills. Dutch farmers moved to Michigan, Iowa, and Wisconsin and Scandinavians to the upper Great Lakes.

Both immigrants and long-time Americans moved west. They carried with them the time-honored American traits of democracy, equality of opportunity, optimism, and individualism. There was low-cost land and abundant soil in the West. Separation of church and state had become a fixed principle. Education was something that every American could strive for and possibly obtain.

Following the Civil War the United States paused long enough to celebrate its centennial in Philadelphia (1876). There were 40 million Americans—many caught up in the country's material progress and with national pride. The typewriter, elevator, and telephone were born. 'Tom Sawyer' was published. Phineas T. Barnum displayed his traveling circus. Americans played croquet, tennis, and baseball. There were the Grant scandals and the disputed Tilden-Hayes election. It was the year that Susan B. Anthony issued her "Declaration of Rights for Women" and Helen Hunt Jackson wrote "A Century of Dishonor"— her discourse on the plight of the American Indians. It was also the year of George Custer's last stand.

In 1876 there were perhaps three Americas. One east of the Mississippi River—civilized and urbane—

where most of the people lived; the frontier area west of the Mississippi, where relatively few people lived; and the large wilderness area in the remote West— still largely unsettled and untapped. Alaska had only recently been purchased from the Russians, and the Hawaiian Islands were still independent. For the Europeans all of America was a frontier—a new, sparkling, and teeming place where life would be better.

In 1884 Frederic Bartholdi's creation, the Statue of Liberty, was presented by the people of France to the people of the United States. At the base—17 years later—Emma Lazarus' words, "Give me your tired, your poor, Your huddled masses yearning to breathe free, . . ." were affixed (see Liberty, Statue of). The immigrants came—from new sources—in the late 19th and early 20th centuries: Italians from southern Italy, Jews from the empire of the czars, and immigrants from the Austro-Hungarian Empire. A million arrived in 1905, another million in 1906, and a million and a quarter in 1907. They brought new vigor to the land.

During the 1920s immigration was severely restricted. A Congressional act in 1921 introduced the quota system. Each year there was to be admitted of each nationality a number equal to 3 percent of those in the country in 1910. The act served to restrict immigration to about 350,000 each year. It favored immigrants from Northern Europe and discriminated against those from Eastern and Southern Europe. In 1927 further restrictions were introduced, and immigration was limited to 150,000. Emma Lazarus' words and thoughts had been relegated to the scrap heap. The Great Depression and World War II helped to restrict immigration even further.

Not until 1965 did the United States abandon the discriminatory features of its national origins quota system. Legislation, however, restricted annual immigration from the Eastern Hemisphere to 170,000, of

Tigua Indians dance to celebrate one of their festivals at the Ysleta Mission in El Paso, Tex.

Courtesy of the Texas Tourist Agency; photo, Richard Reynolds

149

whom no more than 20,000 could come from any single country. Ceilings were also placed on immigrants from the Western Hemisphere—up to 120,000 (1968).

Meanwhile the country had liberalized its policy toward refugees from other lands. When the Russians suppressed the Hungarian revolution in 1956, more than 30,000 Hungarians were admitted to the United States. In the 1960s and 1970s more than 650,000 anti-Castro Cubans arrived. Between 1975 and 1980, about 360,000 Vietnamese found their way to the United States. Legal and illegal immigrants continue to come north from Mexico. For a period the illegals could appeal under the law for citizenship. The United States has continued to welcome "boat people"—the Haitians are an example.

Among the American people today about 60 percent owe their origins to Northern Europe, with Germany, Great Britain, Ireland, Scandinavia, and The Netherlands having made the largest contributions. Southern and Eastern Europe contributed another 16 percent. Blacks, originally from Africa, total 10.5 percent; Hispanics, largely from the Western Hemisphere, about 4 percent; American Indians nearly 3 percent. There are others—Americans all—but with ethnicity retained. Certainly this is one of the great strengths of the nation.

LANGUAGE

An overwhelming majority of Americans speak English. It is the first language in the schools, in the media, and in the marketplace. Spanish, however, is the everyday tongue among the Cubans in Florida and Mexican Americans in Texas, California, and the Southwest. Puerto Ricans have also retained the Spanish language. French is still heard in parts of New England, in Cajun Louisiana, and among the Haitians in Florida. Second- and third-generation Americans, however, tend to drop their mother tongues and concentrate on English. Yiddish, widely spoken on New York City's streets early in the 20th century, is fast disappearing. Jewish children, even in their religious schools, are not likely to learn Yiddish. They concentrate on Hebrew, the language of Jewish law and the State of Israel. There are also small enclaves of people, mostly in the cities, who still speak the Eastern and Southern European languages—Polish, Czech, Hungarian, Greek, Italian, and others.

Of special concern is the lack of linguistic competence in the United States. Except for the foreign-born, few Americans have mastered a second language. School requirements have been dropped or lowered over the decades since 1945. This trend stands in stark contrast to students in Europe and the Far East, who struggle to master English and other languages. Another failure in the United States is the increasing number of those who cannot read or write, even among adults (*see* Literacy). Efforts are being made to increase foreign language studies in American schools and colleges, and there are new programs for teaching adults and school dropouts to read.

RELIGION

The Christian religion predominates in the United States—64 percent of the American people are Protestants, 25 percent Roman Catholics. Jews represent only 2 percent of religious adherents, and there are small percentages of other faiths. At least 7 percent of the American people have no religious ties.

Of the Protestant denominations the Baptists are the largest with 33 percent. The Methodists number 19 percent, Lutherans 12 percent, Presbyterians 7 percent, and Episcopalians 4 percent.

Of the blacks in the country, 88 percent are Protestants—69 percent Baptists, an indication of Southern

Every spring, descendants of the original Dutch settlers in Holland, Mich., celebrate Tulip Time with a parade featuring folk costumes and music.

Joe Viesti—Viesti Associates, Inc.

Japanese folk dancers (above) take part in the annual Cherry Blossom Festival in San Francisco. A Hispanic dance troupe (right) in San Antonio, Tex., performs in a local public festival. San Antonio is the heart of a very large Mexican-American population.

beginnings. The Irish are 55 percent Protestant, 34 percent Roman Catholic. The large Protestant figure is attributable to the early Scots-Irish immigration, the Roman-Catholic figure to immigration in the 19th and 20th centuries. The former chose to live in rural settings, the latter for the most part in the large cities of the Middle Atlantic Region and New England. Cubans, Mexican Americans, and Haitians are predominantly Roman Catholic. Marriages within a faith remain strong, though marriages between different faiths are increasing. Conversions are not infrequent.

ARTS AND LITERATURE

Early in the 19th century someone asked, "Who reads an American book?" The implication was that no one in the United States wrote anything of merit. By mid-century this was no longer true. Edgar Allan Poe, Ralph Waldo Emerson, Nathaniel Hawthorne, Herman Melville, Walt Whitman, Emily Dickinson, and many other writers of note were flourishing. Toward the end of the century the writings of Mark Twain were gaining large audiences.

The 20th century continued this vigorous trend in literature. John Dos Passos viewed American society between 1900 and 1930 in his trilogy 'U.S.A.' James T. Farrell portrayed the Irish slums of Chicago in 'Studs Lonigan'. Sinclair Lewis criticized small town, Protestant morality in 'Main Street' and other books. Ernest Hemingway went to Europe after World War I and wrote his best early work, including 'The Sun Also Rises'. Another expatriate, F. Scott Fitzgerald, published 'The Great Gatsby' and other novels. John Steinbeck tells in 'The Grapes of Wrath' how a down-and-out Oklahoma family joined the migrant workers in California, downtrodden, beaten, and angry. William Faulkner reported on life in the South in his make-believe Yoknapatawpha County. (See also American Literature.)

Americans have also made their mark in painting, sculpture, architecture, music, dance, theater, photography, and filmmaking. In each field the mainstream is primarily a continuation and development of Western European traditions. In addition, American Indians made contributions in ceramics, stonework, metals, painting, and music. Blacks brought sculpture, metalworking, and weaving from their African roots. In the new America they developed song, dance, music, and poetry. They created a black renaissance. Hispanic and Asian immigrants and their descendants have influenced American arts. Museums, theaters, and galleries across the country display the general excellence of American arts.

HEALTH AND EDUCATION

In a world much distressed by poverty and disease, the United States is a relatively wealthy and healthy land. The standard of living and the quality of life are high. The average white American can anticipate a life span of more than 70 years (77 for females). For other Americans the life span is a bit lower—70 for females, 65 for males. Incomes in the United States are high and have risen substantially since the 1940s. From $5,583 in 1941 the median family income rose to $12,840 in 1974. By 1980 it had increased to $16,515 in Tampa-St. Petersburg, Fla.; $20,887 in Sacramento, Calif.; $23,412 in Newark, N.J.; $24,118 in Detroit, Mich.; $25,482 in Anaheim-Santa Ana-Garden Grove, Calif. Americans own cars and homes. Unlike most people in the world, they depend on machines—dishwashers, garbage disposals, clothes dryers, food freezers, steam irons, and vacuum cleaners. Their diet is dominated by meat, dairy products, fruits, and vegetables and is undoubtedly the most varied in the world. In spite of the affluence, poverty and unemployment are well known—especially in urban areas.

151

Diseases that cause pain and death are also prevalent. The chief causes of death are heart disease, cancer, and the cerebrovascular diseases. Research on all three continues.

Education is an aid in the struggle. It is available to Americans (both private and public) from pre-kindergarten through graduate school. All Americans do not or cannot take advantage of these opportunities, but enrollment in colleges has increased remarkably. In 1940 nearly 1.5 million students were enrolled in American colleges. In 1973 the figure was more than 8,370,000. Today about half of the American population between the ages of 18 and 21 are enrolled in college programs—a feat of incredible dimensions.

INTERNATIONAL RELATIONS

Since World War II the United States has been one of the world's leading powers—in essence a superpower. It is one of the five permanent members of the Security Council of the United Nations (*see* United Nations).

To protect its own territory and the territory of the free world, the United States is a member of the North Atlantic Treaty Organization (NATO). The United States maintains its armed forces in a number of NATO countries (*see* North Atlantic Treaty Organization).

The United States is also a member of the Organization of American States (OAS), formed to defend the sovereignty of the nations of the Western Hemisphere

(*see* Organization of American States). It is much interested in the Caribbean Community and Common Market (CARICOM), designed to promote unity in the Caribbean area.

As one of the wealthiest nations in the world, the United States administers aid to the world community through its Agency for International Development (AID). Most of this aid goes to the Near East, South and East Asia, and Europe with lesser amounts to Latin America and Africa.

The United States is among the leading trading nations in the world. Major exports include machinery and transportation equipment (computers, electrical apparatus, motor vehicles and parts, and aircraft, parts, and accessories), chemicals, mineral fuels, beverages, tobacco, and food (wheat and corn). The United States receives in return machinery and transportation equipment (electrical apparatus, automobiles, and parts), chemicals, mineral fuels, beverages, paper, metals, textiles, clothing and footwear, and food (meat, fish, coffee, tea, and bananas). The leading trading partners are Canada, Japan, Saudi Arabia, Mexico, Great Britain, and West Germany.

The United States has penetrated deeply into the Canadian economy. The relationship between the two countries is excellent, and many American multinational corporations have large investments in Canada. Mining and smelting, petroleum and natural gas, and much of the manufacturing enterprise is dominated by American firms.

The choir at the Antioch Missionary Baptist Church, in Chicago, sings during a Sunday service. Baptists form the single largest segment within American Protestantism.

Brent Jones

The Pennfylvania Packet, *and Daily Advertifer.*

[Price Four-Pence.]   WEDNESDAY, September 19, 1787.   [No. 2690.]

WE, the People of the United States, in order to form a more perfect Union, eftablifh Juftice, infure domeftic Tranquility, provide for the common Defence, promote the General Welfare, and fecure the Bleffings of Liberty to Ourfelves and our Pofterity, do ordain and eftablifh this Conftitution for the United States of America.

A R T I C L E I.

Sect. 1. ALL legiflative powers herein granted fhall be vefted in a Congrefs of the United States, which fhall confift of a Senate and Houfe of Reprefentatives.

Sect. 2. The Houfe of Reprefentatives fhall be compofed of members chofen every fecond year by the people of the feveral ftates, and the electors in each ftate fhall have the qualifications requifite for electors of the moft numerous branch of the ftate legiflature.

No perfon fhall be a reprefentative who fhall not have attained to the age of twenty-five years, and been feven years a citizen of the United States, and who fhall not, when elected, be an inhabitant of that ftate in which he fhall be chofen.

The American people had an opportunity to read the United States Constitution two days after it was signed. The historic text was published by a Philadelphia newspaper, *The Pennsylvania Packet, and Daily Advertiser.*

History

1. The New World Is Settled, 1492–1763

AMERICAN COLONIES

OTHER BRITISH TERRITORY

SPANISH TERRITORY

RUSSIAN AND UNCLAIMED TERRITORY

THE HISTORY of the United States began with the discovery of North America by a European. On Oct. 12, 1492, Christopher Columbus landed in the Americas. He was searching for an all-water route from Europe to the Far East. This chance finding of a large continent was one of the great events in the history of the world.

Columbus made his discovery while sailing under the flag of Spain. Later, daring sea captains from several European countries sailed across the Atlantic to explore the New World. In 1497 John Cabot reached the coast of present-day Canada in an English ship. The Spanish adventurer Ponce de León landed on what is now Florida in 1513.

In 1519 Ferdinand Magellan's ships left Spain. They crossed the Atlantic Ocean and then the Pacific. Three years later one of his ships returned to Spain after completely circling the world. North America was now known to be a separate continent between two large oceans. (*See also* America, Discovery and Colonization of; North America.)

Rising Interest in the New World

At this time Europeans were not very interested in the New World itself. They only wanted to find a water passage through it to the Far East. France sent out Jacques Cartier to find such a route in 1534. He explored along the Saint Lawrence River. France then laid claim to part of North America.

The first land journey far into the interior of the continent was made by Hernando de Soto. In 1539 he landed in Florida with about 600 Spanish soldiers. They worked their way north- and then westward. They discovered the Mississippi River near the site of Memphis in 1541.

The Spanish were interested in the New World. In 1565 Pedro Menéndez de Acilés made a landing in Florida and began building a fortified city. He named it St. Augustine. This was the first permanent settlement in what is now the United States. Meanwhile from Mexico the Spanish pressed northward into the New Mexico region. In 1541 Coronado led an ex-

153

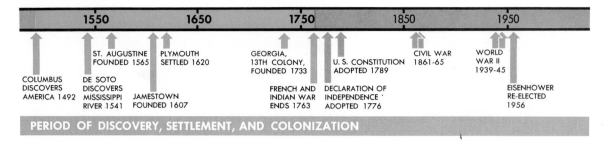

PERIOD OF DISCOVERY, SETTLEMENT, AND COLONIZATION

pedition as far as the Arkansas River in present Kansas. The first permanent settlement in this area was the city of Santa Fe. Pedro de Peralta founded it in 1610. Despite this start the Spanish had little to do with the early development of the United States.

Beginning early in the 1600's, three other nations —France, the Netherlands, and England—showed great interest in the New World. To support the claims established by Cartier, France sent Samuel de Champlain on 11 trips to northern America. In 1608 he founded Quebec on the St. Lawrence River. In 1609 he discovered Lake Champlain.

CHIEF EVENTS, 1492–1763

1492. Christopher Columbus, sailing under the Spanish flag, discovers America, October 12.

1497. John Cabot, representing England, explores Atlantic coast of what is now Canada.

1513. Ponce de León of Spain lands in Florida and gives that region its name.

1519–22. Magellan's Spanish ship—the *Vittoria*—is the first to sail around the world.

1541. Hernando de Soto of Spain discovers Mississippi River near site of Memphis.

1565. St. Augustine, oldest permanent settlement in the United States, founded by Spaniards.

1607. English make first permanent settlement in New World at Jamestown; Virginia becomes first of 13 English colonies.

1619. First representative assembly in America, the House of Burgesses, meets in Virginia; first blacks land in Virginia.

1620. Pilgrims from ship *Mayflower* found settlement at Plymouth.

1649. Act Concerning Religion passed by Maryland legislature is first law of religious toleration in English colonies.

1682. La Salle explores lower Mississippi Valley and claims entire region for France.

1733. Georgia, 13th and last of English colonies in America, is founded.

1754. Both England and the colonies reject Albany Plan of Union to unite colonies. Decisive French and Indian War between France and England begins in America.

1763. Treaty of Paris ends French and Indian War; England becomes supreme power in America.

Additional information about the persons, places, and events of this period will be found in other articles. To find them easily look in the Fact-Index.

That same year (1609) Henry Hudson of the Dutch East India Company sailed his ship the *Half Moon* up the Hudson River. He went as far as the site of Albany. A party of Dutch fur traders built a temporary trading post at this place in 1614. They called it Fort Nassau.

The first English attempts to establish a colony in the New World failed. In July 1587 a party under John White landed at Roanoke Island off the coast of North Carolina. Here a grandchild of White's, Virginia Dare, was born Aug. 18, 1587. She was the first English child born in what is now the United States. The following week White sailed back to England. When he returned three years later the entire settlement had disappeared. No one knows what had happened to Virginia Dare and the other colonists. (*See also* North Carolina.)

Founding of the 13 Colonies

The first permanent English settlement in North America was organized by the London (later called Virginia) Company. On May 14, 1607, a group of 105 colonists landed in Virginia. They called the place Jamestown. Here they built huts for homes, a storehouse, a church, and a fort. The strong leadership of Capt. John Smith protected the colony from starvation and unfriendly Indians. One of Virginia's chief sources of wealth was the growing of tobacco. This started in 1612.

By 1619 Virginia was secure enough to organize the first representative assembly in America. This was the House of Burgesses (or citizens). Its 22 members passed local laws. To further strengthen the colony a shipload of young women arrived in 1619. The settlers then selected wives from among these newcomers. The year 1619 is also notable for the arrival of the first blacks in the American Colonies.

The second English colony to be established in America was Plymouth, in 1620. On December 21, a group of more than 100, including many Puritans, landed at what is now Massachusetts. They were under the military leadership of Capt. Miles Standish. Their ship was the *Mayflower*. Before they left the ship, the Plymouth settlers adopted the first plan for self-government in the New World. This was the Mayflower Compact. (*See also* 'Mayflower'.)

Three years later permanent settlements were made in what is now New Hampshire. New York was founded next, in 1624, by Dutch families. It was called New Netherland until England took control in

1664. The fifth American colony was Maryland. It was settled in 1634. This colony made an important contribution in 1649. It passed the first act of religious toleration in the American Colonies.

The founding of the New England colonies was soon completed. Settlements were established in Connecticut in 1635 and in Rhode Island in 1636. To the south Delaware was settled by Swedes in 1638. It came under English rule in 1664. New Jersey had its first permanent settlement the same year. Pennsylvania, the middle colony of the original 13, was settled by Quakers in 1681. North Carolina was settled in 1653; South Carolina, in 1670. The Carolinas were a single colony, however, until 1730. Georgia, the last of the 13 colonies, was settled in 1733 by Gen. James Oglethorpe with about 150 followers.

The Bettmann Archive

The first permanent English settlement in North America was Jamestown, built along the James River in Virginia in 1607.

Life in the American Colonies

In the scattered settlements along the Atlantic coast there was steady, if sometimes slow, progress. Gains were made in religious freedom, education, travel, communication, and self-government. The population increased rapidly. Colonial families were generally large, often with 10 to 12 children. At the same time settlers from Europe continued to find homes in the New World.

Most of the early immigrants were English. Then came many from Scotland, Ireland, Germany, and France. In 1690 there were about 250,000 people in the 13 colonies. By 1776, when independence was declared, the population had increased to about 2,500,000.

The most powerful force that drew the colonies together was the threat of New France. French people settled in the St. Lawrence Valley, the Great Lakes region, and the Mississippi Valley. The English and French soon came into conflict over fishing rights, the fur trade, and Indian alliances. There was also bitter hostility between France and England in Europe. Between 1689 and 1748 the two powers waged three separate wars. These were fought both in Europe and in America.

The first strong attempt to unite the colonies was a farseeing plan adopted by the so-called Albany Congress in 1754. It was largely the work of Benjamin Franklin. The plan was rejected by both the colonies themselves and Great Britain.

The Decisive French and Indian War

Most of the fighting in America in the first three wars between England and France was centered in the New England-New York areas. A new front, the upper Ohio Valley was now open. Here the important French and Indian War began in 1754. Two years later the New World conflict spread to Europe, where it was known as the Seven Years' War.

In 1759 the English general James Wolfe captured the French stronghold of Quebec. In 1760 Montreal surrendered. This ended French resistance in Canada, and France faced certain defeat. It then secretly ceded to Spain the city of New Orleans and all territory west of the Mississippi River (*see* French and Indian War).

The Treaty of Paris, signed in 1763, formally ended the French and Indian War in America and the European conflict. The treaty had far-reaching effects on the future United States. Great Britain was granted Canada and all French territory east of the Mississippi River. It also received Florida from Spain. These terms ended French power in the New World and made Great Britain supreme. It was now certain that English speech and customs would prevail in the future United States.

New England Mutual Life Insurance Co.

The Pilgrims' first winter in America was harsh. In the spring, Samoset, a friendly Indian, welcomed them to the New World.

2. The United States Wins Its Independence, 1763–1789

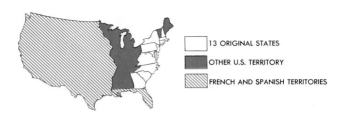

13 ORIGINAL STATES

OTHER U.S. TERRITORY

FRENCH AND SPANISH TERRITORIES

THE YEAR 1763 marked the high point in friendly relations between Great Britain and the American Colonies. The long series of wars against the French had tied the two countries closely together. The colonists wanted and received the help of British armies. They needed protection from New France and its Indian allies. At the same time Britain needed colonial soldiers and supplies to carry on its activities in the New World.

For more than 150 years the colonies had been developing their own society, economic life, and some self-government. The mother country had offered little direction and almost no interference in colonial affairs. After the Treaty of Paris in 1763 the policy changed. Britain began enforcing restrictions on American trade and on manufacturing. Direct taxes were levied on the colonists. The Americans resented the new policies. They felt that only their own colonial assemblies had the right to tax them.

Almost every year after 1763 brought increasing trouble between Britain and the colonies. For a long time the colonists did not ask for independence. They asked only for their rights and liberties as Englishmen. King George III and his ministers answered by passing ever stricter measures. They sent over more troops to enforce these laws. Gradually many of the colonists began to realize that the only solution lay in complete independence.

British Laws Anger the Colonists

The British Parliament passed the first law directly aimed at collecting money from the colonies in 1764. It was the Sugar Act. This raised the duties on certain imports and added many products to the taxed list. Later that year another measure regulated currency in the colonies. Leading citizens in Massachusetts founded a Committee of Correspondence to unify opposition to these laws.

In 1765 two laws brought even greater resentment. A Quartering Act forced Americans to furnish housing and supplies for British troops in the colonies. A Stamp Act levied a direct tax on newspapers, licenses, legal documents, and other business papers. James Otis of Massachusetts and Patrick Henry of Virginia raised their voices against these measures. A Stamp Act Congress representing nine colonies met in New York City. It protested against taxation by the British Parliament in which the colonies were not represented.

The Stamp Act was repealed in 1766 but new taxes were enacted the next year. These were the Townshend duties, levying taxes on glass, lead, paint, paper, and tea imported into the colonies. Again, Americans protested heatedly, particularly John Dickinson of Pennsylvania and Samuel Adams of Massachusetts. In 1770 all the Townshend duties were repealed except the tax on tea.

Meanwhile new trouble flared up in Massachusetts and elsewhere. There was increasing friction between Americans and British soldiers. In Boston red-coated troops fired on a crowd, killing five people. This was the so-called Boston Massacre of 1770.

Steps Leading to War

In 1771 and 1772 tension between the colonies and the mother country relaxed somewhat. Then in 1773 began the chain of events that led directly to war. Early in the year the British Parliament passed a new tea act. This refueled the fires of colonial opposition. In New York City and Philadelphia the people refused to accept tea shipped into these ports. On December 16, Boston patriots dressed as Indians boarded British ships in the harbor. They dumped 342 chests of tea into the water. The Boston Tea Party marked the first act of open resistance to British rule.

To punish the colonies Britain passed five coercive acts, called the Five Intolerable Acts, in 1774. These measures closed the port of Boston; limited self-government in Massachusetts; allowed British officials accused of crimes in America to stand trial in Britain; ordered the colonies to furnish additional quarters for

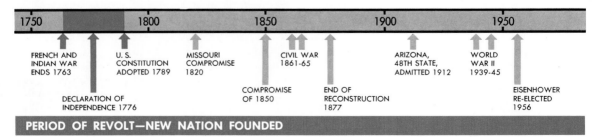

1750   1800   1850   1900   1950

FRENCH AND INDIAN WAR ENDS 1763

U. S. CONSTITUTION ADOPTED 1789

MISSOURI COMPROMISE 1820

CIVIL WAR 1861-65

ARIZONA, 48TH STATE, ADMITTED 1912

WORLD WAR II 1939-45

COMPROMISE OF 1850

END OF RECONSTRUCTION 1877

EISENHOWER RE-ELECTED 1956

DECLARATION OF INDEPENDENCE 1776

PERIOD OF REVOLT—NEW NATION FOUNDED

British troops; and extended the southern boundary of Quebec to the Ohio River.

The colonies bitterly protested these acts. In the fall they sent representatives to the First Continental Congress at Philadelphia. Peyton Randolph of Virginia became chairman. The Congress declared the Coercive Acts unjust and unconstitutional. It planned to meet again the next year if further action became necessary.

The War Begins, 1775

The first battle of the Revolutionary War took place April 19, 1775, in Massachusetts. On the night of April 18, British troops left Boston to seize colonial military supplies stored at Concord, 21 miles away. Warned by Paul Revere and others, colonial minutemen assembled with their guns along the route of march. Early in the morning the British forces killed eight patriots at Lexington and wounded ten more. They then marched on to Concord. The supplies were destroyed but here the Americans fought back. The war was started (see Lexington and Concord, Battle of).

CHIEF EVENTS, 1763–1789

1763. Treaty of Paris ends French and Indian War. Britain wins control of New World; Louisiana ceded to Spain; Florida, to Britain.

1765. Stamp Act angers Americans; nine colonies represented at Stamp Act Congress.

1772. Committees of Correspondence organized in almost all colonies.

1773. Boston Tea Party is first action in chain leading to war with Britain.

1774. First Continental Congress meets at Philadelphia; protests Five Intolerable Acts.

1775. Battles of Lexington and Concord, Bunker Hill; Second Continental Congress meets.

1776. Declaration of Independence is adopted. Washington crosses Delaware to fight at Trenton.

1777. Americans capture General Burgoyne and large British force at Saratoga, N. Y.

1778–79. General George Rogers Clark leads victorious expedition into Northwest Territory.

1781. Washington accepts surrender of Cornwallis at Yorktown, Va. Articles of Confederation become government of the United States.

1783. Treaty of peace with Great Britain signed at Paris, formally ending Revolutionary War.

1786–87. Shays' Rebellion in Massachusetts shows weaknesses of Confederation government.

1787. Northwest Territory organized by Congress. Convention meets to draft new constitution.

1788. United States Constitution is ratified by necessary nine states to insure adoption.

1789. New United States government goes into effect. Washington inaugurated president; First Congress meets in New York City.

Additional information about the persons, places, and events of this period will be found in other articles. To find them easily look in the Fact-Index.

The next month Ethan Allen and Benedict Arnold captured Fort Ticonderoga at the foot of Lake Champlain. That same day, May 10, the Second Continental Congress met at Philadelphia to take charge of the war. The Congress appointed George Washington commander in chief of the Continental forces.

Before Washington reached Boston, British troops had defeated American soldiers at Bunker Hill, outside the city. The colonial forces won fame, however, for the courage and skill they showed against the trained troops of England. (For details of the fighting, see Revolution, American.)

The Declaration of Independence

Along with the early military action came a growing feeling for a complete break with Britain. One of the first to make an open call for independence was Thomas Paine of Philadelphia. His sharp attacks on George III in his pamphlet 'Common Sense' did much to arouse public opinion. In April North Carolina instructed its delegates to the Congress to vote for independence. Virginia did the same in May. On July 2, 1776, Congress voted for independence. Two days later it adopted one of the greatest documents in history—the Declaration of Independence. The document had been prepared chiefly by Thomas Jefferson (see Declaration of Independence).

In 1777 the British started a major plan to cut off New England from the rest of the colonies. A force of about 7,500 British and German troops was put under Gen. John Burgoyne. They marched southward from Canada into upper New York. The Americans stopped the attack in three battles. On October 17 Burgoyne was forced to surrender at Saratoga. This was the turning point in the Revolutionary War and was one of the decisive battles of the world.

Washington's forces spent the winter of 1777–78 at Valley Forge, Pa. Their sufferings made the winter the darkest period of the war (see Valley Forge).

Final Victory at Yorktown

During the next three years, 1778 to 1781, American and British forces seesawed back and forth. Neither side could gain a distinct advantage. The colonies won several notable victories—they secured an alliance with France; John Paul Jones fought well at sea; and George Rogers Clark took control of the Northwest. There were also severe setbacks—an attack on Newport, R. I., failed; Savannah, Ga., and Charleston, S. C., fell to the British; and Benedict Arnold turned traitor.

Finally, in the summer of 1781, a decisive battle began to take shape in Virginia. Lord Cornwallis moved his large British army up from the Carolinas to Yorktown. Here Washington and the French commander Lafayette concentrated their land forces. At sea help came from the French fleet under Admiral DeGrasse. Together they bottled up the British in the peninsula between the York and the James rivers. On October 19, after a siege of several weeks, Cornwallis surrendered. This ended the fighting and se-

The American Revolution virtually ended when Lord Cornwallis surrendered to Washington at Yorktown, Va., Oct. 19, 1781.
Brown Brothers

cured the freedom of the United States (*see* Yorktown).

The peace treaty, drawn up at Paris, France, was accepted by both nations in 1783. The terms recognized the full independence of the United States. It established the nation's boundaries as Canada on the north, the Mississippi River on the west, and Florida on the south. Florida had been ceded back to Spain by Great Britain.

The United States now faced the problem of establishing a just and stable government of its own. The strength of the new nation rested almost entirely upon the 13 state governments. The only central government agency had been the Continental Congress. It had depended upon the co-operation and support of the state governments. In 1781 this organization was replaced by the first true national government. It was called "The United States in Congress Assembled." This was organized under the Articles of Confederation, which had been ratified by all the states (*see* Articles of Confederation).

Government Under the Confederation

In the new national government each state had one vote in Congress. Nine votes were necessary to pass a law. Law enforcement and the administration of justice were left to the states. The states also received all powers not specifically granted to Congress. The lack of a strong central authority made the government only a league of loosely tied states.

Congress could not collect taxes, regulate commerce, or settle disputes among the states. Its work was further handicapped by the people's lack of feeling for national unity. Most Americans still owed their first loyalties to their home state. In addition, the almost 4 million residents of the new nation were widely scattered from Maine to Georgia. Transportation and communication were poor between settlements and worse between states.

Discontent with the Confederation soon increased. The country suffered a business depression following the Revolution. The prices of farm products fell 20 per cent, money was scarce, and local taxes high. In western Massachusetts Daniel Shays led an uprising against the government (*see* Shays' Rebellion).

To solve the government's weaknesses, 55 statesmen met at Independence Hall in Philadelphia, May 25, 1787. All the states were represented but Rhode Island. This was the Constitutional Convention. It drafted the document under which the United States has been governed ever since (*see* United States Constitution). The convention adjourned in September. By June 1788 nine states had ratified the Constitution, making it the new law of the land.

Despite its weaknesses the Articles of Confederation carried the United States through a critical period in its history. It also solved one of the major problems of the time—how to deal with the western lands between the Appalachians and the Mississippi River. The states themselves provided help. They ceded to Congress most of their claims to western territories. Congress then disposed of the lands by the Ordinance of 1785. This law divided government-owned land into townships six miles square. The townships in turn were subdivided into 36 numbered sections of one square mile (640 acres) each. These lands were then sold at auction at a minimum price of one dollar an acre.

Government for the region was provided by the Ordinance of 1787, or Northwest Ordinance. This document ranks next in importance to the Declaration of Independence and the Constitution. It created the "Territory North West of the Ohio." From this region three, four, or five states could be created (*see* Northwest Territory). Congress was less successful in dealing with the Indians there. Attempts to obtain land by treaty failed. Only a series of battles in the 1790's brought peace to the Northwest.

The first permanent settlement north of the Ohio River was made at Marietta, Ohio, in 1788 by veterans of the Revolution.
The Bettmann Archive

3. Growth of American Democracy, 1789–1850

FROM 1789 to 1850 the United States established itself as one of the great democracies in the world. It increased in population from less than 4 million to more than 23 million. At the same time it more than tripled its area to include almost 3 million square miles.

The growing strength of the nation was shown by the addition to the Union of 18 states. In 1789 there were 13 struggling states along the Atlantic seaboard. By 1850 the United States was a nation of 31 states, stretching across the continent from the Atlantic to the Pacific. During this period 13 presidents served the nation—from George Washington in 1789 to Millard Fillmore in 1850.

The First President—George Washington

The 11 states which had ratified the Constitution chose presidential electors early in 1789. All 69 electors voted for George Washington for president. John Adams was named vice-president. On April 30 the nation's first president was inaugurated in New York City. Meanwhile the House of Representatives and the Senate were holding their first sessions.

Washington did much to establish a strong central government. He was aided by his secretary of the treasury, Alexander Hamilton. Hamilton launched a series of measures to put the nation on a sound economic basis. In foreign affairs Washington worked with Secretary of State Thomas Jefferson. They set up a policy of neutrality and fairness in dealing with other nations.

During this time the first ten amendments to the Constitution—the Bill of Rights—went into effect. The date was 1791. That same year President Washington personally helped select the site of the new capital, named for him (see Washington, D. C.). The young republic was growing in other ways. In 1791 Vermont was admitted to the Union as a state. It was the first state added to the original 13. Across the Appalachian Mountains, Kentucky became the first "western" state admitted to the Union, in 1792.

Tennessee also became a state during Washington's presidency, in 1796.

John Adams and Thomas Jefferson, 1797–1809

At the end of his second term as president, Washington refused to run for a third term. This established a tradition unbroken until 1940. Washington's successor was John Adams, his vice-president. Adams was a brave, able man but he lacked the personal popularity of Washington. Opponents criticized the administration of Adams. His Federalist party then enacted the very unpopular alien and sedition laws (see Alien and Sedition Laws).

Adams sought re-election in 1800 but was defeated by Thomas Jefferson. Before leaving office Adams appointed John Marshall chief justice of the Supreme Court. It was largely Marshall who gave the Supreme Court the dignity and influence it has today (see Supreme Court; Courts of Justice).

During the 1790's about 94 per cent of the people lived on farms. There were definite signs, however, that the nation would develop an industrial economy. In 1790 Samuel Slater opened America's first successful cotton mill in Pawtucket, R. I. Three years later Eli Whitney invented the cotton gin. Whitney also started the assembly line system when he began making guns in his factory in New Haven, Conn.

In 1801 Thomas Jefferson became the third president of the United States. His election began 28 consecutive years of rule by the Democratic-Republican

LARGEST CITIES IN 1790	
New York	33,131
Philadelphia	28,522
Boston	18,038
Charleston	16,358
Baltimore	13,503
Salem	7,921
Newport	6,716

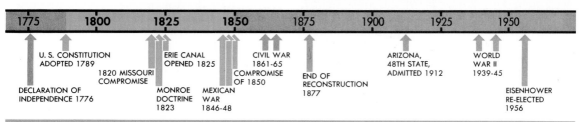

party (later called Democratic). Jefferson was re-elected in 1804. His two administrations increased his reputation as one of the chief builders of American democracy. He also did much to push back the western frontier of the United States. In 1803 he ordered Meriwether Lewis and William Clark to make an overland journey to the Pacific coast. That same year he carried through the famous Louisiana Purchase. In 1803 also, Ohio was admitted to the Union. It was the first of five states carved out of the Northwest Territory.

During Jefferson's administrations two other events helped to guide the long-range course of the nation. In 1803 in the case of Marbury vs. Madison the Supreme Court declared an act of Congress unconstitutional. This established the important principle of judicial review of legislation. The second event was Congressional action halting the importation of slaves into the United States after 1807.

Foreign affairs caused the United States much concern during the early 1800's. Pirates from the Barbary States of North Africa warred on American ships. They were finally defeated in the war against Tripoli in 1801–5. In Europe war between England and France interfered with American shipping. It threatened to draw the United States into combat.

War and Peace, 1809–29

James Madison succeeded Jefferson in the White House in 1809. Madison also tried to keep peace. However, "war hawks" from the new West and South helped to bring on the War of 1812 against Great Britain. The United States suffered some setbacks—the loss of Fort Dearborn (Chicago) and Detroit, the defeat at Bladensburg, Md., and the burning of Washington, D. C. Its chief successes were naval battles—Capt. Oliver H. Perry's victory on Lake Erie and Capt. Thomas Macdonough's triumph on Lake Champlain. The biggest battle of the war took place at New Orleans in 1815. It was fought after the signing of the peace terms (see War of 1812).

The Treaty of Ghent ended the war without deciding any of the issues involved. There was an important political result, however. Late in 1814 the Federalists held a convention at Hartford, Conn. They opposed the war so bitterly that the party fell into disfavor and soon died out.

Madison had won re-election during the War of 1812. In 1817 he was succeeded by James Monroe. The growth of national unity during Monroe's two terms led to the phrase "era of good feeling."

During this time the nation made several notable advances in foreign affairs. In 1818 the United States and Canada agreed upon their boundary from the Lake of the Woods westward to the Rocky Mountains. It was the 49th parallel. The Convention of 1818 also won an agreement with Great Britain on a joint occupation of the Oregon Territory.

The United States completed its southeastern expansion in 1819, when Spain gave up East Florida. West Florida had been annexed earlier, in 1810–13.) The nation then turned to the problem of European influence in North and South America. To block further interference in the American continents President Monroe proclaimed the Monroe Doctrine in 1823 (see Monroe Doctrine).

Meanwhile five new states had been admitted to the Union—Louisiana (1812), Indiana (1816), Mississippi (1817), Illinois (1818), and Alabama (1819). This brought the total number to 22. They were evenly divided between free states and slave states. Then Missouri asked for admission. This raised the question of maintaining the political balance between the North and South. After much debate Congress passed the Missouri Compromise in 1820. This measure permitted Missouri to enter as a slave state and Maine as a free state (see Missouri Compromise).

The presidential campaign of 1824 was a bitter contest among Henry Clay, John Quincy Adams, William Crawford, and Andrew Jackson. None of the candidates received a majority of the electoral votes. Thus the election fell to the House of Representatives. Adams was named president, much to the disgust of Jackson and his followers.

CHIEF EVENTS, 1789–1850

1789. Federal government begins operation under new United States Constitution. Washington becomes president; Congress holds first session.

1791. Bill of Rights added to Constitution. Vermont is first new state admitted to Union.

1793. Eli Whitney invents cotton gin, which leads to large-scale cotton growing in the South.

1800. National capital moved from Philadelphia to Washington, D. C.

1803. Louisiana purchased from France. Supreme Court makes Marbury vs. Madison decision.

1807. Robert Fulton's steamboat makes successful journey from New York City to Albany.

1812–14. United States maintains its independence in conflict with Britain, War of 1812.

1818. United States-Canada boundary dispute settled; agree on open border between countries.

1820. Missouri Compromise settles problem of slavery in new states for next 30 years.

1823. Monroe Doctrine warns European nations that United States will protect the Americas.

1825. Erie Canal, from Hudson River to Great Lakes, becomes great water highway to Middle West.

1829. Inauguration of President Andrew Jackson introduces era of Jacksonian Democracy.

1836. Texas wins its independence from Mexico.

1846. Oregon boundary dispute is settled with Britain. Mexican War begins.

1848. Mexican War ends; United States gains possession of California and New Mexico regions.

1850. Compromise of 1850 admits California as free state; postpones war between North and South.

Additional information about the persons, places, and events of this period will be found in other articles. To find them easily look in the Fact-Index.

In 1803 the American flag was raised in New Orleans, signaling the transfer of Louisiana from France to the United States.

In the early part of the 1800's the United States made great advances in transportation. In 1807 Robert Fulton launched the first successful steamboat, the *Clermont*, in the Hudson River. Five years later the *New Orleans* became the first steamboat to navigate the Mississippi River. Meanwhile, in 1811, the Cumberland Road (National Pike) was started westward from Cumberland, Md. (*see* Roads and Streets). Also important was the Erie Canal, which was completed in 1825. This great waterway linked the Hudson River with the Great Lakes. (*See also* Transportation.)

Jacksonian Democracy, 1829–45

Andrew Jackson was inaugurated president in 1829. He introduced a new era in American politics. He was the first president from the new west. He became the symbol of the political power of the common people in the United States. Most of his supporters were members of the renamed Democratic party, founded originally by Thomas Jefferson.

Jackson was a strong leader. He helped to strengthen the power of the national government at the expense of states' rights. He was re-elected in 1832 with little opposition. Four years later he secured the election of another Democratic president, Martin Van Buren. A severe depression followed. This enabled the newly formed Whig party to elect their first president, William Henry Harrison, in 1840.

President Harrison died a month after taking office. He was succeeded by his vice-president, John Tyler. Tyler helped to settle the Maine-Canada boundary dispute by arranging the Webster-Ashburton Treaty. More important, however, was the beginning of large-scale migrations to the Oregon Territory in 1843 (*see* Oregon Trail).

During this time the nation was making progress in many fields. Railroads were being built, telegraph lines completed, and more canals opened. In 1844 Charles Goodyear patented a process for vulcanizing rubber. One year later Elias Howe invented the sewing machine.

The Mexican War and Its Results, 1845–50

James Polk led the Democrats back into power in 1845. He had campaigned on a platform of annexing Texas and of taking over all Oregon. His slogan was "fifty-four forty ($54°40'$) or fight!" These aims were part of the national feeling that the United States should expand across the continent. This was called "manifest destiny."

Despite some opposition Texas was annexed and admitted as a state in 1845. This Oregon question was settled the following year. Great Britain and the United States agreed to divide the territory along the line of the 49th parallel.

Meanwhile the annexation of Texas led to trouble. The United States and Mexico disagreed over the boundary separating the two nations. This brought a declaration of war May 13, 1846. In less than a year and a half American forces conquered California, the New Mexico region, and northern Mexico (*see* Mexican War). The treaty of Guadalupe-Hidalgo ended the war in 1848. Mexico accepted the Rio Grande as the international border. It ceded New Mexico and California to the United States.

The acquisition of new territory in the West again raised the critical problem of slavery. By now six more states had been admitted to the Union. Three

The Erie Canal was opened in 1825 when Gov. DeWitt Clinton of New York poured a keg of Lake Erie water into the Atlantic Ocean.

were slave states—Arkansas (1836), Florida (1845), and Texas (1845); and three were free—Michigan (1837), Iowa (1846), and Wisconsin (1848). This preserved the even balance between the North and South. Each had 15 states. After the gold rush of 1849, however, California had enough people to become a state. Should it be free or slave?

The settlement of this problem fell to Zachary Taylor. He was the hero of the Mexican War and the newly elected Whig president. Before a solution could

be reached Taylor died. He was succeeded by Millard Fillmore. Just when the slavery issue threatened to break up the Union, Congress passed the Compromise of 1850. It provided that California be admitted as a free state and that New Mexico and Utah be organized as territories without mention of slavery. The Compromise included a stronger fugitive slave law and abolished slavery in the District of Columbia. These measures postponed war between the North and South for ten years (see Compromise of 1850).

4. The Nation's Westward Advance, 1789–1850

☐ 13 ORIGINAL STATES

☐ OTHER STATES AND TERRITORIES

☐ OREGON TERRITORY

☐ CALIFORNIA AND OTHER LANDS WON FROM MEXICO

DURING MOST of its history the United States has been a pioneering nation. For about 250 years Americans pushed steadily westward. They drove out the Indians, built homes, and laid out farms. With the advancing frontier went new local governments, and eventually new states were formed. The march from the Atlantic to the Pacific was finally completed in 1850. In that year California was admitted to the Union as the 31st state.

The Three Great Frontiers

The first American frontier was the eastern seaboard. It stretched inland to the crest of the Appalachians. Here John Smith, Miles Standish, and others conquered the wilderness. They established the 13 colonies which later became the United States.

The second frontier was the "west" of early America —the region lying between the Appalachians and the

Mississippi. French explorers and colonizers had been the first to enter this region. Their hold was broken by Americans crossing the mountains from the East. These men included such frontiersmen as Daniel Boone, George Rogers Clark, and John Sevier. By 1789 the United States was ready to complete its advance to the Mississippi.

The third frontier was the Great West, stretching from the Mississippi to the Pacific coast. There was a Spanish settlement at Santa Fe as early as 1609. Spain could not hold the region, however. This frontier also would be conquered from the East—by Americans armed with rifles, axes, and plows. (See also Frontier.)

Settling the First "West"

The government of the United States had hardly been launched when the Indians in the Northwest Ter-

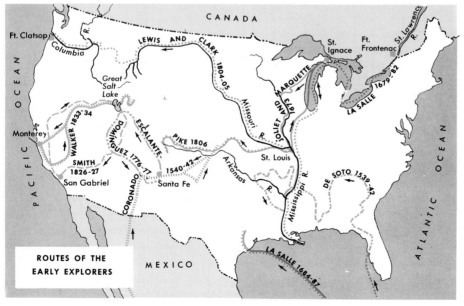

ROUTES OF THE EARLY EXPLORERS

Knowledge of the Mississippi River and the vast region to the west came from the explorers of three nations — Spain, France, and the United States. De Soto, Coronado, Domínguez, and Escalante were Spanish explorers. La Salle and Joliet and Marquette were pioneer Frenchmen. Lewis and Clark, Pike, Smith, and Walker were Americans.

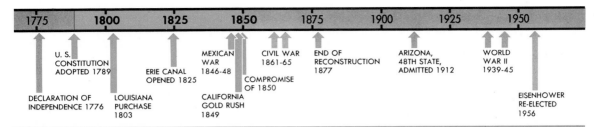

| 1775 | 1800 | 1825 | 1850 | 1875 | 1900 | 1925 | 1950 |

U. S.
CONSTITUTION
ADOPTED 1789

ERIE CANAL
OPENED 1825

MEXICAN
WAR
1846-48

CIVIL WAR
1861-65

END OF
RECONSTRUCTION
1877

ARIZONA,
48TH STATE,
ADMITTED 1912

WORLD
WAR II
1939-45

COMPROMISE
OF 1850

DECLARATION OF
INDEPENDENCE 1776

LOUISIANA
PURCHASE
1803

CALIFORNIA
GOLD RUSH
1849

EISENHOWER
RE-ELECTED
1956

PERIOD OF WESTWARD EXPANSION TO THE PACIFIC

ritory took the warpath in 1789. Many pioneer families were killed, their cabins and crops destroyed. Peace was not restored until 1794. In that year Gen. Anthony Wayne crushed the Indians' power in the battle of Fallen Timbers near the site of Maumee, Ohio.

Pioneers south of the Ohio River also faced hostile Indians. The Spaniards in New Orleans and Florida presented another problem. After years of trouble President Jefferson solved the biggest problem. He bought New Orleans and all the Louisiana territory from France in 1803. This paved the way for further expansion westward (*see* Louisiana Purchase).

During this time thousands of settlers flooded into the first "west." In large numbers they bought farm land from the government. This activity added a new phrase to American speech—"doing a land office business." During the War of 1812 renewed Indian attacks slowed the westward movement. The Indians were soon routed, however, by armies led by two future presidents. They were William Henry Harrison, north of the Ohio River, and Andrew Jackson, in the South. Another popular Indian fighter of the time was Davy Crockett.

After the War of 1812 there was a steady rush of immigration into what is now the Midwest. Small farmers populated the lake plains in the North. Cotton planters set up plantations in the Gulf plains in the South. The Mississippi Valley attracted both kinds of farmers. By 1850 the eastern half of the continent was well settled. Thousands more had poured across the Mississippi River into Iowa, Missouri, Arkansas, and Louisiana.

The Frontier Crosses the Mississippi

By 1800 Spain's hold on western America was a thin line of forts and missions. The outposts curved from east Texas west and north to San Francisco Bay. It had taken Spain two centuries of work to erect this protective wall across the north of Mexico. Within less than 50 years all this area was won by the westward expanding United States.

The first Americans to cross the vast region west of the Mississippi were Meriwether Lewis and William Clark. In 1804–5 they journeyed overland from St. Louis to the Pacific Ocean (*see* Lewis and Clark Expedition). After 1807 hardy fur trappers and traders worked their way into and beyond the Rocky Mountains. They sought valuable beaver pelts. The first trails were blazed by such Mountain Men as Jim Bridger, William Ashley, and Thomas Fitzpatrick. These men made possible the later movement to the Pacific coast. Beyond South Pass (Wyoming) in the Rockies lay the Snake River route to Oregon and the Humboldt River way to California.

When the United States declared its independence in 1776 it was only one fourth its present size. By negotiation, purchase, annexation, and war it extended its boundaries from the Atlantic to the Pacific by 1853. This map shows the acquisitions and the dates the areas were added. Alaska and Hawaii, added in 1959, are not shown.

163

Other bold Americans began trading with the Spanish commercial center of Santa Fe in the Southwest. A brisk business followed the opening of the Santa Fe Trail from Missouri to New Mexico. It had been blazed by William Becknell in 1821. Americans soon discovered that the best southern route from Santa Fe to California was along the Gila River.

The pioneers pushing toward the Southwest and the Pacific coast braved the hostility of foreign powers. Mexico owned both Texas and California and the British had a strong claim to Oregon. In each case the Americans first penetrated and then won complete control of the area.

The first conquest was that of Texas. Stephen Austin had founded an American colony there which grew rapidly. A revolt against Mexican rule in 1836 brought Texas independence. Nine years later it was annexed to the United States. Texas was the 28th state.

The Oregon country was the next region to be taken over by Americans. In the 1830's missionaries and farmers began settling the fertile Willamette Valley. Then in 1843 long, covered-wagon trains started over the Oregon Trail to the Pacific Northwest (see Oregon Trail). This heavy migration won the region for the United States. In 1846 the 49th parallel to the Pacific

The log cabin in a clearing was the symbol of frontier America as pioneers pushed steadily westward across the continent. New and rich farm land always attracted new settlers.

was agreed on as the boundary line between Canada and the United States.

Another area was settled in 1847. This was the establishment of a Mormon colony by Brigham Young in Salt Lake Valley, Utah. Meanwhile western expansion had leaped over the Great Basin and taken root in Mexican California.

The Conquest of California

The first overland trails to California were blazed by Jedediah Smith in 1826 and Joseph Walker in 1833. Organized parties of American settlers began crossing the Sierra Nevada into California in 1841. Five years later Americans at Sonoma revolted against Mexican rule. They set up the Bear Flag, or California, Republic. Their uprising soon merged into the overall American cause in the Mexican War. In this conflict California was conquered by the invading Army of the West, commanded by Gen. Stephen Watts Kearny. The peace treaty of 1848 awarded California to the United States. Mexico also ceded the whole region north of the Gila River and the Rio Grande. The nation's boundaries were now nearly fixed. The final addition, except for Alaska and Hawaii, was the Gadsden Purchase. Bought from Mexico in 1853, this was a triangle of land south of the Gila River wanted for a railroad right-of-way to southern California.

Once California became United States land it developed rapidly. In 1848 James Marshall discovered gold near Coloma. The following year tens of thousands of newcomers made up the historic gold rush of '49. By the end of the year a state constitution had been adopted. California began asking for admission into the Union as a free state. After months of debate Congress admitted California as a free state. This was under the terms of the Compromise of 1850 (see Compromise of 1850). The American frontier had finally crossed the continent to reach the Pacific.

CHIEF EVENTS OF THE WESTWARD ADVANCE, 1789–1850

1789. Federal government begins operation under new United States Constitution.

1792. Kentucky, first state west of Appalachians, admitted to the Union. Captain Robert Gray discovers mouth of Columbia River.

1803. Ohio, first of Northwest Territory states, admitted. Louisiana purchased from France.

1804–6. Lewis and Clark blaze overland trail to the Pacific and return.

1815. General Jackson's victory over British at New Orleans makes him new hero of the West.

1820. Missouri Compromise bans slavery from Louisiana Purchase land north of the line 36° 30'.

1821. William Becknell opens Santa Fe Trail from Missouri to Spanish city in New Mexico.

1825. Erie Canal, great water highway from Hudson River to Great Lakes, completed.

1836. Texas becomes independent republic after successful revolt against Mexico.

1843. First great migration begins on Oregon Trail. American government organized in Oregon.

1845. Texas annexed as 28th state.

1846. Treaty with Great Britain settles Oregon boundary dispute. War with Mexico begins.

1847. Brigham Young leads party of Mormons into Salt Lake Valley, Utah.

1848. War with Mexico ends; United States gains New Mexico region and California.

1849. Gold rush to California.

1850. Compromise of 1850 admits California as free state; frontier reaches the Pacific.

Additional information about the persons, places, and events of this period will be found in other articles. To find them easily look in the Fact-Index.

5. The Nation Divides and Reunites, 1850–1877

31 STATES IN 1850

7 STATES ADDED

FEDERAL TERRITORIES

IN 1850 the United States was a nation of more than 23 million people. For the first time it was now a truly continental nation. It stretched from the Atlantic to the Pacific and included a solid block of 3 million square miles. Its boundaries had been firmly established except for the small Gadsden Purchase area added three years later.

The United States was now so large that it had varied types of climate, natural resources, industries, and social structures. It was held together by a system of governments that had not yet been fully tested. Only matters of general interest were entrusted to the federal government in Washington, D. C. Local affairs, ordinary life, and business were controlled by the states. Each state governed in its own way. There was little interference with governments of neighboring states. Much of this was due to the difficulties of communication and transportation between states.

The continued growth of the nation gradually led to sharp differences of opinion among states on several basic questions of policy. One example was the tariff issue. Such issues affected the entire country. They would have to be settled by the federal government, if they were to be settled at all.

The most explosive issue was slavery. Slavery had never been profitable on the frontier or in the North. Slaves were employed profitably, however, on the cotton and tobacco plantations of the South. The plantation owners of that region were able to make use of all the slaves that could be imported.

Meanwhile many people in the North were becoming critical of slaveholding. They began talking of abolishing the institution in the name of humanity. Such people were called "abolitionists." The antislavery campaign aroused many Southerners. They feared that Northern votes in Congress might exclude slavery from all federal territories. Such action might in time lead to restrictions on slavery in all the states. These Southern fears were eased only temporarily by the Compromise of 1850. During the next ten years slavery and the related question of states' rights be-

came the chief national issues. These issues were to increase the tension between the North and South.

Events Leading to War

President Fillmore's support of the Compromise of 1850 cost him most of his political followers. In 1852 Franklin Pierce, a Democrat from New Hampshire, was elected the 14th president of the United States. The most important event in Pierce's administration was the passage of the inflammable Kansas-Nebraska Act in 1854. This measure led directly to the organization of the antislavery Republican party (see Kansas-Nebraska Act; Political Parties).

The split between the North and South became wider during the next administration, that of James Buchanan, a Democrat. Much of this was due to the Supreme Court's Dred Scott Decision, which angered the North, in 1857; and John Brown's raid on Harpers Ferry, which frightened the South two years later (see Dred Scott Decision). The South was also alarmed by the admission of three new states. They were Minnesota (1858), Oregon (1859), and Kansas (1861). Each of the newcomers was opposed to slavery.

In 1860 Abraham Lincoln, a Republican, was elected president. The South then took action. South Carolina seceded (withdrew) from the Union, Dec. 20, 1860. Six other states seceded early in 1861—Mississippi, Florida, Alabama, Georgia, Louisiana, and Texas. In February representatives from these states organized a new government. It was called the Confederate States of America. Jefferson Davis was elected president. War broke out two months later (see Confederate States of America).

First Two Years of War, 1861–63

The actual fighting began April 12, 1861. Confederate batteries at Charleston, S. C., fired on Union-held Fort Sumter in the harbor of the city. President Lincoln called the attack a rebellion against the government. He asked for 75,000 volunteers for military service. This action enraged four Southern states—

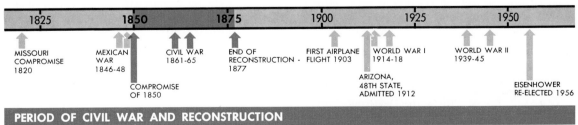

1825	1850	1875	1900	1925	1950

MISSOURI COMPROMISE 1820

MEXICAN WAR 1846-48

CIVIL WAR 1861-65

END OF RECONSTRUCTION 1877

FIRST AIRPLANE FLIGHT 1903

WORLD WAR I 1914-18

WORLD WAR II 1939-45

COMPROMISE OF 1850

ARIZONA, 48TH STATE, ADMITTED 1912

EISENHOWER RE-ELECTED 1956

PERIOD OF CIVIL WAR AND RECONSTRUCTION

165

Virginia, North Carolina, Tennessee, and Arkansas. They too seceded from the Union and joined the Confederacy (*see* Civil War, American).

In July 1861 Confederate forces routed the Union army at Bull Run (Manassas), Va. This was the first major battle of the war. The following year the North and South fought a series of hard but indecisive engagements in Virginia and Maryland. These were the Seven Days battles and the battles of Second Bull Run, Antietam, and Fredericksburg.

Meanwhile in the West, Union campaigns proved more successful. In 1862 Gen. Ulysses S. Grant captured two Southern forts—Fort Henry on the Tennessee River and Fort Donelson on the Cumberland. He then advanced to Shiloh in southwestern Tennessee. Here his forces beat back a strong Confederate attack. The way to the deep South was now open.

In the fall of 1862 Gen. Braxton Bragg led a Confederate counterattack into central Kentucky. He retreated southward after the battle of Perryville. Later that year another savage but inconclusive battle was fought at Stones River (Murfreesboro) in central Tennessee.

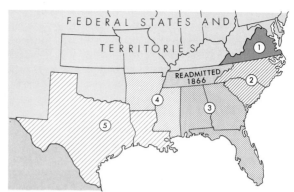

In March 1867 Congress provided "for the more efficient government of the Rebel States" by organizing 10 of the 11 former Confederate states into five military districts.

Last Two Years of War, 1863–65

In 1863 Confederate Gen. Robert E. Lee won a victory at Chancellorsville, Va. He then marched northward into Pennsylvania. At Gettysburg the Southern thrust was crushed in the most important engagement of the war. Lee retreated into Virginia, where both sides maneuvered without advantage.

Meanwhile Grant attacked the Confederate stronghold at Vicksburg, Miss. After a siege of seven weeks the city surrendered July 4. It was the day following the great Union victory at Gettysburg. The North had now split the Confederacy in two by winning control of the Mississippi River.

After his victory at Vicksburg, Grant took over the Union forces bottled up in Chattanooga. The Northern troops had fallen back into this city after a sharp defeat at Chickamauga Creek in Georgia. By the end of November 1863 Grant's new command had driven the Confederate forces back into Georgia.

Early in the spring of 1864 Grant was put in charge of all the Federal armies. He moved his headquarters to Virginia. Here the Army of the Potomac began a cruel, grinding drive for Richmond. Savage battles were fought at the Wilderness, Spotsylvania Court House, and Cold Harbor. The Confederate forces were pinned to defensive lines east of Richmond and Petersburg. Meanwhile Gen. William T. Sherman directed his Federal army southward. He captured Atlanta and then marched across Georgia to Savannah on the Atlantic coast.

In Virginia Grant continued to press against Lee's troops. Finally the Confederates were forced to abandon Richmond and Petersburg on the evening of April 2, 1865. One week later Lee surrendered his retreating forces to Grant at Appomattox Court House. Sherman had been driving northward from Georgia. On April 26, final terms were reached and Sherman accepted the surrender of Gen. Joseph Johnston's remaining Confederate troops near Durham Station, N. C.

Peace and Reconstruction

During the four long years of warfare there were important national advances in other fields. In 1861 the first telegraph connection was established across

---

CHIEF EVENTS, 1850–1877

1850. Compromise of 1850 postpones war between North and South ten years.

1853. Gadsden Purchase adds 45,535 square miles to what is now southern Arizona and New Mexico.

1854. Kansas-Nebraska Act reopens slavery issue, leads to organization of Republican party.

1857. Dred Scott Decision of Supreme Court declares Missouri Compromise illegal.

1860. Lincoln elected president; South Carolina secedes from the Union.

1861. Confederate States of America formed. Civil War begins; Union forces routed at Bull Run, Va. Telegraph links New York City with San Francisco.

1862. Grant launches Union attack in the West; Confederate invasion of Maryland halted at Antietam. Homestead Act grants 160 acres to each settler.

1863. Federal forces win decisive battles at Gettysburg, Vicksburg, and Chattanooga. Emancipation Proclamation takes effect.

1864. Sherman captures Atlanta and marches across Georgia. Grant closes in on Richmond, Va.

1865. Lee surrenders to Grant at Appomattox Court House, Va., ending Civil War. Lincoln is assassinated.

1867. Reconstruction acts impose military rule on South. Alaska purchased from Russia.

1869. First transcontinental railroad completed as two lines meet at Promontory, Utah.

1876. Telephone is invented. Centennial Exposition in Philadelphia celebrates 100th birthday of the United States.

Additional information about the persons, places, and events of this period will be found in other articles. To find them easily look in the Fact-Index.

Union Pacific Railroad

The first railroad across the continent was completed in 1869. The Central Pacific Railway was built eastward from California; the Union Pacific Railroad, westward from Omaha. The two lines met at Promontory, Utah, where a gold spike was used to fasten together the two sets of tracks.

36th state the following year.

Lincoln won re-election in 1864 with Andrew Johnson of Tennessee as the new vice-president. To the great dismay of the entire nation Lincoln was shot and killed only three weeks after his second inauguration. The assassination proved to be particularly tragic for the South. The new president, Johnson, could not provide the leadership necessary for an orderly change from war to peace.

Johnson quarreled bitterly with Congress. He escaped conviction on impeachment charges by the margin of a single vote in the Senate. Meanwhile Congress imposed a series of four Reconstruction laws on the South. Federal troops were sent back into former Confederate states. This action left that section embittered against the Republican party for many years. Reconstruction state governments dealt with the task of rebuilding the war-damaged South (see Reconstruction Period).

During Johnson's administration the 13th and 14th Amendments were added to the Constitution. These measures abolished slavery and established civil rights for all. Nebraska entered the Union in 1867. Alaska was purchased from Russia the same year.

Ulysses S. Grant, Northern hero of the Civil War, was the successful Republican candidate for president in 1868. He was re-elected four years later. While

the continent. The following year the Homestead Act did much to open the West. It granted 160 acres of land to each qualified settler. In 1863 President Lincoln's Emancipation Proclamation took effect. This freed about 3 million slaves (see Emancipation Proclamation).

Two states were added to the Union during the war. West Virginia, a free state carved out of Virginia, was admitted in 1863. Nevada became the

The Bettmann Archive

The nation's westward expansion brought years of conflict with the Indians. To help enforce the laws the government set up a series of Indian agencies in the West. This is the Crow Creek Indian Agency in Dakota Territory soon after the Civil War.

167

Grant was president the first transcontinental railroad was completed across the United States; the 15th Amendment was ratified, giving blacks the right to vote; and Colorado became the 38th state.

Although Grant's honesty was never questioned, his administrations were marred by political fraud. The Crédit Mobilier bribed Congressmen with railroad stock. The Whiskey Ring violated revenue laws. These scandals helped to bring on the postwar business panic of 1873. During the next five years the nation suffered hard times. When Grant left office in 1877 the depression was almost over. The United States was now ready to enter a new period of its history, a period of great industrial expansion.

6. Building an Industrial Nation, 1877–1914

38 STATES IN 1877

10 STATES ADDED

PRESIDENT HAYES took office in 1877. The nation was just recovering from the business depression that struck during Grant's second administration. During the next 16 years the United States carried out a vast industrial expansion. Hayes was a strong president and did much to help the rise in national wealth and power. One of his first official acts was to withdraw the last of the Federal troops from the South. This was the formal end of the troubled reconstruction period.

The reunited country was tied together even more firmly by great advances in communication and transportation. The telegraph, telephone, and new processes in printing made it possible to spread news and information rapidly to all parts of the nation. Railroads were equally valuable to development. In 1880 there were less than 100,000 miles of trackage in the United States. By 1910 this figure had grown to almost 250,000.

The new railroads to the West carried settlers into the last remaining territories of the conterminous United States. In 1889 North Dakota, South Dakota, Montana, and Washington were all admitted to the Union. Idaho and Wyoming followed in 1890. There were only six more areas to be admitted as states: Utah (1896), Oklahoma (1907), New Mexico (1912), Arizona (1912), Alaska (1959), and Hawaii (1959). During this period the nation's population doubled. At the time of the outbreak of World War I in Europe, the United States had over 90 million people.

Progress on Many Fronts

Once the United States had been made up largely of farms. Now it was becoming a nation of growing cities, busy with manufacturing and commerce. A striking example of this growth was the development of Chicago. In 1880 the city had a half million residents; ten years later it had more than a million; and by 1910 it had passed the 2 million mark.

Much of the nation's population rise came from millions of immigrants. They sought new jobs and new homes in a prosperous land. For a while more than a million a year were entering the United States. Until about 1880 most of these newcomers were from such northwestern European countries as Ireland, Germany, Sweden, and Norway. After that time the majority of immigrants were from southern and eastern Europe—largely Italy, Poland, Greece, and Russia. The newer class of immigrants settled chiefly in the cities where they found work in factories. In many cases their working and living conditions were very bad. Attempts to improve their lot led to strikes and to the labor movement (see Migration of People; Labor Movements).

Swift growth and change brought problems as well as prosperity. In business some corporations became so large they were able to squeeze out all rivals in their field. The size of these trusts seemed to threaten democracy itself. Early government efforts to control big business resulted in the Interstate Commerce Act (1887) and the Sherman Anti-Trust Act (1890). The nation also suffered from occasional periods of corruption in government—federal, state, and local. Civil service reform was begun under President Hayes and strengthened under President Arthur. It helped to correct this condition. Another aid was the general broadening of education. This was the period of great growth in universities and in high schools.

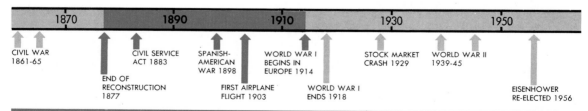

| 1870 | 1890 | 1910 | 1930 | 1950 |

CIVIL WAR 1861-65

CIVIL SERVICE ACT 1883

SPANISH-AMERICAN WAR 1898

WORLD WAR I BEGINS IN EUROPE 1914

STOCK MARKET CRASH 1929

WORLD WAR II 1939-45

END OF RECONSTRUCTION 1877

FIRST AIRPLANE FLIGHT 1903

WORLD WAR I ENDS 1918

EISENHOWER RE-ELECTED 1956

PERIOD OF GROWTH IN INDUSTRY, WEALTH, AND WORLD POWER

Each year more children could stay in school instead of going to work. More of the high-school graduates could go on to college.

Republicans Dominate Political Field

In politics the war-weakened Democrats could not match the strength of the newer Republican party. The Republicans began as a party of human rights. They stayed in power during the long period of industrial growth. As a result they came to be regarded as the party of business and wealth and the protector of industry through a protective (high) tariff. Hayes was succeeded by James Garfield in 1881. When Garfield died of an assassin's bullet later that year, Chester A. Arthur became president.

Grover Cleveland, a Democrat, won the presidential election of 1884. This ended a period of 24 years of Republican rule. Four years later Cleveland lost to Republican Benjamin Harrison. In 1892 Cleveland again entered the White House, winning over the same opponent. He thus became the only president in American history to serve two nonconsecutive terms.

Cleveland had just taken office for the second time

The Pittsburgh area became a center of steel manufacturing in the 1870's. This early mill at Homestead made armor plate.

when a business panic hit the nation. The agricultural West suffered particularly. Farmers made a strong demand for control of trusts and higher prices through free silver and other changes in the money of the country. A new political party was formed, the Populists. Both the Populists and the Democrats nominated William J. Bryan for president in 1896. Bryan was defeated, however, by William McKinley. This began another long period (16 years) of Republican control of the White House.

Prosperity at Home, Trouble Abroad

At the end of the 1800's and during the early years of the 1900's the nation enjoyed another great business boom. It was accompanied by high tariffs and sound money based on a gold standard. President McKinley was re-elected on a "full dinner-pail" platform in 1900. The following year he was assassinated. His vice-president, Theodore Roosevelt, completed the term. Roosevelt then won election in his own right in 1904.

When Roosevelt took office he was 42 years old, the youngest president in the nation's history. A colorful and forceful leader, Roosevelt directed a progressive movement called the Square Deal. It aimed at social justice, the conservation of natural resources, and the regulation of business trusts. Other advances were made in tightening control over railroads and protecting the purity of food and drugs. Roosevelt helped his friend William H. Taft win the presidency in 1908.

Meanwhile a half century of peace with other nations was broken in 1898 by the Spanish-American War. The conflict grew out of public sentiment against Spain. The Spanish government had been trying to put down a revolt in Cuba. Although the United States was unprepared for the war, it won a quick victory. Peace was made eight months later. The United States gained possession of former Spanish colonies in the Philippines and Puerto Rico.

CHIEF EVENTS, 1877–1914

1877. Withdrawal of last Federal troops from South ends reconstruction period. Railroad workers begin first nationwide strike.

1879. First practical electric light is invented by Thomas A. Edison.

1883. Pendleton Civil Service Act provides for examinations as basis of appointment to some government positions.

1884–85. First skyscraper, the Home Insurance Building, is erected in Chicago.

1886. American Federation of Labor is organized; first president is Samuel Gompers.

1887. Interstate Commerce Act adopted to control railroads that cross state lines.

1889–90. First Pan American Conference is held in Washington, D. C.

1890. Sherman Anti-Trust Act is passed in effort to curb growth of monopolies.

1896. Henry Ford's first car is driven on streets of Detroit.

1898. United States wins Spanish-American War; gains Philippines, Puerto Rico, Guam.

1903. Air age begins with successful airplane flight by Wright brothers.

1906. Federal Food and Drug Act passed to protect public from impure food and drugs.

1912. New Mexico and Arizona, 47th and 48th states, admitted to the Union.

1913. Federal income tax authorized by 16th Amendment; 17th Amendment provides for popular election of United States senators.

1914. Panama Canal opened. World War I breaks out in Europe.

Additional information about the persons, places, and events of this period will be found in other articles. To find them easily look in the Fact-Index.

Hawaii was annexed, and Cuba was promised aid in setting up its own government. World power had come to the United States almost overnight (*see* Spanish-American War; Dewey).

World power brought a new series of international problems. In the Far East uprisings had to be put down in the Philippines and in China. In building the Panama Canal it became necessary for the United States to keep peace in Central America and around the Caribbean Sea. At the same time enforcing the Monroe Doctrine involved the nation in the affairs of Latin American republics and European powers.

The Democrats Return to Power

In 1912 Taft was renominated by the Republican party over Roosevelt. The former president had re-entered the political field after four years of retirement. Roosevelt then ran for president as the candidate of a third party called the National Progressives, or Bull Moose. Because of this split in Republican ranks the Democrats were able to elect Woodrow Wilson president.

Wilson had a Democratic majority in both houses of Congress. He immediately launched a program his party had been supporting since 1896. A tariff bill lowering duties was passed in 1913. New banking and currency systems were created under the control of the Federal Reserve Board (*see* Federal Reserve System). These measures were followed in 1914 by the passage of the Clayton Act, which regulated trusts. The Federal Trade Commission was founded to administer the laws and control certain business practices (*see* Federal Trade Commission).

Two other measures of long-range importance went into effect. During the last days of President Taft's administration the 16th Amendment permitted a federal income tax. Congress now adopted a graduated income tax law. The second measure was the

The first steel-skeleton skyscraper was the Home Insurance Building, erected in Chicago in 1884-85. Designed by William LeBaron Jenney, it stood in the Loop until torn down in 1931.

ratification of the 17th Amendment. This provided for the election of senators by direct popular vote.

Wilson's broad program of legislation was still incomplete when war broke out in Europe. The United States tried to remain neutral. The conflict involved so many countries and so great an area that it was called the World War (now World War I). Within three years the United States was drawn into it. A new period of American history had begun.

7. World War I and Its Results, 1914-1929

1) PANAMA CANAL OPENED
2) U.S. IN WORLD WAR I
3) NAVAL TREATY WITH JAPAN

EARLY IN President Wilson's first term foreign affairs took on ever greater importance. In the Western Hemisphere the nation watched the opening of the Panama Canal in 1914 and the long series of frictions with Mexico. Overshadowing all was the spreading war in Europe. It began with the assassination of Austrian archduke Francis Ferdinand, June 28, 1914. Soon the Central Powers—Germany, Austria-Hungary, Turkey, and Bulgaria—were fighting against 23 Allied nations led by France and Britain.

President Wilson asked Americans to be "neutral in both thought and deed." At the same time he insisted upon the right of the United States to trade with both sides. This was in accordance with inter-

national law governing neutral nations in wartime.

At the start of the war few people in the United States wanted to take sides in the conflict. Gradually, however, the Allies gained favor while the Central Powers lost support. Both sides seized American shipping but Britain offered to pay damages and to submit disputes to arbitration. Germany became unpopular largely because of its use of submarines to raid commerce. Other factors promoted friendly feelings toward the Allies. There was a profitable trade carried on with Britain and France, and large loans were made to those countries. Between 1914 and 1917, the American people bought about 2,300 million dollars in bonds from the Allies. Only about

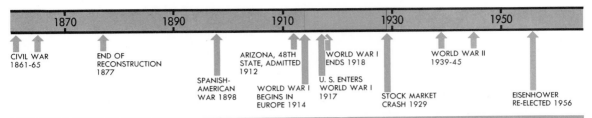

CIVIL WAR
1861-65

END OF
RECONSTRUCTION
1877

SPANISH-
AMERICAN
WAR 1898

ARIZONA, 48TH
STATE, ADMITTED
1912

WORLD WAR I
BEGINS IN
EUROPE 1914

U. S. ENTERS
WORLD WAR I
1917

WORLD WAR I
ENDS 1918

STOCK MARKET
CRASH 1929

WORLD WAR II
1939-45

EISENHOWER
RE-ELECTED 1956

PERIOD OF WORLD WAR I AND POSTWAR PROSPERITY

20 million dollars in German bonds were purchased.

Opposition to Germany flamed high in 1915. The British liner *Lusitania* was sunk by a submarine, with a loss of 124 American lives. Wilson protested strongly. Germany then promised to protect the lives of noncombatants. War was avoided for the moment. Wilson won re-election in 1916, helped in large part by the slogan—"He kept us out of war."

The United States Goes to War

Early in 1917 Germany launched unrestricted submarine warfare against the Allies and neutrals. The hope may have been to end the war before the United States could engage in ground action in Europe. Opposition to Germany grew strong. On April 6, 1917, a joint Congressional resolution declared war on the German Empire (*see* World War I).

The United States embarked upon a great crusade to "make the world safe for democracy." More than 2 million men were sent to Europe in 1917 and 1918. The Navy rushed into action alongside the fleets of Britain and France. Nearly 10 billion dollars were loaned to the Allies to help them carry on the war. American industry mobilized for war. The people made many willing sacrifices in the hope that this would end all wars. President Wilson became the spokesman of the common people all over the world.

General John J. Pershing took command of the American Expeditionary Forces (A.E.F.) in France. Fighting as a separate unit the A.E.F. went into action in the spring of 1918. It fought at Cantigny and on the Marne. It was used in the counteroffensive launched by the French commander Marshal Foch in July. The A.E.F. also fought at Saint-Mihiel in September. Later that month American soldiers fought in the greatest battle the nation had known up to that time—the Meuse-Argonne. The success of the A.E.F. helped to force Germany to ask for an armistice Nov. 11, 1918.

Peace and the League of Nations

Early in 1918 President Wilson had announced his "Fourteen Points" as the basis for a satisfactory peace settlement. These aims were received enthusiastically at home and abroad. Unfortunately, the seemingly endless peace conference in Paris did much to kill the high spirit of the crusade. Wilson had to accept compromise after compromise to win adoption of his chief plan, the Covenant of the League of Nations.

Meanwhile in the November elections the Repub-

licans captured majorities in both houses of Congress. Opposition to the League of Nations increased steadily. In working for its adoption Wilson's health failed. The Versailles peace treaty, including provisions for the League, was finally brought to a vote in the Senate. It was defeated, 55 to 39. The crusade was over and Wilson's hopes were crushed.

During the bitter debates over peace terms two amendments were added to the Constitution. In 1919 the 18th Amendment established national prohibition. The following year the 19th Amendment provided for woman suffrage.

CHIEF EVENTS, 1914–1929

1914. World War I breaks out in Europe. President Wilson appeals for neutrality in the United States.

1915. German submarine sinks *Lusitania* with loss of 124 American lives. Telephone line established coast to coast.

1917. Germany begins open submarine warfare; United States declares war against Germany.

1918. President Wilson proposes "Fourteen Points" as basis for peace. Americans fight at Chateau-Thierry, Belleau Wood, Saint-Mihiel, Argonne Forest. Armistice ends war.

1918–19. President Wilson attends Paris Peace Conference of victorious nations.

1919. United States Senate rejects League of Nations. Navy pilots make first flight across Atlantic. Prohibition established by 18th Amendment.

1920. Right to vote given women by 19th Amendment. Pittsburgh radio station, KDKA, begins broadcasting.

1921. Immigration restricted according to national quotas.

1921–22. Washington Conference restricts warship construction among chief naval powers.

1924. Army plane *Chicago* makes first flight around the world.

1927. Charles A. Lindbergh makes first nonstop solo flight across Atlantic.

1928. United States signs Kellogg-Briand Pact to outlaw war.

1929. Stock market reaches new high, then crashes. Panic marks beginning of great depression.

Additional information about the persons, places, and events of this period will be found in other articles. To find them easily look in the Fact-Index.

Lend *the way they* Fight

Buy Bonds *to your* UTMOST

The United States entered World War I in 1917. To help finance the war and to curb inflation Americans were asked to buy government bonds (left). Crowds thronged Wall Street in New York City (right) during the stock market crash of 1929. This was the start of the great depression.

The Republicans and the 1920's

From his sickroom President Wilson called for a "solemn referendum" on the treaty in the presidential election of 1920. The Republicans nominated an antitreaty senator from Ohio, Warren G. Harding. Harding won the election by a big margin over the Democratic candidate, James M. Cox.

President Harding died in 1923, just when the administration was shaken by grave scandals in government circles. Calvin Coolidge succeeded to the presidency and then won election in his own right in 1924. He defeated Democrat John W. Davis. Republican domination continued with the election of Herbert Hoover in 1928 over Alfred E. Smith. In none of these elections during the 1920's did the Democrats provide a close contest.

After the hardships and losses of World War I, Americans hoped for a long period of peace and prosperity. There was a marked difference of opinion, however, as to the best means of reaching these happy objectives. In foreign affairs many believed that the United States should support the League of Nations and join the World Court (*see* League of Nations). Others held that the nation should keep apart from the disputes of other nations. The isolationist view won out in large part. The United States returned to the foreign policies that had guided it since the Civil War.

In affairs at home many believed that the best course was to follow the progressive policies of Presidents Theodore Roosevelt and Wilson. Others declared that the government should interfere with economic life as little as possible. The policy of limited government action won out. Throughout the 1920's the objective was a return to what was called "normalcy."·

The Prosperity of the 1920's

For nearly ten years the United States enjoyed prosperous times. A rigid economy reduced the national debt and allowed taxes to be cut again and again. Manufacturing was favored by a series of protective tariff laws. Business operated on a mass-production basis that reduced costs. New industries were built on new products—radios, automobiles, refrigerators, talking motion pictures, and airplanes. Most of the country felt that permanent prosperity had been achieved.

This era of prosperity had brought a sharp rise in standards of living and culture. With immigration limited there was more demand for available laborers. Workers now began to share in employers' profits. Good roads, built by combined national and state effort, lifted whole regions out of the mud. The automobile made life easier. Radios became almost a household necessity, giving the country news, entertainment, and education. American films were the best in the world and were shown in the finest motion-picture theaters.

A building boom gave the nation great skyscrapers, such as the Empire State Building in New York City. It also provided many thousands of better-designed homes. These homes were filled with new conveniences—electricity, modern plumbing, refrigerators, and many laborsaving appliances.

More books were sold and more magazines and newspapers read. New equipment and better educational methods improved schools. Most states raised the age of compulsory school attendance to 16 or 18 years. Almost all youths began receiving at least some high-school training. Colleges and universities expanded, with attendance rising from about a quarter million in 1920 to about three quarter million by 1930. There was progress made against illiteracy, poverty, ignorance, malnutrition, and slum housing. (*See also* Education.)

This general prosperity had three unhappy aspects, however. First, it was spotty. Coal mining and textile manufacturing failed to recover from the war. Farmers suffered from cheap prices for agricultural products and high costs for what they had to buy. Second, the reaction to the heroism and sacrifices of World War I was a wave of dishonesty and class hatred. Business frauds and get-rich-quick schemes were common. The Ku Klux Klan fostered racial and religious conflict. Third, government corruption and graft were widespread. The nation was shocked by scandals in the leasing of government oil reserves (such as Teapot Dome), by the handling of the Veterans' Bureau, and by the conduct of the attorney general's office under President Harding. In cities such as New York and Chicago unsuccessful attempts to enforce prohibition accounted for much of the bribing of officials.

Meanwhile the air age was beginning. In 1919 United States Navy pilots made a nonstop flight across the Atlantic. In 1924 Army fliers circled the world, and a New York City to San Francisco airmail service began. Charles A. Lindbergh won the respect of the world in 1927 by flying alone across the Atlantic.

Foreign Policy Proves Weak

After World War I the United States, working with other nations, sought to establish a permanent peace. They tried treaties, world organizations, and similar devices. All these attempts proved ineffective.

An international conference in Washington, D. C., in 1921–22 did agree upon a limitation of naval armaments. It also drew up two treaties, signed by four and nine nations respectively. The aim was to preserve peace in the Pacific. These agreements established Japan as a naval power second only to Britain and the United States.

After some hesitation the United States gave support to the nonpolitical activities of the League of Nations. It worked to stop the narcotics trade, to promote public health activities, and to improve the world-wide position of labor. American experts also aided in dealing with the problem of German reparations after the war. Despite the efforts of Presidents Harding, Coolidge, and Hoover, the Senate kept the United States out of the World Court.

The statesmen of the 1920's had the idea that war might be "outlawed." After much work the United States and France set up the Kellogg-Briand Pact in 1928. This agreement promised to exclude war as an instrument of national policy. The pact was signed by 62 nations, but there was no way of enforcing it.

President Hoover had been in office only six months when the stock market crashed in October 1929. This financial panic is usually considered the end of the decade called the "roaring '20's." From this point on the United States was plunged steadily into the great economic depression which engulfed the whole world.

8. World-Wide Depression and War, 1929–1945

① ASIATIC-PACIFIC THEATER OF OPERATIONS

② AMERICAN THEATER OF OPERATIONS

③ EUROPEAN-AFRICAN-MIDDLE EASTERN THEATER OF OPERATIONS

THE STOCK MARKET crash of 1929 surprised the American people. It had been widely believed prosperity had come to stay. Now a financial panic gripped the nation. The wheels of industry stopped, prices collapsed, unemployment spread rapidly. The United States plunged into the greatest depression in its history. The situation was made worse by the fact that the depression was almost world-wide.

Strong, positive measures were required to treat the sick economy. President Hoover failed to move as fast and as far as Americans demanded. As the depression became more and more critical, the people lost confidence in the administration. One indication of their disapproval was the adoption of the 20th Amendment. This did away with six weeks of "lame duck" time served by Congress and the president after the

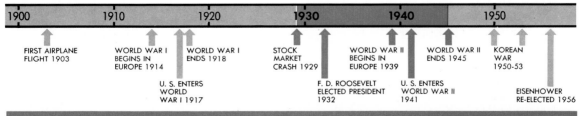

1900	1910	1920	1930	1940	1950
FIRST AIRPLANE FLIGHT 1903	WORLD WAR I BEGINS IN EUROPE 1914	WORLD WAR I ENDS 1918	STOCK MARKET CRASH 1929	WORLD WAR II BEGINS IN EUROPE 1939	WORLD WAR II ENDS 1945	KOREAN WAR 1950-53
		U. S. ENTERS WORLD WAR I 1917		F. D. ROOSEVELT ELECTED PRESIDENT 1932	U. S. ENTERS WORLD WAR II 1941	EISENHOWER RE-ELECTED 1956

PERIOD OF DEPRESSION AND WORLD WAR II

November elections. The newly elected officials were to take office in January instead of in March.

President Hoover was badly defeated for reelection by a rebuilt and stronger Democratic party headed by Franklin Delano Roosevelt. The new president won reelection even more decisively four years later. He defeated Republican Alfred M. Landon.

Presidential leadership reached a new high under Roosevelt's New Deal. During the first 99 days of the new administration, a record number of bills were passed to provide relief for the nation. Then at a somewhat slower pace other laws were enacted. They sought to relieve poverty, cut unemployment, and speed economic recovery. Despite these national efforts industrial and business unemployment continued on a wide scale year after year.

The administration was more successful with its agriculture and labor programs. These provided agricultural subsidies and gave American workers a guaranteed minimum of social security. The administration also helped to win ratification of the 21st Amendment. This repealed the 18th Amendment and ended the 14-year experiment with prohibition.

CHIEF EVENTS, 1929–1945

1929. Stock market crash begins worldwide depression; millions of workers are unemployed.

1932. Franklin Delano Roosevelt elected president.

1933. New Deal launched; gold standard suspended; National Recovery Act passed; bank deposits insured; Tennessee Valley Authority organized. 21st Amendment repeals prohibition.

1934. Congress tightens control over securities; passes first Reciprocal Trade Agreement Act; launches federal housing program.

1935. National Labor Relations (Wagner) Act guarantees collective bargaining to labor. Social Security Act passed. CIO founded.

1936. Hoover Dam (Boulder Dam) completed across Colorado River.

1938. Fair Labor Standards Act provides federal yardstick for wages and hours of workers.

1939. Germany invades Poland to start World War II. United States declares neutrality.

1940. United States begins huge rearmament program; first peacetime draft takes effect.

1941. Lend-Lease Act passed. Atlantic Charter signed. Japanese attack on Pearl Harbor brings United States into World War II.

1942. Americans launch counteroffensive in Pacific. Allies invade North Africa.

1943. Allied invasion of Italy is first landing on European continent.

1944. Allies launch greatest sea-to-land assault in history in invasion of France. Allies invade Philippines. "GI Bill of Rights" passed.

1945. Germany surrenders, May 8; Japan surrenders, September 2. United Nations organized.

Additional information about the persons, places, and events of this period will be found in other articles. To find them easily look in the Fact-Index.

Foreign Problems Become Critical

During the time of bold legislation at home, storm clouds were forming abroad. Italy accepted Fascist rule under Benito Mussolini. Fascism meant force, war, and imperial expansion. In Germany Adolf Hitler and the Nazi party came to power. They suppressed liberty and persecuted Jews and other minorities. The Nazis demanded "living room" in the form of more territory. Equally alarming were events in Asia. Japan came under the complete control of military chiefs. They attacked Manchuria, then the remainder of China. These three nations—Italy, Germany, and Japan—encouraged one another in their acts of aggression. They finally formed a formal alliance called the Axis.

The United States was forced to pay more and more attention to the threats and deeds of the Axis Powers. Most Americans hoped to stand apart from the new world war that was plainly being prepared. Congress hastily passed a series of neutrality acts. At the same time Congress began to build up the national defense.

After 1937 the shadow of war deepened. Never before had Americans been so stirred by what was happening overseas. They saw one small nation after another struck down—Ethiopia, Austria, Czechoslovakia, and Albania. Many came to believe that the United States would be in terrible danger if the Axis conquered all the countries of Europe and Asia.

The United States took two great steps for its own security before World War II actually began. In 1938 it rallied all the nations of the two Americas, including Canada, to act together for the defense of the Western Hemisphere. It also began to strengthen its military forces and to stockpile imported strategic materials.

Hitler plunged Europe into war in the fall of 1939. Congress then repealed the arms embargo act. This made it possible for the United States to send vital supplies to Britain and France. In the spring of 1940 President Roosevelt asked Congress to provide funds for 50,000 airplanes and a two-ocean navy. During the summer the National Guard was called into service. In September Congress adopted the first peacetime military draft law in American history. That same month Roosevelt gave Great Britain 50 destroyers. In exchange the United States received the right to build naval and air bases on Atlantic islands from Newfoundland to British Guiana.

While these feverish preparations for war were going on, the nation faced a critical presidential election. Defying tradition Roosevelt accepted nomination for a third term. The Republicans named Wendell L. Willkie as their presidential candidate. Despite the strongest opposition Roosevelt had yet faced, he was reelected. He thus became the only president to serve more than two terms.

Year of Decision—1941

United States aid to the free nations steadily increased. The country became the great "arsenal of democracy." Ships, guns, and airplanes were turned

Despite bursts of antiaircraft fire, American Flying Fortresses (B-17s) drop their explosive bombs on German targets. Allied air power played a decisive part in shattering Germany's strength. Bombers also made savage raids on Japan.

out at a rapidly increasing rate. Soon a new problem arose—Great Britain and other friendly nations could not pay the United States for all the military supplies they needed. To clear this hurdle President Roosevelt proposed and Congress adopted the far-reaching Lend-Lease Act. Before the war was over this measure provided about 50 billion dollars in aid to the Allied nations.

The gigantic speedup in war production sharply reduced the number of unemployed in the United States. The New Deal was set aside as the nation's attention and energies became fastened on the war in Europe. Seventeen million men had been enrolled in the draft. Almost a million at a time were taking military training.

There was a definite change in the people's attitude. Isolationism seemed to be dying. Most Americans applauded the Atlantic Charter, signed on Aug. 14, 1941, by President Roosevelt and British Prime Minister Winston Churchill. This was a joint declaration of principles to govern the final peace treaty. It promised a "permanent system of general security."

Meanwhile there was mounting tension between the United States and Japan. A high-handed military government in Japan continued to attack neighboring nations. It was trying to establish a "new order in east Asia." On the morning of Dec. 7, 1941, the Japanese attacked the United States naval base of Pearl Harbor, Hawaii. Italy and Germany at once joined Japan in declaring war on the United States. This was part of their Axis agreement.

The attack on Pearl Harbor was only the first of a series of military disasters for the United States at

the beginning of World War II. Wake Island and Guam were lost within a month. The Philippine Islands were isolated and fell four months later. Allied naval power in the Pacific Ocean was all but crushed.

War at Home and Abroad

The series of military defeats spurred the American people to put forth the greatest efforts in their history. As much as 100 billion dollars was spent in a single year to build a war machine. Between 1939 and 1945 employment increased from 45 to 65 million. Whole industries were converted to make war materials instead of peacetime products. More ships, airplanes, tanks, and guns were turned out than was believed possible. Basic industries worked around the clock to manufacture such products as synthetic rubber, aluminum, magnesium, and steel. New government agencies were created to manage the nation's economy and to direct war production.

In 1942 the Axis Powers lost the offensive to the United Nations—the new name given the United States and its Allies. The United Nations fought and won major victories in the Pacific, Egypt, and the Soviet Union. Then on November 8 a powerful Anglo-American force invaded North Africa. It was under the supreme command of Gen. Dwight D. Eisenhower. The Allied troops pushed steadily forward until the Axis forces were driven from the continent.

In 1943 came the capture of Sicily, the invasion of Italy, and the downfall of Mussolini. Meanwhile British and United States air forces were attacking

Shoppers wave meat-coupon books on the last day of rationing. Sacrifices on the home front included the rationing of meat, sugar, and gasoline.

Nazi Europe from British bases. They smashed factories, ports, airfields, railways, and power plants.

Rome, an Axis capital, fell on June 4, 1944. Two days later United States, British, and Canadian forces landed on the beaches of Normandy, France. This was the greatest amphibious operation in history. The success of D-Day was the beginning of the end. The Allies drove steadily eastward; the Soviet armies advanced toward the west. Germany was caught in a giant pincers movement. Its armies and air forces were shattered. On this front peace came on V-E Day (for Victory in Europe), May 8, 1945.

Victory in the Pacific

Admiral Chester Nimitz and Gen. Douglas MacArthur led the counterattack in the Pacific. In 1942 there were United States victories in the Coral Sea at Midway and in the Solomon Islands. In 1943 United States troops overran the Gilbert and Marshall islands and New Guinea. Saipan and Guam in the Marianas were captured and the Philippine Islands were invaded in 1944. During this campaign the Japanese navy was so decisively defeated in its counterattack that Japan ceased to be a major sea power.

The final act in the long bitter drama came in 1945. The Philippines were liberated, and Iwo Jima and Okinawa were conquered. Air fleets of B-29s (Superfortresses) blasted Japanese cities on an increasingly large scale. The Navy moved in close enough to bombard coastal cities. Then on August 6 the first atomic bomb was dropped on the city of Hiroshima. Japan's

subsequent request for peace was granted on August 14 (August 15 in Japan). The formal terms were signed on September 2, celebrated as V–J Day (Victory over Japan). (*See also* World War II.)

Roosevelt, Truman, and the United Nations

In the last full year of World War II (1944), President Roosevelt won reelection to a fourth term. The defeated candidate was Republican Thomas E. Dewey. Roosevelt had served less than three months of this term when he died on April 12, 1945. Vice-President Harry S. Truman was sworn in as the 33rd president later that day. He presided over the victory in Europe, gave the order to drop the first atomic bomb, and accepted the Japanese surrender.

One of President Truman's first big decisions was to continue efforts to establish a United Nations organization. The Atlantic Charter of 1941 had promised the peoples of the world a new and better world order. In 1944 representatives of the United States, Great Britain, China, and the Soviet Union met at the Dumbarton Oaks conference in Washington, D.C. A plan for an international peace organization was drawn up to replace the weak League of Nations. All members of the informal United Nations were asked to send representatives to a conference at San Francisco on April 25, 1945. The meeting took place as planned, less than two weeks after Roosevelt's death. After 52 days of discussion a United Nations Charter was adopted. Before the war ended the new United Nations was well under way (*see* United Nations).

9. Leadership in the Postwar World, 1945–1958

1. U.S. JOINS NATO NATIONS
2. U.S. FIGHTS WITH UNITED NATIONS IN KOREA
3. U.S. JOINS SEATO NATIONS

WITH THE end of World War II, the United States entered a new period in its history. It was now the strongest nation in the world. It ranked first in productive capacity, in naval strength, and in air power. It also had the atomic bomb. No longer could the United States hope to remain aloof from world affairs. Republican and Democratic leaders both realized that it was not possible to return to isolationism.

Americans did not at once realize their new responsibilities. The soldiers overseas wanted to return.

People at home asked Congress to have them brought back immediately. The nation had the problem of keeping up its military strength and of maintaining occupation troops in both Germany and Japan. As a result the government was forced to continue the Selective Service System until March 31, 1947.

Shifts from War to Peace

During the war Americans lived under a controlled economic system. The government rationed scarce

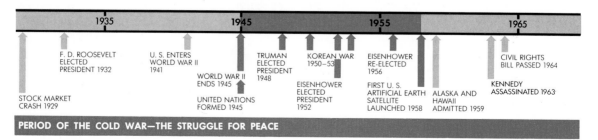

1935   1945   1955   1965

STOCK MARKET CRASH 1929

F. D. ROOSEVELT ELECTED PRESIDENT 1932

U. S. ENTERS WORLD WAR II 1941

WORLD WAR II ENDS 1945

UNITED NATIONS FORMED 1945

TRUMAN ELECTED PRESIDENT 1948

KOREAN WAR 1950–53

EISENHOWER ELECTED PRESIDENT 1952

EISENHOWER RE-ELECTED 1956

FIRST U. S. ARTIFICIAL EARTH SATELLITE LAUNCHED 1958

ALASKA AND HAWAII ADMITTED 1959

KENNEDY ASSASSINATED 1963

CIVIL RIGHTS BILL PASSED 1964

PERIOD OF THE COLD WAR—THE STRUGGLE FOR PEACE

foods and articles, subsidized farm products, fixed prices and wages, and forbade strikes.

The people were now eager to return to a free economy. They protested against government restrictions. Rationing was abandoned. By late 1946 almost all price controls were dropped except ceilings on rent.

Labor was once more free to strike. Workers had put in from 48 to 52 hours a week during the war. Now unions demanded the same take-home pay for a 40-hour week. Beginning late in 1945 a series of strikes crippled the nation's economy. Major walkouts took place among automobile and packinghouse employees, soft-coal miners, steelworkers, and those in the maritime industry. A single strike in a key industry often affected the entire industrial system. For example, coal strikes caused shutdowns in steel; lack of steel tied up the automobile industry.

The strikes generally resulted in higher wages, especially for the workers in large unions. At the same time these gains were largely offset by price increases. Government borrowing and spending had

---

CHIEF EVENTS, 1945–1958

1945. At end of World War II Cold War begins between United States and Soviet Union. United Nations (UN) formally launched on October 24.

1946. Philippines granted independence by United States. Atomic Energy Commission created.

1947. Senate passes Truman Doctrine. Taft-Hartley labor law enacted. Department of Defense consolidates Army, Navy, and Air Force.

1948. European Recovery Program enacted. Truman elected president.

1949. Fair Deal program announced. United States and its allies force Soviet Union to lift Berlin blockade. North Atlantic Treaty Organization (NATO) founded.

1950. United States and several other members of UN send military forces to aid of Republic of Korea; bitter war develops.

1951. Two-term limit put on presidency by ratification of 22nd Amendment to Constitution.

1952. United States and allies end occupation of West Germany. Election of Eisenhower ends 20 years of Democratic rule.

1953. Korean War ends. Department of Health, Education, and Welfare becomes 10th Cabinet post.

1954. Racial segregation of public schools declared illegal by Supreme Court. Southeast Asia Treaty Organization (SEATO) founded.

1955. Two largest labor organizations merge into one group—the AFL-CIO. Salk poliomyelitis vaccine is proved successful.

1956. Eisenhower reelected president. Democrats win control of Congress.

1957. Eisenhower Doctrine to strengthen United States position in Middle East is adopted.

1958. First United States artificial Earth satellite launched. United States joins the International Atomic Energy Agency.

Additional information about the persons, places, and events of this period will be found in other articles. To find them easily look in the Fact-Index.

---

tripled the amount of money in circulation. Since some goods were still scarce, the increased money supply pushed the price level higher. During the war the cost of living had been held in check by wage and price fixing. With the return to free markets, prices shot up. At the end of 1946 the consumer was paying nearly twice as much for food and clothing as such items had cost in 1939.

Rents were still held down by government controls. The housing shortage was so acute that returning veterans had difficulty finding homes. The government launched a program to stimulate home building. It was years, however, before low- and moderate-priced housing was in good supply.

Republicans Gain Control of Congress

Since 1933 the Democratic party had held a strong majority in both houses of Congress. Now it failed to solve the problems of strikes, high prices, and housing shortages. Voters turned away from Democratic leadership. In the mid-term elections of 1946, the Republicans won a majority in both House and Senate. During the Franklin Roosevelt era the president's power had overshadowed Congress. The influence of Congress now increased greatly.

Over President Truman's veto Congress passed the Taft-Hartley labor law. The new measure made labor unions liable to suit for contract violations. It also outlawed the closed shop and provided that, before they could strike, workers must first vote by secret ballot. Another major law enacted in 1947 provided for the unification of the nation's armed forces under a single secretary of defense.

Despite shortages in materials and the stoppages caused by strikes, production and employment began reaching new highs. Agriculture as well as industry benefited from technological improvements developed during the war. There was increased use of laborsaving machinery and better seeds, plants, and fertilizers. These aids raised the nation's food production by roughly one third above the prewar level. Millions of tons of grains and other foodstuffs were shipped to the hungry people of other countries.

Foreign Affairs After the War

On July 4, 1946, the Philippine Islands were given their full independence. The following year the Security Council of the United Nations granted the United States trusteeship over the Pacific islands that had formerly been under mandate to Japan. The trusteeship included hundreds of small islands in the Marianas, the Marshall Islands, and the Caroline Islands.

The United States, Britain, and Canada still held the secret of atomic energy; but it was a secret that could not long be kept. Month after month the question of atomic control was fought over in the United Nations. The United States demanded a thorough system of international inspection and controls. The Soviet Union rejected the plan.

During the war a unity of purpose held the great powers together. With peace it became clear that the

177

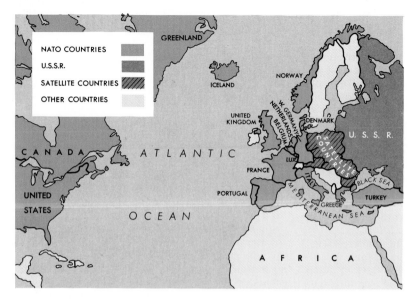

To strengthen themselves against possible Communist aggression, 12 nations formed the North Atlantic Treaty Organization (NATO) in 1949. Greece and Turkey joined in 1952, West Germany in 1955, and Spain entered in 1982.

victors were split into two hostile camps. On one side were the Western nations, or democracies; on the other, the Soviet Union and its Eastern European allies. In the United Nations and elsewhere the Soviet Union worked to block peace and reconstruction. On V-J Day the Soviet Union had dominated more than half of Europe and a large part of Asia. Now it tried to expand farther. Its agents infiltrated foreign governments and stirred up civil war in such places as Greece and China.

President Truman became alarmed at the spread of Communism. In 1947 he called on the United States to take over active world leadership of democratic nations. He pointed out that America's peace and security were endangered by all aggression, either direct or indirect. To aid threatened nations he proposed that the United States provide economic and military assistance. Congress responded to this Truman Doctrine by appropriating funds to aid Greece and Turkey in their struggle against Communism.

The United States had been pouring food, supplies, and money credits into war-torn Europe to stave off collapse. Now Secretary of State George C. Marshall proposed that European nations set up their own program of reconstruction. The plans were to be used as a condition for further American aid. Western Europe quickly accepted the Marshall Plan, renamed the European Recovery Program (ERP). The Soviet Union objected and tried to incite unrest throughout the continent. The United States, however, was now aware of its new responsibilities. It helped to block Communism in Italy, increased aid to Greece, and enlarged the ERP into the Foreign Assistance Act. In the first ten years after World War II, the United States furnished to foreign countries about 53 billion dollars in grants and credits.

Another accomplishment of 1947 was the signing of peace treaties with Italy, Hungary, Bulgaria, and Romania. The Soviet Union stalled all efforts to make treaties with Germany and Austria (see World War II, "The Peace Treaties").

President Truman Elected

In 1948 President Truman waged a vigorous election campaign. He swept to victory in an amazing political upset over Thomas E. Dewey, who had lost four years earlier to Roosevelt. The Democratic party also won control of both houses of Congress.

President Truman began his second term by pledging a Fair Deal for all. He asked Congress to enact a broad program of social legislation. Much of this action had to be postponed when the nation became more deeply involved in foreign affairs.

In Europe the conflict between the Soviet Union and the Western Allies grew into the Cold War (see Cold War). The Allies thwarted a Soviet land blockade of Berlin. The Allies used an airlift to fly supplies into the blockaded city. In May 1949 the Soviets ended the 11-month siege. Two months later the United States ratified the North Atlantic Treaty. It joined with Canada and ten nations of Western Europe in promising a common defense against aggression for 20 years. One feature of the treaty was an agreement to build a collective armed force. This organization was placed under the command of Gen. Dwight D. Eisenhower. Key non-Communist countries outside the North Atlantic Treaty Organization (NATO) were to receive American arms.

United States Fights in Korea

Communist troops invaded South Korea on June 25, 1950. This brought swift action by the United States and the United Nations. The Security Council of the United Nations issued a cease-fire order. President Truman ordered American military forces to take police action against the North Korean invaders. He also ordered the United States Navy to guard the strategic island of Taiwan (see Korean War).

In November 1950 large forces of Chinese entered the fight and stopped the United Nations drive to repel the North Korean forces. In February 1951 the United Nations denounced China as an aggressor. China answered by rejecting all cease-fire proposals.

The 82nd Congress, which convened in 1951, was concerned chiefly with the defense of the United States and its Allies. The problem of what steps to take provoked bitter debate in Congress and throughout the nation. It was finally decided to send more American troops to strengthen NATO in Europe.

In Korea, meanwhile, the prospect of a military stalemate developed. This led to widespread criticism of the United Nations policy of limiting the fighting to the Korean peninsula. The supreme commander in the Far East, Gen. Douglas MacArthur, and others wanted to attack China itself with sea and air power. They wanted to make use of Nationalist Chinese land forces from Taiwan. After much arguing President Truman relieved MacArthur of his Far East commands (*see* MacArthur).

In the summer of 1951 the Soviets surprisingly proposed a cease-fire in Korea. Representatives of the United States, North Korea, and China opened truce negotiations. No early agreement could be reached. The conference dragged on for two more years while the fighting continued.

Foreign Affairs

During the Korean War the United States helped bring World War II to an official end. In September 1951 delegates from 48 nations met in San Francisco to sign a peace treaty with Japan. The Senate ratified the treaty the following year. The Senate also approved security alliances with Japan, the Philippines, Australia, and New Zealand.

A formal peace treaty with Germany was still blocked by the Soviet Union. To help restore German independence, President Truman ended the state of war between the United States and Germany in October 1951. The next year the United States, Great Britain, and France signed a "peace contract" with the Federal Republic of Germany. This ended Allied occupation of West Germany. The Senate also approved a plan to include West Germany in NATO.

The United States was also concerned about the security of the Southwest Pacific. In 1952 the foreign ministers of Australia and New Zealand met in Hawaii with the United States secretary of state to discuss mutual defense problems. The alliance that grew out of the meeting was called ANZUS—the initials of the three member nations (*see* ANZUS Treaty).

First Republican President in 20 Years

In 1952 President Truman refused to seek reelection. The Democrats nominated Adlai Stevenson, governor of Illinois, as their presidential candidate. To oppose Stevenson the Republicans chose General Eisenhower, World War II hero and first commander of NATO's military forces, with Richard M. Nixon as his running mate for vice-president. The American vot-

ers elected Eisenhower by an overwhelming margin, ending 20 years of Democratic administrations. The Republicans also won control of the 83rd Congress, though their majority in each house was small.

One of President Eisenhower's first official acts was to create a tenth Cabinet post. This was the Department of Health, Education, and Welfare. It united five government agencies under one head.

In 1953 the United States Army introduced the use of atomic artillery shells. Atomic energy was also put to use by the Navy. The first nuclear-powered submarine, the *Nautilus,* was launched in 1954.

Eisenhower's chief accomplishment abroad was the signing of a truce in Korea on July 27, 1953. The truce talks had lasted 2 years and 17 days, the longest peace negotiations in history. All prisoners who wanted to go home were repatriated. Among those taken by the United Nations forces, 22,000 refused repatriation. Some 350 members of the United Nations forces, including 21 Americans, chose to stay with their captors. For the United States, casualties in the Korean War were exceeded only by those it had suffered in the Civil War and the two world wars. (For casualty figures, *see* table in Korean War.)

The United States Supreme Court raised a serious issue in 1954. It voted unanimously that racial segregation in public schools was unconstitutional. The verdict affected 17 states in which segregation was compulsory. The following year the Court ruled that segregation problems should be handled by federal district courts and by local school authorities.

In foreign affairs the United States agreed to join with Canada in constructing the St. Lawrence Seaway. It added strength to the Western Hemisphere's defenses by securing the passage of an anti-Communist resolution at the 10th Inter-American Conference, which met at Caracas, Venezuela. In order to meet the increasing threat of Communist aggression in

Dwight D. Eisenhower, right, was inaugurated as the 34th president in 1953, ending 20 years of Democratic party rule. He was sworn in by Chief Justice Frederick M. Vinson.

UPI—Bettmann Archive

179

the Far East, the United States and seven other nations formed the Southeast Asia Treaty Organization (SEATO) in 1954. (It was dissolved in 1977.)

In 1955 earlier large-scale tests of Jonas Salk's poliomyelitis vaccine were pronounced successful. In the same year most labor-union members were merged into one organization, the AFL-CIO. Abroad, the nation made progress toward solving some problems but lost ground in other areas. It helped restore full sovereignty to Austria and West Germany. At Geneva, Switzerland, President Eisenhower held a summit meeting with the heads of the Soviet Union, Great Britain, and France, but the conference failed to produce a lasting climate of peace.

During the elections of 1954 the Democrats regained control of both houses of Congress. Eisenhower subsequently suffered a heart attack from which he

recovered. He ran for reelection in 1956 against Adlai Stevenson, again the Democratic candidate.

The election was a decisive victory for Eisenhower's moderate Republicanism. His margin of victory was the largest ever given up to that time to a Republican candidate for president. The Democrats, however, retained control of both houses of Congress, and they increased their control in the election of 1958.

The United States, Britain, and the Soviet Union discussed disarmament and proposed bans on nuclear tests, but little was accomplished. In January 1958 the United States launched its first successful artificial Earth satellite, Explorer 1. In May it began a new series of nuclear tests in the Pacific. The United States also joined the International Atomic Energy Agency, which promoted the use of nuclear power for peaceful purposes. (*See also* Guided Missile; Space Travel.)

10. The Nation in the Space Age, 1958 to Present

① U.S. ENGAGES IN VIETNAM WAR

② OPEC BEGINS UPWARD PRICE SPIRAL FOR PETROLEUM

③ WATERGATE SCANDAL FORCES NIXON TO RESIGN

THE SATELLITE Sputnik 1 had been launched by the Soviets, on Oct. 4, 1957, and they had sent another into orbit a month later. Americans were electrified. A year later the Soviets pushed their advantage by issuing an ultimatum that the Western Allies evacuate Berlin. Next came a proposal that Berlin become a free city. There were fears that the Cold War of coexistence could escalate into a world war. The West resisted, but the Soviets never officially withdrew their threat. Before long, however, Premier Nikita Khrushchev and other Soviet officials were visiting the United States. President Eisenhower was invited to Moscow. A four-power summit was announced.

The summit collapsed in its opening session, and the invitation to Eisenhower was withdrawn. On May 1, 1960, an American U-2 reconnaissance plane was shot down over Sverdlovsk inside the Soviet Union. Khrushchev, thoroughly incensed, called for a United States apology. Unless such overflights were stopped, the Soviets threatened to launch atomic missiles against United States bases. Eisenhower did not apologize, but the U-2 flights over the Soviet Union were canceled.

Meanwhile in Cuba Fidel Castro had led a revolution against the dictator Fulgencio Batista from 1953 to 1959. After Castro became the premier, he quickly courted the Soviet Union. In 1960 he negotiated a trade treaty that brought sugar to the Soviets at bargain prices after the United States had reduced its quota of Cuban sugar.

In November 1960 Vice-President Nixon, running with the support of President Eisenhower, lost the presidential election in a close race to Senator John F. Kennedy of Massachusetts. When Kennedy took office in January 1961, Cuba became one of his immediate problems. In one of Eisenhower's last acts as president he had broken off diplomatic relations with Cuba. Anti-Castro Cuban refugees were preparing for an invasion of the island. With the president's approval, the invasion was begun at the Bay of Pigs in April 1961. Poor planning and little support resulted in failure—a major setback for the new president.

There was another problem area—Berlin. When Khrushchev renewed his attempts to get the Western powers out of the city, Kennedy promised to defend West Berlin. To halt the flow of refugees to the West

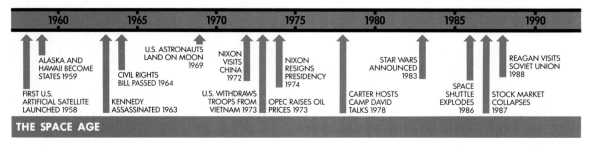

1960	1965	1970	1975	1980	1985	1990

ALASKA AND HAWAII BECOME STATES 1959

U.S. ASTRONAUTS LAND ON MOON 1969

NIXON VISITS CHINA 1972

NIXON RESIGNS PRESIDENCY 1974

STAR WARS ANNOUNCED 1983

REAGAN VISITS SOVIET UNION 1988

CIVIL RIGHTS BILL PASSED 1964

FIRST U.S. ARTIFICIAL SATELLITE LAUNCHED 1958

KENNEDY ASSASSINATED 1963

U.S. WITHDRAWS TROOPS FROM VIETNAM 1973

OPEC RAISES OIL PRICES 1973

CARTER HOSTS CAMP DAVID TALKS 1978

SPACE SHUTTLE EXPLODES 1986

STOCK MARKET COLLAPSES 1987

THE SPACE AGE

CHIEF EVENTS, 1958 TO THE PRESENT

1958. United States launches artificial Earth satellite.

1959. Alaska becomes 49th state, Hawaii the 50th.

1960. United States reconnaissance plane shot down over Soviet Union.

1961. CIA is involved in unsuccessful invasion of Cuba at Bay of Pigs. 23rd Amendment to Constitution gives Washington, D.C., residents right to vote in presidential elections. First American makes space flight. American troops sent to defend West Berlin.

1962. Cuban missile crisis erupts; Soviets remove missiles from Cuba on United States urging.

1963. March on Washington takes place. President John F. Kennedy is assassinated in Dallas, Tex. Nuclear test-ban treaty is signed.

1964. 24th Amendment to Constitution bans poll taxes in federal elections. Civil-rights bill is passed. Supreme Court makes possible reapportionment.

1965. United States combat forces fight in Vietnam. Voting-rights bill and Medicare act signed. Department of Housing and Urban Development becomes 11th Cabinet post.

1966. Department of Transportation becomes 12th Cabinet post.

1967. 25th Amendment to Constitution provides for presidential succession.

1968. Assassinations of Martin Luther King, Jr., and Robert F. Kennedy provoke race riots.

1969. United States astronauts become the first men to land on the moon.

1970. Four students at Kent State University in Ohio killed by National Guard during anti-Vietnam War protest.

1971. 26th Amendment to Constitution gives 18-year-olds right to vote in all elections.

1972. President Richard M. Nixon visits China and Soviet Union.

1973. United States withdraws troops from Vietnam. Vice-President Spiro T. Agnew resigns. OPEC raises price of petroleum 400 percent.

1974. Watergate scandal and threat of impeachment force Nixon to resign.

1977. Department of Energy becomes new Cabinet post. Treaty altered to return Panama Canal to Panama by year 2000.

1978. President Jimmy Carter hosts Camp David talks between Israel's Menachem Begin and Egypt's Anwar el-Sadat.

1979. Strategic Arms Limitation Talks (SALT II) signed by United States and Soviet Union. Militants seize 66 American hostages in takeover of United States Embassy in Iran.

1980. Department of Health, Education, and Welfare is separated into Department of Health and Human Services and Department of Education.

1981. President Ronald Reagan wounded in assassination attempt. Major tax cut and increased defense spending pass Congress. Sandra Day O'Connor is appointed first woman Supreme Court justice.

1983. Reagan announces Star Wars program. United States invades Grenada.

1985. Summit conference between Reagan and Soviet leader Mikhail Gorbachev held in Geneva, Switzerland.

1986. Space Shuttle *Challenger* explodes shortly after lift-off. United States bombs targets in Libya. Summit conference in Iceland fails. Iran-*contra* affair revealed.

1987. Iran-*contra* hearings held. Stock market collapses. Reagan and Gorbachev sign INF treaty.

1988. Fourth Reagan-Gorbachev summit held in Moscow.

Additional information about the persons, places, and events of this period will be found in other articles. To find them easily look in the Fact-Index.

the Soviets built a wall of concrete and barbed wire that divided East and West Berlin.

Meanwhile the Soviets had placed a group of nuclear missiles in Cuba capable of ranges that included portions of the United States and Central and South America. The president reported on Oct. 22, 1962, that he had ordered a blockade on ships carrying military equipment to Cuba and that the United States was prepared to take action if a missile was launched from Cuba. Kennedy was supported unanimously by the Organization of American States. The Soviets recalled vessels that were headed for Cuba and agreed to dismantle the missile installations.

Civil Rights

On the home front Kennedy, who had been elected with black support, faced the problems of civil rights. Freedom Rides were organized in 1961. Recruits—both black and white—from Northern cities traveled to the South to test the desegregation of travel facilities, restaurants, and waiting rooms. When local police protection was denied, the president sent federal marshals to ensure the safety of the riders. In 1962 James Meredith tried to become the first known black to enter the University of Mississippi, but he was barred by the governor of the state. He was later admitted with the aid of federal marshals. When the marshals were attacked by a local mob, the president called in the Mississippi National Guard.

The year 1963—the centennial of the Emancipation Proclamation—was a significant one for the civil-rights movement. There was a massive campaign for desegregation and fair-employment practices in Birmingham, Ala. Demonstrations took the form of marches for freedom, picketing, sit-ins, and pray-ins. To control the demonstrators police used attack dogs and high-pressure water hoses. There were bombings, shootings, and other violence. Medgar W. Evers, the field secretary of the Mississippi branch of the National Association for the Advancement of Colored People (NAACP), was fatally shot in an ambush outside his home in Jackson.

President Kennedy submitted a civil-rights bill to Congress on June 19, 1963. On August 28 the March on Washington for Jobs and Freedom brought more than 200,000 demonstrators to the Mall near the Lincoln Memorial. The highlight of the interracial civil-rights rally was the memorable "I Have a Dream" address by Martin Luther King, Jr.

On November 22 President Kennedy was fatally shot in Dallas while on a tour of Texas. Vice-President Lyndon B. Johnson became the 36th president of the United States. Despite a filibuster by Southern senators, the controversial civil-rights legislation was passed on Feb. 17, 1964. An income-tax reduction and an antipoverty law were also passed. The Supreme Court, ruling on the apportionment of state legislatures, decided that all districts in each house must be substantially equal—that is, one man, one vote. Previously seat distribution had favored rural areas over the growing cities and suburbs.

181

UNITED STATES

In 1965 Martin Luther King, Jr. (third from left front), led a march in Alabama from Selma to the capital at Montgomery to petition for black voting rights in that state.

In the presidential election of 1964, Johnson defeated Barry Goldwater, the conservative Republican senator from Arizona. Using his unique political skills, Johnson won Congressional approval of the Medicare bill to provide health insurance for most persons aged 65 and more. He sought assistance for the elementary and secondary schools and for colleges and universities. He fought for more money for the war on poverty, including legislation to allot funds for the development of Appalachia and other distressed areas. He was active on civil-rights issues.

Vietnam War

After reports that North Vietnamese torpedo boats attacked a United States destroyer in the Gulf of Tonkin in early August 1964, the president ordered retaliatory bombing raids. To bolster the United States position in Vietnam, combat troops were sent to the area. By the year's end 184,000 Americans were in the field, by 1968, more than 538,000.

At home, meanwhile, tensions and frustrations in the black ghettos had exploded into violence. In 1965 Watts, a district of Los Angeles, had been the scene of 34 deaths, 900 reported injuries, and property damage estimated at 40 million dollars. In 1966 and again in 1967 the ghettos were still in turmoil. There were large-scale riots in Newark, Detroit, and some smaller cities, with looting and burning, many deaths, and charges of police brutality. President Johnson sent federal troops to establish order in Detroit, where the rioting was the most violent.

The president also appointed a commission, headed by Governor Otto Kerner of Illinois, to study the reasons for the riots. The report concluded that the United States was splitting into two nations—one black, the other white. It recommended changes in American society, in government, and in business, but it was generally ignored. In the spring of 1968 there was another rash of riots in the black ghettos. Martin Luther King, Jr., was killed by a sniper's bullet in Memphis in April. Robert F. Kennedy, a brother of the former president and an ardent supporter of civil rights, was shot and killed in Los Angeles in June.

Early in 1968 North Vietnam and the Viet Cong launched the Lunar New Year, or Tet, offensive. They struck at cities and towns and United States bases. They captured Hue and fought their way into Saigon. So devastating was the onslaught that Johnson admitted that he could no longer unify the country and keep the war out of politics. He chose, therefore, not to run for reelection in 1968. Vice-President Hubert H. Humphrey of Minnesota became the Democratic candidate. His Republican opponent was Richard M. Nixon, who won the election handily.

Vietnam continued to be an issue. President Nixon proposed a phased withdrawal of United States forces. He favored a policy of "Vietnamization," or turning the defense over to the South Vietnamese. In June and September of 1969 he announced successive withdrawals of 25,000 and 35,000 troops. But the actions were too little, and the protests mounted. Vietnam moratorium days were organized by college students. Early in 1970 the news that an American unit had massacred civilians—including women and children—at My Lai in 1968 further provoked the protesters. When President Nixon ordered troops into Cambodia (now Kampuchea) and resumed the bombing of North Vietnam, many college campuses exploded with riots.

At home Nixon had called for the building of an antiballistic-missile system and the adoption of a tax-reform bill. On July 20, 1969, astronauts from Apollo 11 were the first men to land on the moon. In 1970 the United States Postal Service was established as an independent agency of the executive branch and the voting age was lowered to 18 under the 26th Amendment to the Constitution.

In 1972 the president visited both China and the Soviet Union. The first visit helped to develop economic and cultural exchanges with the Chinese, and the second resulted in a treaty limiting the use of strategic weapons. By October the United States and North Vietnam had agreed to a cease-fire in Vietnam, the return of American prisoners of war, and the withdrawal of all United States forces.

In November 1972 Nixon decisively defeated Senator George S. McGovern in the presidential race. In December, as the United States resumed the bombing of North Vietnam, the president claimed that the enemy had not bargained in good faith. But in January 1973 the North Vietnamese agreed to release their prisoners within 60 days. The United States withdrew all of its troops by the end of March. More than 47,000 Americans had been killed and more than 300,000 wounded. The war may have cost some 200 billion dollars. (See also Vietnam War.)

Some events of 1973 caused new problems for Nixon. The price of wheat on the world market increased considerably. Vice-President Spiro T. Agnew, accused of income-tax evasion and accepting bribes while governor of Maryland, resigned his position in October. He was replaced by Congressman Gerald R. Ford of Michigan—the nation's first appointed vice-president. Earlier in October war broke out between

Israel and the Arab states. The fighting was brief, and an acceptable United Nations cease-fire was worked out. But the Arabs, in an effort to get land concessions from the Israelis, imposed a petroleum boycott on the United States, Japan, and the countries of Western Europe. The Organization of Petroleum Exporting Countries (OPEC) then raised the price from about three dollars per barrel to nearly twelve dollars, and the cost of gasoline at the pump skyrocketed.

Watergate Scandal

Agents hired by the Committee for the Re-Election of the President broke into the Democratic National Committee headquarters at the Watergate complex in Washington, D.C., on June 17, 1972. They had penetrated the files and installed listening devices. The president repeatedly denied that anyone in his administration was involved in the break-in. In 1973 several of Nixon's closest advisers resigned. When it was revealed that White House conversations and telephone calls had been recorded, Congress subpoenaed the tapes, but Nixon refused to release them. In 1974 a special prosecutor called for the tapes. Claiming executive privilege, the president refused to release all of the White House recordings. The Supreme Court ruled that the president must give up the additional tapes, and he surrendered some that implicated him in the cover-up of the Watergate break-in. It was also revealed that he owed more than 400,000 dollars in unpaid income taxes. Public opinion against Nixon continued to mount, and arrangements were made for his impeachment and trial by the Senate.

On Aug. 8, 1974, Nixon appeared on television to resign the presidency, and the next day Vice-President Ford became president. Ford pardoned the ex-president for any and all offenses he might have committed against the United States.

President Lyndon B. Johnson signs the Medicare bill in the presence of former President Harry S. Truman, who proposed the measure. Standing, left to right, are Mrs. Johnson, Vice-President Hubert H. Humphrey, and Mrs. Truman.

AP/Wide World

Ford Administration

Soon after the controversial pardon the new president proclaimed a conditional amnesty for those who had resisted service during the Vietnam War. Ford's decision that they would have to serve the country in a civilian capacity for two years, rather than receive unconditional amnesty, was not a popular one.

Inflation, recession, and unemployment—holdovers from the Nixon years—plagued the new president. Ford called on people to wear WIN (Whip Inflation Now) buttons to draw attention to the economic problem. But the economy slumped, and unemployment soared to more than 9 percent. Taxes were cut to stimulate business activity, and social programs—designed to help the urban poor—were also cut.

Meanwhile the situation in the Far East had deteriorated. Saigon, the capital of South Vietnam, fell to the North Vietnamese in April 1975. A pro-American government in Cambodia had already been toppled, and on May 12 Cambodian forces seized the American merchant ship *Mayaguez* in the Gulf of Thailand. Calling it an act of piracy, Ford ordered United States Marines to attack Tang Island, where the *Mayaguez* was held. The Cambodians claimed they had already released the ship when the Marines struck, but the crew had been removed. After the assault 18 servicemen were reported killed or missing, and the *Mayaguez* and its crew were recovered.

In August 1976 Ford was nominated for president on the first ballot at the Republican national convention in Kansas City, Mo. In the November election he was beaten by his Democratic opponent, former Georgia Governor Jimmy Carter.

Carter Administration

President Carter spearheaded the reorganization of the government's departments and agencies. The functions of the Department of Health, Education, and Welfare were divided between a new Department of Education and a renamed Department of Health and Human Services. Much concerned about energy sources and the problems generated by the country's growing dependency on foreign oil, the president helped to create a new Department of Energy.

In November 1977 Anwar el-Sadat of Egypt was the first Arab head of state to visit Jerusalem. He was prepared to recognize the state of Israel in exchange for the Israeli-held Sinai and a promise of peace for the Palestinians. At that point Carter seized the mediator's role. In 1978 he invited Israel's Prime Minister Menachem Begin and President Sadat to Camp David, the American president's retreat. The talks there led to a 1979 treaty between the former enemies.

Treaties were signed by the United States to turn the Panama Canal over to the Panamanians by the year 2000. Carter strengthened ties with China by entering into full diplomatic relations with Peking in 1979. He talked constantly of human rights and the rights of Soviet dissidents, thereby inviting Soviet anger. Yet on June 15, 1979, he signed the agreement

President Richard M. Nixon boards a helicopter to leave the White House, en route to his home in California on Aug. 9, 1974, the day after announcing to the American people his resignation. Vice-President and Mrs. Gerald R. Ford and members of the Nixon family stand beside the helicopter. Nixon's resignation became effective later in the day as his plane crossed the country.

J.P. Laffont—Sygma

on the Strategic Arms Limitation Talks (SALT II) with Soviet leader Leonid I. Brezhnev.

Iran

President Carter's apparent strength in foreign affairs was shaken in late 1979. Iranian revolutionaries in Tehran had put an end to the regime of the shah in January. The government was turned over to the fundamentalist and anti-American Ayatollah Ruhollah Khomeini, who referred to the United States as the "great Satan." When Carter permitted the exiled shah to come to New York City for medical treatment, Iranian anger exploded. On November 4 a mob broke into the American Embassy in Tehran and took everyone hostage. The Iranian captors wanted the United States to send the shah back to Iran to stand trial for crimes against the state.

In response Carter froze all Iranian assets in the United States and banned trade with Iran until the hostages were set free. The Iranians did not change their demands, and months passed without any progress. In frustration Carter decided on military action—a team of commandos was to fly secretly to Tehran to free the hostages in April 1980. The action was aborted when two of the rescue aircraft collided in the desert south of the Iranian capital. The commandos had to be withdrawn. (The last hostages were released on Jan. 20, 1981.)

In December 1979 Soviet forces invaded Afghanistan in a surprise attack. The Afghans resisted from their mountain hideaways, waging guerrilla warfare. Many fled the Soviet advance and moved as refugees into Pakistan. Carter immediately denounced the invasion. He cut off grain exports and the sale of high-technology equipment to the Soviet Union. He cut off debate on the ratification of Salt II. He would not permit American athletes to compete in the Summer Olympic Games in Moscow.

Carter began to lose support on the domestic front. Inflation had started to run in double digits in 1979, petroleum prices were on the rise, and poor harvests sent food costs upward. Carter asked the Federal Reserve Board to push up interest rates, hoping to slow the money flow and thereby curb inflation, but money became more expensive. Unemployment increased. By the spring of 1980, the United States was entering a mild recession period.

Carter did not campaign actively for the presidential nomination in 1980. The president nevertheless won his party's nomination on the first ballot. The downturn in the economy, the hostage situation in Iran, and the invasion of Afghanistan all affected the outcome of the election. Carter was overwhelmingly defeated by Ronald Reagan. The Republicans also took control of the Senate and cut deeply into the Democratic majority in the House of Representatives.

Reagan Presidency Begins

From the outset the president took a tough anti-Soviet stance and was concerned about Communist expansion in the Americas. Amid much criticism—and pressure, particularly from Israel—he persuaded Congress to support the sale of arms, including AWACS electronic surveillance aircraft, to Saudi Arabia in October 1981. When Argentina invaded the British-controlled Falkland Islands in April 1982, Reagan attempted to remain neutral, but he supported the British position when diplomacy failed and the British counterattack began.

The president had difficulties with the NATO allies. They wanted a reduction in nuclear arms. They refused to comply with United States sanctions against the sale of equipment to the Soviets for the construction of the Siberian natural-gas pipeline. Reagan lifted the bans in November 1982, shortly after the death of Soviet leader Brezhnev.

On the home front, a 35-billion-dollar cutback in federal spending for 1981–82 was pushed through Congress along with reductions in personal and business income taxes. Unfortunately the economy did not respond. Interest rates remained high, there was a slump in investments, and increased tax money failed to appear in government coffers. In July 1982 the unemployment figure reached 9.8 percent. The president changed his tactics by calling for a 98-billion-dollar tax increase, which passed Congress with the help of the Democratic leadership.

Star Wars

On March 23, 1983, Reagan appealed for a defense system that would make nuclear weapons "impotent and obsolete." His proposed Strategic Defense Initiative (SDI) was designed to protect the populations of the United States, its allies, and the Soviet Union from nuclear holocaust. The cost for American taxpayers was estimated at 26 billion dollars over a five-year period. Critics dubbed the project Star Wars to indicate that SDI was nothing more than a futuristic plan that would never work. Many NATO allies viewed SDI as an initiative that would accelerate the arms race, as well as a move by the United States to check its decline in high technology.

In Europe there was a rising fear of the capability of the superpowers to destroy the world through nuclear missiles. Protesters against further deployment of American medium-range missiles in Europe blockaded United States military bases in West Germany. There were massive demonstrations in other European countries and in the United States. In the Americas there was a notable buildup of Soviet matériel on the island of Grenada in the Caribbean. An American invasion was ordered in October 1983.

In 1984 the president visited China and Ireland. Agreements with the Chinese limited China's tax on United States corporations doing business in China. Areas of nuclear cooperation were defined, and cultural exchanges with writers, artists, sports teams, and performers were expanded. The Ireland trip included a stop at Ballyporeen, the site of Reagan's family roots. On Nov. 8, 1984, Reagan was reelected president in a landslide victory over the candidate of the Democratic party, former Vice-President Walter F. Mondale of Minnesota.

After six years of belligerency the Soviets and Americans sat down to talk in November 1985 at a summit conference in Geneva, Switzerland. The Soviet leader, Mikhail Gorbachev, considered Star Wars the central issue separating the two nations, while Reagan's position on SDI was nonnegotiable. Gorbachev pointed out that SDI could never be 100 percent effective but might give the United States the opportunity to deliver a first strike against the Soviet Union. Both sides supported a 50 percent reduction in nuclear arms but disagreed on which of the systems to scale back. They signed accords on cultural and scientific exchanges and the resumption of civil-aviation ties. There was no progress on arms control. There were no agreements on the world's problem areas: Afghanistan, Ethiopia, Angola, Nicaragua, and Kampuchea. There was no real agreement on human rights.

Reagan met with Gorbachev again in 1986, this time in Reykjavík, Iceland. The meeting fell apart on October 12 after vehement disagreement over the Star Wars program. Gorbachev went to Washington, D.C., in December 1987, the first Soviet leader to visit the United States since 1973.

He and Reagan signed an intermediate-range nuclear-forces (INF) treaty. Years in the making, it provided for unprecedented on-site inspection and was the first so-called disarmament treaty to reduce arms instead of limiting them. Senate approval of the treaty was delayed because of problems with its on-site-verification provisions. Reagan made a return trip to Moscow at the end of May 1988 to discuss reductions in long-range nuclear weaponry.

Other Events of the Late 1980s

Two air tragedies marked the end of 1985 and the beginning of 1986. On Dec. 12, 1985, a chartered DC-8 carrying 248 American soldiers home for Christmas—after peacekeeping duties in the Sinai—crashed after takeoff near Gander, Newf. All eight crew members and all the soldiers were killed. On Jan. 28, 1986, after several delays, the Space Shuttle *Challenger* was launched at Cape Canaveral, Fla. About 73 seconds after lift-off the vehicle disintegrated when the booster rockets exploded. On board were five astronauts, an engineer, and a teacher-in-space participant. The United States space program was temporarily grounded as a result of the accident.

In April 1986 United States military aircraft bombed Libyan cities in retaliation for Libya's alleged involvement in terrorist acts, particularly a West Berlin nightclub bombing in which an American serviceman had been killed.

An extraordinary record was compiled by Congress in 1986 on domestic legislation. The tax code was revised more extensively than at any time since World War II. The immigration laws were rewritten, and the most far-reaching environmental bills since the 1970s were passed.

The United States stock market suffered its greatest drop in history on Oct. 19, 1987—since known as Black Monday. Although the drop was nearly twice that of the famous collapse in October 1929, it did not bring on the feared recession. Stock markets in other parts of the world, however, suffered dramatic losses as a result of the Wall Street panic.

During the Reagan years the national debt increased from 1.8 trillion to 2 trillion dollars. In 1985, though it had been the largest creditor nation in the world, the United States became a debtor nation for the first time since World War I. Between 1978 and 1988 household debt was tripled to nearly 3 trillion dollars. In April 1988 the unemployment rate fell to 5.4 percent—the lowest level since June 1974. This created fears of more inflation and higher interest rates.

There was more trouble in the Persian Gulf in 1987 and 1988. The Navy frigate USS *Stark* was attacked by Iraqi missiles, killing 37 sailors on May 17, 1987. United States destroyers bombarded two Iranian oil platforms in the gulf on October 19 in retaliation for Iranian attacks on ships in the gulf—some carrying the United States flag. United States warships and planes sank or disabled six Iranian vessels in a series of clashes on April 18, 1988. On July 3 the cruiser USS *Vincennes* shot down an Iranian commercial airliner, mistaking it for a hostile fighter plane and killing all 290 people aboard. Iran sought condemnation from the UN Security Council, which instead repeated its call for a cease-fire in the Iran-Iraq war. The United States offered to compensate the victims' families.

Iran-*Contra* Affair

Reagan considered Nicaragua to be a "cancer" in the Western Hemisphere, a Soviet "beachhead" in Central America. The Sandinistas' regular army was trained by Cuban advisers. The Soviets supplied weapons and helicopters. In February 1986 Reagan asked for 100 million dollars in aid for the *contras*—whom he called freedom fighters—who were battling the leftist regime of Daniel Ortega Saavedra. Congress turned down the president's request.

In November there was astonishing news that the United States had secretly supplied Iran with arms despite a formal embargo on such sales. A few weeks later it was learned that some of the profits from the sales to Iran had been diverted to Swiss bank accounts controlled by the *contras*. This had apparently taken place while military aid to the Nicaraguan guerrillas was forbidden by law.

House and Senate special committees held hearings on the Iran-*contra* affair in the summer of 1987. Attempts to find presidential involvement in a cover-up failed, and the president denied having knowledge of the affair. The final report on the investigation was highly critical of the administration.

Reagan put forth an alternative peace proposal for Central America in 1987, but his initiative was overshadowed by the peace plan proposed by the presidents of five Central American nations, including Nicaragua. Under the peace accord, talks were held in early 1988 between the Nicaraguan government and the *contras.* In an attempt to end the civil war, a two-month truce was signed on March 23. Official United States aid to the *contras* had ended on February 29, and Congress refused further support except for 48 million dollars in humanitarian aid. Also in March 3,200 United States support troops were sent to Honduras.

An additional 1,300 troops were sent to Panama in April to improve the security of American bases. Reagan froze Panamanian funds in the United States in an attempt to force the leader of Panama, General Manuel Antonio Noriega, to resign. (*See also* Supreme Court; United States Constitution; United States Government; articles on individual states, cities, and geographic features.)

BIBLIOGRAPHY FOR UNITED STATES

Batteau, Allen, ed. Appalachia and America (Univ. Press of Ky., 1983).
Bedell, G.C. Religion in America, 2nd ed. (Macmillan, 1982).
Bergheim, L.A. Weird Wonderful America: the Nation's Most Offbeat and Off-the-Beaten-Path Tourist Attractions (Macmillan, 1988).
Billington, R.A. Land of Savagery, Land of Promise: the European Image of the American Frontier in the 19th Century (Norton, 1981).
Birdsall, S.S. and Florin, J.W. Regional Landscapes of the United States and Canada (Wiley, 1985).
Boorstin, D.J. The Americans: the Democratic Experience (Random, 1985).
Boorstin, D.J. The Americans: the National Experience (Random, 1985).
Commager, H.S. The American Mind: an Interpretation of American Thought and Character Since the 1880s (Yale Univ. Press, 1987).
Cooke, Alistair. Alistair Cooke's America (Knopf, 1987).
Current, R.N. The Essentials of American History (Knopf, 1986).
Demos, J.P. Entertaining Satan: Witchcraft and the Culture of Early New England (Oxford, 1982).
Ehrlich, Eugene. The Oxford Illustrated Literary Guide to the United States (Oxford, 1982).
Encyclopaedia Britannica, Inc. The Annals of America (EB Inc., 1976).
Gabriel, R.H. and others, eds. Pageant of America: a Pictorial History of the United States, 15 vols. (U.S. Publishers, 1987).
Garreau, Joel. The Nine Nations of North America (Houghton, 1981).
Georgia, Lowell. Into the Wilderness (National Geographic, 1978).
Glennon, T.J. Backroads, USA: the Middle Atlantic States (Macmillan, 1988).
Hart, W.B. The United States and World Trade (Watts, 1985).
Hine, R.V. The American West: an Interpretive History (Little, 1984).
House, J.W. United States Public Policy (Oxford, 1983).
Kehoe, A.B. North American Indians (Prentice, 1981).
King, R.H. A Southern Renaissance: the Cultural Awakening of the American South, 1930–1955 (Oxford, 1980).
Kronenwetter, Michael. Capitalism versus Socialism: Economic Policies of the USA and the USSR (Watts, 1986).
Lavender, David. The Great West (American Heritage, 1985).
Lavender, David. The Southwest (Harper, 1987).
Luebke, F.C. and others, eds. Mapping the North American Plains (Univ. of Okla. Press, 1987).
McPhee, John. Basin and Range (Farrar, 1981).
Meining, D.W. The Shaping of America (Yale Univ. Press, 1986).
Mikva, A.J. The American Congress: the First Branch (Watts, 1983).
Morison, S.E. A Concise History of the American Republic (Oxford, 1983).
Muller, P.O. Contemporary Suburban America (Prentice, 1981).
Myers, Joan and Simmons, Marc. Along the Santa Fe Trail (Univ. of N.M. Press, 1986).
National Geographic Society. Preserving America's Past (National Geographic, 1983).
Peirce, N.R. and Hagstrom, Jerry. The Book of America: Inside Fifty States Today (Warner, 1984).
Redfern, Ron. The Making of a Continent (Times Books, 1983).
Reeves, Richard. The Reagan Detour (Simon & Schuster, 1985).
Rierden, A.B. Reshaping the Supreme Court: New Justices, New Directions (Watts, 1988).
Robbins, W.G. and others, eds. Regionalism and the Pacific Northwest (Ore. State Univ. Press, 1983).
Savage, W.W. The Cowboy Hero: His Image in American History and Culture (Univ. of Okla. Press, 1987).
Schneider, H.W. A History of American Philosophy, 2nd ed. (Columbia Univ. Press, 1987).
Schwartz, S.I. and Ehrenberg, R.E. The Mapping of North America (Abrams, 1980).
Scott, J.A. The Story of America: a National Geographic Picture Atlas (National Geographic, 1984).
Smith, B.C. After the Revolution: the Smithsonian History of Everyday Life in the 18th Century (Pantheon, 1985).
Tanner, H.H., ed. Atlas of Great Lakes Indian History (Univ. of Okla. Press, 1987).
Tindall, G.B. America: a Narrative History (Norton, 1984).
Watson, J.W. The United States (Longman, 1983).
Wolverton, Ruthe and Walter. America's National Seashores (Woodbine, 1988).
Yeats, M. and Garner, B. The North American City (Harper, 1980).

THE FIFTY STATES

State	Area* (sq mi)	Area* (sq km)	Rank in Area	Population (1980 census)	Rank in Population	Capital	Year Admitted to Union
Alabama	51,609	133,667	29	3,890,061	22	Montgomery	1819
Alaska	586,412	1,518,800	1	400,481	50	Juneau	1959
Arizona	113,909	295,023	6	2,717,866	29	Phoenix	1912
Arkansas	53,104	137,539	27	2,285,513	33	Little Rock	1836
California	158,693	411,013	3	23,668,562	1	Sacramento	1850
Colorado	104,247	269,998	8	2,888,834	28	Denver	1876
Connecticut	5,009	12,973	48	3,107,576	25	Hartford	1788
Delaware	2,057	5,328	49	595,225	47	Dover	1787
Florida	58,560	151,670	22	9,739,992	7	Tallahassee	1845
Georgia	58,876	152,488	21	5,464,265	13	Atlanta	1788
Hawaii	6,450	16,705	47	965,000	39	Honolulu	1959
Idaho	83,557	216,412	13	943,935	41	Boise	1890
Illinois	56,400	146,075	24	11,418,461	5	Springfield	1818
Indiana	36,291	93,993	38	5,490,179	12	Indianapolis	1816
Iowa	56,290	145,790	25	2,913,387	27	Des Moines	1846
Kansas	82,264	213,063	14	2,363,208	32	Topeka	1861
Kentucky	40,395	104,623	37	3,661,433	23	Frankfort	1792
Louisiana	48,523	125,674	31	4,203,972	19	Baton Rouge	1812
Maine	33,215	86,026	39	1,124,660	38	Augusta	1820
Maryland	10,577	27,394	42	4,216,446	18	Annapolis	1788
Massachusetts	8,257	21,386	45	5,737,037	11	Boston	1788
Michigan	58,216	150,779	23	9,258,344	8	Lansing	1837
Minnesota	84,068	217,735	12	4,077,148	21	St. Paul	1858
Mississippi	47,716	123,584	32	2,520,638	31	Jackson	1817
Missouri	69,686	180,486	19	4,917,444	15	Jefferson City	1821
Montana	147,138	381,086	4	786,690	44	Helena	1889
Nebraska	77,227	200,017	15	1,570,006	35	Lincoln	1867
Nevada	110,540	286,297	7	799,184	43	Carson City	1864
New Hampshire	9,304	24,097	44	920,610	42	Concord	1788
New Jersey	7,836	20,295	46	7,364,158	9	Trenton	1787
New Mexico	121,666	315,113	5	1,299,968	37	Santa Fe	1912
New York	49,576	128,401	30	17,557,288	2	Albany	1788
North Carolina	52,586	136,197	28	5,874,429	10	Raleigh	1789
North Dakota	70,665	183,022	17	652,695	46	Bismarck	1889
Ohio	41,222	106,764	35	10,797,419	6	Columbus	1803
Oklahoma	69,919	181,089	18	3,025,266	26	Oklahoma City	1907
Oregon	96,981	251,180	10	2,632,663	30	Salem	1859
Pennsylvania	45,333	117,412	33	11,866,728	4	Harrisburg	1787
Rhode Island	1,214	3,144	50	947,154	40	Providence	1790
South Carolina	31,055	80,432	40	3,119,208	24	Columbia	1788
South Dakota	77,047	199,551	16	690,178	45	Pierre	1889
Tennessee	42,244	109,411	34	4,590,750	17	Nashville	1796
Texas	267,338	692,402	2	14,228,383	3	Austin	1845
Utah	84,916	219,931	11	1,461,037	36	Salt Lake City	1896
Vermont	9,609	24,887	43	511,456	48	Montpelier	1791
Virginia	40,817	105,716	36	5,346,279	14	Richmond	1788
Washington	68,192	176,616	20	4,130,163	20	Olympia	1889
West Virginia	24,181	62,629	41	1,949,644	34	Charleston	1863
Wisconsin	56,154	145,438	26	4,705,335	16	Madison	1848
Wyoming	97,914	253,596	9	470,816	49	Cheyenne	1890

*Total land and inland water area, excluding Great Lakes, Lake St. Clair, and coastal areas under state jurisdiction. Great Lakes area is divided as follows: Illinois, 1,526 sq mi (3,952 sq km); Indiana, 228 sq mi (591 sq km); Michigan, 38,575 sq mi (99,909 sq km; includes area in Lake St. Clair); Minnesota, 2,212 sq mi (5,729 sq km); New York, 3,627 sq mi (9,394 sq km); Ohio, 3,457 sq mi (8,954 sq km); Pennsylvania, 735 sq mi (1,904 sq km); Wisconsin, 10,062 sq mi (26,060 sq km).

HOW FEDERAL GOVERNMENT EXPENDITURES HAVE GROWN

Period or Fiscal Year	Total Expenditures	Military Services (Including Civil Activities)	Veterans' Expenditures (Incl. Pensions)	Interest on Public Debt	Other Expenditures	Per Capita Expenditure
1789–1800	$ 5,776,000*	$ 2,209,000*	$ 82,000*	$ 2,629,000*	$ 856,000*	$ 1.25*
1851–1860	60,163,000*	27,781,000*	1,531,000*	2,776,000*	28,074,000*	2.10*
1901–1905	535,559,000*	219,649,000*	140,114,000*	27,849,000*	147,947,000*	6.63*
1916–1920	8,065,333,000*	4,094,552,000*	187,143,000*	375,371,000*	3,408,267,000*	77.33*
1930	3,440,269,000	839,019,000	446,956,000	659,348,000	1,494,946,000	27.95
1939	8,965,555,000	1,367,978,000	557,000,000	940,540,000	6,100,037,000	68.50
1945	98,702,525,000	80,537,254,000	2,060,000,000	3,616,686,000	12,488,585,000	707.11
1980	563,600,000,000	130,400,000,000	20,800,000,000	73,300,000,000	339,100,000,000	2,488.25

*Average annual expenditures for period.
Source: U.S. government reports.

United States Fact Summary

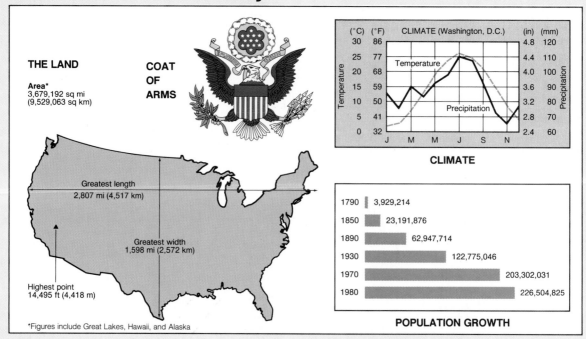

THE LAND

Area*
3,679,192 sq mi
(9,529,063 sq km)

COAT OF ARMS

CLIMATE (Washington, D.C.)

CLIMATE

Greatest length
2,807 mi (4,517 km)

Greatest width
1,598 mi (2,572 km)

Highest point
14,495 ft (4,418 m)

*Figures include Great Lakes, Hawaii, and Alaska

Year	Population
1790	3,929,214
1850	23,191,876
1890	62,947,714
1930	122,775,046
1970	203,302,031
1980	226,504,825

POPULATION GROWTH

Official Name: United States of America.

Capital: Washington, D.C.

Coat of Arms: Shield represents Congress and states; eagle signifies authority of Congress; 13 olives, leaves, arrows, and stars symbolize original 13 states; arrows symbolize military readiness; olive branch symbolizes peace; motto, *E Pluribus Unum* (One Out of Many), on scroll. Adopted 1782.

Flag: 13 equal horizontal red and white stripes represent the original 13 states; a blue field at the hoist has 50 white stars, one for each state (*see* Flags of the World).

Motto: *In God we trust.*

Anthem: 'The Star-Spangled Banner'.

NATURAL FEATURES

Borders: *Coast*—including Alaska and Hawaii, 12,383 miles (19,928 kilometers); *land frontier*—6,000 miles (9,656 kilometers).

Natural Regions: *Mainland*—Atlantic and Gulf Coastal Plain, Appalachian Highlands, Central Lowlands, Interior Highlands, Lake Superior Uplands, Great Plains, Rocky Mountains, Cordilleran Plateaus, Pacific Mountain System; *Alaska*—Pacific Mountain System, Alaska Interior, Arctic Central Plain; *Hawaii*—consists of a chain of shoals, reefs, islands.

Major Ranges: Rocky Mountains; Sierra Nevada; Cascade Range; Appalachian Highlands, including Adirondack, Allegheny, Blue Ridge, Cumberland, and Great Smoky mountains; Aleutian, Alaska, and Brooks ranges in Alaska; Koolau Range in Hawaii.

Notable Peaks: McKinley, 20,320 feet (6,194 meters); North Peak, 19,370 feet (5,904 meters); Foraker, 17,400 feet (5,304 meters); Bona, 16,500 feet (5,029 meters); Blackburn, 16,390 feet (4,996 meters); Sanford, 16,237 feet (4,949 meters); Vancouver, 15,700 feet (4,785 meters); Fairweather, 15,300 feet (4,663 meters); Hubbard, 15,015 feet (4,577 meters), all in Alaska.

Major Rivers: Arkansas, Brazos, Colorado, Columbia, Mississippi, Missouri, Ohio, Red, Rio Grande, Snake, Yukon.

Major Lakes: Erie, Great Salt, Huron, Iliamna, Michigan, Okeechobee, Ontario, Pontchartrain, Superior.

Climate: *Coterminous United States*—tropical savanna, humid subtropical, humid continental warm summer, humid continental cool summer, steppe, desert, western high areas, mediterranean, marine west coast; *Alaska*—subarctic, tundra; *Hawaii*—oceanic.

THE PEOPLE

Population (1987 estimate): 243,773,000; 66.3 persons per square mile (25.6 persons per square kilometer); 73.7 percent urban, 26.3 percent rural.

Vital Statistics (rate per 1,000 population): *Births*—15.5; *deaths*—8.9; *marriages*—9.7.

Life Expectancy (at birth): *White males*—72.0 years; *black males*—65.5 years; *white females*—78.9 years; *black females*—73.6 years.

Major Language: English (official).

Ethnic Groups: German, British, Irish, Scandinavian, Dutch, Southern and Eastern European, black, Hispanic, American Indian.

Major Religions: Protestantism, Roman Catholicism.

MAJOR CITIES (1980 census)

New York, N.Y. (7,071,030): trade and financial center; publishing; clothing; United Nations; Statue of Liberty; Lincoln Center for the Performing Arts; World Trade Center (*see* New York, N.Y.).

Chicago, Ill. (3,005,072): industrial and commercial center; railroad hub of the United States; world's largest grain market; Great Lakes port; Sears Tower; Art Institute; Adler Planetarium (*see* Chicago).

Los Angeles, Calif. (2,966,763): seaport; center for television, motion-pictures, recording, aviation, and petroleum refining; Exposition Park; University of Southern California (*see* Los Angeles).

Philadelphia, Pa. (1,688,210): port city; manufacturing and banking center; United States mint; Independence Hall; Carpenters' Hall; Museum of Art; University of Pennsylvania (*see* Philadelphia).

Houston, Tex. (1,594,086): industrial, medical, and educational center; seaport on ship channel; petroleum refineries; chemical plants; Lyndon B. Johnson Space Center (*see* Houston).

Detroit, Mich. (1,203,339): Great Lakes port; automobile manufacturing; steel; robots; computers; Cranbrook Academy (*see* Detroit).

Dallas, Tex. (904,078): financial, industrial, and fashion center; cotton market; petroleum corporations; insurance company headquarters; aircraft and missile parts; electronics (*see* Dallas).

San Diego, Calif. (875,504): resort; seaport; naval installations; aircraft; tuna packing; agriculture; San Diego Zoo (*see* San Diego).

Phoenix, Ariz. (789,704): state capital; resort city; meat-processing center; electronics (*see* Phoenix).

188

United States Fact Summary

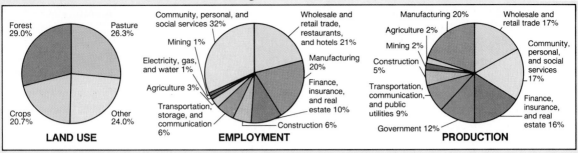

LAND USE
- Forest 29.0%
- Pasture 26.3%
- Crops 20.7%
- Other 24.0%

EMPLOYMENT
- Community, personal, and social services 32%
- Mining 1%
- Electricity, gas, and water 1%
- Agriculture 3%
- Transportation, storage, and communication 6%
- Wholesale and retail trade, restaurants, and hotels 21%
- Manufacturing 20%
- Finance, insurance, and real estate 10%
- Construction 6%

PRODUCTION
- Manufacturing 20%
- Agriculture 2%
- Mining 2%
- Construction 5%
- Transportation, communication, and public utilities 9%
- Government 12%
- Wholesale and retail trade 17%
- Community, personal, and social services 17%
- Finance, insurance, and real estate 16%

Baltimore, Md. (786,775): historic and industrial city; seaport on Patapsco River; automobile assembly; metals; chemicals; printing; shipping, insurance, and financial center (*see* Baltimore).

ECONOMY

Chief Agricultural Products: *Crops*—alfalfa, apples, barley, beans, cabbages, citrus fruits, corn, cotton, dairy products, grains, grapes, hay, lettuce, milo, oats, peaches, peanuts, pears, peas, pecans, potatoes, rice, sorghum, soybeans, squash, sugar beets, sugarcane, sweet potatoes, tobacco, tomatoes, wheat. *Livestock and fish*—cattle, pigs, poultry, sheep, freshwater fish and seafood.

Chief Mined Products: Bauxite, carnotite, clays, coal, copper, crushed stone, gold, iron ore, lead, limestone, mercury, molybdenum, natural gas, nickel, petroleum, phosphate, platinum, salt, sand and gravel, silver, sulfur, tungsten, uranium, zinc.

Chief Manufactured Products: Airplanes, asphalt, automobiles, beverages, buses, cement, chemicals, cigars and cigarettes, clothing, electric and electronic equipment, farm equipment, fertilizers, freeze-dried foods, furniture, heavy machinery, iron, lumber, metals, newspaper, pharmaceuticals, plastics, processed foods, pulp and paper, radios, railroad cars, refined petroleum, rubber, ships, steel, telephones, televisions, textiles, transmitting equipment, transportation equipment, trucks.

Chief Imports: Electrical apparatus, automobiles and parts, chemicals, mineral fuels, beverages, paper, metals, textiles, clothing, footwear, meat, fish, coffee, tea, bananas.

Chief Exports: Electronic and electrical apparatus, motor vehicles, aircraft, chemicals, mineral fuels, beverages, tobacco, wheat, corn.

Chief Trading Partners: Canada, Japan, Mexico, United Kingdom, West Germany, Saudi Arabia.

Monetary Unit: 1 United States dollar = 100 cents.

EDUCATION

Schools: Free and compulsory education for children ages 7 to 16; administered by local communities in accord with state and federal statutes. System composed of 12 years of schooling broken into 2 levels: elementary (lasting from 6 to 8 years) and secondary (lasting from 4 to 6 years); in some systems 3 years of junior high school are included.

Literacy: 95.5 percent of population.

Leading Universities: Brown University, Providence, R.I.; Claremont Colleges, Claremont, Calif.; Columbia University, New York, N.Y.; Dartmouth College, Hanover, N.H.; Harvard University, Cambridge, Mass.; Johns Hopkins University, Baltimore, Md.; Massachusetts Institute of Technology, Cambridge; Princeton University, Princeton, N.J.; Rice University, Houston, Tex.; Smith College, Northampton, Mass.; Stanford University, Stanford, Calif.; United States Military Academy, West Point, N.Y.; University of Pennsylvania, Philadelphia; Wellesley College, Wellesley, Mass.; Williams College, Williamston, Mass.; Yale University, New Haven, Conn.

Notable Libraries: Beinecke Rare Book and Manuscript Library and Sterling Memorial Library at Yale University, New Haven, Conn.; Library of Congress, National Archives, Washington, D.C.; National Library of Medicine, Bethesda, Md.; Newberry Library, Chicago, Ill.; Widener Memorial Library, Cambridge, Mass.

Notable Museums and Art Galleries: Metropolitan Museum of Art, Museum of Modern Art, New York N.Y.; Art Institute of Chicago, Museum of Science and Industry, Chicago, Ill.; California Museum of Science and Industry, Los Angeles, Calif.; Museum of Fine Arts, Boston, Mass.; The Fine Arts Museums of San Francisco, San Francisco Museum of Modern Art, San Francisco, Calif.

GOVERNMENT

Form of Government: Federal republic.

Constitution: Ratified 1788.

Head of State and Government: President; elected, term, 4 years.

Cabinet: 13 heads of departments, appointed by the president and confirmed by the Senate.

Legislature: Congress, composed of Senate and House of Representatives; annual sessions. *Senate*—100 elected members, term, 6 years. *House of Representatives*—435 elected members, term, 2 years.

Judiciary: *Supreme Court*—chief justice and 8 associate justices; selected by president and confirmed by Senate; term, life. Other federal courts are Courts of Appeals, District Courts, Legislative courts.

Political Divisions: 50 states and 1 district.

Voting Qualification: Age 18.

PLACES OF INTEREST

Appalachian Highlands: dominating feature of the landscape of the Eastern seaboard (*see* Appalachian Highlands).

Bunker Hill: north of Boston, Mass.; site of the first major battle of the American Revolution.

Everglades National Park: in southern Florida; only large subtropical area in the continental United States; swamps, marsh animals.

Glacier Bay National Park and Preserve: in Alaska; tidewater glaciers amid magnificent mountain peaks; at least 16 active glaciers.

Grand Canyon: immense gorge cut by the Colorado River into the high plateaus of northwestern Arizona; fantastic shapes and colors.

Great Salt Lake: in northern Utah; largest inland body of salt water in the Western Hemisphere.

Hawaii Volcanoes National Park: on island of Hawaii; dominated by two active volcanoes; tropical trees; rare birds.

Mount Rushmore National Memorial: near Keystone, S.D.; sculptures of the heads of Presidents George Washington, Thomas Jefferson, Theodore Roosevelt, and Abraham Lincoln carved into mountain.

Mount Vernon, Va.: near Washington, D.C.; estate and burial place of George Washington (*see* Mount Vernon).

Muir Woods National Monument: in northwestern California; grove of redwoods, the world's tallest trees.

Orlando, Fla.: one of world's most popular tourist destinations; Cape Canaveral aerospace center nearby; Walt Disney World; Epcot Center; Sea World marine park; citrus fruit center (*see* Orlando).

Plymouth, Mass.: in eastern Massachusetts; site where the Pilgrims landed in New England Plymouth Colony (*see* Plymouth, Mass.).

Rocky Mountains: mountain system that dominates the western North American continent; stretches from Canada to Mexico.

Saint Augustine, Fla.: on northern Florida's Atlantic coast; the oldest continuous settlement in North America.

Statue of Liberty: on Liberty Island in the Upper Bay of New York Harbor; colossal statue that commemorates the friendship of the peoples of the United States and France.

Washington, D.C.: capital of the United States; White House; Jefferson and Lincoln memorials (*see* Washington, D.C.).

Williamsburg, Va.: restored village of 18th century colonial America; College of William and Mary (*see* Williamsburg).

Yellowstone National Park: in northwestern Wyoming and parts of Montana and Idaho; geysers, hot springs, boiling clay pools.

189

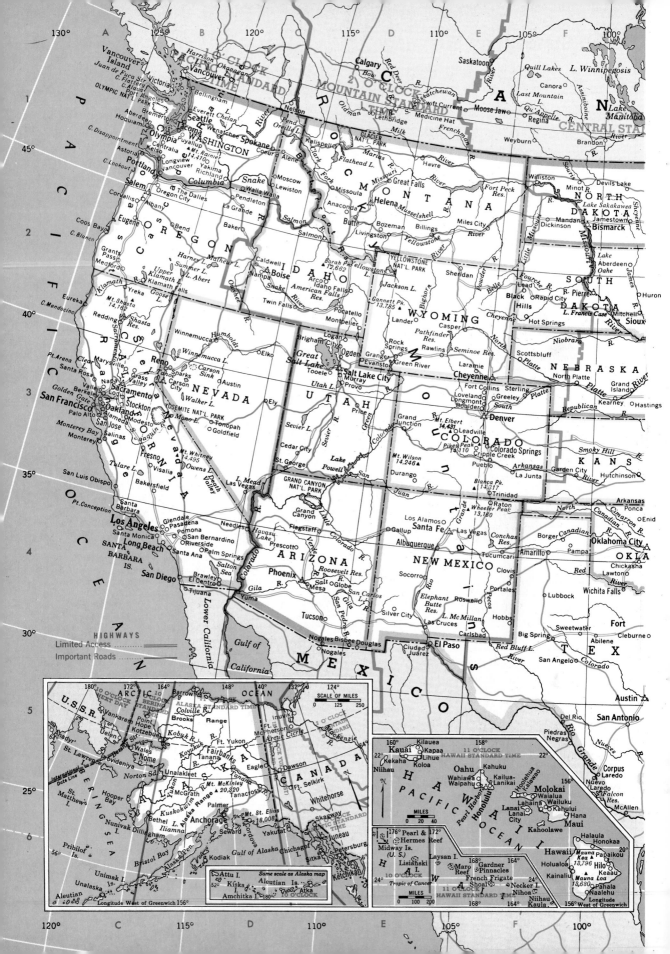

UNITED STATES

POLYCONIC PROJECTION

SCALE OF MILES

0 50 100   200   300   400

SCALE OF KILOMETRES

0   100   200   300   400

Capitals of Countries ⋯⋯⋯⋯ ☆
State Capitals ⋯⋯⋯⋯⋯⋯⋯ ⌂
International Boundaries ⋯⋯⋯

Copyright by C. S. Hammond & Co., N.Y.

Longitude   95°   West of   H   Greenwich   90°

UNITED STATES

STATES

Alabama, 3,890,061 J 4
Alaska, 400,481 C 5
Arizona, 2,717,866 D 4
Arkansas, 2,285,513 H 3
California, 23,668,562 B 3
Colorado, 2,888,834 E 3
Connecticut, 3,107,576 M 2
Delaware, 595,225 L 3
Florida, 9,739,992 K 5
Georgia, 5,464,265 K 4
Hawaii, 965,000 F 5
Idaho, 943,935 D 2
Illinois, 11,418,461 J 3
Indiana, 5,490,179 J 3
Iowa, 2,913,387 H 2
Kansas, 2,363,208 G 3
Kentucky, 3,661,433 J 3
Louisiana, 4,203,972 H 4
Maine, 1,124,660 N 1
Maryland, 4,216,446 L 3
Massachusetts, 5,737,037 M 2
Michigan, 9,258,344 J 1
Minnesota, 4,077,148 H 1
Mississippi, 2,520,638 J 4
Missouri, 4,917,444 H 3
Montana, 786,690 E 1
Nebraska, 1,570,006 F 2
Nevada, 799,184 C 3
New Hampshire, 920,610 M 2
New Jersey, 7,364,158 M 3
New Mexico, 1,299,968 E 4
New York, 17,557,288 L 2
North Carolina, 5,874,429 L 3
North Dakota, 652,695 F 1
Ohio, 10,797,419 K 2
Oklahoma, 3,025,266 G 3
Oregon, 2,632,663 B 2
Pennsylvania, 11,866,728 L 2
Rhode Island, 947,154 M 2
South Carolina, 3,119,208 K 4
South Dakota, 690,178 F 2
Tennessee, 4,590,750 J 3
Texas, 14,228,383 G 4
Utah, 1,461,037 D 3
Vermont, 511,450 M 2
Virginia, 5,346,279 L 3
Washington, 4,130,163 B 1
West Virginia, 1,949,644 K 3
Wisconsin, 4,705,335 J 2
Wyoming, 470,816 E 2

CITIES and TOWNS

Aberdeen, S.D., 25,956 G 1
Aberdeen, Wash., 18,739 B 1
Abilene, Tex., 98,315 G 4
Ada, Okla., 15,902 G 4
Akron, Ohio, 237,177 K 2
Akron, Ohio (met. area), 660,328 K 2
Alameda, Calif., 63,852 B 3
Albany (cap.), N.Y., 101,727 M 2
Albany-Schenectady-Troy, N.Y., (met. area), 795,019 M 2
Albany, Ore., 26,678 B 2
Albuquerque, N.M., 331,767 E 3
Alexandria, La., 51,565 H 4
Alexandria, Va., 103,217 L 3
Allentown, Pa., 103,758 L 2
Allentown-Bethlehem-Easton, Pa., (met. area), 635,481 L 2
Alton, Ill., 34,171 J 3
Altoona, Pa., 57,078 L 2
Amarillo, Tex., 149,230 F 3
Anaconda, Mont., 12,518 D 1
Anchorage, Alaska, 174,431 D 6
Anderson, Ind., 64,695 J 2
Anderson, S.C., 27,313 K 4
Annapolis (cap.), Md., 31,740 L 3
Ann Arbor, Mich., 107,966 K 2
Anniston, Ala., 29,523 J 4
Appleton, Wis., 59,032 J 2
Arco, Idaho, 1,241 D 2
Ardmore, Okla., 23,689 G 4
Arkansas City, Kan., 13,201 G 3
Asheville, N.C., 53,583 K 3
Ashland, Ky., 27,064 K 3
Astoria, Ore., 9,998 B 1
Atchison, Kan., 11,407 G 3
Athens, Ga., 42,549 K 4
Atlanta (cap.), Ga., 425,022 K 4
Atlanta, Ga., (met. area), 2,029,710 K 4
Atlantic City, N.J., 40,199 M 3
Auburn, Me., 23,128 M 2
Auburn, N.Y., 32,548 L 2
Augusta, Ga., 47,532 K 4
Augusta (cap.), Me., 21,819 N 2
Austin, Minn., 23,020 H 2
Austin, Nev., 300 C 3
Austin (cap.), Tex., 345,496 G 4
Austin, Tex., (met. area), 536,688 G 4
Baker, Ore., 9,471 C 2
Bakersfield, Calif., 105,611 C 3
Baltimore, Md., 786,775 L 3
Baltimore, Md., (met. area), 2,174,023 L 3
Bangor, Me., 31,643 N 2
Barrow, Alaska, 2,207 C 5
Baton Rouge (cap.), La., 219,844 H 4
Battle Creek, Mich., 35,724 J 2
Bay City, Mich., 41,594 K 2
Beatrice, Neb., 12,891 G 2
Beaumont, Tex., 118,102 H 4
Belleville, Ill., 41,580 J 3
Bellingham, Wash., 45,794 B 1
Beloit, Wis., 35,207 J 2
Bend, Ore., 17,263 B 2
Berkeley, Calif., 103,328 B 3
Berlin, N.H., 13,084 M 2
Bessemer, Ala., 31,729 J 4
Bethel, Alaska, 3,576 C 6
Biddeford, Me., 19,638 N 2
Big Spring, Tex., 24,804 F 4
Billings, Mont., 66,842 E 1
Biloxi, Miss., 49,311 J 4
Binghamton, N.Y., 55,860 L 2
Birmingham, Ala., 284,413 J 4
Birmingham, Ala., (met. area), 847,360 J 4
Bisbee, Ariz., 7,154 E 4
Bismarck (cap.), N.D., 44,485 G 1
Bloomington, Ill., 44,189 J 2
Bluefield, W. Va., 16,060 K 3
Blytheville, Ark., 23,844 H 3
Bogalusa, La., 16,976 H 4
Boise (cap.), Idaho, 102,160 C 2
Borger, Tex., 15,837 F 3
Boston (cap.), Mass., 562,994 M 2
Boston, Mass., (met. area), 2,763,357 M 2
Boulder, Colo., 76,685 E 2
Bowling Green, Ky., 40,450 J 3
Bozeman, Mont., 21,645 D 1
Brainerd, Minn., 11,489 H 1
Brawley, Calif., 14,946 C 4
Bremerton, Wash., 36,208 B 1
Bridgeport, Conn., 142,546 M 2
Brigham City, Utah, 15,596 D 2
Bristol, Tenn., 23,986 K 3
Bristol, Va., 19,042 K 3
Brownsville, Tex., 84,997 G 5
Brunswick, Ga., 19,585 K 4
Bryan, Tex., 44,337 G 4
Buffalo, N.Y., 357,870 L 2
Buffalo, N.Y., (met. area), 1,242,826 L 2
Burlington, Iowa, 29,529 H 2
Burlington, Vt., 37,712 M 2
Butte, Mont., 37,205 D 1
Cairo, Ill., 5,931 J 3
Calais, Me., 4,262 N 1
Caldwell, Idaho, 17,699 C 2
Calumet, Mich., 1,103 J 1
Camden, N.J., 84,910 M 3
Canton, Ohio, 93,077 K 2
Cape Girardeau, Mo., 34,361 H 3
Caribou, Me., 9,916 N 1
Carlsbad, N.M., 25,496 F 4
Carson City (cap.), Nev., 32,022 C 3
Casper, Wyo., 51,016 E 2
Cedar City, Utah, 10,972 D 3
Cedar Rapids, Iowa, 110,243 H 2
Centralia, Wash., 11,555 B 1
Champaign, Ill., 58,267 J 2
Charleston, S.C., 69,510 L 4
Charleston (cap.), W. Va., 63,968 K 3
Charlotte, N.C., 314,447 L 3
Charlotte-Gastonia, N.C., (met. area), 637,218 L 3
Charlottesville, Va., 45,010 L 3
Chattanooga, Tenn., 169,565 J 3
Cheboygan, Mich., 5,106 K 1
Cheyenne (cap.), Wyo., 47,283 E 2
Chicago, Ill., 3,005,072 J 2
Chicago, Ill., (met. area), 7,102,328 J 2
Chickasha, Okla., 15,828 G 4
Cincinnati, Ohio, 385,457 K 3
Cincinnati, Ohio, (met. area), 1,401,491 K 3
Clarksburg, W. Va., 22,371 K 3
Clarksdale, Miss., 21,137 J 4
Clarksville, Tenn., 54,777 J 3
Cleburne, Tex., 19,218 G 4
Cleveland, Ohio, 573,822 K 2
Cleveland, Ohio (met. area), 1,898,720 K 2
Clinton, Iowa, 32,828 J 2
Clovis, N.M., 31,194 F 4
Coeur d'Alene, Idaho, 19,913 C 1
Coffeyville, Kan., 15,185 G 3
Colorado Springs, Colo., 215,150 F 3
Columbia, Mo., 62,061 H 3
Columbia (cap.), S.C., 101,208 K 4
Columbia, Tenn., 26,571 J 3
Columbus, Ga., 169,441 K 4
Columbus, Miss., 27,383 J 4
Columbus (cap.), Ohio, 564,871 K 3
Columbus, Ohio (met. area), 1,093,293 K 3
Concord (cap.), N.H., 30,400 M 2
Coos Bay, Ore., 14,424 A 2
Cordova, Alaska, 1,879 D 6
Corpus Christi, Tex., 231,999 G 5
Corsicana, Tex., 21,712 G 4
Corvallis, Ore., 40,960 B 2
Council Bluffs, Iowa, 56,449 G 2
Covington, Ky., 49,574 J 3
Cripple Creek, Colo., 655 F 3
Crookston, Minn., 8,628 G 1
Cumberland, Md., 25,933 L 3
Dallas, Tex., 904,078 G 4
Dallas-Fort Worth, Tex., (met. area), 2,974,878 G 4
Danville, Ill., 38,985 J 3
Danville, Va., 45,642 L 3
Davenport, Iowa, 103,264 H 2
Dayton, Ohio, 193,044 K 3
Dayton, Ohio (met. area), 830,070 K 3
Daytona Beach, Fla., 54,176 K 5
Decatur, Ill., 93,896 J 3
Del Rio, Tex., 30,034 F 5
Denison, Tex., 23,884 G 4
Denton, Tex., 48,063 G 4
Denver (cap.), Colo., 491,396 F 3
Denver, Colo., (met. area), 1,619,921 F 3
Des Moines (cap.), Iowa, 191,003 H 2
Detroit, Mich., 1,203,339 K 2
Detroit, Mich., (met. area), 4,227,762 K 2
Devils Lake, N.D., 7,442 G 1
Dickinson, N.D., 15,924 F 1
District of Columbia, 638,333 L 3
Dillingham, Alaska, 1,563 C 6
Dothan, Ala., 48,750 J 4
Douglas, Ariz., 13,058 E 4
Dover (cap.), Del., 23,512 L 3
Dubuque, Iowa, 62,321 H 2
Duluth, Minn., 92,811 H 1
Durango, Colo., 11,649 E 3
Durant, Okla., 11,972 G 4
Durham, N.C., 100,831 L 3
Durham-Raleigh (met. area), 530,673 L 3
Eagle, Alaska, 110 D 5
Eastport, Me., 1,982 N 2
East Saint Louis, Ill., 55,200 J 3
Eau Claire, Wis., 51,509 H 2
El Centro, Calif., 23,996 C 4
El Dorado, Ark., 25,270 H 4
Elgin, Ill., 63,668 J 2
Elkhart, Ind., 41,305 J 2
Elko, Nev., 8,758 C 2
Elmira, N.Y., 35,327 L 2
El Paso, Tex., 425,259 E 4
Ely, Nev., 4,882 D 3
Emporia, Kan., 25,287 G 3
Enid, Okla., 50,363 G 3
Erie, Pa., 119,123 K 2
Eugene, Ore., 105,624 B 2
Eureka, Calif., 24,153 B 2
Evanston, Wyo., 6,421 D 2
Evansville, Ind., 130,496 J 3
Everett, Wash., 54,413 B 1
Fairbanks, Alaska, 22,645 D 5
Fairmont, W. Va., 23,863 K 3
Fall River, Mass., 92,574 M 2
Fargo, N.D., 61,383 G 1
Faribault, Minn., 16,241 H 2
Fayetteville, Ark., 36,608 H 3
Fayetteville, N.C., 59,507 L 3
Flagstaff, Ariz., 34,743 D 3
Flint, Mich., 159,611 K 2
Flint, Mich., (met. area), 521,589 K 2
Florence, Ala., 37,029 J 4
Florence, S.C., 30,062 L 4
Fond du Lac, Wis., 35,863 J 2
Fort Collins, Colo., 65,092 E 2
Fort Dodge, Iowa, 29,423 H 2
Fort Madison, Iowa, 13,520 H 2
Fort Myers, Fla., 36,638 K 5
Fort Scott, Kan., 8,893 H 3
Fort Smith, Ark., 71,626 H 3
Fort Wayne, Ind., 172,349 J 2
Fort Worth, Tex., 385,164 G 4
Fort Worth-Arlington, Tex., (met. area), 973,138 G 4
Fort Yukon, Alaska, 619 D 5
Frankfort (cap.), Ky., 25,973 K 3
Freeport, Ill., 26,266 J 2
Fremont, Neb., 23,979 G 2
Fresno, Calif., 218,202 C 3
Fresno, Calif., (met. area), 514,621 C 3
Gadsden, Ala., 47,565 J 4
Gainesville, Fla., 81,371 K 5
Galesburg, Ill., 35,305 H 2
Gallup, N.M., 18,167 E 3
Galveston, Tex., 61,902 H 5
Garden City, Kan., 18,256 F 3
Gary, Ind., 151,953 J 2
Gary-Hammond-East Chicago, Ind., (met. area), 642,751 J 2
Gastonia, N.C., 47,333 K 3
Georgetown, S.C., 10,144 L 4
Glendale, Calif., 139,060 C 4
Globe, Ariz., 6,708 D 4
Goldfield, Nev., 500 C 3
Goldsboro, N.C., 31,871 L 3
Grand Canyon, Ariz., 1,348 D 3
Grand Forks, N.D., 43,765 G 1
Grand Island, Neb., 33,180 G 2
Grand Junction, Colo., 27,956 E 3
Grand Rapids, Mich., 181,843 K 2
Grand Rapids, Mich., (met. area), 601,680 K 2
Granger, Wyo., 177 D 2
Grants Pass, Ore., 15,032 B 2
Grass Valley, Calif., 6,697 B 3
Great Falls, Mont., 56,725 D 1
Greeley, Colo., 53,006 F 2
Green Bay, Wis., 87,899 J 2
Green River, Wyo., 12,807 E 2
Greensboro, N.C., 155,642 K 3
Greensboro-Winston-Salem-High Point, N.C., (met. area), 827,385 K 3
Greenville, Miss., 40,613 H 4
Greenville, S.C., 58,242 K 4
Greenville, S.C., (met. area), 568,758 K 4
Greenville, Tex., 22,161 G 4
Greenwood, S.C., 21,613 K 4
Gulfport, Miss., 39,676 J 4
Guthrie, Okla., 10,312 G 3
Hagerstown, Md., 34,132 L 3
Halaula, Hawaii G 5
Hamilton, Ohio, 63,189 K 3
Hana, Hawaii, 643 F 5
Hannibal, Mo., 18,811 H 3
Harlingen, Tex., 43,543 G 5
Harrisburg (cap.), Pa., 53,264 L 2
Hartford (cap.), Conn., 136,392 M 2
Hartford, Conn., (met. area), 726,114 M 2
Hastings, Neb., 23,045 G 2
Hattiesburg, Miss., 40,829 H 4
Havre, Mont., 10,891 E 1
Helena (cap.), Mont., 23,938 D 1
Hibbing, Minn., 21,193 H 1
High Point, N.C., 63,380 K 3
Hilo, Hawaii, 35,269 G 6
Hobbs, N.M., 29,153 F 4
Holualoa, Hawaii, 1,243 F 6
Honokaa, Hawaii, 1,936 G 5
Honolulu (cap.), Hawaii, 365,048 F 5
Honolulu, Hawaii (met. area), 762,565 F 5
Hoolehua, Hawaii, 1,090 F 5
Hooper Bay, Alaska, 627 C 5
Hoquiam, Wash., 9,719 B 1
Hot Springs, S.D., 4,742 F 2
Hot Springs National Park, Ark., 35,781 H 4
Houghton, Mich., 7,512 J 1
Houlton, Me., 5,730 N 1
Houston, Tex., 1,594,086 G 5
Houston, Tex., (met. area), 2,905,350 G 5
Huntington, W. Va., 63,684 K 3
Huntsville, Ala., 142,513 J 4
Huron, S.D., 13,000 G 2
Hutchinson, Kan., 40,284 G 3
Idaho Falls, Idaho, 39,734 D 2
Indianapolis (cap.), Ind., 700,807 J 3
Indianapolis, Ind., (met. area), 1,166,929 J 3
International Falls, Minn. 5,611 H 1
Iowa City, Iowa, 50,508 H 2
Jackson, Mich., 39,739 J 2
Jackson (cap.), Miss., 202,895 J 4
Jackson, Tenn., 49,131 J 3
Jacksonville, Fla., 540,898 K 4
Jacksonville, Fla., (met. area), 737,519 K 4
Jamestown, N.Y., 35,775 L 2
Jamestown, N.D., 16,280 G 1
Janesville, Wis., 51,071 J 2
Jefferson City (cap.), Mo., 33,619 H 3
Johnstown, Pa., 35,496 L 2
Joliet, Ill., 77,956 J 2
Jonesboro, Ark., 31,530 H 3
Joplin, Mo., 39,023 H 3
Juneau (cap.), Alaska, 19,528 E 6
Kahuku, Hawaii, 935 F 5
Kahului, Hawaii, 12,978 F 5
Kainaliu, Hawaii, 512 F 6
Kalamazoo, Mich., 79,722 J 2
Kalispell, Mont., 10,648 C 1
Kankakee, Ill., 30,141 J 2
Kansas City, Kan., 161,148 G 3
Kansas City, Kan., (met. area), 1,327,020 G 3
Kansas City, Mo., 448,159 H 3
Kansas City, Mo., (met. area), 1,327,020 H 3
Kapaa, Hawaii, 4,467 E 5
Keaau, Hawaii, 775 G 6
Kearney, Neb., 21,158 G 2
Kekaha, Hawaii, 3,260 E 5
Kelso, Wash., 11,129 B 1
Keokuk, Iowa, 13,536 H 2
Ketchikan, Alaska, 7,198 E 6
Key West, Fla., 24,382 K 6
Kilauea, Hawaii, 895 E 5
Klamath Falls, Ore., 16,661 B 2
Knoxville, Tenn., 175,030 K 3
Kodiak, Alaska, 4,756 D 6
Kokomo, Ind., 47,808 J 2
Koloa, Hawaii, 1,457 E 5
Kotzebue, Alaska, 2,054 C 5
La Crosse, Wis., 48,347 H 2
Lafayette, Ind., 43,011 J 2
La Grande, Ore., 11,354 C 1
La Grange, Ga., 24,204 K 4
Lahaina, Hawaii, 6,095 F 5
La Junta, Colo., 8,338 F 3
Lake Charles, La., 75,226 H 4
Lakeland, Fla., 47,406 K 5
Lanai City, Hawaii, 2,092 F 5
Lancaster, Pa., 54,725 L 2
Lander, Wyo., 7,867 E 2
Lansing (cap.), Mich., 130,414 K 2
Laramie, Wyo., 24,410 E 2
Laredo, Tex., 91,449 G 5
Las Cruces, N.M., 45,086 E 4
Las Vegas, Nev., 164,674 C 3
Las Vegas, N.M., 14,322 E 3
Laurel, Miss., 21,897 J 4
Lawrence, Kan., 52,738 G 3
Lawrence, Mass., 63,175 M 2
Lawton, Okla., 80,054 G 4
Lead, S.D., 4,330 F 2
Leadville, Colo., 3,879 E 3
Leavenworth, Kan., 33,656 G 3
Lewiston, Idaho, 27,986 C 1
Lewiston, Me., 40,481 N 2
Lexington, Ky., 204,165 K 3
Lihue, Hawaii, 4,000 E 5
Lima, Ohio, 47,827 K 2
Lincoln (cap.), Neb., 171,932 G 2
Little Rock (cap.), Ark., 158,461 H 4
Livingston, Mont., 6,994 D 1
Lodi, Calif., 35,221 B 3
Logan, Utah, 26,844 D 2
Long Beach, Calif., 361,334 C 4
Longmont, Colo., 42,942 E 2
Longview, Tex., 62,762 G 4
Longview, Wash., 31,052 B 1
Los Alamos, N.M., 11,039 E 3
Los Angeles, Calif., 2,966,763 C 4
Los Angeles-Long Beach, Calif., (met. area), 7,477,657 C 4
Louisville, Ky., 298,694 J 3
Louisville, Ky., (met. area), 905,749 J 3
Loveland, Colo., 30,215 E 2
Lowell, Mass., 92,418 M 2
Lubbock, Tex., 173,979 F 4
Lynchburg, Va., 66,743 L 3
Macon, Ga., 116,896 K 4
Madison (cap.), Wis., 170,616 H 2
Manchester, N.H., 90,936 M 2
Mandan, N.D., 15,513 F 1
Manistee, Mich., 7,665 J 2
Mankato, Minn., 28,646 H 2
Mansfield, Ohio, 53,927 K 2
Marion, Ind., 35,874 J 2
Marion, Ohio, 37,040
Marquette, Mich., 23,288
Marshall, Tex., 24,921
Marshalltown, Iowa, 26,938
Marysville, Calif., 9,898
Mason City, Iowa, 30,144
McAlester, Okla., 17,255
McAllen, Tex., 66,281
McGrath, Alaska, 355
McKeesport, Pa., 31,012
Meadville, Pa., 15,544
Medford, Ore., 39,603
Memphis, Tenn., 646,356
Memphis, Tenn., (met. area), 912,887
Meridian, Miss., 46,577
Mesa, Ariz., 152,453
Miami, Fla., 346,865
Miami, Fla., (met. area), 1,625,979
Miami Beach, Fla., 96,298
Middlesboro, Ky., 12,251
Miles City, Mont., 9,602
Milwaukee, Wis., 636,212
Milwaukee, Wis., (met. area), 1,397,142
Minneapolis, Minn., 370,951
Minneapolis-Saint Paul, Minn. (met. area), 2,113,533
Minot, N.D., 32,843
Missoula, Mont., 33,388
Mitchell, S.D., 13,916
Moberly, Mo., 13,418
Mobile, Ala., 200,452
Modesto, Calif., 106,602
Moline, Ill., 46,278
Monroe, La., 57,597
Monterey, Calif., 27,558
Montgomery (cap.), Ala. 178,857
Montpelier, Idaho, 3,107
Montpelier (cap.), Vt., 8,241
Moorhead, Minn., 29,998
Moscow, Idaho, 16,513
Muncie, Ind., 77,216
Murray, Utah, 25,750
Muscatine, Iowa, 23,467
Muskegon, Mich., 40,823
Muskogee, Okla., 40,011
Naalehu, Hawaii, 1,168
Nampa, Idaho, 25,112
Napa, Calif., 50,879
Nashua, N.H., 67,865
Nashville (cap.), Tenn., 455,651
Nashville, Tenn., (met. area), 850,505
Natchez, Miss., 22,015
Needles, Calif., 4,120
New Albany, Ind., 37,103
Newark, N.J., 329,248
Newark, N.J., (met. area), 1,965,969
New Bedford, Mass., 98,478
New Bern, N.C., 14,557
Newburgh, N.Y., 23,438
New Castle, Pa., 33,621
New Haven, Conn., 126,109
New London, Conn., 28,842
New Orleans, La., 557,927
New Orleans, La., (met. area), 1,187,073
Newport, Ky., 21,587
Newport, R.I., 29,259
Newport News, Va., 144,903
Newton, Iowa, 15,292
New York, N.Y., 7,071,030
New York, N.Y., (met. area), 9,119,737
Niagara Falls, N.Y., 71,384
Nogales, Ariz., 15,683
Nome, Alaska, 2,301
Norfolk, Neb., 19,449
Norfolk, Va., 266,979
Norfolk-Virginia Beach-Portsmouth, Va., (met. area), 806,951
North Platte, Neb., 24,509
Oakland, Calif., 339,288
Oak Ridge, Tenn., 27,662
Ogden, Utah, 64,407
Ogdensburg, N.Y., 12,375
Oil City, Pa., 13,881
Oklahoma City (cap.), Okla., 403,136
Oklahoma City, Okla., (met. area), 834,088
Okmulgee, Okla., 16,263
Olympia (cap.), Wash., 27,447
Omaha, Neb., 313,911
Omaha, Neb., (met. area), 569,614

Oregon City, Ore., 14,673 . . . B 1
Orlando, Fla., 128,291 . . . K 5
Orlando, Fla., (met. area), 700,699 . . . K 5
Oshkosh, Wis., 49,620 . . . J 2
Oskaloosa, Iowa, 10,989 . . . H 2
Oswego, N.Y., 19,793 . . . L 2
Ottumwa, Iowa, 27,381 . . . H 2
Owensboro, Ky., 54,450 . . . J 3
Paducah, Ky., 29,315 . . . J 3
Pahala, Hawaii, 1,619 . . . G 6
Palestine, Tex., 15,948 . . . H 4
Palm Beach, Fla., 9,729 . . . L 5
Palmer, Alaska, 2,141 . . . D 5
Palm Springs, Calif., 32,359 . . . C 4
Palo Alto, Calif., 55,225 . . . B 3
Pampa, Tex., 21,396 . . . F 3
Panama City, Fla., 33,346 . . . K 4
Papaikou, Hawaii, 1,567 . . . G 6
Paris, Tex., 25,498 . . . G 4
Parkersburg, W. Va., 39,967 . . . K 3
Parsons, Kan., 12,898 . . . G 3
Pasadena, Calif., 118,072 . . . C 4
Paterson, N.J., 137,970 . . . M 2
Pendleton, Ore., 14,521 . . . C 1
Pensacola, Fla., 57,619 . . . J 4
Peoria, Ill., 124,160 . . . J 2
Petersburg, Alaska, 2,821 . . . E 6
Petersburg, Va., 41,055 . . . L 3
Phenix City, Ala., 26,928 . . . J 4
Philadelphia, Pa., 1,688,210 . . . M 2
Philadelphia, Pa., (met. area), 4,716,818 . . . M 2
Phoenix (cap.), Ariz., 789,704 . . . D 4
Phoenix, Ariz., (met. area), 1,508,030 . . . D 4
Pierre (cap.), S.D., 11,973 . . . F 2
Pine Bluff, Ark., 56,636 . . . H 4
Pittsburgh, Pa., 423,959 . . . L 2
Pittsburgh, Pa., (met. area), 2,263,894 . . . L 2
Pittsfield, Mass., 51,974 . . . M 2
Pocatello, Idaho, 46,340 . . . D 2
Point Hope, Alaska, 464 . . . C 5
Pomona, Calif., 92,742 . . . C 4
Ponca City, Okla., 26,238 . . . G 3
Pontiac, Mich., 76,715 . . . K 2
Portales, N.M., 9,940 . . . F 4
Port Angeles, Wash., 17,311 . . . B 1
Port Arthur, Tex., 61,251 . . . H 5
Port Huron, Mich., 33,981 . . . K 2
Portland, Me., 61,572 . . . N 2
Portland, Ore., 366,383 . . . B 1
Portland, Ore., (met. area), 1,242,594 . . . B 1
Portsmouth, N.H., 26,254 . . . N 2
Portsmouth, Ohio, 25,943 . . . K 3
Portsmouth, Va., 104,577 . . . L 3
Prescott, Ariz., 20,055 . . . D 4
Price, Utah, 9,086 . . . D 3
Providence (cap.), R.I., 156,804 . . . M 2
Providence-Pawtucket-Warwick (met. area), 919,216 . . . M 2
Provo, Utah, 74,108 . . . D 2
Pueblo, Colo., 101,686 . . . F 3
Puyallup, Wash., 18,251 . . . B 1
Quincy, Ill., 42,554 . . . H 3
Racine, Wis., 85,725 . . . J 2
Raleigh (cap.), N.C., 150,255 . . . L 3
Rapid City, S.D., 46,492 . . . F 2
Raton, N.M., 8,225 . . . F 3
Rawlins, Wyo., 11,547 . . . E 2
Reading, Pa., 78,686 . . . L 2
Redding, Calif., 41,995 . . . B 2
Reno, Nev., 100,756 . . . C 3
Richland, Wash., 33,578 . . . B 1
Richmond (cap.), Va., 219,214 . . . L 3
Richmond, Va., (met. area), 632,015 . . . L 3
Riverside, Calif., 170,876 . . . C 4
Roanoke, Va., 100,220 . . . K 3
Rochester, Minn., 57,890 . . . H 2
Rochester, N.Y., 241,741 . . . L 2
Rochester, N.Y., (met. area), 971,879 . . . L 2
Rockford, Ill., 139,712 . . . J 2
Rock Hill, S.C., 35,344 . . . K 4
Rock Island, Ill., 46,928 . . . J 2
Rock Springs, Wyo., 19,458 . . . E 2
Rocky Mount, N.C., 41,283 . . . L 3
Rome, Ga., 29,654 . . . K 4
Rome, N.Y., 43,826 . . . M 2
Roswell, N.M., 39,676 . . . E 4
Rumford, Me., 6,256 . . . M 2
Rutland, Vt., 18,436 . . . M 2
Sacramento (cap.), Calif., 275,741 . . . B 3
Sacramento, Calif., (met. area), 1,014,002 . . . B 3
Saginaw, Mich., 77,508 . . . K 2
Saint Augustine, Fla., 11,985 . . . K 5
Saint Cloud, Minn., 42,566 . . . H 1
Saint George, Utah, 11,350 . . . D 3
Saint Joseph, Mo., 76,691 . . . H 3
Saint Louis, Mo., 453,085 . . . H 3
Saint Louis, Mo., (met. area), 2,355,276 . . . H 3
Saint Paul (cap.), Minn., 270,230 . . . H 1
Saint Petersburg, Fla., 238,647 . . . K 5
Salem (cap.), Ore., 89,233 . . . B 1
Salina, Kan., 41,843 . . . G 3
Salinas, Calif., 80,479 . . . B 3
Salmon, Idaho, 3,308 . . . D 1
Salt Lake City (cap.), Utah, 163,033 . . . D 2
Salt Lake City, Utah, (met. area), 936,255 . . . D 2
San Angelo, Tex., 73,240 . . . F 4
San Antonio, Tex., 785,410 . . . G 5
San Antonio, Tex., (met. area), 1,071,954 . . . G 5
San Bernardino, Calif., 118,794 . . . C 4
San Bernardino-Riverside-Ontario, Calif., (met. area), 1,558,182 . . . C 4
San Diego, Calif., 875,504 . . . C 4
San Diego, Calif., (met. area), 1,861,846 . . . C 4
Sandusky, Ohio, 31,360 . . . K 2
Sanford, Fla., 23,176 . . . K 5
San Francisco, Calif., 678,974 . . . B 3
San Francisco-Oakland, Calif., (met. area), 3,252,721 . . . B 3
San Jose, Calif., 636,550 . . . B 3
San Jose, Calif., (met. area), 1,295,071 . . . B 3
San Luis Obispo, Calif., 34,252 . . . B 3
Santa Ana, Calif., 203,713 . . . C 4
Santa Ana-Anaheim-Garden Grove, Calif., (met. area), 1,932,709 . . . C 4
Santa Barbara, Calif., 74,414 . . . C 4
Santa Fe (cap.), N.M., 48,953 . . . E 3
Santa Monica, Calif., (met. area), 88,314 . . . C 4
Santa Rosa, Calif., 83,320 . . . B 3
Sault Sainte Marie, Mich., 14,448 . . . J 1
Savannah, Ga., 141,390 . . . K 4
Schenectady, N.Y., 67,972 . . . M 2
Scottsbluff, Neb., 14,156 . . . F 2
Scranton, Pa., 88,117 . . . L 2
Scranton, Pa., (met. area), 640,396 . . . L 2
Seattle, Wash., 493,846 . . . B 1
Seattle-Everett, Wash., (met. area), 1,606,765 . . . B 1
Sedalia, Mo., 20,927 . . . H 3
Selma, Ala., 26,684 . . . J 4
Seward, Alaska, 1,843 . . . D 6
Shawnee, Okla., 26,506 . . . G 3
Sheboygan, Wis., 48,085 . . . J 2
Sheridan, Wyo., 15,146 . . . E 2
Sherman, Tex., 30,413 . . . G 4
Shreveport, La., 205,820 . . . H 4
Silver City, N.M., 9,887 . . . E 4
Sioux City, Iowa, 82,003 . . . G 2
Sioux Falls, S.D., 81,343 . . . G 2
Sitka, Alaska, 7,803 . . . D 6
Socorro, N.M., 7,173 . . . E 4
South Bend, Ind., 109,727 . . . J 2
Sparks, Nev., 40,780 . . . C 3
Spartanburg, S.C., 43,968 . . . K 4
Spokane, Wash., 171,300 . . . C 1
Springfield (cap.), Ill., 100,054 . . . H 3
Springfield, Mass., 152,319 . . . M 2
Springfield-Chicopee-Holyoke, Mass., (met. area), 530,668 . . . M 2
Springfield, Mo., 133,116 . . . H 3
Springfield, Ohio, 72,563 . . . K 2
Sterling, Colo., 11,385 . . . F 2
Steubenville, Ohio, 26,400 . . . K 2
Stockton, Calif., 149,779 . . . B 3
Superior, Wis., 29,571 . . . H 1
Sweetwater, Tex., 12,242 . . . F 4
Syracuse, N.Y., 170,105 . . . L 2
Syracuse, N.Y., (met. area), 642,375 . . . L 2
Tacoma, Wash., 158,501 . . . B 1
Tallahassee (cap.), Fla., 81,548 . . . K 4
Tampa, Fla., 271,523 . . . K 5
Tampa-Saint Petersburg (met. area), 1,569,492 . . . K 5
Tanacross, Alaska, 117 . . . D 6
Tanana, Alaska, 388 . . . D 5
Taylor, Tex., 10,619 . . . G 4
Temple, Tex., 42,354 . . . G 4
Terre Haute, Ind., 61,125 . . . J 3
Terrell, Tex., 13,269 . . . G 4
Texarkana, Ark., 21,459 . . . H 4
Texarkana, Tex., 31,271 . . . H 4
The Dalles, Ore., 10,820 . . . B 1
Thomasville, Ga., 18,463 . . . K 4
Toledo, Ohio, 354,635 . . . K 2
Toledo, Ohio (met. area), 791,599 . . . K 2
Tonopah, Nev., 1,952 . . . C 3
Tooele, Utah, 14,335 . . . D 2
Topeka (cap.), Kan., 115,266 . . . G 3
Traverse City, Mich., 15,516 . . . K 2
Trenton (cap.), N.J., 92,124 . . . M 2
Trinidad, Colo., 9,663 . . . F 3
Troy, N.Y., 56,638 . . . M 2
Tucson, Ariz., 330,537 . . . D 4
Tucson, Ariz., (met. area), 531,263 . . . D 4
Tucumcari, N.M., 6,765 . . . F 3
Tulsa, Okla., 360,919 . . . G 3
Tulsa, Okla., (met. area), 689,434 . . . G 3
Tuscaloosa, Ala., 75,211 . . . J 4
Twin Falls, Idaho, 26,209 . . . C 2
Tyler, Tex., 70,508 . . . H 4
Unalakleet, Alaska, 623 . . . C 5
Unalaska, Alaska, 1,322 . . . C 6
University City, Mo., 42,738 . . . H 3
Utica, N.Y., 75,632 . . . M 2
Valdosta, Ga., 37,596 . . . K 4
Vallejo, Calif., 80,303 . . . B 3
Vancouver, Wash., 42,834 . . . B 1
Vicksburg, Miss., 25,434 . . . H 4
Victoria, Tex., 50,695 . . . G 5
Virginia, Minn., 11,056 . . . H 1
Visalia, Calif., 49,729 . . . C 3
Waco, Tex., 101,261 . . . G 4
Wahiawa, Hawaii, 16,911 . . . F 5
Wahpeton, N.D., 9,064 . . . G 1
Waialua, Hawaii, 30 . . . F 5
Wailuku, Hawaii, 10,260 . . . F 5
Waipahu, Hawaii, 29,139 . . . F 5
Wales, Alaska, 133 . . . C 5
Walla Walla, Wash., 25,618 . . . C 1
Washington, D.C. (cap.), U.S., 638,333 . . . L 3
Waterbury, Conn., 103,266 . . . M 2
Waterloo, Iowa, 75,985 . . . H 2
Watertown, N.Y., 27,861 . . . M 2
Watertown, S.D., 15,649 . . . G 1
Waterville, Me., 17,779 . . . N 2
Wausau, Wis., 32,426 . . . J 2
Waycross, Ga., 19,371 . . . K 4
Wenatchee, Wash., 17,257 . . . B 1
West Palm Beach, Fla., 63,305 . . . K 5
Wheeling, W. Va., 43,070 . . . K 2
Wichita, Kan., 279,835 . . . G 3
Wichita Falls, Tex., 94,201 . . . G 4
Wilkes-Barre, Pa., 51,551 . . . L 2
Williamsport, Pa., 33,401 . . . L 2
Williston, N.D., 13,336 . . . F 1
Wilmington, Del., 70,195 . . . L 3
Wilmington, Del., (met. area), 523,221 . . . L 3
Wilmington, N.C., 44,000 . . . L 4
Winnemucca, Nev., 4,140 . . . C 2
Winona, Minn., 25,075 . . . H 2
Winston-Salem, N.C., 131,885 . . . K 3
Worcester, Mass., 161,799 . . . M 2
Yakima, Wash., 49,826 . . . B 1
Yakutat, Alaska, 449 . . . D 6
Yankton, S.D., 12,011 . . . G 2
York, Pa., 44,619 . . . L 3
Youngstown, Ohio, 115,436 . . . K 2
Youngstown-Warren, Ohio (met. area), 531,350 . . . K 2
Yreka, Calif., 5,916 . . . B 2
Yuma, Ariz., 42,433 . . . D 4
Zanesville, Ohio, 28,655 . . . K 3

OTHER FEATURES

Abert (lake), Ore. . . . C 2
Alabama (riv.), Ala. . . . J 4
Alaska (gulf), Alaska . . . D 6
Alaska (pen.), Alaska . . . C 6
Alaska (range), Alaska . . . C 6
Alava (cape), Wash. . . . A 1
Albemarle (sound), N.C. . . . L 3
Aleutian (isls.), Alaska . . . D 6
Altamaha (riv.), Ga. . . . K 4
Amchitka (isl.), Alaska . . . D 6
American Falls (res.), Idaho . . . D 2
Apalachee (bay), Fla. . . . K 5
Appalachian (mts.) . . . K 3
Arena (pt.), Calif. . . . B 3
Arkansas (riv.) . . . H 3
Atka (isl.), Alaska . . . D 6
Attu (isl.), Alaska . . . D 6
Barkley (lake) . . . J 3
Belle Fourche (riv.) . . . F 2
Bering (sea), Alaska . . . C 6
Bering (str.), Alaska . . . C 5
Bighorn (riv.) . . . E 2
Big Sioux (riv.), S.D. . . . G 2
Bitterroot (range) . . . D 1
Black Hills (mts.) . . . F 2
Blanca (peak), Colo. . . . F 3
Blanco (cape), Ore. . . . A 2
Borah (peak), Idaho . . . D 2
Brazos (riv.), Tex. . . . G 4
Bristol (bay), Alaska . . . C 6
Brooks (range), Alaska . . . C 5
Canadian (riv.) . . . F 3
Canaveral (cape), Fla. . . . L 5
Cape Fear (riv.), N.C. . . . L 4
Carson Sink (depr.), Nev. . . . C 3
Cascade (range) . . . B 1
Cedar (riv.), Iowa . . . H 2
Champlain (lake) . . . M 2
Charles (cape), Va. . . . L 3
Charlotte (harb.), Fla. . . . K 5
Chattahoochee (riv.) . . . K 4
Chelan (lake), Wash. . . . B 1
Chesapeake (bay) . . . L 3
Cheyenne (riv.) . . . F 2
Chichagof (isl.) Alaska . . . D 6
Chickamauga (lake), Tenn. . . . J 3
Chippewa (riv.), Wis. . . . H 1
Cimarron (riv.) . . . G 3
Clark Fork (riv.), Mont. . . . D 1
Clear (lake), Calif. . . . B 3
Coast (ranges) . . . B 2
Cod (cape), Mass. . . . N 2
Colorado (riv.) . . . D 4
Colorado (riv.), Tex. . . . G 4
Columbia (riv.) . . . B 1
Colville (riv.), Alaska . . . C 5
Conception (pt.), Calif. . . . B 4
Conchas (res.), N.M. . . . F 3
Connecticut (riv.) . . . M 2
Corpus Christi (bay), Tex. . . . G 5
Cumberland (riv.) . . . J 3
Death Valley (depr.), Calif. . . . C 3
Delaware (bay) . . . M 3
Des Moines (riv.) . . . H 2
Disappointment (cape), Wash. . . . A 1
Elbert (mt.), Colo. . . . E 3
Elephant Butte (res.), N.M. . . . E 4
Erie (lake) . . . K 2
Everglades, The (swamp), Fla. . . . K 5
Falcon (res.), Tex. . . . G 5
Fear (cape), N.C. . . . L 4
Flathead (lake), Mont. . . . D 1
Flattery (cape), Wash. . . . A 1
Flint (riv.), Ga. . . . K 4
Florida (bay), Fla. . . . K 6
Florida (keys), Fla. . . . K 6
Florida (strs.), Fla. . . . K 6
Fort Peck (res.), Mont. . . . E 1
Francis Case (lake), S.D. . . . F 2
French Frigate (shoal), Hawaii . . . F 6
Frenchman (riv.), Mont. . . . E 1
Galveston (bay), Tex. . . . H 5
Gannett (peak), Wyo. . . . D 2
Gardner Pinnacles (isls.), Hawaii . . . F 6
Gila (riv.) . . . D 4
Glacier Nat'l Park, Mont. . . . D 1
Golden Gate (chan.), Calif. . . . B 3
Goose (lake) . . . B 2
Grand (lake), La. . . . H 4
Grand Canyon Nat'l Park, Ariz. . . . D 3
Great Salt (lake), Utah . . . D 2
Green (bay) . . . J 1
Green (riv.) . . . D 3
Harney (lake), Ore. . . . C 2
Hatteras (cape), N.C. . . . M 3
Havasu (lake) . . . D 4
Hawaii (isl.), Hawaii . . . F 6
Humboldt (riv.), Nev. . . . C 2
Huron (lake), Mich. . . . K 2
Iliamna (lake), Alaska . . . C 6
Illinois (riv.), Ill. . . . H 2
Iowa (riv.), Iowa . . . H 2
Jackson (lake), Wyo. . . . E 2
James (riv.) . . . G 2
Juan de Fuca (str.), Wash. . . . A 1
Kahoolawe (isl.), Hawaii . . . F 5
Kansas (riv.), Kan. . . . G 3
Kauai (isl.), Hawaii . . . E 5
Kaula (isl.), Hawaii . . . F 6
Kennedy (cape), Fla. . . . L 5
Kentucky (lake) . . . J 3
Kiska (isl.), Alaska . . . D 6
Klamath (riv.), Calif. . . . B 2
Kobuk (riv.), Alaska . . . C 5
Koyukuk (riv.), Alaska . . . C 5
Kuskokwim (riv.), Alaska . . . C 6
Lanai (isl.), Hawaii . . . F 5
Laysan (isl.), Hawaii . . . E 6
Leech (lake), Minn. . . . G 1
Lisianski (isl.), Hawaii . . . E 6
Little Colorado (riv.), Ariz. . . . D 3
Little Missouri (riv.) . . . F 1
Lloyd (res.), Ga. . . . K 4
Long (isl.), N.Y. . . . M 2
Lookout (cape), N.C. . . . L 4
Lookout (cape), Ore. . . . B 1
Madre (lag.), Tex. . . . G 5
Malheur (lake), Ore. . . . C 2
Marias (riv.), Mont. . . . D 1
Marion (lake), S.C. . . . K 4
Maro (reef), Hawaii . . . F 6
Martha's Vineyard (isl.), Mass. . . . N 2
Matagorda (bay), Tex. . . . G 5
Maui (isl.), Hawaii . . . F 5
Mauna Kea (mt.), Hawaii . . . G 6
Mauna Loa (mt.), Hawaii . . . G 6
May (cape), N.J. . . . M 3
McKinley (mt.), Alaska . . . D 5
McMillan (lake), N.M. . . . F 4
Mead (lake) . . . D 3
Mendocino (cape), Calif. . . . A 2
Mexico (gulf) . . . J 5
Michigan (lake) . . . J 2
Midway (isls.) . . . E 6
Milk (riv.), Mont. . . . D 1
Mille Lacs (lake), Minn. . . . H 1
Minnesota (riv.), Minn. . . . G 2
Mississippi (riv.) . . . H 4
Mississippi (delta), La. . . . J 5
Missouri (riv.) . . . H 3
Mitchell (lake), Ala. . . . J 4
Mitchell (mt.), N.C. . . . K 3
Mobile (bay), Ala. . . . J 5
Molokai (isl.), Hawaii . . . F 5
Mono (lake), Calif. . . . C 3
Monterey (bay), Calif. . . . B 3
Moultrie (lake), S.C. . . . K 4
Murray (lake), S.C. . . . K 4
Musselshell (riv.) . . . E 1
Nantucket (isl.), Mass. . . . N 2
Necker (isl.), Hawaii . . . F 6
Neosho (riv.) . . . G 3
Nihoa (isl.), Hawaii . . . F 6
Niihau (isl.), Hawaii . . . E 5
Niobrara (riv.), Neb. . . . F 2
Norris (lake), Tenn. . . . K 3
North Canadian (riv.) . . . G 3
North Platte (riv.) . . . F 2
Norton (sound), Alaska . . . C 5
Nueces (riv.), Tex. . . . G 5
Nunivak (isl.), Alaska . . . C 6
Oahe (lake), S.D. . . . F 1
Oahu (isl.), Hawaii . . . F 5
Ohio (riv.) . . . J 3
Okeechobee (lake), Fla. . . . K 5
Olympic Nat'l Park, Wash. . . . A 1
Ontario (lake), N.Y. . . . L 2
Osage (riv.) . . . H 3
Ouachita (riv.) . . . H 4
Owens (lake), Calif. . . . C 3
Owyhee (riv.) . . . C 2
Ozark (mts.) . . . H 3
Padre (isl.), Tex. . . . G 5
Pamlico (sound), N.C. . . . L 3
Pathfinder (res.), Wyo. . . . E 2
Pearl (riv.) . . . J 4
Pearl (harb.), Hawaii . . . F 5
Pearl and Hermes (reef), Hawaii . . . E 5
Pecos (riv.) . . . F 4
Pend Oreille (lake), Idaho . . . C 1
Pikes (peak), Colo. . . . E 3
Platte (riv.), Neb. . . . G 2
Pontchartrain (lake), La. . . . J 5
Potomac (riv.) . . . L 3
Powder (riv.) . . . E 2
Powell (lake) . . . D 3
Pribilof (isls.), Alaska . . . C 6
Rainier (mt.), Wash. . . . B 1
Rainy (lake), Minn. . . . H 1
Rainy (riv.), Minn. . . . H 1
Red (riv.) . . . H 4
Red (lake), Minn. . . . H 1
Red Bluff (lake), Tex. . . . F 4
Red River of the North (riv.) . . . G 1
Republican (riv.) . . . F 2
Rio Grande (riv.) . . . F 5
Roanoke (riv.) . . . L 3
Rocky (mts.) . . . E 3
Roosevelt (res.), Ariz. . . . D 4
Royale (isl.), Mich. . . . J 1
Sabine (riv.) . . . H 4
Sable (cape), Fla. . . . K 5
Sacramento (riv.), Calif. . . . B 3
Saginaw (bay), Mich. . . . K 2
Saint Clair (lake), Mich. . . . K 2
Saint Croix (riv.) . . . H 1
Saint Elias (mt.), Alaska . . . D 5
Saint John (riv.), Me. . . . N 1
Saint Lawrence (riv.), N.Y. . . . N 2
Saint Matthew (isl.), Alaska . . . C 5
Sakakawea (lake), N.D. . . . F 1
Salmon (riv.), Idaho . . . C 1
Salt (riv.), Ariz. . . . D 4
Salton Sea (lake), Calif. . . . C 4
San Carlos (lake), Ariz. . . . E 4
San Joaquin (riv.), Calif. . . . C 3
San Juan (riv.) . . . E 3
San Pedro (riv.), Ariz. . . . D 4
Santa Barbara (isls.), Calif. . . . C 4
Santee (riv.), S.C. . . . L 4
Sardis (lake), Miss. . . . J 4
Savannah (riv.) . . . K 4
Seminoe (res.), Wyo. . . . E 2
Sevier (lake), Utah . . . D 3
Sevier (riv.), Utah . . . D 3
Shasta (mt.), Calif. . . . B 2
Shasta (res.), Calif. . . . B 2
Sheynne (riv.), N.D. . . . G 1
Sierra Nevada (mts.) . . . B 3
Smoky Hill (riv.) . . . G 3
Snake (riv.) . . . C 1
Souris (riv.), N.D. . . . F 1
South Platte (riv.) . . . F 2
Summer (lake), Ore. . . . C 2
Superior (lake) . . . J 1
Tahoe (lake) . . . C 3
Tampa (bay), Fla. . . . K 5
Tanana (riv.), Alaska . . . D 5
Tennessee (riv.) . . . J 3
Ten Thousand (isls.), Fla. . . . K 5
Texoma (lake) . . . G 4
Tombigbee (riv.) . . . J 4
Trinity (riv.), Tex. . . . G 4
Tulare (lake), Calif. . . . B 3
Unimak (isl.), Alaska . . . C 6
Upper Klamath (lake), Ore. . . . B 2
Utah (lake), Utah . . . D 2
Verde (riv.), Ariz. . . . D 4
Vermilion (lake), Minn. . . . H 1
Wabash (riv.) . . . J 3
Walker (lake), Nev. . . . C 3
Wheeler (lake), Ala. . . . J 4
Wheeler (peak), N.M. . . . F 3
White (riv.), Ark. . . . H 3
Whitney (mt.), Calif. . . . C 3
Wilson (mt.), Colo. . . . E 3
Winnemucca (lake), Nev. . . . C 2
Wisconsin (riv.), Wis. . . . H 2
Woods (lake), Minn. . . . G 1
Yazoo (riv.), Miss. . . . H 4
Yellowstone (riv.) . . . E 1
Yellowstone (lake), Wyo. . . . E 2
Yellowstone Nat'l Park, Wyo. . . . E 2
Yosemite Nat'l Park, Calif. . . . C 3
Yukon (riv.), Alaska . . . C 5

This version of the signing of the United States Constitution is from a mural painted by Albert Herter. The mural is located in the Wisconsin State Capitol in Madison.

UNITED STATES CONSTITUTION

UNITED STATES CONSTITUTION. Many people think of the United States as a young country. Yet it has the oldest written constitution among the major nations of the world.

Soon after the 3 million people who lived in the United States had won the Revolutionary War, various groups among them became discontented with the Articles of Confederation (*see* Articles of Confederation). The government under the Confederation seemed too weak to control the people at home or to make the new republic respected abroad. One difficulty was that Congress lacked sufficient power to raise money: it could only make requests of the states. It was always poor, while generous states such as New York and Pennsylvania complained that they paid more than their share. Congress also had no authority to regulate commerce. When some of the states began laying tariffs and other burdens on the shipping trade of their neighbors, it caused heavy losses.

All states were supposed to abide by the Articles of Confederation; yet some states violated them. They made treaties with the Indians and agreements with each other. They ignored foreign treaties made by Congress and regulated the value of money.

Need for a Stronger Government

By 1785 it seemed to many patriotic citizens that the Confederation was a failure. Washington, Hamilton, Jay, Madison, and other leaders repeatedly declared that the government ought to be strengthened. In 1782 the assembly of New York, and in 1785 the legislature of Massachusetts, voted in favor of a constitutional convention.

Some Americans had special reasons for wanting a stronger government. One group was made up of the Westerners, who after the American Revolution moved into Kentucky, Tennessee, and the new Northwest Territory. They wanted a powerful federal government to protect them from the Indians, Spaniards, and British. Others who speculated in western lands believed that a strong government would make these lands more valuable. Another group consisted of merchants, traders, and shipowners who suffered from tariff wars among the states and from injurious British laws. Other men, who had lent money to the government during the war or just after it, felt a stronger government would be more likely to repay them.

Perhaps the most important group was made up of well-to-do men who owned mortgages and notes. They feared that state legislatures controlled by poor debtors would issue huge sums of worthless paper money or would protect debtors who refused to pay their debts. They wanted a strong national government to take complete control of the currency and to prevent any state laws impairing the obligation of contracts. In 1786 the money issue flared into riots in Vermont and New Hampshire and caused Shays's Rebellion in Massachusetts (*see* Shays's Rebellion).

Pre-Convention Activity

The convention that wrote the Constitution was prepared for by a number of small steps. The first was a meeting in 1785 between representatives of Virginia and Maryland, called the Alexandria Conference, to settle disputes over the navigation of the Potomac River. Washington and Madison took

194

the lead in having this meeting called. It proved so successful that Maryland went a step further and proposed that Pennsylvania, Delaware, Maryland, and Virginia should all appoint commissioners to meet and adopt a uniform commercial system. The shrewd Madison saw the opportunity of doing something still more important. He proposed a convention not of four states, but of all the states, to discuss the commercial conditions of the time and to devise an amendment to the Articles of Confederation. This convention was to meet in Annapolis in 1786.

When the time came only five states sent representatives to the convention in Annapolis, and their opinions were far from harmonious. But Madison and Hamilton were both present and looking toward the future. They persuaded the representatives before adjourning to issue a call for a general convention of all the states to meet in Philadelphia on the second Monday of May 1787. This was to be the Constitutional Convention. But because many people were suspicious of any such action, the call had to be made cautiously. It proposed that the gathering should "take into consideration the situation of the United States," and devise improvements in the government. Congress, after some hesitation, finally endorsed the plan, declaring that the states should send delegates for the sole and express purpose of revising the Articles of Confederation.

The plan for the convention had the warm support of Washington, Franklin, and other eminent men. Virginia was the first state to choose delegates, and contributed greatly to the success of the undertaking by selecting Washington. Before the date set, 11 states had named their delegates. New Hampshire did not send its members until the work was well begun. Rhode Island refused to send any at all. The legislatures, not the people, chose the delegates.

A Notable Assembly

The convention was not a large gathering, for only 55 men, from first to last, attended. But it was a body of very remarkable ability. Any American who, in the summer of 1787, happened to be in the city of Philadelphia, with its broad leafy streets and red brick buildings, would have seen such a collection of statesmen as could hardly then be matched in any other country. He would have seen Washington striding at the head of the Virginia group—James Madison, Edmund Randolph, George Mason, George Wythe, John Blair, and James McClurg. He would have noticed Benjamin Franklin talking with three of the other Pennsylvania delegates—James Wilson, who was one of the ablest lawyers in America, Robert Morris, the financial leader of the Revolution, and Gouverneur Morris.

New York contributed, along with two "States' Rights" delegates who soon withdrew, the brilliant Alexander Hamilton. From South Carolina came John Rutledge, Charles Pinckney, and C. C. Pinckney. Massachusetts sent Elbridge Gerry and Rufus King; and Connecticut sent Roger Sherman and

Oliver Ellsworth. It was a body of men well fitted to produce a great document. Many were lawyers. Most of them had had experience in government. Nearly all of them were either men of large property interests or close to men who had such interests.

Pass Rule for Secrecy

The convention opened tardily on May 25, in the brick State House in Philadelphia, where the Declaration of Independence had been signed. Washington was unanimously elected to preside, a fact which prevented him from taking active part in the debates. Three principal rules were adopted. The votes were to be taken by states, each state having one vote; seven states were to constitute a quorum; and strict secrecy was to be preserved. The delegates wished to be safe from outside criticism or pressure. The official journal kept was the merest record of motions and votes, and was not published till 1819.

These rules having been adopted, the delegates turned to a task upon which there was no general agreement. The overshadowing question was whether they should merely revise the Articles of Confederation, or should make a new constitution. Most delegates had been elected upon the understanding that they were merely to revise the existing government, and some had specific instructions to that effect. But Washington advised against "temporizing expedients." Within a week the convention resolved in committee of the whole that "a national government ought to be established consisting of a supreme legislative, executive, and judiciary," and such leaders as Madison and Hamilton calmly assumed that this meant a complete new constitution.

This done, the convention faced two problems which loomed up above all others. If a strong federal government was established, how was it to be given authority? Was it to be permitted to coerce the different states? If so, just how? In the second place, how was power to be adjusted between the large states, like Pennsylvania, and the small states, like Delaware? As the work progressed, other questions arose and had to be settled by a process of give and take. The Constitution in its final form was a bundle of compromises, but the great compromise was that between the large and the small states.

Two important plans shortly came before the convention. One was the so-called Virginia plan. Largely the work of Madison, it was presented to the convention by Edmund Randolph. The other was the New Jersey plan, a series of seven resolutions submitted by William Paterson of New Jersey. The Virginia plan represented the standpoint of the large states and involved writing an entirely new constitution; the New Jersey plan represented the ideas of the small states and was simply a set of amendments to the old Articles of Confederation.

Under the Virginia plan there was to be a national legislature, or Congress of two chambers, in which the states should be represented in proportion either to their money contributions or to their free populations. The members of the lower house were to be elected by the people and were to choose the upper house out of lists submitted by the state legislatures. The chief executive was to be elected by the national Congress, for a single term, and there were to be a Supreme Court and a system of lower courts.

The New Jersey plan provided for a national congress of one house, each state to have a single vote. The chief executive was to be chosen by Congress, and there was to be a system of federal courts.

Still another plan was presented by Charles Pinckney; but the draft of this plan has been lost, and so historians do not agree on the extent of Pinckney's influence on the Constitution. Hamilton also offered suggestions. His "propositions" indicated a very powerful central government, with a chief executive and a senate chosen for life terms and with the states reduced to a very weak position. Of all the schemes, however, the Virginia plan was the most important.

The Constitutional Convention of 1787 met in the State House of Pennsylvania, now called Independence Hall. Earlier the building had been the home of the Continental Congress.

The Great Compromise

The debate on the Virginia and New Jersey plans revealed the dangerous jealousy between the large states, demanding representation according to population, and the small states, insisting upon equal representation. Men on each side repeatedly threatened to break up the convention and go home. The large states were the stronger and carried a resolution against equal representation in the lower house of Congress. Thereupon the Connecticut delegates brought forward a successful compromise. They proposed that the states be equally represented in the Senate and represented according to population in the lower chamber or House. After much grumbling the large states accepted this scheme.

Then followed a series of minor compromises. In computing the population of the states for representation in the lower chamber, should slaves be counted? The Southern states naturally demanded that they should, while the Northern states wished them passed over as mere property. Fortunately the Continental Congress had already provided a method of settling this dispute. In 1783 it had proposed an amendment to the Articles of Confederation by which the money requisitions upon the states were to be based upon population, with three fifths of the slaves counted. This amendment had been accepted by 11 states. It was now decided that in determining representation in the House of Representatives, five slaves should count for three free persons.

Another compromise dealt with the federal regulation of commerce. The Northern states, which had suffered from commercial chaos, wished to give Congress ample powers to regulate business activities. In the Southern states, however, farmers feared that Congress might lay an export tax upon their cotton and tobacco. The result was that Congress was given wide powers over navigation, foreign and interstate trade, and custom duties, but it was specifically forbidden to levy export duties.

Still another compromise had to do with the importation of Negroes from Africa. Though slavery was not yet a sectional issue, some Northerners would gladly have seen this cruel slave trade abolished. Moreover, Virginia and Maryland bred slaves for the market and wished to stop the African competition. When Georgia and the Carolinas protested, a compromise provided that Congress might stop the importation in 1808 but not sooner.

Little by little, as the summer wore on, a strong central government was hammered out on the forge of the convention. The now familiar features—the representatives chosen for two years and the senators for six; the president serving four years, with possible re-election; and the federal judges appointed for life—were agreed on. One striking feature of the new Constitution was the large power given to Congress over economic and financial affairs. Not only was Congress authorized to regulate commerce, but it was given the right to raise money by taxation, to borrow on the national credit, and to coin money and regulate its value. Strict provisions were inserted forbidding the states to issue paper money or to pass laws impairing the obligation of contracts. These clauses reflected the unhappy recent history of some states. The debts contracted under the Confederation were recognized as valid. The unanimity of opinion on these features was striking. There was no struggle in the convention between creditor groups and debtor groups, between representatives of the poor and of the wealthy.

The great problem of how to give the federal government proper authority was finally solved with surprising ease. This was done by providing that the new government should operate not upon the states, but directly upon the people. Its mandates were to be carried out not by orders and demands upon a set of semi-independent state governments but by the quiet activity of its own administrative officers, attorneys, marshals, and courts.

The Virginia plan, the New Jersey plan, and the Pinckney plan had all proposed some method of coercing the states. All schemes for state coercion, however, were obviously dangerous and futile. They would be sure to break down. Madison wisely saw that it would be sufficient to give the new federal government the power to proceed against individuals all over the nation. The two systems, state and federal, would for the most part operate on parallel lines. Whenever they did come into conflict, the Constitution would define their respective powers.

The Constitution Is Drafted

By September the work was nearly done. The essentials of the Constitution, based on the Virginia plan, had first been thrashed out in committee of the whole. The work of this body was reported to the convention for full debate and amendment. Then near the end of July, the draft of the Constitution was handed over to a committee on detail, which gave it many finishing touches. As a final step, Gouverneur Morris went over the completed Constitution to put it in the clearest and most precise English. On Sept. 17, 1787, it was signed by 39 members and was ready for the people to approve or reject.

At the outset it seemed doubtful whether the Constitution would be ratified by the nine states that the convention declared would suffice to make it effective. For almost a year the American people were interested in nothing so much as whether the "new roof" would be accepted. It was discussed in taverns, in shops, and on the streets. Everyone knew that most of the rich folk who owned fine houses and estates were for it; so were the professional men—most of the lawyers, doctors, and ministers; and so were nearly all the merchants. The creditors both of the state governments and of the Confederation strongly favored it. On the other hand, the poor people, the workingmen, farmers, and many backwoodsmen, were in large part suspicious of it. Such leaders as Patrick Henry and Samuel Adams, who were attached to local liberty, showed hostility because they feared an undue concentration of authority. Many people declared, and with reason, that the Constitution was faulty because it contained no guarantee of the simplest human rights—freedom of speech, of the press, of assemblage, and of worship.

Fight for Ratification

If the Federalists, as the advocates of the Constitution were called, had not used the cleverest tactics, they would have been defeated. One by one the states held conventions to debate the instrument. A favorable impression was produced when the first five conventions readily voted for ratification. Delaware came under the "new roof" on Dec. 7, 1787; Pennsylvania on December 12; New Jersey on December 18; and within the first two weeks of 1788, Georgia and Connecticut. In other states, however, hard fighting was required. In Massachusetts a majority of the delegates was at first unfriendly, and the convention wrangled for almost a month. The Federalists were led by Rufus King, Gen. Benjamin Lincoln, and others. By determined argument, by bringing special influences to bear on the influential Samuel Adams and John Hancock, and by consenting to nine suggested amendments, they finally won. The minimum number of nine states was assured when New Hampshire ratified the Constitution June 21, 1788.

Of the four remaining states, however, two were considered vital to success—Virginia and New York. In Richmond, Patrick Henry and George Mason argued against the Constitution while James Madison, John Marshall, and George Washington skillfully directed the Federalist forces. Finally, on June 25, 1788, Virginia voted for ratification by a close margin.

The hardest battle of all occurred in New York, where only the genius of Alexander Hamilton won the victory. He hit upon the happy idea of publishing in the New York newspapers a series of essays explaining and defending the Constitution. These were later issued in book form under the title 'The Federalist.' Madison and John Jay contributed some of them, but Hamilton wrote the great majority. No better exposition of the Constitution has ever been penned. When the convention met in Poughkeepsie, the Anti-Federalists had a two-thirds majority. Opposed to them were Hamilton and his able lieutenants Jay and Robert R. Livingston. Their irresistible arguments were helped by the fact that all but two other states had already ratified, and it was a question of union or disunion. On July 26, 1788, by a vote of 30 to 27, New York accepted.

The Constitution which thus became the supreme law of the land seemed then to contain marked imperfections. Later it was realized that the Convention of 1787 had done its work better than it knew.

The strength and symmetry of its handiwork have been the admiration of the world ever since and have had a profound influence in many parts of the globe. The British statesman William Gladstone paid tribute to the Constitution, though in somewhat mistaken terms, as "the most wonderful work ever struck off at a given time by the brain and purpose of man."

It is true that in some respects the makers of the Constitution miscalculated. Their greatest error, hardly avoidable because of public opinion, was their refusal to define more precisely the sphere and rights of the states, including the so-called "right of secession." This contributed later to the catastrophe of the Civil War. The careful plan for indirect election of the president by an electoral college was shortly nullified by the growth of political parties, and custom has made the electors mere nonentities. No one saw at the time what a powerful place would be occupied by the Supreme Court. Although a majority of the leading men of the convention seem to have believed that the Court would possess the right to pass upon the constitutionality of acts of Congress, there was no explicit statement to that effect.

There were also grave questions the Constitution failed to treat. It contained no provision regarding the future annexation of territory, nor did it grant clear title to the offshore areas of coastal states. Naturally, many commercial questions which arose in later generations could not have been foreseen by the authors of the Constitution. They did not expect the federal government to become as strong, at the expense of the states, as it has become. On the whole, the "fathers of the Constitution" did well.

Its Deep-Rooted Origins

One reason for the success of the Constitution lay in the fact that it was not really, as Gladstone said, "struck off at a given time," but was rather the result of generations of growth. It was a noble tree which rose from the two great taproots of English and colonial self-government. Almost everything in it can be traced back to earlier sources—the balance between the legislative, executive, and judicial departments; the special duties and powers assigned to each; the methods of operation prescribed; even such features as the electoral college, which was borrowed from Maryland. In particular, the convention profited by the work of the states in making their own constitutions. Between 1775 and 1787 every state except Rhode Island and Connecticut (which took over their colonial charters) had written at least one constitution, and some had adopted two or three. These experiments by the states furnished many lessons of profit to the men who met in Philadelphia.

Even before all the states had ratified, the machinery of the new government was put in motion. During September, Congress fixed the dates for the choice of presidential electors, the election of the president, and the inauguration of the machinery of administration. Although there was some delay, it was not serious. On Feb. 4, 1789, Washington was elected president. On April 30 he took the oath of office, and the government was in running order. Soon afterward North Carolina and Rhode Island, the two laggard states, ratified the Constitution, and the circle of the original 13 colonies was completed.

No constitution can long exist without change and growth. Some of the most important alterations in the American Constitution have taken place quietly and without the adding or dropping of a single phrase. They were changes in custom and interpretation. Other changes were made by formal amendment for which the Constitution provides several different methods. The government had hardly been launched before the first ten amendments were adopted.

The Bill of Rights

These first ten amendments form the so-called Bill of Rights. The makers of the Constitution had considered it unnecessary to forbid some of the elementary invasions of personal liberty and property rights. Many of the people, however, wanted just such reassurances. They remembered the long struggle in England to secure these rights and the difficulty in America of protecting them against the crown and the royal governors. Virginia and other states, in ratifying the Constitution, made it plain that they expected a bill of rights to be added, and Madison led the movement in the first Congress.

Twelve amendments were proposed and all but the first two were ratified in time to go into effect on Dec. 15, 1791. They provided for freedom of speech, of the press, and of worship; for the right of the states to establish militia; for the security of people in their homes against unreasonable search and seizure; and for trial by jury. Some of these amendments were destined to be important. Particularly so was the tenth amendment, declaring that powers not delegated to the United States or prohibited to the states should be reserved to the states or to the people. (*See also* Bill of Rights.)

The next two amendments, made within ten years, furnished a remedy for defects which experience had brought to light. In 1793 the Supreme Court had held that a citizen of one state could sue another state in the federal courts. This shocked everyone who held strong states' rights views, for it seemed a violation of state sovereignty. In 1798 the 11th amendment was adopted, declaring that no citizen of a state and no foreigner could bring a state government into the federal courts to be sued. The 12th amendment met a much more serious flaw in the Constitution. It had been provided that the presidential electors should meet in their respective states and vote for two persons, and that the one having the most votes (if a majority) should be president, and the one with the second largest number should be vice-president. This led in 1800 to a tie between Jefferson and Burr, both Democrats, for the presidency, though everyone had understood that Jefferson was to be president and Burr vice-president. The 12th amendment, ratified in 1804, therefore provided that the

The National Archives was created in 1934 to select and preserve the Constitution and other valuable documents of the federal government. The building stands on Constitution Avenue in Washington, D.C. It was designed by John R. Pope.

electors should vote for president on one ballot, and for vice-president on another.

Amendments After the Civil War

Until 1865 the country functioned well with these 12 amendments. The end of the Civil War, however, made it necessary for the United States to deal with a group of questions about slavery and black Americans. The blacks' freedom had to be assured. Their rights as citizens had to be guaranteed. Many Northerners believed that blacks should be given the vote. The result was the ratification of three amendments that defined the place of the black freedmen in national life. The first, the 13th amendment, declared simply that neither slavery nor involuntary servitude, except as punishment for a crime, should ever exist in the United States. The South, except for the state of Mississippi, ratified the amendment, and it was proclaimed on Dec. 18, 1865.

The 14th amendment—the so-called civil rights amendment—was much more complicated, and was accepted with far greater reluctance. Many Northerners feared that despite the abolition of slavery blacks would soon be reduced to their former position—to serfdom or peonage. This fear increased when several Southern states passed laws that greatly restricted the rights of blacks. Congress therefore drafted an amendment that declared that no state should abridge the rights of any citizen of the United States, or "deprive any person of life, liberty, or property without due process of law," or deny any person the equal protection of the laws. In short, the amendment was intended to make sure that black citizens would have the same civil rights as white citizens. This amendment, which also excluded certain supporters of the Confederacy from holding office, was bitter medicine to the South. Nevertheless it was ratified and became a part of the Constitution in July 1868.

Meanwhile, the growth of radical feeling in the North on the question of reconstruction and the desire of the Republicans to gain the black vote made Congress insist that the Southern states must give blacks the ballot. They had to do this before they were allowed to send representatives to sit in Congress. It was generally believed, however, that the South planned to circumvent this provision. In 1869, therefore, Congress passed the 15th amendment, which declared that the right of citizens to vote should

U.S. CONSTITUTION

not be denied on account of race, color, or previous condition of servitude. Much to the anger of most Southern whites, this became a part of the Constitution in March 1870.

Many years passed without further amendment. Then within a decade, in the Taft and Wilson administrations, four more were added. One, the 16th, enabled Congress to impose an income tax. Such taxes had actually been levied during the Civil War. When Congress passed a new income tax law in the early 1890s, however, the Supreme Court declared it unconstitutional. This produced much indignation, especially in the West. The agitation for an amendment authorizing such a law grew until it became part of the Constitution in February 1913. In the same year the 17th amendment provided that United States senators should be elected by vote of the people instead of the legislatures. It was believed that this would give the country abler and more honest senators.

The 18th and 19th amendments were the products of great popular movements extending over many decades. The 18th amendment, prohibiting the manufacture and sale of intoxicating liquor for beverage purposes, was ratified in January 1919 and went into effect a year later. The 19th amendment, giving women the vote, was proclaimed in August 1920.

In 1933 two more amendments were added. The 20th changed the dates when the president and members of Congress take office, thus eliminating the so-called "lame duck" sessions of Congress. The 21st repealed the prohibition amendment (the 18th).

The 22nd amendment was added in 1951. It limited the president to two terms or to a maximum of ten years in office. The 23rd amendment, added in 1961, granted residents of Washington, D.C., the right to vote in presidential elections. The 24th, or antipoll-tax amendment, added in 1964, provided that citizens could not be denied the right to vote in presidential or congressional elections because of failure to pay a tax. The 25th amendment, added in 1967, established procedures for the appointment of a vice-president if that office should fall vacant and for the vice-president to become acting president if the president should prove unable to perform his duties. In 1971 the 26th amendment reduced the voting age to 18 years.

In the United States there are two methods, other than amendment, of adjusting the Constitution to new conditions. One is by custom. It was custom, for example, that established a method of electing presidents different from that laid down in the Constitution.

The Supreme Court and the Constitution

The other method of adjustment is through the Supreme Court's interpretations of the Constitution. Since the days of John Marshall, the fourth chief justice, the Supreme Court has been helping the Constitution to meet new demands arising from national growth and changes in public opinion.

The Constitution is a written document whose words cannot be changed except by the process of amendment described in Article V. But the meaning of the words is not always interpreted in the same way by members of opposing political parties or by persons engaged in lawsuits over property or human rights. Thus it has been necessary for someone to interpret it—that is, to determine what it means in any controversy. This duty is entrusted to the Supreme Court. It provides that the Constitution and the laws made "in pursuance thereof, shall be the supreme law of the land."

Invalidating Acts of Congress

The Supreme Court therefore has two kinds of duties: one, to decide cases of law; the other, to decide what the Constitution means. Sometimes people who have been dissatisfied with decisions made by the Supreme Court have said that the power to determine the meaning of the Constitution ought to be exercised by Congress; but since a law inconsistent with the Constitution cannot be a valid law, it must not be enforced. Only the court before which the enforcement of such a law comes can easily make the decision. Early in its history the Supreme Court was obliged to face this situation. In the case of Marbury *vs.* Madison (1803) the Court declared an act of Congress void because the act was incompatible with the Constitution. The power has not often been exercised, but it indicates the difference between the United States government, with a fixed basic law, and a constitutional government such as that of Britain, in which the constitution at any moment consists of all the laws that have been passed.

The Constitution has twice been amended because the people did not like the interpretation given it by the Supreme Court. After the decision in Chisholm *vs.* Georgia (1793), in which the Court ruled that a state might be sued by a private citizen of another state, the 11th amendment was promptly adopted forbidding this sort of suit. Governments, in general, do not permit themselves to be sued as though they were private individuals. Again, when the income tax of 1894 was declared unconstitutional in Pollock *vs.* Farmers Loan and Trust Company (1895), the 16th amendment was brought forward to authorize such an income tax.

On a third occasion it might have been necessary to amend the Constitution if the Supreme Court had not taken a broad view of its meaning. Jefferson thought the Louisiana Purchase was unconstitutional because the right to acquire territory is not enumerated in the Constitution. The Supreme Court decided, however, in American Insurance Company *vs.* Canter (1828) that the right to annex territory may be derived from either the power to declare war or the power to conclude treaties. Later, when the annexation of the Philippines raised the question of the right to govern them, the decision in the Insular Cases (1901) upheld the authority of the government.

John Marshall, while chief justice, made many of the most significant constitutional decisions because the problems that came before the Supreme Court in his day were new, like the nation itself (*see* Mar-

200

shall, John). One of these concerned the power of Congress to create a national bank. In McCulloch vs. Maryland (1819), his judgment contained what is perhaps the most important interpretation of the meaning of the Constitution: "Let the end be legitimate, let it be within the scope of the Constitution, and all means which are appropriate, which are plainly adapted to that end, which are not prohibited, but consist with the letter and spirit of the Constitution, are constitutional." This is called the doctrine of "implied powers."

Some Historic Court Decisions

In this spirit the federal courts have made several historic decisions in interpreting the clause giving Congress power "to regulate commerce with foreign nations and among the several states." As a result of these decisions Congress has exerted wide controls over business. The decision in Gibbons vs. Ogden (1824) forbade the states to take action interfering with the free use of rivers and harbors. The right to regulate railroad rates by law was established after the decision in Munn vs. Illinois (1877). In Wabash, St. Louis, and Pacific R. R. vs. Illinois (1886) the Court decided that no such regulation by a state could be sustained if it incidentally fixed part of a rate for an interstate transaction. In the Northern Securities Case (1904) a great railroad combination was broken up because its organization was inconsistent with the acts of Congress passed to regulate interstate commerce.

Sometimes the decisions of the Supreme Court have occurred when party feeling has run high. In Dred Scott vs. Sandford (1857) the right of a black to sue as a citizen was denied. In this case the justices expressed opinions, not essential to the case itself (dicta they are called), that made this Dred Scott Decision a means of inflaming opinion before the Civil War (see Dred Scott Decision). The Court has been attacked because it upheld the power of Congress to issue the "greenbacks" of the Civil War, in the Legal Tender Cases (1871). It was criticized by some when, in Fletcher vs. Peck (1810), it upheld the obligation of contracts, and refused to permit even a state to repudiate such an obligation.

It was for this reason, so that judges might be independent, and not fearful that unpopular decisions might result in their dismissal, that the Constitution provides federal judges shall hold office for life. They can be removed only after impeachment and conviction for "treason, bribery, or other high crimes and misdemeanors."

The Constitution and the New Deal

A crisis in the history of judicial review was reached in 1937 when President Franklin D. Roosevelt threatened to "pack" the Supreme Court by adding new members because the "nine old men" had invalidated New Deal legislation. His proposal failed; but deaths and resignations enabled him to appoint men more in accord with his philosophy of government.

Since then the court has usually validated acts favorable to social welfare and labor. In 1954 it ruled that racial segregation in public schools violated the 14th amendment. In 1960 it upheld the constitutionality of the union shop. (See also Supreme Court.)

Text of the United States Constitution*

We the People of the United States, in Order to form a more perfect Union, establish Justice, insure domestic Tranquility, provide for the common defence, promote the general Welfare, and secure the Blessings of Liberty to ourselves and our Posterity, do ordain and establish this Constitution for the United States of America.

Article. I.

Section. 1. All legislative Powers herein granted shall be vested in a Congress of the United States, which shall consist of a Senate and House of Representatives.

Section. 2. The House of Representatives shall be composed of Members chosen every second Year by the People of the several States, and the Electors in each State shall have the Qualifications requisite for Electors of the most numerous Branch of the State Legislature.

No Person shall be a Representative who shall not have attained to the Age of twenty five Years, and been seven Years a Citizen of the United States, and who shall not, when elected, be an Inhabitant of that State in which he shall be chosen.

Representatives and direct Taxes shall be apportioned among the several States which may be included within this Union, according to their respective Numbers, which shall be determined by adding to the whole Number of free Persons, including those bound to Service for a Term of Years, and excluding Indians not taxed, three fifths of all other Persons. The actual Enumeration shall be made within three Years after the first Meeting of the Congress of the United States, and within every subsequent Term of ten Years, in such Manner as they shall by Law direct. The Number of Representatives shall not exceed one for every thirty Thousand, but each State shall have at Least one Representative; and until such enumeration shall be made, the State of New Hampshire shall be entitled to chuse three, Massachusetts eight, Rhode-Island and Providence Plantations one, Connecticut five, New-York six, New Jersey four, Pennsylvania eight, Delaware one, Maryland six, Virginia ten, North Carolina five, South Carolina five, and Georgia three.

When vacancies happen in the Representation from any State, the Executive Authority thereof shall issue Writs of Election to fill such Vacancies.

The House of Representatives shall chuse their Speaker and other Officers; and shall have the sole Power of Impeachment.

Section. 3. The Senate of the United States shall be composed of two Senators from each State, chosen by the Legislature thereof, for six Years; and each Senator shall have one Vote.

Immediately after they shall be assembled in Consequence of the first Election, they shall be divided as

* Text taken from the literal print issued by the Department of State.

equally as may be into three Classes. The Seats of the Senators of the first Class shall be vacated at the Expiration of the second Year, of the second Class at the Expiration of the fourth Year, and of the third Class at the Expiration of the sixth Year, so that one third may be chosen every second Year; and if Vacancies happen by Resignation, or otherwise, during the Recess of the Legislature of any State, the Executive thereof may make temporary Appointments until the next Meeting of the Legislature, which shall then fill such Vacancies.

No Person shall be a Senator who shall not have attained to the Age of thirty Years, and been nine Years a Citizen of the United States, and who shall not, when elected, be an Inhabitant of that State for which he shall be chosen.

The Vice President of the United States shall be President of the Senate, but shall have no Vote, unless they be equally divided.

The Senate shall chuse their other Officers, and also a President pro tempore, in the Absence of the Vice President, or when he shall exercise the Office of President of the United States.

The Senate shall have the sole Power to try all Impeachments. When sitting for that Purpose, they shall be on Oath or Affirmation. When the President of the United States is tried the Chief Justice shall preside: And no Person shall be convicted without the Concurrence of two thirds of the Members present.

Judgment in Cases of Impeachment shall not extend further than to removal from Office, and disqualification to hold and enjoy any Office of honor, Trust or Profit under the United States: but the Party convicted shall nevertheless be liable and subject to Indictment, Trial, Judgment and Punishment, according to Law.

Section. 4. The Times, Places and Manner of holding Elections for Senators and Representatives, shall be prescribed in each State by the Legislature thereof; but the Congress may at any time by Law make or alter such Regulations, except as to the Places of chusing Senators.

The Congress shall assemble at least once in every Year, and such Meeting shall be on the first Monday in December, unless they shall by Law appoint a different Day.

Section. 5. Each House shall be the Judge of the Elections, Returns and Qualifications of its own Members, and a Majority of each shall constitute a Quorum to do Business; but a smaller Number may adjourn from day to day, and may be authorized to compel the Attendance of absent Members, in such Manner, and under such Penalties as each House may provide.

Each House may determine the Rules of its Proceedings, punish its Members for disorderly Behaviour, and, with the Concurrence of two thirds, expel a Member.

Each House shall keep a Journal of its Proceedings, and from time to time publish the same, excepting such Parts as may in their Judgment require Secrecy; and the Yeas and Nays of the Members of either House on any question shall, at the Desire of one fifth of those Present, be entered on the Journal.

Neither House, during the Session of Congress, shall, without the Consent of the other, adjourn for more than three days, nor to any other Place than that in which the two Houses shall be sitting.

Section. 6. The Senators and Representatives shall receive a Compensation for their Services, to be ascertained by Law, and paid out of the Treasury of the United States. They shall in all Cases, except Treason, Felony and Breach of the Peace, be privileged from Arrest during their Attendance at the Session of their respective Houses, and in going to and returning from the same; and for any Speech or Debate in either House, they shall not be questioned in any other Place.

No Senator or Representative shall, during the Time for which he was elected, be appointed to any civil Office under the Authority of the United States, which shall have been created, or the Emoluments whereof shall have been encreased during such time; and no Person holding any Office under the United States, shall be a Member of either House during his Continuance in Office.

Section. 7. All Bills for raising Revenue shall originate in the House of Representatives; but the Senate may propose or concur with Amendments as on other Bills.

Every Bill which shall have passed the House of Representatives and the Senate, shall, before it become a Law, be presented to the President of the United States; If he approve he shall sign it, but if not he shall return it, with his Objections to that House in which it shall have originated, who shall enter the Objections at large on their Journal, and proceed to reconsider it. If after such Reconsideration two thirds of that House shall agree to pass the Bill, it shall be sent, together with the Objections, to the other House, by which it shall likewise be reconsidered, and if approved by two thirds of that House, it shall become a Law. But in all such Cases the Votes of both Houses shall be determined by yeas and Nays, and the Names of the Persons voting for and against the Bill shall be entered on the Journal of each House respectively. If any Bill shall not be returned by the President within ten Days (Sundays excepted) after it shall have been presented to him, the Same shall be a Law, in like Manner as if he had signed it, unless the Congress by their Adjournment prevent its Return, in which Case it shall not be a Law.

Every Order, Resolution, or Vote to which the Concurrence of the Senate and House of Representatives may be necessary (except on a question of Adjournment) shall be presented to the President of the United States; and before the Same shall take Effect, shall be approved by him, or being disapproved by him, shall be repassed by two thirds of the Senate and House of Representatives, according to the Rules and Limitations prescribed in the Case of a Bill.

Section. 8. The Congress shall have Power To lay and collect Taxes, Duties, Imposts and Excises, to pay the Debts and provide for the common Defence and general Welfare of the United States; but all Duties, Imposts and Excises shall be uniform throughout the United States;

To borrow Money on the credit of the United States;

To regulate Commerce with foreign Nations, and among the several States, and with the Indian Tribes;

To establish an uniform Rule of Naturalization, and uniform Laws on the subject of Bankruptcies throughout the United States;

To coin Money, regulate the Value thereof, and of foreign Coin, and fix the Standard of Weights and Measures;

To provide for the Punishment of counterfeiting the Securities and current Coin of the United States;

To establish Post Offices and post Roads;

To promote the Progress of Science and useful Arts, by securing for limited Times to Authors and Inventors the exclusive Right to their respective Writings and Discoveries;

To constitute Tribunals inferior to the supreme Court;

To define and punish Piracies and Felonies committed on the high Seas, and Offences against the Law of Nations;

To declare War, grant Letters of Marque and Reprisal, and make Rules concerning Captures on Land and Water;

To raise and support Armies, but no Appropriation of Money to that Use shall be for a longer Term than two Years;

To provide and maintain a Navy;

To make Rules for the Government and Regulation of the land and naval Forces;

To provide for calling forth the Militia to execute the Laws of the Union, suppress Insurrections and repel Invasions;

To provide for organizing, arming, and disciplining, the Militia, and for governing such Part of them as may be employed in the Service of the United States, reserving to the States respectively, the Appointment of the Officers, and the Authority of training the Militia according to the discipline prescribed by Congress;

To exercise exclusive Legislation in all Cases whatsoever, over such District (not exceeding ten Miles square) as may, by Cession of particular States, and the Acceptance of Congress, become the Seat of the Government of the United States, and to exercise like Authority over all Places purchased by the Consent of the Legislature of the State in which the Same shall be, for the Erection of Forts, Magazines, Arsenals, dock-Yards, and other needful Buildings;—And

To make all Laws which shall be necessary and proper for carrying into Execution the foregoing Powers, and all other Powers vested by this Constitution in the Government of the United States, or in any Department or Officer thereof.

Section. 9. The Migration or Importation of such Persons as any of the States now existing shall think proper to admit, shall not be prohibited by the Congress prior to the Year one thousand eight hundred and eight, but a Tax or duty may be imposed on such Importation, not exceeding ten dollars for each Person.

The Privilege of the Writ of Habeas Corpus shall not be suspended, unless when in Cases of Rebellion or Invasion the public Safety may require it.

No Bill of Attainder or ex post facto Law shall be passed.

No Capitation, or other direct, Tax shall be laid, unless in Proportion to the Census or Enumeration herein before directed to be taken.

No Tax or Duty shall be laid on Articles exported from any State.

No Preference shall be given by any Regulation of Commerce or Revenue to the Ports of one State over those of another: nor shall Vessels bound to, or from, one State, be obliged to enter, clear, or pay Duties in another.

No Money shall be drawn from the Treasury, but in Consequence of Appropriations made by Law; and a regular Statement and Account of the Receipts and Expenditures of all public Money shall be published from time to time.

No Title of Nobility shall be granted by the United States: And no Person holding any Office of Profit or Trust under them, shall, without the Consent of the Congress, accept of any present, Emolument, Office, or Title, of any kind whatever, from any King, Prince, or foreign State.

Section. 10. No State shall enter into any Treaty, Alliance, or Confederation; grant Letters of Marque and Reprisal; coin Money; emit Bills of Credit; make any Thing but gold and silver Coin a Tender in Payment of Debts; pass any Bill of Attainder, ex post facto Law, or Law impairing the Obligation of Contracts, or grant any Title of Nobility.

No State shall, without the Consent of the Congress, lay any Imposts or Duties on Imports or Exports, except what may be absolutely necessary for executing it's inspection Laws: and the net Produce of all Duties and Imposts, laid by any State on Imports or Exports, shall be for the Use of the Treasury of the United States; and all such Laws shall be subject to the Revision and Controul of the Congress.

No State shall, without the Consent of Congress, lay any Duty of Tonnage, keep Troops, or Ships of War in time of Peace, enter into any Agreement or Compact with another State, or with a foreign Power, or engage in War, unless actually invaded, or in such imminent Danger as will not admit of delay.

Article. II.

Section. 1. The executive Power shall be vested in a President of the United States of America. He shall hold his Office during the Term of four Years, and, together with the Vice President, chosen for the same Term, be elected, as follows

Each State shall appoint, in such Manner as the Legislature thereof may direct, a Number of Electors, equal to the whole Number of Senators and Representatives to which the State may be entitled in the Congress: but no Senator or Representative, or Person holding an Office of Trust or Profit under the United States, shall be appointed an Elector.

The Electors shall meet in their respective States, and vote by Ballot for two Persons, of whom one at least shall not be an Inhabitant of the same State with themselves. And they shall make a List of all the Persons voted for, and of the Number of Votes for each; which List they shall sign and certify, and transmit sealed to the Seat of Government of the United States, directed to the President of the Senate. The President of the Senate shall, in the Presence of the Senate and House of Representatives, open all the Certificates, and the Votes shall then be counted. The Person having the greatest Number of Votes shall be the President, if such Number be a Majority of the whole Number of Electors appointed; and if there be more than one who have such Majority, and have an equal Number of Votes, then the House of Representatives shall immediately chuse by Ballot one of them for President; and if no Person have a Majority, then from the five highest on the List the said House shall in like Manner chuse the President. But in chusing the President, the Votes shall be taken by States, the Representation from each State having one Vote; A quorum for this Purpose shall consist of a Member or Members from two thirds of the States, and a Majority of all the States shall be necessary to a Choice. In every Case, after the Choice of the President, the Person having the greatest Number of Votes of the Electors shall be the Vice President. But if there should remain two or more who have equal Votes, the Senate shall chuse from them by Ballot the Vice President.

The Congress may determine the Time of chusing the Electors, and the Day on which they shall give their Votes; which Day shall be the same throughout the United States.

No Person except a natural born Citizen, or a Citizen of the United States, at the time of the Adoption of this Constitution, shall be eligible to the Office of President; neither shall any Person be eligible to that Office who shall not have attained to the Age of thirty five Years, and been fourteen Years a Resident within the United States.

In Case of the Removal of the President from Office, or of his Death, Resignation, or Inability to discharge the Powers and Duties of the said Office, the Same shall devolve on the Vice President, and the Congress may by Law provide for the Case of Removal, Death, Resignation or Inability, both of the President and Vice President declaring what Officer shall then act as President, and such Officer shall act accordingly, until the Disability be removed, or a President shall be elected.

The President shall, at stated Times, receive for his Services, a Compensation, which shall neither be encreased nor diminished during the Period for which he shall have been elected, and he shall not receive within that Period any other Emolument from the United States, or any of them.

Before he enter on the Execution of his Office, he shall take the following Oath or Affirmation:—"I do solemnly swear (or affirm) that I will faithfully execute the Office of President of the United States, and will to the best of my Ability, preserve, protect and defend the Constitution of the United States."

Section. 2. The President shall be Commander in Chief of the Army and Navy of the United States, and of the Militia of the several States, when called into the actual Service of the United States; he may require the Opinion, in writing, of the principal Officer in each of the executive Departments, upon any Subject relating to the Duties of their respective Offices, and he shall have Power to grant Reprieves and Pardons for Offences against the United States, except in Cases of Impeachment.

He shall have Power, by and with the Advice and Consent of the Senate, to make Treaties, provided two thirds of the Senators present concur; and he shall nominate, and by and with the Advice and Consent of the Senate, shall appoint Ambassadors, other public Ministers and Consuls, Judges of the supreme Court, and all other Officers of the United States, whose Appointments are not herein otherwise provided for, and which shall be established by Law: but the Congress may by Law vest the Appointment of such inferior Officers, as they think proper, in the President alone, in the Courts of Law, or in the Heads of Departments.

The President shall have Power to fill up all Vacancies that may happen during the Recess of the Senate, by granting Commissions which shall expire at the End of their next Session.

Section. 3. He shall from time to time give to the Congress Information of the State of the Union, and recommend to their Consideration such Measures as he shall judge necessary and expedient; he may, on extraordinary Occasions, convene both Houses, or either of them, and in Case of Disagreement between them, with Respect to the Time of Adjournment, he may adjourn them to such Time as he shall think proper; he shall receive Ambassadors and other public Ministers; he shall take Care that the Laws be faithfully executed, and shall Commission all the Officers of the United States.

Section. 4. The President, Vice President and all civil Officers of the United States, shall be removed from Office on Impeachment for, and Conviction of, Treason, Bribery, or other high Crimes and Misdemeanors.

Article. III.

Section. 1. The judicial Power of the United States, shall be vested in one supreme Court, and in such inferior Courts as the Congress may from time to time ordain and establish. The Judges, both of the supreme and inferior Courts, shall hold their Offices during good Behaviour, and shall, at stated Times, receive for their Services, a Compensation which shall not be diminished during their Continuance in Office.

Section. 2. The judicial Power shall extend to all Cases, in Law and Equity, arising under this Constitution, the Laws of the United States, and Treaties made, or which shall be made, under their Authority;—to all Cases affecting Ambassadors, other public Ministers and Consuls;—to all Cases of admiralty and maritime Jurisdiction;—to Controversies to which the United States shall be a Party;—to Controversies between two or more States;—between a State and Citizens of another State;—between Citizens of different States,—between Citizens of the same State claiming Lands under Grants of different States, and between a State, or the Citizens thereof, and foreign States, Citizens or Subjects.

In all Cases affecting Ambassadors, other public Ministers and Consuls, and those in which a State shall be Party, the supreme Court shall have original Jurisdiction. In all the other Cases before mentioned, the supreme Court shall have appellate Jurisdiction, both as to Law and Fact, with such Exceptions, and under such Regulations as the Congress shall make.

The Trial of all Crimes, except in Cases of Impeachment, shall be by Jury; and such Trial shall be held in the State where the said Crimes shall have been committed; but when not committed within any State, the Trial shall be at such Place or Places as the Congress may by Law have directed.

Section. 3. Treason against the United States, shall consist only in levying War against them, or in adhering to their Enemies, giving them Aid and Comfort. No Person shall be convicted of Treason unless on the Testimony of two Witnesses to the same overt Act, or on Confession in open Court.

The Congress shall have Power to declare the Punishment of Treason, but no Attainder of Treason shall work Corruption of Blood, or Forfeiture except during the Life of the Person attainted.

Article. IV.

Section. 1. Full Faith and Credit shall be given in each State to the public Acts, Records, and judicial Proceedings of every other State. And the Congress may by general Laws prescribe the Manner in which such Acts, Records and Proceedings shall be proved, and the Effect thereof.

Section. 2. The Citizens of each State shall be entitled to all Privileges and Immunities of Citizens in the several States.

A Person charged in any State with Treason, Felony, or other Crime, who shall flee from Justice, and be found in another State, shall on Demand of the executive Authority of the State from which he fled, be delivered up, to be removed to the State having Jurisdiction of the Crime.

No Person held to Service or Labour in one State, under the Laws thereof, escaping into another, shall, in Consequence of any Law or Regulation therein, be discharged from such Service or Labour, but shall be delivered up on Claim of the Party to whom such Service or Labour may be due.

Section. 3. New States may be admitted by the Congress into this Union; but no new State shall be formed or erected within the Jurisdiction of any other State; nor any State be formed by the Junction of two or more States, or Parts of States, without the Consent of the Legislatures of the States concerned as well as of the Congress.

The Congress shall have Power to dispose of and make all needful Rules and Regulations respecting the Territory or other Property belonging to the United States; and nothing in this Constitution shall be so construed as to Prejudice any Claims of the United States, or of any particular State.

Section. 4. The United States shall guarantee to every State in this Union a Republican Form of Government, and shall protect each of them against Invasion; and on Application of the Legislature, or of the Executive (when the Legislature cannot be convened) against domestic Violence.

Article. V.

The Congress, whenever two thirds of both Houses shall deem it necessary, shall propose Amendments to this Constitution, or, on the Application of the Legislatures of two thirds of the several States, shall call a Convention for proposing Amendments, which, in either Case, shall be valid to all Intents and Purposes, as Part of this Constitution, when ratified by the Legislatures of three fourths of the several States, or by Conventions in three fourths thereof, as the one or the other Mode of Ratification may be proposed by the Congress; Provided that no Amendment which may be made prior to the Year One thousand eight hundred and eight shall in any Manner affect the first and fourth Clauses in the Ninth Section of the first Article; and that no State, without its Consent, shall be deprived of its equal Suffrage in the Senate.

Article. VI.

All Debts contracted and Engagements entered into, before the Adoption of this Constitution, shall be as valid against the United States under this Constitution, as under the Confederation.

This Constitution, and the Laws of the United States which shall be made in Pursuance thereof; and all Treaties made or which shall be made, under the Authority of the United States, shall be the supreme Law of the Land; and the Judges in every State shall be bound thereby, any Thing in the Constitution or Laws of any State to the Contrary notwithstanding.

The Senators and Representatives before mentioned, and the Members of the several State Legislatures, and all executive and judicial Officers, both of the United States and of the several States, shall be bound by Oath or Affirmation, to support this Constitution; but no religious Test shall ever be required as a Qualification to any Office or public Trust under the United States.

Article. VII.

The Ratification of the Conventions of nine States, shall be sufficient for the Establishment of this Constitution between the States so ratifying the Same.

done in Convention by the Unanimous Consent of the States present the Seventeenth Day of September in the Year of our Lord one thousand seven hundred and Eighty seven and of the Independence of the United States of America the Twelfth In witness whereof We have hereunto subscribed our Names,

Attest WILLIAM JACKSON Secretary   G^o. WASHINGTON—Presid^t and deputy from Virginia

New Hampshire	{ JOHN LANGDON NICHOLAS GILMAN }
Massachusetts	{ NATHANIEL GORHAM RUFUS KING }
Connecticut	{ W^M SAM^L JOHNSON ROGER SHERMAN }
New York	ALEXANDER HAMILTON
New Jersey	{ WIL: LIVINGSTON DAVID BREARLEY. W^M PATERSON. JONA: DAYTON }
Pennsylvania	{ B FRANKLIN THOMAS MIFFLIN ROB^T MORRIS GEO. CLYMER THO^S FITZSIMONS JARED INGERSOLL JAMES WILSON GOUV MORRIS }

Delaware	{ GEO: READ GUNNING BEDFORD jun JOHN DICKINSON RICHARD BASSETT JACO: BROOM }
Maryland	{ JAMES M^CHENRY DAN OF S^T THO^S JENIFER DAN^L CARROLL }
Virginia	{ JOHN BLAIR— JAMES MADISON Jr. }
North Carolina	{ W^M BLOUNT RICH^D DOBBS SPAIGHT. HU WILLIAMSON }
South Carolina	{ J. RUTLEDGE CHARLES COTESWORTH PINCKNEY CHARLES PINCKNEY PIERCE BUTLER. }
Georgia	{ WILLIAM FEW ABR BALDWIN }

Amendments to the Constitution

Articles in addition to, and Amendment of, the Constitution of the United States of America, proposed by Congress, and ratified by the Legislatures of the several States, pursuant to the fifth Article of the Original Constitution.

THE TEN ORIGINAL AMENDMENTS

The first ten amendments to the Constitution were proposed by Congress Sept. 25, 1789, and became effective Dec. 15, 1791. Together they are known as the Bill of Rights, though only the first eight amendments guarantee individuals specific rights and liberties.

Amendment 1

Congress shall make no law respecting an establishment of religion, or prohibiting the free exercise thereof; or abridging the freedom of speech, or of the press; or the right of the people peaceably to assemble, and to petition the Government for a redress of grievances.

Amendment 2

A well regulated Militia, being necessary to the security of a free State, the right of the people to keep and bear Arms, shall not be infringed.

Amendment 3

No Soldier shall, in time of peace be quartered in any house, without the consent of the Owner, nor in time of war, but in a manner to be prescribed by law.

Amendment 4

The right of the people to be secure in their persons, houses, papers, and effects, against unreasonable searches and seizures, shall not be violated, and no Warrants shall issue, but upon probable cause, supported by Oath or affirmation, and particularly describing the place to be searched, and the persons or things to be seized.

Amendment 5

No person shall be held to answer for a capital, or otherwise infamous crime, unless on a presentment or indictment of a Grand Jury, except in cases arising in the land or naval forces, or in the Militia, when in actual service in time of War or public danger; nor shall any person be subject for the same offence to be twice put in jeopardy of life or limb; nor shall be compelled in any criminal case to be a witness against himself, nor be deprived of life, liberty, or property, without due process of law; nor shall private property be taken for public use, without just compensation.

Amendment 6

In all criminal prosecutions, the accused shall enjoy the right to a speedy and public trial, by an impartial jury of the State and district wherein the crime shall have been committed, which district shall have been previously ascertained by law, and to be informed of the nature and cause of the accusation; to be confronted with the witnesses against him; to have compulsory process for obtaining witnesses in his favor, and to have the Assistance of Counsel for his defence.

Amendment 7

In Suits at common law, where the value in controversy shall exceed twenty dollars, the right of trial by jury shall be preserved, and no fact tried by a jury, shall be otherwise re-examined in any Court of the United States, than according to the rules of the common law.

Amendment 8

Excessive bail shall not be required, nor excessive fines imposed, nor cruel and unusual punishments inflicted.

Amendment 9

The enumeration in the Constitution, of certain rights, shall not be construed to deny or disparage others retained by the people.

Amendment 10

The powers not delegated to the United States by the Constitution, nor prohibited by it to the States, are reserved to the States respectively, or to the people.

LATER AMENDMENTS

An amendment to the Constitution becomes effective when three fourths of the states have ratified it. The dates given for the following amendments are the days on which the certificates of adoption (formerly called proclamations) were published.

Amendment 11 (Jan. 8, 1798)

The Judicial power of the United States shall not be construed to extend to any suit in law or equity, commenced or prosecuted against one of the United States by Citizens of another State, or by Citizens or Subjects of any Foreign State.

Amendment 12 (Sept. 25, 1804)

The Electors shall meet in their respective states, and vote by ballot for President and Vice-President, one of whom, at least, shall not be an inhabitant of the same state with themselves; they shall name in their ballots the person voted for as President, and in distinct ballots the person voted for as Vice-President, and they shall make distinct lists of all persons voted for as President, and of all persons voted for as Vice-President, and of the number of votes for each, which list they shall sign and certify, and transmit sealed to the seat of the government of the United States, directed to the President of the Senate;—The President of the Senate shall, in the presence of the Senate and House of Representatives, open all the certificates and the votes shall then be counted;—The person having the greatest number of votes for President, shall be the President, if such number be a majority of the whole number of Electors appointed; and if no person have such majority, then from the persons having the highest numbers not exceeding three on the list of those voted for as President, the House of Representatives shall choose immediately, by ballot, the President. But in choosing the President, the votes shall be taken by states, the representation from each state having one vote; a quorum for this purpose shall consist of a member or members from two thirds of the states, and a majority of all the states shall be necessary to a choice. And if the House of Representatives shall not choose a President whenever the right of choice shall devolve upon them, before the fourth day of March next following, then the Vice-President shall act as President, as in the case of the death or other constitutional disability of the President.—The person having the greatest number of votes as Vice-President, shall be the Vice-President, if such number be a majority of the whole number of Electors appointed, and if no person have a majority, then from the two highest numbers on the list, the Senate shall choose the Vice-President; a quorum for the purpose shall consist of two thirds of the whole number of Senators, and a majority of the whole number shall be necessary to a choice. But no person constitutionally ineligible to the office of President shall be eligible to that of Vice-President of the United States.

Amendment 13 (Dec. 18, 1865)

Section 1. Neither slavery nor involuntary servitude, except as a punishment for crime whereof the party shall have been duly convicted, shall exist within the United States, or any place subject to their jurisdiction.

Section 2. Congress shall have power to enforce this article by appropriate legislation.

Amendment 14 (July 28, 1868)

Section 1. All persons born or naturalized in the United States, and subject to the jurisdiction thereof, are citizens of the United States and of the State wherein they reside. No State shall make or enforce any law which shall abridge the privileges or immunities of citizens of the United States; nor shall any State deprive any person of life, liberty, or property, without due process of law; nor deny to any person within its jurisdiction the equal protection of the laws.

Section 2. Representatives shall be apportioned among the several States according to their respective numbers, counting the whole number of persons in each State, excluding Indians not taxed. But when the right to vote at any election for the choice of electors for President and Vice-President of the United States, Representatives in Congress, the Executive and Judicial officers of a State, or the members of the Legislature thereof, is denied to any of the male inhabitants of such State, being twenty-one years of age, and citizens of the United States, or in any way abridged, except for participation in rebellion, or other crime, the basis of representation therein shall be reduced in the proportion which the number of such male citizens shall bear to the whole number of male citizens twenty-one years of age in such State.

Section 3. No person shall be a Senator or Representative in Congress, or elector of President and Vice-President, or hold any office, civil or military, under the United States, or under any State, who, having previously taken an oath, as a member of Congress, or as an officer of the United States, or as a member of any State legislature, or as an executive or judicial officer of any State, to support the Constitution of the United States, shall have engaged in insurrection or rebellion against the same, or given aid or comfort to the enemies thereof. But Congress may by a vote of two thirds of each House, remove such disability.

Section 4. The validity of the public debt of the United States, authorized by law, including debts incurred for payment of pensions and bounties for services in suppressing insurrection or rebellion, shall not be questioned. But neither the United States nor any

State shall assume or pay any debt or obligation incurred in aid of insurrection or rebellion against the United States, or any claim for the loss or emancipation of any slave; but all such debts, obligations and claims shall be held illegal and void.

Section 5. The Congress shall have power to enforce, by appropriate legislation, the provisions of this article.

Amendment 15 (March 30, 1870)

Section 1. The right of citizens of the United States to vote shall not be denied or abridged by the United States or by any State on account of race, color, or previous condition of servitude—

Section 2. The Congress shall have power to enforce this article by appropriate legislation.

Amendment 16 (Feb. 25, 1913)

The Congress shall have power to lay and collect taxes on incomes, from whatever source derived, without apportionment among the several States, and without regard to any census or enumeration.

Amendment 17 (May 31, 1913)

The Senate of the United States shall be composed of two Senators from each State, elected by the people thereof, for six years; and each Senator shall have one vote. The electors in each State shall have the qualifications requisite for electors of the most numerous branch of the State legislatures.

When vacancies happen in the representation of any State in the Senate, the executive authority of such State shall issue writs of election to fill such vacancies: *Provided,* That the legislature of any State may empower the executive thereof to make temporary appointments until the people fill the vacancies by election as the legislature may direct.

This amendment shall not be so construed as to affect the election or term of any Senator chosen before it becomes valid as part of the Constitution.

Amendment 18 (Jan. 29, 1919; repealed Dec. 5, 1933)

Section 1. After one year from the ratification of this article the manufacture, sale, or transportation of intoxicating liquors within, the importation thereof into, or the exportation thereof from the United States and all territory subject to the jurisdiction thereof for beverage purposes is hereby prohibited.

Section 2. The Congress and the several States shall have concurrent power to enforce this article by appropriate legislation.

Section 3. This article shall be inoperative unless it shall have been ratified as an amendment to the Constitution by the legislatures of the several States, as provided in the Constitution, within seven years from the date of the submission hereof to the States by the Congress.

Amendment 19 (Aug. 26, 1920)

The right of citizens of the United States to vote shall not be denied or abridged by the United States or by any State on account of sex.

Congress shall have power to enforce this article by appropriate legislation.

Amendment 20 (Feb. 6, 1933)

Section 1. The terms of the President and Vice-President shall end at noon on the 20th day of January, and the terms of Senators and Representatives at noon on the third day of January, of the years in which such terms would have ended if this article had not been ratified; and the terms of their successors shall then begin.

Section 2. The Congress shall assemble at least once in every year, and such meeting shall begin at noon on the third day of January, unless they shall by law appoint a different day.

Section 3. If, at the time fixed for the beginning of the term of the President, the President elect shall have died, the Vice-President elect shall become President. If a President shall not have been chosen before the time fixed for the beginning of his term, or if the President elect shall have failed to qualify, then the Vice-President elect shall act as President until a President shall have qualified; and the Congress may by law provide for the case wherein neither a President elect nor a Vice-President elect shall have qualified, declaring who shall then act as President, or the manner in which one who is to act shall be selected, and such person shall act accordingly until a President or Vice-President shall have qualified.

Section 4. .The Congress may by law provide for the case of the death of any of the persons from whom the House of Representatives may choose a President whenever the right of choice shall have devolved upon them, and for the case of the death of any of the persons from whom the Senate may choose a Vice-President whenever the right of choice shall have devolved upon them.

Section 5. Sections 1 and 2 shall take effect on the 15th day of October following the ratification of this article.

Section 6. This article shall be inoperative unless it shall have been ratified as an amendment to the Constitution by the legislatures of three fourths of the several States within seven years from the date of its submission.

Amendment 21 (Dec. 5, 1933)

Section 1. The eighteenth article of amendment to the Constitution of the United States is hereby repealed.

Section 2. The transportation or importation into any State, Territory, or possession of the United States for delivery or use therein of intoxicating liquors, in violation of the laws thereof, is hereby prohibited.

Section 3. This article shall be inoperative unless it shall have been ratified as an amendment to the Constitution by conventions in the several States, as provided in the Constitution, within seven years from the date of the submission hereof to the States by the Congress.

Amendment 22 (March 1, 1951)

Section 1. No person shall be elected to the office of the President more than twice, and no person who has held the office of President, or acted as President, for more than two years of a term to which some other person was elected President shall be elected to the office of the President more than once. But this Article shall not apply to any person holding the office of President when this Article was proposed by the Congress, and shall not prevent any person who may be holding the office of President, or acting as President, during the term within which this Article becomes operative from holding the office of President or acting as President during the remainder of such term.

Section 2. This article shall be inoperative unless it shall have been ratified as an amendment to the Constitution by the legislatures of three fourths of the several States within seven years from the date of its submission to the States by the Congress.

Amendment 23 (April 3, 1961)

Section 1. The District constituting the seat of Government of the United States shall appoint in such manner as the Congress may direct:

A number of electors of President and Vice-President equal to the whole number of Senators and Representatives in Congress to which the District would be entitled if it were a State, but in no event more than the least populous State; they shall be in addition to those appointed by the States, but they shall be considered, for the purposes of the election of President and Vice-President, to be electors appointed by a State; and they shall meet in the District and perform such duties as provided by the twelfth article of amendment.

Section 2. The Congress shall have power to enforce this article by appropriate legislation.

Amendment 24 (Feb. 4, 1964)

Section 1. The right of citizens of the United States to vote in any primary or other election for President or Vice-President, for electors for President or Vice-President, or for Senator or Representative in Congress, shall not be denied or abridged by the United States or any State by reason of failure to pay any poll tax or other tax.

Section 2. The Congress shall have power to enforce this article by appropriate legislation.

Amendment 25 (Feb. 10, 1967)

Section 1. In case of the removal of the President from office or his death or resignation, the Vice-President shall become President.

Section 2. Whenever there is a vacancy in the office of the Vice-President, the President shall nominate a Vice-President who shall take the office upon confirmation by a majority vote of both houses of Congress.

Section 3. Whenever the President transmits to the President pro tempore of the Senate and the Speaker of the House of Representatives his written declaration that he is unable to discharge the powers and duties of his office, and until he transmits to them a written declaration to the contrary, such powers and duties shall be discharged by the Vice-President as Acting President.

Section 4. Whenever the Vice-President and a majority of either the principal officers of the executive departments, or of such other body as Congress may by law provide, transmit to the President pro tempore of the Senate and the Speaker of the House of Representatives their written declaration that the President is unable to discharge the powers and duties of his office, the Vice-President shall immediately assume the powers and duties of the office as Acting President.

Thereafter, when the President transmits to the President pro tempore of the Senate and the Speaker of the House of Representatives his written declaration that no inability exists, he shall resume the powers and duties of his office unless the Vice-President and a majority of either the principal officers of the executive department, or of such other body as Congress may by law provide, transmit within four days to the President pro tempore of the Senate and the Speaker of the House of Representatives their written declaration that the President is unable to discharge the powers and duties of his office. Thereupon Congress shall decide the issue, assembling within 48 hours for that purpose if not in session. If the Congress, within 21 days after receipt of the latter written declaration, or, if Congress is not in session, within 21 days after Congress is required to assemble, determines by two-thirds vote of both houses that the President is unable to discharge the powers and duties of his office, the Vice-President shall continue to discharge the same as Acting President; otherwise, the President shall resume the powers and duties of his office.

Amendment 26 (June 30, 1971)

Section 1. The right of citizens of the United States, who are eighteen years of age or older, to vote shall not be denied or abridged by the United States or any state on account of age.

Section 2. The Congress shall have power to enforce this article by appropriate legislation.

UNITED STATES GOVERNMENT.

The federal government of the United States was created by the Constitution, which went into operation in 1789 when the first Congress convened and George Washington took the oath of office as president. The government is called federal because it was formed by a compact (the Constitution) among 13 political units (the states). These states agreed to give up part of their independence, or sovereignty, in order to form a central authority and submit themselves to it. Thus, what was essentially a group of 13 separate countries under the Articles of Confederation united to form one nation under the Constitution (see Articles of Confederation; United States Constitution).

When the Declaration of Independence was issued in 1776, it used the term United States of America.

Until the Constitution was adopted and ratified, however, the 13 states did not really form one nation. They each held on to so many powers individually, including conducting foreign policy and trade negotiations, that the Continental Congress could only do what the states allowed. The Articles were never the law of the land to the extent that the Constitution is. It can therefore be concluded that the United States as a nation did not come into existence until the Constitution began to function as the framework of the government.

Once the Constitution was in place, tension between the states and the federal government did not automatically cease. There was a point of view held by many political thinkers that the states were really the supreme authority. Consequently it was thought that states could nullify acts of the federal government that were disagreeable to them. One of the strongest proponents of this view was John C. Calhoun, senator from South Carolina (see Calhoun). His chief opponent was Chief Justice John Marshall (see Marshall, John). Calhoun's position, called states' rights, has persisted to the present. It was seriously undermined, however, by the American Civil War. Since that war the federal government has gained much power at the expense of the states (see States' Rights).

OBJECTS OF GOVERNMENT

The Preamble to the Constitution lists six purposes for which the new government was established: to form a more perfect union, establish justice, insure domestic tranquility, provide for the common defense, promote the general welfare, and secure the blessings of liberty. In composing the Preamble the framers of the Constitution were making a statement unprecedented in the history of governments. In the past, apart from Great Britain, governments were not in the habit of issuing lists of objectives—they simply governed. And government was usually an exercise of power over subjects, not citizens. The wording of the Preamble asserts that the people—not the states—are creating the government and are granting it certain powers for fixed purposes.

Two of these purposes are common to all governments: the police power (domestic tranquility) and defense against outside enemies. The other objectives arose from the political thought of the Enlightenment and from the experience of the United States in its relations with Britain. The goal of union stemmed in part from the failure of the Articles of Confederation. The insistence on justice and liberty was in part a reaction against the injustices perpetrated by king and Parliament prior to the American Revolution.

The general welfare phrase was new. Like the other objectives, its purpose was to serve the common good, but its meaning has always been subject to dispute. No sooner was the Constitution ratified than James Madison and Thomas Jefferson began to disagree with Alexander Hamilton on the meaning of the term general welfare in both the Preamble and in Article 1, section 8. For Madison and Jefferson the term was a

The House of Representatives and the Senate meet in the Capitol, the lawmaking heart of the government. The white-columned building in the upper left is the Supreme Court. The buildings of the Library of Congress are in the upper right.

H. Armstrong Roberts

fairly empty one, referring to all the powers listed in section 8. To Hamilton it seemed an open invitation to unlimited governmental authority, since almost anything the government wanted to do could be categorized as belonging to the general welfare.

It is not likely that the phrase promote the general welfare was intended to refer either to limited or unlimited powers of government. If the phrase is to make sense, it must have a significance of its own on a level with the other five objectives. It is probable that its meaning was best stated by Abraham Lincoln in his "Fragment on Government" in 1854: "The legitimate object of government is to do for a community of people whatever they need to have done, but cannot do at all, or cannot so well do for themselves in their separate capacities." There are many things that government can more easily do than individuals or groups. Among them are building roads and highways, canals, airports, and port facilities. Supporting public schools is another.

While the Preamble is remarkable for what it says, it is more so for what it fails to say. There is no reference in it to government operation of the economy. For the first time in history this was specifically excluded as a government function. Government stood aside from direct provision of the basic human needs of food, clothing, and shelter as well as from all other forms of production. By the late 20th century this situation had changed markedly, with the establishment of a welfare state and a vast involvement by

the federal government in economic functions (see Welfare State).

SEPARATION OF POWERS

It has proved true, historically, that there is a natural tendency of governments to assume as much power as possible. To prevent this from happening in the United States, the framers of the Constitution divided the functions of the federal government among three branches: the lawmaking branch, the executive branch, and the judiciary. This separation of powers is in direct contrast to the government in Britain. There Parliament is the single governing unit. Members of the executive—the Cabinet and the prime minister—are members of Parliament. The highest court of appeal is the House of Lords (see Cabinet Government; Parliament).

The separation of powers was also in contrast to the government under the Articles of Confederation. The Articles provided for no separate executive branch. The president was the presiding officer of the Congress. There was no national court system at all.

The framers of the Constitution decided on a government in which the three main functions would be held by three separate branches. The Congress was empowered to make laws. The president was empowered, through the departments and agencies of the executive branch, to enforce the laws. The president is thus the head of the bureaucracy—the nonelected officials of government. The Supreme Court was es-

209

tablished as the highest judicial authority. This three-part arrangement was referred to by John Adams as a system of checks and balances.

In addition to distributing power among the three branches of the federal government, the Constitution also distributes it among the states and the people. The Tenth Amendment specifically reserves all "powers not delegated to the United States" to the "States respectively, or to the people." Within each state there are many other governmental units. Each local government, from the smallest village to the largest city, has its necessary powers. There are taxing bodies, such as school districts, that have the authority they need in order to operate. (*See also* Municipal Government; Taxation.)

CONGRESS: THE LEGISLATIVE BRANCH

One of the most difficult debates in the Constitutional Convention of 1787 centered on representation. The large states desired representation in proportion to population in the proposed national legislature. This would, of course, have allowed them to control legislation because they would have had more legislators than small states. The small states, conversely, wanted equal representation. On June 11, 1787, delegate Roger Sherman of Connecticut proposed the plan that eventually adopted. It called for a bicameral, or two-house, legislature in which one house has proportional representation and the other equal representation. Thus the small states were placated by having equal representation and the large states with proportional representation. After much wrangling among the delegates, the plan was adopted on July 16.

The Congress was created by Article I, section 1, of the Constitution: "All legislative powers herein shall be vested in a Congress of the United States, which shall consist of a Senate and House of Representatives." The first Congress was due to meet in New York City on March 4, 1789, but bad weather and worse roads delayed the members. By April 6, enough Congressmen had assembled to begin preliminary business. The Senate had only 20 members, since two states had not yet ratified the Constitution, and New York did not elect its senators until the following July. The House membership was also short—it had only 59 members.

Until the adoption of the 20th Amendment in 1933, members of Congress took office on March 4 in the year following their election. They did not meet in session, however, until the following December—more than a year after the election—unless the president called a special session. It thus became possible for a session meeting from December 3 of an even-numbered year until the next March 4 to be controlled by "lame ducks"—members who had been defeated in the previous election. To eliminate this situation the 20th Amendment was adopted. Members of Congress now take office on January 3 in the year following an election. Congressional terms extend from each odd-numbered year to the next odd-numbered year

because elections are held in November of even-numbered years. Dates of adjournment are voted by the membership.

At the beginning of a regular session, the president delivers a State of the Union address to a joint session of Congress. In years when there is an outgoing president and an elected president waiting to be sworn in, two such addresses are possible. Congress must also convene in special session every four years in December to count the electoral votes naming the new president (*see* Electoral College). Joint sessions are also held when the president or a foreign dignitary addresses both houses. Joint sessions are not legislative sessions.

Enacting laws does not consume most of the time of members of Congress. Most of the work of the two houses is done in committees. There are 16 standing committees in the Senate and 22 in the House. There are also subcommittees, special committees, congressional commissions, and joint congressional commissions. Each house may appoint special investigating committees such as those that conducted hearings on the Watergate scandal in 1973–74 and the Iran-*contra* affair in 1987.

The committee systems of Congress developed largely by accident, and many committees created for specific purposes outlived their usefulness. In 1921 the Senate reorganized its committee structure and greatly reduced their number. The House did the same in 1927.

Committees of each house are controlled by the political party that has a majority of members in that house. Appointments to committees are mostly based on seniority. The ranking, or most senior, member normally becomes chairman.

In addition to its committee and lawmaking activities, Congress also exercises a general legal control over all government employees. It may also exercise political control through the Senate's power of approving presidential nominations. Congress cannot remove officials from office except by its power of impeachment. In an impeachment proceeding the House acts as a grand jury, gathering evidence and securing an indictment. The Senate then becomes the court in which the case is tried. There has only been one complete presidential impeachment proceeding in American history—that of Andrew Johnson—and he was acquitted. A bill of impeachment was voted against Richard M. Nixon, but he resigned before a Senate trial could begin. (*See also* Impeachment.)

Among Congress' nonlegislative powers is that of initiating amendments to the Constitution, though the states also have this power. Congress may determine whether the states should vote on amendments by special conventions, which is how the Constitution was ratified, or through their legislatures.

In matters of legislation, all bills and joint resolutions must be passed in identical form by both houses and signed by the president. The exception is an amendment to the Constitution, which is not signed by him. Should the president veto a bill, it may be enacted over his veto by a two-thirds vote of both houses. Failure to repass in either house kills it. If a bill is not signed or returned by the president, it becomes law after ten days (excluding Sundays). If the president does not return a bill and Congress has adjourned in the meantime, however, the bill does not become law. This procedure is called a pocket veto (see Veto).

Bills introduced in either house are first sent to the committee having jurisdiction over them. A committee can kill a bill, bury it, or amend it. If the bill is reported favorably out of committee, it is sent to the floor of the respective house for debate and passage—with or without amendments. A bill passed by one house is sent to the other for consideration. There it may be passed intact, it may be amended and passed, or it may be defeated. If one house does not accept the version of a bill passed by the other house, the bill is sent to a conference committee composed of members of both houses. After final passage the bill is signed by the speaker of the House and the vice-president (who is the presiding officer of the Senate) and sent to the president for his signature.

The powers of Congress are specified in Article I, section 8, of the Constitution. Chief among them is the power to assess and collect taxes, for it is this authority that makes running the whole government, including the other two branches, possible. The power to decide how to spend money lies in both houses, but only the House of Representatives has the authority to originate bills for raising revenue.

Each house, because it is the judge of the "qualifications of its own members," may punish its members for misbehavior. Members can be expelled by a two-thirds vote. Actions of certain members have occasionally resulted in some form of rebuke. Senator Joseph R. McCarthy of Wisconsin was censured on Dec. 2, 1954 (see McCarthy). Representative Adam Clayton Powell of New York was excluded from the 90th Congress by a House vote in 1967.

The proceedings of the Congress are published daily in the *Congressional Record*. Publication of this journal began on March 4, 1873. The *Record* is a generally accurate account of daily proceedings, but the speeches of house members may be heavily edited for readers. Occasionally speeches included in the *Record* were never actually delivered on the floor of either house but are inserted to impress voters in home districts.

House of Representatives

The House of Representatives was intended by the framers of the Constitution to reflect the popular will. Its members therefore are directly elected by the people. The number of representatives from each state is proportional to the size of the state's population. No state, however, has less than one representative. Representation is reapportioned after every census. After the states receive their quota of seats, the states themselves determine the boundaries of the congressional districts. In 1964 the Supreme Court ruled that population sizes within each district must

Each January Congress meets in joint session in the House chamber to hear the president deliver the State of the Union message. Senators and cabinet members occupy the front rows of seats.

THE GOVERNMENT OF THE UNITED STATES

THE CONSTITUTION
"We the People . . ."

LEGISLATIVE
THE CONGRESS

SENATE   HOUSE
OF
REPRESENTATIVES

Architect of the Capitol
United States Botanic Garden
General Accounting Office
Government Printing Office
Library of Congress
Office of Technology
  Assessment
Congressional Budget Office
Copyright Royalty Tribunal

EXECUTIVE
THE PRESIDENT

White House Office
Office of Management and
  Budget
Council of Economic Advisers
National Security Council
Office of Policy Development
Office of the United States Trade
  Representative
Council on Environmental Quality
Office of Science and
  Technology Policy
Office of Administration
Office of the Vice-President

JUDICIAL
THE SUPREME COURT
OF THE UNITED STATES

United States Courts of Appeals
Unites States Court of Appeals
  for the Federal Circuit
United States District Courts
United States Claims Court
United States Court of
  International Trade
United States Court of Military
  Appeals
United States Tax Court
Temporary Emergency Court of
  Appeals

be approximately equal. The special powers of the House are two: the right to originate revenue bills and the right to begin impeachment proceedings.

By the time it adjourned the first House had 65 members. Today the House has 435 members, a number reached in 1912. This number was made official in a law of 1941. Two representatives were added when Alaska and Hawaii became states, but the number was returned to 435 after the next census. House members must be 25 years of age, be citizens of the United States for at least seven years, and must reside in the state that is represented. The whole membership of the House stands for election every two years.

Other members of the House are a resident commissioner from Puerto Rico and delegates from American Samoa, Guam, the Virgin Islands of the United States, and the District of Columbia. These individuals may take part in floor debates, but they have no vote.

The Constitution does not specify the organization of the House other than to stipulate the selection of a speaker and other officers. As presently organized, the House has kept some ancient parliamentary offices, including the speaker, clerk, sergeant at arms, and doorkeeper. Two other officers are the postmaster and the chaplain. The speaker of the House presides over its sessions. He is a member of the majority party controlling the House at a given session and is elected by his fellow party members. He is therefore his party's leader in the House.

Each party has a House leader—the majority leader and the minority leader—and under these are the majority whip and minority whip. The whips, as their name implies, try to keep party members in line for crucial votes. The committee chairmen also have considerable party influence. The central unit of a party in the House is the conference, or caucus. Its purpose is to develop the basic party organization that is responsible for carrying on the work of the House. Party control of the membership has declined, and considerable latitude is allowed members of both parties.

The clerk is the chief administrative officer of the House, responsible for keeping its journal, taking votes, certifying passage of bills, and processing legislation. The clerk prepares the House budget and disburses funds and is in charge of purchasing furnishings and supplies.

Senate

The makeup and general rules for the "world's most exclusive club," as it is often called, are detailed in Article I, section 3, of the Constitution. The Senate has 100 members, two for each state. Since 1913, when the 17th Amendment was ratified, senators have been directly elected by the people. Prior to that year they were elected by state legislatures. When vacancies occur between elections, state governors appoint replacements.

The Senate has some special powers not accorded to the House. It approves or disapproves of presidential appointments; it can approve treaties, by a two-thirds vote; and it is the court for impeachment trials.

To become a senator an individual must be at least 30 years of age, a citizen of the United States for nine years, and a resident of the state from which elected. The full term of a senator is six years. The terms of one third of the members expire every two years.

The presiding officer of the Senate is the vice-president of the United States. It is the only duty for that official prescribed by the Constitution. In his absence the presiding officer is the president pro tempore, meaning "for the time being," who is elected by the membership. As in the House, there is a majority leader and a minority leader. The Senate majority leader is often a powerful figure in government, especially if the president is of the other party.

The functions of the secretary of the Senate are similar to those of the House clerk. The chief executive officer of the Senate is the sergeant at arms, who supervises all departments and is, as well, the chief law enforcement officer. Duties include rounding up absent senators when a quorum is needed and when votes are being taken and conducting many ceremonial functions, including escorting the president for addresses to joint sessions of Congress.

The Senate, in its floor debates, has more freedom of action than does the House. As a rule, debate on a measure continues until every senator has had a chance to say everything he wishes on it. Freedom of debate is occasionally abused by a filibuster, a device

The main reading room of the Library of Congress is open to the public without charge.

by which a senator can talk endlessly to prevent a bill from coming to a vote. Senate rules provide for stopping a filibuster by the application of cloture, or closing debate, which requires the support of two thirds of the members present and voting. The cloture rule was adopted in 1917.

Agencies of Congress

The common interests of both houses are served by a number of agencies responsible to Congress or to joint committees of Congress. These agencies are the Architect of the Capitol, the United States Botanic Garden, the General Accounting Office, the Government Printing Office, the Library of Congress, the Office of Technology Assessment, the Congressional Budget Office, and the Copyright Royalty Tribunal.

The Architect of the Capitol is an office created in 1793 to oversee the construction of the Capitol Building. Today the agency is charged with the care and maintenance of the Capitol and grounds, which include 208.7 acres (84.5 hectares) of landscaping, parks, streets, and parking spaces. The office is also responsible for the structural care of the Library of Congress and the Supreme Court Building in addition to a variety of other duties.

The United States Botanic Garden was founded in 1820 but did not remain in continuous operation. It was revived in 1842, when the government had to find space to accommodate collections brought to Washington, D.C., from the South Seas by the United States Exploring Expedition led by Captain Charles Wilkes. The Botanic Garden is under the direction of the Joint Committee of the Library. Annual appropriations for it are provided by Congress.

The General Accounting Office (GAO) was established in 1921 to provide independent audits of government agencies. The GAO also assists Congress by providing information on all matters of pending legislation. It assists members of Congress in investigations and studies. Under the leadership of the comptroller general, the GAO has the authority to verify energy-related information for Congress. Its auditing authority extends to all departments of government. The GAO provides legal services and makes final determination on the legality of actions taken in the spending of federal funds. It also settles claims against the United States and collects debts.

The Government Printing Office (GPO) is one of the world's largest publishers. It was established in June 1860 to print documents for Congress and all departments of the federal government. The GPO also sells thousands of publications to the public through its bookstores and by mail order.

The Library of Congress, established in 1800 as a research facility for Congress, is today one of the world's largest libraries. In addition to its huge collection of books, the library is also responsible for copyrights. The library operates an extension service through its interlibrary loan system and numerous other services. The American Folklife Center, founded in 1976, is part of the library.

The Office of Technology Assessment was created in 1972 as another research facility to serve Congress. The primary task of the office is to identify the effects of technology on society.

The Congressional Budget Office was established in 1974 as an agency to help Congress oversee the federal budget process, aid in fiscal policy, review tax policies, and study the allocation of federal funds. It performs economic analysis by studying the effects of federal spending on the national economy and by projecting cost estimates of legislation passed by Congress.

The Copyright Royalty Tribunal, established in 1976, sets royalty rates for transmission and other use of copyrighted materials. These include books, records, and cable television programs.

EXECUTIVE BRANCH

Just as the delegates to the Constitutional Convention had differences over the nature of Congress, so too were there sharp disagreements on the nature of the Executive Office. Should there be one president or three? Should he serve for life or for a limited term? Was he eligible for reelection? Should he be elected by the people, by the governors of the states, or by Congress?

The outcome of the debates was Article II of the Constitution, outlining the office of the president. The presidency would consist of one individual holding office for four years but eligible for reelection. Because the delegates did not trust the people to elect a president directly, they established an indirect method. Electors chosen by state legislatures (and eventually by the voters) voted for candidates for the presidency (*see* Electoral College). To be eligible for the presidency a person must be a native-born citizen, 35 years of age, and must have lived in the United States for at least 14 years.

Based on the example set by George Washington, successive presidents did not seek more than a second term until Franklin D. Roosevelt ran for office and was elected four times, beginning in 1932. The 22nd Amendment, ratified in 1951, limits the term of office for presidents.

The Constitution gives many specific powers to the president. Other powers have accrued to the office through laws passed by Congress, through interpretations of laws by the courts, and through the president's position as leader of his party.

The president is charged with enforcing all federal laws and with supervising all federal administrative agencies. In practice these powers are delegated to subordinates. The president's principal helpers include the White House staff, specialized agencies of the Executive Office, and the heads of executive departments and their agencies and bureaus. Except for the White House staff, the individuals in charge of agencies and departments are appointed by the president, subject to approval by the Senate. The president nominates all officials, administrative or judicial, who are not civil-service employees.

The Constitution gives the president the power to grant reprieves and pardons to persons convicted of crimes against the United States. This power is denied only in the case of an individual convicted on impeachment.

The president exercises far-reaching powers in the conduct of foreign policy. In most cases he acts through the secretary of state and the Department of State. The president negotiates treaties, mostly through subordinates. These are subject to confirmation by a two-thirds vote in the Senate. He nominates ambassadors, ministers, and consuls to represent the United States abroad (*see* Diplomacy). He takes the lead in recognizing new regimes or withholding official recognition.

Closely related to his foreign policy authority is the president's role as commander in chief of all the armed forces. He appoints all commissioned officers of the Army, Navy, Air Force, and Marines. During wartime he may become involved in planning strategy.

Proper functioning of the government depends in great measure on the president's relations with Congress. It is his responsibility to keep Congress informed of the need for new legislation. He must also submit an annual budget for all the government expenditures. The departments and agencies are required to send Congress periodic reports of their activities, and members of departments and agencies are often required to testify before committees of Congress on matters of pending legislation or other issues.

In times of war or other national crisis, Congress usually grants the president emergency powers. These powers include the authority to issue orders regulating most phases of national life and war effort, to organize special agencies of government, and to make appointments without confirmation.

In normal times, as well as during emergencies, Congress may pass laws establishing a policy but leaving the details to be worked out by the Executive Office. The president then publishes an executive order that has the force of law.

The only official duty of the vice-president is to preside over the Senate, though he does not take part in its deliberations. He casts a deciding vote in case of a tie. In the president's absence he presides over meetings of the Cabinet (*see* Cabinet Government). Originally there were no candidates for this office. The man receiving the second largest number of votes for president became vice-president. In 1801 Thomas Jefferson and Aaron Burr each received 73 electoral votes, and the House of Representatives had to decide between the two candidates. After 36 ballots Jefferson became president and Burr vice-president. As the party system developed, separate candidates were nominated for each office on the same ticket.

Party politics in the 20th century has dictated that the vice-president be a consistent supporter of presidential policies no matter what his personal opinions. This was not always true a century earlier. Political tensions between North and South frequently divided

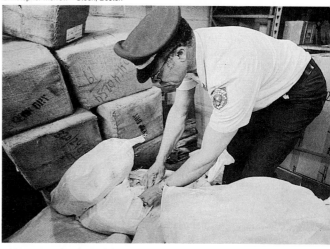

A Customs agent examines a load of freight that has arrived at Logan Airport in Boston, Mass.

parties. John C. Calhoun, vice-president to Andrew Jackson, resigned in 1832 in a dispute with Jackson.

Since the time of President Harry S. Truman, there has been an attempt to involve vice-presidents in the activities of the Executive Office by granting them membership on the National Security Council and in performing other tasks. Article II of the Constitution provides for the succession of the vice-president to the presidency in case of the death, resignation, or removal of the president. The 25th Amendment, ratified in 1967, provides that he also serve as acting president if the president is temporarily incapacitated. (For tables of presidential elections and vice-presidents, *see* Fact-Index.)

DIVISIONS OF THE EXECUTIVE BRANCH

Congress functions primarily in Washington, D.C. The executive branch of government operates throughout the United States, its possessions, and in all foreign nations with which the United States has diplomatic relations. Immediately subject to the president is the White House Office. Also closely associated with him is the Executive Office of the President, which includes several agencies transferred to the office by the Reorganization Act of 1939 and subsequent legislation. Next are the 13 departments: Agriculture, Commerce, Defense, Education, Energy, Health and Human Services, Housing and Urban Development, Interior, Justice, Labor, State, Transportation, and Treasury. Next are a large number of independent commissions, boards, corporations, and agencies. Among them are the Securities and Exchange Commission, the Federal Trade Commission, the General Services Administration, and the Federal Home Loan Bank Board. (*See also* Government Agencies.)

The White House Office consisted of about 85 individuals in the late 1980s. These people, headed by the chief of staff, are the president's personal advisers on all matters of policy, including relations with

Congress and the media. These advisers are hired by the executive branch and are not subject to approval by the Senate.

The Executive Office consists of agencies that deal in foreign and domestic policy for the president. Heads of these agencies are nominated by him, subject to confirmation by the Senate. These agencies are the Office of Management and Budget, the Council of Economic Advisers, the National Security Council, the Office of Policy Development, the Office of the United States Trade Representative, the Council on Environmental Quality, the Office of Science and Technology Policy, the Office of Administration, and the Office of the Vice-President. The secretaries of the departments make up the president's Cabinet.

Departments

Each federal department is headed by a secretary, who has several specialized undersecretaries responsible to him. These officials are nominated by the president subject to confirmation by the Senate.

The Department of State was established in 1789 and is therefore the oldest and highest ranking Cabinet office. It is headed by the secretary of state, who acts on behalf of the president in relations between the United States and foreign governments. With its many field agents in the Foreign Service, the department is a vital link between the United States and other countries. It is also a valuable source of information for the president in foreign policy decisions.

The department speaks for the United States in the United Nations through the United States Mission to the United Nations.

The secretary of state is assisted by a deputy secretary and undersecretaries of state for political affairs, economic affairs, security assistance, and management. The department has five regional bureaus: African Affairs, European and Canadian Affairs, East Asian and Pacific Affairs, Inter-American Affairs, and Near Eastern and South Asian Affairs. The other 11 bureaus are Economic and Business Affairs, Intelligence and Research, International Organization, Legal Adviser, Public Affairs, Consular Affairs, Politico-Military Affairs, Oceans and International Environmental and Scientific Affairs, Protocol, Human Rights and Humanitarian Affairs, and the Bureau for Refugee Programs.

The Department of the Treasury, established in 1789, is the second-ranking executive department. The Treasury is the custodian and manager of the public purse. It collects taxes, duties, and other revenues. It borrows money for the government on short-term notes and long-term bonds. It is responsible for management of the debt. It disburses federal funds. It controls the coinage and making of paper money, enforces revenue laws, and makes reports on the nation's finances.

Agencies with the Treasury are the Bureau of Alcohol, Tobacco, and Firearms; the Office of the Comptroller of the Currency; the United States Cus-

The Pentagon, headquarters for the Department of Defense, is located in Arlington County, Va. It was built between 1941 and 1943 and is the largest office building in the world.

Fairchild Aerial Surveys, Inc.

toms Service; the Bureau of Engraving and Printing; the Federal Law Enforcement Training Center; the Financial Management Service; the Internal Revenue Service; the United States Mint; the Bureau of the Public Debt; the United States Savings Bond Division; and the United States Secret Service. Members of the Secret Service are assigned to protect the president and his family, former presidents and their families, and the vice-presdent and his family.

The Department of Defense was established in 1949 to integrate the policies and procedures for all agencies relating to defense. Its three major components are the departments of the Army, Navy, and Air Force.

Earlier the military forces of the United States had been represented by the Department of War, established in 1789, and the Department of the Navy, created in 1798. Each had been headed by a secretary with Cabinet rank. The Defense Department is now headed by a civilian secretary of defense, who has direction and control of the service branches. Each service has a secretary without Cabinet rank. Next in command are the Joint Chiefs of Staff, representing the armed forces. In terms of personnel, the Defense Department is the largest government agency, as it includes all members of the armed forces.

The Armed Forces Policy Council advises the secretary of defense on policy matters. The council is made up of the deputy secretary of defense; the secretaries of the Army, Navy, and Air Force; the undersecretaries of defense for policy and for research and engineering; the chairman of the Joint Chiefs of Staff; the chiefs of the Army and the Air Force; the chief of naval operations; and the commandant of the Marine Corps. (*See also* Air Force; Army; Marines; Navy; and Warfare.)

The Department of Justice was established in 1870. It provides the means for enforcement of federal laws, furnishes legal counsel in federal cases, affords legal opinions to the president and heads of departments, and directs federal prisons. The head of the department is the attorney general, a Cabinet member since 1789.

The deputy attorney general coordinates the operation of the department and supervises the federal district attorneys and marshals. Presidential appointments of federal judges, attorneys, and marshals clear through the deputy attorney general.

The solicitor general represents the government in cases before the Supreme Court and in any other court if the attorney general thinks it advisable. Each type of case is handled by a division headed by an assistant attorney general. The divisions are: Antitrust, Civil, Civil Rights, Criminal, Land and Natural Resources, and Tax. The assistant attorney general for legislative affairs is the chief liaison officer with Congress.

Bureaus within the Justice Department are: the Federal Bureau of Investigation, the Bureau of Prisons, the United States Marshals Service, the International Criminal Police Organization-United States National Central Bureau, the Immigration and Nat-

Realistic war games are tracked by computer at a military installation in Colorado Springs, Colo.

uralization Service, the Drug Enforcement Administration, and the Justice Assistance Act Agencies. The Justice Assistance Act of 1984 established programs of financial and technical assistance to the states and local governments. The new agencies created under the act are: the Office of Justice Programs, the Bureau of Justice Assistance, the National Institute of Justice, the Bureau of Justice Statistics, and the Office of Juvenile Justice and Delinquency Prevention. Boards within the Justice Department are: the Executive Office for Immigration Review, the United States Parole Commission, the Foreign Claims Settlement Commission of the United States, and the National Drug Policy Board.

The Department of the Interior was established in 1849. Since its inception the department has served two contrasting purposes. During the westward movement of the frontier, it freely granted the resources of the nation to individuals and groups to hasten the growth of the United States. At the time unoccupied land, minerals, timber, and wildlife were abundant and were regarded as expendable.

Today the department's functions are the opposite. It is the government's chief conservation agency. Minerals, public lands, waterpower, fish, wildlife, scenic wonders, and recreation areas are all under the custodianship of the department for the benefit of the American people.

The department is headed by the secretary of the interior. There is an undersecretary, along with assistant secretaries for fish and wildlife and parks; water and science; land and minerals management; Indian affairs; policy, budget, and administration; and territorial and international affairs.

Bureaus within the department are: the United States Fish and Wildlife Service, the National Park Service, the Bureau of Mines, the Geological Survey, the Office of Surface Mining Reclamation and Enforcement, the Bureau of Indian Affairs (originally part of the War Department, 1824–49), Minerals Man-

Guarding the public's health is one task of an inspector for the Department of Agriculture as he checks poultry quality (left). A sick duck at a migratory bird refuge is inoculated with antitoxin (right) by an agent of the Fish and Wildlife Service of the Department of the Interior.

agement Service, the Bureau of Land Management, and the Bureau of Reclamation.

The Department of Agriculture was established in 1862. Until 1889 it was administered by a commissioner of agriculture. The divisions of the department are: Small Community and Rural Development, Marketing and Inspection Services, Food and Consumer Services, International Affairs and Commodity Programs, Science and Education, Natural Resources and Environment, and Economics.

The Small Community and Rural Development division includes the Farmers Home Administration, the Rural Electrification Administration, and the Federal Crop Insurance Corporation. The Marketing and Inspection Services include the Agricultural Cooperative Service, the Agricultural Marketing Service, the Animal and Plant Health Inspection Service, the Federal Grain Inspection Service, the Food Safety and Inspection Service, the Office of Transportation, and the Packers and Stockyards Administration.

Food and Consumer services is divided into the Food and Nutrition Service, the Human Nutrition Information Service, and the Office of the Consumer Advisor. The International Affairs and Commodity Programs comprises the Agricultural Stabilization and Conservation Service, the Commodity Credit Corporation, the Foreign Agricultural Service, and the Office of International Cooperation and Development.

The Science and Education division includes the Agricultural Research Service, the Cooperative State Research Service, the Extension Service, the National Agricultural Library, and the Office of Grants and Programs Systems. The Natural Resources and Environment division includes the Forest Service and the Soil Conservation Service. Included in the Economics division is the Economic Research Service, the National Agricultural Statistics Service, the Eco-

nomic Analysis Staff, the Office of Energy, the World Agricultural Outlook Board, and the Economics Management Staff.

A Department of Commerce was proposed by Gouverneur Morris in 1787, as the Constitution was being debated. It did not become a reality until 1903, when it was established as the Department of Commerce and Labor. In 1913 the Department of Labor became independent.

The Department of Commerce fosters the nation's business, trade, and industry. It grants patents, conducts environmental research, provides weather forecasts, takes censuses, maintains measurement standards, and performs numerous other tasks related to its basic functions. Its divisions are: the National Technical Information Service, the Bureau of the Census, the Bureau of Economic Analysis, the Economic Development Administration, the International Trade Administration, the Minority Business Development Agency, the National Bureau of Standards, the National Oceanic and Atmospheric Administration, the National Telecommunications and Information Administration, the Patent and Trademark Office, and the United States Travel and Tourism Administration.

The Department of Labor, established as a separate division in 1913, had the distinction of having as secretary of labor the first woman to achieve Cabinet rank—Frances Perkins. She held office from 1933 until 1945. The largest division within the department is the Employment and Training Administration. It has within it the Office of Employment Security, the Unemployment Insurance program, the Employment Service, the Office of Trade Adjustment Assistance, the Office of Job Training Programs, the Senior Community Service Employment Program, the Apprenticeship and Training programs, the Office of Strategic Planning and Policy Development, the

Office of Financial and Administrative Management, and the Office of Regional Management.

The other divisions are: the Office of Labor-Management Standards, the Office of Pension and Welfare Benefits Administration, the Bureau of Labor-Management Relations and Cooperative Programs, the Employee Standards Administration, the Occupational Safety and Health Administration, the Mine Safety and Health Administration, the Bureau of Labor Statistics, and the Veterans' Employment and Training Service.

The Department of Health and Human Services (HHS) was, until 1953, the Federal Security Agency. It was then renamed the Department of Health, Education, and Welfare (HEW) and raised to Cabinet status. Its current name was adopted in 1979, when responsibility for education was transferred to a new department. HHS promotes social and economic security, national health, and child welfare. The programs administered under HHS by the Social Security Administration are retirement and survivors insurance; disability insurance; supplemental security income for the aged, blind, and disabled; and Aid to Families with Dependent Children (*see* Social Security; Welfare State).

Divisions of HHS, in addition to the Social Security Administration, are: the Office of Human Development Services, the Public Health Service, the Health Care Financing Administration, and the Family Support Administration.

The Department of Housing and Urban Development (HUD) was established as part of President Lyndon Johnson's Great Society program in 1965. It was created to oversee programs that provide housing assistance backed by federal funds. HUD's program areas are: Community Planning and Development, Fair Housing and Equal Opportunity, Housing, Public and Indian Housing, the Government National Mortgage Association, and the Office of Policy Development and Research.

The Department of Transportation was created by Congress in 1966 to promote transportation safety, develop a national transportation policy, and prepare guidelines for federal spending in transportation facilities and equipment. Its divisions are: the Federal Aviation Administration, the Federal Highway Administration, the Federal Railroad Administration, the National Highway Traffic Safety Administration, the Urban Mass Transportation Administration, the Maritime Administration, the Saint Lawrence Seaway Development Corporation, the Research and Special Programs Administration, and the United States Coast Guard.

The Department of Energy was established in 1977 to provide the framework for a comprehensive, balanced national energy policy. Its divisions are: the

(Left) A worker for the Commerce Department's Bureau of the Census conducts an interview in Baltimore, Md., during the 1980 census. (Right) An agent of the National Oceanic and Atmospheric Administration checks a rain gauge in Texas.

(Left) Ellis Herwig—Stock, Boston; (right) Bob Daemmrich—Stock, Boston

Energy Information Administration, the Economic Regulatory Commission, and the Federal Energy Regulatory Commission.

The Department of Education was established in 1980 to coordinate more than 150 federal programs in education, ranging from college loans to telecommunications. The department absorbed several functions that had belonged to HEW. The department has a director of Bilingual Education, a Civil Rights director, and assistant secretaries for Elementary and Secondary Education, Educational Research and Improvement, Vocational and Adult Education, Special Education and Rehabilitative Services, and Postsecondary Education. The department also supplies funds to the American Printing House for the Blind in Louisville, Ky.; Gallaudet College in Washington, D.C.; Howard University in Washington, D.C.; and the National Technical Institute for the Deaf at Rochester Institute of Technology, at Rochester, N.Y.

FEDERAL COURT SYSTEM

Article III of the Constitution provides for a Supreme Court and "such inferior courts as the Congress may from time to time ordain and establish." Since that statement was written in 1787, Congress has established a multilevel national court system along with several special tribunals.

Below the Supreme Court are the United States Courts of Appeals. Next are the United States District Courts. Special courts created by Congress are: the Temporary Emergency Court of Appeals, the United States Claims Court, the United States Court of International Trade, the United States Court of Military Appeals, and the United States Tax Court. The Federal Judicial Center is a research agency.

Supreme Court

"We are under a Constitution, but the Constitution is what the judges say it is." This extraordinary, but accurate, remark by former Chief Justice Charles Evans Hughes (served 1930–41) highlights the most significant role the Supreme Court plays in American life. The power of judicial review—the authority to rule on the constitutionality of federal and state laws—has played a vital role in shaping the development of law and public policy in the United States (*see* Constitutional Law).

The Supreme Court is the highest judicial tribunal in the United States and perhaps the most powerful court in the world. It is the court of final appeal, and its rulings are law for the president, Congress, and the states as well as for individual citizens.

The Judiciary Act passed by Congress on Sept. 24, 1789, provided for a Supreme Court with a chief justice and five associate justices. The Court itself was organized on Feb. 2, 1790, with John Jay as the first chief justice. In 1807 the membership of the Court was increased to seven and in 1837 to nine. A statute of 1863 raised it to ten, but in 1869 it was changed back to nine—its present number. A proposal by President Franklin D. Roosevelt in 1937 to reorganize the Court

Workers ready a house for painting. They are paid through a loan made possible by the federal government. Rehabilitation of old buildings is among the many programs of the Department of Housing and Urban Development.

and add six new justices—called the "court-packing scheme"—was defeated in Congress. All justices are appointed by the president, subject to confirmation by the Senate.

Justices remain on the Court, and on all federal courts, for life "during good behavior." Only one justice—Samuel Chase in 1805—has ever been impeached, but he was acquitted. Associate justice Abe Fortas resigned under pressure in 1969, accused of a conflict of interest.

The Court has two types of jurisdiction—original and appellate. Original jurisdiction refers to cases tried directly before it without involving the lower courts. The Constitution gives the Court original jurisdiction in controversies between states, between a state and the federal government, between a state and citizens of another state, and in cases affecting ambassadors, other public ministers, and consuls. The Court also hears the rare cases of admiralty and maritime jurisdiction. Sessions of the Court begin on the first Monday in October and end in June or July.

Most cases reach the Court under its appellate jurisdiction—the power to review decisions made by lower courts, both federal and state. These cases come before the Court either by appeals or by certiorari.

Appeals cases are those that challenge a state or federal law as being inconsistent with the Constitution. They invoke an obligatory jurisdiction of the Court. If the losing party in a lower-court case believes the decision against him was based on an unconstitutional statute, he may appeal to the Supreme Court. The Court is obligated to grant a preliminary hearing. If one justice finds merit in the appeal, a full trial is granted. The Court may dismiss an appeal if the question involved is considered insubstantial.

Certiorari cases are reviews of lower-court decisions undertaken at the discretion of the Supreme Court. The Court receives thousands of petitions each year that do not qualify as appeals cases. It is free to choose those it will consider. Review by certiorari procedure is granted only in unusual cases—for example, those involving constitutional interpretation, conflicting interpretations of law by lower courts, or the decision by a state court on a point of federal law. A certiorari case is accepted if four justices agree that it merits review. The Court may not rule on a federal or state law, however, no matter how unconstitutional it may seem, unless the issue is brought before it in a case. The Court does not act in an advisory capacity.

Persons seeking a Court review of a decision must first have exhausted review procedures in their highest state court or in a federal appeals court. Unless the case qualifies as an appeals case, which the Court is obliged to hear, a petition for review by certiorari is then made to the Court. If the petition is granted, specially qualified lawyers are assigned to the case. After briefs have been filed, each side is allowed one hour to present oral arguments. If the federal government has an interest in the case, it is represented by the solicitor general or another government lawyer. A minimum of six justices must be present when any case is argued.

After the Court hears a series of cases, it recesses for research and reflection. Decisions are reached in private conferences. A judgment must be concurred in by a majority of the justices hearing the case. If no decision is reached, a rehearing may be called.

If the chief justice agrees with the majority, he assigns a justice to write the opinion of the Court. If he disagrees, the senior associate justice assigns the opinion. The opinion, which gives the ruling and the reasoning behind it, is read at a subsequent session of the Court. Judges who disagree with the ruling may write dissenting opinions. In the history of the Court, Oliver Wendell Holmes, Jr., was known as "the great dissenter." Many of his dissents subsequently became majority rulings.

Other Federal Courts

The Supreme Court sits atop a three-tiered structure. Below it are the federal appeals courts and the district courts. The latter have original jurisdiction in federal cases. There are also other specialized courts created by Congress.

Courts of Appeals. The Circuit Court of Appeals Act, passed by Congress on March 3, 1891, created intermediate courts to relieve the Supreme Court of its heavy appeals case load. The United States was divided into 12 judicial circuits, plus the District of Columbia. The term circuit is used because the justices of the Supreme Court once rode the circuits of their court responsibilities in addition to being present at sessions of the Supreme Court itself. The 1891 act relieved the judges of this task.

Each circuit has a federal appeals court. Each of the 50 states is assigned to one of the circuits, and the territories are assigned to the first, third, and ninth circuits. Each appeals court has from six to 28 judges, depending on the amount of casework in the circuit. The number of judges can be changed by Congress. Each court of appeals normally hears cases by panels of three judges, but the court may also sit with all its judges present. Cases are sent to an appeals court from a federal district court or from a state court.

Court of Appeals for the Federal Circuit. The Federal Courts Improvement Act of 1982 established the Court of Appeals for the Federal Circuit as the successor to the Court of Customs and Patent Appeals and the Court of Claims. It has national jurisdiction and accepts appeals in patent, trademark, and copyright cases and appeals from the United States Claims Court and from the United States Court of International Trade. It also reviews administrative rulings by the Patent and Trademark Office, the International Trade Commission, the Merit Systems Protection Board, and the secretary of commerce. The court has 12 judges and normally sits in panels of three on a case.

District courts are federal trial courts with original jurisdiction in cases involving federal law. Each state has at least one district court, and large states have as many as four. There are also district courts in the territories. The number of judges in a district ranges from two to 27. One judge usually hears a case, but on occasion three judges may be required.

Temporary Emergency Court of Appeals. The Economic Stabilization Act Amendments of 1971 created the Temporary Emergency Court of Appeals to have jurisdiction over appeals from district courts in cases arising under economic stabilization and energy conservation laws. The court is situated in the District of Columbia and has functioned since February 1972.

Claims Court. Congress established the Claims Court on Oct. 1, 1982, to succeed the Court of Claims. Its cases concern such money judgments against the United States as taking property, contract obligations, claims by government employees for back pay, and claims for refunds from income taxes. The court can also render judgments in cases charging the government with patent or copyright infringement.

Court of International Trade was known as the Board of United States General Appraisers when it was established in 1890. The present court was constituted in 1980. As its name implies, the court has jurisdiction over claims against the government on import transactions, including antidumping charges and customs duties.

Court of Military Appeals, established in 1950, is the appellate tribunal for reviewing court-martial proceedings of the armed services. It has three civilian judges. Its rulings are subject to certiorari review by the Supreme Court.

The Tax Court was created in 1924 as an independent agency of the executive branch. It was given its present name in 1942. Composed of 19 judges, it hears cases about income, gift, and estate taxes.

UNIVERSE *see* COSMOLOGY.

© Mike Yamashita—West Light

The colleges of England's University of Cambridge make up one of the world's best schools. Of special note is King's College and its beautiful Gothic chapel, right, built of white limestone.

UNIVERSITIES AND COLLEGES

UNIVERSITIES AND COLLEGES. Higher education is the schooling that begins at about age 18 after the completion of secondary school. In the past higher education was much more narrowly defined than it is today. It originally meant the schooling that was provided to men entering the professions, and these were limited to law, medicine, and religion. Today the term profession has gained a much broader definition than a calling and has become almost synonymous with career or occupation.

Beginning in about the 11th century, the institutions that provided schooling for the professions were colleges and universities. Now, in addition to these, there are trade schools, technical institutes, military academies, and other organizations in which individuals may prepare for a career. Nevertheless, colleges and universities have remained the dominant institutions throughout the world for the pursuit of higher education.

In these institutions different levels of schooling are provided. Students coming from secondary schools—called high schools or preparatory schools in the United States—normally take a four-year course leading to a diploma called a bachelor's degree. The schooling that leads to the bachelor's degree is called undergraduate work. Students may then proceed to more advanced schooling. This may consist of study at a professional school such as a college of law or engineering, or it may involve graduate school at a university—the pursuit of a master's or doctor's degree in a chosen field of study. After earning an advanced degree, it is possible to continue at a university in a research capacity to earn further credentials in one's field of study. Advanced degrees are gener-

ally required before anyone can teach at a college or university in the United States.

Origin of the College

The terms college and university originally had very similar meanings. Only with the passing of centuries did university come to signify an educational institution composed of more than one college. The word college means literally "union formed by law," or a group of people associated in some common function. The ancient Roman craft guilds were called *collegia.* The closest parallel today is the corporation, a business organization chartered by a government.

During the Middle Ages students at the universities of Paris, Oxford, and Cambridge found it convenient to rent houses and share expenses instead of living in private apartments. By the 13th century these "houses of scholars" were becoming legally recognized corporate institutions. At Oxford the earliest of these corporations were University College, founded in 1249 by William of Durham; Balliol College, founded by John Balliol in 1263; and Merton College, founded about 1264 by Walter de Merton. A similar development took place at Cambridge.

At Paris the university was divided into faculties of canon law, theology, medicine, and the arts. The arts faculty, which was the undergraduate college of its day, was further divided into four nations, which included both teachers and students. Nations at medieval universities were groups primarily of students from a specific region or country who banded together for mutual protection in a foreign land. On the Continent these nations were the forerunners of colleges. In some universities the nations were responsible

222

for teaching and examining students. The division of students into nations first occurred at the university in Bologna, Italy.

In the United States the word college is used in a variety of ways. It most commonly refers to four-year institutions that admit students from secondary schools and grant a bachelor's degree after a general course of studies. Usually called liberal arts colleges, they are often completely independent of any university connection.

A college may also be a school for specialized training that takes place after receiving the bachelor's degree—such as a college of law or medicine. Schools specializing in theological training may be called seminaries or schools instead of colleges. A university normally consists of a group of colleges—one for the liberal arts or general studies and others for engineering, law, medicine, education, and business. Some of these colleges are for advanced study, while the college of liberal arts is the institution in which one earns a bachelor's degree.

There are many schools offering training in secretarial skills, business, accounting, computer programming, and other courses for high-school graduates. Many of these are called colleges, though they do not confer degrees. The United States has many two-year institutions called junior colleges or community colleges. Course work in junior colleges is equivalent to the first two years of a four-year liberal arts college. In a few universities the student residence halls are called colleges.

Origin of the University

During the Middle Ages the Latin word *universitas* referred to any type of community. When used in its modern sense as a place for advanced learning, it usually required the addition of other words such as "masters and scholars." The term that was normally used to describe a legally chartered school of teachers and students was *studium generale,* meaning a place of study open to students from all parts. The *universitas* was a group of teachers or students (or perhaps both) within the *studium.* A *studium* was quite similar to a guild in both origin and composition. The beginners were essentially apprentices, called bachelors, while the teachers were the masters.

The *studium* probably emerged when the bishop of a diocese or some other authority gave a teacher permission to operate a school other than the local cathedral or monastery school. It is likely that a license to teach was granted to a master after a formal examination. The *studium* itself became a school that granted a teaching license to its scholars after they completed a prescribed course of study and passed examinations.

By the 11th or 12th century no *studium generale* could be started without a license from either a church or governmental official. Teachers and students, who were mostly either clergy or future clergy, enjoyed certain privileges. In 1158 the emperor Frederick I Barbarossa granted those in his jurisdiction protection from unjust arrest, the right of trial before their peers, and permission to dwell in security. Such privileges were gradually enlarged to include protection from extortion in financial dealings and the right to stop attending lectures as a protest against grievances or outside interference with established rights.

Gradually certain schools—especially Bologna and Paris—gained international recognition, and students flocked to them from all parts of Europe. Their reputations allowed graduates of those schools to teach anywhere else. To promote the quality of certain schools, the popes and emperors granted special licenses or charters. In 1233, for example, Pope Gregory IX issued a document to the school at Toulouse allowing anyone who had been admitted to a doctorate at the school to teach anywhere without further examination. By the end of the 14th century the term *universitas* had displaced *studium* and was used by itself to describe the better-known schools of Europe.

Yale University in New Haven, Conn., seen in an 1836 view, was the third institution of higher learning founded in the British colonies of North America.

Vassar College, founded in New York State in 1861, was for more than a century one of the most prestigious women's colleges in the United States. It is now coeducational.

The Granger Collection

Degrees and Diplomas

A student graduating from a four-year college in the United States today normally receives a B.A. or B.S. degree, meaning Bachelor of Arts and Bachelor of Science. Should the student wish further education, a graduate school at a university may be selected. (Colleges of the type offering bachelors' degrees do not normally offer graduate courses.) This is a level of study for those who have graduated from college, as the name suggests. Further study of one or two years can earn a master's degree, and beyond that a student may earn a doctorate, normally a Ph.D., or Doctor of Philosophy. This degree, contrary to its name, may be earned in a variety of subjects, not just the field of philosophy.

Besides graduate school there are other options for further study. Among them are medical school, law school, and theological seminary in keeping with the traditional professions as they were known in the Middle Ages. There are today several other choices as well, including business school, architectural school, engineering school, school of veterinary medicine, school of fine arts, school of journalism, and many other forms of specialized training leading to specific careers. Large universities have colleges in all of these fields. The degrees given by these schools vary with the profession and occasionally with the school. A graduate of a medical school, for instance, earns a Doctor of Medicine degree, or M.D., while three years at a seminary brings a master of theology.

The modern degree structure is more complex than that originating in about the 13th century. Then there were only three levels of attainment. The bachelor's degree represented the first stage of academic life in a university. It had its counterpart in the apprenticeships for young members of a guild. The degree allowed the scholar to study to earn a licentiate, comparable to a craft journeyman. This degree, as its name suggests, was a license permitting him to teach and to study further to earn a doctorate or a master's degree, which were the same at that time. The doctorate admitted the scholar into full membership in the teachers' guild and certified him as a full-time lecturer at the university. It was comparable to becoming a master in a craft guild. (*See also* Guild.)

In Great Britain the bachelor's is given as the first degree in arts or sciences after a three-year course in most cases. The Master of Arts degree, or M.A., is earned by examination, except at Cambridge and Oxford. Those universities grant it only after a period of residence dating from a student's commencement of studies at the schools. At Cambridge it is awarded without examination six years after the end of a student's first term of residence, but it does not represent additional academic achievement. It confers seniority in the school, however, and membership in its senate. Other higher earned degrees comparable to a master's in the United States are designated as either a bachelor's or a master's, depending on the field of study. There is also a doctorate of philosophy in all fields. Some advanced degrees are open only to graduates of Oxford or Cambridge.

In continental Europe, with some exceptions, the giving of bachelor's and master's degrees has been abandoned. In France, for example, the usual degrees are *licence* and doctorate. The *licence* is earned after four semesters at the university, while the doctorate takes from four to seven years. In Germany the doctorate is the only degree granted. Students who do not pursue a doctorate are given diplomas in specialized fields after examinations.

Curriculum

The most dramatic change in universities since their beginning has taken place in the courses of study. The early European schools offered a core curriculum for all students based on the seven liberal arts: grammar, logic, rhetoric, geometry, arithmetic, astronomy, and music. Students then proceeded to study under one of the professional faculties of law, medicine, or religion. Some universities were renowned for specializing in one profession—for example, Paris was highly regarded for its theological school, Bologna for law, and Salerno for medicine. Other schools were more diverse, and in time all of them broadened their courses of study considerably.

This classical course of studies was modified somewhat over the centuries, but it was not abandoned until the 19th century. In the United States it was set aside in favor of a much wider array of courses—modern languages were added to the basic Latin and

Greek, for example. New science courses were added. Students were given electives from which to choose. As new disciplines—such as sociology, psychology, and economics—were formulated, they too were introduced into the colleges and universities. Today the range of courses given in higher education is virtually unlimited, especially in the United States.

Early Universities

The first university in Europe was at Salerno, Italy. It became known as a school of medicine as early as the 9th century. As its fame spread, students were drawn to it from all over Europe. In 1231 it was licensed by Frederick II, Holy Roman emperor, as the only school of medicine in his Kingdom of Naples. The school never developed a curriculum beyond medicine.

The second university emerged at Bologna, Italy, during the 11th century at about the same time as the famed Muslim school, El Azhar University, in Cairo, Egypt. Bologna developed into a widely respected school of canon and civil law. The emperor Frederick I Barbarossa gave it his special protection. In about 1200 the faculties of medicine and philosophy (the seven liberal arts) were added to the law faculty. At Bologna the masters formed themselves into organizations called *collegia* for the conferring of degrees. Other Italian universities founded from the 13th to the 15th century include Padua (1222), Siena (1241), Piacenza (1248), Rome (1303), Perugia (1308), Pisa (1343), Florence (1349), Pavia (1361), and Turin (1405).

North of Italy the first great universities were those at Paris in France and at Oxford and Cambridge in England. The University of Paris grew out of theological schools associated with Notre Dame Cathedral. Shortly after 1100 William of Champeaux, a theologian and philosopher, opened a school in the cathedral for teaching dialectic—a type of logical argumentation. Early in the 13th century some of the school's masters placed themselves under the authority of the abbot of the Church of Sainte-Geneviève on the Left (or south) Bank of the Seine. It was the granting of a *licence,* or master of arts degree, by the chancellor of the cathedral, however, that prompted the development of the school into a university. The degree implied a master's formal entrance into the duties of a licensed teacher. It was also an emancipation from his state of bachelorhood, or apprenticeship.

The University of Paris as a formal institution actually emerged between 1150 and 1170, though its written statutes were not set down until about 1208. Recognition as a legal corporation came in 1215 from Pope Innocent III. His support made the school the center for orthodox teaching north of Italy.

About 1253 the theologian Robert de Sorbon began teaching at Paris. In about 1257 he founded the Maison (house) de Sorbonne as a theological school for poor students. His school received the pope's official recognition in 1259, and it soon became one of the colleges around which the University of Paris grew. The Sorbonne is still one of the chief schools of

the university. Other noted French universities were founded at Montpellier (1220), Toulouse (1229), Orléans (1306), Aix-en-Provence (1409), Poitiers (1431), and Caen (1432).

The University of Paris served as a model for the creation of other schools in Northern Europe. In England the first two were Oxford and Cambridge. Of the two Oxford seems to have been the earlier. It probably began about 1167–68 when English students, masters, and scholars returned from Paris.

There was a school taught by clergy at Cambridge after 1112, but the elements of a university did not appear until students migrated there from Oxford in 1209. In 1224 the Franciscan Order established itself in the town, and the Dominicans arrived a few decades later. In 1231 and 1233 letters from the king and the pope indicated that Cambridge was a university with a chancellor at its head. The first of its colleges, Peterhouse, was founded in 1284.

The first university in Scotland was Saint Andrews, founded in 1411 by Bishop Henry Wardlaw. The University of Glasgow was founded in 1451 to preserve and defend the Catholic faith. One of its distinguished alumni was John Knox, the reformer of the church of Scotland in the 16th century. The University of Aberdeen was founded in 1495. The fourth university of Scotland, at Edinburgh, was not started until 1583, after the Reformation.

In Germany the University of Heidelberg received its charter from Pope Urban VI in 1386. Its founder was the elector Rupert I. The University of Erfurt was established in 1379 and refounded by Urban VI in 1389 because its original charter had been issued by an antipope (*see* Papacy). Other early German schools included Leipzig (chartered 1409), Freiburg (1455), Tübingen (1477), Trier (1450), Mainz (1476), and Wittenberg (1502).

In what is now Belgium the University of Louvain was founded in 1425. It was controlled by the town instead of the church, and the wealth of the city en-

The main entrance to the Sorbonne, part of the University of Paris, is one of the most striking parts of the school.

© Mike Yamashita—West Light

abled it to attract outstanding faculty members from the beginning. By the 16th century Louvain ranked second only to Paris in reputation and size. It had 28 colleges and a very active press. Its press is still one of the world's best for producing scholarly books.

The Reformation and After

The Protestant Reformation of the 16th century and the Roman Catholic reaction against it affected the universities in different ways. In Germany, where Protestant universities were founded and older schools were taken over by Protestants, they became mainly centers for theological propaganda and dispute. The pursuit of new learning was discouraged. The German schools almost ceased to be centers of learning. They were devoted primarily to defending and promoting correct doctrine.

The situation was similar in Roman Catholic schools. The Counter-Reformation had little impact on the older schools. They remained centers of theology and traditional learning and were not receptive to the interest in science that was sweeping Europe. Reform of education took place outside the universities. The Collège de France, for example, was founded in 1530 by Francis I as a counterbalance to the backwardness of the University of Paris at the time.

Emergence of the Modern University

Bitter religious controversies and wars resulting from the Reformation lasted well into the 17th century. Only at their close was it possible to restore the universities as places of learning. By this time the Enlightenment had begun to pervade much of Europe (see Enlightenment). New scientific discoveries were undermining the centuries-old truths of religion, and leading scholars in all countries were pressing for new trends in education.

The modern university was born at Halle in Germany as a reaction against rigid Lutheran dogmatism.

A graduate student in marine biology feeds protein pellets to fish at the University of Florida in Miami.

© Robert Holland

The University of Halle was founded in 1694. Although a center of Lutheranism, it was an advocate of a different variety. The founders of the school were Pietists, believers who rejected the notion that correct doctrine was sufficient for the Christian life. Two of Halle's early teachers, Christian Thomasius and August Hermann Francke, had been driven from the University of Leipzig because of their liberal views. At the University of Halle philosophy was taken away from the theological faculty and allowed to flourish on its own. It was also the first university where teachers lectured in German instead of the traditional Latin.

The University of Göttingen was founded in 1737 under a very broad charter from the elector of Hanover, who was also George II of England. It had a brilliant faculty and a large new library to attract students from all over Germany.

Gradually in the 18th century, and with accelerated speed in the 19th, religion was displaced as the dominant force in European universities. The new sciences, the Industrial Revolution, and more worldly ways of thinking all cooperated to transform the universities into institutions of modern learning and research. Students stayed in school longer, and primary and secondary schooling became available for more people.

Modern University Systems

Models of higher education as developed in France, Germany, Great Britain, the United States, and the Soviet Union have had powerful influences on the growth of college and university systems in other places. The distinctive qualities of these 20th-century models are traced in the following sections.

France. The French Revolution marked the temporary end of higher education in France as it had been known for centuries. On Sept. 15, 1793, the National Convention abolished all universities and colleges throughout France, including all faculties of law, medicine, theology, and the arts. Thus the whole system of higher education remained suspended until Napoleon became emperor. In 1808 he published a plan that made the whole educational system—primary, secondary, and higher—subject to state control. With modifications the French system of higher education has kept the essential features of Napoleon's arrangement.

France was divided, for educational purposes, into regions called académies, all of which are larger than the political divisions called départements. Each académie is headed by a rector, who is in charge of the whole educational system in his region. He is also the president of its university. The rector, who is appointed by the president of France, is a representative of the national Ministry of Education.

Higher education in France is open to all students who have passed their secondary-school requirements, specifically the baccalauréat examination. The first year at the university ends with a difficult examination, which serves as a weeding-out process. Usually more than half of the students fail it. Those who fail can continue their education at a two-year university college and obtain diplomas upon completion of their courses. Those who pass the examination continue their university work for three or four years to obtain the *licence,* or university degree.

Apart from the university system, there are other institutions of higher education—called *grandes écoles* (great schools)—for advanced training in the professions and technology. Students are recruited for these schools by competitive examinations from among those who have completed their secondary-school requirements. The course work in these schools is rigorous, and their diplomas have a higher standing than the *licences* from the universities. Notable among these schools are the École Nationale Polytechnique (national technical school) and the École des Beaux-Arts (school of fine arts).

West Germany. The universities of West Germany are operated as agencies of the *Länder* (states), not of the federal government at Bonn. Late in the 19th century several technical and vocational schools, modeled on the great École Polytechnique in Paris, were given college and university status. Those who pursue technical or professional courses receive diplomas rather than the doctorate, which is reserved for students who do extensive research and present dissertations. Administration of the university is in the hands of a curator appointed by the state minister of education. University senates have long been the custodians of school policy. Financial aid to the schools from the federal government since World War II has allowed the federal ministry of education to play a role in setting policy.

Teachers are recruited from assistants to professors. Once an assistant completes postgraduate work, he receives an award called the *Habilitation.* He then must do a research thesis and fulfill other requirements before being given the rank of *Privatdozent,* comparable to an associate or assistant professor in the United States. The highest rank of teacher is the titular professor. There are also lecturers appointed to teach special subjects.

Admission to West German universities is based on requirements similar to those in France, but West Germany has a different system of secondary education. There are three kinds of secondary schools. Students who take the nine-year *Gymnasium* program instead of course work at the other high schools are eligible for entrance to universities.

Patterns of attendance at the general universities are markedly different from those in most countries. German students and teachers have always been wanderers, and this tradition persists. Students customarily attend from two to four universities during their undergraduate years. There is thus little of the personal school loyalty that develops among graduates of American or British universities. West German students must meet minimum requirements but otherwise are free to arrange their own courses of study and length of time in school. Written papers and essay tests are done along the way, and the quality of these

must be high for a student to be admitted to final examinations. The first degree awarded by German universities is the doctorate.

In addition to the universities, West Germany has several colleges of education, along with technical and vocational colleges; colleges of art, music, and economics; military colleges; and theological seminaries.

Great Britain. Degrees in Great Britain are granted either by the universities or by the Council for National Academic Awards. The organization grants degrees to students who attend colleges that are not affiliated with a university. About 70 percent of all first degrees and 95 percent of advanced degrees are granted by universities.

The universities and their colleges are independent, self-governing institutions, while other colleges are maintained by local authorities. At Oxford and Cambridge each college is an independent unit, and the colleges together control the university. In the other universities self-government is vested in a senate and council.

Students are admitted to a university after completing secondary school and passing competitive examinations. A college course leading to the Bachelor of Arts normally takes three years. About 80 percent of undergraduates follow what is called an honors course in one, or sometimes two, subjects. There are examinations at the end of the first year and again at the end of the course. National uniform standards are achieved by the use of external examiners: after tests are marked at a particular institution, the results are sent to examiners at another institution. External examiners serve for a fixed period of years.

The Open University was established in 1969. Its purpose is to offer higher education opportunities to adults who do not have time to attend school full-time. It is also a means of continuing education for graduates. There are no formal entrance requirements. Courses are conducted on a part-time basis through radio and television lectures, correspondence courses, private tutoring, and some residential course work.

United States. The United States is the home of the independent four-year college. Many of the early colleges—such as Harvard (founded 1636), Yale, Princeton, King's College (now Columbia University), and others—became full-fledged universities in time. Others, such as the College of William and Mary (founded in 1693), remained four-year institutions. After the American Revolution, as the frontier moved rapidly westward, hundreds of four-year colleges were founded, mostly by Christian denominations. Although there had been two-year colleges for women— the oldest is Lasell Junior College, established in Massachusetts in 1851—the community college is a product of the 20th century.

Colleges and universities are either private or state-operated. Every state has a state-supported university. Some state university systems are quite large. California's state university, for example, has nine campuses, and other colleges are supported by the state. There is no national university, though plans for one have been put forth since shortly after the Constitution was adopted. Apart from public universities, states also support colleges and vocational, technical, and agricultural schools. Many cities and towns support two-year colleges.

One of the distinctive features of higher education in the United States is the land-grant college or university. The Morrill Act of 1862 granted each state 30,000 acres (12,140 hectares) of federal land for each member in Congress from the state. The lands were sold, and states used the money to establish one or more schools to teach "agriculture and the mechanic arts" to meet the needs of a rapidly industrializing nation. Among the best-known land-grant schools are Massachusetts Institute of Technology, Cornell University, Ohio State University, and the universities of Illinois, Wisconsin, and Minnesota.

The diversity of higher-education opportunities available in the United States is enormous, but the standard is the four-year bachelor's degree, often followed either by graduate studies or professional training. Far more secondary-school graduates pursue degree programs in the United States than in European nations because the general level of American entrance requirements is far lower. Some colleges demand no more than a high-school diploma. Others require high scores on college-entrance examinations such as the Scholastic Aptitude Test (SAT).

There are no standards mandated by government for degree courses, so the quality of colleges varies considerably. Some—such as Harvard, Yale, Princeton, the University of Chicago, Stanford, and the University of California at Berkeley—are among the best in the world. Others are little more than good high schools. There are voluntary agencies and accrediting bodies that monitor quality in the nation's colleges and universities. Accrediting may be done by regional associations—for example, the North Central Association of Colleges and Schools, the New England Association of Schools and Colleges, and the Western

Association of Schools and Colleges. Accrediting is also done by specialized organizations for the various professions. One of the best known of these is the American Bar Association.

Soviet Union. Higher education in the Soviet Union, as in prerevolutionary Russia, is in the service of the state. There was no background of medieval universities devoted to learning for its own sake. The first university was founded in Moscow in 1755 by the linguist M.V. Lomonósov. In the next 50 years universities were established at Vilnius, Kharkov, Kazan, and Saint Petersburg. Powerful influences from Germany slowly brought the Russian schools close to standards of European schools, but that trend ended with the Revolution of 1917.

The Soviet Union puts a strong emphasis on higher education, and the system is very competitive. There are basically three types of schools: universities, institutes, and polytechnic institutes. The major universities teach the arts and pure sciences. In the universities of some republics there are also courses in agriculture, medicine, and technology.

The institutes make up the largest group of schools. They are specialized—they train students in a single field such as law, economics, art, drama, or agriculture. In some ways they resemble university colleges in the United States. The polytechnic institutes teach the same subject matter as the institutes, but they are not specialized in one area of study.

Students wishing to attend an institution of higher education must take competitive examinations. Once in school it takes them from four to six years to earn the first degree. The state examining commission conducts examinations. Candidates for a degree must present and defend a thesis based on original research.

There are graduate-level courses in all three types of schools. The highest degree awarded is the doctorate. All students are supported by government grants.

Canada. Two levels of higher education exist in Canada: degree-granting schools—which are the universities; and nondegree-granting institutions—community colleges, technical schools, colleges of agriculture, colleges of art, and schools of nursing. Most of the community colleges have been built since the late 1960s. They offer two-year programs of university-level courses, after which a student may transfer into one of Canada's 68 universities. The community colleges also offer specialized vocational training. Admission policies are flexible in the colleges. A high-school diploma may be required for some courses, but otherwise admission is open.

Except in Quebec, admission to a university demands a high-school diploma. The University of Quebec requires a two-year college-preparatory course. As in Britain, each university sets its own educational policies. The Bachelor of Arts degree is a three- or four-year program, though an honors degree takes an extra year or more.

The oldest schools in Canada were founded by Christian denominations, and they were purposely modeled either on the University of Paris (if founded

Soviet students in basic chemistry fill an undergraduate lecture hall at Leningrad's Technological Institute.

Tass/Sovfoto

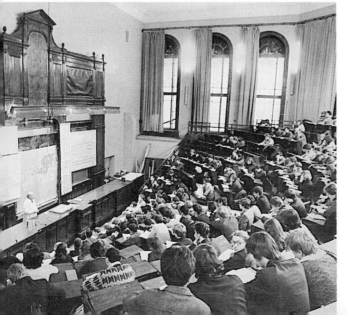

by French settlers) or on Oxford and Cambridge. The French established the first schools. Laval University in Quebec developed out of the Seminary of Quebec, founded in 1663. The University of Montreal was founded in 1876 as a branch of Laval, but it became independent in 1920.

Emigrants from the United States founded three Church of England colleges: King's College in Windsor, N.S., opened in 1789 but moved in 1923 to the Dalhousie University campus in Halifax, which had been founded in 1818; King's College at York, Ont. (1827), later became the University of Toronto; and King's College in Fredericton, N.B. (1828), became the University of New Brunswick. McGill University in Montreal (founded 1821) and Dalhousie were nondenominational schools from the beginning. In the four western provinces the universities patterned their development after the successful land-grant program in the United States by offering extension services and community programs.

Japan. The system of higher education in Japan, as elsewhere, includes universities, colleges, junior colleges, and schools for vocational and technical training. The modern system was established after the Meiji Restoration of 1868 and was consciously modeled on higher education in Europe and the United States. The University of Tokyo was founded in 1877 to take the lead in modernizing the nation's educational system. Today Japan has a system of national, state, and private universities and colleges. The state schools include city colleges. In the 1980s there were about 450 colleges and universities. All degree-granting institutions must meet standards set by the University Accreditation Association.

The degree-granting schools are ranked according to prestige. Examinations to get into the better schools are fiercely competitive. Those students who fail the examination study hard to take it again rather than settle for a less desirable school. The courses of study are considered mild compared to the effort it takes to pass the entrance examination. Once accepted, students normally spend their whole college career in one school, even in one department of the school.

Japanese higher education is directly related to employment and to the way the Japanese economy functions. Schooling is meant to support ongoing development and change in the economy. Specialization in scientific and technological studies is encouraged. Employment after graduation is rarely a problem.

Getting into College

Anyone planning to go to college needs specific sources of information on which school to attend, entrance requirements, and financing. If career goals are decided before leaving high school, the selection process is easier. The problem of financing is most pressing in the United States, which probably has the most expensive higher education in the world. There are reliable sources of information, many of which are published annually and are readily available in libraries and bookstores.

Among the publications giving general information about colleges, universities, and other postsecondary schools are: 'Barron's Profiles of American Colleges', 'Lovejoy's College Guide', 'Peterson's Guide to Four-Year Colleges', 'The College Handbook', 'American Community, Technical, and Junior Colleges', and 'The Directory of Postsecondary Institutions' of the United States Department of Education. For colleges and universities of the United Kingdom and other Commonwealth nations, there is the 'Commonwealth Universities Yearbook'.

A school's standing can be learned from 'Accredited Institutions of Postsecondary Education' published by the American Council on Education. The College Entrance Examination Board publishes 'Guide to Financial Aid for Students and Parents'. 'Peterson's College Money Handbook' offers similar help. Once a school has been selected, its catalog of requirements, courses, faculty, living accommodations, and costs is needed. Many libraries have collections of up-to-date college catalogs, and colleges will send them without cost to prospective students.

URAL MOUNTAINS. Rising almost precisely on the meridian of 60° east longitude, the Ural Mountains in the Soviet Union extend for about 1,250 miles (2,000 kilometers) from the Kara Sea in the north to the Ural River in the south. The mountains have served to mark the traditional boundary between Europe and Asia.

The range may be divided into five sections from north to south. The northernmost Polar Urals are typically Alpine, but the Nether-Polar Urals, the next section southward, contain the highest peaks. The loftiest of these is Mount Narodnaya, at 6,214 feet (1,894 meters). Both of these sections are strewn with glaciers. In the third section, the Northern Urals, peaks rise to between 3,000 and 5,000 feet (900 and 1,500 meters). The flattened summits are remnants of ancient plains that were uplifted by land movements.

Mount Kachkanar, at more than 3,000 feet (900 meters), towers above its neighboring summits in the Central Urals. Heights here rarely exceed 1,600 feet (500 meters). In the Southern Urals the mountains form several parallel ridges that are slightly higher than those of the Central Urals, but remain generally below 4,000 feet (1,200 meters). Yamantau is the highest peak here at 5,374 feet (1,638 meters).

The Urals receive more rain than the surrounding plains. In the north they are almost completely covered with forests. Because of the forests' density, this area is nearly uninhabited. In the south the grassy mountain slopes and fertile valleys provide rich pasture.

The Urals are rich in mineral resources including major deposits of copper, nickel, chromite, gold, and platinum. Nonmetallic mineral resources include asbestos, talc, and fireclay. Amethyst, topaz, and emerald are among the gems and precious stones found in the Urals. Much of the Soviet Union's rich supplies of bituminous coal and lignite are also found here.

URANIUM

URANIUM. In 1789 the German chemist Martin Klaproth discovered the chemical element uranium. For approximately 150 years following that, uranium was to have some of the most wide-reaching effects of any element in history. Above all, it would be put to use in nuclear reactors and nuclear weapons.

Uranium is present in only two to four parts per million in the Earth's crust, and there are few deposits in which uranium ore is present in amounts greater than about 0.2 percent. Nevertheless, hundreds of minerals contain uranium. Uraninite and carnotite, for example, are abundant minerals that contain relatively high concentrations of uranium. Pitchblende, known for its use in the early research of radioactive elements, is a variety of uraninite.

Uranium is widely dispersed in the Earth's crust, though not in large quantities. The United States has large deposits of uranium, as does Canada—a major supplier of the element. Australia has rich uranium deposits in its Northern Territory, and South Africa has also been a chief supplier of uranium.

Properties

Uranium is a silvery metal that is very dense—more than 19 times denser than water. One of the most distinctive properties of uranium is its radioactivity, which was discovered by the French physicist Antoine-Henri Becquerel in 1896. Radioactive isotopes of uranium decay to other elements or isotopes at well-defined rates called half-lives. Each isotope has a unique and characteristic half-life. (*See also* Nuclear Energy; Nuclear Physics; Radioactivity.)

Uranium has an atomic number of 92 and an atomic weight of 238.029 (*see* Chemical Elements). The naturally occurring isotopes of uranium are U-234, U-235, and U-238. Other major isotopes not found in nature but produced in nuclear reactions, such as those that occur in reactors, include U-232, U-233, and U-236. The isotopes U-235 and U-233 are especially useful because they can undergo fission when struck by neutrons. The isotope U-238 turns into plutonium (Pu-239) when it captures a neutron. Because of these properties, both U-235 and U-238 are used in the manufacture of atomic bombs (*see* Nuclear Energy; Nuclear Weapons).

Uranium reacts quite readily with other atoms because it gives up from three to six of its outer electrons rather easily. (*See also* Periodic Table.) When uranium gives up one or more of its outer electrons, it is said to be oxidized. Because of its many possible oxidation states, uranium has a rich chemistry and can form many chemical compounds. Chief among these are the oxides and the halides. Oxides, such as

UO_2, U_3O_8, and UO_3, are formed when uranium reacts with oxygen. Halides result when uranium reacts with any of the halide elements: fluorine, chlorine, bromine, or iodine. Uranium also reacts with oxygen to form a uranyl ion, UO_2^{2+}. The uranyl ion combines with other chemical substances to form molecules such as uranyl nitrate, $UO_2(NO_3)_2$, which is used in the purification of uranium.

Uranium hexafluoride, UF_6, and uranium tetrafluoride, UF_4, are the two principal halides of uranium. They are used in industrial processes such as uranium purification and uranium enrichment.

Many uranium compounds can be dissolved in water or acids. Uranyl nitrate is produced by dissolving any of the oxides of uranium in nitric acid. Uranium can be highly purified by using acidic uranyl nitrate solutions in a process called solvent extraction. The uranyl nitrate is removed, or extracted, from the aqueous phase and enters the organic phase, leaving behind most impurities. This behavior of uranyl nitrate forms the basis of many modern, large-scale uranium purification operations.

Extraction and Processing

With the first large-scale use of uranium in nuclear power reactors, the search for substantial deposits of uranium ore grew. Much of the prospecting in the United States was done in the Western states, primarily in Colorado, Utah, Arizona, and Wyoming, where deposits were already known to exist.

In the United States, uranium ores exist in greatest abundance in sandstone deposits. There are also some vein deposits which are, in general, of a considerably higher grade than those in sandstone. Because uranium ores typically contain very little uranium compared to the amount of sand and other minerals, the uranium processing plants, called mills, must be located near the mines to reduce ore shipping costs.

The first step in the production of uranium is to crush and grind the ores to produce a coarse, gravel-like material. The ground ores are then dissolved in leaching solutions of either sulfuric acid or a mixture of sodium carbonate and sodium bicarbonate, depending on the impurities in the ores. If there is more than about 15 percent of limestone (calcium carbonate) in the ore, the carbonate mixture is used because the limestone would consume too much acid. When the ores are dissolved, a uranyl compound is formed: if a sulfuric acid leaching solution is used, uranyl sulfate is formed; if the carbonate mixture is used, uranyl tricarbonate is formed.

The uranyl salts are selectively removed from the leaching solutions by special materials called ion exchange resins or by solvent extraction with any of several organic solvents. In either case, the uranium compound is physically removed from the original solution leaving many impurities behind. By repeating the ion exchange or solvent extraction process, it is possible to obtain a very pure uranium product.

Next, the uranium undergoes precipitation, drying, and packaging in preparation for shipping in the

PROPERTIES OF URANIUM	
Symbol . . . . U	Specific Gravity at 68° F
Atomic Number 92	(20° C) 18.95
Atomic Weight	Boiling Point
. . . . 238.029	. . . . 6,904° F (3,818° C)
Group in Periodic	Melting Point
Table . . . . VIb	. . . . . 2,070° F (1,132° C)

1. mining

2. crushing and grinding

3. leaching

sulfuric acid

4. solvent extraction

8. shipping

5. precipitation   6. drying   7. packaging   yellow cake

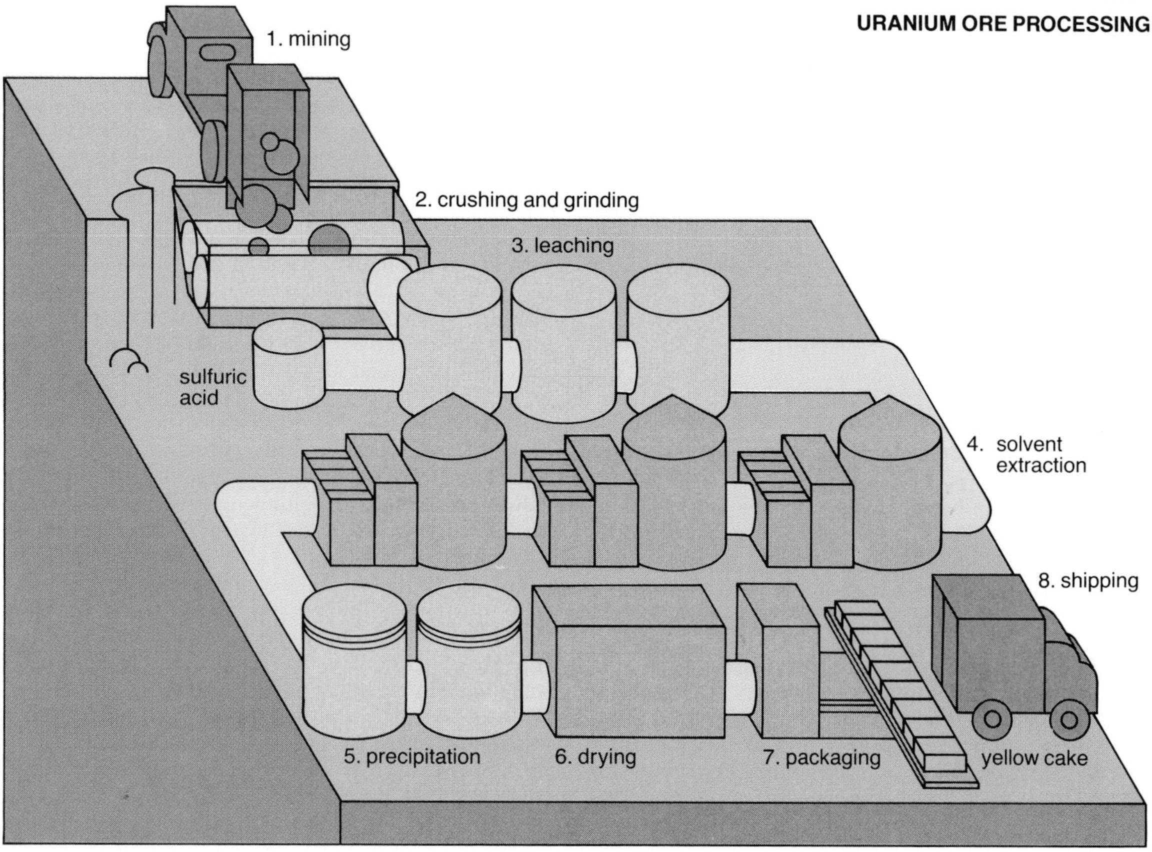

In one uranium production process, the ore is first crushed and ground, then dissolved in leaching solutions of either sulfuric acid or a carbonate mixture. Uranyl salts formed during leaching may be removed by repeated solvent extraction. The uranium compound is precipitated from the solution, and the resulting solid, called yellow cake, is dried, packaged, and shipped.

form of a yellow cake. The yellow cake is often transported to a separate plant for further processing. In the second plant a final purification may be made by converting the uranium to uranium hexafluoride gas and selectively distilling it away from impurities. When this is done, the uranium is often prepared for use as nuclear reactor fuel. In this case, it undergoes a process designed to concentrate the isotope U-235, a procedure called isotopic enrichment.

A very large number of physical and chemical processes will separate the isotopes of uranium; however, few are practical on a large scale. One of the earliest uranium isotope separation methods used banks of large electromagnetic machines called Calutrons. The Calutron process was eventually replaced with the gaseous diffusion process, which is the principal process in use today.

In the gaseous diffusion process, uranium hexafluoride gas is pumped into metal tubes made of a highly porous metal. About half of the gas flows, or effuses, through the walls of the tubes. The effused gas and the remaining gas are pumped into separate tubes identical to the first, and the process is repeated. Each time the gas effuses through the tube wall, it is concentrated, or enriched, in the isotope U-235; the

enriched uranium is called the product. The remainder, the gas that has been depleted of U-235 is referred to as the tails. The collection of tubes and pumps required for carrying out a single separation process is called a stage. Many thousands of stages are required for sufficient enrichment of the uranium, and this collection of stages is referred to as a cascade. (For diagram of gaseous diffusion, see Nuclear Energy.)

In another enrichment process called gas centrifugation, uranium hexafluoride gas (UF_6) is put into large, vertically mounted, spinning cylinders called centrifuges. The molecules of $^{238}UF_6$ are heavier than those of $^{235}UF_6$ and so are preferentially slung to the wall of the centrifuge while the lighter $^{235}UF_6$ molecules are concentrated closer to the center. A specially designed scoop inside the centrifuge scoops up that part of the uranium hexafluoride gas with the higher concentration of $^{235}UF_6$. As in the gaseous diffusion process, one such separation operation is called a stage, and a collection of stages is called a cascade. Gas centrifugation is used in parts of Europe.

In still another enrichment process, called atomic vapor laser isotope separation, or AVLIS, uranium metal is vaporized in a large chamber and irradiated with laser light of precisely controlled wavelengths.

231

Frank Hoffman—U.S. Department of Energy

Cylindrical casings house vertically mounted gas centrifuges that spin at high speeds to separate uranium isotopes.

A photon of light will ionize, or remove an electron from a U-235 atom in the vapor, but leave the U-238 atoms relatively unaffected. The ionized U-235 atoms can then be collected on electrically charged surfaces, while the U-238 atoms are condensed on separate surfaces. In this process, a very high degree of enrichment can be obtained in a single stage.

There are also two chemical processes that show promise for use in uranium isotope separation. These are solvent extraction and ion exchange, both of which have been extensively developed, the former in France and the latter in Japan.

The degree of separation achieved in a given process is called the separation factor. In general, the separation factor obtained in a single stage of a chemical process is less than that for a physical process, and many stages are required to achieve the desired degree of separation. The energy required to achieve this separation is measured in separative work units, abbreviated SWUs.

Uses of Uranium

The widest use of uranium is in nuclear reactor fuels. Uranium dioxide is the chemical form most commonly used in large, modern reactors. However, some metallic uranium is still used in older reactors. In general, uranium used as fuel is in the form of small cylinders that are encased in a metal tube called cladding. The cladding is most commonly an alloy of zirconium metal, chosen because it does not react readily with neutrons. Aluminum is often used as a fuel cladding in smaller research reactors; in such cases, the fuel itself is often an alloy of aluminum and uranium. The enrichment of uranium in power reactor fuels is usually about 3 percent. Uranium enriched to greater than 90 percent is used in nuclear weapons. (*See also* Nuclear Energy; Nuclear Weapons.)

The high density of uranium metal makes it useful as a radiation shield. It is sometimes used for this purpose in the transport of highly radioactive spent fuel elements from nuclear reactors to storage sites. Its high density also gives uranium metal great penetrating power when it is used in projectiles. It may also serve as ballast when a great deal of weight is required in a small volume.

Solutions of uranyl oxalate have been used for many years as actinometers, instruments used to measure the number of photons present in a beam of light. The light energy absorbed by the uranyl ion causes highly reproducible chemical and physical reactions. (*See also* Metal and Metallurgy.)

URBAN, Popes. There have been eight popes named Urban in the Roman Catholic Church.

Urban I (died 230, pope 222–30) was the son of a Roman noble. He belonged to the period before Christianity was tolerated by the Roman Empire. He was martyred in 230.

Urban II (born 1035?, pope 1088–99) is chiefly remembered as the pope who launched the First Crusade in 1095. He was born to a noble family in the Champagne region of France. After his studies he was an archdeacon at Reims from 1055 until 1067. He then became a monk at Cluny, the leading reform monastery in Europe. Sent to Rome on a mission in 1079, he was made a cardinal by Pope Gregory VII. He was elected pope in 1088. Urban preached the powerful sermon at Clermont, France, that ignited enthusiasm for the Crusades (*see* Crusades).

Urban III (died 1187, pope 1185–87) and Emperor Frederick I had serious conflicts over the division of authority between church and state.

Urban IV (born 1200, pope 1261–64) was the son of a French shoemaker. As pope, he started the feast of Corpus Christi.

Urban V (born 1310, pope 1362–70) was a French pope during the period known as the "Babylonian captivity." In 1367 he decided to restore the papal seat (then at Avignon, France) to Rome. He found Rome in such a ruined condition after the 60-year absence of the popes that he went back to Avignon.

Urban VI (born 1318, pope 1378–89) succeeded Gregory XI, who had brought the papacy back to Rome and died there. When the cardinals met to elect a new pope to succeed Gregory, a Roman mob threatened the cardinals with bodily harm if they did not elect a Roman or Italian pope. Although they elected Urban VI, some of the cardinals later declared the election illegal. They elected an antipope, Clement VII. Clement VII set up his court at Avignon. This began the Great Schism (1378–1417), in which half of Western Europe was loyal to Urban VI and his successors at Rome, and the other half to Clement VII and his successors at Avignon. (*See also* Hus.)

Urban VII (born 1521, pope 1590) died 12 days after his election and was never consecrated.

Urban VIII (born 1568, pope 1623–44) was a civic-minded pope who sponsored public works in Rome.

The Australian-American Memorial, center, and Administrative Offices are part of the government complex in the completely planned city of Canberra, Australia's federal capital.

URBAN PLANNING. The growth and development of cities may be random and haphazard or planned. During the Industrial Revolution old cities in Great Britain and new ones in North America mushroomed rapidly in size and became congested and slum-ridden. The designing of whole cities is the exception rather than the rule, though there are some outstanding 20th-century examples. Canberra, the capital of Australia, and Brasília, the capital of Brazil, were planned from their beginnings. Philadelphia, Pa., designed by William Penn in the 1680s, is an early example of an American planned city. Washington, D.C., also originated as a thoroughly planned capital city.

City planning today refers less often to the total design of new cities than to the redevelopment and revitalization of older ones. In this sense city planning means urban renewal. Beginning in the 1950s, many cities—especially in the United States—underwent major redevelopment. Expressways were cut through them, displacing old neighborhoods. Slums were cleared and replaced by high-rise public housing complexes. Old downtown office buildings were torn down to make room for new office towers.

City planning, whether the design of new cities or the redevelopment of old ones, has traditionally been launched by governments. Since the early 1970s there has been another type of urban development prompted instead by economic expansion. This has been the emergence of urban villages in areas that were thinly populated as recently as the 1960s. Examples include north Dallas, Tex.; the Oak Brook-Naperville corridor west of Chicago, Ill.; and Orange County, Calif. These areas have become sizable commercial and industrial expanses amid what were originally suburban populations. In many cases the number of jobs in these urban villages exceeds those in nearby older city centers.

Modern urban planning is a product of the late 19th century. The first planners, unhappy with the way cities were decaying under the influence of industrialization, wanted to use master plans to overhaul them completely. One example is the industrial city plan in 1904 by French architect Tony Garnier. A few years later Daniel Burnham presented his celebrated plan for Chicago.

Success in such total redesign of cities did not always work well, and in the late 20th century the objectives of planners were more modest. Instead of trying to create the ideal city, they focused instead on a few attainable goals. These include the orderly arrangement of all parts of a city so each can function with a minimum of interference from the others; efficient means of local transportation and circulation of traffic; the development of each part of the city, with adequate residential space, parking facilities, outdoor recreational areas, and businesses; provision of an adequate water supply, sewerage system, utilities, garbage pickup, and public services; provision of schools and other community services; and the construction of housing to meet the needs of all segments of a city's population. (*See also* City.)

Historical Background

There is strong evidence of city planning even in the most ancient civilizations of China, India, and the Middle East. Mohenjo-daro in the Indus River valley, for example, was one of two large centers of a thriving civilization in the 3rd millennium BC. The city was laid out in a grid plan with a series of rectangular blocks of buildings separated by wide, unpaved streets and subdivided by narrow lanes (*see* Indus Valley Civilization). Many ancient cities were divided into areas of specialized functions. Palaces and temples were centrally located. There were systems of fortification, water supply, and drainage.

URBAN PLANNING

In contrast to Mohenjo-daro, Rome—a much later city—had a minimum of planning in its earliest centuries. Planning in Rome, as in other ancient cities of the Mediterranean region, focused on the activities of government. Public buildings, including temples, were well designed, but residential areas were often left to develop on their own. The original population of Rome settled on and near the seven hills near the Tiber River. As population increased, settlement spread away from the river in both directions.

With the passage of time the Romans became adept as town planners. When they built new towns they used a traditional plan that called for a square in a grid layout. At or near the center of a town was the forum, the public gathering place. Buildings were erected on the edge of the forum for commercial, governmental, and religious purposes. During the empire a new town forum might be laid out in a single comprehensive architectural design. A large city might have several forums, some for administrative purposes and others for commerce.

During the early Middle Ages there was little city building in Europe. When towns began to grow, they centered on a local church, the protection of a lord and his castle, or on markets. These early towns were irregular in layout, and they had poor sanitation. As populations grew in size, these old walled towns became congested and unsafe. People therefore went outside the walls to live. As it became customary to allot certain sections of towns to specific trades and to different nationalities, the cities became even more congested. Disease, especially the recurrent incidences of plague, often killed more than half of a local population (*see* Plagues and Epidemics).

Towns of the late Middle Ages usually started as villages with a single street and a crossroad. The population spread in a circular fashion from this center, often in quite irregular patterns. This irregularity is still apparent in many European cities today—it is often impossible to walk around a rectangular block,

A model of 4th-century Rome shows little evidence of city planning in the area around the Circus Maximus.

A. Trapani—M. Grimoldi

as one can in most North American cities, because streets angle off in all directions. Early streets were merely footpaths. Paris in 1184 was the first major city to get paved streets. Other cities followed slowly.

From the 16th through the 18th century, there was a conscious attempt to plan some features of cities. Parts of some small cities and many large ones were laid out in monumental splendor to glorify kings and nobles. The results were often stunning in terms of monuments and palatial buildings.

The few cases of city planning in the colonies of North America, and in the United States after 1776, were victimized by the European Renaissance concepts of public grandeur. Washington, D.C., designed by Pierre L'Enfant in 1791 to be a national capital, is a chief example. His model was the radial arrangement of Paris, France, in which streets stretch from a common center like spokes on a wheel. The monumentality that the city achieved is unrelated to the efficiency of traffic, residential patterns, and the growth of industry and commerce.

William Penn's Philadelphia, though laid out more than a century earlier, is more of a prototype for American cities. Penn used a grid, or checkerboard, pattern of streets. This grid pattern was used across the United States by later settlers. It provides the easiest way to survey land and divide it. It also allows city planning to continue far from the city itself by land developers and speculators.

Grid-pattern cities were usually laid out in north-south and east-west directions. This did not always prove possible. Minneapolis, Minn., grew along the Mississippi River. A grid pattern was laid out to conform to the flow of the river. As the city grew, another grid pattern emerged to the north and south of the downtown area at an angle to that of the original. Thus the city today is comprised of two separate grids.

Another influence on town development in the United States was the New England pattern. Towns were built around central squares. These squares were originally used to graze livestock out of range of Indian attack. In time they became a commons, a focus of community life. The town hall, village church, stores, tavern, and other businesses were located around it. Often, after the need for grazing had passed, a bandstand was built in the commons.

New England also inspired the free-standing house, set back from the street in a large yard. This became the standard for residential development throughout the United States—even in large cities. In some East coast cities, however, the European tradition of joined town houses that form a solid block was perpetuated.

The effect of industrialization on cities during the 19th century was enormous. First in Britain, then later on the Continent, masses of unemployed individuals left failing rural areas to seek jobs in factories and mines. In the United States immigrants arrived by the millions beginning in the early 19th century, and most of them settled where there were economic opportunities. On both continents municipal and state governments failed to grasp the problems posed

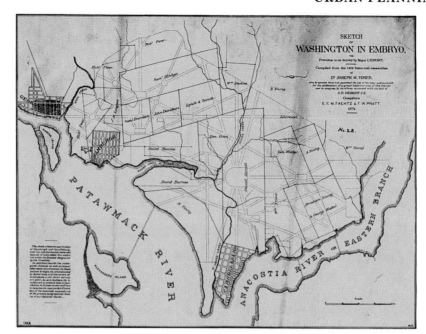

SKETCH
OF
WASHINGTON IN EMBRYO,
VIZ.
Previous to its Survey by Major L'ENFANT.
Compiled from the rare historical researches
of
Dr. JOSEPH M. TONER.

An early sketch for the plan of
Washington, D.C., shows the
boundaries of some of the original
estates that once occupied land
along the Potomac River. The
multiple centers, from which
streets radiate as spokes on a
wheel, were the heart of Pierre
L'Enfant's plan.

Library of Congress

by extremely rapid city growth. City governments,
moreover, were not accustomed to spending funds on
housing and slum clearance.

There was no lack of evidence depicting city decay.
Social critics and reformers published vivid details
of city life and the dire poverty of slum dwellers.
Friedrich Engels, an associate of Karl Marx, published
'The Condition of the Working Class in England' in
1845. In the United States the Danish-born newspa-
perman Jacob Riis published 'How the Other Half
Lives' in 1890. This exposé of New York City's worst
tenement areas led to the first organized efforts at
slum clearance in North America.

Progress in restructuring American cities was slow.
The extraordinary political corruption of city administrations, as revealed by Lincoln Steffens in 'The
Shame of the Cities' (1904), was a chief reason. Another was the inability of the poor to pay for decent
housing, thus making it unprofitable for anyone to
build or maintain it. There were some improvements
in public health with better water supplies and sewerage systems. Parks were built to add beauty to cities
and to provide recreation areas.

In Europe the need to revitalize cities was more
readily accepted during the late 19th century. The
long tradition of palatial structures, cathedrals, public buildings, monuments, and large plazas endured.
In Paris especially there was a huge amount of reconstruction. One of the great city planners of the
century, Georges-Eugène Haussmann, designed the
magnificent system of *grands boulevards* that cross
the city as well as the beautiful parks, the Bois de
Boulogne and the Bois de Vincennes. He built the market of Les Halles (now gone) and the Paris Opéra. His
'Memoirs' (1890–93) significantly influenced modern
urban planners.

Origins of Modern Planning

Much of today's city planning has its origins in a
dislike of cities and a preference for rural life. One of
the most potent influences on modern planning was
Ebenezer Howard, founder of the English garden-city
movement. Howard came to dislike the crowded and
dirty streets of London, and he believed it was necessary to reverse the trend of population movement
from rural areas to cities and towns.

In 1898 he published 'Tomorrow: a Peaceful Path to
Social Reform' (reissued in 1902 as 'Garden Cities of
Tomorrow'). In it he proposed the founding of garden
cities. Each was to be a self-sufficient city with a
population limited to 30,000. The cities would have
industry and commerce and would be surrounded
by an agricultural belt. Groups of garden cities, he
believed, would provide all the good qualities of large
cities and none of the bad. During his lifetime he
succeeded in persuading businessmen to finance two
such cities. Letchworth was founded in 1903 and
Welwyn Garden City in 1920. These served as models
for towns that the British government founded after
World War II.

During the first decades of the 20th century, new
towns were built in many parts of the Western
world. Most of them derived their inspiration from
the garden-city movement. In the United States,
Kingsport, Tenn., was built by industrial interests.
Radburn, N.J., was modeled on Howard's concept in
1928, but it gave more consideration to traffic flow.
Radburn pioneered the "superblock" concept for
residences. Superblocks, as the name indicates, are
very long residential blocks instead of small blocks
interrupted by cross streets. A later attempt to create
a preplanned self-sufficient community is Reston,

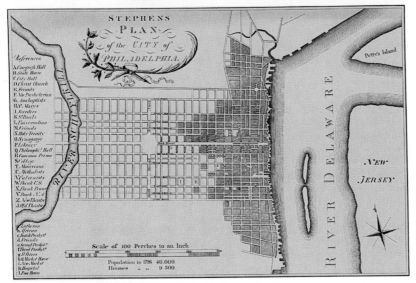

William Penn, third from right (above), talks to the team that is surveying and planning the layout of Philadelphia. By 1796 the city (left) was expanding outside its original grid plan, mostly to the north and south along the Delaware River.

Va., developed after 1962. The overall community aims to be self-sustaining with residences, schools, industries, shopping centers, and cultural facilities. Reston, however, has become basically a suburb of Washington, D.C., where many of its residents work.

At the heart of Howard's planning ideas is the determination to decentralize cities and to segment functions and keep them from each other. Industry, commerce, housing, public buildings, and museums are not mixed together as they are in older cities. Each stands separately. Howard's followers expanded the decentralization movement by attempting to disperse the functions of cities over wider geographic areas, preferably into the equivalents of small towns.

The second great influence on planning came from the Swiss-born architect Le Corbusier (Charles-Édouard Jeanneret-Gris). His vision, 'The Radiant City' (1935), was derived in part from the garden-city movement but was also a radical departure from it. The decentralizers wanted small cities of low buildings with dispersed populations. For Le Corbusier the city should consist mainly of skyscrapers in a parklike setting. By using skyscrapers he hoped to achieve population densities as high as 1,200 persons per acre (3,000 per hectare), leaving 95 percent of the land free of construction. He also differed from the garden-city planners in making room for ample automobile traffic on large expressways that cut through cities. (*See also* Le Corbusier.)

A less significant influence outside the United States was the Burnham plan for the beautification of cities. Daniel Burnham's plan for Chicago was drawn with the aid of Edward H. Bennett and published in 1909. It provided for a ring of forest preserves around the edge of the city and a green belt along the lakefront. This plan was carried out in Chicago, though it was not suitable for all other large cities.

One effect of Burnham's plan carried beyond Chicago: the isolation of civic or cultural centers as clusters of monumental buildings in classical design away from other structures. In this Burnham followed the ancient custom of the Greeks and Romans with their agoras and forums. As municipal functions grew in scope, the idea of a central location for all gov-

236

ernmental buildings gained appeal. The government center complex in Boston, Mass., is an example of such design.

After World War II the garden-city and radiant-city movements gradually merged into today's city planning. Le Corbusier's influence was probably greater in the inner cities, where old neighborhoods were torn down and replaced by high-rise projects. Many of these projects were built for the urban poor, who were former slum tenants. But some have been constructed for the wealthy. In both cases neighborhoods as traditionally understood were obliterated. The projects that replaced them are mainly for housing, and they are situated in great areas of open space with all other neighborhood functions kept at a distance.

Outside cities the garden city influenced the development of new suburbs. Large tracts of land were covered with dispersed housing surrounded by greenery. Commercial and industrial areas were clustered away from residential areas in low buildings. One of the first such developments in the United States was Levittown, N.Y., built between 1946 and 1951. It consists of thousands of low-cost homes, with schools, parks, shopping centers, playgrounds, and community centers. It lacks, however, the garden-city goal of self-sufficiency. It is not surrounded by a productive agricultural belt, nor does it have its own industries.

In such locations as Pasadena, Calif., and the north side of Atlanta, Ga., where business expansion led to urban village developments, the influence of Le Corbusier was again felt in the building of skyscrapers, mostly for commercial use. This transformation of what were originally residential areas into citylike business complexes was aided by government, especially through zoning policies.

Role of Government

Urban planning and renewal have been recognized as functions of government since the first decade of the 20th century. The first town planning act was passed in Great Britain in 1909. In the same year the first national conference on city planning was held in the United States. Sweden, Germany, and some other European nations adopted planning administrations at that time.

Because the cities for which plans were being made could not just be swept away and replaced, it was soon realized that no new overall design was possible. Plans had to be flexible, allowing the incorporation of the parts of cities that could not be easily modified. Governments also came to realize that changes and growth in cities result from the initiative of industries, banks, land developers, and other private interests, as well as from government intervention.

Zoning. One power that government took for itself is zoning—the regulation of land use and buildings—which affects population densities and the height, size, spacing, and use of structures. One function of zoning makes it possible to segregate industrial and commercial buildings from residential neighborhoods. Zoning has been used in Sweden and Germany

The green belt along Chicago's lakefront was part of Daniel Burnham's farsighted plan for the city.

since 1875 to control land use and building height in areas around old city centers.

Britain's zoning regulations stem from passage of the Town Planning Act of 1909. The regulations related almost entirely to new construction. They were effective in controlling industrial locations and in setting standards for residential buildings. They were later displaced by direct government action in building new towns and public housing projects.

In the United States the first comprehensive zoning ordinance was passed by New York City in 1916. It intended to ensure that new skyscrapers would not block out light and air from neighboring buildings. The ordinance also established what is called the planning concept of zoning. This means that zoning can be

Levittown, N.Y., was the first American postwar suburb planned in accordance with the garden city concept.

used to promote the overall welfare of communities by guiding growth through orderly development.

Among the objectives of zoning generally accepted throughout the United States are: reduction of fire hazards by building codes, control of population densities in neighborhoods, assurance of adequate light and air, stabilization of property values, consolidation of commercial districts, control of the height and size of buildings, and provision of off-street parking.

Metropolitan area planning. Larger cities today are ringed with suburbs. Most of them have their own governments. The existence of many independent jurisdictions within one limited geographic area has proved a barrier to wide-area metropolitan planning, even where common problems exist for all the communities. Some European countries have moved toward the concept of metropolitan planning and development, with particular success in Great Britain, Scandinavia, Germany, and The Netherlands. In 1953 a metropolitan government was established for Toronto, Ont. Such efforts in the United States, however, are still limited. The governments of Miami, Fla., and Dade County are united into a metropolitan area, as are Jacksonville, Fla., and most of Duval County.

Future of Urban Planning

By the end of the 20th century more of the world's people will be living in cities than in the countryside. It has been projected by United Nations population specialists that by 2025 there will be 93 metropolitan areas with populations greater than 5 million. Most of these will be in what are now called developing countries—in Latin America, Africa, and Asia. Many city populations are expected to exceed 15 million. Mexico City is projected to have more than 30 million people and Cairo, Egypt, only slightly fewer. These enormous populations will be living for the most part in cities that do not have thriving economies. For this reason the number and quality of city services will lag behind those of cities in North America and Europe.

City planning on a local scale will be difficult to achieve in some areas. Many of these enormous cities will become the focus of national planning instead. Some proposed solutions to making mammoth cities livable include the creation of new economic development zones to draw population away from large cities; the reorganization of large cities into smaller zones or centers to provide city services; the development of green belts outside cities to hamper urban expansion; the construction of completely new cities (being done in Egypt during the 1980s); the use of prefabricated housing; and drastic energy-conservation policies to ensure adequate supplies of electricity and water.

BIBLIOGRAPHY FOR URBAN PLANNING

Barnett, Jonathan. An Introduction to Urban Design (Harper, 1982).
Catanese, A.J. and Snyder, J.C. Urban Planning, 2nd ed. (McGraw, 1988).
Hanmer, T.J. The Growth of Cities (Watts, 1985).
Toynbee, Arnold. Cities on the Move (Oxford, 1970).
Wright, F.L. The Living City (Horizon, 1984).
(See also bibliographies for **City; Civilization**.)

UREY, Harold Clayton (1893–1981). The American scientist Harold Clayton Urey won the Nobel prize for chemistry in 1934 for his discovery of the heavy form of hydrogen known as deuterium. He was a key figure in the development of the atomic bomb and made fundamental contributions to a theory of the origin of the Earth and other planets that is now widely accepted.

Urey was born on April 29, 1893, in Walkerton, Ind. He earned a bachelor's degree in 1917 from Montana State University in Missoula. In Copenhagen, Denmark, from 1923 to 1924, Urey assisted in Niels Bohr's basic research on the theory of atomic structure. Urey taught at Johns Hopkins University in Baltimore, Md., from 1924 to 1929 and at Columbia University in New York City from 1929 to 1945. From 1945 to 1981 he held a series of professorships at the Institute for Nuclear Studies, the University of Chicago, and the University of California in San Diego.

Urey's deuterium research began in the 1920s when he distilled some liquid hydrogen, concentrating its deuterium form. In 1931 he and his associates announced their discovery of heavy water, composed of an atom of oxygen and two atoms of deuterium. He also separated radioactive isotopes of carbon, oxygen, nitrogen, and sulfur, and examined their properties.

During World War II he directed a research program at Columbia that became a vital part of the Manhattan Project, which developed the atomic energy program in the United States. Urey's group provided the fundamental information for the separation of the fissionable isotope uranium-235 from the more abundant isotope uranium-238 and investigated methods for concentrating heavy hydrogen and separating boron isotopes.

After the war his work with the heavy isotope oxygen-18 led him to devise methods for determining ocean temperatures as long as 180,000,000 years ago. This led him to study the relative abundances of the elements on Earth and to develop a theory of the origin of the elements and of their abundances in the sun and other stars.

Urey theorized that the early atmosphere of the Earth was probably like the atmosphere now present on Jupiter—rich in ammonia, methane, and hydrogen. One of his students, Stanley Miller, working in his laboratory at the University of Chicago, demonstrated that when exposed to an energy source, such as ultraviolet radiation, these compounds and water might react to produce compounds essential for the formation of living matter (see Extraterrestrial Life).

Urey suggested that the planets of the solar system may have developed from a gaseous disk rotating around the sun and that the disk, in combination with gases from the sun, may have broken into fragments and begun to condense. In 1952 he published his theory in 'The Planets: Their Origin and Development'.

In 1960 Urey made recommendations in support of space exploration to determine the origin of the solar system and the possibility of life on other planets. He died on Jan. 5, 1981, in La Jolla, Calif.

URINARY SYSTEM. The various activities of the body create waste by-products that must be expelled in order to maintain health. To excrete certain fluid wastes, the body has a specialized filtering and recycling system known as the urinary system. Solid wastes are ultimately expelled through the large intestine (*see* Digestive System).

In most mammals, including humans, wastes are flushed away from tissues by the passing bloodstream and are swept into one of two identical organs called kidneys. In the kidneys, wastes and excess water are removed from the blood as urine (*see* Kidneys). The urine then passes through tubes, called ureters, into a saclike organ called the bladder. From the bladder the urine passes out of the body through another tube called the urethra.

The Human Urinary System

In the kidneys, water and useful blood components such as amino acids, glucose, and other nutrients are reabsorbed into the bloodstream, leaving a concentrated solution of waste material called final, or bladder, urine. It consists of water, urea (from amino-acid metabolism), inorganic salts, creatinine, ammonia, and pigmented products of blood breakdown, one of which (urochrome) gives urine its typically yellowish color. Any unusual substances that cannot be reabsorbed into the blood remain in the urine.

From the kidneys, urine is carried through the ureters by waves of contractions in the ureteral walls. The ureters pass urine to the bladder for temporary storage. The bladder is a muscular organ at the bottom of the abdomen that expands like a sack as it fills. The bladder of an average adult human is uncomfortably distended when it holds a volume of about ⅓ quart (320 milliliters) of urine. When the bladder is full, nerve endings in the bladder wall are touched off. Impulses from the nerve endings are carried to the brain, triggering the bladder walls to contract and the sphincter, a ringlike muscle that guards the entrance from bladder to urethra, to relax. The response to the nerve signals is part involuntary and part learned and voluntary. Now urination can take place through the urethra, a tube lined with mucous membranes. The male urethra ends at the tip of the penis; the female urethra ends just above the entrance to the vagina. Normally the bladder empties completely. (*See also* Anatomy, Human.)

Urinary Systems of Other Species

The composition of urine and the manner in which it is expelled varies from animal to animal. Urine's composition tends to mirror the water needs of the organism. Freshwater animals usually excrete very dilute urine. Marine animals tend to combat water loss to their salty environment by excreting concentrated urine. Terrestrial animals usually retain water and secrete a highly concentrated urine.

In most birds, reptiles, and terrestrial insects, the end product of amino-acid metabolism is not water-soluble urea but insoluble uric acid. The urine of birds

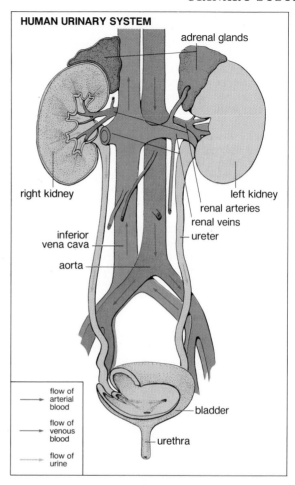

HUMAN URINARY SYSTEM

adrenal glands

right kidney

left kidney

renal arteries

renal veins

inferior vena cava

ureter

aorta

flow of arterial blood

flow of venous blood

flow of urine

bladder

urethra

and reptiles is a whitish, aqueous suspension of uric-acid crystals that is passed into an internal chamber called the cloaca. Here the urine is mixed with fecal material before it is expelled. The urine of terrestrial insects is solid and in some cases instead of being expelled is stored as pigment in the body.

In most vertebrates, except birds, the organ for the temporary storage of urine from the kidneys is the bladder. The urinary bladders of amphibians are simply pockets in the cloaca. The urinary bladders of fishes are expandable parts of the urinary duct.

Disorders

The urinary system, like any other part of the body, is occasionally subject to breakdowns. One disorder of the urinary system is a blockage in the urethra, bladder, or ureters. Disorders of this type, called urinary tract obstruction, cause urine to be dammed up in the kidneys. The condition may be congenital (existing from birth) or it may be caused by tumors, mineral deposits that form stones, or other physical disorders. Other urinary-system disorders include malfunction or disease of the kidneys, which can lead to an accumulation of wastes in the body—a condition called uremia.

URUGUAY. The smallest and most compact country in South America, the Republic of Uruguay (República Oriental del Uruguay) is a buffer between Latin America's two largest and most powerful republics. Covering an area of about 68,000 square miles (176,000 square kilometers), the nation is dwarfed by its giant neighbors Brazil to the north and Argentina to the west and south. The Atlantic Ocean on the east and the estuary of the Río de la Plata on the south create a maritime influence that somewhat modifies climatic extremes. They also give Uruguay immediate access to international trade. Roughly triangular in shape, Uruguay stretches less than 350 miles (560 kilometers) from north to south and about 300 miles (480 kilometers) from west to east.

Land and Climate

Uruguay's primary landform is an undulating plain composed of low, rolling, grass-covered hills divided by broad river valleys. Occupying roughly two thirds of the country's total area, it is dotted with outcrops of crystalline rocks, particularly along ridge crests. These outcrops often create long ridge lines, known as *cuchillas,* which act as watershed divides.

There are two other landscape types. Almost featureless coastal plains extend as a narrow fringe along the Uruguay River, the Río de la Plata, and the eastern lagoon area, occupying about 15 percent of the country. Their fertile sedimentary soils and low relief give them high agricultural potential. Beautiful sand beaches along the coast east of Montevideo are major attractions for tourists.

Uruguay's third major physical region, the *serranías,* is a series of low mountains that stretch in a gentle arc from north-northeast to south-southwest in the eastern third of the country. Mostly no more than large hills, their southern tip is the Mirador Nacional. At only 1,644 feet (501 meters) in elevation, it is the highest point in the nation.

Uruguay is surrounded on three sides by rivers. In the north the Guareim River forms the border with Brazil for more than 175 miles (282 kilometers). The Uruguay, from which the country took its name, forms the western boundary and is by far the largest and most picturesque of the country's rivers. The Uruguay is navigable as far north as Salto, more than 200 miles (322 kilometers) from its union with the Río Paraná. On the southern margin is the Río de la Plata, the large estuary formed by the union of the Uruguay and Paraná rivers.

This article was contributed by Ernst Clark Griffin, Professor of Geography, San Diego State University, San Diego, Calif.

The largest river system within the country is the Río Negro. With headwaters in southernmost Brazil, it crosses Uruguay from northeast to southwest. The damming of the Río Negro provides a source of hydroelectric energy as well as a huge artificial lake, the Embalse del Río Negro, the nation's only large standing body of fresh water.

Uruguay is the only country in Latin America completely outside the tropics. With its maritime location and nearly 500 miles (800 kilometers) of coastline, extreme temperatures are reduced in both summer and winter. In Montevideo, the capital, the average annual temperature is 61° F (16° C), with a winter monthly low of 51° F (11° C) in June and a summer high average of about 80° F (27° C) in January. Temperature ranges are slightly greater in the interior, and the warmest conditions prevail in the northwest. Annual precipitation, which is more or less uniformly distributed throughout the year, ranges from a high of nearly 50 inches (127 centimeters) in the northwest to about 40 inches (102 centimeters) in the south.

The apparent uniformity of climatic conditions is deceiving, however, as Uruguay is subject to extremes from the interaction of different air masses and frontal systems. For anyone who has lived in the country, the hot summer days and cold winter nights make a mockery of the statistical averages. Temperatures of 100° F (38° C) are common during the summer months, while freezing temperatures occur frequently during the winter. Periods of both major flooding and drought have occurred in Uruguay during every decade since the 1880s.

Prairie grasses and herbaceous plants dominate the landscape and represent the nation's single major source of natural wealth. Covering more than 90 percent of the country, the grass-dominated scenery is broken only by *montes,* scrub woodlands that cover rocky hills and ridges, and planted eucalyptus windbreaks and forest lots.

Aside from its rich agricultural potential, Uruguay is almost devoid of natural physical resources. Sand, amethyst, granite, and marble are the only mineral products mined in the country.

People

Throughout its early history Uruguay lacked the things Spanish conquerors dreamed of: gold and converts to Christianity. For 200 years after it was first seen by Europeans in the early 1500s, the area of present-day Uruguay remained little more than a huge natural pasture inhabited by wild cattle, hostile Charrúa Indians, and occasional bands of gauchos, or cowboys. Lacking even a name, the area was simply referred to as the Banda Oriental del Uruguay (the east bank of the Uruguay River). Therefore Uruguayans are still known as *orientales.*

The country's population totals about 3 million, and Uruguay has the slowest annual population growth rate in Latin America—averaging less than 0.6 percent per year. The overwhelming majority of Uruguayans live in the southern and western coastal

Karl Kummels—Shostal Associates

The Palacio Salvo, with a transmitter on top, borders on the Plaza Independencia in Montevideo, Uruguay. The building was renovated in the early 1980s.

margins, and more than 85 percent are urban. Montevideo is home to more than 1.2 million people, or nearly half the nation's total. Montevideo's predominance over the country's second largest city, Salto, makes it an outstanding example of a primate city. (*See also* Montevideo.)

From the earliest period of settlement, Uruguay's economy was dominated by extensive grazing activities overseen by a relatively small number of gauchos. Thus rural areas have always had few employment opportunities. Much of the countryside remains very sparsely settled. Broad areas have population densities of less than 2 persons per square mile (0.8 per square kilometer), and large areas are essentially devoid of people.

Nearly 98 percent of the people trace their ancestry to Europeans. Most Uruguayans are descended from immigrants who arrived in the country after 1870. People of Spanish origin make up the bulk of inhabitants, but more than a third are of Italian origin. The original Charrúa Indians were literally exterminated by the Spanish and Portuguese prior to Uruguayan independence, leaving the nation devoid of an indigenous population. Blacks, originally imported as slaves to work in the country's ports, form an extremely small but distinctive part of Montevideo's population.

Unlike all other Latin American republics except Argentina, Uruguay has developed a social class structure in which the middle classes are numerically dominant. Free public education and subsidized health-care systems have resulted in extremely high literacy levels (more than 95 percent), high life expectancy at birth (more than 70 years), low infant mortality

rates, and a relatively high per capita gross domestic product (GDP) when compared to other nations of the region. In appearance, behavior, and life-styles, Uruguayans are much more like Western Europeans than are most Latin Americans.

Uruguay has no official state religion. While the majority of Uruguayans are Roman Catholics, the country is highly secular in its daily life. The separation of church and state is complete. Civil marriage and divorce have been legal since the early 1900s.

Economy

Although it contributes only slightly more than 9 percent to the country's GDP, agriculture remains the basis of the Uruguayan economy. Nearly 10 million cattle and more than 20 million sheep occupy about three fourths of the agricultural land. Most livestock operations are extensive, substituting land for technical improvements. Raw wool and beef are the major commodities produced. These two items represent only about a third of exports by value, but sheep and cattle products provide the raw materials for the many industries that produce more than 90 percent of Uruguayan exports. The country is heavily dependent on agriculture for tax revenue to support government spending programs and employment in other sectors of the economy.

For the second half of the 20th century, Uruguay's terms of trade, the relative value of exports to imports, have been highly unfavorable. The nation has been excluded from selling fresh or chilled beef in some overseas markets, ostensibly because of the presence of anthrax (hoof-and-mouth disease) within the country. As a result Uruguay's agricultural production has been stagnant, with a severe effect on the entire economy. Some attempts have been made to develop new markets to replace traditional ones,

241

but these have generally turned out to be unstable and less profitable. The leading area of expansion in the agricultural sector has been processed dairy products—especially milk, cheese, and ice cream, which have found a ready market in Brazil.

More than three fifths of Uruguay's GDP is produced through the service sector, mainly in public administration and tourism. Nontraditional export-oriented industrialization is encouraged by the government in an effort to diversify the employment and export base. Historically industry has been costly and inefficient but has survived because of protective tariff barriers and government subsidies. Because of its attractive coastal amenities, increased tourism is seen as a means of improving economic conditions over the long term. The government owns and operates the railroads, a national airline, a shipping fleet, the telephone and telegraph system, petroleum refining and processing, the cement industry, and a number of other activities. Privatization, however, has become a major policy consideration of the government. Severe inflation during the early 1970s and mid-1980s and an excessive foreign debt, largely caused by increased oil prices and unwise spending during the military dictatorship of 1973 to 1984, left Uruguay's economy in a precarious position.

History and Government

The area that is now Uruguay was discovered by Juan Díaz de Solís in 1516, but it remained largely devoid of European population until the Portuguese established the town of Colonia opposite Buenos Aires in 1680. Montevideo was founded in 1726 by a handful of Spanish colonists in an effort to contain Portuguese influence. In 1776 the Banda Oriental del Uruguay became a part of the Spanish viceroyalty of Río de la Plata.

In 1811 Uruguay's national hero, José Gervasio Artigas, rallied the *orientales* against Spanish rule and organized a gaucho army to win independence from Spain. Although Artigas defeated the Spanish at the battle of Las Piedras and laid siege to Montevideo, his successes were foiled by the entry of Portuguese troops and Brazil's subsequent occupation of the area. Artigas led his followers in an exodus to Paraguay and after 1820 never again set foot in Uruguay. (*See also* Artigas.)

In 1825 Brazil's domination of its newly acquired Cisplatine Province was challenged by the *Treinta y Tres Orientales*—33 patriots led by Juan Antonio Lavalleja and aided by Argentina. With British commercial intervention and the agreement of Brazil and Argentina, the República Oriental del Uruguay was established in 1828. After a constitution was adopted in 1830, there were 70 years of nearly continuous civil war. The antagonists, identified by the color of their headbands worn in battle, were the *Colorados* (Reds), representing liberal urban interests, and the *Blancos* (Whites), led by conservative landowners. Uruguay's major political parties today are the Colorado and the Blanco, officially the National party.

The country's last civil war was fought in 1904 during the first presidency of José Batlle y Ordóñez, Uruguay's most notable political figure and leading citizen. Batlle was largely responsible for the advanced social legislation and democratic traditions of modern Uruguay.

During the first half of the 20th century, despite several constitutional changes, Uruguay became a very wealthy and egalitarian nation-state, admired throughout the world for its social programs and democratic liberties. This prosperity was based on the expanding exportation of wool and beef to Europe and a slow growth in population. In the 1950s, however, the Uruguayan economy stagnated. It was followed by political unrest in the 1960s and culminated in a military dictatorship inaugurated in 1973.

The military takeover was broadly supported by most segments of the population. They felt that firm leadership was needed to end urban guerrilla terrorism, which had beset the country since the mid-1960s, and to right an economy that was on the verge of collapse. The military crushed the "internal state of war" and sought to revitalize the economy by reducing the government's role and by creating free-market mechanisms. While initially successful, the military government was viewed as increasingly repressive and antithetical to the Uruguayan political tradition of open and free democracy.

In 1984 a freely elected civilian government replaced the military dictatorship. Severe economic problems remain, but the restoration of democracy was enthusiastically received by Uruguayans.

Facts About Uruguay

Official Name: Oriental Republic of Uruguay.

Capital: Montevideo.

Area: 68,037 square miles (176,215 square kilometers).

Population (1987 estimate): 3,058,000; 45.3 persons per square mile (17.5 persons per square kilometer); 86.2 percent urban, 13.8 percent rural.

Major Language: Spanish (official).

Major Religion: Roman Catholicism.

Literacy: 95.3 percent.

Highest Peak: Mirador Nacional.

Major Rivers: Guareim, Negro, Río de la Plata, Uruguay.

Form of Government: Republic.

Head of State and Government: President.

Legislature: General Assembly.

Voting Qualification: Age 18.

Political Divisions: 19 departments.

Major Cities (1985 estimate): Montevideo (1,246,500), Salto (77,400), Paysandú (75,200), Las Piedras (61,300), Rivera (55,400).

Chief Manufactured and Mined Products: Textiles, chemicals, cement, processed food, refined petroleum, beverages, shoes, transport equipment, sand, amethyst, granite, marble.

Chief Agricultural Products: *Crops*—sugarcane, wheat, rice, sugar beets, sorghum, potatoes, grapes, corn. *Livestock*—cattle, sheep.

Flag: *Colors*—blue, white, gold (*see* Flags of the World).

Monetary Unit: 1 Uruguayan new peso = 100 centésimos.

Utah Travel Council

Utah's capital and largest city is Salt Lake City. It lies in the valley of the Great Salt Lake. Overlooking the city are the rugged, snowcapped peaks of the Wasatch Range.

UTAH

UTAH. The settlement and growth of Utah were the best organized of all the Western states. As late as 1847 there were only a few fur trappers and scattered Indian tribes in the area. Then on July 21, 1847, a party of Mormons arrived in Great Salt Lake Valley seeking freedom to practice their religion. Under the able leadership of Brigham Young, the Mormons worked in cooperative groups to turn the desert valley into a garden spot of fertile cropland.

The hardy Mormon colony grew swiftly, spreading north- and southward from the site of Salt Lake City. In 1850 the population of Utah was about 11,000. By 1880 it had multiplied more than 12 times. Almost all this development was directed by the Mormon church (*see* Mormons; Young, Brigham).

Since 1880 the introduction of mining and manufacturing has attracted many non-Mormons (or gentiles, as they are called by Mormons). Today nearly three fourths of the state's people are Mormons, or members of the Church of Jesus Christ of Latter-day Saints. This church is still the most active social and political force in Utah. It owns much property and manages many cooperative enterprises.

Utah is named from a Ute Indian word *eutaw,* meaning "in the tops of the mountains." Its nickname

Population (1980): 1,461,037—rank, 36th state. Urban, 84.4%; rural, 15.6%. Persons per square mile, 17.8 (persons per square kilometer, 6.9)—rank, 42nd state.

Extent: Area, 84,916 square miles (219,931 square kilometers), including 2,820 square miles (7,304 square kilometers) of water surface (11th state in size).

Elevation: Highest, Kings Peak, 13,498 feet (4,114 meters), in Duchesne County; lowest, Beaver Dam Wash at southwest corner of state, 2,180 feet (664 meters); average, 6,100 feet (1,859 meters).

Geographic Center: 3 miles (4.8 kilometers) north of Manti.

Temperature: Extremes—lowest, −69° F (−56° C), Peter's Sink, Feb. 1, 1985; highest, 117° F (47° C), Saint George, July 5, 1985. Averages at Milford—January, 25.7° F (−3.5° C); July, 73.9° F (23.3° C); annual, 49.2° F (9.6° C). Averages at Salt Lake City—January, 27.0° F (−2.8° C); July, 76.9° F (24.9° C); annual, 51.2° F (10.7° C).

Precipitation: At Milford—annual average, 8.39 inches (213 millimeters). At Salt Lake City—annual average, 13.95 inches (354 millimeters).

Land Use: Crops, 4%; pasture, 44%; forest, 29%; other, 23%.

For statistical information about Agriculture, Education, Employment, Finance, Government, Manufacturing, Mining, Population Trends, and Vital Statistics, see UTAH FACT SUMMARY.

243

Josef Muench

Monument Valley lies in the Navajo reservation of southeastern Utah. Many buttes tower hundreds of feet above the valley floor.

is Beehive State, from its coat of arms. An early Mormon name for the area was Deseret, meaning "honeybee" in the Book of Mormon.

A Survey of Utah

The Beehive State lies in the Rocky Mountain region of the United States. It is bordered on the northeast and north by Wyoming and Idaho. To the west is Nevada. Arizona is to the south and Colorado to the east. In the southeast Utah forms a square corner with Arizona, New Mexico, and Colorado. This is the only point in the nation where four states meet.

Utah's greatest length, from north to south, is 345 miles. Its greatest width is 275 miles. The area of the state is 84,916 square miles, including 2,820 square miles of inland water surface.

Three Large Natural Regions

The surface of Utah is very uneven. The state has high mountain ranges, vast desert basins, broad plateaus, deep canyons, and fertile river valleys.

The **Rocky Mountains** occupy an L-shaped area in the northeastern part of the state. One spur of the Rockies, the Wasatch Range, extends southward into Utah from Idaho. The range ends in Sanpete County. On the western slope of the Wasatch are the largest cities of the state. The bottom leg of the "L" is formed by the Uinta Mountains. In this range is Kings Peak (13,498 feet), the highest point in the Beehive State.

The **Colorado Plateau** in southeastern Utah is a huge broken tableland covering about one third of the state. It is a region of colorful mesas, cliffs, buttes, and other highlands. Here are the deep gorges of the Green and Colorado rivers.

The **Great Basin** extends the length of the state in western Utah. The eastern part of the Basin and Range region of the United States, it is a land of

vast deserts, salt flats, and block mountains. The chief features of the Great Basin are Great Salt Lake and the Great Salt Lake Desert. Great Salt Lake as well as Utah and Sevier lakes are the remains of ancient Lake Bonneville, which covered this area thousands of years ago (see Great Salt Lake). The rivers of this region generally have no outlet to the sea. In the southwest, however, the Virgin River and its branches flow out of Utah to enter the Colorado River and, finally, the Gulf of California. Along the Beaver Dam Wash, a tributary of the Virgin River, is the lowest point in the state, 2,000 feet.

Climate and Weather

Utah has a dry, continental climate with warm summers and cold winters. In the northern mountain regions of the state the average annual temperature is about 42° F.; in the south it is about 60°. The growing season varies from more than 200 days a year along parts of the southern border to only about 60 days a year high in the Rocky Mountains.

The climate is dry because the lofty Sierra Nevada to the west robs the prevailing winds of their moisture. The high, north-central region of the state receives the most moisture—about 40 inches a year. Parts of the Great Salt Lake Desert receive less than 5 inches a year.

Natural Resources and Conservation

Because of inadequate rainfall, many of Utah's agricultural areas are irrigated or dry-farmed. Other sections are suitable for grazing and support herds of cattle or sheep. There are some barren regions in the state where little grows except cactus, creosote bushes, and greasewood.

More than one fourth of the state is forested. Some pine, spruce, and fir is of commercial value. Although more timber is replaced each year than is harvested, the timber industry in Utah has developed slowly, due in part to marketing problems.

Utah's mineral deposits are among the richest in the West. Its most valuable mineral products are copper, petroleum, coal, and uranium. The world's greatest oil shale deposit extends from eastern Utah into adjacent areas in Colorado and Wyoming. Sand and sandstone deposits contain another important source of petroleum energy.

The most important natural resource in the state is water. In 1847 the Mormons began the first systematic irrigation in the United States. Since then many reservoirs have been built to collect water and distribute it where needed. Such projects include the Strawberry, on the Strawberry River; Deer Creek, on the Provo; Piute and Sevier Bridge, on the Sevier; Echo, on the Weber; Scofield, on the Price; and Flaming Gorge, on the Green. In 1952 a 6-mile tunnel was completed through the mountains to carry the waters of the Duchesne River westward to the Provo River.

Conservation work is directed by the Department of Natural Resources. The divisions of the department include Water Resources; Parks and Recreation; and Oil, Gas, and Mining.

People of Utah

The first explorers of the Utah country found the region inhabited by three major Indian tribes—the Ute, Paiute, and Shoshone. In general these Indians lived by hunting small animals and gathering seeds. Trouble between the white settlers and the Indians broke out periodically until the Ute were settled on the Uinta and Ouray Reservation in 1871. This reservation, most of which is in Duchesne County, is the largest in the state.

Utah's first band of Mormon pioneers—143 men, 3 women, and 2 children—came in 1847. By the end of the year the Great Salt Lake colony had grown to 1,700 people. During the next 50 years most of Utah's settlers were Mormons from the Eastern states and Europe. The Mormon church directed the extensive irrigation projects that produced rich farmlands. To encourage commerce the church founded Zion's Cooperative Mercantile Institution in 1868. This is a large chain of retail stores. The church also helped establish the state's transportation system.

During the 1900s the number of non-Mormons in Utah increased considerably. Most of the state's population is concentrated near the original Mormon settlement along the western edge of the Wasatch Range. Foreign-born residents number about 3 percent of the population, chiefly Germans, Canadians, and Mexicans. The nonwhite population totals about 5 percent, made up almost entirely of Asians and Pacific Islanders, American Indians, and blacks.

Products of the Land

Utah's mining industry yields an annual income among goods-producing industries second only to

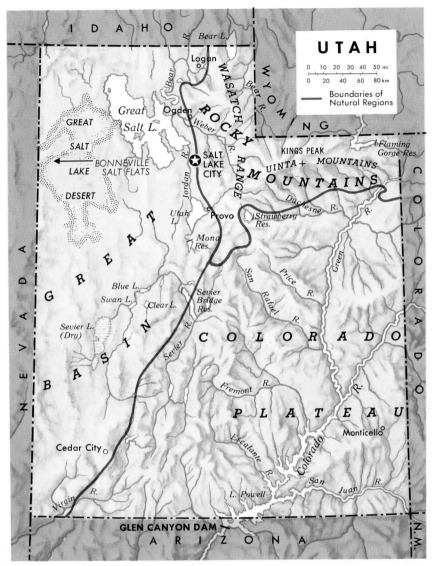

that produced by manufacturing. The largest open-pit copper mine in the United States is at Bingham Canyon. It produces more than 10 percent of the nation's copper. The Bingham Canyon area, called the West Mountain District, is also the state's chief source of lead, gold, silver, and zinc. This mineral-rich region includes the counties of Salt Lake, Davis, Morgan, Toole, and Weber. Petroleum has become the state's most valuable mineral as a result of oil discoveries beginning in 1956.

The other two major mining areas in Utah are Park City and Tintic (near Eureka). Coal is produced chiefly in Carbon County and iron and iron ore in Iron County. Uranium ores are mined in the desolate southeastern corner of the state.

The Beehive State has about 13,500 farms. The average farm consists of approximately 825 acres. More than a million acres of farmland are irrigated. Most of the irrigated land is sowed to grain and to grasses such as alfalfa for feeding livestock and poultry. The remainder produces truck crops, onions, potatoes, other vegetables, and fruits. Wheat is grown by dry-farming methods.

The vast grazing areas of the state support about 750,000 cattle and more than 400,000 sheep. They also support a herd of deer.

Utah ranks among the top ten states in the production of wool. Some of the state's other valuable agricultural products include cattle, hay, milk, sheep, turkeys, and eggs.

Manufacturing and Cities

The manufacturing of machinery ranks first in industry and produces such goods as office equipment. The next ranking industry is the production of transportation equipment, including guided missiles and space vehicles. Other major industries are food processing; primary metals industries such as steel products; electrical and electronic equipment; printing and publishing; and fabricated metals. The production of stone, glass, and clay items and medical instruments and supplies is also vital to the state's economy.

Utah's capital, Salt Lake City, is one of the largest cities in the region between Denver, Colo., and the Pacific coast. Because of its historical sites and magnificent setting—near Great Salt Lake and the Wasatch Range—the city draws many visitors during the year (see Salt Lake City).

Ogden, 32 miles to the north of Salt Lake City, is a transportation center in a rich farming area. It turns out many food products. Provo lies about 40 miles south of Salt Lake City. Its chief industries are steel and clothing. Logan serves the Bear River country in the extreme northern part of the state. Orem, near Provo, is known for its many fruit orchards.

Transportation

The historic Mormon migration was carried out largely by covered wagons drawn by oxen and by handcarts limited to a load of 17 pounds each. The Mormon Trail generally followed the Oregon Trail westward to Fort Bridger, Wyo., then branched southwestward to Salt Lake City. (See also Frontier; Roads and Streets).

Transportation remained primitive until the coming of the railroad. During the Civil War the Union Pacific Railroad began building westward from the Missouri River, the Central Pacific eastward from California. The two lines met at Promontory on May 10, 1869, to provide the nation's first railroad service across the continent. The completion of the Lucin Cutoff across Great Salt Lake in 1903 bypassed the original line through Promontory. Today the state is served by a number of major railroads and airlines. Its network of highways includes Interstate 15, 70, and 80.

Recreation in the Beehive State

Utah attracts several million tourists yearly. Zion, Bryce Canyon, Arches Capitol Reef, and Canyonlands are national parks (see National Parks). Their campgrounds offer excellent facilities. Alta, near Brighton; Brighton; Ogden Snow Basin, near Ogden; and Park City are noted for winter sports. Near the western edge of the Great Salt Lake Desert are the Bonneville Salt Flats, used as an automobile speedway. Hunting and fishing are popular. Among Utah's wildlife are ducks, deer, elk, and mountain lions.

Utah Department of Publicity and Industrial Development

Electric shovels have carved these huge stairsteps out of a mountain of copper ore. The mine has yielded more than 15 billion pounds of ore.

Josef Muench

The busy Geneva Steel Mill stands in the shadows of the Wasatch Range near Provo. It was built in 1943 at a cost of 200 million dollars.

Education in Utah

Beginning as early as 1847 (the year the Mormons arrived in Utah) many settlements established their own schools. As non-Mormons settled in the territory, they established sectarian missionary schools. In 1855 the University of Deseret (now the University of Utah) was directed to supervise the schools. However, the great distances between communities and the scarcity of financial resources hindered the development of public education.

The first free public school in Utah Territory opened at American Fork in 1868. In 1890 a school law providing for a "uniform system of free schools" was passed. Provision for tax-supported high schools was authorized by the state legislature in 1910.

State-supported schools of higher education include the University of Utah, at Salt Lake City. Utah State University, at Logan; Weber State College, at Ogden; Southern Utah State College, at Cedar City; and two-year colleges in Price, Saint George, Ephraim, Provo, and Salt Lake City are the other institutions in the state-supported higher education system. Other educational institutions include Brigham Young University, at Provo, with a branch in the state of Hawaii, and Westminster College, at Salt Lake City.

Government and Politics

Salt Lake City has served as capital of the State of Deseret, 1849–50; of Utah Territory, 1850–96, except 1851–56 (Fillmore) and 1858–59 (Parowan); and of the state since 1896. Utah is governed under the constitution adopted in 1895.

The governor is the state's chief executive officer. The Senate and the House of Representatives make the laws. The Supreme Court heads the judiciary.

In state and Congressional elections Utah has supported Republicans slightly more often than Democrats. In presidential elections the state has likewise cast its electoral votes more often for the Republican candidates.

HISTORY OF UTAH

Utah was part of the territory ceded to the United States by Mexico in 1848 through the Treaty of Guadalupe-Hidalgo. In the spring of 1849 the Mormons organized the State of Deseret, a territory extending from the Rocky Mountains to the Sierra Nevada. It included parts of Arizona, California, Colorado, Idaho, New Mexico, Oregon, and Wyoming, as well as all of Utah and Nevada. A few months later the Mormons petitioned the United States Congress for admission to the Union, but the request was denied. Five more times Utah asked for admission as a state, but each time Congress refused, chiefly because of the Mormon practice of polygamy (having more than one wife). Finally, in 1890, Wilford Woodruff, the president of the Mormon church, forbade polygamy. A state constitution was framed five years later, and in 1896 Utah became the 45th state. The following sections tell the history of Utah.

Brigham Young's first view of the Great Salt Lake Valley is commemorated by a monument recalling his words, "This is the place." It is in Pioneer Trail State Park.

Exploration and the Fur Trade

According to tradition, the first white men to enter what is now Utah were a party sent by Coronado to search for the "seven cities of Cibola" in 1540 (*see* Coronado). More than 200 years later, in 1776, two Franciscan priests, Silvestre Vélez de Escalante and Francisco Domínguez, explored parts of southern Utah. Part of the course they followed became the Old Spanish Trail.

Early in the 1800's the riches of the fur trade brought hardy adventurers into the Utah country. Jim Bridger is credited with having discovered Great Salt Lake in 1824 (*see* Bridger), though similar claims have been made for Étienne Provost, Jedediah Smith, and Peter Skene Ogden. William L. and Milton Sublette were others who explored the region.

The Great Mormon Migration

The real history of Utah's settlement began with the arrival of the Mormons in 1847. Driven from the Middle West, they migrated to the Great Salt Lake Valley. The first of the Mormon "pilgrims" entered the valley on July 21. Most of the original band arrived on July 23, and that same day the pioneers began to plow the desert and to irrigate it with water from City Creek. On July 24 Brigham Young, who had been ill, arrived with the remaining members of the group. The date of his arrival is now celebrated throughout the state as Pioneer Day, Utah's most important state holiday. In November the Mormons bought Fort Buenaventura (now in Ogden), which Miles Goodyear had built in 1844–45.

Despite their hard work the Mormons were threatened with disaster in 1848 when a swarm of crickets descended upon their crops. Then a huge flock of sea gulls appeared and ate the insects. The Mormons considered this an answer to their prayers and erected a monument to the sea gulls in thanks.

Utah—Territory and State

In 1849 the Mormons formed the State of Deseret, with Young as governor and a council of 12 high priests. Congress ignored this state and in 1850 created Utah Territory, naming Young the first territorial governor.

The Mormons' thorough organization made for a diversified economy unheard of in other frontier states. By 1850, 85 different occupations were practiced in Utah. In addition to meeting its own needs, the state was able to supply a variety of goods to neighboring states whose economic activities were more specialized. Mining, of great importance to other Western states, did not develop in the Mormon society since it was forbidden by Brigham Young.

When many non-Mormons began settling in the territory, conflicts arose over the religious and social customs of the Mormons. The gentiles appealed to President James Buchanan, who sent troops to take control in 1857. Young was removed from office. Congress passed several antipolygamy bills but they were difficult to enforce.

The Mormon leaders who followed Young gradually changed some of the church practices and customs.

The doctrine of polygamy was given up in 1890 and Utah was admitted as a state six years later.

During the 1900's the newer, gentile settlers generally took up business, mining, and stock raising. Open-cut mining operations began at Bingham in 1907. This copper-rich deposit had been yielding small quantities of ore since the first claim was registered by George Ogilvie in 1863.

During and after World War II, Utah's mining industry increased enormously. New mines were opened to supply metals for war needs. The Geneva steel plant, opened in 1943, continued to be one of the largest producers in the West. Between 1947 and 1957 Utah's manufacturing showed a growth rate of 269 percent. The mining of uranium added millions to the state's income. Utah became a center for defense industries, both for research and for manufacturing. Computers, electronic devices, aircraft, and rocketry are among the newer products being developed and produced since World War II. Another factor in its growing prosperity was the development of the tourist trade. Additional electric power and irrigation water were assured for Utah by the Colorado River storage project, authorized in 1956.

In the late 1960's the development of brine extraction projects and the exploration of vast oil shale resources promised further expansion of Utah's minerals industries. (*See also* United States, sections "Western Basins and Plateaus" and "Rocky Mountains"; individual entries in the Fact-Index on Utah persons, places, products, and events.)

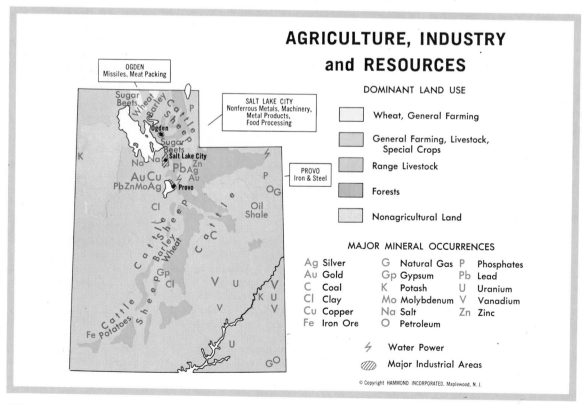

AGRICULTURE, INDUSTRY and RESOURCES

OGDEN
Missiles, Meat Packing

SALT LAKE CITY
Nonferrous Metals, Machinery,
Metal Products,
Food Processing

PROVO
Iron & Steel

DOMINANT LAND USE

Wheat, General Farming

General Farming, Livestock, Special Crops

Range Livestock

Forests

Nonagricultural Land

MAJOR MINERAL OCCURRENCES

Ag	Silver	G	Natural Gas	P	Phosphates
Au	Gold	Gp	Gypsum	Pb	Lead
C	Coal	K	Potash	U	Uranium
Cl	Clay	Mo	Molybdenum	V	Vanadium
Cu	Copper	Na	Salt	Zn	Zinc
Fe	Iron Ore	O	Petroleum		

⚡ Water Power

▨ Major Industrial Areas

© Copyright HAMMOND INCORPORATED. Maplewood, N. J.

Notable Events in Utah History

1540—García L. de Cárdenas and party are probably first white men to sight Utah.

1776—Fathers Silvestre de Escalante and Francisco Domínguez seek route from New Mexico to California; explore Utah.

1821—Mexico wins independence from Spain; claims Utah.

1824—Gen. William H. Ashley sends trappers to northern Utah. **Jim Bridger discovers Great Salt Lake.**

1826—Jedediah Smith leads first American overland expedition to California; returns to Utah in 1827.

1832—Antoine Robidou builds Uinta Basin trading post.

1841—Capt. John Bartleson leads first wagon train of settlers across Utah to California.

1843—John C. Frémont and Kit Carson explore Salt Lake area; Frémont's reports attract settlers.

1844–45—Miles Goodyear builds Fort Buenaventura.

1847—First party of Mormon pioneers arrives in Great Salt Lake Valley; communal irrigation organized.

1848—**Sea gulls stop invasion of crickets.** Mexico cedes Utah to U. S. in Treaty of Guadalupe-Hidalgo.

1849—Mormons organize State of Deseret; capital, Salt Lake City.

1850—University of State of Deseret (University of Utah) chartered at Salt Lake City. Territory of Utah created; capital, Salt Lake City (Fillmore, 1851–56; Parowan, 1858–59); governor, Brigham Young.

1852—Mormons avow plural marriage as rule of church.

1853—Mormon Temple at Salt Lake City begun; completed in 1893. Walker War with Ute Indians begins over slavery among Indians; settled in 1854.

1854—First of grasshopper plagues endangers crops.

1856–60—Pioneers travel with handcarts to Utah.

1857—President James Buchanan removes Young from governorship; Mormons attack U. S. troop trains; peace made in 1858, before troops reach Utah.

1862—Congress rejects new State of Deseret constitution.

1863—Mining of silver and lead begins in Bingham Canyon. Dry farming succeeds near Bear River City.

1865–68—Ute-Black Hawk War ends major Indian conflicts in Utah.

1869—Union Pacific and Central Pacific railroads complete transcontinental line at Promontory.

1887—Antipolygamic Edmunds Act (1882) continues attack on Mormons; church disincorporated.

1890—Wilford Woodruff, Mormon church president, forbids polygamy. Public school system established.

1896—Utah becomes 45th state, January 4; capital, Salt Lake City; governor, Heber Wells.

1907—**Open-cut copper mining begins at Bingham Canyon.**

1911—Strawberry Reservoir completed.

1914—Auto racing begins at Bonneville Salt Flats.

1915—State Capitol completed.

1919—Zion National Park created.

1928—Bryce Canyon National Park established.

1943—Geneva steel plant begins operation near Provo.

1952—Six-mile Duchesne Tunnel completed for irrigation.

1956—Congress creates Colorado River storage project.

1964—Flaming Gorge Dam on Green River dedicated. Arizona's Glen Canyon Dam creates Lake Powell, the nation's second largest man-made lake, in Glen Canyon National Recreation Area.

1965—Canyonlands National Park opened.

1966—Three bridges—Colorado River, Dirty Devil River, and White Canyon—built in 6-mile radius.

1977—Gary Mark Gilmore is first person executed in U. S. in ten years, at state prison.

1824

1848

1907

STATE FLOWER:
Sego Lily

STATE TREE:
Blue Spruce

STATE BIRD:
Sea Gull (Unofficial)

STATE SEAL: On shield are beehive
and sego lilies; state motto;
date 1847, when Mormons
arrived.

Utah Profile

FLAG: *See* **Flags of the United States.**
MOTTO: Industry.
**SONG: 'Utah, We Love Thee'—words
and music by Evan Stephens.**

To the 19th-century American pioneers who pushed westward seeking pastureland and timberland the canyon country of Utah offered little promise. Its settlement began with a wagon train of religious exiles who sought a place no one else wanted where they could worship in their own way. On July 24, 1847, these Mormons, or Latter-Day Saints, chose a site at the foot of the Wasatch mountains as their promised land. From that day on, Utah with its organized and orderly development wrote a unique chapter in the history of the West. Almost as soon as the spot was chosen, streets were laid, irrigated crops were planted, and schools were set up as the early settlers prepared the way for the great Mormon migration. In the next few years Mormons came by thousands, some on wagons, some dragging handcarts.

By feeding the Indians rather than fighting them, the Mormons maintained relative peace with the red man. However, polygamy and other practices peculiar to the Mormon way of life created difficulties between the Saints and the United States government. In 1869, when the last spike of the first transcontinental railway was driven at Promontory, a steady influx of non-Mormons began. In 1896 Utah was admitted to the Union, just a few years after the Mormons ceased to practice polygamy.

Today Utah's breathtaking scenery makes it a favorite tourist center. Since World War II, its location in the heart of the West and its good transportation facilities have also made it a choice area for defense plants. Cattle and sheep graze near missile test sites, and Indians live in primitive huts next to working oil wells. The bleak, apparently unyielding, land produces a wealth of minerals. But some things have not changed. Water is still scarce; religion is still a part of everyday life; and hard work remains a cardinal virtue in the Beehive State.

The Mormon Temple stands in Salt Lake City's Temple Square, two ten-acre plots on which all the city's major Mormon structures have been erected. Begun in 1853, the temple was dedicated in 1893. It is open only to Mormons.

The University of Utah, at Salt Lake City, was incorporated as the University of Deseret in 1850. It closed two years later and was reopened in 1867. The first buildings on the present site were completed in 1901. This is the Park Building.

The State Capitol of Utah stands on a bench of the Wasatch foothills on the northern edge of Salt Lake City. It was built in 1914–15. Salt Lake City became the territorial capital of Utah in 1850 and the state capital in 1896.

251

Lake Powell has transformed a wilderness into one of Utah's favorite vacation spots. Created in 1963 by Arizona's Glen Canyon Dam, the lake's waters provide a route to otherwise forbidding regions of Utah's canyon country.

During the 1870's, Mormon leader and colonizer Brigham Young spent some time at this winter home in St. George. It stands in one of the three units of Dixie State Park in southwestern Utah. Dixie is one of about 30 state parks in Utah.

The Municipal Park Gardens, located in the heart of Ogden, is one of the showplaces of the city. Ogden, an industrial and transportation center, was incorporated in 1861 and named for Peter Ogden, an explorer and fur trader.

Kayaking on the Colorado River is one way to explore Canyonlands National Park. On the park's towering spires are petroglyphs carved by prehistoric Indians. One of Utah's five national parks, Canyonlands was established in 1964.

Cattle are herded in Monument Valley on the Arizona-Utah border. The area is famous for its fantastic red sandstone formations, some more than 1,000 feet high. It contains the Navajo Indians' Monument Valley Tribal Park.

One of Utah's important winter sport centers is Park City, located in the mountains near Salt Lake City. A number of ski meets are held here each year.

High on the plateau that stretches through southern Utah and northern Arizona is Bryce Canyon National Park. The colors of its dramatic rock structures range from red through orange and gold.

The Horn Silver Mine brought a short-lived boom to the town of Frisco in the 1880's. Copper is now Utah's chief mineral.

To commemorate the coming of the Mormon pioneers in 1847, celebrations are held in major Utah cities each July 24. The festivities open with parades like the one shown here.

Bonneville Salt Flats, west of Salt Lake City, is the fastest speedway in the world. The hard, crystallized flats provide an ideal surface for both racing and endurance runs.

UTAH FACT SUMMARY

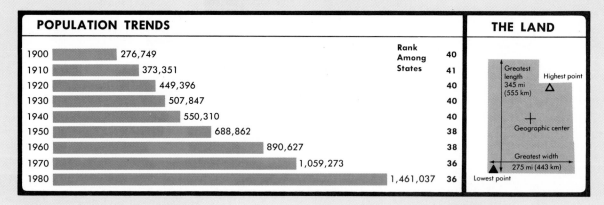

POPULATION TRENDS

Year	Population	Rank Among States
1900	276,749	40
1910	373,351	41
1920	449,396	40
1930	507,847	40
1940	550,310	40
1950	688,862	38
1960	890,627	38
1970	1,059,273	36
1980	1,461,037	36

THE LAND

Greatest length 345 mi (555 km)
Highest point
Geographic center
Greatest width 275 mi (443 km)
Lowest point

LARGEST CITIES (1980 census)

Salt Lake City (163,033): state capital; transportation, distribution, and manufacturing center; food processing; stockyards; smelters; University of Utah; Mormon Temple (1893) and Tabernacle (1867); Sea Gull Monument (*see* Salt Lake City).

Provo (74,108): manufacturing city on Provo River amid mines and irrigated farms and orchards; large steel plant nearby; Brigham Young University; headquarters for nearby Uinta National Forest.

West Valley City (72,378): southwestern suburb of Salt Lake City; Bonneville Raceway; aerospace test facility.

Ogden (64,407): railroad, industrial, and canning center in irrigated area; Hill Air Force Base; Goodyear Cabin (1841); Mormon Tabernacle; Weber State College.

Orem (52,399): fruit orchards irrigated by Provo River; steel plant; shopping centers.

Sandy City (50,546): suburb 13 miles (21 kilometers) south of Salt Lake City, west of Wasatch Range; Little Cottonwood Canyon nearby.

Bountiful (32,877): in irrigated agricultural area north of Salt Lake City; grain, fruits, vegetables, turkeys; second settlement in state.

West Jordan (27,192): on Jordan River; 12 miles (19 kilometers) south of Salt Lake City; rodeo.

Logan (26,844): industrial city in irrigated Cache Valley; Mormon Temple and Tabernacle; Utah State University; Wasatch-Cache National Forest nearby.

VITAL STATISTICS 1985 (per 1,000 population)

Birthrate:	23.4
Death Rate:	5.7
Marriage Rate:	10.4
Divorce Rate:	5.2

GOVERNMENT

Capital: Salt Lake City (since 1896).

Statehood: Became 45th state in the Union on Jan. 4, 1896.

Constitution: Adopted 1895; amendment may be passed by two-thirds vote of both legislative houses or by initiative action of the people, ratified by majority voting on it in an election.

Representation in U.S. Congress: Senate—2. House of Representatives—3. Electoral votes—5.

Legislature: Senators—29; term, 4 years. Representatives—75; term, 2 years.

Executive Officers: Governor—term, 4 years; may succeed self. Other officials—lieutenant governor, attorney general, treasurer, auditor; all elected; terms, 4 years.

Judiciary: Supreme Court—5 justices; term, 10 years. District Court—29 judges; term, 6 years.

County: 29 counties; governed by boards of commissioners; members elected for 2- and 4-year terms.

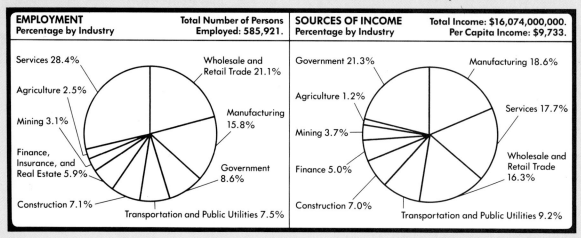

EMPLOYMENT
Percentage by Industry — Total Number of Persons Employed: 585,921.

- Services 28.4%
- Agriculture 2.5%
- Mining 3.1%
- Finance, Insurance, and Real Estate 5.9%
- Construction 7.1%
- Transportation and Public Utilities 7.5%
- Government 8.6%
- Manufacturing 15.8%
- Wholesale and Retail Trade 21.1%

SOURCES OF INCOME
Percentage by Industry — Total Income: $16,074,000,000. Per Capita Income: $9,733.

- Government 21.3%
- Agriculture 1.2%
- Mining 3.7%
- Finance 5.0%
- Construction 7.0%
- Transportation and Public Utilities 9.2%
- Wholesale and Retail Trade 16.3%
- Services 17.7%
- Manufacturing 18.6%

MAJOR PRODUCTS

Agricultural: Barley, wheat, alfalfa, corn, oats, potatoes, cattle, sheep, dairy products, turkeys.

Manufactured: Machinery; transportation equipment; food and beverages; stone, glass, and clay products; petroleum and coal products; fabricated metal products.

Mined: Copper, gold, petroleum, coal, uranium, sand and gravel, silver, stone, lead, zinc.

EDUCATION AND CULTURE

Universities and Colleges: Brigham Young University, Provo; University of Utah, Salt Lake City; Utah State University, Logan; Weber State College, Ogden; Southern Utah State College, Cedar City; Westminster College, Salt Lake City.

Libraries: Logan Library; Davis County Library, Farmington; Brigham City Library; Church of Jesus Christ of Latter-Day Saints Library-Archives and Genealogical Library, Salt Lake City Public Library, Utah State Historical Society Library, Utah State Library, all at Salt Lake City.

Notable Museums: Ute Tribal Museum, Fort Duchesne; Ogden Union Station Museums; Brigham Young Art Museum, Monte L. Bean Life Science Museum, Museum of Peoples and Cultures, all at Provo; Hansen Planetarium, Salt Lake Art Center, Utah Museum of Fine Arts, Utah Museum of Natural History, all at Salt Lake City.

PLACES OF INTEREST

Alpine Scenic Loop Road: from American Fork around Mount Timpanogos; 45-mile (72-kilometer) spectacular drive.

Alta: near Brighton; old mining camp, now a winter resort.

Arches National Park: near Moab; arches, spires, windows, pinnacles formed by erosion; views across gorge of Colorado River and of La Sal Mountains; hiking; wildlife sanctuary.

Bear Lake State Recreation Area: near Garden City; boating; picnicking.

Bingham Canyon: near Salt Lake City; large open-pit copper mine.

Bonneville Salt Flats Speedway: near Wendover; cementlike natural salt; scene of automobile speed records.

Brigham Young Home Historic State Park: in St. George; two-story adobe home; period furnishings.

Brighton: year-round alpine mountain resort.

Bryce Canyon National Park: in Bryce Canyon; unusual Gothiclike colored rock formations; Pink Cliffs of Wasatch limestone; hiking; horseback riding; camping.

Camp Floyd State Park: in Fairfield; remnants of camp; old Stagecoach Inn.

Canyonlands National Park: near Moab; colorful wilderness with spectacular rock formations; Green River joins the Colorado.

Capitol Reef National Park: near Torrey; 20-mile (32-kilometer) ridge of geologic history; white sandstone domes resemble U.S. Capitol.

Cedar Breaks National Monument: near Cedar City; huge amphitheater eroded into cliffs.

Dinosaur National Monument: in Utah and Colorado, near Jensen; quarry of reptile fossils; camping; picnicking; fishing; river rafting; backpacking.

Flaming Gorge Dam and National Recreation Area: on Green River, near Dutch John; 502-foot- (153-meter-) high dam; picnicking; boating; camping.

Glen Canyon National Recreation Area: in Utah and Arizona; Lake Powell.

Golden Spike National Historic Site: in Promontory; transcontinental railroad completed (1869).

Goosenecks of the San Juan State Park: near Mexican Hat; view of eroded river gorge; picnicking.

Great Salt Lake: except for Dead Sea, world's saltiest body of water; about 25 percent salt.

Green River State Recreation Area: on Green River; boating; picnicking.

Hot Springs: near Midway; limestone craters.

Hovenweep National Monument: in Utah and Colorado, near Bluff; Cliff dwellings.

Hyrum Reservoir State Park: near Hyrum; boating; picnicking.

Jacob Hamblin Home Historic State Park: in Santa Clara; home of Mormon missionary.

Monument Valley: in southeast; colorful cliffs, sandstone needles.

Natural Bridges National Monument: near Blanding; three great stone bridges; eroded, colorful terrain; Anasazi Indian ruin; wildlife sanctuary; camping.

Newspaper Rock State Park: near Monticello; Indian petroglyphs.

Ogden Snow Basin: near Ogden; recreation area; downhill skiing; cross-country ski trails.

Old State House State Park: in Fillmore; territorial capital; now a museum for Indian and pioneer relics.

Pioneer Trail State Park: near Salt Lake City; This Is the Place Monument; Old Deseret living-history museum.

Piute Reservoir State Park: near Marysvale; boating.

Rainbow Bridge National Monument: near Arizona border; world's largest natural bridge.

St. George: Mormon Temple (1877).

Timpanogos Cave National Monument: near American Fork; limestone caves in mountain.

Utah Field House of Natural History: in Vernal; exhibits of archaeology, fossils, and geology.

Utah Lake: large freshwater lake; fishing.

Wasatch Mountain State Park: near Midway; picnicking.

Zion National Park: near Springdale; deep, sheer-walled canyon carved by erosion; colorful sandstone; Temple of Sinawava, natural amphitheater surrounded by cliffs.

BIBLIOGRAPHY FOR UTAH

Barnes, F.A. Canyon Country Exploring (Wasatch, 1978).

Carpenter, Allan. Utah, rev. ed. (Children's, 1979).

Federal Writers' Project. Utah: a State Guide (Somerset, 1941).

Fitzgerald, J.D. Great Brain (Dial, 1967).

Fradin, Dennis. Utah: In Words and Pictures (Children's, 1980).

Hemingway, D.W., ed. Utah and the Mormons (Colourpicture, 1983).

May, Dean. Utah: a People's History (Univ. of Utah Press, 1987).

Penfield, Thomas. Treasure Guide to Utah (Carson, 1974).

Thompson, G.A. Some Dreams Die: Utah's Ghost Towns and Lost Treasures (Dream Garden, 1982).

Wharton, Tom. Utah: a Family Travel Guide (Wasatch, 1987).

All Fact Summary data are based on current government reports.

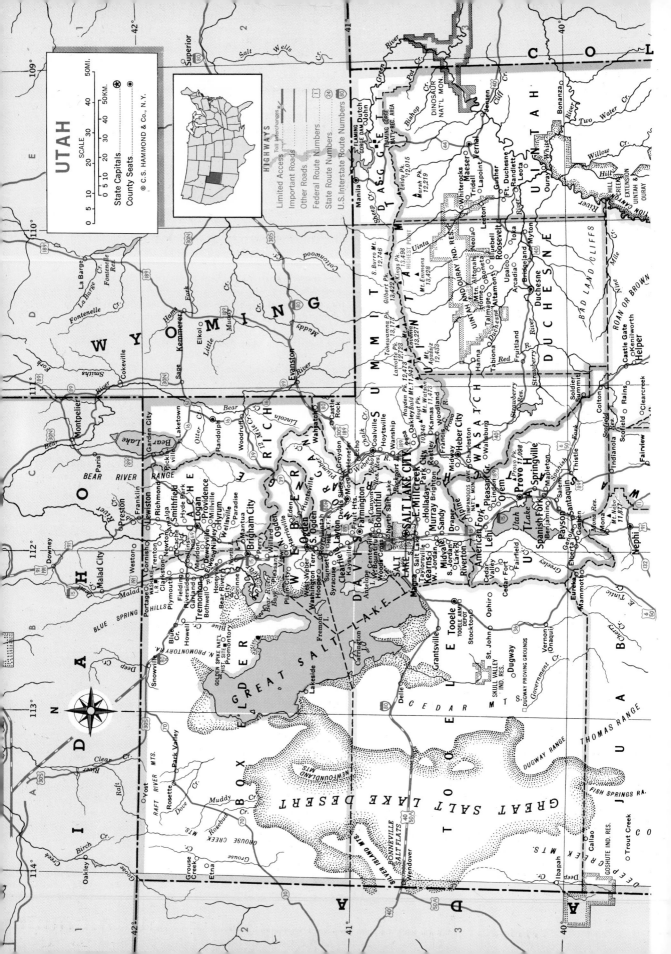

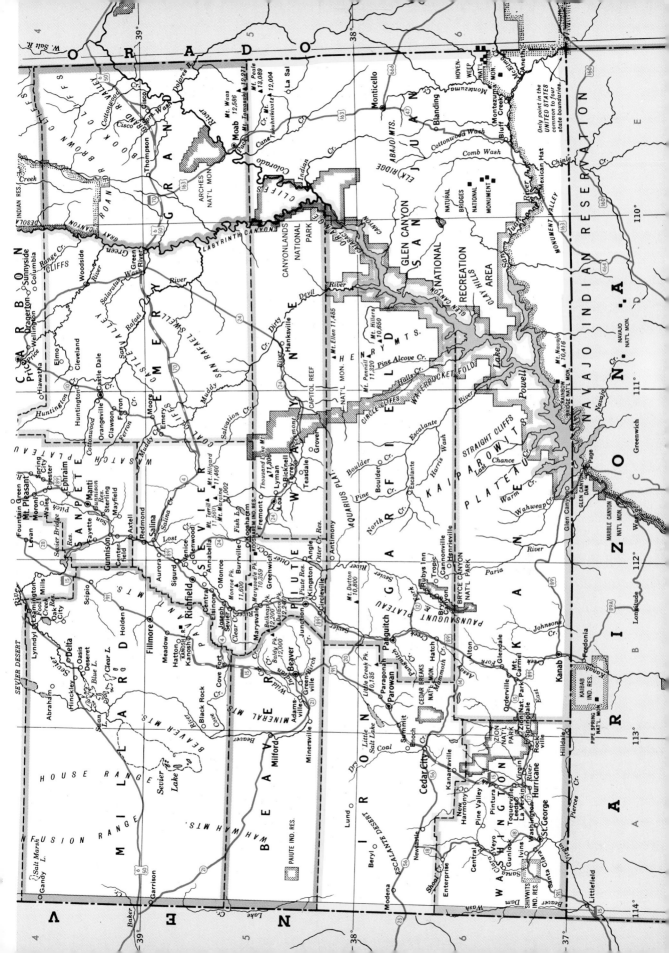

UTAH

COUNTIES

Beaver, 4,378 .... A 5
Box Elder, 33,222 .... A 2
Cache, 57,176 .... C 2
Carbon, 22,179 .... D 4
Daggett, 769 .... E 3
Davis, 146,540 .... B 3
Duchesne, 12,565 .... D 3
Emery, 11,451 .... D 4
Garfield, 3,673 .... C 6
Grand, 8,241 .... E 5
Iron, 17,349 .... A 6
Juab, 5,530 .... A 4
Kane, 4,024 .... B 6
Millard, 8,970 .... A 4
Morgan, 4,917 .... C 2
Piute, 1,329 .... B 5
Rich, 2,100 .... C 2
Salt Lake, 619,066 .... B 3
San Juan, 12,253 .... E 6
Sanpete, 14,620 .... C 4
Sevier, 14,727 .... C 5
Summit, 10,198 .... D 3
Tooele, 26,033 .... A 3
Uintah, 20,506 .... E 3
Utah, 218,106 .... C 3
Wasatch, 8,523 .... C 3
Washington, 26,065 .... A 6
Wayne, 1,911 .... C 5
Weber, 144,616 .... B 2

CITIES AND TOWNS

Alpine, 2,649 .... C 3
Altamont, 247 .... D 3
Altonah, 150 .... D 3
Amalga, 323 .... C 2
American Fork, 12,693 .... C 3
Aneth, 250 .... E 6
Annabella, 463 .... B 5
Antimony, 94 .... C 5
Arcadia, 35 .... D 3

Aurora, 874 .... B 5
Axtell, 150 .... C 4
Bear River City, 540 .... B 2
Beaver, 1,792 .... B 5
Benjamin, 650 .... C 3
Bicknell, 296 .... C 5
Blanding, 3,118 .... E 6
Bluebell, 275 .... D 3
Bluff, 119 .... E 6
Bonanza, 150 .... E 3
Bothwell, 410 .... B 2
Bountiful, 32,877 .... B 3
Bridgeland, 40 .... D 3
Brigham City, 15,596 .... C 2
Brighton, 150 .... C 3
Bryce Canyon, 229 .... B 6
Cannonville, 134 .... B 6
Castle Dale, 1,910 .... D 4
Castle Gate, 205 .... D 4
Cedar City, 10,972 .... A 6
Cedar Fort, 269 .... B 3
Cedar Valley, 286 .... B 3
Centerfield, 653 .... C 4
Centerville, 8,069 .... C 3
Central, 154 .... B 5
Charleston, 320 .... C 3
Circleville, 445 .... B 5
Clarkston, 562 .... B 2
Clearfield, 17,982 .... B 2
Cleveland, 522 .... D 4
Coalville, 1,031 .... C 3
Columbia, 280 .... D 4
Corinne, 512 .... B 2
Cornish, 181 .... B 2
Delta, 1,930 .... B 4
Deseret, 215 .... B 4
Deweyville, 311 .... B 2
Dragerton, 1,614 .... D 4
Draper, 5,521 .... C 3
Duchesne, 1,677 .... D 3
Dugway, 1,646 .... B 3
Dutch John, 230 .... E 3
E. Millcreek, 24,150 .... C 3
Eden, 421 .... C 2
Elberta, 400 .... B 4

Elmo, 300 .... D 4
Elsinore, 612 .... B 2
Elwood, 481 .... B 2
Emery, 372 .... C 5
Enoch, 678 .... A 6
Enterprise, 905 .... A 6
Ephraim, 2,810 .... C 4
Escalante, 652 .... C 6
Eureka, 670 .... B 4
Fairview, 916 .... C 4
Farmington, 4,691 .... C 3
Ferron, 1,718 .... C 4
Fielding, 325 .... B 2
Fillmore, 2,083 .... B 5
Ft. Duchesne, 300 .... E 3
Fountain Green, 578 .... C 4
Francis, 371 .... C 3
Fremont, 250 .... C 5
Fruit Hts., 2,728 .... C 2
Garden City, 259 .... C 2
Garland, 1,405 .... B 2
Genola, 630 .... C 4
Glendale, 237 .... B 6
Glenwood, 447 .... C 5
Goshen, 582 .... C 4
Grantsville, 4,419 .... B 3
Green River, 1,048 .... D 4
Gunnison, 1,255 .... C 4
Gusher, 250 .... E 3
Hanksville, 250 .... D 5
Hanna, 135 .... D 3
Harrisville, 1,371 .... C 2
Hatch, 121 .... B 6
Heber City, 4,362 .... C 3
Helper, 2,724 .... D 4
Henefer, 547 .... C 2
Henrieville, 167 .... C 6
Hiawatha, 249 .... D 4
Hilldale, 1,009 .... B 6
Hinckley, 464 .... B 4
Holden, 364 .... B 4
Holladay, 22,189 .... C 3
Honeyville, 915 .... B 2
Hooper, 700 .... B 2
Howell, 176 .... B 2

Hoytsville, 500 .... C 3
Huntington, 2,316 .... C 4
Huntsville, 557 .... C 2
Hurricane, 2,361 .... A 6
Hyde Park, 1,495 .... C 2
Hyrum, 3,952 .... C 2
Ibapah, 135 .... A 3
Ioka, 115 .... D 3
Ivins, 600 .... A 6
Jensen, 750 .... E 3
Joseph, 217 .... B 5
Junction, 151 .... B 5
Kamas, 1,064 .... C 3
Kanab, 2,148 .... B 6
Kanarraville, 255 .... A 6
Kanosh, 435 .... B 5
Kaysville, 9,811 .... B 2
Kearns, 21,353 .... B 3
Kenilworth, 335 .... D 4
Kingston, 146 .... B 5
Koosharem, 183 .... C 5
Laketown, 271 .... C 2
Lapoint, 430 .... E 3
Lark, 728 .... B 3
La Sal, 665 .... E 5
La Verkin, 1,174 .... A 6
Layton, 22,862 .... C 2
Leamington, 113 .... B 4
Leeds, 218 .... A 6
Lehi, 6,848 .... C 3
Levan, 453 .... C 4
Lewiston, 1,438 .... C 2
Lindon, 2,796 .... C 3
Loa, 364 .... C 5
Logan, 26,844 .... C 2
Lyman, 210 .... C 5
Lynndyl, 90 .... B 4
Maeser, 2,216 .... E 3
Magna, 13,138 .... B 3
Manila, 272 .... E 3
Manti, 2,080 .... C 4
Mantua, 484 .... C 2
Mapleton, 2,726 .... C 3
Marysvale, 359 .... B 5
Mayfield, 397 .... C 4

Desert winds and wind-blown sand have carved this formation out of red sandstone in the Colorado Plateau region's Arches National Monument.

Josef Muench

258

UTAH

Meadow, 265 .... B 5
Mendon, 663 .... B 2
Mexican Hat, 250 .... E 6
Midvale, 10,146 .... B 3
Midway, 1,194 .... C 3
Milford, 1,293 .... A 5
Millville, 848 .... C 2
Minersville, 552 .... B 5
Moab, 5,333 .... E 5
Mona, 506 .... C 4
Monroe, 1,476 .... C 4
Montezuma Creek, 500 .... E 6
Monticello, 1,929 .... E 6
Morgan, 1,896 .... B 3
Moroni, 1,086 .... C 4
Mountain Home, 140 .... D 3
Mt. Pleasant, 2,049 .... C 4
Murray, 25,750 .... C 3
Myton, 500 .... D 3
Neola, 600 .... D 3
Nephi, 3,285 .... C 4
Newcastle, 350 .... A 6
Newton, 623 .... B 2
Nibley, 1,036 .... C 2
No. Ogden, 9,309 .... C 2
No. Salt Lake, 5,548 .... C 2
Oak City, 389 .... B 4
Oakley, 470 .... C 3
Oasis, 170 .... B 4
Ogden, 64,407 .... C 2
Ophir, 42 .... B 3
Orangeville, 1,309 .... C 4
Orderville, 423 .... B 6
Orem, 52,399 .... C 3
Ouray, 100 .... E 3
Panguitch, 1,343 .... B 6
Paradise, 542 .... C 2
Paragonah, 310 .... B 6
Park City, 2,823 .... C 3
Park Valley, 170 .... A 2
Parowan, 1,836 .... B 6
Payson, 8,246 .... C 3
Peoa, 250 .... C 3
Perry, 1,084 .... C 2
Pickleville, 106 .... C 2
Plain City, 2,379 .... B 2
Pleasant Grove, 10,833 .... C 3

Pleasant View, 3,983 .... B 2
Plymouth, 238 .... B 2
Portage, 196 .... B 2
Price, 9,086 .... D 4
Providence, 2,675 .... C 2
Provo, 74,108 .... C 3
Provo-Orem (met. area), 218,106 .... C 3
Randlett, 500 .... E 3
Randolph, 659 .... C 2
Redmond, 619 .... C 4
Richfield, 5,482 .... B 5
Richmond, 1,705 .... C 2
Riverside, 250 .... B 2
Riverton, 7,293 .... B 3
Rockville, 126 .... A 6
Roosevelt, 3,842 .... D 3
Roy, 19,694 .... C 2
St. George, 11,350 .... A 6
Saint John, 350 .... B 3
Salem, 2,233 .... C 3
Salina, 1,992 .... C 5
Salt Lake City (cap.), 163,033 ..... B 3
Salt Lake City (met. area), 936,255 ... B 3
Sandy City, 50,546 .... C 3
Santa Clara, 1,091 .... A 6
Santaquin, 2,175 .... C 4
Scipio, 257 .... B 4
Sigurd, 386 .... B 5
Smithfield, 4,993 .... C 2
Snowville, 237 .... B 2
So. Jordan, 7,492 .... C 3
So. Ogden, 11,366 .... C 2
So. Salt Lake, 10,413 .... C 3
Spanish Fork, 9,825 .... C 3
Spring City, 671 .... C 4
Springdale, 258 .... B 6
Springville, 12,101 .... C 3
Sterling, 199 .... C 4
Stockton, 437 .... B 3
Summit, 200 .... B 6
Sunnyside, 611 .... D 4
Sunset, 5,733 .... B 2
Syracuse, 3,702 .... B 2
Tabiona, 152 .... D 3
Talmage, 180 .... D 3
Taylorsville, 17,448 .... B 3
Teasdale, 125 .... C 5

Tooele, 14,335 .... B 3
Toquerville, 277 .... A 6
Tremonton, 3,464 .... B 2
Trenton, 447 .... B 2
Tridell, 212 .... E 3
Tropic, 338 .... B 6
Uintah, 439 .... C 2
Upalco, 280 .... D 3
Venice, 220 .... C 5
Vernal, 6,600 .... E 3
Vernon, 181 .... B 3
Veyo, 144 .... A 6
Virgin, 169 .... A 6
Wallsburg, 239 .... C 3
Wanship, 175 .... C 3
Washington, 3,092 .... A 6
Washington Terrace, 8,212 .... B 2
Wellington, 1,406 .... D 4
Wellsville, 1,952 .... C 2
Wendover, 1,099 .... A 3
W. Bountiful, 3,556 .... B 3
West Jordan, 27,192 .... B 3
West Weber, 750 .... B 2
Whiterocks, 500 .... E 3
Willard, 1,241 .... C 2
Woodland, 340 .... C 3
Woodruff, 222 .... C 2
Woods Cross, 4,263 .... B 3
Zion National Park, 80 .... B 6

OTHER FEATURES

Arches Nat'l Mon. .... E 5
Bear (lake) .... C 2
Bear (riv.) .... B 2
Bonneville (salt flats) .... A 3
Book (cliffs) .... E 4
Bryce Canyon Nat'l Park .... B 6
Canyonlands Nat'l Park .... D 5
Capitol Reef Nat'l Mon. .... C 5
Cedar Breaks Nat'l Mon. .... B 6
Colorado (riv.) .... C 7
Dinosaur Nat'l Mon. .... E 3
Dirty Devil (riv.) .... D 5
Dolores (riv.) .... E 5
Duchesne (riv.) .... D 3

Dugway Proving Grounds .... B 3
Escalante (riv.) .... C 6
Flaming Gorge Nat'l Rec. Area .... E 3
Fremont (riv.) .... C 5
Glen Canyon Nat'l Rec. Area ...... D 6
Golden Spike Nat'l Hist. Site .... B 2
Goshute Ind. Res. .... A 4
Great Salt (lake) .... B 2
Great Salt L. (des.) .... A 3
Green (riv.) .... D 4
Hill A.F.B. .... C 2
Hill Ck. Ext., Uintah & Ouray
    Ind. Res. .... E 4
Hovenweep Nat'l Mon. .... E 6
Jordan (riv.) .... C 3
Kaiparowits (plat.) .... C 6
Kanosh Ind. Res. .... B 5
Kings (peak) .... D 3
Koosharem Ind. Res. .... C 5
Malad (riv.) .... B 1
Monument (vall.) .... D 6
Natural Bridges Nat'l Mon. .... E 6
Navajo Ind. Res. .... D 7
Nebo (mt.) .... C 4
Paiute Ind. Res. .... A 5
Paria (riv.) .... B 6
Powell (lake) .... D 6
Price (riv.) .... D 4
Rainbow Bridge Nat'l Mon. .... C 6
San Juan (riv.) .... D 6
San Rafael (riv.) .... D 4
Sevier (lake) .... A 5
Sevier (riv.) .... B 4
Shivwits Ind. Res. .... A 6
Skull Valley Ind. Res. .... B 3
Strawberry (riv.) .... D 3
Timpanogos Cave Nat'l Mon. .... C 3
Uinta (mts.) .... D 3
Uinta (riv.) .... D 3
Uinta & Ouray Ind. Res. .... D 3
Utah (lake) .... C 3
Virgin (riv.) .... A 6
Wasatch (plat.) .... C 4
Wasatch (range) .... C 3
Washakie Ind. Res. .... B 2
Weber (riv.) .... C 3
Zion Nat'l Park .... A 6

The Mormons erected this monument in Salt Lake City in honor of the sea gulls which saved their crops from crickets in 1848.

Utah Department of Publicity and Industrial Development

UTOPIAN LITERATURE.

UTOPIAN LITERATURE. The Greek term *ou topos* means "no place." From it Sir Thomas More derived the word utopia to describe an ideal human society. His book 'Utopia' was published in Latin in 1516 and in English translation in 1551 (*see* More). More wrote at a time when the social institutions that held society together during the Middle Ages were beginning to break down. New economic undertakings were laying the foundations of capitalism. Thousands of people in England had been driven from their villages by land enclosures to make room for sheep raising.

More realized that a way of life was passing and that a new, uncertain one was being forged. He wrote 'Utopia' as a protest against the breakdown of the old order. To make his protest effective he described an ideal commonwealth in which people only have to work six hours a day, leaving plenty of time for leisure. Everyone lives in a pleasant home surrounded by a garden. Communities have good schools and hospitals. Education is compulsory, and every student learns at least one trade. Food is given out at public markets and community dining halls. Children, after their earliest years, leave home and are brought up by public authorities. The rulers are selected by secret ballot from among the best-educated citizens. Lawyers are unnecessary because there are so few laws.

More's book shares two primary characteristics of all utopian literature. It criticizes the present as an unhappy time, and it proposes an alternative society in which the state is exalted over the individual.

His book is fiction, but, coming so soon after the discovery of the Americas, utopia soon began to take on the sense of a real place, a new Garden of Eden in the West where humanity could begin anew. (It was no accident that the book's island Utopia is situated near the Western Hemisphere.) In later centuries utopian literature often presented what were then regarded as realistic programs for ideal human societies. This was especially true during the 19th century with its diversity of socialist doctrines (*see* Socialism). In the United States many of these programs were put into practice in hundreds of planned communities based mostly on socialist writings (*see* Communal Living). Other utopias were based on religion, politics, and science and technology.

More's 'Utopia' was not the first book of its kind, nor was it the last. In ancient Greece Hesiod, in 'Works and Days', (about 800 BC), locates his utopia in a long-past Golden Age. The Bible also locates it in the past—in the Garden of Eden. A few centuries after Hesiod the philosopher Plato's 'Republic' describes a state ruled by philosopher kings. In his 'Critias' Plato uses the myth of the undersea kingdom of Atlantis to describe an ideal commonwealth. The legend of Atlantis was taken up by other writers and has persisted in literature to the present.

A century after Plato the Greek writer Euhemerus (about 300 BC) wrote of a utopian island in his 'Sacred History'. The historian Plutarch, in his 'Lives', describes the Greek city-state of Sparta under Lycurgus in utopian terms. The Latin author Lucian (2nd century AD) satirizes earlier utopias in his 'True Story'.

During the Middle Ages, under the influence of Christianity, utopian literature disappeared in Europe. Attention was instead focused on the afterlife, the city of God, or on a time of bliss on Earth during a millennium.

More's 'Utopia' was written just after the end of the Middle Ages, and its popularity prompted imitation. Antonio Francesco Doni edited an Italian translation of 'Utopia' in 1548, and four years later he published his own book, 'The Worlds', about a perfect city in which marriage has been abolished. This was followed in 1553 by Francesco Patrizi's 'The Happy City'.

In 1602 Tommaso Campanella published 'The City of the Sun'. In his utopia everyone's work contributes to the welfare of the whole community. Private property, great wealth, and poverty do not exist. His ideas were taken up by 19th-century socialists. Johann Valentin Andreae proposes a Christian commonwealth in 'Christianopolis' (1619), and Gerrard Winstanley advocates a political and economic ideal in 'The Law of Freedom' (1652). 'Oceana' (1656) by James Harrington calls for redistribution of land as an economic goal. Francis Bacon's 'The New Atlantis' (1627) lays out a program for the new science within a Christian society.

One of the first writers to project a utopia far in the future was Louis Sébastien Mercier in his 'The Year 2440' (1772). Much of today's science fiction deals with similar themes, criticizing present society and proposing better alternatives (*see* Science Fiction).

In the 19th century G.A. Ellis's 'New Britain' (1820) and Étienne Cabet's 'Voyage in Icaria' (1840) were utopian socialist works relating to communal experiments in North America. Two other influential 19th-century economic utopias are Edward Bellamy's 'Looking Backward: 2000–1887' (1888), one of the most significant such books by an American, and Theodor Hertzka's 'A Visit to Freeland' (1894). The great science-fiction writer H.G. Wells produced 'A Modern Utopia' in 1905.

Utopian ideals were not without critics. Jonathan Swift satirizes them in 'Gulliver's Travels' (1726). Samuel Butler's 'Erewhon' (1872) foreshadows the satirical utopias and anti-utopias of the 20th century. His title is a rearrangement of the letters in the word nowhere. The 20th-century anti-utopias have been more than satirical. They are powerful attacks on the notion of utopianism itself. The anti-utopian novel was created by the Russian satirist Yevgeny Zamyatin in 'We' (1924), a parody of the communist state. It was followed by Aldous Huxley's 'Brave New World' (1932), a savage criticism of the scientific future. George Orwell's 'Animal Farm' (1944) shows his disillusionment with the communist paradise, and his 'Nineteen Eighty-four' (1949) projects a totalitarian world. Readers interested in learning more about the subject should consult 'Utopian Thought in the Western World' by F.E. and F.P. Manuel (Belknap Press, 1979).

UTRECHT, The Netherlands. Utrecht has long
been a center of politics, culture, and religion in The
Netherlands. The city is situated at the point where
the Rhine River divides into two branches, the Old
Rhine and the Vecht. The Romans called the city Tra-
jectum ad Rhenum, or "ford on the Rhine." Its name
became Oude Trecht, or "old ford," which evolved
into Utrecht. It is the capital of Utrecht Province and
is the fourth largest city in The Netherlands.

Utrecht is crossed by two canals that are spanned by
more than 90 bridges. The roadways lie high above the
surface of the canals. Steps connect the two levels. In
the 19th century the old ramparts were converted into
pleasant parks and walks, bounded by watercourses.
A focal point of central Utrecht is the enormous Hoog
Catharijne shopping district. This covered and air-
conditioned complex to the west of the old city center
was completed in 1980. It houses the railway and bus
stations, several parking facilities, a hotel, and more
than 180 stores, theaters, and restaurants.

In the center of the old city stands the Domkerk,
a cathedral that was begun in the 13th century and
completed in the 16th century. It occupies the site of
the church founded by Saint Willibrord, the Anglo-
Saxon apostle of the Frisians, in the 7th century. This
once was one of the finest and largest churches in
The Netherlands. In 1674 a storm destroyed the nave,
and it was never rebuilt. The transept and tower, the
tallest church tower in The Netherlands at about 370
feet (113 meters), are all that remain of the cathedral. Graceful Gothic cloisters connect the cathedral
with the State University of Utrecht, the largest state
university in The Netherlands. The building known
as the Pope's House was completed in 1523 for the
only Dutch pope, Adrian VI.

Utrecht has numerous museums, including the
Central Museum with collections of art, history, and
archaeological findings. The city is also home to a
number of museums with more specialized collections, including The Netherlands Railway Museum;
The Netherlands Gold and Silver Museum; the Museum of Modern Religious Art; and the National
Museum From Music Box to Barrel Organ, a unique
collection of mechanical musical instruments.

Utrecht is the headquarters of The Netherlands'
railroads. It has a vegetable, fruit, and cattle market
and is a financial and insurance center and site of the
national mint. The city's industries include construction, steelworking, and printing. Among Utrecht's
manufactured products are chemicals, clothing, aluminum, and furniture. The Royal Dutch Industries
Fair, founded in 1916, is the best known of the famous
international trade fairs that are held in Utrecht each
spring and autumn.

The site that is now Utrecht was a fortified Roman
settlement around AD 48. St. Willibrord founded a
bishopric here in the late 7th century. The city was a
frequent residence of early German emperors, and it
was chartered in 1122 and had a city council as early
as 1304. Under the protection of the Roman Catholic
bishops and the Holy Roman Empire the city became

the capital of a powerful principality and a medieval
ecclesiastical, cultural, commercial, and industrial
center. It lost some of its prominence in the 15th
century to Amsterdam when that city began to prosper. The archbishopric of Utrecht was established in
1559, suppressed in 1580, and revived in 1851.

In 1579 the seven northern provinces of the Spanish Netherlands—the future Dutch republic—formed
the Union of Utrecht to revolt against the political
and religious tyranny of Spain. The city was the site
of the negotiations of 1713–14 that ended with the
signing of the Treaty of Utrecht. This treaty ended
the War of the Spanish Succession and gave the
southern Netherlands (Belgium) to Austria. Utrecht
was occupied by the French from 1795 to 1813 and
was the residence of Napoleon's brother Louis, king
of Holland from 1806 to 1810. Population (1986 estimate), city, 229,900; (1983 estimate), metropolitan
area, 498,900.

UTRILLO, Maurice (1883–1955). A French
painter noted especially for his paintings of the Montmartre district of Paris, Maurice Utrillo was mostly
self-taught. Through strict perspective he created the
illusion of depth, and he had an unerring sense of
color relationships.

Utrillo was born in Paris on Dec. 25, 1883, the il-
legitimate son of Suzanne Valadon, an artist's model
who became a successful painter. He took the name
Utrillo in 1891 from his mother's friend, the Spanish
art critic Miguel Utrillo y Molins. Even as a schoolboy,
young Utrillo was addicted to alcohol, and he was
placed in an institution in 1900. When he was released his mother encouraged him to take up painting
as therapy. His first paintings, with rough textures
and dark colors ('Roofs', 1906–07), soon revealed a
great talent.

Influenced initially by the impressionists, he gradually used brighter colors, and his drawing became
firmer. His best years were his so-called white period from about 1908 to 1914. His milky whites with
grays, pale blues and greens, and flashes of vermilion are notable ('Place du Tertre', 1911–12; 'Church

'View of Montmartre', an oil on canvas painting done by
Utrillo in 1910, depicts a quiet section in the north of Paris.

261

of Mourning', or 'Little Communicant', 1912). He was frequently confined to sanatoriums during these years, but he kept on painting. He produced literally thousands of oils. In 1923 he was commissioned by Sergei Diaghilev to design the sets and costumes for his ballet 'Barabau'.

Utrillo married Lucie Valore in 1934, who installed him in a comfortable villa where she kept him healthy and content. He continued to paint, but his output was drastically reduced. His later works were often no more than imitations of his earlier canvases. Utrillo died in Le Vésinet, France, on Nov. 5, 1955.

UZBEK SOVIET SOCIALIST RE-PUBLIC.

A republic of the Soviet Union, the Uzbek republic, also known as Uzbekistan, is a Muslim cultural center. It is bordered on the north and northwest by the Kazakh Soviet Socialist Republic, on the east and southeast by the Kirgiz and Tadzhik Soviet socialist republics, on the southwest by the Turkmen Soviet Socialist Republic, and on the south by Afghanistan. Its area is 172,700 square miles (447,400 square kilometers).

Nearly four fifths of the area is a flat sun-baked lowland. The republic lies between the Amu-Dar'ya and Syr-Dar'ya rivers, and the delta of the Amu-Dar'ya spreads over a portion of the land. The waters, however, are used up by irrigation, filtration, and evaporation as they flow through the dry lowlands. Most rivers disappear into the sands. Many natural tributaries are captured for mechanized irrigation before they reach the main riverbed. Efforts to water the land have been successful, and the desert is slowly receding. Uzbekistan's climate is very dry and

distinctly continental. Summers are long and warm and winters are short with occasional severe frosts.

There are about 60 different ethnic groups in Uzbekistan. About two thirds of the residents are Uzbeks, who live mainly in rural areas. Russians, Tatars, and Kazakhs make up high percentages of the urban population with lesser numbers of Tadzhiks, Kara-Kalpaks, Ukrainians, and Jews.

Tashkent is the capital of Uzbekistan and is Central Asia's largest metropolis. The republic's oldest and second largest city is Samarkand, which is located in the Zeravshan Valley. It dates back at least 2,500 years. These and the other ancient cities of Bukhara, Khiva, and Kokand, began as irrigated areas or on caravan trade routes. Such younger towns as Chirchik, Angren, Bekabad, Almalyk, and Navoi were established near rich mineral resources. Yangiyul, Gulistan, and Yangiyer began as cotton, silkworm, or fruit-processing centers on more recently developed areas of land.

Many Uzbek cities were famed for centuries as educational centers. Thousands of students came each year from many parts of the Muslim East to attend seminaries. The Uzbek Academy of Sciences, established in 1943 as a branch of the central academy in Moscow, is the leader in Uzbekistan's research with some 200 institutes and centers. Over the centuries Uzbekistan has been noted as a center of Muslim culture. The 'Uthman Koran, an original transcription of the Koran, is kept in the Tashkent Museum of the History of the Peoples of Uzbekistan.

Uzbekistan is the chief source of the Soviet Union's cotton supply and the third largest cotton producer in the world. It is the Soviet Union's major region for the raising of Karakul sheep and silkworms. Cattle raising, orchards, and fur farming also help the economy.

Uzbekistan is the main producer of machines and heavy equipment in Central Asia. Its chemical industry is closely connected with the Uzbek cotton industry and produces fertilizers for the cotton fields. The republic is one of the leading centers of the Soviet natural gas industry. Large reserves of petroleum and coal and a variety of metallic ores are also found here. In the Kuramin Range are deposits of copper, zinc, lead, tungsten, and molybdenum. There is also potential for the development of an aluminum industry. Gold is found in the Kyzyl-Kum Desert.

The Supreme Soviet is the legislative body of the republic. The Communist Party of Uzbekistan selects a single slate of candidates for a four-year term, and the slate is ratified in a general election. The Supreme Soviet appoints a Presidium to act between sessions, and a Council of Ministers, or cabinet.

Traces of human habitation date back some 55,000 to 70,000 years. Beginning in the 6th century BC, a succession of invaders swept over the region. From the 13th to 16th centuries the area was part of the empire of Timur Lenk, or Tamerlane, and his successors. Various dynasties ruled until Russia conquered the region in the 19th century. The republic was founded in 1924. Population (1986 estimate) 18,487,000.

Women tend cotton plants on a collective farm in Tashkent oblast, Uzbek Soviet Republic.

Jacques Jangoux—Photo Researchers/EB Inc.

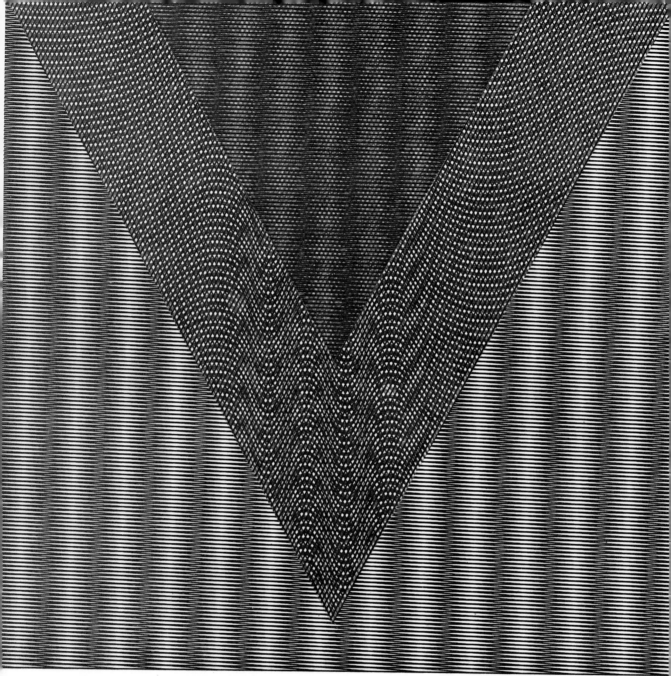

The letter V

probably started as a picture sign for a branched supporting pole or prop, as in Egyptian hieroglyphic writing (1). Descendants of this letter are F, U, W, and Y. About 1000 B.C., in Byblos and in other Phoenician and Canaanite centers, the same sign was used, but its top part was rounded (2). In the Semitic languages the sign was called *waw,* meaning "prop." It had the sound of the "w" in "wine." The Greeks used the sign in two forms. One form (3) was called *digamma* for the consonantal "w," which disappeared in later Greek. This form led to the Latin sign F. Another form (4), called *upsilon,* meaning "bare u," was used for the vocalic "u."

The Romans eliminated the bottom tail (5) and used it for two sounds, consonantal "w" (later "v") and vocalic "u." Consonantal "v" passed into English writing. The English small "v" is a copy of the capital, except that in handwriting it is connected to adjoining letters.

Y	Y
1	2
F	Y
3	4

V

5

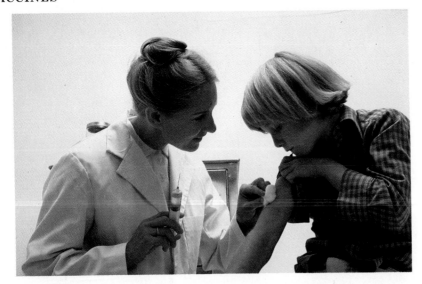

A grade-school child is immunized against whooping cough and the other six major childhood diseases. Such precautions are taken in school systems throughout the United States and in many other nations.

Jeff Reed—Medichrome/The Stock Shop

VACCINES. In 1921 there were 206,939 cases of diphtheria reported in the United States, mostly among children. In 1983 only five people came down with the disease. In 1941 measles claimed 894,134 victims; in 1983 there were only 1,497 cases. The main reason for the dramatic decline in these serious diseases has been the development and use of vaccines.

A vaccine is a substance administered to humans or animals to protect them from serious diseases. The process of administering a vaccine is called vaccination. The process of protecting a person or animal from diseases is called immunization. Through the use of vaccines, humanity has been able to protect itself against many deadly and crippling diseases. Researchers are working to develop new vaccines against other health threats such as Acquired Immune Deficiency Syndrome (AIDS) (see AIDS).

The first vaccine was developed by the English physician Edward Jenner in 1796 to protect against smallpox, a disease that disfigured and killed thousands of people each year. Jenner knew that dairy workers who caught the mild disease cowpox did not get smallpox. Jenner took material from a cowpox sore and scratched it into the arm of a healthy 8-year-old boy. As expected, the child developed cowpox. Jenner then scratched material from a smallpox sore into the boy's arm. The child remained healthy. Jenner named the material from the cowpox sore vaccine, and the process in which he used it, vaccination. Both words are from the Latin *vaccinus,* meaning "from cows." (*See also* Jenner.) Use of the vaccine spread quickly; within 200 years smallpox had been eliminated from the world.

Vaccines are now available for a variety of diseases (see table). The list is likely to grow as new techniques are used to develop safer, less costly vaccines.

Vaccines are used for several purposes. Their widest use is to immunize large groups of people or animals against serious diseases common in areas where they live. Travelers often receive vaccines to protect them from diseases found in the countries they will be visiting. A third use of vaccines is to protect high-risk groups, such as the elderly and the very young, who are at greater risk should they contract a contagious disease.

How Vaccines Work

The principle of vaccination is to cause the immune system to behave as if the body has contracted a disease. This sets in motion the body's defense system without risking the damage that may be caused by the disease itself (*see* Immune System). Immunization can be either active or passive.

In active immunization, the components of the vaccine teach the individual's immune system to recognize a specific toxin, virus, or bacteria. Each pathogen, or disease-causing agent, is identified by antigens, or marker molecules, on its surface. The immune system has cells called B-lymphocytes that detect these antigens and respond by manufacturing molecules called antibodies. Each antibody is made specifically to attack one type of antigen. The antibody combines with the antigen—like a key fitting a lock—and enables the immune system to destroy it. If the same type of pathogen enters the body again in the future, its antigens will be recognized, specific antibodies will be rapidly manufactured, and the organism that could cause a disease will be destroyed.

The protection against specific diseases conferred by active immunization generally lasts for years. If the antibodies formed after a vaccination decrease significantly over time, the individual can be revaccinated. So-called booster shots cause antibodies to be formed more quickly than they are by the first shot.

Passive immunization involves injecting antibodies made by one person or animal into the bloodstream of another. This type of immunization may be used if active immunization is not available; if an individual has already been exposed to a disease and does not have time to manufacture antibodies; or if an individual's own immune system is not working properly. Passive immunization protects an individual for only a few weeks or months.

There are still many diseases for which it has not been possible to create vaccines. In some cases, this is because of the complexity of the pathogen. For example, the one-celled parasite that causes malaria occurs in three different forms, each with its own antigens. None of these antigens seems to cue the immune system to produce antibodies.

Other diseases, such as influenza, are caused by organisms that have the ability to change their antigens from time to time. A new influenza vaccine must be prepared each year to protect against the forms of the flu viruses that researchers predict will strike the population during the flu season.

A third category of organisms has the capacity to hide from the immune system. Some members of the herpes virus family, which cause cold sores, genital sores, chicken pox, and mononucleosis, live in nerve roots where they can avoid detection by the blood-borne B-lymphocytes. The body's immune system cannot distinguish between the nerve root and the pathogen.

In addition to characteristics of the pathogens themselves, technical problems have hindered the development of vaccines. Research is expensive, and the outcome is by no means assured. Vaccines have side effects that can be quite serious for some individuals. Drug companies may be reluctant to produce vaccines because of the threat of lawsuits from those who may be harmed by these side effects. Even many existing vaccines have not been widely used in developing countries because of their production costs and the technical problems of storing and administering the doses.

Administration and Side Effects

Many vaccines can be given only by injection, because passage through the gastrointestinal tract would destroy them. The vaccine may be injected into a muscle, or intramuscularly; beneath the skin, or subcutaneously; or between the skin layers, or intradermally. Some vaccines are effective when given orally, such as the Sabin polio vaccine, and some are sprayed into the nose or mouth.

Vaccines made with live organisms, such as those against measles, mumps, and rubella, need be given only once to confer lifelong immunity. Vaccines made from inactivated or killed organisms or toxoids often must be given several times to stimulate an immune response. Even then antibody production may decline after a time, leaving the individual vulnerable to the disease again.

Booster shots may be required at regular intervals to raise immunity to protective levels. For instance, the diphtheria and tetanus immunizations are given initially at two-month intervals for a total of three doses. Immunity begins to decline after a few years, and booster shots are then administered periodically to ensure protection.

Not every individual will respond to vaccination by developing long-lasting immunity. Much depends on the person's age, state of health, and ability to manufacture antibodies. Physicians believe, however, that if most of the population is immunized against common diseases, these illnesses will occur less frequently. As a result, individuals who are not immunized will have less chance of being exposed.

Adverse reactions, or side effects, have been reported for all existing vaccines. These reactions may range from a sore arm at the injection site to mild fever, joint pains, rash, or nausea, normally lasting only a short time. In some cases, however, severe reactions may occur. Oral polio vaccines, in which live virus is used, have been known to cause mild to crippling paralysis in some people who received the vaccines. However, the incidence of serious problems is rare—approximately one case of paralytic polio per 9 million doses of vaccine. The medical community generally considers vaccines to be among the safest and most beneficial preventive drugs available.

Types of Vaccine

Until recently, vaccines have been made from naturally occurring viruses or bacteria or from the products of these pathogens. Vaccines may be prepared from live pathogens that have been weakened,

SOME COMMONLY USED VACCINES

Disease	Vaccine Type	Who Is Immunized
Diphtheria	Toxoid	Children at age 2, 4, and 6 months. Booster at age 18 months and 4–6 years. Booster every 10 years thereafter.
Tetanus	Toxoid	Same as diphtheria.
Pertussis	Killed bacteria	Same as diphtheria; no booster after 4–6 years.
Measles	Live virus	
Mumps	Live virus	Children at age 15 months.
Rubella	Live virus	
Poliomyelitis	Killed virus (Salk)	Children at age 2, 4, and 6 months.
	Live virus (Sabin)	Booster at 18 months and 4–6 years.
Hepatitis B	Inactivated virus	Adults at risk through occupational exposure.
	Recombinant vaccine	
Tuberculosis	Live bacteria	Those in close contact with untreated patients. In some countries, given to all infants at birth.
Influenza	Inactivated virus	Children and adults at high risk of developing problems if they had the disease because of age or state of health.
Rabies	Inactivated virus	Veterinarians, animal handlers, some laboratory workers, persons living in or visiting countries where rabies is a constant threat.

Sources: American Academy of Pediatrics, American College of Physicians, U.S. Dept. of Health and Human Services

VACCINES

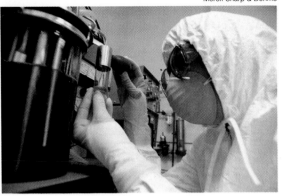

A scientist draws a sample from a fermentation unit used in the development of the first genetically engineered human vaccine. The vaccine protects against the hepatitis B virus, which causes liver disease.

or attenuated, in some way. This technique prevents the pathogen from causing serious disease while still stimulating the immune system to produce antibodies. The antibodies formed against live pathogens last longer; however, the vaccine may not be as safe as one made from killed microorganisms. Vaccines made from weakened microorganisms include those for polio and yellow fever.

The second type of vaccine may consist of dead viruses or bacteria. If the pathogens can be killed so that their chemical makeup changes very little, they will still cause the body to produce antibodies. While these vaccines are among the safest, the antibodies may not be as numerous as with live-pathogen vaccines and may not last very long. Diseases in which killed pathogens are used for the vaccine include typhoid fever, rabies, and whooping cough.

A third type of vaccine produces antibodies that fight against the poisons, or toxins, generated by pathogens rather than against the pathogens themselves. These vaccines contain chemically changed toxins, called toxoids, and are considered safe and highly effective. The diphtheria and tetanus vaccines are made in this manner.

Finally, some vaccines, like Jenner's vaccine, consist of viral or bacterial particles that do not cause serious disease but resemble their disease-causing counterparts. These impostors can fool the immune system into producing antibodies against both diseases.

The advent of genetic engineering has enabled scientists to apply new techniques to the manufacture of vaccines. One approach is to use the recombinant DNA method to remove the disease-causing portion of a microbe without affecting its ability to stimulate antibody production (*see* Genetic Engineering). A recombinant vaccine against hepatitis B has been in common use since 1986. A second approach is simply to manufacture antigens artificially, without using any portion of the pathogen. Antigens are composed of building blocks called amino acids, assembled in a specific order. Scientists have learned how to string together amino acids in the proper order to elicit an antibody response without risking disease.

Genetic engineering has modified Jenner's original vaccine, which was made from the vaccinia virus. This large and fast-growing organism can be changed, using the recombinant DNA method, so that it produces antigens against not one but a number of diseases. If successful, it could be the basis of a so-called supervaccine with a number of advantages. It would be cheap and easy to produce, because many countries have experience in producing the smallpox vaccine. It could be freeze-dried and thus easy to store without refrigeration; one inoculation could provide protection against many diseases; and administration of the supervaccine, like the smallpox vaccine, would leave a small scar, identifying protected individuals without requiring written records.

The new genetic techniques may provide ways to create vaccines for previously resistant diseases, such as malaria and herpes viruses, and perhaps for noninfectious diseases, such as those caused by parasites.

History of Vaccines

When Jenner performed his historic vaccination in 1796, he did not know why the process prevented smallpox. It was left to other scientists to discover the mechanisms of infection and immunity. Over the next 100 years, Robert Koch, a German physician, and others demonstrated that disease was caused by microbes. In 1879 French chemist Louis Pasteur was growing the microbes that caused fowl cholera. He left the cultures in his laboratory while he went on vacation. On his return, he injected some chickens with the old cultures and found that they became only slightly ill. Furthermore, on recovery, they were immune to fowl cholera. He named his attenuated culture vaccine in honor of Jenner. Pasteur eventually developed an effective vaccine against rabies. The French scientist was the first to apply scientific principles to the manufacture of vaccines (*see* Pasteur).

After Pasteur published his findings, other researchers began to develop vaccines. In the late 19th century, Émile Roux, a student of Pasteur, and Emil von Behring, a German physician, found that the killer in diphtheria was not the disease microbe itself but a toxin it produced. They laid the groundwork for the tetanus and diphtheria toxoid vaccines in the early 20th century.

Wilhelm Kolle, a German bacteriologist, developed the typhoid and cholera vaccines in 1896. His method employed killed organisms that nonetheless were able to stimulate an immune response and to protect against disease.

In the mid-20th century, Jonas Salk, an American physician, used the techniques of culturing viruses in living tissue in the laboratory to produce a vaccine against poliomyelitis. The polio vaccine, licensed in 1955, has virtually ended a disease that once killed or crippled thousands of children around the world each year. In the future the names of genetic engineers will undoubtedly be added to the list of those who have made significant contributions to the prevention of disease through the use of vaccines.

VACUUM. A total, or "perfect," vacuum would be a space from which all matter has been removed. This includes solids, liquids, and gases (including air). It would be a space that contains "nothing." Since there is no method or device that can remove *all* matter from an enclosed space, a perfect vacuum is unknown and has only theoretical meaning. It was once thought that a perfect vacuum might exist in outer space. Now scientists know that the apparently empty space between the stars contains a large mass of gas which is mostly hydrogen.

An incomplete, or "partial," vacuum can be created with vacuum pumps. When a very high percentage of gas is removed from a space, it is called a high vacuum and is equal to a very low pressure.

Partial vacuums are common. The vacuum bottle has a partial vacuum between double walls. The vacuum keeps liquids near their original temperature by preventing heat conduction. A partial vacuum must be created in the cylinder of an automobile engine in order to form the air-gas mixture essential to combustion (*see* Automobile). The vacuum cleaner, vacuum coffee maker, and suction plunger depend upon partial vacuums for their operation. Electric-light bulbs have air removed so that the hot filament will not burn up in the oxygen in the air. The piston movement of a lift pump creates a vacuum, allowing water to rise (*see* Pump and Compressor).

The Vacuum in Industry

In the past 50 years industry has developed many profitable vacuum processes. Liquids under vacuum boil at a temperature lower than the normal boiling temperature. This fact has been useful to food and pharmaceutical manufacturers. Solutions of milk, sugar, and fruit and vegetable juices are concentrated under vacuum. This permits the water to boil off at a low temperature and prevents scorching of the product. Vitamins and antibiotics are processed under vacuum to avoid chemical changes that would occur at higher temperatures.

In 1906, the audion vacuum tube was developed by Lee DeForest. This specially built, evacuated glass tube could increase the power of an electric signal by many times the original amount (*see* Radio; Electron). It introduced the age of electronic communication that gave us radio, television, and radar. Vacuum tubes perform vital tasks in the operation of photoelectric cells, electron microscopes, and hundreds of other types of electronic equipment.

The Scientist's Interest in Vacuum

In a very high vacuum almost all gas molecules have been removed from an enclosed space. A particle passing through it moves a relatively long distance before colliding with another particle. A physicist can control and study a single particle without interference. He uses electrical and magnetic fields to guide a stream of electrons or neutrons to a particular target. The cyclotrons in nuclear laboratories are simply machines for speeding particles around a carefully

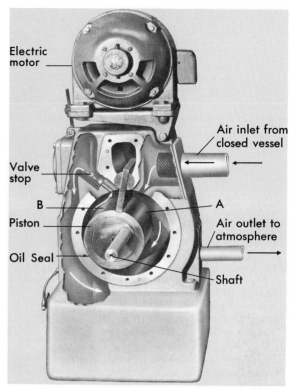

The piston rotates in a clockwise direction in the chamber of a rotary vacuum pump. Air enters the increasing space A from the vessel. The moving piston compresses air in space B until it forces the valve stop open and the air escapes to the exhaust. The valve stop closes again after the piston passes it. Another cycle begins when the piston passes the inlet tube and traps a new volume of air in A.

planned route in a vacuum. Such studies provide results that help scientists to solve the mysteries of molecular structure (*see* Nuclear Energy).

The Operation of Vacuum Pumps

The history of progress in the study of vacuum is the history of vacuum-pump design. Before 1900, vacuums were produced by crude, hand-operated pumps. In this century the rotary oil pump, the molecular pump, the vapor condensation pump, and the oil diffusion pump have been developed. These pumps have made a high vacuum possible for the first time. With modern techniques all but one of every million million molecules in a container can be removed. Pressure can be reduced to 0.00000000001 millimeter of mercury as compared to normal atmospheric pressure of 760 millimeters (*see* Barometer).

The air of our atmosphere exerts great pressure to enter an enclosed space which is under high vacuum. It attempts to equalize pressure inside and outside. Dissolved gas molecules diffuse through solids and enter the evacuated space. Slow evaporation of solid materials, such as the container walls, also takes place. When molecules evaporate into a container as fast as other molecules are removed from it, a practical limit is reached, preventing a perfect vacuum.

Robert Frerck—Odyssey Productions

The Miguelete Tower, Valencia's most outstanding bell tower, adjoins the cathedral, which was completed in 1482.

VALENCIA, Spain. The capital of Valencia province, the city of Valencia has been an agricultural and industrial center throughout its history. It is located on the Mediterranean Sea at the mouth of the Turia River in a region surrounded by orchards. It is Spain's third largest city.

Valencia has been called the city of the 100 bell towers. With its broad streets and new buildings it is also one of Spain's most modern communities. A new University City complex houses many branches of the University of Valencia, which was founded in 1501. The city's picturesque old buildings include the cathedral, La Seo, begun in 1262 on the site of a Muslim mosque; the 15th-century Silk Exchange; the 16th-century Royal Government Palace; and the 18th-century Palace de Dos Aguas, now a ceramics museum. Botanical gardens, sandy beaches, and annual festivals also attract thousands of visitors to the city.

Large quantities of almonds, oranges, lemons, figs, dates, melons, vegetables, sugarcane, and grain are produced. A marshy coastal strip yields some of the finest rice in the world. Thriving mulberry trees contribute to a prosperous silk industry. Other industries include shipbuilding and the manufacture of chemicals, textiles, ceramics, and furniture.

Valencia was taken by the Visigoths in 413 and in 714 by the Moors. In 1021 it became the seat of the newly established independent Moorish kingdom of Valencia. The Spanish soldier-hero El Cid fought for the city from 1089 until 1094. The Moors recovered the city in 1102. In 1238 it became part of the Kingdom of Aragon. It developed rapidly in the late 15th century and was a center for the arts. During the Spanish Civil War it was the loyalist capital from 1936 to 1939. Population (1986 estimate), 763,900.

VALÉRY, Paul (1871–1945). A poet to whom poetry was not especially interesting—that was Paul Valéry's assessment of himself. In the France of his day he was considered the greatest of poets. His real interest, however, was in the workings of the human mind—in the unlimited possibilities for thought in relation to the imperfections of action.

Valéry was born on Oct. 30, 1871, in Cette (now Sète), France, a port on the Mediterranean Sea. He attended school in Montpellier, where he studied law and developed an interest in poetry. He wrote poetry for a few years before abandoning it for mathematics, philosophy, and the physical sciences. In 1892 he moved to Paris. He worked for the French War Office (1897–1900) and then for 22 years was secretary to the head of a news agency. In 1912 Valéry started work on a poem planned as a valediction, or farewell, to a group of his earlier works that his friend André Gide had asked him to revise for publication. This poem, published in 1917 as 'The Young Fate', established Valéry as France's leading poet. The other poems finally appeared in 1920 as 'Album of Ancient Verses'.

After publishing another collection, 'Charmes' (1922), Valéry essentially abandoned poetry. He was elected to the French Academy in 1925. In 1933 he became head of the Mediterranean University Center in Nice. In 1937 he was appointed professor of poetry at the College of France. Valéry died in Paris on July 20, 1945. His best-known poem—'The Graveyard by the Sea' (1920)—is about the cemetery in Sète. He also wrote several collections of essays.

VALLEJO, Mariano G. (1808–90). The city of Vallejo, Calif., is on land once owned by Mariano G. Vallejo. He was a native-born Californian who, while the region was still a Mexican colony, wanted to make it a self-governing territory. Before his goals could be achieved, however, the Americans arrived from the East, and California was annexed to the United States.

Mariano Guadalupe Vallejo was born in Monterey on July 7, 1808. At 15 he became a soldier and remained in the service most of his life. In 1831–32 and 1835–36 he supported rebellions against the Mexican authorities. His nephew, Juan Bautista Alvarado, led the revolt in 1836 that made California virtually free of Mexico and became the new governor. Vallejo became commander of the provincial military forces in 1838 and was stationed at Sonoma.

When the Bear Flag Revolt took place in 1846, Vallejo was taken prisoner and held for two months. He was released when American military forces took the province. In 1849 he was a delegate to the state constitutional convention, and he served a term in the first state Senate. In 1851 he gave part of his estate as land for a state capital, though it was used as such only briefly. Beginning with statehood the fortunes of the native-born Hispanics began to decline, as large numbers of Anglos arrived from the East. During the last decades of his life, Vallejo remained on his estate at Sonoma collecting material for a history of California. He died there on Jan. 18, 1890.

VALLEY. Like other land forms, river valleys are always changing. At the same time that the river is deepening its bed, other forces—rain, frost, wind, and the atmosphere—are loosening material on the valley walls. This material falls into the stream and is carried away. The form of a valley depends upon the rate at which deepening and widening go on.

At first the deepening proceeds rapidly. However, when the level of the stream bed nears the level of the body of water into which the river empties, the stream grows more sluggish and deepening is halted. A slow stream aids the widening process by swinging from side to side when there are obstacles in the channel, thereby eroding the valley walls.

Not all valleys are formed by rivers. Those that are typically are V-shaped. Other valleys were formerly occupied by glaciers and are characteristically U-shaped. As the huge bodies of ice moved along, they carved the valleys as they passed, carrying away giant boulders and huge amounts of debris. At one time, all valleys were thought to be great chasms in the Earth that were opened up by cataclysmic tectonic events. However, depressions formed in this way are not true valleys, though they are often called such; examples are Death Valley and the Great Valley of California.

Very narrow, deep valleys cut in resistant rock and having steep, almost vertical sides are called canyons (*see* Canyon). They may reach depths of several thousand feet. Smaller valleys of similar appearance are called gorges. Both types are commonly cut in flat-lying layers of rock, but they may occur in other types of geologic situations as well. (*See also* Earth, "The Changing Earth"; River.)

VALLEY FORGE, Pa. An area about 20 miles (32 kilometers) northwest of Philadelphia, Pa., Valley Forge served as the headquarters of General George Washington and the encampment of the Continental Army in the winter of 1777–78, during the American Revolution. The major portions of the original camp are now part of Valley Forge National Historical Park, along the Schuylkill River in southeastern Pennsylvania. The 3,465-acre (1,402-hectare) park includes Washington's headquarters, re-creations of log buildings, fortifications, and a memorial arch.

The Continental Army of about 11,000 encamped there in December 1777 after the battles of Brandywine and Germantown. The site was chosen partly because of its strategic location between the British army in Philadelphia and the Continental Congress, which was temporarily quartered in York, Pa. Thousands of soldiers were barefoot and without adequate clothing in the bitter cold. Many died of exposure, and more than 2,000 deserted. Horses starved to death. Congress was unable to provide help despite Washington's pleas in this darkest period of the Revolutionary War. Yet the troops did not lose their courage or morale. Under Baron Frederick William von Steuben the soldiers received instruction in military drill. When spring came, the troops emerged as a well-disciplined and efficient fighting force.

VALPARAÍSO, Chile. A major international shipping port, Valparaíso is located on the mountainous shoreline of a broad ocean bay in central Chile. It is the capital of Valparaíso province and region. The city's commercial quarter and port works occupy reclaimed land near the bay as do the administrative buildings grouped around the Plaza Sotomayor. The cathedral, parks, boulevards, theaters, cafes, and a few colonial buildings, notably the church of La Matriz, are also concentrated in this lower part of the city. On the surrounding hills and cliffs stand the Chilean naval academy and residential areas. Cable railways, elevators, and zigzag roads connect the lower city with the upper. Beaches, mountains, and cultural diversity attract tourists and residents to the city and nearby resort area, Viña del Mar. The city is the home of the Federico Santa María Technical University, the Catholic University of Valparaíso, and museums of natural history and fine arts.

Most of Chile's imports enter through Valparaíso's port. Here are foundries and factories that produce chemicals, textiles, sugar, paints, clothing, leather goods, and vegetable oils. A petroleum refinery is in nearby Concón. The city is the western terminus of the Transandine railway and has direct overland access with the cities of Buenos Aires and Mendoza, Argentina. State railways, good highways, and internal airlines grant easy access to other cities and ports, including the nation's capital, Santiago.

Founded in 1536, Valparaíso was named after the birthplace of conquistador Juan de Saavedra. Pirate raids, severe storms, and fires destroyed most of the early settlement. After Chile's independence in 1818 the city's mercantile strength grew, boosted and protected by the presence of the Chilean navy. A severe earthquake in 1906, however, made it necessary to rebuild much of the city. Another quake in 1971 damaged many buildings. Population (1987 estimate), 278,800.

VALVE. A device that regulates the flow of a fluid in a pipe or other enclosure is called a valve. Valves control flow by means of a movable part that opens to allow the fluid to flow, closes to block the fluid, or partially obstructs an opening in a passageway to slow the fluid's flow. The human heart, for example, has valves that control the flow of blood to and from the heart and lungs and through the body.

Industrial valves are designed in many types to do thousands of jobs in factories, stores, and homes. Common types include the globe, gate, check, and relief valves. To regulate flow closely, a globe valve is one of the most efficient types. The movable element may be a tapered plug or a disk that fits a seat on the valve body. The disk may carry a replaceable rubber or leather washer, as in a household water faucet.

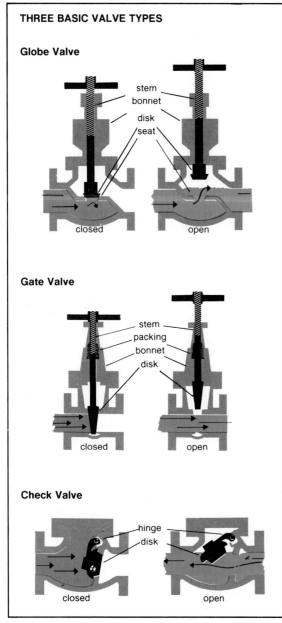

THREE BASIC VALVE TYPES

Globe Valve

stem
bonnet
disk
seat

closed   open

Gate Valve

stem
packing
bonnet
disk

closed   open

Check Valve

hinge
disk

closed   open

The globe valve, top, is used primarily to control the flow of fluids in one direction. The gate valve, center, operates at right angles to a flow either to close or open a passageway to liquids. The check valve, or nonreturn valve, bottom, is a built-in safeguard to prevent backflow.

The seating design of the globe valve changes the direction of flow and increases resistance to flow.

One of the most common industrial valves is the gate valve. Its name comes from its movable element—a wedge-shaped, gatelike disk that is seated against two tapered faces in the valve body. The disk is positioned at right angles to the path of flow and is used for opening and closing a passageway. A similar type of valve, the needle valve, has a long tapered needle that fits in a tapered seat.

Some valves operate automatically. Check, or non-return, valves, for example, allow flow in one direction only and are used to prevent backflow. The valve disk closes automatically if the flow is reversed. A relief, or poppet, valve has a weight or spring to hold it shut. When the pressure in a tank becomes dangerously high, the valve opens automatically and permits the fluid to escape. When the pressure falls to a safe level, the valve closes again.

VAN, LAKE. The largest inland body of water in Turkey is Lake Van. This salt lake is located 5,640 feet (1,720 meters) above sea level in the region of eastern Anatolia near the Iranian border. It has an area of 1,443 square miles (3,737 square kilometers) and is about 80 miles (130 kilometers) across at its widest point. Lake Van is roughly triangular in shape and has two parts. The main body of water is connected by a narrow passage with a shallower northern extension. The shores of the lake are steep and lined with cliffs. The lake is dotted with islands. These include Gadir in the north, which is the largest; Çarpanak in the east; and Aktamar and Atrek in the south.

Lake Van lies in the lowest part of a vast, high basin. The basin is bordered by high mountains to the south, by plateaus and mountains to the east, and by a complex of volcanic cones to the west. The lake is fed by underwater sulfur springs and has no apparent outlet. Rain, melted snow, and four rivers also add to the lake's salty waters. The Bendimahi and Zilan rivers feed the lake from the north and the Karasu and Micinger rivers feed it from the east. The lake rarely freezes due to its high salt content, and the waters are unsuitable for drinking or irrigation. There is some fishing for freshwater fish called *darekh,* which have adapted to the saline environment. On the southwestern shore of Lake Van there is a small shipyard at Tuğ. Passenger-boat service is available between several of the coastal towns.

Van, a town located on the eastern shore, was the capital of the Urartu kingdom, which flourished between the 9th and 8th centuries BC. Much of the area around the lake is desolate and sparsely populated.

VANADIUM. The 22nd most abundant element in the Earth's crust, vanadium is found in combined form in coal, petroleum, and other minerals. South Africa is the largest producer of vanadium. Most of the vanadium produced is used in the manufacture of tool steels, high-strength structural steels, and wear-resistant cast irons.

Vanadium is a silvery-white soft metal of Group Vb of the periodic table. Natural vanadium consists of two isotopes: stable vanadium-51, which accounts for roughly 99 percent of the metal, and weakly radioactive vanadium-50. More than half a dozen artificial radioactive isotopes have been produced. Vanadium does not dissolve in sodium hydroxide, hydrochloric acid, or dilute sulfuric acid nor does it tarnish easily. When heated it combines with oxygen, nitrogen, carbon, or sulfur.

PROPERTIES OF VANADIUM

Symbol V	Specific Gravity at 65.7° F
Atomic Number 23	(18.7° C) 6.11
Atomic Weight	Boiling Point
.... 50.9415	...... 6,116° F (3,380° C)
Group in Periodic	Melting Point
Table .... Vb	...... 3,434° F (1,890° C)

When combined with other substances, vanadium enhances their properties. For example, vanadium improves the alloying qualities of steel and increases the metal's tensile strength, making it more resistant to shock and metal fatigue. The addition of 0.15 percent vanadium strengthens cast iron by 10 to 25 percent. Vanadium compounds are used as catalysts in the manufacture of sulfuric acid and also as driers in paints and inks. Vanadium metal, sheet, strip, foil, bar, wire, and tubing are used in high-temperature applications in the chemical industry and in bonding other metals.

Ores with small amounts of vanadium are widely distributed, but ores containing high concentrations of vanadium are rare. Most vanadium ore in the United States comes from Arkansas and Idaho. Other sources are the Soviet Union and China. The most common ores are carnotite (also an ore of uranium), vanadinite, patronite, and roscoelite. Commercial sources include vanadium-bearing magnetite and flue dust from smokestacks of power plants that burn Venezuelan oil.

Vanadium was first discovered in 1801 by the Spanish mineralogist Andrés Manuel del Río, who believed it was merely impure chromium. The metal was rediscovered and named by the Swedish chemist Nils G. Sefström in 1830. He named the element for the Scandinavian goddess Vanadis because of the beautiful colors of the metal's compounds in solution. Henry Enfield Roscoe, an English chemist, first isolated the metal in 1867; and two chemists in the United States, John Wesley Marden and Malcolm N. Rich, obtained a 99.7 percent pure sample by reduction of vanadium pentoxide with calcium metal. (*See also* Chemical Elements).

VAN ALLEN, James A. (born 1914).

One of the major discoveries made by space probes in the late 1950s was information leading to the discovery of two huge belts of intense radiation encircling the Earth. The belts are doughnut-shaped; the inner zone is made up of high-energy protons; the outer zone, of high-energy electrons and other particles. The belts are part of the magnetosphere, the tear-shaped magnetic region around the Earth. The inner zone is separated from the outer zone by a slot, or an area of less intense radiation. The bands start at an altitude of several hundred miles from the Earth and extend for several thousand miles into space. These radiation belts were named for James A. Van Allen, whose work helped bring about their discovery.

James Alfred Van Allen was born on Sept. 7, 1914, in Mount Pleasant, Iowa. His father was an attorney.

Van Allen was a studious boy, with a great interest in science. In 1931 Van Allen entered Iowa Wesleyan College, in Mt. Pleasant, and began his studies in physics and chemistry. He received his bachelor of science degree there. He was awarded his master's degree and his doctorate at the University of Iowa. From 1939 to 1942 he was a research scientist at the Carnegie Institution in Washington, D.C. During World War II Van Allen served as a naval officer and helped develop the radio proximity fuze for naval artillery shells.

After the war Van Allen was made head of high-altitude research at the Applied Physics Laboratory of Johns Hopkins University. There he worked with captured German V-2 rockets and led in the design of the Aerobee rocket, used for upper atmosphere exploration. Out of a scientific conference that was held at his home in 1950 were developed the first plans for the International Geophysical Year (IGY) program of 1957–58.

Van Allen returned to the University of Iowa in 1951 and was named chairman of the physics department. There he conducted many cosmic-ray studies. He launched his rockets from balloons already 10 to 15 miles (16 to 24 kilometers) up in the atmosphere. Van Allen also designed and built the instrument payloads for the American satellites launched under the International Geophysical Year. These sent radio reports on outer space conditions back to listening stations on Earth. On Jan. 31, 1958, the first United States artificial Earth satellite, Explorer 1, went into orbit. It was equipped with Van Allen instruments. So were the others of the Explorer series that followed. The Pioneer series of moon probes also carried his instruments. These instruments detected the two radiation belts.

Van Allen later participated in the development of numerous space probes built to study planetary and solar physics. He was elected to the National Academy of Sciences in 1959 and became president of the American Geophysical Union in 1982. (*See also* Space Travel.)

The doughnut-shaped Van Allen belts are shown cut away to expose the Earth, which is at their center. They are part of a large area of radiation called the magnetosphere.

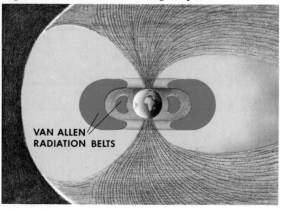

VAN ALLEN RADIATION BELTS

MARTIN VAN BUREN—
8th President of
the United States

thinking and persuasion that he learned in his law work. These skills, enriched by his warm friendliness, helped to make him a master politician—the first "practical politician" to become president.

Descended from Dutch Colonists

Martin Van Buren was born Dec. 5, 1782, at Kinderhook, a village 20 miles south of Albany, N. Y. The first Van Buren, Cornelis—Martin's great-great-great grandfather—had come from Holland in 1631. Martin was the third of the five children of Abraham and Maria Hoes Van Buren.

Abraham owned a popular inn-tavern and, with the help of slaves, he also farmed. He was too generous however, and the family had trouble making ends meet. Young Martin learned never to waste a penny. He went to the village school, then to Kinderhook Academy. After classes he usually had to deliver farm produce or help in the inn. His smiling cheerfulness made him a favorite among the customers. He listened eagerly as they argued American politics in Dutch.

Begins Law Career and Marries

Graduating from school at 14, he was apprenticed to a village lawyer. Mat swept out the office, lit the log fire, ran errands, patiently read law books, and eagerly read every journal he could find on Jeffersonian politics (see Jefferson, Thomas). By the time he was 18 years old his precise legal thinking brought him local renown. He still took time to campaign so successfully for Jefferson that he was sent as delegate to a regional caucus. In 1801 he entered a New York City law office, barely earning a living.

He was admitted to the bar at Kinderhook in 1803. By 1807 he was earning enough to marry his childhood sweetheart, Hannah Hoes, a distant cousin. They had four sons—Abraham, John, Martin Jr., and Smith.

VAN BUREN, Martin (1782–1862; president 1837–1841). Young "Mat" Van Buren rose in the little courtroom to face an amazed jury in a village near Kinderhook, N. Y. He reviewed the evidence with great care. Little wonder the jury was surprised to see him enter the law case. He was only 15 years old—slim, short, yellow-haired—with only one year's experience as a law clerk, but he helped to win the case.

This boyhood success was Martin Van Buren's start in public life—the beginning of a career that carried him to the presidency of the United States. In all that he did throughout life, Van Buren showed the careful

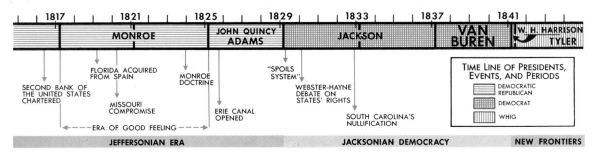

1817	1821	1825	1829	1833	1837	1841
	MONROE		JOHN QUINCY ADAMS	JACKSON	VAN BUREN	W. H. HARRISON TYLER

FLORIDA ACQUIRED FROM SPAIN

MONROE DOCTRINE

"SPOILS SYSTEM"

SECOND BANK OF THE UNITED STATES CHARTERED

WEBSTER-HAYNE DEBATE ON STATES' RIGHTS

MISSOURI COMPROMISE

ERIE CANAL OPENED

SOUTH CAROLINA'S NULLIFICATION

- - - ERA OF GOOD FEELING - - -

TIME LINE OF PRESIDENTS, EVENTS, AND PERIODS

DEMOCRATIC REPUBLICAN

DEMOCRAT

WHIG

JEFFERSONIAN ERA   JACKSONIAN DEMOCRACY   NEW FRONTIERS

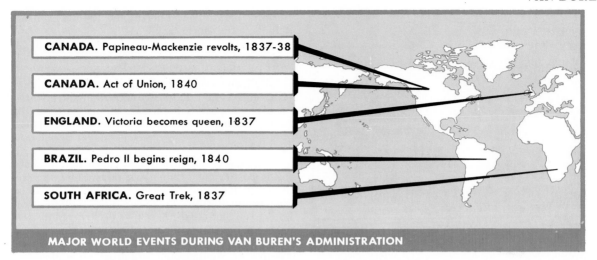

CANADA. Papineau-Mackenzie revolts, 1837-38

CANADA. Act of Union, 1840

ENGLAND. Victoria becomes queen, 1837

BRAZIL. Pedro II begins reign, 1840

SOUTH AFRICA. Great Trek, 1837

MAJOR WORLD EVENTS DURING VAN BUREN'S ADMINISTRATION

Van Buren was close to his family, and they were devoted to him. When Hannah died in 1819, he placed the boys with relatives but supervised their schooling and wrote to them constantly. Abraham later went to the United States Military Academy at West Point and John to Yale. When Van Buren became president, they became his aides—and Abraham's wife, Angelica Singleton Van Buren, agreed to serve as the White House hostess.

Starts Long Political Career

Van Buren soon became a well-to-do lawyer, but politics remained his chief interest. From his first public office as surrogate in 1808, he moved up rapidly through state politics. He became a leader of the so-called "Albany Regency," the political machine that ran the state. He never let anger distort his judgment or warp his manner. He always led by persuasion, often by careful scheming. His enemies called him the Fox of Kinderhook and the Little Magician. Only 5 feet 6 inches tall and slender, he stood erect and liked to be handsomely dressed.

In 1821 he was elected United States senator and was reelected in 1827. An enthusiastic supporter of Andrew Jackson, he helped guide his presidential campaign. Van Buren resigned from the United States Senate to become governor of New York in 1828 but served only three months before he resigned to become secretary of state in Jackson's Cabinet.

From his experiences in New York politics Van Buren knew the political power of the spoils system—in which the workers for the victorious party were appointed to the public offices held by the defeated party. Van Buren helped Jackson extend the system to the federal government (see Jackson, Andrew).

In 1831 Van Buren resigned as secretary of state to become minister to Great Britain. In January 1832, however, the Senate rejected the appointment. He and his son John then toured Europe, often accompanied by Washington Irving, who was an attaché in London. He wrote: "The more I see of Mr. Van Buren the more I have a strong personal regard for him."

When Jackson was reelected president in 1832, Van Buren became vice-president. In 1835 Jackson ordered his Democratic party to nominate Van Buren as president, and he was elected in 1836.

Difficult Administration Followed by Defeat

Van Buren's administration was beset by trouble. Almost at once a financial panic struck the nation. Bankers begged Van Buren for aid, but he pointed out that the crisis was due to ruinous speculation. He insisted that government manipulation would only further weaken the economic structure. As a step to guard the nation's own money, he repeatedly pressed Congress to set up an independent treasury. It was voted in 1840 but repealed in 1841.

Van Buren also inherited from Jackson the Seminole Indian War in Florida (1835–42). The conflict, during which thousands of lives were lost, cost the government between 40 and 60 million dollars.

Meanwhile Van Buren had to handle the undeclared Aroostook War, a dispute between Maine and New Brunswick, Canada, over Maine's northeast boundary on the Aroostook River (see Maine). Maine called out troops in 1839, but Van Buren managed to have the quarrel settled by Britain and the United States.

Van Buren's calm approach to problems angered people who demanded quick action. Despite heated public opinion he carefully weighed both sides of

---

VAN BUREN'S ADMINISTRATION
1837–1841

Financial panic (1837)
Seminole Indian War continued (1837–41)
Aroostook War between Maine and Canada
(1838–39)
First photograph taken in America (1839)
Vulcanized rubber discovered (1839)
Subtreasury established (1840)
Hard Cider campaign results in Whig
victory (1840)

Brown Brothers

Martin Van Buren, eighth president of the United States, was born in a frame house in the village of Kinderhook, N.Y.

any question. Today he is regarded as having been a sound statesman in a troubled era.

Memories of the financial crisis defeated Van Buren in 1840. William Henry Harrison was elected president (*see* Harrison, William H.). Van Buren was again nominated for president in 1848 but was decisively defeated. On July 24, 1862, Martin Van Buren died at Lindenwald, his estate near Kinderhook.

BIBLIOGRAPHY FOR MARTIN VAN BUREN

Beard, C.A. The Presidents in American History, rev. ed. (Messner, 1981).

Cole, D.B. Martin Van Buren and the American Political System (Princeton Univ. Press, 1984).

DeGregorio, W.A. The Complete Book of U.S. Presidents (Dembner, 1984).

Graff, H.F., ed. The Presidents: a Reference History (Scribner, 1984).

Whitney, D.C. The American Presidents, 6th ed. (Doubleday, 1986).

Wilson, M.L. The Presidency of Martin Van Buren (Univ. Press of Kansas, 1984).

VANCOUVER, B.C.

Located just north of the United States-Canada border, Vancouver is the industrial, commercial, and financial center of British Columbia. Greater Vancouver is Canada's third-largest metropolitan area after Toronto and Montreal. It

is located on a peninsula that projects into the Strait of Georgia, an arm of the Pacific Ocean. Vancouver is 140 miles (225 kilometers) north of Seattle, Wash. Extending over an area of 44 square miles (114 square kilometers), metropolitan Vancouver contains almost half of British Columbia's population.

The city spreads to the east opposite Vancouver Island in the southwestern corner of the British Columbia mainland and occupies a site facing the sea and the mountains. At an elevation of 1,394 feet (425 meters), the city is flanked by the tall peaks of Grouse Mountain, Mount Seymour, and Mount Hollyburn.

Burrard Inlet is to the north, and the Fraser River delta is to the south.

The average January temperature is 37° F (2.8° C), and winter temperatures seldom drop below 35° F (1.7° C). The average summer temperature is 60° F (15.6° C), and annual precipitation is about 40 inches (102 centimeters). Extensive forests in surrounding areas provide raw materials for numerous sawmills, plywood factories, and paper-manufacturing plants.

Landscape

The majority of Vancouver's historic buildings are in the Gastown and Chinatown areas. Older sections of the city have undergone considerable change since 1960, when downtown high-rise office buildings and hotels were built. False Creek—a decaying industrial area with sawmills, rail yards, and small shops—was transformed into a residential development project. Another successful example of urban renewal is Gastown, the original heart of the city that was restored in the 1880s style with antique stores and boutiques.

With more than 130 parks, Vancouver is noted for its recreational facilities. Stanley Park occupies more than 1,000 acres (400 hectares) of the downtown area near the harbor entrance, which is crossed by the Lion's Gate Bridge. It includes an arboretum, gardens, lagoons, lakes, an aquarium, a theater, a zoo, and 50 miles (80 kilometers) of trails. Famous for its forests of centuries-old Douglas firs and red cedars, the park overlooks the entrance to Burrard Inlet. Exhibition Park holds the annual Pacific National Exhibition. Other parks include Mount Seymour Provincial Park, Queen Elizabeth Park, and Lynn Park. Nearby Grouse Mountain, 3,974 feet (1,211 meters) high, provides excellent ski slopes in the winter. The mountain top can be reached by an aerial tramway.

People and Culture

Vancouver is largely British in character with some Chinese influence. Almost three fourths of the population are of British ancestry. The Chinese, French, Japanese, and East Indians are the largest among other ethnic groups.

Vancouver became more cosmopolitan after World War II, when waves of emigrants came for better job opportunities. Its Chinatown is the second largest in North America, after San Francisco, Calif. Large residential suburbs extend to the south and east along the Fraser River, including the satellite towns of New Westminster, Port Moody, and Port Coquitlam. The city's northern and western suburbs extend up to 5,000 feet (1,500 meters) on the steep mountain slopes.

Noted educational institutions are the University of British Columbia (1908), Simon Fraser University (1963), and several regional colleges such as Vancouver Community College (1965) and the British Columbia Institute of Technology (1964). The city has long been noted for its varied cultural activities. Major institutions are the MacMillan Planetarium, Centennial and Maritime museums, Opera House,

Queen Elizabeth Theatre, Vancouver Art Gallery, and Vancouver Aquarium. Robson Square has provincial government offices, a skating rink, multilevel shopping and food facilities, and the British Columbia Place sports stadium with a seating capacity of 60,-000. The Robson Square Conference Center and the Provincial Court House buildings are noted for their modern architectural style.

Industry

Sometimes called Canada's gateway to the Pacific, Vancouver is linked by shipping services with Pacific ports of the United States, China, Japan, Australia, and New Zealand. Through the Panama Canal it is linked with Atlantic ports of the Americas and Europe. Trade and transportation are the city's chief functions. Products of Western Canada's farms, ranches, forests, mines, and industries are sent by rail to Vancouver and then by water to the ports of the world.

The natural, ice-free harbor is one of the world's largest. With extensive docks and grain-elevator facilities, it is one of the busiest ports of Canada, ranking first in tonnage handled. The Roberts Bay terminal (1970) to the south of Vancouver is used for shipping coal.

Vancouver's major industries are wood, fish, and food processing, fruit and vegetable canning, sugar refining, shipbuilding and repairing, metal fabricating, and printing and publishing. Other industries produce beverages, tobacco, leather goods, machinery, transport equipment, furniture, petroleum and coal products, and electrical, rubber, chemical, and plastic products. Low-cost electricity and natural gas for its industries are provided by nearby hydroelectric plants and pipelines from Alberta. Exports include wheat, grains, lumber, fish and fish products, metals, manufactured items, and minerals.

The Trans-Canada Highway and major railroads connect Vancouver with other Canadian cities. It is also well connected by roads and railways with cities in the United States. Sea Island at the mouth of the Fraser River is the site of Vancouver International Airport. Regular ferry service connects the city with Vancouver Island.

History

Archaeological evidence indicates that the city site was inhabited by coastal Indians around 400 BC. The first permanent white settlement began in 1866, when a saloon was built near a small sawmill. The settlement developed in the 1870s as a community called Granville. In April 1886, with a population of 2,500 and some 300 wooden houses, it was incorporated as a city and renamed to honor Captain George Vancouver of the Royal Navy who had navigated the coast in 1792. A disastrous fire almost destroyed the city in June 1886, but it was quickly rebuilt. The next year Vancouver became the terminus of the Canadian Pacific Railway, the first trans-Canada railroad. The Hudson's Bay Company department store and the Vancouver Hotel opened in 1887.

Queen Elizabeth Park in Vancouver has an arboretum and the Bloedel Conservatory of tropical plants.

The depression of the mid-1890s halted Vancouver's growth, but the city soon prospered again and displaced Victoria, the provincial capital, as the leading trade and commercial center of Canada. The opening of the Panama Canal in 1914 greatly boosted Vancouver's position as a seaport. The canal facilitated exports of fish, grain, and lumber from Vancouver to Europe as well as to the eastern coasts of the United States and Canada. Fish- and wood-processing industries also provided job opportunities for emigrant workers.

The metropolitan area continued to expand, and nearby Point Grey and South Vancouver were annexed in 1929. By the 1930s Vancouver had become Canada's third largest city and its principal port on the Pacific coast. During World War II the city was a center for war industries, particularly shipbuilding and repairing. A world's fair was held in Vancouver in 1986. Population (1981 census), city proper, 414,281; metropolitan area, 1,268,183.

VANCOUVER ISLAND. The top of a partially submerged mountain system, Vancouver Island is the largest island on the Pacific coast of North America. It is part of the Canadian province of British Columbia and is situated near the province's southern border. The straits of Georgia and Queen Charlotte separate the island from the Canadian mainland.

With a beautiful mountainous terrain, Vancouver Island is 285 miles (460 kilometers) in length and from 40 to 80 miles (65 to 130 kilometers) in width. Several peaks rise higher than 7,000 feet (2,100 meters). The tallest of these is Golden Hinde. The coastline, especially on the west, is deeply indented with fjords, and on the eastern side is a coastal plain. Forests cover most of the island. Designated park areas include the immense Strathocona Provincial Park in the central part of the island, Pacific Rim

National Park in three sections along the west coast, and Cape Scott Provincial Park at the northern tip.

Lumbering; tourism; agriculture; fishing; and coal, gold, and copper mining are major industries. Victoria, the capital of British Columbia, is the chief city (*see* Victoria, B.C.).

The island was named for George Vancouver, who charted its coast in 1792. It was made a British Crown Colony in 1849. In 1866 it was united with the mainland colony of British Columbia, which became a province in 1871.

VANDALS. Looted churches and wrecked buildings marked the path of the Vandals in the early Middle Ages. These Germanic tribes plundered so wantonly that the word vandal is still used to describe a person who recklessly destroys property.

At the beginning of the 5th century AD the Vandals—pursued by the Huns—left their home on the Baltic and trekked toward the southwest. Crossing the Rhine River, they invaded Gaul (now France). They were defeated in a battle with the Franks and in 409 fled across the Pyrenees Mountains into Spain. They remained there for about 20 years, until Genseric (Gaiseric) became king.

In 429 Genseric moved his people across the Strait of Gibraltar into Africa. A discontented governor in the African provinces of Rome is believed to have invited him. In 439 Genseric conquered Carthage, the leading Roman city in North Africa. He established an independent Vandal Kingdom. Genseric sailed northward and captured the city of Rome in 455. He ruled the conquered territories until his death in 477.

Under Genseric's successors the Vandals continued to be a source of terror for the Romans because of their aggression and their persecution of the orthodox Christians. The Vandals themselves followed a variant form of Christianity called Arianism. In 533 Emperor Justinian ordered Belisarius, his great general, to subdue the Vandals. After severe fighting Belisarius accomplished his mission. Most of the Vandal men were made slaves of the Romans. Within a few years the Vandals had disappeared from history.

VANDERBILT FAMILY. Beginning with the efforts of Cornelius Vanderbilt in the early 19th century, the Vanderbilt family amassed a fortune in the shipping and railroad industries. They became one of the wealthiest and most prominent families in the United States.

Cornelius Vanderbilt (1794–1877) was born on May 27, 1794, in Port Richmond, Staten Island, N.Y. The son of a farmer, Vanderbilt left school at age 11 and at age 16 borrowed money from his parents to buy his first boat. He used the boat to ferry passengers between New York City and Staten Island and during the War of 1812 ferried provisions to government outposts around the city.

In 1829 he formed a steamboat company. During the next decade Vanderbilt beat out competitors on the Hudson River by cutting his fares and transforming his steamboats into luxury vessels. His competitors finally paid him handsomely to relocate. He moved his business to the Northeastern seaboard, and by 1846 "Commodore" Vanderbilt was a millionaire. In 1847 he formed a company to transport passengers from New York City and New Orleans to San Francisco via Nicaragua. He was just in time to make a fortune from the California gold rush.

In the 1850s Vanderbilt began to extend his empire. He purchased a number of railroads and in 1873 offered the first New York–Chicago rail connection. Vanderbilt ordered the construction of the Grand Central Terminal in New York City, and during the Panic of 1873 his project provided jobs for thousands of the unemployed. When Vanderbilt died in New York City on Jan. 4, 1877, he left behind a fortune of about 100 million dollars. He contributed a large sum of money to Central University (renamed Vanderbilt University) in Nashville, Tenn.

William Henry Vanderbilt (1821–85), the only son of Cornelius Vanderbilt, was born on May 8, 1821, in New Brunswick, N.J. Although he had eight sisters, William inherited the bulk of his father's estate. William was at first judged unworthy to assist his father in business and was sent to live on a farm on Staten Island, N.Y. William surprised his father by making the farm, and later a bankrupt railroad, profitable. When his father died, William expanded the Vanderbilt railroad empire with further acquisitions. He used his power to participate in rate wars and gave special rates to favored shippers. William vigorously opposed regulation of the railroads, proclaiming, "The public be damned." When he retired in 1883, he had nearly doubled his father's fortune. He died in New York City on Dec. 8, 1885, leaving eight children, including three sons: Cornelius, William Kissam, and George Washington.

Cornelius Vanderbilt (1843–99) was born on Nov. 27, 1843, on a farm on Staten Island, N.Y. Of William Henry's three sons, Cornelius was by far the most devoted to furthering the family's business and investment interests. After his father's death, Cornelius took charge of the various railroads, corporations, and philanthropic activities. His gifts built the Vanderbilt Clinic for the College of Physicians and Surgeons at Columbia University. He died in New York City on Sept. 12, 1899.

William Kissam Vanderbilt (1849–1920). Born on Dec. 12, 1849, on Staten Island, William Kissam was far less interested in business than were his brother, father, and grandfather. In 1903 he turned over management of the family's railroads to an outside firm in order to devote himself to his philanthropic, social, and sporting interests. He was deeply involved in yacht racing, and in 1895 he retained the America's Cup for the United States. He died in Paris, France, on July 22, 1920.

George Washington Vanderbilt (1862–1914), born on Nov. 14, 1862, on Staten Island, was the least involved of William Henry's three sons with the family businesses and investments. He built a huge estate, named Biltmore, near Asheville, N.C. There he carried out experiments in scientific farming, forestry, and stock breeding. He died in Washington, D.C., on March 6, 1914, after an operation for appendicitis.

Of the fourth generation of the Vanderbilt family, Cornelius' son Cornelius III (1873–1942) was a financier. Harold Stirling Vanderbilt (1884–1970), son of William Kissam, was notable as the inventor of the game of contract bridge and as a three-time winner of the America's Cup.

VAN DYCK, Anthony (1599–1641).

The Flemish painter Anthony Van Dyck left a valuable historical record of the colorful age in which he lived. He is known chiefly for his portraits of Europe's kings and queens and other dignitaries, particularly those of the English court in the time of Charles I.

Van Dyck was born in Antwerp, Belgium, on March 22, 1599. The boy was apprenticed to a local painter when he was 10, and at 16 Van Dyck had pupils of his own. At 20 he was living in the house of the Flemish painter Peter Paul Rubens and was completely under his influence. He painted not only in the same style as Rubens but also often the same subjects, possibly as a collaborator.

Young Van Dyck went to London in 1620, but whether he painted anything there on this first visit is unknown. The next year he left Antwerp again, this time for Italy, where he spent about six years. There he was influenced by the works of Titian, the great Venetian colorist. In this period Van Dyck painted scores of pictures on religious and mythological subjects as well as some portraits of Genoese patricians.

In 1627 Van Dyck was back in Antwerp, where by that time he had become a famous and fashionable painter. For five years he remained there, painting portraits and religious pictures and occasionally visiting other European cities to execute commissions. By this time he had formed his own style.

Then came an invitation to the English court. On Van Dyck's arrival in 1632, the king knighted him and gave him a house in London. Within a few months the king gave him a pension. (For picture, *see* Charles, Kings of England, Scotland, and Ireland.)

Charles I and his queen were the painter's first sitters. Soon the lords and ladies of the court were demanding portraits. So popular did the artist become that he set up a large studio like Rubens'. Assistants blocked in the paintings on the required scale from Van Dyck's small sketches. Then, in a few hours, Van Dyck completed the works.

The artist gave subjects an aristocratic bearing, refined features, and long tapering fingers. The same characteristics appear in his many self-portraits. His style influenced Flemish and English artists for more than a century after his death, particularly Thomas Gainsborough and Joshua Reynolds.

Van Dyck did not marry until two years before his death, when, at the king's suggestion, he married Mary Ruthven, a lady of the court. Van Dyck died in London on Dec. 9, 1641.

VAN EYCK, Jan (1390?–1441).

The Flemish painter who perfected the new technique of painting in oils, Jan van Eyck produced mostly portraits and religious subjects on wooden panels. His works often contain disguised religious symbols.

Van Eyck was probably born in Maaseik, now in Belgium, before 1395. From 1422 to 1425 he was in the service of John of Bavaria, count of Holland, in The Hague. For the rest of his life he served Philip the Good, duke of Burgundy.

Only nine of Van Eyck's paintings are signed and only ten are dated. His masterpiece, 'The Adoration of the Lamb' altarpiece in Ghent's Saint-Bavon Cathedral, is dated 1432, but it also has a questionable 16th-century inscription that introduces Hubert van Eyck, supposedly his brother, as its principal master. There are no other references to the brother, but a "Master Hubert, the painter" who died in 1426 is mentioned in city records.

Van Eyck moved from a heavy, sculptural realism to a more delicate pictorial style. This development can be traced most notably in 'Portrait of a Young Man' (1432); 'Madonna of Autun' (1433); 'The Marriage of Giovanni Arnolfini and Giovanna Cenami' (1434) (*see* Painting); 'Madonna with Chancellor Rolin' (1435); 'Madonna with Canon van der Paele' (1436); 'Saint Barbara' (1437); and 'Madonna at the Fountain' (1439). His paintings are known for the beauty of their colors and their special qualities of light. Said the French writer Chateaubriand when he saw the Ghent altarpiece: "Where did the Flemish painters steal their light . . . What ray of Greece has strayed to the shores of Holland?" Van Eyck died in Brugge and was buried on July 9, 1441, in the Church of Saint-Donatian, which was destroyed in 1799.

'Madonna with Chancellor Rolin' is an oil on wood painting by Van Eyck painted in about 1435. It measures 66 centimeters by 82 centimeters and is on display at the Louvre in Paris.

SCALA—Art Resource/EB Inc.

VAN GOGH, Vincent

VAN GOGH, Vincent (1853–90). One of the four great postimpressionists (along with Paul Gauguin, Georges Seurat, and Paul Cézanne), Vincent van Gogh is generally considered the greatest Dutch painter after Rembrandt. His reputation is based largely on the works of the last three years of his short ten-year painting career, and he had a powerful influence on expressionism in modern art. He produced more than 800 oil paintings and 700 drawings, but he sold only one during his lifetime. His striking colors, coarse brushwork, and contoured forms display the anguish of the mental illness that drove him to suicide.

Vincent Willem van Gogh was born on March 30, 1853, in Zundert in the Brabant region of The Netherlands. He was the eldest son of a Protestant clergyman. At the age of 16 Van Gogh was apprenticed to art dealers in The Hague, and he worked for them there and in London and Paris until 1876.

Van Gogh disliked art dealing, and, rejected in love, he became increasingly solitary. He began to prepare for the ministry, but he failed the entrance examinations for seminary and became a lay preacher. In 1878 he went to the impoverished Borinage district in southwestern Belgium to do missionary work. He was dismissed in 1880 over a disagreement with his superiors. Penniless and with his faith broken, he sank into despair and began to draw. He soon realized the limitations of being self-taught and went to Brussels to study drawing. In 1881 he moved to The Hague to work with the Dutch landscape painter Anton Mauve, and the next summer Van Gogh began to experiment with oil paints. His urge to be "alone with nature" took him to Dutch villages, and his subjects—still life, landscape, and figure—all related to the peasants' daily hardships and surroundings. In 1885 he produced his first masterpiece, 'The Potato Eaters'.

Feeling too isolated, he left for Antwerp, Belgium, and enrolled in the academy there. He did not respond well to the school's rigid discipline, but while in Antwerp he was inspired by the paintings of Peter Paul Rubens and discovered Japanese prints. He was soon off to Paris, where he met Henri de Toulouse-Lautrec and Gauguin and discovered the impressionists Camille Pissarro, Seurat, and others. Van Gogh's two years in Paris shaped his personal style of painting—more colorful, less traditional, with lighter tonalities and distinctive brushwork.

Tired of city life, Van Gogh left Paris in 1888 for Arles in the south of France. He rented and decorated a "yellow house" in which he hoped to found a community of "impressionists of the South." Gauguin joined him in October, but their relations deteriorated, and in a quarrel on Christmas Eve Van Gogh cut off part of his own left ear. Gauguin left, and Van Gogh was hospitalized. Exhibiting repeated signs of mental disturbance, Van Gogh asked to be sent to an asylum at Saint-Rémy-de-Province. After a year of confinement he moved to the home of a physician-artist in Auvers-sur-Oise for two months. On July 27, 1890, Van Gogh shot himself; he died two days later.

Despite his deteriorating mental condition, Van Gogh's year at Arles, another in the asylum, and two months at Auvers proved to be his greatest productive periods. At Arles he painted sun-drenched fields and flowers with great bursts of energy; at St-Rémy the colors of his paintings were more muted, but the lines were bolder and the whole more visionary; in the northern light of Auvers he adopted pale, fresh tonalities, a broader and more expressive brushwork, and a lyrical vision of nature. Van Gogh's paintings include many self-portraits and 'Sunflowers in a Vase'. (*See also* Painting.)

VANILLA

VANILLA. For centuries before Hernando Cortez' arrival in Mexico in the 1500s, the Aztecs had been flavoring their beverages with a sweet-smelling extract made from the fermented pods of an orchid. The flavoring was introduced into Europe and soon became popular. The Spaniards called it *vainilla,* or *vanilla,* meaning "little pod."

Today vanilla is among the most common of the flavoring extracts. It is used in a variety of sweet foods and beverages and in the manufacture of perfumes. Vanilla beans of commerce are the cured, unripe fruit of primarily one species of climbing orchid—the Mexican, or Bourbon, vanilla of the tropical Americas. The plant has a long, fleshy climbing stem and oblong leaves. Its numerous yellowish flowers bloom briefly. Because of their dainty structure, the blossoms can be naturally pollinated only by a small bee of Mexico. In other countries the flowers are pollinated artificially with a wooden needle as soon as they open.

The beans are without odor or flavor until they are cured. This is done by alternately warming them in the sun and putting them into sweat boxes at night to ferment. During this curing process the volatile oil vanillin is formed. The beans are then dried. To make vanilla extract, the cured, dried vanilla beans are crushed and the vanillin is extracted with alcohol. Vanilla flavor is made from a concentration of vanilla extract, alcohol, and water. The scientific name of the Mexican vanilla plant is *Vanilla planifolia.*

'The Starry Night', an oil on canvas painted by Van Gogh in 1889, is one of the artist's boldest and most imaginative paintings. It measures 73.7 centimeters by 92.1 centimeters.

VANUATU. The Republic of Vanuatu consists of 12 islands and 60 islets that form a Y-shaped chain in the southwestern Pacific Ocean. Formerly known as New Hebrides, it is situated about 1,200 miles (1,900 kilometers)

east of Australia. Vanuatu's total land area is 4,600 square miles (11,900 square kilometers). The capital and largest city, Vila, is on Efate, the main island.

Mountainous interiors, narrow coastal plains, and offshore coral reefs characterize the islands. There are several active volcanoes, and the islands are subject to frequent earthquakes. Rainfall ranges from 90 inches (230 centimeters) in the south to 155 inches (395 centimeters) in the north.

The largest ethnic group is Melanesian. There are small minorities of Europeans, Chinese, and Polynesians. The languages spoken are French, English, and Bislama, a Melanesian pidgin.

Agriculture, fishing, and cattle raising are the major occupations. Chief crops are copra, cocoa, coffee, bananas, yams, taro, and breadfruit. Large-scale commercial fishing of tuna and bonito is conducted with Japanese and Australian assistance. Some manganese is mined. Manufacturing includes meat packing, fish freezing, and the production of soft drinks and furniture. A lack of direct taxation fostered Vanuatu's development as a financial and banking center.

First sighted by a Portuguese navigator in 1606, the islands were named in 1774 by the English explorer James Cook after the Scottish Hebrides Islands. During World War II they were a major Allied base. The islands became independent under the name of Vanuatu in 1980. Population (1987 estimate), 145,000.

VARANASI, India. Located in northern India, Varanasi is revered by Hindus as a most sacred city. Situated on the northern bank of the Ganges River, Varanasi is bounded by the river's two tributaries, Varuna on the north and Asi on the south. Each year more

than 1 million Hindu pilgrims visit the city.

The Ganges River frontage has miles of ghats, or steps, for religious bathing. The older city sections are a maze of narrow streets full of little shops. The semicircular Panchakosi Road around the city has been used by pilgrims since ancient times.

Also known as the "city of a thousand temples," Varanasi's most venerated is the Visvanatha Temple. It is dedicated to the god Shiva. The ruins of ancient Buddhist monasteries and temples are in nearby Sarnath, where Buddha delivered his first sermon in the 6th century BC.

Varanasi has been renowned as a city of learning for many centuries. There are numerous schools and centers imparting traditional religious education. Brahman pandits, or learned men, are responsible for the continuation of traditional learning. The Banaras Hindu University is one of the most prominent educational institutions in India. The observatory on the Manmandir Ghat dates from about AD 1600.

Varanasi is a center of arts, crafts, music, and dance, and its musicians and dancers have gained international fame. The major traditional handicraft is weaving silk brocades with gold and silver threadwork. Other handicrafts include wooden toys, glass bangles, ivory work, jewelry, and brass ware.

A contemporary of Thebes and Babylon, Varanasi is probably one of the oldest existing cities in the world. Originally known as Kasi, it was the capital of the kingdom of Kasi during the 6th century BC. It gained prominence as a center of education and artistic activities during the 4th through the 6th century AD. Under Muslim occupation beginning in 1194, Varanasi's prosperity declined, and most of its ancient temples were destroyed. Because of this destruction very few of the shrines left in Varanasi were built earlier than the 18th century. The city was ceded to the British in 1775. In 1910 the British made Varanasi a new Indian state. In 1949, after India's independence, the Varanasi, or Benares state became part of the state of Uttar Pradesh. Population (1981 census), 708,647.

VARGAS, Getúlio (1883–1954). From 1930 to 1954, Getúlio Vargas was the dominant political force in Brazil. Although he seized power through a revolution, he governed well during his first years as president (1930–45). During this period the landholding system was revolutionized, the tax structure revised, and the nation industrialized. During World War II Brazil contributed huge quantities of raw materials to the Allied cause.

Getúlio Dorneles Vargas was born in São Borja, Rio Grande do Sul, Brazil, on April 19, 1883. He entered the army at age 16, and after his military service he attended the University of Pôrto Alegre. After graduation in 1908 he practiced law and worked in state government. In 1922 he was elected to the national legislature. For two years (1926–28) Vargas served as finance minister. Then in 1928 he was elected governor of Rio Grande do Sul.

Vargas used this office unsuccessfully to campaign for the presidency in 1930. Failing to win, he and his followers staged a revolution and took power. In November 1937 he abolished the constitutional government entirely. On Oct. 29, 1945, he was overthrown by a military revolt. Although in semiretirement, Vargas remained popular with the workers and was again elected president in 1950. The overwhelming opposition of the armed forces drove him to suicide on Aug. 24, 1954. He died in Rio de Janeiro.

VARNISH *see* PAINT AND VARNISH.

The dome of Saint Peter's Basilica, designed by Michelangelo, dominates Vatican City and the skyline of Rome. The huge square in front of the basilica was designed by Giovanni Lorenzo Bernini.

VATICAN CITY. The official residence of the Roman Catholic church's pope is Vatican City (Città del Vaticano). It is one of the smallest independent states in the world and lies entirely within the confines of Rome, Italy, on the west, or right, bank of the Tiber River. Here the pope directs the government of his church, which has more than 750 million adherents.

To all intents and purposes Vatican City as the territorial base of the Holy See, or the government of the Roman Catholic church, is a theocracy—that is, a state governed by divine guidance or by people who are believed to be divinely guided. It remains, at the same time, a recognized secular state because it possesses territory, population, and government.

The official name of the papal territory, which has an area of ⅙ square mile (0.4 square kilometer), is the State of Vatican City. More often it is called the Vatican or the Holy See. (*See also* Papacy.)

Within the City Walls

An ancient Roman wall marks the boundaries of Vatican City on all sides except the southeast. Here Saint Peter's Square, designed by Giovanni Lorenzo

This article was contributed by Allan Rodgers, Professor of Geography, Pennsylvania State University, University Park.

Bernini, serves as a stately entrance to the Vatican. Vatican City contains some of the most famous buildings in Christendom. Foremost are St. Peter's Basilica, to which pilgrims have journeyed for centuries, and the Vatican Palace, the home of popes since the 14th century. These two buildings preserve an extraordinary record of history and art—both religious and secular.

St. Peter's Basilica is the largest Christian church in the world and a splendid example of Renaissance architecture. It is built on the site of a 4th-century basilica—dating from the time of Constantine—that is believed to enclose the tomb of St. Peter, the founder of the church. The present structure was consecrated in 1626 after more than a century of building. Notable architects directed the construction. Among them were Donato Bramante, Raphael, and, perhaps most important, Michelangelo (for pictures, *see* Architecture). Michelangelo designed the great dome, which rises more than 400 feet (122 meters) above the floor. It can be seen from all districts of Rome.

Many celebrated Renaissance artists contributed to the rich ornamentation of the interior. Above the high altar, where traditionally the pope alone may celebrate mass, is the well-known baldachin sculpted by Bernini. It is a gleaming bronze canopy 95 feet (29 meters) high with striking twisted pillars. The world-famous sculptor also designed St. Peter's throne behind the high altar and crafted many of the wall decorations and the colored pavement of the floor (for pictures, *see* Bernini; Europe). The statue of St. Peter, by an unknown artist, has been an object of devotion for centuries. It is argued that the kisses of countless pilgrims have worn down one foot of this bronze statue. In one of the many side chapels of St. Peter's is Michelangelo's 'Madonna della Pietà', the only work he is reputed ever to have signed (for picture, *see* Michelangelo).

Vatican Palace. In 1377 Pope Gregory XI began to reside in a house on Vatican Hill. The popes who followed made repeated additions. Thus gradually the house became a palace. Today the Vatican Palace is a collection of buildings of different periods that cover 13½ acres (5.5 hectares) and contain more than 1,400 rooms. Much of the surrounding area consists of formal gardens. Only a small portion, on the southeast side, however, is taken up by the apartments of the pope, the secretary of state, and other officials. The remainder is given over to the vast library and to the many museums that house great art treasures.

The most celebrated section of the palace is the Sistine Chapel with magnificent frescoes by Michelangelo. On the ceiling are nine scenes that depict the story of Genesis from the creation to the flood. On the wall behind the altar is his fresco, 'The Last Judgment', painted from 1533 to 1541. In the late 1980s the frescoes were being restored—among much controversy in artistic circles. The small chamber, which is crowded with tourists every day, is also the scene of the most intimate of Vatican affairs. It is the private chapel of the pope and the meeting place of the conclave of cardinals during the election of a new pope. The second major chapel is called the Pauline. It is the parish church of the Vatican.

The Pinacoteca (Picture Gallery) houses hundreds of paintings by Giotto, Fra Angelico, Leonardo da

PLACES OF INTEREST IN VATICAN CITY

1. Picture Gallery
2. Museums
3. Vatican Gardens
4. Library
5. Belvedere Palace
6. Vatican Radio Offices
7. Academy of Sciences
8. Belvedere Courtyard
9. Post Office
10. Papal Printing Office
11. Church of St. Anne
12. Electric Power Plant
13. Sistine Chapel
14. Papal Apartments
15. Barracks of the Swiss Guard
16. Ethiopian Seminary
17. Government Palace
18. St. Peter's Square
19. Obelisk
20. Radio Station
21. Mosaic Studio
22. St. Peter's Basilica
23. Sacristy
24. Museum of St. Peter
25. Railway Station
26. Square of St. Martha
27. Palace of the Holy Office

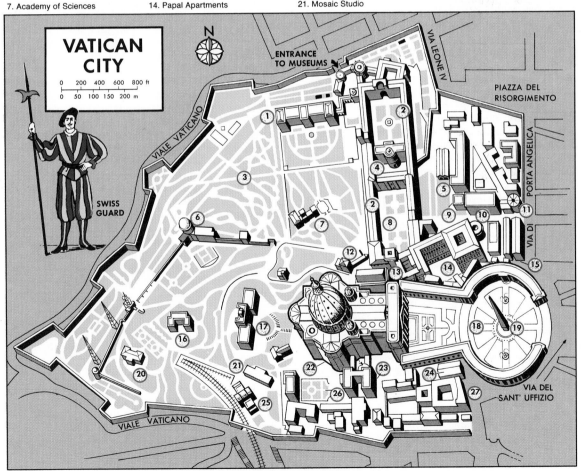

© Robert Frerck—Odyssey Productions

The Vatican Library, a work of art in itself, contains some of the most valuable ancient manuscripts in the world.

Vinci, Titian, Sandro Botticelli, Perugino, Pinturic-chio, Correggio, Guido Reni, and other masters. The collection of classical sculpture, one of the foremost in the world, is displayed in the museums east of the library—the Chiaramonti and the Pio-Clementino. Masterful frescoes and remarkable paintings are found on the walls of the Borgia Apartments and the Raphael Rooms.

The Vatican museums also contain records of great historical value. Large collections of relics are displayed from Egyptian, Etruscan, and Roman times and from early Christian days. The immense archives contain records of the Holy See dating back to the 13th century. Equally important to scholars is the collection of manuscripts and early printed books in the library, one of the great libraries of the world. There is also a major geographic chart collection. Other buildings include the Propaganda, Cancelleria, Dateria, and Vicareate.

Service facilities. Within the city walls all normal public services are maintained. These include a telephone and telegraph system, a 900-foot (274-meter) railway that connects with the main Italian line, electric power and water services from Rome supplemented by a local water supply, and a small electric power plant. The city has a post office that issues its own stamps and a bank that issues currency as well as Vatican automobile license plates. Its flag is yellow and white with the papal coat of arms on the white stripe. (For picture, *see* Flags of the World.) The Vatican has its own elementary school, a pharmacy, a medical staff and infirmary, a mosaic factory, and a printing plant. This facility prints a vast array of literature produced by the papacy. Other structures include an astronomical observatory.

The Vatican radio station HVJ each week broadcasts some 400 programs in more than 30 languages. There are daily news bulletins in seven languages. The first radio station began operation in 1931. It has since been enlarged, and in 1957 powerful trans-mitters were built northwest of Rome. Besides papal messages and addresses, the station broadcasts news, general information, and cultural programs.

The Vatican newspaper, *L'Osservatore Romano* (The Roman Observer), also has a worldwide audience. It is published daily by the Vatican Publishing House. This division of the Vatican press also publishes liturgical and juridical works of the Holy See and Roman Curia as well as works pertaining to the government of the state. In addition it publishes the official bulletin, 'Acta Apostolicae Sedis' (Acts of the Apostolic See), and the papal yearbook and directory, 'Annuario Pontificio'.

Government

Vatican City is an absolute monarchy, with the pope as sovereign. Upon his election as supreme pontiff of the Roman Catholic church, he assumes complete civil and political authority in the state. The pope, however, does not personally carry out the functions of a temporal sovereign. He delegates his temporal governing power to the Pontifical Commission for Vatican City, confining himself to the spiritual leadership of the church.

Citizenship in Vatican City is regulated by the terms of the Lateran Treaty of 1929. It is given to all persons and their families whose offices require that they live in the territory. It is ended when their office or residence is terminated. Vatican citizenship does not necessarily preclude citizenship in other countries but may suspend such citizenship temporarily. It is never acquired by birth but is always voluntary.

Although the population of Vatican City is about 700, the number of citizens is actually somewhat greater. Certain prelates and Vatican diplomats reside outside the city. The great majority of the population are Italians, and Italian is the official language. Latin is used in official documents. Clergymen, lay people, and the Vatican military are included in the population. The military consists of the Swiss Guard, which protects the person of the pope.

Neutrality. Vatican City is pledged by the Lateran Treaty to permanent neutrality in international relations. It is bound not to wage war or to enter alliances that might lead to war. Unless a direct appeal is made to the Vatican, it may not take part in international attempts to settle disputes among nations.

Diplomatic relations. The right of the Holy See to send and receive diplomats is recognized in the Lateran Treaty. It guarantees the Vatican full communication with other governments—even those at war with Italy. Complications arose over this guarantee during World War II. While Italy remained an active opponent of the Allies, Vatican envoys from Western countries moved to cramped quarters within Vatican City. When Rome was occupied in 1944 by the Allies, envoys from the Axis powers in turn moved to the neutral Vatican territory.

In the diplomatic relations that the pope maintains with some 50 governments, his representative is a papal nuncio. This Vatican diplomat has the rank of full ambassador and traditionally is dean of the diplomatic corps in the country where he serves. A papal representative without diplomatic status is the apostolic delegate. He serves as an intermediary between the Vatican and Roman Catholics of the country to which he is assigned.

History

The Vatican was established as the state of the pope by the Lateran Treaty and the Concordat of Feb. 11, 1929—an agreement between the Holy See and the Italian government. In 1870 the former Papal States, which had existed since the 8th century, were dissolved. By the 19th century these papal territories extended through central Italy and covered 17,000 square miles (44,000 square kilometers). These states included Rome, which was the seat of papal power from the time the popes returned from Avignon, France, in 1377.

To protest their incorporation into a unified Italy, each pope thereafter remained a "voluntary prisoner of the Vatican," never leaving the small papal grounds. This situation lasted nearly 60 years. Finally the Fascist government of Italy under Benito Mussolini began negotiations with the Holy See. The outcome of these sessions was the Lateran Treaty and the Concordat. (*See also* Italy, "History.")

The treaty established a territory of 109 acres (44 hectares) on Vatican Hill as an independent state with the pope as absolute sovereign. In doing so it recognized that complete freedom from all secular political authority was vital to the papacy. The treaty guarantees that the boundaries of the Vatican state are fixed and unchangeable.

Outside Vatican City the popes also have jurisdiction over certain areas where the church functions or has historic interests. These extraterritorial areas include the buildings that house the pontifical ministries; certain key historical churches—the basilica of St. John Lateran, Santa Maria Maggiore and St. Paul Outside the Walls; the Catacombs; and Castel Gondolfo, the summer residence of popes since the 17th century located about 6 miles (10 kilometers) southeast of Rome.

On June 10, 1946, Italy adopted a republican form of government. Its new constitution, adopted in December 1947, provided for the continuance of the Lateran Treaty and the Concordat, which had worked well since their inception in 1929. The Concordat, which established Roman Catholicism as the official religion of Italy, was revoked in 1985.

BIBLIOGRAPHY FOR VATICAN CITY

Fellucci, Mario. The Masterpieces of the Vatican (Amer. Classical College Press, 1975).
Hebblethwaite, Peter. In the Vatican (Adler and Adler, 1986)
Heuzinger, Lutz and Mancinelli, Fabrizio. The Sistine Chapel (Scala, 1984).
Lo Bello, Nino. Nino Lo Bello's Guide to the Vatican (Chicago Review, 1987).
Packard, J.M. Peter's Kingdom: Inside the Papal City (Scribner, 1985).
Walsh, M.J. Vatican City State (ABC-Clio, 1983).

VATICAN COUNCILS. Ecumenical councils are meetings of the leaders of the whole Christian church (*see* Church Councils). The Roman Catholic church recognizes 21 such councils, the first being the Council of Nicaea, which met in 325. The 20th and 21st such gatherings were the First and Second Vatican Councils, so called because they assembled in Saint Peter's Basilica in Vatican City.

Vatican I, convened by Pope Pius IX, was a reaction against the modern world—that is, the emergence of popular democracy, the materialism spawned by the Industrial Revolution, and all the ferment of new ideas in the 19th century. Vatican II, convened by Pope John XXIII, was an earnest attempt to deal with the 20th-century world at a time when religious faith no longer had a commanding place in society, when developing countries were in the throes of revolution, and when the church itself appeared to be out of touch with the lives of the faithful.

Pius IX's goal was to reassert the authority of the church in the strongest possible terms and to build defenses against the outside world. His Vatican Council took place during the decade of the struggle for reunification of Italy, and the survival of Vatican City itself was in question. Approximately 1,050 bishops and other leaders were eligible to attend, but only about 700 were at the official opening on Dec. 8, 1869. Altogether, 774 took part in deliberations. Four working sessions were held up to July 18, 1870. On Oct. 20, 1870, the pope suspended the council indefinitely because Rome had been occupied by troops intent on making the city the capital of a united Italy.

On April 24, 1870, Vatican I approved a decree on the relation between faith and reason. The issue that dominated the council, however, was the authority of the pope in the church. In spite of some objections, the dogma of papal infallibility was adopted on July 18 in a decree entitled 'Pastor Aeternus' (Eternal Shepherd). It declared that the pope has supreme authority over the whole church and that in his pronouncements on faith and morals he cannot be in error.

Sessions of Vatican II were held in four successive autumns from 1962 to 1965. The opening session was on Oct. 11, 1962, and the adjournment was on Dec. 8, 1965. Of the 2,908 churchmen eligible to attend, 2,540 took part in the first public session. In addition, there were nonvoting observers from all the major Protestant and Eastern Orthodox denominations. Altogether, the council enacted 16 texts. Of these the most significant were on the nature of the church and revelation, the revision of the liturgy, the work of the clergy, the role of lay people, and the role of the church in the world today. The most immediate result of Vatican II was the revision of the liturgy, which included changing the language of the liturgy from Latin to the languages of the people. Another prominent outcome was increased openness to other religions and denominations and cooperation with them.

VAUDEVILLE *see* PERFORMING ARTS.

VAUGHAN WILLIAMS, Ralph (1872–1958).
The dominant English composer of the early 20th century was Ralph Vaughan Williams. He broke the ties with continental Europe that for two centuries—notably through Handel and Mendelssohn—had made Britain virtually a musical province of Germany.

Vaughan Williams was born on Oct. 12, 1872, in Down Ampney, Gloucestershire, England, the son of a clergyman. He was educated at Trinity College in Cambridge University and the Royal College of Music in London. After receiving his doctorate from Cambridge in 1901, he became organist of Saint Barnabas' Church in London.

From 1904 to 1906 he was editor of 'The English Hymnal', for which he wrote his celebrated tune 'Sine Nomine' for the hymn 'For All the Saints'. His first major composition was the cantata 'Toward the Unknown Region' (1905). He had begun to collect folk songs about 1903, and between 1905 and 1906 he wrote three 'Norfolk Rhapsodies' based on melodies from that region. He began work on 'A Sea Symphony' for voices and orchestra. Dissatisfied with the music he had written, he went to Paris in 1909 to work with Maurice Ravel, even though he was three years older than his teacher. The following year Vaughan Williams completed his first significant composition, the popular 'Fantasia on a Theme by Thomas Tallis' for strings. This was followed by his second symphony, 'A London Symphony' (1914, later rewritten).

After artillery service in World War I, Vaughan Williams became professor of composition at the Royal College of Music and conductor of London's Bach Choir. He continued to compose until his death in London on Aug. 26, 1958. He wrote cantatas, including 'Dona Nobis Pacem' and 'Hodie'; 'Mass in G Minor' and 'Te Deum in G Major' for double chorus; and the frequently performed motet 'O Clap Your Hands'. Other works include nine symphonies, songs, chamber music, ballets, and operas—'The Pilgrim's Progress' and 'Hugh the Drover' are the best known.

VEBLEN, Thorstein (1857–1929).
The American economist and social critic Thorstein Veblen, in his popular book 'The Theory of the Leisure Class', used Charles Darwin's theory of evolution to analyze the modern industrial system. He claimed that industry demands diligence, efficiency, and cooperation among businessmen. What he saw instead were companies run by selfish predators interested in making money and displaying their wealth in what he termed "conspicuous consumption." Veblen's other books include 'The Theory of Business Enterprise' (1904), 'The Instinct of Workmanship and the State of the Industrial Arts' (1914), and 'Imperial Germany and the Industrial Revolution' (1915).

Thorstein Bunde Veblen was born to Norwegian immigrant parents in Manitowoc County, Wis., on July 30, 1857, and was brought up in rural Minnesota. He graduated from Carleton College in 1880 and did graduate work at Johns Hopkins and Yale universities before earning his doctorate at the latter in 1884. Unable to find a teaching position, he returned home, where he engaged in farm work and reading for seven years. He was finally accepted as a teacher at the University of Chicago, where he taught political economy until 1906.

From Chicago Veblen moved to Stanford University, then to Missouri. He worked for the Food Administration in Washington, D.C., during World War I. After the war he was a contributor to *Dial* magazine and a lecturer at the New School for Social Research in New York City. Veblen gave up teaching in 1926 and returned to California. He died in his cabin near Menlo Park on Aug. 3, 1929.

VEGA, Lope de (1562–1635).
In the golden age of Spanish literature the playwright and poet Lope de Vega was one of his country's brightest lights and its truest representative. He is credited with an enormous output of drama and lyric poetry. An early biographer claims that Lope wrote a total of 1,800 plays, but titles are known for only 723 dramas and 44 religious works. Lope's compositions in lyric poetry total 1,587, and texts survive of 468 plays. He developed the dramatic form called *comedia*—not comedy in the modern sense but a dramatic blend of tragedy and comedy.

Lope Félix de Vega was born on Nov. 25, 1562, in Madrid. He studied under the poet Vicente Espinel and attended the Theatine College in Madrid. Lope was pressured to study for the priesthood at Alaclá de Henares, but he soon left and spent about two years at the University of Salamanca (1580–82). In 1583 he participated in a Spanish expedition against the Azores, and for the next four years he worked for the marqués de Las Navas.

Apart from his writing, most of Lope's adult life was spent in a series of tempestuous and scandalous love affairs. In 1588 he was banished from Madrid for libeling his mistress. He then abducted the daughter of the king's herald, married her, and sailed off on the Armada to invade England (*see* Armada). Afterward he spent 18 months in Valencia, where he was profoundly influenced by the dramatist Cristóbal de Virués. It was then that Lope began writing for a living. He worked successively for the duke of Alba, the marqués de Sarría, and finally—from 1635 until his death—he enjoyed the patronage of the duke of Sessa.

Meanwhile Lope's wife had died in 1595, and he remarried in 1598. This wife died in 1613, and Lope underwent a brief religious crisis that prompted him to become a priest. Nevertheless, he was soon involved in new scandalous relationships. His last affair lasted from 1619 until the woman's death in 1632. Further saddened by the deaths of most of his children and the abduction of his youngest daughter, Lope died on Aug. 27, 1635, in Madrid.

Apart from short religious plays, Lope's dramas were of two types: heroic dramas based on national legends, or stories and comedies of intrigue and manners. His best-known drama outside Spain is 'All Citizens Are Soldiers'.

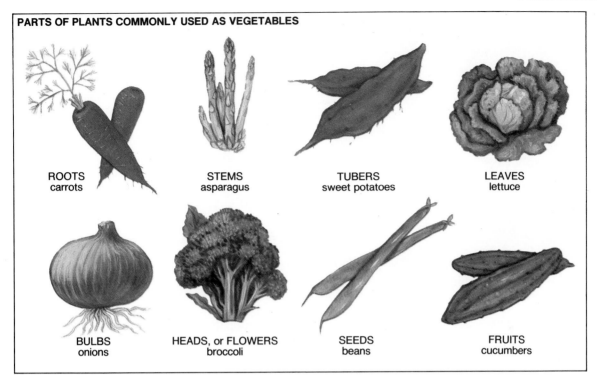

PARTS OF PLANTS COMMONLY USED AS VEGETABLES

ROOTS
carrots

STEMS
asparagus

TUBERS
sweet potatoes

LEAVES
lettuce

BULBS
onions

HEADS, or FLOWERS
broccoli

SEEDS
beans

FRUITS
cucumbers

VEGETABLES. In about 10,000 to 5000 BC, the first farmers prepared the earth for planting, and since then cultivated vegetables have been a major part of the human diet. Vegetables may someday be grown in space stations and taken on extraterrestrial voyages.

Vegetables are eaten fresh or are prepared in a number of ways. They are good sources of vitamins, particularly vitamins A and C, and of minerals, especially calcium and iron (*see* Food and Nutrition). In addition to their primary value as food crops for people, vegetables have a variety of uses both in their natural form and as processed products. They provide feed for cattle, sheep, pigs, and poultry. Vegetable oils are widely used in cooking. Refined vegetables provide sugar and starch, which are added to other food products. Nonnutritive food coloring and additives, alcoholic beverages, and fibers are also made from some vegetables.

Some of the most popular garden vegetables in the Western world are corn, potatoes (white and sweet), beans, peas, tomatoes, carrots, onions, lettuce, and cabbage. Others include melons, cucumbers, asparagus, turnips, spinach, broccoli, brussels sprouts, beets, rutabagas, eggplants, squashes, and garlic.

In the broadest sense, any kind of plant is "vegetable matter." In common, narrow usage, however, the term vegetables usually refers to the fresh, ed-

This article was contributed by Roy E. Cameron, Ph.D. in Plant Science and member of the United States Department of Agriculture National Agriculture Research and Extension Users Advisory Board.

ible parts of herbaceous plants. Herbaceous plants are distinguished from other plants by stems that are generally softer and less fibrous than the woody stems of trees, shrubs, and bushes (*see* Plant).

In horticulture, the branch of agriculture concerned with growing fruits and vegetables, fruits are the edible parts of plants that contain the plants' seeds, whereas vegetables are considered to be edible roots, tubers, stems, leaves, fruits, seeds, flower clusters, and other softer plant parts. In common usage, however, there is no exact distinction between a vegetable and a fruit. A tomato, for example, is a fruit because it is fleshy and contains seeds, but it is commonly eaten as a vegetable. Similar fruits that contain seeds surrounded by pulp, but that are eaten as vegetables, include cucumbers, peppers, eggplants, okra, melons, and squashes. The classification of plants and plant parts as vegetables is largely determined by custom, culture, and usage.

Kinds of Vegetables

In strict scientific circles, vegetables, like any other plant, are grouped according to their botanical characteristics and are identified by their Latin binomial names (that is, genus and species) and horticultural variety, if applicable (for example, the mustard green *Brassica juncea* variety *crispifolia*). The variety may also include strains, such as a pest-resistant strain.

More loosely, vegetables are classified according to the particular edible part that is harvested for food. According to this scheme there are root vegetables; stem vegetables; tubers, or underground stems; leaf and leafstalk vegetables; bulb vegetables; and head,

Celery is harvested by machinery near Belle Glade, Fla.

Frederick Myers—CLICK/Chicago

or flower, vegetables. Scientists are working on developing plants, such as the winged bean, in which all the parts can be eaten.

Root vegetables include such plants as beets, carrots, parsnips, radishes, and turnips. These plants have a round or elongated fleshy root that ends in a thin "tail"; above ground they are topped by thick or lacy leaves. Roots taste best when picked while young and tender; they get fibrous, pithy, and bitter with age.

Beets (*Beta vulgaris*) are characterized by a large, globe-shaped red root, with red stalks that continue above ground and form veins through the large green leaves. Originally only the leaves of the beet were eaten; beet root was first mentioned as a food in Germany in 1550. Beets are most extensively grown in temperate to cool regions.

Carrots (*Daucus carota*) are long, smooth, straight, orange roots topped by fernlike, bright green foliage. The wild carrot is called Queen Anne's lace (*see* Queen Anne's Lace). Carrots were cultivated in the Mediterranean region before the Christian Era and in China and northwestern Europe by the 13th century. Today carrots are grown extensively throughout the temperate zones of the world.

Parsnips (*Pastinaca sativa*) were common in Europe by the 16th century and were brought to North America by the early colonists. They look like carrots but are pale in color and have a sweeter flavor. Only garden-grown parsnips should be eaten; in the wild it is difficult to distinguish parsnips from the poisonous water hemlock. Parsnips grow on roadsides and in open places in Great Britain and throughout Europe and temperate Asia.

The radish (*Raphanus sativus*) has a crisp white, red, purple, or black root. There are two basic varieties: a quick-growing small plant and a large, winter plant with a more hearty flavor. The common radish is probably of Oriental origin.

The turnip (*Brassica rapa*) has a large, purple and white globular root and young, tender leaves that can be eaten. The turnip probably originated in middle and eastern Asia and by cultivation has spread throughout the Temperate Zone. Swedish turnips, or rutabagas (*B. napobrassica*), resemble turnips but have white or yellow flesh and smooth, waxy leaves, while turnips are white, with leaves that grow rough and hairy when older. The rutabaga was developed during the Middle Ages from a cross between turnips and cabbage. The plant is extensively cultivated in Canada, Great Britain, and Northern Europe, and to a lesser extent in the United States.

Horseradish (*Armoracia lapathifolia*) is a plant with large, glossy-green leaves. The fleshy root is so hot to the taste buds that it is peeled, grated, and used only in small quantities to flavor other foods. It is native to Mediterranean lands and is grown throughout the Temperate Zone.

Stem vegetables. In some plants, such as asparagus and kohlrabi, only the aboveground stems are used as food. Garden asparagus (*Asparagus officinalis*) is cultivated for its succulent stalks. They are long, straight, and green, with arrowhead-shaped bud clusters on top. Garden asparagus is cultivated in most temperate and subtropical parts of the world, particularly in France, Italy, and the United States.

Kohlrabi (*Brassica oleracea*) looks like a green turnip. Its most distinctive feature is its swollen globular base—actually the plant's greatly enlarged stem just above the soil. The flesh of the stem resembles that of the turnip but is sweeter and milder. The young tender leaves are sometimes eaten as greens. Kohlrabi was first described in the 16th century and is of European origin. It is not widely grown commercially.

Tubers. Plants with tubers, or underground stems, produce blossoms above ground. Each bud on the knobby, edible, underground portions of the plant is capable of producing a new plant. Tubers include potatoes, Jerusalem artichokes, and taro.

Both the white potato (*Solanum tuberosum*) and the sweet potato (*Ipomoea batatas*) are native to South America. They were introduced into Europe during the 16th century, and their cultivation spread to Africa, Asia, China, and then to the United States. The white potato is one of the main food crops of the world. (*See also* Potato; Sweet Potato.)

The tubers of the Jerusalem artichoke (*Helianthus tuberosus*) are thin-skinned with white, crisp flesh. The plant originated in eastern North America and its cultivation spread to Europe. The plant may have gotten its unusual name because its original name, girasole, sounded like "Jerusalem."

Taro (*Colocasia esculenta*) has become a staple crop cultivated primarily for its large, starchy, spherical tubers, though the leaves are also eaten. Taro leaves and tubers are poisonous if eaten raw; the poison they contain must first be destroyed by heating. Taro is probably native to southeastern Asia and spread from there to the Pacific islands.

Leaf and leafstalk vegetables. Depending on the variety, leafy vegetable plants may have loose, separate leaves or leaves that are tightly or loosely folded over each other, forming round "heads." The entire plant may be dug from the ground, or individual leaves or stalks may be cut off and used. Leaf and leafstalk vegetables include lettuce, chard, watercress, and cabbage.

Lettuce (*Lactuca sativa*) was cultivated more than 2,500 years ago. In their shape lettuce leaves may be frilly, crinkled, or lobed; their color may be light or dark green or bronze; and their flavor varies with the variety (*see* Lettuce).

Chard (*Beta vulgaris* variety *cicla*) is a very early form of the beet in which the leaves and leafstalks, instead of the roots, have become greatly developed. Watercress (*Nasturtium officinale*) is a hardy aquatic plant that has been grown in Europe as a source of both food and medicine for about 2,000 years. It is native to Eurasia and naturalized throughout North America.

The leaves of endive (*Cichorium endiva*) develop a bitter taste if they are allowed to grow naturally in the light. Endive is believed to have originated in Egypt and Indonesia and has been cultivated in Europe since the 16th century.

Celery (*Apium graveolens*) is most often grown for its tall, fleshy, green or yellow leafstalks, but its leaves can also be eaten. Native to the Mediterranean areas and the Middle East, celery was used as a flavoring by the ancient Greeks and Romans and as a medicine by the ancient Chinese.

The bright red or green leafstalks of the rhubarb plant (*Rheum rhaponticum*) are fleshy and tart. Rhubarb is generally cultivated only for its leafstalks; its dark green leaves are poisonous. However, they are cooked and eaten in certain parts of the world. The plant originated in Asia and is best adapted to cooler parts of the Temperate Zone (*see* Rhubarb).

The cabbage plant has many forms. The varieties cultivated as leaf vegetables include brussels sprouts, collards, kale, savoy cabbage, and the tightly folded, firm, green head of the most widely known variety, common cabbage (*Brassica oleracea* variety *capitata*). These various forms are said to have been developed by long cultivation from the wild, or sea, cabbage found near the seacoast in various parts of England and continental Europe (*see* Cabbage).

Bulb vegetables have relatively large, usually globe-shaped, underground buds, or bulbs, with overlapping leaves arising from a short stem. Common bulb vegetables include onions and garlic.

The many types of tart, pungent bulbs known as onions (*Allium cepa*) are among the world's oldest cultivated plants. They were probably known in India, China, and the Middle East before recorded history. American Indians and early American settlers ate the wild onions growing in the prairies. The green onion tops grow best in cool weather; the underground yellow, white, or red bulbs grow in warm weather. When the bulbs are ripe, the tops lose their color and fall over. (*See also* Onion.)

A relative of the onion, garlic (*A. sativum*), is used as a seasoning in many national cuisines. The membranous skin of the bulb contains about ten—and sometimes as many as 20—small, edible bulblets called cloves. Garlic is native to Asia and also grows wild in Italy and southern France (*see* Garlic).

Head, or flower, vegetables, such as broccoli, cauliflower, and artichokes, are grown for their flower heads or buds. Broccoli (*Brassica oleracea*, italica group) bears dense green clusters of flower buds. Broccoli is native to the eastern Mediterranean and Asia Minor and is cultivated in Italy, England, and the United States. In cauliflower (*B. oleracea*, botrytis group), the edible buds form a large head that may be white, green, or purple. (*See also* Cabbage.)

Artichokes (*Cynara scolymus*) are primarily cultivated for the immature flower heads (the fleshy parts

A group of Illinois farmers and seed retailers tour fields to examine varieties of experimental corn.

© Steve Leonard—CLICK/Chicago

287

are considered a delicacy), though the leaves may also be eaten. The plant is native to the western and central Mediterranean. In ancient times, the young leaves rather than the flower heads were eaten. The modern, edible-flower form was first recorded in Italy about 1400. Today it is extensively cultivated in the United States (particularly in California), France, Belgium, the Mediterranean countries, and other regions with rich soil and a mild, humid climate.

Vegetable Farming

Modern vegetable farming ranges from small-scale, low-technology production and local sale to vast commercial operations utilizing the latest advances in automation and technology. Vegetable production includes all the operations required for planting; growing; weed, pest, and disease management; harvesting; storage; and marketing.

Planting and general care. The time of planting depends on the crop. The large majority of vegetables are planted by seeding in the fields, but occasionally they are germinated in a nursery or greenhouse and transplanted as seedlings to the field.

During the growing season herbicides, pesticides, and fungicides are commonly used to inhibit damage by weeds, insects, and diseases, respectively. In the continental United States, growing seasons vary in length from about 75 days or less to 200 days and may begin in late March. Farmers select their vegetable crops according to the plants' temperature tolerance. It is essential to know whether the vegetable is hardy and can withstand extreme temperatures, or if it is tender and can only survive within a limited temperature range.

Cool-season crops are those adapted to temperature ranges of approximately 55° to 70° F (13° to 21° C) and may include plants that can tolerate some frost at maturity. Those that can tolerate frost include cabbages, turnips, parsnips, beets, onions, leeks, asparagus, chard, celery, and spinach. Those that are damaged by frost include lettuces, endive, white potatoes, peas, cauliflower, carrots, and artichokes.

Warm-season crops are those that are readily damaged by frost. Crops grown in temperatures between about 65° and 80° F (18° and 27° C) include squash, cucumbers, pumpkins, tomatoes, peppers, and sweet corn. Plants requiring longer growing seasons and temperatures above about 70° F include such sensitive plants as eggplant, okra, and sweet potatoes.

Harvesting and marketing. Harvesting operations are usually mechanized in developed nations, but the practice of harvesting by hand is still employed in some areas or is used in conjunction with machine operations. After harvesting the vegetables, the farmer may store them. Storage may require both large bins and silos as well as refrigerated facilities.

The length of time between harvest and transport to market and the handling and storage conditions are critical factors in vegetable marketability. Vegetables have a high water content—80 to 90 percent—and perish quickly if they are not maintained at the proper temperature and relative humidity. Some crops, such as white potatoes, sweet potatoes, onions, beets, turnips, parsnips, and carrots, may be stored at temperatures between about 45° and 55° F (7° and 13° C) for weeks or months. Others, such as many leaf and stem vegetables, will not last longer than a few weeks under even the best storage conditions. Storage temperature and length of storage also affect the speed with which certain natural chemical changes occur in plants—the conversion of sugar to starch in corn, for example.

Before vegetables are marketed, they are put through such processes as washing, trimming, waxing, grading, and packaging. Vegetables such as beets, carrots, celery, lettuce, radishes, spinach, and turnips are trimmed before washing to remove discolored leaves or to cut back the green tops. Some vegetables, including cucumbers, peppers, and tomatoes are waxed to give them a bright appearance and to control shriveling due to moisture loss. The vegetables are graded, packaged, and sold through various retail and wholesale markets. (See also Agriculture; Farming.)

World production. The leading producer of the world's vegetable crop is China, followed by India and the Soviet Union. Other major producers are the United States, Italy, and Spain. Leading vegetable-producing states in the United States include California (particularly the Imperial, San Joaquin, and Salinas valleys), Illinois, Iowa, Minnesota, Missouri, Arizona (in the Salt River valley), Texas (along the Rio Grande), and southern Florida.

NUTRITIONAL VALUE OF SELECTED VEGETABLES

Vegetable*	Vitamin A (international units)	Vitamin C (milligrams)	Calories
Asparagus	900	26	20
Beets	20	6	32
Broccoli	2,500	90	26
Brussels sprouts	520	87	36
Cabbage	130	33	20
Carrots	10,500	6	31
Cauliflower	60	55	22
Celery	240	9	17
Cucumbers	250	11	15
Eggplant	10	3	19
Green beans	540	12	25
Green peppers	420	128	22
Lettuce (head)	330	6	13
Lettuce (leaf)	1,900	18	18
Mustard greens	5,800	48	23
Okra	490	20	29
Onions	40	10	38
Peas (garden)	540	20	71
Radishes (raw)	322	26	17
Scallions	2,000	32	36
Spinach	8,100	28	23
Sweet corn (yellow)	400	9	91
Sweet potatoes	8,100	22	141
Tomatoes	1,000	24	26

*Figures are for 100-gram (about ½-cup) samples of cooked vegetables, unless normally eaten raw.
Source: 'Gardening for Food and Fun' (U.S. Dept. of Agriculture, 1977).

VEGETARIANISM.

VEGETARIANISM. The practice of vegetarianism involves eating vegetable products and eliminating meat, fish, and, in many instances, eggs and dairy products from the diet for ethical, religious, or nutritional reasons. Some vegetarians trace the term to the Latin *vegetus,* meaning "active, vigorous." Vegetarianism traditionally has been associated with the philosophy of living a more peaceful life in harmony with natural laws and principles. Some aspects of the vegetarian diet currently are regarded as healthy alternatives to the modern diet consumed in many Western countries, which is high in animal fat and low in vegetable fiber.

In general, a vegetarian diet consists of vegetables, fruits, grains, nuts, and seeds. Strict vegetarians, known as vegans, avoid all foods from the animal kingdom, including eggs and dairy products. Less strict vegetarians who consume milk and milk products are known as lactovegetarians, while those who include eggs in their diet are called ovovegetarians. Some consider themselves to be vegetarians if they eliminate only red meat from their diets. Vegetarians tend to prefer food in its most natural state, opposing the use of chemicals in growing or harvesting food and avoiding processed or canned foods.

Vegetarianism probably was first practiced in connection with religious purification rituals. The idea of a fleshless diet for normal use arose in India and eastern Mediterranean lands around the 1st millennium BC. From Plato onward, many Greek and Roman philosophers and writers advocated vegetarianism as part of an ethical way of life. Hindu and Buddhist sects also considered all animal life sacred and taught that human beings should avoid harming animals.

Some Jewish and Christian groups followed the principles of vegetarianism and considered eating flesh gluttonous, cruel, and wasteful. In the Roman Catholic church, Trappist monks have practiced vegetarianism since 1666. Among Protestants, the Seventh-day Adventists observe strict vegetarian guidelines. Although Muslims in general do not advocate fleshless diets, some Sufi mystics (who are among the chief guides of Muslim spiritual life) recommend a vegetarian diet for spiritual seekers. In the 19th century, members of the Bible Christian sect established the first vegetarian groups in England and in the United States. In 1847 the Vegetarian Society was founded, and in 1908 the International Vegetarian Union held the first of its regular meetings.

In nutritional terms, the vegetarian diet has been recognized as having some value in reducing the risk of heart disease, certain types of cancers, and other diet-related ailments. Single vegetable products generally lack the essential amino acids found in animal products, but these amino acids can be included in a vegetarian diet by combining foods, such as beans and rice, that provide complementary amino acids (*see* Food and Nutrition; Malnutrition). Care must be exercised in a strict vegetarian diet to make sure that there is sufficient vitamin B_{12} (*see* Vitamins). Those who practice vegetarianism also claim that it is less costly to grow vegetable crops than it is to raise animals to feed a population. They maintain that converting grazing land to cropland could make more food available to the world.

VELASQUEZ, Diego (1599–1660). Spain's greatest painter was also one of the supreme artists of all time. A master of technique, highly individual in style, Diego Velasquez may have had a greater influence on European art than any other painter.

Diego Rodriguez de Silva Velasquez was born in Seville, Spain, presumably shortly before his baptism on June 6, 1599. His father was of noble Portuguese descent. In his teens he studied art with Francisco Pacheco, whose daughter he married. The young Velasquez once declared, "I would rather be the first painter of common things than second in higher art." He learned much from studying nature. After his marriage at the age of 19, Velasquez went to Madrid. When he was 24 he painted a portrait of Philip IV, who became his patron.

The artist made two visits to Italy. On his first, in 1629, he copied masterpieces in Venice and Rome. He returned to Italy 20 years later and bought many paintings—by Titian, Tintoretto, and Paolo Veronese—and statuary for the king's collection.

Except for these journeys Velasquez lived in Madrid as court painter. His paintings include landscapes, mythological and religious subjects, and scenes from common life, called genre pictures. Most of them, however, are portraits of court notables that rank with the portraits painted by Titian and Anthony Van Dyck.

Duties of Velasquez' royal offices also occupied his time. He was eventually made marshal of the royal household, and as such he was responsible for the royal quarters and for planning ceremonies.

A portrait in oil of Pope Innocent X was painted by Diego Velasquez in 1649. It measures 120 centimeters by 140 centimeters.

In 1660 Velasquez had charge of his last and greatest ceremony—the wedding of the Infanta Maria Theresa to Louis XIV of France. This was a most elaborate affair. Worn out from these labors, Velasquez contracted a fever from which he died on August 6.

Velasquez was a modest, sincere, kindly genius who has been called "the noblest and most commanding man among the artists of his country." He was a master realist, and no painter has surpassed him in the ability to seize essential features and fix them on canvas with a few broad, sure strokes. "His men and women seem to breathe," it has been said; "his horses are full of action and his dogs of life."

Because of Velasquez' great skill in merging color, light, space, rhythm of line, and mass in such a way that all have equal value in a balanced composition, he has been called "the painter's painter." Since the day he befriended and taught the young Bartolomé Murillo, Velasquez has directly or indirectly led painters to make original, even revolutionary, contributions to the development of art. Among those who have been noticeably influenced by him are Francisco de Goya, Camille Corot, Gustave Courbet, Édouard Manet, and James McNeill Whistler.

Velasquez' famous paintings include 'The Surrender of Breda', an equestrian portrait of Philip IV, 'The Spinners', 'The Maids of Honor' (*see* Painting), 'Pope Innocent X', 'Christ at Emmaus', and a portrait of the Infanta Maria Theresa (*see* Dress).

VENDA. Located in the southern part of Africa, Venda covers an area of 2,448 square miles (6,340 square kilometers). It consists of an enclave within Transvaal, inside South Africa, just south of Zimbabwe. Venda shares a boundary to the southeast with the non-independent black state of Gazankulu, South Africa. The Limpopo River flows just to the north of and parallel to the northern border of Venda. Kruger National Park borders Venda on the northeast.

Venda has few natural resources and no large towns. The grazing of livestock is the major livelihood. Crops include corn (maize), peanuts (groundnuts), beans, peas, sorghum, wheat, fruits, and vegetables. There are large supplies of stone for construction. Small-scale industries include carpentry, leather working, welding, upholstering, sawmilling, and clothing manufacturing. Most citizens work outside Venda as migrant contract workers in the Republic of South Africa, Venda's major trade partner.

In 1962 South Africa made Venda a homeland for the Venda-speaking people, and a territorial authority was established. The territory was granted partial self-government in 1973. On Sept. 13, 1979, South Africa declared Venda an independent republic and Thohoyandou became the capital—replacing the former capital at Sibasa. Construction of the capital city began in 1979. It is expected eventually to accommodate about 125,000 people. Among the member states of the United Nations, Venda is recognized as an independent republic only by South Africa. Population (1987 estimate), 516,000.

VENDING MACHINE. In schools, factories, office buildings, and other public places, food and beverages are often provided in vending machines. The word vending comes from the Latin verb *vendere,* meaning "to sell."

Vending machines are operated by coin. Older machines required exact change, but today most accept different-sized coins and are able to make change. Some have electronic components that provide a digital display of the amount of money required and change owed. The machines verify coins by weight, size, or magnetic properties. Some machines also accept paper money.

Modern vending machines dispense a large variety of food products—including sandwiches, desserts, snacks, soft drinks, candy bars, chewing gum, milk, coffee, tea, and soups. There are also vending machines that sell cigarettes, toiletries, and other items. Some vending machines have refrigeration units to keep products cold, while others are able to heat liquids. Microprocessors and controllers are revolutionizing vending machines, enabling them to take their own inventories and to detect mechanical problems. This information is relayed to a master computer at the vending company.

Vending machines are usually owned by the vending companies, which distribute them to other firms. The vending companies keep the machines filled and provide maintenance and service. There is usually little or no charge to the establishment where the machines are located.

According to the ancient mathematician Hero of Alexandria, Egyptian temples in about 215 BC had devices from which one could get a squirt of holy water for a few small coins. Today's vending machines, however, have their origins in coin-operated dispensers of tobacco and snuff in 18th-century England. These were called honor boxes, because when a coin was inserted the top opened, laying bare the supply. Customers were on their honor to take their entitled amount and then close the lid so that the next person could pay.

Vending machines more similar to those in use today made their first appearance in the United States in 1888. They were installed on elevated train platforms in New York City to sell chewing gum. The machines remained penny-gum-and-candy vendors until the modern cigarette machine was introduced in 1926. Cigarette machines were the first to make change. The first soft-drink machine appeared in 1937.

World War II gave great impetus to the vending-machine industry. The machines were installed in factories as a convenient way to provide coffee for workers on long shifts. The machines' services improved morale and helped raise productivity. By the 1960s their use had expanded considerably. In the same decade they became a major factor in Japan's product-distribution system.

VENEREAL DISEASE *see* SEXUALLY TRANSMITTED DISEASE.

Chip and Rosa Maria Peterson

The high valleys of the Cordillera de Mérida, a branch of the Andes Mountains, have a climate that makes them one of the finest coffee-growing regions in the world.

VENEZUELA. When the explorer Alonso de Ojeda first saw the Indian villages built on stilts along the swampy shores of Lake Maracaibo in 1499, he named the site Venezuela (Little Venice). Today the country is known for its crude oil production— 4 percent of the world's

output. This is greater than that of any other Third World country outside the Middle East.

Venezuela is a coastal, mountain, and plains republic. Its 1,748-mile (2,813-kilometer) Caribbean coastline provides tourist beaches and connects the country to its island neighbors. Some of these— Trinidad and Tobago, Costa Rica, Honduras, and Puerto Rico—were the focus of economic assistance from Venezuela for industrial development projects in the 1960s and 1970s.

The Andes originate in northeastern Venezuela and stretch 750 miles (1,210 kilometers) westward to Colombia, where they turn southward and increase in length and width in Colombia, Ecuador, Peru, and Bolivia. They reach 16,427 feet (5,007 meters) in Pico Bolívar in the western Andes. The Andean states of Venezuela account for some two thirds of the population, reflecting the original Spanish colonists' preference for the temperate uplands. Venezuela is a

This article was contributed by Richard C. Jones, Associate Professor of Geography, University of Texas at San Antonio.

member of the Andean Pact, within which it supports its less economically advanced Andean neighbors.

Venezuela has vast tropical plateaus and plains, stretching southward to occupy more than half the national territory. This region is sparsely populated. The territory of Amazonas has a population density that is one seventh that of Alaska.

Venezuela's 18.3 million people (1987 estimate) make it the sixth largest Latin American country in population. With an area of 352,144 square miles (912,050 square kilometers), its population density is 51.9 per square mile (20.0 per square kilometer). Its rate of natural increase (excess of births over deaths) was 2.7 percent in 1986, the highest of any Latin American country its size. Venezuela's overall population growth is greater, however, because of the migration of from 25,000 to 50,000 undocumented Colombians across its western border each year. The per capita income of 3,330 dollars is the highest of any Latin American country except for several oil- and tourist-supported Caribbean islands.

Venezuela's location is generally east of the United States—the longitude of Caracas (67° W), the capital, is east of any point in the United States. Miami, Fla., is the closest major United States city. Venezuela extends through 14 degrees of longitude and 11 degrees of latitude, but because of the country's proximity to the equator, this latitudinal spread results in minimal temperature differences in the winter.

Venezuela before 1959 was governed by a string of military dictatorships. Although oil wealth from the 1920s onward provided capital for many government projects, economic development was strongly concentrated in the capital region, and most of the rural population lived in poverty. In 1959 Venezuela

VENEZUELA

- ⊛ CAPITAL
- ▲ HIGH POINT
- ▬▪▬▪ INT'L BOUNDARY

0   50   100   150 mi
0 50 100 150 200 km

elected a civilian president and in succeeding years established a two-party system in which presidents are elected from each party in alternating five-year terms. This representative democratic system remains strong despite economic setbacks after 1978.

Physical Regions and Their Economic Bases

Venezuela can be divided into four regions with different elevations and topographic features. These regions are the Andes, the Guiana Plateau, the Orinoco Llanos, and the Maracaibo Basin.

Andes. The Venezuelan Andes are chiefly sedimentary, with an exposed crystalline core (igneous and metamorphic rocks) in the higher elevations. They run east-west instead of north-south as in the rest of South America (see Andes). This results from the eastward push of the gigantic Caribbean plate that borders the country to the north. This slow but irresistible process bends the Andean mountain chain toward the east, creates volcanoes in the islands of the eastern Caribbean, and causes earthquakes along its southern margin as the plate slips past the westward-moving South American plate. In 1967 a quake in Caracas killed hundreds, and in 1755 and 1812 much stronger quakes totally destroyed the city.

The Andes can themselves be divided into four subregions. The Cordillera de Mérida, extending from the Colombian border to the city of Trujillo, is the highest

and most rugged. In this subregion climate and land use are determined by elevation. Up to an elevation of 2,950 feet (900 meters) is the *tierra caliente* (hot zone), with the raising of sugarcane, tropical fruits, and rice. The *tierra templada* (temperate) extends from 2,950 to 5,900 feet (900 to 1,800 meters), and is the zone of coffee, still a major export product. The *tierra fría* (cold), from 5,900 to 9,850 feet (1,800 to 3,000 meters), is where wheat and potatoes are raised on a limited scale. A striking scene is the yellow wheat fields near Apartaderos on the Trans-Andean Highway at harvesttime in March. Up to the snow line at about 15,000 feet (4,600 meters) is the *páramo*—a treeless, cloud-enshrouded realm where such thick-leaved succulents as the agavelike *frailejón,* alpine shrubs, and lichens prevail. These carpet the mountains with white and yellow blossoms at the beginning of the rainy season in March. The government is actively reforesting the lower *páramo* between Santo Domingo and Mérida to protect the watershed from floods, landslides, and the silting of reservoirs.

The population of this subregion is clustered in basins around such cities as Mérida, Valera, and San Cristóbal. Mérida is the capital of the high Andes, with a pleasant climate (64° F, or 18° C, average yearly temperature). Snowcapped peaks near Mérida provide skiing, mountain climbing, and the highest cable-car system in the world. San Cristóbal is the center of the Venezuelan coffee region and maintains strong ties with Colombia.

The Segovia Highlands subregion extends from Trujillo to Puerto Cabello and centers on Barquisimeto, a city that specializes in agricultural processing and light manufacturing for the commercial grain and cattle area of the western Llanos (plains). The mountains are lower and drier here than they are around Mérida. From the 1960s sugarcane has been raised in the mixed forest-grassland region around San Felipe. Petrochemical refining around the cities of Morón and Cardon capitalize on good harbors for shipping. Puerto Cabello, the major port serving the industries in Valencia and Maracay, benefits from the same ideal harbor conditions.

The Central Highlands form the key cultural, economic, and population center of the country. They stretch from Puerto Cabello to near Barcelona. Their central portion rises abruptly from the coast to form a mountain barrier 9,067 feet (2,764 meters) high in Píco Naiguatá, which provides a spectacular green backdrop of broadleaf and coniferous forests for the capital city of Caracas but which limits growth northward. A series of national parks protects the Andean summit watersheds from Mérida to east of Caracas. Elevations are generally from 650 to 6,500 feet (200 to 2,000 meters) in this subregion, with the population concentrated in the upper *tierra caliente* and lower *tierra templada*. The climate is ideal for human settlement. The subregion is composed of a coastal range, a series of interior valleys carved by the Tuy and Aragua rivers and the tributaries of Lake Valencia, and a lower interior chain of hills and mountains to the south, grading into the Llanos.

Caracas, in the *tierra templada* at about 3,300 feet (1,000 meters), has average temperatures that range from 64° to 72° F (18° to 22° C) and an average rainfall of 32 inches (81 centimeters). With a population of 1.2 million (3.2 million in the metropolitan area, 1987 estimate), it is the center of national life in every sense. It is the headquarters of the petroleum industry and the center of manufacturing, with 30 percent of the firms and 40 percent of the workers. Downtown Caracas is only 10 miles (16 kilometers) from the Caribbean by freeway. Caracas has spread 15 miles (24 kilometers) from east to west in its narrow valley and some 8 miles (13 kilometers) southward into the canyons of the interior range. (*See also* Caracas.)

A major goal of the government in the 1970s was to decentralize population growth toward the south in the Tuy River valley around such new towns as Ocumare del Tuy, some 37 miles (60 kilometers) from the capital. Some food-processing industries and water-supply projects have been located here, but the residential subdivisions laid out by the government architects lie largely unoccupied because of the long commuting distance to jobs in the capital.

Thirty miles (48 kilometers) west of Caracas, atop the coastal mountain ridge at 6,200 feet (1,890 meters) elevation, is the picturesque German village, Colonia Tovar. Established in 1843, it maintains its traditional agricultural economy and German language, offering delightful food and lodging for Caraqueños and other tourists on weekend outings.

Besides Caracas, two other major cities are found in the Central Highlands—Valencia, which is the country's third largest city, and Maracay. These cities are the centers of durable consumer-goods manufacturing—automobiles, appliances, furniture, kitchenware, and textiles—and they have benefited from government decentralization policies since 1970. They are located at either end of the fertile Lake Valencia basin—traditionally the country's richest agricultural zone, with sugarcane, cotton, coffee, sesame, and dairying. Production here was eclipsed by that in the western Llanos in the 1970s.

The Sierra de Cumaná, the last of the four Andean subregions, stretches from Barcelona to the Paria Peninsula. It is a dry zone with low hills and mountains, resembling the Segovia Highlands. The economy revolves around its attractive tourist beaches and the oil shipping through Barcelona from the eastern Venezuelan oil fields. Cumaná, the first city founded in Venezuela (1523), is a major service city for its agricultural hinterland to the south.

Guiana Plateau. Southeast of the Orinoco River and encompassing more than a third of the national area, the Guiana Plateau is part of a huge metamorphic-igneous shield—the center of the old supercontinent Pangaea—that covers much of Brazil and Africa. In the deeply incised tributary canyons the rock is more than a billion years old, but in between are younger *tepuís* (sandstone mesas) that rise spectacularly from their riverbeds. One of these, the Auyán-Tepuí, is more than 270 square miles (700 square kilometers) in extent. It collects enough rainfall to feed rivers on its surface. One plunges 3,212 feet (979 meters) to form Angel Falls, the highest waterfall in the world (*see* Angel Falls). The Guiana Plateau reaches more than 10,000 feet (3,000 meters) in elevation at its southern margin in Amazonas territory.

Where the sedimentary cover is stripped away, as on the northern rim, the mining of iron ore, bauxite, and precious stones takes place. Ciudad Guayana is the industrial center of eastern Venezuela. Its steel and aluminum mills produce for domestic markets and export. Some 50 miles (80 kilometers) to the south, the Guri Dam provides power for these industries as well as more than half the country's electrical needs.

Orinoco Llanos. Comprising about a third of Venezuela, the Orinoco Llanos runs parallel to and south of the Andes region across the length of the country. Its tropical wet and dry climate brings rainfall favorable to the growing of corn and dryland rice in the wet season (April to October) and to paddy rice, tobacco, and sesame in the dry season (November to March).

The government successfully colonized the western Llanos with, in progression, German, Spanish, Polish, and other immigrant settlers. It built the Guárico Dam south of Caracas in the late 1950s. In the 1970s irrigation and drainage projects on the Bocono and

The Altamira section of Caracas, with its wide plaza and obelisk, is a modern residential, business, and shopping area. It is normally closed to vehicular traffic, so shoppers can use it as a pedestrian mall.

Chip and Rosa Maria Peterson

Tucupido rivers further extended cultivation. By 1975 more than two thirds of the country's rice, half of its corn, and 90 percent of its oilseeds were grown in the western Llanos. This new breadbasket is centered on Acarigua. Farther west the city of Barinas is the northern and eastern outlet for a great tropical forest and cattle-grazing area.

Since 1976, when the petroleum industry was nationalized, the eastern Llanos (Orinoco Delta) has been the focus of heavy oil exploitation. This "liquid coal"—a low-grade oil emulsion—is in demand for United States and Canadian power plants because its price is less than that of conventional crude oil.

The Maracaibo Basin in northwestern Venezuela has the country's highest average temperatures. Climatically it ranges from desert in the north to tropical rain forest in the south. Isolation limits the south to subsistence agriculture and cattle grazing, but northward are Venezuela's major petroleum fields, especially the Bolívar field on the northeastern shores of Lake Maracaibo. Before 1955 most Venezuelan oil was refined overseas or offshore on Curaçao, but government development of refineries at Morón, Cardon, and ultimately Maracaibo (in the 1970s) changed this. The region focuses economically on Maracaibo, Venezuela's second largest city. It is a modern and progressive city but climatically oppressive, with an average annual temperature of 82° F (28° C). (*See also* Maracaibo, Venezuela; Maracaibo, Lake.)

People and Culture

In racial composition 69 percent of the Venezuelan people are of mixed Indian and European descent, 20 percent are of European descent, 9 percent are of black descent, and 1 percent are Indian. Those of mixed Indian and European heritage are spread throughout the country, but the other groups tend to be more concentrated—the whites in the largest cities, the blacks along the Caribbean, and the Indians toward

the farthest reaches of the Llanos, Guiana Plateau, and Maracaibo Basin.

Venezuela's high natural increase of population—2.7 percent per year—reflects a relatively progressive economy and a comparatively hands-off policy toward birth control by the government. This contrasts with the active family-planning programs in other countries of the region. Because of the large numbers of illegal Colombians who cross the western border for work, net immigration is about equal to natural increase, resulting in an overall population growth rate of more than 5 percent per year.

In 1985, 85.7 percent of the Venezuelan population were classified as urban—the highest such rate in all of tropical South America. In the period from 1960 to 1980, secondary urban areas—those with populations of between 250,000 and 1 million—were growing at faster rates than either Caracas or smaller cities. More than 90 percent of internal migration is now from one urban area to another, with only 10 percent from rural to urban areas.

Education. Venezuela channels a higher portion of its budget into education than do other large Latin American countries such as Mexico and Brazil. As a result its literacy rate is considerably higher—88 percent. Primary and secondary education is free and compulsory. Higher education at state universities is tuition free, but places in the best institutions—such as the Central and Simón Bolívar universities in Caracas—are limited. Better students can get government scholarships for overseas study under the Reca de Ayacucho program, the best of its kind in Latin America. The government funded many new vocational high schools in the 1970s to provide technicians for the emerging manufacturing industries.

Health care. Venezuela also spends well above the Latin American average on health facilities and programs. The average life expectancy of 68 years is higher than in Mexico and Brazil, indicating the effectiveness of programs to control contagious diseases. New hospitals were directed to such peripheral regions as the western Andes, the Segovia Highlands, and Sierra de Cumená in the 1970s. The birthrate in the mid-1980s was 33 per thousand.

Religion and language. Venezuela is nominally 96 percent Roman Catholic, with less than 2 percent Protestant. Spanish is the predominant language except in a few enclaves of blacks and among the Indians, who speak more than 25 different languages.

Arts and letters. Venezuelan art, music, and letters are well advanced and respected in Latin America, especially for a country its size. Simón Bolívar, the liberator, was himself a poet and essayist. One of the best-known Venezuelan novelists, Rómulo Gallegos, went on to become president of his country. The leading *vanguardista* writer was Andriano González Léon. (*See also* Latin American Literature.)

Economy

The recent history of the Venezuelan economy has been one of diversification. It has moved away from petroleum dominance toward food self-sufficiency and import-substituting industrialization.

Petroleum provides some two thirds of total government revenue, more than 90 percent of exports, and 23 percent of total gross national product. In 1981–82 curtailment of production—in keeping with OPEC policies—resulted in a drop of 50 percent in production. (Venezuela is a founding member of the Organization of Petroleum Exporting Countries, or OPEC.) This had disastrous effects on government programs. Production has since rebounded, aided by heavy petroleum development in the Monagas province in eastern Venezuela.

Agriculture and manufacturing have been the beneficiaries of the Venezuelan policy of "sowing the petroleum"—diversification with the help of government oil taxes and royalties—since the Rómulo Betancourt administration began in the late 1950s. These policies culminated in the administration of Carlos Andrés Pérez Rodriquez in the 1970s with extensive credit, extension, and rural-road programs in agriculture and with steel, aluminum, and petroleum-refining projects in manufacturing. These policies suffered setbacks from the low oil prices in the early 1980s, but they have been restored. Agricultural production grew 20 percent faster in 1986 than in 1985 with bumper harvests of rice, corn, and sorghum. Food imports declined from 60 percent in 1983 to 20 percent in 1986. In the manufacturing sector production is focused on the processing of raw materials that were formerly exported. The decentralization policy has led to a shift in the location of industrial jobs. From 1970 to 1985 the Caracas region lost manufacturing jobs, while the low-income regions (other Andean regions, Llanos, and Guiana) gained jobs. This is the result of policies instituted in 1976 to provide tax relief and loans to industries that located in certain specified peripheral zones. As a result of government decentralization policies in agriculture, industry, and

social services, the traditionally high differences in income that existed between Venezuelan regions at last began to decline in the 1970s.

Transportation in Venezuela is highly variable. The air network is well developed between Caracas and all other cities. The road network is dense along the Andean spine, with an *autopista,* or superhighway, connecting Barquisimeto to Caracas by way of Valencia and Maracay and with good rural roads radiating from this main axis into the western Andes and Llanos. There are few roads in the rest of the Llanos and the Maracaibo Basin, however, and practically none in the Guiana region. Although Venezuela's road mileage is low compared with Mexico, Brazil, and Argentina, the Caracas–Valencia and Caracas–Maiquetía *autopistas* are among the best engineered in Latin America.

Government and History

Venezuela is a federal republic divided into 20 states, two federal territories, the federal district, and some 72 island territories. The constitution of 1961 declares Venezuela a federal republic with "autonomous states," but in fact nearly all power is held by the national government. The president is elected by direct vote for a single five-year term. Congress consists of the Senate and Chamber of Deputies. Voting is compulsory for persons 18 years of age and older.

The Venezuelan coast was first sighted by Christopher Columbus in 1498, and the land was settled shortly thereafter by the Spanish. For more than three centuries the people were under Spanish rule. In 1811 revolutionary forces led by Francisco de Miranda declared a republic, but the revolution was soon crushed. The struggle continued under the leadership of Bolívar, who finally defeated the Spanish in 1821 (*see* Bolívar). For a few years Venezuela was part of the republic of Colombia, but it seceded and became an independent republic in 1830. After that the country was ruled by a series of dictators, including Antonio Guzmán Blanco (1870–88), Cipriano Castro (1899–1908), and General Juan Vicente Gómez (1908–35).

Boundary disputes with British Guiana (now Guyana) came to a head in 1895. Great Britain threatened to use force. United States President Grover Cleveland sent a message to Congress, stating that any attempt by Britain to enforce its claims without recourse to arbitration would be considered a violation of the Monroe Doctrine and might lead to war with the United States. (The dispute was settled by arbitration.) In 1903 Castro's overbearing violation of foreign rights led Britain, Germany, and Italy to declare a blockade of Venezuelan ports. When United States President Theodore Roosevelt protested that this violated the Monroe Doctrine, Britain and Italy consented to refer the dispute to arbitration. Germany declined to arbitrate until Roosevelt announced his intention of sending an American fleet to the Caribbean. (*See also* Monroe Doctrine.)

Castro plunged his country into new difficulties in 1908, and the offended nations paralyzed Venezuelan commerce by quarantining the ports. Castro then fled. When General Gómez became president he built roads and schools, began to develop oil resources, and paid off the national debt, but his rule was so tyrannical that his death in 1935 was welcomed.

The oil boom of the 1940s and 1950s paid the government huge royalties. These funds were used for public works, but strong-man rule continued.

Betancourt was the first elected president to serve his full term (1959–64). His liberal programs led to social and economic advancement. His administration—as did those of Raúl Leoni (1964–67) and Rafael Caldera (1969–74)—attempted to decentralize economic growth and to make Venezuela more visible internationally by taking stronger prosocialist stances and by espousing economic independence from the United States. (See also Betancourt.)

Under Pérez Rodriquez (1974–79), the country went through a period of intense economic nationalism spurred by huge oil profits after the Arab embargo—the nationalization of the steel (1975) and petroleum (1976) industries; the buying of foreign companies by incentives and coercion; and "sowing the petroleum" in a wide variety of domestic programs. This economic pharaoism backfired. The oil earnings could not be-

gin to finance all the projects, so the government borrowed massive amounts of foreign capital at high rates of interest, thereby greatly increasing the national debt. Inefficiency in project design and administration resulted from the lack of skilled engineers, economists, and industrial foremen. Corruption and graft were endemic.

President Luis Herrera Campins (1979–84) inherited huge debts, half-completed projects, and bureaucratic corruption, exacerbated by the oil price drops of 1981–82. Under President Jaime Lusinchi, whose five-year term began in 1984, the problems began to be solved. In 1986 oil production, agricultural harvests, and industrial output all increased markedly over previous years.

BIBLIOGRAPHY FOR VENEZUELA

Dalton, L. Venezuela (Gordon, 1976).
Lieuwen, Edwin. Venezuela (Greenwood, 1986).
Lombardi, J.V. Venezuela: the Search for Order, the Dream of Progress (Oxford, 1982).
Lye, Keith. Take a Trip to Venezuela (Watts, 1988).
Marsland, W.D. and A.L. Venezuela Through Its History (Greenwood, 1976).
Martz, John, ed. Venezuela, 2nd rev. ed. (Praeger, 1986).
Venezuela in Pictures (Lerner, 1987).

Venezuela Fact Summary

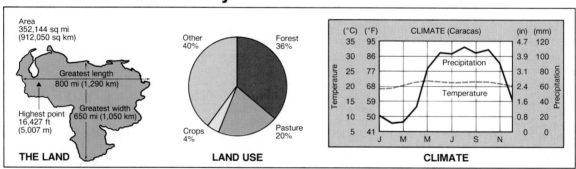

THE LAND — Area 352,144 sq mi (912,050 sq km); Greatest length 800 mi (1,290 km); Greatest width 650 mi (1,050 km); Highest point 16,427 ft (5,007 m)

LAND USE — Other 40%, Forest 36%, Crops 4%, Pasture 20%

CLIMATE (Caracas)

Official Name: Republic of Venezuela.
Capital: Caracas.

NATURAL FEATURES

Principal Physical Features: Andes Mountains, Guiana Plateau, Orinoco Llanos, Maracaibo Basin.
Mountain Ranges: Andes, Cordillera de Mérida.
Highest Peak: Pico Bolívar, 16,427 feet (5,007 meters).
Major Rivers: Apure, Arauca, Brazo Casiquiare, Meta, Negro, Orinoco, Ventuari.
Largest Lake: Maracaibo.

PEOPLE

Population (1987 estimate): 18,272,200; 51.9 persons per square mile (20.0 persons per square kilometer); 85.7 percent urban, 14.3 percent rural.
Major Cities (1987 estimate): Caracas (1,246,700), Maracaibo (1,124,-400), Valencia (856,500), Barquisimeto (661,300), Maracay (496,-700).
Major Religion: Roman Catholicism.
Major Language: Spanish (official).
Literacy: 88.4 percent.
Leading Universities: Central University of Venezuela, Open University, Simón Bolívar University, Caracas; University of Carabobo; University of Zulia, Maracaibo.

GOVERNMENT

Form of Government: Republic.
Head of State and Government: President.
Legislature: Congress; consists of Senate with 47 members and Chamber of Deputies with 200 members; popularly elected; five-year terms.
Voting Qualification: Age 18.
Political Divisions: 20 states and 4 federally-controlled areas.
Flag: Three equal horizontal stripes of yellow, blue, and red with the coat of arms and an arc of white stars (see Flags of the World).

ECONOMY

Chief Agricultural Products: Crops—coffee, sugarcane, tropical fruits, rice, wheat, potatoes, cotton, sesame, dairy products, corn, tobacco, oilseeds, sorghum. Livestock—cattle.
Chief Mined Products: Crude petroleum, iron ore, bauxite, precious stones.
Chief Manufactured Products: Refined petroleum, automobiles, appliances, furniture, kitchenware, textiles, steel, aluminum.
Chief Exports: Petroleum, coffee, steel, aluminum.
Chief Imports: Agricultural equipment, industrial machinery, consumer goods.
Monetary Unit: 1 bolívar = 100 céntimos.

The area around Piazza San Marco is the center of Venice. The Doges' Palace (right foregound), in late Gothic style, is now a museum. In the background can be seen the ornate Byzantine-style Basilica of Saint Mark.

Jadwiga Lopez—CLICK/Chicago

VENICE, Italy.

Once a city-state that as a great maritime power served as a bridge between East and West, Venice is now one of the great pleasure centers of Europe. It attracts thousands of tourists each year. It serves as the capital of the province of Venice (Venezia) and the Veneto region.

The historic center of Venice is built on a group of islets and mudbanks in the middle of Laguna Veneta, a crescent-shaped lagoon separated from the Adriatic Sea by a barrier of narrow islands and peninsulas. The modern city embraces the whole 90-mile (145-kilometer) perimeter of the lagoon and includes ten principal islands in addition to those of the mother city and two industrial boroughs of Mestre and Marghera on the mainland.

The main core includes the islands La Giudecca; San Giorgio Maggiore, with its famous 16th-century church of the same name by the architect Andrea Palladio; and San Michele. Other islands include Lido, with its casino, hotels, and beaches; Murano, noted for its glassworks; Burano, famous for its lace; and Torcello, site of the remains of the Santa Maria Assunía Cathedral.

Venice is separated from the sea by natural and artificial breakwaters, but flooding (*acqua alta*) is common from November through March of each year. During the season the Venetian squares and streets are floored by thick planks and the local people wear high waterproof boots for protection.

This article was contributed by Allan Rodgers, Professor of Geography, Pennsylvania State University, University Park.

Venice is world renowned as a city of canals and bridges. These facilitate internal transportation and have a beauty and charm that draw countless visitors each year. Chief among these arteries is the S-shaped Canale Grande—the Grand Canal which starts at the railway station and parking garage on Piazza Roma and ends at Piazza San Marco (Saint Mark's Square). Altogether there are more than 180 canals, which are literally the streets and avenues of Venice. Crossing the waterways are about 400 bridges, the most famous of which is probably the Rialto. Others include the Scalzi, the Accademia, and the infamous Bridge of Sighs, which leads from the upper story of the Doges' Palace to the republic's prison. Centuries ago countless prisoners went over it to their secret and often tortured deaths.

The center is connected to the mainland by viaducts, which carry a major highway and a double-track rail line. Large cruise vessels and freighters move to the Stazione Marittima (marine station) nearby. Within the Venetian islands, canals, and lagoons, commodities move by barges and tugs, while passenger movement is primarily by vaporetti (motorboats). The world-famous black gondolas, powered by men, are narrow with high prows and sterns and are used mainly for short canal passages. They are mainly the vehicles of merchants, politicians, and tourists.

Historic Venice

Lining the canals are noteworthy architectural monuments. Through the centuries Venetian artists created magnificent examples of Byzantine, Renaissance, and Gothic architecture. They also developed a style that is distinctively Venetian. Paintings and sculpture are housed in churches, palaces, museums, and public buildings, and Venice's libraries hold priceless manuscripts and relics.

VENICE

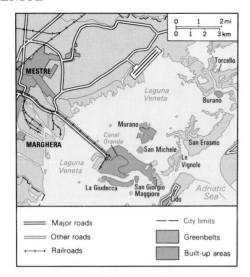

Major roads — City limits
Other roads — Greenbelts
Railroads — Built-up areas

St. Mark's. Central Venice is dominated by the Piazza San Marco. It is the city's political, religious, and artistic nucleus—the setting for seeing and understanding both medieval and modern Venice. The square is enclosed by the three *Procuratie,* lined with sheltered walkways and shops. These buildings were once the residences of the chief magistrates of the old republic. On the eastern side of the piazza lies the Basilica of St. Mark, one of the world's great churches. It is the seat of the patriarch of Venice and reputedly contains the remains of its patron saint. The cathedral is topped by five gilded domes, clearly in the Byzantine tradition. The basilica was built from the 9th to 11th century, in part with relics brought from Alexandria and Constantinople. The extraordinary wealth of the East was drawn into its construction to enhance its beauty. Rare gemstones and marble were

brought from the Indies. Columns from the ruins of Muslim mosques and Byzantine churches were incorporated into the building. Outside the basilica there are replicas of four Hellenic bronze horses brought from Constantinople, but their origins date from the time of the Roman emperor Nero.

Inside its five-arched portals St. Mark's is awesomely rich. The inner shape is that of a Greek cross. In every direction there are chapels, ornamented ceilings, decorated panels, and mosaics in profusion. The main treasure is the 'Pala d'Oro', a golden altarpiece encrusted with jewels, mosaics, and enamel.

Doges' Palace. South of the basilica is the 16th-century Doges' Palace. It houses many famous paintings, pieces of sculpture, and historical relics. There is a series of paintings by Tintoretto, including 'Paradise', and others by Veronese, including 'Rape of Europa'. Paintings by Titian and the Bellini family were destroyed by fire. The Council of Ten met here, and it was the residence of the various doges, the magistrates who ruled the republic. They lived in private, richly furnished apartments.

Campanile. Facing the palace is the imposing Campanile of San Marco, once called the Landlord of Venice. The 324-foot (99-meter) bell tower is a reconstruction of the original that collapsed in 1902. Other related structures are the clock tower and, in the *piazzetta,* two marble and granite columns that face the Grand Canal—the winged lion that is the symbol of St. Mark and a representation of St. Theodore. It was here that political and criminal prisoners were executed.

Along the Grand Canal. The main artery of historic Venice is the Grand Canal, crisscrossed with vaporetti and gondolas. It is spanned by bridges and lined with palaces, public buildings, and churches. Among the churches are Santa Maria della Salute, across the

(Left) The Bridge of Sighs was so named because convicts were taken across it from the Doges' Palace on the left to the prison. (Below) The Rialto, crossing the Grand Canal, is the best known of Venice's main bridges.

Photos, Robert Frerck—CLICK/Chicago

298

Grand Canal from St. Mark's; the Franciscan church of Santa Maria Gloriosa dei Frari; San Salvatore; and San Zanipòlo (the Dominican church of San Giovanni and San Paolo).

Many of the other architectural treasures are now museums. Probably the most famous collection of paintings is in the Accademia. The collection in Ca'd'-Oro (house of gold) includes works by Giorgione, Andrea Mantegna, Titian, and Anthony Van Dyck. The Peggy Guggenheim Collection focuses on modern art, including the works of Marc Chagall, Pablo Picasso, and Jackson Pollock. Farther down the canal is the Rezzonico Museum, which specializes in Renaissance art and design. Other painters represented in Venice's art collections are Giovanni Bellini, Giovanni Battista Tiepolo, and Jacopo Sansovino. They adapted their paintings to the quasi-Byzantine setting of Venice.

Historical Venice is a maze of squares, streets, alleys, and passageways. The most notable shopping street is the Mercerie, and the Rialto zone is also lined with shops. La Fenice is a distinguished theater where operas, concerts, and ballets by noted artists are performed. In addition Venice hosts a spectacular spring carnival with masked balls, a Summer Biennale, a film festival that rivals the one in Cannes and a regatta centered on the Lido.

People

In the mid-1980s Venice had a population of about 333,000. Its area is roughly 120 square miles (310 square kilometers). The central core accounts for only 2 percent of the area and about a third of the population. The remaining inhabitants live on the mainland.

The historic core of the city has lost a large share of its population from flooding, coupled with sinking and excessively high population densities. The center of Venice has become virtually a museum of inhabitants who service hotels and restaurants for the tourist trade and work in retail and wholesale establishments. Artisan workshops, however, are still in abundance. Many of those who left have moved to the adjoining mainland, where commerce and industry flourish, and to Padua, Milan, and Turin in the Po Valley. Migration to Western Europe is also a continuing phenomenon.

Marghera is the industrial heart of the commune (administrative district). It is also the third-ranked Italian port. Its industries include steel and nonferrous metals, aluminum, machinery, petroleum refining, petrochemicals, plastics, and nondurable consumer goods. Mestre is also an industrial center, but is primarily a focus of commerce. The district is described as a deteriorating residential suburb for the industrial core. Roughly 20,000 commuters move into the center of Venice each day.

History

With the fall of the Roman Empire, barbarian states—Goths, Ostrogoths, and later Lombards—swept over Italy in the 5th and 6th centuries AD. People who had lived on or near the northwest Adri-

The Campanile (with a corner of the Doges' Palace in the foreground) was rebuilt after its collapse in 1902.

atic coast found shelter on the scores of offshore islets in the Venetian lagoons, which had previously been inhabited by small numbers of fishermen. The political climate of that era was so unstable that the early inhabitants were ready to move into the swamps and lagoons, building their houses on pilings on the partially flooded islands. The main centers of settlement lay between the Piave River on the north and the Adige River on the south.

Over the centuries Venice grew into a great maritime power because of the astuteness of its merchants and rulers as well as its location in relation to the East. This city-state was never part of the old Teutonic empires. For centuries its main political, military, and commercial ties were clearly with Byzantium (Constantinople, now Istanbul).

Early Venice was a society ruled by its doges. Often despots, they were first elected in 727. They were chosen by the Council of Ten, which was elected by nobles and rich merchants who accounted for only 6 percent of the population.

The city-state's chief competitor was Genoa, but Venice had the advantage of easier access through low Alpine passes to the heart of Western and Central Europe. The Crusades were especially advantageous for Venice. During the Fourth Crusade Constantinople was conquered in 1204 and Venetian trade flourished (*see* Crusades). Its imports were spices, incense, grain, salt, sugar, and silk; these were balanced by exports of silver, copper, woolens, and linen cloth.

Berlitz—CLICK/Chicago

The church of Santa Maria della Salute (1687) was built on a foundation of more than 1 million wooden pilings.

After years of bitter conflict Genoa was defeated in 1381. The Venetians trapped its fleet inside the Chioggia lagoons south of the city and forced its surrender. At the height of the republic's power Venice controlled Corfu, Crete, and the Peloponnesus. On the mainland it had acquired the land westward almost to Milan. The Black Sea and the eastern Mediterranean were now open for Venetian vessels.

From the 16th century on there was a sharp decline. The population of Venice was decimated over three centuries by outbreaks of plague. In one, from 1347 to 1349, three fifths of its inhabitants died. The Turks, who had captured Constantinople in 1453, began to strip Venice of its Greek possessions. Venice later was defeated by the League of Cambrai (1508) but temporarily rose again. The opening of the cape route around Africa was devastating for the spice trade. In 1797 the city was conquered by Napoleon and later ceded to Austria. There was an unsuccessful revolt against the Austrians in 1848. Because of the domination of Austria's Trieste, further stagnation set in until Venice became part of a unified Italy in 1866. With the opening of the Suez Canal in 1869, the city regained a direct route to the East, but it never fully recovered its commercial supremacy.

As the land subsides, Venice has been sinking into the sea at an alarming rate. The core is plagued by flooding. A 6-foot (1.8-meter) tide engulfed the area in 1966. Heavy rains and southeast winds backed up flooding rivers, giving Venice its highest-known tide

in recent history. Waves lashed against the Lido and St. Mark's basilica.

To prevent new floods additional breakwaters were added and new gates raised to close Venice's three mouths to the sea. Plans to build a new tanker canal were abruptly cancelled. One partial solution, the capping of artesian wells, brought some improvement but no permanent solution. Occasional untreated sewage is a constant problem.

Air pollution is another problem, especially for Venice's art treasures. One of the causes has been the burning of coal and, later, fuel oil. Heating is now mainly by natural gas, which has eased but not solved the problem. The United Nations Educational, Scientific, and Cultural Organization (UNESCO) has a major ongoing project to save Venice from pollution and flooding, but the effort has yielded only minimal results—far below expectations. (*See also* Italy.) Population (1981 census), 332,775.

BIBLIOGRAPHY FOR VENICE

Lauritzen, Peter. Venice Preserved (Adler, 1986).
Macadam, Alta. Venice, 3rd ed. (Norton, 1986).
Martineau, Jane and Hope, Charles, eds. The Genius of Venice: 1500–1600 (Abrams, 1984).
Morris, James. The World of Venice, rev. ed. (Harcourt, 1985).
Norwich, J.J. A History of Venice (Knopf, 1982).
Ventura, Piero. Venice: Birth of a City (Putnam, 1988).
Zorzi, Alvise. Venice (Abbeville, 1983).

VENTRILOQUISM. The practice, or art, of speaking so that the voice seems to come from a source other than the speaker's vocal organs is called ventriloquism. It is sometimes used by entertainers who pretend to carry on a conversation with a "dummy" or puppet (*see* Puppet).

The popular expression "throwing one's voice" is inaccurate. The sounds continue to come from the speaker's throat. The ventriloquist produces the illusion that the voice originates elsewhere by moving the lips as little as possible, by using a different voice sound, and by skillfully directing the audience's attention to the supposed source of the voice.

The speech used by ventriloquists is a somewhat muffled vocal sound produced by slowing the rate at which the breath is exhaled and by retracting the tongue so that only the tip moves. As much as possible the ventriloquist avoids such words as beam or lamp. Instead such words as king or girl, which do not require lip movement, are used.

During ancient times ventriloquism may have been used to demonstrate "divine" power. It was mentioned by Confucius in the 6th century BC. The first known ventriloquist was Louis Brabant, a member of the court of French king Francis I. In the 20th century Edgar Bergen, with his wooden "dummy" Charlie McCarthy, was an internationally known ventriloquist and comedian. Today the art is still practiced by the Zulus of Africa, by the Maoris of New Zealand, and by Eskimo of North America. (*See also* Voice.)

VENUS *see* MYTHOLOGY; PLANETS.

VENUS'S-FLYTRAP. One of the best known of the meat-eating plants is the Venus's-flytrap. At the end of each leaf it has a pair of hinged lobes, or jaws, edged with spines. When an insect or other small animal alights on a lobe, the jaws fold together and trap it.

This small plant is found in the wild only in eastern North and South Carolina, where it is common in damp, mossy areas. The plant bears a round cluster of small white flowers at the tip of an erect stem that grows from 8 to 12 inches (20 to 30 centimeters) tall. The leaves are 3 to 5 inches (8 to 13 centimeters) long and form a rosette. Each leaf ends in two lobes that form a trap. Crimson glands give the lobes a red, flowerlike appearance to attract insects. The plant's traps are "set" only when the sun shines.

On the surface of each lobe are three highly sensitive hairs. In normal daytime temperatures, when these hairs are stimulated by an insect or by any other means, the lobes snap shut in about half a second. The spines along the edges interlock to hold fast the captive, and the glands on the lobes' surface secrete an acidic fluid that digests the insect's

Jack Dermid

Venus's-flytrap (*Dionaea muscipula*)

body. About ten days are required for digestion, then the leaf reopens. A leaf rarely captures more than three insects in its lifetime. The scientific name of the Venus's-flytrap is *Dionaea muscipula*. (*See also* Pitcher Plants; Sundew.)

VERACRUZ, Mexico. One of the country's principal seaports and a communications center for the surrounding area, Veracruz is situated in east-central Mexico, on the Bay of Campeche, about 180 miles (290 kilometers) east of Mexico City.

For nearly a mile the city curves along the waters of the bay and its sandy beaches. The narrow streets of Veracruz are lined with low buildings tinted red, yellow, blue, and green. The Government Building stands on the attractive Main Square. Situated just

Carl Frank—Photo Researchers

The 17th-century Town Hall of Veracruz is on the Plaza de Armas, a colonnaded square near the waterfront.

above sea level, the area has a very warm climate, but many shady plazas throughout the city afford relief from the sun.

Veracruz is a significant manufacturing city, known especially for the production of cigars. Because of its proximity to the ocean, Veracruz has long been a vital trade link between Mexico and other countries. Access to the interior cities of Mexico is made possible by several railways, highway routes, and air transport. The city houses the Regional Technical Institute of Veracruz.

The harbor was once a shallow lagoon, dreaded by seamen because it afforded no protection from storms that sweep the bay. For centuries, moreover, Veracruz was known as "the city of the dead" because of the outbreaks of yellow fever and malaria that devastated it.

Landscaping efforts and engineering technology, however, have greatly improved conditions and saved the city from decline and desertion. The surrounding swamps where disease-carrying mosquitoes bred were filled in, and a modern sewage and water-supply system was constructed. The harbor was deepened, and modern docking, cargo-handling, and storage facilities, as well as a dry dock, were built.

Hernando Cortez landed near the site of the present city in 1519. There he founded the first Mexican municipality, La Villa Rica de la Veracruz, meaning "Rich Town of the True Cross." The site was twice abandoned because of its rainy, humid, and unhealthful conditions. The present city dates from about 1599. Both the 1857 and 1917 Mexican constitutions were proclaimed here.

The city was attacked and captured repeatedly through the years since its founding. In the 17th and 18th centuries Veracruz was twice raided by pirates. Their raids led to the building of Fort San Juan de Ulúa on one of the small islands in the harbor. The French held the port in 1838 and again in 1861. In

1847 United States troops under General Winfield Scott captured Veracruz in the Mexican War. In 1914, following an incident in which United States sailors were arrested, United States Marines occupied the city for a brief time. Population (1980 census), 284,822.

VERB see GRAMMAR.

VERDI, Giuseppe (1813–1901). One of the leading composers of Italian operas in the 19th century was Giuseppe Verdi. His 'Rigoletto' (1851), 'Il Trovatore' and 'La Traviata' (both 1853), and 'Aïda' (1871) will be staged as long as operas are performed. Verdi was born on Oct. 10, 1813, in Le Roncole, a little village near Parma in northern Italy's Po River valley. The child of a poor family, Verdi showed unusual musical talent at an early age. A local musician named Antonio Barezzi helped him with his education. Verdi was sent to Milan at Barezzi's expense when he was 18. He stayed in Milan for three years then served as musical director in Busseto for two years before returning to Milan. By 1840, just as he had established a reputation and had begun to make money, personal tragedy befell Verdi. Within a three-year period his wife and both of his children died.

With his opera 'Ernani', in 1844, Verdi's fame and fortune were made. The right to publish one opera brought him 4,000 dollars. Later he received 20,000 dollars for the first night's performance of 'Aïda'. Verdi's last opera, 'Falstaff', was produced just be-

Giuseppe Verdi, in a portrait by Giovanni Boldini in 1886

SCALA—Art Resource/EB Inc.

fore his 80th birthday. Thousands of music lovers journeyed to Milan from all parts of Italy for its first performance, and the ovation the old composer received has seldom been equaled in musical history. He died in Milan on Jan. 27, 1901. A Verdi museum has been established in La Scala opera house in Milan to honor his work there.

In his nearly 30 operas, Verdi's music shapes and advances the dramatic action. He often links musical themes and motifs with specific characters and events, especially in such late masterpieces as 'Otello' (1887) and 'Falstaff' (1893). The emotional impact, drama, and soaring melodies that characterize his operas are also found in such nonoperatic works as his 'Requiem' and 'Four Sacred Pieces'. (See also Opera.)

VERDUN, France. An ancient fortress town, Verdun was the site of a major World War I battle. The city stands in the fertile valley of the Meuse River, surrounded by forests in the Lorraine region of northeastern France. Situated on the Meuse River, Verdun is about 50 miles (80 kilometers) from the German border.

One of the oldest cities in France, Verdun was nearly destroyed in World War I, but has been rebuilt with wide streets and modern buildings. The city has two sections: the older part, known as the Heights, is built on a hill and the newer section, with offices and residential and public buildings, spreads along the banks of the Meuse. Narrow stairs lead up to the Heights from Main Street in the newer section. Notable in the Heights is the 11th-century Romanesque-style Notre Dame Cathedral. Once the seat of a Bishopric, it has a Gothic cloister, a treasury, and an 18th-century bishop's residence. The cathedral, situated at the town's highest point, was badly damaged during the war, but has been restored to its original style. The Citadel is an old fortress that has been restored as a war museum. It stands on 4 miles (6.5 kilometers) of underground tunnels, and can still be reached by underground passages.

The city and its countryside are full of monuments commemorating the war. A symbol of French courage and resistance, the battle of Verdun was fought to save the crucial fortress, which protected the road to Paris. The battlefields extend in a semicircle to the north of town. Of the 1 million soldiers who died here, only one fourth have been identified. The unidentified soldiers are buried in the Ossuaire de Douaumont. There are more than 70 cemeteries in the area. Major monuments include the Lion Monument, which marks the spot where the German offensive was stopped; the Victory Monument, which contains a book with the names of people who took part in the fighting; and the Bayonet Trench, which marks the place where a section of French infantry was buried alive during fierce bombardment. A memorial pillar is at Butte de Montfaucan, the highest point of the region. The site was taken over by Germany in September 1914 and was strongly fortified. The American army retook it in September 1918. The war museum at the restored 17th-century Hôtel de Ville, or Town Hall, exhibits numerous decorations conferred upon the city.

Verdun is a strategic communications center and a railroad junction. Its chief industries are food processing, metal production, and hardware and furniture making. The surrounding region is largely agricultural.

The battle of Verdun, in which France repulsed a major German offensive, is considered one of the most devastating engagements of World War I. During March and April 1916 the hills and ridges on the east and west of the Meuse River were bombarded, attacked, counterattacked, taken, and retaken. By July, Germany realized that their plans to take Verdun had failed. The failure at Verdun cost the German army tremendous casualties and materials. Some 300,000

French soldiers died here, but for France and its allies it was a turning point in the war. In Germany's drive against France during World War II, Verdun was taken in a single day, and remained in German hands from 1940 until September 1, 1944, when it was freed by the Allies. The city was heavily bombed by Germany after its liberation by the United States.

Verdun is an ancient city dating back to the Roman Empire. Known as Virodunum in Roman times, the most notable event in its early history was the signing of the Treaty of Verdun in 843, which divided the former empire of Charlemagne among his three grandsons. The treaty laid the foundations of several states of modern Europe, including France and Germany. Verdun was conquered by German invaders in the 10th century and was later linked with Metz and Toul to form the Three Bishoprics territory. France took possession of Verdun in 1552, but confirmed the ownership by the Peace of Westphalia in 1648. The city remained under Prussian control from 1870 to 1873. Population (1982 census), 21,170.

VERLAINE, Paul (1844–96). The French lyric poet Paul Verlaine is known for the musical quality of his verse. Associated early in his life with the group of French poets called the Parnassians, he later became the leader of the symbolists, a group of writers who sought freedom from the rigid conventions of French poetry. His 'Songs Without Words', published in 1874, is one of the masterpieces of the symbolist movement. Verlaine, along with Stéphane Mallarmé and Arthur Rimbaud, also belonged to a group of poets called the decadents, who believed that the rules of everyday life do not apply in art.

Paul-Marie Verlaine was born on March 30, 1844, in Metz, France. He graduated from the Lycée Bonaparte in Paris in 1862 and began associating with poets and writers. His first published poem, 'Monsieur Prudhomme', appeared in 1863. His first volume of poetry, 'Poèmes saturniens', came out in 1866.

Verlaine was married in 1870, but the following year he became infatuated with the young poet Arthur Rimbaud. Verlaine abandoned his wife and son, and the two poets traveled in France, Belgium, and England. The relationship with Rimbaud was a stormy one—in 1873 Verlaine shot and wounded Rimbaud and was sent to prison. After his release Verlaine taught for several years in England. After the death of a close friend in 1883 and of his mother in 1886, Verlaine abandoned any attempt to reform his life. He continued to write, but he became dissipated and the quality of his work suffered. His admirers and friends helped him by publishing his writings and providing support. He died in Paris on Jan. 8, 1896.

VERMEER, Jan (1632–75). One of the greatest 17th-century Dutch painters, Jan Vermeer is known for his light-drenched genre pictures—scenes from everyday life. They are both realistic and poetic, conveying the sense that Vermeer saw beauty in the simplest object.

'Allegory of Painting', a self-portrait in oil by Vermeer, was painted in about 1665. It measures 1 meter by 1.2 meters and is on display at Vienna's Art History Museum.

He was baptized in Delft, the Netherlands, on Oct. 31, 1632. His father dealt in art, kept a tavern, and designed and sold *caffa,* a type of silk cloth. Nothing further is known of Vermeer's first 20 years. The marriage register at Delft records his wedding on April 5, 1653, to Catharina Bolnes.

When he was 21, Vermeer was enrolled as a master painter in the Guild of Saint Luke, which regulated the arts in Delft. Only a few of Vermeer's paintings were dated. The dates of his other works have been deduced mainly from the brush strokes, which grew progressively more refined. Working with painstaking care, Vermeer painted fewer than 40 pictures in his lifetime. The exact number is disputed. Like his father, he also dealt in art.

Vermeer died in 1675, when his finances were at their lowest. Staggering under defense taxes imposed after France declared war on the Netherlands in 1672, the Dutch no longer had money for art. Vermeer's widow petitioned the town council for a bankruptcy ruling. She struggled to keep her husband's work intact despite grasping creditors.

Nine years after Catharina died in 1687, there were 21 paintings by Vermeer listed in the catalog of an Amsterdam auction. This was the last time for nearly 200 years that his work received serious attention. In the mid-19th century artists began to recognize that he was unique in his understanding and rendering of light and shade. Characteristic of Vermeer's paintings are 'Allegory of Painting'; 'Officer and Laughing Girl'; 'View of Delft'; 'Girl with the Red Hat'; and 'Young Woman with a Water Jug' (*see* Painting).

The quiet, rustic charm of such villages as Burke Hollow characterizes Vermont and attracts many visitors to the state. The spired meetinghouse remains as it was when built in 1825.

VERMONT

VERMONT. The state of Vermont has long been noted for its hardy, independent people. Its first settlers were New England pioneers. They built farms and villages on the rocky, forested land of the Green Mountains. For years this land was claimed by both New Hampshire and New York. In 1777, however, Vermont declared itself an independent state and adopted a constitution. It was admitted to the Union as the 14th state in 1791. Vermont was thus the first state to be added to the original 13 colonies that formed the United States.

Vermont is one of the smallest states in the Union. It ranks only 43rd in area and 48th in population. Despite its small size, the state has contributed fully to the growth of the nation. The Vermont dairy industry is one of the most significant in the Northeast. Vermont is one of the nation's leading producers of maple sugar and syrup. The state is also a valuable source of granite and marble.

The list of famous people born in Vermont is headed by two presidents of the United States—Chester A. Arthur and Calvin Coolidge. An unsuccessful pres-

Population (1980): 511,456—rank, 48th state. Urban, 33.8%; rural, 66.2%. Persons per square mile, 55.2 (persons per square kilometer, 21.3)—rank, 29th state.

Extent: Area, 9,609 square miles (24,887 square kilometers), including 342 square miles (886 square kilometers) of water surface (43rd state in size).

Elevation: Highest, Mount Mansfield, 4,393 feet (1,339 meters), near Underhill; lowest, Lake Champlain, 95 feet (29 meters); average, 1,000 feet (305 meters).

Geographic Center: 3 miles (5 kilometers) east of Roxbury.

Temperature: Extremes—lowest, −50° F (−45.6° C), Bloomfield, Dec. 30, 1933; highest, 105° F (40.6° C), Vernon, July 4, 1911. Averages at Burlington—January, 18.6° F (−7.4° C); July, 70.4° F (21.3° C); annual, 45.2° F (7.3° C).

Precipitation: At Burlington—annual average, 33.80 inches (859 millimeters).

Land Use: Crops, 10%; pasture, 5%; forest, 77%; other, 8%.

For statistical information about Agriculture, Education, Employment, Finance, Government, Manufacturing, Mining, Population Trends, and Vital Statistics, see VERMONT FACT SUMMARY.

idential candidate was Stephen A. Douglas. Ethan Allen was one of the first heroes of the American Revolution. In the Spanish-American War, Admiral George Dewey won fame at Manila Bay. Vermont inventors include John Deere, who made the first steel plowshare, and Thomas Davenport, who devised the first electric motor. John Dewey, a noted educator, changed many school practices.

The early name of the region was New Hampshire Grants. In 1777 it was named New Connecticut. This was later changed to Vermont at the suggestion of Dr. Thomas Young of Philadelphia. The name comes from two French words, *vert* and *mont,* meaning "green mountain." The nickname Green Mountain State comes from the chief range in the state.

Survey of the Green Mountain State

Vermont lies in the New England region of the United States. It is bordered on the north by the Canadian province of Quebec. To the east the Connecticut River forms the boundary with New Hampshire. Massachusetts is the state to the south. On the west is New York, separated from Vermont for about 100 miles (160 kilometers) by Lake Champlain.

The state's greatest length from north to south is 159 miles (256 kilometers). Its greatest width is 89 miles (143 kilometers) from east to west. Its narrowest width is 37 miles (60 kilometers). Vermont's total area is 9,609 square miles (24,887 square kilometers), including 342 square miles (886 square kilometers) of inland water surface.

Five Natural Regions

The crest of the Green Mountains runs through the center of the state from the Massachusetts boundary northward into Canada. This highland is sometimes said to divide the state into eastern and western sections. There are five distinct natural regions, however.

The Champlain Valley covers all the northwestern part of the state as far south as the Poultney River and Bomoseen Lake. It is a narrow lowland wedged between Lake Champlain on the west and the Green Mountains on the east. Along Lake Champlain is the state's lowest point—95 feet (29 meters). Draining into the lake are Vermont's three longest streams—the Lamoille and Winooski rivers and Otter Creek.

The Taconic Mountains rise south of Brandon and extend southward along the New York border into Massachusetts. The highest peak in this narrow range is Mount Equinox at 3,816 feet (1,163 meters). It is located a few miles west of Manchester. At the eastern edge of the Taconics is the Valley of Vermont, which separates this region from the Green Mountains.

The Green Mountains, part of the Appalachian Highlands, form the backbone of Vermont. They extend the length of the state and vary in width from about 21 miles (34 kilometers) in the north to some 36 miles (58 kilometers) in the south. These highlands are heavily forested. Near Underhill is Mount Mansfield, the highest point in the state at 4,393 feet (1,339 meters).

The New England Upland borders the Green Mountains on the east for the entire length of the state. This plateaulike region, sharply cut by streams, is sometimes called the Vermont Piedmont. The Upland is the lake region of the state.

The White Mountains Region in northeastern Vermont is an extension of a larger highland region in New Hampshire. Located mainly in Essex County, it is a thinly populated, mountainous wilderness.

Climate and Weather

Vermont's climate is characterized by wide temperature ranges, even distribution of precipitation, short summers, and long winters. Variations throughout the state in temperature and precipitation are due mainly to elevation.

Average January temperatures range from 16° F (−8.9° C) in the northeast to 20° F (−6.7° C) in the Champlain Valley. Average July temperatures range from 67° F (19° C) in the northeast and southeast to 70° F (21° C) in the Champlain Valley. Precipitation, heaviest in summer, ranges from an annual average of 52 inches (132 centimeters) in the south to 32 inches (81 centimeters) in the northwest. Snowfall varies from 55 inches (140 centimeters) yearly in the west and in the Connecticut Valley to 125 inches (318 centimeters) elsewhere. The growing season is 130 to 150 days in the Lake Champlain and Connecticut Valley areas and 100 to 130 days in the rest of the state.

Natural Resources and Conservation

Much of the soil in Vermont is too thin and rocky for general farming. The most valuable agricultural resource is extensive pasturage for the state's dairy industry. There are about 4,400,000 acres (1,780,680 hectares) of commercial forest land. The most valuable tree is the sugar maple. The white pine is valuable in the Connecticut River valley. Groves of sugar maples supply lumber and sap for maple sugar and syrup (*see* Maple).

Greater Vermont Association

A hiker prepares a meal in a trail shelter in Mount Mansfield State Forest, one of more than 30 state forests in Vermont.

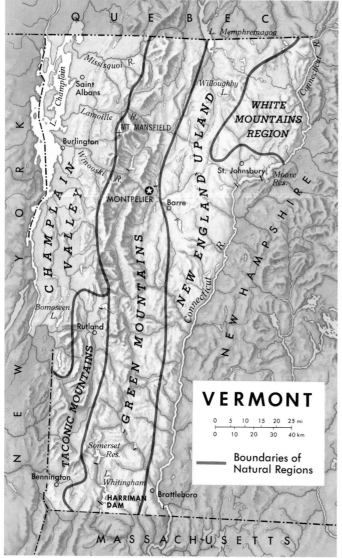

Stone, particularly marble and granite, is the most valuable mineral. The chief commercial resources are the state's lakes, mountains, and climate, which attract many tourists. Some mountain rivers are dammed and used for hydroelectric power. The highest dam (275 feet; 84 meters) is Ball Mountain Dam, completed in 1961, on the West River.

The major conservation agencies of the state were created in 1947. They are the departments of Fish and Wildlife; Forests, Parks, and Recreation; and Water Resources and Environmental Engineering. The Vermont Development Commission was established in 1945 to promote the interests of the state.

People

Before the arrival of Europeans, the Indians entered what is now Vermont only to hunt and fish. The first colonists in the area came from New Hampshire to the east and New York to the west. Because it had little manufacturing, few immigrants from foreign lands settled in the state. The largest foreign group has been made up of French-Canadian farmers who have crossed the border to settle in the northern counties.

Today the great majority of the people are of English background. Vermont's population is 99 percent white—the highest percentage of any state. About 4 percent of the state's people are foreign born. Most of these are from Canada.

About two thirds of the people live in small villages and on farms. The rest live in towns and cities with a population of 2,500 or more. Only three communities have more than 15,000 residents each.

Manufacturing and Cities

In comparison with other states Vermont has little manufacturing. After the services industry, however, manufacturing employs more workers than does any other occupation in the state.

The chief manufacturing industry is the making of electrical and electronic equipment. The second most valuable industry is fabricated metal products. The manufacture of nonelectrical machinery is third in value. Paper and allied products rank fourth. Printing and publishing is also significant. Food products, transportation equipment, and lumber and wood products are also made.

Burlington, the largest city, is a port on Lake Champlain and the chief manufacturing center. The second largest city is Rutland in the south-central part of the state. It is noted for its marble quarries. Barre in central Vermont is a great granite center. Brattleboro in the southeast is noted for printing and publishing.

The state capital is Montpelier (*see* Montpelier). The chief regional trading centers are Saint Albans in the northwest, Bennington in the southwest, and St. Johnsbury in the northeast.

Products of the Land

Vermont has about 6,000 farms, of which about 40 percent are full-time dairy farms. The most valuable agricultural product is milk. It is sold in markets as far away as Boston, Mass., and New York City. Hay, the most valuable crop, is cut and stored to feed dairy herds during the winter.

The major farming areas are in the Champlain Basin and the Connecticut River valley. These regions produce corn, potatoes, oats, and truck crops. Apples are the most valuable cash crop and are grown chiefly along the shores of Lake Champlain. Franklin County in northwestern Vermont is the largest producer in the state-wide maple-sugar industry, in which Vermont is

Ewing Galloway

a national leader. Other agricultural products are beef and veal, eggs, chickens, turkeys, sheep, and wool.

The state's most valuable mineral product is dimension stone. Marble is quarried west of the Green Mountains. A valuable product since the first quarry was opened in Dorset in 1785, Vermont marble has been used in many buildings. Granite is taken from the Barre region and from other quarries on the east slopes of the Green Mountains. The slate industry is centered in Rutland County.

Vermont ranks third among the states in talc production. Sand and gravel are also valuable mineral products. The state was once a leader in asbestos production, but health concerns related to the effects of asbestos fibers in the lungs have caused severe cutbacks in the industry.

Transportation

Because of the Green Mountain barrier through the center of the state, most transportation routes run in a generally north-south direction. The first main road extended northwestward from Springfield to Chimney Point on Lake Champlain. This was the Crown Point Military Road, constructed in 1759–60.

Today Vermont has nearly 14,000 miles (22,530 kilometers) of federal, state, and local highways. The main north-south highways are US 7 in the Vermont Valley west of the mountains and US 5 in the Connecticut Valley east of the mountains. The chief east-west highways are US 2 in the north and US 4 across central Vermont. Two interstate highways pass through Vermont. Interstate 91

Across Lake Champlain from Crown Point, N.Y., rise the Green Mountains in western Vermont. In the foreground are the ruins of Crown Point Fort, famous in American Revolution fighting.

parallels the Connecticut River and US 5. Interstate 89 runs across Vermont from White River Junction to Highgate Township.

In 1848 the first railroad in the state, the Vermont Central, was opened between White River Junction and Bethel. This line was later completed across the state to Burlington. Today the state is served by a dozen railroad lines. In addition six airlines provide regularly scheduled service. Shipping is significant on Lake Champlain.

Popular Vacationland

Vermont's cool climate, mountain lakes, and fine scenery have made the state a tourist attraction of

Curtis Publishing Company

From the village of Stowe can be seen the crest of the thickly wooded Green Mountains. At the far left is Mount Mansfield, Vermont's highest peak.

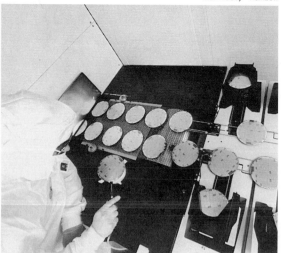

A technician at an IBM plant in Burlington, Vt., inspects silicon wafers as they come out of diffusion ovens.

growing popularity. Lake Champlain lures thousands every summer for boating and other water sports. Lake Memphremagog, shared with Canada, is lined with summer homes. The most popular hiking route is the Long Trail, which follows the crest of the Green Mountains for more than 260 miles (418 kilometers).

Many winter visitors come for downhill and cross-country skiing. There are 20 major downhill ski areas, including Killington, Stowe, Stratton, Dover, Warren, Sugarbush, and Jay Peak.

Education

Vermont's pioneers put up log schoolhouses almost as soon as they built their cabins. The constitution of 1777 called for state-supported schools from the elementary grades through the college level. A town school-district system of education developed. In the 1840s the public high school began to compete with the state's many private academies.

Today the public school system is managed by the Department of Education. It is directed by a board of education appointed by the governor. A commissioner of education administers its policies.

The largest institution of higher learning is the University of Vermont and State Agricultural College. The university, located at Burlington, was chartered in 1791 and opened to students in 1800. Other state-supported schools are Vermont Technical College at Randolph Center and colleges at Castleton, Johnson, and Lyndonville.

Other schools of higher education are Middlebury College at Middlebury, Norwich University at Northfield, Saint Michael's College at Winooski, Goddard College at Plainfield, Trinity College at Burlington, Bennington College at Bennington, Marlboro College at Marlboro, and Green Mountain College at Poultney. There are also junior colleges located in Burlington and Montpelier.

Government and Politics

Montpelier has been Vermont's capital since 1805. Before that time the capital was at various places—including Windsor and Rutland. The state is governed under a constitution adopted in 1793.

The chief executive officer is the governor, elected every two years. The General Assembly consists of the Senate and the House of Representatives. The judiciary is headed by the Supreme Court. The major element in local government is the town meeting. All voters must take the Freeman's Oath: "You solemnly

A Vermont farmer picks up hay bales from his field. Hay is the state's most valuable crop. It is cut and stored to be used as feed for dairy herds during the winter.

swear (or affirm) that whenever you give your vote or suffrage, touching any matter that concerns the State of Vermont, you will do it so as in your conscience you shall judge will most conduce to the best good of the same, as established by the Constitution, without fear or favor of any person."

In national and local politics Vermont was for many years strongly Republican. Except in 1964, the state cast its electoral votes for the Republican candidate for president in every election since 1856. During the late 20th century a balance between the two major political parties began to develop in state politics.

HISTORY

What is now Vermont was included in several different grants of land made by British kings. The charter of Massachusetts Bay of 1629 laid claim to most of the land west of the Connecticut River. New York claimed the region on the basis of grants first made to the duke of York in 1664. A third claim was made by New Hampshire following a decree of King George II in 1740. After Vermont declared itself an independent state in 1777, the other states finally agreed to recognize its boundary claims. Massachusetts adjusted its differences in 1781, New Hampshire in 1782, and New York in 1790. This paved the way for the admission of Vermont to the Union in 1791. The following sections tell the history of the state from settlement to the present.

Exploration and Settlement

The first Europeans to see the Green Mountains were Samuel de Champlain and his party of French explorers. They paddled up the lake named for Champlain in 1609 (*see* Champlain). For nearly 150 years more the area remained unsettled.

Old First Church in Bennington is typical of the old New England architecture preserved in Vermont. Built in 1806, the church is still in use today.

In 1666 the French built Fort St. Anne on Isle La Motte as part of their Lake Champlain fortifications. The settlement was short-lived. The British made the first permanent settlement at Ft. Dummer in 1724. It was built by Massachusetts Colony to protect its people in the Connecticut Valley. The town of Brattleboro later grew up around the fort.

The close of the French and Indian War in 1763 gave the British possession of the Lake Champlain area. Lord Jeffrey Amherst had built a strong fort at Crown Point, N.Y., and a military road through the wilderness to the Connecticut River. After the war many settlers entered the region.

Beginning in 1749 the governor of New Hampshire had issued grants of land for new towns in the Vermont region. Settlers on these New Hampshire grants cleared forests, built cabins, and planted crops. By 1754, 16 grants had been made.

Green Mountain Boys

After 1764 the New York governor granted charters to land already occupied under the New Hampshire grants. Many settlers could not pay additional fees for their hard-won acres. In 1770 Ethan Allen recruited the Green Mountain Boys to protect the interests of New Hampshire settlers in the western part of the territory. Others in this daring band included his brother Ira Allen and Seth Warner.

A New York judge was sent to Westminster to open court in March 1775, but enraged citizens took over the courthouse. A sheriff's posse fired on the settlers, killing William French and Daniel Houghton in the Westminster massacre. When the American Revolution broke out, however, the Green Mountain patriots joined with vigor in the larger cause.

On May 10, 1775, Ethan Allen led his band in the capture of Ft. Ticonderoga in New York. Seth Warner helped take Crown Point the next day. Under the leadership of Benedict Arnold, Americans gained control of Lake Champlain. Many Green Mountain Boys followed Allen in a futile attack on Montreal. Others followed Arnold in his unsuccessful attempt against Quebec. (*See also* Allen; Revolution, American.)

Separate State Is Organized

In January 1777 a convention of Vermonters met at Westminster and set up a state independent of both New Hampshire and New York. Another convention met at Windsor in July and adopted a state constitution. It was the first American constitution to give suffrage to all men and to forbid slavery.

In July 1777 the British general John Burgoyne sent a force to capture military supplies stored at Bennington. On August 16 this force was routed west of Bennington by patriots under General John Stark. This victory started the series of defeats that led to the vital surrender of Burgoyne at Saratoga in October.

Vermont asked the Continental Congress for recognition but failed to get it largely because of the disputed boundaries with neighboring states. There were even some attempts to unite with Canada. Finally, after all the boundary arguments were settled, Vermont was admitted to the Union on March 4, 1791.

Civil War to the Present

During the Civil War, Confederates raided Saint Albans, robbing the town's banks of more than $200,000. They escaped to Canada where they were brought to trial and freed.

The first president from Vermont was Chester A. Arthur, born at Fairfield. He became the nation's 21st president when James A. Garfield was assassi-

nated in 1881. In 1923 the death of Warren G. Harding made Calvin Coolidge of Plymouth president of the United States. The new president was sworn in at Plymouth by his father, a notary public.

From 1970 to 1980 the population of Vermont increased by 66,724, or 15 percent. This was above the national average of 11.4 percent, and it was more than the total increase for the state from 1920 to 1980. (*See also* United States, section "New England"; individual entries in Fact-Index on Vermont persons, places, products, and events.)

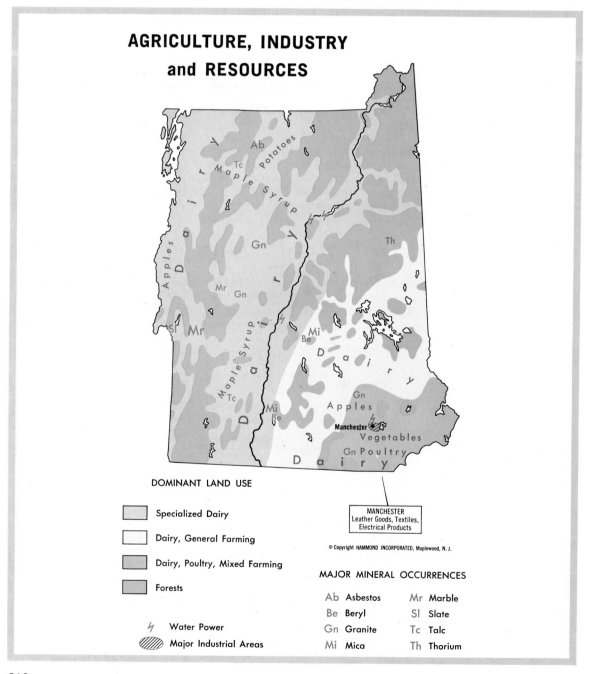

AGRICULTURE, INDUSTRY and RESOURCES

DOMINANT LAND USE

- Specialized Dairy
- Dairy, General Farming
- Dairy, Poultry, Mixed Farming
- Forests

⚡ Water Power
▨ Major Industrial Areas

MANCHESTER
Leather Goods, Textiles,
Electrical Products

© Copyright HAMMOND INCORPORATED, Maplewood, N. J.

MAJOR MINERAL OCCURRENCES

Ab	Asbestos	Mr	Marble
Be	Beryl	Sl	Slate
Gn	Granite	Tc	Talc
Mi	Mica	Th	Thorium

Notable Events in Vermont History

1609—Samuel de Champlain discovers lake later named for him.

1666—French erect Fort St. Anne on Isle La Motte.

1690—English establish outpost at Chimney Point.

1724—Massachusetts colonists build Fort Dummer near Brattleboro to fight French and Indians; is first permanent white settlement in Vermont.

1749—Benning Wentworth, governor of New Hampshire, issues land grants in Vermont.

1759—In French and Indian War British drive French from Lake Champlain region. Crown Point Military Road through Vermont built in 1759–60.

1763—France cedes all claims to area to Great Britain.

1764—King George III sustains New York claim to "New Hampshire grants" made to duke of York in 1664.

1770—Ethan Allen organizes Green Mountain Boys to drive out New York authorities.

1775—New York officials clash with settlers at Westminster courthouse. Allen and Green Mountain Boys, with Benedict Arnold, capture Fort Ticonderoga from British; Seth Warner and his men take fort at Crown Point.

1777—Gen. John Burgoyne captures Fort Ticonderoga. Americans lose battle of Hubbardton; win battle of Bennington. Vermont declares itself independent state; adopts first state constitution to provide universal manhood suffrage and to ban slavery.

1778—Thomas Chittenden elected first governor.

1785—First marble quarry opened at Dorset.

1791—Vermont becomes 14th state, March 4; University of Vermont chartered at Burlington.

1793—Present state constitution adopted.

1805—Montpelier chosen as state capital; present Statehouse completed in 1859.

1814—Americans win battle of Plattsburg on Lake Champlain in War of 1812.

1823—First normal school in U. S. opened at Concord Corner. Champlain Canal links Lake Champlain with Erie Canal.

1834—Thomas Davenport, blacksmith, invents the world's first electric motor at Brandon.

1837—State enacts antislavery Vermont Resolutions; provokes ire of South; Congress passes "gag rule."

1864—Confederate guerrillas raid Saint Albans.

1866–70—Fenians (Irish rebels) try invasion of Canada.

1881—Vice-president Chester A. Arthur, born 1830 at Fairfield, becomes 21st president of U. S.

1898—Com. George Dewey, born 1837 at Montpelier, leads U. S. fleet in defeat of Spanish in Manila Bay; becomes 3d U. S. admiral.

1923—Vice-president Calvin Coolidge, born 1872 at Plymouth, becomes 30th president of U. S.

1927—Floods devastate large part of Vermont.

1947–53—Warren R. Austin, born 1877 in Highgate township, is head of U. S. delegation to United Nations.

1950—Hydroelectric plant opened at Wilder.

1953—Vermont Development Credit Corporation organized to seek new industries for the state.

1961—Ball Mountain Dam completed on West River.

1962—Vermont elects first Democratic governor in more than 100 years.

1964—Lyndon B. Johnson is first Democratic presidential candidate to receive state's electoral votes.

1974—Vermont French Cultural Commission organized to promote language and culture of French Americans, state's largest ethnic minority.

1609

1724

1785

1834

STATE FLOWER:
Red Clover

STATE TREE:
Sugar Maple

STATE BIRD:
Hermit Thrush

STATE SEAL: Pine tree rises from
forest; grain sheaves, cow in
background; clouds at top;
state motto below scene.

Vermont Profile

FLAG: *See* **Flags of the United States.**
MOTTO: Freedom and Unity.
**SONG: 'Hail, Vermont!'—words and
music by Josephine Hovey-Perry.**

Vermont has been called a piece of America's past. In no other state has natural beauty been so untouched by modern development or the small farms and towns of a century ago been so well preserved. Vermont lacks the urban sprawl of many other parts of the nation. A refuge for city dwellers, perhaps its greatest asset is its peaceful beauty.

Vermont owes its rugged New England character to inhospitable terrain. The granite spine of its forested Green Mountains makes large-scale farming difficult. Except for Lake Champlain, its many rivers and lakes offer no harbors for commerce. Nonetheless, Vermont's mountains and rivers sustain its people. In winter, the mountains are a skier's paradise. The rocky foundation provides the nation's foremost marble and granite quarries. In the river valleys dairying flourishes and vacationists come to play.

Vermont was first explored by Champlain in 1609, when he sailed into the vast lake now bearing his name. After permanent settlers came in 1724, the Indians, the colonial powers France and Britain, and the American colonists fought for this land. However, in 1777 Vermont declared itself an independent republic. Only after the Revolutionary War, in 1791, did Vermont join the Union. It was the first state to adopt a constitution prohibiting slavery. Always a state of farmers, Vermont today produces dairy goods, hay, and cattle. Food and paper products and machinery are made in the state's small cities.

Vermont's rural population and the number of its farms have declined drastically in recent years, and its textile and lumber industries have been losing ground. Although the state has succeeded in attracting new industries, the supply of skilled labor and housing has not been sufficient to meet their needs. Yet there seems to be little doubt that the development of industry as well as tourism probably offers the most promise for Vermont's future.

On Aug. 16, 1777, American troops defeated the British at Bennington. The Bennington Battle Monument, marking the event, was dedicated in 1891 during Vermont's centennial year. The 412 steps of the 306-foot tower lead to an observation platform.

The gold leaf dome of Vermont's State Capitol is visible for miles around Montpelier. The Capitol, built of Barre granite in the Greek Revival style, was completed in 1859. Montpelier, conveniently situated in the center of the state, became the capital city in 1805.

On the eastern shore of Lake Champlain lies Burlington, the chief manufacturing center of Vermont and its largest and most cosmopolitan city. The Queen City of Vermont was chartered in 1763, settled in 1773, and incorporated as a city in 1865.

The modern Guy W. Bailey Memorial Library of the University of Vermont, at Burlington, stands on one of the nation's oldest campuses. The university was chartered in 1791 and offered its first classes in 1800. The Bailey library was opened in 1961.

Vermont picture profile

Granite quarrying was begun near Barre early in the 19th century. Today this area in central Vermont produces more granite than any other region in the world. The Rock of Ages operation alone covers over 20 acres.

Vermont's appeal to tourists is largely due to the peace and charm of its countryside, much of which has remained unchanged for more than a century. This gristmill stands near Waterbury, in the heart of the Green Mountains. It dates from the 1840's.

The old Constitution House at Windsor is called the birthplace of Vermont. At this house, then a public tavern, the state's first constitution was adopted in 1777. Now restored, the building has been open to the public since 1961 as a historical shrine.

Vermont is a leading producer of maple syrup and maple sugar. The industry's largest plant is at St. Johnsbury. Other agricultural products include milk, hay, livestock, eggs, and apples.

In the village of Plymouth Notch stands the Coolidge Homestead, once the home of President Calvin Coolidge. Here, in 1923, Coolidge took the presidential oath of office, which his father administered. The house has been restored to its condition at that time.

HORSESHOE BARN

SHELBURNE MUSEUM ENTRANCE

The Shelburne Museum, near Burlington, is a unique exhibit of the architecture, arts and crafts, and ways of life of early New England. Many of its old homes, barns, shops, and other buildings were moved from their original sites. The museum was established in 1947.

DUTTON HOUSE

WEBB MEMORIAL BUILDING

The slopes and trails of the Green Mountains have made Vermont the leading ski center east of the Rockies. The first ski tow in the United States was built near Woodstock in 1933. The Smuggler's Notch ski area near Jeffersonville is one of about three dozen in the state.

Vermont's long winters and numerous rivers provide ample opportunity for ice skating. These skaters are on the First Branch of the White River near Tunbridge. The covered bridge is one of nearly one hundred such bridges on Vermont's public roads.

VERMONT FACT SUMMARY

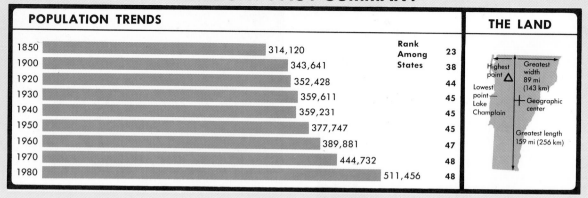

POPULATION TRENDS

Year	Population		Rank Among States
1850	314,120		23
1900	343,641		38
1920	352,428		44
1930	359,611		45
1940	359,231		45
1950	377,747		45
1960	389,881		47
1970	444,732		48
1980	511,456		48

THE LAND

Highest point △

Lowest point — Lake Champlain

Greatest width 89 mi (143 km)

Geographic center

Greatest length 159 mi (256 km)

LARGEST CITIES (1980 census)

Burlington (37,712): commercial, financial, and transportation center of state; aircraft armaments; computer components; business machines; structural steel; concrete products; Lake Champlain port; Ethan Allen burial place; University of Vermont; Burlington College.

Rutland (18,436): commercial and manufacturing hub; marble; scales; castings; plywood; machinery; airplane parts; service center for nearby ski areas; College of St. Joseph the Provider.

Bennington (15,815): industrial village on Walloomsac River between Taconic and Green mountain ranges; furniture; textiles; batteries; dairy products; apples; maple sugar; poultry; tourism; ski areas nearby; Bennington Battle Monument; Old First Church (1806); Bennington Museum; Bennington College.

Essex (14,392): industrial town on Winooski River; electronics.

Colchester (12,629): agricultural community in Burlington area; water sports recreation center for Lake Champlain.

Brattleboro (11,886): resort and manufacturing town on Connecticut River; commercial center for southeastern part of state; printing; paper; lumber products; optical goods; handbags; School for International Training; Austine School for the Deaf.

South Burlington (10,679): commercial, residential, and manufacturing community adjacent to Burlington; suburban community with South Burlington Village; computer manufacturing.

Springfield (10,190): center of state's machine-tool industry; state's oldest schoolhouse (1785).

Barre (9,824): industrial city; granite center; electrical equipment.

Montpelier (8,241): state capital on Winooski River; granite; insurance; plastics; wood and concrete products; machinery; ski areas nearby; Vermont College of Norwich University (*see* Montpelier).

VITAL STATISTICS 1985 (per 1,000 population)

Birthrate:	14.8
Death Rate:	9.0
Marriage Rate:	10.5
Divorce Rate:	4.3

GOVERNMENT

Capital: Montpelier (since 1805).

Statehood: Became 14th state in the Union on March 4, 1791.

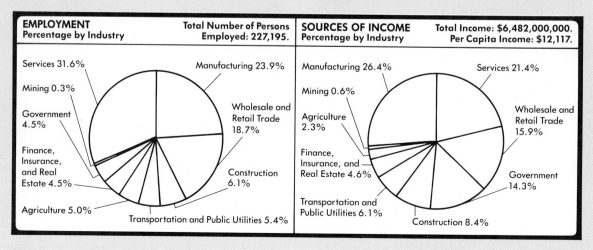

EMPLOYMENT
Percentage by Industry
Total Number of Persons Employed: 227,195.

Services 31.6%
Mining 0.3%
Government 4.5%
Finance, Insurance, and Real Estate 4.5%
Agriculture 5.0%
Manufacturing 23.9%
Wholesale and Retail Trade 18.7%
Construction 6.1%
Transportation and Public Utilities 5.4%

SOURCES OF INCOME
Percentage by Industry
Total Income: $6,482,000,000.
Per Capita Income: $12,117.

Manufacturing 26.4%
Mining 0.6%
Agriculture 2.3%
Finance, Insurance, and Real Estate 4.6%
Transportation and Public Utilities 6.1%
Services 21.4%
Wholesale and Retail Trade 15.9%
Government 14.3%
Construction 8.4%

Constitution: Adopted 1793; amendment may be passed by two-thirds vote of the Senate and majority vote of the House; majority vote of each house at next session; ratified by majority voting on it in an election.

Representation in U.S. Congress: Senate—2. House of Representatives—1. Electoral votes—3.

Legislature: Senators—30; term, 2 years. Representatives—150; term, 2 years.

Executive Officers: Governor—term, 2 years; may succeed self. Other officials—lieutenant governor, secretary of state, attorney general, treasurer; all elected; terms, 2 years.

Judiciary: Supreme Court—5 justices; term, 6 years. Superior courts—10 judges; term, 6 years. District courts—14 judges; term, 6 years.

County: 14 counties; supervised by 2 assistant judges of county courts; elected for 2-year terms.

MAJOR PRODUCTS

Agricultural: Milk, hay, corn, potatoes, oats, apples, maple sugar, beef and veal, eggs, chickens, turkeys, sheep, wool.

Manufactured: Electrical and electronic equipment, fabricated metal products, nonelectrical machinery, paper and allied products, printing and publishing, food products, transportation equipment, lumber and wood products.

Mined: Dimension stone, construction sand and gravel, crushed stone, talc, asbestos.

EDUCATION AND CULTURE

Universities and Colleges: Bennington College, Bennington; Green Mountain College, Poultney; Lyndon State College, Lyndonville; Marlboro College, Marlboro; Middlebury College, Middlebury; Norwich University, Northfield; St. Michael's College, Winooski; University of Vermont, Burlington; Vermont College, Montpelier.

Libraries: Bailey-Howe Memorial Library at the University of Vermont, Burlington; Brooks Memorial Library, Brattleboro; Crossett Library at Bennington College, Bennington; Middlebury College libraries, Middlebury; Vermont Department of Libraries, Montpelier.

Notable Museums: Bennington Museum, Bennington; Brattleboro Museum and Art Center, Brattleboro; Fairbanks Museum and Planetarium, St. Johnsbury; Johnson Gallery of Middlebury College, Middlebury; Robert Hull Fleming Museum, Burlington; Shelburne Museum, Shelburne; Wilson Castle, Proctor.

PLACES OF INTEREST

Allis State Park: near Brookfield; scenic views from summit.

Ascutney State Park: near Ascutney; parkway up Ascutney Mountain; foot trails; camping, snowmobile trails.

Branbury State Park: near Brandon; sandy beach on Lake Dunmore, nature trails, scenic views.

Brighton State Park: near Island Pond; scenic; white sand beach; swimming; fishing; nature trails.

Button Bay State Park: near Panton, on Lake Champlain; recreational area; boating; fishing; camping.

Constitution House: in Windsor; where Vermont's first constitution was written in 1777.

Coolidge Birthplace: in Plymouth; birthplace and boyhood home of former president.

Crystal Lake State Park: near Barton; white sand beach.

D.A.R. State Park: near Bridport, on Lake Champlain; boating; fishing; playground; picnicking area.

Dorset: homes of many writers and artists.

Dutton Pines State Park: near Brattleboro; picnic area in pine grove.

Elmore State Park: near Elmore; beach; sugar maples; Elmore Mountain; camping; swimming; fishing; boating; hiking.

Emerald Lake State Park: near Dorset; picnicking; camping.

Gifford Woods State Park: near Sherburne; sugar maples.

Grand Isle County: summer resort area on island group in Lake Champlain; apple orchards.

Grand Isle State Park: near South Hero; scenic views of lake; picnicking; camping.

Jamaica State Park: near Jamaica; picnicking; fishing.

Lake St. Catherine State Park: near Poultney; wooded area on Lake St. Catherine; swimming; picnicking; nature museum and trail.

Long Trail: footpath extends length of state.

Manchester: resort; golf, skiing; art center.

Marble Exhibit: in Proctor; large display of many varieties of marble and granite and their uses, massive marble factory.

Middlebury: resort; Middlebury College; annual winter carnival; Morgan Horse Farm nearby.

Molly Stark State Park: near Wilmington; fire tower on Mount Olga; scenic views; picnicking.

Molly Stark Trail: between Bennington and Brattleboro; scenic road through Green Mountains.

Mount Philo State Park: near Burlington; panoramic views; picnicking; hiking.

St. Albans Bay State Park: in St. Albans Bay; beach on Lake Champlain; picnicking; fishing; boating.

Sand Bar State Park: near Burlington; beach on Lake Champlain; swimming; boating; picnicking.

Smuggler's Notch: on Mount Mansfield, near Morrisville; pass used to smuggle goods from Canada in War of 1812; skiing.

Weston: restoration of pioneer village.

Wilgus State Park: near Ascutney; hiking trails; picnicking.

Wolcott: last railroad covered bridge in use in Vermont.

BIBLIOGRAPHY FOR VERMONT

Bruhn, Paul and Milens, Sanders. Vermont's Historic Architecture: a Second Celebration (Preservation Trust of Vermont, 1986).

Budbill, David. Snowshoe Trek to Otter River (Bantam, 1984).

Cheney, Cora. Vermont, the State with the Storybook Past, rev. ed. (New England Press, 1986).

Curtis, Jane and others. Green Mountain Adventures: Vermont's Long Trail (Curtis Lieberman, 1985).

Guyette, Elise. Vermont: a Cultural Patchwork (Cobblestone, 1986).

Jellison, C.A. Ethan Allen: Frontier Rebel (Syracuse Univ. Press, 1983).

Jennison, Keith. Vermonters and the State They're In (New England Press, 1985).

Lasky, Kathryn. Sugaring Time (Macmillan, 1986).

Morrisey, C.T. Vermont (Norton, 1981).

Vermont Heritage Press. Vermont in the Victorian Age: Continuity and Change in the Green Mountain State (1985).

All Fact Summary data are based on current government reports.

VERMONT

COUNTIES

Addison, 29,406 .... A 2
Bennington, 33,345 .... A 4
Caledonia, 25,808 .... C 1
Chittenden, 115,534 .... A 2
Essex, 6,313 .... D 1
Franklin, 34,788 .... B 1
Grand Isle, 4,613 .... A 1
Lamoille, 16,767 .... B 1
Orange, 22,739 .... C 3
Orleans, 23,440 .... C 1
Rutland, 58,347 .... A 3
Washington, 52,393 .... B 2
Windham, 36,933 .... B 5
Windsor, 51,030 .... B 4

CITIES AND TOWNS

Addison, *889 .... A 2
Albany, *705 .... C 1
Alburg, *1,352 .... A 1
Andover, *350 .... B 4
Arlington, *2,184 .... A 4
Arlington, 1,309 .... A 4
Ascutney, 274 .... C 4
Bakersfield, *852 .... B 1
Barnard, *790 .... B 3
Barnet, *1,338 .... C 2
Barre, 9,824 .... C 2
Barton, *2,990 .... C 1
Barton, 1,062 .... C 1
Bartonsville, 300 .... B 4
Beebe Plain, 950 .... C 1
Beecher Falls, 950 .... D 1
Bellows Falls, 3,456 .... C 4
Belvidere, *218 .... B 1
Bennington, *15,815 .... A 5
Bennington, 9,349 .... A 5
Benson, *739 .... A 3
Berkshire, *1,116 .... B 1
Bethel, *1,715 .... B 3
Bolton, *715 .... B 2
Bomoseen, 700 .... A 3
Bradford, *2,191 .... C 3
Braintree, *1,065 .... B 3
Brandon, *4,194 .... A 3
Brandon, 1,925 .... A 3
Brattleboro, *11,886 .... C 5
Brattleboro, 8,596 .... C 5
Bridgewater, *867 .... B 3
Bridgewater Corners, 84 ..... B 3
Bridport, *997 .... A 3
Bristol, *3,293 .... A 2
Bristol, 1,793 .... A 2
Brookfield, *959 .... B 2
Brownington, *708 .... C 1
Brownsville, 75 .... C 4
Burke, *1,385 .... D 1
Burlington, 37,712 .... A 2
Cabot, *958 .... C 2
Calais, *1,207 .... B 2
Cambridge, *2,019 .... B 1
Canaan, *1,196 .... D 1
Castleton, *3,637 .... A 3
Cavendish, *1,355 .... B 4
Center Rutland, 465 .... A 2
Charlotte, *2,561 .... A 2
Chelsea, *1,091 .... C 2
Chelsea, 525 .... C 2
Chester, *2,791 .... B 4
Chester Depot, 1,267 .... B 4
Chittenden, *927 .... B 3
Colchester, *12,629 .... A 1
Concord, *1,125 .... D 2
Corinth, *904 .... C 3
Cornwall, *993 .... A 2
Coventry, *674 .... C 1
Craftsbury, *844 .... C 1
Craftsbury Common, 55 ..... C 1
Cuttingsville, 200 .... B 3
Danby, *992 .... A 4
Danville, *1,705 .... C 2
Derby (Derby Center), 598 .. C 1
Derby Line, 874 .... C 1
Dorset, *1,648 .... A 4
Duxbury, *877 .... B 2
E. Arlington, 600 .... A 4
E. Barre, 2,172 .... C 2
E. Berkshire, 200 .... B 1
E. Burke, 150 .... D 1
E. Calais, 170 .... C 2
E. Concord, 140 .... D 2
E. Dorset, 550 .... A 4
E. Fairfield, 150 .... B 1
E. Hardwick, 200 .... C 1
E. Haven, 350 .... D 1
E. Jamaica, 200 .... B 4
E. Middlebury, 550 .... A 3
E. Montpelier, *2,205 ...... B 2
E. Poultney, 450 .... A 3
E. Randolph, 180 .... C 3
E. Richford, 150 .... C 1
E. Ryegate, 210 .... D 2
E. Thetford, 30 .... C 3
E. Wallingford, 500 .... B 4
Eden,*612 .... B 1
Eden Mills, 200 .... C 1
Enosburg Falls, 1,207 .... B 1
Essex, *14,392 .... A 2
Essex Jct., 7,033 .... A 2
Fairfax, *1,805 .... B 1
Fairfield, *1,493 .... B 1
Fair Haven, *2,819 .... A 3
Fair Haven, 2,363 .... A 3
Fairlee, *770 .... C 3
Ferrisburg, *2,117 .... A 2
Florence, 250 .... A 3
Forest Dale, 500 .... A 3
Franklin, *1,006 .... B 1
Gaysville, 150 .... B 3
Georgia, *2,818 .... A 1
Georgia Ctr., 225 .... A 1
Gilman, 600 .... D 2
Glover, *843 .... C 1
Grafton, *604 .... B 4
Granby, *70 .... D 1
Grand Isle, *1,238 ..... A 1
Graniteville, 2,172 ..... C 2
Granville, *288 .... B 3
Greensboro, *677 ...... C 1
Groton, *667 .... D 2
Guildhall, *202 .... D 1
Guildhall, 130 .... D 1
Guilford, *1,532 .... B 5
Halifax, *488 .... B 5
Halifax Ctr., 125 ...... B 5
Hancock, *334 .... B 3
Hardwick, *2,613 .... C 2
Hardwick, 1,476 ..... C 2
Hartford, *7,963 ..... C 3
Hartland, *2,396 .... C 3
Hartland Four Corners, 400 ... C 3
Highgate Ctr., 350 ... B 1
Highgate Falls, 400 .. A 1
Highgate Sprs., 100 .. A 1
Hinesburg, *2,690 ... A 2
Hubbardton, *490 ... A 3
Huntington, *1,161 .. A 2
Huntington Ctr., 140 .. B 2
Hyde Park, *2,021 ... B 1
Hyde Park, 475 ...... B 1
Hydeville, 500 .... A 3
Irasburg, *870 ...... C 1
Island Pond, 1,216 .. D 1
Isle La Motte, *393 .. A 1
Jacksonville, 252 ... B 5
Jamaica, *681 ...... B 4
Jay, *302 .... C 1
Jeffersonville, 491 .. B 1
Jericho, *3,575 ..... A 2
Jericho Ctr., 120 ... B 2
Johnson, *2,581 ... B 1
Johnson, 1,393 .... B 1
Jonesville, 300 .... B 2
Killington, 400 .... B 3
Lake Elmore, 250 .. B 1
Lincoln, *870 ...... B 2
Londonderry, *1,510 .. B 4
Lowell, *573 .... C 1
Ludlow, *2,414 .... B 4
Ludlow, 1,352 .... B 4
Lunenburg, *1,138 .. D 2
Lyndon, *4,924 ... C 1
Lyndon Ctr., 246 .. C 1
Lyndonville, 1,401 .. C 1
Maidstone, *100 .. D 1
Manchester, *3,261 .. A 4
Manchester, 563 ... A 4
Manchester Center, 1,719 .. A 4
Manchester Depot, 1,560 .. B 4
Marlboro, *695 .... B 5
Marshfield, *1,267 .. C 2
McIndoe Falls, 140 .. C 2
Middlebury, *7,574 .. A 2
Middlebury, 5,591 ... A 2
Middlesex, *1,235 .. B 2
Middletown Springs, *603 .. A 4
Milton, *6,829 ..... A 1
Milton, 1,411 ...... A 1
Monkton, *1,201 ... A 2
Montgomery, *681 .. B 1
Montgomery Center, 400 .. B 1
Montpelier (cap.), 8,241 .. B 2
Moretown, *1,221 .. B 2
Morgan, *460 ..... D 1
Morrisville, 2,074 .. B 1
Morses Line, 200 .. B 1
Moscow, 250 ..... B 2
Mount Holly, *938 .. B 4
Newbury, *1,699 .. C 2
Newfane, *1,129 .. B 4
Newfane, 119 ..... B 4
New Haven, *1,217 .. A 2
Newport, 4,756 ... C 1
Newport Ctr., 250 .. C 1
N. Bennington, 1,685 .. A 5
N. Clarendon, 750 .. B 3
N. Danville, 200 .. C 2
N. Ferrisburg, 150 .. A 2
Northfield, *5,435 .. B 2
Northfield, 2,033 .. B 2
Northfield Falls, 600 .. B 2
N. Hartland, 500 .. C 3
N. Hero, *442 .... A 1
N. Hero, 60 ...... A 1
N. Hyde Park, 450 .. B 1
N. Montpelier, 188 .. C 2
N. Pomfret, 400 .. B 3
N. Pownal, 700 .. A 5
N. Springfield, 1,200 .. C 4
N. Thetford, 350 .. C 3
N. Troy, 717 ..... C 1
N. Westminster, 310 .. C 4
N. Williston, 300 .. B 2
Norton, *184 ..... C 1
Norwich, *2,398 .. C 3
Old Bennington, 353 .. A 5
Orange, *752 .... C 2
Orleans, 983 .... C 1
Orwell, *901 .... A 3
Panton, *537 ... A 2
Passumpsic, 140 .. C 2
Pawlet, *1,244 .. A 4
Peacham, *531 .. C 2
Perkinsville, 187 .. B 4
Peru, *312 ...... B 4
Pittsfield, *396 .. B 3
Pittsford, *2,590 .. A 3
Plainfield, *1,249 .. C 2
Plymouth, *405 .. B 3
Pomfret, *856 ... B 3
Post Mills, 500 .. C 3
Poultney, *3,196 .. A 3
Poultney, 1,554 .. A 3
Pownal, *3,269 .. A 5
Pownal Ctr., 250 .. A 5
Proctor, *1,998 .. A 3
Proctorsville, 481 .. B 4
Putney, *1,850 .. B 5
Quechee, 900 ... C 3
Randolph, *4,689 .. B 3
Randolph, 2,217 .. B 3
Randolph Ctr., 150 .. B 3
Reading, *647 ... B 4
Readsboro, *638 .. B 5
Richford, *2,206 .. B 1
Richford, 1,527 .. B 1
Richmond, 865 .. A 2
Ripton, *327 .... B 3
Riverton, 250 ... B 2
Rochester, *1,054 .. B 3
Roxbury, *452 .. B 2
Royalton, *2,100 .. B 3
Rupert, *605 ... A 4
Rutland, 18,436 .. B 3
Ryegate, *1,000 .. C 2
St. Albans, 7,308 .. A 1
St. Albans Bay, 350 .. A 1
St. Johnsbury, *7,938 .. D 2
St. Johnsbury, 7,150 .. D 2
St. Johnsbury Center, 400 .. D 2
Salisbury, *881 .. A 3
Saxtons River, 593 .. B 4
Shaftsbury, *3,001 .. A 4
Sharon, *828 ... C 3
Sheffield, *435 .. C 1
Shelburne, *5,000 .. A 2
Sheldon, *1,618 .. B 1
Sheldon Sprs., 300 .. A 1
Shoreham, *973 .. A 3
S. Barre, 1,301 .. C 2
S. Burlington, 10,679 .. A 2
S. Dorset, 200 .. A 4
S. Hero, *1,188 .. A 1
S. Londonderry, 500 .. B 4
S. Newbury, 160 .. C 2
S. Pomfret, 250 .. B 3
S. Royalton, 700 .. C 3
Rupert, 400 ..... A 4
S. Shaftsbury, 650 .. A 4
S. Woodstock, 360 .. B 3
Springfield, *10,190 .. C 4
Springfield, 5,603 .. C 4
Stamford, *773 .. A 5
Starksboro, *1,336 .. A 2
Stockbridge, *508 .. B 3
Stowe, *2,991 .. B 2
Stowe, 531 .... B 2
Strafford, *731 .. C 3
Sudbury, *380 .. A 3
Sutton, *667 ... C 1
Swanton, 2,520 .. A 1
Taftsville, 260 .. C 3
Thetford, *2,188 .. C 3
Thetford Ctr., 180 .. C 3
Tinmouth, *406 .. A 4
Topsham, *767 .. C 2
Townshend, *849 .. B 4
Troy, *1,498 ... C 1
Tunbridge, *925 .. C 3
Underhill, *2,172 .. B 1
Underhill Ctr., 575 .. B 2
Union Village, 161 .. C 3
Vergennes, 2,273 .. A 2
Vernon, *1,175 .. C 5
Vershire, *442 .. C 3
Waitsfield, *1,300 .. B 2
Walden, *575 ... C 2
Wallingford, *1,893 .. A 4
Wardsboro, *505 .. B 4
Warren, *956 ... B 2
Washington, *855 .. C 2
Waterbury, *4,465 .. B 2
Waterbury, 1,892 .. B 2
Waterbury Ctr., 900 .. B 2
Waterville, *470 .. B 1
Webstersville, 700 .. C 2
Wells, *815 .... A 4
Wells River, 396 .. C 2
W. Barnet, 175 .. C 2
W. Brattleboro, 2,795 .. B 5
W. Burke, 338 .. C 1
W. Charleston, 170 .. C 1
W. Cornwall, 350 .. A 3
W. Dover, 550 .. B 5
W. Dummerston, 100 .. B 5
W. Fairlee, *427 .. C 3
Westfield, *418 .. C 1
Westford, *1,413 .. A 1
W. Hartford, 300 .. C 3
Westminster, *2,493 .. C 4
Westminster Station, 200 .. C 4
Westminster West, 400 .. B 4
Westmore, *257 .. C 1
Weston, *627 ... B 4
W. Pawlet, 300 .. A 4
W. Rupert, 300 .. A 4
W. Rutland, *2,351 .. A 3
W. Rutland, 2,169 .. A 3
W. Salisbury, 150 .. A 3
W. Woodstock, 250 .. B 3
Wheelock, *444 .. C 1
White River Junction, 2,582 .. C 3
Whiting, *379 .. A 3
Whitingham, *1,043 .. B 5
Wilder, 1,461 .. C 3
Williamstown, *2,284 .. B 2
Williston, *3,843 .. A 2
Wilmington, *1,808 .. B 5
Windham, *223 .. C 4
Windsor, *4,048 .. C 4
Winooski, 6,318 .. A 2
Wolcott, *986 .. C 1
Woodbury, *573 .. C 2
Woodford, *314 .. A 5
Woodstock, *3,214 .. B 3
Woodstock, 1,178 .. B 3
Worcester, *727 .. B 2

OTHER FEATURES

Ascutney (mt.) .... B 4
Batten Kill (riv.) .... A 4
Bomoseen (lake) .... A 3
Bread Loaf (mt.) .... B 3
Bromley (mt.) .... B 4
Burke (mt.) .... D 1
Camels Hump (mt.) ...... A 2
Champlain (lake) .... A 1
Connecticut (riv.) .... C 5
Dunmore (lake) .... A 3
Equinox (mt.) .... A 4
Green (mts.) .... B 4
Harriman (res.) .... B 5
Jay (peak) .... B 1
Killington (peak) ...... B 3
Lamoille (riv.) .... B 2
Mad (riv.) .... B 2
Mansfield (mt.) ...... B 1
Memphremagog (lake) .. C 1
Missisquoi (riv.) .... B 1
Okemo (mt.) .... B 4
Otter (creek) .... A 2
Pico (peak) .... B 3
St. Catherine (lake) .. A 4
Smugglers Notch (pass) .. B 1
Snow (mt.) .... B 5
Stratton (mt.) ..... A 5
Taconic (mts.) .... A 4
West (riv.) .... B 4
White (riv.) ..... C 3
White Face (mt.) .. B 1
Willoughby (lake) .. D 1
Winooski (riv.) .. B 2

*Population of town (township).

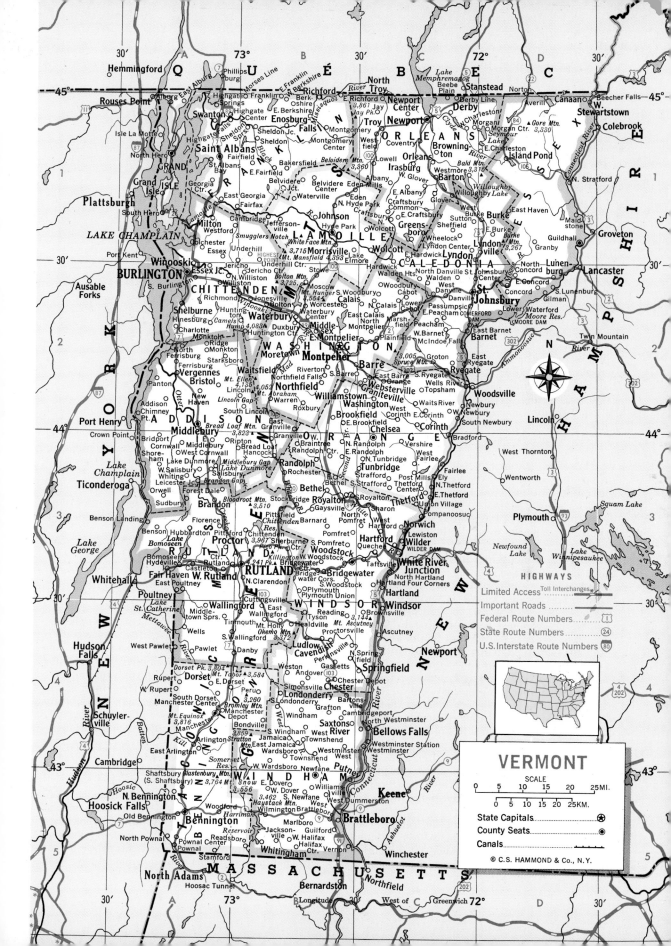

VERMONT

SCALE

0 5 10 15 20 25MI.

0 5 10 15 20 25KM.

State Capitals .... ⊛
County Seats .... ◉
Canals ....

© C.S. HAMMOND & Co., N.Y.

HIGHWAYS

Limited Access   Toll Interchanges ✳

Important Roads ....

Federal Route Numbers .... ▢

State Route Numbers .... ⬡

U.S. Interstate Route Numbers ▥

VERNE, Jules

VERNE, Jules (1828–1905). The startling inventions described in the novels of Jules Verne seemed highly fantastic to the readers of his time. Today he is regarded as a prophet. His dreams of undersea and air travel have come true, and Verne's story 'Around the World in Eighty Days' now seems a record of a leisurely trip.

Jules Verne was born on Feb. 8, 1828, in Nantes, France. With his brother, young Jules sailed on the Loire River, often going down to the sea. To the boy's active imagination the leaky boat was a palatial yacht and every scene an important geographic discovery. His father was a lawyer and wanted Jules to follow the same profession. When Jules was sent to school in Paris, however, he studied literature instead of law.

Verne began to write poetry and plays at an early age, but he had little success until he published 'Five Weeks in a Balloon' in 1863. This fantastic tale delighted readers, both young and old. Its success led Verne to continue writing exciting stories of adventure. He studied geography and science to get ideas for his tales.

Verne's works include many short stories and more than 50 novels. The most popular novels include 'A Journey to the Center of the Earth' (1864); 'From the Earth to the Moon' (1865); 'The Mysterious Island' (1870); 'Twenty Thousand Leagues Under the Sea' (1870); and 'Around the World in Eighty Days' (1872). (*See also* Science Fiction.)

VERONESE, Paolo

VERONESE, Paolo (1528–88). The third of four 16th-century masters of the Venetian school (along with Titian, Tintoretto, and El Greco), Paolo Veronese characteristically painted allegorical, Biblical, or historical subjects set in frameworks of classical architecture. His canvases were usually huge, filled with people, and painted in splendid colors. He excelled at illusionary compositions that extend the eye into the distance. (*See also* Painting.)

Paolo Caliari was born in 1528 in Verona (now in Italy) and became known as Veronese, after his birthplace, when he moved to Venice in 1553. His slightly old-fashioned early training in Verona—faithful to the style of Giovanni Bellini and Andrea Mantegna—instilled in him an attachment to clarity of color and form. Titian and Tintoretto were at the height of their careers, but Veronese retained his own characteristics. He preferred cold atmospheres with transparent light backgrounds so that figures stood out; sumptuous, balanced, somewhat superficial decoration; and scenes full of figures that were controlled and unified without confusion. Veronese's first commission was painting ceiling medallions in the Doges' Palace, which began many years of assignments in the palace. Another long series of works was for the church of Santo Sebastiano, which was to become his burial place.

After a short trip to Rome in 1560, Veronese began the famous frescoes in the villa at Maser, a building that had recently been completed by the architect Andrea Palladio. The first of Veronese's monumental

Paolo Veronese's 'The Adoration of the Kings', an oil painting, was done in 1573. It is on display at the National Gallery in London.

banquet scenes was 'The Marriage at Cana', painted in 1562–63. The best known of the banquets is what was commissioned as 'Last Supper' in 1573. After the painting was completed, Veronese was summoned before the Inquisition to defend the inclusion of such irreverent elements as buffoons, drunkards, a dog, and a jester holding a parrot. Veronese replied that "we painters take the same liberties as poets and madmen take." The problem was solved by renaming the painting 'Feast in the House of Levi'.

As the work of Veronese gained renown, the participation of his studio increased. His brother was his chief assistant, and later his two sons, a nephew, and others made use of Veronese's sketches and drawings. Veronese died in Venice on April 9, 1588.

VERSAILLES, PALACE OF.

VERSAILLES, PALACE OF. About 13 miles (21 kilometers) southwest of Paris, in the city of Versailles, stands the largest palace in France. It was built because of the consuming envy of King Louis XIV, and once completed it became the object of envy of every other monarch in Europe. The Winter Palace in Saint Petersburg (now Leningrad), Schönbrunn in Vienna, and Herrenchiemsee in Bavaria are only three of the royal palaces built in imitation of the Palace of Versailles. Versailles itself served as a royal residence for a little more than a century—from 1682 until 1789, when the French Revolution began. (For photographs, *see* Architecture; France.)

On Aug. 17, 1661, the French superintendent of finances, Nicolas Fouquet, presided over a large celebration in honor of Louis XIV. The festivities took place at Fouquet's magnificent newly completed château, Vaux-le-Vicomte. When Louis saw this palace he was outraged that one of his ministers should have such

Giraudon/Art Resource

The Versailles chapel was begun in 1699 by Jules Hardouin-Mansart and completed in 1710 by Robert de Cotte.

a home, while he did not. He had Fouquet thrown into prison and hired the men who had designed and built the palace to do the same for him at Versailles.

Versailles was not even a town when the king's predecessor, Louis XIII, built a hunting lodge there in 1624. This small structure became the base on which was constructed one of the most costly and extravagant buildings in the world. It was meant to be a home for Louis XIV, known as the Sun King,

who boasted of himself, "I am the state." The men in charge of the project were Louis Le Vau, architect; Charles Le Brun, painter and decorator; and André Le Nôtre, landscape architect.

Work began first on the gardens. About 37,000 acres (15,000 hectares) of land were cleared to make room for tree-lined terraces and walks and thousands of flowering plants. In the center the cross-shaped Grand Canal was laid out. It was 1,737 yards (1,588 meters) long and 67 yards (61 meters) wide. There were 1,400 fountains and 400 pieces of new sculpture.

The beginnings of the palace in 1669 were fairly humble compared to the finished structure. The architect Le Vau enclosed the hunting lodge and gave it the appearance of a small palace. In 1676 another architect, Jules Hardouin-Mansart, was put in charge of redesigning and enlarging the building. Starting with Le Vau's plans, Hardouin-Mansart added a second story and built the magnificent Hall of Mirrors and the north and south wings. Hardouin-Mansart's facade, facing the garden, was 1,903 feet (580 meters) long.

Construction of the palace went on through the next century. More than 36,000 workers were involved in the project, and when the building was completed it could accommodate up to 5,000 people, including servants. About 14,000 soldiers and servants were quartered in annexes and in the town.

Other structures on the palace grounds include the Grand Trianon, Petit (Small) Trianon, and the Carriage Museum. The Grand Trianon is a small château built by Hardouin-Mansart in 1687–88 for Louis XIV. It is now used to house distinguished visitors to France. The Petit Trianon was built by architect Jacques-Ange Gabriel at the direction of Louis XV in 1766 for Madame Du Barry, the last of his famous mistresses.

The lavishly restored bedroom of Louis XIV is next to the Hall of Mirrors. The wood carvings and the balustrade separating the bed from the rest of the room were original appointments. Other decorations are of more recent manufacture.

Giraudon/Art Resource

VERSAILLES

Under Louis XVI it became a favorite residence of his queen, Marie Antoinette. Near the Petit Trianon is the Hamlet, a small farm village constructed for Marie Antoinette. There she and other ladies of the court would occasionally pass time pretending they were peasant women. The Carriage Museum, near the Grand Trianon, contains a collection of state coaches and carriages.

Today the Palace of Versailles is one of France's national monuments. The building is so large, however, that only a small portion of it is open to the public. Many of the rooms are government offices. Visitors are allowed to tour the sections of the north and south wings closest to the center as well as the central section itself.

The north wing contains, on two floors, the Gallery of History, with portraits of the kings and members of their courts. It also contains the chapel designed by Hardouin-Mansart but completed by Robert de Cotte in 1710. Farther on in the north wing is the opera, or theater, added between 1753 and 1770 by Gabriel.

The most striking room in the central part of the palace is the Hall of Mirrors. It was designed by Hardouin-Mansart, and the ceiling paintings were done by Le Brun and his assistants. The hall, on the west facade of the palace facing the gardens, is about 240 feet (73 meters) long and 40 feet (12 meters) high. Along the garden side are 17 large windows with rounded Romanesque arches. Opposite each window is a matching mirror. The glass for the hall was imported from Venice, the leading glassmaking city of Europe at the time. Apart from the glass the walls are decorated with white and colored marble and gilded bronze. On June 28, 1919, the Treaty of Versailles ending World War I was signed in the Hall of Mirrors. (For photograph, *see* Interior Design.)

At either end of the hall is a large square room—the Salon de la Guerre and the Salon de la Paix, or rooms of war and peace, respectively. Behind the Hall of Mirrors are the apartments of Louis XIV. The rooms of his apartments are decorated with paintings of Roman gods. His throne was in the Apollo drawing room. Near the king's apartments are the queen's apartments and other state residential quarters. All of these rooms are richly decorated with paintings and fine furniture.

The south wing contains more of France's historical museums, including the Gallery of Battles. This museum contains busts of famous French generals and paintings of historic battles. The paintings are generally of poor quality except one by Eugène Delacroix, 'The Battle of Taillebourg'.

From 1978 the French government spent the equivalent of more than 37 million dollars in the renovation of the palace and the two Trianons. The Hall of Mirrors, Louis XIV's bedroom, and the opera had been renovated previously, leaving the other rooms looking shabby by comparison. In order to re-create the atmosphere of the 17th and 18th centuries, materials of the time were exactly duplicated. Parts of the palace that had been damaged or rebuilt after the French Revolution were restored to their original design. Some of the original furniture was recovered and brought back to the palace.

Located just outside the front gates of the Palace of Versailles are the royal stables, which once accommodated 2,000 carriages and 2,500 horses and were later converted to military barracks. There is also a military hospital and a school of military engineering and artillery.

The town that grew around the palace was founded in 1671, when construction of the palace was under way. Many of the first residents were people who had come to work on the palace. When Louis XIV died in 1715, after 72 years as king, the town of Versailles had a population of 30,000. Versailles is now a residential suburb of Paris. The palace remains the chief attraction and draws thousands of tourists every year.

The Petit Trianon, on the palace grounds, is a two-story building constructed as a retreat for Louis XV. Designed by Jacques-Ange Gabriel, it was built in 1766. Marie Antoinette used it as a residence later in the 18th century.

Giraudon/Art Resource

VERTEBRATES. Animals with backbones are called vertebrates. They include the most highly developed animals—fishes, amphibians, reptiles, birds, and mammals—among which are human beings, the highest of the primates. The earliest vertebrates developed in the sea and gradually evolved into land animals, though a few species returned to the water. They are distinguished from invertebrates, or backboneless organisms (*see* Invertebrate). Vertebrates typically have bilateral symmetry in their skeleton and in their muscular, respiratory, nervous, circulatory, and urogenital systems. Their two pairs of limbs are adapted for different uses, such as wings for flying or fins for swimming. In most vertebrates, a hollow, jointed backbone and its upper extension, the cranium, protect the spinal cord and brain. Almost all young vertebrates have gill slits in their embryonic stage. In land vertebrates the gills develop into lungs. All vertebrates reproduce sexually, and males and females have distinct characteristics.

Scientific Classification

Scientists have devised a classification system for vertebrates that begins at the lowest level with the concept of species—that is, a group of animals that can breed with one another. Related species are grouped into a genus (plural, genera). Related genera form larger categories, in ascending order, of family, order, class, and phylum (plural, phyla). The domestic dog, for example, belongs to the species and genus of *Canis familiaris,* to the family Canidae, to the order Carnivora (made up of most meat-eating mammals), to the class of mammals, and finally to the phylum Chordata (to which all vertebrates belong).

The phylum Chordata is divided into fishes (Pisces) and four-limbed animals (Tetrapoda). Fishes are further grouped into the classes Agnatha (jawless fish), Placodermi (extinct fish), Chondrichthyes (boneless fish), and Osteichthyes (bony fish) (*see* Fish). Four-limbed animals are divided into the classes Amphibia, Reptilia, Aves (birds), and Mammalia.

Agnatha

The oldest group of fishes are the Agnatha, or jawless fishes. They were prominent in Silurian times some 450 to 400 million years ago. The lamprey and hagfish, known as cyclostomes, trace their ancestry back to the ancient species of this class. Jawless fishes obtain their food by sucking. (*See also* Lamprey.)

Placodermi

The earliest jawed fishes were the Placoderms, which became extinct nearly 350 million years ago. They lived in fresh water during the Silurian period. Many were large, active predators, while others spent their lives on the bottoms of streams or lakes.

This article was contributed by Lorna P. Straus, Professor in the Department of Anatomy and The College, University of Chicago.

Chondrichthyes

The Chondrichthyes, which include sharks, skates, and rays, may have evolved from the earlier Placodermi species. The skeletons of Chondrichthyes contain no bones but instead are made entirely of cartilage. Sharks are voracious predators and powerful swimmers with well-developed paired fins and strong tails. Skates and rays have flattened bodies, and their pectoral fins are greatly expanded.

Osteichthyes

Another of the now-extinct Placodermi also gave rise to the Osteichthyes, or bony fish. This group is divided into the Actinopterygii and the Sarcopterygii. The Actinopterygii, or ray-finned fishes, have been the dominant group since roughly 350 million years ago. There are about 20,000 known species. The ray-finned fishes get their name from the fact that their paired fins are webs of skin supported by rays of bone. Most of these fish belong to the Teleostei group, which has the largest number of species among the vertebrates. Their complex jaw and associated muscles enable them to eat a wide range of foods. They are also highly prolific breeders, with a single female capable of producing up to 9 million eggs in one season.

The Sarcopterygii, though smaller, gave rise to land vertebrates. They were long thought to have become extinct, but in 1938 a representative of this group, a coelacanth, was caught off the coast of Africa. Since then others have been found in the Indian Ocean. Although quite different from their ancient ancestors, they represent the closest living fish relative of land-dwelling vertebrates.

Amphibians

Some 400 million years ago, representatives of the sarcopterygian group of fishes first moved onto land. They developed short legs in place of paired fins and lungs instead of gills. These early land animals became known as amphibians (*see* Amphibian). Modern members of this class still spend the early part of their lives in water and return to it during their reproductive cycle.

The 3,000 species of modern amphibians are divided into frogs and toads (Anura), newts and salamanders (Urodela), and burrowers in the Gymnophiona group. The anuran skeleton is modified to make jumping possible. Salamanders have short, stout bodies with powerful muscles and well-developed tails.

Reptilia

The Reptilia class of vertebrates became the first to live their entire lifespan on dry land (*see* Reptiles). This evolutionary development was made possible by the hard eggshell, which protects the egg from drying out. The egg contains food that sustains the developing young until it hatches. These animals became so successful that during the Permian period, 280 to 230 million years ago, reptiles replaced amphibians as the dominant land-dwelling vertebrates. The Mesozoic

THE RANGE AND RELATIVE ABUNDANCE OF VERTEBRATES OVER TIME

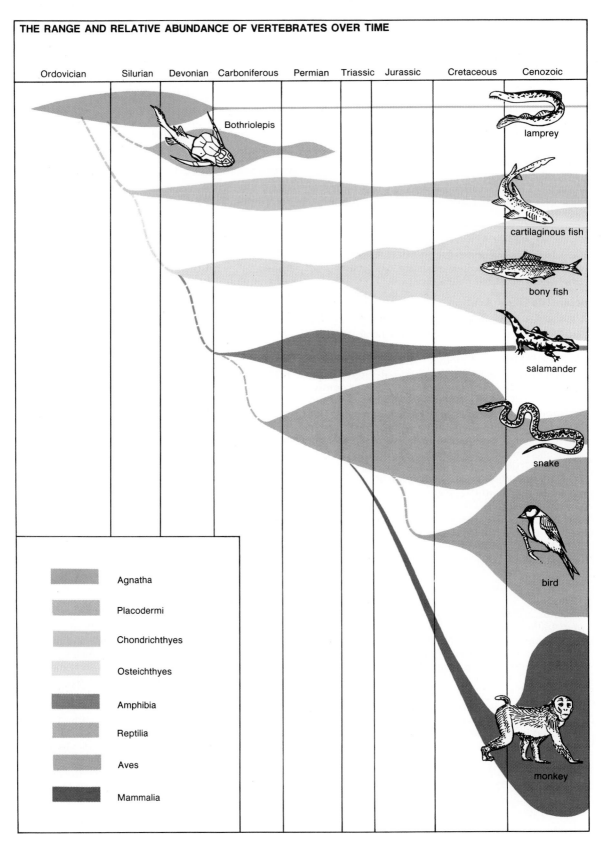

Ordovician Silurian Devonian Carboniferous Permian Triassic Jurassic Cretaceous Cenozoic

Bothriolepis

lamprey

cartilaginous fish

bony fish

salamander

snake

bird

monkey

Agnatha

Placodermi

Chondrichthyes

Osteichthyes

Amphibia

Reptilia

Aves

Mammalia

era, which lasted until 65 million years ago, is known as the Age of Reptiles. At present the Earth supports about 6,000 species of modern reptiles.

The major reptile groups are turtles and tortoises, Squamata (lizards and snakes), and Archosaurs (now-extinct dinosaurs and modern-day alligators and crocodiles). Lizards are widespread in the tropics where they occur in great variety from horned toads to the monitor lizard, which measures up to 13 feet (4 meters) in length, of the East Indies. Snakes developed from early lizards. Their primary characteristics are lack of limbs; movement by undulating the body and tail; a highly flexible skull and jaw that allows them to swallow their prey whole; and, in some families of snakes, poison glands and hollow fangs.

The dinosaurs were prominent between 180 and 75 million years ago and then mysteriously died out (*see* Animals, Prehistoric). Dinosaurs can be divided into Saurischia, Ornithischia, and Crocodilia groups. The Saurischia, or reptilelike dinosaurs, included the huge meat-eater *Tyrannosaurus rex* and the largest plant-eater Diplodocus, a four-legged reptile that weighed up to 50 tons. Some of the Ornithischia were two-legged animals, but most walked on all fours. They were all plant-eaters and had a variety of defenses against the giant carnivores.

Modern-day alligators and crocodiles are the only surviving members of the Archosaurs. These amphibious reptiles use four limbs for locomotion. Alligators live in fresh water and crocodiles in salt water.

Aves

Birds are descended from Archosaurs. Scientists have classified some 8,700 species of birds that inhabit the Earth today. The characteristic features of the class Aves include feathers that form the wing surfaces of modified forelimbs, hollow bones, air sacs distributed throughout the body, a horn bill, and generally small size. Many modern birds eat grain and seeds. Lacking teeth, they have developed a grinding mechanism. They swallow grit or small pebbles, which are held in a gizzard, a part of the digestive tract. There the stony particles grind the seeds so they can be digested. Birds have well-developed nervous systems and demonstrate complex patterns of behavior in courtship, nest building, and rearing their young.

Mammalia

The first mammals appeared by the end of the Mesozoic era. The main features of this class are the presence of mammary glands in the females, the birth of live young, the ability of females to nurse their young, a constant body temperature, the presence of hair, keen senses, an efficient means of locomotion, and superior intelligence and learning capacity compared with other classes of animals. Modern-day mammalian species number about 4,500.

The earliest mammals laid eggs instead of giving birth to live young. The only remaining members of this group, known as monotremes, are the duck-billed platypus and the spiny anteater, both found in Australia. All other mammals, which give birth to live young, are divided into marsupial and placental mammals. Marsupial, or pouched, mammals, such as the kangaroo, give birth to small, immature fetuses. The newborn must complete the next stage of growth in the mother's pouch. Placental mammals are the most diverse and successful of the mammal class. The young, nourished within the mother's body by the placenta, are able to reach a more developed stage before birth.

Mammals have evolved into specialized orders of insectivores (insect eaters), carnivores (meat eaters), and herbivores (plant eaters). Some species are omnivores (meat and plant eaters). The most primitive placental mammals are the insectivores, a group that contains over 60 genera. Shrews, hedgehogs, and moles are common examples of this group. They live in woods and meadows but are extremely shy and are seldom seen. Groups that have developed from the insectivores include Chiroptera (bats); Edentata (tree sloths, anteaters, and armadillos); and the Lago-morphs (hares and rabbits).

The order Rodentia has the most genera (260) of any group. The rodents, or gnawing animals, are identified by a pair of enlarged upper and lower front teeth. Highly adaptable and resilient, these mammals flourish in nearly every known land habitat.

Carnivorous mammals can be divided into three groups: the canine family and related species; the feline, or cat family; and the pinnipeds (seals and walruses). The canine family includes domestic and wild dogs, wolves, foxes, weasels, coyotes, and bears. Related species include badgers, skunks, and otters. The various genera of cats have claws for seizing prey and specialized teeth for ripping and tearing. Seals and walruses probably evolved from land carnivores about 40 million years ago. In this group, limbs have become flippers to aid in swimming.

Herbivorous mammals are divided into three orders: land animals with an odd number of toes (such as the horse); land animals with an even number of toes, or cloven hooves (including cows, deer, and pigs); and the Cetecea (whales and porpoises). Among the Cetecea, the forelimbs have developed into flippers, the hind limbs have disappeared, and the tail has become a powerful aid in swimming. Most members of this group eat some animals such as fish and squid, but the largest whales eat only plankton.

The most advanced group of mammals are the Primates, the group to which human beings belong. The early Primates were agile and had well-developed hands; keen, stereoscopic vision; and a large brain. This group includes lemurs, tarsiers, monkeys, and great apes. Primates use all four limbs for locomotion, and some monkeys have long, prehensile tails that act as a fifth limb.

Homo sapiens is the most recent member of this group. As distinguished from the other Primates, human beings stand and move in an erect posture on their hind limbs, and have hands with opposable thumbs and more highly developed brains.

VESALIUS, Andreas (1514–64). The science of biology and the practice of medicine were revolutionized by the Flemish physician and surgeon Vesalius in the 16th century. By careful and painstaking dissections of cadavers he learned a great deal about the structure of the human body and laid the foundation for modern physiology.

Vesalius was born in December 1514 in Brussels into a family of physicians and pharmacists. He attended the University of Louvain (1529–33) and spent the next three years at the medical school of the University of Paris. In 1536 he returned home to spend another year at Louvain. He received his doctorate in medicine in 1537 and then worked in Padua as a lecturer in surgery. His anatomical studies led him to break with the theories of the Greek physician Galen, whose writings on physiology had long been considered authoritative (*see* Galen). In 1543 Vesalius published his 'Seven Books on the Structure of the Human Body', the most accurate such work on the subject up to that time.

In the same year Vesalius presented a copy of his work to Emperor Charles V, who appointed him court physician. From 1553 to 1556 Vesalius was in Brussels, occupied with a flourishing medical practice. Three years later he went to Madrid to take up an appointment as physician to the court of Philip II. He remained in Madrid until 1564, when he was allowed to make a pilgrimage to Jerusalem. On the way back he became ill, and he died on the Greek island of Zacynthus in June 1564.

VESEY, Denmark (1767?–1822). The self-educated former slave Denmark Vesey is credited with plotting the largest slave revolt in American history. The revolt never took place because the conspirators were caught and executed.

Vesey's early life is mostly unaccounted for. He was probably born on the island of Saint Thomas in the Danish West Indies (now United States Virgin Islands) in about 1767. His real name is unknown. He was sold as a slave in 1781 to the slave trader Joseph Vesey. He settled in Charleston, S.C., with the trader in 1783. In the late 1790s they were in Haiti helping French colonials flee the slave uprising. Back in the United States in 1800, Vesey won 1,500 dollars in a lottery and used 600 dollars of it to buy his freedom. He worked as a carpenter in Charleston and achieved local notoriety for his preaching against slavery—mostly to black audiences. Charleston at the time had a sizeable free black population.

Although the specifics of the conspiracy are uncertain, it is believed that Vesey plotted with city and plantation slaves to stage an uprising. They would attack arsenals to get weapons, kill all whites they encountered, and destroy the city. Word of the plot reached city authorities, and ten slaves were arrested. Their testimony led to the arrest of Vesey. He confessed nothing, saying that he had nothing to gain by freeing slaves. He was convicted and, with five other blacks, was hanged on July 2, 1822. Altogether some 130 blacks were arrested and 67 convicted. Thirty-five were executed and 32 sent into exile. Four white men were also fined and imprisoned for assisting in the plot.

VESPUCIUS, Americus (1454–1512). In a pamphlet printed in 1507, a German cartographer named Martin Waldseemüller suggested that the newly discovered world be named "from Amerigo the discoverer . . . as if it were the land of Americus or America." Waldseemüller created a large map on which the name America appears for the first time, though it is applied only to South America. The extension of the name to North America came later.

Waldseemüller had probably never heard of Columbus. His suggestion resulted in one of the oddities of history—the naming of the New World after a comparatively unknown Florentine merchant who accompanied Spanish or Portuguese expeditions to South America and wrote about them, instead of after Christopher Columbus (*see* Columbus).

Americus Vespucius (or Amerigo Vespucci, as the name is spelled in Italian) was born in Florence, Italy, in 1454. He was in Spain at the time of Columbus' first and second voyages. In a letter, written in 1504 and printed in 1505, he claimed to have made four voyages, on the first of which, in 1497, he explored the South American coast. This would make him the first European to land on the American continent, for at that time Columbus had only reached the outlying islands. Most scholars reject Vespucius' version of this voyage. Vespucius perhaps did accompany a Spanish expedition—that of Alonzo de Ojeda—to South America in 1499, and in 1501 and 1503 he probably went with Portuguese expeditions. Probably he never commanded an expedition himself and, of course, was not the first person to set foot on the continents to which his name is given. Vespucius died in Seville, Spain, in 1512.

VESUVIUS, MOUNT. An active volcano in southern Italy, rising 4,190 feet (1,277 meters) above the Bay of Naples, Mt. Vesuvius is situated on the plain of Campania, about 7 miles (11 kilometers) from the city of Naples. Its fiery eruptions have claimed a high toll in lives and property through the centuries, but the mountainside and surrounding area remain the home of more than 2 million people. There are industrial towns along the bay, and small agricultural centers thrive on the northern slopes. (For photograph, *see* Naples.)

The mountain originated some 200,000 years ago and for a time had only one peak. Now a high, semicircular ridge known as Mt. Somma partly surrounds the main cone of Vesuvius and has a slope of its own, beginning at about 1,970 feet (600 meters) and climbing to 3,714 feet (1,132 meters). The area between the ridge and the cone is known as Valle del Gigante, or Giant's Valley. At the top of the cone is a large crater about 1,000 feet (300 meters) deep and 2,000 feet (600 meters) across.

Volcanic ash has made the soil of Mt. Vesuvius very fertile, and the lower slopes are covered with vineyards and orchards. Up the mountain from the farmlands, the volcano's slopes are cloaked with thickets of oak and chestnut trees. The wooded areas grow to the summit of the northern slope of Mt. Somma, but on the higher western side, the chestnut groves give way to small shrubs on plateau areas at an altitude of 2,000 feet (600 meters). Still higher, the surface of the great cone is almost bare.

The temperature at the mouth of the volcano is measured daily by scientists using sophisticated equipment. Readings far above 1,000° F (540° C) are common. Rising temperatures are one indicator of forthcoming eruptions.

The most famous eruption of Vesuvius occurred in AD 79, when lava and ashes buried the towns of Pompeii, Herculaneum, and Stabiae. Excavations have uncovered parts of the cities (see Pompeii and Herculaneum). Since that disaster, nearly 50 eruptions of varying intensity have been reported. An eruption in 1631 buried villages and blew ashes as far as 150 miles (240 kilometers). Despite the warnings of earthquakes for many months before the eruption, people remained in the area and more than 3,000 were killed. Another great upheaval in 1794 destroyed the village of Torre del Greco for the fourth time.

The eruptions of Mt. Vesuvius are of the highest degree of volcanic explosiveness. In this type of eruption, large volumes of gases boil out of gas-rich magma and generate enormous, nearly continuous jetting blasts. The blasts rip apart and core out the magma column. The volcano's fierce turbulence has caused many changes in the mountain's shape and height. In 1906 an eruption killed hundreds of people and reduced the volcano's height by several hundred feet. In 1944 Vesuvius again hurled out its ashes and lava. The powerful surge raised the height of Vesuvius by about 500 feet (150 meters) and widened the top crater by three times, to its present width.

VETERANS' AFFAIRS. In 1932, during the Great Depression, about 15,000 American war veterans and members of their families converged on Washington, D.C., to persuade Congress to provide them with some economic relief. The proposed legislation failed to pass, but many members of this "bonus army," as it was called, remained near the Capitol, living in huts and shanties until they were driven away by regular Army troops.

The bonus army was a product of America's worst economic crisis. It was seeking money that Congress had already promised, but the payment date was set at 1945. The veterans and their families eventually dispersed, but their presence symbolized the fact that government had always made special provision, either in the form of money or land, for those who had served in combat. Today veterans' programs are an established government policy. In the United States they are operated by the Veterans Administration and in Canada by Veterans' Affairs Canada.

Historical Background

For many centuries veterans had a special status in the societies they served. Military commanders or their governments sought to provide some reward for services. The standard solution was to provide tracts of land for disbanded soldiers. Land grants were also promised as an encouragement for new enlistments, to promote frontier settlements by former soldiers, and to avoid unrest among veterans.

In the United States during the 19th century, there were vast expanses of unsettled land. By 1850 Congress had offered 160 acres (65 hectares) to any veteran who had seen at least 14 days of combat duty in any war since 1776. Under this policy about 47 million acres (19 million hectares) were allotted. Much of the acreage was sold by veterans to land speculators.

After the two world wars other governments adopted similar land policies. In Canada the Soldier Settlement Act of 1918 and the Veterans' Land Act of 1942 made low-interest loans available for the purchase of land. Great Britain, France, and Germany made attempts to get veterans into farming after 1918. They also set up agricultural training schools. By the end of World War II, land-settlement policies were no longer regarded as useful, since most veterans wanted vocations other than farming, and vast amounts of arable land were no longer available.

One type of veterans' benefit that was used early in American history was the pension. Plymouth Colony passed a law in 1636 that provided lifetime support to any soldier who returned from battle maimed. Other colonies passed similar laws. The Continental Congress enacted laws promising money benefits to soldiers who fought in the Revolutionary War, but no funds were ever made available. Congress passed the first national pension law on Sept. 29, 1789. This legislation was followed by other statutes, culminating in the Servicemen's and Veterans' Survivor Benefits Act, which was passed in 1956. Early pension benefits also covered war widows and orphans, and they were granted to veterans with service-connected disabilities. Similar plans were not common in Europe until World War I.

Before the end of World War II, the warring nations enacted legislation to deal with the reemployment and readjustment of returning military personnel. The new programs were far more comprehensive than any previous veterans' legislation. Included were plans to handle employment, educational needs, housing programs, and loans. Medical care had already become an accepted feature of veterans' affairs.

The most far-reaching piece of legislation passed for veterans in the United States was the Servicemen's Readjustment Act of 1944. It is commonly referred to as the GI Bill of Rights. ("GI" was originally an abbreviation for the term government issue and referred to the provisions given to military personnel. In World War II, "GI" came to mean a member or former member of the armed forces of the United States.)

The bill provided unemployment benefits, paid for schooling, and offered low-interest loans for buying homes, farms, or small businesses. Other nations—including Great Britain, the Commonwealth countries, and the Soviet Union—established similar programs. Hospitalization and rehabilitation programs were greatly expanded because of the huge numbers of returning wounded and disabled veterans. In the United States the Selective Training and Service Act of 1940 had already stipulated that returning veterans were entitled to reinstatement in their old jobs. The Veterans' Preference Act of 1944 offered special advantages to veterans who wanted government employment.

In 1966 Congress passed legislation that was seen as a permanent peacetime GI Bill of Rights. It made the provisions of the earlier GI bill valid for service personnel who were part of the large peacetime military establishment during the Cold War. This bill provided for educational costs, housing loans, and medical treatment for personnel whether they had served in a combat zone or not.

Veterans Administration

On July 21, 1930, President Herbert Hoover signed Executive Order 5398 establishing the Veterans Administration (VA) as an independent agency of the federal government, in accordance with legislation passed by Congress on July 3. The act consolidated previous agencies that had handled veterans' affairs.

Pensions had been handled by the Bureau of Pensions since 1833. In 1849 this agency became part of the Department of the Interior. In 1865 Congress created the National Homes for Disabled Volunteer Soldiers. This consisted of a number of homes established in various parts of the country for veterans of the American Civil War. In 1921 the various agencies handling disability compensation, government life insurance, family allotments, vocational rehabilitation, and medical and hospital care were combined in the Veterans Bureau. The Bureau of Pensions, the National Homes for Disabled Volunteer Soldiers, and the Veterans Bureau were merged to form the VA. There is also the Veterans' Employment and Training Service in the Department of Labor.

The VA is divided into the Department of Medicine and Surgery, the Department of Veterans Benefits, and the Department of Memorial Affairs. These departments handle pensions, death and disability payments, burial, education, rehabilitation, home loan guaranty, and a comprehensive medical-care program.

The Department of Medicine and Surgery operates 172 medical centers, 16 soldiers' homes, 228 clinics, and 116 nursing home care units in the United States, Puerto Rico, and the Philippines. Veterans are provided with care in non-VA facilities, and, under terms of the Civilian Health and Medical Program of the VA, dependents of certain veterans are provided with medical care supplied by non-VA facilities.

The Department of Veterans Benefits handles all veterans' compensation and pension plans, vocational education and rehabilitation, the loan guaranty program, insurance programs, and veterans' assistance. The loan guaranty program is a form of credit assistance to ensure more liberal terms on loans than would otherwise be available through commercial lenders. The department supervises a wide range of insurance programs, including group life and the Veterans Mortgage Life Insurance.

The Department of Memorial Affairs supervises the national cemeteries. It also provides headstones and grave markers for plots in both private and national cemeteries. (*See also* National Cemeteries.)

Veterans' Affairs Canada

Veterans' Affairs Canada, or the Department of Veterans Affairs, was established in 1944 to administer pensions, health care, and other benefits for Canadian ex-service personnel. It is headed by the minister for veterans' affairs. During World War II the Canadian Parliament passed the Veterans' Land Act (1942), the Re-establishment in Civil Employment Act (1942), the Veterans' Rehabilitation Act (1944), the Veterans' Insurance Act (1944), and the War Service Grants Act (1944). These pieces of legislation together form the charter under which Veterans' Affairs Canada functions.

A number of other boards operate under the authority of the minister of veterans' affairs: the Army Benevolent Fund, the Bureau of Pensions Advocates, the Canadian Pension Commission, the Commonwealth War Graves Commission, the Pension Review Board, and the War Veterans Allowance Board. Some of these are older than the Department of Veterans Affairs. The War Graves Commission, for instance, was founded in 1917 to maintain graves of Commonwealth service personnel, to build memorials to the dead whose graves are unknown, and to keep records. The commission's work is shared by other Commonwealth nations. It carries out its duties worldwide because so many of the dead have been buried in overseas cemeteries.

The Veterans' Land Act of 1942 replaced the Soldier Settlement Act of 1918. The newer act began by arranging for low-cost loans to buy farms, farm equipment, and livestock. In 1950 it was expanded to include loans for building new homes. This program was terminated in 1977.

VETERANS' ORGANIZATIONS. Of the many patriotic societies in the United States, some of the largest and most influential are the veterans' organizations. The American Legion, the American Veterans Committee, AMVETS, the Disabled American Veterans, and Veterans of Foreign Wars are the best-known such associations in the United States. In Great Britain the Royal British Legion is the association of former servicemen. Many other nations involved in 20th-century wars have similar groups.

There are also some international federations of veterans' organizations. The British Commonwealth Ex-Services League has 17 million members in 47 countries and territories. It was founded in 1921 as

Cathy Melloan—EB Inc.

Veterans' organizations from around the nation marched in a Chicago parade honoring Vietnam veterans on June 13, 1986.

Several societies were founded at the end of the Spanish-American War. The United Spanish War Veterans absorbed the Legion of Spanish War Veterans in 1906 and the Veteran Army of the Philippines in 1908. Most of the active veterans' organizations are a product of the war-torn 20th century.

The American Legion was founded in Paris, France, in March 1919. Founding members were from the American Expeditionary Force called together by Lieutenant Colonel Theodore Roosevelt, Jr. Congress granted the organization a national charter on Sept. 16, 1919. The charter has been amended several times to include veterans from World War II, the Korean War, and the Vietnam War. The Legion has been extremely influential in obtaining benefits for veterans, including the GI Bill of Rights after World War II. The Legion is active in about 14,500 communities throughout the United States.

The British Legion was founded in 1921 to replace four earlier ex-servicemen's organizations—the Comrades of the Great War, the National Association of Discharged Sailors and Soldiers, the National Federation of Discharged and Demobilized Sailors and Soldiers, and the Officers' Association. The Legion was granted a royal charter in 1925. There were about 3,500 branches in the 1980s, some of them overseas. The Legion organizes the annual Poppy Appeal to raise money for needy members. It is comparable to the Poppy Day held every May in the United States near Memorial Day. In addition, the Legion administers residential homes for the aged and convalescent homes.

AMVETS was founded in 1944. The organization's members are veterans of World War II, the Korean War, and the Vietnam War. It has local affiliates in about 1,100 communities in the United States.

Veterans of Foreign Wars of the U.S.A. (VFW) is, after the American Legion, the second largest veterans' association in the United States. It was founded in 1899 for overseas veterans of the Spanish-American War, but its membership has been expanded to include veterans of all wars. The VFW has about 10,000 local affiliates.

The Disabled American Veterans (DAV) was founded in 1921 to accommodate veterans with service-connected disabilities. A DAV Auxiliary was founded in 1922. Both organizations are active in rendering assistance to veterans with free legal counseling, processing claims forms, giving college scholarships to children of disabled veterans, and other services. The DAV is active in all 50 states. There are about 2,500 local affiliates.

There are numerous other veterans' organizations in the United States. Among them are the Jewish War Veterans of the U.S.A. (1896), the Women World War Veterans (1919), the Retired Officers Association (1929), the Military Order of the Purple Heart of the United States of America (1932), the American Veterans Committee (1944), the Paralyzed Veterans of America (1946), and the Navy Seabee Veterans of America (1948). Many of the organizations have women's auxiliaries. (*See also* Patriotic Societies.)

the British Empire Services League. The World Veterans Federation, with headquarters in Paris, was founded in 1950. It represents about 150 national organizations with a combined membership of 20 million. The European War Veterans' Confederation was founded in Paris in 1961 and has national sections in ten countries.

The first organization founded by veterans in the United States was the Society of the Cincinnati. It was formed in 1783 by American officers from the Revolutionary War. French officers of the war organized a branch of the organization in France. It was named after the Roman statesman and military leader Lucius Quinctius Cincinnatus, whose historical reputation rests on his selfless devotion to the Roman republic in the 5th century BC. The objectives of the society were to promote friendship, perpetuate the rights for which they had fought, and aid members and their families in time of need. Today the organization is a hereditary society, made up of male descendants of those who fought in the Revolution.

Men who fought in the War of 1812 did not meet to start an organization until 1854. They then met at a large convention for veterans of all ranks. A few years earlier, in 1847, veterans of the Mexican War had founded the Aztec Club. The American Civil War was followed by the founding of several societies for former servicemen. The Loyal Legion was started in 1865 primarily for officers. A few of the societies were made up of former officers from specific armies in the war: Society of the Tennessee (1865), of the Army of the Cumberland (1868), and of the Potomac (1869). For enlisted men the major organization was the Grand Army of the Republic (GAR), founded in 1866. This was the largest veterans' organization until the end of World War I. The GAR became a powerful political lobby for obtaining veterans' benefits during the ten years after 1880. The GAR had two women's affiliates—the Women's Relief Corps (1883) and the Ladies of the GAR (1886). In the South the United Confederate Veterans was formed in 1889.

VETERINARY MEDICINE

VETERINARY MEDICINE. What physicians are to humans, veterinarians are to animals. Veterinarians prevent, diagnose, and treat animal diseases and manage other animal disorders. They perform surgery and prescribe and administer drugs. Their practice is called veterinary medicine, or veterinary science.

Children growing up in today's cities may think of a veterinarian as a pet doctor who treats sick dogs and cats. In rural communities, however, livestock farmers depend on the veterinarian to keep their animals disease-free, to help the animals breed properly, and to increase the animals' productivity. An epidemic among cattle, pigs, sheep, or poultry can put a farmer out of business.

Today's veterinarians are called upon to do more than manage animal diseases. They are involved in inspecting meat for human consumption, preserving endangered wildlife, keeping exotic zoo animals healthy, looking after valuable racehorses and breeding stock, and caring for laboratory animals used for research. Others may conduct research or teach. In addition, a growing number of veterinarians are concerned with the control of zoonoses, a class of human diseases acquired from or transmitted to other vertebrate animals. (*See also* Disease, Human.) The field of veterinary medicine has become so diverse that graduate veterinarians are becoming increasingly specialized. Most are likely to spend a whole career working in just one of the above areas.

In cities and towns veterinarians diagnose and treat diseases of common household pets and also give them inoculations.

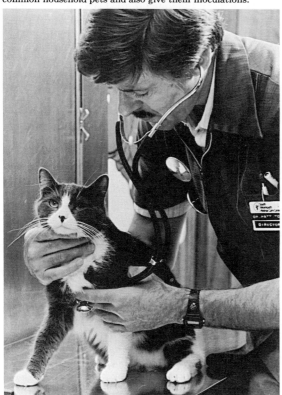

© Julie Houck—Stock, Boston

330

Training

In many countries the degree of doctor of veterinary medicine (D.V.M. or V.M.D.) is awarded after the candidate has successfully completed a formalized course of study. In the United States, candidates must complete a minimum of six years of schooling, consisting of two years of preveterinary study—with a concentration on physical and biological sciences—and a four-year professional degree program. Colleges of veterinary medicine are accredited by the Council on Education of the American Veterinary Medical Association.

In order to practice, veterinarians must obtain a license. Once they have earned their degrees, applicants must pass state tests. Applicants in specialized fields of veterinary medicine may have to meet additional requirements.

Practice

Currently, there are more than 35,000 veterinarians practicing in the United States alone. Of these, most are engaged in private practice, detecting, diagnosing, and treating such pet diseases as distemper. Like physicians they also provide inoculations, offer advice on feeding and care, and use other measures to keep pets healthy. Such veterinarians usually work in animal hospitals and clinics.

Other veterinarians prevent, control, and eradicate diseases in cattle, sheep, swine, and poultry through quarantine, immunization, inspection, and education. Veterinarians work on farms and at marketplaces administering blood tests, giving examinations, and immunizing animals. (*See also* Agriculture, "Twentieth-Century Trends.")

Some veterinarians are research specialists who work in the laboratory to develop better ways to upgrade the genetic quality of milk cows in order to increase their productivity. In addition, recent advances in artificial insemination have helped to ensure the survival of endangered species by improving their reproductive capacities.

History

Veterinary medicine may have been established as a specialty as early as 2000 BC in Babylonia and Egypt. An Egyptian document dated around 1800 BC contains descriptions of treatments for cattle, dogs, birds, and fish. Because these ancient cultures considered the animals sacred, the practice of veterinary science was often limited to external observations only. It was not until the time of the Greeks, 1,000 years later, that the practice of veterinary medicine became a science based on experimentation and observation.

After the fall of the Roman Empire, veterinary science went into a sharp decline. For the next 1,300 years, the care of animals was generally left to farriers, or horseshoers. In the 18th century, when a disease called rinderpest decimated herds of European cattle, colleges of veterinary medicine began to arise in Europe and later elsewhere.

VETO. The word veto comes from the Latin word meaning "I forbid." A veto is the right of an executive to forbid or withhold his assent to acts passed by a lawmaking body.

In the older nations of Europe the king had an absolute veto—that is, by refusing his assent he could prevent acts of the legislature from taking effect. This right still exists in some constitutional monarchies, but in nearly all other nations today the veto power of the chief executive has been limited or abolished.

In the United Nations, each of the five permanent members of the Security Council has the right of absolute veto. (*See also* United Nations.)

In Great Britain the Crown (the king or queen) still has the nominal right of absolute veto, but no British sovereign has vetoed an act of Parliament since 1707. Long after the veto had fallen into disuse in England, however, the king still exercised it to nullify legislation passed in the American Colonies.

The colonial leaders so deeply resented this use of the veto that they listed it as the first of their protests in the Declaration of Independence, saying of the king: "He has refused his Assent to Laws, the most wholesome and necessary for the public good."

The members of the Constitutional Convention feared that Congress might be misled by "Democratic haste and instability" and might encroach on the executive branch. They therefore gave the president the power of a limited veto. Although the word veto is not mentioned in the Constitution, Article I, Section 7 clearly defines the president's right. All bills passed by Congress must be sent to the president. If he approves a bill, he signs it. If he disapproves, he withholds his signature and within ten days returns the bill, with his objections, to the house in which it originated. If the bill is then passed by a two-thirds majority of each house of Congress, it becomes a law over the president's veto. (*See also* United States Constitution.)

The president is allowed by the Constitution to veto only an entire bill and not part of a bill. Congress sometimes makes it difficult for him to veto an unwelcome measure by passing the disputed legislation as a rider, or supplementary clause, in a bill for appropriations. Since appropriation bills are necessary to carry on the work of government, the president thus is almost forced to assent to a measure that he might otherwise veto.

Andrew Jackson was the first president to use the veto aggressively. Not until President John Tyler was a presidential veto overridden by Congress. Andrew Johnson was the most frequently thwarted president. A hostile Reconstruction Congress overrode 15 of the 21 bills he had vetoed. Franklin D. Roosevelt vetoed more bills than any of his predecessors. Since his time the veto has been more carefully used by presidents, who generally prefer to get along with Congress and get their own legislation passed.

Presidents have another tactic at their disposal—the pocket veto. When a bill to which the president objects is sent to him within ten days of an adjournment of Congress, he may nullify it by "pocketing" it, that is, by failing to return it to Congress before the session ends. This effectively kills the legislation.

Although a president may not veto a portion of a bill, this power had been given to governors in more than 40 states by the late 1980s. This power is usually referred to as the line-item veto. The uses of this veto vary among the states, but it generally means that a governor may veto an objectionable portion of a bill, while accepting the remainder. The governor's item vetoes may, however, be overridden. One reason for the success of the line-item veto in state governments is that most of them have a balanced-budget requirement, which the federal government does not.

State legislatures, moreover, generally present appropriations bills in which spending items are clearly separated in order to accommodate the line-item veto power of governors. Congressional bills, by contrast, often contain lump sum payments, without specifying how the money shall be spent.

President Ronald Reagan in January 1984 asked for line-item veto power, and several bills calling for it were entered in Congress. Those favoring it say it will put a stop to appropriation riders. Opponents feel it would get Congress bogged down in dealing with an endless number of item vetoes, each of which would have to be considered on its merits.

VICKSBURG, Miss. The Mississippi River and the Civil War shaped the history of Vicksburg. The city has been called The Gibraltar of the Confederacy. From its high bluffs Confederate soldiers once kept watch over several miles of the Mississippi River.

Fine old Vicksburg homes bear scars of the famous Civil War siege of 1863. The Warren County Courthouse, now known as the Old Court House Museum, and several caves that were occupied during the siege are open to tourists. Vicksburg National Military Park has 1,741 acres (705 hectares) of Civil War fortifications. In Vicksburg National Cemetery are buried more than 16,000 Union soldiers. Confederate soldiers are buried in Cedar Hill Cemetery.

Since its early days Vicksburg has been a strategic river port. Here, through the Yazoo Canal, the Yazoo River joins the Mississippi. Light fixtures, earthmoving machinery, and trailers are among the city's manufactured products. Tourism, shipping, and boatbuilding also help the economy.

The United States Army Corps of Engineers Waterways Experiment Station is located nearby. The station has hundreds of acres of models of hydraulic installations. Vicksburg also is the headquarters of the Mississippi River Commission.

In 1719 the French built Fort Saint Peter on the Yazoo River, several miles north of where Vicksburg now stands. It was destroyed by Indians in 1730. The

Spaniards reestablished an outpost here in 1791. In 1814 the Reverend Newitt Vick, a Methodist minister from Virginia, founded one of the first Mississippi missions nearby. He planned to build a town. It was finally established after Vick's death in 1819 by his son-in-law, John Lane. Vicksburg was officially named in Vick's honor in 1825. The town prospered as a port. A railroad to the Big Black River was completed in 1838 and extended to Jackson by 1840.

In 1876 the Mississippi River cut a new path westward, eliminating the hairpin bend that passed Vicksburg. The Yazoo Canal, completed in 1902, reestablished port facilities. In 1953 a tornado caused 25 million dollars in damage, killed 30 persons, and left 1,200 homeless. Vicksburg has a commission form of government. It is the seat of Warren County. (*See also* Mississippi.) Population (1980 census), 25,434.

VICO, Giambattista (1668–1744). A major figure in European intellectual history, Giambattista Vico influenced the writings of such notable thinkers as Goethe, Auguste Comte, and Karl Marx. In his 'New Science', published in 1725, he developed a remarkable philosophy of history. Human societies, he claimed, pass through predictable stages of growth and decay. They go from the level of beasts to be ruled by superstition. Then they stabilize and divide into classes. Class conflict follows, in which the lower classes attain equal rights. This leads to corruption, dissolution, and a return to being beasts as security and money become life's goals.

Vico was born in Naples, Italy, on June 23, 1668, to a poor family. He had some schooling but was mostly self-educated. In 1699 he was named professor of rhetoric at the University of Naples, a post he retained until his death there on Jan. 23, 1744. During his lifetime Vico sought in vain to have his ideas read and considered. But it was only in the decades after his death that they began to gain notice. Goethe praised 'The New Science' for containing "prophetic insights . . . based on sober meditation about life and about the future." Marx's economic interpretation of history owes a good deal to Vico. Many scholars now see Vico as a source of anthropology and ethnology because of his perceptive views on human nature.

VICTOR EMMANUEL, Kings of Italy. The royal family of Italy is called the House of Savoy. Three Savoy rulers were named Victor Emmanuel. The first (1759–1824) was king of Sardinia before the unification of Italy.

Victor Emmanuel II (1820–1878) was the first king of a united Italy. He was born in Turin. During the reign of his father, Charles Albert (1798–1849), the island kingdom of Sardinia was united with the kingdom of Piedmont on the Italian mainland. This was the first step toward the unification of Italy.

Much of northern Italy was at this time under the rule of the Austrian Empire. Charles Albert wanted to drive the Austrians out of Italy. He went to war in 1848 and was disastrously defeated at the battle of Novara in 1849. Charles Albert abdicated, and his son became king of Sardinia–Piedmont as Victor Emmanuel II.

The new king was faced with many difficulties. He made a temporary peace with Austria, but the army was disorganized, the treasury was empty, and the people were weary of war. Victor Emmanuel, however, with the aid of the brilliant statesman and diplomat Camillo Benso Cavour, finally restored order in the kingdom.

Cavour arranged an alliance between Sardinia and Napoleon III of France. War with Austria broke out again in the spring of 1859. Victor Emmanuel, with the support of French troops, made a new effort to regain Italian territories held by Austria. He was victorious in the battles of Magenta and Solferino and conquered the province of Lombardy. Then Napoleon abandoned his Italian ally and signed the Treaty of Villafranca, leaving Austria still in possession of Venetia. Cavour wanted to continue the struggle alone, but the king refused. (*See also* Cavour.)

After the war Sardinia–Piedmont, already enlarged by the conquest of Lombardy, was joined by the states of Tuscany, Parma, Modena, and Romagna. To appease Napoleon III Sardinia ceded to France the territories of Nice and Savoy.

Through Giuseppe Garibaldi's activities in the south, Sicily and Naples were added to Victor Emmanuel's kingdom (*see* Garibaldi). In 1861 Victor Emmanuel II was proclaimed king of a united Italy. Venice and the Papal States were still outside his kingdom. These two, however, finally joined the Italian union—Venice in 1866 and the Papal States in 1871. The pope withdrew into the Vatican and refused to recognize the king as ruler of Italy (*see* Papacy).

Victor Emmanuel, in a long military procession, entered Rome on July 2, 1871. The Eternal City then became his capital. The unification of Italy was complete. (*See also* Italy, section on History.)

Victor Emmanuel III (1869–1947) came to the throne suddenly upon the assassination of his father, Umberto I, in 1900. The new king had been born in Alexandria, Egypt, and received a military education. As king he believed in a constitutional monarchy and had liberal views.

His chief interest was in the development of the economy, and he left political policies to his ministers. But when strains developed in the parliamentary system because of World War I, he was unable to prevent the seizure of power by Benito Mussolini and his fascists (*see* Fascism; Mussolini).

From then on he was no more than a figurehead in Italy's government. But in 1943, after Mussolini's fall from power, he had the dictator arrested and replaced as premier. Following the war Victor Emmanuel relinquished power in favor of his son Umberto, and in 1946 he abdicated so Umberto could become king. But a plebiscite that year ended the monarchy. Both Umberto and his father went into exile when the republic was proclaimed. Victor Emmanuel made his home in Alexandria, where he died on Dec. 28, 1947.

VICTORIA (1819–1901). On June 22, 1897, as cheering throngs massed in the streets, cannon roared, and the bells of London rang, a carriage pulled up to the steps of Saint Paul's Cathedral. The greatest empire on Earth was paying tribute to Victoria, the queen-empress, on her Diamond Jubilee.

Alexandrina Victoria of the House of Hanover was born at Kensington Palace in London on May 24, 1819. Her father, the Duke of Kent, was the fourth son of George III. Her mother was a German princess.

Victoria became queen when her uncle William IV died in 1837. She was 18 years old. She was crowned at Westminster Abbey on June 28, 1838.

Queen Victoria's first prime minister was the Liberal Lord Melbourne. He also played the part of father and secretary to the young queen. Melbourne took great pains to further Victoria's political education. As Victoria grew older and wiser, however, her ministers began more and more to follow her advice and suggestions. Toward the end of her reign her influence was enormous.

The young Victoria met and fell in love with her first cousin Prince Albert of Saxe-Coburg-Gotha. They were married in 1840 after Victoria had decided that as queen it was her right to propose to Albert. It was a happy marriage. Albert loved art, music, and literature. He was devoted to his family. His political life, however, was difficult. The queen had insisted that he be given the title of prince consort. But the government and many of the people were critical. They objected to any part the prince took in advising the queen on affairs of state.

Victoria and Albert had nine children. They devoted as much time as possible to them, and their home life became an example for all Britain. Victoria arranged her children's marriages. Her eldest daughter became empress of Germany and mother of William II. A granddaughter was the last empress of Russia. By the end of the 19th century, Victoria had so many royal relatives that she was called the "grandmother of Europe."

After Albert's untimely death in 1861, Victoria went into seclusion. She avoided London and spent most of her time at Balmoral Castle in Scotland, at Osborne House on the Isle of Wight, and at Windsor.

In the early years of her reign, guided by Lord Melbourne, the queen was partial to the Liberals (Whigs). One prominent Liberal, however, annoyed the queen. When Lord Palmerston was foreign secretary, he received several severe rebukes from Victoria because he followed his own policies without heeding her opinions. He was finally forced to resign. When Benjamin Disraeli became prime minister, Victoria, pleased with his personality, supported the Conservatives (Tories). She never got along with Disraeli's great political rival, the Liberal William Gladstone. (*See also* Disraeli; Gladstone.)

In 1875, while Disraeli was in office, Britain gained control of the Suez Canal, and Victoria was proclaimed empress of India in 1876. Disraeli's fall from power in 1880 was a blow to the queen. After his death

Queen Victoria, dressed for a state occasion, was rarely seen by the public for many years after Prince Albert's death.

her favorite advisers were Lord Robert Salisbury and Joseph Chamberlain (*see* Chamberlain, Joseph).

The years went by, and the "widow of Windsor" in her self-imposed isolation became an almost legendary figure. Then, as the 19th century drew to a close, the queen began to appear more frequently in public. The last years of her reign, the longest in British history (64 years), were marked with the glitter and pageantry of her Golden Jubilee in 1887 and her Diamond Jubilee in 1897.

Victoria was not a great ruler or a particularly brilliant woman. She was fortunate through most of her reign in having a succession of politically able Cabinet ministers. She happened, however, to be queen of Great Britain for most of the 19th century—a century with more changes than any previous period in history. The queen became the living symbol of peace and prosperity. Governments rose and fell. Industry expanded beyond everyone's wildest dreams. Science, literature, and the arts found new meaning. Through all these long years of peaceful change, there was always the queen. Victoria had lived from the dissolute days of George III to the beginning of the 20th century. She made the Crown a symbol of "private virtue and public honor." Victoria died on the Isle of Wight on Jan. 22, 1901, but the Victorian Age continued until 1914, when Europe was plunged into World War I. She was succeeded on the throne by her son Edward VII. (*See also* England; Edward VII.)

VICTORIA, Australia. The smallest state on the mainland of the Commonwealth of Australia is Victoria. It has an area of 87,884 square miles (227,619 square kilometers). The capital is Melbourne.

Victoria has a rich variety of landscapes and can be divided into three geographical regions. Most of the state's forest is in the central uplands. There is some mixed farming in the sheltered valleys. Most of the northern plains consist of the infertile Mallee region, which supports Mallee eucalyptus and little else. There is a narrow fertile strip, however, adjoining the Murray River. The river separates Victoria from New South Wales. On that strip wheat is grown and Merino sheep and prime lambs are raised. The southern plains are grazed to support the wool, beef, and dairy industries. Most of Victoria's workers are in manufacturing, commerce, farming, construction, and transport. Most of the factories are in Melbourne, which is also the major port and the hub of rail, air, and road systems.

Victoria supplies about one third of Australia's vegetables. Broccoli, brussels sprouts, celery, cauliflower, lettuce, and potatoes are the major crops. Other products include processed beans, sweet corn, and tomatoes. There is a small export market, mostly to Southeast Asia, which includes onions, potatoes, broccoli, celery, and cauliflower.

The Victorian Arts Centre near Melbourne includes art galleries, courtyards for theatrical productions, a convention center and concert hall, a display center, and a hall for state receptions. There are several other art galleries at different centers, including Geelong and Bendigo. Melbourne also has an orchestra. Universities include the University of Melbourne, Monash University, and La Trobe University.

Victoria had its first permanent settlers in the 1830s. It became a prosperous pastoral community during the 1840s and 1850s. The population increased as herders drove their flocks to Victoria from New South Wales and British migrants came from Tasmania. Originally a colony of New South Wales, Victoria became a separate colony in 1851. That same year gold was discovered and brought in many miners. The gold rush was short-lived, though it laid the foundation for Victoria's development. In 1855 Victoria installed a government with a parliament of two houses, a Legislative Assembly and a Legislative Council. Victoria became a state of the Commonwealth of Australia in 1901. (*See also* Australia.) Population (1983 estimate), 4,037,600.

VICTORIA, B.C. One of the province of British Columbia's oldest communities and its capital, Victoria has the atmosphere of an English seaport. A major commercial and distribution center of the province, it is also a popular tourist resort and retirement community as a result of its pleasant climate. Gardens

enclosed by clipped hedges, ivy-covered walls, and shops in Tudor style add to the city's charm.

Victoria is situated at the southeastern end of Vancouver Island on the Juan de Fuca Strait. It lies on low hills that provide magnificent views of the sea. Across the strait to the south can be seen the Olympic Mountains in the state of Washington. Victoria is a major Pacific coast port with a naval base and dockyard. It is connected to mainland Canada and the United States by air and ferry service and to the rest of the island by railroad and highway.

The climate is mild, like that of southern England. Ocean breezes cool Victoria in summer and warm it in winter. Summer temperatures average about 60° F (16° C); winter temperatures, about 39° F (4° C). Rainfall, averaging 26 inches (66 centimeters) annually, keeps lawns green throughout the year. The city is both a summer and winter resort.

Manufacturing focuses on the forest products industry and also includes shipbuilding and food processing. The city is the business center of a lumbering, mining, fishing, farming, and tourist region. Minerals are coal, iron ore, and copper. Agricultural output includes dairy products, fruits, and vegetables. About one fifth of the working population is employed in governmental services. The city is the site of the University of Victoria and Royal Roads, an armed forces training college. The Art Gallery of Greater Victoria, the British Columbia Provincial Museum, and an astrophysical observatory are also in the city.

Among Victoria's handsome structures, the massive Parliament Buildings are outstanding. They overlook the Inner Harbor and yacht basin. Also notable are the Anglican and Roman Catholic cathedrals. Near the Parliament Buildings are Beacon Hill Park and Thunderbird Park, which is famous for its totem poles. On the outskirts of the city are the noted Butchart Gardens. The Marine Drive skirts Beacon Hill Park and the southern shoreline of the city.

Victoria was founded in 1843 as a Hudson's Bay Company fur-trading post, which was known as Fort Camosun. It was later renamed Fort Victoria in honor of the British queen. The town served as the capital of the colony of Vancouver Island from 1848. When gold was discovered in the area about 1856, Victoria served as the supply center for thousands of prospectors. It became the capital of British Columbia in 1868. Population (1981 census), 64,379.

VICTORIA, LAKE, or **VICTORIA NYANZA.** Africa's largest lake is on the equator. It is bordered by Kenya, mainland Tanzania, and Uganda. At its longest, it stretches 210 miles (338 kilometers) across the East African plateau. Its greatest width is 150 miles (241 kilometers). Its area is about 26,418 square miles (68,422 square kilometers). Its shores, except on the west, are deeply indented. Lake Superior in North America is the world's only larger body of fresh water in surface area.

Lake Victoria's chief tributary is the Kagera River. The flow of water from the lake, through the Victoria Nile and into the White Nile, is controlled by the great Owen Falls Dam in Uganda. (*See also* Nile River.) The dam provides electricity for the region. Steamers cross Lake Victoria on regular schedules, and the Kenya-Uganda Railway links the lake with the Indian Ocean at Mombasa. (For map, *see* Africa.) The surrounding region is one of the most densely populated in Africa.

An English explorer, John H. Speke, was the first European to see Lake Victoria in 1858. He named the lake in honor of Queen Victoria. Speke later explored part of its southern shores. In 1874 Sir Henry Morton Stanley sailed around it.

VICTORIA FALLS. One of the world's mightiest waterfalls is in east-central Africa, on the border between Zambia and Zimbabwe (formerly Rhodesia). Here the Zambezi River spreads out into an island-studded channel that extends to more than 5,500 feet (1,680 meters) wide and drops abruptly some 355 feet (108 meters) into a deep cleft set squarely across the current. The turbulent waters emerge through a narrow gorge leading to a steep-walled, zigzag canyon. (For picture, *see* Waterfall.)

The gorge is spanned by a steel arch railway and highway bridge 657 feet (200 meters) long and 420 feet (128 meters) above highwater level. When it was opened in 1905, the Falls Bridge was the highest in the world. Also in the area are Victoria Falls National Park in Zimbabwe and Livingstone Game Park in Zambia.

Victoria Falls is about twice as wide and twice as high as Niagara Falls in North America. It is divided by islands into four main cataracts, or waterfalls. The mist from the falling water is especially dense during the rainy first half of the year and is visible for miles.

In 1855 British explorer David Livingstone was the first European to see Victoria Falls. He named it after Queen Victoria of Great Britain.

VIDEO RECORDING. When video recording was developed in the 1960s, it caused the greatest change in television and home entertainment since the introduction of color television in the 1950s. Video recorders are devices that allow a user to record television transmissions, view home television movies, or play commercially produced videotapes. They also provide viewers with greater control over what they watch on television and when they watch it. The technology embodied in video recording led to significant advances in data recording for both computers and audio recording. (*See also* Computer; Tape Recorder.)

Video recording involves the use of two different types of technology: videotape recording and videodisc recording. The more widespread technology is videotape recording. Here, the video image is recorded as a series of signals in regions of a magnetic tape, the operating principles of which are qualitatively identical to those of audio tapes. The videotape recorders initially had stationary heads, requiring large amounts of tape and bulky equipment carried in large trucks and vans. Since the late 1970s

videocassettes, in which the tape is stored in a self-contained cassette rather than on reels, have been the dominant form of videotape. The advantage in videotape recording is that the same equipment is used both to record and to play the magnetic tapes, and videotapes can be reused many times.

In videodisc recording, the video image, converted to signals, is recorded on a disc by a laser, which vaporizes tiny holes or indentations in the disc. When the disc is played, these holes are detected by another, less powerful laser. Like videotape recording, videodisc recording has its drawbacks and advantages. The laser used to optically produce the master disc is more powerful than the laser used to play it, so each can be recorded only once. More information, however, is stored in a physically smaller area. In addition, information located anywhere on the disc can be accessed quickly. Videodiscs are more suitable for some applications, but the recording abilities and reusability of cassette tapes contributed to their popularity in the home-video market during the 1980s.

Another development in the videodisc recording industry is a system that combines the advantages of optical and magnetic recording. In these magneto-optical systems, the magnetic domains on the disc are changed when a spot is heated by a laser. Another laser is used to detect the domains during playback. Like magnetic tapes, magneto-optical discs are reusable, and the same equipment can be used for recording and for playback. The discs are also extremely compact. Magneto-optical discs are being developed primarily for storage of computer data.

The principal use of video recording is in home videocassette recorders (VCRs), also called videotape recorders (VTRs). Commercially introduced on a major scale in 1979, VCRs were in half of the homes in the United States by the mid-1980s. VCR users can record television shows and then view them at more convenient times or repeatedly. It is also possible to record one show while watching another. Videotapes of motion pictures or tapes produced specifically for VCRs, such as exercise tapes or educational tapes, can be rented or purchased. In addition, linked to video cameras, VCRs are used to produce home video movies. Since hours of material can be recorded on a single cassette that, unlike film, requires no special processing, video cameras and VCRs are rapidly replacing 8-millimeter equipment for home movies.

In the 1960s videotape recording became a standard method of recording, and later editing, television shows or news events. The development of compact cassette recorders in the 1970s replaced the earlier bulky models and made video recorders more portable. This aided television news organizations and, at the same time, the cassette recorder's lower cost made the technology available to home users.

This article was contributed by Eric J. Lerner, writer on scientific and technical subjects and electronics editor of *Aerospace America*.

HOW A VHS TAPE RECORDER WORKS

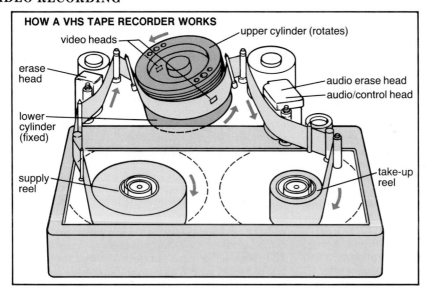

video heads

upper cylinder (rotates)

erase head

audio erase head

audio/control head

lower cylinder (fixed)

supply reel

take-up reel

During playback (left), magnetic video signals on the cassette tape are turned into electric signals, which then become pictures and sound. The supply reel rotates, and the tape moves at an angle past two or more heads on a drum. As the drum's upper cylinder rotates, the heads read the magnetic signals along paths, called tracks, until all of the tape is wound onto the take-up reel. The device has other components with heads to erase the video or audio signals on the tape and signal the beginning of a track. The key to VHS compactness is in the design of its magnetic recording system (below). The signals on the A and B tracks are arranged so that each head can read only its corresponding track, even if there is some track overlap. This means that video head A reads only track A and video head B reads only track B.

Source: Maxell Corporation of America

Optical videodiscs are not as widely used because they are not designed for home recording. To a limited extent, videodisc players are used to view the same sort of prerecorded material as is available on videotapes. Videodiscs are also incorporated into some arcade video games. They are also used for commercial education, such as in equipment training for technicians. Videodisc players provide quick access to a specific area of the disc instead of having to scan through an entire tape.

Optical discs are used extensively outside the video field. Very small optical discs that are used to make audio recordings of extremely high quality and fidelity are called compact discs, or CDs (see Compact Disc). These discs are also widely used in computer systems to store large amounts of information, both text and graphics. As many as 3 billion words—the equivalent of a 10,000-book library—can be stored on one optical disc.

VCR technology has also been applied to the audio field. In the late 1980s digital tape recording provided quality equal to that of compact discs. It also improved on repeat-recording capabilities.

How Videotape Recorders Work

Videotape recorders function on principles similar to those of audiotape recorders. To record, an image is converted to electronic signals in the form of a varying electric current. This current lies in close proximity to a moving magnetic tape. As the signal changes, an electromagnet generates a varying magnetic field, which magnetizes the magnetic particles in the moving tape in a pattern corresponding to the strength of the signals.

To play the tape, the magnetic particles on the tape move past a head, inducing an electrical current. These currents are identical to the initial electrical signal used to record the tape.

The difference between video and audio recording is in the sources and destinations of the signals. In

PATTERN OF VHS MAGNETIC RECORDING

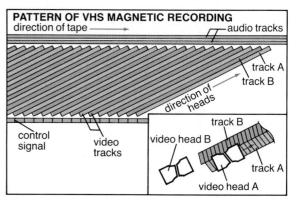

direction of tape

audio tracks

track A

track B

direction of heads

control signal

video tracks

track B

video head B

track A

video head A

audio the signals come from a microphone and return in playback to a speaker. In video recording they come from a camera or from a television broadcast and return in playback to a television receiver.

Since there is more information in a video signal than in an audio signal, a compact way of recording was developed for the VCR. The key to this compactness is writing speed—the speed at which the tape moves across the head. The higher the speed, the higher the frequency of signal recorded for a given size of magnetic particle. This presented another problem: as the speed of the tape moving past the head increased, the length of tape eventually became unwieldy. The solution in the VCR was to move the recording heads as well as the tape so that the combined speed is increased without increasing the tape length. Two or more recording heads are mounted in a VCR on a rapidly rotating drum. The drum revolves about 30 times per second. The tape is wrapped around the drum at an angle, forming a helix. Without this method of recording, called helical scanning, the tape would have to run about 100 times faster than it does. As the video heads rotate, the tape contacts the heads on a diagonal path as shown. The heads record diagonal strips alternately across the tape, with one head starting one strip just as the other head finishes another strip. Each pair of strips, or tracks, contains the signal from a single frame or video image. One strip has the even-numbered lines of the image and the other track has the the the odd-numbered lines. This interlaced scanning prevents flicker since images are presented 60 times per second, as in a conventional television broadcast, even though the drum spins only 30 times per second.

The moving drum common to all VCR formats gives them several capabilities not shared with ordinary television. A single frame can be "frozen" on the screen by stopping the tape and moving the heads repeatedly over the same video tracks. Similarly, the heads can move from track to track, creating a slow-motion image. Much more commonly used is the ability to "fast forward"—move the tape at an accelerated rate while still viewing the image. Fast forwarding allows the viewer to skip over undesired portions of tape, such as advertisements. The same capability, available in rewind, allows repeat viewing.

VCRs come equipped with small microprocessors. Users can program these microprocessors to record a

transmission at times when they are not present or while they watch another show.

Initially, two VCR formats were introduced: Beta and VHS (Video Home System). Both used 1½-inch-wide tape but differed in the size of the drum and in other secondary features. In the late 1980s VHS and Beta were joined by a third format, which uses a more compact 8-millimeter-wide recording tape.

The 8-millimeter tape uses metal particles, instead of metal oxide particles, to record the magnetic field. Since these particles are smaller, a more compact tape is possible. In addition, the tape allows the audio signal to be recorded in digital form as a sequence of pulses. This provides extremely high-quality recordings and also makes it possible to use the 8-millimeter videotapes in high-fidelity digital audiotape equipment. The 8-millimeter format is especially suited for use in camcorders—combination home-video cameras and VCRs. Camcorder sales in the late 1980s approached a million units per year, surpassing sales of conventional movie cameras.

How Videodiscs Work

Just as a VCR works on the same principles as a conventional tape recorder, the technology used in an optical disc resembles that used in making a vinyl phonograph recording. There are, however, major differences. The optical recording of a video signal on a disc begins in a factory with production of a master disc. The signal is first converted to a series of digitized pulses. These pulses are then fed to a laser. For each pulse, the laser burns a small pit into the surface of the master disc. The pits are arranged in a spiral pattern, much like the grooves on a phonograph, but more closely spaced—about one micron apart. A micron is equal to 1 millionth of a meter (39 millionths of an inch).

The master is used to produce a stamp from which millions of videodisc copies are pressed. The discs

VIDEODISC COMPOSITION

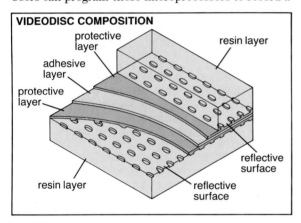

The microscopic pits of the videodisc's reflective layers (above) represent the signals recorded by a laser beam. In the videodisc playback system (right), a laser beam is created by the laser diode and passes through a sophisticated optical system to focus the beam on the disc. The system includes a variety of lenses, mirrors, a grating, and a prism; a wavelength plate adjusts the wavelength of the laser beam. The tracking and tangential mirrors together move the beam across the signal track on the disc during playback. Once the beam has been modulated by the signal pits on the disc, it is rerouted through the objective lens and reflected back through the wavelength plate, prism, and a lens. It is then reflected to the photodiode, which converts the laser signal to an electronic signal that creates the picture and sound.

Source: Pioneer Electronics (USA) Inc.

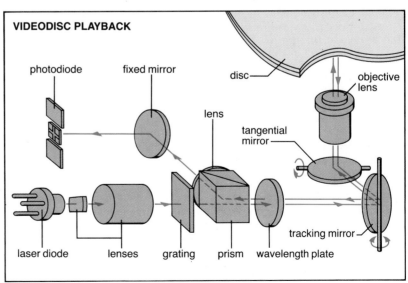

VIDEODISC PLAYBACK

consist of three layers on each side, sandwiched by an adhesive layer. These three layers are the substrate layer, a reflective film layer with the pits, and a protective layer of transparent plastic to prevent damage to the tiny pits. Each side of the disc carries information of up to 54,000 video frames, the individual pictures that make up the moving image at 30 frames per second.

Unlike a conventional phonograph, which is played back by a fine needle in physical contact with the phonograph, a videodisc is played back by a laser beam, involving no actual contact. As the disc spins, a laser beam is focused on the series of pits and the gaps between pits, called lands. When the laser strikes a land, the light is reflected to a photodiode detector. When it strikes a pit, the light scatters, reflecting much less light to the detector. The result is a series of flashes of light corresponding to the initial pulses of the digitized video signal. The detector converts these laser light pulses into a digitized electrical signal and sends it to other circuits that re-create the original video and feed it to a television.

The identical operating principles are used to record extremely high-quality audio recordings on what are called compact discs (see Compact Disc). This type of system can also be used for high-speed memory storage for data from a computer.

The optical disc is the most widely used type of videodisc. The use of another type, a capacitive disc, is less common. In the capacitive discs very fine metallic grooves are used to encode the video signals. A fine needle contacts the disc to read the grooves by detecting changes in their height. The optical disc is considered generally superior to the capacitive disc because the absence of physical contact with the laser discs avoids wear and makes them last almost indefinitely.

VIENNA, Austria. The capital of Austria, Vienna was once one of the most important political and cultural centers of the world. For more than 2,000 years a gateway between East and West, Vienna was the seat of the Holy Roman Empire from 1558 to 1806 and the capital of the Austro-Hungarian Empire until 1918 (see Austria-Hungary).

Renowned for its music and architecture, the modern city has retained a style that reflects its elegant and ornate past. It is the least spoiled of the great, old Western European capitals, and much of the urban landscape remains as it was designed centuries ago by royal gardeners and architects.

Vienna is in northeastern Austria on the Danube River. It has an area of 160 square miles (415 square kilometers). The city is built on the slopes of the Vienna Woods, which descend to the Danube in a series of four semicircular terraces. On the north side of the river, the countryside gives way to the broad Pan-

nonian Basin of Eastern Europe. The Danube Canal, a channelized branch of the Danube, was completed in 1600 and winds through the oldest part of the city. The average yearly temperature hovers around 51° F (11° C), and rainfall, heaviest in the spring months, is approximately 20 inches (50 centimeters) a year.

The base of the Viennese economy is trade and industry. Vienna produces almost a third of Austria's gross national product, including most of the Austrian-made electrical appliances, nearly half of the paper and clothing, and a large portion of the machine tools. Government on all levels is a major employer, and tourism is a growing economic factor.

Description

The old city of Vienna is encircled by a grand boulevard known as the Ringstrasse. The Ringstrasse coincides with the old city walls and was laid out when the walls were torn down in 1857. Some of Vienna's finest buildings are on either side of this thoroughfare. Within the Ring is Vienna's most famous landmark, Saint Stephen's Cathedral. St. Stephen's was begun in Romanesque style in 1147 and reconstructed in Gothic style between 1304 and 1450. The church's southern tower is 446 feet (136 meters) high and dominates the city's skyline. The northern tower was never completed.

Near St. Stephen's Cathedral is the Hoher Markt, the oldest square in Vienna. When Rome controlled Vienna, the forum and commander's palace stood in this area. The Roman emperor Marcus Aurelius is said to have died here. Another old square, Am Hof, is nearby. It was the site of the first palace built by the ruling Babenberg family in the 12th century. The major site on the square today is the Church of the Seven Choirs of Angels, dating from the 14th century. The announcement of the dissolution of the Holy Roman Empire in 1806 was made from the balcony of this church.

The largest complex of buildings within the Ringstrasse is the Hofburg, the former Hapsburg royal palace. The oldest part of this complex dates from the 13th century, the newest from the late 19th. Covering an area of more than 47 acres (19 hectares), the Hofburg has magnificently furnished private and state apartments and also houses the imperial treasury of the Holy Roman and Austrian empires, the Austrian National Library, the Albertina and several other museums, and the Winter (or Spanish) Riding School. The Vienna Boys' Choir sings for mass in the chapel at the Hofburg every Sunday from September to June. The Austrian government's executive branch is now housed within the Hofburg.

Also within the Ring is Austria's national theater. Called the Burg Theater, it was founded in 1751 and has been in its current home since 1888. The Staatsoper, or Vienna State Opera House, completed in 1869, is also in the Ring. The Vienna Philharmonic, when not functioning as the orchestra for the opera, performs in the Musikvereinsgebäude, just south of the Ring.

Austria's Greek-revival style Parliament Building, right, is opposite the huge Hofburg Palace, left. On the right, beyond parliament, are the twin museums of natural history and art.

Opposite the Burg Theater and just outside the Ring is the Town Hall. Completed in 1883, it is the seat of the municipal government. Opposite the Hofburg are the twin museums of natural history and art history. They were built in the late 19th century on either side of Maria Theresa Square.

Outside the Ring are the two Belvedere palaces, now the Austrian Gallery museums, and the Schönbrunn palace—all in the baroque style. The Schönbrunn has a park of nearly 500 acres (200 hectares).

Culture and Education

For many years Vienna was the musical capital of the world, and music remains a Viennese passion. Some of the city's famous composers include Haydn, Mozart, Beethoven, Schubert, Brahms, Bruckner, the Strausses, Mahler, and Schoenberg.

There are 16 state museums, 12 city museums, and special exhibition halls in such places as the National Library. The Albertina has renowned Dürer and Rembrandt engravings. The Museum of Fine Arts houses the superb Hapsburg collection of old masters. Three houses in which Beethoven lived and worked have been preserved as museums, as have former residences of Mozart, Haydn, and Schubert. In 1971 the Sigmund Freud museum was opened in the apartment that had served as Freud's home and office for nearly 50 years. Vienna is also the home of the University of Vienna, founded in 1365, and schools of agriculture, commerce, veterinary medicine, and applied art.

The People

When Vienna was the capital of the Austro-Hungarian Empire it was a cosmopolitan city. By 1900 more than 60 percent of the residents were non-German speaking, and by 1910 Vienna was at its most populous with more than 2 million inhabitants. The city has lost population continuously since the 1930s. Most residents are Austrian citizens; the largest immigrant group is Yugoslavian, followed by Turkish. More than 70 percent of the population is Roman Catholic.

Government

Vienna is both a capital city and a province. It is divided into 23 districts, each with an appointed magistrate and an elected chairman and representatives. The mayor of the city is also the deputy of the province. The Town Senate acts as the provincial government, while the city council acts as the legislative branch for both city and province. Vienna has elected a socialist government at every free municipal election since 1918.

History

Vienna has been inhabited since Neolithic times, about 4,000 years ago. It was a Celtic settlement when the Romans annexed it in the 1st century BC. During Roman times it was known as Vindobona and grew in population to 15 or 20 thousand by about the 3rd century AD. The Romans were swept away in the turmoil of the 5th century, but enough of Vindobona remained to serve as the beginning of the medieval city.

Charlemagne conquered the area around Vienna in the late 8th century, and by 881 the name Wenia appeared for the first time. In 1137 Vienna received a city charter. The dukes of Babenberg made Vienna their capital in 1156, and in 1276 the first of the long line of Hapsburg rulers was installed. The Hapsburgs acquired territories through marriage, and by the 16th century Vienna was one of the great capitals of the world.

The city was besieged by the Ottoman Turks in 1529 and again in 1683; both times they were repelled. In response an outer circle of defenses, the Linienwall, was built. The wall has been replaced by a boulevard known as the Gürtel. The prizes taken from the Turks following their defeat can still be seen in the Museum of Army History. It was from the Turks that coffee was introduced to Vienna. After the defeat of the Turks, Vienna developed into a splendid baroque city.

Between 1792 and 1815 Austria fought several wars against France. Napoleon twice occupied Vienna, once in 1806, when he forced the dissolution of the Holy Roman Empire, and again in 1809. After Napoleon's exile to Elba, the Congress of Vienna met from 1814 to 1815 and decided the political fate of Europe.

In 1848 rioting broke out in Vienna. The revolt was led by students and intellectuals interested in securing a more democratic and liberal government, but by 1849 the revolt had failed. The victorious Hapsburg monarchy launched another building boom in Vienna by ordering the old city walls to be torn down in 1857. The resulting Ringstrasse buildings and parks were not completed until 1913, just one year before the outbreak of World War I and five years before the end of the Austro-Hungarian Empire.

The Nazis took Austria in 1938, and when World War II ended in 1945 Vienna was occupied by the four Allied powers: Great Britain, France, the United States, and the Soviet Union. This occupation came to an end in 1955. Since then Vienna has regained international status by becoming the home for several international organizations, including the United Nations High Commission for Refugees, the United Nations Industrial Development Organization, the International Atomic Energy Agency, and the Organization of Petroleum Exporting Countries. Important American-Soviet summit meetings in 1961 and 1979 were held in Vienna. Population (1984 estimate), 1,505,800.

Saint Stephen's Cathedral, a combination of Romanesque and Gothic styles, is in the center of old Vienna.

Bernard G. Silberstein—Rapho/Photo Researchers

VIENNA, CONGRESS OF. Except for minor conflicts, Europe was at peace from 1815 until 1914. This century of relative stability owed a great deal to the Congress of Vienna. This gathering of statesmen was convened by the powers that had defeated Napoleon: Austria, Russia, Prussia, and Great Britain. It met from September 1814 until June 1815, and its purpose was to redraw the map of Europe after Napoleon's rampages and to re-establish conservative political order. It succeeded in both respects.

The leading statesmen in attendance were Prince Metternich of Austria, Czar Alexander I of Russia, Frederick William III and Prince Karl von Hardenberg of Prussia, Viscount Castlereagh of Great Britain, and Talleyrand (Charles Maurice de Talleyrand-Périgord) of France, one of the ablest politicians in the history of Europe. The congress established a balance of power in Europe that endured until Germany was unified in 1871. A powerful Germany in the center of Europe gradually destroyed the work of the congress.

VIENTIANE, Laos. The capital city of Laos, Vientiane is also the administrative center of the Vientiane province. The city's industries include brewing, lumber processing, and the manufacture of brick, tile, textiles, cigarettes, matches, detergents, plastic bags, rubber sandals, and iron and steel. Soil in the area is good, and farmers grow rice and corn and raise livestock. There are unmined copper and gold deposits.

Until 1975 Vientiane was the principal livestock shipping and slaughtering center of the country. It is Laos's main port of entry. There is an international airport, and highways link Vientiane with other major cities. The Mekong River is navigable only by small boat at Vientiane, and passage across it is by ferry. The Nam Ngum Dam north of Vientiane provides enough hydroelectric power for surrounding areas and for export to Thailand.

Sisavangvong University offers study in agriculture, art, education, forestry and irrigation, and medicine. Fa-Ngum College, Lycée Vientiane, Polytechnic, and Pali and Sanskrit institutes are also in Vientiane. Ho Phakeo, the national museum, is located there, as are the Dongsaphangmeuk Library and the Bibliothèque Nationale.

Although it has government offices, foreign embassies, schools, and a radio station, Vientiane still maintains some of its older wooden structures. Its most outstanding building is the That Luang, a temple founded in 1586. The temple has a four-sided brick and stucco base with a tall four-sided dome. The dome is crowned with an ornate spire and is encircled by a row of spires. The monument is enclosed in a court.

Vientiane was founded during the late 13th century. In 1778 it came under Siamese control and in 1828 was destroyed when the Laotian king revolted against Siamese dominance. From 1899 to 1953, except during Japanese occupation in 1945, Vientiane was the seat of the French governor or served as the French administrative capital. Population (1978 estimate), 200,000.

Many Vietnamese rural communities depend upon fishing for survival. Here in the Dong Hoi region people often row with their feet.

© Philip J. Griffiths—Magnum

VIETNAM.

The Socialist Republic of Vietnam consists of the former Democratic Republic of Vietnam (North Vietnam) and the former Republic of Vietnam (South Vietnam). The division of the country resulted from the defeat of the French by Communist-inspired nationalists in 1954. A prolonged civil war resulted in a victory for the Communist north, and reunification occurred in mid-1976.

Physical Setting

Vietnam has an area of 127,207 square miles (329,-465 square kilometers) and is located in Southeast Asia. The country has a coastline of nearly 1,440 miles (2,317 kilometers), much of which fronts on the South China Sea. Border countries are China, Kampuchea, and Laos. The latter two countries, along with Vietnam, constituted the former French Indochina.

Northern Vietnam is quite mountainous, especially the extreme north and northwest. The Red River (Song Koi), which originates in China's Yunnan Province, is the principal river of the north and is about 725 miles (1,167 kilometers) in length. The major lowland area is a delta that has been created by deposits from the Red River as it enters the South China Sea. The river passes through the capital city of Hanoi. For more than 2,000 years the Tonkin Lowland, considered the cradle of Vietnamese civilization, has been the scene of considerable water control efforts in the form of canals and dikes.

The southernmost portion of the country is dominated by another lowland that is much more extensive than that in the north. This lowland has essentially been created by the Mekong River (Song Cuu Long) and its various tributaries. Just north of Ho Chi Minh City (formerly Saigon) the landscape becomes more varied and rolling with forested hills.

This article was contributed by Thomas R. Leinbach, Professor of Geography and International Affairs, University of Kentucky, Lexington, and author of 'Mobility and Employment in Urban Southeast Asia' (1987) and 'Development and Environment in Peninsular Malaysia' (1982).

The central portion of Vietnam varies in width but is only 35 miles (56 kilometers) at its narrowest point. This region has only a narrow coastal strip in contrast to the rest of the coastline, where wider lowlands exist. The westernmost portion of the area is dominated by the Annamese, or Annamite, Cordillera, a major mountain chain, which forms the spine of the country from north to south. Along with the two major rivers, there are many shorter rivers that drain the highlands and flow eastward to the South China Sea. The country also has six island groups, 14 separate mountain ranges, and three large lakes.

The climate of Vietnam is largely tropical, though the north may be distinguished as subtropical. Differences in humidity, rainfall, and temperature are caused largely by changes in elevation. The north has a hot and humid five-month-long wet season lasting from May through September. The remainder of the year is relatively warm and rainfree, but humid. A prolonged period of fog, cloudiness, and drizzle occurs from December through April in the central zone and coastal lowlands. The south is characterized by a monsoon-type climate dominated by a changing wind pattern that brings rainfall. The rainy period is shorter than in the north.

In the north maximum rainfall occurs in July and August, while in the south these peaks are in June and September. Average rainfall at Hanoi is 72 inches (183 centimeters) per year, at Hue 117 inches (297 centimeters), and at Ho Chi Minh City 81 inches (206 centimeters). In the higher elevations of the Annamese mountain chain, rainfall can exceed 175 inches (455 centimeters). The region is subject to typhoons, which may occur from July through November. Daily temperatures in the south range between 64° and 92° F (18° and 33° C), while in the north the climate is considerably cooler. Average summer temperatures are approximately 82° F (28° C) with the winter average at 63° F (17° C).

People and Culture

The population of Vietnam in the late 1980s was estimated at more than 62 million. Birth- and death

341

rates respectively were 34 and 8 per thousand. The natural rate of increase per year is 2.3 percent. If this rate continued, the population of the country would double within 30 years. Family planning services, including contraception and abortion, are widely available. A major goal is to reduce the rate of population growth to less than 2 percent per year. The infant mortality rate of 69 per 1,000 live births is close to that of the Philippines but considerably higher than that of Malaysia. The average life expectancy is 60 years in contrast to 75 years in the United States.

Given the contrasting landforms of the country, the distribution of the population is very uneven. Major concentrations are found in the Red and Mekong river deltas, where densities may exceed 2,000 persons per square mile (772 per square kilometer). The average density, however, is much lower—488 persons per square mile (188 per square kilometer).

A major element of current development planning is the forced relocation of more than 10 million Vietnamese into new economic zones that are scattered throughout the country. Earlier movements of people occurred largely in response to war activity, with refugees migrating from north to south and subsequently into urban areas. In the mid-1970s there also was an evacuation effort carried out by the United States that took more than 135,000 Vietnamese to that

country. Movement out of Vietnam in small fishing vessels continues. These migrants seek destinations largely in other Southeast Asian countries.

As a result of a United Nations effort, a coordinated orderly departure program has been in place since 1980. Ethnic Chinese and children of American and Asian (Amerasian) descent are conspicuous in this program because they are the objects of discrimination if they remain in Vietnam. Illegal emigration continues but at a reduced rate, as the penalty when caught is severe. Property confiscation and hard labor and reeducation camps are common punishments.

The urban population in Vietnam is 19 percent of the total, comparable to that of Thailand and Burma. The largest cities are Ho Chi Minh City in southern Vietnam and Hanoi in the north. Other large cities are Haiphong (the major port for Hanoi), Da Nang, Bien Hoa, Can Tho, Nha Trang, Qui Nhon, Hue, and Cam Ranh. The latter is the site of the Soviet naval fleet, which occupies the facility built by the United States during the Vietnam War. (*See also* Hanoi; Ho Chi Minh City.)

The Vietnamese are descended from both Chinese and Thai peoples. Originating in southern China, the Vietnamese people pushed southward over the course of several hundred years to occupy much of the current area of Vietnam. A strong sense of national identity was produced as a result of the struggle for political independence from China. Vietnamese culture, however, still reflects the strong influence of Chinese civilization. Nearly 100 years of French rule instilled many European cultural traits, but the Vietnamese continue to attach great importance to the family and observe rites honoring their ancestors.

Although 90 percent of the population is Vietnamese, there are several significant minorities. The largest of these is the Chinese, who number about 4.1 million and constitute nearly 7 percent of the total population. The Chinese minority is concentrated largely in urban areas, especially the Cholon section of Ho Chi Minh City. The Chinese have long played major roles in the Vietnamese economy, being active in rice trade and milling, real estate, banking, shopkeeping, stevedoring, and mining.

Another minority group, known collectively as Montagnards, is made up of two main ethnic-linquistic groups—Malayo-Polynesian and Mon-Khmer. More than 25 tribes of various cultures and dialects are spread throughout the hill areas of the country. Still another minority group is the Khmer Krom, or Kampucheans. These people, perhaps numbering 1 million, are concentrated in the southern provinces near the Kampuchean border and at the delta of the Mekong River. Commonly they are farmers.

Government policy appears to be directed toward the assimilation of minorities. There are attempts to place ethnic Vietnamese among minority peoples in order to strengthen control. A further emphasis is the encouragement of minorities to emigrate, as noted above. Ethnic Chinese are often denied official employment and educational opportunities.

© Christine Spengler—Sygma

Bicycles have been the chief means of transportation in Hanoi, even before the capital was impoverished by war.

The three traditional religions are Buddhism, Taoism, and Confucianism. Buddhism was brought into Vietnam from China in the 2nd century AD and has the largest number of followers. About 32 million Vietnamese follow Buddhism, and most of these followers are Mahayana Buddhists (*see* Buddhism). Both Mahayana and Theravada Buddhism are practiced. Most of Vietnam's Theravada Buddhists are Khmer Krom. They number about 900,000 and live in southern and southwestern Vietnam. It is this group that has supplied the Vietnamese army in Kampuchea with interpreters and staff for its government there. Confucianism serves as a means of forming social patterns. Rules for social interaction, the cult of ancestor worship, and the male-dominated family structure are by-products of the religion. Roman Catholicism was introduced into Vietnam in the 16th century and flourished especially under the French. There are about 2 million followers of the religion today.

The government tolerates religion and permits religious services but restricts conversion activities and growth in general. Reports indicate that the Roman Catholic church is a special target for control, and as a result church membership has begun to dwindle. Since 1975 government authorities have attempted to suppress and intimidate the Mahayana Buddhist leaders. Temples have been closed, and monks have been forced into reeducation camps. Travel is also severely restricted.

The official language of the country is Vietnamese. It is monosyllabic and belongs to the Mon-Khmer family. There is considerable borrowing from Chinese in the vocabulary. Of the numerous other languages spoken, Thai, Sino-Tibetan and Miao-Yao are the most widespread. Once widely spoken, French has fallen from use. Given the American intervention in Vietnamese affairs, English is not encouraged. Russian is of some importance because of the strong aid from and trade connection with the Soviet Union. Both Russian and Chinese are taught in the schools.

Education in Vietnam is universal and compulsory for children ages 6 to 11. The educational system has been altered somewhat since reunification. This basically involves the use of new texts in the south to conform to those in the north. In addition many teachers in the south have undergone political indoctrination programs. Private schools are now under government control. The school year extends from September to May. Primary and secondary education accounts for more than 12,600 schools, 566,000 teachers, and 15.8 million students. There were more than 80 institutions of higher learning with a total enrollment of 160,000 in the mid-1980s.

Health services and facilities are being refurbished and expanded to make up for wartime destruction. Yet expenditures on health services are grossly inadequate. It is estimated that only 15 percent of the population have access to safe water. The government appears to have eliminated such major diseases as tuberculosis, smallpox, malaria, leprosy, and bubonic plague. In the early 1980s there were approximately 11,000 hospitals and 14,000 physicians in the country.

Vietnamese cooking has been influenced by Chinese, French, and Malay food preparation. The Vietnamese cuisine in upper-class homes has a rich sophistication that rivals Chinese and Thai cooking. A fermented fish sauce called *nuoc mam* is used in many prepared dishes. Rice, the staple food, is usually eaten with cooked leafy green vegetables or in soup. Rice is grown wherever possible in irrigated rice fields. Rice is supplemented by corn, sweet potatoes, and cassavas. Many people raise fruits and vegetables. Meat is only consumed at festivals or sacrifices. Fresh fish and dried fish, however, are readily available. Red chili is used in most meals in some form, and occasionally boiled maize is eaten as a snack. Agriculture in the south-central coastal plain and on the Kampuchean border has been historically dominated by market gardening rather than wet rice agriculture.

Economy

Vietnam is viewed by the World Bank as one of 37 low-income countries. It has a centrally planned economy in which the dominant sector is public. Very few current statistics are available because no financial or production information is reported to outside agencies. Gross national product was estimated for 1982 at 9 billion dollars, with a per capita income of 175 dollars. The economy has evolved in phases that have attempted to eliminate capitalism, elevate state control and planning, and deal with financial indebtedness and weak resources. Efforts to redistribute land in the north were coupled with an attempt to implement a cooperative movement. Cooperative land has been contracted to families or production teams to meet production targets. Excess production above a quota may be sold by peasants on the open market. Individual land ownership is still widespread in the south. Similarly, private enterprise in the south has only gradually changed and continues to play a significant role.

The economy is guided by a five-year development plan model that corresponds to the Soviet and Eastern European planning cycle. During the 1970s emphasis

The port of Ho Chi Minh City is on the Saigon River about 50 miles (80 kilometers) inland from the South China Sea. Although its economy was severely undermined by the war, the city's recovery was more rapid than that of Hanoi.

moved from heavy industry to agriculture and light industry in order to improve material living standards within Vietnam as well as develop exports to earn foreign exchange. The south was viewed as the main food basket and supplier for the nation as well as a producer of light industrial goods.

The plan was built on the assumption of United States aid after normalization of ties. Little aid from the United States was delivered, and foreign aid in general was reduced in reaction to Vietnam's invasion of Kampuchea. Conflict with China further drained resources. It is estimated that more than 40 percent of the country's budget is being spent on defense.

A new plan not yet implemented emphasizes small practical projects in agriculture, consumer goods, energy, and communications. The new domestic economic policy, which was announced in early 1988, in effect abandoned centralized planning in favor of managerial decision making at the factory level in state enterprises. Worker incentives, quality control, shareholding, an expanded banking industry, and wage scales linked to productivity were part of this sweeping reform.

In 1976 Vietnam joined the International Monetary Fund, World Bank, and Asian Development Bank, but no requests for loans have been honored since 1978. Most aid has come from the United Nations Development Program, France, Japan, and the Scandinavian countries. The Soviet Union has assisted with major development projects.

Agriculture—the mainstay of the economy—employs 60 percent of the labor force. It accounts for an estimated 45 percent of the gross domestic product. Only 17 percent of the total land area is cultivated. The deltas of the Red and Mekong rivers, as well as other lowland areas, are the prime rice-growing regions. Multiple cropping is common in the north, accomplished through an extensive system of irrigation. Single cropping is the rule in the south because of dry conditions half of each year and an inadequate water supply. High-yielding varieties of rice are commonly used. Elsewhere such dry crops as corn, sweet potatoes, cassavas, and pulse plants are grown.

Before 1980 chronic food shortages consistently caused widespread malnutrition. Natural disasters as well as collectivist policies were responsible for the food deficits. Food production improved as a result of production contracts and increased prices. Mechanization of agriculture is thwarted by the lack of fuel, so the raising of draft animals is encouraged. In the absence of adequate local fertilizer production, there is increased use of green and natural fertilizers in rice terraces. Commercial forest production was affected by the war, but more than 800 million cubic feet (22.7 million cubic meters) of valuable hardwoods were harvested in 1982.

There is considerable potential for the fishing industry in the rich offshore fishing grounds. A variety of fish species are caught in addition to prawns,

The delta of the Mekong River, near Ho Chi Minh City, is southern Vietnam's most fertile rice-growing region.

lobsters, and crayfish. The collective model has been employed in this industry and has adversely affected the annual catch and fishermen's incomes. Refugee movements have gradually removed vessels from the fishing fleet, and this, too, has hurt the industry.

The heavy industrial base of Vietnam is concentrated in the north. Productive capacity rebounded after the destruction of the war period. Machine tools, iron and steel, and fertilizer operations contribute to the industrial output. Light manufacturing and processed agricultural products are focused in the south. Industrial production is difficult to monitor, but apparently growth rates have been stronger in locally run and handicraft industries and weaker in large-scale industries. Consumer industries too often require imported components or materials that are difficult to obtain because of inadequate foreign exchange. Emigration has seriously affected the industrial sector, as management expertise is conspicuously uneven. Vietnamese industry continues to be troubled by power shortages, which affect both plant capacity and output.

The north is endowed with mineral resources that include coal, tin, chrome, and phosphate. The coal mines of Hong-Quong are quite large and produced more than 800,000 tons of coal in 1982.

The railway system includes more than 1,700 miles (2,700 kilometers) of track. Since 1976 a trans-Vietnam railway links the two largest cities. There are more than 22,500 miles (36,200 kilometers) of roads, of which only 15 percent are paved. Human-powered three-wheel vehicles are more common than motorized vehicles. Major ports are at Haiphong, Ho Chi Minh City, Nha Trang, Da Nang, Qui Nhon, and Hon Gai. Vietnam's national airline, Hang Khong Vietnam, has an old fleet of DC-4 aircraft along with some newer Soviet aircraft that operate primarily on domestic routes.

Telephones are a rare luxury in Vietnam. In the early 1980s only 118,000 were in operation.

Trade figures for 1984 show that imports far exceeded exports: 596 million dollars and 254 million dollars, respectively. Manufactured goods, handicrafts, and agricultural products are the major export goods and are sold principally to Japan, Hong Kong, the Soviet Union, and Singapore. Imported goods consist of fuels, raw materials, machinery, and food products. Some 60 percent of these come from the Soviet Union, Japan, India, Singapore, and Hong Kong.

History

In the 2nd century BC the northern area of Vietnam and part of southern China were conquered by the army representing the Han Dynasty of China. Chinese rule lasted for more than 1,000 years until AD 939, when the Vietnamese managed to throw off their conquerors. A southward expansion continued over the following 800 years, reaching as far as the Gulf of Siam (now the Gulf of Thailand). Internal strife, however, produced a struggle that lasted more than two centuries. Essentially Vietnam was divided

near the 17th parallel with two states—Tonkin in the north and Cochinchina in the south. Following a civil war the country was reunited briefly in 1802.

Political weakness permitted French intervention and expansion. Cochinchina became a French colony in 1867, and Annam and Tonkin became French protectorates in 1883. Later all three were merged with Laos and Cambodia (now Kampuchea) to form French Indochina. Throughout the period of French rule, strong nationalist and revolutionary movements were present. During World War II the French yielded Indochina to Japan. After the Japanese surrender in 1945, a nationalist coalition known as the Viet Minh, led by Ho Chi Minh, proclaimed the Democratic Republic of Vietnam (see Ho Chi Minh). French resistance to the Viet Minh led to a war that lasted eight years. After a crucial battle at Dienbienphu, a cease-fire agreement was signed in 1954 (see Dienbienphu, Battle of). The cease-fire provided for a partitioned Vietnam, the south becoming the Republic of Vietnam under Ngo Dinh Diem. This anti-Communist southern regime was opposed by a growing resistance movement that became known as the Viet Cong.

Just prior to the overthrow of Diem in the south, the United States joined the conflict between north and south. Ground forces were committed, and bombing was carried out against the north from 1965 to 1968. Peace negotiations began between the Hanoi government and the United States in 1969; the Paris accord was signed on Jan. 27, 1973. More than 47,000 American troops were killed before the last forces departed in March 1973. Two years later the National Liberation Front forces of the north pushed southward and captured Saigon. The three-decade war produced a toll of 2 million Vietnamese dead with

A girl in the province of Vinh Phu plants a tree as part of a postwar forestry school project.

© Philip J. Griffiths—Magnum

345

another 4 million critically injured. More than half of the population were left homeless, and large areas of cultivated land and infrastructure were devastated. (*See also* Vietnam War.)

Vietnam was admitted to the United Nations in 1977. Close cooperation has existed with the Soviet Union, and a quest for authority over Laos and Kampuchea has been maintained. More than 40,000 Vietnamese troops are permanently based in Laos. Kampuchean resistance to Vietnamese demands led to full-scale warfare and Vietnamese occupation of the country. This conquest has made it necessary for Vietnam to deploy troops on the Chinese and Thai borders in addition to maintaining armies of occupation in both Kampuchea and Laos.

Governmental ties and commercial relations have now been established with all members of the Association of Southeast Asian Nations (ASEAN). Vietnam also has close ties to India. More significant is the restoration of relations with France. The settlement of many issues, including compensation for the seizure of French property, has opened the way for French development aid. Vietnam and the United States have no diplomatic relations, though discussions continue on the subject of armed forces personnel missing in action. This matter and the occupation of Kam-

puchea remain obstacles to the resumption of any relationship.

Vietnam continues to violate human rights and to suppress freedom. Restrictions include close surveillance over religious groups, the necessity of seeking official approval for all internal and external travel, discrimination against the Chinese, and confiscation of international mail. The widely publicized relocation of millions of people to new economic zones in virgin or unproductive areas in order to expand agricultural production has involved extensive coercion. Conditions in the zones are generally acknowledged to be poor at best and are often life threatening, as basic services are absent. The government continues to hold large numbers of people in reeducation camps without trial or charge. The purpose is to remove dissident elements and produce conformity through hard labor and confinement.

BIBLIOGRAPHY FOR VIETNAM

Fincher, E.B. The Vietnam War (Watts, 1980).
Huynh Quang Nhuong. The Land I Lost (Harper, 1986).
Karnow, Stanley. Vietnam: a History (Viking, 1983).
Page, Tim. Ten Years After: Vietnam Today (Knopf, 1987).
Sharma, Ritu. Vietnam (Apt, 1987).
Summers, H.G. Vietnam War Almanac (Facts on File, 1985).
Taylor, K.W. The Birth of Vietnam (Univ. of Calif. Press, 1983).

Vietnam Fact Summary

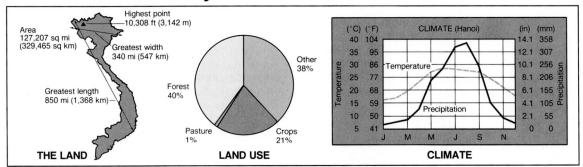

THE LAND — Area 127,207 sq mi (329,465 sq km); Highest point 10,308 ft (3,142 m); Greatest width 340 mi (547 km); Greatest length 850 mi (1,368 km).

LAND USE — Other 38%, Forest 40%, Crops 21%, Pasture 1%.

CLIMATE (Hanoi)

Official Name: Socialist Republic of Vietnam.

Capital: Hanoi.

NATURAL FEATURES

Principal Physical Features: Annamese Cordillera, Mekong Delta, Red River delta, Tonkin Lowland.
Mountain Ranges: Annamese Cordillera.
Highest Peak: Fan Si Pan, 10,308 feet (3,142 meters).
Major Rivers: Mekong, Red.

PEOPLE

Population (1987 estimate): 62,468,000; 487.8 persons per square mile (188.4 persons per square kilometer); 19 percent urban, 81 percent rural.
Major Cities (1979 census): Ho Chi Minh City (2,441,185), Hanoi (2,961,000, 1985 estimate), Haiphong (330,755), Da Nang (318,655), Bien Hoa (190,086).
Major Religions: Buddhism, Taoism, Confucianism.
Major Language: Vietnamese (official).
Literacy: 94 percent.
Leading Universities: College of Pharmacy, Hanoi; Hanoi University; Technical University of Hanoi; Technical University of Ho Chi Minh City; University of Ho Chi Minh City; University of Hue.

GOVERNMENT

Form of Government: People's Republic.
Chief of State: President.
Head of Government: Premier.
Legislature: National Assembly; one legislative house of 496 members; four-year terms.
Voting Qualification: Age 18.
Political Divisions: 36 provinces, 3 municipalities, and 1 special zone.
Flag: Red with a five-pointed yellow star in the center (*see* Flags of the World).

ECONOMY

Chief Agricultural Products: *Crops*—rice, corn, sweet potatoes, cassavas, pulse plants, sugarcane, cotton, tobacco, yams, peanuts. *Fish*—freshwater fish and seafood.
Chief Mined Products: Coal, tin, chrome, phosphate.
Chief Manufactured Products: Machine tools, iron and steel, fertilizers, processed agricultural products, handicrafts.
Chief Exports: Manufactured goods, handicrafts, agricultural products, fish and shellfish.
Chief Imports: Fuels, raw materials, machinery, food products.
Monetary Unit: 1 dong = 10 hao = 100 xu.

VIETNAM WAR

VIETNAM WAR. Four countries have been divided since World War II as the result of global Communist strategy: China, Germany, Korea, and Vietnam. Until formal reunification in 1976, Vietnam was split at the 17th parallel of latitude into North Vietnam, with a Communist government, and South Vietnam, with a republican government.

Much of Vietnam had been controlled by France for over a century as part of French Indochina. Following World War II a bloody seven-and-a-half-year struggle raged between Communist Vietnamese and the French for control of the land. Finally a peace conference was held at Geneva, Switzerland, to determine the fate of Indochina. Concluding in July 1954, the conference determined that French rule would be ended in Vietnam and that the country would be temporarily divided politically.

Neighboring Laos and Cambodia (now Kampuchea), comprising the rest of Indochina, were prohibited from making military alliances. Foreign military bases were barred from their territory and from Vietnam. (*See also* Laos; Kampuchea; Indochina.)

Rebels Raid South Vietnam

Not long after the 1954 partition, United States military advisers assumed the task of training the South Vietnamese army. At the same time, Ho Chi Minh, president of North Vietnam, pledged to "liberate" South Vietnam.

Communist guerrillas, known as the Viet Cong, infiltrated across the border and by way of Laos in large numbers, supplementing bands of native Red terrorists in the south. A chief objective of these rebels—who were directly controlled by the Vietminh, North Vietnam's governing faction—was to disrupt South Vietnamese social and economic improvement programs. The assassination of local administrators was one of the ways in which guerrillas sought to bring this about. Guerrilla bands also raided industrial plants, plantations, military installations, and entire villages. Frequently they attacked at night, withdrawing afterward to the security of the forest. Seldom were the South Vietnamese forces able to fight them in the open.

The struggle in Vietnam was never concentrated along a single front. Patches and strips of Red-held territory spread gradually across the map of South Vietnam. By 1965 much of the coastline and nearly all borderlands had fallen to the rebels. Most of the Mekong Delta, Vietnam's vital rice-growing area, had also been seized.

South Vietnam Government Loses Support

Rebel gains coincided with the waning popularity of South Vietnam's president, Ngo Dinh Diem. Elected in 1955, Diem enjoyed great popularity at first, but public support, as well as that of military officers and cabinet ministers, gradually disappeared. This stemmed largely from the fact that Diem's brother and closest adviser, Ngo Dinh Nhu, was able to manipulate officers and military units at his discretion. Madame Ngo Dinh Nhu, Diem's bitterly outspoken sister-in-law, also played a unique and important role in arousing the disfavor of Vietnamese and foreigners alike.

In October 1961 President John F. Kennedy sent his military adviser, Gen. Maxwell D. Taylor, to

South Vietnam to evaluate that country's economic and military condition. General Taylor reported that infiltration of the Viet Cong from the north was increasing, that South Vietnam's economy had suffered drastically, and that better and more equipment was needed. American aid was stepped up. During the next two years more than 16,000 military advisers were sent to South Vietnam, and some 400 million dollars was provided in military aid alone. For the time being, Viet Cong successes were halted.

A serious setback occurred in May 1963, when President Diem, a Roman Catholic, prohibited the flying of the Buddhist flag. Thousands of Buddhists were arrested, and some were tortured or killed. Buddhist priests publicly burned themselves to death in protest; national morale was badly shaken. The Viet Cong attacked with greater fervor. Casualties and desertions from the South Vietnamese army rose sharply as public displeasure with the Diem regime mounted. In November Diem and Nhu were assassinated. A military junta assumed control. The gov-

ernment remained unstable, however, with a marked absence of popular support.

United States Warships Attacked

On Aug. 2, 1964, the United States was drawn further into the conflict when the USS *Maddox*, a destroyer cruising in the Gulf of Tonkin, was attacked by North Vietnamese patrol boats 30 miles off the coast of North Vietnam. Two days later the *Maddox* and another destroyer were attacked; two North Vietnamese patrol boats were sunk by return fire. President Lyndon B. Johnson ordered retaliatory air attacks.

The continuing instability of the Vietnamese government made United States assistance more difficult. Coups, attempted coups, or government shake-ups occurred almost monthly. The State Department warned that unless Vietnamese army officers kept out of politics, American aid might be discontinued. Mass demonstrations by Buddhist groups alternated with those of Catholics, depending upon which of these groups was in power at the time.

Terrorist attacks upon American installations in South Vietnam became frequent. These were calculated to discourage the United States into complete withdrawal from Vietnam. Their immediate effect, however, was to increase the tempo of air raids by American aircraft against North Vietnam. Principal targets were highways and bridges. In neighboring Laos, bombers also struck the Ho Chi Minh Trail, an important Viet Cong supply line. United States warships shelled North Vietnamese coastal installations.

Peace Bids; Civil War Threatens

In April 1965 President Johnson proposed that "unconditional discussions" be held for a settlement of the conflict. His peace move was ignored by North Vietnam. The North Vietnamese insisted that United States forces first be withdrawn from South Vietnam. They also stipulated that the United Nations must not intervene and that the internal affairs of South Vietnam would have to be settled in accordance with the program of the National Liberation Front, the political arm of the Viet Cong. Johnson maintained that these matters could not be discussed prior to a peace conference. In June he urged the United Nations to seek a solution.

An era of relative stability in South Vietnam's government began in June when a new military regime was installed. The new regime was led by a ten-man military junta, which called itself the National Leadership Committee. Air Force Commander Vice-Marshal Nguyen Cao Ky, a member of the council, was named premier.

Ky's first crisis in office followed his dismissal of Lieut. Gen. Nguyen Chanh Thi in

UPI

These South Vietnamese refugee children have just been airlifted from territory threatened by Viet Cong guerrillas. The giant Chinook helicopter that evacuated them also serves as a troop carrier.

Wide World

These American soldiers are attacking a Viet Cong position northwest of Bien Hoa. In this operation the entire unit was landed by helicopter.

United States Role Accelerates

During 1965 the United States became even more deeply committed to South Vietnam's struggle for freedom. In February it was officially revealed that planes raiding North Vietnam were being flown by American personnel. In June it was acknowledged that United States troops were engaged in combat with the Viet Cong. By midyear the size of the United States force in South Vietnam exceeded 50,000 troops, having doubled in less than six months. Although contingents had also arrived from South Korea, Australia, and New Zealand, the military situation in South Vietnam continued to deteriorate. Military observers theorized that 1965 was the year scheduled by the Reds for total victory. With the approach of the summer rainy season and an anticipated Viet Cong offensive, Ky asked for more American ground forces. Between July and November a fighting force of an additional 100,000 men was transferred from military bases in the United States to Vietnam.

The first major American victory took place in August at Chu Lai, where more than 5,000 United States troops defeated an estimated 2,000 Viet Cong. In November American forces won a decisive victory over a large North Vietnamese force in the Ia Drang Valley. It was the first time that a major Viet Cong or North Vietnamese force had abandoned hit-and-

March 1966 from the military council and from his post as a regional army commander. Thi had established himself as virtual warlord of several provinces in northern South Vietnam. He had also aligned himself with politically powerful Buddhists, including Thich Tri Quang. When followers of General Thi publicly protested his dismissal, Tri Quang encouraged further antigovernment demonstrations. The Buddhists demanded that civilians be represented on the governing council and that elections be held for a national assembly.

Civil war threatened as fighting erupted between government forces and troops loyal to Thi. Riots instigated by the Buddhists, notably Tri Quang, broke out in Saigon, Hue, and Da Nang. Again, as in 1963, Buddhists publicly burned themselves to death. In April Premier Ky acceded to most of the Buddhist demands; elections were scheduled for later in the year. The unrest continued, however, as militant Buddhists called for Ky's resignation. Meanwhile government troops won back control of the cities which had been taken over by Thi's followers. By mid-1966 the rioting had also subsided.

UPI

A family of displaced South Vietnamese flees from a Viet Cong-held area as a column of American tanks rolls forward to attack positions held by North Vietnamese forces.

run guerrilla tactics for open combat. Ia Drang was the bloodiest battle of the war to that date.

In January 1966 some 20,000 American, South Vietnamese, and South Korean troops encircled four enemy regiments south of Da Nang. A successful allied sweep through the central coastal province of Binh Dinh took place in the spring.

In February 1965 United States bombers attacked North Vietnam in retaliation for a Viet Cong raid on the United States helicopter base at Plei Ku. The Viet Cong bombing raids continued, however.

In May the air strikes against the North were suspended for five days, following President Johnson's invitation in April to "unconditional discussions" of peace. The raids were again suspended in late December 1965 and throughout January 1966 as a so-called "peace offensive" was launched by President Johnson and other world leaders. The North Vietnamese failed to respond to these overtures.

In June 1966 United States bombers made their first attack on the industrial outskirts of North Vietnam's two largest cities—Hanoi, the capital, and Haiphong, the chief port. Subsequent American bombing raids were made on these as well as other industrial centers and on MiG air bases in North Vietnam.

United States forces—increased from 190,000 in January 1966 to more than 500,000 by early 1968—used "search-and-destroy" tactics to expel National Liberation Front (NLF) forces from the South. In 1967 and 1968, American troops raided NLF troop concentrations in the demilitarized zone.

In January 1968 the NLF launched a large-scale offensive throughout the South during Tet, the Vietnamese Lunar New Year holiday. The targets included about 30 provincial capitals.

On March 31 President Johnson—faced with increasing antiwar sentiment at home and abroad—announced a halt in all bombing north of the 20th parallel and offered to negotiate for peace with North Vietnam. Peace talks began in Paris in May, but were quickly deadlocked. After the United States stopped bombing North Vietnam in early November, the North Vietnamese agreed not to escalate the war. In January 1969 South Vietnam and the NLF joined the talks.

On April 29, 1970, American and South Vietnamese ground forces began an assault on North Vietnamese and NLF sanctuaries in Cambodia. Similar action was taken by the South Vietnamese on targets in Cambodia and Laos in 1971. (In 1973 the United States government admitted that it had conducted secret bombing missions inside Cambodia in 1969, and in Laos in 1970.) American troop withdrawals, which had begun in the summer of 1969, left fewer than 200,000 Americans in South Vietnam at the end of 1971.

In April 1972 the United States bombed civilian dwellings and military targets in Hanoi and Haiphong. In May, in response to a drive by the North Vietnamese forces into the South, President Richard M. Nixon ordered the mining of harbors off North Vietnam. Both the bombing and the mining provoked sustained antiwar protests within the United States.

The End of the Conflict

On Jan. 27, 1973, a cease-fire was signed in Paris by the United States, South Vietnam, North Vietnam, and the Provisional Revolutionary Government of the NLF. A Four-Party Joint Military Commission was set up to implement such provisions as the withdrawal of foreign troops and the release of prisoners. An International Commission of Control and Supervision was established to oversee the cease-fire.

United States ground troops left Vietnam by the end of March 1973. Fighting continued, however, as the North and the South accused each other of truce violations. A second cease-fire was signed in June, but the hostilities continued through 1974.

The ultimate fall of South Vietnam began with the capture of Phuoc Long Province in January 1975. Soon more inland provinces were under North Vietnamese control and the major coastal cities had fallen, with little resistance from Southern troops. The war in Cambodia ended on April 16, and the South surrendered on April 30, 1975, as enemy troops entered Saigon. (*See also* Vietnam; Ho Chi Minh.)

VIGNY, Alfred de (1797–1863). One of the foremost French romantic writers was the poet, dramatist, and novelist Alfred de Vigny. He introduced into France the poem in the style of Lord Byron and Thomas Moore and the novel in the style of Sir Walter Scott.

Alfred-Victor Vigny was born on March 27, 1797, in Loches, France. He grew up in Paris and, while studying at a preparatory school, developed an "inordinate love for the glory of bearing arms." At the age of 17 he became a second lieutenant in the king's guard. In spite of consistent promotions, he became bored with peacetime garrison duty and found refuge in a literary career. In 1820 his first poem, "Le Bal," was published, and two years later he published his first collection of verse. In 1826 the poet also revealed his narrative talent with the publication of a historical novel, 'Cinq-Mars'. After several leaves of absence, Vigny finally abandoned military life in 1827.

The repeated failures of the French monarchy, culminating in the Revolution of 1830, disillusioned Vigny. His political torment was revealed in his work—especially 'Stello' (1832), three stories that represent the isolation of the poet. Three years later he wrote 'Chatterton', the triumph of his career as a playwright. It dramatized the misfortune of the poet in a materialist and pitiless society. The last half of Vigny's life was passed in melancholy and disappointment. He almost completely withdrew from society. He helped lead a campaign to establish literary copyrights, and he tried to serve the republic in an ambassadorial role, but both efforts failed.

Vigny left numerous unedited works of exceptional interest. Although he did not receive the recognition he merited during his lifetime, succeeding generations—including such writers as Charles Baudelaire and André Breton—have revered his memory and his message. Vigny died on Sept. 17, 1863, in Paris.

Henry C. Pitz

Henry C. Pitz

A Norse chief sits on the high seat in his home, beneath his shields. The entertainer is a skald, or minstrel poet. The small harp he plays was probably brought from Ireland by a Viking raider.

VIKINGS. Late in the 8th century AD strange ships began appearing in the bays along the coasts of Europe. Some of these ships were quite long for that era. They were strongly built of oak, and from 40 to 60 oarsmen sat on the rowers' benches. Each ship had a single mast with a square sail that was often striped in brilliant colors. Bright shields overlapped along the gunwale. The ships were pointed at each end so that they could go forward or backward without turning around. They had tall curved prows, usually carved in the shapes of dragons.

These dragon ships, as they were often called, usually appeared in a bay at about dawn. As soon as the ships reached the beach, tall blond men jumped out, shouting battle cries. Armed with swords and battle-axes, they attacked the sleeping villagers. They killed many of them, captured some of the youths and maidens, and gathered all the loot that their ships could carry. Then they sailed away.

These marauders, or pirates, came from Scandinavia—what is now Denmark, Norway, and Sweden. The people who lived there were Norsemen, or Northmen. Those Norsemen who took part in these swift, cruel raids along the coast were called Vikings. Their expression for this type of warfare was to "go a-viking." *Vik* in Norse means "harbor" or "bay." The Vikings came to be the most feared raiders of their time and were the only Norsemen with whom most Europeans came in contact. Their name was given to the era that dated from about AD 740 to about 1050—the Viking Age.

Conquests and Settlements

At first these Viking attacks were made by small bands. Later there were more men and more ships, which roamed farther and farther from their homelands. To the north and east they attacked the Lapps, Finns, and Russians. To the west they conquered and held for generations large parts of Britain and Ireland. To the south they occupied northern France. The Norsemen did not actually conquer any country south of France, but their ships sailed along the coasts of Spain and Portugal. They plundered Sicily and the northern shores of Africa and attacked Constantinople, the capital of the Eastern Roman Empire.

To the west the Vikings did not stop with the British Isles but crossed the Atlantic Ocean to take Iceland away from the Irish monks who had settled there. In 874 they began to colonize Iceland, and during the years that followed, many freedom-loving people came to Iceland as settlers. In about the year 982 Eric the Red sailed westward from Iceland. He

VIKINGS

Henry C. Pitz

The Vikings made sea voyages in narrow, high-prowed boats. These ships were sturdy enough to cross the Atlantic Ocean.

landed on the coast of Greenland and gave the island its name. Later he founded the first colony there. His son, Leif Ericson, sometimes called Leif the Lucky, is believed by most historians to have been the first explorer to reach the North American mainland. About the year 1000 he landed at a place that he called Vinland. Vinland was identified as Newfoundland in 1963 when archaeologists uncovered the remains of a Viking settlement at the extreme northern tip of the island. (*See also* Ericson; Eric the Red.)

While the Vikings were discovering lands and waging war, they were telling each other adventure tales that later were known as sagas, from the Icelandic word for story (*see* Saga). Poets also were singing the praises of Norse heroes and gods and describing the Norse way of life. In this way the Norsemen preserved major parts of the early history of the Scandinavian countries and of Russia, Germany, Britain, and Ireland.

Why the Vikings Were Powerful

The Vikings probably were descended from blue-eyed and blond invaders from the south of Scandinavia. There they found and conquered a short, dark-haired race. Long-limbed and muscular, with flaxen or red hair hanging below their shoulders, Norsemen were trained from childhood to be strong and self-reliant. Running, jumping, and wrestling took the place of reading, writing, and arithmetic. Their other subjects were skating, skiing, snowshoeing, swimming, rowing,

and riding horseback. As soon as a youngster could carry a weapon, he was taught to thrust a sword, to swing a battle-ax, and to throw a spear.

A part of their success was due to their religion, for the Norsemen's gods were warriors too. Thor the Thunderer made constant war against the ice and snow giants of the North. The chief god, Odin, presided over Valhalla, the warrior's heaven. Death in battle was considered the most honorable death. Only by that death could a Norseman enter Valhalla. So the Norsemen battled unafraid and joyful, calling upon their gods to help them. (*See also* Mythology.)

The Norsemen were the most skilled and daring seamen of their day. Because the compass was still unknown, they navigated by sun and star. When fog hid the stars, their ships drifted until the weather cleared. Not fearing death, they took great chances. Their experiences and discoveries were therefore many.

The Norsemen dared not risk open fires aboard their wooden ships, and in those days there were no stoves. So, unless they were on a long sea voyage, they would anchor in a quiet bay each evening. Then they pitched tents on the shore, kindled fires, and cooked their food. Porridge with dried meat or fish was the usual diet. Sometimes they had bread, butter, and cheese. If they spent the night aboard ship, they unrolled their skin sleeping gear and stretched out on the rowers' benches. A successful Viking expedition might bring fortune, fame, and, perhaps, noble rank to those who took part. So by the time they were 15 or 16, Norse boys were eager to try their luck in battle.

Trade Is Developed

The early Viking voyages were mostly raids in which Christian churches and monasteries were robbed and burned and peaceful villages were plundered. But in later times piracy was often combined with trading. A pirate expedition might stop off to do a little quiet trading, and a trading expedition might turn to a little pirating.

As time went on, trade among the Scandinavian countries and with the rest of Europe grew. Norway sent herring and salt to Sweden. Denmark received sheep from the Faeroe Islands. Greenland imported timber from Labrador and grain and iron from Europe. It paid for these in walrus and narwhal ivory, furs, live falcons, and even live polar bears.

Norwegian Viking expeditions started in the spring after the seed was sown or in the autumn when crops were harvested. At home the Norsemen were mainly farmers and stockmen. They also hunted and fished. After a successful voyage or two, many retired from the sea and were often succeeded by their sons.

During wars and raids, villagers who were not killed by the Vikings were often taken as slaves. These slaves, called thralls, were usually Irish, Finns, Germans, or Slavs. A free Norseman might be enslaved for a debt or crime, but this was rare. Many slaves were voluntarily freed by their masters, especially after the introduction of Christianity, and there was much intermarriage.

The Norsemen at Home

The houses of the Norsemen differed according to the resources of each country. In Norway houses were built of rough pine logs. The roofs were usually covered with turf or straw. In Iceland, which had few trees, houses were built of turf, rocks, and driftwood. Both in Iceland and Greenland heavy timbers needed for the frames of buildings were brought from Norway and later from North America.

A house had only one room and was built with a pitched roof. A poor man might have two or three huts. The estate of a rich man had so many buildings that it looked like a village. In later centuries, several of these buildings were often connected by passageways.

The houses were plain on the outside. All the decoration was indoors, where most of the woodwork was carved, painted, and touched with gilt. On festive occasions, brightly embroidered tapestries would be hung on the walls, and long tables were set up for feasting.

The Norsemen had a great variety of foods and beverages. Mutton and beef were plentiful. Until its use was forbidden, the favorite meat was horse meat. The Norsemen also used fish and cereals, eggs from wild and domestic fowl, and milk products. They had few vegetables. Honey was the only sweet, and bees were kept to supplement the wild honey. Meat and fish were often dried, smoked, or pickled. Many foods were preserved in brine or in sour whey, a preservative still in use among Scandinavians. Butter was never salted. It was eaten fresh or was fermented for use like cheese.

Norsemen liked both fresh and sour milk and buttermilk too. The favorite drink was whey. They had a food named *skyr* that was much like cottage cheese. Apples and berries were their only fruits. Porridge was cooked in enormous kettles over an open fire. Although boiling was favored for most foods, meat was sometimes baked in hot ashes. Bread was baked in ashes or in clay ovens.

At feasts the Norse drank quantities of ale. From honey they made a fermented drink called mead, and wealthy Norsemen imported wine from France. There were long and sometimes rowdy drinking festivals, at which sagas were told and poems were recited.

All wealthy Norsemen dressed lavishly for events like weddings and funerals and for *things,* as the assemblies were called. Skins and furs of tame and wild animals were used, but the most common material was a woven woolen cloth, called *vadmal.* Dyes were expensive, so poorer people wore the cloth in its natural color. The rich wore it in bright colors, often striped and patterned. Silk and linen, which were imported and costly, were used mostly for underwear.

Since the Vikings traded with so many countries, they often brought home new ideas for dress and adornment. The native dress of both sexes in early times was similar. The main garment was a long buttonless tunic, which might be narrow or wide. If wide, it was gathered around the waist with a belt. It had an opening that was slipped over the head and tightened with a brooch. The custom was to wear a gown of one color and a cloak of another. A man's tunic was usually sleeveless, perhaps to show off his muscles and gold arm rings. Young women wore their hair long and caught around the forehead with a band, sometimes made of pure gold. Noble and wealthy men also wore their hair long with a band to keep it in place.

The young Norsemen loved games, especially those that helped to develop their bodies. They played ball games on the ground and on ice. Wrestling and fencing were popular sports. Young Norsemen used skates made of the bones of animals. According to a Norwegian historian, an unusual sport involved walking on oar blades while a boat was being rowed. In another game two or three small swords were thrown in the air and then caught; to play with three swords at once without injuring oneself required great skill.

Norsemen loved music and dancing. They had a *fidla,* or fiddle, a horn made from a buck's horn, and also a kind of harp. The high point at a feast was the performance of a skald, or professional poet.

Education

There were no public schools. All education was given at home, with a parent, nurse, or visitor acting as teacher. Children were often sent to the home of a rich man, sometimes a relative, to be educated. Both girls and boys learned to sing, to recite and compose poetry, and to tell sagas.

The Vinland colony in North America was established by Thorfinn Karlsefni, three years after Leif Ericson's discovery.

Henry C. Pitz

ᚠᚢᚦᚨᚱᚲᚺᚨᛁᚾᛊᛏᛞᛈᛒᛗᛚᛦ
f u t h o r k h a i n s t,d p,b m l r(y)

The 16 letters of the later runic alphabet were well suited to carving in wood or stone. The runic letters are shown here with their modern English equivalents.

Girls, even those of noble birth, were also given lessons in how to spin, weave, and dye wool; to sew, knit, and embroider; to wash and to cook; and to make butter and cheese.

Some girls and most boys learned to read and cut runes, which were the letters of the ancient alphabet used by the Norsemen. Just as the English alphabet is often called the ABCs, that of the Norsemen was called *futhork* after the first letters. The early Norse alphabet had 24 letters. The later Norse alphabet had 16.

At first runes were used for scratching names on personal belongings or for simple memorials. Later, as the art developed, these memorials grew more elaborate. Thousands of these memorial stones have been found on the Scandinavian peninsula and in Denmark. North of Upernivik, in Greenland, the discovery of a little rune stone was considered proof that Vikings had traveled more than 400 miles north of the Arctic Circle. Others carved runes on the statue of a lion in Athens, Greece.

Government

In the early history of the Norsemen there were no nations in the modern sense. People lived in what might be called tribal communities. These communities were independent of one another, and banded together only for some common purpose.

When the title *konungr* (king) was given to the chief of a community, it did not carry the meaning that it has now. There were many kings. Often one would rule over a small section of land no larger than a county, and some of the kings were war chiefs who had no land.

Each community had a *thing* (assembly), which acted as a court and legislative body. Only those who owned land could be members. A king could hold his position only as long as the people wanted him. Before a new king could take office, he had to have the consent of the members of the assembly.

Next in rank were the jarls, nobles who often had about as much power and land as the kings. Both kings and jarls had to rule according to law. No laws were written down until around 1100. Before then the laws were really traditions and opinions of the majority of the people. The people elected lawmen who had to know these unwritten laws and explain them to the rulers.

Later in Sweden and in Denmark people began to unite under one king. In 872 Norway had a single king, known as Harald Fairhair. But Harald undid much of Norway's unity by giving each of his numerous sons the title of king. Norway therefore remained divided for some time.

When Harald became king, some dissidents went to Iceland and founded a colony there. While the

The Dybeck sword of about AD 1000 (top left), from Dybeck in Skåne, Sweden, has a silver hilt. A hand-carved Viking cart (bottom left) was found at Oseberg, Norway, during excavations made in 1904. The Gokstad ship (right), excavated in Norway in 1880, is made of oak and measures 22.3 meters long by 5.3 meters wide. The wagon and ship are on display in the Viking Ship Museum in Oslo.

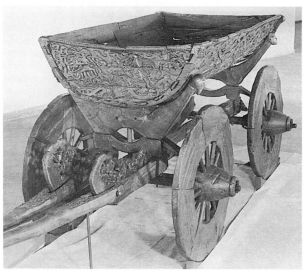

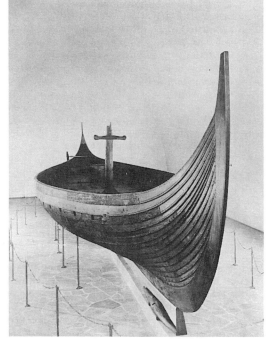

people of Iceland did not unite under one king at that time, Iceland was the only country to form a national assembly during the Viking Age. Called the Althing, it first met in 930 and is the oldest national assembly in the world.

Religion

A young Viking, King Olaf Tryggvason of Norway, became a convert to the Christian religion some time before AD 1000. His passion for the new religion was backed by a military force that threatened all who refused baptism. Some Norsemen had already become Christians, mainly through Irish influence, though on the whole the Vikings were content with their own gods. Gradually Norway was Christianized, then the Faeroe Islands and Iceland, and finally Greenland. The first Christian missionaries in Greenland were brought there from Norway by Leif Ericson.

A Viking chieftain was buried with everything he might need to get to Valhalla. One third of his property might be used in this way. (Another third went to his widow and the remainder to his children.) The goods buried included money, tools, changes of clothing, weapons, horses, chariots, boats, and even ships. Women's graves contained many of the things they might need in afterlife, such as needles and thread, looms, kitchen utensils, and cooking vessels.

Sometimes a dead warrior would be placed aboard his ship, which was set afire and allowed to drift out to sea. Sometimes people were buried in boat-shaped coffins, which were covered with earth mounds. Fortunately, ships were not always burned, and a few have been preserved.

Next to the sagas, graves have been the best source of information about the Norsemen. In Scandinavian museums there are examples of almost every art known to the Viking Age. Among these are jewelry, weapons, furniture, and bronze and silver utensils. Most have survived because they were made of such durable materials as stone, metal, and hardwood. But woolen clothes in good condition have been found in parts of Greenland where they had lain in the frozen soil for centuries.

History from the Sagas

The Norsemen, like the Greeks of Homer's time, were storytellers and poets. At all assemblies, weddings, and funerals, those skilled at storytelling and reciting verses would perform.

When Christianity came to the mainland of Scandinavia, folk poems and stories were frowned upon by the clergy. But Iceland was protected by distance from the influence of Europe. So, long after Christianity became the official religion, the Icelandic people struggled to preserve their historical and literary heritage. Their religious leaders enjoyed the storytelling and found no offense in it.

During the 12th and 13th centuries, the clergy and scholars of Iceland wrote many manuscripts. All were written as the saga tellers related them. Some were true and some were pure fiction. Among the serious

Orient and Occident Photo Service

Runic stones at Jelling, Denmark, are from the Christian era. A carving of Jesus Christ is visible on the larger of the two stones, along with some pre-Christian religious symbols.

historical records are sagas that tell of the kings and of Viking conquests. They tell of their discovery and colonization of Iceland and Greenland and their discovery of the American mainland.

Two significant manuscripts dealing with the religion and philosophy of the Norsemen were written in Iceland—the Elder Edda (in poetry) and the Younger Edda (in prose). Much of what is known of early Norse mythology came from the Eddas. (*See also* Saga; Scandinavian Literature.)

In Iceland much of the old Norse language has been retained. In Norway, Sweden, and Denmark the languages are as different from the old Norse as modern English is from early Anglo-Saxon.

BIBLIOGRAPHY FOR VIKINGS

Atkinson, Ian. The Viking Ships (Lerner, 1980).
Benchley, Nathaniel. Beyond the Mists (Harper, 1975).
Donovan, F.R. The Vikings (Harper, 1964).
Irwin, Constance. Strange Footprints on the Land: Vikings in America (Harper, 1980).
Logan, F.D. The Vikings in History (B & N Imports, 1983).
Magnusson, Magnus. Vikings! (Dutton, 1980).
Magnusson, Magnus. The Vinland Sagas: the Norse Discovery of America (Noontide, 1988).
Martell, Hazel. The Vikings (Watts, 1986).
Sawyer, P.H. Kings and Vikings (Methuen, 1982).

Pancho Villa led his followers on raids into the southwestern part of the United States in 1916.

VILLA, Pancho (1878–1923). A Mexican bandit and guerrilla leader who became a folk hero, Pancho Villa led brutal attacks on American citizens in Mexico and the American Southwest. In 1916 a United States military expedition pursued Villa across the Mexican state of Chihuahua in retaliation for raids on Santa Isabel, where 16 Americans were executed, and on Columbus, N.M. This invasion of Mexico was bitterly resented, and Villa was never captured.

Pancho Villa, whose original name was Doroteo Arango and who was also known as Francisco Villa, was born on June 5, 1878, in Hacienda de Río Grande, San Juan del Río, Mexico. He was orphaned at an early age. In revenge for an assault on his sister, he killed one of the owners of an estate on which he worked. Forced to flee to the mountains, he spent his adolescence as a fugitive bandit leader.

In 1909 Villa joined Francisco Madero's successful revolution against the dictator Porfirio Díaz. He was condemned to death in 1912 by his commanding officer, General Victoriano Huerta, but Madero had him imprisoned instead and Villa escaped.

After Madero's assassination in 1913 Villa formed a military band of several thousand men that became famous as the Division of the North. Combining his force with that of another revolutionary, Venustiano Carranza, Villa revolted against the increasingly repressive dictatorship of General Huerta. In December 1913 Villa became governor of the state of Chihuahua and with Carranza won a decisive victory over Huerta in June 1914. Together they entered Mexico City as victorious revolutionary leaders. Rivalry led to a break between the two, however, and Villa fled in December 1914 to the northern mountains with another revolutionary leader, Emiliano Zapata.

In order to demonstrate that Carranza did not control this region, Villa launched his attacks on the Americans in 1916. Villa continued his guerrilla activities until Carranza was overthrown in 1920. He then agreed to retire from politics. On June 20, 1923, Villa was assassinated on his ranch in Parral.

VILLA-LOBOS, Heitor (1887–1959). One of the foremost Latin American composers of the 20th century, Heitor Villa-Lobos wrote operas, ballets, symphonies, concertos, symphonic suites, and solo pieces in a style that was influenced by J. S. Bach, French composers, and Richard Wagner. His style was also characterized by an original use of Brazilian percussion instruments and Brazilian rhythms.

Heitor Villa-Lobos was born on March 5, 1887, in Rio de Janeiro, Brazil. A cellist in his youth, he left home at the age of 18 because his widowed mother opposed a musical career. During years as a musical vagabond, he played popular music on the cello and guitar. Meanwhile, he began to absorb Brazilian folk music and incorporate it into his own works.

He eventually returned to Rio, where his career received a vital boost with the publication in 1915 of some of his music. In 1919 Villa-Lobos met the renowned pianist Artur Rubinstein, who played Villa-Lobos' music throughout the world, bringing the composer increasing recognition.

Villa-Lobos composed endlessly—about 2,000 works are credited to him. By the time of his first trip to Europe in 1923 he had compiled a long list of compositions in every form.

In 1932 Villa-Lobos took charge of musical education throughout Brazil. He founded the Brazilian Academy of Music in 1945. For several years he traveled widely in the United States and Europe as an orchestra conductor.

One of his most characteristic works is 'Bachianas brasileiras', a set of nine pieces for various instrumental and vocal groups in which a Bach-like contrapuntal technique is applied to themes of Brazilian origin. A similar series of 14 works is titled 'Chôros', a Brazilian country dance. Villa-Lobos' 12 symphonies, written between 1920 and 1958, are mostly associated with historic events or places. The composer died in Rio de Janeiro on Nov. 17, 1959.

VILLON, François (1431–after 1463). One of the greatest French lyric poets, François Villon was also a criminal who spent much of his life in prison or in banishment from medieval Paris. His emotional poems speak of love and death, revealing a deep compassion for human suffering, and they express in an unforgettable way his remorse for his sins.

The poet was born François de Montcorbier or François des Loges in Paris in 1431. While he was still a child, his father died and he was brought up by the chaplain of Saint-Benoît, Guillaume de Villon. He studied at the University of Paris.

In June 1455 he was involved in a violent quarrel with drinking companions and a priest, whom Villon killed with a sword. He was banished from Paris but received a royal pardon in January 1456. By the end of the year Villon was implicated in a theft and banished again. Meanwhile he had written 'Le Petit Testament', which he called "bequests" for his friends and acquaintances before he left them and the city.

Villon traveled through France for several years. He composed more poetry but was often imprisoned for various crimes and then pardoned. Free in 1461, he wrote his longest work, 'Le Grand Testament'. It reviews Villon's life and expresses his horror of sickness, prison, and old age, and his fear of death. It is from this work especially that his poignant regret for his wasted youth and talent is known.

More prison terms followed—in 1462, for robbery, and in 1463, for a street brawl. Villon was condemned to be hanged, but on Jan. 5, 1463, his sentence was commuted to banishment from Paris for ten years. He was never heard from again.

VINE. Any plant whose main stem is too weak to grow erect without support is called a vine. In the wild, vines may trail over the ground or they may climb on trees, plants, rocks, or other structures.

The term vine encompasses a wide range of plants—herbaceous and woody, deciduous and evergreen, annual and perennial. A number are found in temperate regions of the world, but most thrive in the humid tropics. Many are popular garden and landscape plants. They may be grown for food (grapes, blackberries, melons, squashes, garden peas), for their showy flowers (trumpet vines, passionflowers, morning glories, bougainvillea), or to prevent soil erosion. On the basis of their growth habits, vines may be divided into two types—clamberers and climbers.

Clamberers lack any holdfasts—the structures that allow the plant to cling to objects—and merely scramble or trail over surrounding vegetation, debris, or bare ground. They include certain blackberries, or dewberries, and some wild and rambler roses.

Climbers ascend by clinging to other objects for support. Climbing vines may use aerial roots, twining tendrils, twining leafstalks, tendrils tipped with adhesive disks, or some variation of these structures.

Vines that climb by means of aerial roots include poison ivy, many English ivies, and the common pepper vine. The aerial roots emerge on the side of the stem opposite the source of light and penetrate cracks in the supporting structure.

A second and larger group of climbing plants includes those that support themselves by means of tendrils or leaves. A tendril is sensitive to contact. When it brushes against an object, it turns toward it and, when possible, wraps around it. A strong tissue then develops in the tendrils, rendering them strong enough to support the weight of the plant.

Leaf climbers, which include the common nasturtium, may have coiling leaf petioles—leaves in which the last third is reduced to a tendril—or compound leaves whose leaflets are transformed into hooks or tendrils. In the garden pea some of the lower leaflets become twining tendrils.

Adhesive-disk climbers constitute a very small group of commonly cultivated tendril-producing vines, including the Virginia creeper, or woodbine, and Boston ivy. After they have been irritated by friction against a surface, the tendril tips expand into small disks. These disks produce a resinous, sticky substance and attach to the surface.

Twining vines, such as the hop, bean, and bindweed, have slender stems that, as they grow, circle in the air until they touch a support. When a stem makes contact, it spirals around the support in loose coils. In some woody twining vines, the thickening stem exerts so great a pressure that it strangles the supporting tree or shrub. Examples include the climbing honeysuckle and some species of tropical figs called strangler figs. (*See also* Plant.)

VINEGAR. "Sour wine" is the meaning of the word vinegar, for, as a commercial product, vinegar was probably first made from wine. Vinegar is a sour liquid produced by acetic-acid fermentation of any of the numerous dilute alcoholic liquids. When the liquids are exposed to air, the alcohol gradually changes to acetic acid. (*See also* Fermentation.) Any of a variety of materials may be used to make vinegar: apples or grapes (cider or wine vinegar); malted barley or oats (malt vinegar); and industrial alcohol (distilled white vinegar). There are also vinegars made from beer, sugars, rice, and other substances.

The sharp, sour vinegar taste comes from acetic acid, which makes up from 4 to 12 percent of the vinegar volume. The thick scum sometimes seen in the vinegar bottle is mother of vinegar, a form of the bacteria that help to change the alcohol to acetic acid.

Vinegar is used chiefly to flavor foods and to preserve, or pickle, meat products, fish, fruits, and vegetables. It is also mixed with oils and seasonings to make the dressing known as vinaigrette.

VIOLET. Under a blanket of leaves in the meadows and damp woods, the wild violets lie dormant all winter. Then, in early spring, they cover the earth with flowers of blue, violet, lilac, reddish purple, yellow, or white. Violets are also popular garden and house plants.

Violets grow throughout the world. In North America the common blue, or meadow, violet grows to 8 inches (20 centimeters) tall. It has heart-shaped leaves with finely toothed margins, and its flowers range from light, or even white, to deep violet in color. The bird's-foot violet, named for its deeply cleft leaves, has flowers colored in various combinations of lilac and purple. Other species, such as the sweet white violet and the Canada violet, also grow wild in North America. The pansy is a cultivated form of a European species of violet (*see* Pansy).

The flower of the violet grows singly on a stalk and has five unequal petals. The leaves are large, dark green, and heart shaped. They may grow on the same stalk as the flower or on separate stalks. About 500 species of violets constitute the genus *Viola*. The common blue violet is *Viola papilionacea;* the bird's-foot violet is *V. pedata*. (*See also* Flowers, Garden; Flowers, Wild.)

VIOLIN FAMILY *see* STRINGED INSTRUMENTS.

VIPER *see* SNAKE.

VIRCHOW, Rudolf (1821–1902). One of the most prominent physicians of the 19th century, German scientist and statesman Rudolf Virchow pioneered the modern concept of the pathological processes of disease. He emphasized that diseases arose, not in organs or tissues in general, but primarily in individual cells. Virchow also contributed to the development of anthropology as a modern science.

Rudolf Carl Virchow was born on Oct. 13, 1821, in Schivelbein, Prussia. He studied at the University of Berlin and graduated as a doctor of medicine in 1843. As a young intern, Virchow published a paper on one of the two earliest reported cases of leukemia; this paper became a classic. In 1849, Virchow was appointed to the chair of pathological anatomy at the University of Würzburg—the first chair of that subject in Germany. In 1856 Virchow became director of the Pathological Institute at the University of Berlin.

Virchow's concept of cellular pathology replaced the existing theory that disease arose from an imbalance of the four fluid humors of the body (blood, phlegm, yellow bile, and black bile). He applied the cell theory to disease processes and stated that diseased cells arose from preexisting diseased cells (*see* Cell). In 1859 Virchow was elected to the Berlin City Council on which he dealt mainly with such public health matters as sewage disposal, the design of hospitals, meat inspection, and school hygiene. He also designed the new Berlin sewer system. Virchow was elected to the Prussian National Assembly in 1861 and to the German Reichstag in 1880.

Virchow's work in pathological anatomy had led him to begin anthropological work with studies of skulls. He was the organizer of German anthropology, and in 1869 he founded the Berlin Society for Anthropology, Ethnology, and Prehistory. Virchow died on Sept. 5, 1902, in Berlin, Germany.

VIREO. The small, active songbirds called vireos are found only in the Western Hemisphere. Many winter in the tropics and then migrate in the spring to North America to breed. Vireos live in woodlands and thickets; some live only in trees, others in dense shrubbery. They feed primarily on berries and insects.

Vireos are plain olive green or gray above and whitish or buff yellow below. The slightly notched and hook-tipped bill is stout but narrow, with fine bristles at the base. The birds range in length from 4 to 7 inches (10 to 18 centimeters). Most species repeat loud, short phrases over and over.

The best-known and most widely distributed species is the red-eyed vireo, which breeds from southern Canada to Argentina. It has ruby red eyes and a white eye stripe, outlined in black, that contrasts with the bird's gray crown. Similar in range and general appearance is the white-eyed vireo. The warbling vireo is a melodious singer found in shade trees and open woods from Alaska to Mexico.

About 38 species of vireos make up the genus *Vireo* of the family Vireonidae. A number of species are called greenlets—a name once applied to all vireos. The red-eyed vireo is *Vireo olivaceus;* the white-eyed vireo, *V. griseus;* and the warbling vireo, *V. gilvus*. (*See also* Birds.)

VIRGIL, or VERGIL (70–19 BC). The greatest of the Roman poets, Publius Vergilius Maro, was not a Roman by birth. His early home was on a farm in the village of Andes, near Mantua. His father was a farmer, prosperous enough to give his son the best education. The young Virgil was sent to school at Cremona and then to Milan. At the age of 17 he went to Rome to study. There he learned rhetoric and philosophy from the best teachers of the day.

After the civil war between Julius Caesar and Pompey, the family farm was seized. The loss, however, proved to be a blessing in disguise, for it brought Virgil powerful friends. They introduced Virgil to the friends of Octavian, who was soon to become the emperor Augustus. Maecenas, the chief imperial minister of Augustus, became Virgil's best friend and his influential patron. Through his generosity Virgil was freed from financial worries and was able to devote himself entirely to literature.

Virgil studied the Greek poets. Following Theocritus as a model, he wrote his 'Eclogues'. These are pastoral poems describing the beauty of Italian scenes. At the suggestion of Maecenas he wrote a more serious work on the art of farming and the charms of country life called the 'Georgics'. This established his fame as the foremost poet of his age.

The year after the 'Georgics' was published, he began his great epic, the 'Aeneid'. He took as his hero the Trojan Aeneas, supposed to be the founder of the Roman nation. He had devoted more than ten years to this work when, on a visit to Greece, he contracted a fatal fever. On his deathbed he begged to have the 'Aeneid' destroyed, saying that it needed three years' work to make it perfect, but Augustus saved for the world one of its epic masterpieces.

The poem, published after Virgil's death, exercised a tremendous influence upon Latin literature, prose as well as poetry. Even the Christian church regarded him as divinely inspired. Thus his influence continued through the Middle Ages and into modern times. Dante revered him as his master and represented him as his guide in the 'Divine Comedy'. Chaucer, Spenser, Milton, and Tennyson owed much to him. Superstitious people of medieval times looked upon his tomb at Naples with religious veneration. (*See also* Latin Literature.)

Virginia Division of Tourism

Historic Mount Vernon, built in about 1735, was the plantation home of George Washington from 1759 to 1799. Also on the estate is the tomb of the first president and his wife, Martha.

VIRGINIA

VIRGINIA. No state has played a more significant role in American history than Virginia. Four of the first five presidents of the United States came from Virginia. They were George Washington, Thomas Jefferson, James Madison, and James Monroe. Since then four other Virginia-born men have served as president. They were William Henry Harrison, John Tyler, Zachary Taylor, and Woodrow Wilson. This is the greatest number of presidents from one state and gives Virginia the title Mother of Presidents.

The first permanent English settlement in North America was made at Jamestown in 1607. Twelve years later Jamestown was the meeting place of America's first representative assembly. During the American Revolution Virginia gave the colonies such leaders as Washington, Patrick Henry, and George Rogers Clark.

During the long and bitter Civil War, Virginia was the chief battleground, and Richmond served as the capital of the Confederacy. Four Virginia-born generals won wide respect for their military leadership— Confederate generals Robert E. Lee, Stonewall Jackson, and Jeb Stuart and Union general George Thomas. (*See also* biographies of these famous Virginians.)

Population (1980): 5,346,279—rank, 14th state. Urban, 66.0%; rural, 34.0%. Persons per square mile, 134.4 (persons per square kilometer, 51.9)—rank, 16th state.

Extent: Area, 40,817 square miles (105,716 square kilometers), including 1,037 square miles (2,686 square kilometers) of water surface (36th state in size).

Elevation: Highest, Mount Rogers, 5,729 feet (1,746 meters), near Trout Dale; lowest, sea level; average, 950 feet (290 meters).

Geographic Center: 5 miles (8 kilometers) southwest of Buckingham.

Temperature: Extremes—lowest, −30° F (−34° C), Mountain Lake Biological Station, Jan. 22, 1985; highest, 110° F (43° C), Balcony Falls, July 15, 1954. Averages at Norfolk— January, 42.1° F (5.6° C); July, 78.8° F (26.0° C); annual, 60.1° F (15.6° C). Averages at Roanoke—January, 38.2° F (3.4° C); July , 76.1° F (24.5° C); annual, 56.8° F (13.8° C).

Precipitation: At Norfolk—annual average, 44.91 inches (1,141 millimeters). At Roanoke—annual average, 41.53 inches (1,055 millimeters).

Land Use: Crops, 19%; pasture, 7%; forest, 62%; other, 12%.

For statistical information about Agriculture, Education, Employment, Finance, Government, Manufacturing, Mining, Population Trends, and Vital Statistics, see VIRGINIA FACT SUMMARY.

359

Virginia Beach, in the southeastern corner of the state, is dotted with high-rise hotels facing the Atlantic Ocean.

Today Virginia is chiefly a manufacturing state. Its industrial plants turn out large quantities of transportation equipment, textiles, and electrical and electronic equipment. Other sources of income are agriculture, fishing, mining, lumbering, and the tourist industry.

Virginia is named for the "virgin queen," Elizabeth I of England. Its nickname of Old Dominion dates back to 1660, when Charles II of England placed the arms of Virginia on the royal shield. This gave the American colony equal rank with the other dominions—England, Scotland, and Ireland.

Survey of Virginia

The Old Dominion is in the southeastern part of the United States. It is shaped roughly like a triangle with its southern boundary the base. Virginia is bordered on the east by the Atlantic Ocean for 112 miles. Two of its eastern counties—Northampton and Accomack—are on the Delmarva Peninsula. The name of the peninsula was formed from letters of the three states—*Del*aware, *Mar*yland, and *V*irgini*a*—that occupy the area. This region is separated from the main body of the state by Chesapeake Bay (*see* Chesapeake Bay).

On the northeast, Virginia is separated from Maryland and the District of Columbia by the Potomac River. The boundary line runs not in midstream but along the right (west) bank of the river. The entire river is in Maryland (*see* Potomac River). To the northwest and west are West Virginia and Kentucky. Tennessee and North Carolina are the border states to the south of Virginia.

Virginia's greatest length (east to west) is 440 miles along its southern border. (North Carolina is the only Atlantic coast state with a greater length.) The state's greatest width (north to south) is 196 miles. The total area is 40,817 square miles, including 1,037 square miles of inland water surface.

Five Natural Regions

From east to west the surface of Virginia rises from sea level to mountain peaks more than 5,000 feet high. Within this range of elevation are five distinct natural regions.

The Coastal Plain covers all the eastern part of Virginia, including the two counties on the Delmarva Peninsula. This is the so-called Tidewater section of the state. It extends inland about 100 miles to a line running north and south through Arlington, Richmond, and Emporia. The average elevation here is 200 to 300 feet above sea level. Some parts of the Coastal Plain are low and wet—the 750-square-mile Dismal Swamp, for instance, which extends southward into North Carolina. Along the western shore of Chesapeake Bay are three peninsulas cut out by the long, wide mouths of the Potomac, Rappahannock, York, and James rivers.

The Piedmont Plateau lies west of the Coastal Plain. It is a region of low rolling hills. They reach from the Blue Ridge to the fall line, the place where rivers descend, often in rapids, from higher and geologically older regions onto the flatter coastal plains. This region is about 40 miles wide in the north and 165 miles wide along the southern border.

The Blue Ridge crosses the whole state in a northeast-southwest direction. It extends about 300 miles. These highlands are widest near the North Carolina border. In the north the Potomac and Shenandoah rivers join to cut a deep notch through the Blue Ridge Mountains at Harpers Ferry, W. Va. To the southwest are the headwaters of the state's great Tidewater rivers—the Rappahannock (and its branch, the Rapidan), the York, and the James. Still farther south rises the Roanoke River, which crosses into North Carolina. On the border of Smyth and Grayson counties is Mount Rogers. At 5,729 feet, it is the highest point in the state.

The Valley and Ridge region covers most of western Virginia. Its outstanding feature is the Shenandoah Valley, a part of the Great Appalachian Valley. It stretches for about 150 miles between the Alleghenies of West Virginia and the Blue Ridge. The limestone soils of the valley make it one of the most fertile parts of the state. The ridges of this region include the Massanutten, North, Shenandoah, and Cumberland. In the extreme west where Virginia, Kentucky, and Tennessee meet is the Cumberland Gap through the Appalachians.

The Appalachian Plateau covers a small part of Virginia in Wise, Dickenson, and Buchanan counties. The elevation here is from 2,700 to 3,000 feet. Streams

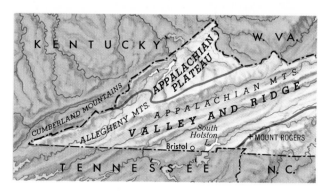

have channeled the region into a maze of deep ravines and winding ridges. (*See also* Appalachian Highlands.)

Climate and Weather

Virginia's climate is generally mild and pleasant. There are marked differences in temperatures, however, between the eastern and western parts of the state. The southeastern Tidewater section, tempered by ocean breezes, has an even climate throughout most of the year. In the west the Appalachian Highlands have cold winters and cool summers. Average annual temperatures vary from 54° F in the southwestern mountains to about 59° along the coast. The average annual precipitation (rain and snow) varies from 50 inches in the extreme southeastern section to about 35 inches in the northwestern part of the state.

The western shore of Chesapeake Bay around Norfolk has the longest growing season in the state—some 250 days. At the other extreme are parts of Tazewell County with about 140 frost-free days a year.

Natural Resources and Conservation

Virginia soils are suitable for growing tobacco, grain, and fruit. The southwestern part of the state has good grazing land. The industrial resources are minerals, fisheries, waterpower, and lumber. The chief commercial trees are pine in the Coastal Plain, hardwoods in the mountains, and mixed pine and hardwoods in the Piedmont. The state's commercial resources include Tidewater ports, navigable rivers, and scenic and historic attractions for tourists.

Much of the soil in the Tidewater and Piedmont regions was worn out by intensive tobacco growing. Today this land is being rebuilt by crop rotation and other conservation practices. Virginia's two largest flood-control and hydroelectric projects—Philpott Dam on the Smith River and John H. Kerr Dam on the Roanoke—were completed during the 1950s.

Most of the conservation work is directed by the State Department of Conservation and Historic Resources. Other agencies are the Marine Resources Commission and the Commission of Game and Inland Fisheries.

People

At the time of the founding of Jamestown, the largest group of Indians in the area was the Powhatan confederacy. These were Woodland Indians led by Chief Powhatan. After several years of warfare against the whites, the Indians became peaceful when Powhatan's daughter Pocahontas married John Rolfe in 1614 (*see* Pocahontas).

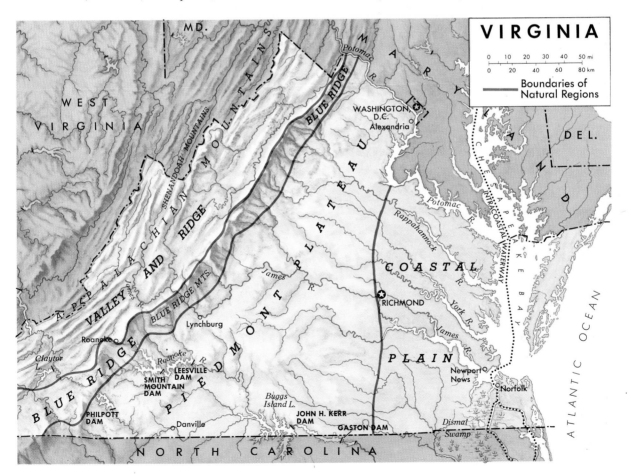

In 1622 and in 1644 the Powhatans attacked the white settlements. They were defeated in each attempt, and by 1684 the confederacy had almost disappeared.

Most of the white population of Virginia stems from two immigrant groups. In the Tidewater section nearly all the early settlers were English colonists. The other group consisted of Germans and Scots-Irish who had pushed down into the Shenandoah Valley from Pennsylvania beginning about 1730. Today only about 3 percent of the people are foreign born. They come chiefly from Germany, the Philippines, Korea, England, and Canada.

The first black indentured servants arrived in Virginia in 1619. Today black people constitute almost a fifth of the state's population.

Virginia Department of Conservation and Historic Resources

One of the delights of Richmond is Monument Avenue, a beautiful, treelined thoroughfare. It features monuments to five Confederate leaders. Richmond, the capital, is Virginia's third largest city.

Newport News Shipbuilding, a Tenneco Company

The aircraft carrier USS *John F. Kennedy* (in the foreground) is tied up at the docks at Newport News, on the James River.

Manufacturing and Employment

During the 1900s the Old Dominion steadily became a "new dominion" of manufacturing. Today the income from manufacturing is almost eight times the total income from Virginia's farms, mines, forests, and fisheries. About one fifth of Virginia's workers are employed in industrial plants.

The largest industry is the manufacture of transportation equipment, including shipbuilding and repair and motor-vehicle assembly. The second largest industry is textiles. Electrical and electronic equipment rank third, with communications equipment the industry's most valuable sector. Food is the fourth largest industry, and the making of chemicals ranks fifth.

The state's forest resources provide the basis for tremendous pulp, paper, and paperboard production. Virginia's lumber industry usually ranks among the first ten states, with nearly 1 billion board feet cut each year.

A major source of employment in the state is public administration, accounting for about 20 percent of the working force. Included are civilian and military federal government personnel and those employed at state and local levels. Most of the federal government employees work in the Washington, D.C., and Norfolk areas.

Cities of the Old Dominion

Norfolk, Virginia's chief city, is a port on Hampton Roads at the site where the James River enters Chesapeake Bay. This natural harbor is the location of both naval and air bases (*see* Norfolk). The state capital and Virginia's third largest city is Richmond, which is one of the leading industrial cities of the South (*see* Richmond). The state's second largest city is Virginia Beach.

Newport News and Hampton are ports on the peninsula between the York and the James rivers. Roanoke, the largest city of western Virginia, stands at the southern end of the Shenandoah Valley (*see* Roanoke). Portsmouth, southwest of Norfolk, is a port on Hampton Roads. Alexandria, on the Potomac, is a residential city. Valuable tobacco markets are Lynchburg on the upper James River; Danville, near the southern border; and Petersburg, south of Richmond.

Products of Land and Sea

The early history of Virginia centered around tobacco growing. Today this crop is still one of the most valuable in the state. Virginia ranks with the two Car-

A small electric train hauls bituminous, or soft, coal from a mine in southwestern Virginia. Coal is Virginia's chief mineral product.

olinas and Kentucky as one of the nation's chief sources of tobacco. Most of the crop is grown in the southern Piedmont region.

Other valuable agricultural products are milk, cattle, poultry, pigs, and eggs. In addition to tobacco, the leading crops are soybeans, corn, peanuts, wheat, and potatoes. Apples are a major crop in the Shenandoah Valley. Virginia has about 50,000 farms. The average size of farms in the state is some 190 acres.

Virginia's most valuable mineral is bituminous coal. Millions of tons are dug each year from the Pocahontas fields in the southwest. Other chief minerals are stone, sand and gravel, and calcined lime.

The Old Dominion is one of the major fishery states. The commercial catch is significant. The leading finfish catches are menhaden, flounder, croaker, scup, and sea trout.

Transportation

The first transportation system in what is now Virginia was based on the waters of Chesapeake Bay and its river tributaries. During the early 1800s canals were dug along the Potomac and James rivers as far inland as the mountains. These interior waterways gradually lost traffic with the coming of railroads and modern highways.

Land travel was chiefly on a north-south axis until the late 1700s when the emphasis changed to an east-west course. Two of the leading east-west routes of pioneer days were the Little River Turnpike and the Wilderness Road (see Roads and Streets). Today Virginia maintains about 54,000 miles of primary and secondary state roads. In addition the state is served by a system of federal and interstate highways. Interstates 95, 81, and 77 are major north-south routes; Interstates 64 and 66 cross the state from east to west.

Virginia's first railroad was a horse-drawn line that hauled coal from Chesterfield County to Richmond beginning in 1831. The first steam-powered railroad connected Petersburg with Weldon, N.C. During the

A sprawling plant on the New River in Giles County makes synthetic fibers, a valuable manufacturing industry in the state. In the background are the wooded ridges of the Appalachian Highlands.

Christ Church at Alexandria was built between 1767 and 1773. George Washington and, later, Robert E. Lee attended services here.

National Park Service

In the McLean House at Appomattox Court House, General Lee surrendered his army to General Grant on April 9, 1865.

Civil War the railroads suffered great damage. Later many of the smaller lines were absorbed by the major railroads that serve the state today. Dulles International, one of the world's largest airports, and Washington National Airport—both in northern Virginia—serve Washington, D.C.

Scenic and Historic Attractions

The tourist industry is valuable to Virginia. Especially popular are such scenic routes as the 105-mile Skyline Drive and the Blue Ridge Parkway on the top of the western mountains. Iron markers along the highways point out the state's many historic spots. These include battlefields of the Revolutionary and Civil wars, famous mountain routes, and the homes of such national figures as George Washington, Thomas Jefferson, James Monroe, Woodrow Wilson, Robert E. Lee, and John Marshall. (*See also* National Parks.)

Of particular historical interest is the peninsula between the York and James rivers. Here are located Jamestown, the first permanent English settlement in America; Williamsburg, the restored colonial capital of Virginia; and Yorktown, the site of Cornwallis' surrender in the American Revolution (*see* Jamestown; Williamsburg; Yorktown).

Education

The first free school in colonial Virginia was founded in Hampton in 1634. Virginia's first college, William and Mary, was chartered in Williamsburg in 1693. It was the second college to be founded in the colonies. Only Harvard, dating from 1636, is older.

First to advocate a free public educational system was Thomas Jefferson. The present public school system, however, was not established until 1870.

The state system of higher education was started in 1819 when Jefferson founded the University of Virginia in Charlottesville. It has a branch campus in Wise. Mary Washington College, formerly the women's division of the university in Fredericksburg, became an independent coeducational school in 1974.

Other state-supported schools are Virginia Polytechnic Institute and State University in Blacksburg; Virginia Commonwealth University in Richmond; Old Dominion University in Norfolk; College of William and Mary in Williamsburg; and a former branch, Christopher Newport College, in Newport News; Virginia State University in Petersburg; Norfolk State University in Norfolk; Radford University in Radford; James Madison University in Harrisonburg; Virginia Military Institute in Lexington; Longwood College in Farmville; and George Mason University in Fairfax.

The state is also the site of the University of Richmond in Richmond; Virginia Union University in Richmond; Hampton University in Hampton; Washington and Lee University in Lexington; and Lynchburg College in Lynchburg. Other Virginia colleges include Randolph-Macon College in Ashland; Randolph-Macon Woman's College in Lynchburg; Sweet Briar College in Sweet Briar; and Hampden-Sydney College in Hampden-Sydney.

Government and Politics

When Virginia was a British colony, its first capital was Jamestown. In 1699 the seat of the colonial government was moved to Williamsburg. Richmond has been the state capital since 1779. The state, or commonwealth, as it calls itself, is governed under a constitution adopted in 1970.

The chief executive officer of the state is the governor. Lawmaking is in the hands of the General Assembly, which is made up of the Senate and the House of Delegates. The judicial branch is headed by the Supreme Court.

Virginia has been strongly Democratic in state and local politics since Reconstruction. Voters supported the Democratic presidential candidate in all elections until 1968 except those held in 1928, 1952, 1956, and 1960.

HISTORY OF VIRGINIA

In addition to being called the Mother of Presidents, Virginia is also known as the Mother of States. The original charter of colonial Virginia covered so much territory that the western part was carved into the present states of Kentucky, Ohio, Illinois, Indiana, Wisconsin, and part of Minnesota. The bitter conflict over secession from the Union in 1861 reduced the size of Virginia still more. Fifty counties in the northwest broke away to form the state of West Virginia in 1863. Despite these losses of territory the population of the state has steadily increased. Today Virginia ranks 14th among the states in population although it is only 36th in area. The following sections tell the development of the Old Dominion.

The Jamestown Settlement

On May 13, 1607, during the reign of James I of England, three ships arrived along a marshy peninsula 30 miles inland from Chesapeake Bay. The men who went ashore the next day founded the first permanent English settlement in America. The community was named Jamestown, for the English king.

The tiny colony established by the Virginia Company of London almost failed during its first years. The new governor, Lord de la Warr (Delaware), arrived with supplies in 1610, just as the colony was being deserted. The pioneers fared better after 1612, when John Rolfe introduced the growing of tobacco. (*See also* America, Discovery and Colonization of.)

In 1619 a new charter allowed each free colonist 50 acres of land. A House of Burgesses was established to provide local government for the Virginia planters. This was the first representative assembly formed in America. In that same year the first Negro indentured servants were landed. The year 1620 is memorable for the arrival of the young women who were to become brides of the colonists. Each man paid 120 pounds of tobacco for his future wife's passage.

In 1624 the settlement became a royal colony. One of the king's governors was William Berkeley. When the Indians went on the warpath Berkeley failed to protect the small farmers in the Piedmont. Finally in 1675 the western settlers under Nathaniel Bacon defeated the Indians and then revolted against the governor in 1676 (*see* Bacon's Rebellion).

Virginia—Colony and State

As the years went by tobacco crops made the Tidewater plantation owners wealthy. Most of the work was done by Negro slaves. Farther west in the Pied-

Thomas Lee, the first native-born Virginia governor, built Stratford Hall about 1727. Here Robert E. Lee, the Confederate commander, was born.

Full-scale replicas of the three ships that brought the first English settlers to Virginia are exhibited at Jamestown. This is a model of the lead ship.

mont, farms were smaller and the number of slaves few. The prosperity of Virginia led to heavy tax collections. As new taxes were added after 1764 the House of Burgesses protested until the governor ordered it dissolved. Patrick Henry's ringing speech against the Stamp Act in 1765 echoed far and wide through the colonies (*see* Henry, Patrick).

Virginia patriots organized opposition to Great Britain. In May 1776 they asked the Continental Congress for a declaration of independence. The Virginia delegate, Richard Henry Lee, introduced the resolution that was adopted July 2, 1776. The declaration was written largely by another Virginian, Thomas Jefferson (*see* Declaration of Independence).

Meanwhile Virginia adopted a state constitution, including George Mason's bill of rights. The state then passed Thomas Jefferson's acts for religious freedom and the outlawing of entail, or laws that restricted the inheritance of land and other wealth to one line of descendants. On the battlefront of the Revolution, the American army was directed by George Washington, assisted by such other Virginia generals as George Rogers Clark, Light-Horse Harry Lee, and Daniel Morgan. The actual fighting ended at Yorktown in 1781 (see Revolution, American).

When the national Constitution was drafted in 1787 much of it was based on the Virginia Plan of organization (see United States Constitution). Later the state provided one of the nation's greatest jurists, John Marshall. Other men from the Old Dominion who won national fame are explorers William Clark and Meriwether Lewis, inventor Cyrus McCormick, Gen. Winfield Scott, surgeon Walter Reed, and Arctic explorer Richard Byrd. (See also biographies of each of these men.)

Civil War and After

In 1859 John Brown's raid on Harpers Ferry (now in West Virginia) helped bring on the Civil War (see Brown; Harpers Ferry; Civil War, American). Virginia seceded from the Union and joined the Confederacy in 1861. The Confederate capital was moved from Montgomery, Ala., to Richmond in May–June 1861. Richmond remained the capital of the Confederate States until 1865 (see Confederate States of America).

In the semicircle around Richmond—north, east, and south—occurred some of the bloodiest fighting of the war. Besides Robert E. Lee, Stonewall Jackson, and Jeb Stuart, Virginia also contributed such Confederate generals as Jubal Early, Joseph E. Johnston, and George Pickett. After the fighting ended near Appomattox in 1865, Virginians had to rebuild private homes, public structures, farm buildings, and railroad tracks on their war-torn land (see Reconstruction Period).

Modern State

During the 1900s Virginia made steady progress, especially in manufacturing. It now ranks as one of the top industrial states of the South with about 50 billion dollars in annual manufacturing shipments. Shipbuilding in the Hampton Roads area is the largest single manufacturing sector.

In 1960 Virginia created the Natural Areas System, designed to preserve small wilderness areas in the state. Better inland freight connections for Hampton Roads' shipping terminals were made possible when the Chesapeake Bay Bridge-Tunnel opened in 1964.

A new city, Reston, was dedicated in 1966. Reston was the first of 20 planned satellite cities of Washington, D. C., designed to relieve the pressure of urban population and to prevent suburban sprawl. (See also United States.)

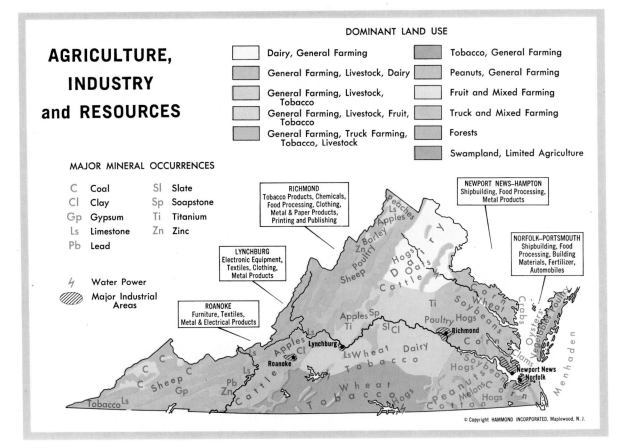

© Copyright HAMMOND INCORPORATED, Maplewood, N. J.

Notable Events in Virginia History

1606—King James I charters two companies to colonize Virginia.

1607—Jamestown founded; first permanent English settlement in North America; John Smith becomes leader of colony.

1610—Colonists abandon Jamestown.

1612—John Rolfe begins cultivation of tobacco.

1619—**House of Burgesses created; first representative assembly in America meets at Jamestown.** First black indentured servants arrive.

1622—Indians massacre many colonists.

1624—King revokes Virginia Company's charter.

1676—Nathaniel Bacon leads revolt against governor.

1693—William and Mary chartered at Williamsburg.

1699—Capital moved from Jamestown to Williamsburg.

1716—First theater in U. S. built at Williamsburg.

1775—Patrick Henry delivers "liberty or death" oration in St. John's Church, Richmond.

1776—Virginia declares its independence.

1778—State authorizes Northwest expedition by George Rogers Clark, born 1752 near Charlottesville.

1779—Richmond becomes state capital.

1781—**Lord Cornwallis surrenders at Yorktown.**

1784—Virginia cedes its northwestern lands to U. S.

1787—Constitutional Convention adopts Virginia Plan.

1788—Virginia is 10th state to ratify U. S. Constitution, June 26.

1789—George Washington, born 1732 near Oak Grove, becomes first president of U. S.; other presidents born in Virginia: Thomas Jefferson, James Madison, James Monroe, William H. Harrison, John Tyler, Zachary Taylor, and Woodrow Wilson.

1792—State Capitol completed.

1801—John Marshall, born 1755 in Fauquier County, appointed chief justice of U. S.

1819—State university founded at Charlottesville.

1831—Nat Turner leads slave rebellion at Southampton. **Cyrus McCormick invents successful reaper near Steeles Tavern.**

1846—Two Virginians, Zachary Taylor and Winfield Scott, command the chief American armies during Mexican War.

1859—John Brown seizes arsenal at Harpers Ferry.

1861—Virginia secedes from Union. Gen. Robert E. Lee heads Virginia troops. Richmond made Confederate capital; first major battle at Bull Run.

1862—*Monitor* and *Merrimack* battle in Hampton Roads. Gen. "Stonewall" Jackson defeats Union forces in Shenandoah Valley. Lee recalled to Richmond.

1863—Virginia loses territory by admission of West Virginia to the Union.

1865—**Lee surrenders to Gen. Ulysses S. Grant near Appomattox, ending Civil War.**

1870—Virginia readmitted to the Union.

1908—Staunton is first city in U. S. with a city manager.

1915—Virginia-West Virginia debt dispute settled.

1926—John D. Rockefeller, Jr., restores Williamsburg.

1951—SS *United States*, largest ocean liner constructed in U. S., launched at Newport News.

1952—John H. Kerr Dam on Roanoke River completed.

1964—Chesapeake Bay Bridge-Tunnel completed.

1966—Supreme Court rules Virginia's poll tax unconstitutional, thus outlawing tax in all states.

1967—Court unanimously rules state's antimiscegenation law unconstitutional.

1970—Present state constitution adopted.

1972—Tropical storm Agnes produces worst floods in Virginia's history.

1619

1781

1831

1865

STATE FLOWER:
Dogwood

STATE BIRD:
Cardinal

**STATE SEAL: Virtus represents
Commonwealth; holds spear and
sword; rests foot upon Tyranny.**

Virginia Profile

FLAG: *See* **Flags of the United States.**
**MOTTO: Sic Semper Tyrannis (Thus
    Ever to Tyrants).**
**SONG: 'Carry Me Back to Old Virginia'
    —words and music by James A. Bland.**
TREE: None official.

In 1607 the first permanent English settlement in North America was established on the shores of Virginia. From that time on Virginia's place in American history was assured. During the Revolutionary War it contributed such leaders as George Washington, Patrick Henry, and Thomas Jefferson to the cause of freedom. After the United States won its independence, the state earned the name Mother of Presidents because of the outstanding number of Virginians who served in the nation's highest office.

Two of the greatest conflicts fought on United States soil came to a close in Virginia. The Revolutionary War virtually ended at Yorktown, when Lord Cornwallis surrendered his British army to Gen. George Washington. Less than a hundred years later, the great Virginian commander of the Confederate forces, Gen. Robert E. Lee, presented his sword to Union Gen. Ulysses S. Grant at Appomattox—thus ending the Civil War. Some of the bloodiest Civil War battles—Bull Run, Fredericksburg, Chancellorsville— were fought within Virginia.

The terrible conflict between the North and the South left Virginia's cities and countryside in ruins. However, the devastated state managed to solve the problems of reconstruction and to lay the foundations of its modern era. Today the huge cotton and tobacco plantations are gone, but in their place modern farms produce a diversified and abundant quantity of crops. From Richmond to Norfolk the state's riverbanks and coast are lined with busy ports and prosperous shipyards. Its cities support giant industrial complexes. Its coal mines extract new riches from the earth.

Despite the prosperity of many Virginians, poverty is widespread among families living in the mountain regions. The issue of civil rights has also presented a major challenge to the state. Although numerous monuments and markers memorialize the past, Virginians are not unaware of the needs and difficulties of the present. Their state will continue to make history as it finds solutions to the new problems of the Old Dominion.

The University of Virginia, founded by Thomas Jefferson in 1819, is situated on a tree-shaded campus at Charlottesville. Jefferson designed some of the university's first buildings.

Reminiscent of a Greek temple, the State Capitol of Virginia graces Capitol Square in downtown Richmond. The main building was completed in 1792; the steps and wings, in 1905. The Confederate Congress met here during the Civil War.

These costumed horsemen add a 17th-century air to the Adam Thoroughgood House near Norfolk. Built in the mid-1600's, it is thought to be the oldest brick home in America.

The United States naval base and air station at Norfolk is the world's largest naval installation. Norfolk is the home port for ships and planes of the Mediterranean Fleet and for about 200 craft of the Atlantic Fleet.

Virginia picture profile

Besides operating about two dozen state parks, Virginia helps maintain Breaks Interstate Park on the Virginia-Kentucky border. Here Russell Fork River, a branch of the Big Sandy, has cut the "Grand Canyon of the South" through Pine Mountain.

The Revolutionary War was brought to a close at Yorktown on Oct. 19, 1781, when Lord Cornwallis surrendered to Gen. George Washington. Redoubt No. 10 was captured five days earlier by Lieut. Col. Alexander Hamilton and 400 soldiers after ten minutes of fighting.

Royal governors of colonial Virginia resided in the Governor's Palace at Williamsburg. Today, the colonial capital—restored to its 17th-century appearance—is a living memorial to the past.

At the Glasshouse in Jamestown, glassblowers in 17th-century costumes exhibit their craft and sell their wares to 20th-century tourists. The original Glasshouse was built in 1608, one year after the first permanent English settlement in the New World was established at Jamestown. Colonial Parkway, a scenic drive, connects Jamestown to Williamsburg and the battlefield at Yorktown.

Tobacco, which first brought riches to Virginia's colonists, is still important in the economy of the modern state. Virginia is a leading state in both the growing and the processing of tobacco.

One of about 20 national park areas in Virginia, Shenandoah National Park occupies a strip along the crest of the Blue Ridge Mountains. Hawksbill Mountain is the highest point in the park.

Rough-cut rail fences border the Blue Ridge National Parkway as it traces the contours of Virginia's countryside. The highway stretches nearly 500 miles through North Carolina and Virginia.

Although manufacturing accounts for much of Virginia's income, farming remains important. Peanuts and corn are leading farm products.

This replica of a pre-Civil War slave cabin is in Booker T. Washington National Monument near Rocky Mount. The famous Negro educator was born of slave parents in 1856 on a Franklin County plantation.

371

VIRGINIA FACT SUMMARY

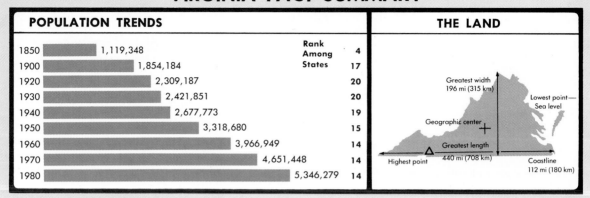

POPULATION TRENDS

Year	Population	Rank Among States
1850	1,119,348	4
1900	1,854,184	17
1920	2,309,187	20
1930	2,421,851	20
1940	2,677,773	19
1950	3,318,680	15
1960	3,966,949	14
1970	4,651,448	14
1980	5,346,279	14

THE LAND

Greatest width 196 mi (315 km)
Lowest point— Sea level
Geographic center
Greatest length 440 mi (708 km)
Highest point
Coastline 112 mi (180 km)

LARGEST CITIES (1980 census)

Norfolk (266,979): port on Hampton Roads; United States naval base; seafood, shipbuilding and repair, truck assembly, food products; Norfolk Botanical Gardens; Virginia Zoological Park; Hermitage Foundation Museum; Douglas MacArthur Memorial; Norfolk State University; Old Dominion University (*see* Norfolk).

Virginia Beach (262,199): resort area on Atlantic Ocean; steel, furniture, food products; Seashore State Park; Cape Henry Lighthouse; Association for Research and Enlightenment; Virginia Marine Science Museum.

Richmond (219,214): state capital on James River; tobacco products, printing and publishing, paper, food, fabricated metal products, apparel, chemicals, rubber, plastics; Richmond National Battlefield; Edgar Allan Poe Museum; White House of the Confederacy; Virginia Museum of Fine Arts; University of Richmond; Virginia Commonwealth University (*see* Richmond).

Arlington County (152,599): residential area on Potomac River opposite Washington, D.C.; Arlington National Cemetery; Pentagon.

Newport News (144,903): port; shipyard; bakery and dairy products; mica and manganese ore processing; Mariners' Museum; Virginia Living Museum; War Memorial Museum of Virginia; Christopher Newport College.

Hampton (122,617): historic port on Hampton Roads; food products; diesel truck production; NASA Langley Center; Fort Wool; Fort Monroe; Hampton University.

Chesapeake (114,486): industrial and residential city; fiberglass and steel products; cement; fertilizer; lumber; Chesapeake Planetarium.

Portsmouth (104,577): Hampton Roads port; food products; machinery parts; Portsmouth Naval Shipyard Museum.

Alexandria (103,217): historic Potomac River port; book publishing; chemical products; Marketplace Square; Gadsby's Tavern (1752); Carlyle House (1752).

Roanoke (100,220): industrial city; textile products; plastics; metal pipe manufacturing; electrical and electronic equipment; Virginia Museum of Transportation; Roanoke Museum of Fine Arts; Roanoke College (*see* Roanoke).

VITAL STATISTICS 1985 (per 1,000 population)

Birthrate:	14.6
Death Rate:	7.8
Marriage Rate:	11.7
Divorce Rate:	4.2

GOVERNMENT

Capital: Richmond (since 1779).

Statehood: Became 10th state in the Union on June 26, 1788.

Constitution: Adopted 1970; amendment may be passed by majority vote of General Assembly at two consecutive sessions; ratified by the voters or by constitutional convention and ratified by the voters.

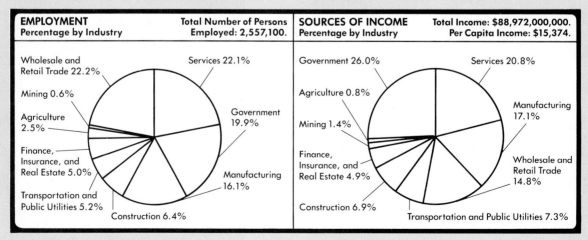

EMPLOYMENT — Percentage by Industry — Total Number of Persons Employed: 2,557,100.

- Wholesale and Retail Trade 22.2%
- Mining 0.6%
- Agriculture 2.5%
- Finance, Insurance, and Real Estate 5.0%
- Transportation and Public Utilities 5.2%
- Construction 6.4%
- Manufacturing 16.1%
- Government 19.9%
- Services 22.1%

SOURCES OF INCOME — Percentage by Industry — Total Income: $88,972,000,000. Per Capita Income: $15,374.

- Government 26.0%
- Agriculture 0.8%
- Mining 1.4%
- Finance, Insurance, and Real Estate 4.9%
- Construction 6.9%
- Transportation and Public Utilities 7.3%
- Wholesale and Retail Trade 14.8%
- Manufacturing 17.1%
- Services 20.8%

Representation in U.S. Congress: Senate—2. House of Representatives—10. Electoral votes—12.

Legislature: Senators—40; term, 4 years. Delegates—100; term, 2 years.

Executive Officers: Governor—term, 4 years; may not succeed self. Other officials—lieutenant governor, attorney general; both elected; terms, 4 years.

Judiciary: Supreme Court—7 justices; term, 12 years. Court of Appeals—10 judges; term, 8 years. Circuit courts—122 judges; term, 8 years.

County: 95 counties; most governed by boards of supervisors and county administrators.

MAJOR PRODUCTS

Agricultural: Tobacco, cattle and dairy products, chickens, turkeys, soybeans, corn, pigs, peanuts.

Manufactured: Transportation equipment, textiles, electrical and electronic equipment, food products, chemicals, printing and publishing.

Mined: Coal, stone, sand and gravel, calcined lime, feldspar, gypsum.

EDUCATION AND CULTURE

Universities and Colleges: College of William and Mary, Williamsburg; George Mason University, Fairfax; Hampden-Sydney College, Hampden-Sydney; Hollins College, Hollins College; James Madison University, Harrisonburg; Old Dominion University, Norfolk; Radford University, Radford; Randolph-Macon Woman's College, Lynchburg; University of Virginia, Charlottesville; Virginia Military Institute, Washington and Lee University, Lexington; Virginia Polytechnic Institute and State University, Blacksburg.

Libraries: Fairfax County Library, Fairfax; Old Dominion University Library, Norfolk; Richmond City Library, Richmond; University of Virginia Library, Charlottesville; Virginia Beach City Library, Virginia Beach; Virginia Polytechnic Institute and State University Library, Blacksburg; Virginia State Library, Richmond.

Notable Museums: Casemate Museum, Fort Monroe; Chrysler Museum, Norfolk; Colonial Williamsburg, Williamsburg; Mariners' Museum, Newport News; Museum of the Confederacy, Richmond; New Market Battlefield Park, New Market; Peninsula Nature and Science Center, Newport News; Roanoke Museum of Fine Arts, Roanoke; Valentine Museum, Richmond; Virginia Museum of Fine Arts, Richmond; VMI Museum, Lexington; Woodrow Wilson Birthplace Foundation, Staunton.

PLACES OF INTEREST

Appomattox Court House National Historical Park: near Appomattox; where Lee surrendered to Grant in 1865.

Arlington National Cemetery: Tomb of the Unknown Soldier; Custis-Lee Mansion; amphitheater.

Ash Lawn: near Charlottesville; estate of President James Monroe; beautiful box hedges.

Booker T. Washington National Monument: near Rocky Mount; birthplace of black educator and reformer.

Colonial National Historical Park: near Williamsburg; Cape Henry; Jamestown, first permanent English settlement; Yorktown; Colonial Parkway.

Cumberland Gap National Historical Park: historic pioneer pass in Virginia, Kentucky, and Tennessee; spectacular views.

Fredericksburg: James Monroe's law office; homes of George Washington's mother and sister.

Fredericksburg and Spotsylvania County Battlefields Memorial National Military Park: major Civil War battlefields.

Fredericksburg National Cemetery: Civil War cemetery.

George Washington Birthplace National Monument: near Oak Grove; mansion and gardens.

George Washington Memorial Parkway: landscaped riverfront parkway; Washington landmarks in Virginia and Maryland.

Hungry Mother State Park: near Marion; woods; swimming.

Jamestown Island and Festival Park: original site of the first permanent English settlement in America; ruins of settlement; reproductions of ships.

Lee Chapel Museum: in Lexington; statue and family tomb at Washington and Lee University.

MacArthur Memorial: in Norfolk; tomb and memorabilia of Gen. Douglas MacArthur.

Manassas National Battlefield Park: in Manassas; battles of Bull Run (1861, 1862).

Mariners' Museum: near Newport News; ship models and other nautical exhibits.

Monticello: near Charlottesville; mansion and tomb of President Thomas Jefferson; filled with original furnishings.

Mount Vernon: George Washington's home on the Potomac River (*see* Mount Vernon).

National Capital Parks: in Washington, D.C., Maryland, and Virginia; more than 300 parks.

Petersburg National Battlefield: near Petersburg; longest siege in United States history, 1864–65.

Pohick Church: near Fort Belvoir (1774); Washington was vestryman.

Shenandoah National Park: in Blue Ridge Mountains; scenic Skyline Drive along crest.

Stratford Hall Plantation: near Stratford; ancestral estate and birthplace of Robert E. Lee.

Williamsburg: restored colonial city; Colonial Capitol; Governor's Palace (*see* Williamsburg).

Woodrow Wilson's Birthplace: in Staunton.

Yorktown National Cemetery: near Yorktown.

BIBLIOGRAPHY FOR VIRGINIA

Beeman, R.R. The Old Dominion and the New Nation (Univ. Press of Ky., 1972).

Billings, W.M., ed. The Old Dominion in the Seventeenth Century (Univ. of N.C. Press, 1975).

Chesson, M.B. Richmond After the War, 1865–1890 (Va. State Library, 1981).

Cooper, Weldon and Morris, T.R. Virginia Government and Politics: Readings and Comments (Univ. Press of Va., 1976).

Dabney, Virginius. Virginia: the New Dominion (Univ. Press of Va., 1971).

Friddell, Guy. We Began at Jamestown (Dietz, 1968).

Heinemann, R.L. Depression and New Deal in Virginia: the Enduring Dominion (Univ. Press of Va., 1983).

Rubin, L.D., Jr. Virginia: a History (W.W. Norton, 1977).

Tate, T.W. and others. Colonial Virginia: a History (Kraus, 1986).

Ward, H.M. Richmond: an Illustrated History (Windsor, 1985).

All Fact Summary data are based on current government reports.

VIRGINIA

SCALE

0 5 10   20   30   40MI.

0 5 10   20   30   40 KM.

National Capital .... ✪

State Capitals .... ✪

County Seats .... ◉

Canals ....

© C.S. HAMMOND & Co., N.Y.

VIRGINIA

COUNTIES

Accomack, 31,268 N 5
Albemarle, 50,689 G 5
Alleghany, 14,333 D 5
Amelia, 8,405 H 6
Amherst, 29,122 F 5
Appomattox, 11,971 G 6
Arlington, 152,599 K 3
Augusta, 53,732 F 4
Bath, 5,860 E 4
Bedford, 34,927 E 6
Bland, 6,349 B 6
Botetourt, 23,270 E 5
Brunswick, 15,632 J 7
Buchanan, 37,989 D 1
Buckingham, 11,751 G 5
Campbell, 45,424 F 6
Caroline, 17,904 K 4
Carroll, 27,270 C 7
Charles City, 6,692 K 6
Charlotte, 12,266 G 6
Chesterfield, 141,372 J 6
Clarke, 9,965 H 2
Craig, 3,948 D 6
Culpeper, 22,620 H 3
Cumberland, 7,881 H 6
Dickenson, 19,806 D 2
Dinwiddie, 22,602 J 6
Essex, 8,864 L 5
Fairfax, 596,901 K 3
Fauquier, 35,889 J 3
Floyd, 11,563 D 7
Fluvanna, 10,244 H 5
Franklin, 35,740 E 6
Frederick, 34,150 H 2
Giles, 17,810 C 6
Gloucester, 20,107 L 6
Goochland, 11,761 J 5
Grayson, 16,579 B 7
Greene, 7,625 H 4
Greensville, 10,903 J 7
Halifax, 30,418 G 7
Hanover, 50,398 J 5
Henrico, 180,735 K 6
Henry, 57,654 E 7
Highland, 2,937 E 4
Isle of Wight, 21,603 L 7
James City, 22,763 L 6
King and Queen, 5,968 L 5
King George, 10,543 K 4
King William, 9,327 K 5
Lancaster, 10,129 M 5
Lee, 25,956 B 2
Loudoun, 57,427 J 2
Louisa, 17,825 J 5
Lunenburg, 12,124 H 7
Madison, 10,232 H 4
Mathews, 7,995 M 6
Mecklenburg, 29,444 H 7
Middlesex, 7,719 M 5
Montgomery, 63,516 D 6
Nelson, 12,204 G 5
New Kent, 8,781 L 5
Northampton, 14,625 N 6
Northumberland, 9,828 M 5
Nottoway, 14,666 H 6
Orange, 17,827 H 4
Page, 19,401 H 3
Patrick, 17,585 D 7
Pittsylvania, 66,147 F 7
Powhatan, 13,062 J 5
Prince Edward, 16,456 H 6
Prince George, 25,733 K 6
Prince William, 144,703 K 3
Pulaski, 35,229 C 6
Rappahannock, 6,093 H 3
Richmond, 6,952 L 5
Roanoke, 72,945 D 6
Rockbridge, 17,911 F 5
Rockingham, 57,038 G 4
Russell, 31,761 E 2
Scott, 25,068 D 2
Shenandoah, 27,559 G 3
Smyth, 33,345 A 7
Southampton, 18,731 K 7
Spotsylvania, 34,435 J 4
Stafford, 40,470 K 4
Surry, 6,046 L 6
Sussex, 10,874 K 7
Tazewell, 50,511 B 6
Warren, 21,200 H 3
Washington, 46,487 E 2
Westmoreland, 14,041 L 4
Wise, 43,863 C 2
Wythe, 25,522 B 7
York, 35,463 L 6

CITIES AND TOWNS

Abingdon, 4,318 E 2
Accomac, 522 N 5
Achilles, 525 M 6
Afton, 350 G 4
Alberene, 200 G 5
Alberta, 394 J 7
Alexandria, 103,217 L 3
Alleghany, 48 D 5
Allisonia, 325 C 7
Altavista, 3,849 F 6
Alton, 500 F 7
Amelia Court House, 500 J 6
Amherst, 1,135 F 5
Amissville, 150 H 3
Amonate, 350 A 6
Andersonville, 45 G 6
Andover, 180 C 2
Annandale, 49,524 K 3
Appalachia, 2,418 C 2
Appomattox, 1,345 G 6
Ararat, 500 C 7
Arlington, 152,599 L 3
Arrington, 500 G 5
Arvonia, 500 H 5
Ashburn, 345 K 2
Ashland, 4,640 J 5
Atkins, 1,352 B 7
Augusta Springs, 600 F 4
Austinville, 750 B 7
Axton, 540 E 7
Aylett, 100 K 5
Bacons Castle, 78 L 6
Ballsville, 150 H 6
Balty, 50 K 5
Bandy, 200 F 1
Banner, 3,271 D 2
Barboursville, 600 H 4
Barren Springs, 125 C 7
Bassett, 2,034 E 7
Bastian, 600 B 6
Batesville, 575 G 5
Bealeton, 200 J 3
Beaverdam, 500 J 5
Beaverlett, 200 M 6
Bedford, 5,991 E 6
Bellbluff, 390 J 6
Belle Haven, 6,520 N 5
Belleview, 8,299 K 3
Ben Hur, 400 B 2
Benhams, 100 D 2
Benns Church, 50 L 7
Bent Creek, 68 G 5
Bent Mountain, 140 D 6
Bentonville, 500 H 3
Bergton, 150 G 3
Berryville, 1,752 H 2
Big Island, 500 F 5
Big Rock, 900 D 1
Big Stone Gap, 4,748 C 2
Birchleaf, 650 D 1
Birdsnest, 736 N 6
Bishop, 600 A 6
Blackridge, 32 H 7
Blacksburg, 30,368 D 6
Blackstone, 3,624 J 6
Blackwater, 130 C 3
Blairs, 500 F 7
Bland, 950 B 6
Bloxom, 407 N 5
Bluefield, 5,946 B 6
Blue Grass, 200 E 3
Bluemont, 200 J 2
Blue Ridge, 2,347 E 6
Boissevain, 975 B 6
Bolar, 135 E 4
Bon Air, 16,224 J 5
Boones Mill, 303 E 6
Boonesville, 56 G 4
Boston, 400 H 3
Bowling Green, 665 K 4
Boyce, 401 H 2
Boydton, 486 H 7
Boykins, 791 K 7
Bracey, 106 H 7
Branchville, 174 K 7
Brandy Station, 400 J 4
Breaks, 550 D 1
Bremo Bluff, 200 H 5
Bridgewater, 3,289 F 4
Brightwood, 100 H 4
Bristol, 19,042 D 3
Bristow, 98 J 3
Broadford, 500 F 2
Broadway, 1,234 G 3
Brodnax, 492 J 7
Brooke, 245 K 4
Brookneal, 1,454 G 6
Brownsburg, 300 F 5
Browntown, 300 H 3
Brucetown, 250 H 2
Bryce Mtn., 205 G 3
Buchanan, 1,205 E 5
Buckhorn, 75 L 7
Buckingham, 200 G 5
Buena Vista, 6,717 F 5
Buffalo Junction, 300 G 7
Bumpass, 110 J 5
Burgess, 200 M 5
Burkes Garden, 267 B 6
Burkeville, 606 H 6
Burnsville, 140 E 4
Callands, 102 E 7
Callao, 500 L 5
Callaway, 225 D 7
Calverton, 500 J 3
Cana, 168 C 7
Cape Charles, 1,512 M 6
Capeville, 325 M 6
Capron, 238 K 7
Cardwell, 200 J 5
Carrsville, 300 L 7
Carson, 500 K 6
Cartersville, 100 H 5
Carysbrook, 40 H 5
Casanova, 370 J 3
Cascade, 835 E 7
Castlewood, 2,420 D 2
Catawba, 350 D 6
Catlett, 500 J 3
Cedar Bluff, 1,550 E 2
Cedar Springs, 200 B 7
Cedarville, 200 H 3
Center Cross, 360 L 5
Ceres, 200 B 6
Champlain, 160 K 4
Chancellorsville, 40 J 4
Chantilly, 12,259 K 3
Charles City, 5 K 6
Charlotte Court House, 568 G 6
Charlottesville, 45,010 H 4
Chase City, 2,749 H 7
Chatham, 1,390 F 7
Check, 75 D 6
Cheriton, 695 M 6
Chesapeake, 114,486 M 7
Chester, 11,728 K 6
Chesterfield, 950 J 6
Chester Gap, 400 H 3
Chilhowie, 1,265 F 2
Chincoteague, 1,607 O 5
Christiansburg, 10,345 D 6
Chuckatuck, 500 L 7
Chula, 150 J 6
Church Road, 100 J 6
Church View, 200 L 5
Churchville, 250 F 4
Cismont, 25 H 4
Claremont, 380 L 6
Clarksville, 1,468 H 7
Claudville, 180 D 7
Clay Bank, 200 L 6
Clayville, 200 J 6
Clear Brook, 300 H 2
Cleveland, 360 E 2
Clifford, 150 F 5
Clifton Forge, 5,046 E 5
Clinchburg, 250 E 2
Clinchco, 900 D 1
Clinchport, 89 C 2
Clintwood, 1,369 D 2
Clover, 215 C 7
Cloverdale, 850 E 6
Cluster Springs, 350 G 7
Cobbs Creek, 700 M 6
Coeburn, 2,625 D 2
Coleman Falls, 250 F 6
Coles Point, 100 L 4
Collierstown, 300 E 5
Collinsville, 7,517 E 7
Colonial Bch., 2,474 L 4
Colonial Heights, 16,509 K 6
Columbia, 111 H 5
Columbia Furnace, 60 G 3
Concord, 500 F 6
Copper Hill, 50 D 6
Copper Valley, 425 C 7
Courtland, 976 K 7
Covesville, 475 G 5
Covington, 9,063 D 5
Craigsville, 845 E 4
Crandon, 250 C 6
Crewe, 2,325 H 6
Crimora, 450 G 4
Cripple Creek, 200 B 7
Critz, 125 D 7
Crockett, 200 B 7
Cross Junction, 125 H 2
Crozet, 2,553 G 4
Crozier, 300 J 5
Crystal Hill, 475 G 7
Cullen, 725 G 6
Culpeper, 6,621 H 4
Cumberland, 500 H 6
Dahlgren, 950 K 4
Dale City, 33,127 K 3
Daleville, 450 E 6
Damascus, 1,330 E 2
Dante, 1,083 D 2
Danville, 45,642 E 7
Darlington Hts., 102 G 6
Davenport, 230 D 2
Dayton, 1,017 G 4
Deerfield, 500 F 4
Delaplane, 100 J 3
Deltaville, 1,082 M 5
Dendron, 307 L 6
Denniston, 200 G 7
Dewitt, 140 J 6
Dillwyn, 637 H 5
Dinwiddie, 500 J 6
Disputanta, 800 K 6
Doe Hill, 30 F 4
Doswell, 50 J 5
Drakes Branch, 617 G 7
Draper, 276 C 7
Drewryville, 200 K 7
Drill, 192 E 2
Driver, 250 L 7
Dryden, 400 C 2
Dry Fork, 200 F 7
Dublin, 2,368 C 6
Duffield, 148 C 2
Dugspur, 50 C 7
Dumfries, 3,214 K 3
Dundas, 200 H 7
Dungannon, 339 D 2
Dunnsville, 800 L 5
Eagle Rock, 750 E 5
Earlysville, 210 H 4
East Stone Gap, 240 C 2
Eastville, 238 M 6
Ebony, 400 J 7
Eclipse, 295 M 7
Edgehill, 100 K 4
Edgerton, 75 J 7
Edinburg, 752 H 3
Eggleston, 350 C 6
Elberon, 25 L 6
Elk Creek, 100 B 7
Elk Garden, 25 E 2
Elkton, 1,520 G 4
Elliston, 1,172 D 6
Emory, 2,292 E 2
Emporia, 4,840 J 7
Esmont, 950 G 5
Esserville, 750 C 2
Ettrick, 4,890 K 6
Evergreen, 300 G 6
Evington, 175 F 6
Ewing, 800 B 2
Exmore, 1,300 N 5
Faber, 125 G 5
Fairfax, 19,390 K 3
Fairfield, 465 F 5
Fairlawn, 1,794 C 6
Fairport, 175 M 5
Falls Church, 9,515 K 3
Falls Mills, 800 B 6
Falmouth, 3,271 K 4
Fancy Gap, 200 C 7
Farmville, 6,067 H 6
Farnham, 150 L 5
Ferrum, 200 D 7
Fieldale, 1,190 D 7
Fincastle, 282 E 6
Fishersville, 975 F 4
Flint Hill, 750 H 3
Floyd, 411 D 7
Forest, 497 F 6
Forks of Buffalo, 99 F 5
Fork Union, 350 H 5
Fort Blackmore, 150 C 2
Fort Defiance, 600 G 4
Fort Mitchell, 125 H 7
Fosters Falls, 100 C 7
Foxwells, 400 M 5
Franklin, 7,308 L 7
Franktown, 500 N 6
Fredericksburg, 15,322 J 4
Fredericks Hall, 50 J 4
Free Union, 121 G 4
Fries, 758 B 7
Front Royal, 11,126 H 3
Fulks Run, 130 G 3
Gainesboro, 101 H 2
Gainesville, 600 J 3
Galax, 6,524 C 7
Garrisonville, 200 K 4
Gasburg, 150 J 7
Gate City, 2,494 C 3
Georges Fork, 200 C 2
Gibson Station, 150 B 3
Gladehill, 150 E 7
Glade Spring, 1,722 E 2
Gladstone, 74 G 5
Gladys, 500 F 6
Glasgow, 1,259 F 5
Glen Allen, 6,202 J 5
Glen Lyn, 235 C 6
Glen Wilton, 190 E 5
Glenwood, 2,276 F 7
Gloucester, 700 L 6
Gloucester Point, 5,841 M 6
Goldbond, 250 C 6
Goldvein, 500 J 4
Goochland, 800 J 5
Goode, 200 F 6
Gordonsville, 1,421 H 4
Gore, 500 H 2
Goshen, 134 F 5
Grafton, 500 L 6
Greenbackville, 300 O 5
Green Bay, 500 H 6
Greenbush, 200 N 5
Greenville, 400 F 5
Greenwood, 800 G 4
Gretna, 1,255 F 7
Grottoes, 1,369 G 4
Groveton, 18,860 K 3
Grundy, 1,699 D 1
Guinea, 75 K 4
Gum Spring, 125 J 5
Gwynn, 205 M 5
Hacksneck, 111 N 5
Hague, 425 L 4
Halifax, 772 G 7
Hallwood, 243 N 5
Hamilton, 598 J 2
Hampden-Sydney, 1,011 C 6
Hampton, 122,617 M 6
Handsom, 60 K 7
Hanover, 500 K 5
Harborton, 200 N 5
Hardy, 325 E 6
Harman-Maxie, 650 D 1
Harrisonburg, 19,671 F 4
Hartfield, 700 M 5
Haymarket, 230 J 3
Haynesville, 500 L 5
Haysi, 371 D 1
Head Waters, 35 F 4
Healing Sprs., 175 E 5
Healys, 30 M 5
Heathsville, 300 L 5
Henry, 300 E 7
Herndon, 11,449 K 3
Highland Springs, 12,146 K 5
Hightown, 15 E 4
Hillsboro, 94 J 2
Hillsville, 2,123 C 7
Hiltons, 300 D 2
Hiwassee, 250 C 7
Hoadly, 400 K 3
Hobson, 800 L 7
Holland, 400 L 7
Hollins College, 12,295 E 6
Honaker, 1,475 E 2
Hopeton, 100 N 5
Hopewell, 23,397 K 6
Hopkins, 100 N 5
Horntown, 400 O 5
Hot Springs, 300 E 4
Howardsville, 55 G 5
Huddleston, 200 F 6
Hume, 350 J 3
Hurley, 850 E 1
Hurt, 1,481 F 6
Independence, 1,112 B 7
Indian Neck, 40 K 5
Indian Valley, 300 C 7
Ingram, 71 F 7
Iron Gate, 620 E 5
Irvington, 567 M 5
Isle of Wight, 185 L 7
Ivanhoe, 900 C 7
Ivor, 403 L 7
Ivy, 900 G 4
Jamestown, 12 L 6
Jamesville, 500 N 5
Jarratt, 614 K 7
Java, 100 F 7
Jefferson, 40 J 5
Jeffersonton, 300 J 3
Jericho, 2,438 L 7
Jetersville, 110 H 6
Jewell Ridge, 600 E 1
Jonesville, 874 B 2
Keeling, 680 F 7
Keezletown, 975 C 4
Keller, 236 N 5
Kenbridge, 1,352 H 7
Kents Store, 130 H 5
Keokee, 300 C 2
Keswick, 300 H 4
Keysville, 704 H 6
Kilmarnock, 945 M 5
Kimballton, 50 C 6
King George, 575 K 4
King & Queen Court House, 500 L 5

VIRGINIA

King William, 100 K 5
Kinsale, 250 L 4
Konnarock, 300 E 2
Lacey Spring, 140 G 3
La Crosse, 734 H 7
Ladysmith, 360 J 4
Lafayette, 350 D 6
Lakeside, 12,289 J 5
Lambsburg, 800 C 7
Lancaster, 110 M 5
Lanesville, 30 L 5
Laurel Fork, 300 C 7
Lawrenceville, 1,484 J 7
Lebanon, 3,206 E 2
Lebanon Church, 300 G 2
Leesburg, 8,357 J 2
Leesville, 100 F 6
Lennig, 38 G 7
Lewisetta, 125 M 4
Lexington, 7,292 E 5
Lightfoot, 120 L 6
Linden, 320 H 3
Linville, 500 G 3
Lithia, 105 E 6
Little Plymouth, 195 L 5
Littleton, 15 K 7
Lively, 400 L 5
Lloyd Place, 2,367 L 7
Locustville, 75 N 5
Long Island, 80 F 6
Loretto, 150 K 4
Lorton, 5,813 K 3
Louisa, 932 H 4
Lovettsville, 613 J 2
Lovingston, 600 G 5
Lowesville, 500 F 5
Lowmoor, 700 E 5
Lowry, 100 F 6
Lucketts, 500 J 2
Lunenburg, 13 H 7
Luray, 3,584 H 3
Lynchburg, 66,743 F 6
Lynchburg (met. area), 153,260 F 6
Lynch Station, 500 F 6
Machipongo, 400 N 6
Madison, 267 H 4
Madison Hts., 14,146 F 6
Maidens, 100 J 5
Manakin-Sabot, 200 J 5
Manassas, 15,438 K 3
Manassas Park, 6,524 K 3
Mannboro, 175 J 6
Manquin, 576 K 5
Mappsville, 700 O 5
Marion, 7,287 A 7
Markham, 300 J 3
Marshall, 800 J 3
Martinsville, 18,149 E 7
Massaponax, 50 K 4
Massies Mill, 225 F 5
Mathews, 500 M 6
Matoaca, 1,967 J 6
Mattaponi, 300 L 5
Maurertown, 158 G 3
Max Meadows, 782 C 6
McClure, 300 D 2
McCoy, 600 C 6
McDowell, 110 E 4
McGaheysville, 600 G 4
McKenney, 473 J 7
McLean, 35,664 K 3
Meadows of Dan, 150 D 7
Meadowview, 875 E 2
Mechanicsburg, 350 C 6
Mechanicsville, 9,269 K 5
Meherrin, 400 H 6
Melfa, 391 N 5
Mendota, 375 D 2
Middlebrook, 125 F 4
Middleburg, 619 J 3
Middletown, 841 H 2
Midland, 600 J 3
Midlothian, 950 J 6
Milford, 650 K 4
Millboro, 400 E 5
Millboro Springs, 200 E 4
Millwood, 400 J 2
Mineral, 399 J 4
Mine Run, 450 J 4
Mitchells, 88 J 4
Mobjack, 210 M 6
Modest Town, 225 O 5
Mollusk, 800 L 5
Moneta, 300 E 6
Monroe, 500 F 6
Monterey, 247 F 4
Montross, 5,349 L 4
Montvale, 900 E 6
Morattico, 225 L 5
Moseley, 210 J 6
Mount Crawford, 315 G 4
Mount Holly, 200 L 4
Mount Jackson, 1,419 G 3
Mount Sidney, 500 F 4
Mount Solon, 124 F 4
Mount Vernon, 24,058 K 3
Mouth of Wilson, 400 B 7
Mustoe, 150 E 4
Narrows, 2,516 C 6
Naruna, 175 G 6
Nassawadox, 630 N 6
Nathalie, 200 G 7
Natural Bridge, 200 E 5
Natural Bridge Sta., 450 F 5
Naxera, 300 M 6
Nellysford, 290 G 5
New Baltimore, 125 J 3
New Canton, 96 H 5
New Castle, 213 D 5
New Church, 427 N 5
New Hope, 200 G 4
New Kent, 25 L 5
New Market, 1,118 G 3
Newport, 600 D 6
Newport News, 144,903 L 6
Newport News-Hampton (met. area), 364,449 L 6
New River, 500 C 6
Newsoms, 368 K 7
Nickelsville, 464 D 2
Nokesville, 520 J 3
Nora, 550 D 2
Norfolk, 266,979 M 7
Norfolk–Virginia Beach–Portsmouth (met. area), 806,951 M 7
Norge, 750 L 6
North Garden, 200 G 5
North Pulaski, 1,315 C 6
Norton, 4,757 C 2
Norwood, 60 C 5
Nottoway, 170 H 6
Oak Grove, 100 K 4
Oak Hall, 221 N 5
Oakpark, 150 H 4
Oakwood, 715 E 1
Occoquan, 512 K 3
Onancock, 1,461 N 5
Onley, 526 N 5
Orange, 2,631 H 4
Oriskany, 116 E 5
Owenton, 400 K 5
Oyster, 200 N 6
Paint Bank, 235 D 5
Painter, 321 N 5
Palmyra, 250 H 5
Pamplin, 273 G 6
Pardee, 190 C 1
Paris, 90 J 3
Parksley, 979 N 5
Parrott, 750 C 6
Partlow, 35 J 4
Patrick Springs, 800 D 7
Patterson, 500 E 1
Peaks, 500 K 5
Pearisburg, 2,128 C 6
Pedlar Mills, 50 F 5
Pembroke, 1,302 C 6
Pendletons, 100 J 5
Penhook, 500 E 7
Pennington Gap, 1,716 C 2
Perrin, 250 M 6
Petersburg, 41,055 J 6
Petersburg–Colonial Hts.–Hopewell (met. area), 129,296 J 6
Phenix, 250 G 6
Philomont, 265 J 2
Pilot, 360 D 6
Piney River, 778 G 5
Pittsville, 600 F 7
Pleasant Hill, 2,277 L 7
Pleasant Valley, 150 G 4
Pocahontas, 708 B 6
Poquoson, 8,726 M 6
Port Republic, 75 G 4
Port Richmond, 130 L 5
Port Royal, 291 K 4
Portsmouth, 104,577 M 7
Potomac Beach, 200 L 4
Pound, 1,086 C 2
Pounding Mill, 399 E 2
Powhatan, 600 J 5
Prince George, 150 K 6
Prospect, 275 G 6
Providence Forge, 500 L 6
Pulaski, 10,106 C 6
Pungoteague, 500 N 5
Purcellville, 1,567 J 2
Purdy, 350 J 7
Quantico, 7,121 K 3
Quicksburg, 160 G 3
Quinby, 350 N 5
Quinton, 121 K 5
Radford, 13,225 C 6
Radiant, 250 H 4
Randolph, 150 G 7
Raphine, 500 F 5
Rapidan, 176 H 4
Raven, 4,000 E 2
Rawlings, 200 J 7
Rectortown, 225 J 3
Red Ash, 300 E 2
Red House, 150 G 6
Red Oak, 250 G 7
Reedville, 400 M 5
Rehoboth, 100 H 7
Reliance, 150 H 3
Remington, 425 J 3
Republican Grove, 125 F 7
Reston, 36,407 K 3
Rice, 194 H 6
Rich Creek, 746 C 6
Richlands, 5,796 E 2
Richmond (cap.), 219,214 K 5
Richmond (met. area), 632,015 K 5
Ridgeway, 858 E 7
Riner, 360 D 6
Ringgold, 150 F 7
Ripplemead, 600 C 6
Riverton, 500 H 3
Rixeyville, 150 H 3
Roanoke, 100,220 D 6
Roanoke (met. area), 224,341 D 6
Rockville, 290 J 5
Rocky Gap, 200 B 6
Rocky Mount, 4,198 E 7
Rosedale, 760 E 2
Rose Hill, 700 B 3
Roseland, 300 F 5
Round Hill, 510 J 2
Rowe, 150 D 2
Ruby, 188 J 3
Rural Retreat, 1,083 B 7
Rushmere, 1,070 L 6
Rustburg, 650 F 6
Ruther Glenn, 200 K 5
Ruthville, 300 L 6
Saint Charles, 241 C 2
Saint Paul, 973 D 2
Saint Stephens Church, 500 K 5
Salem, 23,958 D 6
Saltville, 2,376 E 2
Saluda, 150 L 5
Sandston, 8,071 K 5
Saratoga Place, 1,245 L 7
Saxe, 110 G 7
Saxis, 415 N 5
Schuyler, 250 G 5
Scottsburg, 335 G 7
Scottsville, 250 G 5
Seaford, 2,500 M 6
Sealston, 200 K 4
Sebrell, 160 K 7
Sedley, 523 L 7
Selma, 500 E 5
Seven Mile Ford, 425 A 7
Shanghai, 150 L 5
Sharps, 100 L 5
Shawsville, 950 D 6
Shenandoah, 1,861 G 4
Shiloh, 150 K 4
Shipman, 350 G 5
Simpsons, 150 D 6
Singers Glen, 155 F 3
Skippers, 150 K 7
Smithfield, 3,718 L 7
Snell, 300 J 4
Somerset, 200 H 4
South Boston, 7,093 G 7
South Hill, 4,341 H 7
Sparta, 485 K 4
Speedwell, 650 B 7
Spencer, 500 E 7
Sperryville, 500 H 3
Spotsylvania, 350 J 4
Springfield, 21,435 K 3
Springwood, 120 E 5
Stacy, 100 E 1
Stafford, 750 K 4
Stanardsville, 284 G 4
Stanley, 1,204 G 3
Stanleytown, 1,761 D 7
Star Tannery, 500 G 2
Staunton, 21,857 F 4
Steeles Tavern, 200 F 5
Stephens City, 1,179 H 2
Sterling, 16,080 K 2
Stevensburg, 125 J 4
Stonega, 275 C 2
Stony Creek, 329 J 7
Strasburg, 2,311 H 3
Stratford, 30 L 4
Stuart, 1,131 D 7
Stuarts Draft, 1,776 G 4
Studley, 4,674 K 5
Suffolk, 47,621 L 7
Sugar Grove, 1,027 B 7
Surry, 237 L 6
Susan, 500 M 6
Sussex, 75 K 7
Sutherlin, 180 F 7
Sweet Briar, 900 F 5
Sweet Chalybeate, 65 D 5
Swords Creek, 315 E 2
Sylvatus, 200 C 7
Syria, 75 H 4
Tabb, 2,466 M 6
Tacoma, 150 C 2
Tangier, 771 M 5
Tappahannock, 1,821 K 5
Tazewell, 4,468 B 6
Temperanceville, 400 O 5
Tetotum, 75 L 4
Thaxton, 450 E 6
The Plains, 382 J 3
Thornburg, 135 J 4
Timberville, 1,510 G 3
Tiptop, 175 B 6
Toano, 950 L 6
Toms Brook, 226 G 3
Toms Creek, 100 D 2
Townsend, 525 M 6
Trammel, 459 D 2
Triangle, 4,770 K 3
Triplet, 300 J 7
Trout Dale, 248 B 7
Troutville, 496 E 6
Tunstall, 34 K 5
Turbeville, 50 F 7
Tye River, 80 G 5
Tyro, 125 F 5
Union Hall, 125 E 6
Union Level, 100 H 7
Unionville, 500 J 4
Upperville, 250 J 2
Urbanna, 518 L 5
Valentines, 400 J 7
Vanderpool, 68 E 4
Vansant, 2,708 D 1
Vera, 150 G 6
Vernon Hill, 250 F 7
Verona, 2,782 F 4
Vesta, 350 D 7
Vesuvius, 500 F 5
Victoria, 2,004 H 6
Vienna, 15,469 K 3
Vinton, 8,027 E 6
Virgilina, 212 G 7
Virginia Beach, 262,199 M 7
Volney, 105 B 7
Wachapreague, 404 N 5
Waidsboro, 55 E 7
Wakefield, 1,355 K 7
Walkerton, 985 K 5
Ware Neck, 100 M 6
Warfield, 100 J 7
Warm Springs, 325 E 4
Warrenton, 3,907 J 3
Warsaw, 771 L 5
Washington, 247 H 3
Waterford, 350 J 2
Water View, 265 L 5
Waverly, 2,284 K 6
Waynesboro, 15,329 F 4
Weber City, 1,543 D 3
Weems, 500 L 5
Weirwood, 300 N 6
West Augusta, 325 F 4
West Point, 2,726 L 5
Weyers Cave, 300 G 4
Whaleyville, 332 L 7
White Hall, 250 G 4
White Plains, 60 H 7
White Post, 85 H 2
White Stone, 409 M 5
Whitetop, 860 A 7
Wicomico Church, 500 M 5
Wilderness, 200 J 4
Williamsburg, 9,870 L 6
Willis, 170 D 7
Willis Wharf, 360 N 5
Wilsons, 102 J 6
Winchester, 20,217 H 2
Windsor, 985 L 7
Winterpock, 100 J 6
Wirtz, 500 E 6
Wise, 3,894 C 2
Wolftown, 350 H 4
Woodberry Forest, 450 H 4
Woodbridge, 24,004 K 3
Woodlawn, 1,689 C 7
Woodstock, 2,627 G 3
Woodville, 200 H 3
Woodway, 400 C 2
Woolwine, 150 D 7
Wylliesburg, 213 G 7
Wytheville, 7,135 C 7
Yale, 115 K 7
Yorktown, 550 M 6
Zepp, 100 G 3
Zuni, 300 L 7

OTHER FEATURES

Allegheny (mts.) D 5
Appalachian (mts.) E 5
Appomattox (riv.) H 6
Appomattox C. H. Nat'l Hist. Pk. F 6
Assateague I. Nat'l Seashore O 4
Banister (riv.) F 7
Big North (mts.) H 1
Blackwater (riv.) K 6
Blue Ridge (mts.) E 6
Booker T. Washington Nat'l Mon. E 6
Buggs I. (lake) H 7
Bull Run (creek) J 3
Camp A. P. Hill K 4
Charles (cape) M 6
Chesapeake (bay) M 5
Chesapeake and Ohio Canal Nat'l Mon. K 2
Chincoteague (bay) O 4
Claytor (lake) C 6
Clinch (riv.) D 2
Colonial Nat'l Hist. Park L 6
Cowpasture (riv.) E 4
Cumberland (mt.) B 2
Cumberland Gap Nat'l Hist. Pk. A 3
Dan (riv.) F 7
Dismal (swamp) M 8
Drummond (lake) L 7
Ft. Belvoir K 3
Ft. Eustis L 6
Ft. Hunt K 3
Ft. Lee K 6
Ft. Monroe M 6
Ft. Myer K 3
Ft. Story N 7
Gaston (lake) H 8
Geo. Washington Birthplace Nat'l Mon. L 4
Hampton Roads (estuary) M 7
Henry (cape) M 7
Holston, N. Fork (riv.) D 2
Jackson (riv.) E 4
James (riv.) K 6
Langley A.F.B. M 6
Leesville (lake) E 6
Manassas Nat'l Battlef. Park F 3
Massanutten (mt.) G 3
Mattaponi (riv.) K 5
Mattaponi Ind. Res. L 5
Maury (riv.) F 5
Meherrin (riv.) H 7
New (riv.) B 8
Norfolk Naval Air Sta. M 7
Norfolk Naval Base M 7
Nottoway (riv.) K 7
Oceana Naval Air Sta. N 7
Pamunkey (riv.) K 5
Pamunkey Ind. Res. L 5
Philpott (res.) D 7
Pocomoke (sound) N 5
Potomac (riv.) K 4
Powell (riv.) B 3
Quantico Marine Air Sta. K 4
Rapidan (riv.) H 4
Rappahannock (riv.) L 4
Richmond Nat'l Battlef. Park K 6
Rivanna (riv.) H 5
Roanoke (riv.) J 8
Rogers (mt.) A 7
Shenandoah (mt.) F 3
Shenandoah (riv.) J 2
Shenandoah Nat'l Park G 3
Smith (riv.) E 7
Smith Mtn. (lake) E 6
S. Holston (lake) E 3
Staunton (Roanoke) (riv.) F 7
Tangier (isl.) M 5
Tangier (sound) N 5
Vint Hill Farm Mil. Res. J 3
Wallops (isl.) O 5
York (riv.) L 6

VIRGIN ISLANDS, BRITISH.

Located about 50 miles (80 kilometers) east of Puerto Rico in the eastern Caribbean Sea, the British Virgin Islands consist of 36 picturesque islands and islets. They are part of an island chain that is continued by the United States Virgin Islands to the west. The major islands are Tortola, Anegada, Virgin Gorda, and Jost Van Dyke. The chief town and port is Road Town on Tortola, the largest island. The total area is 59 square miles (153 square kilometers). The pleasant subtropical climate has year-round temperatures between 70° and 90° F (21° and 32° C). The variety of scenic physical features includes steep hills, lagoons with coral reefs, and landlocked harbors.

The majority of the population is of black African descent. About 80 percent of the total population lives on Tortola. The official language is English.

Tourism is the economic mainstay. Cottage industries produce handmade items. Manufactured goods are rum, paint, and building materials. Fishing is a growing export industry. Agriculture focuses on livestock, though some tropical fruits and vegetables are exported.

A colony of the United Kingdom with a representative government, the islands are administered under a constitution dating from 1977. The governor is appointed by the British monarch.

Christopher Columbus landed in the area in 1493, and Spain sent an invasion force to claim the islands in 1555. The islands were an early haunt of pirates. Dutch buccaneers held Tortola until English planters took control in 1666. In 1872 the islands became part of the Colony of the Leeward Islands. In 1956 they were made a separate colony. Population (1986 estimate), 12,000.

VIRGIN ISLANDS, UNITED STATES.

Composed of three large islands and some 50 islets, the Virgin Islands of the United States are located in the northeastern Caribbean Sea about 40 miles (64 kilometers) east of Puerto Rico. They cover an area of 136 square miles (352 square kilometers). Saint Croix, the largest of the islands, has an area of 84 square miles (218 square kilometers). The capital of the Virgin Islands, Charlotte Amalie, is on St. Thomas, the second largest island. The third major island is St. John.

The islands are covered mostly with steep hills. St. Croix's northern hills, however, give way in the south to a plain that varies from rolling to level. The lofty hills and deep valleys of Virgin Islands National Park cover nearly three fourths of St. John. Native tropical forests are found only on St. Thomas. Only 5 percent of the land on the islands is forested, though

Charlotte Amalie harbor on St. Thomas island is a free port and thus a popular destination for cruise ships in the Caribbean.

the government has replanted parts of St. Croix and St. Thomas. All of the islands are surrounded by coral reefs.

Tourism is a leading industry. Visitors are attracted by the pleasant tropical climate, beautiful scenery, beaches, and sport fishing. Close proximity to the United States mainland and free-port status also attract tourists. In addition to the traditional rum-distilling industry, chemicals, pharmaceuticals, and clothing are manufactured on a small scale, and watches are assembled. In the 1980s the petroleum-refining and alumina industries on St. Croix were expanded. Exports from the islands are shipped mainly to the United States, Puerto Rico, and the British Virgin Islands. Ferries and seaplanes travel between the islands and to Puerto Rico. There are deepwater ports at Charlotte Amalie and Frederiksted on St. Croix.

Since the 1970s the island's agriculture industry has expanded from its reliance on sugarcane to cultivation of a variety of crops. Citrus fruits, tamarinds, mangoes, bananas, and vegetables are the primary nonexport food crops. Cattle, goats, sheep, and pigs are the principal livestock.

Nearly 80 percent of the people on the islands are descended from black Africans. About 15 percent of the people are descended from white Europeans. There is a significant Hispanic heritage in both groups and in the remainder of the population. Residents are United States citizens and elect their own governor, local legislature, and a nonvoting representative to the United States Congress. The islanders do not vote in United States national elections.

Christopher Columbus landed on St. Croix in 1493. The islands were controlled by a series of countries until becoming a colony of Denmark in 1754. The Danes planted sugarcane, first using convicted criminals and then African slaves for labor. The sugar industry declined in the early 1800s, and slave revolts shook the economy. In 1848 slavery was abolished. The United States bought the territory from Denmark in 1917. Population (1986 estimate), 114,000.

VIRUS. The composition of a virus is relatively simple, and its size is extremely small. It cannot even properly be called an organism because it is unable to carry on life processes outside a living cell of an animal, plant, or bacteria. Yet its method of entering and "enslaving" a living cell is so ingenious that the virus has been humankind's deadly enemy for thousands of years and continues to resist the most advanced efforts of modern science to eliminate it.

Millions of people throughout the world suffer each year from virus-produced diseases such as polio, measles, chicken pox, mumps, acquired immune deficiency syndrome (AIDS), and the common cold. Viruses also produce such illnesses as foot-and-mouth disease in cattle, distemper in dogs, panleukopenia in cats, hog cholera, and parrot fever. The viruses that infect bacteria are called bacteriophages. (*See also* Disease, Human; Bacteria.)

Structure and Composition

Viruses are exceedingly small; they range in size from about 0.02 to 0.25 micron in diameter (1 micron = 0.000039 inch). By contrast, the smallest bacteria are about 0.4 micron in size. As observed with an electron microscope, some viruses are rod-shaped, others are roughly spherical, and still others have complex shapes consisting of a multisided "head" and a cylindrical "tail." A virus consists of a core of nucleic acid surrounded by a protein coat called a capsid; some viruses also have an outer envelope composed of fatty materials and proteins. The nucleic-acid core is the essential part of the virus—it carries the virus's genes. The core consists of either deoxyribonucleic acid (DNA) or ribonucleic acid (RNA), substances that are essential to the transmission of hereditary information (*see* Genetics, "Genes and the Genetic Code"). The protein capsid protects the nucleic acid and may contain molecules that enable the virus to enter the host cell—that is, the living cell infected by the virus.

The multisided "head" and cylindrical "tail" of a bacteriophage are clearly visible when observed with an electron microscope.

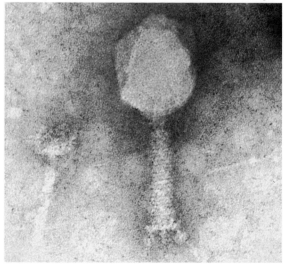

Cycle and Patterns of Infection

Outside of a living cell, a virus is a dormant particle. It exhibits none of the characteristics generally associated with life—namely, reproduction and metabolic processes such as growth and assimilation of food (*see* Metabolism). Unlike bacteria and other microorganisms, viruses cannot live in body fluids. Thus, great numbers of viruses may be present in a body and yet not produce a disease because they have not invaded the body's cells. Once inside a host cell, however, the virus becomes an active entity capable of taking over the infected cell's metabolic machinery. The cellular metabolism becomes so altered that it works solely for the virus, helping to produce thousands of new viruses.

The virus's developmental cycle begins when it succeeds in introducing its nucleic acid, and in some cases its protein coat, into a host cell. Bacterial viruses attach to the surface of the bacterium and then penetrate the rigid cell wall, transmitting the viral nucleic acid into the host. Animal viruses enter host cells by a process called endocytosis. Plant viruses enter through wounds in the cell's outer coverings—through abrasions made by wind, for example, or through punctures made by insects.

Once inside the host cell, the virus's genes usually direct the cell's production of new viral protein and nucleic acid. These components are then assembled into new, complete, infective virus particles called virions, which are then discharged from the host cell to infect other cells.

Among bacterial viruses, or bacteriophages, the new virions are released by bursting the host cell—a process called lysing, which kills the cell. Sometimes, however, bacteriophages form a stable association with the host cell. The virus's genes are incorporated into the host cell's genes, replicate as the cell's genes replicate, and when the cell divides, the viral genes are passed on to the two new cells. (For details of cell division, *see* Cell.)

In such cases no progeny virions are produced, and the infecting virus seems to disappear. Its genes, however, are being passed on to each new generation of cells that stem from the original host cell. These cells remain healthy and continue to grow unless, as happens occasionally, something triggers the latent viral genes to become active. When this happens, the normal cycle of viral infection results: the viral genes direct viral replication, the host cell bursts, and the new virions are released. This pattern of infection is called lysogeny.

Closely related to lysogeny is the process known as transduction, whereby a virus carries bacterial genes from one host to another. This occurs when genes from the original host become incorporated into a virion that subsequently infects another bacterium.

Viral infections of plant and animal cells resemble those of bacterial cells in many ways. The release of new virions from plant and animal cells does not, however, always involve the bursting of the host cell

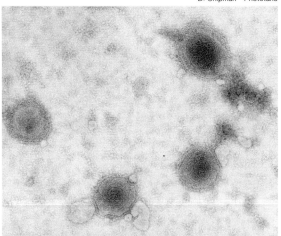

An electron micrograph of stained viruses reveals the folded protein coats surrounding the particles' nucleic-acid cores. The viruses also have outer layers of proteins and carbohydrates.

as it does in bacteria. Particularly among animal viruses, the new virions may be released by budding off from the cell membrane, a process that does not necessarily kill the host cell.

In general, a viral infection produces one of four effects in a plant or animal cell: inapparent effect, in which the virus remains dormant in the host cell; cytopathic effect, in which the cell dies; hyperplastic effect, in which the cell is stimulated to divide before its death; and cell transformation, in which the cell is stimulated to divide, take on abnormal growth patterns, and become cancerous (see Cancer).

Viral infections in animals can be localized or can spread to various parts of the body. Some animal viruses produce latent infections: the virus remains dormant much of the time, but becomes active periodically. This is the case with the herpes simplex viruses that cause cold sores.

Natural Defenses, Immunization, and Treatment

Animals have a number of natural defenses that may be triggered by a viral infection. Fever is a general response; many viruses are inactivated at temperatures just slightly above the host's normal body temperature. Another general response of infected animal cells is the secretion of a protein called interferon. Interferon inhibits the reproduction of viruses in noninfected cells. (See also Genetic Engineering, "Protein and Peptide Production.")

Fever and interferon production are general responses to infection by any virus. In addition, humans and other vertebrates can mount an immunological attack against a specific virus. The immune system produces antibodies and sensitized cells that are tailor-made to neutralize the infecting virus. These immune defenders circulate through the body long after the virus has been neutralized, thereby providing long-term protection against reinfection by that virus (see Immune System).

Such long-term immunity is the basis for active immunization against viral diseases. A weakened or inactivated strain of an infectious virus is introduced into the body. This virus does not provoke an active disease state, but it does stimulate the production of immune cells and antibodies, which then protect against subsequent infection by the virulent form of the virus. Active immunizations are now routine for such viral diseases as measles, mumps, poliomyelitis, and rubella. In contrast, passive immunization is the injection of antibodies from the serum of an individual who has already been exposed to the virus. Passive immunization is used to give short-term protection to individuals who have been exposed to such viral diseases as measles and hepatitis. It is useful only if provided soon after exposure, before the virus has become widely disseminated in the body (see Vaccines).

The treatment of an established viral infection usually is restricted to relieving specific symptoms. There are few drugs that can be used to combat an infecting virus directly. The reason for this is that viruses use the machinery of living cells for reproduction. Consequently, drugs that inhibit viral development also inhibit the functions of the host cell. Nonetheless, a small number of antiviral drugs are available for specific infections.

The most successful controls over viral diseases are epidemiological. For example, large-scale active immunization programs can break the chain of transmission of a viral disease. Worldwide immunization is credited with the eradication of smallpox, once one of the most feared viral diseases. Because many viruses are carried from host to host by insects or contaminated food, insect control and hygienic food handling can help eliminate a virus from specific populations.

History of Virus Research

Historic descriptions of viral diseases date back as far as the 10th century BC. The concept of the virus,

An HIV, or AIDS, virus penetrates a white blood cell. Once inside its host cell, the virus becomes an active entity capable of directing the cell to produce new viruses.

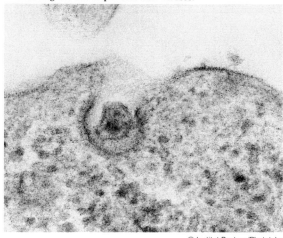

however, was not established until the last decade of the 19th century, when several researchers obtained evidence that agents far smaller than bacteria were capable of causing infectious diseases. The existence of viruses was proved when bacteriophages were discovered by independent researchers in 1915 and 1917. The question of whether viruses are actually microorganisms (similar to very tiny bacteria) was resolved in 1935, when the virus responsible for causing mosaic disease in tobacco was isolated and crystallized; the fact that it could be crystallized proved that the virus was not a cellular organism.

Bacteriophages are a valuable research tool for molecular biologists. Studies of bacteriophages have helped to illuminate such basic biological processes as genetic recombination, nucleic-acid replication, and protein synthesis.

VISTULA RIVER. Winding from the Carpathian Mountains of southern Poland to form a giant letter S, the Vistula River flows 664 miles (1,069 kilometers) to its delta near Gdańsk on the Baltic Sea. With its branches, including the Bug, Wieprz, San, Nida, Pilica, Brda, and Wierzyca rivers, the Vistula drains a basin of 75,022 square miles (194,306 square kilometers).

The river flows eastward and then northward. It first travels through rich mining and industrial areas. Near the ancient city of Kraków it passes great salt mines. In the central section it threads through agricultural country. Beyond the city of Warsaw the Vistula enters vast timber forests before meeting more fertile farming areas at the delta.

Despite dredging and diking efforts in the delta region, accumulations of silt and shifting sandbars continue to plague navigation. Floods are frequent and dangerous. Thus the Vistula is not a major traffic artery. Canals connect the Vistula with the Oder River to the west and, via the Bug, a major tributary, with the Pripyat River to the east, providing a link with the vast inland waterway system of the Soviet Union.

VITAMINS. All living things, plant or animal, need vitamins for health, growth, and reproduction. Yet vitamins are not a source of calories and do not contribute significantly to body mass. The body uses vitamins as tools in processes that regulate chemical processes in the body and use basic food elements—carbohydrates, fats, and proteins—to form bones and tissues and to produce energy.

Vitamins can be used over and over, and only tiny amounts are needed to replace those that are lost. Nevertheless, vitamins are essential in the diet be-

This article was contributed by Manisha Harisingh Maskay, Ph.D., R.D., Health Education Coordinator and Clinical Nutritionist, University of Chicago.

cause the body does not produce enough of them or, in many cases, does not produce them at all.

Thirteen different vitamins have been identified: A, eight B-complex vitamins, C, D, E, and K. Some substances, such as carnitine and choline, behave like vitamins but are made in adequate amounts in the human body.

Vitamins were originally placed in categories based on their function in the body and were given letter names. Later, as their chemical structures were revealed, they were also given chemical names. Today, both naming conventions are used.

Daily Requirements

With a few exceptions, the body is unable to make vitamins; they must be supplied in the daily diet or through supplements. One exception is vitamin D, which can be produced in the skin when the skin is exposed to sunlight. Another vitamin, vitamin K, is not made by the human body but is formed by microorganisms that normally flourish in the intestinal tract. In some cases, however, these vitamins are not made in large enough quantities to fill the body's needs.

The body's vitamin requirements are expressed in terms of recommended dietary allowances, or RDA. These allowances are the amount of essential nutrients that, if acquired daily, are considered to be sufficient to meet the known nutritional needs of most healthy persons. In the United States, the RDA values are established by the Food and Nutrition Board of the National Research Council. In addition, two agencies of the United Nations—the Food and Agriculture Organization and the World Health Organization—have collaborated with several countries to develop RDA for different population groups.

In the past, the strength of a vitamin, or the amount of the vitamin necessary to produce a certain effect in the body, was often expressed in terms of international units, abbreviated IU. The unit corresponds to a weight of the purified vitamin, and its value differs from one vitamin to another. Today, the strength of a vitamin is generally expressed directly in metric weights—micrograms or milligrams.

How Vitamins Work

In the body, proteins, carbohydrates, and fats combine with other substances to yield energy and build bones and tissue. These chemical reactions are catalyzed, or accelerated, by specific vitamins and take place in specific parts of the body.

The vitamins needed by humans are divided into two categories: water-soluble vitamins (the B vitamins and vitamin C) and fat-soluble vitamins (A, D, E, and K). The water-soluble vitamins are absorbed by the intestine and carried by the circulatory system to the specific tissues where they will be put into use. The B vitamins act as coenzymes, compounds that unite with a protein component called an apoenzyme to form an active enzyme (*see* Enzymes). The enzyme then acts as a catalyst in the chemical reactions that

VITAMINS

In a balanced diet there are four basic food groups, and each has its own nutritional value: fruits and vegetables, top left; potatoes, breads, and other starches, top right; dairy products, bottom right; and meats and nuts, bottom left.

Runk/Schoenberger—Grant Heilman

transfer energy from the basic food elements to the body. It is not known whether vitamin C acts as a coenzyme. (*See also* Digestive System; Metabolism.)

When a person takes in more water-soluble vitamins than are needed, small amounts are stored in body tissue, but most of the excess is excreted in urine. Because water-soluble vitamins are not stored in the body in appreciable amounts, a daily supply is essential to prevent depletion.

Fat-soluble vitamins seem to have highly specialized functions. The intestine absorbs fat-soluble vitamins, and the lymph system carries these vitamins to the different parts of the body. Fat-soluble vitamins are involved in maintaining the structure of cell membranes. It is also believed that fat-soluble vitamins are responsible for the synthesis of certain enzymes.

The body can store larger amounts of fat-soluble vitamins than of water-soluble vitamins. The liver provides the chief storage tissue for vitamins A and D, while vitamin E is stored in body fat and to a lesser extent in reproductive organs. Relatively little vitamin K is stored. Excessive intake of fat-soluble vitamins, particularly vitamins A and D, can lead to toxic levels in the body.

Many vitamins work together to regulate several processes within the body. A lack of vitamins or a diet that does not provide adequate amounts of certain vitamins can upset the body's internal balance or block one or more metabolic reactions.

Sources of Vitamins

Vitamins, though they are available from a variety of sources, are unevenly distributed in natural sources. For example, some vitamins, such as vitamins A and D, are produced only by animals, whereas other vitamins are found only in plants. (For natural sources of vitamins, *see* table.) All vitamins can be synthesized, or produced commercially, from foods and other sources, and there is no evidence that natural vitamins are superior to those that are synthetically derived.

Some foods are fortified with vitamins—that is, vitamins that are not normally present in the food, or that have been removed during processing, are added to the food before it is sold. Milk, for example, is fortified with vitamin D, and vitamins that have been lost from flour during processing are often replaced.

Although vitamin supplementation is generally unnecessary for otherwise well-nourished persons, there are times when the body's vitamin requirements may increase and when vitamin supplementation may be essential. Those likely to require such supplements include pregnant women, the elderly, and the chronically ill. Excessive intakes of supplemental vitamins should be avoided, however, because of the possibility of toxicity. (*See also* Food and Nutrition.)

Kinds of Vitamins

Vitamin A, also called retinol, is a fat-soluble vitamin that is readily destroyed upon exposure to heat, light, or air. The vitamin has a direct role in vision and is a component of a pigment present in the retina of the eye. It is essential for the proper functioning of most body organs and also affects the functioning of the immune system.

Vitamin A deficiency results in various disorders that most commonly involve the eye and the epithelial tissues—the skin and the mucous membranes lining the internal body surfaces. An early symptom of vitamin A deficiency is the development of night blindness, and continued deficiency eventually results in loss of sight. If deficiency is prolonged, the

Squibb Corporation, Princeton, N.J.; photo, Joseph Salenetri

skin may become dry and rough. Vitamin A deficiency may also result in defective bone and teeth formation.

Excessive intake of vitamin A causes a toxic condition. The symptoms may include nausea, coarsening and loss of hair, drying and scaling of the skin, bone pain, fatigue, and drowsiness. There may also be blurred vision and headache in adults, and growth failure, enlargement of the liver, and nervous irritability in children.

Vitamin B complex consists of several vitamins that are grouped together because of the loose similarities in their properties, distribution in natural sources, and physiological functions. All the B vitamins are soluble in water. Most of the B vitamins have been recognized as coenzymes, and they all appear to be essential in facilitating the metabolic processes of all forms of animal life. The complex includes B_1 (thiamine), B_2 (riboflavin), niacin (nicotinic acid), B_6 (a group of related pyridines), B_{12} (cyanocobalamin), folic acid, pantothenic acid, and biotin.

Vitamin B_1, or thiamine, helps the body convert carbohydrates into energy and helps in the metabolism of proteins and fats. Vitamin B_1 deficiency affects the functioning of gastrointestinal, cardiovascular, and peripheral nervous systems. Beriberi and Wernicke-Korsakoff syndrome (often seen in alcoholics) are the primary diseases related to thiamine deficiency. General symptoms of beriberi include loss of appetite and overall lassitude, digestive irregularities, and a feeling of numbness and weakness in the limbs and extremities.

Vitamin B_2, or riboflavin, is required to complete several reactions in the energy cycle. Reddening of the lips with cracks at the corners of the mouth, inflammation of the tongue, and a greasy, scaly in-

A worker checks a freshly coated batch of vitamin tablets at a vitamin manufacturing facility. The tablets are covered with an inert film that makes them easier to swallow.

flammation of the skin are common symptoms. In children, poor growth is likely.

Niacin, or nicotinic acid, helps the metabolism of carbohydrates. Prolonged deprivation leads to pellagra, a disease characterized by skin lesions, gastrointestinal disturbance, and nervous symptoms.

A form of Vitamin B_6 is a coenzyme for several enzyme systems involved in the metabolism of proteins, carbohydrates, and fats. No human disease has been found to be caused by a deficiency of this vitamin. Chronic use of large doses of vitamin B_6 can create dependency and cause complications in the peripheral nervous system.

Vitamin B_{12}, or cyanocobalamin, is a complex crystalline compound that functions in all cells, but especially in those of the gastrointestinal tract, the nervous system, and the bone marrow. It is known to aid in the development of red blood cells in higher animals. Deficiency most commonly results in pernicious anemia (see Blood, "Some Blood Disorders").

Folic acid is necessary for the synthesis of nucleic acids and the formation of red blood cells. Folic-acid deficiency most commonly causes folic-acid-deficiency anemia. Symptoms include gastrointestinal problems, such as sore tongue, cracks at the corners of the mouth, diarrhea, and ulceration of the stomach and intestines. Large doses of folic acid can cause convulsions and other nervous-system problems.

Pantothenic acid promotes a large number of metabolic reactions essential for the growth and well-being of animals. Deficiency in experimental animals leads to growth failure, skin lesions, and graying of the hair. A dietary deficiency severe enough to lead to clear-cut disease has not been described in humans.

Biotin plays a role in metabolic processes that lead to the formation of fats and the utilization of carbon dioxide. Biotin deficiency results in anorexia, nausea, vomiting, inflammation of the tongue, pallor, depression, and dermatitis.

Severe illness can result from vitamin deficiencies. The effects of malnutrition are evident in a rat fed a diet deficient in biotin (top left) and in a chick whose diet lacks pantothenic acid (bottom left). After several weeks on diets with adequate amounts of these vitamins, the health of both animals is markedly improved (top right and bottom right).

Courtesy of The Upjohn Company, Kalamazoo, Michigan

383

U.S. RECOMMENDED DIETARY ALLOWANCE (RDA) FOR VITAMINS

	Unit of Measurement	Children Under Four Years of Age	Adults and Children Older than 4	Major Dietary Sources
vitamin A (retinol)	IU	2,500	5,000	fish and fish-liver oils, liver, butter
vitamin B₁ (thiamine)	mg	0.7	1.5	cereal grains, pork, nuts
vitamin B₂ (riboflavin)	mg	0.8	1.7	milk, eggs, kidney, liver
niacin (nicotinic acid)	mg	9	20	liver, kidney
vitamin B₆	mg	0.7	2	cereal grains, liver, fish
vitamin B₁₂ (cyanocobalamin)	mcg	3	6	eggs, meat, milk
folic acid	mg	0.2	0.4	liver, green leafy vegetables, wheat bran and germ
pantothenic acid	mg	5	10	liver, kidney, eggs
biotin	mg	0.15	0.3	beef liver, eggs, yeast
vitamin C	mg	40	60	citrus fruits, green peppers, broccoli, cantaloupe
vitamin D	IU	400	400	fish-liver oils, eggs, milk enriched with vitamin D
vitamin E	IU	10	30	vegetable oils, margarine, cereal grains
vitamin K	*	*	*	green leafy vegetables, vegetable oils

IU = international unit; mg = milligram; mcg = microgram
*no data available
Source for RDA data: U.S. Department of Health, Education, and Welfare

Vitamin C, or ascorbic acid, is water-soluble and easily destroyed. It is essential in wound healing and in a variety of metabolic functions, including the formation of collagen, a protein important in the formation of healthy skin, tendons, bones, and supportive tissues. Deficiency results in defective collagen formation and is marked by joint pains, irritability, growth retardation, anemia, shortness of breath, and increased susceptibility to infection. Scurvy is the classic disease related to deficiency. Symptoms peculiar to infantile scurvy include swelling of the lower extremities, pain upon flexing them, and lesions of the growing bones. Excessive ascorbic-acid intake can cause kidney stones, gastrointestinal disturbances, and red-blood-cell destruction.

Vitamin D is a fat-soluble compound essential for calcium metabolism in animals and therefore important for normal mineralization of bone and cartilage. The skin forms vitamin D when exposed to sunlight, but in some circumstances sunlight may lack sufficient amounts of ultraviolet rays to bring about adequate production of the vitamin.

Deficiencies cause many biochemical and physiological imbalances. If uncorrected, faulty mineralization of bones and teeth causes rickets in growing children and osteomalacia (progressive loss of calcium and phosphorus from the bones) in adults. Common early symptoms of rickets include restlessness, profuse sweating, lack of muscle tone in the limbs and abdomen, and delay in learning to sit, crawl, and walk. Rickets may produce such conditions as bowlegs and knock-knees. Deficiency may also cause osteoporosis, a bone condition characterized by an increased ten-

dency of the bones to fracture. Large doses of vitamin D are toxic, and symptoms include weakness, loss of appetite, nausea, vomiting, diarrhea, excessive thirst, and weight loss.

Vitamin E is a fat-soluble compound. The metabolic roles of this vitamin are poorly understood. Its primary role appears to be as an inhibitor of oxidation processes in body tissues. Deficiency is rare but may impair neuromuscular function. Although serious toxicity has not been attributed to large doses of vitamin E, adverse effects have been reported.

Vitamin K is fat-soluble and essential for the synthesis of certain proteins necessary for the clotting of blood. Deficiency, though relatively uncommon, results in impaired clotting of the blood and internal bleeding. (*See also* Disease, "Metabolic and Deficiency Diseases"; Malnutrition.)

Vitamin-like substances include a number of compounds that resemble vitamins in their activity but are normally synthesized in the human body in adequate amounts. They are often classified with the B vitamins because of similarities in function and distribution in foods. Their status as essential nutrients remains uncertain. Choline is found in all living cells and plays a role in nerve function and various metabolic processes. Myoinositol is a water-soluble compound; its significance in human nutrition is not established. Para-aminobenzoic acid is an integral part of folic acid but its role in human nutrition has not been documented. Carnitine has an essential role in the transport of fatty substances. Lipoic acid seems to have a coenzyme function similar to that of thiamine; however, because it is synthesized in the human liver and kidneys, it is not considered a vitamin. Bioflavinoids are a group of substances that affect the permeability of capillaries but do not normally have to be added to human diets.

History

The value of certain foods in maintaining health was recognized long before the first vitamins were actually identified. In the 18th century, for example, it had been demonstrated that the addition of citrus fruits to the diet would prevent the development of scurvy. In the 19th century it was shown that substituting unpolished for polished rice in a rice-based diet would prevent the development of beriberi.

In 1906 the British biochemist Frederick Hopkins demonstrated that foods contained necessary "accessory factors" in addition to proteins, carbohydrates, fats, minerals, and water. In 1911 the Polish chemist Casimir Funk discovered that the anti-beriberi substance in unpolished rice was an amine (a type of nitrogen-containing compound), so Funk proposed that it be named vitamine—for "vital amine." This term soon came to be applied to the accessory factors in general. It was later discovered that many vitamins do not contain amines at all. Because of its widespread use, Funk's term continued to be applied, but the final letter e was dropped.

In 1912 Hopkins and Funk advanced the vitamin hypothesis of deficiency, a theory that postulates that the absence of sufficient amounts of a particular vitamin in a system may lead to certain diseases. During the early 1900s, through experiments in which animals were deprived of certain types of foods, scientists succeeded in isolating and identifying the various vitamins recognized today. (*See also* Health.)

VIVALDI, Antonio (1678–1741). The most influential and innovative Italian composer of his time, Antonio Vivaldi was an accomplished violinist who wrote music for operas, solo instruments, and small ensembles. His finest work was thought to be his concerti in which virtuoso solo passages alternate with passages for the whole orchestra. He orchestrated in new, unique ways and prepared the way for the late baroque concerto.

Antonio Lucio Vivaldi was born on March 4, 1678, in Venice, Italy. When he was born he looked so frail that the midwife baptized him immediately. He grew to love the violin and played along with his father at Saint Mark's Basilica. Young Vivaldi studied for the priesthood and was ordained in 1703. The same year he was given a teaching position at the Pio Ospedale della Pietà, where he gave music lessons to those among the resident orphan girls who showed musical aptitude. Their Sunday concerts, for which Vivaldi composed many orchestral and choral works, gained renown, until no visit to Venice was considered complete without hearing a performance.

Vivaldi taught there until 1709, when for financial reasons the school voted not to renew his post. Two years later he was reappointed, and he remained as a teacher until 1716, when he was appointed to the higher position of maestro. In his later years Vivaldi traveled widely, living for extended periods in Vienna and Mantua, where he was the court composer for Prince Philipp. He probably also performed and composed in Prague, Dresden, and Amsterdam. His popularity declined at the end of his life, and he died in Vienna on July 28, 1741.

Early in his life Vivaldi's operas were performed throughout Italy and in Vienna. More than 750 works are known to exist, and researchers have long struggled with the task of identifying and cataloguing them. Vivaldi's original musical style had wide influence on later composers, including Johann Sebastian Bach, who transcribed some of Vivaldi's concertos for keyboard. His operas are seldom heard now, but his orchestral and chamber music are performed frequently, as is his popular sacred 'Gloria'.

VLADIVOSTOK, U.S.S.R. A city whose name means "ruler of the east," Vladivostok plays a major role as a port and naval base in the Soviet Far East. It is situated on the western side of a peninsula that separates Amur and Ussuri bays on the Sea of Japan.

The city is the chief educational and cultural center of the Soviet Far East. It is home to the Far Eastern Scientific Center, the Far Eastern State University, and several other foundations of higher education, including medical, art-education, polytechnic, trade, and marine-engineering institutions. Vladivostok has amateur and professional theaters as well as a Philharmonic society and a symphony orchestra. It also has a number of libraries and museums of local history and of the history of the Pacific fleet.

A key port and distribution center for the Soviet Union's foreign trade, Vladivostok is also the Soviet Union's naval, submarine, and air base for the Pacific Ocean area. Merchant shipping, both passenger and cargo, is a leading function. Daily air service connects the city with Moscow, some 6,000 miles (9,660 kilometers) to the west. The railroad from Leningrad to Vladivostok is the world's longest and includes the Trans-Siberian Railroad.

Industry is diversified and includes ship repair yards, railway workshops, a mining-equipment plant, light industry, and food processing. Principal exports are petroleum, coal, and grain. Petroleum products and fish are the main imports. The port is also a receiving point for processed fish arriving from other Far Eastern ports and intended for inland distribution. One of the Soviet Union's two Antarctic whaling fleets is based here.

Vladivostok was founded in 1860 as a military outpost. In 1872 the main Russian naval base on the Pacific was transferred here, and in 1880 it was given city status. Population (1986 estimate), 608,000.

Guillaume de Machaut, at right, found patrons in the royalty and clergy of his day. As depicted in a miniature from 'Oeuvres de Guillaume de Machaut' (about 1370–80), they lavished praise upon him as one of the best of 14th-century French composers in the Ars Nova style of the period.

Courtesy, Bibliotheque Nationale, Paris

VOCAL MUSIC. A term that refers to the wide variety of music composed for the voice, vocal music can be written for one or more voices alone or scored for the human voice and one or more instruments. It can be monophonic (a single line of melody) or polyphonic (two or more melodic lines). It can be modest and personal in its emotional expression, as are many sacred works and art songs, or lavish and extroverted, as in operas and musical comedies.

Plainsong

Among the earliest forms of vocal music—and one that had a deep influence on later traditions—is plainsong, also called Gregorian chant. This form of monody, which was written for use in the rites of the Roman Catholic church, is melodically simple and austere. It was taken to France from Rome between about AD 750 and 850 and was most highly developed by Parisian masters from about 1000 to 1150.

Especially significant during this period of the development of plainsong were the ways in which different types of liturgical poetry, such as hymns and sequences, were organized into musical settings with regular stanzas and rhymes—features widely employed by later composers of both sacred and secular music. Although plainsong continues to be sung

This article was contributed by George Gelles, Executive Director, Philharmonia Baroque Orchestra, San Francisco, Calif.; Consulting Editor, 'Britannica Book of Music'; and contributor to 'New Grove Dictionary of Music and Musicians'.

today, other types of chant that also developed have become extinct. These include Gallician, Mozarabic, Ambrosian, and Coptic chant.

Early Solo Song

Among the earliest types of secular music in Western Europe were the monodic songs composed and performed by wandering minstrels called troubadours in southern France (from the late 11th to the early 13th century), trouvères in northern France (from the mid-12th through the 13th century), and minnesingers in Germany (from the mid-12th to the late 15th century). Instrumentalists and poets from all classes of society, these musicians performed primarily for the nobility until the 13th century, when patronage shifted to the middle class and the clergy. Most often their songs concerned courtly love and chivalry, though songs also addressed certain occasions and political events.

Some monophonic songs resembled plainsong, with their long-spun flowing melodies. Others used major scales and short symmetrical phrases. Dancelike songs were performed in stricter rhythm than were songs that had many embellishments. Although instrumental accompaniments were not called for in the original manuscripts, they are often appropriate and probably were added in an improvisatory way.

Songs of this sort spread throughout Europe—to the courts of England, Spain, and Italy. During the 14th century the form declined because of the loss of aristocratic patronage, because of a newfound interest in polyphonic (many-voiced) compositions, and because of the new domination in art of theoretical rules over free instinct.

Polyphonic songs first gained wide popularity in French chansons, or songs. Chansons usually were written for three voices and most often contained two principal sections. These songs flourished in the 14th and 15th centuries, and leading composers included Guillaume de Machaut, Guillaume Dufay, and Jean d'Okeghem. These composers were most active in the courts of France and Burgundy, though they traveled to Spain and Italy as well. Their travels inspired the invention of local forms of song, among them the madrigal in Italy, the romance in Spain, and the carol in England. While instruments undoubtedly accompanied these songs, there is no certain knowledge of how instruments and voices were combined.

By the late 16th century there was a widespread change in attitude among composers and performers. No longer was it felt appropriate for a vocal composition to be performed by any possible combination of voices and instruments, which often destroyed the sense of the text. This concern led to the development of solo songs that presented their texts with uncluttered clarity. The major types of this new genre were the English lute songs, the finest composer of which was John Dowland, and Italian monody. In these types of song, texts often were declaimed in speechlike recitation, and significant words were emphasized with harmonic colorations, melodic elaboration, and rhythmic alterations.

Art Songs

From the 17th century to the present, songs have reflected an awareness of the special relationship between music and literature. The greatest composers of song seem to mirror the essence of the poetry they set to music. Often this means that in addition to matching the verse's character, they are able through their musical intuitions to discover new meaning in the words. In part because of their poetic qualities and the skills with which they blend words and music, settings for solo voice and instrumental accompaniment, as they developed from the 17th through the 20th century, are known as art songs.

Settings often have been made not simply of single poems but of entire groups of poems. Such song cycles have been written by many of the greatest composers, including Ludwig van Beethoven ('An die ferne Geliebte', 1815–16), Franz Schubert ('Die Winterreise', 1827), and Robert Schumann ('Frauenliebe und Leben', 1840).

From the 17th through the 18th century, solo songs were most often accompanied by simple figurations for keyboard—harpsichord, fortepiano, or piano. Earlier examples of songs of this sort had accompaniments that offered little of their own in the way of musical substance or emotional interest. The keyboard simply provided a harmonic framework in which the song was heard. Later songs, however, made imaginative and extensive use of the keyboard. Classical and Romantic composers embellished and enhanced the meaning of their texts with inventive keyboard parts. The overall sense of their songs could be intensified, and individual words could be highlighted, by imaginative accompaniments. Often the vocal part was set in a larger musical framework that offered its own commentary on the text. Schubert, perhaps, was the most accomplished of the great song composers in enhancing the emotional meaning of his songs with deft and sensitive accompaniments—most often for keyboard alone but sometimes for keyboard and such wind instruments as horn ('Auf dem Strom', 1828) or clarinet ('Der Hirt auf dem Felsen', 1828).

National schools of solo songs developed—each with its particular melodic and rhythmic profile. German solo songs, or lieder, were first written by the 17th-century composer Adam Krieger and the 18th-century composer George Frideric Handel. Later in the 18th century, Wolfgang Amadeus Mozart and Joseph Haydn wrote songs, though neither composer can be said to have specialized in the genre. The flowering of German lieder is represented by Schubert and Schumann, who along with Johannes Brahms ('Four Serious Songs', 1896) and Hugo Wolf ('Songs to Poems by Eduard Mörike', 1888; 'Spanish Songbook', 1889–90) created a repertoire that many feel has never been surpassed. In the 20th century major Austrian song composers include Arnold Schoenberg and his disciple Alban Berg, both of whom wrote songs with lush and lavish orchestral accompaniments.

The French tradition was slower to develop. In the 17th and 18th centuries, songs were written on both serious and frivolous topics, but they lacked the depth of feeling of their German or English counterparts. Despite the presence in France of such supremely gifted opera composers as Jean-Baptiste Lully ('Atys', 1676; 'Armide', 1686) and Jean-Philippe Rameau ('Les Indes galantes', 1735; 'Platée', 1745), French song came into its own only in the 19th century. It was championed by, among other composers, Hector Berlioz, whose cycle for soprano and orchestra, 'Les Nuits d'eté' (1843–56), is considered a masterpiece of poetic evocation. Equally significant song composers were Gabriel Fauré ('La Bonne chanson', 1891–92) and Henri Duparc ('Chanson triste', 1868; 'L'Invitation au voyage', 1870–71). Composers who continued this tradition in the 20th century include Maurice Ravel ('Histoires naturelles', 1906), Darius Milhaud ('Le Voyage d'été', 1946) and Francis Poulenc ('The Bestiary', 1918–19).

In England few song composers were as accomplished as John Dowland, master of lute songs. At the end of the 17th century, Henry Purcell wrote brilliantly for voice—most often in operas, less often in solo songs. After Purcell England did not produce a song composer of comparable quality until the 20th century, when Benjamin Britten wrote not only masterful operas ('Peter Grimes', 1945; 'Billy Budd', 1951) but equally fine song cycles ('Seven Sonnets of Michelangelo', 1940; 'Winter Words', 1953; 'Les Illuminations', 1939).

The Mormon Tabernacle Choir of Salt Lake City, Utah, is one of the most noted choral groups in the United States. Widely known through radio broadcasts and phonograph records, it is highly regarded for its presentations of all types of religious works, from hymns and carols to oratorios.

Tony Ray Jones—Magnum

The art song in the United States first flourished in the 20th century. Although such 19th-century composers as George Whitefield Chadwick and Edward MacDowell wrote many songs, they were heavily influenced by a conservative strain of German Romanticism. Charles Ives, with his bold musical language and highly personal poetic vision, can be considered the first major American song composer, and other distinguished song composers include Aaron Copland, Leonard Bernstein, and Ned Rorem.

Another national tradition was found in Russia. The leading song composers included Modest Musorgski, Peter Ilich Tchaikovsky, and Sergei Rachmaninoff. In Spain the primary composers included Enrique Granados, Manuel de Falla, and Joaquín Turina. Edvard Grieg, Jean Sibelius, and Carl Nielsen were the leading song composers in Scandinavia.

Choral Music

Broadly defined, choral music refers to music sung by a choir, which usually is a collection of men and women, the mixed choir, or of boys and men. There are also choirs of all-treble voices and of all-lower voices. Choirs can be modest in size. A chamber choir can contain between a dozen and two dozen voices, while a massive choir, such as that assembled for the Handel festivals in 19th-century England, can number in the thousands.

Mass. Choral music long has been associated with the church. Although choirs existed in Europe throughout the Middle Ages, their role was restricted to unison performances of plainsong. By the 15th century the mass was normally performed by a choir. Among the earliest mass settings is that by the 14th-century composer Guillaume de Machaut, which probably was conceived for performance by solo voices but is often performed chorally. Motets were also sung, but not as part of the ordinary mass text.

Renaissance composers often based their mass settings on tunes found outside the liturgy, as in Josquin's setting of the mass, 'L'Homme armé', which takes its title from the secular song that it employs. Secular tunes also were used by the Flemish composers Orlando di Lasso and Heinrich Isaac, though other composers, such as the Englishmen William Byrd and Thomas Tallis, avoided this procedure. Mass settings were also based on motets. The Italian Giovanni Pierluigi da Palestrina was a notable exponent. An instrumental element was added to the choral mass by Italian composers Giovanni Gabrieli and Claudio Monteverdi, both of whom on occasion used multiple choirs in antiphonal effects.

Among the many masses of the baroque period, none is grander than Johann Sebastian Bach's 'Mass in B Minor', which, unlike masses of the Renaissance, was never intended for performance during a liturgical service. Bach's mass has brilliant instrumental and choral effects and has five-, six-, and even eight-part choral writing.

Mozart, Haydn, and Beethoven all wrote significant masses. Mozart's 'Coronation Mass', Haydn's 'Mass in Time of War', and Beethoven's 'Missa Solemnis', are masterpieces of the genre. Later 19th-century composers of masses include Schubert, Anton Bruckner, and Carl Maria von Weber.

The requiem, or funeral, mass has also been set by various composers. Mozart's 'Requiem' (1791) was completed after his death by a pupil, Franz Xaver Süssmayr. Giuseppe Verdi's 'Requiem' (1873) honored his friend Alessandro Manzoni. Johannes Brahms set additional poetry from the Psalms in his 'German Requiem' (1868), and Benjamin Britten used the requiem text along with poetry by Wilfred Owen in his 'War Requiem' (1962).

Vespers and anthems. Second to the mass in liturgical importance was the service called vespers, which included psalms, hymns, antiphons, and the Magnificat. Renaissance composers who set parts of this liturgy include Josquin, Lasso, Gabrieli, and Heinrich Schütz. Bach's 'Magnificat' setting is one of the best-known baroque representatives of this category. Anthems were a specialty of English musicians—above all Tallis and Byrd—both of whom developed an animated and lucid style that enhanced the meaning of both music and words.

Cantata and oratorio. The cantata is another form of devotional music. Developed in northern Germany in the 17th century, it was given its greatest stature by Johann Sebastian Bach. In some 200 cantatas written for liturgical use throughout the church year, Bach explored a wide range of instrumental, solo vocal, and choral effects. He also used the chorus to great effect in his settings of the 'Passion According to Saint John' and the 'Passion According to Saint Matthew'.

Another major genre of choral music is the oratorio, which was developed early in the 17th century in Italy by Giacomo Carissimi and Antonio Vivaldi, among other composers. Later composers to refine the form include Handel (whose oratorio 'Messiah' is perhaps the best-known work of its kind), Haydn (whose oratorios 'The Creation' and 'The Seasons' are perhaps the finest examples of the genre from the late 18th and early 19th centuries), Felix Mendelssohn (whose setting of 'Elijah' has proved enduring), Berlioz ('The Childhood of Christ'), and, in the 20th century, Edward Elgar ('Dream of Gerontius'), Arthur Honegger ('King David'), and William Walton ('Belshazzar's Feast'). (*See also* Oratorio.)

Other works for chorus and orchestra were written to commemorate special occasions. Among these are the 'Madrigals of War and Love' by the early baroque master Claudio Monteverdi, the several odes for Queen Mary's birthday by Purcell, a cantata honoring the election of the Leipzig town councillors by Bach, and the 'Cantata on the Death of the Emperor Joseph II' by Beethoven.

Beethoven also wrote one of the best known of symphonic works employing a chorus, his Symphony No. 9 in D Minor, whose final movement presents a choral setting of the 'Ode to Joy' by the German poet Friedrich Schiller. Works written after, and inspired by, Beethoven's 'Ninth' include 'Faust' by Franz Liszt, 'The Damnation of Faust' by Berlioz, 'Rhapsody' by Brahms, and three of the symphonies by Gustav Mahler. (*See also* Music, Classical.)

Opera

The most comprehensive of art forms, opera unites music, drama, dancing, stagecraft, and the scenic arts. Above all, however, opera is a vocal art. It relies on one or usually many more singers, who are participants in the opera's drama. Often a chorus is also employed to participate in the work.

The genre was invented in the late 16th century by a group of Italian musicians, poets, scholars, and connoisseurs, who believed they were creating a work of art that mirrored the tragic drama of antiquity.

The Florentine Camerata, as this group was known, inspired several works, the most significant of which was 'Orfeo' by Claudio Monteverdi. Opera quickly became popular throughout Europe in the baroque era. In France major works were written by Lully and Rameau, in England by Purcell and Handel, and in Germany by Reinhard Keiser.

Classical masters of the genre include Mozart and Christoph Willibald Gluck, who restored a stylistic rigor and purity to the form. Romantic operas were written in Germany by Beethoven, Weber, and Richard Wagner, whose massive cycle 'Der Ring des Nibelungen' (1869–76) expanded the genre to its limits.

In the early part of the 19th century Italy produced Gioacchino Rossini, whose operas were admired for their musical sparkle and verve. In the middle and later years of the century the most admired operas were those of Giuseppi Verdi. Contemporaneous French composers included Georges Bizet and Charles Gounod. In Russia major operas were written late in the 19th century by Modest Musorgski and Tchaikovsky. Czech operas include those by Bedřich Smetana and, in the 20th century, Leoš Janáček. Other modern operas were written by Claude Debussy of France, Béla Bartók of Hungary, Alban Berg of Austria, and Hans Werner Henze of Germany.

Twentieth-century opera in England is best exemplified by the works of Britten. While operas have been written in the United States since the 19th century, the major works are those of George Gershwin ('Porgy and Bess', 1935) and Igor Stravinsky ('The Rake's Progress', 1951). (*See also* Opera.)

Operetta and Musical Comedy

Operetta in the 17th century referred simply to a short opera. In the 19th century, and especially in France, it was used to describe a play with an overture, songs, dances, and other musical interludes. Eventually it connoted a lighter form of opera, with an emphasis placed on frothy melodies, frank and simple harmonies, and uncomplicated stories. The works of Gilbert and Sullivan are prime examples. Designed for an expanding audience that was more interested in entertainment than in high and serious art, operettas nonetheless can be skillfully crafted and musically rewarding. (*See also* Operetta.)

An invention primarily of the 20th-century United States and of England, musical comedy is a popular form of musical theater modeled on the European operetta—with spoken dialogue, songs, dances, and other incidental interludes. The roots of the genre can be found in such American entertainments as 19th-century minstrel shows and vaudeville. (*See also* Musical Comedy.)

BIBLIOGRAPHY FOR VOCAL MUSIC

Miller, K.E. Vocal Music Education (Prentice, 1988).
Moe, Daniel. Basic Choral Concepts (Augsburg, 1972).
Monahan, B.J. The Art of Singing (Scarecrow, 1978).
Robinson, Ray, ed. Choral Music: Norton Historical Anthology (W.W. Norton, 1978).
Ulrich, Homer. A Survey of Choral Music (Harcourt, 1973).

A high school guidance counselor shows a student a variety of materials on vocational planning and post-high school training.

Cathy Melloan—EB Inc.

VOCATION

VOCATION. For many people their lifework, or vocation, is a matter of chance rather than choice. Yet there is great variety in the world of work. The task of selecting the right work from the thousands of available choices takes vocational planning. Individuals need to know many things about themselves and many things about the world of work. After they have this information in hand, the requirements of the work can be matched against the present and potential qualifications of each individual, and a choice can be made. This procedure requires time, effort, and study, but the rewards are great.

CHOICE VS. CHANCE

Anyone who works regularly has a vocation. Making a choice, however, offers the opportunity to have a vocation that is satisfying and rewarding. Decisions on education and training that are more appropriate to that vocation can also be made, saving time and money. The alternative is a job that is a matter of chance, depending only on what can be found easily. This happens when little or no thought is given to abilities and desires. Any job that comes along is accepted regardless of how well it fits needs or abilities. Leaving the choice to chance generally proves unsatisfactory and leads to boredom with work and difficulty in performing the job well.

Everyone concerned benefits when a worker chooses a vocation instead of accepting one by chance. It is best for the worker's happiness and contentment with the job. It is to the employer's advantage as well because the worker who has chosen a job is likely to be better at it, to be more efficient, and to stay at it

This article was contributed by Ray D. Ryan, Executive Director, the National Center for Research in Vocational Education, The Ohio State University, Columbus.

longer. If one works eight hours a day for a period of 50 weeks a year over 20 years, that person will have spent about 40,000 hours at work. The same amount of time will be spent by all who work, but it is far better spent if enjoyment and fulfillment can be found in the job.

Factors Involved in Choice

There are several factors to be considered when choosing a vocation. Each is essential to making a good vocational choice.

Aptitudes. What kinds of aptitudes does the individual have? What does one do well and enjoy doing? Is working with plants or animals, for example, or dealing with people a pleasant experience? Some people prefer to work alone. What seems easy for some may be difficult for others. The assessment of aptitudes helps to define what kind of vocation is appropriate. There are several different kinds of aptitude inventories available—tests that help to identify special talents and abilities. They can usually be taken under the direction of a school counselor or an employment service.

Interests. Another factor to consider is the individual's interests. What school subjects does one like? What hobbies does a person have? Are sports, politics, history, or science especially enjoyable? Is there an interest in collecting stamps, drawing, working with a computer, or cooking? These factors are clues to knowing the type of job to consider.

Education and training. A third factor is education and training. How much education does the individual have and how much additional studying is one willing or able to do? To be a physician, for example, requires not only a college degree but also a number of years of additional schooling and training in order to practice. To be a medical assistant, on the other hand, may require only two years of college or technical training. Many jobs require only a high school diploma.

Wages and salaries. Some jobs pay more than others. The more training a position requires, the more likely it is to pay a higher salary. Occupations that have a labor shortage tend to pay higher salaries than those for which there are many able candidates.

Physical demands. Choosing a vocation should also be done with a realistic attitude toward its physical demands in relation to one's own physical attributes. Is there a love of the outdoors, or does one prefer indoor activities? Jobs that require great physical strength cannot be done by everyone. The pursuit of a vocation is no time for wishful thinking or trying to reach far beyond one's range of talents, experiences, and aptitudes. Vocational choice, however, is an opportunity to grow, improve oneself, and make a contribution to society.

OCCUPATIONAL INFORMATION

A major resource for making an appropriate vocational decision is current occupational information—the nature of a vocation, its physical and educational requirements, salary range, and job outlook. It can also lead to information about related occupations and provide suggestions about where to look further. While this information provides an overall view, it varies with how an organization or company defines particular positions.

Occupational information can be found in many ways. Talking with someone who works in a particular vocation can be helpful. For example, a great deal can be learned about nursing by discussing the field with a nurse. It is also useful to observe someone doing a job.

Another way is to read books or other materials about occupations. There are good books about most major vocations, and there are also such things as videotapes and other media materials. One of the

An employee of the Bethlehem Steel Corporation learns welding under the supervision of an experienced instructor.

most useful and up-to-date sources of information on the current and future job market is the employment section of big city newspapers.

Talking to a school counselor is still another way to get occupational information. Counselors have a great deal of material and many resources that can assist in making vocational choices. They often have access to computerized occupational lists with required attributes and aptitudes. Some computerized systems list employers in a community, state, or region with available positions. By using this technology it is possible to plan a hypothetical career, beginning with an education and training program, a vocation, and an employer.

Making a career plan does not mean that a specific series of events will occur. Employers' needs often change. An occupation may become obsolete. A school may change a course of study. Because the economy changes, so will the job outlook for a particular occupation. A career plan can give a picture, however, of the way that training, education, and vocational choice fit together to provide a satisfying and productive career.

One of the most widely known sources of occupational information is the 'Occupational Outlook Handbook' (OOH). Compiled by the United States Department of Labor's Bureau of Labor Statistics, it provides information about job families—groups of occupations that have similar features and that require some of the same skills. For a more comprehensive list of occupations, the 'Dictionary of Occupational Titles' provides a listing of more than 10,000 occupational names. The OOH, on the other hand, provides a range of information about groups of similar occupations organized by the type of work. The job families and a representative range of occupations within them are listed on the next few pages.

An instructor teaches a drafting trainee how to make the lines and symbols of the precise craft he has chosen.

Accountant

Inspector

Personnel manager

Surveyor

(Top) © Donald Dietz—Stock, Boston;
(others) Richard Younker

392

EXECUTIVES, ADMINISTRATORS, AND MANAGERS

Managers and administrators are needed in every organization. They plan, organize, direct, and control the organization's major functions.

Bank officers and managers coordinate the activities of a banking institution's departments or regional offices. Almost every banking institution—whether a commercial bank, savings and loan association, or personal credit institution—has one or more vice presidents who act as general managers. Financial managers oversee the branches.

Health services managers are responsible for facilities, services, programs, staff, budgets, and relations with other organizations. They may hold many different positions, but all help plan, organize, and coordinate care.

Hotel managers and assistants are responsible for the profitable operation of their establishments. They manage front-office, housekeeping, food-service, and recreational activities and oversee the accounting, marketing and sales, personnel, security, and maintenance departments. They also satisfy the needs of guests and handle problems.

School principals and assistant principals provide leadership and management required for a school's smooth operation. Principals plan and organize, coordinate, direct, and evaluate the activities of school personnel.

MANAGEMENT-SUPPORT OCCUPATIONS

Management-support workers gather, process, and analyze data and develop information that enables management to formulate policies, improve procedures, oversee daily operations, and attain the organization's goals.

Accountants and auditors prepare, analyze, and verify financial reports that furnish up-to-date financial information to managers. There are four major fields—public, management, government accounting, and internal auditing.

Construction and building inspectors make sure that the construction, alteration, or repair of highways, streets, sewer and water systems, dams, bridges, buildings, and other structures complies with codes, ordinances, zoning regulations, and contract specifications.

Inspectors and compliance officers enforce laws and regulations that protect the public from health and safety hazards, prohibit unfair trade and employment practices, control immigration, prevent entry of prohibited matter, regulate business practices, and raise revenue.

Personnel, training, and labor relations specialists assist in recruiting employees and matching them to the jobs within an organization that they can do best.

Purchasing agents see to it that the goods, materials, supplies, and services purchased for internal use by an organization are of suitable quality, sufficient quantity, priced right, and available when needed.

Underwriters analyze information in insurance applications, reports from loss-control consultants, medical reports, and actuarial studies (reports that describe the probability of insured loss) in order to determine risk.

Wholesale and retail buyers purchase for resale the best available merchandise at the lowest possible prices and expedite delivery from the producer to the consumer.

ENGINEERS, SURVEYORS, AND ARCHITECTS

Engineers, surveyors, and architects plan and design. Engineers design machines, processes, systems, and structures. Surveyors measure and lay out land and building boundaries. Architects design buildings and other structures as well as outdoor areas. (*See also* Engineering.)

Aerospace engineers design, develop, and test commercial and military aircraft, missiles, and spacecraft. They develop new technologies in commercial aviation, defense systems, and space exploration.

Chemical engineers work in many phases of the production of chemicals and chemical products. They design equipment and plants and determine and test methods of manufacturing. They also work in such areas as electronics manufacturing and biotechnology.

Civil engineers design and supervise the construction of roads, airports, tunnels, bridges, water-supply and sewage systems, and buildings.

Electrical and electronics engineers design, develop, test, and supervise the manufacture of electrical and electronic equipment.

Industrial engineers determine the most effective ways for an organization to use the factors of production—people, machines, materials, and energy. They are more concerned with people and methods of organization than are engineers in other specialties.

Mechanical engineers are concerned with the use, production, and transmission of mechanical power and heat. They design and develop such power-producing machines as internal-combustion engines, steam and gas turbines, and jet and rocket engines. They also design and develop power-using machines.

Metallurgical, ceramics, and metals engineers develop new types of metals and other materials tailored to meet specific requirements—for example, materials that are heat resistant, strong yet lightweight, or highly malleable.

Mining engineers find, extract, and prepare minerals for use in manufacturing industries. They design open-pit and underground mines, supervise the construction of mine shafts and tunnels, and devise methods for transporting minerals to processing plants.

Nuclear engineers design, develop, monitor, and operate nuclear-power plants used to generate electricity and to power ships. They also conduct research on nuclear energy and radiation.

Petroleum engineers explore and drill for oil and gas. They work to achieve the maximum profitable recovery of oil and gas from a petroleum reservoir by determining and developing the most efficient production methods.

Architect

Civil engineers

NATURAL SCIENTISTS AND MATHEMATICIANS

Natural and mathematical scientists seek knowledge of the physical world through observation, study, and experimentation. Their research is used to develop new products, increase productivity, provide greater defense capabilities, protect the environment, and improve health care.

Actuaries design insurance and pension plans and make sure that they are maintained on a sound financial basis. They calculate probabilities of death, sickness, injury, disability, unemployment, retirement, and property loss from accident, theft, fire, and other hazards. From this information they determine expected losses.

Computer systems analysts plan and develop methods for computerizing business and scientific tasks or improving computer systems already in use.

Mathematicians are engaged in a wide variety of activities, ranging from the development of new theories to the translation of scientific and managerial problems into mathematical terms.

Statisticians devise and carry out surveys and experiments and interpret the numerical results, applying knowledge of statistical methods to particular subject areas.

Chemists search for and put to practical use new knowledge about substances. Most chemists work in research and development.

Geologists and geophysicists study the physical aspects and history of the Earth. They also identify rocks, minerals, and fossils, conduct geological surveys, construct maps, and measure the Earth's gravity and magnetic field.

Meteorologists study the atmosphere's physical characteristics, motions, and processes and the way the atmosphere affects the environment. Their research includes air-pollution control, fire prevention, agriculture, air and sea transportation, and climate.

Agricultural scientists study farm crops and animals and develop ways of improving their quantity and quality. They look for ways to increase yields with less labor, control pests and weeds more effectively, and conserve soil and water.

Biological scientists study all aspects of living organisms and the relationship of animals and plants to the environment.

Foresters and conservation scientists manage, develop, and protect forests, rangelands, and other natural resources. These provide habitats for wildlife, serve as sites for recreational activities, and supply lumber, livestock forage, minerals, and water.

Computer systems analyst

Mathematician

Lawyer with client

Urban planner

Clergyman

SOCIAL SCIENTISTS, SOCIAL WORKERS, RELIGIOUS WORKERS, AND LAWYERS

People in the areas of social and religious work must be tactful, compassionate, and sensitive to the needs of others. Their manner must inspire trust and confidence. Other workers in this section conduct basic and applied research in the social sciences. They deal primarily with data and things rather than people.

Lawyers, also called attorneys, serve as a link between the legal system and society. They must understand the world around them and be sensitive to the numerous aspects of society that the law touches. They must comprehend not only the words of a particular statute but also the human circumstances that the statute addresses.

Economists study the way society uses such scarce resources as land, labor, raw materials, and machinery to provide goods and services. They determine the costs and benefits of making, distributing, and using resources.

Psychologists study human behavior and mental processes to understand and explain people's actions. Some investigate the physical, emotional, or social aspects of human behavior. Others may counsel and conduct training programs, do market research, or provide health services in hospitals or clinics.

Sociologists study human society and social behavior by examining groups and social institutions. They study the behavior and interaction of groups, trace their origins and growth, and analyze the influence of group activities on individual members.

Urban and regional planners, often called city planners, develop programs to provide for future growth and revitalization of urban, suburban, and rural communities and their regions. They help local officials make decisions on social, economic, and environmental problems.

Social workers, through direct counseling, referral to other services, or policy-making and advocacy, help individuals, families, and groups cope with problems. They also help people understand how social systems operate and propose ways of bringing about needed change in such things as health services, housing, and education.

Recreation workers plan, organize, and direct activities that help people enjoy and benefit from leisure hours. These workers hold a wide range of jobs that bring them in contact with people of all ages, socioeconomic levels, and degrees of emotional and physical health.

Clergy lead their congregations in worship services and administer such rites as baptism, confirmation, marriage, and Holy Communion. They deliver sermons during services, give religious instruction, and counsel parishioners.

TEACHERS, COUNSELORS, LIBRARIANS, ARCHIVISTS, AND CURATORS

Teaching, librarianship, and counseling are people-oriented fields that involve helping others to learn, acquire information, or gain insight into themselves. Archivists and curators are involved with preserving and identifying historical and cultural artifacts.

Kindergarten and elementary schoolteachers introduce children to the basics of mathematics, language arts, the sciences, and social studies.

Secondary schoolteachers instruct students in specific subjects. They may teach a variety of related courses.

Adult- and vocational-education teachers generally teach courses related to their fields of specialization. Teaching methods vary by subject, but usually teachers try to promote students' active involvement in learning.

College and university faculty members provide instruction at an advanced level in particular fields of study. They generally teach several different courses in the same field. They often advise individual students and supervise research in their specialized fields.

Counselors help individuals deal with personal, social, educational, and career problems and concerns.

Librarians make information available. They link the public and the millions of sources of information by selecting and organizing materials and making them accessible.

Curator

HEALTH PRACTITIONERS

Health practitioners diagnose, treat, and strive to prevent illness and disease. They differ in methods of treatment and areas of specialization.

Chiropractors use the principle that a person's health is determined largely by the nervous system and that interference with this system impairs normal functions and lowers resistance to disease.

Dentists examine teeth and tissues of the mouth to diagnose and treat diseases or abnormalities.

Optometrists examine people's eyes to diagnose vision problems and to detect signs of disease and other abnormal conditions.

Physicians perform medical examinations, diagnose illnesses, and treat people suffering from injury or disease. They also advise patients about good health.

Podiatrists diagnose and treat diseases and disorders of the feet.

Surgeons are physicians who specialize in performing surgical procedures.

Veterinarians diagnose medical conditions, perform surgery, and prescribe and administer drugs for sick and injured animals.

Teacher

REGISTERED NURSES, PHARMACISTS, DIETITIANS, THERAPISTS, AND PHYSICIAN'S ASSISTANTS

Health professionals care for the sick, help the disabled, and advise individuals and communities on ways of maintaining and improving their health.

Dietitians and nutritionists counsel, set up and supervise food-service systems for institutions, and promote sound eating habits through education and research.

Occupational therapists treat people who are mentally, physically, developmentally, or emotionally disabled. They provide their patients with specialized activities that help them master the skills to perform daily tasks.

Pharmacists dispense drugs and medicines prescribed by physicians, podiatrists, and dentists.

Physical therapists plan and administer treatment to restore mobility, relieve pain, and prevent or limit permanent disability for those with injury or disease.

Physician's assistants perform such routine procedures as physical examinations, provide postoperative care, and assist with complicated medical procedures.

Recreational therapists provide services to people who are mentally, physically, or emotionally disabled. They use recreational and leisure activities in treatment.

Registered nurses observe, assess, and record symptoms, reactions, and progress; administer medications; assist in convalescence and rehabilitation; instruct patients and their families in proper care; and help people improve or maintain their health.

Respiratory therapists treat patients with cardiopulmonary problems.

Speech pathologists and audiologists assist people by evaluating their speech, language, or hearing abilities and by providing treatment.

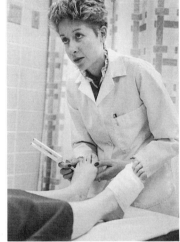
Podiatrist

Veterinarian

HEALTH TECHNOLOGISTS AND TECHNICIANS

Many jobs in the health field owe their existence to the development of new laboratory procedures, diagnostic techniques, and treatment methods. To keep pace, there are a variety of health technologists and technicians.

Clinical laboratory technologists and technicians provide laboratory services that range from routine tests to highly complex analyses.

Dental hygienists provide direct patient care, remove deposits and stains from teeth, and develop and examine X-ray film.

Dispensing opticians fill optometrists' prescriptions for lenses.

Electrocardiograph (EKG) technicians operate the equipment that produces tracings of heartbeats for review by a physician.

Electroencephalographic (EEG) technologists and technicians perform tests to aid in diagnosis.

Emergency medical technicians respond to accidents and emergencies that require immediate medical attention.

Licensed practical nurses help care for the physically or mentally ill and infirm.

Nurses

Designer

Artist

Singer

Salesman

(Top, center bottom) Cathy Melloan—
EB Inc.; (others) Richard Younker

Medical-record technicians manage information systems to meet medical, administrative, ethical, and legal requirements.

Radiologic technologists operate radiologic equipment and provide pertinent information to physicians to aid in diagnosis and treatment.

WRITERS, ARTISTS, AND ENTERTAINERS

Creativity, imagination, and talent are prerequisites for a career as a writer, artist, or entertainer. People in these fields use a variety of media to express ideas and emotions and to describe and interpret the human experience.

Public-relations specialists help business, government, and other organizations build positive relationships with the public.

Radio and television announcers and newscasters.

Reporters and correspondents.

Writers and editors.
Designers.
Graphic and fine artists.
Photographers and camera operators.
Actors, directors, and producers.
Dancers and choreographers.
Musicians.

TECHNOLOGISTS AND TECHNICIANS

Technologists and technicians perform much of the detailed technical work necessary in engineering, scientific, computer, library, legal, broadcasting, and other professional activities. They focus on the practical elements, operating and maintaining technical equipment and systems or providing skilled help with the research, design, testing, and creation of the end product.

Drafters prepare detailed drawings based on rough sketches, specifications, and calculations made by scientists, engineers, architects, and designers.

Electrical and electronics technicians develop, manufacture, and service equipment and systems.

Engineering technicians use their knowledge of science, engineering, mathematics, machinery, and technical processes in research and development, manufacturing, sales, and customer service.

Science technicians use their knowledge of science, mathematics, and technical processes to assist scientists in research and development.

Air traffic controllers have safety as their first concern, but they also must direct planes efficiently to minimize delays. Some regulate airport traffic; others regulate flights between airports.

Broadcast technicians operate and maintain electronic equipment used to record and transmit radio and television programs.

Computer programmers write the detailed instructions that list in a logical order the steps the machine must follow to organize data, solve problems, or do other tasks.

Legal assistants work directly with a lawyer. They perform all the functions of a lawyer other than accepting clients, setting legal fees, giving legal advice, or presenting a case in court.

Library technicians assist in acquiring, organizing, and making materials accessible to users.

MARKETING AND SALES OCCUPATIONS

Sales work offers a wide range of career opportunities. In some sales jobs people are their own bosses and set their own schedules, with their earnings depending entirely on their performance. Other jobs are more routine, with structured work schedules and guaranteed hourly wages.

Cashiers keep records of cash transactions, receipts, and disbursements in a business.

Insurance salespeople sell policies that provide financial protection against loss.

Manufacturers' salespeople sell mainly to other businesses and institutions. They inform buyers about the products they sell.

Real estate agents and brokers have a thorough knowledge of the real estate market in their communities and assist individuals in buying or selling homes and other real estate.

Retail salespeople, in addition to selling, make out sales checks, receive cash payments, and give change and receipts.

Securities and financial-services salespeople assist investors with securities, sales, buying and selling stocks, bonds, shares in mutual funds, and other financial products.

Travel agents arrange transportation and housing for travelers.

ADMINISTRATIVE-SUPPORT OCCUPATIONS

Workers in this group prepare and keep records; operate office machines; arrange schedules and make reservations; collect, distribute, and account for money, material, mail, and messages; or perform similar administrative duties. Administrative-support jobs can be found in virtually all industries.

Bank tellers perform services for bank customers by receiving deposits, paying out withdrawals, and crediting or debiting customers' accounts. They record daily trans-actions and balance accounts.

Bookkeepers and accounting clerks maintain journals and ledgers to provide up-to-date records of ac-counts and business transactions.

Computer and peripheral equipment operators monitor the controls and outputs of computers.

Data-entry keyers type data from documents.

Mail carriers and postal clerks.

Receptionists and information clerks.

Reservation and transportation ticket agents and travel clerks.

Secretaries.

Statistical clerks.

Stenographers.

Teachers' aides.

Telephone operators.

Traffic, shipping, and receiving clerks.

Typists.

Fireman

SERVICE OCCUPATIONS

Guarding and cleaning buildings, preparing and serving food, cutting and styling hair, and caring for children and elderly persons are types of jobs performed by service workers.

Corrections officers.
Fire-fighting occupations.
Guards.
Police and detectives.
Bartenders.
Chefs and cooks.

Waiters and waitresses.
Janitors and cleaners.
Barbers.
Child-care workers.
Cosmetologists and related workers.
Flight attendants.

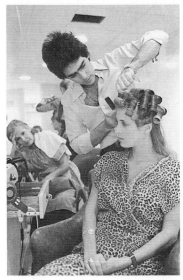
Hairdresser

AGRICULTURAL, FORESTRY, AND FISHING OCCUPATIONS

Workers in agriculture, forestry, and fishing are involved in the gathering, development, production, and distribution of basic food, clothing, shelter, and industrial products. Agricultural workers raise crops and livestock that provide food as well as material for clothing. Forestry workers harvest trees that provide lumber for buildings as well as material for paper products. Fishing workers gather sea, lake, and river life that provide food, fertilizer, and other products.

MECHANICS AND REPAIRERS

In high-technology societies, machines touch almost all aspects of living. Mechanics and repairers maintain and repair these machines.

Aircraft mechanics and engine specialists.
Automotive and motorcycle mechanics.
Automotive-body repairers.
Diesel mechanics.
Farm-equipment mechanics.
Mobile heavy-equipment mechanics.
Commercial and industrial electronic-equipment repairers.
Communications-equipment mechanics.
Computer-service technicians.
Electronic home-entertainment equip-ment repairers.

Home-appliance and power-tool repairers.
Line installers and cable splicers.
Telephone installers and repairers.
General maintenance mechanics.
Heating, air-conditioning, and refrigera-tion mechanics.
Industrial-machinery repairers.
Millwrights.
Musical-instrument repairers and tuners.
Vending-machine servicers and repairers.

Fisherman
(Top) Cathy Melloan—EB Inc.; (others) Richard Younker

Carpenter

Watch repairman

Bus driver

Photos, Richard Younker

CONSTRUCTION AND EXTRACTIVE OCCUPATIONS

Construction and extractive workers use labor-saving machinery and tools, but the work in general is physically demanding.

Bricklayers and stonemasons.
Carpenters.
Carpet installers.
Concrete masons and terrazzo workers.
Drywall workers and lathers.
Electricians.
Glaziers.
Insulation workers.

Painters and paperhangers.
Plasterers.
Plumbers and pipe fitters.
Roofers.
Sheet metalworkers.
Structural and reinforcing metalworkers.
Tile setters.
Roustabouts.

PRODUCTION OCCUPATIONS

Most production workers are employed in manufacturing plants, but others work in settings as different as shoe-repair shops, jewelry stores, and meat markets. There are thousands of production occupations.

Blue-collar worker supervisors.
Bookbinders.
Butchers and meat cutters.
Compositors and typesetters.
Dental-laboratory technicians.
Jewelers.
Lithographers and photoengravers.
Machinists.
Photographic-process workers.
Tool-and-die makers.

Upholsterers.
Stationary engineers.
Water- and sewage-treatment plant operators.
Metalworking and plastic-working machine operators.
Printing-press operators.
Precision assemblers.
Transportation-equipment painters.
Welders and cutters.

TRANSPORTATION AND MATERIAL-MOVING OCCUPATIONS

People in transportation operate such equipment as trucks, buses, taxicabs, trains, ships, and aircraft. People in material-moving occupations operate such industrial equipment as cranes, power shovels, graders, and industrial trucks. These occupations are concentrated in the transportation industry.

Aircraft pilots.
Bus drivers.

Construction-machinery operators.
Truck and tractor operators.

HELPERS, HANDLERS, EQUIPMENT CLEANERS, AND LABORERS

These workers assist skilled workers and perform the routine tasks required to complete a project. An example is a construction-trades helper.

MILITARY OCCUPATIONS

The military services constitute the single largest employer in the United States. They offer a wide range of employment and training opportunities in managerial and administrative jobs, professional occupations, clerical work, skilled construction trades, electrical and electronic occupations, motor-vehicle repair, and hundreds of other specialties.

JOBS FOR THE FUTURE

Based on the 'Occupational Outlook Handbook', some American occupations are expected to grow in the future, and others are likely to decline sharply. Changes are related to the United States economy.

Fastest-Growing Occupations

The occupational areas expected to be in greatest demand will be in response to changes predicted in American society for the coming years. Employees in the medical profession, for example, will be in demand. Most will be physical and occupational therapists, medical assistants, and medical technicians.

This prediction is based on two significant changes: the technology of medical care continues to change, requiring workers with up-to-date skills, and the population is aging. People born between 1946 and 1956, known as the "baby boomers," constitute the largest group in the American population. As a direct consequence of their aging and the subsequent decrease in the number of babies born, the population as a whole will be older. As people age their need for medical care tends to increase, creating a demand for more workers in the medical profession. The following occupations are expected to have the fastest growth:

Accountants and auditors.
Actuaries.
Computer programmers, operators, and technicians.
Corrections officers.
Electrical and electronic engineers and technicians.
Lawyers and legal assistants.
Medical practitioners and managers.
Public-relations specialists.
Securities and financial analysts.
Tool programmers.
Travel agents.

Declining Occupations

Occupational areas expected to decline include jobs that require manual skills, those that do not rely on computers or other technologies, and those that are unable to respond to changes in society. This does not mean that there will be no jobs in these areas—simply fewer opportunities and fewer workers. They include:

Butchers and meat cutters.
Industrial truck and trailer operators.
Mail carriers and postal clerks.
Statistical clerks.
Stenographers.
Telephone installers and repairers.

THE CHANGING WORKPLACE

Not only will there be changes in technology and the way in which jobs are performed, there will also be changes in where the work is done. Workers will not gather every day at the same location. It will be increasingly possible for them to remain at home and work through computers and telephones. It will also be possible for different aspects of work to be done in various locations around the community, the nation, or even the world.

Another change concerns the composition of the work force. Because of modifications in laws and customs, many jobs once thought to be for men only— such as a police officer or a corporate manager—are now recognized as appropriate for both sexes. Likewise secretarial and clerical positions, the nursing profession, and other occupations once thought to be "women's work," are now increasingly done by men as well. In the years to come, more and more women will enter the work force with increased opportunities.

Similarly, social changes have removed barriers to minorities and the disabled. Because it is now against the law in the United States for an employer to discriminate against a worker because of race, handicap, or ethnic origin, as well as age or sex, the American workplace will increasingly reflect the true variety and diversity of American society.

EMPLOYMENT AND THE ECONOMY

The availability of occupations depends also on shifts in the national economy and increasingly on economic developments worldwide. There are several ways to measure these effects, including the rate of unemployment, the international balance of trade, and the productivity of American workers.

The unemployment rate is a standard measure of joblessness in a community, state, or nation as a whole. Computed by standards set by the United States Department of Labor, the measure is made by taking a random sample of households in an area. It is an estimate of the percentage of people who are not working but are looking for work.

The unemployment rate has been said to underrepresent the actual unemployed because those who have stopped looking for work are not counted. It is a comparable statistic from state to state, however, because it is computed in the same manner. Traditionally an unemployment rate of 4 percent is considered full employment because people quit, change jobs, or are fired regardless of the relative health of the economy. In contrast the national unemployment rate reached as high as 25 percent during the Great Depression of the 1930s.

When unemployment is low, people work and receive payment. They in turn buy goods and services that keep the work force employed and growing. This is an expanding economy. When unemployment is high, there is less money to purchase goods and services because fewer people are working. Fewer goods are sold, and businesses lose money and reduce the number of workers. This is a contracting economy.

The United States government has many safeguards for the economy. It cannot, however, prevent dislocations due to technological change. A manufacturing process can suddenly become obsolete when a new technology is developed. Economic hardship may occur in a region even though the same goods are still being produced. An example is the industrial Midwest in the early 1980s. Increasingly manufacturers, both in the United States and abroad, were using foreign steel to make products. More finished products were also being imported, replacing American-made goods. Many workers were laid off, causing disruption of normal economic activities.

Meanwhile high-tech manufacturing processes were developing elsewhere. California's so-called Silicon Valley, south of San Francisco, became famous for its computer-related goods and computer-assisted design and manufacturing (CAD/CAM) processes. This was of little benefit to workers displaced by the obsolescence of traditional manufacturing. Because of a lack of transferable skills, many could not make the change. Some workers were furloughed indefinitely, forcing them to accept jobs that paid less or imposing upon them essentially permanent unemployment.

Leaders in American business and education are sensitive to these issues. Increasingly concerned with the productivity of the individual worker, business people and educators have formed alliances to save local jobs by improving the work force and by redesigning the curricula of schools and training centers to encourage the development of useful skills. (*See also* Vocational Training.)

VOCATIONAL TRAINING. Colleges and universities offer a wide range of course requirements to their students in their departments of arts and sciences. Vocational training, by contrast, is more narrowly focused. Its aim is a specific job or career. It is training that is comparable to an apprenticeship in a trade such as bricklaying. The student learns precisely what he needs and wants for his chosen field.

Vocational training courses range from accounting to X-ray technology and include automobile repair, court reporting, computer programming, cosmetology, dental hygiene, food service management, forestry, hotel management, plastering, secretarial skills, television repair, travel agency, and welding. These fields differ from studies in aerospace engineering, chemistry, law, teaching, nursing, and pharmacology, which have numerous course requirements, usually demand a college degree, and often call for schooling beyond college (such as law school).

Thus the difference between vocational training and more general schooling lies in the outcome. If a student wants to devote himself to a very specific kind of work, access to such a career is open through vocational training. If, however, he is unsure of future work plans, it is probably better to generalize one's schooling and leave more options open.

Vocational training is available to high school students; high school dropouts who are trying to get into the job market; college-age young people; and adults who want a new career or need retraining because of structural unemployment. (This type of unemployment stems from economic dislocations, resulting in plant closings and farm failures since the early 1970s.)

Apprenticeship is one alternative, and some trades still require it (*see* Apprenticeship). On-the-job training is given by companies to newly hired workers. It is often provided to college graduates as well as those with less schooling. Many corporations are reluctant to offer it, because once a new worker is trained he may go to work for a competing firm at a higher salary. Thus the company has borne the expense of training someone, without reaping the benefits. A specialized kind of on-the-job training is offered by the armed forces, and there is the additional enticement of earning money for school beyond the services.

There are schools that limit themselves to teaching one kind of trade: barber colleges, secretarial schools, beauty colleges, or travel schools, for example. Some schools teach a variety of courses in related fields. A business college, for instance, will teach accounting, bookkeeping, and secretarial skills. Technical institutes offer schooling in radio, television, computers, and similar fields.

Community colleges (formerly called junior colleges) are two-year institutions that once specialized in the liberal arts—preparing their graduates to attend the last two years of a four-year college. They have broadened their curriculums and now offer a variety of programs: automotive technology, child care, data processing, dental hygiene, dietetics, drafting, electronics, food service management, graphic arts, heating and refrigeration, legal secretarial studies, machine tool training, medical laboratory technology, nuclear medicine technology, practical nursing, real estate, printing technology, welding, and more.

Vocational training is a product of the Industrial Revolution and the specialization of work that the factory system entailed. Prior to the 19th century such training was nearly confined to apprenticeship, and some crafts jealously limited the number of trainees. With the rapid growth of industrialization, several European countries—especially Germany—introduced vocational training into their elementary and secondary schools. Opposition to such training persisted in Great Britain until after World War I.

By the early 20th century in the United States vocational programs were limited to manual training courses for boys and home economics for girls. In 1917 Congress passed the Smith-Hughes Act. Other statutes included the George-Barden Act of 1956, the GI Bill of Rights, the Health Amendments Act of 1956, the National Defense Education Act of 1958, the Manpower Development and Training Act of 1962, and—most significant of all—the Vocational Education Act of 1963. The 1963 act clearly defined vocational training and enumerated the purposes for which federal funds could be allotted. The statute was updated by the Vocational Amendments of 1968 and more recent legislation.

VOICE. One of the most widely used methods of communication for both humans and animals is the voice. Nearly all higher vertebrates can make some vocal sounds, such as an owl's hoot or a lion's roar. Only humans, however, can laugh, cry, sing, and speak. Such complex voice sounds require the coordination of many different parts of the body. These parts include sense organs such as the ear and tongue; the brain and the nerves; the lungs and trachea; cavities of the throat, mouth, and nose; and the human voice box, or larynx, which contains the vocal cords that actually produce sounds. (*See also* Brain, "The Brain and Human Language." For diagrams, *see* Anatomy, Human; Lungs.)

A speech analyzer attached to a computer can produce a readout of the word baby as a voiceprint.

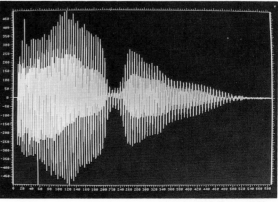

Hank Morgan—Rainbow

The Human Larynx

The larynx sits at the top of the windpipe, or trachea. It helps produce vocal sounds and closes the windpipe during swallowing so that no food particles pass into the lungs (see Respiratory System). In men the larynx is about 1¾ inches (4.4 centimeters) long and about 1½ inches (3.8 centimeters) wide; the larynx is smaller in women. The larynx is held open by a framework of cartilage plates called the thyroid, the cricoid, and the epiglottis. The thyroid cartilage bulges outward to form the Adam's apple in the throat. The smaller cricoid cartilage forms most of the anterior, lateral, and posterior walls of the larynx. The epiglottis, an elastic section of cartilage covered by mucous membrane, covers the windpipe during swallowing.

Two small pairs of tissue flaps in the larynx are called vocal cords. The upper pair are known as false cords because they do not actually produce sound. True vocal cords are white folds of mucous membrane that produce sound as air passes over them. The glottis is the narrow opening of the upper part of the larynx between the vocal cords.

The Mechanics of Speech

As a person inhales, the vocal cords swing outward toward the walls of the larynx. When voice sounds are to be produced, the cords swing inward and the laryngeal muscles contract, causing the cords to become stretched and taut. Air exhaled from the lungs passes over the taut cords and they vibrate, producing sound waves (see Sound).

High-pitched sounds are made when the cords are short and taut. Long and more relaxed cords produce lower pitched sounds. Loudness is determined by how hard the expelled air is forced over the vocal cords. Voice quality depends on the size and shape of certain body cavities called resonators. These include the mouth, nose, sinuses, head, neck, and chest. The lips, tongue, palate, and teeth are used with the vocal cords to produce various speech sounds. Together, they are called the vocal tract.

Sometimes because of disease a person's larynx may have to be removed by surgery. The person must then learn another method of producing speech. In one method, called esophageal speech, the individual swallows air into the stomach and traps it in the upper portion of the esophagus. The air is then expelled by a controlled belch. As the air passes through the mouth, the person uses the lips, tongue, and palate to produce speech sounds.

Why the Voice Changes in Adolescence

Adolescence is the time between childhood and adulthood when many bodily changes take place (see Adolescence). The growth spurt that boys experience enlarges the larynx and causes the vocal cords to become longer and thicker, deepening the voice's pitch. During the early periods of adolescence, boys find that their voices "crack" and that the pitch is

THE VOICE-PRODUCING APPARATUS

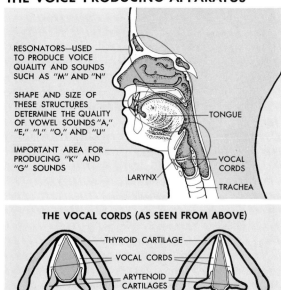

RESONATORS—USED TO PRODUCE VOICE QUALITY AND SOUNDS SUCH AS "M" AND "N"

SHAPE AND SIZE OF THESE STRUCTURES DETERMINE THE QUALITY OF VOWEL SOUNDS "A," "E," "I," "O," AND "U"

IMPORTANT AREA FOR PRODUCING "K" AND "G" SOUNDS

TONGUE

VOCAL CORDS

LARYNX

TRACHEA

THE VOCAL CORDS (AS SEEN FROM ABOVE)

THYROID CARTILAGE

VOCAL CORDS

ARYTENOID CARTILAGES

VOCAL CORDS DURING INHALATION

VOCAL CORDS IN POSITION TO PRODUCE SOUNDS

hard to control. This is because the larynx is still in its growing stages, and the vocal cords have not yet adjusted to the larger voice box holding them.

Production of Sound in Animals

Animals produce sound in various ways. Reptiles such as snakes produce a hissing sound by forcibly expelling air from the lungs. Some snakes have developed a membrane near the opening to the glottis, enabling them to produce a string of short hisses.

Birds have what is known as a syrinx instead of a larynx. The syrinx contains membranes that vibrate when air is passed over them. Muscles in this area contract and expand, enabling the bird to increase or decrease tension in the membranes and vary the quality of sound produced. Parrots and some other birds can be taught to mimic various sounds including human speech, but they cannot use it to communicate.

Mammals such as dogs and cats have a wide range of voice sounds. The cat, in addition to its cries, hisses, and growls, is the only animal that purrs. It does so by vibrating its vocal cords in a continuous hum. Dogs can bark, growl, or whine in a variety of pitches and levels of sound.

Amphibians such as frogs are the lowest order of vertebrates to have a larynx. Air expelled from the lungs passes over the vocal cords and enters the mouth area. In some frogs, vocal sacs under the throat or near the jaw serve as resonators.

Some animals have no vocal cords but are still able to make vocal sounds. Deep inside the nasal passageways of dolphins are two flaps that overlap like valves. Air blown through the nasal passageway causes the flaps to vibrate, producing a wide array of vocal sounds.

Mount Saint Helens in Washington State erupted with tremendous force on May 18, 1980, sending ash and debris over an area of 150 square miles (390 square kilometers).

VOLCANO. A volcano is a vent, or opening, in the surface of the Earth through which magma and associated gases and ash erupt. The term also refers to the form or structure, usually conical, produced by accumulations of erupted material. Volcanoes occur mainly near plate tectonic boundaries and are especially common around the Pacific basin, called the Pacific Ring of Fire (*see* Plate Tectonics).

Humanity has long been awed by this powerful force of nature. The Romans attributed volcanic events to Vulcan, their feared god of fire and metalworking. In 79 BC the eruption of Mount Vesuvius destroyed the Roman cities of Pompeii and Herculaneum. Polynesians believe volcanoes to be ruled by the fire goddess Pele. One of the most spectacular eruptions in recorded history occurred in 1883 with the explosion of Krakatoa, an island near Java (*see* Krakatoa). A more recent example is the dramatic 1980 eruption of Mount Saint Helens in the Cascade Range in Washington State.

This article was contributed by Charles W. Finkl, Jr., Professor of Geology, Florida Atlantic University, Boca Raton, and Executive Director, Coastal Education and Research Foundation, Charlottesville, Va.

Volcano Formation and Eruptions

Volcanic eruptions may be violent, even catastrophic, or relatively mild. The most explosive eruptions are essentially blasts of steam that create spectacular displays. Quieter fissure eruptions occur when molten rock pushes through long cracks in the Earth's crust and floods the surrounding landscape. Such repeated outpourings of lava can fill surrounding valleys and bury low hills, creating thick lava sequences that eventually become plateaus (*see* Plateau).

The origin of molten rock, referred to by geologists as magma, is not clearly understood. About 80 percent of all magma is composed of basalt rock. Geophysical research suggests that volcanic magma forms near the base of the crust and moves upward to a shallow magma chamber before erupting at the surface. Magmas rise because they are less dense than the rocks at lower depth, and their heat probably weakens surrounding rocks. The upward movement of magma may also be due to expanding gases within the molten rock or to chemical reactions that dissolve rocks above the magma. Volcanic material moves toward the surface through channelways, or volcanic conduits, and is extruded through vents at the Earth's surface. (*See also* Lava and Magma.)

Eruptions take different forms depending on the composition of the magma when it reaches the surface. Sudden eruptions are often associated with low viscosity (more fluid) magma where the expanding gases form a froth that becomes a light, glassy rock called pumice. In eruptions of high viscosity (thicker) magmas, the gas pressure shatters the rock into fragments. Pyroclastic rocks, formed by volcanic explosion, are named according to size: volcanic ash if sand-sized or smaller, volcanic bombs if larger. Consolidated ash is called tuff. Quieter, more passive eruptions release fluid basalt lava from dikes or dike swarms (magma intrusions that cut across layers of rock). These eruptions cover large areas and often produce ropy, or pahoehoe, lava flows. Thicker basalt lava breaks into chunks or blocks, forming blocky lava flows, called aa.

The products of volcanism may be classified into two groups: lava and pyroclastics. Lava is the fluid phase of volcanic activity. Pyroclastics (also called tephra) are various-sized particles of hot debris thrown out of a volcano. Whether lava or pyroclastics are being ejected, the eruption is normally accompanied by the expulsion of water and gases, many of which are poisonous. Lava usually forms long, narrow rivers of molten rock that flow down the slopes of a volcano.

Explosive eruptions tend to be spectacular events best observed from a safe distance. Earthquakes, high columns of vapors, lightning, and strong whirlwinds often accompany the explosions. The eruption of Krakatoa unleashed a tsunami, a large seismic sea wave, that swept the coasts of Java and Sumatra and drowned more than 36,000 people. A volcano can grow with frightening speed and often affects territory far beyond the area on which the cone forms. When volcanoes are born in the sea, the eruptions may be more violent than those on land because the contact between molten rock and seawater produces steam.

Volcanoes also create craters and calderas. Craters are formed either by the massive collapse of material during volcanic activity, by unusually violent explosions, or later by erosion during dormancy. Calderas are large, basin-shaped depressions. Most of them are formed after a magma chamber drains and no longer supports the overlying cone, which then collapses inward to create the basin. One of the most famous examples is the still-active Kilauea caldera in Hawaii.

Types of Volcanoes

Volcanoes are usually classified by shape and size. These are determined by such factors as the volume and type of volcanic material ejected, the sequence and variety of eruptions, and the environment. Among the most common types are shield volcanoes, stratovolcanoes, and cinder cones.

Shield volcanoes have a low, broad profile created by highly fluid basalt flows that spread over wide areas. The fluid basalt cannot build up a cone with sides much steeper than 7 degrees. Over thousands of years, however, these cones can reach massive size. The Hawaiian Islands are composed of shield volcanoes that have built up from the sea floor to the surface some 3 miles (5 kilometers) above. Peaks such as Mauna Loa and Mauna Kea rise to more than 13,600 feet (4,145 meters) above sea level. Hawaii is the largest lava structure in the world, while Mauna Loa, if measured from the sea floor, is the world's largest mountain in terms of both height and volume.

Stratovolcanoes (or composite volcanoes) are the most common volcanic form. They are composed of alternating layers of lava and pyroclastic material. When a quiet lava flow ends, it creates a seal of solidified lava within the conduit of the volcano. Pressure gradually builds up below, setting the stage for a violent blast of pyroclastic material. These alternating cycles repeat themselves, giving stratovolcanoes a reputation for violent explosions.

A cinder cone is a conical hill of mostly cinder-sized pyroclastics. The profile of the cone is determined by the angle of repose, that is, the steepest angle at which debris remains stable and does not slide downhill. Larger cinder fragments, which fall near the summit, can form slopes exceeding 30 degrees. Finer particles are carried farther from the vent and form gentle slopes of about 10 degrees at the base of the cone. These volcanoes tend to be explosive but may also extrude some lava. Cinder cones are numerous, occur in all sizes, and tend to rise steeply above the surrounding area. Those occurring on the flanks of larger volcanoes are called parasitic cones.

Volcanic activity typically alternates between short active periods and much longer dormant periods. An extinct volcano is one that is not erupting and is not likely to erupt in the future. A dormant volcano, while currently inactive, has erupted within historic times and is likely to do so in the future. An inactive volcano

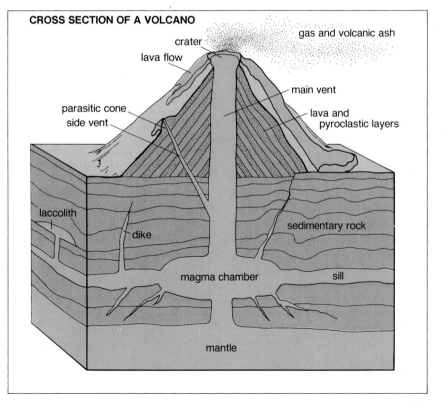

CROSS SECTION OF A VOLCANO

In a typical composite volcano hot magma from the Earth's mantle rises upward and collects in a magma chamber. As the magma rises it begins to lose gas. During an eruption the magma is forced up through the main vent, or conduit. Lava and pyroclastics (or tephra) are ejected from the crater. Pyroclastics are various-sized particles of hot debris. Usually the lava flows out during the quieter periods. The pyroclastics form when explosions spray out liquid lava, which hardens and settles on the sides of the cone. Water and gases are also ejected from the crater. The cone is built up by successive layers of solid lava and pyroclastics. Branches of the main vent, called side vents, are formed as the hot lava creeps between the layers of rock or through cracks. When side vents reach the surface, they sometimes form parasitic cones. Sheets of lava that solidify along fissures are called dikes. A laccolith is a mass of solidified magma that intrudes between sedimentary layers and produces a domelike bulging of the overlying strata.

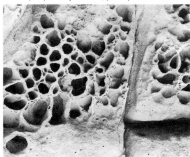

Minor volcanic structures often develop on or near a volcano cone. Such inactive craters (left) in southwestern Washington State near Mount Saint Helens, seen smoldering in the distance, indicate the extensive underground network of volcanic activity. When molten rock rapidly cools, the volcanic gases within it expand and form bubbles. The bubbles then leave cavities (above) in the cooled and solidified rock.

is one that has not been known to erupt within historic times. Such classification is arbitrary, however, since almost any volcano is capable of erupting again.

In the late stages of volcanic activity, magma can heat circulating groundwater, producing hot springs and geysers (see Geyser and Fumarole). A geyser is a hot-water fountain that spouts intermittently with great force. One of the best-known examples is Old Faithful in Yellowstone National Park. Fumaroles are vents that emit gas fumes or steam.

Volcanoes occur along belts of tension, where continental plates diverge, and along belts of compression, where the plates converge. Styles of eruption and types of lava are associated with different kinds of plate boundaries. Most lavas that issue from vents in oceanic divergence zones and from midoceanic vol-

canoes are basaltic. Where ocean plates collide, the rock types basalt and andesite predominate. Near the zone where an ocean plate and continental margin converge, consolidated ash flows are found.

Nearly 800 volcanoes are active today or known to have been active in historical times. Of these, more than 75 percent are situated in the Pacific Ring of Fire. This belt partly coincides with the young mountain ranges of western North and South America, and the volcanic island arcs fringing the north and western sides of the Pacific basin. The Mediterranean-Asian orogenic belt has few volcanoes, except for Indonesia and the Mediterranean where they are more numerous. Oceanic volcanoes are strung along the world's oceanic ridges, while the remaining active volcanoes are associated with the African rift valleys.

The composite volcano, or stratovolcano, has alternating layers of lava and pyroclastic materials. The shield volcano is named for its low, broad shape. It usually has a wide summit crater, or caldera, and several collapse pits. Cinder cones generally have steep slopes consisting mainly of pyroclastics.

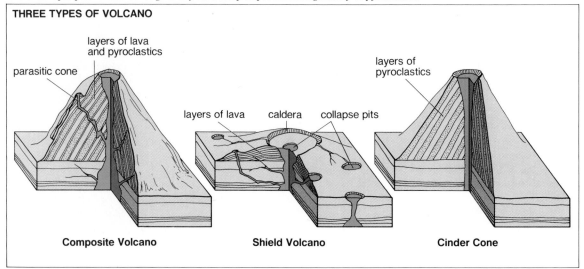

THREE TYPES OF VOLCANO

parasitic cone

layers of lava and pyroclastics

layers of lava   caldera   collapse pits

layers of pyroclastics

Composite Volcano   Shield Volcano   Cinder Cone

Study of Volcanic Eruptions

Volcanology, a branch of geology, is the study of volcanoes and volcanic activity. Although volcanoes are difficult to study because of the hazards involved, volcano observatories have existed for decades.

Active volcanoes are observed to obtain information that might help predict the timing and intensity of eruptions. Sensitive instruments detect changes in temperature, chemical composition of emissions, Earth movements, magnetic fields, gravity, and other physical properties of the volcano. Modern networks of seismographs provide information on the internal structure and activity of volcanoes (*see* Earthquake). The intensity, frequency, and location of earthquakes provide important clues to volcanic activity, particularly impending eruptions. Movements of magma typically produce numerous tremors, sometimes exceeding 1,000 per day. An almost continuous tremor generally accompanies a lava outpouring. Tiltmeters (instruments that measure tilting of the ground) help detect swelling and deflation of the volcano caused by the accumulation and movement of magma. Researchers also monitor variations in the chemistry and petrology of the lavas and the chemistry of emitted gases.

Volcanoes erupt in a wide variety of ways. Even a single volcano may go through several eruption phases in one active period. Eruptions are classified according to the geochemical composition and viscosity of the lavas, nature of the flows or ash release, and associated phenomena. Magmatic eruptions are the most common, but the most violent arise from steam explosions when the fiery magma reaches surface water, ice, or groundwater.

Pelean eruptions, named after the 1902 eruption of Mount Pelée on the Caribbean island of Martinique, are characterized by incandescent flows of rock and pumice fragments. The entrapment of high-temperature gases in these "glowing avalanches," known by the French term *nuée ardente*, is associated with a particularly violent phase of eruption.

Eruptions of intermediate force are typified by Plinian eruptions, named after Pliny the Elder, who witnessed the volcanic destruction of Pompeii and Herculaneum. Plinian eruptions are characterized by both the extrusion of high-viscosity lava flows and the violent explosion of released gases that blast huge quantities of ash, cinders, bombs, and blocks skyward. Volcanic mudflows, landslides, and lahars (flows of volcanic debris) may also follow, particularly if the eruptions are accompanied by rainstorms.

Less violent Hawaiian and Strombolian-type eruptions are associated with fissures that often produce a line of fire fountains. These geyserlike fountains of lava may shoot several hundred meters into the air and form a nearly continuous curtain of fire. The basalt lava is extremely fluid and flows down the mountain sides in torrents. When these streams reach the sea, they form pillow lavas, lobes of stacked lava that resemble a pile of pillows.

The Hawaiian volcano Mauna Loa ("long mountain") is one of the largest single mountain masses in the world.

Volcanoes provide a wealth of natural resources. Emissions of volcanic rock, gas, and steam are sources of important industrial materials and chemicals, such as pumice, boric acid, ammonia, and carbon dioxide. In Iceland most of the homes in Reykjavík are heated by hot water tapped from volcanic springs. Greenhouses heated in the same way can provide fresh vegetables and tropical fruits to this subarctic island. Geothermal steam is exploited as a source of energy for the production of electricity in Italy, New Zealand, the United States, Mexico, Japan, and the Soviet Union. The scientific study of volcanoes provides useful information on Earth processes, particularly how they may be used to benefit society.

IMPORTANT TERMS IN VOLCANOLOGY

Caldera—large, basinlike depression formed by the collapse of an overlying volcanic cone

Cinder cone volcano—conical, usually highly symmetrical hill of pyroplastics

Crater—depression resulting from volcanic collapse or violent explosion, or by gradual erosion

Dike or **dike swarms**—tabular body or bodies of molten rock injected into a fissure

Lahar—debris flows of volcanic materials that often accompany or follow a volcanic eruption

Lava—fluid rock that issues from a volcano or fissure and is composed primarily of basalt, andesite, or rhyolite rock

Magma—molten rock within the Earth

Pyroclastics (tephra)—various-sized particles ejected by volcanic activity

Shield volcano—low, broad-profile volcano built up by outpourings of highly fluid basaltic lava

Stratovolcano (composite volcano)—cone constructed by alternating layers of lava and pyroclastic material

Vent—an opening in the Earth's surface through which gas or lava can escape

Cargo vessels on the Volga passing the city of Gorky are an indication of the river's heavy use as a transportation route in the Soviet Union.

VOLGA RIVER.

Europe's longest river and the principal waterway of the Soviet Union, the Volga arises in the Valdai Hills northwest of Moscow and flows southeastward for 2,325 miles (3,740 kilometers) to empty into the Caspian Sea. Known as "Mother Volga," it is a symbol of Russia and a central theme in songs and stories.

The course consists of three parts: the Upper Volga, from the river's source to its confluence with the Oka River near Gorky; the Middle Volga, from the Oka to the Kama, its major tributary near Kazan; and the Lower Volga, from the junction of the Kama to the mouth of the Volga at Astrakhan. After passing a series of lakes in its upper course, the river heads eastward to Rzhev and Kalinin and through the Rybinsk Reservoir. It then flows southwestward through a narrow valley and crosses an area of plains to Gorky. In its middle portion the river turns southward toward the Kuybyshev Reservoir, where the Kama joins it from the left bank. The Volga veers slightly westward in its lower reaches near the city of Volgograd and its dam. It then flows through the Caspian Depression and reaches its delta on the Caspian Sea at Astrakhan.

The river flows slowly. Considering the Volga's length, it falls only slightly from its source at 748 feet (228 meters) above sea level to its mouth at 99 feet (30 meters) below sea level. Melting snow accounts for 60 percent of the river's drainage. Reservoirs control flooding.

Although it has no direct natural outlet to the oceans, the Volga is joined to the Baltic Sea via the Volga-Baltic Canal and to the White Sea via the Sukhona and Northern Dvina rivers and also by the White Sea-Baltic Canal. The Moskva Canal links it with the Moskva River and Moscow, and the Volga-Don Canal provides access to the Sea of Azov and the Black Sea.

Navigable for most of its length, the Volga is an economically prominent river. The Volga and its tributaries, aided by canal connections, provide transportation, electric power, and irrigation for a region extending almost from Leningrad in the north to the Caspian Sea in the south, and from Moscow in the west to Perm' in the east. The network carries about two thirds of the freight and more than half of the passenger traffic within the Soviet waterway system. The Volga basin covers one third of the European section of the Soviet Union. One quarter of the Soviet population lives in the basin.

The Volga is joined by about 200 tributaries. Eleven large piers and ports are located along its route, and ten dams capture its waters for hydroelectric and irrigation service. Timber accounts for about 25 percent of the total freight carried by the Volga network. Other cargo consists of petroleum and petroleum products, coal, grain, fish, vegetables, salt, watermelons, agricultural machinery, automobiles, chemical apparatus, and fertilizers.

VOLGOGRAD, U.S.S.R.

Formerly known as Stalingrad, Volgograd is a shipping port and industrial center on the Volga River. The city is the administrative center of Volgograd region. Its apartment buildings and factories extend for more than 40 miles (64 kilometers) along the banks of the river.

Volgograd State University was opened in 1978. Steel and aluminum, engineering products, timber goods, building materials, and foodstuffs head a long list of manufactured products. A petroleum refinery was built in 1957, and chemicals have been manufactured since the 1960s. A hydroelectric station provides inexpensive power. Inland waterways and railways link Volgograd to the heavily developed regions to the north and west. Access to Europe is by way of the Volga-Don Canal, the Black Sea, and the Mediterranean Sea.

The city was founded as the fortress of Tsaritsyn in 1589. Its name was changed to Stalingrad in 1925 to honor Joseph Stalin, who successfully directed the city's defense in a major battle against the White Russian armies in the Russian Civil War. In 1942–43, during World War II, Stalingrad was the scene of a long, bitter battle that stopped the penetration of the Soviet Union by German forces. The "hero city" of the nation, however, was reduced to rubble and had to be totally rebuilt. In 1961 the city's name was changed to Volgograd as part of the government's de-Stalinization program. Population (1986 estimate), 981,000.

VOLLEYBALL. Suitable for all ages, volleyball is a year-round sport. The game was invented in 1895 by William G. Morgan of the YMCA in Holyoke, Mass. In 1916 rules were issued by the YMCA and the National Collegiate Athletic Association (NCAA). The United States Volleyball Association (USVBA) was formed in 1928 and is recognized as the sport's national governing body. The Fédération Internationale de Volley Ball (FIVB) oversees the sport on the international level. Volleyball became an Olympic event for both men and women in 1964.

Across the middle of the 30- by 60-foot court is a 3-foot-wide net, the top of which is 8 feet above the ground for men (7 feet 4¼ inches for women). The inflated, leather-covered ball is about 26 inches in circumference and weighs no more than 10 ounces. Each team is made up of six players, who, while volleying the ball over the net, try to make the ball touch the court within the opponents' playing area before it can be returned.

Serves are made underhand or overhand with an open hand or fist. Players may volley the ball with any part of the body above the waist as long as the ball is clearly hit and not held. Following the serve each team may hit the ball up to three times before sending it back over the net. The serving team scores a point if the opponents fail to return the ball or if they hit it out of bounds; if the serving team fails to return the ball, it loses the serve. A winning score is at least 15 points, with at least a 2-point lead.

This portrait of Voltaire by an unknown artist is a copy of a painting by Nicolas de Largillière done in 1718.

VOLTAIRE (1694–1778). In his 84 years Voltaire was historian and essayist, playwright and storyteller, poet and philosopher, wit and pamphleteer, wealthy businessman and practical economic reformer. Yet he is remembered best as an advocate of human rights. True to the spirit of the Enlightenment, he denounced organized religion and established himself as a proponent of rationality (*see* Enlightenment).

Voltaire was born François-Marie Arouet on Nov. 21, 1694, in Paris. At 9 he was sent to the College of Louis-le-Grand. At 16 he left school to become a writer. He wrote witty verse mocking the royal authorities. For this he was imprisoned in the Bastille for 11 months. About this time he began calling himself Voltaire.

Another dispute in 1726 led to exile in England for two years. On his return to Paris he staged several unsuccessful dramas and the enormously popular 'Zaïre'. He wrote a life of Swedish king Charles XII, and in 1734 he published 'Philosophical Letters', a landmark in the history of thought. The letters, denouncing religion and government, caused a scandal that forced him to flee Paris. He took up residence

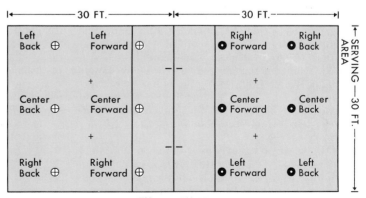

An indoor volleyball court consists of two adjacent squares, each measuring 30 feet on a side and separated by a net. Players advance position with each change of serve. The player at "right back" serves.

in the palace of Madame du Châtelet, with whom he lived and traveled until her death in 1749.

In 1750 Voltaire went to Berlin at the invitation of Prussia's Frederick the Great. Three years later, after a quarrel with the king, he left and settled in Geneva, Switzerland. After five years his strong opinions forced another move, and he bought an estate at Ferney, France, on the Swiss border. By this time he was a celebrity, renowned throughout Europe. Visitors of note came from everywhere to see him. Voltaire returned to Paris on Feb. 10, 1778, to direct his play 'Irene'. His health suddenly failed, and he died on May 30.

'Candide', the strongly anti-Romantic comic novel, is the work by Voltaire most read today. His other writings include 'Zadig' (1747), 'The Century of Louis XIV' (1751), 'Micromégas' (1752), 'The Russian Empire under Peter the Great' (1759–63), 'The Philosophical Dictionary' (1764), and 'Essay on Morals' (1756).

VONNEGUT, Kurt, Jr. (born 1922). Characterized by grim humor and a preoccupation with the hostile forces of science and technology, Kurt Vonnegut, Jr., has written numerous novels in which he pleads for human kindness in the present world and in the dehumanized world he depicts as the future.

Vonnegut was born on Nov. 11, 1922, in Indianapolis, Ind. He attended Cornell University before serving in the United States Air Force in World War II. As a German prisoner of war, Vonnegut was a survivor of the fire bombing of Dresden, Germany, in February 1945. After the war Vonnegut studied anthropology at the University of Chicago and worked as a police reporter and a public relations writer before leaving to write full-time.

Vonnegut began his writing career with short stories for magazines. His first novel, 'Player Piano', was published in 1952, followed by 'The Sirens of Titan' (1959), 'Mother Night' (1961), and 'God Bless You, Mr. Rosewater' (1965). Vonnegut gained attention from the critics and the reading public with 'Cat's Cradle' (1963). His best-known work, 'Slaughterhouse Five, or The Children's Crusade' (1969), is an autobiographical but fictional recreation of the Dresden bombing as experienced by a naive American soldier, Billy Pilgrim, imprisoned in a meat storage cellar below a slaughterhouse.

Later novels include 'Breakfast of Champions' (1973), 'Slapstick' (1976), 'Jailbird' (1979), 'Deadeye Dick' (1982), 'Galápagos' (1985), and 'Bluebeard' (1987). Vonnegut has also written the play 'Happy Birthday, Wanda June' (1970), the collection of short stories 'Welcome to the Monkey House' (1968), and two works of nonfiction, 'Wampeters, Foma & Grandfalloons' (1974) and 'Palm Sunday' (1981).

VOODOO. The religion of most of the population of Haiti is voodoo. Its origins are in Africa, especially in Benin (formerly Dahomey). The term voodoo is from *vodun*, which means "god" or "spirit" in the Fon language of Africa. The beliefs of the African slaves gradually mingled with the Roman Catholicism of the white French plantation owners of Haiti.

Voodoo combines a belief in one god with a belief in various kinds of spirits. The purpose of voodoo is to serve these spirits and keep their good will. The god Bondye (from the French *bon dieu*) is identified with the Christian God. He is considered remote and unapproachable. Real devotion is given to the spirits (*loa,* or *lwa,* in the Yoruba language of Africa). The spirits are not evil. They serve as intermediaries between people and Bondye. Each person is believed to have several souls. After death these souls become spirits that can take possession of another individual. When possessed, a believer does ritual dances, accepts animal sacrifice for the spirit, and offers valuable counsel and advice. Otherwise the role of the spirit combines the functions of guardian angel and patron saint.

Male voodoo leaders are called *hungan* and the females *mambo*. They serve small congregations as counselors, healers, and leaders of the lively voodoo ritual. Annual festivals are held in honor of the major spirits.

There are traditions of private magic and sorcery that have been sensationalized by outsiders—especially stories about zombies. These are presumably soulless bodies raised from the grave to be slaves. It is probable that they are actually persons who have been drugged into insensibility and revived.

VORSTER, John (1915–83). As prime minister of the Republic of South Africa from 1966 to 1978, John Vorster softened some of the worst elements of apartheid—the rigid system of racial discrimination. He promoted cooperation with the leaders of neighboring black African nations. Although he tried to persuade the white leadership of Rhodesia (now Zimbabwe) to share power with blacks, he was completely unwilling to entertain such notions about South Africa.

He was born Balthazar Johannes Vorster on Dec. 13, 1915, in Jamestown, Cape Province. While attending the University of Stellenbosch, he became involved in politics as a student leader of the conservative National party. Because of his support for Germany during World War II, he was imprisoned for 14 months. He was defeated in parliamentary elections in 1948 but won in 1953. He served in the government of Prime Minister Hendrik Frensch Verwoerd as deputy minister of education, and after racial disturbances in 1960 he became minister of justice, police, and prisons.

Vorster became leader of the National party and prime minister in 1966, when Verwoerd was assassinated. He resigned in 1978 for health reasons and became president, a ceremonial position. A financial scandal involving his party forced him to resign on June 4, 1979. He died in Cape Town on Sept. 10, 1983.

VOTING see ELECTIONS; SUFFRAGE.

VULTURE see BIRDS OF PREY.

The letter U

is a descendant of the letter V, which is discussed later in this volume. Relatives of U are F, W, and Y. The original forms of the sign in the Egyptian hieroglyphic, Phoenician, and Greek writings are shown in the illustrations numbered (1), (2), and (3) respectively.

For a time the Romans used one sign (4) for three sounds, namely "u," "v," and "w." For example, they wrote the name "Julius" as IVLIVS.

In late Roman times Latin scribes made the capital letter as V but rounded the small letter (5). People of the Middle Ages chose the pointed form for the consonantal "v" and the rounded form for the vocalic "u." To make the change complete, they added small "v" and capital U to their writing (6). This distinction of the four signs passed into English writing unchanged. The English small "u" is a copy of the capital, except that in handwriting it is connected to adjoining letters.

Y	Y
1	2
V	V
3	4
Vu	vU
5	6

U, radioactive chemical element. see in index Uranium

U2, Irish rock group formed in Dublin 1976; music known for social conscience and religious overtones; performed in Live Aid (1985) and Amnesty International (1986) concerts; albums include *Boy*, *War*, and *The Joshua Tree* M-683

U-2, U.S. observation plane E-142
   United States U-180

U-235, U-238, U-239. see in index Uranium

Uakari, monkey A-504

UAW. see in index International Union, United Automobile, Aircraft & Agricultural Implement Workers of America

Ubangi River (in French, Oubangui), tributary of the Congo (Zaire) River U-2
   Africa, *map* A-118
   Congo C-645
   Congo River C-647

Ubangi-Shari. see in index Central African Republic

Uber Cup, in badminton competition B-17

Ubico, Jorge (1878–1946), president of Guatemala 1931–44; made reputation as soldier and governor of various provinces; resigned presidency due to national strike.

'U-boat' (in German, Unterseeboot), popular name given to German submarines during World War I U-boat

Ucayali River, river in Peru, one of main headstreams of Amazon; flows n. 1,000 mi (1,600 km) to join Marañon River
   Peru P-240
   South America, *map* S-419

Uccello, Paolo (1397–1475), Florentine painter U-2
   'Battle of San Romano, The' P-33, *picture* P-34

Uchatius, Franz von, Austrian inventor; developer of early motion picture projector M-615

Ucle River, in Zaire U-2

Udaipur, former Rajputana princely state in India, now part of Rajasthan state; maharaja's palace dates from about 1570, *map* I-86

Udalfs, soil classification S-372, U-102

Udall, Nicholas (1505–56), English schoolmaster, author of earliest extant English comedy, 'Ralph Roister Doister'.

Udall, Stewart Lee (born 1920), U.S. public official and lawyer, born in St. Johns, Ariz.; U.S. congressman 1955–60; U.S. secretary of the interior 1961–69; chairman of conservation consulting firm from 1969; author of 'The Quiet Crisis' and '1976—Agenda for Tomorrow'.

Udasis, Sikh monastic order M-542

Udine, Italy, capital of Friuli-Venetia Julia Region, 63 mi (101 km) n.e. of Venice; makes silk, velvet; trades in flax and hemp; military base 1915–17; held by Austrians 1917; pop. 86,188, *map* I-404

Udjung Pandang (or Makassar, or Macassar), seaport and largest city of Celebes, Indonesia, on w. coast of s. peninsula of island; source of macassar oil, from seeds of the kusam tree *(Schleichera trijuga)*, so widely used as hair ointment in the 19th century that tidies to protect chair backs are called antimacassars; pop. 497,000, *maps* A-700, I-166

Udones, footwear worn by the Romans H-278

Ueberroth, Peter V. (born 1937), U.S. commissioner of baseball, born in Evanston, Ill.; founded travel agency, First Travel Corp., 1963; president of Los Angeles Olympic Organizing Committee 1979–84; baseball commissioner 1984–89; instituted changes in by-laws of position.

Uele River (or Welle River), one of the headstreams of the Ubangi River; flows through Zaire in w. Africa, navigable for long distances U-2, *map* A-118

Ueno Park, park in Tokyo, Japan T-207, *picture* T-210

Ufa, U.S.S.R., city 715 mi (1,150 km) e. of Moscow; capital of Bashkir Republic; river port, mining; airplanes, cables, typewriters, clothing, leather goods, food processing, clay refactory; Palace of Labor and Art, monument to Lenin; pop. 773,000, *map* E-361
   U.S.S.R., *maps* U-62, 66 world, *map* W-300

Uffizi Palace, palace in Florence, Italy (erected 1560–76); gallery famed for collection of Florentine Renaissance paintings F-190, *picture* F-192
   gallery M-661, 663
   'The Holy Family', *picture* M-352

UFO. see in index Unidentified flying object

Uganda, country in e. Africa n. of Lake Victoria; 93,104 sq mi (241,139 sq km), including water; cap. Kampala; pop. 15,514,000 U-3
   Africa, *map* A-118, *table* A-112
   Amin A-370
   Commonwealth membership C-602
   flag, *picture* F-171
   Kampala K-167
   Obote O-455
   terrorism T-114
   United Nations, *table* U-84 world, *map* W-300

Ugo of Segni. see in index Gregory IX

Ugrians, people
   Siberia S-282

Uhland, Johann Ludwig (1787–1862), German lyric poet, literary historian, and philologist; ballads ('The Luck of Edenhall').

UHT (ultrahigh temperature method), process used in pasteurization of milk and cream D-4

Uinta Mountains, range of n.e. Utah, *map* U-259
   Rocky Mountains R-254

Uitlanders (outlanders), Boer name for foreign residents in South Africa.

Uiyudang (pen name of Lady Kim), Korean writer K-294

Ujiji, Tanzania, former town, now part of Kigoma-Ujiji; in 1871 Stanley found Livingstone here. see also in index Kigoma-Ujiji

'Ujishūi monogatari', Japanese anthology J-81

Ujjain, India, historic city of Gwalior (now in Madhya Pradesh state) on Sipra River; opium trade; one of 7 sacred cities of Hindus; pop. 209,118, *map* I-86

Ujvidek, Yugoslavia. see in index Novi Sad

Ukai Dam, dam in India, on Tapti River. see in index Dam, *table*

'Ukigumo' (The Drifting Cloud), novel by Shimei Futabatei J-82

Ukiyo-e, Japanese art style J-51

'Ukrainian Folk Tales', work by Bloch S-656

Ukrainian language
   Slavic languages S-321

Ukrainians, people U-5

Ukrainian Shield, geographic region in U.S.S.R. U-22

Ukrainian Soviet Socialist Republic (commonly known as the Ukraine), U.S.S.R.; area 233,100 sq mi (601,010 sq km); cap. Kiev; pop. 50,994,000 U-4
   cities. see in index cities below and other cities by name
      Khar'kov K-230
      Kiev K-236
      Russian Civil War R-355
   United Nations, *table* U-84
   U.S.S.R. U-22, *maps* U-62, 66, *picture* U-38

Ukrainian Soviet Socialist Republic Academy of Sciences, in Kiev K-237

Ukulele, small guitar-shaped musical instrument; used by Hawaiians; strummed; has four strings.

Ulaanbaatar (formerly Urga), Mongolia, capital; pop. 488,200 U-6
   Gandan Tekechiling monastery, *pictures* M-541, 543
   Mongolia M-535
   world, *map* W-300

'Ulalume', poem by Poe A-348

Ulanhot, China, city of Inner Mongolian Autonomous Region; pop. 51,400.

Ulanova, Galina (born 1910), Soviet ballerina, born in St. Petersburg, now Leningrad; prima ballerina Bolshoi Theater, Moscow, 1944–61; appeared in United States 1959 ('Giselle'; 'Swan Lake'; 'Romeo and Juliet').

Ulan-Ude (formerly Verkhneudinsk), U.S.S.R., city in s.-central Siberia at junction of Uda and Selenga rivers e. of Lake Baikal; on Trans-Siberian Railroad; builds locomotives and railway cars; pop. 254,000, *map* A-700
   U.S.S.R., *map* U-62 world, *map* W-300

Ulbricht, Walter (1893–1973), East German political leader U-7
   Germany G-127, *picture* G-128

Ulcer, a break in continuity of skin or mucous membrane; caused by death of large numbers of tissue cells U-7
   antiseptic treatment A-495
   psychosomatic disorder theory P-640
   stomach S-630
   therapy T-165

Ulfilas (311?–382?), bishop and missionary to the Goths who reputedly created the Gothic alphabet and wrote the earliest translation of the Bible into a Germanic language G-197

Ulloa, Antonio de (1716–95), Spanish mathematician and traveler; in 1748 identified platinum as an element N-233

Ulloa, Francisco de (died 1540?), Spanish conquistador sent by Cortez to explore the Gulf of California in 1539; established Lower California as a peninsula C-586

Ulm, West Germany, city and river port on Danube 43 mi (69 km) w. of Augsburg; varied manufactures; beautiful Gothic cathedral; pop. 92,943, *map* G-134

Ulmaceae. see in index Elm family

Ulna, inner bone of the forearm S-310

Ulnar nerve, nerve extending from the brachial plexus in the neck to various muscles of the forearm and fingers.

Ulothrix, plant, *picture* L-267

Ulsan, South Korea, seaport town near s.e. coast 33 mi (53 km) n.e. of Pusan; in industrial area; pop. 159,340, *map* K-290

Ulster, a former province of Ireland in n.e. corner of island; consisted of 9 counties; 6 of these now form Northern Ireland, while 3 form Ulster Province (area 3,393 sq mi [10,342 sq km]; pop. 208,303) in Republic of Ireland; name Ulster often used for Northern Ireland, *map* I-283. see also in index Ireland, Republic of; Ireland, Northern

Ultima Thule, name used in ancient times to denote the farthest (in Latin, *ultimus*), or most northerly known land; phrase now used for something far away or unattainable.

Ultisols, soil classification U-102

Ultrahigh temperature method (UHT), process used in pasteurization of milk and cream D-4

Ultralight glider. see in index Hang glider

Ultramarine, a permanent blue pigment originally obtained by powdering lapis lazuli; now made artificially; valued as oil and water color by artists; used in cloth and paper printing, dyeing, ink making.

Ultramicrofiche, type of microfilm M-377

Ultramicroscope, type of microscope M-382

Ultrasaurus, dinosaur A-462

Ultrashort wave. see in index Microwave

Ultrasonic alarm, security system S-164

Ultrasonic machining (USM), a metalworking operation T-226

Ultrasonic wave. see in index Supersonic wave

Ultrasonography, technique for diagnosing disease and for determining size and position of fetus during pregnancy D-127
   genetic disorder detection G-48
   hospital H-282
   multiple birth M-650
   pregnancy P-582

Ultrasound radiation R-42

Ultraviolet light
   photographic application P-335
   radiation R-48

Ultraviolet microscope, type of microscope M-383

Ultraviolet photography. see in index Infrared photography

Ultraviolet radiation, rays R-41, 48
   bee vision B-124
   cancer cause C-132
   light L-194, 201, *diagram* L-202
   lighting types L-206

Ulugh Muztagh, highest peak 25,340 ft (7,720 m) of Kunlun Mountains; in area of n. border of Tibet K-309

Uluru National Park, park in Australia, *picture* N-26

Ulyanov, Vladimir Ilich. see in index Lenin

Ul'yanovsk, U.S.S.R., city on Volga River 430 mi (690 km) s.e. of Moscow; river trade; saw and flour mills, factories; pop. 351,000, *map* E-361
   U.S.S.R., *maps* U-62, 66

Ulysses. see in index Odysseus

'Ulysses', work by Joyce J-145, L-243
   English literature E-281
   naturalism N-414

'Umar I, patriarch of Islam C-54

Umatilla, a Shahaptian people in Oregon; lived along Columbia River; signed treaty with U.S. 1855; Umatilla Indian Reservation (pop. 1,800) just e. of Pendleton, Ore.

Umayyad (or Ommiad, or Omayyad) (661–750), Islamic dynasty I-361
  caliphate C-55
  Iraqi history I-314
  Islamic literature I-365

Umbelliferae. *see in index* Parsley family

Umber, an earthy mineral pigment; contains iron, manganese oxides; mines in U.S. and island of Cyprus; raw umber is dark brown, burnt umber is reddish; used in paints.

Umberto. *see in index* Humbert I; Humbert II

Umbilical cord, a cord that connects the fetus with the placenta, *picture* P-581
  development E-201, *picture* E-199

Umbilicus, part of a mollusk shell, *picture* S-229

Umbo, part of a mollusk shell, *picture* S-229

Umbra, the inner, total shadow cast during an eclipse A-712
  eclipse E-48
  sun S-706, *picture* S-707

Umbrella bird (or dragoon bird), a South American bird *(Cephalopterus ornatus);* size and color of a crow; male has bluish, umbrella-shaped crest and plumed wattle.

Umbrella plant, an East African sedge *(Cyperus alternifolius)* cultivated as a house plant; closely allied to Egyptian papyrus, or paper plant S-165

Umbrella tent, a tent with a vertical pole placed inside T-109

Umbrella tree, a tree *(Magnolia tripetala)* with large white flowers and dark green leaves, often 2 ft (0.6 m) long, crowded into umbrellalike whorls at ends of branches; not evergreen.

Umbria, region in central Italy, until 1860 part of Papal States; area 3,265 mi (8,460 sq km); agriculture and industry; art treasures; pop. 794,745, *map* I-401

Umbriel, moon of Uranus P-413

Ume River, river in Sweden, rises in n. in mountains on the Norway border, flows s.e. more than 280 mi (450 km) to the Gulf of Bothnia; logging route.

Umiak, open Eskimo boat made of a wooden frame covered with hide, usually propelled with broad paddles E-299

Umm al-Qaiwain, one of seven kingdoms comprising the United Arab Emirates U-67

Umm al-Qaiwain, United Arab Emirates, harbor town and urban center of Umm al-Qaiwain kingdom; pop. 14,300.

Umpire, in sports
  baseball B-93

Umtata, town and capital of Transkei, s. Africa; pop. 80,000, *map* A-118

UMW. *see in index* United Mine Workers of America

UN. *see in index* United Nations

Unaka Mountains, range in Appalachian Mountains, along N.C.-Tenn. border, includes Mount Unaka 5,258 ft (1,603 m)

North Carolina, *map* N-355

Unalachtigo, American Indian tribe of the Delaware confederacy; lived on Delaware River in Delaware and possibly in New Jersey.

Unalaska Island, one of Aleutian Islands of Alaska; 75 mi (120 km) long; city of Unalaska (pop. 1,322) is base of U.S. Coast Guard for Bering Sea; Dutch Harbor on adjacent island is a strategic port
Alaska, *map* A-254

Un-American Activities, House Committee on (HUAC), committee organized by the House of Representatives to investigate all subversive activities in U.S.; set up 1938; renamed House Internal Security Committee (HISC) 1969
  Hiss case N-323, *picture* N-322
  Reagan R-112

Unami, American Indian tribe belonging to the Delaware confederacy; lived on Pennsylvania side of Delaware River.

Unamuno, Miguel de (1864–1936), Spanish philosopher, poet, and novelist; rector of Salamanca University after 1900, retired 1934 ('The Tragic Sense of Life'; 'The Agony of Christianity'; 'El Cristo de Velazquez', poem), *picture* S-505
  Spanish literature S-506

'Unanswered Question, The', musical piece by Ives I-406

Unaus, species of two-toed sloth *(Choloepus)* S-324

'Unbearable Bassington, The', work by Saki S-28
  novel N-412

Uncas (originally Wonkus) (1588?–1683?), American Indian chief; in 1635 revolted against Pequots and formed a new group, the Mohegans; fought with British against other American Indians; name used for hero of Cooper's story 'The Last of the Mohicans'.

Uncertainty principle (or indeterminacy principle), in physics
  Heisenberg H-117

Uncia (plural, unciae), in Roman measurement W-138, *table* W-141

Uncial, in handwriting A-318, B-346, C-58

'Uncle Bouqui and Little Malice', Haitian folktale S-644

Uncle Remus, fictional character created by Harris
  American literature A-351
  fable F-4
  folklore F-266, *picture* F-267
  short story S-275
  storytelling S-653

'Uncle Tom's Cabin', novel by Stowe S-664
  American literature A-351
  Beecher family B-131
  cult novel N-411
  short story S-275

'Uncle Tom's Children', novel by Wright W-368

UNCLOS. *see in index* United Nations Conference on the Law of the Sea

Uncompahgre Peak, mountain peak in Colorado Plateau in the United States C-568, *map* C-569
  mountain M-636

Unconscious mind, in psychoanalytic theory P-633
  personality P-234

UNCTAD. *see in index* United Nations Conference on Trade and Development

Undenominational Fellowship of Christian Churches and Churches of Christ, one of three major bodies that split from the Disciples of Christ over doctrinal differences D-164

Underbed irrigation (or subirrigation) I-355

Underclass, social class S-346

Underdeveloped countries. *see in index* Third World

'Under Dogs, The', novel by Azuela L-69

Underemployment E-207

Underfur, of mammals H-7

Undergraduate education, schooling that prepares a person for higher education U-222

Underground, during wartime, a system of espionage, sabotage, and secret communication operated in occupied areas to hamper the enemy
  World War II. *see in index* Resistance movement

Underground economy E-207

Underground film. *see in index* Avant-garde film

Underground mining (or deep mining) M-427
  coal C-521, *diagrams* C-520, 523

Underground Railroad, in U.S. history, escape system for runaway slaves U-7
  abolitionist movement A-10
  black Americans B-290
  Civil War C-472
  Douglass D-235
  Mott M-632
  Rochester, N.Y. R-244
  Tubman T-303

Underground railway. *see in index* Subway

Underground stem. *see in index* Tuber

Underhand mining M-429

Undershot waterwheel W-103

'Understanding Media; the Extensions of Man', work by McLuhan M-22

Understatement, figure of speech F-81

Under the rose. *see in index* Sub rosa

'Under the Volcano', work by Lowry E-282

Underwater navigation N-73

'Under Western Eyes', work by Conrad S-555

Underwood, Oscar Wilder (1862–1929), U.S. statesman, born in Louisville, Ky.; representative and senator from Alabama 1895–1927; chiefly responsible for Underwood-Simmons Tariff Act of 1913; Democratic leader in the Senate 1920–23.

Underwood-Simmons Tariff, in United States W-217

Underwriter, in insurance I-232, 235
  vocation V-392

Undset, Sigrid (1882–1949), Norwegian novelist U-8.
see also in index Nobel Prizewinners, *table*
  Norway N-391
  Scandinavian literature S-89

Undulant fever (or Malta fever), disease with attacks of fever, rheumatic symptoms, weakness, nervousness; caused by *Brucella* organisms, usually from unpasteurized milk. *see also in index* Brucellosis
  infectious disease, *table* D-172

Undy (or wavy line), in heraldry H-136

UNEF (United Nations Emergency Force) U-84

Unemployment E-205. *see also in index* Employment
  black Americans B-301
  child abuse C-319
  depression of 1930s G-242
  factors
    business cycle B-517
    computers C-626
    inflation I-199
    technological machinery A-778
  housing H-296
  Keynes K-229
  labor L-3
  social class S-346
  transportation T-265
  United States U-183
  vocation V-399
  welfare programs W-145
  West Germany G-126

Unemployment compensation, welfare program W-147
  social security S-350

UNESCO. *see in index* United Nations Educational, Scientific, and Cultural Organization

Uneven bars, in gymnastics G-323, *diagram* G-324

Unfederated Malay States. *see in index* Malay States, Unfederated

'Unfinished Symphony', work by Schubert M-672

Ungaretti, Giuseppe (1888–1970), Italian poet I-379

Ungava (or New Quebec), region in Canada, the Quebec area of the Labrador Peninsula; formerly included entire peninsula and was under Hudson's Bay Company; became part of Northwest Territories 1869; made separate district 1895 bounded by that area of Labrador belonging to Newfoundland, *map* C-112
  Labrador L-12
  ore mining O-601
  Quebec Q-13

Ungava Bay, in n. Quebec, inlet of Hudson Strait, *maps* N-351

Ungerer, Tomi (Jean Thomas Ungerer) (born 1931), U.S. author, artist, and cartoonist; born in Strasbourg, France; came to U.S. 1957; wrote and illustrated 'Mellops Go Flying', 'Rufus', 'Ask Me A Question', 'The Beast of Monsieur Racine'.

Unguis, part of hoof H-231

Ungulates, the group of hoofed animals H-231
  antelopes A-478

UNIA. *see in index* Universal Negro Improvement Association and African Communities League

Uniats, Eastern Christians who follow rites of Greek Catholic church but accept supremacy of pope.

Unicameral legislature, one-house legislature N-97, S-594

UNICEF (United Nations Children's Fund) U-86
  Halloween H-17
  malnutrition M-77

Unicellular organisms. *see in index* Radiolaria

Unicoi Mountains, in Appalachian Mountains, on North Carolina-Tennessee border
  North Carolina, *map* N-355

Unicorn, one-horned horse of fable A-458, *picture* A-430
  folklore F-260

Unicorn, a constellation. *see in index* Monoceros

Unicorn plant (or Proboscidea), genus of annual and perennial plants of the Martynia family,

native to tropical America; the tender 6 in (15 cm) seedpods are grown as vegetables and used in pickles.

Unicycle, one-wheeled vehicle circus, *picture* C-431

Unidentified flying object (UFO) U-8

Unification church (full name, Holy Spirit Association for the Unification of World Christianity) U-9

Unified Dairy Cow Score Card, The, guide for evaluating dairy cattle C-225

Unified field theory, relativity R-154

UNIFON, 40-symbol phonetic alphabet based on one symbol for a single basic sound; developed by John Malone, U.S. economist; contains 22 letters of the English alphabet and 18 variants.

Uniformitarianism, in geology Hutton H-336

Uniforms, military U-10. *see also in index* Insignia
  medals M-270

Uniforms, nonmilitary
  laundering L-85

Unimak Island, the largest island of the e. Aleutians in Alaska; 65 mi (105 km) long and 25 mi (40 km) wide; wildlife refuge
  Alaska, *map* A-254

Union, N.J., an urban township 3 mi (5 km) n.w. of Elizabeth; paint, lacquers, aluminum products, and steel; Kean College of New Jersey; pop. 55,593
  New Jersey, *map* N-211

Union, S.C., industrial city located 28 mi (45 km) s. of Spartanburg; textiles, metal stampings; plastic molding; pop. 10,523
  South Carolina, *map* S-437

Union, W. Va., town 18 mi (29 km) s.e. of Hinton; in farming area; lumbering, flour mills; pop. 743
  West Virginia, *map* W-182

Union, a flag badge, *list* F-149

Union, labor. *see in index* Labor unions

Union, Act of. *see in index* Act of Union

Union bagpipe (or musette), wind instrument W-228

Union Carbide Corporation, formed 1917; present name after 1956; makers of carbons, alloys, Bakelite and other plastics, chemicals and gases; diverse nuclear activities; many divisions and subsidiaries in U.S. and Canada; headquarters, New York, N.Y.
  Bhopal I-80

Union City, Calif., city 17 mi (27 km) s. of Oakland; sugar refining; foundry products; pop. 39,406
  California, *map* C-53

Union City, N.J., a city adjoining Jersey City to the n.; embroideries, toiletries, incandescent lamps, and corrugated paper; pop. 58,537
  Hispanic Americans H-163
  New Jersey, *map* N-211

Union City, Tenn., town 32 mi (52 km) n.e. of Dyersburg; footwear, auto parts, dairy products; incorporated 1861; pop. 10,436, *map* T-99

Union College, in Barbourville, Ky.; Methodist; founded 1879; arts and sciences, education; graduate study.

Union College, in Lincoln, Neb.; Seventh-day Adventist; founded 1891; arts and sciences, agriculture, business, education, home economics, music, nursing.

Union College, in Schenectady, N.Y.; part of Union University; formerly for men; founded 1795; arts and sciences, engineering; graduate work; college fraternity system originated here in 1825 N-255. *see also in index* Union University

Uniondale, N.Y., residential community 21 mi (34 km) e. of New York City in Nassau County on Long Island; about 10 mi (16 km) s. of Hempstead Harbor; pop. 22,077.

Union Flag. *see in index* British Union

Union Islands. *see in index* Tokelau

Union Jack. *see in index* British Union

Union of American Hebrew Congregations (U.A.H.C.), main governing body of Reform Judaism in Western Hemisphere; oldest federation of U.S. Jewish congregations, founded 1873; provides administrative, religious, educational, and cultural programs to more than 600 affiliated synagogues; strenuously fights anti-semitism; trains leaders, rabbis, educators; affiliated with World Union for Progressive Judaism.

Union of South Africa. *see in index* South Africa, Republic of

Union of Soviet Socialist Republics (commonly called Soviet Union, formerly Russia), country of e. Europe and of w.-central and n. Asia; area 8,649,798 sq mi (22,402,874 sq km); cap. Moscow; pop. 241,748,000 U-18
  agriculture A-141
    cotton C-735
    poultry P-572
    sugar beet, *chart* B-113
    tobacco T-198
    wheat W-187, 190
  armed forces
    air force A-163
    conscription C-667
    disarmament D-163
    guided missile G-312
    helicopters H-122
    limitations treaties P-163
    military education M-409, 413
    navy N-84, 92
      Mediterranean fleet M-286
      submarines S-686
    nuclear weapons N-434
  arts
    ballet B-34, *picture* B-30
    dance D-28
    folk art F-253
    medals M-272
    motion pictures D-155, M-620, 623
    music
      classical M-674
      folk F-273
      vocal V-388
  cities C-453. *see also in index* cities listed below and other cities by name
    Khar'kov K-230
    Kiev K-236
    Kuybyshev K-308
    Leningrad L-127
    Minsk M-461
    Moscow M-591, 594
    Novosibirsk N-415
    Odessa O-493
    Samarkand S-35
    Sverdlovsk S-722
    Vladivostok V-385
  communications
    newspapers N-236, N-242
    radio R-66
  concentration camps C-638
    genocide G-60
    prisoners of war P-605
  Cossacks C-733
  economics E-61
    banking B-70

industry F-463, I-196
  labor movements L-11
  subsidy S-687
education E-96, 101
  adult education A-52
  bilingual education B-191
  kindergarten K-239, 242
  Kolmogorov K-267
  libraries L-177, 184, *pictures* L-179, 180
  school systems S-94
  universities and colleges U-228
energy
  nuclear energy N-430
  waterpower W-105
flag, *picture* F-171
geography
  Aral Sea A-527
  Arctic region A-571
  Asia, *map* A-700
  Black Sea B-307
  Caspian Sea C-196
  Crimea C-774
  Europe, *map* E-361
  Ladoga Lake L-19
  Mongolia A-278
  Onega Lake O-541
  republics. *see in index* republics by name
  rivers. *see in index* names of rivers
  Siberia A-677, S-280
  Ural Mountains U-229
government A-46, G-199
  censorship C-247
  Communism C-619
  court systems S-714
  espionage E-302
  housing H-298, 302
  intelligence agencies I-236
  Kremlin K-304
  law L-96
    administrative A-46
    courts-martial C-748
    criminal law C-775
    estate and inheritance E-307
    legal system L-96
    prison and punishment P-601
  municipal government M-654
  political assassinations A-704
  prison and punishment P-601, 605
  propaganda P-610
  socialism S-348
  state government S-597
  totalitarianism T-234
  welfare programs W-145
health care H-285
  agencies H-89
  alcoholism P-607
  insurance H-95
history
  expansion F-426
  Holocaust H-205
  Mao Zedong M-112
  Mongol empire M-534
  plague P-403
  rulers and leaders. For Russia's rulers to 1917 *see table in index* following Russia. For leaders of the Soviet Union *see table* following Alexanders, czars A-278
    Andropov A-411
    Brezhnev B-435
    Catherine II, the Great C-222
    Chernenko C-303
    Gorbachev G-195

Ivans, grand dukes and czars I-405
    Khrushchev K-233
    Lenin L-126
    Nicholas, czars N-306
    Peter I, the Great P-247
    Romanov Dynasty R-280
    Stalin S-570
    Sun Yat-sen S-710
  treaties
    North Atlantic Treaty Organization N-352
    Rapallo Treaty G-123
    Southeast Asia Treaty Organization S-454
    Warsaw Pact W-34
  wars
    Crimean War C-774
    Korean War K-295, *chart* K-299
    Napoleonic wars N-16
    Russian Civil War W-319
    Russian Revolution R-354, W-309, *picture* C-619
    Russo-Japanese War R-357
    Seven Years' War S-185
    World War I A-643, W-302, 305, *map* W-304, *picture* W-306
    World War II W-322, *map* W-334
  Zionism S-168, Z-455
international affairs
  Asia
    Afghanistan A-91
    China C-358, 377
    Dardanelles D-35
    Iran I-312
    Korea K-286
    Lüda L-328
    Manchuria M-94
    Ottoman Empire O-618, T-323
    Tianjin T-179
    Vietnam V-342
  Europe
    Austria-Hungary A-830
    Balkans B-29
    Czechoslovakia C-816
    East Germany G-110, 118
    Finland F-91, K-195
    Germany G-124, W-142
    Hungary H-330
    Poland P-494
    Prussia P-628
    Romania R-279
    Sweden S-730
    West Germany G-126
    Yugoslavia Y-438
  Latin America
    Argentina A-579
    Cuba C-801
    Grenada G-284
    Third World T-168
    United Nations U-80, 84
    United States U-143, 176, 180
      Alaska A-278
      California C-41
      embargoes E-197
      Oregon O-581, 586
      Roosevelt R-308
  invention I-278
  irrigation I-356
  land-use control L-29
  literature. *see in index* Russian literature
  migration of people M-400, 407
  mining
    aluminum A-321
    coal C-518
    gold G-180
    manganese M-96

ores O-601, *table* O-600
national anthem, *table* N-64
national parks N-27
nihilism R-282
Olympic games O-541
pageant and parade P-13
pipeline P-390
refugees R-147
religion
  Baptists B-76
  Christianization M-543
  church and state issue C-409
  Russian Orthodox Church E-42
satellites S-71
social class S-344
space travel S-460, 469, 476
transportation
  Trans-Siberian Railroad T-266
  waterway W-108
  weights and measures, *table* W-141
world, *map* W-300
youth organizations Y-427, 431

Union of the Crowns (1603), union of England and Scotland U-68

Union Pacific Railroad, one of links in first transcontinental railroad in United States R-86
  bribery uncovered G-219
  Wyoming W-389

Union party, U.S. political party organized 1861 (after Union defeat at Bull Run) in attempt to save the Union by unifying all Northern antislavery forces; formed by Republicans with support of War Democrats; renominated Lincoln; name also used by minor party in 1936 presidential campaign
  Civil War C-477

Union Stock Yards (or Chicago stockyards), supply depot C-317, *picture* C-316

Union Terminal, railroad station in Cincinnati, Ohio C-415

Uniontown, Pa., a city situated 45 mi (70 km) s.e. of Pittsburgh; coal, textiles, trailer tanks, crushed limestone, lumber, and metal products; pop. 14,510
  Pennsylvania, *map* P-206

Union University, institution comprising Union College at Schenectady, N.Y., and Albany Medical College, Albany Law School, Dudley Observatory, and Albany College of Pharmacy, at Albany, N.Y.; with exception of pharmacy college (founded 1881), all were incorporated as Union University 1873 A-259

Union University, in Jackson, Tenn.; Southern Baptist; founded 1825; present name since 1907; arts and sciences, music.

Unireme, galley ship N-81

Unita and Ouray Reservation, American Indian reservation in Utah U-245

Unita Mountains, mountain range in Utah U-245

Unitarian Church, church in Shorewood Hills, Wis. W-367

Unitarianism, a system of Christian belief that rejects the doctrine of the Trinity, fixed creeds, and all authority in religion; basic beliefs taught since AD 150; first church of Unitarian beliefs organized in Poland about 1587 by Faustus Socinus; first organized Unitarian movement in England 1773; influential in New England from middle of 18th century; in 1961 merged with the Universalists
  England E-233
  Unitarian Universalist Association U-67

Unitarian Universalist Association, formed 1961 by the American Unitarians and the Universalist Church of America U-67

Unitary tax policy, an issue in corporate taxes T-36

Unitas, John (born 1933), U.S. football player, born in Pittsburgh, Pa.; quarterback for Baltimore Colts 1956–72, San Diego Chargers 1973; chosen National Football League's most valuable football player 1957; holder numerous records; author of 'Playing Pro Football to Win' F-296

Unit cell, in crystal structure C-795

United All England Croquet Association (now Croquet Association) C-783

United Arab Emirates (formerly Trucial States, or Trucial Coast), a group of seven states in Arabia, along s. coast of Persian Gulf; area 30,000 sq mi (77,700 sq km); cap. Abu Dhabi; pop. 1,856,000 U-67
  Arabia A-521, *map* A-522
  Asia, *map* A-700, *table* A-694
  flag, *picture* F-171
  United Nations, *table* U-84
  world, *map* W-300

United Arab States E-121

United Artists, U.S. motion-picture company M-620
  Chaplin C-271
  Fairbanks F-11

United Automobile Workers. *see in index* International Union, United Automobile, Aircraft & Agricultural Implement Workers of America

United Brethren. *see in index* Moravians

United Brethren in Christ, Evangelical Christian denomination founded in U.S. under leadership of Philip William Otterbein (1726–1813) of German Reformed church and Martin Boehm (1725–1812), a Mennonite; in 1946 united with Evangelical church to become the Evangelical United Brethren church; in 1968 merged with Methodists to form United Methodist church.

United Church of Canada, religious group
  Methodism M-318
  Presbyterianism P-583

United Church of Christ, founded 1957 by the merger of the Evangelical and Reformed church, with a membership of 774,300, and the General Council of the Congregational and Christian churches, with a membership of 1,342,000 R-142

United Colonies of New England. *see in index* New England Confederation

United Daughters of the Confederacy, organization composed of female descendants of Confederate Civil War veterans; founded 1894 at Nashville, Tenn. W-270

United East India Company. *see in index* Dutch East India

United Empire Loyalists
  Canada C-94
    Hamilton H-23
    New Brunswick N-157
    Ontario O-553
    Saint John S-20

United Farm Workers of America (UFW), U.S. labor union; founded 1962 as National Farm Workers Association by César Chavez; merged with AFL-CIO 1966; re-formed with current name 1971 to achieve collective-bargaining rights

LEADERS OF THE SOVIET UNION

1917–1924	V.I. Lenin
1924–1953	Joseph Stalin
1953–1955	Committee headed by Georgi Malenkov
1955–1964	Nikita Khrushchev
1964	Aleksei Kosygin
1964–1982	Leonid Brezhnev
1982–1984	Yuri Andropov
1984–1985	Konstantin Chernenko
1985–	Mikhail Gorbachev

for U.S. farm workers; seeks to give workers dignity and improve wages and working and safety conditions of migrant farm workers; espouses nonviolence; educates members in political and social arenas.

United Food and Commercial Workers, U.S. labor union L-10

United Fund, U.S. charity F-329
  public relations P-645

United Independent Broadcasters, Inc. see in index Columbia Broadcasting System

United Jewish Appeal, fund-raising organization for Jewish needs overseas, founded 1939; provides humanitarian programs and social services in Israel and many other countries; sponsors cultural programs, exhibitions, workshops, conferences; develops national themes and programs for fund-raising efforts throughout the U.S.

United Kingdom (officially United Kingdom of Great Britain and Northern Ireland); area 94,248 sq mi (244,100 km); cap. London; pop. 56,878,000 U-68. For climate and geology: see in index British Isles; for history before 1801 and individual country information: see in index England. see also in index British Empire; Commonwealth, The; Ireland, Northern; Scotland; Wales
  armed forces. see also in index Royal Air Force; Royal Marines; Royal Navy
    military education M-411
    uniform and insignia U-17
    veterans' organizations V-328
    warfare W-20, 25
  arts
    architecture A-561
    dance D-29
    furniture F-460
    handicrafts H-29
    literature. see in index English literature
    motion pictures M-615, 618, 623
    music
      bands B-55
      opera O-569
      popular M-681
    painting P-45
    performing arts P-219
    Punch and Judy shows P-665
  business and industry I-196
    airlines A-170
    automobile A-866
    brewing B-134
    cartels M-544
    concrete C-641
    garment industry G-35
    hats and caps H-54
    lace L-13, picture L-16

mines and mining M-430
cities C-449, U-234. see also in index cities listed below and other cities by name
    Birmingham B-282
    Canterbury C-142
    Liverpool L-261
    London L-286
    Oxford O-621
    Sheffield S-224
    Stratford-upon-Avon S-667
  citizenship C-442
  communications
    ham radio H-190
    magazine and journal M-33
    mail delivery P-553, 557
    newspapers N-241
    radio R-52
    television T-73
  constitution C-683
  crime C-770
  customs and traditions
    Christmas C-405
    cosmetics C-729
    hairdressing H-10
    Halloween H-17
    marriage M-149
    tea T-45
  East Indian minority M-460
  education E-85, 100
    alternative schools B-321
    school systems S-96
    universities and colleges U-224, 227. see also in index Cambridge University; Eton College; Harrow School; Oxford University; Rugby School
  employment and unemployment E-206
  encyclopedias R-131
  Europe, map E-361
  Fabian Society F-2
  fire fighting F-111
  flags F-161, picture F-172
    British Union F-153, picture F-155
    medieval banner M-384
  foundations and charities F-333, table F-331
  government. see also in index Parliament, subhead United Kingdom
    administrative power A-46
    aviation supervision A-881
    Bill of Rights B-194, picture B-195
    bureaucracy B-506
    cabinet C-4
    democracy D-92
    government agencies G-202
    municipal government M-655
    political parties P-514
    prime ministers. see table following
    socialism S-347
    taxation, table T-35
  gross national product, table P-576
  halfway house H-14
  health care H-285
    agencies H-89
    education H-94
    hospice H-275
  history E-251
    Industrial Revolution I-178
    Munich Pact M-653

slavery S-320
wars and battles
    Afghan Wars A-91
    Battle of Waterloo W-99
    Boer War B-330
    Korean War, table K-296
    Opium Wars O-573, C-369
    Seven Years' War S-185
    War of 1812 W-29
    World War I W-302, map W-303, picture W-306
    World War II A-743, G-309, M-569, W-322
  hostels H-285
  housing H-297, 306
  intelligence agencies I-237
  international relations D-149
    Afghanistan A-91
    Africa A-97, 111
    Asia A-678
    Canada C-87, 99. see also in index Canada Confederation, Fathers of
    East Indies E-45
    Egypt E-121
    France F-363
    Gambia G-8
    Germany G-124
    Ghana G-139
    Greece G-260
    India I-61, 77, map I-79
      Delhi D-88
      Mughal Empire M-645
    Iran I-30
    Iraq I-315
    Ireland I-317, 325
    Kenya K-228
    Kiribati K-250
    Korea K-287
    Libya T-289
    Malawi M-69
    Malaysia M-72
    Malta M-79
    Mauritius M-233
    New Zealand N-282
    Nigeria N-310
    North Atlantic Treaty Organization N-352
    Oregon territory dispute O-581, P-521
    Pakistan B-63
    Palestine P-84
    People's Democratic Republic of Yemen Y-414
    Philadelphia P-281
    Qatar Q-2
    Quebec Q-15
    Seychelles S-198
    South Africa S-398
    Southeast Asia Treaty Organization S-454
    Sudan S-692
    Tibet T-181
    Togo T-202
    trade I-271
    Treaties of Washington T-275
    Trinidad and Tobago T-289
    Uganda U-4
    United Arab Emirates U-67
    United Nations U-80, 83, table U-84
    United States U-170, 174
      Alabama claims A-238
      Civil War C-477
      Detroit D-122
      Roosevelt R-308
    Zimbabwe Z-453
  invention I-278

labor unions L-4, table L-8
language. see in index English language
law
    blue laws B-319
    constitutional law C-685
    corn laws C-723
    courts of justice C-746, S-714
    criminal law C-776
    estate and inheritance E-307
    jury system J-158
    prison and punishment P-604
    welfare programs W-146
    women's rights W-272, 278
  lighthouse maintenance L-205
  mathematics M-216
  medals M-270
  museums. see in index British museum; National Gallery; Victoria and Albert Museum
  national anthem N-65
  national parks N-25
  nobility. see in index Titles of nobility
  nuclear energy N-430
  pageant and parade P-12
  peace movements P-161
  pension plans P-209
  pleasure gardens A-384
  police P-504, P-510. see also in index Scotland Yard
  reformatories R-141
  religion. see also in index Church of England
    Anglican church A-416
    Baptist churches B-77
    church and state issue C-409
    Protestantism P-625
  safety S-5
  social class S-344
  sports
    archery A-541
    boxing B-290
    cricket C-765
    dog racing D-214
    field hockey H-193
    football F-295
    horse racing H-275
    water polo W-102
    wrestling W-366
  stamp, picture S-574
  temperance movements T-80
  territories, colonies, and possessions
    British Virgin Islands V-398
    Channel Islands C-270
    Falkland Islands F-14
    Gibraltar G-143
    Hong Kong H-229
    Isle of Man M-91
    terrorism T-113
    Thames River T-150
    transportation
      canals C-127
      locomotives L-280
    weights and measures W-138, table W-140
  world, map W-300

United Methodist church, Protestant organization formed 1968 by union of Methodist church and Evangelical United Brethren church M-318. see also in index Evangelical

church; Methodist church; United Brethren in Christ

United Mine Workers of America (UMW)
  coal mining history C-526
  Jones J-140
  Lewis L-142

United Nations (UN) U-80. see also index entries beginning with United Nations
  Atlantic charter A-743
  banking
    development banking B-71
    World Bank W-301
  Canada C-104
  China C-374
  cities C-450
  disarmament D-163
  Egypt E-121
  embargo E-198
  Europe E-353
  flag code F-152
  France F-360
  headquarters
    Geneva G-58
    New York City N-258, pictures A-666, N-261
  human rights H-319
  international law I-257
  international relations I-262
  Israel I-372
  Korean War K-295, table K-299
  labor and industrial law L-5
  Latin American programs L-66
  North America N-344
  origin S-47
  Palestine P-86
  parks N-26
  peacekeeping
    Cyprus T-325
    India I-79
    Lebanon L-113
    Pakistan P-83
  peace movements P-161
  prostitution P-619
  protocol E-319
  radio broadcasting R-66
  refugees R-149
  Rockefeller R-249
  Roosevelt R-312
  ship and shipping S-253
  South Africa S-393
  space programs S-480
  Taiwan C-309
  tariff T-30
  Thant T-151
  Truman T-297
  trusteeships. see in index Trusteeships
  United States U-175, 178
  Universal Declaration of Human Rights B-197
  Universal Postal Union B-144
  U.S.S.R. U-54
  veto authority V-331
  Vietnam V-342
  World War II W-355
  Zionism Z-456

United Nations Charter U-80

United Nations Children's Fund. see in index UNICEF

United Nations Commission on Human Rights
  international law I-257

20TH-CENTURY PRIME MINISTERS OF THE UNITED KINGDOM

Name	Term	Party	Name	Term	Party
Marquis of Salisbury	1895–1902	Conservative	Winston Churchill	1940–45	National
Arthur James Balfour	1902–05	Conservative	Clement Attlee	1945–51	Labor
Henry Campbell-Bannerman	1905–08	Liberal	Winston Churchill	1951–55	Conservative
Herbert Henry Asquith	1908–15	Liberal	Anthony Eden	1955–57	Conservative
Herbert Henry Asquith	1915–16	Coalition	Harold Macmillan	1957–63	Conservative
David Lloyd George	1916–22	Coalition	Alexander Douglas-Home	1963–64	Conservative
Andrew Bonar Law	1922–23	Conservative	Harold Wilson	1964–70	Labor
Stanley Baldwin	1923–24	Conservative	Edward Heath	1970–74	Conservative
Ramsay MacDonald	1924	Labor	Harold Wilson	1974–76	Labor
Stanley Baldwin	1924–29	Conservative	James Callaghan	1976–79	Labor
Ramsay MacDonald	1929–31	Labor	Margaret Thatcher	1979–	Conservative
Ramsay MacDonald	1931–35	National			
Stanley Baldwin	1935–37	National			
Neville Chamberlain	1937–40	National			

United Nations Conference on International Organization U-80

United Nations Conference on the Law of the Sea (UNCLOS) I-257
oceanography O-474

United Nations Conference on Trade and Development (UNCTAD)
food supply F-287
international trade I-267

United Nations Development Programme U-83

United Nations Educational, Scientific, and Cultural Organization (UNESCO) U-86
national parks N-26
oceanography commission O-464
space research S-480
Venice V-300

United Nations Emergency Force (UNEF) U-84

United Nations Monetary and Financial Conference I-258

United Nations Operation in the Congo (ONUC, in French, Opération des Nations Unies au Congo) U-85

United Nations Relief and Rehabilitation Administration (UNRRA) W-356
refugees R-148

United Nations War Crimes Commission W-11

United Negro College Fund, an agency offering aid to black students; headquarters, New York, N.Y.

United Nile River. see in index Nile River

United Press International (UPI), news gathering service N-238
football poll F-290

United Provinces. see in index Netherlands, The

United Provinces of Agra and Oudh (or United Provinces), in n. India; formerly province of British India; now part of Uttar Pradesh state.

United Reform church, Protestant denomination England E-233

United Republic of Cameroon. see in index Cameroon

United Republic of Tanzania. see in index Tanzania

United Service Organizations (USO), founded 1941 to conduct recreation centers for U.S. armed forces personnel
Hope H-237
Rockefeller R-249

United Shoe Machinery Corporation, shoe manufacturing S-264

United Sioux of South Dakota, American Indian activists I-154

United Society of Believers in Christ's Second Appearing. see in index Shakers

United Sons of Confederate Veterans. see in index Confederate Veterans, United Sons of

United States, a republic of North America; 3,679,192 sq mi (9,529,063 sq km); cap. Washington, D.C.; pop. 243,773,000 U-89. see also in index entries beginning with United States; also chief topics below
agriculture A-133, F-27
cotton C-736
dairy industry D-3
machinery F-30
margarine M-134
milk M-415
fruit production F-439
livestock. see in index livestock by name
pest control P-244
soil, map S-370
sugarcane S-698
tobacco T-198
vegetables V-288, pictures V-286, 287
wheat W-187, 190
American Indians I-110, 148, 154, maps I-136, 149, picture I-150
amusement parks A-383
art and architecture
architecture A-561. see also in index Colonial architecture; Mission architecture
dance D-29
ballet B-35
folk F-257
design D-111
drama D-247
dress design D-269
folk art F-252
furniture F-458, picture F-457
glassmaking G-162
literature. see in index American literature
motion pictures M-618, 621, 624, 628
music
classical M-674
country M-678
folk F-273
opera O-560, 571
popular M-679
vocal V-388
needlework N-112
painting P-49, R-117
performing arts P-218
pottery and porcelain P-571
puppetry P-666
quilts Q-24
sculpture S-148
theater T-161
Western W-151
assassinations A-704
banks and banking B-66, 73
coinage C-538
money M-531
savings and loan association S-85
bison population B-286
black Americans B-295
business, industry, and mining I-183
beer B-132
cement C-245
cooperatives C-707
fur F-463
garment G-35
insurance I-235
iron and steel I-331
leather L-107
mining M-431
paint and varnish P-16
paper production P-111
pencils P-178
real estate R-115
rubber R-338
rug and carpetmaking R-344
salt S-32
shoe S-265
sports industry S-549
trucking T-292
vending machines V-290
wine W-239
wire W-247
cities. see in index individual cities by name
citizenship C-439
naturalization N-67
passport P-148
communal living C-604, S-347, U-260
communications
ham radio H-190
magazine and journal M-32
mail delivery P-558
newspapers N-235, 239, 242
radio R-51
conscription C-667
Constitution. see in index United States Constitution
crime C-769
customs and traditions
clothing C-505, pictures A-39, F-424, 426
cosmetics C-729
etiquette E-318, 321
Halloween H-17
leisure L-123
Thanksgiving T-150
totemism and taboo T-236
dams D-16, pictures D-12
democracy D-93
Dickens' views D-135
diplomacy D-149, diagram D-150
ecology and environment
acid rain A-19
irrigation and reclamation I-355, R-118
land use L-29
pollution P-526
recycling R-123
economics E-60
Black Friday panic (1869) G-218
depression of 1929. see in index Great Depression
employment and unemployment E-205. see also Fact Summary with each state article
gross national product G-290, table P-576
inflation I-198
monopolies M-543
subsidy S-687
taxation T-35
education E-88
bilingual B-191
kindergarten and nursery school K-239, 242
school systems S-93
special education S-512
universities and colleges U-223, 227
vocational training V-400
Webster, picture A-346
energy
fuel resources and consumption F-443
oil embargo O-606
petroleum P-251
pipeline P-390
solar energy S-372
waterpower resources W-105
espionage E-302
eugenics E-326
family F-15, 19, G-46, diagram F-18
fire fighting F-103
food and beverage F-285
fisheries, diagram F-166
meat consumption M-246, graph M-247
restaurants R-176
tea innovation T-46
foundations and charities F-328, table F-332
geology and physical geography, map E-25
deserts D-105
easternmost point. see in index West Quoddy Head, Me.
fall line F-14
forest F-310, 315
Great Smoky Mountains G-251
Gulf of Mexico M-345
Rio Grande R-225
river R-227
southernmost mainland point. see in index Sable, Cape, Fla.
water W-84, 90
government. see in index United States government
harbors and ports H-36
health and disease D-173. see also in index Public health
agencies H-89
education H-91, 94
halfway house H-14
hospitals H-279, 284
insurance H-95
medicine M-275, 279
pharmacology P-275
physiological research P-370
sports medicine S-552
poisonings P-487
psychology P-638
Red Cross R-125
sexually transmitted disease S-195
vitamins V-381
Hispanic Americans H-162
history
Alaska Purchase A-245
ANZUS treaty A-497
Bacon's rebellion B-11
Civil War. see in index Civil War, American
Confederate States of America C-470, C-642
Constitution U-194
Declaration of Independence D-53
Dred Scott decision D-259
exploration and colonization A-327, E-376, J-21. see also in index America, discovery and colonization of
French and Indian War F-393
Industrial Revolution I-181
Korean War K-295, 300, chart K-299, table K-296
Ku Klux Klan K-78d
mail delivery P-555
Mexican War (1846–48) M-319
Alamo A-238
Mexico M-336
Veracruz V-302
peace movements P-161
prisoners of war P-605
Prohibition P-606
Reconstruction period. see in index Reconstruction period
Revolutionary War. see in index Revolution, American
slavery S-319
abolitionist movement A-9
Missouri Compromise M-507
Spanish-American War S-501
Spanish Civil War S-503
Vietnam War V-347. see also in index Vietnam War
Virginia Declaration of Rights B-196
War of 1812 W-29
westward movement F-419
fur trade F-471
gold rush of 1849 G-183
Louisiana Purchase L-324
World War I W-303
army A-643
Verdun V-302
World War II W-322
Holocaust H-206
Japanese-American internment C-638
Yamamoto Y-409
XYZ affair X-406
hotels and motels M-286
housing H-290, 299, 306
humanism H-318
human rights H-319
international relations I-261
Alabama claims A-238
Alaska boundary dispute A-256
Asia A-692
Atlantic Charter A-743
Canada C-89, 106
Central America C-256
China C-358, 374, 377
Cold War C-545
Cuba C-800, 802
Dominican Republic D-228
Egypt E-121
England E-246
Germany G-124
Greece G-260
Greenland G-282
Grenada G-284
Haiti H-13
Honduras H-227
hostage incident I-310
Israel I-372
Japan J-68, O-520
Korea K-286
Korean jetliner incident I-264
Latin America L-66
Lebanon L-113
Libya L-190
Mediterranean Sea M-286
Mexico M-326, M-329
Monroe Doctrine M-549
Nicaragua N-304
North Atlantic Treaty Organization N-67
Palestine P-85
Panama P-94
Persian Gulf P-232
Philippines P-303, Q-24
Poland P-495
seal hunting S-156
Southeast Asia Treaty Organization S-454
Spain S-485, 499
Taiwan C-309, T-13
Thailand T-149
Third World T-168
trade
Bremen B-316
fairs F-20, 22
United Nations U-80, table U-84
U.S.S.R. E-197, U-54
Vietnam V-342
West Indies W-157
Zionism Z-456
law
food and drug F-274
labor and industrial L-4
women's rights W-272, 279
levees D-146
libraries L-185
mathematics M-216
medals M-270
minerals. see in index minerals listed below and others by name
coal C-518, map C-526
gold G-180
ores, table O-600
sulfur S-701
uranium U-230
museums M-660. see also Fact Summary with each state article
nationalism N-66
national parks N—25, 33
national symbols
anthem N-63. see also in index 'Star-Spangled Banner, The'
bird E-2
flags F-150, picture F-172
Liberty Bell, picture P-198
North America N-334, map N-351
pageant and parade P-12
parks and playgrounds P-134
philosophy P-318
police P-504, 511
population P-538. see table following
census C-247
density, chart J-414
immigration. see in index Immigration, subhead United States
migration M-400, 404
minority groups M-459
Oceania O-468, 472
race and ethnicity R-34
refugees R-147
states. see Fact Summary with each state article
pornography P-543
presidential cabinet C-5. see also in index Presidents and Presidential Candidates, table
printing P-599
religion C-408. see also in index religions and denominations by name
Romanticism R-282
safety S-5
science and technology S-111
atomic bomb N-434
invention I-278
radar R-40
satellites S-72
submarines S-682
sociology S-359
class S-344
retirement R-178
segregation S-168
war on poverty J-472
welfare programs W-145
social security S-350
social settlements S-351
space travel. see in index Space travel
sports
auto racing A-874
baseball B-87
basketball B-97
dog racing D-214
football F-289
golf G-185
ice hockey H-194
rodeo R-257
skiing S-311
soccer S-344
stadiums and arenas S-566
tennis T-108
suffrage S-694
taxation. see in index Tariff; Taxation
television T-69
territories and possessions. see in index territories

UNITED STATES POPULATION GROWTH

Census	Population	Increase	Pct.
1980	226,504,825	23,202,794	11.4
1970	203,302,031	23,978,856	13.4
1960	179,323,175	27,997,377	18.5
1950	151,325,798*	19,656,523	14.9
1940	131,669,275	8,894,229	7.2
1930	122,775,046	17,064,426	16.1
1920	105,710,620	13,738,354	14.9
1910	91,972,266	15,977,691	21.0
1900	75,994,575	13,046,861	20.7
1890	62,947,714	12,791,931	25.5
1880	50,155,783	10,337,334	26.0
1870	39,818,449	8,375,128	26.6
1860	31,443,321	8,251,445	35.6
1850	23,191,876	6,122,423	35.9
1840	17,069,453	4,203,433	32.7
1830	12,866,020	3,227,567	33.5
1820	9,638,453	2,398,572	33.1
1810	7,239,881	1,931,398	36.4
1800	5,308,483	1,379,269	35.1
1790	3,929,214	....	...

*Includes populations of Alaska and Hawaii, though then not states

and possessions listed below and others by name
American Samoa S-35
Puerto Rico P-652
Virgin Islands of the United States V-378
terrorism T-113
transportation T-253, *pictures* T-254, 255, 262, 263, 265
aviation, *chart* A-220
canals. see in index Canals, *subhead* United States
express E-382
railroads R-85
roads and highways R-230, 236, *map* R-234, *pictures* R-232, 233, 235
St. Lawrence Seaway S-21
ships S-249, 253
street railways S-669
waterways W-108
trusteeships. see in index Trusteeships, *table*
urban planning U-233
veterans' organizations V-328
vice-president. see in index Vice-president, *table*
weather W-119, 121, 126
climate C-500
floods F-180, *table* F-181
weights and measures, *table* W-140
women's organizations W-270
world, *map* W-300
youth organizations Y-427, 431
'United States', frigate Washington W-44
'United States', ship, *picture* S-245
United States Advisory Committee on National Illiteracy R-109
United States Air Force A-163. see also in index Aviation, military and naval
fire fighting F-106
flags F-158
gliders G-168
guided missile, *picture* G-309
Korean War K-295, *chart* K-299
national museum, *picture* O-511
navigation N-77
unidentified flying objects U-8
uniform and insignia U-11, *pictures* U-12, 14
women A-133, *picture* A-130
X-15. see in index X-15

United States Air Force Academy, near Colorado Springs, Colo. C-571, 586, *map* C-583, *picture* C-576
Eisenhower E-138
military education M-411
United States Air Forces in Europe (USAFE) A-164
United States Air Service W-309
United States Army A-645, 647
advertising A-60
black Americans B-291, R-119, *list* B-299, *picture* B-292
conscription. see in index Conscription, *subhead* United States
education M-409
firearms F-100, *picture* F-99
fire fighting F-106
guard dogs D-193
guided missiles G-307
helicopter A-580, 577, *picture* A-581
intelligence test I-241, *graph* I-239
Korean War K-295, 300, *chart* K-299
machine gun M-13
military academy. see in index United States Military Academy
signaling S-287
tanks. see in index Tank
uniform and insignia U-11, *pictures* U-12, U-14
Vietnam War V-347, *pictures* V-348, 349
World War I W-313, *pictures* W-302, 309, 310
World War II W-328, 340, 345, *pictures* W-336, 341, 342, 346, 348
Wright W-368
yellow fever eradication M-598

United States Army Corps of Engineers A-646
flood control F-183
Fort Peck Dam M-551
Manhattan District. see in index Manhattan District
United States Army Yellow Fever Commission
Reed R-127
United States Botanic Garden, in Washington, D.C. U-214
United States Business Hall of Fame H-17
United States Catholic Conference (formerly National

Catholic Welfare Conference), an agency to promote welfare of Roman Catholics in U.S.; organized 1919; has four departments: communication, education, social development, and world peace; succeeded National Catholic War Council, founded 1917.
United States Coast Guard. see in index Coast Guard
United States Conciliation Service A-528
United States Constitution U-194
amendments. see in index specific amendments by name; Bill of Rights
American literature A-344
civil rights C-469
Civil War C-470
constitution C-683
Constitutional Convention (1787). see in index Constitutional Convention
copyright guidelines C-713
democracy D-93
electoral college E-148
ethics and morality E-309
federal government G-199, U-208
franchise rights F-373
habeas corpus H-2
human rights H-320
jury system regulations J-159
New Jersey plan N-200
patent laws P-152
police P-504
postal service P-558
revolution R-181
slave trade A-10, B-289
stamps S-573, *picture* S-574
state government S-594
states' rights J-93, S-594, 599
Supreme Court S-711
titles of nobility T-196
United States U-158, *picture* U-153
veto authority V-331
United States Department of the Treasury S-299
United States Employment Service E-205
United States European Command A-646
United States Fencing Association (USFA, formerly Amateur Fencers League of America, AFLA), a nonprofit fencing organization, handles competitions and tournaments at all levels F-54
United States Fire Administration (USFA), U.S. government F-112
United States Fish and Wildlife Service D-288
United States Football League (USFL)
football F-291, 295
United States Golf Association (USGA) G-185, 191
United States government U-208. see also in index Government regulation of industry; Municipal government; State government; United States Constitution
aviation regulation A-880
Bank of the United States B-73
budget B-486
Cabinet. see in index Cabinet
censorship prohibition C-246
census. see in index United States, *subhead* population, census
city C-449
civil disobedience C-463
Communist party C-620
Constitution U-194
courts of justice C-746. see also in index Supreme Court of the United States
disarmament D-163
elections E-145
black Americans B-296, *table* B-298
electoral college E-148
flag procedures F-151

landslides. see in index Landslide
lobbying L-276
president. see in index President, *subhead* election
employment agency E-205
employment and unemployment E-206
executive departments. see in index Agriculture, Department of, etc.
Federal Aviation Administration. see in index Federal Aviation Administration
Federal Reserve System F-51
Federal Trade Commission. see in index Federal Trade Commission
foreign aid F-306
foreign exchange F-307
government G-199
agencies G-200, H-89
bureaucracy B-506
civil service C-469
political science P-518
housing H-295, 302, 305
impeachment I-58
industrial spending I-190
initiative, referendum, and recall I-205
intelligence agencies I-237
international relations I-261
diplomacy D-149, *diagram* D-150
international trade agencies I-368
journalism N-236
jury system J-159
labor movements L-6
law and legal system L-94, 97
administrative law A-46
copyright law C-713
drug laws D-277
estate and inheritance law E-307
prison and punishment P-600
prostitution P-619
Library of Congress. see in index Library of Congress
medical education M-279
NASA. see in index National Aeronautics and Space Administration
national debt. see in index National debt
naturalization N-67
passport P-148
patent laws P-152
pension P-207
police P-512
political parties P-514
postal service P-551
propaganda P-611
property ownership P-613
public utility P-649
securities S-624
social security I-217, S-350
Supreme Court S-711
Tennessee Valley Authority T-100
territories. see in index territories listed below and others by name
American Samoa S-35
Puerto Rico P-652
Virgin Islands of the United States V-378
treaties of Washington W-71
unidentified flying objects U-8
Veterans Administration. see in index Veterans Administration
vocation V-390, 398
Washington, D.C. W-66
United States Ground Observer Corps. see in index Ground Observer Corps
United States Gymnastics Federation (USGF) G-325
United States Hockey Hall of Fame, sports hall of fame in Eveleth, Minn. H-16
United States International Trade Commission I-268
United States International University, in San Diego, Calif.; private control; founded 1952; arts and science, business, education, human behavior,

international and intercultural studies, performing and visual arts; graduate studies, associated campuses in England, Mexico, and Kenya.
United States Jack, flag F-158
United States Marine Band M-137
bands, *picture* B-57
United States Marine Corps M-136
flag F-158
Korean War K-295, *chart* K-299, *pictures* K-296, 297
navy N-88
Parris Island, *picture* S-430
public relations P-646
reserve. see in index Reserves
uniform and insignia U-16, *picture* U-12
United States Marine Corps Women's Reserve M-138
United States Maritime Commission. see in index Maritime Administration of the Department of Commerce
United States Merchant Marine Academy, in Kings Point, Long Island, N.Y.; federal academy for education of officers of U.S. Merchant Marine and Naval Reserve; dedicated Sept. 30, 1943; candidates for appointment must take competitive examination; accredited college-level course of four 11-month years (including one year at sea in merchant ships); graduates receive license as third mate or third assistant engineer, commission of ensign in U.S. Naval Reserve and in U.S. Maritime Service, and B.S. degree N-255, S-250
United States Military Academy M-410
engineering curriculum E-227
United States Mint. see in index Mint, United States
United States National Museum, a depository of government historical and scientific collections in Washington, D.C.; established 1846 as a branch of Smithsonian Institution; present name adopted 1875; two buildings built by Congressional appropriation 1879 and 1903; material relating to North America particularly valuable; includes Museum of History and Technology and Museum of Natural History.
United States Naval Academy M-410
Maryland M-168, *map* M-183, *picture* M-175
United States Naval Observatory N-91
United States Naval Reserve, force to supplement regular Navy forces in time of war or emergency; established 1915; term of enlistment is six years; recruit must be 17 to 41 years old. see also in index Reserves
United States Navy N-80, 84, 87, 91
aircraft carrier. see in index Aircraft carrier
aviation. see in index Aviation, military and naval
Civil War C-480
dirigible B-40
fire fighting F-106
fish research F-127
guided missile G-308
Korean War K-295, *chart* K-299
Marine Corps. see in index United States Marine Corps
navigation N-73, *pictures* N-68, 69

Navy Department. *see in index* Navy, Department of the
nuclear power N-425
reserve. *see in index* Reserves
ships. *see in index* Ships, famous
signaling S-288
submarine. *see in index* Submarine
uniform and insignia U-16, *pictures* U-12, U-15
World War I W-314
World War II W-328, 333, 344, *picture* W-345

United States Open, golf tournament G-191

United States Open, tennis tournament T-104, 108
New York City N-279

United States Pharmacopoeia (USP), in pharmacology P-273

United States Postal Service. *see in index* Postal Service, United States

United States Public Health Service. *see in index* Public Health Service

United States Revolver Association S-268

United States Secret Service P-512, *picture* P-512

United States Shipping Board S-252
World War I W-314

United States Steel Corporation, vertical trust formed 1901 by merger of top steel companies embodying interests of Morgan, Gary, Carnegie, and others; first billion-dollar corporation in U.S.
Carnegie C-170
Morgan M-583
United States U-107, 110, 121

United States Steel Wire Gauge (U.S.S.W.G.), wire W-247

United States Supreme Court. *see in index* Supreme Court of the United States

United States Trade Representative, Office of the
international trade I-268

United States versus One Book Entitled Ulysses, case in U.S. constitutional law
obscenity determination P-543

United States Volleyball Association (USVBA) V-407

United States Weather Bureau. *see in index* National Weather Service

United Steelworkers of America, a labor union affiliated with the AFL-CIO since 1936, with headquarters located in Pittsburgh, Pa.
labor movements L-10

United Steelworkers of America versus Weber (1979), U.S. Supreme Court case, *list* S-712

United Way. *see in index* United Fund

United Workmen, Ancient Order of, fraternal and beneficiary society; provides life insurance for members; founded in Meadville, Pa., 1868.

Unities, the, in drama, the three rules for the structure of a play, derived in part from Aristotle's 'Poetics', and stating that the action must occur in one place within one day
Corneille's plays C-723
drama D-244

Uniting for Peace Resolution, United Nations peace-keeping resolution U-84

Unit record accounting machine C-628

Unit record processing, method of data processing C-627

Units of measurement. *see also in index* Weights and measures
energy units, *table* E-217

Unit train R-94

Unity Temple, in Oak Park, Ill. W-367

Univalve, mollusk with a one-piece shell S-226, *picture* S-229

Universal, in philosophy R-116

'Universal Bibliography', work by Gesner G-136

Universal Copyright Convention (or Geneva Copyright Convention), signed in Geneva, Switzerland, Sept. 6, 1952, by 36 nations to give international copyright protection to literary, artistic, and scientific works; drafted by UNESCO; U.S. participation voted by Congress 1954; in effect 1955 C-713

Universal Declaration of Human Rights, United Nations
bill of rights B-197
human rights H-319
international law I-258

Universal donors and recipients, blood types B-316

Universal education. *see in index* Compulsory education

Universal Exposition of Rome (E.U.R.), in Rome, Italy R-288

Universalists, Christian denomination; beginning in the United States in 1770; believes salvation of all humanity; doctrine of Trinity rejected; in 1961 merged with the Unitarians to form the Unitarian Universalist Association
Unitarian Universalist Association U-67

Universal law, in philosophy K-190

Universal life insurance I-234

Universal Negro Improvement Association and African Communities League (UNIA) B-294
Garvey G-37

Universal Postal Union (UPU, or General Postal Union) P-560
United Nations U-86

Universal Product Code (UPC) A-834
packaging M-142

Universal Studios C-713

Universal time, any designation of time, such as Greenwich time, which is used throughout the world without change for longitude; usually employs 24-hour system from midnight to midnight as fixed at originating point.

Universe (or cosmos). *see also in index* Astronomy; Planet; Relativity; Solar system; Star; entries beginning Aerospace
cosmic rays. *see in index* Cosmic rays
cosmology C-731
physical character A-726
black holes B-306
gravitation G-239
light wave origins L-199
science S-111
space travel. *see in index* Space travel
world W-295

Universe, in statistics
public opinion poll P-543

Universitas, medieval universities U-223

University U-222. *see also in index* College; Teaching; names of universities; names of countries and states, *subhead* education; *see also* Fact Summary with each state article
education E-83, 98
Europe E-338
football stadiums S-566
fraternities and sororities F-388
Greece A-7
India I-72, *picture* I-74
libraries L-149
philosophy P-318
research subsidy S-687
Roman Catholicism R-265
school systems S-92
science S-113
United States U-152
vocation V-394
women's rights W-272

University City, Mo., residential city adjoining St. Louis on w.; incorporated 1906; pop. 42,738
Missouri M-491, 500, *map* M-506

University College, at Oxford University U-222

University Heights, Ohio, city 8 mi (13 km) s.e. of Cleveland; John Carroll University; pop. 15,401
Ohio, *map* O-518

University Hospital, at University of Saskatchewan, Saskatoon, Sask. S-71

University of . . . *see in index* main part of name, as Michigan, University of, except as below

University of California versus Bakke (1979), U.S. Supreme Court case, *list* S-712

University Park, Tex., a city surrounded by the city of Dallas; site of Southern Methodist University; pop. 23,498
Texas, *map* T-137

University Wits, a group of English university men who flourished 1580–95—John Lyly, Thomas Lodge, George Peele, Robert Greene, Thomas Nash, and Christopher Marlowe; influenced growth of Elizabethan drama
Shakespeare S-207, 210

Unknown Soldier, one of a nation's unidentified war dead, buried in a tomb that is made a shrine in memory of all soldiers killed in the war
British tomb L-292
United States tombs N-24, *picture* N-23

Unkpapa, Teton Sioux Indians living in North Dakota; Sitting Bull was famous chief.

Unplanned economy E-61. *see also in index* Capitalism

Unredeemed Italy. *see in index* Italia Irredenta

UNRRA (United Nations Relief and Rehabilitation Administration) W-356

Unruh, Fritz von (1885–1970), German novelist, playwright, and poet; born in Coblenz; made appeal against militarism in prose epic, 'The Way of Sacrifice', based on his experiences in World War I; lived in U.S. 1940–47.

'Unsafe at Any Speed: the Designed-in Dangers of the American Automobile', work by Nader N-2

Unsaturated chemicals, petrochemicals P-249

Unsaturated fats and oils F-48
meat M-247

Unser, Al, Sr. (born 1939), U.S. auto racer, born in Albuquerque, N.M.; began racing 1957; won Indianapolis 500 1970–71, 1978, 1987, also becoming oldest Indianapolis winner, breaking record of brother **Bobby Unser** (born 1934), born in Albuquerque; won Indianapolis 500 1968, 1975, 1981; retired 1983. **Al Unser, Jr.** (born 1962), born in Albuquerque; he and Al, Sr., first father and son to race against each other in Indianapolis 500 (1983).

Unsought goods M-142

'Unswept Floor', mosaic by Sosos M-589

Unter den Linden, street in East Berlin B-168

Untermeyer, Louis (1885–1977), U.S. author and editor, born in New York, N.Y.; noted as anthologist (collections for older readers: 'Modern American Poetry', 'Modern British Poetry', 'Treasury of Great Humor'; collections of poetry for young readers: 'This Singing World', 'Rainbow in the Sky', 'Star to Steer By'); author of biography, 'Makers of the Modern World', 'Lives of the Poets', and autobiography, 'From Another World'; 'Bygones'.

Untermyer, Samuel (1858–1940), U.S. lawyer, born in Lynchburg, Va.; counsel in many financial cases and in reorganization committees of large corporations; aided preparation of federal currency and trust legislation.

Unterseeboot. *see in index* U-boat

Unterwalden, Swiss canton, divided into Nidwalden (Lower Unterwalden) and Obwalden (Upper Unterwalden); area 296 sq mi (767 sq km); pop. 46,600.

Untouchables (or Harijan), Hindu caste I-68, *picture* M-460

U Nu. *see in index* Nu, Thakin

Unweighing, in skiing S-313

Unwin, Nora Spicer (1907–82), British artist and illustrator of children's books, born in Surrey, England; children's books illustrated: 'The Doll Who Came Alive', by Enys Tregarthen; 'The Secret Garden', by Frances H. Burnett; 'Peter Pan', by James M. Barrie; 'The Princess and the Goblin', by George MacDonald.

Up, direction D-157

Upanishads, a group of sacred writings in Hinduism H-157, I-105

'Upapuranas', Hindu encyclopedia I-106

Upas tree, southeast Asian tree T-282

UPC (Universal Product Code) A-834

Updike, Daniel Berkeley (1860–1941), U.S. typographer, born in Providence, R.I.; established Merrymount Press; leader in revival of classical typography in U.S.; lecturer on printing, Harvard University 1910–17; ('Printing Types—Their History, Form and Use' and 'Some Aspects of Printing')
type and typography T-338

Updike, John Hoyer (born 1932), U.S. writer, born in Shillington, Pa. ('Poorhouse Fair'; 'Rabbit, Run'; 'The Centaur'; 'Of the Farm'; 'Couples'; 'Bech: a Book'; 'Rabbit Redux'; 'Picked-Up Pieces'; 'Rabbit Is Rich'; poems and short stories)
American literature A-362

UPI. *see in index* United Press International

Upjohn, Richard (1802–78), U.S. architect, born in England A-561, 569

Upland, Calif., city 35 mi (55 km) n.e. of Los Angeles; citrus fruits, olives; electronic components, metal products; pop. 47,647
California, *map* C-53

Upland-game, in hunting H-331

Upland long-staple cotton, variety of cotton plant, grown chiefly in U.S. C-741

Upland plover (also called Bartramian sandpiper), bird of the family Scolopacidae.

Upland rice, production R-216, *picture* R-215

Uplands, region in Scotland S-125

Upland sandpiper, (also called Bartram's sandpiper, and mistakenly called Upland plover), shorebird *(Bartramia longicanda)* S-41

Upland short-staple cotton, variety of cotton plant *(Gossypium hirsutum);* staples from ⅝ to 1 in. (1.2 to 2.5 cm) long C-741

Upolu, Western Samoa, 2nd largest island of Samoa; area 430 sq mi (1,110 sq km); cacao, rubber, bananas, and coconuts; pop. 105,889.

'Upon the Spiritual in Art', theoretical study by Kandinsky K-171

Upper Amazonia porcupine, rodent of the family Erethizontidae P-542

Upper Arlington, Ohio, city 4 mi (6 km) n.w. of Columbus; mainly residential suburb; Ohio State University nearby; pop. 35,648
Ohio, *map* O-518

Upper Austria, a province of Austria; area 4,625 sq mi (11,980 sq km); cap. Linz; cereals, potatoes, fruit, wine, textiles, and chemicals; pop. 1,131,623.

Upper Canada. *see in index* Ontario

Uppercase letters (or capital letters) T-336

Upper class M-460, S-346

Uppercut, in boxing B-388

Upper Darby, Pa., urban township w. of Philadelphia; residential with some manufacturing; incorporated 1907; pop. 95,910
Pennsylvania, *map* P-206

Upper East Side, a neighborhood in Manhattan, New York, N.Y. N-273, 278

Upper Falls, waterfall in Yellowstone National Park W-97

Upper Fort Garry, now part of Winnipeg, Man., *picture* M-103

Upper Iowa University, in Fayette, Iowa; private control; opened 1857; arts and sciences, education.

Upper Moreland, Pa., urban township n. of Philadelphia in Montgomery County; includes towns of Hatboro and Willow Grove; pop. 24,866
Pennsylvania, *map* P-206

Upper Peninsula, northern section of Michigan M-354, 359

Upper Silesia. *see in index* Silesia

Upper Volga, part of the Volga River V-406

Upper Volta. *see in index* Burkina Faso

Upper West Side, a neighborhood in Manhattan, New York, N.Y. N-273

Uppsala (or Upsala), Sweden, cathedral city, 41 mi (66 km) n. of Stockholm on Fyris River; pop. 103,374
Europe, *map* E-361

Upright piano, musical instrument M-689

Upright vacuum cleaner, appliance H-211

Upsala College, in East Orange, N.J.; Lutheran; founded 1893; arts and sciences, education.

Upsilon particle, heavy, short-lived, neutral subatomic particle with mass about ten times that of a proton; a meson composed of a bottom, or beauty, quark and an antibottom, or antibeauty, quark; discovered 1977 by American physicist Leon Lederman and colleagues; was the first manifestation of the bottom quark and gave rise to speculation about the existence of a sixth kind of quark—the top (also called truth), or t, quark. see also in index Atomic particles; Quark

UPU. see in index Universal Postal Union

Upward Bound, U.S. federal antipoverty program for underprivileged high school students of high potential but poor academic records; helps prepare them for admission to a college or university by summer sessions and tutoring during school year.

Upwelling, in oceanography O-484

Ur, ancient city of s. Babylonia near Euphrates River; site marked by ruin mounds
  Abraham A-12
  archaeological excavation A-532, picture A-530
  board games B-320
  power B-7, map B-4
  Sumerian civilization B-7, map B-4

Ural-Altaic, term broadly used for Finno-Tataric languages and peoples. see also in index Finno-Tatars
  Europe E-336

Uralic language family L-41, diagram L-44
  Asian language patterns A-682
  U.S.S.R. U-32

Ural Mountains, low range in Soviet Union forming part of Europe-Asia boundary; 1,500 mi (2,400 km) long U-229
  Asia, map A-700
  Europe, map E-361
  U.S.S.R. U-19, 23, maps U-62, 66
  Russian S.F.S.R. R-356
  Siberia S-280

Ural River, river in s.e. European Soviet Union and w. Kazakh Soviet Socialist Republic; rises in s. Ural Mountains and flows more than 1,500 mi (2,400 km) to Caspian Sea, map A-700
  U.S.S.R., maps U-62, 66

Uraninite, a radioactive mineral
  minerals M-435
  ore, table O-600
  radium R-82
  uranium U-230

Uranium (U), radioactive chemical element U-230
  atomic bomb B-339
  energy E-216
  nuclear energy N-416, 422
  nuclear fuel F-442
  nuclear weapons N-433
  ores, map O-600, table O-600
  periodic table, list P-226, table P-225
  producing regions
    Africa
      Central African Republic C-252
      Namibia N-9
      Niger N-309
    Australia A-774
    Canada
      Ontario O-551
      Saskatchewan S-64
    United States
      Arizona A-598

New Mexico N-216, map N-218
  radioactivity R-73, S-110
  radiometric dating E-22
  radium R-82
  rock R-245

Uranium City, Sask., city in n.w. corner of province on Lake Athabasca; pop. 2,507 S-64, map S-70

Uranium compounds, nuclear fuels N-423

Uranium hexafluoride, principal halide of uranium U-230

Uranium tetrafluoride, principal halide of uranium U-230

Uranus, in Greek mythology, Uranus, the sky, and Gaea, the Earth, were parents of Cronus and Rhea who became parents of Zeus and the other gods M-700

Uranus, in astronomy, the seventh planet from the sun; discovered in 1781 P-412, picture P-411, table P-413
  astronomy A-714
  Earth, diagram E-9
  Herschel H-144
  solar system S-375, picture S-377, table S-376

Uranyl nitrate, compound of uranium U-230

Urartians, ancient people n. of Assyria; flourished from 1270–750 BC
  writing W-371

Urban I, Saint (died 230), pope 222–230; commemorated as saint May 25 U-232

Urban II (1035–99), pope U-232
  First Crusade C-786
    Middle Ages M-391
  migration of people M-402
  revivalism R-180

Urban III (died 1187), pope U-232

Urban IV (died 1264), pope U-232

Urban V (1310–70), pope U-232

Urban VI (1318–89), pope U-232
  University of Erfurt U-225

Urban VII (1521–90), pope U-232

Urban VIII (1568–1644), pope U-232

Urbana, Ill., city about 125 mi (200 km) s.w. of Chicago; adjacent to Champaign; agricultural center; settled 1822, incorporated 1833; pop. 35,978. see also in index Illinois, University of
  Illinois, map I-53

Urbana, Ohio, city 15 mi (25 km) n.e. of Springfield; metal tools, carbonic products, plastic moldings; pop. 10,762
  Ohio, map O-518

Urbandale, Iowa, town 9 mi (15 km) n.w. of Des Moines; residential suburb; incorporated 1917; pop. 17,869
  Iowa, map I-302

Urban ecology S-360

Urban geography G-68

Urban geology G-72

Urban housing H-291, 299, 304
  urban planning U-233

Urbanization C-550
  Africa A-99
  China C-344, C-366
  endangered species E-212
  Europe E-338
  police P-510
  population P-539
  United States U-114
  urban planning U-233
  U.S.S.R. U-29

Urban League, National. see in index National Urban League

Urban planning U-233
  access for disabled D-163

Fuller F-446
  vocation V-394
  water supply and waterworks W-90

Urban renewal, effort to improve cities by combined attack on such problems as slums, land use, and traffic H-298, 304, list H-305
  Amsterdam A-380
  city C-460
  urban planning U-233

Urban settlement, a settlement that is related to manufacturing and trade
  city C-449
  geography G-66
  urban planning U-233

Urban Transportation Development Corporation, Canadian agency G-202

'Urban Villagers, The', work by Gans S-359

Urchin, sea animal. see in index Sea urchin

Urd (or Urth), in German and Norse mythology F-44

Urdaneta, Andrés de (1498–1568), Spanish explorer S-484

Urdu, language, a form of Hindustani
  India I-67
  Indian literature I-107
  Pakistan P-80

Urea (or carbamide), a colorless, crystalline compound, $CO(NH_2)$; produced in nature chiefly by oxidation of proteins inside animal organisms; found in nearly all body fluids, but mostly in urine; artificially prepared from carbon dioxide and ammonia; used in fertilizers and plastics, and in helping growth of new tissue in wounds
  button manufacture B-530, picture B-532
  inorganic chemistry I-208
  organic chemistry O-601
  Wöhler's discovery S-110

Urea-formaldehyde, plastics, list P-448

Uremia, a condition resulting from kidney failure D-182
  urinary system U-239

Ureter, a long tube conveying urine U-239, picture D-182
  physiology P-369

Urethane, plastic B-491

Urethra, a human duct R-166
  urinary system U-239

Urey, Harold Clayton (1893–1981), U.S. chemist U-238. see also in index Nobel Prizewinners, table
  evolution E-365
  science breakthroughs, list S-116
  Urey and Miller experiment E-386

Urfa, Turkey. see in index Edessa

Urfé, Honoré d' (1567–1625), French novelist, born in Marseilles; wrote 'L'Astrée', pastoral romance.

Urga, Mongolian People's Republic. see in index Ulan Bator

Uri, Swiss canton; 415 sq mi (1,075 sq km); dairying and stock raising; mountainous; scene of William Tell legend; pop. 32,400.

Uriah, in Bible, faithful captain of David, who is betrayed for David's wife Bathsheba D-41
  Hittites H-178

Urial. see in index Sha

Urianghai, people of the Altai Mountains in Siberia
  nomads N-332

Uriburu, Jose Felix (1868–1932), president of Argentina 1930–31 A-583

Urinary system, in anatomy U-239
  cat disorder C-210
  diseases D-182
  kidneys K-235
  pregnancy P-580
  sulfa drugs S-700

Urinary tract obstruction, disorder of the urinary system U-239

Urine, excretion from the kidneys. see also in index Urea
  anatomy A-391
  diagnosis
    disease D-127
    pregnancy P-580
  kidney K-235
  urinary system U-239

Uris, Leon Marcus (born 1924), U.S. novelist, born in Baltimore, Md. ('Battle Cry'; 'The Angry Hills'; 'Exodus'; 'Armageddon'; 'Mila 18', 'QB VII', 'The Haj'); also wrote screenplay for 'Gunfight at the O.K. Corral'.

Urmia, Iran. see in index Rezaieh

Urmia, Lake, shallow body of salt water in n.w. Iran; area ranges seasonally from approximately 1,500 to 2,300 sq mi (3,900 to 6,000 sq km) I-305, maps A-700, I-312

Urochorda, subphylum of marine animals
  phylogenetic tree, diagram Z-468

Urology, medical specialty, table M-277

Uropeltidae, family of snakes S-336

Urostyle, in frog anatomy F-406

Ursa Major, constellation. see in index Great Bear

Ursa Minor, constellation. see in index Little Bear

Ursinia, genus of South African annual and perennial plants of composite family; leaves finely cut; flowers daisylike, yellow or orange.

Ursinus College, in Collegeville. Pa.; United Church of Christ; founded 1869; liberal arts, education.

Ursula, Saint, leader of a group of maidens who, according to legend, went from Britain to Rome and were massacred on their return by Huns near Lower Rhine (various dates given, AD 238, 283, 382, 451); church erected at Cologne in their honor; removed from sainthood by Pope Paul VI in 1969.

Ursuline College, in Cleveland, Ohio; Roman Catholic; for women; founded 1871; arts and sciences, education.

Ursulines, Roman Catholic religious order founded by St. Angela Merici of Brescia (1470–1540) primarily for girls' education; patron St. Ursula.

Ursus, genus of bears B-116

Urth (or Urd), in German and Norse mythology F-44

Urticaceae. see in index Nettle family

Urticaria (or hives), itchy, whitish elevations of the skin D-178

Uru, South American people T-194

Uruguay, smallest of the South American republics; 68,000 sq mi (176,000 sq km); cap. Montevideo; pop. 3,058,000 U-240

cities. see in index
  Montevideo and other cities by name
  flag F-161, picture F-172
  history A-657
  International Wheat Agreement W-190
  Latin American literature L-75
  Montevideo siege M-568
  national anthem, table N-64
  South America S-404, map S-419
  United Nations, table U-84
  world, map W-300

Uruguay River, river in South America, rising in s.e. Brazil and flowing 1,000 mi (1,600 km) to the Río de la Plata; boundary between Argentina on w. and Brazil and Uruguay on e., map A-585
  Argentina A-576
  Brazil, map B-425
  South America S-403, map S-419
  Uruguay U-240
  world, map W-300

Uruk (or Erech), ancient Sumerian city in Mesopotamia (Iraq) on Euphrates about 12 mi (19 km) n.w. of Ur; among its archaeological findings are the libraries and documents of the temple of Ishtar of the 2nd millennium BC B-4, map B-7
  mosaic M-589

Urumiyeh, Iran. see in index Rezaieh

Ürümqi (or Urumchi), China, capital of Xinjiang Uygur Autonomous Region; iron and steel; pop. 320,000, map A-700
  world, map W-300
  Xinjiang Uygur X-402

Urus (or giant ox, or aurochs), extinct forebear (Bos primigenius) of certain European wild cattle C-224
  U.S.S.R. U-29

Urushiol, an oil P-445

'Urvasi Won by Valor', drama by Kalidasa K-167

'U.S.A.', trilogy by Dos Passos A-359

USAFE. see in index United States Air Forces in Europe

Usage clump, in linguistics L-33

'USA Today', national newspaper N-241

Use theory, in semantics S-170

USFA (United States Fencing Association, formerly Amateur Fencers League of America, AFLA) F-54

USFA (United States Fire Administration), U.S. government F-112

USFL (United States Football League)
  football F-291, 295

USGA (United States Golf Association) G-185, 191

USGF (United States Gymnastics Federation) G-325

Usher, James. see in index Ussher, James

Ushuaia, Argentina A-576, map A-585, picture A-579
  South America, map S-419

Uskub, Yugoslavia. see in index Skopje

Uskudar (or Scutari), Turkey, Asian portion of Istanbul; hospital used by Florence Nightingale; famous cemetery; pop. 101,814.

USM (ultrasonic machining), a metalworking operation T-226

USMC. see in index Maritime Administration of the Department of Commerce

Usnea, genus of lichens often called tree mosses because of their branching filaments, which may be yellow or grayish; common beard lichen (*U. barbata*) hangs from branches of trees.

USO. *see in index* United Service Organizations

Usonian, type of housing designed by Wright W-367

USP (United States Pharmacopoeia), in pharmacology P-273

USS, U.S. warships. *see in index* warships by name, as 'Essex'; 'Enterprise'

USS 'Arizona' National Memorial, memorial in Hawaii N-59, *map* N-40

Ussher, James (1581–1656), English theologian and scholar, author of a Biblical chronology printed in margins of Authorized Version; archbishop of Armagh 1625; placed date of world's creation at 4,004 BC.

U.S.S.R. *see in index* Union of Soviet Socialist Republics

Ussuri Lowland, geographic region in U.S.S.R. U-23

Ussuri River, river that flows n. along boundary between Siberia and n.e. part of China; 365 mi (585 km) long; tributary of Amur River, *map* A-700
U.S.S.R. U-23, *map* U-62

U.S.S.W.G. *see in index* United States Steel Wire Gauge

Ustalfs, soil classification U-102

Ústí nad Labem (in German, Aussig), Czechoslovakia, city in Bohemia, on Elbe River, 45 mi (70 km) n.w. of Prague; coal traffic; chemical industries; pop. 66,674.

Ustinov, Peter Alexander (born 1921), British actor, producer, and author; born in London; short stories, 'Add a Dash of Pity'; wrote and starred in play 'Romanoff and Juliet', also wrote, directed, produced, and starred in movie of same name; portrayed Agatha Christie's Hercule Poirot in 'Evil Under the Sun', 'Death on the Nile'; won Emmy awards for performances in 'The Life of Samuel Johnson' (1957),

'Barefoot in Athens' (1966), 'A Storm in Summer' (1970) D-247

Usumacinta River, river flowing through s. Mexico and Guatemala; rises in Guatemala, flows 450 mi (725 km) to Gulf of Mexico; navigable a short distance
Mexico, *map* M-344
North America N-335, *picture* N-336

Usury, term originally applied to all lending of money at interest; now applies mainly to charging of interest in excess of the legal rate, *table* L-93
Renaissance banking R-162

USVBA (United States Volleyball Association) V-407

Utah, a w.-central state of U.S.; 84,916 sq mi (219,931 sq km); cap. Salt Lake City; pop. 1,461,037 U-243
Bingham Canyon Copper Mine, *picture* N-341
cities. *see in index* Salt Lake City and other cities by name
geographic regions N-351
Great Salt Lake G-250
Mormons M-584
national parks N-42, 54, 61, *map* N-40
railroads, *pictures* R-86, 88
state capitals, *list* S-595
state symbols
flag, *picture* F-160
flower, *picture* F-239
tree S-554
Statuary Hall, *table* S-609
taxation, *tables* T-37, 39
United States U-126, 129, 168, *table* U-187
Young Y-424

Utah, University of, in Salt Lake City, Utah; state control; founded 1850 as University of the State of Deseret; letters and science, business, education, engineering, fine arts, law, medicine, mines and mineral industries, nursing, pharmacy, social work; graduate school
Utah, *picture* U-251

Utah Lake, largest freshwater lake in Utah, 30 mi (50 km) s.e. of Great Salt Lake; 23 mi (37 km) long

Utah, *map* U-259

Utah State University, in Logan, Utah; founded 1888; agriculture, business and social sciences, education, engineering and technology, forest, range, and wildlife management, home and family living, humanities and sciences; graduate studies; junior colleges at Ephraim, Price, Provo, Saint George, and Salt Lake City.

Utamaro, Kitagawa (1754–1806), Japanese designer of color prints; called great master of the popular school.

Ute, a group of North American Indians that live in Utah and Colorado
American Indians, *map* I-136, *table* I-139
Carson C-178
Colorado C-569
Utah U-245

Ute Mountain Indian Reservation, reservation in Colorado and New Mexico, *maps* C-583, N-229

Uterine lining (or endometrium), mucous coating of the uterus M-300

Uterus (or womb), female organ for holding and nourishing young during prenatal development
embryology E-199, *picture* E-199
mammal M-81
menstruation M-300
multiple birth M-649
pregnancy and birth, *picture* P-580
reproductive system R-166
sexuality S-191

U Thant. *see in index* Thant, U

Uther, King, Arthurian legends A-655

'Uthman ibn 'Affan (died 656), Islamic caliph C-54, I-361

'Uthman Koran, an original transcription of the Koran U-262

Utica, ancient Phoenician city on n. coast of Africa; sided with Rome in Third Punic War

and succeeded Carthage as leading city of Africa; scene of last stand of Pompeians against Caesar and of younger Cato's suicide (46 BC).

Utica, N.Y., city 45 mi (70 km) e. of Syracuse on Mohawk River and New York State Barge Canal; pop. 75,632
New York N-251, *map* N-269

Utilitarianism, in philosophy, *list* P-319. *see also in index* Bentham, Jeremy

Utilities, public. *see in index* Public utilities

Utility dress, military uniform U-11

Utnapishtim, the Babylonian Noah B-7
flood legends F-185

Uto-Aztecan, language, *tables* I-138, 139

Utopia, a place of ideal perfection
communal living C-604
Romanticism R-283
utopian literature U-260

'Utopia', book by More M-582
utopian literature U-260

Utopian literature U-260
socialism S-346

Utopian socialism S-347

Utrecht, The Netherlands, historic Dutch city on Rhine River; pop. 229,900 U-261
Europe, *map* E-361
The Netherlands N-125, *picture* N-128

Utrecht, Treaty of (1713) U-261, *table* T-275
Austria-Hungary A-829
Canada C-93
Newfoundland N-168
Nova Scotia N-403
Queen Anne's War A-467, Q-23
slave trade S-320

Utrecht, Union of (1579) U-261, *table* T-275
The Netherlands N-130

'Utrecht Te Deum and Jubilate', work by Handel H-28

Utricle, part of the inner ear E-4

Utrillo, Maurice (1883–1955) French modernist painter U-261

Uttar Pradesh, state in n. India; area 113,409 sq mi (293,728 sq km); cap. Lucknow; composed almost entirely of former United Provinces of Agra and Oudh; pop. 88,341,144, *map* I-83

Uvalde, Tex., city 82 mi (132 km) s.w. of San Antonio; agriculture, cotton, livestock, pecans, work clothes; pop. 14,178
Texas, *map* T-137

Uvula, a small, fleshy U-shaped mass hanging down from the soft palate of mouth above root of tongue.

Uxmal, Mexico, ancient ruined Maya city in Yucatán, 40 mi (60 km) s.w. of Mérida; one of continent's most remarkable archaeological sites
Maya M-235, *picture* M-237
Mexico, *map* M-344
Yucatán Peninsula Y-433

Uygurs, a people of China C-345, *picture* C-348
Kunlun Mountains K-309
Turkestan T-317

Uylenborch, Saskia van (fl. 17th century), wife and model of Rembrandt R-158

Uzbek, an individual, or the language, of a Turkic people; socially and politically rather than racially distinct, they were the dominant people in central Asia from the 13th century until the arrival of the Russians in the 19th century
Afghanistan A-89
Turkestan T-317
Turkmen Soviet Socialist Republic T-327
Uzbek Soviet Socialist Republic U-262

Uzbek Soviet Socialist Republic (or Uzbekistan), U.S.S.R.; 172,700 sq mi (447,400 sq km); cap. Tashkent; pop. 18,487,000 U-262
Asia, *map* A-700
Samarkand S-35
U.S.S.R., *map* U-62, *pictures* U-27, 44

The letter V

probably started as a picture sign for a branched supporting pole or prop, as in Egyptian hieroglyphic writing (1). Descendants of this letter are F, U, W, and Y. About 1000 B.C., in Byblos and in other Phoenician and Canaanite centers, the same sign was used, but its top part was rounded (2). In the Semitic languages the sign was called *waw,* meaning "prop." It had the sound of the "w" in "wine." The Greeks used the sign in two forms. One form (3) was called *digamma* for the consonantal "w," which disappeared in later Greek. This form led to the Latin sign F. Another form (4), called *upsilon,* meaning "bare u," was used for the vocalic "u."

The Romans eliminated the bottom tail (5) and used it for two sounds, consonantal "w" (later "v") and vocalic "u." Consonantal "v" passed into English writing. The English small "v" is a copy of the capital, except that in handwriting it is connected to adjoining letters.

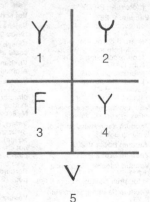

V, chemical element. *see in index* Vanadium

V-1 and V-2, missiles developed by Nazi Germany
guided missiles G-309
jet propulsion J-110
space travel S-460
World War II B-339, W-335, 355

VA. *see in index* Veterans Administration

Vaal River (or Yellow River), river in South Africa, rises on w. slope of Drakensberg; flows w. 500 mi (800 km) to Orange River, *map* A-118

Vaalserberg, mountain, highest point in The Netherlands (1,053 ft; 321 m) N-125

Vaasa (in Swedish, Vasa), Finland, port on Gulf of Bothnia; timber, textiles, sugar, soap, machinery; pop. 42,701.

Vacana, Kannada prose poetry I-106

Vacancy, crystal defect C-798

Vacation activities. *see in index* Amusements; Camping; Games; Hobby; Reading for recreation; Recreation; Sports; Travel and tourism

Vacaville, Calif., city 34 mi (55 km) s.w. of Sacramento; in agricultural area; food processing; pop. 43,367
California, *map* C-53

Vaccination V-264

Vaccines V-264
bacteria B-14
disease prevention D-169
epidemic diseases P-403
genetic engineering G-50
Jenner J-98
microbiology M-376
Pasteur P-151
Salk S-29
sexually transmitted disease S-198
travel and tourism T-272
viruses V-380

Vaccinia, virus V-266

Vacuole, cell structure C-238, *picture* C-237
feeding A-375, A-428
living things L-266, *picture* L-265
protozoan P-626

Vacuum V-267
air evacuation A-147, *picture* A-148
aneroid barometer B-82
black hole theory B-306
food processing F-281
light L-197
microscope M-382
pneumatic device P-476
radiation R-41
sound S-388

Vacuum appliances. *see in index* Pneumatic device

Vacuum aspiration, surgical technique A-11

Vacuum bottle V-267

Vacuum brake R-91

Vacuum cleaner, appliance H-211
industrial design, *picture* I-171

Vacuum flashing, petroleum P-261

Vacuum syringe B-315

Vacuum thermoforming plastics manufacture, *picture* P-452

Vacuum tube. *see in index* Electron tube

Vadmal, cloth used by the Vikings V-353

Vaduz, Liechtenstein, capital, near Rhine s. of Lake Constance; pop. 3,398.

Vagina (or birth canal), structure in female reproductive system R-166, S-191
pregnancy and birth P-580, *picture* P-581
urinary system U-239

Vaginal infection, pathology sexually transmitted disease S-196

Vagrancy Act (1597), in England, authorized government to deport criminal and political offenders M-400

Vagus nerve (or cranial nerve X, or pneumogastric nerve, or tenth cranial nerve), mixed nerve descending from medulla oblongata through the carotid sheath and branching to the various internal organs N-119, *picture* A-384
stomach S-630
therapy T-165

Vail, Alfred (1807–59), U.S. inventor, born in Morristown, N.J.; in 1837 lent money to Samuel F.B. Morse, and for several years worked with him in improving the telegraph
telegraph T-58

Vail, Theodore Newton (1845–1920), U.S. businessman, born in Carroll County, Ohio; president American Telephone and Telegraph Co.; did much to build up telephone industry.

Vaiont Dam, Italy, on Vaiont River; 858 ft (262 m) high, 624 ft (190 m) long; because of landslide overflowed and flooded surrounding country 1963; abandoned as source of electric power D-17

Vair, heraldic fur, *picture* H-136

Vai script, Sierra Leone S-285

Vaisnavism, worship of the Hindu god Vishnu H-159

Vaisya, member of farmer caste among Hindus I-68

Vakhan Corridor, in Afghanistan A-88

Vakhtangov, Eugene (1883–1922), Russian actor, director, and producer, born in Moscow; director of the Moscow Art Theatre A-27

Valais, canton of s.w. Switzerland, 2,021 sq mi (5,234 sq km); minerals and wines, but chiefly pastoral; Alpine peaks; summer and winter resorts; contains Great St. Bernard and Simplon passes; pop. 187,000
masks M-187

Valday Hills, in the U.S.S.R., groups of low hills and

plateaus midway between Leningrad and Moscow; form divide for chief river systems of country; 600 to 1,200 ft (180 to 370 m) above sea level
U.S.S.R. U-22, *map* U-66

Valdemar, kings of Denmark D-99

Valdés, Juan de (1490?–1541), one of foremost Spanish writers of prose; dealt with problems of Biblical interpretation and their bearing on devout life.

Valdez, Pedro de, Spanish naval officer
Drake D-240

Valdez, Alaska, all-year-open port in s.e. on Prince William Sound; gold mining; severely damaged by earthquake 1964; rebuilt 5 mi (8 km) away; pop. 3,079
Alaska, *map* A-254

Valdivia, Chile, port city on Valdivia River about 10 mi (16 km) from Pacific Ocean and 450 mi (725 km) s.w. of Santiago; distributing center for farm, livestock, and lumber district; metal, food, wood, and leather products; pop. 90,942
Chile C-332
South America, *map* S-419
world, *map* W-300

Valdosta, Ga., city in s. center, near Florida line; tobacco, cotton, lumber, livestock center; naval stores, paper and paperboard, concrete pipe; Valdosta State College; pop. 37,596
Georgia, *map* G-101

Valdosta State College, Valdosta, Ga.; founded 1906; arts and sciences, education; graduate studies.

Valdotains, a European people Italy I-384

Valence (ancient Valentia), France, historic town 57 mi (92 km) s. of Lyon on Rhone River; printed fabrics, flour, canned foods; vineyards; pop. 60,662
France, *map* F-372

Valence (or valence number), combining capacity of a chemical element
chemistry C-298
crystals C-796

Valencia, province of Spain, on e. coast; 4,155 sq mi (10,760 sq km); agriculture, fisheries, silk culture; cap. Valencia; pop. 1,429,708.

Valencia, Spain, city; pop. 763,900 V-268
Europe, *map* E-361
Spain S-489

Valencia, Venezuela, city about 20 mi (30 km) s. of its seaport Puerto Cabello and 77 mi (124 km) s.w. of Caracas; with suburbs; trade in sugar, coffee, cacao, corn, tobacco, hides; cotton milling and many other industries; pop. 856,500 V-293
South America, *map* S-419

Valencia orange, citrus fruit *(Citrus sinensis valencia)*, *picture* C-445

Valenciennes, France, industrial town 28 mi (45 km) s.e. of Lille on Scheldt River in coal district; pop. 46,237
France, *map* F-372
lace L-17, *picture* L-16

Valens (328?–378), Byzantine emperor, chosen AD 364 by his brother Valentinian I to rule East; warred with Persians and Goths; with his defeat by the Goths at Adrianople (AD 378) began the decline of the Roman Empire
Roman Empire, *list* R-275

Valentia Island (or Valencia Island), off s.w. coast of Ireland; belongs to County Kerry, Ireland; 7 by 3 mi (11 by 5 km); terminus of cables between America and United Kingdom; pop. 847, *map* U-78

Valentine, Saint, Christian martyr of 3rd century; feast day February 14; dropped from Roman Catholic calendar in 1969.

Valentine, Neb., city in n. part of state; pop. 2,829, *map* N-94

Valentine's Day. *see in index* Saint Valentine's Day

Valentinian I (321–375), Roman emperor, son of humble parents, who rose to high rank in army and was elected emperor AD 364; shared power with brother Valens, giving him eastern part of empire; a firm, impartial, tolerant ruler
Roman Empire, *list* R-275

Valentinian II (372–392), son of Valentinian I, at age of 4 shared empire of the West with his half-brother, Gratian; driven out with his mother by Magnus Maximus, he was restored by Theodosius, emperor of the East; murdered in Gaul
Roman Empire, *list* R-275

Valentinian III (419?–455), Roman emperor, succeeded AD 425; during his reign Africa, Sicily, Gaul, and Britain were lost; murdered Aetius, and was himself murdered the next year A-758
Roman Empire, *list* R-275

Valentino, Rudolph (Rodolfo d'Antonguolla) (1895–1926), U.S. motion-picture actor, born in Castellaneta, Italy; to U.S. 1913; with role of Julio in 'The Four Horsemen of the Apocalypse', became one of most popular of all romantic actors: starred in 'The Sheik', 'Blood and Sand', 'Monsieur Beaucaire'.

Valentinus (fl. 2nd century AD), Egyptian religious philosopher and teacher of Gnosticism, a system of belief in rival deities of good and evil
Gnosticism G-170

Valenzuela, Luisa (born 1938), Argentine writer L-71, *picture* L-75

Valera, Eamon de. *see in index* De Valera

Valera, Juan (1824–1905), Spanish statesman and

eminent man of letters; his 'Pepita Jiménez' marked the renaissance of the Spanish novel.

Valerian (Publius Licinius Valerianus) (died AD 260), Roman emperor 253–260, elected by army when he was over 60; zealous worker but overwhelmed by constant fighting with barbarians and Persians; defeated by Persians AD 260 and held prisoner until his death
Christians persecuted C-401
Roman Empire, *list* R-275

Valerian, perennial herb with opposite leaves and small white or reddish flowers in rounded terminal clusters; thickened and strong-scented root of garden heliotrope, or common valerian *(Valeriana officinalis)*, and of other species yields a volatile oil used in treating hysteria.

Valerian Way, a principal highway of ancient Italy; continued Tiburtina Way (Rome to Tivoli) n.e. to Adriatic.

Valéry, Paul (1871–1945), French poet and essayist V-268

Valhalla, in Norse mythology, hall of slain warriors in heaven M-703
Vikings V-352

Valium (or diazepam), a sedative N-19

Valjean, Jean, character in Hugo's 'Les Misérables' H-316

'Valkyrie, The' (in German, Die Walküre), second opera in Wagner's series 'The Ring of the Nibelungs (Der Ring des Nibelungen) O-568

Valkyries (or Valkyrs, or choosers of the slain), maidens in Norse mythology, sent by Odin to conduct souls of slain heroes to Valhalla M-704

Valladolid, Spain, former capital, 100 mi (160 km) n.w. of Madrid; Columbus died here; birthplace of Philip II; home of Cervantes; textiles, leather, ironware; university; pop. 133,486
Europe, *map* E-361

Vallandigham, Clement Laird (1820–71), U.S. Civil War copperhead, born in New Lisbon, Ohio; Ohio congressman; convicted of sedition by military court 1863; sentence of imprisonment commuted by Lincoln to banishment to Confederate states; subsequently supreme commander Knights of the Golden Circle
Civil War C-478

Vallee, Rudy (popularly known as the Vagabond Lover) (1901–86), U.S. bandleader, saxophonist, and singer; born in Island Pond, Vt.; gained fame as first crooner singing through a megaphone; performed on radio, stage, and screen.

Valle-Inclán, Ramón María del (1866–1936), Spanish writer; finely polished prose, also subtle, delicate verse ('Sonatas'; 'La Guerra carlista'; 'Cofre de sándalo'; 'Tirano Banderas', novels; 'Cara de plata', verse).

Vallejo, Mariano Guadalupe (1808–90), Spanish-American soldier, California pioneer V-268

Vallejo, Calif., city on arm of San Pablo Bay, about 25 mi (40 km) n.e. of San Francisco opposite Mare Island Navy Yard; in agricultural and industrial area; state capital 1851–53; pop. 80,188
California, map C-53
Vallejo V-268

Valles Marineris, valley on Mars P-409

Valletta, Malta, capital and port; trade city and resort built to commemorate a victory in 1565 of the Knights of Malta over the Turks; became capital in 1570; pop. 14,100
Europe, map E-361
Italy, map I-404
Malta M-78

Valley, land form V-269
drowned. see in index
Drowned coasts and valleys
Earth E-15
floods F-180
mountain M-634
river R-227

Valley and Ridge, geographic region, U.S.
Alabama A-223, map A-224
Georgia G-84, map G-85
Maryland M-167, map M-168
Pennsylvania P-184, map P-185
Virginia V-360

Valley breeze, winds W-220, diagram W-221

Valley Caviedes, Juan del (1652–92), Peruvian writer L-75

Valley City, N.D., city on Sheyenne River in s.e. part of state, 58 mi (93 km) w. of Fargo; grain, dairy products; Valley City State College; North Dakota winter show (livestock); pop. 7,774
North Dakota, map N-387

Valley City State College, Valley City, N.D.; founded 1889; arts and sciences, education; junior college affiliated; quarter system.

Valleyfield, Que., port city on St. Lawrence River at head of Beauharnois Canal, 35 mi (55 km) s.w. of Montreal; cotton textiles, chemicals, wood and metal products, canned goods; pop. 30,173, map Q-20
Canada, map C-112

Valley Forge, Pa., village on Schuylkill River 20 mi (30 km) n.w. of Philadelphia V-269
American Revolution R-191
Pennsylvania P-183, 193, map P-206, picture P-192
Washington W-41, picture W-40

Valley Forge National Historical Park, park in s.e. Pennsylvania N-60, map N-40
Valley Forge V-269

Valley glacier, in geology G-150
Ice Age I-6

Valley of California, geographic area in California U-95

'Valley of Fear, The', short story by Doyle M-526

Valley of Fire State Park, Nevada, picture N-142

Valley of Ten Thousand Smokes, volcanic area in Alaska created 1912; discovered by Robert F.

Griggs, 1915–19; part of Katmai National Monument N-52

Valley of the Fallen, memorial to the Spanish Civil War dead, picture S-503

Valley of the Tombs of the Kings, in Egypt
ancient Egypt E-126
Tutankhamen T-331

Valley of Vermont, area in Vermont V-305

Valley quail, bird (Lophortyx californicus) of the family Phasianinae Q-3

Valley Station, Ky., community 11 mi (18 km) s.w. of Louisville; located near bank of Ohio River; mainly residential suburb of Louisville; pop. 24,471
Kentucky, map K-222

Valley Stream, N.Y., residential suburb of New York City on s. shore of Long Island; light industry; pop. 40,413
New York, map N-269

Valley train, a long narrow body of outwash G-151

Vallisneria (also called eelgrass, or wild celery, or tape grass), a water plant (Vallisneria americana); rooted in bottom of shallow ponds and streams; leaves may be 3 ft (1 m) or more long and scarcely ¼ in. (⅔ cm) wide; tiny greenish female flowers, borne singly at ends of long supple stems, float on surface of water; male flowers on short stems near base of plant in clusters of several hundred; as they mature, become detached and bubble of air carries each to the top where it opens and floats until it meets a female flower; masses of male flowers gather around the larger female flower to which the sticky pollen adheres; favorite food of waterbirds; as an aquarium plant grows easily and provides abundant oxygen for animal life
fish camouflage, picture F-127
water plants W-101

Vallombrosa, Italy, summer resort in Apennines 20 mi (30 km) s.e. of Florence; Vallombrosian order of monks, founded 11th century, now extinct.

Valmy, France, village 40 mi (60 km) s.e. of Reims; pop. 267.

Valmy, battle of (1792), warfare, list W-16

Valois, Margaret of. see in index Margaret of Valois

Valois, old district of n. central France now in departments of Oise and Aisne; countship in Middle Ages; later united to crown; home of House of Valois.

Valois, House of, French royal dynasty, branch of Capetian family; reigned 1328–1589; name comes from historic region of France. For list, see in index France, history of, table of rulers
Paris P-132

Valona (in Albanian, Vlorë, or Vlonë), Albania, port city 70 mi (110 km) s.-s.w. of Tiranë; olives, olive oil; held by Italy 1914–20; pop. 41,285.

Valour, Cross of, medal M-272, picture M-271

Valparaíso, Chile, chief U.S. Pacific port s. of Los Angeles; pop. 278,800 V-269
Chile C-332
South America, map S-419
world, map W-300

Valparaiso, Ind., city 40 mi (64 km) s.e. of Chicago, Ill.; largely

residential; electrical insulating materials, permanent magnets, ball and roller bearings; Valparaiso University; pop. 22,247
Indiana, map I-102

Valparaiso University, Valparaiso, Ind.; Lutheran; founded 1859; arts and sciences, business administration, engineering, law, nursing; Christ College, an honors college; graduate studies.

'Valpinçon Bather', oil painting by Ingres, picture I-205

Valtellina, fertile valley of Adda River in n. Italy, fought over by ancient and medieval powers; wines and honey; mineral springs; ruled by Austria 1814–59.

Value, of color C-561
design D-108
dress design D-269

Value added by manufacture, essentially, the difference between the value of a finished product and the value of the raw materials consumed in its manufacture; usually it is determined for industries as a whole, or for groups of industries within a geographic area; this figure is a means for measuring and comparing the economic importance of industries; it is found by subtracting from the value of finished products the cost of materials, supplies, fuel, and power used in their manufacture, as well as resale costs and miscellaneous receipts; it is also adjusted by the net change in finished-products and work-in-progress inventories between the beginning and end of the year.

Value-added tax, a form of sales tax T-37

Valve, a device that stops or regulates the flow of a liquid or gas V-269. see also in index Electron tube
automobile engine A-847
heart H-97, pictures H-98, 99
plumbing P-470
transplant surgery S-719
wind instruments W-230

Vampire, folklore legend F-262
horror story H-245

Vampire bat B-105

Van, Turkey, town on s.e. shore of Lake Van; important city in Assyrian period; famous cuneiform inscriptions; pop. 22,043
Asia, map A-700
Lake Van V-270

Van, motor vehicle A-844

Van, Lake, large salt lake in e. Turkey; about 1,400 sq mi (3,600 sq km) V-270
Turkey T-318, picture T-320

Vanadate mineral, classification M-432, 435

Vanadinite, mineral, picture M-433

Vanadium (V), chemical element V-270
ore, map O-600
periodic table, list P-226, table P-225

Van Allen, James A. (born 1914) V-271

Van Allen belt, in earth's atmosphere V-271

Van Alstyne, Frances Jane. see in index Crosby, Fanny

Van Biesbroeck, George (1880–1974), U.S. astronomer, born in Ghent, Belgium; authority on comets and double stars; became U.S. citizen 1922; professor Yerkes Observatory, Williams Bay,

Wis., 1926–45; measured bending of starlight passing close to sun at times of eclipses, verifying Albert Einstein's predictions.

Van Brocklin, Norman (Dutchman) (1926–83), U.S. football quarterback, born in Eagle Butte, S.D.

Vanbrugh, John (1664–1726), English dramatist and architect, one of leading wits of his day; designed Blenheim Palace and mansions for English nobility A-569

Van Buren, Martin (1782–1862), 8th president of United States V-272
Harrison H-50
Jackson J-9
Martin Van Buren N.H.S. N-53
United States U-161

Van Buren, Steve (born 1920), U.S. football halfback and coach, born in Tecla, Honduras; played for Philadelphia Eagles 1944–51.

Vance, Arthur Charles (Dazzy) (1891–1961), U.S. baseball pitcher, born in Orient, Iowa; with Pittsburgh, N.L., and New York, A.L., 1915, New York, A.L., 1918, Brooklyn, N.L., 1922–32, St. Louis, N.L., 1933, Cincinnati, N.L., and St. Louis, N.L., 1934, Brooklyn, N.L., 1935; won 197 games, lost 140; led N.L. in strikeouts 7 years in a row, 1922–28; had best earned-run average in N.L. 1924, 1928, and 1930; lifetime earned-run average of 3.54; won over 20 games in each of 3 major-league seasons; in 1924, best season, won 28, lost 6; pitched no-hit game against Philadelphia, Sept. 13, 1925.

Vance, Cyrus Roberts (born 1917), U.S. lawyer and government official, born in Clarksburg, W. Va.; general counsel U.S. Department of Defense 1961–62, secretary of the army 1962–64; deputy secretary of defense 1964–67; U.S. president's foreign and domestic troubleshooter 1967–68; deputy U.S. negotiator at Vietnam peace talks in Paris 1968–69; U.S. secretary of state 1977–80.

Vance, Ethel. see in index Stone, Grace Zaring

Vance, Zebulon Baird (1830–94), U.S. statesman, born near Asheville, N.C.; served North Carolina three times as governor and as U.S. senator (Democrat) from 1879 until his death
Statuary Hall, table S-609

Vancouver, George (1758?–98), English navigator, served under Capt. James Cook on 2nd and 3rd voyages; 1791–95 made explorations in Australia, New Zealand, Tahiti, Hawaiian Islands, Vancouver Island, and along n.w. coast of North America ('A Voyage of Discovery to the North Pacific Ocean and Round the World')
British Columbia B-456
Canada C-95
Vancouver Island V-276
Washington W-53

Vancouver, B.C., city on west coast; pop. 414,281, with suburbs 1,268,183 V-275
British Columbia B-450
Canada C-78, map C-109
North America, map N-351
world, map W-300

Vancouver, Wash., port on Columbia River opposite Portland, Ore.; lumber and wood products, aluminum, textiles, chemicals; food

processing; veterans' hospital; incorporated 1857; pop. 42,834
Washington W-50, 60, map W-65

Vancouver, Mount, peak in St. Elias Mountains in s.w. Yukon Territory, near Alaska border, 15,700 ft (4,785 m); on s.e. edge of Seward Glacier.

Vancouver Island, British Columbia, largest island off w. coast of the Americas; 12,408 sq mi (32,136 sq km); pop. 381,297 V-275. see also in index Victoria, B.C.
British Columbia B-452
Canada C-74, 99, map C-109
North America, map N-351
Trans-Canada Highway T-248
Vancouver V-274
world, map W-300

Vandalia, Ill., city on Kaskaskia River, about 65 mi (105 km) n.e. of St. Louis, Mo.; shoes, clothing; state capital 1820–37; pop. 5,338 I-41, map I-53

Vandals, a Germanic tribe V-276
Byzantine Empire B-533
Carthage C-185
Germany G-121
Leo I L-130
Libya L-190
Middle Ages M-384
migration of people M-402
Roman Empire, picture R-276
Spain S-495
Tripoli T-289

Van de Graaff, Robert Jemison (1901–67), U.S. scientist, born in Tuscaloosa, Ala.; associate professor of physics at Massachusetts Institute of Technology 1934–60; inventor of the Van de Graaff generator for producing very high voltage.

Vandegrift, Alexander Archer (1887–1973), U.S. Marine Corps officer, born in Charlottesville, Va.; served in Nicaragua, Mexico, Haiti, China; commander of marines in Solomons 1942–43; commandant U.S. Marine Corps 1944–48
World War II W-345

Vandenberg, Arthur Hendrick (1884–1951), U.S. political leader, born in Grand Rapids, Mich.; U.S. senator 1928–51; Republican leader in the Senate; author of 'The Private Papers of Senator Vandenberg'
Grand Rapids G-213

Vandenberg, Hoyt Sanford (1899–1954), U.S. Air Force general, born in Milwaukee, Wis.; commanded U.S. Ninth Air Force in Europe in World War II; head of Central Intelligence Agency 1946; deputy commander of U.S. Air Force 1947, chief of staff 1948–53.

Vandenberg Air Force Base, near Lompoc, Calif. S-463

Vandenberg Center, multimillion-dollar building complex in Grand Rapids, Mich. G-213

Vanderbilt, Amy (1908–74), U.S. authority on etiquette, born in Staten Island, N.Y.; newspaper column; radio and television programs ('Amy Vanderbilt's Complete Book of Etiquette'; 'Amy Vanderbilt's Complete Cook Book').

Vanderbilt, Cornelius (1794–1877), U.S. capitalist and financier V-276
Nicaragua N-305
Westinghouse W-162

Vanderbilt, Cornelius (1843–99), U.S. capitalist and philanthropist V-276

Vanderbilt, Cornelius (1873–1942), U.S. capitalist

and inventor, born in New York, N.Y.; son of Cornelius Vanderbilt (1843–99); director of railroads and banks; patented many railroading devices.

Vanderbilt, Cornelius (1898–1974), U.S. journalist, author, and lecturer; born in New York, N.Y.; son of Cornelius Vanderbilt (1873–1942).

Vanderbilt, George Washington (1862-1914), U.S. scientist V-276

Vanderbilt, Harold Stirling (1884–1970), U.S. railroad official and sportsman, born in Oakdale, near Sayville, N.Y.; son of William Kissam Vanderbilt; originated game of contract bridge, elected to Bridge Hall of Fame 1964; won America's Cup yacht races 1930, 1934, and 1937 V-277

Vanderbilt, William Henry (1821–85), U.S. capitalist V-276

Vanderbilt, William Kissam (1849–1920), U.S. railroad official, philanthropist, and sportsman V-276
Marble House, picture R-207

Vanderbilt Mansion National Historic Site, site in Hyde Park, N.Y. N-60

Vanderbilt University, Nashville, Tenn.; founded 1873 by Cornelius Vanderbilt; arts and sciences, divinity, engineering, law, medicine, nursing; graduate school.

Vanderdecken, legendary sea captain of 'Flying Dutchman' S-255

Van der Donck, Adriaen (1620–55?), first lawyer of New Netherland and author of first book describing life in the colony; championed people's rights of self-government Yonkers Y-423

Vandergrift, Pa., borough on Kiskiminetas River 27 mi (43 km) n.e. of Pittsburgh; steel foundry products; coal mining; pop. 6,823
Pennsylvania, map P-206

Vanderlip, Frank Arthur (1864–1937), U.S. banker, born in Aurora, Ill.; assistant secretary of treasury 1897–1901; chairman War Savings Committee during World War I; wrote on financial and economic subjects.

Van der Rohe, Ludwig Mies. see in index Mies van der Rohe, Ludwig

Vandervelde, Emile (1866–1938), Belgian Socialist statesman and orator; as foreign minister, influential in negotiations for Versailles Treaty and Locarno Pact.

Van der Waals, Johannes Diderik. see in index Waals, Johannes van der

Van der Waals force, in physics W-2

Van der Weyden, Rogier. see in index Weyden, Rogier van der

Van Devanter, Willis (1859–1941), U.S. jurist, born in Marion, Ind.; associate justice of U.S. Supreme Court 1910–37.

Van de Velde, Henri (1863–1957), Belgian architect A-569
furniture design F-462

Van Diemen's Land. see in index Tasmania

Van Dine, S.S. see in index Wright, Willard Huntington

Van Doren, Carl Clinton (1885–1950), U.S. critic and biographer, born in

Hope, Ill.; taught English, University of Illinois and Columbia University; former literary editor, The Nation and Century; author 'Three Worlds', autobiography; 'Benjamin Franklin', Pulitzer prize biography (1939); 'The Great Rehearsal', story of U.S. Constitution; with brother Mark Van Doren, 'American and British Literature Since 1890'.

Van Doren, Mark (1894–1972), U.S. writer and editor, born in Hope, Ill.; joined faculty Columbia University 1920, professor 1942–59; editor of 'Anthology of World Poetry', 'American Poets 1630–1930'; author of verse: 'Collected Poems, 1922–1938', awarded Pulitzer prize 1940, 'Selected Poems', 'That Shining Place'; biography: 'Nathaniel Hawthorne'; 'Autobiography'; drama: 'The Last Days of Lincoln'; 'Collected Stories'.

Van Dorn, Earl (1820–63), U.S. military leader, born near Port Gibson, Miss.; served in U.S. Army during Mexican War; captain Second Cavalry 1855–61; major general Mississippi militia and Confederate army 1861.

Van Druten, John William (1901–57), U.S. playwright, born in London, England, son of Dutch father and English mother; became U.S. citizen 1944 (plays: 'The Voice of the Turtle', 'I Remember Mama', 'Bell, Book, and Candle', 'I Am a Camera'; autobiographical: 'Playwright at Work', 'The Widening Circle').

Van Dyck, Anthony (1599–1641), Flemish portrait painter V-277
Charles I, picture C-274

Van Dyke, Henry (1852–1933), U.S. Presbyterian clergyman and author, born in Germantown, Pa.; professor of English literature at Princeton University ('The Blue Flower', short stories: 'Fisherman's Luck', essays; 'The Builders, and Other Poems').

Van Dyke, John Charles (1856–1932), U.S. art critic; born in New Brunswick, N.J.; professor history of art, Rutgers College 1889–1932 ('New Guides to Old Masters'; 'Rembrandt and His School').

Vandyke print B-319

Vane, Henry (1613–62), English Puritan statesman, friend of religious liberty; governor of Massachusetts 1636–37; returned to England; active Parliamentarian; imprisoned at Restoration; and beheaded for treason H-336

Vane (or web), a series of locked barbs on a feather F-50

Vane, blade of a waterwheel W-103

Vane pump P-660

Vänern, Lake, in Sweden, largest lake in Scandinavian peninsula and 3rd largest in Europe; 2,141 sq mi (5,545 sq km)
Europe, map E-361

Vanessa, poetical name given by Jonathan Swift to Esther Vanhomrigh (1692–1723) in his serious poem, 'Cadenus and Vanessa', Swift being Cadenus.

Van Eyck, Hubert (1366?–1426), Flemish artist V-277
painting P-30
Renaissance R-161

Van Eyck, Jan (before 1395–1441), Flemish artist V-277

painting P-30
Renaissance R-161

Van Fleet, James Alward (born 1892), U.S. Army officer, born in Coytesville, N.J.; served in World Wars I and II; headed U.S. military mission to Greece 1948–50; Eighth Army commander in Korea April 1951–Jan. 1953; promoted to four-star general July 1951; retired from active military service 1953
Korean War K-298, chart K-299

Van Gogh, Vincent (1853–90), Dutch artist V-278
'Bedroom at Arles' P-54, picture P-57
Netherlands N-127

Van Gulik, Robert (1910–67), writer D-119

Van Hise, Charles Richard (1857–1918), U.S. geologist and educator, born in Fulton, Wis.; president University of Wisconsin 1903–18; authority on geology of Lake Superior iron-bearing region.

Vanhomrigh, Esther. see in index Vanessa

Van Horne, William Cornelius (1843–1915), Canadian railway executive, born in Illinois; after wide experience with U.S. railroads, superintended construction Canadian Pacific Railway, of which he was president 1888–99.

Vanhouttei spirea (or bridal wreath), a flowering shrub S-544

Vanier, Georges Philias (1888–1967), Canadian statesman, born in Montreal, Que.; eminent career as soldier and diplomat; ambassador to France 1944–54; governor-general of Canada 1959–67.

Vanilla, a flavoring V-278
Madagascar M-24
nuts N-449
orchid O-580

'Vanity Fair', novel by Thackeray T-145

Van Loon, Hendrik Willem (1882–1944), U.S. historian and illustrator, born in Rotterdam, The Netherlands ('R.v.R.', fictionized biography of Rembrandt; 'The Arts'; 'Van Loon's Geography'; 'Life and Times of Simon Bolivar' and 'Thomas Jefferson', biographies for young people).

Vann, Robert L. (1887–1940), U.S. publisher, assistant attorney general in administration of Franklin Roosevelt B-294

Vannes, France, historic town 67 mi (108 km) n.w. of Nantes; fabrics, leather, iron; ancient capital of the Veneti, a seafaring people; museum containing prehistoric remains; pop. 36,380
France, map F-372

Vannucci, Pietro. see in index Perugino

Van Paassen, Pierre (1895–1968), U.S. journalist, writer, and Unitarian minister, born in Gorcum, The Netherlands; columnist for New York Evening World 1924–31; ordained Unitarian minister 1946; known as fighter against fascism and for Zionism (autobiography: 'Days of Our Years', 'A Pilgrim's Vow'; 'To Number Our Days'; 'Crown of Fire', biography of Savonarola).

Van Rensselaer, Kiliaen (1595–1644), first Dutch patroon of New York, one of founders of New York and Albany.

Van Rensselaer, Martha (1864–1932), U.S. expert in home economics, born in Randolph, N.Y.; at Cornell University from 1900, director of extension courses that developed into Home Economics College, of which she was head 1911–32.

Van Rensselaer, Stephen (1764–1839), U.S. political leader and soldier, last of Dutch patroons; ardent promoter of Erie Canal; founded Rensselaer Polytechnic Institute, Troy, N.Y.

Van Rijn, Rembrandt Harmenszoon. see in index Rembrandt Harmenszoon van Rijn

Van't Hoff, Jacobus Hendricus (1852–1911), Dutch chemist and physicist, founder of stereochemistry and the first Nobel prizewinner (1901) in chemistry. see also in index Nobel Prizewinners, table osmosis O-611

Van Twiller, Wouter (1580?–1656?), governor of New Netherland, born in Nijkerk, The Netherlands; clerk Dutch West India Co. at Amsterdam; made governor 1633; inept government led to trouble with English and American Indians, as well as with own people; recalled 1637.

Vanua Levu, an island of Fiji; 2,130 sq mi (5,515 sq km); chief town, Lambasa; gold, sugar, rice, copra; pop. 84,892.

Vanuatu (formerly New Hebrides), group of islands e. of n. Australia; pop. 145,000 V-279
Commonwealth membership C-602
flag, picture F-172
United Nations, table U-84
world, map W-300

Van Vactor, David (born 1906), U.S. composer and flutist, born in Plymouth, Ind.; professor in department of fine arts University of Tennessee 1947–76; conductor Knoxville Symphony Orchestra 1947–72; compositions include orchestral works, chamber music, and choral works.

Van Vechten, Carl (1880–1964), U.S. novelist, born in Cedar Rapids, Iowa; assistant music critic New York Times, later on New York Press; composed 'Five Old English Ditties'; a rebel against dullness and standardization ('Peter Whiffle'; 'The Blind Bow-Boy'; 'Spider Boy').

Van Vleck, John Hasbrouck (1899–1980), U.S. physicist, born in Middletown, Conn.; faculty of Harvard University 1922–23 and from 1934, professor 1935–69, professor emeritus 1969–80; study of sources of magnetism in atomic structure.

Van Wagener, Isabella. see in index Truth, Sojourner

Van Wert, Ohio, city 27 mi (43 km) n.w. of Lima; metal tool kits, fiberboard containers, oil seals, work clothes, cheese, electronic lighting equipment; pop. 11,035
Ohio, map O-518

Vanzetti, Bartolomeo. see in index Sacco-Vanzetti case

Vapor, gaseous form of a substance normally solid or liquid. see also in index Evaporation
air A-146
water W-84, 87
weather W-120

Vaporetti, motorboat V-297

Vaporization, process whereby a substance changes from a liquid to a gas M-225
petroleum P-259, picture P-262

Vapor pressure, pressure exerted by a vapor when the vapor is in equilibrium with the liquid or solid form, or both, of the same substance; increases with increasing temperature; the temperature at which the vapor pressure at the surface of a liquid equals the pressure exerted by the surroundings is called the boiling point of the liquid.

Vapor tube, lighting L-206

Vara, Mexican unit of measure, table W-141

Varanasi (or Banaras, or Benares), India, city on Ganges River; pop. 708,647 V-279
Asia, map A-700
Hinduism H-159
India, map I-86
pilgrimage P-384

Vardar River, river in the Balkan Peninsula; empties into Aegean Sea near Salonika, Greece.

Varden, Dolly, character in Charles Dickens' 'Barnaby Rudge', the locksmith's coquettish daughter whose dress of flowered dimity gave her name to fabric so figured.

Vardhamana. see in index Mahavira

Vardon, Harry (1870–1937), British golfer, born in Grouville on island of Jersey, Channel Islands; won British, U.S., and German open championships golf G-189

Varennes, Pierre Gaultier de, sieur de la Vérendrye. see in index Vérendrye, Pierre Gaultier de Varennes, sieur de la

Varennes-en-Argonne, France, town 18 mi (29 km) n.w. of Verdun, on Aire River; taken by U.S. troops on first day of Meuse-Argonne offensive in World War I; pop. 643.

Varèse, Edgar (1883–1965), U.S. composer, born in Paris, France; to U.S. 1916, became citizen 1926; one of most radical of modern composers (chamber music: 'Hyperprism', 'Intégrales')
classical music M-676

Vargas, Getúlio (1883–1954), president and dictator of Brazil V-279
Brazil B-423

Vargas, diamond D-131

Vargas Llosa, Mario (born 1936), Peruvian author L-71

Várhegy (or Castle Hill), central hill of Budapest, Hungary B-479

Variability (or dispersion), in statistics S-605

Variable, in mathematics M-214, 219
algebra A-263
calculus C-21

Variable, in scientific method S-103, S-359

Variable air volume system (VAV), air-conditioning A-152

Variable resistor. see in index Rheostat

Variable star. see in index Eclipsing binary star

Variation, of compass. see in index Declination

'Variation of Animals and Plants under Domestication, The', work by Darwin D-39

'Variations on America', organ piece by Ives I-406

Varicella. see in index Chicken pox

Varicose veins, bulging veins in the leg D-174

Varied bunting, a small bird of the finch family; has purple head and plum-red back and underparts.

'Varieties of Religious Experience, The', work by James J-21

Variety (or music hall), a form of performing arts P-219

'Variety', show business newspaper N-242

Variety store C-513

Varley, John (1778–1842), English landscape painter and art teacher whose instruction laid foundation of an English school of watercolor painting ('Treatise on the Principles of Landscape Design').

Varmint (or pest), in hunting H-331

Varna (formerly Stalin, ancient Odessus), Bulgaria, chief port, on Black Sea; cotton mills; exports cattle, grain, pop. 219,000
Europe, map E-361

Varna, a social class
India I-68

Varnhagen von Ense, Rahel (1771–1833), German author remembered for her letters and for her influence on A. von Humboldt, Goethe, Carlyle, and other literary men; her salon in Berlin was the most important in Germany; her husband, **Karl Varnhagen von Ense** (1785–1858), wrote historical and literary sketches of permanent value.

Varnish. see in index Paint and varnish

'Varqeh o-Golshah', Persian epic, picture I-367

Varro, Marcus Terentius (116–27 BC), Roman historian and soldier, most learned of the Romans; most of writings lost.

Varthema, Lodovico de (1465–1517), Italian adventurer and traveler
history writing H-172

Varuna, god in early Vedic Hindu religion, creator and ruler of the world; later, god of the waters.

Varus, Publius Quintilius, Roman general defeated by Arminius in the Teutoburg Forest (AD 9); disheartened, Varus killed himself, and the Emperor Augustus cried in anguish at the news: "Varus, Varus, give me back my legions!"

Varve, in geology
Ice Age phase measurement I-9
time estimation A-563

Varying hare (or snowshoe rabbit), rodent (Lepus americanus) of the Leporidae family R-30
protective coloration P-620, picture P-619
Swedish history S-730

Vasa, Finland. see in index Vaasa

Vasa, Swedish royal house beginning with Gustavus I Vasa (1523–60) and ending with Christina (1632–54)
Polish history P-494

'Vasa', Swedish warship launched 1628; sank on maiden voyage; raised from Stockholm harbor 1961; black oak hull almost intact; objects aboard included wood carvings, kitchenware, and

bronze cannons; restored; on exhibit in Stockholm.

Vasarely, Victor (born 1908), Hungarian painter
'Mach-C' P-61

Vasari, Giorgio (1511–74), Italian author, painter, and architect (Uffizi Palace, Florence); biographer and 'father of modern art, history and criticism' ('Lives of the Most Eminent Painters, Sculptors, and Architects', a classic despite inaccuracies)
Uffizi Palace gallery M-661

Vasco da Gama. see in index Gama, Vasco da

Vasconcelos, José (1882–1959), Mexican educator and writer, born in Oaxaca; nation's first minister of public education
Latin American literature L-74, picture L-73

Vasconia. see in index Basques; Gascony

Vascular bundles, plant structure P-422
cambium cells C-240

Vascular cryptogram, plant classification P-419

Vascular seed plants plant classification P-419

Vascular system, human. see in index Circulatory system, human

Vas deferens, male reproductive structure R-166

Vase. see also in index Pottery
Greek G-269

Vasectomy, birth control method B-283

Vashti, queen of Ahasuerus, king of Persia, put aside for refusing to come before the king at his command (Bible, Book of Esther).

Vasilyevski Island, U.S.S.R.
Leningrad L-127

Vasopressin (sometimes called an antidiuretic hormone), hormone that raises blood pressure H-240, table H-241
diabetes insipidus D-126

Vasquez, Miguel, circus performer C-433

Vassa, Gustavas (originally Oulaudah Equino) (1745–1801), African antislavery author, born in Benin; entered U.S. as slave at 11; bought freedom and became sailor; settled in England; autobiography, 'The Interesting Narrative of the Life of Oulaudah Equino, or Gustavas Vassa, the African' (1789), spurred abolitionist cause in Europe and U.S.

Vassa, Buddhist monastic retreat B-483

Vassal, in European Middle Ages M-386
feudalism F-69, picture F-68

Vassar, Matthew (1792–1868), U.S. brewer and philanthropist, born in East Tuddingham, England; gave 200 acres of land and $788,000 to found Vassar College.

Vassar College, Poughkeepsie, N.Y.; founded by M. Vassar; incorporated 1861; arts and sciences; graduate study N-255, picture U-224
educational influence E-92

Västeras, Sweden, port city on Lake Mälaren 60 mi (100 km) n.w. of Stockholm; electrical products; medieval cathedral; pop. 110,457
Europe, map E-361

Vasyugan, world's largest bog in western Siberia U-21

Vathek, hero of 'The History of Caliph Vathek', fantastic Oriental romance by William

Beckford, written in style of 'Arabian Nights'.

Vatican, palace of the pope in Italy. see also in index Sistine Chapel; Vatican City
mosaic M-590

Vatican Bank, Italian bank banking scandal I-398

Vatican City, independent state under temporal rule of pope; area 108.7 acres (44 hectares); pop. 1,000 V-280. see also in index Papacy; Roman Catholicism; Rome
Europe, map E-361
flag, picture F-172
Italy I-384, map I-404
Pius XI P-399
St. Peter's. see in index St. Peter's

Vatican Councils, Roman Catholic council V-283
I (1869–70) P-399
II (1962–65)
canon law C-142
church council history C-411
ecumenism E-69
John XXIII J-123
Paul VI P-156
Roman Catholicism R-266

Vatican Museums, in Rome, Italy M-663, picture M-662

Vatican Palace, home of the popes V-281

Vattel, Emmerich von (1714–67), Swiss jurist
Enlightenment E-289

Vättern, 2nd largest lake in Sweden; 733 sq mi (1,898 sq km), map E-361

Vauban, Sébastien le Prestre de (1633–1707), French military engineer; had charge of French fortifications; made marshal 1703
fort and fortifications F-320

Vaudeville, theatrical entertainment composed of songs, sketches, dances, acrobatics; originally meant a lively ballad
Benny B-163
Fields F-80
musical comedy M-685
performing arts P-219
popular music M-684
radio programming R-53

Vaudois. see in index Waldenses

Vaudreuil-Cavagnal, Pierre François de Rigaud, marquis de (1698–1765), last French governor-general of Canada, succeeding Duquesne in 1755; his father, **Philippe de Rigaud** (1643–1725), was appointed governor in 1703.

Vaughan, Henry (1622–95), Welsh poet and mystic, called the Silurist because his native region was that of the Silures, an ancient people of Britain ('The Retreat'; 'The World'; 'Peace'; 'Beyond the Veil').

Vaughan, Herbert, Cardinal (1832–1903), English Roman Catholic prelate, Manning's successor as cardinal and archbishop of Westminster; founded St. Bede's College, Manchester.

Vaughan, Sarah (born 1924), U.S. singer, picture J-85

Vaughan Williams, Ralph (1872–1958) English composer V-284
classical music M-675

Vault, in architecture, a development of the arch principle. see also in index Arch; Dome
Roman A-548
Romanesque A-551

Vault, in gymnastics G-323, diagram G-324

Vault, room for the secure storage of valuables, picture B-70

Vaulting horse, in gymnastics G-323

Vauquelin, Louis Nicolas (1763–1829), French chemist, discovered chromium and beryllium.

Vaux, Calvert (1824–95), British landscape architect, born in London
Central Park N-273

Vaux, James Hardy (1782–died?), English-born Australian convict and writer; disappeared after release from prison in 1841 A-797

Vauxhall Garden, in London, England, amusement center built 1661; closed 1859; mentioned by several English dramatists A-384

VAV. see in index Variable air volume system

Vava'u, a group of islands forming a division of Tonga T-214

VCR. see in index Videocassette recorder

VD. see in index Sexually transmitted disease

Ve, Norse god M-697

Veal, meat M-246
meat industry M-250

Veblen, Thorstein (1857–1929), U.S. economist and social scientist V-284
Minnesota M-444

Vecchio, Tiziano. see in index Titian

Vecht River (or Vechte River), branch of the Rhine River, 18 mi (29 km) long; flows into IJsselmeer
Germany, map G-134

Vector, an organism P-124

Vector, in mechanics M-263, 268

Vector mesons. see in index Boson

Vedalia beetle, insect
pest control P-245

Vedanta, a Hindu philosophy founded on Upanishads, parts of Veda; treats soul and universe in relation to Supreme Spirit
Hinduism H-158
Transcendental Meditation T-249

'Veda of the Chants' (or Samaveda), sacred Indian literature I-105

Vedas, sacred writings of Hinduism H-157
India I-72
Indian literature I-105
readings R-110

V-E Day (Victory in Europe) (May 8), day of German surrender, World War II U-176

Vedder, Elihu (1836–1923), U.S. painter and illustrator, born in New York City; works represented in leading museums of U.S.; murals, Library of Congress, Washington, D.C.; illustrations for Omar Khayyám.

Vedro, Soviet unit of capacity, table W-141

Veery, a bird (Hylocichla fuscescens) of the family Turdidae T-177

Vega, Garcilaso de la (1503–36), Spanish poet S-505

Vega, fixed star S-582, charts S-589, 590

Vega Carpio, Lope Félix de (1562–1635), Spanish dramatist and poet V-284
drama D-243
Spanish literature S-505

Vegan, a strict vegetarian V-289

Vegetable fibers. see in index Fibers, natural, subhead plant

Vegetable ivory (or tagua nut, or corozo nut) I-406
buttons B-530, picture B-529
nuts N-449

Vegetable lamb, legendary animal A-458

Vegetable oils F-47
margarine M-134

Vegetable pear. see in index Chayote

Vegetables, edible plant or plant part V-285. see also in index names of vegetables
cooking C-701
farming procedures F-25
food and nutrition F-278
garden G-20, 25, picture G-23
radiation, picture R-74
truck farming T-293
vegetarianism V-289

'Vegetable Seller', work by Yoshida A-662

Vegetable sponge (or dishcloth gourd), Luffa genus of vine that can be dried and used as a sponge G-198

Vegetable tanning, in leather production L-107

Vegetarianism V-289
food and nutrition F-279
meat M-247

Vegetation. see also in index continents by name, subhead vegetation
jungle environment J-154
Latin America L-59, picture L-65
literature L-75

Vegetative reproduction, form of asexual reproduction R-168
plant P-427
domestication P-439
potato P-562

Veil, Simone (born 1927), French lawyer and political leader, born in Nice; minister of health 1974–77, of health and social security 1977–78, of health and family affairs 1978–79; member European Parliament from 1979, president 1979–82.

Veil, clothing
wedding H-54

Vein, blood vessel B-313
circulatory system C-421
digestive system, diagram D-143, picture D-145
Harvey H-51

Vein, of plant
leaf structure L-100

Vein, type of mineral deposit M-427

Veira, João Bernardo, president of Guinea-Bissau G-315

Vejle, Denmark, seaport in e. Jutland at head of Vejle Fjord; dairying, shipbuilding, ironwork, textiles; pop. 31,362.

Vela (literally "sails"), part of constellation Argo, charts C-682, S-587, 588

Vela, Soviet satellite A-163

Velásquez, Diego (1465?–1522?), Spanish soldier; accompanied Columbus to West Indies on his second voyage; first governor of Cuba, founded Havana (1519)
Cortez C-727
Cuba C-801

Velasquez, Diego (1599–1660), Spanish painter V-289
Infanta Maria Theresa, picture D-264
'Maids of Honor' P-39, picture P-41
Spain S-492

Veliger, larva of marine snails S-328

Vellum B-345
Montgolfier M-569

Velocipede, early form of bicycle B-187

Velocity, in physics, rate of motion, or speed, in a given direction. *see also in index* Speed
energy, *table* E-217
mechanics M-263, 266
planets P-414, *table* P-413
radiation R-42
sound S-389
wind tunnel W-234

Velon, trade name for a synthetic textile fiber made from petroleum and brine; used for automobile seat covers, curtains, handbags, and upholstery; resistant to shrinkage, dirt, water, and acids.

Velour (or velours, French meaning "velvet"), a drapery fabric with a short, thick pile; made of mercerized cotton, silk, or mohair; term also applied to fine woolen fabrics with a soft, velvety nap, and to a velvety felt used for hats.

Velvet, in textiles
rug and carpet R-341, *diagram* R-342

Velvet ant, wasp of the Mutillidae family W-75

Velvet leaf. *see in index* Indian mallow

Vena cava (hollow vein), superior and inferior, the two great blood vessels that carry venous blood to the right atrium of the heart, the superior from head, arms, and upper part of trunk, the inferior from all structures of lower part of body.

Vence, France; town located near Nice; pop. 7,332, *map* F-372
Matisse decorated chapel M-222

Venda, republic in s. Africa, formerly part of South Africa; 2,448 sq mi (6,340 sq km); cap. Thohoyandou; pop. 516,000 V-290
Africa, *map* A-118
African political unit, *table* A-112
flag, *picture* F-172
South Africa S-398

Vendée, maritime department of w. France; 2,709 sq mi (7,016 sq km); center of royalist revolt (1792–93) against French Republic; pop. 450,641
France, *map* F-372

Vendetta, a feud for blood revenge in Italy, often passed from generation to generation, between clans or families.

Vending machine V-290
marketing M-147
soft drinks S-366

Vendôme, France, town 35 mi (55 km) n.e. of Tours; ruins of 11th-century castle of counts of Vendôme; birthplace of Rochambeau; glove making; pop. 15,854
France, *map* F-372

Veneer
brick B-436, B-494
carpentry C-175
forest products F-316
furniture F-453, 458
lumber industry L-332
wood W-281

Venera, Soviet space probe
Venus P-407, *picture* P-408

Venerable Bede, the. *see in index* Bede, Saint

Venereal disease. *see in index* Sexually transmitted disease

Venereal warts. *see in index* Genital warts

Veneti, an ancient people of n. Italy; also a powerful maritime people of w. France around Vannes, conquered by Julius Caesar 56 BC.

Venetia (or Veneto), region in n. Italy between Alps and Adriatic Sea; area 7,095 sq mi (18,375 sq km); ancient Roman province; long ruled by Venice; held by Austria 1797–1866; pop. 3,846,562
Italy I-394

Venetian glass G-164
beadwork B-114

'Venetian Nobleman, A' painting by Titian
painting P-37

Venetian red, iron oxide I-329

Venezia, Italy. *see in index* Venice

Venezuela, republic of South America on the Caribbean Sea; 352,144 sq mi (912,050 sq km); cap. Caracas; pop. 18,272,200 V-291
abolition of slavery A-10
cities. *see in index* cities below and other cities by name
Caracas C-153
Maracaibo M-130
flag, *picture* F-172
geography
Guiana Highlands G-302
Lake Maracaibo M-130
waterfalls A-414
history
Betancourt B-178
Bolívar B-332
Miranda M-464
Roosevelt R-319
national anthem, *table* N-64
North America, *map* N-351
South America S-401, *map* S-419
United Nations, *table* U-84
world, *map* W-300

Venice, Calif., beach resort and residential community along Santa Monica Bay; oil; annexed to Los Angeles 1925; planned after Venice, Italy; pop. 80, 500
California, *map* C-53

Venice (in Italian Venezia, or Republic of Venice), Italy, city built on islands in bay of Adriatic Sea; pop. 332,775 V-297
art and architecture
mosaic M-590
painting P-37
sculpture S-144
banking B-72
Byzantine wars B-536
canals C-127, *picture* C-453
Crusades C-787, N-82
Europe, *map* E-361, *picture* E-349
film festival M-627
Genoa G-59
glassmaking G-162
hairdressing H-9
Italy, *map* I-404
Marco Polo A-329
St. Mark's Cathedral. *see in index* St. Mark's Cathedral
trade
international I-270
Renaissance R-163
textiles T-144

Venice, Gulf of, on the Adriatic Sea A-50
Italy, *map* I-404

Venice of Brazil. *see in index* Recife

Venice of the North. *see in index* Stockholm

Venidium, genus of annual and perennial s. African plants of the composite family; leaves lobed, one lobe much larger than others; flowers solitary, daisy-like, in a wide range of soft colors, with each ray floret darkly blotched at base, and center florets dark.

Vening Meinesz, Felix Andries (1887–1966), Dutch engineer, born in The Hague; inventor of special pendulum.

Venire, legal summons to jury service, writ by this name issued by a court commands that a specified number of qualified citizens act as jurors in the same court.

Venireman, a member of a panel from which jurors are drawn.

Venison, meat of deer D-61

Venizélos, Eleuthérios (1864–1936), Greek statesman; prominent in Greek politics 1910–35; helped unite Crete and Greece G-260

Venn, John (1834–1923), English logician and mathematician, born in Hull; originated Venn diagrams adopted by the new math.

Venn diagram, in mathematics G-74

Venom, poisonous matter normally secreted by some animals
lizard L-272
platypus P-458
snake S-333, S-338
spider S-535

Venous stenosis, medical complication that frequently accompanies surgery S-718

Vent, in plumbing P-471

Vent, opening in Earth's surface V-402, *picture* V-403

Ventilating H-107, 112. *see also in index* Heating
air conditioning A-149
fan F-23

Ventral fin (or pelvic fin), fish, *diagram* F-125
shark S-219

Ventricle, part of the heart H-97, *pictures* H-98, 99

Ventricular fibrillation, abnormal contraction of the ventricles of the heart D-173, H-98

Ventriloquism V-300

Ventris, Michael George Francis (1922–56), English architect and cryptographer, born near St. Albans A-61, A-537

Ventspils, Latvian Soviet Socialist Republic, Baltic port and resort; 100 mi (160 km) n.w. of Riga; exports timber and grain; pop. 27,400 L-83
Europe, *map* E-361
U.S.S.R., *maps* U-62, 66

Ventura (officially San Buenaventura), Calif., city on Pacific Ocean about 60 mi (100 km) n.w. of Los Angeles; petroleum products; citrus fruits, vegetables, walnuts; San Buenaventura Mission established 1782; pop. 74,474
California, *map* C-53

Venture, retail store chain, *picture* M-140

Venturi nozzle, part of jet-ejector pump P-660

Venturi tube A-179

Venue, in law
legal definition, *table* L-92

Venus, Roman goddess of love and beauty, identified with Greek Aphrodite. *see also in index* Aphrodite
Roman mythology M-701

Venus, planet P-407, *picture* P-408, *table* P-413
astronomy A-714
Earth E-7, *diagram* E-9
eclipse E-49
observation O-458
solar system S-375, *picture* S-377, *table* S-376

'Venus and Adonis', poem by Shakespeare S-202, 206
horse H-247

'Venus de Milo', statue A-505, *pictures* A-455, E-335
Greek art G-271
sculpture S-141

Venus-flytrap, plant *(Dionaea muscipula)* V-301
leaf, *picture* L-101
plant P-435, *picture* P-434

Venus's-hairstone. *see in index* Sagenite

Veracruz, Mexico, state in e. on Gulf of Mexico; 28,114 sq mi (72,815 sq km); cap. Jalapa; chief port Veracruz; pop. 4,917,773
Mexico, *map* M-341

Veracruz, Mexico, port on the Gulf of Mexico, e. of Mexico City; pop. 284,822 V-301
Mexico M-336, *map* M-344
North America, *map* N-351
world, *map* W-300

'Vera Vorontzoff', work by Kovalevsky K-302

Verb, in grammar
part of speech G-209
spelling S-526

Verbal scale, in maps M-116

Verbena (also called vervain), genus of annual or perennial herbs of the family Verbenaceae; the many varieties of garden verbenas, with their white, red, and purple flower clusters, are descendants of several South American species. *see also in index* Vervain family
growing conditions G-24
perfume, *table* P-223

Verbenaceae. *see in index* Vervain family

Verbrugghen, Henri (1873–1934), musical conductor, born in Brussels; led orchestras in Scotland, Australia, and the U.S. A-800

Vercel, Roger (1894–1957), French novelist, born in Le Mans; books deal with adventure and the sea ('Captain Conan'; 'Tides of Mont St.-Michel'; 'Easter Fleet').

Verchères, Marie-Madeleine Jarret de (1678–1747), Canadian pioneer heroine; when 14 years old, in absence of parents, defended home fort, about 20 mi s. of Montreal, against Iroquois C-92

Vercingetorix (died 45? BC), chief of the Arverni in Gaul, leader of the great rebellion against Caesar; beheaded by Caesar's order.

Verdandi (or Verthandi), in German and Norse mythology
Fates F-44

Verd antique. *see in index* Serpentine

Verde, Cape. *see in index* Cape Verde

Verde, Cape (in French, Cap Vert), peninsula, Senegal; westernmost point of continent of Africa; site of Dakar, *map* A-118

Verden, West Germany, town 23 mi (37 km) s.e. of Bremen on Aller River; machinery, precision instruments, food processing; pop. 17,233
Germany, *map* G-134

Verde River, river in central Arizona; 190 mi (305 km) long
Arizona, *maps* A-598, 610

Verdi, Giuseppe (1813–1901), Italian composer V-302
bass drums P-216
opera O-566
vocal music V-388

Verdict, in law
criminal law C-776
jury system J-158
legal definition, *table* L-93

Verdigris, a green crystallized substance produced by action of acetic acid on copper; used as pigment in paints, in liniment, in dyeing, and calico printing; name also popularly applied to green rust formed on copper by weathering, chemically a copper carbonate
corrosion C-726

Verdigris River, river that rises in s.e. Kansas and flows s. into Oklahoma; enters Arkansas River near Fort Gibson; about 280 mi (450 km) long
Kansas, *maps* K-175, 186
Oklahoma, *maps* O-522, 537

Verdin, bird *(Auriparus flaviceps)* T-197

Verdun (ancient Virodunum), France, fortified city; pop. 21,170 V-302

Verdun, Que., city and residential suburb of Montreal on St. Lawrence River; incorporated 1921; pop. 68,013, *map* C-112
Quebec, *map* Q-20

Verdun, battle of, World War I W-306, 310
Pétain P-246
Verdun V-302
warfare, *list* W-16

Verdun, Treaty of (or Partition of Verdun) (843), France, divided Charlemagne's empire
Belgium B-149
Europe E-347
Germany G-121
treaty, *table* T-275
Verdun V-303

Vereeniging, Peace of. *see in index* Pretoria, Treaty of

Vérendrye, François, chevalier de la, French Canadian explorer
South Dakota S-442

Vérendrye, Louis Joseph de la, French Canadian explorer
South Dakota S-442

Vérendrye, Pierre Gaultier de Varennes, sieur de la (1685–1749), French Canadian explorer and fur trader, born at Trois-Rivières, Canada; pushed westward in search of the Western Sea; visited Mandan villages on the Missouri; two of his sons, Francois, chevalier de la Vérendrye, and Louis Joseph de la Vérendrye, visited North Dakota and possibly reached the foothills of the Rocky Mountains
Canada C-95
Manitoba M-103
Minnesota M-445, *picture* M-451
North Dakota N-376
fur trade, *picture* F-469

Vereshchagin, Vasili (1842–1904), Russian painter; sought to promote peace by realistic pictures of horrors of war ('The Pyramid of Skulls'; 'Left Behind').

Verga, Giovanni (1840–1922), Italian novelist, born in Catania, Sicily; sketches of Sicilian peasantry I-377

Vergennes, Charles Gravier, comte de (1717–87), French foreign minister under Louis XVI; aided North American colonies during their war for independence
American Revolution R-189

Vergil. *see in index* Virgil

Verhaeren, Emile (1855–1916), Belgian poet and critic; early poems impressionistic in tone; influenced by Flemish artists; later showed patriotic fervor and interest in social problems; glorified the beauty of Flanders.

Verification principle, in semantics S-170

Verisimilitude, in writing
French literature F-395

Verismo (or realism), in Italian opera O-568
Italy I-385

Leoncavallo's technique L-135

Veríssimo, Erico Lopes (1905–75), Brazilian writer B-418

Verkhneudinsk. *see in index* Ulan-Ude

Verkhoyansk, U.S.S.R., village in n.e. Siberia on Yana River; pop. 2,000
Asia, *map* A-700
Siberia S-281
temperature range A-572
U.S.S.R., *map* U-62
world, *map* W-300

Verkhoyansk Range, mountains in n.e. Siberia U-23

Verkolje, Jan (or Jan Verkolye) (died 1763), artist
Leeuwenhoek portrait, *picture* L-117

Verlaine, Paul (1844–96), French lyric poet V-303
Rimbaud R-222

Vermeer, Jan (1632–75), Dutch painter V-303
Netherlands N-127
'Young Woman with a Water Jug' P-44

Vermiculite, hydrous silicates usually derived from alteration of mica; so named because scales, when heated, open out in wormlike forms; used in insulation, fireproofing, and soundproofing materials.

Vermiform appendix. *see in index* Appendix, vermiform

Vermilion, a scarlet pigment used in paint; English vermilion, mercury sulfide, very opaque but not permanent in color; American vermilion, chromate of lead, has good color strength but is blackened by sulfides; because of high price, both the above have been extensively replaced by coal-tar dyes.

Vermilion Range, in Minnesota, underground iron-ore mine M-446, *maps* M-441, 458

Vermillion, S.D., city on Vermillion River, near Missouri River, 33 mi (53 km) n.w. of Sioux City, Iowa; livestock; trade center for agricultural area; pop. 10,136 S-441, *map* S-453

Vermont, a New England state of the U.S.; 9,609 sq mi (24,887 sq km); cap. Montpelier; pop. 511,456 V-304
Arthur's birthplace, *picture* A-654
covered bridges, *picture* B-439
flag, *picture* F-160
Montpelier M-570
North America, *map* N-351
state capitals, *list* S-595
Statuary Hall, *table* S-609
taxation, *tables* T-37, 39
United States U-103, 159, *table* U-187

Vermont and State Agricultural College, University of, Burlington, Vt.; founded 1791; arts and sciences, agriculture and home economics, education, medicine, technology; graduate studies V-308, *picture* V-313

Vermont Piedmont. *see in index* New England Upland

Vermouth, an aromatic wine W-237

Vernal equinox A-718

Verne, Jules (1828–1905), French author V-320. *see also in index* 'Twenty Thousand Leagues Under the Sea'
frontiers F-427
science fiction S-118
space travel S-459

Verneuil process, in making jewels
sapphires and rubies C-796
synthetic gems J-113

Vernier, a scale invented by Vernier
instrumentation I-229
micrometer M-378

Vernis Martin (Martin varnish), a brilliant translucent lacquer developed in the 18th century by the Martin brothers; the secret of making it is now lost and articles decorated with it are in museums.

Vernix, fetal skin covering P-580

Vernon, Dorothy (16th century), daughter and heiress of Sir George Vernon; eloped with Sir John Manners and became ancestress of dukes of Rutland; heroine of Charles Major's novel, 'Dorothy Vernon of Haddon Hall'.

Vernon, Edward (1684–1757), English admiral; captured (1739) Porto Bello, Panama, with a fleet of 6 ships; Mount Vernon, Va., named for him M-639

Vernon, B.C., city near n. end of Okanagan Lake 27 mi (43 km) n.e. of Kelowna; fruit-growing and fruit processing; lumber, poultry, eggs; fishing, hunting; pop. 19,987
Canada, *map* C-109

Vernon, Conn., 11 mi (18 km) n.e. of Hartford; electronic components, chemicals; dairy and truck farms; pop. of township 27,974
Connecticut, *map* C-665

Veron, Tex., city in n. part of state, about 45 mi (70 km) n.w. of Wichita Falls; cotton, wheat, livestock; oil wells; meat-packing; clothing, feed; pop. 12,695
Texas, *map* T-137

Verona, Italy, fortified city 62 mi (100 km) w. of Venice on Adige River; noted art center in Middle Ages; famous art collections and Roman remains; Congress of great European powers 1822; bombarded by Austrian aviators in World War I; scene of 'Romeo and Juliet'; pop. 221,138
Europe, *map* E-361
Italy, *map* I-404, *picture* I-393

Verona, N.J., borough 8 mi (13 km) n.w. of Newark, near Montclair; brushes, hardware; incorporated 1907; pop. 14,166
New Jersey, *map* N-211

Veronese, Paolo (1528–88), painter of Venetian school V-320
'Finding of Moses, The' P-38

Veronica, Saint, legendary woman of Jerusalem, on whose kerchief, used by Jesus to wipe the bloody sweat from his brow on way to Golgotha, his portrait was said to have been miraculously imprinted; festival July 12.

Veronica (popularly called speedwell), genus of plants and shrubs of the figwort family with blue, pink, or white flowers; well-known species is the long-leaved veronica *(Veronica longifolia)*, a tall garden perennial with small violet or blue flowers on erect spikes.

Verrazano-Narrows Bridge, in New York, links Brooklyn and Richmond N-271, *picture* N-263

Verrazzano, Giovanni da (1480–1528), Florentine explorer of North America for France
Canada and Newfoundland C-90
Long Island L-297
New Jersey N-199
New York N-256, N-279
voyage A-333

Verres, Gaius (died 43 BC), corrupt and rapacious Roman quaestor and propraetor (governor) of Sicily 73–71 BC; brought to trial by the people and prosecuted by Cicero; only two of the seven orations that Cicero wrote against him were delivered because Verres fled, knowing conviction was certain.

Verrill, Addison Emery (1839–1926), U.S. natural scientist, born in Greenwood, Me.; studied fauna of Atlantic and Pacific coasts and marine animals of Bermuda Islands.

Verrill, Alpheus Hyatt (1871–1954), U.S. naturalist and explorer, born in New Haven, Conn.; originator of autochrome process of color photography; explorer in Bermuda, West Indies, Panama ('Harper's Book for Young Naturalists'; 'Islands and Their Mysteries'; 'Old Civilizations of the New World').

Verrocchio, Andrea del (1435–88), Italian sculptor, goldsmith, and painter; one of greatest early Renaissance artists; painted famous 'Baptism of Christ'
Leonardo da Vinci L-132
sculpture S-144
statue of Colleoni H-272

Verruca. *see in index* wart

Verruga peruana, stage of Carrion's disease; skin eruption characterized by reddish papules and nodules
Noguchi N-330

Versailles, France, suburb of Paris; pop. 89,035
Europe, *map* E-361
France, *map* F-372
Palace of Versailles V-320

Versailles, Palace of, Versailles, France V-320
architecture A-558, *picture* A-559
court of Louis XIV E-320
fountains F-335
France, *picture* F-351
imitations C-200
interior design I-248
sculpture S-146

Versailles, Treaty of (1919)
China C-372
France F-363
Germany G-122
gliders G-168
Prussia P-629
Weimar Republic W-142
treaty, *table* T-275
United States U-171
warfare W-27
Wilson W-219
World War I W-319

Verschaffelt, Pieter Anton (or Pietro Fiammingo, or Peter the Fleming) (1710–93), Flemish sculptor and architect of rococo style, born in Ghent; trained in Paris and Rome; became court sculptor in Germany.

Verse, a line of poetry; may mean more than one line, a stanza; sometimes applied to poetry in general. *see also in index* Poetry
Indian literature I-105
Shakespeare S-209

Vers libre. *see in index* Free verse

Verst, Soviet measure of length or distance; equal to 0.6629 mi (about ⅔ mi), or 1.0684 km, *table* W-141

Vert, in heraldry, *picture* H-136

Vert, Cap. *see in index* Verde, Cape

Vertebra (plural vertebrae), any one of the segments of the spinal column S-309
bird B-245
development E-201
human A-390

Vertebrata, subphylum of animals with backbones
phylogenetic tree, *diagram* Z-468

Vertebrates, animals with backbones V-323
animal morphology A-422, *picture* A-423
blood systems B-317
embryogeny E-200
frog F-406
hand H-27
invertebrate comparison I-282
joint J-136
lungs L-336
population biology P-541
protective coloration P-622
reproductive system R-166
respiratory system R-174
sensory reception S-176
skeleton, *picture* S-308
sleep S-323
urinary system U-239

Verthandi (or Verdandi), in German and Norse mythology
Fates F-44

Vertical boring mill, a machine tool T-222

Vertical draw, a glass manufacturing method G-163, *picture* G-157

Vertical file, for information storage
libraries L-164

Vertical lift bridge B-442, *picture* B-443

Vertical shaper (or slotter), a tool T-220

Vertical-speed indicator. *see in index* Rate-of-climb indicator

Vertical takeoff and landing (VTOL), aircraft A-80, A-162, A-207
helicopter H-118

Vertigo, a severe form of dizziness resulting from the inability of the body to adapt to abrupt or unexpected motion D-179

Vertisols, soil classification S-372, U-102

Vertumnus, in Roman mythology, a god who watched over plants in their change from blossom to fruit; husband of Pomona.

Verulam, Baron. *see in index* Bacon, Francis

Verulamium, Roman town in what is now Hertfordshire, England; archaeological excavations have revealed a high Roman culture.

Vervain family (or Verbenaceae), family of plants, shrubs, and trees including the hemp tree, verbenas, lantanas, golden dewdrop, lippias, and teak. *see also in index* Verbena

Verviers, Belgium, town 15 mi (25 km) s.e. of Liège; woolen goods, dyes, leather products; suffered severely during German occupation 1914–18; pop. 35,453.

Vervins, Treaty of (1598), *table* T-275

Verwoerd, Hendrik Frensch (1901–66), South African statesman, born in Amsterdam, The Netherlands; chief architect of apartheid; senator 1948–58, minister native affairs 1950–58, prime minister 1958–66
assassination, *list* A-704

Very, Jones (1813–80), U.S. poet, born in Salem, Mass.; wrote religious sonnets and lyrics which he said were inspired directly by the Holy Ghost ('Essays and Poems').

Véry, restaurant in Paris, France R-176

Very, Very Tall, game G-13

Very Large Array (VLA), telescope T-68, *picture* T-65

Very-large-scale integration (VLSI), microprocessor M-379
transistor T-250

Very lights, signals of red, green, or white fire shot from a Very pistol; lights are fired in groups, thus indicating a code; used in Army and Navy; invented 1877 by Edward Wilson Very.

Very Long Baseline Interferometer (VLBI), in astronomical observation O-457

Very pistol, in signaling S-288

Verzuiling (or pillarization), long-entrenched system of religious and ideological strata of Dutch society N-131

Vesalius, Andreas (1514–64), Flemish physician and surgeon V-326
Renaissance R-161
science S-105, *list* S-114
medicine M-283
physiology P-369
zoology Z-470

Vesey, Denmark (1767–1822), U.S. slave revolt leader V-326
black Americans B-290

Vesle, river of n.e. France; rises n. of Châlons-sur-Marne, flows 90 mi (145 km) past Reims to Aisne River 6 mi (10 km) e. of Soissons.

Vespasian (Titus Flavius Vespasianus) (AD 9–79), Roman emperor AD 69–79, father of Titus and Domitian; in his reign Titus captured Jerusalem, the Colosseum was begun, and Agricola extended Roman sway in Britain
Isle of Wight W-202
Roman Empire R-275

Vesper sparrow (or bay-winged bunting), bird *(Pooecetes gramineus)* of the family Fringillidae S-510

Vespucius, Americus (in Italian, Amerigo Vespucci) (1454–1512), Florentine merchant and author V-326
America A-330

Vessel members, a type of plant cell P-422

Vessels. *see in index* Ship and Shipping

Vesta, in Roman mythology, goddess of the hearth and home; Greek counterpart Hestia M-701

Vesta, an asteroid A-706

Vesta, a type of match M-209

Vestal, Stanley (pen name of Walter Stanley Campbell) (1887–1957), U.S. author and educator, born near Severy, Kan.; professor and director of courses in professional writing University of Oklahoma after 1939; noted for carefully documented books on old West (biography; history; novels; ballads; literary manuals).

Vestal Virgins, priestesses in ancient Roman religion
Roman mythology M-702

Vestibular sense S-175

Vestris, Gaetano (1729–1808), ballet dancer and choreographer, born in Florence, Italy; ballet master of Paris Opéra and of King's Theatre, London D-24

Vestris, Madame (1797–1856), British actress and manager who inaugurated tasteful and beautiful stage decor, and set a standard in stage costumes
directing D-154

Vestry, architecture, a room in a church where vestments are kept and where the clergy and choristers robe for services.

Vesuvius, Mount (in Italian, Vesuvio), volcano in Italy V-326
archaeology A-531
Europe, *map* E-361
Italy, *map* I-404
mountain, *picture* M-635
Naples, *picture* N-11
Pompeii and Herculaneum P-533
volcano V-402

Veterans Administration (VA), United States V-328
health agencies H-89
housing H-303
property P-613

Veterans' affairs V-327
disability compensation S-350
pension P-207

Veterans' Affairs Canada (or Department of Veterans Affairs) V-328

Veterans Committee. *see in index* American Veterans Committee

Veterans Day (formerly Armistice Day), annual holiday honoring war dead
national cemeteries N-24

Veterans of Foreign Wars of the U.S.A (VFW), society of veterans who have fought in wars on foreign soil or waters; founded 1913; object to assist needy veterans and dependents, promote comradeship, patriotism V-329

Veterans' organizations V-328

Veterinary Corps, U.S. Army A-577, A-647

Veterinary medicine (from Latin *veterina,* "beast of burden"), the science of caring for diseased or injured domestic animals V-330
pets P-266
vocation V-395
zoo Z-461, 464, *picture* Z-463

Vetiver (or khus-khus), a perennial (*Vetiveria zizanioides*) of the grass family, native to Asia, cultivated in the U.S. for ornamental purposes and for its aromatic roots used in perfumery.

Veto, executive right to withhold consent V-331
Congress U-210
Ford F-303
Jackson J-9, *picture* J-5
state governors S-594
United Kingdom U-71

Vetter, Craig (born 1942), U.S. industrial designer
industrial design contribution I-172, 174

Vetticost. *see in index* Corn salad

Vevey, Switzerland, resort town on n.e. shore of Lake Geneva; Swiss chocolate; condensed milk; pop. 17,900.

Vexillology, scientific study of flag history and symbolism, *list* F-149

Vexillum, Roman cavalry flag F-148

Vézelay, France, historic village 60 mi (100 km) n.w. of Dijon; noted for the 12th-century Church of the Madeleine; pop. 437.

Vézère River, river in s. France; flows 120 mi (190 km) s.w. to the Dordogne at a point 4 mi (6 km) s. of Le Bugue; drives the turbines of a hydroelectric plant at Le Saillant.

VFW. *see in index* Veterans of Foreign Wars of the U.S.A.

VHS (Video Home System) video recording V-337

Via Appia Antica. *see in index* Appian Way

Viadua, river. *see in index* Oder

Viaduct, long bridge for carrying a road or railroad across a valley or another road; usually built of steel or concrete, in a series of small arches.

Viana, Javier de (1868–1926), Uruguayan writer L-70

Vianna da Motta, José (1868–1948), Portuguese pianist and composer, director National Conservatory, Lisbon; chamber music, compositions for orchestra and for piano ('Portuguese Rhapsodies').

Viardot, Pauline (originally Michelle Ferdinande Pauline Garcia) (1821–1910), French operatic mezzo-soprano, *list* O-570

Via Sacra. *see in index* Sacred Way

Viaticum, the Holy Eucharist when administered to the dying in Roman Catholicism; originally, provisions or preparations for a journey.

Via Toledo (or Via Roma), thoroughfare in Naples, Italy N-11

Viaud, Louis Marie Julien. *see in index* Loti, Pierre

Via Vittorio Veneto, street, Rome, Italy V-286

Vibraphone, percussion instrument P-217, *picture* P-215

Vibration, in sound S-388
mechanical radiation R-42
music M-689
radio waves R-58, 68
spider S-534

Vibrissa, type of mammal hair H-7

Viburnum, genus of shrubs or small trees of the honeysuckle family with dense flat-topped clusters of white or pink flowers; includes various species of arrowwood, the maple-leaved viburnum, black haw, wayfaring tree, and high-bush cranberry, of which the snowball is a cultivated form.

Vicar, a person who acts for a superior; in Church of England, a clergyman in charge of a parish in behalf of the rector.

'Vicar of Wakefield, The', novel by Goldsmith (published 1766), portraying the trials of the Rev. Dr. Charles Primrose, a kindly clergyman, thought to represent the author's father, Charles Goldsmith.

Vicente, Gil (1469?–1536?), Renaissance dramatist and lyric poet; plays range from religious to farcical, and depict both the splendor and squalor of the age; wrote in Spanish and Portuguese ('Ignez Pereira'; 'Amadis de Gaula').

Vicenza, Italy, city on Bacchiglione River 40 mi (60 km) w. of Venice; silk, silk goods; birthplace of Palladio, great 16th-century architect; pop. 98,019
Italy, *map* I-404

Vice-president, of the United States U-215. *see table following*
flag F-158, *picture* F-157
U.S. Constitution U-198, 200, 203

Viceroyalties A-334

Viceroy butterfly B-526
mimicry M-423

Vichy, France, town on the Allier River, famous for mineral springs; capital of France, 1940–44; pop. 33,458

Vichy government, French government during World War II W-324

Vickers, Edward (1804–97), British manufacturer
industry I-195

Vicksburg (The Gibraltar of the Confederacy), Miss., manufacturing city on Mississippi River; pop. 25,434 V-331
Grant G-217
Mississippi M-469, *map* M-468, *picture* M-477
North America, *map* N-351
Sherman S-237
United States U-166

Vicksburg National Military Park, site adjacent to Vicksburg, Miss. N-60
Mississippi M-470, *picture* M-475
Vicksburg V-331

Vico, Giambattista (1668–1744), Italian philosopher V-332
history writing H-172

Victimless crime C-771

Victor Emmanuel II (1820–78), king of Italy V-332
Italy I-393
Rome R-285, 291

Victor Emmanuel III (1869–1947), king of Italy V-332
Italy I-394
Mussolini M-694
World War II W-333

Victoria (1819–1901), queen of United Kingdom V-333
British Columbia B-450
Disraeli D-185
Edward VII E-108
Isle of Wight W-202
London memorial L-292, *picture* L-293
medals M-270
United Kingdom E-253
Victorian Age. *see in index* Victorian Age

Victoria, Australia, state in s.e.; 87,884 sq mi (227,619 sq km); cap. Melbourne; pop. 4,141,200 V-334
Australia A-767, *map* A-822
Melbourne M-289
Snowy Mountains S-339

Victoria (or Fort Camosun, or Fort Victoria), B.C., capital of province, at s.e. end of Vancouver Island; pop. 64,379 V-334
Canada, *map* C-109
North America, *map* N-351
Trans-Canada Highway T-248

Victoria, Hong Kong, capital, on island of Hong Kong; primarily center of administration; cotton mills; naval dockyards; university; pop. 996,183
Hong Kong H-228

Victoria, Seychelles, capital, on n.e. coast of Mahé Island; deep water port, business and cultural center; pop. 23,880 S-198

Victoria, Tex., residential city, 110 mi (180 km) s.e. of Austin; livestock, cotton, oil; truck farms, petrochemicals, food processing; Victoria Barge Canal to Intracoastal Waterway; pop. 41,349
Texas, *map* T-137

Victoria, Lake (or Victoria Nyanza), in e.-central Africa, 2nd largest freshwater lake in world; area about 26,418 sq mi (68,422 sq km) W-334
Africa, *map* A-118
Uganda U-3
world, *map* W-300

Victoria, Mount, in s.w. Alberta at boundary of British Columbia, overlooking Lake Louise; height 11,365 ft (3,465 m).

Victoria, Mount, in Wellington, New Zealand; height 643 ft (196 m) W-148

Victoria and Albert Museum (formerly South Kensington Museum), in London, England L-293
museum M-662

Victoria Bridge, bridge, Montreal, Que.; *picture* Q-15

Victoria Cross, chief medal of valor in the United Kingdom M-270, *picture* M-271

Victoria Day (formerly Empire Day), either on or about May 24 (the birthday of Queen Victoria), in the Commonwealth; originated 1897 by Mrs. Clementina Fessenden of Hamilton, Ont., to stimulate patriotism.

Victoria Falls, in Africa, one of world's greatest waterfalls; in Zambezi River, Zimbabwe, and Zambia V-335
Africa, *map* A-118
Livingstone L-263
waterfall W-96, *picture* W-98
Zambezi River Z-446
Zambia Z-447, *picture* Z-448
Zimbabwe Z-452

Victoria Island, in Canada, large island in Arctic Ocean, District of Franklin in the Northwest Territories; irregular coastline; explored in 1838; area 81,930 sq mi (212,200 sq km)
arctic regions A-571
North America, *map* N-351
size, comparative. *see in index* Island, *table*
world, *map* W-300

Victoria Land, in Antarctica, w. of Ross Sea; discovered and named for Queen Victoria by Sir James Clark Ross 1841
world, *map* W-300

Victorian Age
Butler B-519
etiquette E-321

Victorian Arts Centre, arts center in Melbourne, Australia M-289

Victoria Nile, river in Uganda; upper section of the Nile River U-3

Victoria Nyanza. *see in index* Victoria, Lake

Victoria Park, Charlottetown, P.E.I. P-590

Victoria Peak, mountain on Hong Kong Island; 1,825 ft (556 m) high H-228

'Victoria Regina', work by Housman H-307

Victoria River, rises in the w. of Northern Territory, Australia, and flows n. and w. into Indian Ocean by Queen's Channel Australia, *map* A-819

Victoria Theatre, in Sydney, Australia A-799

Victoriaville, Que., manufacturing town and farm center 85 mi (140 km) n.e. of Montreal; furniture, clothing, metal products, maple syrup; pop. 22,047
Canada, *map* C-112
Quebec, *map* Q-20

Victoria water platter lily, plant leaf, *picture* L-101

'Victory', English ship famous ships S-259
Nelson N-115

Victory, Order of, medal M-272

Victory, Temple of. *see in index* Wingless Victory

'Victory at Junin: a Song to Bolivar, The', work by Olmedo O-540
Latin American literature L-68

'Victory Boogie Woogie', painting by Mondrian M-529

Victory Monument, monument in France V-302

Victory of Samothrace. *see in index* 'Winged Victory'

Vicuña, llama-like animal (*Vicugna vicugna* or *Lama vicugna*) of the family Camelidae C-65, *picture* C-63
La Plata region A-582
Peru P-240

Vicuña cloth, a fabric made of vicuña wool; used in high-quality coats, knitwear, robes, blankets, and rugs.

Vidal, Gore (born 1925), U.S. writer, born in West Point, N.Y.; novelist, screenwriter and two-time unsuccessful candidate for Congress; ('The City and the Pillar', 'Washington D.C.', 'Burr', 'Myra Breckenridge', 'Myron', 'Creation', 'Duluth', 'Empire', 'Lincoln').

Videla, Jorge Rafaél (born 1925), Argentinian leader, born in Mercedes; commander in chief of army 1975–76; president 1976–81 A-583

Video arcade, electronic game emporium E-172

Videocassette recorder (VCR, or videotape recorder, or VTR), machine that, when hooked up to a television set, plays material prerecorded on magnetic videotape; can also copy television programs for later viewing; two basic videocassette formats, Beta and VHS; revolutionized home entertainment, spawning multibillion-dollar industry
electronics E-176
hobby H-189
police P-506
television T-76
video recording V-335

Video conference, in telecommunication T-55

Videodisc
phonograph P-326
television T-76
video recording V-335, *picture* V-337

Video display terminal. *see in index* Terminal

Video game E-172
electronics E-179
industry I-194

Video Home System (VHS) video recording V-337

Video recording V-335
hobby H-189
popular music M-683
telecommunication T-55

Video tape T-75
video recording V-335

Videotext, in telecommunication T-56

Vidocq, François-Eugène, (1775–1857) French detective D-118
police P-511

Vidor, King (1895–1982), U.S. film director, born in Galveston, Tex.; directed both silent and sound films ('Billy the Kid'; 'The Wedding Night'; 'The Fountainhead'; 'War and Peace'; autobiography, 'A Tree Is a Tree').

Vidzenie Uplands, mountain range
Latvia L-83

Vienna (in German, Wien), Austria, capital and chief city, on Danube River; pop. 1,505,800 V-338
Austria A-825
Austria-Hungary A-828
Europe, *map* E-361, *picture* E-354
porcelain P-569
world, *map* W-300

Vienna, Va., town 11 mi (18 km) n.w. of Arlington;

VICE-PRESIDENTS OF THE UNITED STATES

Name	Term	State	Party	President
John Adams	1789–1797	Massachusetts	Federalist	George Washington
Thomas Jefferson	1797–1801	Virginia	Democratic Republican	John Adams
Aaron Burr	1801–1805	New York	Democratic Republican	Thomas Jefferson
George Clinton*	1805–1809 1809–1812	New York	Democratic Republican	Thomas Jefferson James Madison
Elbridge Gerry*	1813–1814	Massachusetts	Democratic Republican	James Madison
Daniel D. Tompkins	1817–1825	New York	Democratic Republican	James Monroe
John C. Calhoun	1825–1829 1829–1832†	South Carolina	Democratic Republican	John Quincy Adams Andrew Jackson
Martin Van Buren	1833–1837	New York	Democrat	Andrew Jackson
Richard M. Johnson	1837–1841	Kentucky	Democrat	Martin Van Buren
John Tyler‡	1841	Virginia	Democrat	William Henry Harrison
George M. Dallas	1845–1849	Pennsylvania	Democrat	James K. Polk
Millard Fillmore‡	1849–1850	New York	Whig	Zachary Taylor
William R. King*	1853	Alabama	Democrat	Franklin Pierce
John C. Breckinridge	1857–1861	Kentucky	Democrat	James Buchanan
Hannibal Hamlin	1861–1865	Maine	Republican	Abraham Lincoln
Andrew Johnson‡	1865	Tennessee	Republican§	Abraham Lincoln
Schuyler Colfax	1869–1873	Indiana	Republican	Ulysses S. Grant
Henry Wilson*	1873–1875	Massachusetts	Republican	Ulysses S. Grant
William A. Wheeler	1877–1881	New York	Republican	Rutherford B. Hayes
Chester A. Arthur‡	1881	New York	Republican	James A. Garfield
Thomas A. Hendricks*	1885	Indiana	Democrat	Grover Cleveland
Levi P. Morton	1889–1893	New York	Republican	Benjamin Harrison
Adlai E. Stevenson	1893–1897	Illinois	Democrat	Grover Cleveland
Garret A. Hobart*	1897–1899	New Jersey	Republican	William McKinley
Theodore Roosevelt‡	1901	New York	Republican	William McKinley
Charles W. Fairbanks	1905–1909	Indiana	Republican	Theodore Roosevelt
James S. Sherman*	1909–1912	New York	Republican	William H. Taft
Thomas R. Marshall	1913–1921	Indiana	Democrat	Woodrow Wilson
Calvin Coolidge‡	1921–1923	Massachusetts	Republican	Warren G. Harding
Charles G. Dawes	1925–1929	Illinois	Republican	Calvin Coolidge
Charles Curtis	1929–1933	Kansas	Republican	Herbert Hoover
John N. Garner	1933–1941	Texas	Democrat	Franklin D. Roosevelt
Henry A. Wallace	1941–1945	Iowa	Democrat	Franklin D. Roosevelt
Harry S. Truman‡	1945	Missouri	Democrat	Franklin D. Roosevelt
Alben W. Barkley	1949–1953	Kentucky	Democrat	Harry S. Truman
Richard M. Nixon	1953–1961	California	Republican	Dwight D. Eisenhower
Lyndon B. Johnson‡	1961–1963	Texas	Democrat	John F. Kennedy
Hubert H. Humphrey, Jr.	1965–1969	Minnesota	Democrat	Lyndon B. Johnson
Spiro T. Agnew	1969–1973†	Maryland	Republican	Richard M. Nixon
Gerald R. Ford‡◆	1973–1974	Michigan	Republican	Richard M. Nixon
Nelson A. Rockefeller◆	1974–1977	New York	Republican	Gerald R. Ford
Walter F. Mondale	1977–1981	Minnesota	Democrat	Jimmy Carter
George Bush	1981–1989	Texas	Republican	Ronald Reagan

*Died in office. †Resigned. ‡Succeeded to presidency. §Democrat elected on Republican ticket. ◆Installed under 25th Amendment.

residential; incorporated 1890; pop. 15,469, *map* V-377

Vienna, W. Va., industrial city 5 mi (8 km) n. of Parkersburg on Ohio River; glass industry; pop. 11,549
West Virginia, *map* W-182

Vienna, Congress of (1814–15) V-340
Alexander I A-278
Austria A-830
Germany G-122
Metternich M-319
slave trade S-320
Switzerland S-743
Talleyrand T-17
treaty, *table* T-275

Vienna, Treaties of (1738, 1864), *table* T-275

Vienne, France, ancient town on Rhône River 17 mi (27 km) s. of Lyons; fortified by Caesar 47 BC; Roman antiquities; pop. 26,512, *map* F-372

Vientiane, Laos, capital, on Mekong River; name of former kingdom; pop. 200,000 V-340
Laos L-47

Vieques, Puerto Rico P-652

Viereck, Peter Robert Edwin (born 1916), U.S. author and educator, born in New York City (prose: 'Metapolitics' and 'Conservatism Revisited'; poetry: 'Terror and Decorum', awarded Pulitzer prize 1949, and 'The Persimmon Tree').

Viet Cong, the guerrilla force that fought against South Vietnam (late 1950s–1975) and the United States (early 1960s–1973)
United States U-182
Vietnam V-345
Vietnam War V-347

Viète, François (or François Vieta) (1540–1603), French mathematician, born in Fontenay-le-Comte; credited with founding modern algebra; introduced symbols and decimal notation for fractions mathematics, *table* M-218

Viet Minh, Vietnamese Communist movement V-345
battle of Dienbienphu D-140
Ho Chi Minh H-191
Indochina I-157

Vietnam (officially Socialist Republic of Vietnam), nation in s.e. Asia, formerly divided into North Vietnam and South Vietnam; 127,204 sq mi (329,465 sq km); cap. Hanoi; pop. 62,468,000 V-341. *see also in index* Vietnam, North; Vietnam, South; Vietnam War
Asia, *map* A-700, *table* A-694
China C-378
Communist world, *map* C-619
flag, *picture* F-172
French history F-365
Hanoi H-31
Kampuchea K-170
Laos L-46

Mekong River M-288
national anthem, *table* N-64
post-World War II W-360
spices S-531
storytelling S-644, 655
Thailand T-149
United Nations U-87, *table* U-84
United States U-182
world, *map* W-300

Vietnam, North (officially Democratic Republic of Vietnam), former nation in s.e. Asia; 61,294 sq mi (158,751 sq km); cap. Hanoi V-345
Laos L-48
Vietnam War V-347

Vietnam, South (officially Republic of Vietnam), former nation in s.e. Asia; 65,987 sq mi (170,906 sq km); cap. Ho Chi Minh City V-345
Ho Chi Minh City H-192
Indochina I-157
Laos L-48
Vietnam War V-347
warfare W-17

Vietnam War, war in s.e. Asia V-347
Agent Orange C-293
amnesty A-374
Asia A-693
Australia A-806
battle of Dienbienphu D-140
black Americans B-298
Carter C-184
civil disobedience C-463
conscription C-668

Ford administration F-305
fort and fortification F-320
guerrilla warfare, *picture* G-302
Ho Chi Minh H-191
international relations I-263
Johnson J-133
King K-245
Laos L-47
marines M-139
news coverage N-238, 242
Nixon N-325
peace movement P-162
prisoners of war P-605
Red Cross R-125
refugees R-148
Saigon H-192
Southeast Asia Treaty Organization S-454
United States U-182
U.S. armed forces
Air Force A-160
Army A-648
Vietnam V-345
warfare W-17, 24

Vietnam Veterans Memorial, memorial in Washington, D.C. N-60

'Vietnam War Literature', work compiled by Newman W-28

Vieux Carré. *see in index* French Quarter

Viewfinder, of a camera P-336

'View from Satta Peak, Yui', print by Hiroshige, *picture* H-161

'View of Montmartre', painting by Utrillo, *picture* U-261

'View of Salisbury Cathedral, A', painting by Constable painting P-47, *picture* P-46

'Views of Society and Manners in America', work by Wright W-366

Viganò, Salvatore (1769–1821), Italian dancer, choreographer and composer, born in Naples; noted for themes of heroic nature B-34, *list* D-24

Vigée-Lebrun, Elisabeth (1755–1842), French portrait and landscape painter, born in Paris; portrayed royal family, especially Marie Antoinette.

Vigeland, Adolf Gustav (1869–1943), Norwegian sculptor; early work semi-impressionistic, later style more classic Norway N-391, *picture* N-392

Vigenère tableau, cipher system C-418

Vigili Urbani (or City Watchmen), municipal police in Italy P-505

Vigils, evening devotions; also the evening service preceding certain festivals, or the day before these festivals.

Vigneaud, Vincent du. *see in index* Du Vigneaud, Vincent

Vignemale, Pic de, mountain in France F-343, *map* F-372
Vigny, Alfred de (1797–1863), French poet and dramatist V-350
French literature F-396
Vigo, Spain, seaport and naval station in n.w., on Vigo Bay; fine harbor; flour, paper, soap, leather; pop. 69,249, *map* E-361
Spain S-488, *picture* S-495
Viipuri. *see in index* Vyborg
Vikings (or Norsemen, or Northmen), Scandinavian warrior sailors who raided and colonized the British Isles and mainland Europe between AD 800 and 1100; attacked and plundered coastal settlements from their longships V-351
Denmark D-99
England E-239
Europe E-347
exploration E-373, P-498
Atlantic Ocean A-746
Canada C-76, 89
Newfoundland N-168
North America N-339
invasions
England A-282
Ireland I-325
Middle Ages M-386
migration of people M-402
mythology. *see in index* Norse mythology
naval power N-81
Norway N-394
Russia U-50
Scandinavia S-88
ship S-240
Sweden S-729
Vikings, U.S. spacecraft; space probes launched 1975 from Cape Canaveral, Fla.; consisted of lander, orbiter, and lander support structure; landed on Mars 1976; cameras and other instruments on board used to determine landing site and to map and investigate structure of the planet P-410, *picture* P-409
extraterrestrial life E-386
Viking ships, vessel, *picture* T-262
Vila, Vanuatu, capital and port, on island of Efate; pop. (including suburbs) 17,367.
Vila do Infante, small court created by Henry the Navigator H-134
Vilakazi, Benedict Wallet (1906–47), Zulu educator and writer; taught at University of Witwatersrand, in Johannesburg, South Africa A-122
Vilas, Guillermo (born 1952), Argentine tennis player T-107
Vildrac, Charles (pen name of Charles Messager) (1882–1971), French poet and dramatist, born in Paris (poems: 'A Book of Love'; also one-act plays).
Vili, Nordic god M-697
Villa, Pancho (1878–1923), Mexican revolutionist and bandit V-356
assassination A-704
Carranza C-175
Mexico M-337
Wilson's administration W-218
Villa Cisneros. *see in index* Dakhla
Villa Clara, province in Cuba; sugarcane, tobacco, rice, fruit, black beans, and cattle; pop. 773,565
Cuba, *map* C-802
Villa Concepción. *see in index* Concepción
Villafranca, Italy, town 10 mi (16 km) s.w. of Verona; silk textiles, fishing nets; pop. 19,151
Italy, *map* I-404
treaty (1859), *table* T-275
Villafrancian period, preglacial portion of the Pleistocene epoch M-83
Village, the. *see in index* Greenwich Village
Village, The (post office name Village), Okla., city in n.w. section of Oklahoma City and surrounded by it; pop. 13,695.
'Village Blacksmith, The', lyric poem by Longfellow B-308
Village weaver, bird *(Ploceus cucullatus), picture* W-128
Villa-Lobos, Heitor (1887–1959), Brazilian composer V-356
classical music M-676
'Villa Ludovisi Mars', ancient Greek sculpture, *picture* G-270
Villa Maria College, Erie, Pa.; Roman Catholic; for women; founded 1925; arts and sciences.
Villanelle, verse form derived from the French, consisting of five three-line stanzas (tercets) and a final quatrain and employing only two rhymes; first line closes second and fourth stanzas and appears as second last line of final quatrain; last line of first stanza closes third, fifth, and last stanzas; example: Austin Dobson's 'When I Saw You Last, Rose'.
Villanovans, name given by archaeologists to certain peoples of the early Iron Age in Italy; so called from the village of Villanova, near Bologna, where excavations revealed burial urns of rough pottery and articles of excellent metalwork.
Villanova University, Villanova, Pa.; Roman Catholic; founded 1842; liberal arts, commerce and finance, engineering, law, nursing; graduate study.
Villa Park, Ill., village 18 mi (29 km) w. of Chicago; light industry; fertilizer, beverages; incorporated 1914; pop. 23,185
Illinois, *map* I-53
Villard, Henry (originally Henry Hilgard) (1835–1900), U.S. journalist and financier, born in Speyer, Bavaria; came to U.S. 1853; was correspondent during Civil War and Austro-Prussian War; organized Oregon Railway and Navigation Company and gained control of Northern Pacific; bought controlling interest in *New York Evening Post* and *The Nation*.
Villard, Oswald Garrison (1872–1949), U.S. journalist; born in Wiesbaden, Germany; son of Henry Villard; grandson of William Lloyd Garrison, abolitionist; publisher *New York Evening Post* (1897–1918); editor *The Nation* 1918–33 ('Prophets True and False'; 'Germany Embattled'; 'Fighting Years: Memoirs of a Liberal Editor'; 'Within Germany').
Villarrica, Paraguay, city 80 mi (130 km) s.e. of Asunción, in agricultural region; tobacco, cotton, sugarcane, corn, wine, lumber; pop. 33,553
South America, *map* S-419
Villars, Claude Louis Hector, duc de (1653–1734), marshal of France, one of greatest French generals; commanded against Eugene and Marlborough in War of the Spanish Succession.
Villehardouin, Geoffroi de (1160?–1213?), French historian, known for vivid, human account of Fourth Crusade, in which he took part ('Conquête de Constantinople').
Villein. *see in index* Serf
Villella, Edward (born 1936), U.S. ballet dancer, born in New York City; known for his acting ability and powerful technique; joined New York City Ballet 1957; appeared in George Balanchine's 'Prodigal Son'; created roles of Oberon in 'A Midsummer Night's Dream' (1962) and Harlequin in 'Harlequinade' (1965); was the first non-Danish male to dance with Royal Danish Ballet (1962); retired 1979.
Ville-Marie de Montréal. *see in index* Montreal
Villeneuve, Jean Marie Rodrigue, Cardinal (1883–1947), Canadian prelate, born in Montreal, Que.; ordained Roman Catholic priest 1907; archbishop of Quebec 1931–47; cardinal 1933.
Villi, fingerlike projections on the intestines
digestive system D-146, *picture* D-145
Villiers, Alan John (1903–82), Australian adventurer and writer, born in Melbourne; sailed world's oceans since 1918; skipper of *Mayflower II*, 1957 ('By Way of Cape Horn'; 'Sons of Sinbad'; 'Monsoon Seas'; 'Wild Ocean'; 'The New Mayflower'; 'Give Me a Ship to Sail'; 'Men, Ships and the Sea'; 'The Ocean')
Massachusetts, *picture* M-201
Villiers de l'Isle-Adam, Auguste, comte de (1838–89), French writer, born in St. Brieuc, France; exponent of symbolism ('Sardonic Tales'; 'Axel', drama; 'Isis', novel).
Villon, François (1431–?), French poet V-356
French literature F-394
Vilna (or Vilnius, or Wilno), Lithuanian Soviet Socialist Republic, capital; rail and trade center; pop. 372,000 L-260, *map* E-361
U.S.S.R., *maps* U-62, 66
Vilna Troupe (formerly called the Yiddish Dramatic Actors), Yiddish theater group Y-420
Vimy Ridge, a high ridge 4 mi (6 km) n.e. of Arras, France, scene of World War I battles; taken by Germans 1940.
Viña del Mar, Chile, beautiful seaside resort and residential suburb of Valparaiso; pop. 229,020
South America, *map* S-419
Vinal, fiber, *table* F-72
Vinaya, in Buddhism B-482
Vinca. *see in index* Periwinkle
Vincennes, France, city adjoining Paris on e.; castle, begun 1164, famed as historic state prison; pop. 49,116, *map* F-372
porcelain P-569
Vincennes, Ind., railroad city on Wabash River 55 mi (90 km) s. of Terre Haute; oldest town in state; structural steel, shoes, glass, batteries, paper products; pop. 20,857
Indiana I-92, *map* I-102, *picture* I-99
'Vincennes', U.S. cruiser U-186
'Vincennes', U.S. Navy ship, first to go around the world N-91
Vincennes Trail (or St. Louis Trace), U.S. trail
Illinois I-39
Vincennes Zoo, in Paris, France Z-457
Vincent, Saint (or Saint Vincentius), martyr and deacon of the church; of noble Spanish family; martyred under Emperor Diocletian; festival January 22.
Vincent, George Edgar (1864–1941), U.S. educator, born in Rockford, Ill.; long connected with Chautauqua Institute; president of University of Minnesota 1911–17; president of Rockefeller Foundation until 1929.
Vincent de Paul, Saint (1576–1660), French priest, founder of Lazarists, a missionary order; famed for benevolent work; founded Sisters of Charity; established hospital for galley slaves at Marseilles, two homes for foundlings at Paris; feast day observed July 19.
Vincent's gingivitis. *see in index* Trench mouth
Vinci, Leonardo da. *see in index* Leonardo da Vinci
Vincristine, a medicine P-416
Vin de Consommation Courante, French wine classification W-327
Vindel (or Windel), river in n.w. Sweden; rises near Norwegian border, flows s.e. about 200 mi (320 km) to Ume River.
Vin delimité de Qualité Supérieure, French wine classification W-237
Vin de Pays, French wine classification W-237
Vindhya Mountains, range in central India; about 600 mi (965 km) long; highest point 5,000 ft (1,500 m)
India I-63, *map* I-86
'Vindication of the Rights of Women, A', work by Godwin E-273
women's rights W-276, *list* W-275
Vine, plant V-357
flowering, *picture* F-227
jungle life J-155
melons M-292
morning-glory M-584
Vine family. *see in index* Grape family
Vinegar, fermented liquid V-357
Vinegarroon, large whip scorpion *(Mastigoproctus giganteus)* found in s.w. United States and Mexico; so named because of vinegarlike odor; dark brown; erroneously thought to be venomous.
Vineland, N.J., city 32 mi (52 km) s.e. of Camden; glass, clothing, machinery, food processing; founded 1861, incorporated 1880; pop. 47,399
New Jersey, *map* N-211
Vines, H. Ellsworth, Jr. (born 1911), U.S. tennis player, born in Los Angeles, Calif.; won U.S. singles 1931 and 1932, British singles 1932; member of U.S. Davis Cup team 1932 and 1933; professional 1934–39; later a professional golfer; elected to Tennis Hall of Fame 1962.
Vineyard. *see in index* Grapes, *subhead* vineyard
Vinification, technique of wine production W-236
Vining, Elizabeth G. *see in index* Gray, Elizabeth Janet
Vinland (Wineland), name given by Leif Ericson to that portion of the coast he visited in North America
Canada C-89
Ericson E-297
Vikings V-352, *picture* V-353
Vinson, Frederick Moore (1890–1953), U.S. public official, born in Louisa, Ky.; U.S. congressman 1923–39; associate justice U.S. Court of Appeals for D.C. 1937–43; director economic stabilization 1943–45; later federal loan administrator, director war mobilization and reconversion, and secretary of the treasury; chief justice of the U.S. 1946–53.
Vinson Massif, in the Ellsworth Mountains, Antarctica; height 16,900 ft (5,150 m).
Vinyl
adhesives A-43
flooring F-186
paints P-17
plastics, *list* P-448
Vinylidene chloride, in chemistry
health hazard I-175
synthetic fibers F-74
Vinyon, trade name for a synthetic textile fiber made from a vinyl resin; used for awnings, bathing suits, draperies, fish nets, sails, shower curtains, umbrella fabrics; resistant to fire, water, and acids; thermoplastic, *table* F-72
Viol, family name for stringed musical instruments, predecessors of the modern violin, viola, violoncello, and double bass
orchestra O-576
stringed instruments S-675
Viola, character in Shakespeare's 'Twelfth Night'; wrecked on Illyrian coast, dresses as page and enters service of Duke Orsino, with whom she falls in love.
Viola, genus of mainly perennial plants; most blossom with attractive flowers in spring or early summer; some winter annuals; includes the violet and pansy
growing conditions G-23
Viola, stringed instrument S-675, *picture* S-673
'Violent Land, The', work by Amado L-70
Violet, flower of the family Violaceae V-357
flowers, *picture* F-228
growing conditions, *picture* G-23
seed, *picture* S-166
state flower
New Jersey, *picture* N-202
Rhode Island, *picture* R-204
Wisconsin, *picture* W-256
Violet, color C-558
rainbow, *picture* R-95
Violet cress. *see in index* Ionopsidium
Violet phosphorus (black phosphorus) P-328
Violin, stringed instrument
country music M-678
folk music F-272
Heifetz H-116
Kreisler K-303
sound S-392
Stradivari S-664
stringed instruments S-675, *picture* S-673
Violino piccolo, stringed instrument S-676
Violin spider, arachnid *(Loxosceles reclusa), picture* S-537
Viollet-le-Duc, Eugène Emmanuel (1814–79), French architect, archaeologist, critic, scientist, chief prophet of the Gothic revival in architecture who revealed to the modern world the logic and beauty of the despised "barbarous" medieval construction; restored Carcassonne, France
architecture A-562, *list* A-569

Violoncello. *see in index* Cello
Viperidae, family of snakes S-330, 333, 337
Vipers, a category of snakes S-330, 337
Viper's bugloss (or Echium), genus of plants and shrubs of the borage family with erect hairy stems and showy spikes of blue, violet, red, or white flowers; one common species *(Echium vulgare)* is a weed called blueweed or blue devils, formerly used in medicine.
Viral enteritis (or cat distemper, or panleucopenia, or cat typhoid), most widespread and serious infectious disease of cats C-210
Virchow, Rudolf (1821–1902), German pathologist, anthropologist, and archaeologist V-358
archeology A-875
cell theory C-241
medicine M-284
Vireo, family of birds V-358
Virgil (70–19 BC), Roman poet V-35
'Aeneid'. *see in index* 'Aeneid'
Latin literature L-77
manuscript books preserved B-350
poetry P-486
Roman Empire, *picture* R-269
storytelling S-650
Virgilia. *see in index* Yellowwood
Virgin. *see in index* Virgo
Virginal (or spinet), early harpsicord
'Virgin and Child Between Saints Frediano and Augustin, The', work by Lippi L-233
Virgin archipelago, island group in Caribbean Sea formed by volcanic activity. *see in index* Virgin Islands, British; Virgin Islands of the United States
Virginia. *see in index* Claudius, Appius
Virginia, a Southern state of U.S. on Atlantic; 40,817 sq mi (105,716 sq km); cap. Richmond; pop. 5,346,279 V-359
Boone's Wilderness Road B-365
cities. *see in index* cities below and other cities by name
Hampton H-24
Norfolk N-332
Richmond R-220
Roanoke R-238
Williamsburg W-209
Yorktown Y-423
flag, *picture* F-155
history
Civil War C-473
Confederate States of America C-642
Kentucky K-208
Lee L-115
Reconstruction period R-122
U.S. Constitution U-195
Virginia colony
African indentured servants B-289
Bacon's Rebellion (1676) B-11
Jamestown J-21
Raleigh R-99
Smith S-325
Mount Vernon, *picture* M-639
national parks N-42, 48, 56, *map* N-40
Colonial N.H.P. *see in index* Colonial National Historical Park
Shenandoah N.P. *see in index* Shenandoah National Park
natural features
Appalachian Highlands A-507
Chesapeake Bay C-304
Potomac River P-563
North America, *map* N-351
state capitals, *list* S-595
Statuary Hall, *table* S-609
taxation, *tables* T-37, 39
Tennessee Valley Authority T-100, *map* T-101
United States U-109, 112, 166, *table* U-187
Washington, D.C. W-66
West Virginia W-164
Virginia, Minn., city 55 mi (90 km) n.w. of Duluth on Mesabi iron range; iron mining; ore-processing plant, foundries; outdoor recreational area; pop. 11,056
Minnesota, *map* M-458
'Virginia', ship. *see in index* 'Merrimack'
'Virginia', ship built in North America by European colonists S-250
Maine M-55
Virginia, University of, in Charlottesville, Va.; state control; opened 1825; arts and sciences, architecture, commerce, education, engineering, law, medicine, nursing; graduate studies; branch campus at Wise and Roanoke V-364, *picture* V-369
Virginia and Kentucky Resolutions. *see in index* Kentucky and Virginia Resolutions
Virginia Beach, Va., city just e. and s.e. of Norfolk; Atlantic beach resort; residential and farming area; oyster fisheries; became a city 1952; merged with Princess Anne County 1963; pop. 262,199 V-362, *map* V-377, *picture* V-360
Virginia bluebell. *see in index* Virginia cowslip
Virginia City, Mont., old gold-mining town, 88 mi (142 km) s. of Helena; had great boom in Civil War times; first incorporated town in Montana (1864); was headquarters for notorious gang of outlaws who robbed and murdered miners and held up stagecoaches carrying gold; most of gang were hanged by vigilantes (1864–65); Thompson Museum has relics from early days; pop. 192
Montana M-553, *map* M-565
Virginia City, Nev., town about 20 mi (30 km) s.e. of Reno; once great mining center; much of old town gone; later mining activity has consisted chiefly in working surface ores and old mine waste; pop. 1,500
Nevada N-136, *map* N-148, *picture* N-137
United States U-128
Virginia Commonwealth University, in Richmond, Va.; state control; founded 1838; arts and sciences, art, business, dentistry, education, medicine, pharmacy, social work; graduate school.
Virginia Company of London. *see in index* London Company
Virginia Company of Plymouth. *see in index* Plymouth Company
Virginia Conventions (1774–76), adopted resolutions affecting struggle for independence of the North American colonies
Jefferson J-90
Madison M-26
Virginia cowslip (also called Virginia bluebell, or lungwort), a perennial plant *(Mertensia virginica)* of the borage family with pale-green leaves and clusters of purplish-blue trumpet-shaped flowers; often cultivated in gardens; herbalists once used extract made from leaves to treat lung diseases
botany B-381
flower, *picture* F-235
Virginia creeper (also called American ivy, or woodbine), creeping vine *(Parthenocissus quinquefolia)* of the family Vitaceae
leaflets I-407
Virginia Declaration of Rights B-194
Virginia deer. *see in index* White-tailed deer
Virginia Military Institute, in Lexington, Va.; state control; for men; founded 1839; liberal arts, engineering, sciences.
Virginia Museum of Fine Arts, museum in Richmond, Virginia R-220
Virginian, The, television Western W-153
'Virginian: a Horseman of the Plains, The', work by Wister W-152
'Virginians, The', novel by Thackeray (sequel to 'Henry Esmond') which treats of colonial times; two grandsons of Esmond take part in American Revolution on opposite sides.
Virginia opossum, marsupial mammal *(Didelphis virginiana)* M-156
Virginia Plan, proposal at U.S. Constitutional Convention U-195
Congress U-210
Madison M-26
New Jersey N-200
Virginia Polytechnic Institute and State University, in Blacksburg, Va.; state control; founded 1872; agriculture, arts and sciences, business, engineering, home economics; graduate studies.
Virginia rail, game bird *(Rallus limicola)* R-83
Virginia State College, in Petersburg, Va.; founded 1882; arts and sciences, agriculture, commerce, education, home economics, industries; graduate studies.
Virginia stock. *see in index* Malcomia
Virginia Union University, Richmond, Va.; Baptist; founded 1865; present name 1899; liberal arts; theological seminary.
Virginia Wesleyan College, Norfolk, Va.; United Methodist; chartered 1961, opened 1966; liberal arts, education N-333
Virgin Islands, British, island group in Virgin archipelago belonging to United Kingdom, 59 sq mi (153 sq km); pop. 12,200 V-378
Commonwealth membership C-602
North America, *map* N-351
West Indies W-158, *map* W-159
Virgin Islands, College of the, in St. Thomas, V.I.; public control; chartered 1962; liberal arts, education; graduate study.
Virgin Islands, United States, westernmost part of Virgin archipelago; 136 sq mi (352 sq km); pop. 112,000 V-378
flag, *picture* F-160
national parks N-43, 45, 60, *map* N-40
North America, *map* N-351
West Indies W-157, *map* W-159
Virgin Islands National Park, park on most of the island of St. John N-60, V-378, *map* N-40
Virginius Massacre, execution of 53 men of U.S.-owned vessel *Virginius* by Spanish authorities in 1873 because ship carried arms and men to Cuban rebels; event brought U.S. and Spain close to war; it was later proven that *Virginius* flew U.S. flag unlawfully.
Virgin Mary, The. *see in index* Mary
Virgin of Guadalupe, Shrine of the, in Mexico, holy site for Roman Catholics M-328
'Virgin of the Rocks, The', painting by Leonardo da Vinci, *picture* L-133
Virgin Queen. *see in index* Elizabeth I
Virgo (or Virgin), constellation, *charts* A-708, C-681, S-588
Virgule (also called diagonal, slash, or solidus), punctuation mark P-661
Virion, an entire virus particle—the extracellular infective form of a virus—consisting of an outer protein shell (capsid) and an inner core of nucleic acid (either ribonucleic or deoxyribonucleic acid); in some, the capsid further enveloped by a fatty membrane. *see also in index* Virus V-379
Virodunum. *see in index* Verdun
Viroid, smallest known agent of infectious disease; consists of only an extremely small circular ribonucleic-acid molecule, lacking the protein coat of a virus; an agent of certain plant diseases; uncertain whether viroids also occur in animal cells; of considerable interest because of their subviral nature and obscure mode of action.
Virology, study of viruses microbiology M-375
Virtanen, Artturi Ilmari (1895–1973), Finnish biochemist, born in Helsinki; discovered method of preserving fodder. *see also in index* Nobel Prizewinners, *table*
Virtual image, in optics O-574
Virtue, in philosophy P-315, S-628
Virtues, Seven Cardinal. *see in index* Seven Cardinal Virtues
Virtuoso, in music, *list* M-671
Virus, computer sabotage C-636
Virus, ultramicroscopic organism that may cause diseases of plants, animals, and humans V-379
antibiotics A-488
antiseptic action A-495
bacteriophage. *see in index* Bacteriophage
blood's defense B-314
genetic disorders G-48
genetic engineering G-49
human diseases D-165, *picture* D-166. *see also in index* Mononucleosis
AIDS A-145
arthritis A-650
cancer C-132, *picture* C-133
hepatitis H-134
sexually transmitted disease S-195
skin S-315
wart W-34
living things L-266
microbiology M-375
parasitism P-123
pest P-244
plant diseases P-437
vaccines V-264
Visa, credit card consumer credit C-762
Visa, endorsement on passport
passport P-148
travel and tourism T-272
Visalia, Calif., city about 40 mi (60 km) s.e. of Fresno; orchard, truck, and field crops, dairying; electronic equipment; founded 1852, incorporated 1874; pop. 27,268
California, *map* C-53
Visayas (or Visayan islands), an island group of the Philippines; Bohol, Cebu, Leyte, Masbate, Negros, Panay, and Samar are the major islands P-285
Visby (or Wisby), capital of Swedish island of Gotland in Baltic; a trading post in Stone Age; ironworks in medieval times; member Hanseatic League; remains of 11th to 14th centuries including walls, churches; pop. 19,245
Europe, *map* E-361
Viscacha, a burrowing rodent *(Lagostomus maximus)* of chinchilla family; lives in colonies in Argentine pampas of South America; head and body 20 in. (50 cm) long, tail 7 in. (18 cm); fur is soft, grayish above and white below.
Viscaria (or German catchfly), a perennial plant *(Lychnis viscaria)* of the pink family, native to Eurasia; grows to 18 in. (46 cm); somewhat hairy; gray, with leaves small, narrow; flowers small, flat, red, sometimes white or striped, growing in short-stemmed clusters.
Viscera, the internal organs of the body; particularly those located in the great cavity of the body trunk, such as the heart, lungs, liver, stomach, and intestines.
Visceral mass (or buccal mass)
mollusks M-523
Visceral skeleton M-80
Vischer, Peter, the Elder (1455?–1529), German sculptor, born in Nuremberg; work shows transition from Gothic to Renaissance style; worked with his five sons ('Shrine of St. Sebald' in Nuremberg; 'Theodoric' and 'King Arthur', two statues on tomb of Emperor Maximilian at Innsbruck).
Visconti, Italian family; ruled Milan 1277–1447; created methods of central government used by later rulers; dynasty reached its peak with **Gian Galeazzo Visconti** (1351–1402) who initiated construction of the Milan Cathedral in 1386
Milan M-408
Viscosity, the tendency of all bodies—solids, liquids, or gases—to resist any force tending to change their shape or the arrangement of their parts instantaneously
hydraulics H-339
lubricant quality L-327
Viscount, title of nobility T-196
Vishinsky, Andrei Yanuarievich. *see in index* Vyshinsky, Andrei Yanuarievich
Vishnu, one of the Hindu supreme triad of gods H-157, *picture* H-156
sculpture S-152
Sikhism S-293
Visibility, in aviation A-888
Visible spectrum, color arrangement C-558
Visigoths (or West Goths), a Germanic people who lived in Europe about AD 100–700 G-121
Byzantine Empire B-533
Goths G-197
Huns H-330
migration of people M-402

Spain S-495

Vision. see in index Eye

'Vision, A', work by Yeats Y-412

'Vision of Sir Launfal, The', poem by James Russell Lowell, in which a young knight dreams that after a long search for the Holy Grail it is revealed to him at his own gate when he relieves sufferings of a fellow man A-348

'Vision of Tondalys' ', painting by Bosch
painting P-31, *picture* P-33

'Vision of William Concerning Piers the Plowman, The', work by Langland E-265

'Visit from St. Nicholas, A', book written by Moore S-51

Vista, Calif., community 35 mi (55 km) n. of San Diego; truck crops, commercial flowers, rabbits, poultry; pop. 35,834
California, *map* C-53

Vista House, in Oregon, *picture* O-583

'Vista Vision', motion picture innovation of the 1950s M-623

Vistula River (in Polish, Wisla; in Russian, Visla; in German, Weichsel), river in Poland V-381
Europe, *map* E-361
Krakow K-303
Poland P-489

Visual arts A-661
graphic arts G-230
writing W-373

Visual Auto Teller, banking industry, *picture* P-476

Visual center, part of the brain eye E-389

Visual education, teaching by means of materials which can be seen, other than the printed word. see also in index Audiovisual instruction

Visual flight rules A-216

Visual purple (or rhodopsin), pigment in the eye E-388
color C-562

Visvanatha Temple, Varanasi, India V-279

Vitaceae. see in index Grape family

Vital statistics, birth and death
Africa A-101
insurance mortality tables I-234
population P-538
rates by states. see Fact Summary with each state article
sociology S-360

Vitamin A (also called Retinol) V-382
dandelions W-131
eye E-388
malnutrition M-77
mango M-96
melons M-292

Vitamin B complex V-383
honey H-198

Vitamin B₁ (or Thiamine) V-383
malnutrition M-77

Vitamin B₂ (or Riboflavin) V-383
malnutrition M-77

Vitamin B₁₂ V-383
Hodgkin's study H-198

Vitamin C. see in index Ascorbic acid

Vitamin D V-384
malnutrition M-77
mango M-96
milk M-414, *list* D-6
ultraviolet radiation R-48

Vitamin E V-384

Vitamin K V-381, 384

Vitamins V-381
deficiency diseases D-180
enrichment of
bread B-430
flour F-213
enzyme activity B-203

foods F-277
butter B-520
meat M-247
milk M-414
soft drinks S-367
Hodgkin's study H-198
Hopkins H-238
malnutrition M-77
organic chemistry O-605
plant P-417

'Vita Nuova' (New Life), work by Dante; prose interspersed with short poems; fine verse translation into English by Dante Gabriel Rossetti.

Vitascope, forerunner of modern motion-picture projector M-617

Vitebsk, U.S.S.R., city on Western Dvina River, 325 mi (525 km) s. of Leningrad; railroad center; pop. 231,000
Europe, *map* E-361
U.S.S.R., *maps* U-62, 66

Vitellius, Aulus (AD 15–69), Roman emperor during 69, chosen by army; defeated and slain by troops of Vespasian, *list* R-275

'Vitelloni, I' (1951), motion picture directed by Fellini F-53

Viterbo, Italy, historic walled town 38 mi (61 km) n.w. of Rome; Gothic cathedral and churches with tombs of several popes; sulfur springs, Etruscan antiquities nearby; pop. 50,047
Italy, *map* I-404

Viterbo College, in La Crosse, Wis.; Roman Catholic; formerly for women; founded 1931; arts and sciences, education.

Viticulture, grape growing G-220

Viti Levu, largest island of Fiji; 4,053 sq mi (10,497 sq km); has numerous inactive volcanoes; agricultural products include sugar, rice, cotton and pineapples; pop. 388,645 F-82

Vitis labrusca. see in index Fox grape

Vitis rotundifolia. see in index Muscadine grape

Vitis vinifera. see in index Old World grape

Vitoria, Spain, city in n. center 32 mi (52 km) s.e. of Bilbao; victory of Wellington 1813, freeing Spain from French rule; pop. 65,946.

Vitosha Mountains, Sofia, Bulgaria S-365

Vitreous humor, in eye's anatomy, the clear jellylike substance which fills the space between the lens and the retina E-388

Vitrification, conversion to glass or a glasslike substance by heat and fusion
toxic waste W-76

Vitruvius (Marcus Vitruvius Pollio) (fl. 1st century BC), Roman architect of first century AD; 10-vol. work, 'On Architecture', discovered in 15th century, used as guide in Renaissance

Vittorini, Elio (1908–66), Italian writer and translator I-378

Vitus, Saint, Christian martyr under the Emperor Diocletian; festival day June 15; invoked by sufferers of chorea, or St. Vitus' dance.

Vivace, in music M-691, *list* M-671

Vivaldi, Antonio (1680?–1741), Italian priest, violinist, and composer V-385

Vivekananda (or Narendranath Datta) (1863–1902), Indian Hindu spiritual leader H-159

Viviparous animal R-168
insects I-221, *picture* I-220

lizards L-272
mammals. see in index Mammals

Vivisection, cutting or dissecting of living animals for purposes of scientific research; common subjects are fruit flies, mice, guinea pigs, dogs, and monkeys A-449

Viyella, trade name for lightweight half-wool, half-cotton fabric made in United Kingdom; fibers blended before spinning, woven into twill material; used for shirts, underwear, dresses, and pajamas.

Vizcaíno, Sebastián, 16th-century Spanish merchant-explorer; organized company to explore Gulf of California, reputedly rich in pearls; made several voyages (1594–1603) and visited Monterey Bay; made first maps and first scientific exploration of west coast
California C-40
San Diego S-41

Vizcaíno Casas, Fernando (born 1926), Spanish novelist S-508

Vizier (or wazir), title of high officials in Muslim countries, especially in the former Turkish empire.

Vizla, dog, *picture* D-199

V-J Day (Victory over Japan) (Sept. 2), day of Japanese surrender, World War II U-176

VLA. see in index Very Large Array

Vlaardingen, The Netherlands, port on Maas River 6 mi (10 km) w. of Rotterdam; fishing center; soap, synthetic fertilizer, chocolate; pop. 68,002.

Vlachs, a Latin people of s.e. Europe, n. and s. of the Danube from the Bug River to the Adriatic Sea; includes major element of Romanian population.

Vladimir I (or Saint Vladimir) (956?–1015), grand duke of Kiev, first Christian sovereign of Russia; introduced Greek Orthodox church into Russia U-50

Vladivostok, U.S.S.R., chief seaport of Siberia; pop. 608,000 V-385
Asia, *map* A-700
U.S.S.R., *map* U-62, *picture* U-48
world, *map* W-300

Vlad the Impaler, Walachian ruler
folklore F-262

Vlaminck, Maurice de (1876–1958), French painter, born in Paris; known for richly colored, often somber, landscapes..

VLBI (Very Long Baseline Interferometer), in astronomical observation O-457

Vlissingen. see in index Flushing

Vlonë see in index Valona

VLSI. see in index very-large-scale integration

Vltava River (in German, Moldau), waterway in Bohemia, Czechoslovakia, rises in s.w., flowing generally n. 265 mi (427 km) to Elbe
Prague P-577

V-mail, a mail service in use during World War II; letters to or from U.S. armed forces were reproduced on photographic microfilm for sending outside continental U.S. and enlarged on photographic paper for delivery.

Vneshorgbank, U.S.S.R. B-70

Vocabulary, in language S-316
reading R-108

Vocal cord, in human anatomy respiratory system R-174
sound S-388, S-523
voice V-401

Vocal music V-386
Russia U-36

Vocal tract, human physiology speech S-523
voice V-401

Vocation V-390
arts
design D-107
dress design D-268
graphic arts G-230
handicrafts H-29
interior design I-250
motion pictures M-605
photography P-336
business and industry
advertising A-60
industrial design L-172
insurance I-235
marketing M-140
education
libraries L-166, 169
special education S-519
teaching E-103
universities and colleges U-223
employment and unemployment E-206
fire fighting F-111
guidance G-306
home economics H-214
industry affects I-190
legal professions L-97
occupational health hazards I-175
prophets P-616
safety S-9
sciences
engineering E-224
food and nutrition F-279
health care
dentistry D-102, T-53
eyecare O-575
medicine M-276
nursing N-446
plastic surgery P-455
podiatry P-478
microbiology M-374
oceanography O-474
zoo Z-461
ship and shipbuilding S-250
social class S-344
tests I-242
vocational psychology S-636
vocational training A-512, V-400
women W-274

Vocational Education Act (1963), United States H-214

Vocational guidance G-306

Vocational training (or vocational education) V-400
apprenticeship A-512
black Americans B-292
education, *chart* E-80
guidance G-306
home economics H-214
safety S-7
veterans' affairs V-328

Vo-Dinh (born 1933), Vietnamese author and artist, born in Hue, Vietnam; chief medium is oil but equally adept at gouache, watercolor, ink, acrylics, and woodcuts; wrote and illustrated 'The Toad Is the Emperor's Uncle'.

Vodka, alcoholic beverage, usually made from potatoes, corn, or rye malt; originated in Russia A-276
liquor distribution L-234, 237

Vogau, Boris Andreevich. see in index Pilnyak

Vogel, Hermann Wilhelm (1834–98), German photochemist, born near Berlin.

Vogel, Julius (1835–99), New Zealand politician and businessman, born in London, England; elected to Parliament 1863; opposition leader 1865–68; prime minister

1873–75, 1876; knighted 1875; agent-general for the colony in England 1876–80; leader of Stout administration 1884–87; resigned from Parliament 1889.

Vogelweide, Walther von der. see in index Walther von der Vogelweide

Voice V-400
acting skills A-24
animal. see in index Animal communication
identification P-508
language and expression L-31, 44
sinuses N-396
speech S-523
vocal music V-386

Voice box. see in index Larynx

Voice command
space research contributions S-481

Voice of America, the official propaganda program of the U.S. government; broadcasts programs to other countries R-66, *picture* R-59

Voiceprint (or sound spectrogram), a graphic representation of an individual's speech characteristics imprinted on paper, produced electronically on a spectrogram; each person's speech patterns are unique, *pictures* L-31, V-400

'Voices of Silence, The', work by Malraux M-78

Voile, a transparent, thin fabric of plain weave made of cotton, silk, rayon, or wool; used for clothing. see also in index Ninon

Voir dire, in jury selection J-160

Vokshod, Soviet multiman spacecraft R-476

Volans, constellation, *chart* C-682

Volapük, a universal language interlanguage examples L-39

Volatile oils. see in index Essential oils

Volcanic ash and soil
bentonite B-165

Volcanic belt, in geology
continental development C-690
volcano V-404

Volcanic cone, in geology M-633
volcano V-403

Volcanic island
Iceland I-13
oceans O-461
volcano V-403

Volcanic mountain, in geology M-634

Volcanic peak, in geology O-461

Volcanic plateau, in geology
continental development C-690

Volcanism, volcanic power or action V-402

Volcano V-402
basalt formation B-86
continental development C-690
earth E-33
earthquakes E-39
Europe E-330
Italy I-381
Pompeii and Herculaneum P-533
Vesuvius V-326, *picture* N-11
floods F-182
geyser and fumarole G-138
Great Rift Valley G-250
hydrochloric acid H-340
Indonesia I-158
islands I-368
Japan J-60
Kilimanjaro. see in index Kilimanjaro
Krakatoa K-302

lake formation L-24
Latin America L-60
Central America C-253
El Salvador E-195
Guatemala G-296
Mexico M-321, *picture* N-344
Mexico City M-345
South America S-401
Andes A-410
Peru. *see in index* Misti, El
lava and magma L-89
mountain M-633
New Zealand N-286, *picture* N-285
oceanography O-485
Oceania O-465
Pacific Ocean P-4
planets P-406
plateaus P-456
plate tectonics P-456
soil. *see in index* Volcanic ash and soil
United States
Hawaii H-58
Mount Rainier. *see in index* Rainier, Mount
Mount Saint Helens. *see in index* Saint Helens, Mount
Mount Shasta. *see in index* Shasta, Mount
waves O-487

Volcano House, hotel in Hawaii U-146

Volcano Islands, three small islands (Kita Iwo Jima, Iwo Jima, and Minami Iwo Jima) in w. Pacific s. of Bonin Islands and about midway between Guam and Honshu; mountainous; area 11 sq mi (28 sq km); annexed by Japan 1891; occupied by U.S. 1945; returned to Japan 1968. *see also in index* Iwo Jima
Japan, *map* J-78

Volcanology, study of volcanoes and volcanic activity V-405

Volcker, Paul (born 1927), U.S. economist and government official, born in Cape May, N.J.; economist Chase Manhattan Bank 1957–61; deputy under secretary of the treasury for monetary affairs 1961–65, under secretary 1969–74; president New York Federal Reserve Bank 1975–79; chairman Federal Reserve Board 1979–87.

Volendam, The Netherlands, picturesque village, 12 mi (19 km) n. of Amsterdam on the IJsselmeer; old customs and dress remain; pop. 10,123.

Volga-Don Canal, in the U.S.S.R.
canals C-128

Volga River, in the U.S.S.R., longest river of Europe (2,325 mi; 3,740 km) V-406
cannery, *picture* E-341
commercial port A-707
comparative length. *see in index* River, *table*
Europe, *map* E-361
U.S.S.R. U-23, *maps* U-62, 66, *picture* U-41
Volgograd V-406
world, *map* W-300

Volgograd (originally Tsaritsyn, formerly Stalingrad), U.S.S.R., port on Volga River; pop. 981,000 V-406
Europe, *map* E-361
Germany G-124
Stalin S-571
U.S.S.R., *maps* U-62, 66, *picture* U-54
world, *map* W-300
World War II W-329, 339

Volkhov River, in n.w. U.S.S.R.; from Lake Ilmen flows n.e. 130 mi (210 km) to Lake Ladoga; hydroelectric power station at Volkhov
U.S.S.R., *map* U-66

Volkov, Vladislav N. (1935–71), Soviet cosmonaut, born in Moscow; flight engineer for Soyuz 7 and 11; died during reentry of Soyuz 11 on June 30, 1971, *list* S-477

Volkskammer (People's Chamber), legislature of East Germany G-120

Volkswagen, automobile, *picture* A-869
automobile racing A-874
Brazil T-169
Detroit D-121
West Germany G-117, *picture* G-119

Volley, in tennis T-106

Volleyball V-407
Young Men's Christian Association Y-425

Vólos, Greece, seaport on e. coast 100 mi (160 km) n. w. of Athens; ancient ruins nearby; chief port of Thessaly; industrial and trade center; exports include olive oil and wheat; pop. 51,290
Europe, *map* E-361

Volo Tamarack Bog, Illinois
wildflower conservation F-231
Nixon N-326

'Volpone', comedy by Jonson; social satire of 16th-century Venice E-267

Volscians, ancient Italic people in Latium, s.e. of Rome; gradually disappeared after war with Romans 489–450 BC.

Volstead, Andrew John (1860–1947), U.S. legislator, born in Goodhue County, Minnesota; congressman (Republican) from Minnesota 1903–23; author of the Volstead Act.

Volstead Act (or National Prohibition Act, 1919), U.S. law providing for enforcement of 18th, or prohibition, Amendment; defined intoxicants as drinks containing ½ of 1 percent or more of alcohol
Prohibition P-606

'Volsunga Saga', Icelandic saga S-647

Volsungs, in Norse mythology, heroic people descended from Odin, from which sprang Sigurd; story told in the 'Volsunga Saga' and William Morris' 'Story of Sigurd the Volsung'; 13th-century German epic, 'Song of the Nibelungs', similar except for some names and details. *see also in index* 'Nibelungs, Song of the'

Volt, the unit of electric potential difference or electromotive force.

Volta, Alessandro, Count (1745–1827), Italian physicist, born in Como; noted for inventions in electricity, which include voltaic pile, cell, and battery; volt named for him
battery B-107
electricity E-161, S-109, *list* S-115
physics, *picture* P-365

Volta (or volte), a quick, vigorous dance in triple time with leaps and turns; name Italian for "turn"; variation of the galliard; popular in 16th-century England. *see also in index* Galliard

Volta, Lake, lake in e.-central Ghana, 3,270 sq mi (8,480 sq km) G-139

Volta Basin, geographic region in Ghana G-139

Voltage, in electricity
electric power E-166
electronics E-175
electroreception S-176
instrumentation measures I-230
nervous system N-120, *diagram* N-122
photoelectric device P-332
radar R-39
radio waves, *picture* R-72
thermometer T-167
transformer T-249

Voltaic cell, device for producing electric current chemically B-107

Voltaire (1694–1778), French writer V-407
Châtelet's influence C-281
Enlightenment E-289
French literature F-396, *picture* F-395
satire S-74

Volta Redonda, Brazil, town in Rio de Janeiro state, on Paraíba River; has major steel plant; pop. 83,973.

Volta River, in Ghana, formed by junction of Black Volta and White Volta rivers; 275 mi (440 km) long; flows into Gulf of Guinea G-139
Africa, *map* A-118
Burkina Faso B-507

Volterra, Italy, town 30 mi (50 km) s.w. of Florence; alabaster, salt, chemicals; once powerful Etruscan city; pop. 17,938
Italy, *map* I-404

Voltmeter, an instrument for measuring the voltage or difference of electric potential between two points
electronics E-177
instrumentation I-230
galvanometer G-7

Volturno River, in s. Italy, rises on w. slope of Apennines; flows s.w. 100 mi (160 km) to Tyrrhenian Sea, *map* I-404

Volume, in mathematics
calculus C-21
measurement M-244
weights and measures W-139

Volumetric analysis, in chemistry C-290

Voluntary muscles, in physiology A-390

Volunteers, in military, citizens serving country in military capacity of own free will; idea of large volunteer force originated in England in 1757.

Volunteers of America, a religious and philanthropic organization
halfway house establishment H-14

Volunteer State. *see in index* Tennessee

Volute pump, type of pump, *picture* S-660

Volva, cuplike structure at base of stem of gill fungi; common feature in many poisonous mushrooms M-664

Volvox, a greenish freshwater organism, composed of similar cells gathered into a spherical colony; sphere rotates incessantly
science, *picture* S-121

Volynov, Boris Valentinovich (born 1934), Soviet cosmonaut, flight commander, of Soyuz 5 which docked with Soyuz 4; born in Siberia.

Vomiting, a medical disorder
first aid F-122

Von . . . *see in index* under last name, except as below

Von Békésy, Georg (1899–1972), U.S. physicist, born in Budapest, Hungary; with Harvard University 1947–66, senior research fellow in psychophysics 1949–66; professor of sensory science University of Hawaii after 1966. *see also in index* Nobel Prizewinners, *table*

Vondel, Joost van den (1587–1679), Dutch poet, born in Cologne; best known for tragic dramas on Biblical and historical subjects; also wrote satirical poetry ('Lucifer'; 'Palamedes'; 'Maria Stuart') N-127

Von Drais, Karl (1785–1851), German inventor of velocipede B-187

Vo Nguyen Giap (born 1912), Vietnamese military and political leader, born in An Xa, Vietnam; perfected guerilla tactics used by Viet Minh; member of the Politburo of the Vietnamese Communist party until 1982
battle of Dienbienphu D-140

Von Hayek, Friedrich (born 1899), British economist, born in Vienna, Austria; naturalized 1938; professor London School of Economics 1931–50, University of Chicago 1950–62; advocate of laissez-faire economics; wrote 'The Road to Serfdom'. *see also in index* Nobel Prizewinners, *table*

Vonnegut, Kurt, Jr. (born 1922), U.S. author V-408
American literature A-361

Von Neumann, John (1903–57), U.S. mathematician, born in Budapest, Hungary; to U.S. 1930, became citizen 1937; research professor of mathematics Institute for Advanced Study, Princeton, N.J., after 1933, leave of absence to serve on Atomic Energy Commission 1954–57; made important contribution to H-bomb by developing high-speed calculators; expert on games of strategy and their application to economic behavior; Fermi award 1956 for contributions to atomic energy
computer development C-629

Vonnoh, Bessie Potter (1872–1955), U.S. sculptor, born in St. Louis, Mo.; portrayed mothers and children and young women with delicate skill.

Voodoo, religion of most of the population of Haiti V-408

Voorhees, Stephen Francis (1878–1965), U.S. architect, born in Rocky Hill, N.J.; supervising architect Princeton University 1930–49; chief architect New York World's Fair 1936–40; designed many skyscrapers.

Voorhees College, Denmark, S.C.; Episcopal; opened 1897; liberal arts, education.

Voorhis, Jerry (1901–84), U.S. representative from California, born in Ottawa, Kan.
Nixon N-323

Vorarlberg, province in w. corner of Austria adjoining Switzerland; 1,005 sq mi (2,605 sq km); pop. 226,323.

Vorlage, in skiing, *table* S-311

Voronoff, Serge (1866–1951), French surgeon, born in Russia; experimented in grafting glands from animals, chiefly from monkeys, onto human bodies to rejuvenate them.

Voroshilov, Kliment Yefremovich (1881–1969), military and political leader of U.S.S.R., born in Verkhneye, Ukraine; head of state after death of Joseph Stalin; became member of Politburo 1926; marshal of the Soviet Union 1935; appointed to committee for state defense 1941; supervised establishment of Communist regime in Hungary 1945–47; chairman of Presidium of Supreme Soviet 1953–60.

Vorster, John (Balthazar Johannes Vorster) (1915–83), South African lawyer and political leader V-408

'Vortex, The', work by Rivera L-70

Vorticella (popularly called bell animalcules), genus of bell-shaped Protozoa A-428
living things, *picture* L-267

Vosges, department of France in region called Lorraine; agriculture and forestry; area, 2,279 sq mi (5,903 sq km); pop. 397,957
Alsace-Lorraine A-320
France, *map* F-372

Vosges, mountains of e. France, *map* F-372

Voss, Johann Heinrich (1751–1826), German poet, best known for translations of Homer, Virgil, Shakespeare, and Horace; in 'Luise', one of his famous 'Idylls' and his most famous poem, he expressed a German theme in classical style.

Vostoks, Soviet spacecraft
Gagarin G-2
satellites S-73
space travel S-462, 476

Voting. *see also in index* Elections; Suffrage
Australian system A-803
black Americans B-292, 296
King K-244
Reconstruction period R-120, *picture* R-119
citizenship C-440
franchise F-373
Hispanic Americans H-164
parliamentary law P-146
plebiscite. *see in index* Plebiscite
president. *see in index* President, *subhead* election

Voting machine E-148, *picture* E-147

'Voting of the Greek Chiefs', *picture* D-252

Voting Rights Act (1965), United States B-297, 301
King K-245
suffrage S-694

Voulkos, Peter, U.S. potter
ceramics P-571

Vowels, in alphabet
early writing A-317
Hebrew P-662
language L-31, 40
phonics P-322
spelling S-527

Vox Pop, radio program R-55

'Voyager', experimental aircraft flown by Rutan and Yeager A-208

Voyager, U.S. space probe P-412, *pictures* P-405, 410, 411

Voyageur (French for "traveler"), colonial French Canadian employed to carry men and goods, especially between the fur-trading posts F-471, *picture* F-469

Voyageurs National Park, park in Minnesota N-60, *maps* M-458, N-40

Voysey, Charles (1857–1941), British furniture designer and architect F-462

Voyvodina, district in Yugoslavia, formerly part of Hungary; population a mixture of Slavs, Germans, Magyars, and Romanians.

Voznesensky, Andrei (born 1933), Soviet poet, born in Moscow; known for his experimental style and humanistic themes; traveled widely in Europe and U.S. ('Mozaika'; 'Parabola'; 'The Fifth Ace')
Russian literature R-353

Vredeman de Vries, Hans (1527–1604?), Dutch architect and painter F-457

Vriesland. *see in index* Friesland

VTOL. *see in index* Vertical takeoff and landing

VTR. *see in index* Videocassette recorder

Vuillard, Jean Edouard (1868–1940), French painter, lithographer; impressionistic, influenced by oriental prints; portraits, decorative interiors, still lifes.

Vulcan, in Roman mythology, god of fire and metalworking; identified with Greek Hephaestus M-701. *see also in index* Hephaestus

Vulcanite, rubber hardened by combination with a large proportion of sulfur at high temperatures; used for combs, phonograph records, insulation.

Vulcanization, process in manufacturing rubber R-335

Goodyear I-274, *picture* I-275, *table* I-273

Vulgate, Latin Bible B-185, L-78

Vulpecula, constellation, *chart* C-681

Vulture, a carrion bird B-247, *picture* B-269
  predatory behavior B-280

Vulva, female reproductive structure R-166

Vyborg (in Finnish, Viipuri), U.S.S.R., city and seaport on Gulf of Finland; connected by canal with inland lakes; formerly Finnish, included in U.S.S.R. since 1944; pop. 51,088
  Europe, *map* E-361
  U.S.S.R., *maps* U-62, 66

Vychegda River, river in n. U.S.S.R.; flows w. for 702 mi (1,130 km), *picture* U-40

Vyshinsky, Andrei Yanuarievich (1883–1954), Soviet diplomat and jurist, born in Odessa, U.S.S.R.; became chief state prosecutor 1935, conducted Moscow purge trials 1936–38; first deputy foreign minister 1940–49 and 1953–54, foreign minister 1949–53; head of Soviet delegation to UN General Assembly 1953–54.